D1088017

The Oxford Handbook of Obsessive
Compulsive and Spectrum Disorders

OXFORD LIBRARY OF PSYCHOLOGY

EDITOR-IN-CHIEF

Peter E. Nathan

AREA EDITORS:

Clinical Psychology
David H. Barlow

Cognitive Neuroscience
Kevin N. Ochsner and Stephen M. Kosslyn

Cognitive Psychology
Daniel Reisberg

Counseling Psychology
Elizabeth M. Altmaier and Jo-Ida C. Hansen

Developmental Psychology
Philip David Zelazo

Health Psychology
Howard S. Friedman

History of Psychology
David B. Baker

Industrial/Organizational Psychology
Steve W. J. Kozlowski

Methods and Measurement
Todd D. Little

Neuropsychology
Kenneth M. Adams

Personality and Social Psychology
Kay Deaux and Mark Snyder

OXFORD LIBRARY OF PSYCHOLOGY

Editor-in-Chief **PETER E. NATHAN**

The Oxford Handbook of Obsessive Compulsive and Spectrum Disorders

Edited by

Gail Steketee

OXFORD
UNIVERSITY PRESS

OXFORD
UNIVERSITY PRESS

Oxford University Press, Inc., publishes works that further Oxford University's
objective of excellence in research, scholarship, and education

Oxford New York
Auckland   Cape Town   Dar es Salaam   Hong Kong   Karachi
Kuala Lumpur   Madrid   Melbourne   Mexico City   Nairobi
New Delhi   Shanghai   Taipei   Toronto

With offices in
Argentina   Austria   Brazil   Chile   Czech Republic   France   Greece
Guatemala   Hungary   Italy   Japan   Poland   Portugal   Singapore
South Korea   Switzerland   Thailand   Turkey   Ukraine   Vietnam

Copyright © 2012 by Oxford University Press, Inc.

Published by Oxford University Press, Inc.
198 Madison Avenue, New York, New York 10016
www.oup.com

Oxford is a registered trademark of Oxford University Press
All rights reserved. No part of this publication may be reproduced, stored in a
retrieval system, or transmitted, in any form or by any means, electronic, mechanical,
photocopying, recording, or otherwise, without the prior permission of
Oxford University Press

Library of Congress Cataloging-in-Publication Data

The Oxford handbook of obsessive compulsive and spectrum disorders / edited by Gail Steketee.
   p. cm.
   ISBN 978-0-19-537621-0
   1. Obsessive-compulsive disorder–Handbooks, manuals, etc. 2. Compulsive behavior–Handbooks,
manuals, etc. I. Steketee, Gail.
   RC533.O94 2012
   616.85'227—dc22   2010054116

1 3 5 7 9 10 8 6 4 2

Typeset in Adobe Garamond Pro
Printed in the United States of America on acid-free paper

SHORT CONTENTS

OXFORD LIBRARY OF PSYCHOLOGY

The *Oxford Library of Psychology*, a landmark series of handbooks, is published by Oxford University Press, one of the world's oldest and most highly respected publishers, with a tradition of publishing significant books in psychology. The ambitious goal of the *Oxford Library of Psychology* is nothing less than to span a vibrant, wide-ranging field and, in so doing, to fill a clear market need.

Encompassing a comprehensive set of handbooks, organized hierarchically, the *Library* incorporates volumes at different levels, each designed to meet a distinct need. At one level are a set of handbooks designed broadly to survey the major subfields of psychology; at another are numerous handbooks that cover important current focal research and scholarly areas of psychology in depth and detail. Planned as a reflection of the dynamism of psychology, the *Library* will grow and expand as psychology itself develops, thereby highlighting significant new research that will impact on the field. Adding to its accessibility and ease of use, the *Library* will be published in print and, later on, electronically.

The *Library* surveys psychology's principal subfields with a set of handbooks that capture the current status and future prospects of those major subdisciplines. This initial set includes handbooks of social and personality psychology, clinical psychology, counseling psychology, school psychology, educational psychology, industrial and organizational psychology, cognitive psychology, cognitive neuroscience, methods and measurements, history, neuropsychology, personality assessment, developmental psychology, and more. Each handbook undertakes to review one of psychology's major subdisciplines with breadth, comprehensiveness, and exemplary scholarship. In addition to these broadly conceived volumes, the *Library* also includes a large number of handbooks designed to explore in depth more specialized areas of scholarship and research, such as stress, health and coping, anxiety and related disorders, cognitive development, or child and adolescent assessment. In contrast to the broad coverage of the subfield handbooks, each of these latter volumes focuses on an especially productive, more highly focused line of scholarship and research. Whether at the broadest or most specific level, however, all of the *Library* handbooks offer synthetic coverage that reviews and evaluates the relevant past and present research, and anticipates research in the future. Each handbook in the *Library* includes introductory and concluding chapters written by its editor to provide a roadmap to the handbook's table of contents, and to offer informed anticipations of significant future developments in that field.

An undertaking of this scope calls for handbook editors and chapter authors who are established scholars in the areas about which they write. Many of the nation's and world's most productive and best-respected psychologists have agreed to edit *Library* handbooks or write authoritative chapters in their areas of expertise.

For whom has the *Oxford Library of Psychology* been written? Because of its breadth, depth, and accessibility, the *Library* serves a diverse audience, including graduate students in psychology and their faculty mentors, scholars, researchers, and practitioners in psychology and related fields. Each will find in the *Library* the information they seek on the subfield or focal area of psychology in which they work or are interested.

Befitting its commitment to accessibility, each handbook includes a comprehensive index, as well as extensive references to help guide research. And because the *Library* was designed from its inception as an online as well as a print resource, its structure and contents will be readily and rationally searchable online. Further, once the *Library* is released online, the handbooks will be regularly and thoroughly updated.

In summary, the *Oxford Library of Psychology* will grow organically to provide a thoroughly informed perspective on the field of psychology, one that reflects both psychology's dynamism and its increasing interdisciplinarity. Once published electronically, the *Library* is also destined to become a uniquely valuable interactive tool, with extended search and browsing capabilities. As you begin to consult this handbook, we sincerely hope you will share our enthusiasm for the more than 500-year tradition of Oxford University Press for excellence, innovation, and quality, as exemplified by the *Oxford Library of Psychology.*

Peter E. Nathan
Editor-in-Chief
Oxford Library of Psychology

ABOUT THE EDITOR

Gail Steketee

Dr. Gail Steketee is Dean and Professor at Boston University's School of Social Work. She has conducted numerous research studies on the psychopathology and treatment of anxiety and related problems, especially obsessive compulsive spectrum disorders, including hoarding. She has published over 200 articles and chapters, as well as 12 books. She gives frequent lectures and workshops on hoarding, OCD, and related topics to professional and public audiences in the United States and abroad.

CONTRIBUTORS

Jonathan S. Abramowitz
Department of Psychology
University of North Carolina
Chapel Hill, NC

Gillian M. Alcolado
Department of Psychology
Concordia University
Montreal, Quebec

Mirela A. Aldea
Department of Pediatrics
University of South Florida
Tampa, FL

Diana Antinoro
Department of Psychiatry
University of Pennsylvania School of
Medicine
Philadelphia, PA

O. Joseph Bienvenu
Department of Psychiatry and
Behavioral Sciences
The Johns Hopkins University School
of Medicine
Baltimore, MD

Rebecca K. Blais
Department of Psychology
University of Utah
Salt Lake City, UT

Danielle Bodzin
Department of Pediatrics
University of South Florida
Tampa, FL

John E. Calamari
Department of Psychology
Rosalind Franklin University of Medicine
and Science
Chicago, IL

Cheryl N. Carmin
Department of Psychiatry
University of Illinois at Chicago
Chicago, IL

Catherine M. Caska
Department of Psychology
University of Utah
Salt Lake City, UT

Stephanie E. Cassin
University of Toronto
Toronto, Ontario

Sarah P. Certoma
School of Psychology
University of New South Wales
Sydney, Australia

Heather M. Chik
Department of Psychology
Rosalind Franklin University of Medicine
and Science
Chicago, IL

Anne Chosak
Department of Psychiatry
Massachusetts General Hospital
Harvard Medical School
Boston, MA

Carrie Cuttler
Department of Psychology
University of British Columbia
Vancouver, British Columbia

Brandon L. DeJong
Department of Psychology
Rosalind Franklin University of Medicine
and Science
Chicago, IL

Guy Doron
Interdisciplinary Centre (IDC) Herzilya
Herzilya, Israel

Nicole M. Dorfan
Department of Psychology
University of British Columbia
Vancouver, British Columbia

Darin D. Dougherty
OCD Institute
McLean Hospital/Massachusetts General
Hospital
Department of Psychiatry
Harvard Medical School
Boston, MA

Jane L. Eisen
Department of Psychiatry and Human
Behavior
Alpert Medical School of
Brown University
Providence, RI

Angela Fang
Department of Psychology
Boston University
Boston, MA

Elham Foroughi
University of Melbourne
Swinburne University of Technology
Melbourne, Australia

Martin E. Franklin
Department of Psychiatry
University of Pennsylvania School of
Medicine
Philadelphia, PA

Randy O. Frost
Department of Psychology
Smith College
Northampton, MA

Marco A. Grados
Department of Psychiatry and Behavioral
Sciences
The Johns Hopkins University School of
Medicine
Baltimore, MD

Benjamin D. Greenberg
OCD Research Clinic
Butler Hospital
Department of Psychiatry and Human
Behavior
Alpert Medical School of Brown
University
Providence, RI

Jennifer L. Greenberg
Department of Psychiatry
Massachusetts General Hospital
Harvard Medical School
Boston, MA

Jessica R. Grisham
School of Psychology
University of New South Wales
Sydney, Australia

Michael A. Jenike
OCD Institute
McLean Hospital/Massachusetts General
Hospital
Department of Psychiatry
Harvard Medical School
Boston, MA

Megan M. Kelly
Alpert Medical School of Brown
University
Providence, RI

Michael Kyrios
Brain and Psychological Science Research
Centre (BPsyC)
Swinburne University of Technology
Melbourne, Australia

David Mataix-Cols
Departments of Psychological Medicine
and Psychology
King's College London
London, England

Brian H. McCorkle
Boston University
Boston, MA

Dean McKay
Department of Psychology
Fordham University
Bronx, NY

Nicole C. R. McLaughlin
OCD Research Clinic
Butler Hospital
Department of Psychiatry and
Human Behavior
Alpert Medical School of
Brown University
Providence, RI

Richard Moulding
Brain and Psychological Science Research
Centre (BPsyC)
Swinburne University of Technology
Melbourne, Australia

Jordana Muroff
School of Social Work
Boston University
Boston, MA

Tanya K. Murphy
Departments of Pediatrics and Psychiatry
University of South Florida
Tampa, FL

Maja Nedeljkovic
Brain and Psychological Science Research
Centre (BPsyC)
Swinburne University of Technology
Melbourne, Australia

Melissa M. Norberg
National Drug and Alcohol Research
Centre
University of New South Wales
Sydney, Australia

Raymond L. Ownby
Department of Psychiatry and
Behavioral Medicine
Nova Southwestern University
Ft. Lauderdale, FL

Katharine A. Phillips
Alpert Medical School of Brown
University
Providence, RI

Anthony Pinto
Department of Psychiatry
Columbia University
Anxiety Disorders Clinic
New York State Psychiatric Institute
New York, NY

Elizabeth Planalp
Department of Psychology
Loyola College
Baltimore, MD

Noelle K. Pontarelli
Department of Psychology
Rosalind Franklin University of Medicine
and Science
Chicago, IL

Christine Purdon
Department of Psychology
University of Waterloo
Waterloo, Ontario

Adam S. Radomsky
Department of Psychology
Concordia University
Montreal, Quebec

Omar Rahman
Department of Pediatrics
University of South Florida
Tampa, FL

Jessica L. Rasmussen
School of Social Work
Boston University
Boston, MA

Scott L. Rauch
Department of Psychiatry
McLean Hospital
Harvard Medical School
Boston, MA

Neil A. Rector
Department of Psychiatry
University of Toronto
Toronto, Ontario

Jeannette M. Reid
Department of Pediatrics
University of South Florida
Tampa, FL

Keith D. Renshaw
Department of Psychology
University of Utah
Salt Lake City, UT

Emily J. Ricketts
Department of Psychology
University of Wisconsin-Milwaukee
Milwaukee, WI

Melisa Robichaud
Department of Psychology
University of British Columbia
Vancouver, British Columbia

Camila S. Rodrigues
Department of Psychology
University of Utah
Salt Lake City, UT

Abigail Ross
School of Social Work
Boston University
Boston, MA

Joseph Rothfarb
School of Social Work
Boston University
Boston, MA

Jack F. Samuels
Department of Psychiatry and Behavioral
Sciences
The Johns Hopkins University School of
Medicine
Baltimore, MD

Gail Steketee
School of Social Work
Boston University
Boston, MA

Eric A. Storch
Departments of Pediatrics and Psychiatry
University of South Florida
Tampa, FL

Steven Taylor
Department of Psychiatry
University of British Columbia
Vancouver, British Columbia

David F. Tolin
The Institute of Living
Yale University School of Medicine
New Haven, CT

Odile A. van den Heuvel
Department of Psychiatry
Department of Anatomy & Neurosciences
VU University Medical Center
Amsterdam, The Netherlands

Maureen L. Whittal
Department of Psychology
University of British Columbia
Vancouver, British Columbia

Sabine Wilhelm
Department of Psychiatry
Massachusetts General Hospital
Harvard Medical School
Boston, MA

Douglas W. Woods
Department of Psychology
University of Wisconsin-Milwaukee
Milwaukee, WI

Sheila R. Woody
Department of Psychology
University of British Columbia
Vancouver, British Columbia

CONTENTS

PART 1

Introduction and Overview

Introduction

Gail Steketee

Abstract

The Oxford Handbook of Obsessive Compulsive and Spectrum Disorders reviews current literature on obsessive compulsive disorder (OCD) and its associated spectrum conditions of body dysmorphic disorder (BDD), hoarding, trichotillomania and tic disorders. Authors who are leading researchers in their fields summarize and synthesize the current knowledge about these OC spectrum disorders to provide a road map for the field and open the door to new research and further study. This introduction previews the contents of the book and highlights some of the challenges in current research on epidemiology, features, and diagnosis, as well as biological and psychosocial theories and treatments for these conditions.

Keywords: OCD, obsessive compulsive spectrum, nosology, psychosocial theory, biological theory, therapy

The task of developing a comprehensive and up-to-date reference book on obsessive compulsive disorder (OCD) and obsessive compulsive spectrum disorders (OCSDs) is challenging. Our goal in compiling the chapters for this volume was to summarize and synthesize the current knowledge about these mental health disorders in order to provide a road map for the field and open the door to new research and further study. This volume is part of the *Oxford Library of Psychology*, a landmark series of handbooks that will span the entire field of psychology, from the broad disciplinary level to the focused, in-depth topic level. This *Oxford Handbook of Obsessive Compulsive and Spectrum Disorders* reviews the major psychological disorders of OCD and its associated spectrum conditions with breadth, comprehensiveness, and excellent scholarship by authors who are leading researchers in their fields. This introduction highlights a few of the challenges in deciding what to include and what to place elsewhere in the Oxford handbook series, and how to cover the broad and sometimes uneven knowledge base for each of the spectrum conditions.

Among the first tasks was to determine what disorders would be included and which ones would not. Defined by the U.S.-based *Diagnostic and Statistical Manual of Mental Disorders* (the DSM-IV-TR, APA, 2000) or its World Health Organization (2007) counterpart, the International Classification of Diseases (ICD-10), the conditions described in this book reside in a somewhat informal category of OCSDs that groups together a handful of mental health problems thought to be related to OCD (see also Hollander, 2007). Along with OCD in its many forms or subtypes, we have included body dysmorphic disorder (BDD), hoarding, tic disorders and Tourette's Syndrome, as well as trichotillomania and related habit disorders of skin picking and nail biting. These disorders have traditionally been included in prior writings on OCSD (e.g., Allen, King, & Hollander, 2003; Wetterneck, Teng, & Stanley, 2010). Not included in this book is hypochondriasis or health anxiety, a condition often associated with OC spectrum conditions by virtue of its obsession-like focus on health and bodily concerns and avoidant and compulsive behaviors, such as checking body parts and functions. The rationale for this decision was somewhat arbitrary and partly a function of arranging the coverage of the handbook series where hypochondriasis is covered (Martin Anthony and Murray Stein's *The Oxford Handbook of Anxiety and Related Disorders*, among others). Also omitted were anorexia and bulimia, eating disorders that have been included in Stewart Agras's *The Oxford Handbook of Eating Disorders* and James Lock's *The Oxford Handbook of Developmental Perspectives on Adolescent Eating Disorders*. Other candidates for inclusion might have been the impulse control disorders, which bear some similarity to the habit disorders mentioned above and also to tic disorders. In addition to trichotillomania, which is included in this volume (see Chapters 5 and 23), these include intermittent explosive disorder, kleptomania, pyromania, and pathological gambling, which appear to more closely resemble addictions than OC spectrum conditions. These disorders have been included in Jon Grant's and Marc Potenza's *The Oxford Handbook of Impulse Control Disorders*.

As will be evident in the chapters contained here, these OCSD diagnoses bear some relationship to OCD with regard to nosology and phenomenology, although differences are clearly evident in onset, course, and biological features, as well as strategies for assessment and effective types of treatments. However, sometimes even the nosological relationship to OCD appears tenuous. For example, hoarding disorder appears to be driven by both positive and negative emotional states and to lack the characteristic ritualistic behaviors of OCD (see Chapter 4). The habit disorders often lack the hallmark obsessions of OCD (see Chapter 5). Even the requirement for impairment and distress may vary. DSM diagnoses in general, and OC spectrum conditions in particular, share the requirement of provoking significant distress and impairment in functioning to cross the line between mere subclinical symptoms and a DSM clinical disorder. Perhaps the sole exception to this is hoarding, which is in diagnostic flux at this time. Diagnostic criteria for hoarding have been proposed for the next revision of the DSM (DSM-V, expected in 2012), and these are detailed in Chapter 4. Interestingly, the almost legendary low-insight aspect of hoarding for many sufferers has led diagnosticians to develop criteria that do not require that hoarding sufferers themselves experience distress (as many do not report this), but that the distress might be experienced mainly by others living with and near them. This is a departure from the usual DSM requirement for both distress and impairment typically associated with OCD and other anxiety and mood disorders.

This volume begins with reviews of the diagnostic features, epidemiology, and phenomenology of OCD, BDD, hoarding, tic disorders, and trichotillomania, in Chapters 2 through 5. These chapters provide extensive literature reviews of the prevalence of these conditions, their association with anxiety, mood, and other comorbid disorders, and potential etiological factors. As Calamari, Chik, Pontarelli, and DeJong indicate in Chapter 2 on OCD, clarification of the heterogeneity within disorders like OCD can help advance theories about etiology, as well as research on treatments, and suggest where these and seemingly related conditions lie in our psychiatric disorder nomenclature. These reviews inevitably point to the ongoing debate about what features the OCSDs share, along what dimensions they differ, where each should be placed in the taxonomy of psychiatric disorders, and whether these conditions in fact belong in the broad category of OC spectrum conditions. Figure 1.1 presents a modified map of the dimensions along which several OCSD conditions might vary with regard to mood (euphoria to dysphoria) and behavioral propensities (harm avoidance to impulsivity; see also Lochner et al., 2005; Summerfeldt, Hood, Antony, Richter, & Swinson, 2004). On these dimensions, BDD falls on the most dysphoric and harm-avoidant end, with its frequent suicidal features and poor insight into the irrationality of the fears of imagined ugliness. OCD appears similar, with high rates of depression and avoidant behaviors. In contrast, impulse control disorders rest in the opposing end, with euphoric mood and impulsivity. In between are hoarding and habit disorders like trichotillomania. This figure does not contain reference to a third dimension of cognitive features (beliefs and cognitive processes) that might also help distinguish these conditions, as some chapters in this volume suggest (see Chapters 8, 12 and 18). How biological aspects (genetic, neurobiology) might be represented is yet another missing element.

Among the five chapters outlining symptoms and features of OCSDs, Calamari and colleagues (Chapter 2) point to OCD's heterogeneity. While this may be less true of conditions like BDD and

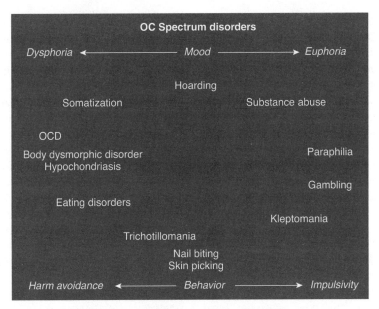

Fig. 1.1. A modified map of the dimensions along which several obsessive-compulsive/spectrum disorder conditions might vary with regard to mood (euphoria to dysphoria) and behavioral propensities (harm avoidance to impulsivity).

trichotillomania, heterogeneity certainly characterizes the larger category of OCSDs. These authors also note the potential value of studying both the subclinical and clinical levels of these conditions, an important point with regard to understanding the critical factors that affect their development and worsening. In Chapter 3, Kelly and Phillips highlight the very serious comorbidity that commonly characterizes BDD, including major depression, hypochondriasis, and psychotic disorders. This underresearched condition is perhaps one of the most severe within the OCSD grouping. Hoarding is the newest member of the spectrum conditions, as its departure from its former diagnostic role as a symptom of obsessive compulsive personality disorder and a subtype of OCD is based on research published within the past decade. Described in detail by Rasmussen and Frost in Chapter 4, it is perhaps one of the more confusing OC spectrum conditions from a nosological and phenomenological point of view. Chapter 5 by Ricketts and colleagues outlines the features of tic disorders and trichotillomania, a repetitive behaviors group sometimes referred to as *habit disorders,* in which symptoms rise and fall with changes in mood. As these authors note, information about crosscultural aspects of these conditions is limited, a statement that also applies to other OCSDs.

Next are three chapters that discuss various biological aspects of OCSDs. In Chapter 6, Samuels and colleagues review more than two decades of research on genetic aspects; findings indicate that specific genes for OCD and these spectrum conditions have not yet been identified, but there is little doubt that genetic linkages play a role. In Chapter 7, Mataix-Cols and van den Heuvel cover the neurobiological aspects of OCSDs and note that it remains unclear how they relate to one another from this perspective, a task complicated by the heterogeneity of OCD and related disorders, especially hoarding. In the third of these chapters on biology, Radomsky and Alcolado (Chapter 8) examine information-processing in OCD and spectrum disorders, describing a variety of experimental methodologies designed to elucidate the both the features and the mechanisms behind symptoms of these conditions. These three chapters do an excellent job of organizing the research findings to better understand OCSDs, just as they point to the great need for further research in these important areas.

Four chapters examine social, family, and personality features, as well as psychological models for understanding OCD and spectrum disorders. In Chapter 9, Renshaw, Caska, Rodrigues, and Blais point to serious patient impairments in social and family functioning, as well as problems among family members who also display distress and relationship problems with their afflicted relatives. Unfortunately, family accommodation and strong negative emotional reactions can contribute to treatment failure among those with OCD, but little is known about family responses in the spectrum conditions. Pinto and Eisen (Chapter 10) review the relationship of OCD to personality disorders, especially OCPD, a long studied but little understood association. They point to the need to examine dimensional personality traits rather than merely categorical groupings of personality disorders in order to inform theoretical models of OCSDs, noting that much remains to be done in this arena. Cassin and Rector (Chapter 11) review the largely untested psychodynamic models, and focus mainly on behavioral models with their 40 years of empirical support for explaining the symptoms of OCD and related disorders. However, as the authors note, these models only partly explain these disorders, and mainly the persistence of symptoms rather than their etiology. In Chapter 12, Taylor, Abramowitz, McKay and Cuttler detail the much more recent cognitive models for understanding OCD and the evidence supporting predictions derived from these models, as well as applications to related OCSDs. As noted for behavioral models in Chapter 11, these authors concur that cognitive theories only partly explain OCSDs. Their recommendations for improving upon the explanatory power of these models include examining special features like disgust, as well as developmental and cultural aspects, and tying dysfunctional beliefs to information-processing and neuroscience findings.

Two chapters focus on assessment methods. Chapter 13, by Dorfan and Woody, focuses mainly on assessing OCD symptoms, whereas Purdon's Chapter 14 covers measurement of comorbidity, insight, family features, and functioning. Assessment methods for determining severity and features of BDD, hoarding, tics, and trichotillomania are not provided in a separate chapter but included within earlier chapters describing research on these conditions.

The largest portion of this volume focuses on treatment, with six chapters on treatments for OCD and three chapters on treatments for OC spectrum disorders. In the first group, Dougherty, Rauch and Jenike review pharmacological treatments in Chapter 15, mainly considering the substantial literature on selective serotonin reuptake inhibitors, or SSRIs, as major first-line treatments for OCD, with other monotherapies and augmentation strategies as second-line medication treatments. McLaughlin and Greenberg (Chapter 16) describe various nonmedication biological interventions, including neurosurgical methods such as cingulotomy, capsulotomy,

leucotomy, and tractotomy, as well as deep brain stimulation. Not surprisingly, given the possibility of serious side effects, they point to the need for caution and careful review required before these methods can be applied. Chapter 17, by Abramowitz, Taylor, and McKay, reviews exposure treatments for OCD, noting that these are among the oldest and most effective methods available. They describe common variants and potential mechanisms of action, as well as comparative efficacy in relation to other methods, and predictors of outcome and strategies for improving outcomes. In Chapter 18, Whittal and Robichaud detail cognitive methods of therapy based on the empirically demonstrated assumption that intrusive thoughts are a universal phenomenon, but when interpreted negatively can become clinical obsessions. They point to the possible mechanisms of action of cognitive interventions that address various types of beliefs. Tolin (Chapter 19) reviews literature on the efficacy of combining medications and cognitive and behavioral therapy (CBT) for OCD, finding that combination therapies that include CBT have a small but significant advantage over single therapies. He points to new strategies for combining therapies to potentiate the mechanisms of CBT. The final chapter in this group by Muroff, Ross, and Rothfarb (Chapter 20) is on complementary and alternative approaches to treating OCD. These authors summarize research on such therapies as yoga, herbal remedies, motivational strategies, and bibliotherapy, as well as alternative methods more closely related to standard CBT, with a special focus on technology-supported treatments.

The next three chapters address treatments specifically developed for body dysmorphic disorder, hoarding, and tic and trichotillomania disorders. With regard to BDD, in Chapter 21, Greenberg Chosak, Fang, and Wilhelm point to the efficacy and limitations of separate and combined medications and cognitive-behavioral therapies. They also note that cosmetic procedures favored by patients are typically ineffective, and that early intervention is critical to limit the morbidity associated with BDD. In Chapter 22, Grisham, Norberg, and Certoma describe treatments for compulsive hoarding as an urgent public health priority. They comment on the poor response to standard pharmacological and psychological treatments, according to mainly retrospective research, and review the somewhat more positive outcomes to CBT that is derived from a model for understanding hoarding. Franklin, Antinoro, Ricketts, and Woods (Chapter 23) describe the methods and outcomes of treatments for tic disorders and trichotillomania. They indicate that cognitive therapy techniques are not typically included in psychosocial treatments, and that behavioral therapies including habit reversal training (HRT) are promising for both conditions.

Three final chapters cover OCD and spectrum conditions in older adults, children and adolescents, and across cultures. In Chapter 24, Carmin, Calamari, and Ownby focus on older adults, noting the need to study interventions for late life OCD that are designed to address possible medical and cognitive limitations, as well as beliefs about intrusive thoughts and compulsive behaviors. On the other end of the developmental spectrum, Storch et al. (Chapter 25) summarize the phenomenology, etiology, and treatment of OCSDs in children and adolescents. They propose novel CBT augmentation methods for OCD using D-cycloserine, as well as other modifications of CBT and medications, and point to the severely limited research on treatments for BDD and trichotillomania in children. Nedeljkovic, Moulding, Foroughi, and Kyrios discuss cultural aspects of OCD and OCSDs in Chapter 26. They consider the role of cultural and religious factors in how OCD symptoms are perceived, assessed, and diagnosed, as well as how patients present for help. Their review of the effects of treatments across countries, and within minority cultures from Western countries, indicates the extremely limited information available about cultural aspects of OC spectrum conditions.

Finally, we (Steketee & McCorkle, Chapter 27) close with a discussion of the topics of most compelling need for further research on obsessive compulsive and spectrum disorders. Here we review a number of the major issues raised in the research summarized across the chapters of this volume, especially as they pertain to the need to better understand the etiology of these conditions, their biological and social contexts, and the biological and psychosocial interventions that derive from these. It is our genuine hope that readers will benefit from the detailed research summaries contained in this book and use them to guide future research and clinical interventions.

References

Allen, A., King, A., & Hollander, E. (2003). Obsessive-compulsive spectrum disorders, *Dialogues Clinical Neuroscience, 5*, 259–271.

American Psychiatric Association. (2000). *Diagnostic and statistical manual of mental disorders* (4th ed., text revision). Arlington, VA: APA.

Hollander, E. (2007). Anxiety and OC spectrum disorders over life cycle. *International Journal of Psychiatry in Clinical Practice*, 11 (Suppl. 2), 5–10.

Lochner, C., Hemmings, S.M.J., Kinnear, C.J., Niehous, D.J.H., Nel, D.G., Corfield, V.A., Moolman-Smook, J.C., Seedat, S., & Stein, D.J. (2005). Cluster analysis of obsessive-compulsive spectrum disorders in patients with obsessive-compulsive disorder: clinical and genetic correlates. *Comprehensive Psychiatry, 46*, 14–19.

Summerfeldt, L.J., Hood, K.E., Antony, M.M., Richter, M.A., & Swinson, R.P. (2004). Impulsivity in obsessive-compulsive disorder: Comparisons with other anxiety disorders and within tic-related subgroups. *Personality and Individual Differences, 36*, 539–553.

Wetterneck, C.T., Teng, E.J., & Stanley, M.A. (2010). Current issues in the treatment of OC-spectrum conditions. *Bulletin of the Menninger Clinic, 74*, 141–166.

World Health Organization. (2007). *International statistical classification of diseases and related health problems, 10th Revision.*

PART 2

Phenomenology and Epidemiology

Phenomenology and Epidemiology of Obsessive Compulsive Disorder

John E. Calamari, Heather M. Chik, Noelle K. Pontarelli, *and* Brandon L. DeJong

Abstract

Obsessive compulsive disorder (OCD) is a complex, often debilitating syndrome that significantly diminishes quality of life. Although the exact prevalence of OCD is unclear, estimates suggest that it is a common form of psychopathology in the West and throughout the world. A challenge to researchers and clinicians is the significant heterogeneity of OCD. Initial heterogeneity research points to important subtypes of the disorder. Elucidation of disorder heterogeneity might advance etiologic theory and treatment research, and suggest where OCD or OCD-like conditions should be placed in a comprehensive psychiatric disorder nosology. OCD more often occurs with other psychiatric disorders, and evaluation of OCD comorbidity will help clarify this condition's relation to anxiety disorders, mood disorders, and conditions posited to be part of a broad OCD spectrum. Despite significant advancements, much work remains before we can fully understand obsessional disorders and the relation of OCD to commonly experienced negative intrusive thoughts.

Keywords: Obsessive compulsive disorder, phenomenology, epidemiology, comorbidity, heterogeneity

Obsessive compulsive disorder (OCD) is a common and often debilitating condition that is defined in the current psychiatric disorder taxonomy by the experience of obsessions or compulsions that cause marked distress and impairment (*Diagnostic and Statistical Manual*, 4th edition, text revision, American Psychiatric Association [APA], 2000 [DSM-IV-TR]). In the current volume, both OCD and obsessive compulsive spectrum disorders are reviewed. Obsessive compulsive spectrum disorders are syndromes posited to be related in important ways to OCD, sharing phenomenological features, etiologic processes, or similar responsiveness to specific interventions. Although we focus in this chapter only on the phenomenology and epidemiology of OCD as currently defined, our review inevitably touches on issues important to the ongoing debate on where OCD should be placed in the psychiatric disorder taxonomy, and whether there

are importantly related disorders that should be incorporated in a broader OCD spectrum category. We review the defining features of OCD and how the syndrome might be similar or different from the anxiety disorders, among which OCD is included in the DSM-IV-TR. Because OCD infrequently occurs without other conditions, we evaluate these regularly seen comorbidities as important to understanding the phenomenology of OCD. We examine the frequency of specific comorbidities, and then consider the implications for understanding OCD as a distinct syndrome or as a disorder with features that might significantly overlap with several other conditions. OCD's relatedness to other syndromes has important implications for where the disorder might be placed in the taxonomy.

A challenge to understanding OCD phenomenology is the disorder's significant heterogeneity (see McKay et al., 2004, for a review). We overview approaches to understanding OCD heterogeneity, including evaluations of symptom differences, demographic factors, and age at onset. Age at onset appears more variable than initially appreciated, and early-onset variants of the disorder might be associated with different comorbidities and patterns of heritability (e.g., Geller et al., 1998). We discuss recent advances in the study of OCD heterogeneity, as well as some of the limitations of the approaches used to study this issue.

We included in our review of OCD heterogeneity an examination of the variability seen in patients' insight into the excessiveness of their obsessional concerns and related neutralizing behaviors. OCD with poor insight, incorporated in the psychiatric classification system in the fourth edition of the Diagnostic and Statistical Manual (APA, 1994 [DSM-IV]), is recognized as a particularly important clinical subgroup because of the possible implications for treatment. We review the challenges to assessing the specific overvalued ideas of obsessional patients. We examine both variability in patient insight, posited to range from complete rationality to delusion (Kozak & Foa, 1994), and discuss whether overvalued ideas appear to be stable over time, variable during the course of OCD, or modifiable in response to specific interventions.

Rachman and De Silva's (1978) seminal study on clinical and nonclinical obsessions, and the related empirical work that followed, can be considered the foundation on which contemporary cognitive theories and therapies of OCD rest. Rachman and De Silva's observation that most healthy individuals experienced obsession-like intrusive thoughts, and that clinical and nonclinical obsessions were difficult for skilled mental health professionals to distinguish based on their content, accelerated the development of cognitive theories and the adaptation of Beck's (1976) cognitive specificity hypothesis to OCD. The development of an OCD-specific cognitive theory and therapy has progressed rapidly (see Frost & Steketee, 2002 for a review; see Salkovskis, 1985; 1989). We briefly review the empirical work on similarities and differences between clinical and nonclinical obsessions, including recent studies suggesting that important content differences might exist (e.g., Rassin & Muris, 2006). This line of investigation has critical implications for understanding OCD phenomenology.

Lastly, we review the epidemiology of OCD and discuss the many challenges to estimating the prevalence of a disorder with highly diverse symptom presentations. The ubiquitous nature of intrusive thought experiences makes distinguishing between a clinical obsessional syndrome and commonly experienced negative thoughts challenging. Although we critically review evidence on OCD prevalence, the available information continues to support understandings of OCD as a common psychiatric condition, rather than the rare disorder it was once posited to be (see Swinson, Antony, Rachman, & Richter, 1998, for review).

The Phenomenology of Obsessive Compulsive Disorder
Early Conceptualizations of Obsessional Syndromes

Obsessional symptoms have been documented throughout written history, suggesting that the disorder has existed for many centuries. Early accounts of individuals' obsessional symptoms reveal that religious authorities were often relied on to explain these difficulties. Obsessional symptoms were understood to reflect the individual's spiritual well being, and interventions congruent with that belief were offered. As Neziroglu and Yaryura-Tobias (1997) and Panksepp (2004) noted in their reviews, people with obsessions and compulsions were sometimes treated using methods reserved for the correction of blasphemy, as their symptoms were seen as signs of possession. Individuals exhibiting thoughts or behaviors that were deemed blasphemous were subjected to exorcisms, which sometimes took the form of torture. The intervention was intended to restore the obsessional individual to normality (Neziroglu & Yaryura-Tobias, 1997).

In later accounts of obsessionality, symptoms remained connected to moral and spiritual issues. At the beginning of the seventeenth century, Shakespeare, in one of his most famous works, wrote of the guilt and accompanying ritualistic handwashing behaviors of Lady Macbeth. Robert Burton, in his *Anatomy of Melancholy* (1621/1847), described obsessions and compulsions as "religious melancholy." He foreshadowed current conceptualizations of obsessions and compulsions when he described a particular individual who "[i]f he be in a silent auditory, as at a sermon, he is afraid he shall speak aloud and unaware, something indecent, unfit to be said" (p. 234).

These early understandings of obsessional symptoms as related to morality might have connected the syndrome to the scrupulosity symptoms described in historical accounts, and now identified as an important variant of OCD (e.g., Nelson, Abramowitz, Whiteside, & Deacon, 2006).

O'Flaherty (1966) described individuals who were "persistently concerned with incident, thought, word, or deed," whose "thoughts caused uneasiness and distress," and who experienced these symptoms while being otherwise "healthy, normal, and free of other pathological disorders," (O'Flaherty, as cited in Rapoport, 1989, p. 312). Earlier, Jeremy Taylor described in *Ductor Dubitantium* in 1660, individuals free of other pathological disorders who experienced religious scruples in excess. He described those people as ". . .[R]epent[ing] when they have not sinned, and accus[ing] themselves without form or matter; their virtues make them tremble, and in their innocence they are afraid; they at no hand would sin, and know not on which hand to avoid it" (1660/1855, p. 263), suggesting that behaviors were repeatedly performed in order to reduce the individual's subjective levels of distress. A similar description was given by Saint Alphonsus Liguori in 1773 (cited in Rapoport, 1989) when he described the scrupulosity he had examined as "[a] groundless fear of sinning that arises from erroneous ideas."

The connecting of OCD symptoms to religiosity continued into the twentieth century. At the behest of the Roman Catholic Church, a study was conducted that examined the pastoral treatment of scrupulosity (Mullen, 1927). In the study, 400 women in a Catholic high school were asked about their scrupulosity symptoms, and about any cleaning and washing habits they felt compelled to perform. Some study participants observed that such symptoms seemed to run in their family. The symptoms reported by participants, including fearing that their analysis of the morality of an action was incorrect, are similar to contemporary conceptualizations of OCD (Rapoport, 1989).

Starting in the 1800s, a shift began from describing obsessive compulsive symptoms in religious terms, toward understanding the syndrome as a medical condition (Krochmalik & Menzies, 2003). Esquirol, in his textbook *Traite des Maladies Mentales* (Esquirol, 1845/1938), presented the case of "Mademoiselle F." He used the term *monomania*, or partial insanity, to describe a physical disease of the brain, which occurred without fever and was characterized by partial lesion of intellect, the emotions, or the will. The affected individual was said to be "chained to actions that neither reason nor emotion have originated, that conscience rejects and will cannot suppress" (Esquirol, cited in Bynum, Porter, & Shepherd, 2005, p. 170). Esquirol indicated that this "disordered intellect" or "disordered will," led to thoughts and rituals that were both recurrent and

unwanted, and that were characterized by magical thinking (Panksepp, 2004). He observed that although the repetitive symptoms were described as irresistible by those with the condition, individuals had insight into the nature of their symptoms, inasmuch as they ". . .[c]arried out actions they considered as bizarre and absurd. . .but were aware of their state, able to talk about it, and longed to be rid of it" (Esquirol, cited in Bynum et al., 2005, p. 170).

By the 1850s, the conceptualization of obsessional disorders as monomania was criticized for several reasons (Bynum et al., 2005). This conceptualization was seen as resulting from an overly mechanistic application of faculty psychology. Here, the mind was viewed as having separate divisions, or modules, which were assigned to carrying out a particular task. These divisions were thought to respond to training, where behaviors could be enhanced through practice or diminished if practice did not occur (Benjamin, 2007). Thus, the mind was treated as if it were a muscle that could be strengthened in order to control the will and emotions. This conceptualization was also rejected for being too broad, attempting to explain many clinical states, and not accounting for variability in individual symptomatology or the subjective experiences of individuals with specific conditions.

Alvarenga et al. (2007) reviewed theories of obsessional disorders in Europe in the 1800s. They described how new theories developed because of the backlash against the monomania concept. Dagonet (1870) considered compulsive behaviors to be impulsions, acts that were irresistible and imposed on the mind, much like hallucinations. Those with obsessive compulsive symptoms were thought to have had their will overcome and their impulsions given form in their obsessions. While Dagonet's (1870) view of obsessional symptoms as disorders of will or emotion were dominant in France in the later 1800s, German physicians of the same period tended to understand obsessive compulsive symptoms as resulting from a disorder of intellect. They posited that irrational thoughts occurred because of physical changes in the brain, which in turn affected cognition. Griesenger published several cases in 1868 of a disorder that involved questioning or rumination that resulted from an "impairment of ideas," and designated them as *Grubelnsucht*, from the Old German *Grubeln,* meaning to "wrack one's brains," and *suchen,* meaning "to seek" (Berrios, 1996). Westphal shared this view, also conceptualizing obsessive compulsive behaviors as arising out of disordered intellectual functioning (Westphal, 1878). Westphal theorized that emotional dysregulation was insufficient by itself to cause obsessional symptoms. Symptoms resulted from difficulties in inhibiting negative intrusive thoughts, the excessive awareness of one's thoughts, and understanding related repetitive actions as being excessive. Westphal also hypothesized that there might be a genetic predisposition for obsessional disorders (Alverenga et al., 2007). Westphal was one of the first to provide a comprehensive description that he designated *Zwangsvorstellung*, translated as "obsession" in Europe and "compulsion" in the United States. His work is credited as leading to the current nomenclature of "obsessive compulsive" (Alverenga et al., 2007).

As conceptualizations of obsessive compulsive symptoms evolved, there was a shift toward more explicitly relating human experience to the disorder (e.g., the increased stress that resulted from urbanization). The term *neurasthenia* was introduced by Beard in 1869 to define a heterogeneous disorder that included obsessional symptoms (Beard, 1869). Neurasthenia, as defined by Beard, included intrusive thought experiences and the performance of rituals, but was also characterized by mental and physical fatigue and muscular weakness (Beard, 1869). Individuals with neurasthenia were thought not to have sufficient psychological tension (nervous energy) to perform more sophisticated mental activities. The nervous energy that these individuals did have was instead redirected toward more primitive functions, precipitating obsessions and compulsions (van der Hart & Friedman, 1989).

Swinson et al. (1998) have reviewed more recent conceptualizations of OCD. At the turn of the twentieth century, there was a movement away from the neurasthenic construct. Janet considered anxiety to be a secondary characteristic of OCD, and introduced the concept of *psychasthenia* (Swinson et al., 1998). Janet believed that a sense of imperfection, or of incompletely achieving an objective, characterized those with obsessive compulsive syndromes. Anxiety was theorized to be a reaction to, rather than a precipitant of, the obsessional symptoms. North American audiences did not as readily embrace Janet's view, a theory that had features that overlapped with the psychoanalytic conceptualization of obsessional disorders. In 1895, Freud (1895/1958) published an article in which he distinguished what he called an *anxiety neurosis* and the concept of neurasthenia. Due to the popularity of psychoanalysis in the late nineteenth and early

twentieth centuries, Freud's conceptualization of OCD became dominant. Freud's ideas continued to be highly influential as the first psychiatric taxonomies were developed in the United States. The first two editions of the *Diagnostic and Statistical Manual* of the American Psychiatric Association, (APA, 1952; 1968) used his psychoanalytic conceptualizations as the basis for disorder classification.

In summary, conceptualizations of obsessive compulsive symptoms, before Freud's highly influential work, pointed to a distinct syndrome that had important phenomenological differences from other forms of psychopathology. Early on, the core phenomenology of the disorder was believed to involve the experience of unwanted thoughts that the individual could exert little control over (Burton, 1621/1847; Esquirol, cited in Bynum et al., 2005; O'Flaherty, 1966; Rapoport, 1989). Compulsive behaviors were likewise identified as a core aspect of the syndrome in early understandings of obsessional conditions (Burton, 1621/1847; Esquirol, cited in Bynum et al., 2005; Dagonet, 1870; Neziroglu & Yaryura-Tobias, 1997). The afflicted individual was again understood to have limited ability to prevent these repetitive actions (Burton, 1621/1847; Esquirol, as cited in Bynum et al., 2005; Mullen, 1927; O'Flaherty, as cited in Rapoport, 1989; J. Taylor, 1660/1855; Westphal, 1878). Thus, in the early descriptions of the syndrome, volitional control of thought and behavior was more often believed to have been lost. The functional relationship between obsessions and compulsions was sometimes recognized in early descriptions of obsessional conditions, with individuals understood to perform their ritualized behaviors to decrease their subjective level of stress (Liguori, as cited in Rapoport, 1989; Taylor, 1660/1855). Compulsive behaviors were not seen as anxiety-reducing in their own right, but as related to intrusive cognition. The ego-dystonic nature of the experienced intrusions was also often recognized (Burton, 1621/1847; Esquirol, as cited in Bynum et al., 2005; O'Flaherty, as cited in Rapoport, 1989). Individuals with the syndrome were seen as often recognizing the excessive nature of their obsessional concerns and behaviors (Esquirol, as cited in Bynum et al., 2005; O'Flaherty, as cited in Rapoport, 1989; Taylor, 1660/1845).

Psychoanalytic Theory and Obsessional Disorders

Freud conceptualized obsessive compulsive symptoms as symbolizing the patient's unconscious struggle over drives that were unacceptable at a conscious level (Freud, 1913/1958). Individuals with obsessional disorders, Freud maintained, had their defensive system, specifically repression, fail, thereby allowing improper or unwanted thoughts to enter into consciousness. As a result, these individuals focused their energy on repeatedly and exactly performing tasks in order to avoid conscious awareness of previously repressed material. That is, they distracted themselves from thinking about what they unconsciously felt they should not think about (Carr, 1974; Rachman, 1963). Psychoanalytic theorists posited that the root cause of obsessional syndromes was the "precocity" of ego development, a mismatch between the development of the libido and the ego. According to the theory, individuals who progress through the psychosexual stages normally develop the libido first, followed by the ego. In the case of those with obsessive compulsive symptoms, the reverse was thought to be true, which predisposed the individual to a pathologically immature and incomplete mode of relating to others. Thus, with respect to object relations, hate would precede love and "obsessional neurotics have to develop a super-morality in order to protect their object-love from the hostility lurking behind it" (Freud, 1913/1958, p. 325). Freud underscored this opposition between love and hate for the object in his analysis of the "Rat Man," one of the first published treatments of an individual with OCD. Here, Freud advanced the opinion that this opposition among psychic forces was the source of the doubting, compulsive behavior, and ambivalence that, he argued, are characteristic of obsessional neurosis (Freud, 1909/1958).

Freud maintained that adults with obsessive compulsive syndromes manifested several broad characteristics. First, they were fixated at the anal-sadistic psychosexual stage of development, preoccupied with a need for control, and exhibited the "anal triad" personality traits of orderliness, parsimony, and obstinacy. Additionally, these individuals had a very rigid and demanding set of external prohibitions, which dictated their behavior. Freud observed that for obsessional patients, having a particular unacceptable thought (e.g., harming an infant), was experienced as intensely distressing, almost as if the person had actually performed the action (Freud, 1909/1958). Freud's observation is congruent with contemporary cognitive theories of OCD emphasizing beliefs in the importance of thought (Rachman, 1997), and dysfunctional meta-cognitive beliefs in thought–action fusion (e.g., thought influencing events in the world, or thought

as a moral act, see Thordarson & Shafran, 2002, for a review).

In Freud's model, the overuse of particular defense mechanisms characterized those with obsessive compulsive symptoms, particularly the use of reaction formation, intellectualization and isolation, and undoing. Freud attributed the syndrome to psychogenic processes; learning and conditioning, neuropathology, and genetic predisposition were not considered.

In psychoanalytic models, the content of compulsive symptoms was related to behaviors that previously served to reduce anxiety, but these behaviors had now become exaggerated and overgeneralized; such as engaging in handwashing to avoid criticism from one's parents (Dollard & Miller, 1950). More contemporary psychoanalytic theorists have used object-relations approaches that focus not only on the patient, but on the patient's impression of the behavior of others (Kempke & Luyten, 2007).

Conceptualizations of Obsessive Compulsive Disorder in the Psychiatric Disorder Taxonomy

Next, we review the evolution of conceptualizations of OCD as reflected in the most influential psychopathology taxonomy, the *Diagnostic and Statistical Manual of Mental Disorders* of the American Psychiatric Association. We examine how the phenomenology of OCD has been described in this classification system since the early 1950s until the present. We briefly review several issues being debated as the next edition of this classification system is being developed.

The First and Second Editions of the Diagnostic and Statistical Manual of Mental Disorders of the American Psychiatric Association

Psychoanalytic theory greatly influenced the classification and treatment of mental disorders in the United States for several decades. The first edition of the DSM (DSM-I; APA, 1952) brought together for the first time descriptions of mental disorders, and placed the identified syndromes in a classification framework. In the first major revision of that taxonomy (DSM-II; APA, 1968), the classification methods, as well as the accompanying text for describing disorders, were drawn from the mental disorders section of the eighth edition of the International Classification of Diseases (World Health Organization, 1965). During this period, psychoanalytic theory continued to dominate the field. In these models, psychopathology was believed to be secondary to the experience of anxiety, which was caused by intrapsychic conflicts. In the DSM-I (APA, 1952), anxiety was described as "a danger signal felt and perceived by the conscious portion of the personality" and "produced by a threat from within the personality" (p. 31). How the individual responded to this anxiety determined the type of reaction (e.g., "obsessive compulsive reaction") in this diagnostic system. In the DSM-II (APA, 1968), anxiety was defined as "anxious over concern extending to panic, commonly associated with somatic symptoms that must be distinguished from normal apprehension, or fear" (p. 39). Psychodynamic theorists posited that mental disorders and the associated symptoms existed on a continuum with nonpathological behavior. All people were seen as experiencing intrapsychic conflicts and the associated anxiety symptoms to an extent, and on an extreme point on the continuum, because of severe unconscious conflict, were those who developed psychoses (Mayes & Horwitz, 2005). Neuroses were described as involving anxiety that was "felt and expressed directly, or controlled unconsciously or automatically by conversion, displacement, and various other psychological mechanisms" (APA, 1952, p. 31). Thus, the different categories of psychopathology were guided by the underlying methods the affected individual was believed to use to deal with internal conflict. This early psychiatric taxonomy was driven by the dominant theory of the time, rather than by the behavioral criteria (e.g., the frequency of certain symptoms; the presence of several defining symptoms from a list of core behaviors) that characterizes the current classification system (First, Frances, & Pincus, 2004).

In the DSM-I, what is currently known as OCD was designated "obsessive compulsive reaction" and was included in a broader category of Psychoneurotic Disorders. The defining characteristic of the Psychoneurotic Disorders was anxiety. Individuals might receive this diagnosis if they experienced ideas that were unwanted, or felt compelled to perform rituals (specified as "touching, counting, ceremonials, hand-washing, or recurring thoughts"), which might be seen by the individual to be excessive or unreasonable (APA, 1952, p. 33). In the DSM-II, OCD was classified as a neurosis, and conditions included in this broad category were characterized by anxiety from which the individual desired relief. The "obsessive compulsive neurosis" was defined in a manner almost identical to that of the "obsessive compulsive reaction" of the DSM-I, with the

addition that "[a]nxiety and distress are often present either if the patient is prevented from completing his compulsive ritual or if he is concerned about being unable to control it himself" (APA, 1968, p. 40).

Obsessive Compulsive Disorder in the Contemporary Psychiatric Taxonomy

A significantly different approach was taken to the classification of psychopathology in the third edition of the DSM (APA; 1980). The often vague and brief descriptions of syndromes in DSM-II resulted in poor diagnostic reliability (Beck, Ward, Mendelson, Mock, & Erbaugh, 1962; Nathan, Andberg, Behan, & Patch, 1969). An attempt was made to define syndromes reliably, and to make such definitions independent of specific etiologic theories of the disorder (Bayer & Spitzer, 1985; Millon, 1983). The result was an atheoretical classification system and a significantly greater number of diagnostic categories. Psychopathology syndromes were largely defined by sets of observable symptoms considered to reflect the core overt phenomenology of specific disorders (Millon, 1983; Spitzer, Williams, & Skodol, 1980). The emphasis placed on behavioral descriptions and symptom clusters and the attempt to maintain a largely descriptive and atheoretical classification system comes with both costs and benefits. Classification systems have several purposes, including the reliable definition of a syndrome to facilitate communication among scientists and clinicians. Additionally, a well-structured classification system should incorporate existing empirical data while promoting ongoing study of unanswered questions.

How well does the current psychiatric disorder nosology address core OCD phenomenology? Abramowitz and Deacon (2005) argued that there are several important limitations. An implied assumption in the DSM, that the presence of obsessions or compulsions is necessary and sufficient to consider the symptom cluster OCD, ignores important OCD phenomenology. This assumption could result in some types of symptoms being considered OCD or OCD-related based on only superficial similarities. Abramowitz and Deacon suggested that this focus ignores the core functional characteristics of the disorder (e.g., negative intrusive thoughts that elevate distress and compulsions undertaken to neutralize this discomfort).

In the DSM-III (APA; 1980), OCD was placed under the broad heading of Anxiety Disorders, specifically, and under the subheading of Anxiety

States. The other Anxiety Sates were panic disorder and generalized anxiety disorder (GAD). The other two subheadings of the Anxiety Disorders were Phobic Disorders, and Post-Traumatic Stress Disorders. Agoraphobia with panic attacks, agoraphobia without panic attacks, social phobia, and simple phobia comprised the Phobic Disorders. Acute and chronic (or delayed) post-traumatic stress disorder (PTSD) stood alone in the Post-Traumatic Stress Disorders category. The hallmark of OCD, according to the DSM-III, was the recurrence of obsessions or compulsions that caused significant distress or "interfere with social or role functioning" (p. 235). Obsessions were defined as "recurrent, persistent ideas, thoughts, images, or impulses that are ego-dystonic. . .and are experienced as senseless or repugnant" (p. 235). Individuals with OCD attempted to ignore or suppress the thoughts, images, or impulses they experienced. Compulsions, on the other hand, were defined as "repetitive and seemingly purposeful behaviors that are performed according to certain rules or in a stereotyped fashion" (p. 235). The behaviors are "designed to produce or prevent some future event or situation. However, either the activity is not connected in a realistic way with what it is designed to produce or prevent, or may be clearly excessive" (p. 235). Further, in the DSM-III, individuals with the disorder were described not as only trying to resist doing the compulsions (at least initially), but they also were understood in general to recognize "the senselessness of the behavior (this may not be true for young children). . ." (p. 235). An additional distinction made between the compulsive behaviors associated with OCD, and other repetitive maladaptive behaviors, was that the affected individual did not perform the behavior to derive pleasure, but rather to experience a release of tension.

The conceptualization of OCD in the psychiatric taxonomy has not changed dramatically since DSM-III, although several issues important to understanding OCD phenomenology are reflected in the modifications to the diagnostic criteria. In DSM-III-R (APA, 1987), the nine diagnoses under the broad heading of Anxiety Disorders were no longer subdivided into Phobic versus Anxiety Neurosis. Emphasis was placed on better defining obsessions and compulsions while also emphasizing the degree of distress and impairment required for the diagnosis. New to this edition was the inclusion of the time-consuming nature of obsessions and compulsions. The DSM-III-R indicated obsessions and compulsions should "take more than an hour

a day" (p. 247). Excellent reliability was reported for a current principal diagnosis of OCD using the Anxiety Disorders Interview Schedule-Revised (ADIS-R; di Nardo, Moras, Barlow, Rapee, & Brown, 1993), but poor reliability was found for the OCD diagnosis when using the Structured Clinical Interview for DSM-III-R (Skre, Onstad, Torgersen, & Kringlen, 1991).

Based on the field trial for the DSM-IV (APA; 1994), two important recommendations were made for improving the criteria of OCD in the DSM-IV (Foa et al., 1995a, 1995b). In the field trial, most individuals with OCD were uncertain about whether their obsessive-compulsive symptoms were unreasonable or excessive, and most had both mental and behavioral compulsions. As a result, the DSM-IV acknowledged the variability in patient insight. A specifier of "with poor insight" was added to the criteria of OCD. Although adults with OCD should, at some point, recognize the excessiveness or unreasonableness of their obsessions and compulsions, the DSM-IV acknowledged that insight is likely to vary between individuals, and to vary over time and situations within individuals. The poor insight specifier is applied when the individual does not recognize the excessiveness or unreasonableness of their obsessions and compulsions most of the time during their current episode (APA; 1994). The insight variability seen in OCD is reviewed in a later section of this chapter. Furthermore, the DSM-IV included mental acts (e.g., praying, counting, repeating words silently) within the definition of compulsions. Further, in the DSM-IV the differentiation of core OCD phenomenology from the symptoms seen in other conditions (e.g., the excessive worries about real-life problems characteristic of generalized anxiety disorder) was clarified.

Finally, the DSM-IV and its text revision (APA; 2000) described a greater number of obsession and compulsion symptoms (i.e., repeated thoughts about contamination, doubts, having things in a particular order, aggressive impulses, sexual imagery, as common obsessions; washing and cleaning, counting, checking, requesting or demanding assurances, repeating actions, and ordering, as compulsions) acknowledging the significant symptom heterogeneity of OCD. Hoarding was not explicitly acknowledged as a variant of OCD.

Obsessive Compulsive Disorder and the Next Psychiatric Disorder Taxonomy

As the next major revision of the psychiatric disorder taxonomy [DSM-V] progresses, we consider in this section what changes in the classification and conceptualization of OCD might occur. These changes will likely emerge from an integration of the extensive empirical work on OCD.

OCD has been classified under the rubrics of anxiety disorders, neuroses, or psychoneurotic disorders for almost a century (Tynes, White, & Steketee, 1990). The more recent classification of OCD as an anxiety disorder has not been without controversy. Although the revisions in the psychiatric taxonomy seen in the DSM-II made the system generally congruent with the eighth edition of the International Classification of Diseases (ICD-8), OCD was no longer classified as an anxiety disorder in the ICD-8 system at that time. The phenomenology of OCD was judged importantly different from the anxiety disorders (Montgomery, 1993). Some taxonomists continue to argue that OCD should not be classified as an anxiety disorder, understanding anxiety symptoms as secondary to core OCD processes (Mataix-Cols, Pertusa, & Leckman, 2007). Further, proponents of this change argue that the neurobiological distinctiveness of OCD from several other anxiety disorders is now better understood, and supports reclassification of the disorder (Bartz & Hollander, 2006). Counterarguments to the reclassification of OCD have included contentions that all the anxiety disorders have defining features in addition to the experience of anxiety, and that although specific neurobiological processes were associated with some anxiety disorders, there are significant overlapping features among these conditions (e.g., striatal involvement; commonalities in the neurotransmitter systems involved; see D. J. Stein, 2008, for a review). Mataix-Cols et al. (2007) surveyed 187 OCD experts and found that 60% believed OCD should be reclassified, while 40% maintained that OCD should remain an anxiety disorder.

A related issue for the DSM-V is the OCD disorder spectrum. Hollander, Braun, and Simeon (2008) advocated removing OCD from the anxiety disorders, and development of a distinct category for OCD and OCD-related disorders—obsessive compulsive spectrum disorders, or sometimes called *obsessive compulsive related disorders* (OCRDs; Hollander et. al 2009). Hollander and colleagues argued that development of an OCRD classification would aid in diagnosis and screening, as well as bring the classification of these disorders in line with that of the World Health Organization ICD system. Hollander et al. (2008) suggested that OCRDs can be conceptualized as lying on a spectrum of compulsivity-impulsivity, with risk-aversive and harm related disorders on one end of this spectrum (e.g., disorders where compulsions are performed to reduce perceived threat or anxiety, such as OCD, body dysmorphic disorder, and anorexia nervosa). Disorders characterized by risk-taking, gratification seeking, and impulsivity were posited to lie at the other end of the compulsivity-impulsivity continuum (e.g., sexual compulsions, pathological gambling, and binge eating). Hollander and colleagues argued that there is significant empirical support for the proposed OCRD classification, including overlapping phenomenology across the conditions proposed for inclusion. Hollander and colleagues contended that OCRDs also have similar comorbidities, commonalities in heritability and associated genetic anomalies, similar brain circuitry and neurotransmitter system involvement, and share a positive response to related treatments.

Storch, Abramowitz, and Goodman (2008) critically reviewed the data often used to support development of the OCRD classification. The authors concluded that reclassification of OCD into a new OCRD category was not well supported and at best premature. Storch et al. (2008) argued that the OCRD category classification is poorly defined, and that there is no easily operationalized cutoff between compulsivity and impulsivity or indication that this conceptualization is useful for elucidating OCD. Further, Storch et al. (2008) noted that there is not a consensus among mental health practitioners that the approach has clinical utility (Mataix-Cols et al., 2007). Storch and colleagues indicated that emphasizing repetitive behaviors as a defining aspect of the spectrum criteria overlooks other, more fundamental phenomenological features of OCD, such as the reduction of obsession-related fears through performance of compulsions. The criticisms directed at the proposed OCD spectrum appear to focus on the limitations of a classification system not guided by well-developed theory (cf. Follette & Houts, 1996).

Disorders proposed for the OCD spectrum category are addictions, autism, body dysmorphic disorder, chronic tic disorders, eating disorders, hypochondriasis, impulse-control disorders (e.g., pathological gambling), and OCD (Hollander & Zohar, 2004; D. J. Stein & Lochner, 2006; Storch, Abramowitz et al., 2008). Again, Bartz and Hollander (2006) argued that the spectrum classification is based on important commonalities in the phenomenology of the proposed disorders, and that these commonalities include similarities in patient characteristics, course of the disorders, comorbidity patterns, neurobiology, and treatment response. Some psychopathologists have recommended that if the spectrum construct is adopted, it should be defined more narrowly and include body dysmorphic disorder, trichotillomania, tic disorders, and hypochondriasis. In this approach, OCD would be treated as a heterogeneous condition, with specifiers for each of its presentations (e.g., contamination/cleaning, symmetry/order/repeating/counting, hoarding, harm, obsessions and checking, and sexual and religious obsessions; Mataix-Cols et al., 2007). Additionally, the hoarding subtype might be specified as a separate OCD-related disorder and have its own diagnostic criteria (Mataix-Cols et al., 2007). Recently, the DSM-V Work Group on obsessive compulsive related disorders came to a consensus to not include addictive disorders, several conditions classified as impulse control disorders (e.g., pathological gambling), and binge eating in the OCRDs (Hollander et. al 2009).

Other issues that may affect OCD as the DSM-V is constructed are proposals that mood and anxiety disorders be collapsed into a broader emotional disorders category (Watson, 2005). Additionally, Fontenelle et al. (2008) advocated that more research be done on a possible spectrum of conditions with common perceptual disturbances, symptoms typically found in psychotic disorders but potentially associated with OCD.

Clearly, there is much empirical work needed to integrate disparate perspectives on where OCD should be placed in a comprehensive nosological system. Changes in the classification of OCD should be driven by the available science on this complex disorder. Any changes in the classification of OCD and conditions posited to be OCD-related should function to promote new research, while enabling mental health professionals to more successfully diagnose and treat these disorders.

Conditions Co-occurring with Obsessive Compulsive Disorder

Understanding comorbidity in OCD is important for several reasons. The co-occurrence of another psychological disorder with OCD is usually associated with greater symptom severity, diminished treatment response, a poorer prognosis (Abramowitz, Franklin, Street, Kozak, & Foa, 2000; Brown & Barlow, 1992; Hansen, Vogel, Stiles, & Götestam, 2007; Masellis, Rector, & Richter, 2003; Storch, Merlo et al., 2008; Tükel, Polat, Ozdemir, Aksut, &

Turksov, 2002), and greater impairment in quality of life (Huppert, Simpson, Nissenson, Liebowitz, & Foa, 2009). Additionally, OCD infrequently occurs without other disorders (e.g., Weissman et al., 1994). The frequent comorbidity of syndromes has significant implications for the classification of emotional disorders (Brown, Campbell, Lehman, Grisham, & Mancill, 2001). For example, the high rates of comorbidity of anxiety and mood disorders has caused Watson (2005) to propose that mood and anxiety disorders should be collapsed into a broader emotional disorders category.

HOW OFTEN DOES OBSESSIVE COMPULSIVE DISORDER CO-OCCUR WITH OTHER PSYCHIATRIC DISORDERS?

High rates of diagnostic comorbidity have been found with OCD, although few surveys involved large-scale epidemiological studies (e.g., Angst et al., 2004; Ruscio, Stein, Chiu, & Kessler, 2010; A. R. Torres et al., 2006; Weissman et al., 1994). Early surveys used the DSM-III definition of OCD, whereas more recent investigations have adopted the DSM-IV diagnostic criteria. Weissman et al. (1994) conducted an epidemiological survey in seven countries and found 49% of individuals diagnosed with OCD experienced a comorbid anxiety disorder and 27% experienced comorbid major depression. DSM-III diagnostic criteria were used in the study. In the recent National Comorbidity Survey Replication study, a nationally representative survey of U.S. adults, Ruscio et al. (2010) reported substantial comorbidity not only with anxiety (75.8%) and mood (63.3%) disorders, but also with impulse control (55.9%) and substance use disorders (38.6%) using DSM-IV diagnostic criteria.

Surveys conducted in anxiety clinics have also used DSM-IV criteria for evaluating comorbidity. In these studies, 48%–64% of OCD patients had at least one additional Axis I diagnosis at the time of evaluation (Antony, Downie, & Swinson, 1998; Brown, Campbell et al., 2001; Denys, Tenney, van Megen, de Geus, & Westenberg, 2004). The most common additional diagnoses were social phobia (3.6%–41.4%) and major depression (20.7%–24.1%), followed by specific phobia (0.95%–20.7%), dysthymic disorder (2.8%–13.8%), panic disorder with/without agoraphobia (4%–11.5%), generalized anxiety disorder (0.95% –12%), somatoform disorders (1% –3.8%), and PTSD (0%–1.6%) (Antony et al., 1998; Brown et al., 2001; Denys et al., 2004). Comorbidity rates with disorders not classified as anxiety or mood disorders were not as high: tic-related disorders (3.6%–13%), eating disorders (2.4% –5%), impulse control disorders such as trichotillomania (4.6%– 9%), and skin picking (15%) (Antony et al., 1998; Denys et al., 2004). When lifetime comorbidity was considered, fewer than 15% of cases had a sole diagnosis of OCD (Brown et al., 2001; Diniz et al., 2004; LaSalle et al., 2004). Furthermore, those with earlier onset OCD typically had more lifetime comorbid psychiatric conditions (de Mathis et al., 2008; LaSalle et al., 2004).

With growing evidence for the heterogeneity of OCD (McKay et al., 2004), recent studies have examined comorbidity patterns for different OCD symptom presentations. To evaluate whether OCD symptom subtypes had different comorbid disorders, Hasler et al. (2005) first factor– and cluster-analyzed both the Yale-Brown Obsessive-Compulsive Scale Symptom Checklist and the Thoughts and Behaviors Inventory, finding support for a four-factor/cluster model. Their Factor I (aggressive, sexual, religious, and somatic obsessions, and checking compulsions) was broadly associated with comorbid major depression and anxiety disorders, including GAD, panic disorder, agoraphobia, social anxiety disorder, specific phobia, and substance use disorders. Factor II (obsession of symmetry, and repeating, counting, and ordering/arranging compulsions) was associated with bipolar disorder and panic disorder/agoraphobia, and substance use disorders. Factor III (contamination obsessions and cleaning compulsions) was positively associated with eating disorders but negatively associated with Tourette's disorder. Interestingly, no associations were found between Factor IV (hoarding obsessions and compulsions) and any other psychiatric conditions.

Hasler et al.'s (2005) findings were incongruent with other studies that found hoarding patients to have significantly more co-occurring disorders than non-hoarding OCD patients (Lochner et al., 2005; Samuels et al., 2007; Wheaton, Timpano, LaSalle-Ricci, & Murphy, 2008). These differences likely result from the method used to define the hoarding subgroup. Hasler et al. (2005) defined their hoarding subgroup based on multivariate analysis of two self-report measures, whereas Lochner et al. (2005), Samuels et al. (2007), and Wheaton et al. (2008) classified their hoarding subgroup based on clinician-administered structured interviews. Lochner et al. (2005) and Samuels et al. (2007) reported increased rates of obsessive compulsive personality disorder (OCPD) among hoarding patients compared to non-hoarding OCD patients. This finding differentiates OCD patients with prominent hoarding symptoms from other OCD patients who have more often been diagnosed with comorbid dependent and avoidant personality disorders (Summerfeldt, Huta, & Swinson, 1998).

Depression and other anxiety disorders occur frequently with individuals who have a primary OCD diagnosis. Yet, when major depression or other anxiety disorders are primary, OCD is infrequently found as a secondary diagnosis even when lifetime rates of comorbidity are considered (Antony et al., 1998; Brown, Campbell et al., 2001; Crino & Andrews, 1996). When the chronology of disorder onset is carefully evaluated, comorbid anxiety disorders tended to precede OCD, whereas comorbid depression tended to occur after the onset of OCD (Brown, Campbell et al., 2001; Ruscio et al., 2010). Comorbid impulse control disorders were also found to begin at an earlier age than OCD (Ruscio et al., 2010). However, findings regarding comorbid substance use disorders are inconsistent; whereas Mancebo et al. (2009) found a majority (70%) of participants reported the onset of OCD preceded substance use disorder, Ruscio et al. (2010) found substance use disorders began at an earlier age than OCD for most (58.9%). After the onset of OCD, an individual remains at elevated risk for developing other anxiety, mood, eating, and tic disorders as long as the episode persists (Yaryura-Tobias et al., 2000).

SPECIFIC COMORBID CONDITIONS – MOOD DISORDERS

The occurrence of a major depressive episode in persons with OCD is high, ranging from 20.7%–24.1%; followed by dysthymia, ranging from 2.8%–13.8% (Brown, Campbell et al., Antony et al., 1998; 2001; Denys et al., 2004). These rates are much higher for comorbid depressive disorder, lifetime (61%–66%), and dysthymia, lifetime (12%–24%) (Brown, Campbell et al., 2001; Diniz et al., 2004; LaSalle et al., 2004). Bipolar disorders (I and II) appear to accompany OCD less frequently, with lifetime comorbidity rates ranging from 9% to 13% (Diniz et al., 2004; LaSalle et al., 2004; Maina, Albert, Pessina, & Bogetto, 2007), although bipolar disorder type II is more frequently associated with OCD than bipolar disorder type I (Maina et al., 2007).

Major depression comorbidity sometimes has a highly detrimental effect on OCD. Obsessional patients with comorbid major depression had more severe OCD symptoms, a greater tendency to misinterpret the significance of intrusive thoughts, poorer insight into the senselessness of their concerns (Abramowitz, Storch, Keeley, & Cordell, 2007), and significantly reduced quality of life (Cassin, Richter, Zhang, & Rector, 2009) compared to patients without comorbid depression. It appears that OCD patients with comorbid major depression do show significant gains in treatment (Abramowitz & Foa, 2000; Rector, Cassin, & Richter, 2009), but their posttreatment symptom level is still significantly greater than symptom levels of OCD patients without concurrent depression (Abramowitz & Foa, 2000). Rector et al. (2009) found that severe levels of depressive symptoms did not substantially interfere with treatment gains from cognitive-behavioral therapy, although additional treatment strategies may be warranted to reduce high treatment dropout rates. Highly depressed OCD patients also appear to be at greater risk for relapse following treatment discontinuation (Abramowitz & Foa, 2000).

The clinical impact of comorbid bipolar disorder in OCD has only recently been investigated. OCD patients with comorbid bipolar disorder were more likely to be male; report more sexual, religious, aggressive, impulsive, and hoarding obsessions, and checking, repeating, ordering, and hoarding compulsions; report more suicide attempts and hospitalizations; and had higher rates of substance use disorders (Diniz et al., 2004; Maina et al., 2007; Perugi et al., 1997; Perugi et al., 2002). In addition, OCD patients with comorbid bipolar disorder have shown significantly higher rates of a Cluster A (42.9%) or B (57.1%) personality disorders, especially narcissistic and antisocial personality disorder. OCD patients without this comorbidity have consistently lower rates of personality disorders (Cluster A: 21.3% versus Cluster B: 29%) (Maina et al., 2007). Taken together, comorbid bipolar disorder in OCD patients might lead to a poor response to, or compliance with, pharmalogical or psychological treatments.

SPECIFIC COMORBID CONDITIONS — ANXIETY DISORDERS

Many individuals with a principal diagnosis of OCD experience additional anxiety symptoms and disorders. The most common comorbid anxiety disorder using DSM-IV diagnostic criteria was social phobia (3.6%–41.4%), followed by specific phobia (0.95%–20.7%), panic disorder with or without agoraphobia (4%–11.5%), GAD (0.95%–12%), somatoform disorder (1%–3.8%),

and PTSD (0%–1.6%) (Antony et al., 1998; Brown, Campbell et al., 2001; Denys et al., 2004). Overall, evidence of symptom overlap and diagnostic co-occurrence of anxiety disorders with OCD suggests that these disorders are sufficiently related to indicate that they may share a common underlying diathesis such as negative affectivity or neuroticism (Brown, 1998). In some cases, trauma appears to have precipitated the OCD symptoms and is likely to require special attention during treatment (de Silva & Marks, 1999), although others found a low rate of trauma-related disorders occurring before (2.9%), or during the same year the OCD began (1.5%) (Grabe et al., 2008). In one study, no significant improvements in OCD and depression were found with patients with comorbid PTSD after a course of behavior therapy (Gershuny, Baer, Jenike, Minichiello, & Wilhelm, 2002). When GAD co-occurs with OCD, it appears to intensify specific OCD-related dysfunctional beliefs with patients experiencing more pathological responsibility and indecisiveness (Abramowitz & Foa, 1998), and these patients may be more likely to drop out of behavior treatment (Chambless & Steketee, 1999).

SPECIFIC COMORBID CONDITIONS — DISORDERS POSITED TO BE PART OF AN OCD SPECTRUM

As previously described, conditions proposed to be part of an OCD spectrum include somatoform disorders (i.e., body dysmorphic disorder [BDD], hypochondriasis), eating disorders (anorexia and bulimia), impulse control disorders (i.e., trichotillomania, kleptomania, pathological gambling), paraphilias and nonparaphilic sexual addictions, and movement disorders such as tics and Tourette's syndrome (Goldsmith, Shapira, Phillips, & McElroy, 1998; Hollander & Wong, 2000).

Similar to OCD, symptoms of BDD include recurrent persistent thoughts and compulsive behaviors (e.g., mirror checking; Wilhelm & Neziroglu, 2002). By contrast, the recurrent thoughts are exclusively appearance-related (Wilhelm & Neziroglu, 2002) and insight is often limited or absent (Eisen, Phillips, Coles, & Rasmussen, 2004). Comorbid BDD within samples of patients with OCD is high (12.9%–19%; Diniz et al., 2004; du Toit, van Kradenburg, Niehaus, & Stein, 2001; Phillips, Gunderson, Mallya, McElroy, & Carter, 1998; Stewart, Stack, & Wilhelm, 2008). OCD patients with comorbid BDD often exhibited greater psychopathology and functional impairment, and more frequently experienced comorbid mental disorders.

These patients experienced earlier onset OCD, had more severe depression, and higher comorbidity with bulimia, substance use disorders, bipolar II disorder, and social anxiety. These patients also reported lower quality of life than those without comorbid BDD (Didie et al., 2007; Frare, Perugi, Ruffolo, & Toni, 2007; Phillips et al., 2007; Stewart et al., 2008). OCD treatment response was found to be unaffected by the presence of BDD, however (Stewart et al., 2008).

Hypochondriasis is characterized by fears of having, or the idea that one has, a serious disease based on misinterpretation of bodily symptoms. Overlaps are evident in the contamination fears and checking and reassurance-seeking behaviors in individuals with hypochondriasis and OCD (Furer, Walker, & Stein, 2007). Prevalence rates of comorbid hypochondriasis range from 2.8%–7.1% (Denys et al., 2004; du Toit et al., 2001). When patients with OCD also exhibit excessive health concerns, they appear to have less insight into their obsessive fears than those without such concerns (Abramowitz, Brigidi, & Foa, 1999), thus potentially interfering with motivation and compliance in treatment.

Significant overlap in phenomenology has been found between eating disorders and OCD. However, the fears and worries of those with anorexia nervosa or bulimia nervosa are focused exclusively on body weight and image (Rothenberg, 1986). At times, the fears of weight gain may lead to compulsive behaviors centered on eating, cooking, and exercise that are similar to OCD rituals (Rothenberg, 1986). Comparisons between OCD and eating disorders suggest shared personality traits such as perfectionism and rigidity (Anderluh, Tchanturia, Rabe-Hesketh, & Treasure, 2003; Jiminez-Murcia et al., 2007), common neuropsychological impairments (Sherman et al., 2006), and similar levels of obsessional beliefs (Lavender, Shubert, De Silva, & Treasure, 2006). In a cross-sectional examination of 815 OCD patients, Sallet et al. (2010) found that comorbid eating disorders were not necessarily associated with greater OCD symptomatology, but suggested that this comorbidity was indicative of more severe general psychopathology (e.g., elevated levels of anxiety and depression, higher frequency of suicide attempts, higher prevalence of several Axis I disorders including impulsecontrol disorders and BDD).

Unlike OCD, the fears in eating disorder patients are generally not ego-dystonic, but are in keeping with the person's belief system regarding the importance of shape and weight (Vitousek, 1996).

When OCD-related contamination fears lead to a reduction in food intake and significant weight loss, patients may be referred for the treatment of an eating disorder, but the psychopathology is that of OCD (Shafran, 2002). Although the similarities between eating disorders and OCD can complicate the symptom picture, they co-occur infrequently. Point prevalence comorbidity rates are relatively low (anorexia: 0.05%–2.4%, bulimia: 1%–3.5%, binge eating: 0%–4.5%) as are lifetime comorbidity rates (anorexia: 2.6%–9%, bulimia: 2.5%–10%, binge eating: 0%–7.9%) (du Toit et al., 2001; LaSalle et al., 2004; Sallet et al., 2010).

Impulse control disorders, including pathological gambling and trichotillomania, are problems that involve repetitive behavior that causes distress, harm, or interference (Radomsky, Bohne, & O'Connor, 2007). Unlike OCD, in which compulsions are usually designed to reduce anxiety or prevent unwanted or catastrophic events from occurring, the repeated behavior in impulse control disorders is commonly carried out to reduce feelings of tension or to generate certain soothing or pleasurable sensations (Radomsky et al., 2007). It is important to distinguish compulsive from impulsive behaviors, as the needed treatment intervention varies depending on this distinction (Radomsky et al., 2007). In particular, habit reversal training (Azrin & Peterson, 1988) is most effective when applied to symptoms of hair-pulling and skin picking, whereas exposure and response prevention (ERP) is most effective when treating symptoms of OCD (Radomsky et al., 2007).

In large OCD clinical samples, comorbidity with impulse control disorders was 16.4%–37% (lifetime), and 3.0%–35.5% for point prevalence (du Toit et al., 2001; Fontenelle, Mendlowicz, & Versiani, 2005; Grant, Mancebo, Pinto, Eisen, & Rasmussen, 2006; Richter, Summerfeldt, Antony, & Swinson, 2003). Ruscio et al. (2010) reported higher lifetime comorbidity with impulse control disorders in their analysis of the National Comorbidity Survey Replication data. In evaluations of OCD clinical samples, the most common lifetime comorbidity for impulse control problems was skin picking (8.9%–15.0%), followed by nail biting (4.1%), and trichotillomania (1.4%–12.9%). The most common concurrently diagnosed impulse control disorders included skin picking (7.8%–13.3%), nail biting (2.4%), trichotillomania (1.0%–7.1%), and pathological gambling (0.3%–2.2%). Individuals with OCD with concurrent impulse control disorders had an earlier age of OCD onset, significantly worse OCD symptom severity, particularly compulsive symptoms, and poorer functioning and quality of life (Fontenelle et al., 2005; Grant et al., 2006). They were also more likely to show poorer treatment response than OCD patients without any history of impulse control disorder (Matsunaga et al., 2005).

Studies show that rates of comorbid Tourette's syndrome are relatively low (2.1%–2.4%) (Denys et al., 2004; du Toit et al., 2001). Yet, in studies of adults with Tourette's syndrome, approximately 30% to 40% experience obsessive compulsive symptoms (Leckman, 1993). During the typical course of Tourette's syndrome, tics appear earlier, and obsessive compulsive behaviors later, often overtaking the tics as the predominant presenting complaint (Bloch et al., 2006). In fact, earlier age of OCD onset (i.e., before 10 years of age) is associated with a significant increase in comorbid tic disorders (Janowitz et al., 2009). It is not uncommon for obsessive compulsive symptoms to persist into adulthood, whereas the tics have dissipated or disappeared (Bloch et al., 2006). Furthermore, tic-related OCD has been associated with higher frequencies of sensory phenomena preceding or accompanying compulsions (Leckman, Walker, Goodman, Pauls, & Cohen, 1994; Miguel et al., 2000). Few studies have tested the effects of CBT in OCD patients with comorbid tic disorder. However, in a recent uncontrolled trial of group CBT, significant improvement in OCD symptom severity was observed with adolescent patients, with and without tic-related OCD, suggesting that the presence of comorbid tic-disorders may not attenuate response to behavioral group treatment with adolescents (Himle, Fischer, van Etten, Janeck, & Hanna, 2003).

SPECIFIC COMORBID CONDITIONS – ALCOHOL AND OTHER SUBSTANCE USE DISORDER

Comorbidity between OCD and substance use disorders is important for several reasons. There is evidence that taking certain substances (e.g., cocaine or methamphetamine) may exacerbate OCD symptoms, while other substances (e.g., opiates) might alleviate OCD symptoms (Koizumi, 1985; Koran et al., 2005; Satel & McDougle, 1991), although little is known regarding the mechanisms involved. OCD patients with comorbid alcohol use disorders have reported that they use alcohol to reduce their obsessive compulsive symptoms (Gentil et al., 2009). Nevertheless, only a few studies have examined the comorbidity between OCD and substance

use problems. Studies have been undertaken with individuals receiving treatment for a substance use disorder (Eisen & Rasmussen, 1989; Fals-Stewart & Angarano, 1994; Riemann, McNally, & Cox, 1992), as well as with individuals receiving treatment for OCD (Denys et al., 2004; Diniz et al., 2004; Mancebo, Grant, Pinto, Eisen, & Rasmussen, 2009; Rasmussen & Eisen, 1998; Yaryura-Tobias et al., 2000).

Estimates made from the Epidemiological Catchment Area (ECA) data put lifetime OCD–alcohol use disorders at 24%, and lifetime OCD–other drug use disorders at 18% (Karno, Golding, Sorenson, & Burnam, 1988). OCD prevalence rates among individuals receiving treatment for a substance use disorder ranged from 6% to 12% (Eisen & Rasmussen, 1989; Riemann et al., 1992), two to six times higher than the prevalence in the general population. Lifetime rates of substance use disorder in individuals treated at OCD specialty clinics and in other psychiatric and mental health settings ranged from 10% to 27% (Diniz et al., 2004; Mancebo et al., 2009; Rasmussen & Eisen, 1998; Yaryura-Tobias et al., 2000).

Only recently have the characteristics of individuals with a primary diagnosis of OCD and comorbid substance use disorder been systematically examined in a large clinical samples (Gentil et al., 2009; Mancebo et al., 2009). Mancebo et al. found that 27% of their sample met lifetime criteria for an alcohol use disorder only (abuse or dependence), 11% met criteria for both an alcohol and a drug use disorder, and 3% met criteria for drug use disorder only. Nearly twice as many individuals met criteria for dependence than abuse. The most commonly abused substances were alcohol, cannabis, and cocaine. However, only 5% of the participants met current (past month) criteria for a substance use disorder. Gentil et al. (2009),reported that only 7.5% of the OCD patients in their sample presented with alcohol use disorders. Participants with comorbid substance use disorders and OCD presented with more severe OCD symptoms, poorer insight regarding their OCD symptoms, poorer quality of life, greater impairment in overall psychosocial functioning, and were more likely to report suicide attempts than those without substance use disorders (Mancebo et al., 2009). Gentil et al. (2009) found that OCD patients with comorbid alcohol use disorders were more likely to be men, to have received previous psychiatric treatment, had greater levels of hoarding symptoms, and higher rates of comorbid GAD, somatization disorders, and compulsive sexual behavior. Comorbid borderline personality disorder was associated with increased risk of alcohol and/or drug use disorder for OCD patients, whereas early onset of OCD (defined as age 15 or younger) was associated with increased lifetime rates of alcohol use disorder only (Mancebo et al., 2009). Gentil et al. also found that more than 80% of their participants with comorbid alcohol use disorders experienced their first obsessive compulsive symptoms during childhood, and alcohol misuse began more often during early adulthood.

SPECIFIC COMORBID CONDITIONS – SCHIZOPHRENIA AND OTHER PSYCHOTIC DISORDERS

The co-occurrence of OCD in patients with schizophrenia and related disorders has been increasingly recognized, with 7.8% to 40% of patients with a primary schizophrenia diagnosis also meeting criteria for OCD (Eisen, Beer, Pato, Venditto, & Rasmussen, 1997; Poyurovsky et al., 2001; Poyurovsky & Koran, 2005; Tibbo, Kroetsch, Chue, & Warneke, 2000). However, only 1.7% to 4% of OCD patients were found to meet criteria for schizophrenia or other psychotic disorders such as schizoaffective disorder (de Haan, Dudek-Hodge, Verhoeven, & Denys, 2009; Denys et al., 2004; Eisen & Rasmussen, 1993). Thus, OCD patients do not appear to be at elevated risk for developing schizophrenia (Poyurovsky & Koran, 2005), whereas the reverse might be more likely. The reasons for the high incidence of OCD in patients with primary schizophrenia is not well understood, although the presence of obsessive compulsive symptomatology appears to be associated with higher global, positive, and negative psychotic symptoms (Cunill, Castells, & Simeon, 2009).

SPECIFIC COMORBID CONDITIONS – OBSESSIVE COMPULSIVE PERSONALITY DISORDER

Obsessive compulsive personality disorder (OCPD) is defined as "a preoccupation with orderliness, perfectionism, and mental and interpersonal control, at the expense of flexibility, openness, and efficiency" (APA; 2000, p. 725). Despite similarity in diagnostic labels, there is little evidence that OCPD is related to OCD. Although personality disorder comorbidity is common (50%–65%), the most common personality disorders with OCD are dependent and avoidant (Summerfeldt et al., 1998). Moreover, OCPD occurs in many people who never develop an Axis I disorder, and more frequently

co-occurs in psychiatric conditions other than OCD (Rasmussen & Eisen, 1992).

In summary, OCD most often occurs with other psychiatric disorders. Often, but not always, OCD onset will precede the development of the frequently seen comorbid anxiety and mood disorders. Given the negative effect comorbid disorders appear to have on symptom severity, treatment response, and the prognosis for OCD patients, clinicians must conduct careful evaluations of each patient to identify comorbid disorders and to make decisions about appropriate treatment. Ledley, Pai, and Franklin (2007) presented a detailed guide for diagnosing OCD and co-occurring anxiety disorders. Ledley and colleagues first called for careful assessment to determine if observed symptoms warrant an additional diagnosis (e.g., unexpected panic attacks, fear of future panic experiences, and a diagnosis of panic disorder), or whether symptoms can subsumed under the individual's OCD (e.g., panic attacks that occur only in response to a feared contaminant). When comorbid conditions do occur, pragmatic considerations will determine whether the condition must be treated first (e.g., severe agoraphobic avoidance interfering with leaving the home), as there has been very limited research on this issue. Ledley et al. suggested that most often OCD can be effectively treated when comorbid conditions are present, and often reductions in the symptoms of OCD will produce positive change in the coexisting anxiety disorders.

Widiger and Clark (2000) concluded in their review that the co-occurrence of mental disorders cannot be explained by either symptom overlap in the diagnostic criteria or specific methodological problems. Widiger and Clark contend that comorbidity patterns reflect underlying commonalities in core processes. Based on comorbidity data, and the important studies completed to date on the structure of emotion with mood and anxiety disorders (e.g., Brown, Chorpita, & Barlow, 1998; Zinbarg & Barlow, 1996),the greatest support exists for OCD's association with anxiety and mood disorders. Studies of the structure of emotion with anxiety disorder patients, as defined in the DSM-IV, offer some support for hierarchical models that address the comorbidity of anxiety and mood disorders and the association of both conditions to higher-order personality dimensions (e.g., negative affectivity; Watson, 2005). Broader evaluations of the structure of emotion and the applications of multivariate analyses are needed, with clinical samples with OCD diagnoses and spectrum diagnoses, to better elucidate relations between these conditions.

Obsessive Compulsive Disorder Heterogeneity

Although commonalities seen in individuals with OCD (e.g., intrusive thoughts and repetitive behaviors) are emphasized in the current psychiatric disorder taxonomy (DSM-IV-TR), the heterogeneous presentation of patients meeting diagnostic criteria distinguishes the syndrome from most other conditions. OCD heterogeneity occurs across multiple dimensions including gender differences in age at onset, different patterns of comorbidity, and the significant variability seen in the obsessional symptoms and compulsive behaviors of patients. More recently, behavioral scientists have attempted to elucidate OCD heterogeneity by examining variability on measures of constructs and processes posited to be importantly related to the etiology of the disorder. This research is often conducted with carefully diagnosed clinical samples, and important differences have been found on several measures of processes posited to be important to the development of OCD (Calamari et al., 2006; Saxena et al., 2004; S. Taylor et al., 2006). We review OCD heterogeneity with the understanding that the issue is essential to elucidating the complex phenomenology of the disorder. Variability in the phenotypic expression of OCD obscures findings from treatment outcome studies, and makes more difficult the elucidation of etiologic processes, including the search for vulnerability genes (Miguel et al., 2005).

Comorbidity and Demographic Variables

Some researchers have focused on patterns of comorbid conditions (see the prior section in this chapter on OCD comorbidity) to elucidate disorder heterogeneity. For example, OCD co-occurring with tic disorders is often associated with symmetry concerns (e.g., Hemmings et al., 2004; Leckman et al., 1995), occurs more often in males (e.g., Geller et al., 1998), and in some studies has been associated with a diminished treatment response to some interventions (e.g., March et al., 2007). Although important relationships between comorbidity patterns and OCD severity and life interference have been reported, McKay et al. (2004), in their review of OCD heterogeneity, concluded that further work was needed on OCD subtyping schemes based on comorbidity patterns before the importance of this variable to understanding OCD heterogeneity could be determined. Nestadt et al. (2009) have more recently used multilevel latent class analysis to determine if important OCD subtypes could be identified based on comorbidity. The presence of eight comorbid psychiatric disorders was evaluated, including anxiety, tic, mood, and somatization disorders. Nestadt et al. found support for a two- or three-class solution. The more descriptive three-class solution was characterized by a subgroup with OCD and major depressive disorder as the most frequent additional condition. A second latent class was characterized "comorbid tic-related conditions and infrequent mood disorders," while the third subgroup often experienced comorbid panic disorder and mood difficulties. Significant gender and OCD symptom differences were found across subgroups.

Evaluation of differences seen in the age at onset of OCD has been a productive line of research. Although OCD was once understood to begin in early adulthood (see Antony et al., 1998, for a review), onset in very young children has been reported (cf. Freeman et al., 2007), and an early-onset variant of the disorder is now well recognized. Careful evaluations of the literature on older adults suggest that a late-onset subgroup might exist who experience OCD for the first time after age 65 (see Carmin et al., Chapter 24, for a review). Although the age-at-onset literature is limited by several methodological issues, including frequent dependence on retrospective self-report (cf. Henry, Moffitt, Caspi, Langley, & Silva, 1994), available evidence indicates that OCD onset is not limited to the early adult years. Initial studies of early-onset OCD suggest it might be an important disorder subtype.

Hanna, Fischer, Chadha, Himle, and Van Etten (2005) evaluated individuals with early- and later-onset OCD. They assessed lifetime OCD symptoms and measured several symptom classes including aberrant grooming behaviors, attention deficit hyperactivity disorder, tic disorders, depressive disorders, and other anxiety disorders. They found that ordering compulsions were significantly more common in early-onset OCD, as were aberrant grooming and skin-picking. Tükel et al. (2005) found more males in their early-onset group, as has been reported previously (e.g., Geller et al., 1998). Symmetry and exactness obsessions, religious obsessions, hoarding and saving obsessions, and hoarding and collecting compulsions were significantly more frequent in the early-onset group (Tükel et al., 2005). Hemmings et al. (2004) evaluated a large South African clinical sample. Early onset was associated with an increased frequency of tics, Tourette's disorder, and trichotillomania. To elucidate age-at-onset differences in OCD, Delorme et al. (2005) used admixture analysis, a method for identifying subgroups. Using this approach, they found evidence for two OCD subtypes, one group with a mean age at onset of 11.1 (4.1) years, and a second group with a mean age of 23.5 (11.1). The early-onset OCD group more frequently had comorbid Tourette's syndrome, and had an increased family history of OCD.

Ulloa, Nicolini, Avila, and Fernández-Guasti (2007) compared children with OCD to adults with late-onset OCD, on their response to a standardized treatment with clomipramine. The children's group had more males and more frequent comorbidities than the adult group. Although adults reported a higher frequency of medication side effects compared to children, adults had better treatment outcome. Differences between early- and late-onset OCD subgroups in response to pharmacotherapy have not always been found though (e.g., Uguz, Askin, Cilli, & Besiroglu, 2006), nor have differences sometimes been found in responsiveness to cognitive-behavioral therapies (e.g., March et al., 2007).

Eapen, Pauls, and Robertson (2006) suggested that although genetic factors are significant in pre-disposing individuals to OCD, not all forms of the disorder appear equally heritable, suggesting that additional explanations for this variability are needed. Differences in age at onset might be an important aspect of OCD heterogeneity for elucidating heritability. In several studies, the early-onset variant of the disorder was found more heritable (e.g., Nestadt et al., 2000; Pauls, Alsobrook, Goodman, Rasmussen, & Leckman, 1995). Chabane et al. (2005) investigated the characteristics of an early-onset OCD clinical sample that included children, adolescents, and adults, all of whom had early-onset OCD. The first-degree biological relatives of the early-onset proband were also evaluated. The average age of onset of OCD was 9.98 (3.2) years, and 44% of the probands had a comorbid tic disorder. First-degree relatives had higher rates of OCD and tic disorders; 32.6% of the probands had a positive family history of OCD. The authors concluded that their findings were consistent with other reports in the literature where elevated rates of OCD were reported in the relatives of individuals with early-onset OCD.

Symptom Heterogeneity

The most frequently used approach for studying OCD heterogeneity has been evaluations of differences seen in obsessions and compulsions (Calamari, Wiegartz, & Janeck, 1999). The approach implicitly assumes that important differences (e.g., etiology, factors maintaining the disorder, response to treatment) underlie the substantial symptom heterogeneity that characterizes OCD. More recent work on OCD symptom heterogeneity suggests this assumption is correct, and there has been a burgeoning of research in this area.

Initial evaluations of OCD symptom heterogeneity focused on patients' major compulsive behavior (checkers versus washers; e.g., Hodgson & Rachman, 1977). Although the approach made significant contributions to understanding OCD, the strategy was limited by several factors (Calamari et al., 1999), including the tendency of patients to present with multiple types of symptoms (e.g., Hodgson & Rachman, 1977) of greater or lesser importance to their OCD. To evaluate these complex symptom patterns, researchers applied several types of multivariate statistics. Factor analysis has most often been used to identify the latent dimensions of several measures of OCD symptoms. Multiple research groups have used the Yale-Brown Obsessive-Compulsive Scale Symptom Checklist (YBOCS-CL; Goodman et al., 1989) to assess OCD symptoms, because this measure lists a broad range of OCD symptoms in 15 obsession and compulsion categories. The use of the YBOCS-CL for this purpose is limited by the largely unknown psychometric properties of the checklist portion of the Yale-Brown Obsessive-Compulsive Scale. Further, factor analysis of the checklist items suggests that specific items might not connect well to the 15 obsessions and compulsion categories (Feinstein, Fallon, Petkova, & Liebowitz, 2003; Summerfeldt, Richter, Antony, & Swinson, 1999).

Other researchers have used cluster analysis to elucidate OCD symptom heterogeneity (e.g., Abramowitz, Franklin, Schawartz, & Furr, 2003; Calamari et al., 1999; Calamari et al., 2004), a technique for forming homogeneous groups within complex data sets (e.g., Borgen & Barnett, 1987). Calamari et al. (2004) suggested that cluster analysis might offer advantages for evaluating OCD symptom heterogeneity. Cluster analysis results in the assignment of each participant to a single subgroup, while in factor analysis, variance is usually partitioned among several sources or factors. In factor analysis, each participant can be assigned a score on each of the identified factors, and these scores might not connect a participant to any of the identified latent dimensions (e.g., a participant might have high or low scores on any combination of the identified latent dimensions). Further, when factor analysis suggests a complex latent structure involving multiple dimensions, evaluation of individuals' scores on these latent dimensions might reveal commonalities between individual profiles suggesting subtypes or clusters.

The superiority of the dimensional versus the categorical (i.e., cluster analysis) approach for understanding OCD symptom heterogeneity remains controversial (see reviews by Leckman, Mataix-Cols, & Rosario-Campos, 2005; and S. Taylor, 2005). Mataix-Cols, Rosario-Campos, and Leckman (2005) proposed a dimensional model of OCD to understand disorder heterogeneity. They argued that replicable symptom dimensions are identified in factor analytic studies, and that the identified symptom dimensions were associated with distinct patterns of comorbidity, genetic transmission, specific neural substrates, and differences in treatment response, validating the approach. Mataix-Cols et al. (2005) concluded that the complex clinical presentation of OCD could be summarized with a few consistently identified and temporally stable symptom dimensions. In a recent meta-analysis of factor analytic evaluations of OCD symptom measures, Bloch, Landeros-Weisenberger, Rosario, Pittenger, and Leckman (2008) concluded that there are four reliably identified dimensions: (1) symmetry—symmetry obsessions and repeating, ordering, and counting compulsions; (2) forbidden thoughts—aggression, sexual, religious, and somatic obsessions and checking compulsions; (3) cleaning—cleaning and contamination; and (4) hoarding—hoarding obsessions and compulsions.

Mataix-Cols et al.'s (2005) model is based on several assumptions that have empirical support in the OCD literature, namely: several types of OCD symptoms often coexist in patients; OCD symptoms are continuous with normal obsessive compulsive phenomena; and OCD symptoms extend beyond the traditional nosological boundaries of OCD. Although dimensional approaches to elucidating OCD symptom heterogeneity have advanced understanding, Calamari (2005) suggested that cluster analysis may offer several advantages over factor analysis in characterizing OCD heterogeneity, and that this categorical approach was not limited in some of the ways Mataix-Cols et al. (2005) suggested. McKay and Neziroglu (2009) critically reviewed methodological approaches for elucidating OCD heterogeneity broadly, and for distinguishing

condition subtypes and condition-related spectrum disorders. McKay and Neziroglu emphasized the importance of a theoretical framework for such studies and posited that no single methodology will be adequate.

Despite the controversies on what analytic approach is best, and the limitations of many of the symptom measures of OCD, symptom heterogeneity studies have resulted in the identification of several replicable dimensions or subgroups. McKay et al. (2004) concluded that contamination/washing, checking, hoarding, and symmetry/ordering emerged from the literature as reliable dimensions or subtypes, a conclusion congruent with Bloch et al. (2008). McKay et al. emphasized that symptom heterogeneity research was limited by the reliance on symptom measures (e.g., the YBOCS-CL) that limit the conceptualization of latent subtypes to largely overt symptoms (e.g., covert compulsions are not adequately assessed). Nevertheless, evaluations of symptom heterogeneity have advanced understanding of OCD. For example, a hoarding subtype of OCD has been reliably identified in symptom heterogeneity studies supporting contentions of the distinctiveness of patients with predominant hoarding difficulties. Researchers have developed comprehensive formulations of the hoarding problem (Frost & Hartl, 1996; Steketee & Frost, 2003) and modifications in treatment for this variant of OCD, developed based on new theories (e.g., Frost & Steketee, 1999; Kyrios, Steketee, Frost, & Oh, 2002). The results of initial evaluations of a model-based cognitive-behavioral therapy for hoarding are promising (Tolin, Frost, & Steketee, 2007), including an Internet-based intervention (Muroff, Steketee, Himle, & Frost, 2010).

OCD heterogeneity researchers have begun to focus on processes that may underlie symptom differences, and which may connect more directly to etiologic mechanisms. For example, Mataix-Cols et al. (2004) evaluated neuropathology differences across OCD symptom dimensions using functional magnetic resonance imaging. Study participants were scanned while viewing alternating blocks of concern-related and neutral pictures. Analyses of covariance, controlling for depression, showed a distinct pattern of activation associated with each symptom dimension in the OCD group. Using whole-brain voxel-based morphometry, van den Heuvel et al. (2009) reported relations between global and regional gray matter and white matter volumes and the symptom dimension scores of OCD patients.

Taylor et al. (2006) and Calamari et al. (2006) evaluated differences in dysfunctional beliefs—beliefs posited to help precipitate OCD in cognitive models. In these studies, two independent, large clinical samples were evaluated with the Obsessional Beliefs Questionnaire, a well-validated measure of OCD-related dysfunctional beliefs (OBQ; Obsessive-Compulsive Cognitions Working Group, 2005). Cluster analysis resulted in identification of two subgroups in both studies: an OCD patient group with elevated dysfunctional beliefs, and an OCD patient group with low dysfunctional beliefs (almost 50% of the clinical sample in both studies). The low-beliefs subgroups scored similarly to a non-clinical sample on the OBQ. The authors concluded that additional dysfunctional beliefs needed to be assessed to capture the concerns of most individuals with OCD, or that other etiologic processes might better explain the development of OCD in the low-beliefs subgroup.

These studies, along with many other evaluations of OCD heterogeneity, demonstrate the significant challenges that researchers face in trying to develop a comprehensive model of OCD as currently conceptualized. As OCD heterogeneity research moves forward, the empirical data needed to better understand OCD phenomenology will become more available, and psychopathologists will have more of the information needed to place this complex disorder in the taxonomy of mental disorders.

Insight Variability in Patients with Obsessive Compulsive Disorder

As described earlier, the specifier "with poor insight" was added to the psychiatric disorder taxonomy in 1994 (DSM-IV; APA, 1994), acknowledging the significant variability in OCD patients' insight into the excessiveness of their obsessional concerns and compulsive behaviors. Although the importance of the variability seen in OCD patient insight is now acknowledged, the issue continues to provide significant challenges for researchers and clinicians. There is disagreement on what constitutes poor insight (Clark, 2004; Veale, 2007), and some maintain that many of the scales currently used to measure insight have not been shown to be reliable or valid for assessing obsessional patients (Clark, 2004; Neziroglu & Stevens, 2002). According to Veale (2007), it is difficult to assess levels of insight, as individuals with OCD can have a difficult time putting into words what the consequences of their action or inaction might be beyond "not quite right" feelings, or the experience of significant negative affect. As he stated, it is "difficult to measure the awfulness of experiencing emotion on scales that measure the conviction of belief" (p. 269).

Despite the challenges and many unresolved issues, advances have been made in studying insight in OCD. Poor insight was associated with more severe symptoms as assessed with the Y-BOCS, elevated depression, and higher-state anxiety (Turksoy, Tukel, Ozdemir, & Karali, 2002). Bellino (2005) found that patients with poor insight had higher scores on the Y-BOCS compulsions subscale, were more likely to have a chronic course of OCD, and OCD occurred more frequently in their first-degree relatives. Catapano et al. (2010) also found that poor insight was associated with an earlier age at onset, a higher rate of schizophrenia spectrum disorder in OCD patients' first-degree relatives, and greater comorbidity with schizotypal personality disorder.

Interest in OCD patient insight has, in part, been motivated by the construct's relationship to treatment response. For example, Foa, Abramowitz, Franklin, and Kozak (1999) found that having poor insight was associated with a diminished treatment response to exposure and response prevention (ERP), although study participants with poor insight did improve significantly. The authors theorized that individuals with poor insight have a more difficult time incorporating new information that is inconsistent with their fixed beliefs (Foa et al., 1999). In several other treatment outcome studies, insight changed (increased) during treatment and was associated with symptom reduction (Alonso et al., 2008; see Clark, 2004, for a review; Eisen et al., 2001). Clark (2004) posited that didactic and experiential elements of cognitive-behavioral therapy for OCD were critical for improving insight and reducing symptom severity. As patients are taught about the nature of negative intrusive thoughts, the appraisal processes they use to understand the experience, and the dysfunctional beliefs they hold, this information will help them begin to challenge their overvalued ideas (Neziroglu & Stevens, 2002). Unfortunately, the very patients that most need treatment will avoid it because poor insight is associated with failure to seek treatment for OCD (Veale, 2007).

Some theorists believe that the insight of most OCD patients is highly variable, and that this occurs independent of involvement in treatment. Clark (2004) maintained that insight in OCD is situationally bound, and that "[f]or most individuals, strength of belief may be unstable and vary across time and situations" (p. 35). That is, the level of insight is seen to fluctuate across the continuum from total awareness to complete denial or delusion. Neziroglu and colleagues believe otherwise. Neziroglu and Stevens (2002) theorized that poor insight is associated with pathological thought processes that lead to overvalued ideas. These overvalued ideas, in turn, "do not fluctuate spontaneously but are fixed and possibly modifiable only if challenged" (p. 186). Neziroglu and Stevens hypothesized that the stability of overvalued ideas in OCD is supported by disorder-related mood change, which helps support specific dysfunctional beliefs, belief domains outlined by the Obsessive Compulsive Cognitions Working Group (OCCWG, 1997; 2001). This process serves to reinforce the overvalued ideas. Neziroglu and Stevens (2002) identified additional factors that affected the stability of patient insight. These factors included limited cognitive abilities, poor memory, affect regulation difficulty, and attentional biases. In addition, they theorized that different levels of insight exist and are relatively stable, and these differences have been associated with particular patterns of scores on clinical assessment instruments, such as the Minnesota Multiphasic Personality Inventory-2 (MMPI-2). Specifically, low scores on scales 5 and 9 on the MMPI-2 "Correlate roughly with intellectual insight" (Neziroglu & Stevens, 2002, p. 189). This "intellectual" level of insight indicates that the individuals understand that their maladaptive behavior is due to their own thoughts, feelings, or behaviors, but do not take steps to alter them nonetheless.

When OCD patient insight into the excessiveness of their concerns has been completely lacking, their overvalued ideas have sometimes been considered delusional. In the DSM-IV, delusion is defined as "erroneous beliefs that usually involve a misinterpretation of perceptions or experiences" (p. 299), and the difficulty of distinguishing delusion from overvalued ideas is acknowledged. As indicated in the DSM-IV, "the distinction between a delusion and a strongly held idea is sometimes difficult to make and depends in part on the degree of conviction with which the belief is held despite clear contradictory evidence regarding its veracity" (APA, 1994, p. 299). Some researchers have tried to better distinguish delusions from overvalued ideas rather than arguing insight is largely continuous. Some theorists hypothesize that the individual who has overvalued ideas is distressed or upset with the repeated performance of a behavior in response to an obsession, whereas the individual who has

delusions is not (Insel & Akiskal, 1986; Kozak & Foa, 1994). Some theorists have suggested that insight is related to symptom severity, and this contention has been supported (Bellino, 2005). OCD patients with severe symptoms might lose their insight and, in turn, abandon their attempts to resist their obsession (Insel & Akiskal, 1986). There is some evidence that patients with a single obsessional theme are more likely to experience delusional levels of obsessive beliefs (Fear, Sharp, & Healy, 2000). See O'Dwyer and Marks (2000) for an extended review of delusional OCD.

Clinical and Nonclinical Obsessions and Compulsions

In this section of the chapter, we examine similarities and differences between clinical and nonclinical obsessions and compulsions. Clark (2004), in his review of nonclinical obsessions, summarized the importance of this line of research. As researchers have attempted to determine whether obsessional disorders are continuous with the ubiquitous experience of negative intrusive thoughts, several processes that might be responsible for transforming a common experience into OCD have been identified. Decades of experimental research make clear that the study of intrusive cognition in nonclinical and clinical samples provides important information relevant to the development of OCD. Although there are important similarities between nonclinical and clinical obsessions and compulsions, there are also important differences. Identification of the overlapping features and core differences between nonclinical and clinical obsessions and compulsions has advanced etiologic theory and treatment, and further elucidation of these differences will increase understanding of OCD phenomenology. Investigations of the different reactions of clinical and nonclinical groups to intrusive cognitions have proved important, and several specific aspects of the appraisal process have been identified that connect intrusive thoughts to obsessional problems. These appraisal differences are related to the initiation of effortful mental control, efforts that are largely counterproductive. We summarize recent studies on these processes and direct the interested reader to several excellent reviews (see Clark, 2004; Clark & O'Connor, 2005; Clark & Rhyno, 2005; Julien, O'Connor, & Aardema, 2007).

Clark and Rhyno (2005) defined clinically relevant intrusive thoughts as "any distinct, identifiable cognitive event that is unwanted, unintended, and recurrent. It interrupts the flow of thoughts, interferes in task performance, is associated with negative affect, and is difficult to control" (p. 4). The experience is attributed to an internal origin, is considered unacceptable or unwanted, is repetitive, captures attentional resources, and detracts the individual from ongoing activity (Clark & Rhyno, 2005). It is important in this line of research to distinguish clinically relevant intrusive thoughts from other cognitive processes that are more associated with different forms of psychopathology (e.g., worry; rumination). As Clark and colleagues summarized (Clark, 2004; Clark & Rhyno, 2005), experimental research completed following Rachman and De Silva's (1978) seminal study on clinical and nonclinical obsessions has largely replicated their initial finding that intrusive thought experiences are common. The majority of nonclinical samples (80%–90%) have reported experiencing obsession-like intrusive thoughts in these studies. Evaluations of the content of nonclinical and clinical obsessions suggest important similarities. Indeed, mental health experts experienced difficulty differentiating nonclinical from clinical obsessions in Rachman and DeSilva's seminal study.

In recent reviews, and in several new studies of nonclinical obsessions, potentially important differences between clinical and nonclinical obsessions have been reported. The negative intrusive thoughts of nonclinical samples occur less frequently, cause less distress, and are perceived as more controllable (see Clark & O'Connor's, 2005 review). Rassin and Muris (2006) reanalyzed Rachman and DeSilva's (1978) data and found that mental health professionals were able to differentiate clinical and nonclinical obsessions beyond chance levels, although not with complete accuracy. In follow-up studies, Rassin and Muris presented nonclinical and clinical obsessions to psychotherapists and psychology students, and both groups were able to distinguish clinical and nonclinical obsessions beyond a chance level. The authors suggested that additional research was needed to identify the content and other characteristics of clinical obsessions that made them recognizable.

Rassin, Cougle, and Muris (2007) presented a student sample with a list of obsessions from clinical and nonclinical groups. Participants reported whether they had ever experienced the particular obsessions listed. Students endorsed significantly more normal than abnormal obsessions. Correlations between the number of endorsed normal and abnormal obsessions and scoring on the short version (van Oppen, Hoekstra, & Emmelkamp, 1995) of the Padua Inventory (PI; Sanvio, 1988) revealed that both kinds of obsessions were significantly related to PI score, (nonclinical obsessions, $r = 0.36$; clinical obsessions, $r = 0.41$). The authors reported that when analyses controlled for the experience of abnormal obsessions, the correlation between normal obsessions and the PI score disappeared.

Morillo, Belloch, and García-Soriano (2007) evaluated the frequency, content, emotional impact, appraisals, and control strategies used when obsessions, or clinically relevant intrusive thoughts, were experienced by OCD patients, depressed patients, non-obsessive anxious patients, and nonclinical controls. As predicted, the main obsession in the OCD group occurred more frequently than the most upsetting clinically relevant intrusive thoughts reported by the other groups, while the depressed and anxious control groups scored significantly higher than the nonclinical group. The OCD group experienced their main intrusive thought as more unpleasant than the other groups. The OCD and clinically depressed groups did not differ on ratings of related guilt experiences, though. Further, significant differences were found on how often specific thought control strategies were used. The OCD patients used overt neutralizing, reasoning with self, seeking reassurance, suppression, saying a prayer, and reassuring self more often than other groups. In an earlier investigation, Muris, Merckelbach, and Clavan (1997) evaluated the ritualistic behavior of a nonclinical sample. The authors reported that while their rituals were less frequent and less intense than the compulsions of a clinical OCD sample, few content differences were found, suggesting that abnormal and normal compulsions might lie on a continuum.

In an investigation of the appraisal of intrusive thought experiences, Corcoran and Woody (2008) evaluated university students' appraisals of the occurrence of unwanted, clinically relevant intrusive thoughts. Participants considered intrusion-related vignettes and rated how personally significant the intrusions were. Appraisals of the vignettes were moderately correlated with OCD symptoms, and associated with the tendency to interpret unwanted intrusive thoughts as socially unacceptable, as an indication of mental instability, or as immoral. Because the study was carefully designed to make the intrusions obsession-like (i.e., not ego-syntonic worries about life problems), the results point to the importance of appraisal processes for obsessional disorders.

Research on nonclinical obsessions has provided important information that has encouraged the development of etiologic theories of OCD and refinements in the treatment of the disorder. Several conclusions can be drawn from these studies. The experience of intrusive thoughts is ubiquitous, although careful evaluations of the most clinically relevant intrusive thought themes suggest that the experience might not be as common as once thought. Nonclinical populations experience intrusive thoughts that are similar to obsessions, but intrusions with ego-dystonic content highly similar to the obsessional themes of OCD patients occur much less often in nonclinical samples (Julien et al., 2007). Researchers continue to demonstrate important relations between specific appraisals of intrusive thoughts and effortful mental control strategies and OCD symptoms. Longitudinal studies are needed, possibly with high-risk populations (e.g., children of parents with more heritable types of OCD) to determine if appraisals and mental control efforts are important to the development of obsessional disorders, or are a consequence of developing OCD. Although much has been accomplished in studies of nonclinical obsessions and compulsions, additional work is needed to explain how intrusive thoughts evolve into obsessional disorders for only a small percentage of the population.

Epidemiology of Obsessive Compulsive Disorder
Prevalence of OCD
In epidemiological research, *disorder prevalence* is understood to be the number of all individuals in a population who are affected by a disorder or illness within a specified period. *Lifetime prevalence* refers to the number of individuals who have met criteria for a diagnosis at any point during their life up to the time of assessment. *Period prevalence* rates may also be reported as the percentage of individuals who met criteria for the disorder during a specified period (e.g., the 12 months prior to assessment). These estimates are often reported as a percentage or a ratio between those affected with the disorder in question and the total number of individuals studied. Lastly, *point prevalence* is a measure of the percentage of people in a population who have a disorder at a particular time point, while *incidence* refers to new cases over a specified period (cf. Davison & Neale, 1994).

Before the 1980s, OCD was considered to occur infrequently, "apparently rare in the general population" (DSM-III; APA, 1980, p. 234). Underestimates of the prevalence of OCD resulted in part from the few attempts to estimate prevalence. As summarized by both Karno, Golding, Sorenson, and Burnam (1988) and Antony, Downie, and Swinson (1998), the few studies that were conducted on the epidemiology of OCD estimated the lifetime prevalence rate to range from a mere 0.05% (Rudin, 1953) to 0.3% (Roth & Luton, 1942). These early studies typically relied on unstandardized clinical observation to determine diagnosis, rather than systematic structured interviewing methods.

Contemporary epidemiologic studies of OCD have used improved methodologies, and prevalence estimates of the disorder have been significantly higher. The World Mental Health (WMH) Survey Initiative conducted the National Comorbidity Survey Replication, a nationally representative survey of adults in the United States (Kessler, Chiu, Demler, Merikangas & Walters, 2005). Ruscio et al. (2010) evaluated the epidemiology of OCD in subsample of 2073 respondents of the National Comorbidity Survey Replication study. The lifetime prevalence of OCD was determined using the Composite International Diagnostic Instrument (CIDI; Robins, Wing, Wittchen, & Helzer, 1988), and a structured version of the Yale–Brown Obsessive Compulsive Scale (Y-BOCS) was used to assess the severity of OCD. Ruscio et al. (2010) found that more than 25% of respondents reported experiencing obsessions or compulsions at some time in their lives, although a relatively small proportion of respondents met full DSM-IV criteria, lifetime (2.3%) or within the 12-month period prior to assessment (1.2%).

Ruscio et al.'s (2010) results were, in general, congruent with earlier reports. The earlier ECA study (Karno et al., 1988) was carried out in five communities in the United States between 1980 and 1984. Face-to-face interviews were conducted in randomly selected households using the Diagnostic Interview Schedule (DIS; Robins, Helzer, Croughan, & Ratcliff, 1981). The lifetime prevalence of OCD was 2.5, a rate 40 to 60 times greater than previously reported (Karno et al., 1988). The 2-week, 1-month, 6-month, and 1-year prevalence rates were 1.2%, 1.3%, 1.5%, and 1.6%, respectively.

Although the ECA study represented a significant advance in epidemiological research, there were several methodological limitations. The DIS was highly structured so it could be used by lay interviewers. The lack of open-ended questions for probing suspected obsessions and compulsions on the DIS might have resulted in an incomplete evaluation of the significance of reported symptoms

(Karno et al., 1988). Follow-up evaluations of the ECA study participants that were conducted by psychiatrists using semistructured interviews found significantly lower rates of OCD diagnoses than were originally reported by the ECA research teams (Anthony et al., 1985; Helzer et al., 1985).

Following the publication of the ECA study results, similar epidemiological surveys were conducted in Edmonton, Alberta, Canada; Puerto Rico; Munich, Germany; Taipei, Taiwan; urban Seoul, rural regions of Korea; and Christchurch, New Zealand. The Cross National Collaborative Group (Horwath & Weissman, 2000; Weissman et al., 1994) compiled the multisite data and found generally consistent lifetime prevalence rates cross-nationally that ranged from 1.9% in Korea to 2.5% in Puerto Rico. Only a 0.4% prevalence rate was reported in Taiwan. Bebbington (1998) reported congruent prevalence estimates (1% in males and 1.5% in females) in the National Psychiatric Morbidity Surveys of Great Britain.

The use of the CIDI (Robins et al., 1988) in recent epidemiologic studies is an important methodological improvement, although some problems remain. The CIDI combines the diagnostic criteria of both the DSM-IV (APA, 1994) and the tenth edition of the International Classification of Diseases (ICD-10; World Health Organization, 1992). Like the DIS, the CIDI is designed to be administered by lay personnel. Studies using the CIDI reported highly variable estimates of the 1-month prevalence of OCD, ranging from as low as 0.3% (Andrade, Walters, Gentil, & Laurenti, 2002) to as high as 3.1% (M. Stein, Forde, Anderson, & Walker, 1997). Fontenelle, Mendlowicz, and Versiani (2006) suggested this variability could be due to several factors, including the brief time frame, the training of the assessors, and the setting in which the evaluation was conducted. Again, use of lay interviewers may have resulted in inflation of prevalence estimates. When Stein et al.'s (1997) participants were reassessed by mental health professionals and diagnoses were made using the Structured Clinical Interview for the DSM-IV Axis I Disorders (SCID; First, Spitzer, Gibbon, & Williams, 1996), the prevalence rate dropped to 0.6%. Among the primary problems with the false positive diagnoses was the tendency for the lay interviewers to label everyday worries and concerns as "obsessions" (M. Stein et al., 1997).

Another challenge for OCD epidemiology research has been the changing diagnostic criteria for the disorder. Although the fifth edition of the DSM-V is currently in preparation, most of the large epidemiologic surveys of prevalence rates relied on the diagnostic criteria of the third edition of the DSM (APA, 1980). Crino, Slade, and Andrews (2005) recently compared prevalence rates of OCD based on the DSM-III versus the DSM-IV. As previously reviewed in this chapter, the newer edition of the DSM defines more explicitly the nature of both clinical obsessions and compulsions, and better quantifies the levels of distress and impairment that must be experienced in order to meet the diagnostic criteria. Using the more descriptive and stringent criteria for OCD in the DSM-IV, Crino et al. (2005) found the 12-month prevalence rate was 0.6%, significantly less than estimates using DSM-III criteria. Nevertheless, Ruscio et al. (2010) reported much higher lifetime (2.3%) or 12-month rates (1.2%) using DSM-IV criteria.

Although the improved diagnostic criteria of the DSM-IV promotes a clearer distinction between clinical and nonclinical obsessions and compulsions, the emphasis placed on the description of symptomatology rather than the functional relations between thoughts and behaviors (cf. Abramowitz & Deacon, 2005) might be problematic for accurately estimating prevalence. Because the functional relationship between negative intrusive thoughts and rituals designed to neutralize distress is not well articulated in the DSM-IV criteria, less frequently observed obsession or compulsion symptoms might go unrecognized (see the prior section in this chapter on OCD symptom heterogeneity).

Age at Onset, Gender, and Ethnicity
WHEN DOES OCD BEGIN?
The typical age of onset for OCD was believed to be late adolescence into early adulthood (Rachman & Hodgson, 1980; see the earlier discussion on age at onset and OCD heterogeneity in this chapter). The majority of individuals with OCD have reported symptom onset prior to age 25, with an increase in incidence during puberty in some studies (Rasmussen & Eisen, 1992). In recent studies, an early-onset variant of OCD has regularly been identified.

As with adults, the earliest estimates of the prevalence of childhood and adolescent OCD indicated that the disorder was rare. As summarized by Swedo, Leonard, Rapoport, Lenane, and Cheslow (1989), as few as six cases in 3000 children admitted to a psychiatric hospital were believed to have OCD (Berman, 1942). Evaluation of a nonreferred sample in England failed to identify any cases in a sample of

2000 children (Rutter, Tizard, & Whitmore, 1970). Judd (1965) identified five children who met criteria for an "obsessive compulsive reaction" within a pool of 405 children, a prevalence rate more congruent with contemporary estimates. Flament et al. (1988) reported a point prevalence of 1.0% and a lifetime prevalence of 1.9%, indicating that OCD in children and adolescence is not rare. Since Flament et al.'s study, several investigations in the United States (Lewinsohn, Hops, Roberts, Seeley, & Andrews, 1993; Reinherz, Giaconia, Lefkowitz, & Pakiz, 1993; Valleni-Basile, Garrison, Jackson, & Waller, 1994), in New Zealand (Douglass, Moffitt, Dar, & McGee, 1995), and in Israel (Apter, Fallon, King, & Ratzoni, 1996; Zohar, Ratzoni, Pauls, & Apter, 1992) have reported lifetime prevalence rates that vary between 0.53% and 2.95% in children and adolescent samples. Rapoport et al. (2000) suggested some of the variability might be due to differences in methodology (e.g., whether a parent or child's report is used to determine the diagnosis; mean age of the sample studied).

Rapoport et al. (2000) analyzed data from the National Institute of Mental Health Methods for the Epidemiology of Child and Adolescent Mental Health study (Lahey et al., 1996) to investigate congruence between parent and child reports of symptoms. They found that when parent and child reports of OCD symptoms leading to a diagnosis where compared, agreement was found for only one case out of a total of 35. Little correspondence was found between child and parent symptom reports and the child's actual diagnostic status. The study included 1,285 pairs of youth and their caregivers from four different areas of the United States. This finding supports Rapoport et al.'s (2000) assertion that children and adolescents are frequently secretive about their OCD symptoms, and parents are uninformed as to what OCD symptoms may look like. These findings suggest that estimates of child and adolescent OCD might be too low if estimates are dependent on parent or child reports.

OCD in late life has been under-studied (see Chapter 24). Perhaps the dearth of literature regarding the occurrence of OCD among older adults is the result of reports where only 15 percent of OCD clinical samples reported that their symptoms began after age 35 (Rasmussen & Tsuang, 1986), results congruent with recent epidemiologic studies (Ruscio et al., 2010). However, anxiety symptomatology might frequently be underestimated with adults aged 65 and older as good assessment tools normed for this age group are lacking (Fuentes &

Cox, 1997). Anxiety disorders in older adults have historically garnered less attention than depressive disorders, despite findings that anxiety disorders are four to eight times more common in this population than depressive disorders (Regier, Boyd, Burke, & Rae, 1988; Weissman et al., 1994; see Carmin et al. in the present volume for an extended discussion of late-life OCD).

GENDER DIFFERENCES

In their review, Lochner and Stein (2001) reported that in clinical samples of OCD (e.g., Rasmussen & Eisen, 1992), equal gender ratios of the disorder are found, while in epidemiological investigations, slightly higher rates of OCD among women were reported (e.g., Karno et al., 1988; Weissman et al., 1994). Interestingly, (Karno et al., 1988) reported sex differences were no longer statistically significant after controlling for the impact of other demographic variables such as employment status in the ECA study.

A number of studies have reported that there are specific types of symptoms that differentially affect men and women (e.g., Castle, Deale, & Marks, 1995; Lensi et al., 1996). For example, women were more likely to present with aggressive obsessions and more cleaning compulsions, while men reported a greater incidence of sexual obsessions and obsessions related to symmetry and exactness (Lensi et al., 1996). As suggested by Lensi and colleagues (1996), these gender differences may indicate that sociocultural factors can influence the expression of OCD symptoms.

RACE AND ETHNICITY

As noted in a later section of this chapter, cross-national epidemiological studies suggest consistent rates of OCD internationally. In the United States, the prevalence of OCD was equivalent among Hispanics and those of European descent, with significantly lower prevalence rates found among African Americans (Karno et al., 1988). Friedman et al. (2003) found that African Americans and Caribbean Americans with OCD were more likely than Caucasians to be misdiagnosed at first with panic disorder. Friedman, Hatch, Paradis, Popkin, and Shalita (1993) suggested that African Americans might be more likely to present to general medical providers rather than to mental health specialists, and that this difference might explain the reported lower prevalence rates. Friedman et al. (1993) found a high rate of OCD in a group of African Americans presenting to a dermatologist. Neighbors (1988) suggested that African Americans typically consult those within their social network, such as friends, family members, and clergy, during times of emotional distress. For several reasons, it seems, few African Americans present to mental health centers for treatment in general, or for the treatment of OCD.

Longitudinal Course of OCD

LONGITUDINAL COURSE IN CLINICAL SAMPLES
In their review of studies examining the natural course of OCD, Eisen and Steketee (1998) evaluated studies that used both prospective methods and retrospective design. Consistent conclusions emerged from their analyses. If OCD is left untreated, individuals will continue to meet full criteria for the disorder or experience significant symptoms for long periods. They concluded that the empirical literature suggested some waxing and waning of OCD symptoms over time, but complete remission was relatively rare. In a retrospective evaluation of 44 patients, Rasmussen and Tsuang (1986) identified three potential courses for OCD. The majority of patients (84%) presented with a continuous course of OCD, while only 14% presented with a deteriorating course. In this sample of previously untreated patients, a mere 2% presented with an episodic course of OCD.

In the longest longitudinal study to date, Skoog and Skoog (1999) followed 144 patients with OCD over approximately 40 years. These inpatients were evaluated between 1954 and 1956, and then again between 1989 and 1993 by the same psychiatrist. The authors reported that while 83% of their sample demonstrated improvement in OCD symptomatology, only 20% showed complete recovery. Almost half of the sample (48%) continued to have clinically significant symptoms of OCD. Over time, only 12% of their sample exhibited the same symptom (i.e., the same obsessional concerns and compulsions). However, in more recent analyses of symptom stability, obsessional concerns or compulsions were observed to be stable within the same symptom dimension or cluster (e.g., Mataix-Cols et al., 2002; see discussion below), symptom groupings that have emerged from OCD heterogeneity research.

Skoog and Skoog's (1999) findings on low rates of full remission in OCD patients who did not receive extensive treatment were replicated in another prospective study of OCD. Steketee, Eisen, Dyck, Warshaw, and Rasmussen (1999) found that out of 100 patients with OCD, only 20% demonstrated full remission of symptoms at a follow-up assessment five years later. Marital status and global severity scores were the only significant predictors of outcome. Individuals with OCD who were married, or who had lower initial GAF scores, were more likely to show improvement (Steketee et al., 1999). In a similar prospective study of untreated OCD, Ravissa, Maina, and Bogetta (1997) compared patients with a chronic course of OCD versus those with an episodic course over a 1-year period. A chronic course was associated with earlier onset, male gender, longer duration of symptoms, a family history of psychiatric illness, and more severe compulsions.

SYMPTOM STABILITY
As previously reviewed in this chapter, the symptoms of OCD are heterogeneous, and grouping individuals based on symptom subtypes, or grouping symptoms into dimensions based on how symptoms co-vary, has proved useful. In Skoog and Skoog's (1999) longitudinal study, the majority of their patient sample experienced qualitative changes in their OCD symptomatology. However, Mataix-Cols and colleagues (2002) recently evaluated symptom stability using a prospective design, and found that although symptom severity within one dimension did vary, individuals' symptoms rarely shifted to a completely different symptom dimension. Rufer, Grothusen, Maszling, Peter, and Hand (2005) also reported that significant shifts between symptom dimension types were rare.

Besiroglu, Uguz, Ozbebit, Guler, Cilli, and Aksin (2007) evaluated changes in symptom profile over time by dividing participants into one of three OCD subtypes based on Lee and Kwon's (2003) subtyping work: those with autogenous obsessions, those with reactive obsessions, and those with mixed obsessions. Autogenous obsessions come into consciousness abruptly without an identified stimulus, while reactive obsessions are provoked by environmental stimuli. The authors found that while individuals may experience changes in specific OCD symptoms, none of the participants shifted between autogenous and reactive obsession subtypes.

LIFE STRESSORS AND THE DEVELOPMENT AND COURSE OF OCD
While the etiology of OCD is not known, researchers frequently report a link between onset and significant life stressors. In an early study of case histories, Pollitt (1960) reported that 62% of patients with OCD believed that the onset of their

symptoms was associated with a specific stressor. More recent investigations have corroborated this early observation. Studies of individuals who have experienced a traumatic event reveal that comorbid OCD can occur in addition to post-traumatic stress disorder (e.g., de Silva & Marks, 1999). In an evaluation of children with OCD, significantly more stressful life events occurred the year prior to the onset of symptoms than was reported by healthy controls (Gothelf, Aharonovsky, & Horesh, 2004). In one of the most comprehensive investigations to date, Cromer, Schmidt, and Murphy (2007) assessed 265 individuals with OCD to determine if traumatic life events were related to OCD symptom severity. They found a significant positive relationship, even after controlling for other factors such as symptoms of depression and other comorbidities (Cromer et al., 2007). Moreover, traumatic life events were most strongly correlated with the OCD symptoms dimensions of "obsessions/checking" and "symmetry/ordering" (Cromer et al., 2007).

Functional Impairment

OCD is the 10th leading cause of disability in the industrialized world (Murray & Lopez, 1996). In the British National Psychiatric Morbidity Survey of 2000, individuals with OCD were significantly more likely than those with other anxiety disorders to be unemployed, unmarried, have a lower income, and lower socioeconomic status (A. Torres et al., 2006).

It was once thought that individuals with OCD had higher intelligence levels and attained better levels of education than average (e.g., Black, 1974; Kringlen, 1965). More recent investigations indicate that this is not the case. No significant differences were found on intelligence tests in several studies (Coryell, 1981; Rasmussen & Eisen, 1992). Similarly, although there are reports that individuals with OCD are more likely to drop out of college (Henderson & Pollard, 1988), more recent surveys find that educational attainment among those with OCD is similar to individuals with other psychiatric disorders, and even nonclinical comparison groups (Karno et al., 1988; Kringlen, Torgersen, & Cramer, 2001).

A survey of members of the Obsessive Compulsive Foundation found that 41% of respondents indicated that they could not work because of their symptoms and had lost, on average, two years of wages (Hollander, Kwon, Stein, & Broatch, 1996). Similarly, approximately one-third of a large OCD clinical sample reported that they were unable to

work due to the disorder (Eisen et al., 2006). At this time, it is unclear whether the poor occupational functioning seen in OCD is worse than the dysfunction seen in other psychiatric disorders. Both higher rates of unemployment and lower income levels have been reported for OCD patients in several studies (Henderson & Pollard, 1988; Steketee, Grayson, & Foa, 1987; A. R. Torres et al., 2006), while others have found that employment status and income level was no worse than what is seen with other anxiety disorders (Antony et al., 1998; Karno et al., 1988). Huppert, Simpson, Nissenson, Liebowitz and Foa (2009) reported that OCD was associated with significantly decreased quality of life and increased functional impairment compared to healthy controls in areas of work, social life, and family life. Individuals with OCD and other comorbid psychiatric diagnoses, particularly comorbid depression, exhibited the lowest quality of life and functioning.

Grabe et al. (2000) found statistically significant differences in unemployment rates between individuals with a diagnosis of OCD and those with subclinical OCD symptoms. Interestingly, Eisen et al. (2006) found that overall quality of life was most negatively impacted by the severity of obsessions, but not compulsions. In contrast, Stengler-Wenzke and colleagues (Stengler-Wenzke, Kroll, Matschinger, & Angermeyer, 2006) reported that compulsion severity reduced patients' quality of life in the specific areas of physical well-being, psychological well-being, and environment. In line with Eisen and colleagues' findings regarding the specific impact of obsessions, Abbey, Clopton, and Humphreys (2007) reported that the severity of obsessions in particular was negatively correlated with intimacy, relationship satisfaction, and self-disclosure. Overall, rates of marital dysfunction, including separation and divorce, are high among individuals with OCD (Coryell, 1981; Emmelkamp & Gerlsma, 1994; Karno et al., 1988; Rasmussen & Eisen, 1992). Additionally, rates of late marriage and nonmarriage are higher among individuals with OCD than the U.S. population average (Steketee, 1997).

Almost two-thirds of relatives of individuals with OCD report some type of life disruption due to OCD, including family problems, deterioration or loss of relationships, and financial problems (Cooper, 1996). The causes of these familial disruptions are diverse. Relatives report distress due to both extensive participation in rituals or accommodations made for the patients' rituals (Rachman &

Hodgson, 1980). Families who refused to participate in rituals were also distressed (Amir, Freshman, & Foa, 2000). Involvement in caregiving was associated with lower quality of life among family members (Stengler-Wenzke et al., 2006). For a more complete discussion of the special issues related to family and social functioning in relation to OCD, see Chapter 9 of this volume.

HEALTH CARE UTILIZATION

Individuals affected by OCD delay seeking treatment from anywhere between 2 and 7 years following symptom onset (Eisen et al., 2006; Rasmussen & Tsuang, 1986). Investigations of both adults and adolescents demonstrate that 35% or less of those with OCD have received specialized mental health treatment (Shapiro, Skinner, & Kessler, 1984; Whitaker, Johnson, & Shaffer, 1990). In a systematic investigation of the factors that may predict help-seeking behavior, Goodwin, Koenen, Hellman, Guardino, and Struening (2002) found that gender, age, and race were all strong predictors of health-seeking behaviors. That is, older, Caucasian females were most likely to seek help. Comorbidity with panic disorder was also a strong predictor of help-seeking behavior. Finally, Goodwin and colleagues (2002) reported that lack of knowledge regarding the availability of treatment was a more robust barrier to seeking help than lack of funds or insurance coverage.

ASSOCIATION WITH SUICIDE

OCD's association with suicidal behavior is not well understood. Among the anxiety disorders, suicide in panic disorder has been better evaluated (Beck, Steer, Sanderson, & Skeie, 1991; Schmidt, Woolaway-Bickel, & Bates, 2001). One of the challenges in determining the specific risk for suicide in OCD is the frequent comorbidity with other conditions. Sareen et al. (2005) found that the presence of an anxiety disorder, including OCD, was a risk factor for subsequent suicidal ideation and attempts. The results of Sareen et al.'s study are congruent with the findings of the ECA study, where uncomplicated OCD was associated with suicide attempts (Weissman et al., 1994).

Crosscultural Differences in Obsessive Compulsive Disorder

There has been limited study of the phenomenology and epidemiology of OCD crossculturally, and most information about the disorder has come from Western industrial nations (Horwath & Weissman, 2000; Weissman et al., 1994). The limited crosscultural information suggests both similarities and potentially important differences between the obsessional problems seen in the West and the manifestations of the syndrome found in other parts of the world.

The prevalence and age at onset of OCD is generally the same internationally. Compared to prevalence estimates, more often reported for the United States, a slightly higher incidence of OCD of approximately 1.9%–2.5% is reported in non-Western countries (Horwath & Weissman, 2000; Weissman et al., 1994). Age-at-onset estimates of OCD are more variable crossculturally. In epidemiologic studies carried out in the West, age-at-onset estimates are often mid- to late-twenties to mid-thirties (although, see the discussion of disorder onset variability in an earlier section of this chapter). The disorder onset reported in some cultures was later than the onset reported in epidemiologic studies in the mainland United States: Puerto Rico, mean age 35.5 (SD = 13.6); Taiwan, 34.6 (14.4); Germany, 30.6 (13.8); and Korea, 29.8 (11.5) (Horwath & Weissman, 2000; Weissman et al., 1994). Reported age-at-onset differences might result from methodology differences or limited study of OCD in youth. In the West, there are data to suggest early- and later-onset subtypes of OCD. Similar analyses have not been conducted with non-Western samples. Additionally, in some age-at-onset research, disorder onset is defined as the time symptoms were first noticed (Rosario-Campos et al., 2001), but in other studies age at onset is considered to have occurred when diagnostic criteria were first met (Fontanelle, Mendlowicz, Marques, & Versiani, 2003). Without a consistent definition of age at onset, different conclusions may be reached even when using the same data set.

Although study has been limited, the core features of OCD (i.e., intrusive, ego-dystonic thoughts one resists, and the performance of rituals) are seen crossculturally (Okasha, Saad, Khalil, El-Dawla, & Yehia, 1994; Weissman et al., 1994). Symptom content, however, may be more culturally influenced (Fontenelle, Mendlowicz, Marques, & Versiani, 2004; Karadag, Oguzhanoglu, Ozdel, Atesci, & Amuk, 2006; Lemelson, 2003; Sica, Taylor, Arrindel, & Sanavio, 2006; Yourlmaz, Yilmaz, & Gencoz, 2004). In the United States and other Western countries, obsessions often focus on themes of contamination and doubt, and compulsions frequently involve washing and checking (Fontenelle et al., 2004), though these symptoms have also been found in non-Western countries (Juang & Liu, 2001). Egyptians, living in a predominantly Muslim society, more often report a high degree of repetition and cleaning compulsions, which are often more ego-syntonic. The connection of these symptoms to strong religious beliefs may be responsible for the limited insight into the excessive nature of the concern (Karadag et al., 2006; Okasha et al., 1994). Sexual obsessions were also more frequent in Egyptian culture, and this might result from cultural differences where religious practices emphasize cleanliness and purity (Karadag et al., 2006; Okasha et al., 1994). This association between obsessional symptoms and religiosity was also noted by Yourlmaz and colleagues (2004). They found that in Turkey, individuals with OCD were more disposed to have thought-action fusion regarding morality (i.e., thought is understood to be a moral act independent of behavior) than in other nations. In the West, thought-action fusion was more likely to take the likelihood form (e.g., thought about an outcome somehow increases the probability of the event; Rassin, Diepstraten, Mercelbach, & Muris, 2001; Rassin, Merkelbach, Muris, & Schmidt, 2001). In another evaluation of cultural differences, individuals with OCD from Bali experienced more frequent "need to know" obsessions than was found in Western cultures (Lemelson, 2003). This difference was hypothesized to result from the high value that is placed on the social network in that culture, where being aware of and being able to react to the identity and status of others is of primary importance (Lemelson, 2003).

Initial studies suggest that culture might influence the dysfunctional beliefs posited to be etiologic in cognitive models of OCD. Personal responsibility, the extent to which one believes that he or she is personally responsible for preventing harm, was identified as a core OCD-related dysfunctional belief in studies with Western samples, and has been associated with the severity of compulsions that serve to prevent harm (see Frost & Steketee, 2002, for a review). Sica (2006) demonstrated that cultural factors that promote a sense of being powerless attenuated the relationship between OCD symptom severity and responsibility beliefs.

Cultural differences also influence help-seeking behavior, including the pursuit of mental health treatment (Sica et al., 2006). Specifically, after obsessive compulsive symptoms manifest, individuals in more conservative or more religious cultures tend to wait to get help until symptoms become more severe, or they attempt to deal with their symptoms through other social support mechanisms. Additionally, in some cultures, core OCD symptoms, obsessing or doubting, are seen in a positive light—indicative of carefulness, orderliness, and faithfulness—further affecting help-seeking behavior (Karadag et al., 2006; Okasha et al., 1994). Weissman et al. (1994), Horwath and Weissman (2000), and Fontenelle et al. (2004) found a predominance of women with OCD, and a higher lifetime prevalence of OCD for women in non-Western cultures. It is unclear whether these differences are the result of gender differences in OCD prevalence, or result from the greater tendency of women to present for assessment and treatment in these cultures.

Chapter Summary and Future Directions

OCD is a very complex psychiatric disorder that is heterogeneous at multiple levels (e.g., patterns of comorbidity, symptom presentation, cognitive processing). Significant advances have been made in understanding the phenomenology of OCD, although much work remains. Some clinical researchers argue that more work on elucidating the phenomenology of OCD is needed before significant changes can be considered for OCD's placement in the psychiatric disorders taxonomy. Others suggest that the increased information realized during the past several decades is sufficient for consideration of OCD and importantly related conditions as components of a new syndromal grouping, OCD Spectrum Conditions.

Two major issues that must be addressed to advance understanding of OCD are disorder heterogeneity, and the commonalities and differences between clinical and nonclinical obsessions. OCD heterogeneity investigations burgeoned over the last two decades and significant gains were made, with important disorder subtypes identified (e.g., predominant clinical hoarding). Nonetheless, additional work is needed including further evaluations of overt symptom differences, and investigations of differences in the core motivations underlying obsessional patient concerns (e.g., harm avoidance and incompleteness; Summerfeldt, 2007). We agree with McKay and Neziroglu (2009) that multiple methodologies will be needed to better understand OCD heterogeneity. The extensive experimental work on nonclinical and clinical obsessions and compulsions has been very important to understanding OCD, and is the foundation for cognitive models of the disorder (e.g., Salkovskis, 1985). Additional work in this area is also critical to understanding how a common experience becomes a debilitating disorder for some.

References

Abbey, R. D., Clopton, J. R., & Humphreys, J. D. (2007). Obsessive-compulsive disorder and romantic functioning. *Journal of Clinical Psychology, 63*, 1181–1192.

Abramowitz, J. S., Brigidi, B. S., & Foa, E. B. (1999). Health concerns in patients with obsessive-compulsive disorder. *Journal of Anxiety Disorders, 13*, 529–539.

Abramowitz, J. S., & Deacon, B. J. (2005). Obsessive-compulsive disorder: Essential phenomenology and overlap with other anxiety disorders. In J. Abramowitz & A. C. Houts (Eds.), *Concepts and controversies in obsessive-compulsive disorder* (pp. 119–135). New York: Springer.

Abramowitz, J. S., & Foa, E. B. (1998). Worries and obsessions in individuals with obsessive-compulsive disorder with and without comorbid generalized anxiety disorder. *Behaviour Research and Therapy, 36*, 695–700.

Abramowitz, J. S., & Foa, E. B. (2000). Does comorbid major depression influence outcome of exposure and response prevention for OCD? *Behavior Therapy, 31*, 795–800.

Abramowitz, J. S., Franklin, M. E., Schawartz, S. A., & Furr, J. M. (2003). Symptom presentation and outcome of cognitive-behavioral therapy for obsessive-compulsive disorder. *Journal of Consulting and Clinical Psychology, 71*, 1049–1057.

Abramowitz, J. S., Franklin, M. E., Street, G. P., Kozak, M. J., & Foa, E. B. (2000). Effects of comorbid depression on response to treatment for obsessive-compulsive disorder. *Behavior Therapy, 31*, 517–528.

Abramowitz, J. S., Storch, E. A., Keeley, M., & Cordell, E. (2007). Obsessive-compulsive disorder with comorbid major depression: What is the role of cognitive factors? *Behaviour Research and Therapy, 45*, 2257–2267.

Alonso, P., Menchon, J. M., Segalas, C., Jaurrieta, N., Jiminez-Murcia, S., Cardoner, N., et al. (2008). Clinical implications of insight assessment in obsessive-compulsive disorder. *Comprehensive Psychiatry, 49*, 305–312.

Alverenga, P. G., Hounie, A. G., Mercadante, M. T., Miguel, E. C., & Conceicao, M. (2007). Obsessive-compulsive disorder: A historical overview. In E. A. Storch, G. R. Geffken & T. K. Murphy (Eds.), *Handbook of child and adolescent obsessive-compulsive disorder* (pp. 1–15). Mahwah, NJ: Lawrence Erlbaum.

American Psychiatric Association. (1952). *Diagnostic and statistical manual of mental disorders* (1st ed.). Washington, DC: Author.

American Psychiatric Association. (1968). *Diagnostic and statistical manual of mental disorders* (2nd ed.). Washington, DC: Author.

American Psychiatric Association. (1980). *Diagnostic and statistical manual of mental disorders* (3rd. ed.). Washington: DC: Author.

American Psychiatric Association. (1987). *Diagnostic and statistical manual of mental disorders* (3rd ed., rev). Washington, DC: Author.

American Psychiatric Association. (1994). *Diagnostic and statistical manual of mental disorders* (4th ed.). Washington, DC: Author.

American Psychiatric Association. (2000). *Diagnostic and statistical manual of mental disorders* (4th ed., text rev). Washington, D.C: Author.

Amir, N., Freshman, M., & Foa, E. B. (2000). Family distress and involvement in relatives of obsessive-compulsive disorder patients. *Journal of Anxiety Disorders, 14*, 209–217.

Anderluh, M. B., Tchanturia, K., Rabe-Hesketh, S., & Treasure, J. (2003). Childhood obsessive-compulsive personality traits in adult women with eating disorders: Defining a broader eating disorder phenotype. *American Journal of Psychiatry, 160*, 242–247.

Andrade, L., Walters, E., Gentil, V., & Laurenti, R. (2002). Prevalence of ICD-10 mental disorders in a catchment area in the city of São Paolo, Brazil. *Social Psychiatry and Psychiatric Epidemiology, 37*, 316–325.

Angst, J., Gamma, A., Endrass, J., Goodwin, R., Ajdacic, V., Eich, D., et al. (2004). Obsessive-compulsive severity spectrum in the community: Prevalence, comorbidity, and course. *European Archives of Psychiatry & Clinical Neuroscience, 254*, 156–164.

Anthony, J. C., Folstein, M., Romanoski, A. J., Von Korff, M. R., Nestadt, G. R., & Chahal, R. (1985). Comparison of the lay diagnostic interview schedule and a standardized psychiatric diagnosis experience in eastern Baltimore. *Archives of General Psychiatry, 42*, 667–675.

Antony, M. M., Downie, F., & Swinson, R. P. (1998). Diagnostic issues and epidemiology in obsessive-compulsive disorder. In R. P. Swinson, M. M. Antony, S. J. Rachman & M. A. Richter (Eds.), *Obsessive-compulsive disorder: Theory, research, and treatment* (pp. 3–32). New York: Guilford Press.

Apter, A., Fallon, T., King, R., & Ratzoni, G. (1996). Obsessive-compulsive characteristics: From symptoms to syndrome. *Journal of the American Academy of Child & Adolescent Psychiatry, 35*, 907–912.

Azrin, N. H., & Peterson, A. L. (1988). Habit reversal for the treatment of Tourette's syndrome. *Behaviour Research and Therapy, 26*, 347–351.

Bartz, J. A., & Hollander, F. (2006). Is obsessive-compulsive disorder an anxiety disorder? *Progress in Neuro-Psychopharmacology and Biological Psychiatry, 30*, 338–352.

Bayer, R., & Spitzer, R. L. (1985). Neurosis, psychodynamics, and DSM-III: A history of the controversy. *Archives of General Psychiatry, 42*, 198–196.

Beard, G. (1869). Neurasthenia, or nervous exhaustion. *The Boston Medical and Surgical Journal, 3*, 217–221.

Bebbington, P. E. (1998). Epidemiology of obsessive-compulsive disorder. *British Journal of Psychiatry, 35*, 2–6.

Beck, A. T. (1976). *Cognitive therapy and the emotional disorders.* New York: International Universities Press.

Beck, A. T., Steer, R. A., Sanderson, W. C., & Skeie, T. M. (1991). Panic disorder and suicidal ideation and behavior: Discrepant findings in psychiatric outpatients. *American Journal of Psychiatry, 148*, 1195–1199.

Beck, A. T., Ward, C. H., Mendelson, M., Mock, J. E., & Erbaugh, J. K. (1962). Reliability of psychiatric diagnoses: II. A study of consistency of clinical judgments and ratings. *American Journal of Psychiatry, 119*, 351–357.

Bellino, S., Patria, L., Ziero, S., & Bogetto, F. (2005). Clinical picture of obsessive-compulsive disorder with poor insight: A regression model. *Psychiatry Research, 136*, 223–231.

Benjamin, L. T. (2007). *A brief history of modern psychology.* Boston: Blackwell Publishing.

Berman, L. (1942). The obsessive-compulsive neurosis in children. *Journal of Nervous and Mental Disease, 95*, 26–39.

Berrios, G. E. (1996). *The history of mental symptoms: Descriptive psychopathology since the nineteenth century*. Cambridge: Cambridge University Press.

Besiroglu, L., Uguz, F., & Ozbebit, O. (2007). Longitudinal assessment of symptom and subtype categories in obsessive-compulsive disorder. *Depression and Anxiety, 24*, 461–466.

Black, A. (1974). The natural history of obsessional patterns. In H. R. Beech (Ed.), *Obsessional states* pp. 19–54). London: Methuen.

Bloch, M. H., Landeros-Weisenberger, A., Rosario, M. C., Pittenger, C., & Leckman, J. F. (2008). Meta-analysis of the symptom structure of obsessive-compulsive disorder. *American Journal of Psychiatry, 165*, 1532–1542.

Bloch, M. H., Peterson, B. S., Scahill, L., Otka, J., Katsovich, L., Zhang, H., et al. (2006). Adulthood outcome of tic and obsessive-compulsive severity in children with Tourette Syndrome. *Archives of Pediatrics & Adolescent Medicine, 160*, 65–69.

Borgen, F. H., & Barnett, D. C. (1987). Applying cluster analysis in counseling psychology research. *Journal of Counseling Psychology, 34*, 456–468.

Brown, T. A. (1998). The relationship between obsessive-compulsive disorder and other anxiety-based disorders. In R. P. Swinson, M. M. Antony, S. J. Rachman & M. A. Richter (Eds.), *Obsessive-compulsive disorder: Theory, research, and treatment* (pp. 207–226). New York: Guilford Press.

Brown, T. A., & Barlow, D. H. (1992). Comorbidity among anxiety disorders: Implications for treatment and DSM-IV. *Journal of Consulting and Clinical Psychology, 60*, 835–844.

Brown, T. A., Campbell, L. A., Lehman, C. L., Grisham, J. R., & Mancill, R. B. (2001). Current and lifetime comorbidity of the DSM-IV anxiety and mood disorders in a large clinical sample. *Journal of Abnormal Psychology, 110*, 585–599.

Brown, T. A., Chorpita, B. F., & Barlow, D. H. (1998). Structural relationships among dimensions of the DSM-IV anxiety and mood disorders and dimensions of negative affect, positive affect, and autonomic arousal. *Journal of Abnormal Psychology, 107*, 179–192.

Burton, R. (1847). *The anatomy of melancholy*. New York: Wiley & Putnam. (Original work published 1621).

Bynum, W. F., Porter, R., & Shepherd, M. (2005). *The anatomy of madness: Essays in the history of psychiatry*. London: Tavistock Publications.

Calamari, J. E. (2005). Understanding the heterogeneity of OCD. *American Journal of Psychiatry, 162*, 2192–2194.

Calamari, J. E., Cohen, R. J., Rector, N. A., Szacun-Shimizu, K., Riemann, B. C., & Norberg, M. M. (2006). Dysfunctional belief-based obsessive-compulsive disorder subgroups. *Behaviour Research and Therapy, 44*, 1347–1360.

Calamari, J. E., Wiegartz, P. S., & Janeck, A. S. (1999). Obsessive-compulsive disorder subgroups: A symptom-based clustering approach. *Behaviour Research and Therapy, 37*, 113–125.

Calamari, J. E., Wiegartz, P. S., Riemann, B. C., Cohen, R. J., Greer, A., Jacobi, D. M., et al. (2004). Obsessive-compulsive disorder subtypes: An attempted replication and extension of a symptom-based taxonomy. *Behaviour Research and Therapy, 42*, 647–670.

Carr, A. T. (1974). Compulsive neurosis: A review of the literature. *Psychological Bulletin, 81*, 311–318.

Cassin, S. E., Richter, M. A., Zhang, K. A., & Rector, N. A. (2009). Quality of life in treatment-seeking patients with obsessive-compulsive disorder with and without major depressive disorder. *Canadian Journal of Psychiatry, 54*, 460–467.

Catapano, F., Perris, F., Fabrazzo, M., Cioffi, V., Giacco, D., De Santis, V., & Maj, M. (2010).Obsessive?compulsive disorder with poor insight: A three-year prospective study. *Progress in Neuro-Psychopharmacology & Biological Psychiatry, 34(2)*, 323–330.

Castle, D., Deale, A., & Marks, I. M. (1995). Gender differences in obsessive compulsive disorder. *Australian and New Zealand Journal of Psychiatry, 29*, 114–117.

Chabane, N., Delorme, R., Millet, B., Mouren, M., Leboyer, M., & Pauls, D. (2005). Early-onset obsessive-compulsive disorder: A subgroup with a specific clinical and familiar pattern? *Journal of Child Psychology and Psychiatry, 46*, 881–887.

Chambless, D. L., & Steketee, G. (1999). Expressed emotion and behavior therapy outcome: A prospective study with obsessive-compulsive and agoraphobic outpatients. *Journal of Consulting and Clinical Psychology, 67*, 658–665.

Clark, D. A. (2004). *Cognitive behavior therapy of OCD*. New York: Guilford Press.

Clark, D. A., & O'Connor, K. P. (2005). Thinking Is believing: Ego-dystonic intrusive thoughts in obsessive-compulsive disorder. In D. A. Clark (Ed.), *Intrusive thoughts in clinical disorders: Theory, research, and treatment* (pp. 145–174). New York: Guilford Press.

Clark, D. A., & Rhyno, S. (2005). Unwanted intrusive thoughts in nonclinical individuals: Implications for clinical disorders. In D. A. Clark (Ed.), *Intrusive thoughts in clinical disorders: Theory, research, and treatment* (pp. 1–29). New York: Guilford Press.

Cooper, M. (1996). Obsessive-compulsive disorder: Effects on family members. *American Journal of Orthopsychiatry, 66*, 296–304.

Corcoran, K. M., & Woody, S. R. (2008). Appraisals of obsessional thoughts in normal samples. *Behaviour Research and Therapy, 46*, 71–83.

Coryell, W. (1981). Obsessive-compulsive disorder and primary unipolar depression. *Journal of Nervous and Mental Disease, 169*, 220–224.

Crino, R. D., & Andrews, G. (1996). Obsessive-compulsive disorder and Axis I comorbidity. *Journal of Anxiety Disorders, 10*, 37–46.

Crino, R. D., Slade, T., & Andrews, G. (2005). The changing prevalence and severity of obsessive-compulsive disorder criteria from DSM-III to DSM-IV. *American Journal of Psychiatry, 162*, 876–882.

Cromer, K. R., Schmidt, N. B., & Murphy, D. L. (2007). An investigation of traumatic life events and obsessive-compulsive disorder. *Behaviour Research and Therapy, 45*, 1683–1691.

Cunill, R., Castells, X., & Simeon, D. (2009). Relationships between obsessive-compulsive symptomatology and severity of psychosis in schizophrenia: A systematic review and meta-analysis. *Journal of Clinical Psychiatry, 70*, 70–82.

Dagonet, H. (1870). Des impulsions dans la folie et de la folie impulsive. *Annales Médico-Psychologiques, 4*, 5–32.

Davison, G. C., & Neale, J. M. (1994). *Abnormal psychology* (6th ed.). New York: Wiley & Sons.

de Haan, L., Dudek-Hodge, C., Verhoeven, Y., & Denys, D. (2009). Prevalence of psychotic disorders in patients with obsessive-compulsive disorder. *CNS Spectrums, 14*, 415–417.

de Mathis, M. A., do Rosario, M. C., Diniz, J. B., Torres, A. R., Shavitt, R. G., Ferrão, Y. A., et al. (2008). Obsessive-compulsive disorder: Influence of age at onset on comorbidity patterns. *European Psychiatry, 23*, 187–194.

de Silva, P., & Marks, I. M. (1999). The role of traumatic experiences in the genesis of obsessive-compulsive disorder. *Behaviour Research and Therapy, 37*, 941–951.

Delorme, R., Golmard, J.-L., Chabane, N., Millet, B., Krebs, M.-O., Mouren-Simeoni, M. C., et al. (2005). Admixture analysis of age at onset in obsessive-compulsive disorder. *Psychological Medicine, 35*, 237–243.

Denys, D., Tenney, N., van Megen, H. J. G. M., de Geus, F., & Westenberg, H. G. M. (2004). Axis I and II comorbidity in a large sample of patients with obsessive-compulsive disorder. *Journal of Affective Disorders, 80*, 155–162.

di Nardo, P. A., Moras, K., Barlow, D. H., Rapee, R. M., & Brown, T. A. (1993). Reliability of DSM-III-R anxiety disorder categories: Using the Anxiety Disorders Interview Schedule-Revised (ADIS-R). *Archives of General Psychiatry, 50*, 251–256.

Didie, E. R., Pinto, A., Mancebo, M., Rasmussen, S. A., Phillips, K. A., Walters, M. M., et al. (2007). A comparison of quality of life and psychosocial functioning in obsessive-compulsive disorder and body dysmorphic disorder. *Annals of Clinical Psychiatry, 19*, 181–186.

Diniz, J. B., Rosario-Campos, M. C., Shavitt, R. G., Curi, M., Hounie, A. G., Brotto, S. A., et al. (2004). Impact of age of onset and duration of illness on the expression of comorbidities in obsessive-compulsive disorder. *Journal of Clinical Psychiatry, 65*, 22–27.

Dollard, J., & Miller, N. E. (1950). *Personality and psychotherapy: An analysis in terms of learning, thinking, and culture.* New York: McGraw-Hill.

Douglass, H., Moffitt, T., Dar, R., & McGee, R. (1995). Obsessive-compulsive disorder in a birth cohort of 18-year-olds: Prevalence and predictors. *Journal of the American Academy of Child & Adolescent Psychiatry, 34*, 1424–1431.

du Toit, P. L., van Kradenburg, J., Niehaus, D. J. H., & Stein, D. J. (2001). Comparison of obsessive-compulsive disorder patients with and without comorbid putative obsessive-compulsive spectrum disorders using a structured clinical interview. *Comprehensive Psychiatry, 42*, 291–300.

Eapen, V., Pauls, D. L., & Robertson, M. M. (2006). The role of clinical phenotypes in understanding the genetics of obsessive-compulsive disorder. *Journal of Psychosomatic Research, 61*, 359–364.

Eisen, J. L., Beer, D. A., Pato, M. T., Venditto, T. A., & Rasmussen, S. A. (1997). Obsessive-compulsive disorder inpatients with schizophrenia or schizoaffective disorder. *American Journal of Psychiatry, 154*, 271–273.

Eisen, J. L., Mancebo, M., Pinto, A., Coles, M., Pagano, M., Stout, R., et al. (2006). Impact of obsessive-compulsive disorder on quality of life. *Comprehensive Psychiatry, 47*, 270–275.

Eisen, J. L., Phillips, K. A., Coles, M. E., & Rasmussen, S. A. (2004). Insight in obsessive compulsive disorder and body dysmorphic disorder. *Comprehensive Psychiatry, 45*, 10–15.

Eisen, J. L., & Rasmussen, S. A. (1989). Coexisting obsessive compulsive disorder and alcoholism. *Journal of Clinical Psychiatry, 50*, 96–98.

Eisen, J. L., & Rasmussen, S. A. (1993). Obsessive-compulsive disorder with psychotic features. *Journal of Clinical Psychiatry, 54*, 373–379.

Eisen, J. L., Rasmussen, S. A., Phillips, K. A., Price, L. H., Davidson, J., Lydiard, R. B., et al. (2001). Insight and treatment outcome in obsessive-compulsive disorder. *Comprehensive Psychiatry, 42*, 494–497.

Eisen, J. L., & Steketee, G. (1998). Course of illness in obsessive-compulsive disorder. In L. J. Dickstein, M. B. Riba & J. M. Oldham (Eds.), *Review of Psychiatry (Vol. 16)* (pp. III–73–III–95). Washington, DC: American Psychiatric Press.

Emmelkamp, P. M. G., & Gerlsma, C. (1994). Marital functioning and the anxiety disorders. *Behavior Therapy, 25*, 407–429.

Esquirol, J. E. D. (1845/1938). *Mental maladies: A treatise on insanity. (E.K. Hunt, Trans.).* Philadelphia, PA: Lea & Blanchard.

Fals-Stewart, W., & Angarano, K. (1994). Obsessive-compulsive disorder among patients entering substance abuse treatment: Prevalence and accuracy of diagnosis. *The Journal of Nervous and Mental Disease, 182*, 715–719.

Fear, C., Sharp, S., & Healy, D. (2000). Obsessive-compulsive disorder with delusions. *Psychopathology, 33*, 55–61.

Feinstein, S., Fallon, B. A., Petkova, E., & Liebowitz, M. R. (2003). Item-by-item factor analysis of the Yale-Brown Obsessive Compulsive scale symptom checklist. *The Journal of Neuropsychiatry and Clinical Neurosciences, 15*, 187–193.

First, M. B., Frances, A., & Pincus, H. A. (2004). *DSM-IV-TR guidebook.* Washington, DC: American Psychiatric Publications.

First, M. B., Spitzer, R. L., Gibbon, M., & Williams, J. B. W. (1996). *Structured Clinical Interview for DSM-IV Axis 1 Disorders-Patient Edition (SCID-I/P, Version 2.0).* New York: Biometrics Research Department of the New York State Psychiatric Institute.

Flament, M., Whitaker, A., Rapoport, J., & Davies, M. (1988). Obsessive compulsive disorder in adolescence: An epidemiological study. *Journal of the American Academy of Child & Adolescent Psychiatry, 27*, 764–771.

Foa, E. B., Abramowitz, J. S., Franklin, M. E., & Kozak, M. J. (1999). Feared consequences, fixity of belief, and treatment outcome in patients with obsessive-compulsive disorder. *Behavior Therapy, 30*, 717–724.

Foa, E. B., Kozak, M. J., Goodman, W. K., Hollander, E., Jenike, M. A., & Rasmussen, S. A. (1995a). DSM-IV field trial: Obsessive-compulsive disorder. *American Journal of Psychiatry, 152*, 90–96.

Foa, E. B., Kozak, M. J., Goodman, W. K., Hollander, E., Jenike, M. A., & Rasmussen, S. A. (1995b). "DSM-IV field trial: Obsessive-compulsive disorder": Correction. *American Journal of Psychiatry, 152*, 654.

Follette, W. C., & Houts, A. C. (1996). Models of scientific progress and the role of theory in taxonomy development: A case study of the DSM. *Journal of Consulting and Clinical Psychology, 64*, 1120–1132.

Fontanelle, L. F., Mendlowicz, M. V., Marques, C., & Versiani, M. (2003). Early- and late-onset obsessive-compulsive disorder in adult patients: An exploratory clinical and therapeutic study. *Journal of Psychiatric Research, 37*, 127–133.

Fontenelle, L. F., Lopes, A. P., Borges, M. C., Pacheco, P. G., & Versiani, M. (2008). Auditory, visual, tactile, olfactory, and bodily hallucinations in patients with obsessive-compulsive disorder. *CNS Spectrums, 13*, 125–130.

Fontenelle, L. F., Mendlowicz, M., & Versiani, M. (2006). The descriptive epidemiology of obsessive-compulsive disorder.

Progress in Neuro-Psychopharmacology & Biological Psychiatry, 30, 327–337.

Fontenelle, L. F., Mendlowicz, M. V., Marques, C., & Versiani, M. (2004). Trans-cultural aspects of obsessive-compulsive disorder: A description of a Brazillian sample and a systematic review of international clinical studies. *Journal of Psychiatric Research, 38,* 403–411.

Fontenelle, L. F., Mendlowicz, M. V., & Versiani, M. (2005). Impulse control disorders in patients with obsessive-compulsive disorder. *Psychiatry and Clinical Neurosciences, 59,* 30–37.

Frare, F., Perugi, G., Ruffolo, G., & Toni, C. (2007). Obsessive-compulsive disorder and body dysmorphic disorder: A comparison of clinical features. *European Psychiatry: The Journal of the Association of European Psychiatrists, 19,* 292–298.

Freeman, J. B., Choate-Summers, M. L., Moore, P. S., Garcia, A. M., Sapyta, J. J., Leonard, H. L., et al. (2007). Cognitive behavioral treatment for young children with obsessive-compulsive disorder. *Biological Psychiatry, 61,* 337–343.

Freud, S. (1909). Notes Upon a Case of Obsessional Neurosis. (J. Strachey, Trans.). In J. Strachey (Ed.), *The Standard Edition of the Complete Works of Sigmund Freud, Vol. 10.* (pp. 151–249). London: Hogarth Press. (Original work published 1958).

Freud, S. (1913). The disposition to obsessional neurosis: A contribution to the problem of choice of neurosis (J. Strachey, Trans.). In J. Strachey (Ed.), *The standard edition of the complete works of Sigmund Freud, Vol. 12* (pp. 311–326). London: Hogarth Press. (Original work published 1958).

Freud, S. (1958). Uber die Berechtigung, von der Neurasthenie einen bestimmten Symptomen-komplex als "Angstneurose" abzutrennen. (J. Strachey, Trans.). In J. Strachey (Ed.), *The standard edition of the complete works of Sigmund Freud, Vol. 3* (pp. 90–115). London: Hogarth Press. (Original work published 1895).

Friedman, S., Hatch, M. L., Paradis, C., Popkin, M., & Shalita, A. R. (1993). Obsessive compulsive disorder in two Black ethnic groups: Incidence in an urban dermatology clinic. *Journal of Anxiety Disorders, 7,* 343–348.

Friedman, S., Smith, L., Halpern, B., Levine, C., Paradis, C., Viswanathan, R., et al. (2003). Obsessive-compulsive disorder in a multi-ethnic urban outpatient clinic: Initial presentation and treatment outcome with exposure and ritual prevention. *Behavior Therapy, 34,* 397–410.

Frost, R. O., & Hartl, T. (1996). A cognitive behavioral model of compulsive hoarding. *Behaviour Research and Therapy, 34,* 341–350.

Frost, R. O., & Steketee, G. (1999). Issues in the treatment of compulsive hoarding. *Cognitive and Behavioral Practice, 6,* 397–407.

Frost, R. O., & Steketee, G. (2002). *Cognitive approaches to obsessions and compulsions: Theory, assessment, and treatment* (1st ed.). Amsterdam; New York: Pergamon.

Fuentes, K., & Cox, B. (1997). Prevalence of anxiety disorders in elderly adults: A critical analysis. *Journal of Behavior Therapy and Experimental Psychiatry, 28,* 269–279.

Furer, P., Walker, J. R., & Stein, M. B. (2007). *Treating health anxiety and fear of death: A practitioner's guide.* New York: Springer.

Geller, D., Biederman, J., Jones, J., Park, K., Schwartz, S., Shapiro, S., et al. (1998). Is juvenile obsessive-compulsive disorder a developmental subtype of the disorder? A review of the pediatric literature. *Journal of the American Academy of Child & Adolescent Psychiatry, 37,* 420–427.

Gentil, A. F., De Mathis, M. A., Torresan, R. C., Diniz, J. B., Alvarenga, P., Do Rosario, M. C., et al. (2009). Alcohol use disorders in patients with obsessive-compulsive disorder: The importance of appropriate dual-diagnosis. *Drug and Alcohol Dependence, 100,* 173–177.

Gershuny, B. S., Baer, L., Jenike, M. A., Minichiello, W. E., & Wilhelm, S. (2002). Comorbid posttraumatic stress disorder: Impact on treatment outcome for obsessive-compulsive disorder *American Journal of Psychiatry, 159,* 852–854.

Goldsmith, T., Shapira, N. A., Phillips, K. A., & McElroy, S. L. (1998). Conceptual foundations of obsessive-compulsive spectrum disorders. In R. P. Swinson, M. M. Antony, S. J. Rachman & M. A. Richter (Eds.), *Obsessive-compulsive disorder: Theory, research, and treatment* (pp. 397–425). New York: Guildford Press.

Goodman, W. K., Price, L. H., Rasmussen, S. A., Mazure, C., Fleischmann, R. L., Hill, C. L., et al. (1989). The Yale-Brown Obsessive Compulsive Scale. I. Development, use, and reliability. *Archives of General Psychiatry, 46,* 1006–1011.

Goodwin, R., Koenen, K. C., Hellman, F., Guardino, M., & Struening, E. L. (2002). Helpseeking and access to mental health treatment for obsessive-compulsive disorder. *Acta Psychiatrica Scandinavica, 106,* 143–149.

Gothelf, D., Aharonovsky, O., & Horesh, N. (2004). Life events and personality factors in children and adolescents with obsessive-compulsive disorder and other anxiety disorders. *Comprehensive Psychiatry, 45,* 192–198.

Grabe, H. J., Meyer, C., Hapke, U., Rumpf, H. J., Freyberger, H. J., Dilling, H., et al. (2000). Prevalence, quality of life and psychosocial function in obsessive–compulsive disorder and subclinical obsessive–compulsive disorder in northern Germany. *European Archives of Psychiatry and Clinical Neuroscience, 250,* 262–268.

Grabe, H. J., Ruhrmann, S., Spitzer, C., Josepeit, J., Ettelt, S., Buhtz, F., et al. (2008). Obsessive-compulsive disorder and posttaumatic stress disorder. *Psychopathology, 41,* 129–134.

Grant, J. E., Mancebo, M. C., Pinto, A., Eisen, J. L., & Rasmussen, S. A. (2006). Impulse control disorders in adults with obsessive compulsive disorder. *Journal of Psychiatric Research, 40,* 494–501.

Hanna, G. L., Fischer, D. J., Chadha, K. R., Himle, J. A., & Van Etten, M. L. (2005). Familial and sporadic subtypes of early-onset obsessive-compulsive disorder. *Biological Psychiatry, 57,* 895–900.

Hansen, B., Vogel, P. A., Stiles, T. C., & Götestam, K. G. (2007). Influence of co-morbid generalized anxiety disorder, panic disorder and personality disorders on the outcome of cognitive behavioural treatment of obsessive-compulsive disorder. *Cognitive Behaviour Therapy, 36,* 145–155.

Hasler, G., LaSalle-Ricci, V. H., Ronquillo, J. G., Crawley, S. A., Cochran, L. W., Kazuba, D., et al. (2005). Obsessive-compulsive disorder symptom dimensions show specific relationships to psychiatric comorbidity. *Psychiatry Research, 135,* 121–132.

Helzer, J. E., Robins, L. N., McEvoy, L. T., Spitznagel, E. L., Stoltzman, R. K., Farmer, A., et al. (1985). A comparison of clinical and diagnostic interview schedule diagnoses: Physician reexamination of lay-interviewed cases in the general population. *Archives of General Psychiatry, 42,* 657–666.

Hemmings, S. M. J., Kinnear, C. J., Lochner, C., Niehaus, D. J. H., Knowles, J. A., Moolman-Smook, J. C., et al. (2004).

Early- versus late-onset obsessive-compulsive disorder: Investigating genetic and clinical correlates. *Psychiatry Research, 128,* 175–182.

Henderson, J., & Pollard, C. (1988). Three types of obsessive compulsive disorder in a community sample. *Journal of Clinical Psychology, 44,* 747–752.

Henry, B., Moffitt, T. E., Caspi, A., Langley, J., & Silva, P. A. (1994). On the "remembrance of things past": A longitudinal evaluation of the retrospective method. *Psychological Assessment, 6,* 92–101.

Himle, J. A., Fischer, D. J., van Etten, M. L., Janeck, A. S., & Hanna, G. L. (2003). Group behavioral therapy for adolescents with tic-related and non-tic-related obsessive-compulsive disorder. *Depression and Anxiety, 17,* 73–77.

Hodgson, R. J., & Rachman, S. (1977). Obsessional-compulsive complaints. *Behaviour Research and Therapy, 15,* 389–395.

Hollander, E., Braun, A., & Simeon, D. (2008). Should OCD leave the anxiety disorders in DSM-V? The case for obsessive-compulsive related disorders. *Depression and Anxiety, 25,* 317–329.

Hollander, E., Kim, S., Braun, A., Simeon, D., & Zohar, J. (2009). Cross-cutting issues and future directions for the OCD spectrum. *Psychiatry Research, 170,* 3–6.

Hollander, E., Kwon, J., Stein, D., & Broatch, J. (1996). Obsessive-compulsive and spectrum disorders: Overview and quality of life issues. *Journal of Clinical Psychiatry, 57,* 3–6.

Hollander, E., & Wong, C. M. (2000). Spectrum, boundary, and subtyping issues: Implications for treatment-refractory obsessive-compulsive disorder. In W. K. Goodman, M. V. Rudorfor & J. D. Maser (Eds.), *Obsessive-compulsive disorder: Contemporary issues in treatment* (pp. 3–22). Mahwah, NJ: Erlbaum.

Hollander, E., & Zohar, J. (2004). Beyond refractory obsessions and anxiety states: Toward remission. *Journal of Clinical Psychiatry, 14,* 3–5.

Horwath, E., & Weissman, M. M. (2000). The epidemiology and cross-national presentation of obsessive-compulsive disorder. *Psychiatric Clinics of North America, 23,* 493–507.

Huppert, J. D., Simpson, H. B., Nissenson, K. J., Liebowitz, M. R., & Foa, E. B. (2009). Quality of life and functional impairment in obsessive-compulsive disorder: A comparison of patients with and without comorbidity, patients in remission, and healthy controls. *Depression & Anxiety, 26,* 39–45.

Insel, T. R., & Akiskal, H. S. (1986). Obsessive-compulsive disorder with psychotic features: A phenomenologic analysis. *American Journal of Psychiatry, 143,* 1527–1533.

Janowitz, D., Grabe, H. J., Ruhrmann, S., Ettelt, S., Buhtz, F., Hochrein, A., et al. (2009). Early onset of obsessive-compulsive disorder and associated comorbidity. *Depression & Anxiety, 26,* 1012–1017.

Jiminez-Murcia, S., Fernandez-Guasti, A., Raich, R. M., Alonso, P., Krug, I., Jaurrieta, N., et al. (2007). Obsessive-compulsive and eating disorders: Comparison of clinical and personality features. *Psychiatry and Clinical Neurosciences, 61,* 385–391.

Juang, Y., & Liu, C. (2001). Phenomenology of obsessive-compulsive disorder in Taiwan. *Psychiatry and Clinical Neurosciences, 55,* 623–627.

Judd, L. L. (1965). Obsessive compulsive neurosis in children. *Archives of General Psychiatry, 12,* 136–143.

Julien, D., O'Connor, K. P., & Aardema, F. (2007). Intrusive thoughts, obsessions, and appraisals in obsessive-compulsive disorder: A critical review. *Clinical Psychology Review, 27,* 366–383.

Karadag, F., Oguzhanoglu, N. K., Ozdel, O., Atesci, F. C., & Amuk, T. (2006). OCD symptoms in a sample of Turkish patients: A phenomenological picture. *Depression and Anxiety, 23,* 145–152.

Karno, M., Golding, J. M., Sorenson, S. B., & Burnam, A. (1988). The epidemiology of obsessive-compulsive disorder in five US communities. *Archives of General Psychiatry, 45,* 1094–1099.

Kempke, S. K., & Luyten, P. L. (2007). Psychodynamic and cognitive-behavioral approaches of obsessive-compulsive disorder: Is it time to work through our ambivalence? *Bulletin of the Menninger Clinic, 71,* 291–311.

Kessler, R. C., Chiu, W. T., Demler, O., Merikangas, K. R., & Walters, E. E. (2005). Prevalence, severity, and comorbidity of 12-month DSM-IV disorders in the National Comorbidity Survey Replication. *Archives of General Psychiatry, 62,* 617–627.

Koizumi, H. M. (1985). Obsessive-compulsive symptoms following stimulants. *Biological Psychiatry, 20,* 1332–1333.

Koran, L. M., Aboujaoude, E., Bullock, K. D., Franz, B., Gamel, N., & Elliott, M. (2005). Double-blind treatment with oral morphine in treatment-resistant obsessive-compulsive disorder. *Journal of Clinical Psychiatry, 66,* 353–359.

Kozak, M. J., & Foa, E. B. (1994). Obsessions, overvalued ideas, and delusions in obsessive-compulsive disorder. *Behaviour Research and Therapy, 32,* 343–353.

Kringlen, E. (1965). Obsessional neurotics. A long-term follow-up. *British Journal of Psychiatry, 111,* 709–722.

Kringlen, E., Torgersen, S., & Cramer, V. (2001). A Norwegian psychiatric epidemiological study. *American Journal of Psychiatry, 158,* 1091–1098.

Krochmalik, A., & Menzies, R. G. (2003). The classification and diagnosis of obsessive-compulsive disorder. In R. G. Menzies & P. d. Silva (Eds.), *Obsessive-compulsive disorder* (pp. 3–20). Chichester: Wiley.

Kyrios, M., Steketee, G., Frost, R. O., & Oh, S. (2002). Cognitions of compulsive hoarding. In R. O. Frost & G. Steketee (Eds.), *Cognitive approaches to obsessions and compulsions* (pp. 269–289). Amsterdam, Netherlands: Pergamon/Elsevier.

Lahey, B. B., Flagg, E. W., Bird, H. R., Schwab-Stone, M. E., Canino, G., Dulcan, M. K., et al. (1996). The NIMH methods for the epidemiology of child and adolescent mental disorders (MECA) study: Background and methodology. *Journal of the American Academy of Child and Adolescent Psychiatry, 35,* 855–864.

LaSalle, V. H., Cromer, K. R., Nelson, K. N., Kazuba, D., Justement, L., & Murphy, D. L. (2004). Diagnostic interview assessed neuropsychiatric disorder comorbidity in 334 individuals with obsessive-compulsive disorder. *Depression and Anxiety, 19,* 163–173.

Lavender, A., Shubert, I., De Silva, P., & Treasure, J. (2006). Obsessive-compulsive beliefs and magical ideation in eating disorders. *British Journal of Clinical Psychology, 45,* 331–342.

Leckman, J. F. (1993). Tourette's syndrome. In E. Hollander (Ed.), *Obsessive-compulsive-related disorders* (pp. 113–137). Washington, DC: American Psychiatric Press.

Leckman, J. F., Grice, D. E., Barr, L. C., de Vries, A. L., Martin, C., Cohen, D. J., et al. (1995). Tic-related vs. non-tic-related obsessive compulsive disorder. *Anxiety, 1,* 208–215.

Leckman, J. F., Mataix-Cols, D., & Rosario-Campos, M. C. (2005). Symptom dimensions in OCD: Developmental and evolutionary perspectives. In J. S. Abramowitz & A. C. Houts (Eds.), *Concepts and controversies in obsessive-compulsive disorder* (pp. 3–25). New York: Springer.

Leckman, J. F., Walker, D. E., Goodman, W. K., Pauls, D. L., & Cohen, D. J. (1994). "Just right" perceptions associated with compulsive behavior in Tourette's syndrome. *American Journal of Psychiatry, 151*, 675–680.

Ledley, D. R., Pai, A., & Franklin, M. E. (2007). Treating comorbid presentations: Obsessive-compulsive disorder, anxiety disorders, and depression.

Lee, H. J., & Kwon, S.-M. (2003). Two different types of obsession: Autogenous obsessions and reactive obsessions. *Behaviour Research and Therapy, 41*, 11–29.

Lemelson, R. (2003). Obsessive-compulsive disorder in Bali: The cultural shaping of a neuropsychiatric disorder. *Transcultural Psychiatry, 40*, 377–408.

Lensi, P., Cassano, G. B., Correddu, G., Ravagli, S., Kunovac, J. L., & Akiskal, H. S. (1996). Obsessive-compulsive disorder: Familial-developmental history, symptomatology, comorbidity and course with special reference to gender-related differences. *British Journal of Psychiatry, 169*, 101–107.

Lewinsohn, P., Hops, H., Roberts, R., Seeley, J., & Andrews, J. (1993). Adolescent psychopathology: I. Prevalence and incidence of depression and other DSM-III–R disorders in high school students. *Journal of Abnormal Psychology, 102*, 133–144.

Lochner, C., Kinnear, C. J., Hemmings, S. M. J., Seller, C., Niehaus, D. J. H., Knowles, J. A., et al. (2005). Hoarding in obsessive-compulsive disorder: Clinical and genetic correlates. *Journal of Clinical Psychiatry, 66*, 1155–1160.

Lochner, C., & Stein, D. (2001). Gender in obsessive-compulsive disorder and obsessive compulsive spectrum disorders. *Archives of Women's Mental Health, 4*, 19–26.

Maina, G., Albert, U., Pessina, E., & Bogetto, F. (2007). Bipolar obsessive-compulsive disorder and personality disorders. *Bipolar Disorders, 9*, 722–729.

Mancebo, M., Grant, J. E., Pinto, A., Eisen, J., & Rasmussen, S. A. (2009). Substance use disorders in an obsessive compulsive disorder clinical sample. *Journal of Anxiety Disorders, 23*, 429–435.

March, J. S., Franklin, M. E., Leonard, H., Garcia, A., Moore, P., Freeman, J., et al. (2007). Tics moderate treatment outcome with sertraline but not cognitive-behavior therapy in pediatric obsessive-compulsive disorder. *Biological Psychiatry, 61*, 344–347.

Masellis, M., Rector, N. A., & Richter, M. A. (2003). Quality of life in OCD: Differential impact of obsessions, compulsions, and depression comorbidity. *Canadian Journal of Psychiatry, 48(2)*, 74–77.

Mataix-Cols, D., Do Rosario, M. C., & Leckman, J. F. (2005). A multidimensional model of obsessive-compulsive disorder. *American Journal of Psychiatry, 162*, 228–238.

Mataix-Cols, D., Pertusa, A., & Leckman, J. F. (2007). Issues for DSM-V: How should obsessive-compulsive and related disorders be classified? *American Journal of Psychiatry, 164*, 1313–1314.

Mataix-Cols, D., Rauch, S., Baer, L., Eisen, J., Shera, D., Goodman, W., et al. (2002). Symptom stability in adult obsessive-compulsive disorder: Data from a naturalistic two-year follow-up study. *American Journal of Psychiatry, 159*, 263–268.

Mataix-Cols, D., Wooderson, S., Lawrence, N., Brammer, M. J., Speckens, A., & Phillips, M. L. (2004). Distinct neural correlates of washing, checking, and hoarding symptom dimensions in obsessive-compulsive disorder. *Archives of General Psychiatry, 61*, 564–576.

Matsunaga, H., Kiriike, N., Matsui, T., Oya, K., Okino, K., & Stein, D. J. (2005). Impulsive disorders in Japanese adult patients with obsessive-compulsive disorder. *Comprehensive Psychiatry, 46*, 43–49.

Mayes, R., & Horwitz, A. V. (2005). DSM-III and the revolution in the classification of mental illness. *Journal of the History of the Behavioral Sciences, 41*, 249–267.

McKay, D., Abramowitz, J. S., Calamari, J. E., Kyrios, M., Radomsky, A., Sookman, D., et al. (2004). A critical evaluation of obsessive-compulsive disorder subtypes: symptoms versus mechanisms. *Clinical Psychology Review, 24*, 283–313.

McKay, D., & Neziroglu, F. (2009). Methodological issues in the obsessive-compulsive spectrum. *Psychiatry Research, 170*, 61–65.

Miguel, E. C., Leckman, J. F., Rauch, R. L., Do Rosario, M. C., Hounie, A. G., Mercadante, M. T., et al. (2005). Obsessive-compulsive disorder phenotypes: Implications for genetic studies. *Molecular Psychiatry, 10*, 258–275.

Miguel, E. C., Rosário-Campos, M. C., Prado, H. S., Valle, R. V., Rauch, R. L., Coffey, B. J., et al. (2000). Sensory phenomena in obsessive-compulsive disorder and Tourette's disorder. *Journal of Clinical Psychiatry, 61*, 150–156.

Millon, T. (1983). The DSM-III: An insider's perspective. *American Psychologist, 38*, 804–814.

Montgomery, S. A. (1993). Obsessive compulsive disorder is not an anxiety disorder. *International Clinical Psychopharmacology, 8(Suppl. 1)*, 57–62.

Morillo, C., Belloch, A., & García-Soriano, G. (2007). Clinical obsessions in obsessive-compulsive patients and obsession-relevant intrusive thoughts in non-clinical, depressed and anxious subjects: Where are the differences? *Behaviour Research and Therapy, 45*, 1319–1333.

Mullen, J. (1927). *Psychological factors in the pastoral treatment of scruples: Studies in psychology and psychiatry*. Washington, DC: Catholic University of America Publishers.

Muris, P., Merckelbach, H., & Clavan, M. (1997). Abnormal and normal compulsions. *Behaviour Research and Therapy, 35*, 249–252.

Muroff, J., Steketee, G., Himle, J., & R. F. (2010). Delivery of internet treatment for compulsive hoarding (D.I.T.C.H.). *Behaviour Research and Therapy, 48*, 79–85.

Murray, C. J. L., & Lopez, A. D. (1996). *The global burden of disease*. Cambridge, MA: Harvard University Press.

Nathan, P. E., Andberg, M. M., Behan, P. O., & Patch, V. D. (1969). Thirty-two observers and one patient: A study of diagnostic reliability. *Journal of Clinical Psychiatry, 25*, 9–15.

Neighbors, H. W. (1988). The help-seeking behavior of Black Americans. *Journal of the National Medical Association, 80*, 1009–1012.

Nelson, E. A., Abramowitz, J. S., Whiteside, S. P., & Deacon, B. J. (2006). Scrupulosity in patients with obsessive-compulsive disorder: Relationship to clinical and cognitive phenomena. *Journal of Anxiety Disorders, 20*, 1071–1086.

Nestadt, G., Di, C. Z., Riddle, M. A., Grados, M. A., Greenberg, B. D., Fyer, A. J., et al. (2009). Obsessive–compulsive disorder: subclassification based on co-morbidity. *Psychological Medicine, 39*, 1491–1501.

Nestadt, G., Samuels, J. F., Riddle, M. A., Bienvenu, O. J., 3rd, Liang, K.-Y., LaBuda, M., et al. (2000). A family study of obsessive-compulsive disorder. *Archives of General Psychiatry, 57*, 358–363.

Neziroglu, F., & Stevens, K. P. (2002). Insight: its conceptualization and assessment. In R. O. Frost & G. Steketee (Eds.), *Cognitive approaches to obsessions and compulsions: Theory, assessment, and treatment* (pp. 183–193). Oxford: Elsevier Science.

Neziroglu, F., & Yaryura-Tobias, J. A. (1997). *Over and over again: Understanding obsessive-compulsive disorder.* San Fransisco, CA: Jossey-Bass.

O'Dwyer, A., & Marks, I. M. (2000). Obsessive-compulsive disorder and delusions revisited. *British Journal of Psychiatry, 176*, 281–284.

O'Flaherty, V. M. (1966). *How to cure scruples.* Milwaukee: Bruce.

Obsessive-Compulsive Cognitions Working Group. (2005). Psychometric validation of the Obsessive Beliefs Questionnaire and the Interpretation of Intrusions Inventory–Part 2: Factor analyses and testing of a brief version. *Behaviour Research and Therapy, 43*, 1527–1542.

Obsessive Compulsive Cognitions Working Group. (1997). Cognitive assessment of obsessive compulsive disorder. *Behaviour Research and Therapy, 35*, 667–687.

Obsessive Compulsive Cognitions Working Group. (2001). Development and initial validation of the Obsessive Beliefs Questionnaire and the Interpretation of Intrusions Inventory. *Behaviour Research and Therapy, 39*, 987–1005.

Okasha, A., Saad, A., Khalil, A. H., El-Dawla, A., & Yehia, N. (1994). Phenomenology of obsessive-compulsive disorder: A transcultural study. *Comprehensive Psychiatry, 35*, 191–197.

Panksepp, J. (2004). *Textbook of biological psychiatry.* Hoboken, NJ: Wiley-Liss.

Pauls, D. L., Alsobrook, J. P., Goodman, W., Rasmussen, L., & Leckman, J. F. (1995). A family-study of obsessive-compulsive disorder. *American Journal of Psychiatry, 152*, 76–84.

Perugi, G., Akiskal, H. S., Pfanner, C., Presta, S., Gemignani, A., Milanfranchi, A., et al. (1997). The clinical impact of bipolar and unipolar affective comorbidiy on obsessive-compulsive disorder. *Journal of Affective Disorders, 46*, 15–23.

Perugi, G., Toni, C., Frare, F., Travierso, M. C., Hantouche, E., & Akiskal, H. S. (2002). Obsessive-compulsive-bipolar comorbidity: A systematic exploration of clinical features and treatment outcome. *Journal of Clinical Psychiatry, 63*, 1129–1134.

Phillips, K. A., Gunderson, C. G., Mallya, G., McElroy, W., & Carter, W. (1998). A comparison study of body dysmorphic disorder and obsessive compulsive disorder. *Journal of Clinical Psychiatry, 59*, 568–575.

Phillips, K. A., Pinto, A., Menard, W., Eisen, J. L., Mancebo, M., & Rasmussen, S. A. (2007). Obsessive-compulsive disorder versus body dysmorphic disorder: A comparison study of two possibly related disorders. *Depression and Anxiety, 24*, 399–409.

Pollitt, J. D. (1960). Natural history studies in mental illness: A discussion based on a pilot study of obsessional states. *Journal of Mental Science, 106*, 93–113.

Poyurovsky, M., Hramenkov, S., Isakov, V., Rauchverger, B., Modai, I., Schneidman, M., et al. (2001). Obsessive-compulsive disorder in hospitalized patients with chronic schizophrenia. *Psychiatry Research, 102*, 49–57.

Poyurovsky, M., & Koran, L. M. (2005). Obsessive-compulsive disorder (OCD) with schizotypy vs. schizophrenia with OCD: Diagnostic dilemmas and therapeutic implications. *Journal of Psychiatric Research, 39*, 399–408.

Rachman, S. J. (1963). *Critical essays on psychoanalysis.* London: Pergamon Press.

Rachman, S. J. (1997). A cognitive theory of obsessions. *Behaviour Research and Therapy, 35*, 793–802.

Rachman, S. J., & de Silva, P. (1978). Abnormal and normal obsessions. *Behaviour Research and Therapy, 16*, 233–248.

Rachman, S. J., & Hodgson, R. J. (1980). *Obsessions and compulsions.* Englewood Cliffs, NJ: Prentice-Hall.

Radomsky, A. S., Bohne, A., & O'Connor, K. P. (2007). Treating comorbid presentations: Obsessive-compulsive disorder and disorders of impulse control. In M. M. Antony, C. Purdon & L. J. Summerfeldt (Eds.), *Psychological treatment of obsessive-compulsive disorder: Fundamentals and beyond* (pp. 295-309). Washington, DC: American Psychological Association.

Rapoport, J. L. (1989). *Obsessive-compulsive disorder in children and adolescents.* Washington, DC: American Psychiatric Press.

Rapoport, J. L., Inoff-Germain, G., Weissman, M. M., Greenwald, S., Narrow, W. E., Jensen, P. S., et al. (2000). Childhood obsessive-compulsive disorder in the NIMH MECA Study: Parent versus child identification of cases. *Journal of Anxiety Disorders, 14*, 535–548.

Rasmussen, S. A., & Eisen, J. L. (1992). The epidemiology and clinical features of obsessive compulsive disorder. *Psychiatric Clinics of North America, 15*, 743–758.

Rasmussen, S. A., & Eisen, J. L. (1998). Epidemiology and clinical features of obsessive-compulsive disorder. In M. A. Jenike & L. Baer (Eds.), *Obsessive-compulsive disorders: Practical Management* (3 ed., pp. 12–43). Boston: Mosby.

Rasmussen, S. A., & Tsuang, M. T. (1986). Clinical characteristics and family history in DSM-III obsessive-compulsive disorder. *American Journal of Psychiatry, 143*, 317–322.

Rassin, E., Cougle, J., & Muris, P. (2007). Content difference between normal and abnormal obsessions. *Behaviour Research and Therapy, 45*, 2800–2803.

Rassin, E., Diepstraten, P., Mercelbach, H., & Muris, P. (2001). Thought-action fusion and thought suppression in obsessive-compulsive disorder. *Behaviour Research and Therapy, 39*, 757–764.

Rassin, E., Merkelbach, H., Muris, P., & Schmidt, H. (2001). The thought-action fusion scale: Further evidence for its reliability and validity. *Behaviour Research and Therapy, 39*, 537–544.

Rassin, E., & Muris, P. (2006). Abnormal and normal obsessions: A reconsideration. *Behavioural Research and Therapy, 45*, 1065–1070.

Ravissa, L., Maina, G., & Bogetta, F. (1997). Episodic and chronic obsessive-compulsive disorder. *Depression & Anxiety, 6*, 154–158.

Rector, N. A., Cassin, S. E., & Richter, M. A. (2009). Psychological treatment of obsessive-compulsive disorder in patients with major depression: A pilot randomized controlled trial. *Canadian Journal of Psychiatry, 54*, 846–851.

Regier, D. A., Boyd, J., Burke, J., & Rae, D. (1988). One-month prevalence of mental disorders in the United States: Based on five epidemiologic catchment area sites. *Archives of General Psychiatry, 45*, 977–986.

Reinherz, H., Giaconia, R., Lefkowitz, E., & Pakiz, B. (1993). Prevalence of psychiatric disorders in a community population of older adolescents. *Journal of the American Academy of Child & Adolescent Psychiatry, 32*, 369–377.

Richter, M. A., Summerfeldt, L. J., Antony, M. M., & Swinson, R. P. (2003). Obsessive-compulsive spectrum conditions in obsessive-compulsive disorder and other anxiety disorders. *Depression and Anxiety, 18*, 118–127.

Riemann, B. C., McNally, R. J., & Cox, W. M. (1992). The comorbidity of obsessive-compulsive disorder and alcoholism. *Journal of Anxiety Disorders, 6*, 105–110.

Robins, L., Helzer, J., Croughan, J., & Ratcliff, K. (1981). National Institute of Mental Health diagnostic interview schedule: Its history, characteristics, and validity. *Archives of General Psychiatry, 38*, 381–389.

Robins, L., Wing, J., Wittchen, H., & Helzer, J. (1988). The Composite International Diagnostic Interview: An epidemiologic instrument suitable for use in conjunction with different diagnostic systems and in different cultures. *Archives of General Psychiatry, 45*, 1069–1077.

Rosario-Campos, M. C., Leckman, J. F., Mercadante, M. T., Shavitt, R. G., Prado, H. S., Sada, P., et al. (2001). Adults with early-onset obsessive-compulsive disorder. *American Journal of Psychiatry, 158*, 1899–1903.

Roth, W. F., & Luton, F. H. (1942). The mental health program in Tennessee. *American Journal of Psychiatry, 99*, 662–675.

Rothenberg, A. (1986). Eating disorder as a modern obsessive-compulsive syndrome. *Psychiatry and Clinical Neurosciences, 153*, 6–15.

Rudin, E. (1953). Ein beitrag zur frage der zwangskrainheit insebesondere ihere hereditaren beziehungen. *Archiv für Psychiatrie und Nervenkrankheiten, 191*, 14–54.

Rufer, M., Grothusen, A., Mass, R., Peter, H., & Hand, I. (2005). Temporal stability of symptom dimensions in adult patients with obsessive-compulsive disorder. *Journal of Affective Disorders, 88*, 99–102.

Ruscio, A. M., Stein, D. J., Chiu, W. T., & Kessler, R. C. (2010). The epidemiology of obsessive-compulsive disorder in the National Comorbidity Survey Replication. *Molecular Psychiatry, 15*, 53–63.

Rutter, M., Tizard, J., & Whitmore, K. (1970). *Education, health, and behavior*. London: Longman.

Salkovskis, P. M. (1985). Obsessional-compulsive problems: A cognitive-behavioural analysis. *Behaviour Research and Therapy, 23*, 571–583.

Salkovskis, P. M. (1989). Cognitive-behavioural factors and the persistence of intrusive thoughts in obsessional problems. *Behaviour Research and Therapy, 27*, 677–682; discussion 683–674.

Sallet, P. C., de Alvarenga, P. G., Ferrão, Y., de Mathis, M. A., Torres, A. R., Marques, A., et al. (2010). Eating disorders in patients with obsessive-compulsive disorder: prevalence and clinical correlates. *International Journal of Eating Disorders, 43*, 315-325.

Samuels, J. F., Bienvenu, O. J., 3rd, Pinto, A., Fyer, A. J., McCracken, J. T., Rauch, S. L., et al. (2007). Hoarding in obsessive-compulsive disorder: Results from the OCD Collaborative Genetics Study. *Behaviour Research and Therapy, 45*, 673–686.

Sanvio, E. (1988). Obsessions and compulsions: The Padua Inventory. *Behaviour Research and Therapy, 26*, 169–177.

Sareen, J., Cox, B. J., & Afifi, T. O. (2005). Anxiety disorders and risk for suicidal ideation and suicide attempts: A population-based longitudinal study of adults. *Archives of General Psychiatry, 62*, 1249–1257.

Satel, S. L., & McDougle, C. J. (1991). Obsessions and compulsions associated with cocaine abuse. *American Journal of Psychiatry, 148*, 947.

Saxena, S., Brody, A. L., Maidment, K. M., Smith, E. C., Zohrabi, N., Katz, E., et al. (2004). Cerebral glucose metabolism in obsessive-compulsive hoarding. *American Journal of Psychiatry, 161*, 1038–1048.

Schmidt, N. B., Woolaway-Bickel, K., & Bates, M. (2001). Evaluating panic-specific factors in the relationship between suicide and panic disorder. *Behaviour Research and Therapy, 39*, 635–649.

Shafran, R. (2002). Eating disorders and obsessive compulsive disorder. In R. O. Frost & G. Steketee (Eds.), *Cognitive approaches to obsessions and compulsions: Theory, assessment, and treatment* (pp. 215–231). Oxford, UK: Elsevier Science.

Shapiro, S., Skinner, E. A., & Kessler, L. G. (1984). Utilization of health and mental health services. *Archives of General Psychiatry, 41*, 971–978.

Sherman, B. J., Savage, C. R., Eddy, K. T., Blais, M. A., Deckersbach, T., Jackson, S. C., et al. (2006). Strategic memory in adults with anorexia nervosa: are there similarities to obsessive compulsive spectrum disorders? *International Journal of Eating Disorders, 39*, 468–476.

Sica, C., Taylor, S., Arrindel, W. A., & Sanavio, E. (2006). A cross-cultural test of the cognitive theory of obsessions and compulsions: A comparison of Greek, Italian, and American individuals–a preliminary study. *Cognitive Therapy Research, 30*, 585–597.

Skoog, G., & Skoog, I. (1999). A 40-year follow-up of patients with obsessive compulsive disorder. *Archives of General Psychiatry, 56*, 121–127.

Skre, I., Onstad, S., Torgersen, S., & Kringlen, E. (1991). High interrater reliability for the Structured Clinical Interview for DSM-III-R Axis I (SCID-I). *Acta Psychiatrica Scandinavica, 84*, 167–173.

Spitzer, R. L., Williams, J. B., & Skodol, A. E. (1980). DSM III: The major achievements and an overview. *American Journal of Psychiatry, 137*, 151–164.

Stein, D. J. (2008). Is disorder X in category or spectrum Y? General considerations and application to the relationship between obsessive-compulsive and anxiety disorders. *Depression & Anxiety, 25*, 330–335.

Stein, D. J., & Lochner, C. (2006). Obsessive-compulsive spectrum disorders: A multidimensional approach. *Psychiatric Clinics of North America, 29*, 343–351.

Stein, M., Forde, D., Anderson, G., & Walker, J. R. (1997). Obsessive-compulsive disorder in the community: An epidemiologic survey with clinical reappraisal. *American Journal of Psychiatry, 154*, 1120–1126.

Steketee, G. (1997). Disability and family burden in obsessive-compulsive disorder. *The Canadian Journal of Psychiatry, 42*, 919–928.

Steketee, G., Eisen, J., Dyck, I., Warshaw, M., & Rasmussen, S. A. (1999). Predictors of course in obsessive-compulsive disorder. *Psychiatry Research, 89*, 229–238.

Steketee, G., & Frost, R. O. (2003). Compulsive hoarding: Current status of the research. *Clinical Psychology Review, 23*, 905–927.

Steketee, G., Grayson, J. B., & Foa, E. B. (1987). A comparison of characteristics of obsessive compulsive disorder and other anxiety disorders. *Journal of Anxiety Disorders, 1*, 325–335.

Stengler-Wenzke, K., Kroll, M., Matschinger, H., & Angermeyer, M. C. (2006). Subjective quality of life of patients with obsessive-compulsive disorder. *Social Psychiatry and Psychiatric Epidemiology, 41,* 662–668.

Stewart, S. E., Stack, D. E., & Wilhelm, S. (2008). Severe obsessive-compulsive disorder with and without body dysmorphic disorder: Clinical correlates and implications. *Annals of Clinical Psychiatry, 20,* 33–38.

Storch, E. A., Abramowitz, J. S., & Goodman, W. K. (2008). Where does obsessive-compulsive disorder belong in DSM-V? *Depression and Anxiety, 25,* 336–347.

Storch, E. A., Merlo, L. J., Larson, M. J., Geffken, G. R., Lehmkuhl, H. D., Jacob, M. L., et al. (2008). Impact of comorbidity on cognitive-behavioral therapy response in pediatric obsessive-compulsive disorder. *Journal of the American Academy of Child and Adolescent Psychiatry, 47,* 538–592.

Summerfeldt, L. J. (2007). Treating Incompleteness, Ordering, and Arranging Concerns. In Antony, Martin M. (Ed); Purdon, Christine; Summerfeldt, Laura J. (Ed), *Psychological treatment of obsessive-compulsive disorder: Fundamentals and beyond.* (pp. 187–207). Washington, DC: American Psychological Association.

Summerfeldt, L. J., Huta, V., & Swinson, R. P. (1998). Personality and obsessive-compulsive disorder. In R. P. Swinson, M. M. Antony, S. J. Rachman & M. A. Richter (Eds.), *Obsessive-compulsive disorder: Theory, research, and treatment.* (pp. 79–119). New York: Guilford Press.

Summerfeldt, L. J., Richter, M. A., Antony, M. M., & Swinson, R. P. (1999). Symptom structure in obsessive-compulsive disorder: A confirmatory factor-analytic study. *Behaviour Research and Therapy, 37,* 297–311.

Swedo, S. E., Rapoport, J. L., Leonard, H., Lenane, M., & Cheslow, D. (1989). Obsessive-compulsive disorder in children and adolescents. Clinical phenomenology of 70 consecutive cases. *Archives of General Psychiatry, 46,* 335–341.

Swinson, R. P., Antony, M. M., Rachman, S. J., & Richter, M. A. (1998). *Obsessive-compulsive disorder: Theory, research, and treatment.* New York: Guilford Press.

Taylor, J., Herber, H., &, Page Eden, C. (1855). *Ductor dubitantium.* London. (Original work published 1621). The Whole Works of the Right Rev. Jeremy Taylor, Reginald Heber and, Charles Page Eden: Ductor Dubitantium, Part 1, Books I and II. Charleston, S.C: Nabu Press.

Taylor, S. (2005). Dimensional and subtype models of OCD. In J. S. Abramowitz & A. C. Houts (Eds.), *Concepts and controversies in obsessive-compulsive disorder* (pp. 27–41). New York: Springer.

Taylor, S., Abramowitz, J. S., McKay, D., Calamari, J. E., Sookman, D., Kyrios, M., et al. (2006). Do dysfunctional beliefs play a role in all types of obsessive-compulsive disorder? *Journal of Anxiety Disorders, 20,* 85–97.

Thordarson, D. S., & Shafran, R. (2002). Importance of thoughts. In R. O. Frost & G. Steketee (Eds.), *Cognitive approaches to obsessions and compulsions: Theory, assessment and treatment* (pp. 15–28). Oxford: Elsevier.

Tibbo, P., Kroetsch, M., Chue, P., & Warneke, L. (2000). Obsessive-compulsive disorder in schizophrenia. *Journal of Psychiatric Research, 34,* 139–146.

Tolin, D. F., Frost, R. O., & Steketee, G. (2007). *Buried in treasures: Help for compulsive acquiring, saving, and hoarding:* Oxford University Press: New York.

Torres, A. R., Prince, M. J., Bebbington, P. E., Bhugra, D., Brughy, T. S., Farrell, M., et al. (2006). Obsessive-compulsive disorder: Prevalence, comorbidity, impact, and help-seeking in the British National Psychiatric Morbidity Survey of 2000. *American Journal of Psychiatry, 163,* 1978–1985.

Tükel, R., Ertekin, E., Batmaz, S., Alyanak, F., Sözen, A., Aslantaş, B., et al. (2005). Influence of age of onset on clinical features in obsessive-compulsive disorder. *Depression & Anxiety, 21,* 112–117.

Tükel, R., Polat, A., Ozdemir, O., Aksut, D., & Turksov, N. (2002). Comorbid conditions in obsessive-compulsive disorder. *Comprehensive Psychiatry, 43,* 204–209.

Turksoy, N., Tukel, R., Ozdemir, O., & Karali, A. (2002). Comparison of clinical characteristics in good and poor insight obsessive-compulsive disorder. *Anxiety Disorders, 16,* 413–423.

Tynes, L. L., White, K., & Steketee, G. S. (1990). Toward a new nosology of obsessive-compulsive disorder. *Comprehensive Psychiatry, 31,* 465–480.

Uguz, F., Askin, R., Cilli, A. S., & Besiroglu, L. (2006). Comparison of treatment responses and clinical characteristics of early-onset and late-onset obsessive-compulsive disorder. *International Journal of Psychiatry in Clinical Practice, 10,* 291–296.

Ulloa, R. E., Nicolini, H., Avila, M., & Fernandez-Guasti, A. (2007). Age onset subtypes of obsessive compulsive disorder: Differences in clinical response to treatment with clomipramine. *Journal of Child and Adolescent Psychopharmacology, 17,* 85–96.

Valleni-Basile, L., Garrison, C., Jackson, K., & Waller, J. (1994). Frequency of obsessive compulsive disorder in a community sample of young adolescents. *Journal of the American Academy of Child & Adolescent Psychiatry, 33,* 782–791.

van den Heuvel, O. A., Remijnse, P. L., Mataix-Cols, D., Vrenken, H., Groenewegen, H. J., Uylings, H. B., et al. (2009). The major symptom dimensions of obsessive-compulsive disorder are mediated by partially distinct neural systems. *Brain, 132,* 853–868.

van der Hart, O., & Friedman, B. (1989). A reader's guide to Pierre Janet on dissociation: A neglected intellectual heritage. *Dissociation, 2,* 3–16.

van Oppen, P., Hoekstra, R. J., & Emmelkamp, P. M. G. (1995). The structure of obsessive-compulsive symptoms. *Behaviour Research and Therapy, 33,* 15–23.

Veale, D. (2007). Treating obsessive-compulsive disorder in people with poor insight and overvalued ideation. In M. M. Antony, C. Purdon & L. J. Summerfeldt (Eds.), *Psychological treatment of obsessive-compulsive disorder: Fundamentals and Beyond* (pp. 267–280). Washington, DC: American Psychological Association.

Vitousek, K. M. (1996). The current status of cognitive-behavioral models of anorexia nervosa and bulimia nervosa. In P. M. Salkovskis (Ed.), *Frontiers of cognitive therapy* (pp. 383–418). New York: Guilford.

Watson, D. (2005). Rethinking the mood and anxiety disorders: A quantitative hierarchical model for DSM-V. *Journal of Abnormal Psychology, 114,* 522–536.

Weissman, M. M., Bland, R. C., Canino, G. J., Greenwald, S., Hwu, H.-G., Lee, C. K., et al. (1994). The cross national epidemiology of obsessive compulsive disorder. The Cross National Collaborative Group. *Journal of Clinical Psychiatry, 55 Suppl,* 5–10.

Westphal, K. (1878). Ueber Zwangsvorstellungen. *Archiv Fur Psychiatrie und Nervenkrankheiten, 8,* 734–750.

Wheaton, M., Timpano, K. R., LaSalle-Ricci, V. H., & Murphy, D. (2008). Characterizing the hoarding phenotype in individuals with OCD: Associations with comorbidity, severity and gender. *Journal of Anxiety Disorders, 22,* 243–252.

Whitaker, A., Johnson, J., & Shaffer, D. (1990). Uncommon troubles in young people. *Archives of General Psychiatry, 47,* 487–496.

Widiger, T. A., & Clark, L. A. (2000). Toward DSM-V and the classification of psychopathology. *Psychological Bulletin, 126,* 946–963.

Wilhelm, S., & Neziroglu, F. (2002). Cognitive theory of body dysmorphic disorder. In R. O. Frost & G. Steketee (Eds.), *Cognitive approaches to obsessions and compulsions: Theory, assessment, and treatment* (pp. 203-214). Oxford, UK: Elsevier Science.

World Health Organization. (1965). *International classification of diseases* (8th ed.). Geneva: Author.

World Health Organization. (1992). *The tenth revision of the International Classification of Diseases and Related Health Problems* (10th ed.). Geneva: WHO.

Yaryura-Tobias, J. A., Grunes, M. S., Todaro, J., McKay, D., Neziroglu, F. A., & Stockman, R. (2000). Nosological insertion of Axis I disorders in the etiology of obsessive-compulsive disorder. *Journal of Anxiety Disorders, 14,* 19–30.

Yourlmaz, O., Yilmaz, A. E., & Gencoz, T. (2004). Psychometric properties of the Thought-Action Fusion Scale in a Turkish sample. *Behaviour Research and Therapy, 42,* 1203–1214.

Zinbarg, R. E., & Barlow, D. H. (1996). The structure of anxiety and the DSM-III-R anxiety disorders: A hierarchical model. *Journal of Abnormal Psychology, 105,* 181–193.

Zohar, A., Ratzoni, G., Pauls, D., & Apter, A. (1992). An epidemiological study of obsessive compulsive disorder and related disorders in Israeli adolescents. *Journal of the American Academy of Child & Adolescent Psychiatry, 31,* 1057–1061.

Phenomenology and Epidemiology of Body Dysmorphic Disorder

Megan M. Kelly *and* Katharine A. Phillips

Abstract

Body dysmorphic disorder (BDD) is an often severe DSM-IV disorder characterized by distressing or impairing preoccupations with imagined or slight defects in appearance. Individuals with BDD suffer from time-consuming obsessions about their bodily appearance and excessive repetitive behaviors (for example, mirror checking, excessive grooming, and skin picking). Functioning and quality of life are typically very poor, and suicidality rates appear markedly elevated. While prevalence data are still limited, they suggest that BDD affects 0.7% to 2.4% of the population; however, BDD typically goes unrecognized in clinical settings. In this chapter we discuss demographic and clinical features of BDD, prevalence, and morbidity. In addition, we discuss BDD's relationship to obsessive compulsive disorder, hypochondriasis, and psychotic disorders.

Keywords: Body dysmorphic disorder, dysmorphophobia, delusional disorder, clinical features, epidemiology

Definition of BDD

Body dysmorphic disorder (BDD) is an often severe, distressing, and impairing disorder characterized by preoccupations with nonexistent or slight defects or flaws in physical appearance in a person who is normal appearing. If a slight physical defect is observable, the person's concern about the perceived defect must be markedly excessive (APA, 2000). If a bodily defect is readily apparent and significant (for example, an individual who is preoccupied with facial scars actually has marked scarring, or a person preoccupied with hair loss is actually bald), the person would not meet DSM-IV criteria for BDD. It is unclear, however, which diagnosis they would qualify for, as DSM does not include a category that covers problematic concerns such as these. For BDD to be diagnosed, the appearance concerns must also cause clinically significant impairment in psychosocial functioning (for example, in social, academic, or occupational functioning) or cause clinically significant distress. This criterion (in addition to the requirement for preoccupation) differentiates BDD from normal appearance concerns, which are quite common in the general population (e.g., Cash, Winstead, & Janda, 1986). Furthermore, to qualify for a diagnosis of BDD, the appearance concerns cannot be better accounted for by another psychiatric disorder, such as anorexia nervosa.

History and Classification

BDD is classified as a somatoform disorder in DSM-IV and as a type of "hypochondriacal disorder" in ICD-10 (WHO, 1992). It was first described in 1886 by Morselli, an Italian physician, who called it *dysmorphophobia* (Morselli, 1891; Phillips, 1991). As Morselli wrote, "The dysmorphophobic patient is really miserable; in the middle of his daily routines, conversations, while reading, during meals, in fact everywhere and at any time, is overcome by the fear of deformity. . .which may reach a very painful intensity, even to the point of weeping and desperation" (Morselli, 1891). Kraepelin and Janet are among other prominent psychopathologists who subsequently described this disorder (Janet, 1903; Kraepelin, 1901–1915; Phillips, 1991). Over the past century, BDD has largely been neglected by clinicians and researchers alike, perhaps because many patients do not reveal their symptoms (because they are too ashamed, fear being judged negatively [e.g., as vain] for having such concerns, or fear their clinician won't understand them) (Conroy et al., 2008; Grant, Kim, & Crow, 2001). In recent years, however, BDD has received far greater attention and systematic research, and much has been learned about its clinical features, epidemiology, and relationship to other disorders.

BDD was included in DSM-III as an example of an atypical somatoform disorder under the rubric *dysmorphophobia*. In DSM-III-R, its name was changed to *body dysmorphic disorder*, and it was made a separate diagnostic category (APA, 1987). BDD has a delusional form that DSM-IV classifies in the psychosis section of the manual, as a type of delusional disorder, somatic type. As discussed below, however, BDD's delusional and nondelusional forms appear to have more similarities than differences, although the delusional variant appears to be more severe. Thus, these two variants appear to constitute the same disorder, which encompasses good insight, poor insight, and delusional beliefs about one's appearance.

Examples of Patients with BDD
Amy—Preoccupation with the Appearance of Her Eyebrows

Amy, a 45-year-old woman, was obsessed with her eyebrows. She believed she had too few eyebrow hairs, that they were too gray, and that their shape was abnormal. She was also preoccupied with the appearance of her hair, believing that it always looked "messy." Amy spent hours each day thinking about her eyebrows, staring at them in the mirror and examining them with a magnifying mirror, and plucking any hairs that were gray or not in the desired shape. As she stated, "My eyebrows are like a map—I know every single hair." Amy had electrolysis done to reshape her eyebrows and believed that this process irreparably damaged them. She felt intensely angry over the perceived damage and wanted the electrolysist to "feel the despair" that Amy felt about her eyebrows. She was so angry that she stalked her electrolysist, who pressed harassment charges and obtained a restraining order against Amy. Amy also tried minoxidil to make her eyebrow hairs grow back, but believed this did not help.

Because she thought she looked so bad, Amy had few social contacts, and when she did interact socially, she worried about how others perceived her appearance. She had difficulty holding a job and worked part-time selling beauty products in a mall. She sought this job because she could get a discount on products that she hoped would improve how her eyebrows looked. Amy finally sought psychiatric treatment at the suggestion of a surgeon from whom she had sought treatment for further "eyebrow repair." She stated that she recognized that her appearance concerns were severely interfering with her ability to hold jobs and maintain relationships, and that her anger over the "damage" to her eyebrows was still consuming her years after the procedure had been done.

John—A Case of Muscle Dysmorphia

John, a 50-year-old man, presented with concerns about his muscles not being "big enough." He was actually fairly muscular, because he worked out for several hours a day at the gym. John was frequently worried that he looked "shriveled and puny." He constantly felt anxious about what others thought of how he looked. Despite experiencing significant social anxiety because he thought he looked so bad, John was able to work as a grocery clerk. However, his anxiety prevented him from maintaining friendships and interactions with family members. John's appearance concerns led him to repeatedly check the mirror, compare himself to other men in body building magazines and on television, and seek products on the internet that he hoped would make him more muscular. He spent about an hour each day in the health food store searching for nutritional supplements to help him "bulk up." He had considered taking anabolic steroids to make himself bigger, but he was concerned about potential health risks. John sought treatment after seriously considering suicide because he believed his co-workers mocked and rejected him because of how he looked.

Epidemiology

BDD appears to be relatively common. Six epidemiologic studies have examined BDD's prevalence, with a reported prevalence of 0.7%–2.4% in the general population (Faravelli et al., 1997; Bienvenu et al., 2000; Buhlmann, et al., 2010; Koran, Abujaoude, Large, & Serpe, 2008; Otto, Wilhelm, Cohen, & Harlow, 2001; Rief, Buhlmann, Wilhelm, Borkenhagen, & Brähler, 2006). The three largest studies were population-based surveys in the United States (n=2,048) and Germany (n=2,552 and n=2,510), which found a point prevalence of 2.5% of women vs 2.2% of men, 1.9% of women and 1.4% of men, and 2.0% of women and 1.5% of men, respectively (Koran et al., 2008; Rief et al., 2006; Buhlmann et al., 2010). Gender ratios have varied across epidemiologic and clinical studies, but these findings suggest that BDD may be somewhat more common in women than in men. Of importance, BDD clearly does not occur only in women, as is sometimes assumed.

In both of the German nationwide surveys (n=2,552 and n=2,510), which examined selected demographic and clinical features, individuals with BDD were more likely to report suicidal ideation and suicide attempts due to appearance concerns than individuals without BDD (Rief et al., 2006; Buhlmann et al., 2010). Those with BDD also had higher somatization scores, lower income, were less likely to be living with a partner, and were more likely to be unemployed.

Epidemiologic studies have great value in their ability to screen large samples and determine the prevalence of mental disorders, like BDD, in the general population. These studies also have some limitations, however, one of which is the inability to do in-depth clinical interviews that can obtain more detailed information about symptoms, clarify ambiguities in participant responses, and use clinical judgment regarding information that is obtained. In some studies (including some of those below), self-report questionnaires have been used without confirmation of the diagnosis via interview. This is a particularly important issue for BDD, as appearance concerns are common in the general population, and clinical judgment is helpful in differentiating normal concerns from BDD.

Studies have also been done in smaller nonclinical student samples, many of which used self-report measures. The prevalence of BDD in these studies ranged from 2%–13% (Biby, 1998; Bohne et al., 2002; Cansever, Uzun, Donmez, & Ozsahin, 2003; Mayville, Katz, Gipson, & Cabral, 1999; Taqui et al., 2008). In a recent study in a student sample in China, a prevalence of 1.3% was reported, which is lower than that in other studies, perhaps because individuals who reported significant weight concerns on the BDDQ (a widely used self-report BDD screening measure [Phillips, 2005a]) were considered not to have BDD (Liao et al., 2009). However, the BDDQ item that assesses weight concerns is included to ensure that individuals with a primary diagnosis of an eating disorder are not misidentified as having BDD. Indeed, a notable proportion of

those with BDD have clinically significant preoccupation with their weight that reflects BDD rather than an eating disorder; figures were 29% in one BDD sample (Kittler, Menard, & Phillips, 2007) and 14% in another (Phillips & Diaz, 1997). The complex differential diagnosis between BDD and eating disorders in some cases highlights the importance of obtaining diagnostic information via clinical interviews if possible, to verify the BDD diagnosis.

A majority of individuals with BDD seek and receive dermatologic treatment, cosmetic surgery, and other types of cosmetic treatments in an attempt to "fix" their perceived appearance flaws (Crerand, Phillips, Menard, & Fay, 2005; Hollander, Cohen, & Simeon, 1993; Phillips, Grant, Siniscalchi, & Albertini, 2001; Veale et al., 1996). Thus, the prevalence of BDD tends to be higher in these settings than in epidemiologic studies. In dermatology settings, a prevalence of 9%–12% has been reported (Calderón et al., 2009; Phillips, Dufresne, Wilkel, & Vittorio, 2000; Uzun et al., 2003). In cosmetic surgery settings in the U.S., 7%–8% of patients have been found to have BDD (Crerand et al., 2004; Sarwer, Wadden, Pentschuk, & Whitaker, 1998). In international cosmetic populations, the prevalence ranges from 2.9%–53% (Aouizerate et al., 2003; Bellino et al., 2006; Castle, Molton, Hoffman, Preston, & Phillips, 2004; Harth & Linse, 2001; Ishigooka et al., 1998; Vargel & Ulusahin, 2001; Vindigni et al., 2002; Vulink et al., 2006). In a sample of 91 cosmetic dental patients, 9.5% were diagnosed with BDD (De Jongh, Aartman, Parvaneh, & Ilik, 2009), and in a sample of 40 adult orthodontic patients, 7.5% met diagnostic criteria for BDD (Hepburn & Cunningham, 2006). Methodological limitations such as small sample sizes, selection biases, and differences in study design (including different methods for diagnosing BDD) may account for these varied findings. These findings are important because the dermatology, surgery, and psychiatry literature emphasize that BDD usually responds poorly to cosmetic treatments, and that these patients may be at risk for suicide or violence toward the surgeon because of dissatisfaction with the cosmetic outcome (Cotterill, 1981; Cotterill & Cunliffe, 1997; Crerand et al., 2005; Koblenzer, 1985; Phillips, 1991; Phillips, Grant, et al., 2001; Phillips, McElroy, and Lion, 1992; Tignol, Biraben-Gotzamanis, Martin-Guehl, Grabot, & Aouizerate, 2007; Veale et al., 1996).

Studies similarly suggest that BDD is relatively common in various outpatient mental health settings, including among patients with obsessive compulsive disorder (OCD), social phobia, trichotillomania, and atypical major depressive disorder (e.g., Brawman-Mintzer et al., 1995; Hollander et al., 1993; Nierenberg et al., 2002; Phillips, Gunderson, Mallya, McElroy, & Carter, 1998; Perugi et al., 1998; Phillips, Nierenberg, Brendel, & Fava, 1996; Phillips, Pinto, et al., 2007; Soriano et al., 1996; Wilhelm, Otto, Zucker, Pollack, 1997). In a study of atypical major depressive disorder, the prevalence of BDD (42%) was higher than that for OCD, social phobia, generalized anxiety disorder, bulimia, and substance use disorders (Perugi et al., 1998).

Two studies have been done in psychiatric inpatient settings. In a study of 122 general inpatients, 13% (95% CI=6.9%–19.3%) (n=16) had BDD, making BDD more common than many other disorders, including schizophrenia, OCD, post-traumatic stress disorder, and eating disorders (Grant et al., 2001). In another study in a general adult inpatient setting, BDD was diagnosed in 16.0% (95% CI=8.7%–23.3%) (n=16) of patients. In the first study, inpatients with BDD had significantly lower scores on the Global Assessment of Functioning scale (GAF) and twice the lifetime rate of suicide attempts as patients without BDD (Grant et al., 2001). In the second study, a high proportion of BDD patients reported that their BDD symptoms were a major reason or "somewhat of a reason" for their suicidal thinking (50% of subjects), suicide attempts (33%), or substance use (42%) (Conroy et al., 2008).

Two studies of prevalence in youth have been published. Among 566 high school students, BDD's current prevalence was 2.2%, based on a self-report questionnaire (Mayville et al., 1999). Among adolescent psychiatric inpatients, using the self-report BDDQ (which has a sensitivity of 100% and a specificity of 89% in a clinical setting [Phillips, 2005a]), 4.8% of 208 patients had definite BDD, and an additional 1.9% had probable BDD (Dyl, Kittler, Phillips, & Hunt, 2006). In the latter study, youth with BDD had significantly greater anxiety, depression, and suicide risk on standardized measures than those without significant body image concerns.

Despite the above findings, which indicate that BDD may be relatively common, BDD usually goes undiagnosed in clinical settings. In all five studies that examined this issue in adults, no patient who was identified as having BDD by the investigators had the diagnosis recorded in their clinical record (Conroy et al., 2008; Grant et al., 2001; Phillips,

McElroy, Keck, Pope, & Hudson, 1993; Phillips et al., 1996; Zimmerman & Mattia, 1998). These findings highlight the importance of screening specifically for BDD in clinical settings.

Demographics
Gender
Studies in adults yield somewhat varying findings on gender ratio. The above-noted population-based surveys in Germany (n=2,552, n=2,510) and the United States (n=2,048) found that BDD was somewhat more common in women, with 1.9% of women and 1.4% of men, 2.5% of women vs 2.2% of men, and 2.0% of women and 1.5% of men, respectively, meeting DSM-IV criteria for current BDD (Koran et al., 2008; Rief et al., 2006). In a smaller community study in Italy (n=673), which did not use a standardized diagnostic measure, 1.4% of women but no men were identified as having BDD during the preceding year. In contrast, another community study in the United States (n=373) found a slightly higher point prevalence of BDD in men (1.2%) than in women (1.0%). Taken together, these epidemiologic studies suggest that BDD may affect somewhat more female than male adults.

Studies in clinical samples of adults have had widely varying proportions of males and females. Some have contained more females (e.g., Phillips, Menard, & Fay, 2006; Rosen & Reiter, 1996; Veale et al., 1996), whereas others have contained an equal proportion of females and males (Phillips & Diaz, 1997) or more males than females (e.g., Hollander et al., 1993; Neziroglu & Yaryura-Tobias, 1993; Perugi et al., 1997). In some cases, these differences may have been attributable to recruitment methods. In the two largest published series of individuals with BDD, 49% of 188 subjects in a clinical setting, and 64% of a largely clinical sample (n=200), were female (Phillips & Diaz, 1997; Phillips, Menard, & Fay, 2006).

Marital Status
In two of the three nationwide epidemiologic studies, individuals with BDD were less likely to be married than those without BDD (36.2% vs 55.5% and 21.4% vs 52.7%) (Koran et al., 2008; Rief et al., 2006). In the U.S. study, a significantly higher proportion of those with BDD were separated (10.6% vs 1.5%) or never married (34.0% vs 17.5%). While the U.S. study did not find a higher divorce rate among those with BDD (10.6% of both groups; Koran et al., 2008), the German study found that a higher proportion of individuals with

BDD were divorced (28.6% vs 9.9%; Rief et al., 2006). Clinical impressions indicate that BDD symptoms often negatively impact a person's ability to pursue, take part in, or effectively manage relationships (although such a causal relationship cannot be confirmed in cross-sectional studies such as these).

In the largest clinical samples of individuals ascertained for BDD, a majority were not married (81% of 200 subjects in one study, and 80% of 293 subjects in the other) (Gunstad & Phillips, 2003; Phillips, Menard, Fay, & Weisberg, 2005). Furthermore, in a clinical sample, 55.7% of adults with BDD reported that they did not currently have a primary relationship. Subjects who reported this were significantly more likely to be male, younger, and less educated than those with a primary relationship (Didie et al., 2006).

Socioeconomic Status

In one of the two German epidemiologic samples, those with BDD were significantly more likely to be unemployed than those without BDD (21.4% vs 6.8%; Rief et al., 2006). In a largely clinical sample of 200 individuals with BDD, 39.0% of subjects reported that they did not work for at least one consecutive week in the past month due, at least in part, to psychopathology (BDD was the primary diagnosis for most of this sample); 32.6% of this adult sample reported that they wanted to be in school (at least part-time) but were not enrolled in school solely because of psychopathology, or because of psychopathology plus some other reason (Didie, Menard, Stern, & Phillips, 2008). Twenty-three percent were currently receiving disability payments (Didie et al., 2008). In a study of 200 individuals with lifetime BDD, the mean Hollingshead score was approximately 4 (Phillips, Menard, Fay, & Weisberg, 2005). Overall, it appears that socioeconomic status can be severely impacted by the presence of BDD.

Clinical Features

Preoccupation with Perceived Appearance Flaws

Individuals with BDD are preoccupied with perceived appearance defects, thinking that some aspect of their appearance is ugly, unattractive, abnormal, deformed, or defective (Phillips, 2009). Concerns range from looking "not right" or "unattractive" to looking "hideous" or like "a monster" (Phillips, 2009). Appearance concerns can focus on any part of the body. Most commonly, they focus on the skin

(e.g., acne, marks, scars, lines, wrinkles, or pale skin), hair (e.g., too thin, too thick, balding, excessive body or facial hair), or nose (e.g., size or shape) (Fontenelle et al., 2006; Hollander et al., 1993; Perugi et al., 1997; Phillips & Diaz, 1997; Phillips, Menard et al., 2005; Phillips, McElroy, Keck, et al., 1993; Veale et al., 1996). Most patients are preoccupied with several body areas, with the lifetime number of areas in the range of 3–4 in one sample (n=188; Phillips & Diaz, 1997) and 6 in another sample (n=200; Phillips, Menard, Fay & Weisberg, 2005). Some patients, however, are concerned with only one body area, whereas others dislike virtually everything about how they look (Phillips, 2005a).

The appearance preoccupations are time-consuming, occurring on average for 3–8 hours a day (Phillips, 2009; Phillips, Gunderson, Mallya, McElroy, & Carter, 1998). Clinical studies of BDD typically require that the preoccupations are present for at least one hour a day in order to differentiate BDD from more normal appearance concerns. It is typically difficult for patients with BDD to resist or control these preoccupations (Phillips, 2005a; Phillips et al., 1998). Appearance concerns are often associated with significant anxiety and social anxiety (see below; Kelly, Walters, & Phillips, 2010; Pinto & Phillips, 2005) as well as depression (Conroy et al., 2008; Phillips, 1999; Phillips, Siniscalchi, & McElroy, 2004; Veale, Kinderman, Riley, & Lambrou, 2003), low self-esteem (Buhlmann, Teachman, Naumann, Fehlinger, & Rief, 2009; Phillips, Pinto, & Jain, 2004), and fear of rejection and embarrassment (Veale et al., 1996).

Insight/Delusionality of BDD Beliefs

Prior to effective treatment, most individuals with BDD do not recognize that they actually look normal. Studies (some of which have used the Brown Assessment of Beliefs Scale; Eisen et al., 1998) have found that insight is typically poor or absent. In other words, a majority of patients believe that their view of their appearance is probably or definitely accurate (Mancuso, Knoesen, & Castle, 2010; Phillips, 2004; Phillips, Menard, Pagano, Fay, & Stout, 2006). However, insight can range from good to fair to poor to absent (i.e., delusional beliefs, or complete conviction that they look abnormal, ugly, unattractive, or deformed; Phillips, 2004).

Studies have found that 36%–60% of patients are currently delusional (Phillips, 2004; Eisen, Phillips, Coles, & Rasmussen, 2004; Mancuso et al., 2010; Phillips, Menard, Pagano, et al., 2006). Clinical impressions suggest that poor insight or delusional BDD beliefs can interfere with patients' willingness to engage in, and remain in, psychiatric treatment, as they do not recognize that their appearance concerns are attributable to a mental illness (Eisen, Phillips, Coles, & Rasmussen, 2004; Phillips, 2005a).

Studies have found more similarities than differences between delusional and non-delusional patients across a range of variables, suggesting that these BDD variants constitute the same disorder (Mancuso, Knoesen, & Castle, 2010; Phillips, McElroy, Keck, Pope, & Hudson, 1994; Phillips, Menard, Pagano, Fay, & Stout, 2006). Delusional patients tend to have more severe BDD symptoms, lower educational attainment, more impairment in social functioning and quality of life on some (but not all) measures, higher levels of perceived stress, anxiety, depression, and anger-hostility, and higher suicide attempt rates (DeMarco, Li, Phillips, & McElroy, 1998; Mancuso et al., 2010; Phillips, 2000; Phillips et al., 1994; Phillips, Menard, Pagano, et al., 2006; Phillips, Menard, Fay, & Pagano, 2005; Phillips, Siniscalchi, & McElroy, 2004). However, when controlling for BDD symptom severity, fewer differences are found between these groups (Mancuso et al., 2010; Phillips, Menard, Pagano, et al., 2006).

Many patients with BDD have ideas or delusions of reference, believing that other people take special notice of them or mock them because of their appearance (Eisen et al., 2004; Phillips, 2004). Clinical experience suggests that such symptoms may contribute to the social morbidity experienced by many individuals with BDD. For example, they may be less willing to leave the house if they believe people will mock them because they are "ugly."

Compulsive and Safety Behaviors

Repetitive, compulsive behaviors are not required for the diagnosis of BDD, but virtually all individuals with this disorder engage in them (Phillips & Diaz, 1997; Phillips, Menard, Fay, & Weisberg, 2005). The intent of these behaviors is to reduce anxiety about their appearance by fixing it, hiding it, or obtaining reassurance that they look acceptable (Phillips, 2005a). Like appearance preoccupations, BDD-related behaviors are typically time consuming and difficult to resist or control (Phillips, 2005a; Phillips et al., 1998). One typical behavior is comparing their appearance with that of others, including people in newspapers, magazines, or on television. Other compulsive behaviors include repeated checking of mirrors and other reflective surfaces (e.g., windows), checking the "flawed" body part by looking at it directly (if visible, such as "hairy" arms), excessive grooming (e.g., makeup application, hair styling, shaving, hair combing or plucking), reassurance seeking, and excessive exercise or weightlifting. Some people with BDD engage in excessive tanning (for example, to try to minimize the appearance of acne or wrinkles, or darken "pale" skin), repetitive clothes-changing in an attempt to better camouflage the perceived defects or find a more flattering outfit, and compulsive shopping (e.g., for beauty products or clothes) (Phillips, 2005a; Phillips, Conroy, et al., 2006; Phillips & Diaz, 1997; Phillips, Menard, Fay, & Weisberg, 2005). Many patients perform other, often idiosyncratic behaviors, such as repeatedly checking to see if their hair is "breaking."

Compulsive skin-picking that occurs as a symptom of BDD is worth highlighting. Studies have found that 27%–45% of BDD patients have lifetime skin-picking as a symptom of BDD (Grant et al., 2006; Phillips & Taub, 1995). The intent of this behavior is to improve perceived flaws in the appearance of one's skin by making it smoother or removing tiny blemishes (Phillips and Taub, 1995). However, because this behavior is typically time consuming and difficult to control, it often causes irritation, scabbing, or scarring, and can cause skin infections and rupture blood vessels, which is occasionally life-threatening (Grant, Menard, & Phillips, 2006; O'Sullivan, Phillips, Keuthen, Wilhelm, 1999; Phillips & Taub, 1995).

The compulsive behaviors described above resemble OCD compulsions in a number of ways. First, the behaviors are performed intentionally, in response to an obsession-like preoccupation with appearance, and the acts are not pleasurable. Furthermore, the intent is to reduce anxiety or distress and prevent an unwanted event (e.g., being rejected by others or looking "ugly"), and most of these behaviors are repetitive, time-consuming, and excessive. Furthermore, they may be rule bound or done in a rigid manner (Phillips & Kaye, 2007). While compulsions can be conceptualized as a type of avoidance behavior (Kozak & Foa, 1997; Maltby & Tolin, 2003), many BDD behaviors involve an increased focus on perceived flaws, and appear to immediately fuel BDD preoccupations (Phillips, 2009). In addition, a developmental and evolutionary perspective emphasizes the highly conserved nature of compulsive behaviors such as compulsive grooming (Feusner, Hembacher, & Phillips, 2009; Leckman & Mayes, 1998).

One common BDD behavior that may be conceptualized as avoidant in nature is camouflaging. Most people with BDD camouflage body areas of concern—for example, they may cover disliked areas with makeup, clothing, a hat, hair, sunglasses, or posture. Some refuse to participate in activities if it requires them to stop camouflaging (e.g., remove a hat for a wedding). Camouflaging can, however, be done repeatedly, resembling a compulsive behavior (for example, reapplying makeup 30 times a day).

Distraction techniques are another common BDD behavior (Phillips, 2009; Phillips, Menard, Fay, & Weisberg, 2005). The purpose of such behaviors is to distract other people from noticing the "defective" body areas. For example, wearing flamboyant makeup, unusual clothing, or a dramatic hairstyle may be an attempt to draw attention to that feature so that the disliked body areas will go unnoticed.

Anxiety

Anxiety, including social anxiety, is an aspect of BDD that is receiving increased research attention. Clinical observations indicate that many individuals with BDD suffer from intense anxiety because of how they think they look, which can be problematic in their daily lives (Phillips, 2005a). In a study that used the Symptom Questionnaire (Kellner, 1987), a validated self-report measure, 75 outpatients with BDD had markedly elevated scores on the anxiety scale compared to published norms for normal subjects, and they had higher anxiety scores than norms for psychiatric outpatients. BDD subjects' scores indicated severe distress and psychopathology in the anxiety domain. Greater anxiety was associated with greater BDD severity (r=0.32, p=0.006). In a study of psychiatric inpatients, 16 patients with BDD had levels of anxiety, as assessed with the Beck Anxiety Inventory (BAI; Beck, Epstein, Brown & Steer, 1988), in the moderate to severe range, which was higher, but not significantly higher, than inpatients without BDD (Conroy et al., 2008). In an adolescent inpatient study, individuals with BDD had significantly higher levels of anxiety on the MASC-10 (March, 1997) than those without BDD (Dyl et al., 2006).

Recent preliminary findings suggest that many patients with BDD experience panic attacks resulting from BDD symptoms (Phillips KA, et al., unpublished data). In this study, 30.4% of 56 participants reported lifetime cued panic attacks triggered by BDD symptoms. Among this group, the most common triggers of such attacks were feeling that other people were looking at/scrutinizing the perceived appearance flaws (64.3%), looking in the mirror (26.7%), and being in bright light (14.3%). Such panic attacks were associated with greater severity of BDD and depressive symptoms, functional impairment, suicidal ideation, and hospitalization.

Social anxiety also appears common in persons with BDD. Levels of social anxiety range from 1.3–1.7 standard deviations higher than normative samples (Kelly et al., 2010; Pinto & Phillips, 2005; Veale et al., 1996). Social anxiety is significantly correlated with BDD severity (Pinto & Phillips, 2005), including in those without concurrent social phobia (Kelly et al., 2010). In one BDD study (n=81), higher levels of social anxiety were also associated with greater depressive symptoms and comorbid avoidant personality disorder (Pinto & Phillips, 2005).

The majority of participants (62%) in a sample of 108 individuals with BDD but without comorbid social phobia had clinically significant social anxiety (Kelly et al., 2010). However, only 14% endorsed clinically significant social anxiety that was *not* related to appearance concerns, suggesting that much of the social anxiety in this sample may have been secondary to BDD symptoms. Social anxiety was associated with significant functional impairment both cross-sectionally and prospectively, with greater social anxiety predicting subsequent impairment in psychosocial functioning (Kelly et al., 2010). These findings suggest that anxiety and social anxiety are important to assess in individuals with BDD.

Forms of BDD

BDD symptoms are generally quite similar across patients; however, BDD can have different forms (Phillips, 2009). Here we discuss two important forms of BDD.

Muscle Dysmorphia

Muscle dysmorphia is a form of BDD that occurs almost exclusively in males (Phillips & Diaz, 1997). Muscle dysmorphia consists of preoccupation with the idea that one's body is insufficiently muscular or lean, or is "too small" (Phillips, O'Sullivan, & Pope, 1997; Pope, Gruber, Choi, Olivardia, & Phillips, 1997; Pope, Phillips, & Olivardia, 2000). In reality, these men look normal or may even be very muscular. One of the cases presented above illustrates this form of BDD. Many men with muscle dysmorphia adhere to a meticulous diet and time-consuming workout schedule, which can cause bodily damage (Phillips, O'Sullivan, & Pope, 1997; Pope et al., 1997; Pope et al., 2000; Pope et al., 2005). In addition, many use anabolic-androgenic steroids and other substances in an attempt to get bigger (Hitzeroth, Wessels, Zungu-Dirwayi, Oosthuizen, & Stein, 2001; Olivardia, Pope, & Hudson, 2000; Pope et al., 2005).

A BDD study (n=63) that compared men with and without muscle dysmorphia (86% of whom had additional non–muscle appearance concerns) found similarities in demographic features, BDD severity, delusionality of BDD beliefs, and number of non–muscle related body parts of concern (Pope et al., 2005). However, men with muscle dysmorphia were significantly more likely to lift weights excessively (71% vs 12%), diet (71% vs 27%), and exercise excessively (64% vs 10%). Those with muscle dysmorphia also had significantly poorer quality of life and higher lifetime rates of suicide attempts (50% vs 16%) and substance use disorders (86% vs 51%), including anabolic steroid abuse/dependence (21% vs 0%). Thus, this form of BDD appears to be associated with severe psychopathology.

BDD by Proxy
Individuals with this form of BDD are preoccupied with what they perceive to be defects or flaws in the appearance of another person, such as a family member (Atiullah & Phillips, 2001; Phillips, 2005a). In one case, a man in his 50s was so distressed by his conviction that he had caused his daughter to go bald (she actually looked normal), which he thought made her look ugly, that he committed suicide (Atiullah & Phillips, 2001). There are few reports of BDD by proxy in the literature, but this form of BDD may be more common than is recognized.

Age of Onset and Course of Illness
BDD tends to have an early onset, typically during adolescence. In the largest clinical BDD sample (n=293) and in a largely clinical sample (n=200), BDD's mean age at onset was 16.0 ± 6.9 (range 4–43) and 16.4 ± 7.0 years (range 5–49), respectively (Gunstad & Phillips, 2003; Phillips, Menard, Fay & Weisberg, 2005). The mode was 13 in both samples, and approximately two thirds of cases had onset of BDD before age 18. In the latter sample, the mean age of onset of subclinical body

dysmorphic disorder was 12.9 years (SD=5.8) (Phillips, Menard, Fay & Weisberg, 2005). In a sample of patients ascertained for major depressive disorder (MDD) who had lifetime or current BDD, the mean age of onset of BDD was 17.5 years (SD=10.0) (Nierenberg et al., 2002).

BDD is often a chronic condition. In the only prospective study of BDD's course, the Longitudinal Interval Follow-Up Evaluation (LIFE; Keller et al., 1987) obtained data on weekly BDD symptom status and treatment received over one year for 183 broadly ascertained subjects. The probability of full remission from BDD over one year of follow-up was only 0.09, and the probability of partial remission was 0.21 (Phillips, Pagano, Menard, & Stout, 2006). Mean BDD severity scores during this year reflected full DSM-IV criteria for BDD, and the mean proportion of time that subjects met full BDD criteria was 80%. More severe BDD at intake, longer BDD duration, and a comorbid personality disorder predicted a lower likelihood of partial or full remission from BDD (Phillips, Pagano et al., 2005).

In the same study, psychosocial functioning was poor at baseline and was significantly associated with more severe BDD symptoms (Phillips, Menard, Fay, & Pagano, 2005). Psychosocial functioning continued to be stably poor over one to three years of follow-up (Phillips, Quinn, & Stout, 2008). Only 5.7% of participants attained functional remission on the GAF (score of 70 or higher for at least 2 consecutive months), and only 10.6% attained functional remission on the Social and Occupational Functioning Assessment Scale (same definition of remission) during the follow-up period. Greater BDD symptom severity predicted poorer psychosocial functioning over time. More delusional BDD symptoms also prospectively predicted poorer functioning, but this finding was no longer significant when controlling for BDD severity.

Comorbidity
BDD is commonly comorbid with a number of disorders. In the largest BDD studies in a clinical sample (n=293) and a largely clinical sample (n=200), the most common comorbid disorder was MDD, with three quarters of both samples having lifetime MDD; BDD usually began before MDD (Gunstad & Phillips, 2003; Phillips, Menard, Fay & Weisberg, 2005). In these samples, 37%–39% had lifetime social phobia, and 32%–33% had lifetime OCD. Substance use disorders were also common, with lifetime rates of 50% and 30%

(the latter rate was in a more representative subset of the sample). In one of these studies, nearly 70% of subjects with a substance use disorder said that BDD contributed to their substance use, with 30% of them citing BDD as the main reason or a major reason (Grant, Menard, Pagano, Fay, & Phillips, 2005).

Studies in smaller clinical samples have found much broader ranges of comorbidity rates, from 6%–78% for OCD, 12%–69% for social phobia, 6%–69% for MDD, and 2%–22% for substance use disorders (Hollander et al., 1993; Perugi et al., 1997; Veale et al., 1996; Zimmerman & Mattia, 1998). The wide variation in rates might be explained in part by the fact that not all studies used a standard assessment instrument such as the SCID.

When other disorders (e.g., OCD, social phobia, MDD, substance use disorders) are comorbid with BDD, individuals tend to have more severe BDD symptoms (Phillips, Didie, & Menard, 2007; Phillips, Pinto, et al., 2007; Ruffolo, Phillips, Menard, Fay, & Weisberg, 2006), more suicidality (Phillips, Didie, & Menard, 2007; Phillips, Pinto, et al., 2007), and greater functional impairment (Coles et al., 2006; Grant et al., 2005; Phillips, Didie, & Menard, 2007). They are also more likely to have sought mental health treatment (Phillips, Didie, & Menard, 2007; Ruffolo, Phillips, Menard, Fay, & Weisberg, 2006) and to have a lifetime history of psychiatric hospitalization (Grant et al., 2005; Ruffolo et al., 2006).

Functional Impairment and Quality of Life

Functioning and quality of life in BDD, as in other disorders, ranges from moderately to very poor, although on average it is notably poor (Hollander et al., 1999; Phillips, 2000; Phillips & Diaz, 1997; Phillips, Menard, Fay & Pagano, 2005; Phillips, Quinn, and Stout, 2008). Some people with BDD are able to work or attend school, although most report some impairment in these areas, such as poor concentration, decreased productivity, or missing work or school. Some are able to initiate and maintain relationships, although some avoidance of social activities, difficulty with intimacy, and conflict in the relationship because of BDD symptoms appears common. In severe cases, impairment is marked, and may include inability to work or go to school, inability to maintain a job, substantial or complete social avoidance, and being housebound (Didie et al., 2008; Phillips, 2009).

Social Adjustment scores on the SAS-SR are more than two standard deviations (SD) below community norms (Phillips, Menard, Fay & Pagano, 2005). Similarly, Social Functioning scores on the SF-36 are 1.7–2.2 SD units below community norms and 0.4–0.7 SD units poorer than for depression (Phillips, 2000; Phillips, Menard, et al., 2005). People with BDD often feel embarrassed and ashamed of their appearance, and fear they will be rejected by others because of their "ugliness." Thus, they tend to have high rates of social avoidance (Kelly et al., 2010), which can lead to few friendships and romantic relationships, as well as overall poor functioning (Kelly et al., 2010; Phillips, 2009). In addition, individuals with BDD often find it difficult to leave their homes—two studies found that 31% of 188 people with BDD and 27% of 200 people with BDD had been completely housebound for at least one week because of their BDD symptoms (Phillips & Diaz, 1997; Phillips, Menard, Fay, & Weisberg, 2005). Social functioning can improve, but still tends to be impaired, after successful treatment for BDD (Phillips, Albertini, & Rasmussen, 2002).

BDD is associated with high lifetime rates of psychiatric hospitalization in adults (48%) and adolescents (44%) (Phillips, Didie, et al., 2006; Phillips & Diaz, 1997). Impairment in academic or occupational functioning is common (Didie et al., 2008). In a sample of 200 adults, most of whom had a primary diagnosis of BDD, 32% wanted to attend school but were unable to because of psychopathology (Phillips, Menard, Fay, & Pagano, 2005). And, in a sample of 33 youth with BDD, 18% had dropped out of elementary school or high school primarily because of BDD symptoms (Albertini & Phillips, 1999). Furthermore, 39% of the adult sample reported not working in the past month because of psychopathology; fewer than half were working full time, and a significant proportion (23%) were receiving disability benefits (Didie et al., 2008). Those who were not working had more chronic and severe BDD symptoms. They were also more likely to be male, and had less education and more severe depressive symptoms (Didie et al., 2008). These subjects were also more likely to have been psychiatrically hospitalized and had a higher lifetime rate of suicidal ideation and attempted suicide.

Physical functioning and physical health-related quality of life also appear to be poor in individuals with BDD. In a study of 176 individuals, physical functioning as assessed by the SF-36 was 0.7 SD units poorer in BDD than U.S. population norms (Phillips, Kelly, & Menard, 2009). Poorer physical functioning was associated with longer BDD duration, older age, receiving disability benefits, and greater social anxiety. Physical health-related quality of life as assessed by the Q-LES-Q was 1.9 SD units poorer than community norms, and was associated with more severe BDD symptoms, a greater number of comorbid Axis I disorders, and receiving disability benefits. The association of more severe BDD and social anxiety with poorer physical functioning and quality of life is consistent with clinical observations that many people with BDD avoid medical care because they don't want their body to be seen by a physician.

Suicide Risk

Suicidal ideation and attempts appear very common in persons with BDD (Phillips, 2007). In clinical cross-sectional samples, lifetime rates of suicidal ideation (78%–81%) and suicide attempts (24%–28%) are very high (Perugi et al., 1997; Phillips, 2007; Phillips, Coles, et al., 2005; Phillips & Diaz, 1997; Veale et al., 1996). The lifetime suicide attempt rate in BDD is an estimated 6–23 times higher than in the U.S. population (Moscicki, 1997; Moscicki, O'Carroll, & Locke, 1989). In a logistic regression analysis using cross-sectional/retrospective data, more severe lifetime BDD was independently associated with an increased risk of lifetime suicidality (Phillips, Coles, et al., 2005). For each 1 point increase on a 9-point BDD severity scale, the odds of experiencing lifetime suicidal ideation increased by 1.48 (p=0.003), and the odds of a suicide attempt increased by 1.59 (p=0.005). Lifetime suicidal ideation was also independently associated with comorbid MDD, and lifetime suicide attempts were also independently associated with a comorbid substance use disorder or PTSD (Phillips, Coles, et al., 2005). In a nationwide epidemiologic study (n=2,510), 31.0% of subjects had had thoughts about committing suicide specifically because of their appearance concerns, and 22.2% had attempted suicide due to their appearance concerns (Buhlmann et al., 2010).

Preliminary results from the only published prospective study of individuals ascertained for BDD indicate that the annual rate of completed suicide appears to be very high (0.3%; Phillips & Menard, 2006) and higher than annual rates of completed suicide for other psychiatric disorders (Harris & Barraclough, 1997). In a retrospective study in two dermatology practices over 20 years, most patients who suicided had acne or BDD (Cotterill & Cunliffe, 1997).

Although research has not examined risk factors for suicide in BDD, many factors may potentially contribute to this risk, including high rates of suicidal ideation and attempts; high rates of psychiatric hospitalization; high comorbidity with depression, substance use disorders, and eating disorders; poor self-esteem; a history of abuse; high rates of unemployment and being on disability; being single or divorced; and poor social support, all of which are characteristic of many individuals with BDD (Didie, Tortolani, Pope, et al., 2006; Gunstad & Phillips, 2003; Phillips, 2005a; Phillips, Coles et al., 2005; Phillips & Diaz, 1997; Phillips & Menard, 2006; Phillips, Menard, Fay, & Pagano, 2005; Phillips, Menard, Fay, & Weisberg, 2005; Phillips, Pinto, & Jain, 2004; Veale et al., 1996; Perugi et al., 1997). In addition to these somewhat nonspecific risk factors, we theorize that BDD patients' often-delusional beliefs that they look deformed causes severe distress and self-loathing. This distress is further fueled by time-consuming, intrusive obsessions about the "defect" and a belief that others mock and reject them because of how they look (Phillips, 2004), which in turn can fuel suicidal thinking and behavior.

BDD in Children and Adolescents

As noted above, BDD typically begins during adolescence. However, only a few studies have systematically examined a broad range of BDD's clinical features in youth. One study examined a clinical sample of 33 children and adolescents with BDD, and another study compared BDD's clinical features in a more broadly ascertained (but largely clinical) sample of 36 adolescents to 164 adults who were clinically interviewed (Albertini & Phillips, 1999; Phillips, Didie, et al., 2006). Like adults, youth reported prominent, distressing, and time-consuming appearance preoccupations, as well as prominent appearance-related compulsive behaviors. Nearly all youth experienced impairment in psychosocial functioning that was attributed primarily to BDD symptoms. In the study of 33 children and adolescents (Albertini & Phillips, 1999), 94% experienced social interference and 85% reported that their appearance concerns interfered with school, job, or social functioning. Eighteen percent had dropped out of elementary school or high school primarily because of BDD symptoms. In the other study, 22% of 36 youth had dropped out of school primarily because of BDD (Phillips, Didie, et al., 2006). Such difficulties may be particularly problematic during adolescence because they may substantially interfere with important adolescent developmental transitions, such as completing school and developing social and romantic relationships (Albertini & Phillips, 1999; Phillips, Atala, & Albertini, 1995; Phillips, 2009).

Although data are limited, preliminary findings suggest that BDD appears largely similar in youth and adults across most domains that have been examined, but that youth may differ from adults in several clinically important ways. In the study that directly compared youth to adults, these groups were largely similar across most domains, including body areas of concern, frequency and types of compulsive behaviors, comorbidity rates, and levels of functional impairment (Phillips, Didie et al., 2006). However, as expected, adolescents had an earlier age of BDD onset than adults. In addition, compared to adults, adolescents had more delusional beliefs about their appearance, more severe BDD symptoms at a trend level, and a significantly higher rate of current substance use disorders (30.6% vs 12.8%; Phillips, Didie et al., 2006). Lifetime rates of comorbidity and functional impairment were similar in youth and adults, even though youth had had fewer years over which to have developed these problems.

Suicidality is a significant concern among youth with BDD. In the study of 33 youth, 67% reported a history of suicidal ideation, and 21% had attempted suicide (Albertini & Phillips, 1999). In the study of 36 adolescents, 80.6% reported a history of suicidal ideation, and 44.4% had attempted suicide (Phillips, Didie et al., 2006). In the latter study, the suicide attempt rate among youth was significantly higher than the rate among adults (44.4% vs 23.8%). In an adolescent inpatient study, adolescents with BDD (n=14) scored higher (p<0.001) than those without clinically significant body image concerns (n=140) on the Suicide Probability Scale, which reflects suicide risk (Cull & Gill, 1982; Dyl et al., 2006).

Risk for suicidal behavior is illustrated by a 17-year-old female who was seen by the second author when the patient was hospitalized after attempting suicide (Phillips, Atala, & Albertini, 1995). She stated that she thought about her "large" nose, "small" breasts, and "ugly" hair "every second of every day," and she checked mirrors for hours a day. Her BDD symptoms caused her to avoid all social interactions and dating, fail her courses, and drop out of school. She described her preoccupations with her appearance concerns as "very, very distressing—an obsession. They're so horrible I get suicidal; it's why I overdosed. . . ."

Aggression/violence is another risk behavior that appears common in youth with BDD. In the series of 33 cases, 38% reported a history of aggressive/violent behavior that was attributed primarily to BDD symptoms (e.g., breaking objects or causing property damage due to anger over being "ugly"; Albertini & Phillips, 1999). In the series of 36 cases, 36.1% reported a history of violence or aggression, and 22.2% reported violence or aggression that was attributed primarily to BDD symptoms (Phillips KA, unpublished data).

Thus, it is important to recognize that BDD can occur in youth, and that treatments for this age group need to address possible differences in clinical features, including risk behaviors, as well as BDD's effects on developmental transitions and tasks.

Gender Similarities and Differences

Three published studies with sample sizes ranging from 58 to 200 have directly compared females and males with BDD (Perugi et al., 1997; Phillips & Diaz, 1997; Phillips, Menard, & Fay, 2006). These three studies found that females and males had more similarities than differences across a number of domains. The two groups were similar in terms of most demographic and clinical characteristics, such as which body areas were disliked, types of compulsive BDD behaviors, BDD severity, suicidality, and comorbidity. Of note, males were as likely as females to seek and receive cosmetic treatment, such as surgery, for their BDD concerns, whereas this is not the case in the general population (American Society for Aesthetic Plastic Surgery, 2008).

However, all three studies found some gender-related differences (Perugi et al., 1997; Phillips & Diaz, 1997; Phillips, Menard, & Fay, 2006). In all three studies, females were more likely to have a comorbid eating disorder, and males were more likely to be preoccupied with their genitals. Two of the three studies found the following differences: females were more likely to be preoccupied with their weight, hips, breasts, legs, and excessive body hair, and were more likely to hide their perceived defects with camouflaging techniques, to check mirrors, and to pick their skin as a symptom of BDD. In contrast, males were more likely to have muscle dysmorphia, be preoccupied with thinning hair, be single, and have a substance-related disorder. Males also had significantly worse scores on one measure of psychosocial functioning, were less likely to be working because of psychopathology (for most, BDD was the primary diagnosis), and were more likely to be receiving disability payments (because of BDD symptoms or for any reason).

As noted above, muscle dysmorphia is a form of BDD that occurs almost exclusively in males. Muscle dysmorphia appears to be particularly severe and to have some unique features, such as association with use of anabolic steroids, which potentially have health risks (Brower, 2002; Pope et al., 2005). Our clinical impression is that cognitive-behavioral treatment approaches (see Chapter 21 in this volume) may need to be modified to treat this form of BDD.

Cultural Factors

Sociocultural factors likely play an important role in the development of appearance concerns; however, little research has evaluated the contribution of such factors to the pathogenesis of BDD. It has been posited that cultural messages, such as the association of physical attractiveness with positive outcomes, benefits, or rewards may contribute to increased focus on physical attributes (Neziroglu, Khemlani-Patel, & Veale, 2008).

Although there is evidence that some cultures tend to focus more on appearance than others (e.g., Americans may focus more on their appearance than some European or Asian cultures) (Bohne, Keuthen, Wilhelm, Deckersbach, & Jenike, 2002; Crystal, Watanabe, Weinfurt, & Wu, 1998), there is no evidence to suggest that BDD is more prevalent in some cultures than others, although this topic has not been well studied.

To our knowledge, no studies have directly compared BDD's clinical features across cultures. A qualitative comparison of case reports and case series of BDD from around the world suggested more similarities than differences (Phillips, 2005a). Similarities across cultures included gender ratio and other demographic features, which body areas were disliked, what aspects of appearance were disliked, types of compulsive BDD behaviors, and levels of BDD-related distress and impairment in social and occupational functioning. Thus, BDD may be largely invariant across cultures. Indeed, BDD may in part have an evolutionary basis (e.g., desire to attract mates or avoidance of social ostracism), and thus marked differences across cultures would not be expected (Feusner et al., 2009; Phillips, 2009; Stein, Carey, & Warwick, 2006). Yet, the above-noted comparison suggested that cultural values and preferences may influence BDD symptoms to some degree (Phillips, 2005a). For example, in Japan but not in Western countries, eyelid concerns and worry about displeasing others by being unattractive appear more common (Choy, Schneier, Heimberg, Oh, & Liebowitz, 2008; Phillips, 2005a).

Indeed, BDD is well known in Japan, where it is considered a form of *taijin kyofusho* (*shubo-kyofu*—"the phobia of a deformed body; Suzuki, Takei, Kawai, Minabe, & Mori, 2003). *Taijin kyofusho*, or anthropophobia (fear of people), refers to a fear of interpersonal relations (Choy et al., 2008; Kleinknecht, Dinnel, Kleinknecht, Hiruma, & Harada, 1997; Maeda & Nathan, 1999). Thus, in Japan, BDD is considered closely related to social phobia, whereas in Western countries, BDD's likely relationship to OCD has received more emphasis (see below).

Health Care Utilization

Little is known about health care utilization among individuals with BDD. In an epidemiologic study, 40% of those with BDD had sought treatment from a psychiatrist and 20% from a general practitioner, 20% had sought psychotherapy, and 40% had sought no treatment for their BDD symptoms (Faravelli et al., 1997).

As discussed above, a majority of those with BDD seek and receive cosmetic treatment for their appearance concerns (Crerand et al., 2005; Hollander et al., 1993; Phillips, Grant, et al., 2001; Veale et al., 1996), and, conversely, a substantial proportion of persons seeking dermatologic treatment, cosmetic surgery, and other cosmetic procedures have BDD (see epidemiology section). In two general population samples in Germany, 7.2% and 15.6% of those with BDD had received cosmetic surgery, compared to only 2.8% and 2.0%, respectively, of those without BDD (Buhlmann et al., 2010; Rief et al., 2006). The psychiatry, surgery, and dermatology literatures note that some patients with BDD pursue large amounts of cosmetic treatment, including repeat treatments for "failed" procedures (Cotterill, 1996; Koblenzer, 1994; Crerand et al., 2004). This is particularly concerning, given the poor outcomes that can occur. In a survey of plastic surgeons, 40% said a BDD patient had threatened them legally and/or physically (Sarwer, 2002). Indeed, surgeons have been sued by BDD patients in high-profile cases (Kaplan, 2000). Occasional dissatisfied patients even murder the physician (Cotterill, 1996; Ladee, 1966; Phillips, 1991; Phillips et al., 1992).

In one BDD sample that was broadly ascertained from many sources, both clinical and nonclinical,

96% of subjects had a history of mental health treatment, but this proportion is almost certainly not broadly representative (Phillips, Didie, et al., 2006). BDD is commonly comorbid with certain psychiatric disorders and relatively common in psychiatric samples (as previously discussed), but it is unclear how many of these patients seek treatment for BDD specifically. It appears that individuals with BDD only rarely bring up their BDD symptoms with their health care providers. For instance, in two inpatient studies, 0%–0.6% of patients mentioned their BDD symptoms to their providers (Conroy et al., 2008; Grant et al., 2001). This reticence appeared to be primarily due to embarrassment about BDD symptoms, fear of being negatively judged (e.g., as "vain"), and fear that the clinician would not understand their concerns (Conroy et al., 2008). This was the case even though in the first study, 81% of patients with BDD said that BDD was their major or biggest problem (Grant et al., 2001). Our clinical impression is that BDD is often misdiagnosed as another disorder (e.g., OCD, depression, social phobia, schizophrenia, trichotillomania), which may lead to ineffective treatment (Phillips, 2005a).

Relationship to Other Disorders

BDD appears to be a distinct disorder that nonetheless shares some clinical features with, and may be closely related to, certain other psychiatric disorders. BDD is widely considered an obsessive compulsive spectrum disorder, and a number of studies have directly compared BDD's clinical features to those of OCD. Therefore, below we discuss BDD's relationship to OCD. We also discuss BDD's relationship to hypochondriasis, because ICD-10 classifies BDD as a type of hypochondriacal disorder. Finally, we discuss BDD's relationship to psychotic disorders, because BDD's delusional variant is currently classified as a psychotic disorder (a type of delusional disorder). BDD's relationship to other disorders, such as social phobia, major depressive disorder, and eating disorders, is discussed elsewhere (Phillips, 2009).

OCD

For more than a century, BDD has been considered to be closely related to OCD (Janet, 1903; Morselli, 1891; Phillips, 1991; Stekel, 1949). Currently, BDD is widely conceptualized as an obsessive compulsive spectrum disorder (Abramowitz & Deacon, 1995; Brady, Austin, & Lydiard, 1990; Cohen, Stein, Simeon, & Hollander, 1997; Goldsmith,

Shapira, Phillips et al, 2010; Phillips & McElroy, 1998; Hollander, 1993; Jaisoorya, Reddy, & Srinath, 2003; Mataix-Cols, Pertusa, & Leckman, 2007; Phillips, 2002; Simeon, Hollander, Stein, Cohen, & Aronowitz, 1995; Solyom, DiNicola, Phil, Sookman, & Luchins, 1985). Three studies have directly compared BDD and OCD across a broad array of clinical and demographic variables (Frare, Perugi, Ruffolo, & Toni, 2004; Phillips et al., 1998; Phillips, Pinto, et al., 2007), and smaller studies have directly compared these disorders on selected variables (see below). Data from a number of validators—including phenomenology, family history, comorbidity, and treatment response—indicate that BDD and OCD have similarities and may be related disorders. At the same time, some data suggest that these disorders have important differences. Here, we briefly summarize some of these findings; more detailed reviews can be found elsewhere (e.g., Phillips, 2009; Phillips & Kaye, 2007; Phillips et al., 2010).

A notable similarity is that both BDD and OCD are characterized by obsessional preoccupation and repetitive behaviors (Phillips & Kaye, 2007). The preoccupations and behaviors focus on perceived appearance flaws in BDD, and various non–appearance related themes in OCD. Preoccupations/obsessions and compulsive behaviors in both disorders are intrusive, time-consuming, and difficult to resist or control (Phillips & Kaye, 2007); they are also unwanted and not pleasurable (Phillips, McElroy, Hudson, & Pope, 1995; Phillips, McElroy, & Keck, 1994). In studies that directly compared BDD to OCD using the Yale-Brown Obsessive Compulsive Scale (Y-BOCS; Goodman et al., 1989) and a slightly modified version of this scale for BDD (Phillips, Hollander, et al., 1997), total score and/or individual item scores did not significantly differ for BDD and OCD preoccupations/obsessions and compulsive behaviors in terms of time spent preoccupied, resulting distress and functional impairment, resistance, and control (Phillips et al., 1998, Phillips, Pinto, et al., 2007). This finding suggests notable similarities in cognitions and compulsive behaviors.

One difference, however, is that BDD-related beliefs (e.g., "I am ugly") are more likely than OCD-related beliefs (e.g., "If I don't check the stove, the house will burn down") to be characterized by poor insight or delusional thinking (Eisen et al., 2004; McKay, Neziroglu, Yaryura-Tobias, 1997; Phillips, Pinto, et al., 2007). Approximately 2% of OCD patients are currently delusional compared to

27%–60% of BDD patients (Eisen et al., 2004; Mancuso et al., 2010; McKay, Neziroglu, & Yaryura-Tobias, 1997; Phillips et al., 1998; Phillips, Pinto, et al., 2007). Regarding specific components of delusionality, BDD patients are more convinced than those with OCD that their underlying belief (e.g., "I am ugly and deformed") is accurate, more likely to think that others agree with their belief, less willing to consider that their belief is inaccurate, and less likely to recognize that their belief has a psychiatric/psychological cause (Eisen et al., 2004). Another possible difference between BDD and OCD is that some BDD compulsions (e.g., mirror checking) do not appear to follow a simple model of anxiety reduction, which commonly occurs in the compulsive checking of OCD (Veale & Riley, 2001).

The three studies that directly compared BDD to OCD found many similarities—for example, in terms of many demographic features, gender ratio, age of disorder onset, disorder severity, course of illness (retrospectively assessed), and most comorbidity (Frare et al., 2004, Phillips et al., 1998; Phillips, Pinto, et al., 2007). However, in two of the three studies, BDD subjects were significantly younger and less likely to be married than OCD subjects (Frare et al., 2004; Phillips et al., 1998), and in one study, those with BDD had lower educational attainment (Frare, 2004). One study found that BDD patients were more likely than those with OCD to have an occupation or education in art and design (20% vs 3%), raising the possibility that an interest in aesthetics may contribute to BDD's development (Veale, Ennis, & Lambrou, 2002).

Individuals with BDD and OCD both tend to be more perfectionistic and more concerned about making mistakes than healthy controls (Buhlmann, Etcoff, & Wilhelm, 2008). In a study of evaluations of facial photographs, BDD subjects did not differ from OCD subjects or controls in their ratings of physical attractiveness across faces of varying attractiveness; however, BDD participants rated attractive faces as more attractive than these other groups (Buhlmann et al., 2008). In addition, BDD participants had stricter ratings for their own attractiveness than controls or OCD participants did (Buhlmann et al., 2008).

BDD and OCD are both associated with high rates and levels of functional impairment (Didie et al., 2007), although impairment may be somewhat worse in BDD than in OCD in education, employment, and other domains (Didie et al., 2007,

Frare et al., 2004; Phillips et al., 1998). Several studies suggest that individuals with BDD may be more likely to have comorbid MDD or a substance use disorder, and that BDD may be associated with higher rates of suicidality than OCD (Frare et al., 2004; Phillips, Pinto, et al., 2007, Phillips et al., 1998).

Recent studies have begun to investigate neurocognitive functioning in BDD. Several studies suggest that individuals with BDD and OCD may have similar deficits, including more deficits in executive functioning than healthy controls (Deckersbach et al., 2000; Hanes, 1998). People with BDD also tend to have more negative and threatening interpretations of ambiguous social information (for both appearance-related and social scenarios) compared to those with OCD (Buhlmann, Wilhelm, et al., 2002). Thus, individuals with BDD and OCD may differentially process social cues and environmental information. Several structural and functional neuroimaging studies have been conducted in BDD, with some results, but not others, suggesting some similarities between BDD and OCD (Atmaca et al., 2009; Feusner et al., 2010; Feusner, Townsend, Bystritsky, & Bookheimer, 2007; Rauch et al., 2003). Further research is needed to confirm and extend these findings.

High rates of comorbidity between BDD and OCD suggest that they may be related disorders. Lifetime rates of BDD in patients with OCD range from 3%–37%, with an average of about 17% across studies (e.g., Brawman-Mintzer et al., 1995; Diniz et al., 2004; Hollander et al., 1993; Jaisoorya et al., 2003; Phillips et al., 1998; Simeon et al., 1995; Wilhelm et al., 1997). Conversely, about one-third of individuals with BDD have comorbid OCD (see above) (Gunstad & Phillips, 2003; Phillips, Menard, Fay, & Weisberg, 2005). Despite such high rates of comorbidity, prospective comorbidity data suggest that BDD and OCD are not identical disorders. In a prospective study of the course of BDD, among subjects with comorbid OCD an improvement in OCD symptoms predicted subsequent BDD remission, but improvement in BDD symptoms did not predict subsequent OCD remission (Phillips & Stout, 2006). Furthermore, BDD symptoms continued to persist in about half of subjects whose OCD remitted (Phillips & Stout, 2006). If BDD were simply a symptom of OCD, improvement in BDD would be expected to predict OCD remission, and BDD would not be expected to persist after OCD symptoms remitted.

A family study found an elevated rate of BDD in first-degree relatives of OCD probands compared to first-degree relatives of control probands (Bienvenu, Samuels, Riddle, Hoehn-Saric, Liang, Cullen, 2000). These findings were recently replicated in a different, larger sample (Bienvenu et al., unpublished data), indicating that OCD and BDD may be related disorders.

While no studies have directly compared treatment outcome in BDD versus OCD, pharmacotherapy approaches have many similarities. BDD, like OCD, appears to preferentially respond to serotonin-reuptake inhibitors (SRIs) but, unlike OCD, BDD may not respond well to antipsychotic augmentation of SRIs (although findings regarding the latter are very limited for BDD) (Hollander et al., 1999; Phillips, 2005b, 2005c; Phillips & Hollander, 2008). Psychotherapeutic approaches for these disorders have notable similarities but also some differences (see Chapter 21).

Taken together, direct comparison studies of BDD and OCD are still limited, but the growing literature on this topic suggests that BDD and OCD have many similarities as well as some important differences, and that they are probably closely related but distinct disorders.

Hypochondriasis

The ICD-10 Classification of Mental and Behavioural Disorders classifies both BDD and hypochondriasis as a type of "hypochondriacal disorder" (WHO, 1992). However, some of ICD-10's criteria for hypochondriacal disorder are not suitable for BDD. For example, ICD-10's criteria B and C (which specify that the patient must seek medical treatment and refuse to accept medical advice, and that there is no adequate physical cause for the symptoms or physical abnormality) do not seem applicable to BDD. As discussed above, not all individuals with BDD seek medical care for their appearance concerns, and when they do, they do not necessarily divulge these concerns. Nonetheless, they do have BDD.

No studies have directly compared BDD and hypochondriasis. However, one apparent similarity is that both BDD and hypochondriasis are characterized by preoccupations and compulsive behaviors that focus on the body (Abramowitz & Braddock, 2006; Phillips et al., 1993), and sufferers of both disorders frequently seek nonpsychiatric medical treatment (Crerand et al., 2005; Escobar et al., 1998; Magariños, Zafar, Nissenson, & Blanco, 2002; Phillips, Grant, et al., 2001).

However, preoccupation with being ugly or unattractive is quite different from the belief that one has a serious disease. In addition, only 15.5% of individuals with BDD have ever believed that their body was malfunctioning in some way, and few with this belief focus specifically on having a disease (Phillips KA, unpublished data). Furthermore, a study that used the Symptom Questionnaire found that BDD subjects (n=75) had markedly elevated scores on the somatic/somatization symptom scale compared to norms for normal controls but lower scores than published norms for psychiatric outpatients (Phillips, Siniscalchi, & McElroy, 2004). Thus, somatization may not be particularly characteristic of BDD.

Comorbidity data also suggest that BDD may not be closely related to hypochondriasis. In two studies of BDD (n=200 and n=293), comorbid hypochondriasis was much less common (4.8% lifetime in one study and 1.5% currently in the other study) than comorbidity with many other psychiatric disorders (Gunstad & Phillips, 2003; Phillips, Menard, Fay, & Weisberg, 2005; see comorbidity section above). Comparison of treatment response is limited by the relatively small number of studies in both disorders. However, whereas BDD appears to respond preferentially to SRIs (Hollander et al., 1999; Phillips & Hollander, 2008), hypochondriasis may respond to a broader range of psychotropic medications (Fallon & Barsky, 2007).

Psychotic Disorders

DSM-IV and ICD-10 classify BDD's delusional form (which applies to patients who are completely convinced that their view of their appearance is accurate) as a psychotic disorder (a type of delusional disorder, somatic type). DSM-IV allows patients with delusional BDD to additionally receive a diagnosis of BDD. In other words, delusional BDD beliefs can be considered a symptom of two different disorders (i.e., double coded). Several studies indicate that there are many more similarities than differences between delusional and nondelusional BDD across a broad range of features (Mancuso et al., 2010; Phillips et al., 1994; Phillips, Menard, Pagano, et al., 2006). Delusional and nondelusional BDD have been shown to not significantly differ in terms of most demographic features, core BDD symptoms (preoccupations and compulsive behaviors), most measures of functional impairment and quality of life, comorbidity, and family history. Two studies found that on a number of measures, delusional subjects evidenced greater morbidity; however, this finding appeared to be accounted for by greater BDD symptom severity (Mancuso et al., 2010; Phillips, Menard, Pagano, et al., 2006).

Of clinical importance, pharmacotherapy studies have consistently found that delusional BDD responds as robustly as nondelusional BDD does to SRI monotherapy (Hollander et al., 1999; Phillips, Albertini, & Rasmussen, 2002; Phillips & Hollander, 2008; Phillips, McElroy, Dwight, Eisen, & Rasmussen, 2001). Data on response to antipsychotics are very limited, but it appears that antipsychotics may not be efficacious as SRI augmenters for either delusional or nondelusional BDD (Phillips, 2005b, 2005c; Phillips & Hollander, 2008). The role of insight in predicting treatment response is discussed further in Chapter 21 in this volume.

In summary, available data suggest that there are far more similarities than differences between delusional and nondelusional BDD, and that BDD appears to encompass both delusional and nondelusional beliefs. Future editions of DSM and ICD may benefit from combining the delusional and nondelusional forms of this disorder into a single disorder and indicating that BDD may be characterized by a range of insight, including good, fair, poor, and absent insight (i.e., delusional thinking).

Our clinical experience indicates that BDD is sometimes misdiagnosed as schizophrenia because BDD beliefs can be delusional and patients can have prominent delusions of reference. However, BDD beliefs are usually not bizarre, nor is BDD characterized by other psychotic symptoms or formal thought disorder. Nor does BDD appear to be closely related to schizophrenia when considering other validators, such as comorbidity, family history, or treatment response (Phillips, 2005a).

Conclusion

BDD is a common, distressing, and often severely impairing disorder. Knowledge of BDD has advanced dramatically over the past 20 years, but this disorder remains much less researched than most other psychiatric disorders. Further investigation is needed on all aspects of BDD, including its prevalence, clinical features, pathogenesis, and relationship to other disorders. Such research is expected to improve detection, treatment, and prevention of this often disabling disorder.

Future Directions

Knowledge of BDD's phenomenology is greatly advancing; however, BDD is still under-studied compared to other mental disorders, and much more research is needed on its clinical features. One important area to address is the similarities and differences between delusional and nondelusional BDD. Research on BDD is especially limited and greatly needed in children, adolescents, the elderly, and in different cultural contexts. Another important research area is to understand why and how frequently BDD is under-recognized in mental health and other settings.

Very little research has been conducted on BDD's pathogenesis. This type of research, particularly on BDD's neurobiological and genetic underpinnings, may ultimately lead to improved treatment and perhaps even prevention of this severe mental illness. Another major avenue of future research should focus on the relationship between BDD and other disorders. A number of direct comparison studies have examined BDD's relationship to OCD, but because social anxiety and panic attacks appear to be prominent features of BDD, future studies should investigate BDD's relationship to other anxiety disorders. In addition, given the overlap between BDD and eating disorders in terms of body image distortion and dissatisfaction, more research is necessary to understand the commonalities and differences between these disorders.

Finally, little is known about the course of BDD. To date, there has been only one prospective longitudinal observational study of the course of BDD (Phillips, Pagano, Menard & Stout, 2006; Phillips, Quinn, & Stout, 2008). More research is necessary to understand the longitudinal course of BDD, particularly with regard to morbidity and mortality. In summary, much more research is necessary to further our understanding of this common and severe disorder.

Related Chapters

Chapter 21. Treatment of Body Dysmorphic Disorder

References

Abramowitz, J. S., & Braddock, A. E. (2006). Hypochondriasis: Conceptualization, treatment, and relationship to obsessive-compulsive disorder. *Psychiatric Clinics of North America, 29*, 503–519.

Abramowitz, J. S., & Deacon B. J. (2005) Obsessive-compulsive disorders: Essential phenomenology and overlap with other anxiety disorders. In J. S. Abramowitz, A. C. Houts (Eds.), *Concepts and controversies in obsessive-compulsive disorder* (pp. 141–149). New York: Springer.

Albertini, R. S., & Phillips, K. A. (1999). Thirty-three cases of body dysmorphic disorder in children and adolescents.

Journal of the American Academy of Child and Adolescent Psychiatry, 38, 453–459.

American Psychiatric Association. (1987). *Diagnostic and statistical manual of mental disorders* (3rd ed., revised). Washington, DC: American Psychiatric Association.

American Psychiatric Association. (2000). *Diagnostic and statistical manual of mental disorders* (4th ed., text revision). Washington, DC: American Psychiatric Association.

American Society for Aesthetic Plastic Surgery (2008). *Cosmetic Surgery National Data Bank statistics.* New York: American Society for Aesthetic Plastic Surgery.

Aouizerate, B., Pujol, H., Grabot, D., Faytout, M., Suire, K., Braud, C., et al. (2003). Body dysmorphic disorder in a sample of cosmetic surgery applicants. *European Psychiatry, 18,* 365–368.

Atiullah, N., & Phillips, K. A. (2001). Fatal body dysmorphic disorder by proxy (letter). *Journal of Clinical Psychiatry, 62,* 204–205.

Atmaca, M., Bingol, I., Aydin, A., Yildirim, H., Yildirim, M. A., Mermi, O., et al. (2010). Brain morphology of patients with body dysmorphic disorder. *Journal of Affective Disorders, 123,* 258–263.

Beck, A. T., Epstein, N., Brown, G., & Steer, R. A. (1988). An inventory for measuring clinical anxiety: Psychometric properties. *Journal of Consulting and Clinical Psychology, 56,* 893–897.

Bellino, S., Zizza, M., Paradiso, E., Rivarossa, A., Fulcheri, M., & Bogetto, F. (2006). Dysmorphic concern symptoms and personality disorders: A clinical investigation in patients seeking cosmetic surgery. *Psychiatry Research, 144,* 73–78.

Biby, E. L. (1998). The relationship between body dysmorphic disorder and depression, self-esteem, somatization, and obsessive-compulsive disorder. *Journal of Clinical Psychology, 54,* 489–499.

Bienvenu, O. J., Samuels, J. F., Riddle, M. A., Hoehn-Saric, R., Liang, K. Y., Cullen, B. A., et al. (2000). The relationship of obsessive-compulsive disorder to possible spectrum disorders: Results from a family study. *Biological Psychiatry, 48,* 287–293.

Bohne, A., Keuthen, N. J., Wilhelm, S., Deckersbach, T., & Jenike, M. A. (2002). Prevalence of symptoms of body dysmorphic disorder and its correlates: A cross-cultural comparison. *Psychosomatics, 43,* 486–490.

Bohne, A., Wilhelm, S., Keuthen, N. J., Florin, I., Baer, L., Jenike, M. A. (2002). Prevalence of body dysmorphic disorder in a German college student sample. *Psychiatry Research, 109,* 101–104.

Brady, K. T., Austin, L., Lydiard, R. B. (1990). Body dysmorphic disorder: The relationship to obsessive-compulsive disorder. *Journal of Nervous and Mental Disease, 178,* 538–540.

Brawman-Mintzer, O., Lydiard, R. B., Phillips, K. A., Morton, A., Czepowicz, V., Emmanuel, N., et al. (1995). Body dysmorphic disorder in patients with anxiety disorders and major depression: A comorbidity survey. *American Journal of Psychiatry, 152,* 1665–1667.

Brower, K. (2002). Anabolic steroid abuse and dependence. *Current Psychiatry Reports, 4,* 377–383.

Buhlmann, U., Glaesmer, H., Mewes, R., Fama, J.M., Wilhelm, S., Brähler, E., Rief, W (2010). Updates on the prevalence of body dysmorphic disorder: a population-based survey. *Psychiatry Research, 178,* 171–175.

Buhlmann, U., Teachman, B. A., Naumann, E., Fehlinger, T., & Rief, W. (2009). The meaning of beauty: Implicit and explicit self-esteem and attractiveness beliefs in body dysmorphic disorder. *Journal of Anxiety Disorders, 23,* 694–702.

Buhlmann, U., Wilhelm, S., McNally, R. J., Tuschen-Caffier, B., Baer, L., & Jenike, M. A. (2002). Interpretative biases for ambiguous information in body dysmorphic disorder. *CNS Spectrums, 7,* 441–443.

Calderón, P., Zemelman, V., Sanhueza, P., Castrillón, M. A., Matamala, J. M. & Szot, J. (2009). Prevalence of body dysmorphic disorder in Chilean dermatological patients. *Journal of the European Academy of Dermatology and Venereology, 23,* 1328.

Cansever, A., Uzun, O., Donmez, E., Ozsahin, A. (2003). The prevalence and clinical features of body dysmorphic disorder in college students: a study in a Turkish sample. *Comprehensive Psychiatry, 44,* 60–64.

Cash, T. F., Winstead, B. A., Janda, L. H. (1986). The great American shape-up: body image survey report. *Psychology Today, 20,* 30–37.

Castle, D. J., Molton, M., Hoffman, K., Preston, N. J., & Phillips, K. A. (2004). Correlates of dysmorphic concern in people seeking cosmetic enhancement. *Australian and New Zealand Journal of Psychiatry, 38,* 439–444.

Choy, Y., Schneier, F. R., Heimberg, R. G., Oh, K. S., & Liebowitz, M. R. (2008). Features of the offensive subtype of Taijin-Kyofu-Sho in US and Korean patients with DSM-IV social anxiety disorder. *Depression and Anxiety, 25,* 230–240.

Cohen, L.J., Stein, D.J., Simeon, D., & Hollander, E. (1997). Obsessive-compulsive spectrum disorders. In D. J. Stein (Ed.), *Obsessive-compulsive disorders* (pp. 47–74). New York: Marcel Dekker.

Coles, M. E., Phillips, K. A., Menard, W., Pagano, M. E., Fay, C., Weisberg, R. B., et al. (2006). Body dysmorphic disorder and social phobia: Cross-sectional and prospective data. *Depression and Anxiety, 23,* 26–33.

Conroy, M., Menard, W., Fleming-Ives, K., Modha, P., Cerullo, H., & Phillips, K. (2008). Prevalence and clinical characteristics of body dysmorphic disorder in an adult inpatient setting. *General Hospital Psychiatry, 30,* 67–72.

Cotterill, J. A. (1981). Dermatological non-disease: a common and potentially fatal disturbance of cutaneous body image. *British Journal of Dermatology, 104,* 611–619.

Cotterill, J. A. (1996). Body dysmorphic disorder. *Dermatology Clinics, 14,* 457–463

Cotterill, J. A., & Cunliffe, W. J. (1997). Suicide in dermatological patients. *British Journal of Dermatology, 137,* 246–250.

Crerand, C. E., Phillips, K. A., Menard, W., & Fay, C. (2005). Non-psychiatric medical treatment of body dysmorphic disorder. *Psychosomatics, 46,* 549–555.

Crerand, C. E., Sarwer, D. B., Magee, L., Gibbons, C., Lowe, M., Bartlett, S., et al. (2004). Rate of body dysmorphic disorder among patients seeking facial plastic surgery. *Psychiatric Annals, 34,* 958–965.

Crystal, D. S., Watanabe, H., Weinfurt, K., & Wu, C. (1998). Concepts of human differences: A comparison of American, Japanese, and Chinese children and adolescents. *Developmental Psychology, 34,* 714–722.

Cull, J. G., & Gill, W. S. *Suicide Probability Scale (SPS) Manual.* Los Angeles, CA: Western Psychological Services, 1982.

Deckersbach, T., Savage, C. R., Phillips, K. A., Wilhelm, S., Buhlmann, U., Rauch, S. L., et al. (2000). Characteristics of memory dysfunction in body dysmorphic disorder.

Journal of the International Neuropsychological Society, 6, 673–681.

De Jongh, A., Aartman, I. H. A., Parvaneh, H., & Ilik, M. (2009). Symptoms of body dysmorphic disorder among people presenting for cosmetic dental treatment: a comparative study of cosmetic dental patients and a general population sample. *Community Dentistry and Oral Epidemiology, 37,* 350–356.

DeMarco, L. M., Li, L. C., Phillips, K. A., & McElroy, S. L. (1998). Perceived stress in body dysmorphic disorder. *Journal of Nervous and Mental Disease, 186,* 724–726.

Didie, E. R., Menard, W., Stern, A. P., & Phillips, K. A. (2008). Occupational functioning and impairment in adults with body dysmorphic disorder. *Comprehensive Psychiatry, 49,* 561–569.

Didie, E. R., Walters, M. M., Pinto, A., Menard, W., Eisen, J. L., Mancebo, M., et al. (2007). A comparison of quality of life and psychosocial functioning in obsessive-compulsive disorder and body dysmorphic disorder. *Annals of Clinical Psychiatry, 19,* 181–186.

Didie, E. R., Tortolani, C. C., Pope, C. G., Menard, W., Fay, C., Phillips, K. A. (2006). Childhood abuse and neglect in body dysmorphic disorder. *Child Abuse and Neglect, 30,* 1105–1115.

Didie, E. R., Tortolani, C. C., Walters, M., Menard, W., Fay, C., & Phillips, K. A. (2006). Social functioning in body dysmorphic disorder: Assessment considerations. *Psychiatric Quarterly, 77,* 223–229.

Diniz, J. B., Rosario-Campos, M. C., Shavitt, R. G., Curi, M., Hounie, A. G., Brotto, S. A., et al. (2004). Impact of age at onset and duration of illness on the expression of comorbidities in obsessive-compulsive disorder. *Journal of Clinical Psychiatry, 65,* 22–27.

Dyl, J., Kittler, J., Phillips, K. A., & Hunt, J. I. (2006). Body dysmorphic disorder and other clinically significant body image concerns in adolescent psychiatric inpatients: prevalence and clinical characteristics. *Child Psychiatry and Human Development, 36,* 369–382.

Eisen, J. L., Phillips, K. A., Baer, L., Beer, D. A., Atala, K. D., & Rasmussen, S. A. (1998). The Brown Assessment of Beliefs Scale: reliability and validity. *American Journal of Psychiatry, 155,* 102–108.

Eisen, J. L., Phillips, K. A., Coles, M. E., & Rasmussen, S. A. (2004). Insight in obsessive compulsive disorder and body dysmorphic disorder. *Comprehensive Psychiatry, 45,* 10–15.

Escobar, J. I., Gara, M., Waitzkin, H., Cohen Silver, R., Holman, A., & Compton, W. (1998). DSM-IV hypochondriasis in primary care. *General Hospital Psychiatry, 3,* 155–159.

Fallon, B. A., & Barsky, J. A. (2007). The treatment of hypochondriasis. In G. Gabbard (ed.), *Treatments of DSM-IV-TR psychiatric disorders*. Washington, DC: American Psychiatric Publishing, Inc.

Faravelli, C., Salvatori, S., Galassi, F., Aiazzi, L., Drei, C., & Cabras, P. (1997). Epidemiology of somatoform disorders: A community survey in Florence. *Social Psychiatry and Psychiatric Epidemiology, 32,* 24–29.

Feusner, J. D., Hembacher, E., & Phillips, K. A. (2009). The mouse who couldn't stop washing: pathologic grooming in animals and humans. *CNS Spectrums, 14,* 503–513.

Feusner, J. D., Moody, T., Hembacher, E., Townsend, J., McKinley, M., et al. (2010). Abnormalities of visual processing and fronto-striatal systems in body dysmorphic disorder. *Archives of General Psychiatry, 67,* 197–205.

Feusner, J. D., Townsend, J., Bystritsky, A., & Bookheimer, S. (2007). Visual information processing of faces in body dysmorphic disorder. *Archives of General Psychiatry, 64,* 1417–1425.

Fontenelle, L. F., Telles, L. L., Nazar, B. P., de Menezes, G. B., do Nascimento, A. L., Mendlowicz, M. V., et al. (2006). A sociodemographic, phenomenological, and long-term follow-up study of patients with body dysmorphic disorder in Brazil. *International Journal of Psychiatry Medicine, 36,* 243–259.

Frare, F., Perugi, G., Ruffolo, G., & Toni, C. (2004). Obsessive-compulsive disorder and body dysmorphic disorder: A comparison of clinical features. *European Psychiatry, 19,* 292–298.

Goldsmith, T., Shapira, N. A., Phillips, K. A., & McElroy, S. L. (1998). Conceptual foundations of obsessive-compulsive spectrum disorders. In M. M. Antony, S. Rachman, M. A. Richer, & R. P. Swinson (Eds.), *Obsessive-compulsive disorder: Theory, research and treatment*. New York: Guilford Press.

Goodman, W. K., Price, L. H., Rasmussen, S. A., Mazure, C., Delgado, P., Heninger, G. R., et al. (1989). The Yale-Brown Obsessive Compulsive Scale II: validity. *Archives of General Psychiatry, 46,* 1012–1016.

Grant, J. E., Kim, S. W., & Crow, S. J. (2001). Prevalence and clinical features of body dysmorphic disorder in adolescent and adult psychiatric inpatients. *Journal of Clinical Psychiatry, 62,* 517–522.

Grant, J. E., Menard, W., Pagano, M. E., Fay, C., & Phillips, K. A. (2005). Substance use disorders in individuals with body dysmorphic disorder. *Journal of Clinical Psychiatry, 66,* 309–311.

Grant, J. E., Menard, W., & Phillips, K. A. (2006). Pathological skin picking in individuals with body dysmorphic disorder. *General Hospital Psychiatry, 28,* 487–493

Gunstad, J., & Phillips, K. A. (2003). Axis I comorbidity in body dysmorphic disorder. *Comprehensive Psychiatry, 44,* 270–276.

Hanes, K. R. (1998). Neuropsychological performance in body dysmorphic disorder. *Journal of the International Neuropsychological Society, 4,* 167–171.

Harris, E. C., & Barraclough, B. (1997). Suicide as an outcome for mental disorders: A meta-analysis. *British Journal of Psychiatry, 170,* 205–228.

Harth, W., & Linse, R. (2001). Botulinophilia: Contraindication for therapy with botulinum toxin. *International Journal of Clinical Pharmacology and Therapeutics, 39,* 460–463.

Hepburn, S., & Cunningham, S. (2006). Body dysmorphic disorder in adult orthodontic patients. *American Journal of Orthodontic and Dentofacial Orthopedics, 130,* 569–574.

Hitzeroth, V., Wessels, C., Zungu-Dirwayi, N., Oosthuizen, P., & Stein, D. J. (2001). Muscle dysmorphia: A South African sample. *Psychiatry and Clinical Neuroscience, 55,* 521–523.

Hollander, E. (1993). Introduction. In E. Hollander (ed.), *Obsessive-compulsive related disorders* (pp. 1–16). Washington, DC: American Psychiatric Press Inc.

Hollander, E., Allen, A., Kwon, J., Aronowitz, B., Schmeidler, J., Wong, C., et al. (1999). Clomipramine vs desipramine crossover trial in body dysmorphic disorder: Selective efficacy of a serotonin reuptake inhibitor in imagined ugliness. *Archives of General Psychiatry, 56,* 1033–1039.

Hollander, E., Cohen, L. J., & Simeon, D. (1993). Body dysmorphic disorder. *Psychiatric Annals, 23,* 359–364.

Ishigooka, J., Iwao, M., Suzuki, M., Fukuyama, Y., Murasaki, M., & Miura, S. (1998). Demographic features of patients seeking cosmetic surgery. *Psychiatry and Clinical Neurosciences, 52,* 283–287.

Jaisoorya, T. S., Reddy, Y. C., & Srinath, S. (2003). The relationship of obsessive-compulsive disorder to putative spectrum disorders: Results from an Indian study. *Comprehensive Psychiatry, 44,* 317–323.

Janet, P. (1903). *Les obsessions et al psychasthenie.* Paris: Feliz Alcan.

Kaplan, R. (2000). What should plastic surgeons do when crazy patients demand work? *The New York Observer,* March 7, 2000:1

Keller, M. B., Lavori, P. W., Friedman, B., Nielsen, E., Endicott, J., McDonald-Scott, P., et al. (1987). The longitudinal interval follow-up evaluation: A comprehensive method for assessing outcome in prospective longitudinal studies. *Archives of General Psychiatry, 44,* 540–548.

Kellner, R. (1987). A symptom questionnaire. *Journal of Clinical Psychiatry, 8,* 268–274.

Kelly, M. M., Walters, C., & Phillips, K. A. (2010). Social anxiety and its relationship to functional impairment in body dysmorphic disorder. *Behavior Therapy, 41,* 143–153.

Kittler, J. E., Menard, W., & Phillips, K. A. (2007). Weight concerns in individuals with body dysmorphic disorder. *Eating Behaviors, 8,* 115–120.

Kleinknecht, R. A., Dinnel, D. L., Kleinknecht, E. E., Hiruma, N., & Harada, N. (1997). Cultural factors in social anxiety: A comparison of social phobia symptoms and Taijin Kyofusho. *Journal of Anxiety Disorders, 11,* 157–177.

Koblenzer, C. S. (1985). The dysmorphic syndrome. *Archives of Dermatology, 121,* 780–784.

Koblenzer, C. S. (1994). The broken mirror: Dysmorphic syndrome in the dermatologists's practice. *Fitz Journal of Clinical Dermatology, March/April,* 14–19.

Koran, L. M., Abujaoude, E., Large, M. D., & Serpe, R. T. (2008). The prevalence of body dysmorphic disorder in the United States adult population. *CNS Spectrums, 13,* 316–322.

Kozak, M. J., & Foa, E. B. (1997). *Mastery of obsessive-compulsive disorder: A cognitive behavioral approach.* San Antonio, TX: The Psychological Corporation.

Kraeplin, E. (1909–1915). *Psychiatrie,* 8th ed. Leipzig: JA Barth.

Ladee, G.A. (1966). *Hypochondriacal syndromes.* Amsterdam: Elsevier.

Leckman, J. L., & Mayes, L. C. (1998). Understanding developmental psychopathology. How useful are evolutionary accounts. *Journal of the American Academy of Child and Adolescent Psychiatry, 37,* 1011–1021.

Liao, Y., Knoesen, N. P., Deng, Y., Tang, J., Castle, D. J., Bookun, R., et al. (2010). Body dysmorphic disorder, social anxiety and depressive symptoms in Chinese medical students. *Social Psychiatry and Epidemiology, 45,* 963–971.

Maeda, F., & Nathan, J. H. (1999). Understanding Taijin Kyofusho through its treatment, Morita therapy. *Journal of Psychosomatic Research, 46,* 525–530.

Maltby, N., & Tolin, D. F. (2003). Overview of treatments for obsessive-compulsive disorder and spectrum conditions: Conceptualization, theory, & practice. *Brief Treatment and Crisis Intervention, 3,* 127–144.

Mancuso, S. G., Knoesen, N. P., & Castle, D. J. (2010). Delusional versus nondelusional body dysmorphic disorder. *Comprehensive Psychiatry, 51,* 177–182.

March, J. S. (1997). *Multidimensional anxiety scale for children short version* (MASC-10). New York: Multi-Health Systems.

Magariños, M., Zafar, U., Nissenson, K., & Blanco, C. (2002). Epidemiology and treatment of hypochondriasis. *CNS Drugs, 16,* 9–22.

Mataix-Cols, D., Pertusa, A., & Leckman, J. F. (2007). Issues for DSM-V: How should obsessive-compulsive and related disorders be classified? *American Journal of Psychiatry, 164,* 1313–1314.

Mayville, S., Katz, R. C., Gipson, M. T., Cabral, K. (1999). Assessing the prevalence of body dysmorphic disorder in an ethnically diverse group of adolescents. *Journal of Child and Family Studies, 8,* 357–362.

McKay, D., Neziroglu, F., & Yaryura-Tobias, J. A. (1997). Comparison of clinical characteristics in obsessive-compulsive disorder and body dysmorphic disorder. *Journal of Anxiety Disorders, 11,* 447–454.

Morselli, E. (1891). Sulla dismorfofobia e sulla tafefobia. *Bolletinno Della R Accademia Di Genova, 6,* 110–119.

Moscicki, E. K. (1997). Identification of suicide risk factors using epidemiologic studies. *Psychiatric Clinics of North America, 20,* 499–517.

Moscicki, E. K., O'Carroll, P., & Locke, B. Z. (1989). Suicidal ideation and attempts: The Epidemiologic Catchment Area Study. In *Alcohol, drug abuse, and mental health administration: Report of the Secretary's Task Force on Youth Suicide, Vol. 4: Strategies for the Prevention of Youth Suicide* (DHHS Publication No [ADM]89–1624). Washington, DC: US Government Printing Office.

Neziroglu, F. A., Khemlani-Patel, S., & Veale, D. (2008). Social learning theory and cognitive-behavioral models of body dysmorphic disorder. *Body Image, 5,* 28–38.

Neziroglu, F. A., & Yaryura-Tobias, J. A. (1993). Body dysmorphic disorder: Phenomenology and case descriptions. *Behavioural Psychotherapy, 21,* 27–36.

Nierenberg, A. A., Phillips, K. A., Petersen, T. J., Kelly, K. E., Alpert, J. E., Worthington, J. J., et al. (2002). Body dysmorphic disorder in outpatients with major depression. *Journal of Affective Disorders, 69,* 141–148.

Olivardia, R., Pope, H. G., & Hudson, J. I. (2000). Muscle dysmorphia in male weightlifters: a case-control study. *American Journal of Psychiatry, 157,* 1291–1296.

O'Sullivan, R. L., Phillips, K. A., Keuthen, N. J., & Wilhelm, S. (1999). Near fatal skin picking from delusional body dysmorphic disorder responsive to fluvoxamine. *Psychosomatics, 40,* 79–81.

Otto, M. W., Wilhelm, S., Cohen, L. S., & Harlow, B. L. (2001). Prevalence of body dysmorphic disorder in a community sample of women. *American Journal of Psychiatry, 158,* 2061–2063.

Perugi, G., Akiskal, H. S., Giannotti, D., Frare, F., Di Vaio, S., & Cassano, G. B. (1997). Gender-related differences in body dysmorphic disorder (dysmorphophobia). *Journal of Nervous and Mental Disease, 185,* 578–582.

Perugi, G., Akiskal, H. S., Lattanzi, L., Cecconi, D., Mastrocinque, C., Patronelli, A., et al. (1998). The high prevalence of "soft" bipolar (II) features in atypical depression. *Comprehensive Psychiatry, 39,* 63–71.

Phillips, K. A. (1991). Body dysmorphic disorder: The distress of imagined ugliness. *American Journal of Psychiatry, 148,* 1138–1149.

Phillips, K. A. (1999). Body dysmorphic disorder and depression: Theoretical considerations and treatment strategies. *Psychiatric Quarterly, 70,* 313–331.

Phillips, K. A. (2000). Quality of life for patients with body dysmorphic disorder. *Journal of Nervous and Mental Disease, 188,* 170–175.

Phillips, K. A. (2002). The obsessive compulsive spectrums. *Psychiatric Clinics of North America, 25,* 791–809.

Phillips, K. A. (2004). Psychosis in body dysmorphic disorder. *Journal of Psychiatric Research, 38,* 63–72.

Phillips, K. A. (2005a). *The broken mirror: Understanding and treating body dysmorphic disorder.* (revised and expanded text). New York: Oxford University Press.

Phillips, K. A. (2005b). Placebo-controlled study of pimozide augmentation of fluoxetine in body dysmorphic disorder. Am J Psychiatry 2005;162:377–379.

Phillips, K. A. (2005c). Olanzapine augmentation of fluoxetine in body dysmorphic disorder (letter). Am J Psychiatry 2005;162:1022–1023.

Phillips, K. A. (2007). Suicidality in body dysmorphic disorder. *Primary Psychiatry, 14,* 58–66.

Phillips, K. A. (2009). *Understanding body dysmorphic disorder: An essential guide.* New York: Oxford University Press.

Phillips, K. A., Albertini, R. S., & Rasmussen, S.A. (2002). A randomized placebo-controlled trial of fluoxetine in body dysmorphic disorder. *Archives of General Psychiatry, 59,* 381–388.

Phillips, K. A., Atala, K. D., & Albertini, R. S. (1995). Body dysmorphic disorder in adolescents. *Journal of the American Academy of Child and Adolescent Psychiatry, 34,* 1216–1220.

Phillips, K. A., Coles, M. E., Menard, W., Yen, S., Fay, C., & Weisberg, R. B. (2005). Suicidal ideation and suicide attempts in body dysmorphic disorder. *Journal of Clinical Psychiatry, 66,* 717–725.

Phillips, K. A., Conroy, M., Dufresne, R. G., Menard, W., Didie, E. R., Hunter-Yates, J. et al. (2006). Tanning in body dysmorphic disorder. *Psychiatric Quarterly, 77,* 129–138.

Phillips, K. A., & Diaz, S. (1997). Gender differences in body dysmorphic disorder. *Journal of Nervous and Mental Disease, 185,* 570–577.

Phillips, K. A., Didie, E. R., & Menard, W. (2007). Clinical features and correlates of major depressive disorder in individuals with body dysmorphic disorder. *Journal of Affective Disorders, 97,* 129–135.

Phillips, K. A., Didie, E. R., Menard, W., Pagano, M. E., Fay, C., & Weisberg, R. B. (2006). Clinical features of body dysmorphic disorder in adolescents and adults. *Psychiatry Research, 141,* 305–314.

Phillips, K. A., Dufresne, R. G., Wilkel, C. S., & Vittorio, C. C. (2000). Rate of body dysmorphic disorder in dermatology patients. *Journal of the American Academy of Dermatology, 42,* 436–441.

Phillips, K. A., Grant, J. E., Siniscalchi, J., & Albertini, R. S. (2001). Surgical and nonpsychiatric medical treatment of patients with body dysmorphic disorder. *Psychosomatics, 42,* 504–510.

Phillips, K. A., Gunderson, C. G., Mallya, G., McElroy, S. L., & Carter, W. (1998). A comparison study of body dysmorphic disorder and obsessive-compulsive disorder. *Journal of Clinical Psychiatry, 59,* 568–575.

Phillips, K. A., & Hollander E. (2008). Treating body dysmorphic disorder with medication: Evidence, misconceptions, and a suggested approach. *Body Image, 5,* 13–27.

Phillips, K. A., Hollander E., Rasmussen, S. A., Aronowitz, B. R., Decaria, C., & Goodman, W. K. (1997). A severity rating scale for body dysmorphic disorder: development, reliability, and validity of a modified version of the Yale-Brown Obsessive Compulsive Scale. *Psychopharmacology Bulletin, 33,* 17–22.

Phillips, K.A., Stein, D.J., Rauch, S.L., Hollander, E., Fallon, B.A., Barsky, A., Fineberg, N., Mataix-Cols, D., Ferrão, Y.A., Saxena, S., Wilhelm, S., Kelly, M.M., Clark, L.A., Pinto, A., Bienvenu, O.J., Farrow, J., & Leckman, J. (2010). Should an obsessive-compulsive spectrum grouping of disorders be included in DSM-V? *Depression and Anxiety, 27,* 528–555.

Phillips, K. A., & Kaye, W. (2007). The relationship of body dysmorphic disorder and eating disorders to obsessive compulsive disorder. *CNS Spectrums, 12,* 347–358.

Phillips, K. A., Kelly, M. M., & Menard, W. (2009). Physical functioning and physical health-related quality of life in body dysmorphic disorder. Poster session presented at annual meeting of the American Psychiatric Association, San Francisco, CA.

Phillips, K. A., McElroy, S. L., Hudson, J. I., & Pope, H. G. (1995). Body dysmorphic disorder: An obsessive-compulsive spectrum disorder, a form of affective spectrum disorder, or both? *Journal of Clinical Psychiatry, 56,* 41–51.

Phillips, K. A., McElroy, S. L., & Keck, P. E. (1994). Obsessive compulsive spectrum disorder. *Journal of Clinical Psychiatry, 55,* 33–51.

Phillips, K. A., McElroy, S. L., Dwight, M. M., Eisen, J. L., & Rasmussen, S. A. (2001). Delusionality and response to open-label fluvoxamine in body dysmorphic disorder. *Journal of Clinical Psychiatry, 62,* 87–91.

Phillips, K. A., McElroy, S. L., Keck, P.E., Pope, H. G., & Hudson, J. I. (1993). Body dysmorphic disorder: 30 cases of imagined ugliness. *American Journal of Psychiatry, 150,* 302–308.

Phillips, K. A., McElroy, S. L., Keck, P. E., Pope, H. G., & Hudson, J. I. (1994). A comparison of delusional and nondelusional body dysmorphic disorder in 100 cases. *Psychopharmacology Bulletin, 30,* 179–186.

Phillips, K. A., McElroy, S. L., & Lion, J. R. (1992). Body dysmorphic disorder in cosmetic surgery patients (letter). *Plastic and Reconstructive Surgery, 90,* 333–334

Phillips, K. A., & Menard, W. (2006). Suicidality in body dysmorphic disorder: A prospective study. *American Journal of Psychiatry, 163,* 1280–1282.

Phillips, K. A., Menard, W., & Fay, C. (2006). Gender similarities and differences in 200 individuals with body dysmorphic disorder. *Comprehensive Psychiatry, 47,* 77–78.

Phillips, K. A., Menard, W., Fay, C., & Pagano, M. E. (2005). Psychosocial functioning and quality of life in body dysmorphic disorder. *Comprehensive Psychiatry, 46,* 254–260.

Phillips, K. A., Menard, W., Fay, C., & Weisberg, R. (2005). Demographic characteristics, phenomenology, comorbidity, and family history in 200 individuals with body dysmorphic disorder. *Psychosomatics, 46,* 317–325.

Phillips, K. A., Menard, W. & Fay, C. (2006). Gender similarities and differences in 200 individuals with body dysmorphic disorder. *Comprehensive Psychiatry, 47,* 77–87.

Phillips, K. A., Menard, W., Pagano, M. E., Fay, C., & Stout, R. L. (2006). Delusional versus nondelusional body dysmorphic disorder: Clinical features and course of illness. *Journal of Psychiatric Research, 40,* 95–104.

Phillips, K. A., Nierenberg, A. A., Brendel, G., & Fava, M. (1996). Prevalence and clinical features of body dysmorphic disorder in atypical major depression. *Journal of Nervous and Mental Disease, 184,* 125–129.

Phillips, K. A., O'Sullivan, R. .L, & Pope, H. G. (1997). Muscle dysmorphia (letter). *Journal of Clinical Psychiatry, 58,* 361.

Phillips, K. A., Pagano, M. E., Menard, W., Fay, C. &, Stout, R. L. (2005). Predictors of remission from body dysmorphic disorder: A prospective study. *Journal of Nervous and Mental Disease, 193,* 564–567.

Phillips, K. A., Pagano, M. E., Menard, W., &, Stout, R. L. (2006). A 12-month follow-up study of the course of body disorder. *American Journal of Psychiatry, 163,* 907–912.

Phillips, K. A., Pinto, A., & Jain, S. (2004). Self-esteem in body dysmorphic disorder. *Body Image, 1,* 385–390.

Phillips, K. A., Pinto, A., Menard, W., Eisen, J. L., Mancebo, M., & Rasmussen, S. A. (2007). Obsessive-compulsive disorder versus body dysmorphic disorder: A comparison study of two possibly related disorders. *Depression and Anxiety, 24,* 399–409.

Phillips, K. A., Quinn, E., & Stout, R. L. (2008). Functional impairment in body dysmorphic disorder: A prospective, follow-up study. *Journal of Psychiatric Research, 42,* 701–707.

Phillips, K.A., & Rasmussen, S.A (2004). Change in psychosocial functioning and quality of life of patients with body dysmorphic disorder treated with fluoxetine: a placebo-controlled study. *Psychosomatics, 45,* 438–444.

Phillips, K. A., Siniscalchi, J. M., & McElroy, S. L. (2004). Depression, anxiety, anger, and somatic symptoms in patients with body dysmorphic disorder. *Psychiatric Quarterly, 75,* 309–320.

Phillips, K. A., & Stout, R. L. (2006). Associations in the longitudinal course of body dysmorphic disorder with major depression, obsessive-compulsive disorder, and social phobia. *Journal of Psychiatric Research, 40,* 360–369.

Phillips, K. A., & Taub, S. L. (1995). Skin picking as a symptom of body dysmorphic disorder. *Psychopharmacology Bulletin, 31,* 279–288.

Pinto, A., & Phillips, K. A. (2005). Social anxiety in body dysmorphic disorder. *Body Image, 2,* 401–405.

Pope, H. G., Gruber, A. J., Choi, P. Olivardia, R., & Phillips, K. A. (1997). Muscle dysmorphia: An underrecognized form of body dysmorphic disorder. *Psychosomatics, 38,* 548–557.

Pope, H. G., Phillips, K. A., & Olivardia, R. (2000). *The Adonis complex: The secret crisis of male body obsession.* New York: The Free Press.

Pope, C. G., Pope, H. G., Menard, W., Fay, C., Olivardia, R., & Phillips, K. A. (2005). Clinical features of muscle dysmorphia among males with body dysmorphic disorder. *Body Image, 2,* 395–400.

Rauch, S. L., Phillips, K. A., Segal, E., Makris, N., Shin, L. M., Whalen, P. J., et al. (2003). A preliminary morphometric magnetic resonance imaging study of regional brain volumes in body dysmorphic disorder. *Psychiatry Research: Neuroimaging, 20,* 13–19.

Rief, W., Buhlmann, U., Wilhelm, S., Borkenhagen, A., & Brähler, E. (2006). The prevalence of body dysmorphic disorder: A population-based survey. *Psychological Medicine, 36,* 877–885.

Rosen, J. C., & Reiter, J. (1996). Development of the body dysmorphic disorder examination. *Behaviour Research and Therapy, 34,* 755–766.

Ruffolo, J. S., Phillips, K. A., Menard, W., Fay, C., & Weisberg, R. B. (2006). Comorbidity of body dysmorphic disorder and eating disorders: Severity of psychopathology and body image disturbance. *International Journal of Eating Disorders, 39,* 11–19.

Sarwer, D. B. (2002). Awareness and identification of body dysmorphic disorder by aesthetic surgeons: Results of a survey of American Society for Aesthetic Plastic Surgery members. *Aesthetic Surgery Journal, 22,* 531–535.

Sarwer, D. B., Wadden, T. A, Pertschuk, M. J., & Whitaker, L. A. (1998). Body image dissatisfaction and body dysmorphic disorder in 100 cosmetic surgery patients. *Plastic and Reconstructive Surgery, 101,* 1644–1649.

Simeon, D., Hollander, E., Stein, D. J., Cohen, L., & Aronowitz, B. (1995). Body dysmorphic disorder in the DSM-IV field trial for obsessive-compulsive disorder. *American Journal of Psychiatry, 152,* 1207–1209.

Solyom, L., DiNicola, V. F., Phil, M., Sookman, D., & Luchins (1985). Is there an obsessive psychosis? Aetiological and prognostic factors of an atypical form of obsessive-compulsive neurosis. *Canadian Journal of Psychiatry, 30,* 372–380.

Soriano, J. L., O'Sullivan, R. L., Baer, L., Phillips, K. A., McNally, R. J., & Jenike, M. A. (1996). Trichotillomania and self-esteem: A survey of 62 female hair pullers. *Journal of Clinical Psychiatry, 57,* 77–82.

Stein, D. J., Carey, P. D., & Warwick, J. (2006). Beauty and the beast: psychobiologic and evolutionary perspectives on body dysmorphic disorder. *CNS Spectrums, 11,* 419–422.

Stekel, W. (1949). *Compulsion and doubt.* Translated by E. A. Gutheil. New York: Liveright.

Suzuki, K., Takei, N., Kawai, M., Minabe, Y., & Mori, N. (2003). Is taijin kyofusho a culture-bound syndrome? *American Journal of Psychiatry, 160,* 1358.

Taqui, A. M., Shaikh, M., Gowani, S. A., Shahid, F., Khan, A., Tayyeb, S. M., et al. (2008). Body dysmorphic disorder: Gender differences and prevalence in a Pakistani medical student population. *BMC Psychiatry, 8,* 20.

Tignol, J., Biraben-Gotzamanis, L., Martin-Guehl, C., Grabot, D., & Aouizerate, B. (2007). Body dysmorphic disorder and cosmetic surgery: Evolution of 24 subjects with a minimal defect in appearance 5 years after their request for cosmetic surgery. *European Psychiatry, 22,* 520–524.

Uzun, O., Basoglu, C., Akar, A., Cansever, A., Ozsahin, A., Cetin, M., et al. (2003). Body dysmorphic disorder in patients with acne. *Comprehensive Psychiatry, 44,* 415–419.

Vargel, S., & Ulusahin, A. (2001). Psychopathology and body image in cosmetic surgery patients. *Aesthetic Plastic Surgery, 25,* 474–478.

Veale, D., Boocock, A., Gournay, K., Dryden, W., Shah, F., Willson, R., et al. (1996). Body dysmorphic disorder: A survey of fifty cases. *British Journal of Psychiatry, 169,* 196–201.

Veale, D., Ennis, M., & Lambrou, C. (2002). Possible association of body dysmorphic disorder with an occupation or education in art and design. *American Journal of Psychiatry, 159,* 1788–1790.

Veale, D., Kinderman, P., Riley, S., & Lambrou, C. (2003). Self-discrepancy in body dysmorphic disorder. *British Journal of Clinical Psychology, 42,* 157–169.

Veale, D., & Riley, S. (2001). Mirror, mirror on the wall, who is the ugliest of them all? The psychopathology of mirror gazing in body dysmorphic disorder. *Behaviour Research and Therapy, 39,* 1381–1393.

Vindigni, V., Pavan, C., Semenzin, M., Granà, S., Gambaro, F. M., Marini, M., et al. (2002). The importance of recognizing body dysmorphic disorder in cosmetic surgery patients: Do our patients need a preoperative psychiatric evaluation? *European Journal of Plastic Surgery, 25,* 305–308.

Vulink, N. C., Sigurdsson, V., Kon, M., Bruijnzeel-Koomen, C. A., Westenberg, H. G., & Denys, D. (2006). Body dysmorphic disorder in 3–8% of patients in outpatient dermatology and plastic surgery clinics. *Nederlands Tijdschrift Voor Geneeskunde, 150,* 97–100.

Wilhelm, S., Otto, M. W., Zucker, B. G., & Pollack, M. H. (1997). Prevalence of body dysmorphic disorder in patients with anxiety disorders. *Journal of Anxiety Disorders, 11,* 499–502.

World Health Organization (1992). *The ICD-10 classification of mental and behavioural disorders.* Geneva: World Health Organization.

Zimmerman, M., & Mattia, J. I. (1998). Body dysmorphic disorder in psychiatric outpatients: Recognition, prevalence, comorbidity, demographic, and clinical correlates. *Comprehensive Psychiatry, 39,* 265–270.

CHAPTER 4

Phenomenology and Characteristics of Compulsive Hoarding

Randy O. Frost *and* Jessica L. Rasmussen

Abstract

This chapter discusses current understanding of the phenomenology and characteristics of compulsive hoarding. The disorder is conceptualized within a cognitive-behavioral framework that includes excessive acquisition, difficulties with discarding, and clutter/disorganization. Information-processing deficits, emotional attachments, beliefs about possessions, and perfectionism are examined as underlying etiological factors. Characteristics of the disorder such as prevalence, onset and course, demographics and comorbidity are discussed. It is suggested that the distinctive features of compulsive hoarding, including unique neural and genetic substrates, warrant diagnostic classification as a separate disorder. Methodological problems with existing research are identified.

Keywords: hoarding, difficulty discarding, excessive acquisition, phenomenology, clutter, information-processing deficits, diagnostic classification

Introduction
Phenomenology and Characteristics of Compulsive Hoarding

Until recently, little attention has been paid to hoarding as a clinical phenomenon. Freud (1908) mentioned the hoarding of money as evidence of one part of the "anal triad." Jones (1912) suggested that hoarding objects was part of the parsimony leg of the triad. Fromm (1947) hypothesized that some people hold a "hoarding orientation" and that their sense of security comes from collecting and saving things. Salzman (1973) described hoarding as an attempt to exert control over one's environment and to "perfectly" control threat. In addition to these speculations, several case reports of hoarding have described the behavior in more detail (Greenberg, 1987; Leonard, Goldberger, Rapoport, Cheslowe, & Swedo, 1990). By and large, these accounts linked hoarding to obsessive compulsive disorder. However, little attention was given to defining the phenomenon or developing ways of measuring it.

Frost and Gross (1993) provided the first systematic definition of hoarding, "the acquisition of and failure to discard (p. 367)" a large number of possessions. Frost and Hartl (1996) suggested that in order to be considered clinically significant, the hoarding behavior must result in clutter that made living areas unusable and caused significant distress or impairment. They identified three major manifestations of the problem: excessive acquisition, difficulty discarding, and clutter or gross disorganization.

Excessive Acquisition

Frost and Gross (1993) first reported a tendency among hoarders to buy excessive amounts of extra items. Frost et al. (1998) found elevated levels of compulsive buying among members of a hoarding self-help group, as well as a tendency to collect free things. A number of subsequent studies have reported significantly greater levels of acquisition (either buying or free items) among hoarders compared to nonhoarders (Frost, Steketee, & Grisham, 2004; Frost, Steketee, Tolin, & Renaud, 2008), and significant correlations between excessive acquisition and both difficulty discarding and clutter (Frost et al., 2004; 2008; Frost, Kyrios, McCarthy, & Matthews, 2007). In a recent survey of a large sample of hoarders, 85%–95% acquired excessively, either through buying or acquiring for free, or both (Frost, Tolin, Steketee, Fitch, & Selbo-Bruns, 2009). The link between hoarding and compulsive or excessive acquisition has been observed in samples of people suffering from compulsive buying as well (Frost, Steketee, & Williams, 2002; Mueller et al., 2007). While it appears that the vast majority of hoarders engage in excessive acquisition, a somewhat smaller proportion of compulsive buyers display hoarding problems. Mueller et al. (2007) reported that only about half of their compulsive buying sample had high scores on the clutter and difficulty discarding dimensions of the Saving Inventory Revised.

The most frequent form of acquiring in hoarding is excessive buying followed by the excessive acquisition of free things. Nearly 75% of hoarders engage in excessive buying, while just over half excessively acquire free things. Many do both, but very few hoarders only acquire free things (Frost et al., 2009). Little research has been done on the excessive acquisition of free things, though it appears to operate somewhat differently from compulsive buying. For instance, while compulsive buying is strongly correlated with materialism, the acquisition of free things is not (Frost et al., 2007). Both excessive buying and acquisition of free things predicted significant and independent variance in hoarding severity; while buying was negatively correlated with age (younger people bought more), excessive acquisition of free things predicted an earlier age of onset of hoarding and was negatively correlated with income (Frost et al., 2009). Anecdotal reports of stealing and kleptomania in people who hoard suggest a third and rarer form of excessive acquisition in hoarding (Frost et al., 2009). While we have seen hoarding cases in which clients deny excessive acquisition, in many of these cases their excessive acquisition surfaces later in treatment when they stop avoiding situations that trigger acquisition. In other cases, clients who deny current acquisition problems describe excessive acquisition in the past. At present, it is unclear just how many hoarding cases acquire possessions solely through passive means.

Difficulty Discarding
The hallmark of hoarding is the difficulty discarding or letting go of possessions for which the person has little use or need. This behavior can sometimes appear almost delusional if the item is obviously useless or disgusting, such as bodily products (e.g., urine, tampons, nail clippings, etc) or rotten food. The description of hoarding in the diagnostic criteria for obsessive compulsive personality disorder (APA, 2004) emphasizes the worthless and worn out aspect of hoarded items. However, closer inspection of the nature of items collected has revealed that hoarders collect and save virtually everything, often filling their homes with recently purchased items that never leave their original packaging (Frost & Gross, 1993). Such things are often mixed with trash or other seemingly worthless items. When asked why they save such things, the reasons tend to fall into three broad categories: sentimental, instrumental, or intrinsic (Frost & Hartl, 1996). Sentimental saving results from the attachment of emotional significance or personal meaning to objects, often due to their connection with important people, places, or events. Instrumental saving refers to reasons having to do with utility and cost, while intrinsic saving refers to saving items for aesthetic reasons (Frost, Hartl, Christian, & Williams, 1995). Interestingly, the nature of the items saved by people who hoard, and the reasons they give for doing so, are strikingly similar to those of people who do not hoard (Frost & Gross, 1993). The difference seems to be in the number and variety of objects that get assigned such value.

Clutter/Disorganization
When the excessive acquisition and saving behavior results in living spaces so cluttered that they can't be used for their intended purposes, the hoarding has reached clinical significance (Frost & Hartl, 1996). People with hoarding problems report being unable to cook in the kitchen, eat at a table, sleep in their bed, or even walk through their house. Rooms that once served as living spaces have been given over to storage. For the majority of people with hoarding problems, clutter reflects difficulties with organization as well as acquisition and difficulty discarding. Piles of seemingly random objects have no apparent organizational scheme. Candy wrappers and old newspapers may cover the title to the car or important insurance papers. In some cases, the clutter may be limited by a spouse or partner who takes control of the living space. In other cases, especially when the person has lived alone for a long time, objects may be stacked to the ceiling, often with only narrow passageways, or sometimes with no way to navigate the room.

Such conditions can make hoarding dangerous, putting people at risk for fire, falling, and poor sanitation. In a survey of health department officials in cities throughout Massachusetts regarding their most recent complaints about hoarding, hoarding posed substantial risks to the person's health. In 6% of the cases, hoarding was judged to contribute directly to the person's death in a house fire (Frost, Steketee, & Williams, 2000). In one case, the local health department spent $16,000, most of their budget, cleaning out one home, only to return 18 months later to the same problem. Housing officials also face tremendous difficulties with hoarding cases that present health and safety problems for neighbors as well as those who hoard (Frost, Steketee, Youngren, & Mallya, 1999).

Some hoarding cases are characterized by "squalid" or unsanitary conditions (Frost et al., 2000). Squalor has been defined in a number of ways including, "social breakdown of the elderly" and as a primary symptom in "Diogenes Syndrome" (Clark, Manikikar & Gray, 1975; Shaw, 1957; Snowdon, Shah & Halliday, 2007). The primary characteristics of squalor include domestic neglect and a lack of personal hygiene (Snowdon et al., 2007). Historically, squalor has been observed in elderly populations recruited from nursing or disability services. These cases have not been referred for primary hoarding assessment or treatment, but rather for a lack of personal hygiene or dirty/unsanitary living conditions in the home (Gannon & O'Boyle, 1992; Shah, 1990; Snowdon et al., 2007; Snowdon & Halliday, 2009). Individuals in these studies have typically been over the age of 60, living alone and unmarried (Gannon & O'Boyle, 1992; Shah, 1990; Snowdon et al., 2007). However, a study conducted by Halliday, Banjaree, Philpot and MacDonald (2000) examined 74 individuals living in squalid conditions that had been referred by a cleaning service, and found that a significant portion of cases were under the age of 30.

While the majority of studies on squalor have not focused on a population primarily referred for hoarding assessment or treatment, hoarding behaviors have been frequently observed in these cases (Clark et al., 1975; Shaw, 1957; Snowdon et al., 2007). In a study conducted by Snowdon (1987), 72% of participants with squalor were observed to have significant levels of hoarding. In another study, Halliday et al. (2000) reported that up to 51% of squalor cases evidenced minimal, moderate, or severe hoarding.

While hoarding has been frequently described in cases of squalor, few descriptions exist of squalid conditions in those with a primary disorder of hoarding. Winsberg, Cassic, and Koran (1999) noted that clutter inhibited normal activities of daily living—including personal hygiene. A few studies have provided more direct indications of squalor in hoarding. Frost et al.(2000) surveyed health department officers who reported 38% of their hoarding cases to be "heavily cluttered with filthy environment, overwhelming." Kim, Steketee, and Frost (2001) focused on cleanliness ratings of the personal appearance and the homes of 62 elderly hoarders. In their sample, 17% were described as "extremely filthy" and 33% of residences were rated as "extremely filthy and dirty." Severe domestic squalor has also been observed within the context of animal hoarding (Patronek, 1999).

The etiology of squalor appears to have numerous pathways (Snowdon et al., 2007). Psychiatric disorders (ranging from psychotic spectrum to alcohol and substance abuse disorders), organic deterioration, and personality disorders all have been hypothesized as factors in the development of squalor (Shah, 1990; Snowdon et al., 2007). In recent years, there has been a more specialized focus on hoarding behaviors, otherwise thought of as obsessive compulsive disorder, in squalid conditions (Snowdon et al., 2007). Despite this association, researchers in the field have cautioned that it is important to distinguish that not all cases of squalor result from hoarding behaviors. Rather, they have proposed that there are three potential scenarios: (1) some individuals have hoarding (from difficulties with discarding or excessive acquisition) that results in squalid conditions; (2) some individuals collect ritualistically as stereotypic behavior in disorders such as Asperger's Syndrome; and (3) some individuals are unable to dispose of their rubbish, and accumulate filth because they are unable to attend to it (e.g., dementia, substance abuse, physical disabilities; see Maier, 2004; Snowdon et al., 2007).

Until recently, standardized measures of squalor were lacking and research relied mainly on case studies and observational techniques (Snowdon et al., 2007). The only standardized measure of squalor, known as the Environmental Cleanliness and Clutter Scale (ECCS), is a 10-item scale designed to measure aspects of environmental uncleanliness and clutter (Halliday & Snowdon, 2009). The scale showed good reliability and limited validity in a sample of individuals who had been referred to an old-age psychiatry service. While the ECCS does contain some items pertaining to the measurement of clutter, the number of items is limited and a standardized assessment of hoarding is lacking. Additionally, while the scale showed moderately strong psychometric properties in a sample of individuals referred to an old-age psychiatry clinic, it was not tested in a sample of individuals who were assessed or primarily treated for hoarding (Halliday & Snowdon, 2009). It is possible that individuals with hoarding present with squalor differ based on their unique living situation, and thus need a scale to measure squalor specifically developed and tailored toward this population. Furthermore, when assessing squalor in those with compulsive hoarding, it appears that there would be a need for a scale that solely assesses the presence of squalor separate from the hoarding itself.

The Home Environment Index (HEI) is a 15-item scale developed solely to measure the presence of squalor in individuals with compulsive hoarding (Rasmussen, Steketee, Frost, Tolin & Brown, under review). The scale was developed from observational data on squalid conditions in hoarding, and contains some items that are found on the ECCS and are common in the domestic squalor literature. This includes questions concerning such things as the presence of rotten food, animal/human waste, and odor of the house. It also includes items that may be more specific to squalid conditions in hoarding, including the presence of a fire hazard (Rasmussen et al., under review). The scale was tested in an Internet sample of 793 self-identified individuals with compulsive hoarding, and was found to have moderately strong reliability and validity. Interestingly enough, as opposed to studies of domestic squalor, age was negatively correlated with level of squalor. The HEI was most strongly correlated with a standardized measure of compulsive hoarding, the Hoarding Rating Scale-Self-Report (HRS-SR) (Tolin, Frost & Steketee, 2010) but also correlated to a moderate extent with measures of depression, anxiety, and stress (Rasmussen et al., under review).

In addition to the risks associated with the physical conditions in the home, hoarding has been found to be associated with other problems. Higher levels of depression and poor adaptive functioning have been reported in hoarding OCD patients compared to nonhoarding OCD patients (Frost, Steketee, Williams, & Warren, 2000; Wheaton, Timpano, LaSalle-Ricci & Murphy, 2008). Social functioning appears to be severely affected as well.

Several studies have found reported lower rates of marriage (Frost & Gross, 1993; Kim et al., 2001; Wheaton et al., 2008) and higher rates of social phobia (Samuels et al., 2002; Steketee, Frost, Wincze, Greene, & Douglass, 2000; Wheaton et al., 2008).

Hoarding also carries a heavy economic and general health burden. In a large survey of people with hoarding problems (Tolin, Frost, Steketee, Gray, & Fitch, 2008), participants who met criteria for a serious hoarding problem averaged 7.0 work impairment days in the past month. This level of impairment was significantly greater than that reported by National Comorbidity Survey (NCS) participants with any other anxiety, mood, or substance use disorders (Kessler et al., 1994). Work impairment was predicted by the severity of hoarding symptoms even after controlling for age, sex, and nonpsychiatric medical conditions. In addition, hoarding participants reported significantly more severe and chronic medical conditions than NCS participants. Hoarding participants were also more overweight than family members.

Families often suffer from the hoarding symptoms of loved ones. A large Internet survey of family members of people with hoarding problems revealed elevated distress and family strain in children of hoarding parents (Tolin et al., 2008). In addition, family members reported high levels of patient rejection and hostility, higher than those reported in studies of OCD patients. Children whose homes were cluttered before the age of 10 rated their childhoods as less happy. Also, they reported having friends over less often, and more difficulty making friends. They described their relationship with their parents as more strained, and expressed more hostility toward them than children of hoarders whose homes were not cluttered until after they were 10 years old.

People who hoard are widely considered to lack insight into the nature of their problem (Greenberg, 1987; Steketee & Frost, 2003). They appear to lack an awareness of the severity of their behavior, often rationalizing their acquiring and saving as necessary, or not out of the ordinary. Sometimes they deny having any problem and resist attempts to intervene (Christensen & Griest, 2001). Research on insight in this population suggests that many hoarders do not consider their behavior unreasonable (Frost & Gross, 1993; Frost et al., 2000); they receive low ratings from clinicians on the insight item of the Y-BOCS compared to nonhoarding OCD patients (DeBerardis et al., 2005; Frost et al., 1996;

Matsunaga et al., 2002; Samuels et al., 2007), and higher scores on measures of poor insight (Kishore, Samar, Reddy, Chandrasekhar, & Thennarasu, 2004). Studies of informants suggest more extreme problems with insight. Kim et al. (2001) surveyed elder-service caseworkers, who reported that only 15% of their hoarding clients definitely acknowledged the irrationality of their hoarding behavior, even though the vast majority had no significant cognitive deficits. More than half of a large sample of friends and family members of people with hoarding problems (n =558) described their hoarding family member as having "poor insight" or "lacks insight/delusional" (Tolin et al., 2008). Poor insight was associated with excessive acquisition and difficulty discarding, but not severity of clutter. Hoarders who were described as not being distressed about their hoarding were judged to have poorer insight.

Not all reports of insight in hoarding have been consistent, however. Samuels et al. (2008) found poor insight in only 14%–20% of OCD hoarding participants, which did not differ from people with OCD but not hoarding, while Nakata et al. (2007) found hoarding to be associated with better insight among OCD patients. It is important to note that with respect to insight, people's responses to questions about their behavior may depend heavily on the context. In the Tolin et al. (2008) study of economic burden of hoarding, 85% of the hoarding participants stated that they would seek therapy for their hoarding behavior if it were available, suggesting a clear recognition of the problem. Furthermore, more severe hoarding was associated with a higher likelihood of attending therapy for the problem. The exact nature of the insight problem in compulsive hoarding is as yet unclear.

A cognitive-behavioral model of hoarding (Frost & Hartl, 1996; Steketee & Frost, 2003) hypothesizes that the disorder results from (1) information processing deficits, (2) abnormal attachments to and beliefs about possessions, and (3) emotional distress and avoidance behaviors that develop as a result. Information-processing deficits include problems with attention, categorization, memory and decision making. Hartl, Duffany, Allen, Steketee, and Frost (2005) found higher levels of inattention and hyperactivity, both in childhood and currently, among a group of hoarders solicited from a self-help organization for clutterers compared to a group of community controls. Hoarders in this study also scored significantly higher on the cognitive failures questionnaire (Broadbent, Cooper, FitzGerald, &

Parkes, 1982), which measures everyday failures in concentration, memory, perception, and motor function. Moll et al. (2000) reported more hoarding behaviors among ADHD children than among community controls or a control group of children with tic disorders.

Wincze, Steketee, and Frost (2007) found that on a categorization (sorting) task, hoarders took more time, created significantly more categories, and were significantly more anxious than nonpsychiatric controls. They also took more time and created more categories than OCD patient controls, but only when the items were personally relevant. Luchian, McNally, and Hooley (2007) replicated the findings in a nonclinical population. Nonclinical hoarders rated the categorization task as more difficult and stressful. They took longer and created more categories than the nonhoarding control group. With respect to memory, Hartl et al. (2004) found that hoarders recalled less information on delayed recall in the Rey-Osterrieth Complex Figure Test (RCFT) and the California Verbal Learning Test. They also used less effective organizational strategies on the RCFT.

Early case reports described an association between hoarding and problems making decisions (Warren & Ostrom, 1988). Subsequent studies have found significant correlations between hoarding and indecisiveness (Frost & Gross, 1993; Frost & Shows, 1993). These accounts led Frost and Hartl (1996) to speculate that indecisiveness may be a key characteristic of people with hoarding problems. Since then, a number of studies have reported correlations between decision-making deficit measures and compulsive hoarding measures in adults (Frost et al., 2007; Samuels et al., 2002; 2007) as well as children (Mataix-Cols, Nakatani, Micali, & Heyman, 2008). Findings using the Iowa Gambling Task (Bechara, Damasio, Damasio & Anderson, 1994), which requires participants to maximize long-term gain by sacrificing immediate rewards, has been equivocal, with one study finding poorer performance by hoarders (Lawrence et al., 2006) and one finding no such difference (Grisham, Brown, Savage, Steketee, & Barlow, 2007). Samuels et al. (2002; 2007) found hoarding OCD patients to have more difficulty making decisions than nonhoarding OCD patients. In addition, Samuels et al. (2007) found relatives of hoarding OCD patients had more decision-making difficulty than relatives of nonhoarding OCD patients. Steketee, Frost, and Kyrios (2003) also found compulsive hoarders to report significantly more indecisiveness than nonhoarding OCD patients or community controls. Furthermore, indecisiveness accounted for significant variance in hoarding symptoms independent of hoarding-related beliefs about possessions.

In a recent survey of a very large sample of self-identified hoarders, 84% of those meeting criteria for diagnosis of hoarding scored greater than one standard deviation above the mean of community controls on the Frost Indecisiveness Scale (Frost & Shows, 1993). Indecisiveness remained significantly correlated with hoarding severity, compulsive acquisition, and work impairment due to hoarding after controlling for depression and obsessive compulsive symptoms (Oh, Frost, Tolin, Steketee, & Fitch, 2008). Frost et al. (2007) also found indecisiveness to be associated with compulsive buying and buying-related cognitions. Difficulties with decision making may be gender-specific. Samuels, et al. (2008) found that women with OCD who hoarded reported more difficulty starting and finishing tasks than women with OCD who didn't hoard. Men with OCD who did or didn't hoard showed no such difference.

These information-processing deficits may reflect abnormalities in brain function. Several investigations have noted abnormalities in glucose metabolization, blood flow, and brain injury in prefrontal regions of the brain, and in particular the cingulated cortex (Anderson, Damasio, & Damasio, 2005; Mataix-Cols et al., 2004; Saxena et al., 2004; Tolin, Kiehl, Worhunsky, Book, & Maltby, 2009). Portions of the cingulated cortex control the same processes that have been observed to be problematic for people who hoard, including executive control, focused attention, problem solving, detecting errors, and decision making (Saxena et al., 2004). Decision-making deficits in hoarding may be associated with hemodynamic activity in the lateral orbitofrontal cortex and parahippocampal gyrus (Tolin et al., 2009).

In addition to information-processing deficits, emotional attachments and beliefs about possessions are hypothesized to play a role in hoarding (Steketee & Frost, 2003). Although the DSM-IV suggests that hoarding is defined by items that have no sentimental value (APA, 2004), numerous investigations indicate that people who hoard develop strong emotional bonds with their possessions (Frost & Gross, 1993; Frost et al., 1995; Hartl et al., 2005; Kellett & Knight, 2003). People who hoard have been found to endorse statements such as, "I love my belongings the way I love some people" and, "Throwing something away would feel like part of

me dying" to a greater extent than people who do not hoard. Frost and colleagues (1995) systematically examined the nature of emotional attachment to possessions in a sample of college students and community volunteers. Ratings of hoarding severity were associated with greater emotional attachment to possessions, reliance on possessions for emotional comfort, and an inflated sense of responsibility for the well-being of their possessions. Recent findings suggest that the emotional attachments hoarders form to their possessions are strong and immediate, and don't depend on prolonged use or ownership (Grisham et al., 2009).

Closely related to these emotional attachments are feelings of safety and comfort that are provided by possessions. As mentioned, several investigations have noted such attachments among people who hoard (Frost & Gross, 1993; Hartl et al., 2005). Early theorizing about compulsive hoarding (Frost & Hartl, 1996) suggested that hoarded objects may provide signals of safety and security in individuals who feel threatened and vulnerable. Hartl et al. (2005) reported significantly higher scores among hoarders on a scale designed to measure the extent to which possessions provide protection, comfort, and security. Consistent with this observation, Grisham, Frost, Steketee, Kim, and Hood (2006) observed that individuals who reported a stressful life event at the time of onset tended to have a later age of onset, suggesting that some individuals may develop hoarding behaviors in response to such an event. Similarly, Hartl et al. (2005) reported a higher frequency of self-reported traumatic events among hoarders compared to nonhoarding community controls. In a follow-up, Cromer, Schmidt, and Murphy (2007) found that traumatic life events (TLEs) were associated with the frequency and severity of hoarding, and that the relationship between TLEs and hoarding was independent of depression, OCD symptoms, and comorbidity with mood and anxiety disorders. Interestingly, the association was accounted for almost exclusively by the clutter dimension of hoarding.

Other beliefs about responsibility for possessions, and the necessity of maintaining strict control over possessions, also characterize people with hoarding problems (Steketee et al., 2003). In addition to memory deficits, hoarders have demonstrated poorer confidence in their memory, which is independent of their actual memory abilities (Hartl et al., 2005).

Frost and Hartl (1996) describe hoarders as perfectionistic and worried about making mistakes, which may lead them to avoid making decisions. Frost and Gross (1993) found significant correlations between perfectionism and hoarding in nonclinical populations, and that people with hoarding problems scored significantly higher on measures of perfectionism than did community controls. Other evidence also supports an association between perfectionism and hoarding. Steketee et al. (2003) reported significant correlations between hoarding beliefs and subscales of the obsessional beliefs questionnaire (OBQ), including perfectionism. Tolin, Brady, and Hannan (2008) found that hoarding scores on the Obsessive Compulsive Inventory-Revised (OCI-R) were predicted only by the perfectionism/uncertainty subscale of the OBQ. In addition, Kyrios, Frost, and Steketee (2004) reported significant correlations between perfectionism and compulsive buying, as well as the excessive acquisition of free things.

Animal Hoarding

A special case of hoarding occurs when an individual accumulates a large number of animals and fails to provide adequate living conditions (HARC, 2000). Although animal hoarding is much less prevalent than the hoarding of objects, its impact is more dramatic and extreme, sometimes affecting the lives of hundreds of animals (Patronek, 1999). Animal hoarding cases pose significant health risks for the individual and those living nearby (Frost, Steketee, & Williams, 2000). In addition, their resolution is more complicated and expensive.

Unfortunately, not much is known about animal hoarding. Most of the literature is in the form of interviews with animal care caseworkers who come in contact with people who hoard animals. Information from these studies suggests that most animal hoarders are middle-aged or older, female, and often unmarried or widowed (Patronek, 1999). Cats and dogs are the most frequently collected animals, usually 30 to 40 at a time but sometimes up into the hundreds. Animal hoarders are usually very reluctant to part with their animals and, remarkably, fail to recognize the poor health and living conditions. In severe cases the floors and walls are covered with animal feces and urine, and dead animals are present (Patronek, 1999). Most animal hoarders claim great affection and attachment to their animals, and often claim to have special powers allowing them to communicate or understand their pets at a level not possible for others. It is not yet clear how this compares with similar sentiments expressed by object hoarders about their possessions.

A recent paper described a series of interviews conducted with former animal hoarders, as well as multiple pet owners who did not hoard (Gibson, Alabiso, Steketee, & Frost, 2008). Compared to multiple pet owners, animal hoarders had histories of chaotic or traumatic childhoods characterized by poor family relationships and ambivalent parenting. For these individuals, animals may have provided stable emotional relationships, as well as comfort and support, in an otherwise unpleasant world.

Prevalence

Accurate prevalence estimates for compulsive hoarding are hampered by the limited insight sometimes displayed by people who hoard. Researchers predicted that because hoarding occurs in approximately 30% of people with OCD, and the population prevalence of OCD is 1%–2%, that the prevalence of compulsive hoarding in the community would be around 0.4% (Steketee & Frost, 2003). However, researchers acknowledged that this figure was most likely an underestimate, as it excluded those individuals with compulsive hoarding who did not present with other symptoms of OCD (Steketee & Frost, 2003).

Several epidemiological studies of hoarding over the past several years have suggested a relatively higher prevalence rate than was previously thought. The National Comorbidity Catchment Study (NCCS) found a lifetime hoarding prevalence of 14% in the U.S. population (Ruscio, Stein, Chiu & Kessler, 2010). Samuels et al. (2008) estimated the prevalence of hoarding at 5.3% after interviewing 742 individuals from the Baltimore Epidemiologic Catchment Area (ECA) Follow-Up Survey. Another study conducted by Mueller, Mitchell, Crosby, Glaesmer, and de Zwann (2009) used the German version of the Savings Inventory-Revised (SI-R) to assess the prevalence rate of hoarding and compulsive buying in 2,307 German individuals. Results suggested a point prevalence rate of 4.6% for hoarding. In contrast, the most recently conducted epidemiological studies of hoarding have found smaller prevalence rates. A twin study (Iervolino et al., 2009) of 5,022 individuals in the general population found that 2.3% met criteria for hoarding. In addition, the European version of the National Cormorbidity Catchment Study showed a 2.6% lifetime prevalence rate in the general population (Fullana et al., 2010)

Samuels et al. (2008) found that the prevalence of hoarding was two times greater in men (5.6%) than women (2.6%), and Iervolino et al. (2009)

also found a greater prevalence of hoarding in men versus women. Mueller et al. (2009) found no difference in the prevalence of hoarding for males versus females. Samuels et al. (2008) also found that prevalence increased with age, from 2.3% in the youngest age group to 6.2% in the oldest, and was greater in those who were widowed compared to those who were currently married. Samuels et al. (2008) found no significant differences in prevalence by education, living arrangement, or race/ethnicity. Those in the poorest financial group were four times more likely to hoard compared to those in the wealthy group.

Rates of hoarding appear to be higher in specialty populations. Mataix-Cols et al. (2008) recently reported that 7% of a homeless population endorsed significant current difficulties with discarding and excessive acquisition of possessions. Nearly 5% reported difficulties due to clutter, and 1.2% and 3.6% reported significant distress and impairment due to their hoarding. With regard to lifetime rates, 11% reported difficulty discarding at some point in their lives, while 15% reported excessive acquisition of possessions, 6% reported distress and 11% had impairment due to hoarding.

Onset and Course

Onset of hoarding has been reported to occur in adolescence or childhood (Frost & Gross, 1993; Grisham et al., 2006; Samuels et al., 2002; 2007; Seedat & Stein, 2002). In a careful assessment of onset and intensity of hoarding dimensions, Grisham et al. (2006) reported that among 51 self-identified hoarders, mild hoarding symptoms began by age 12 for 60% of participants, and by age 18 for 80%. Although mild symptoms of acquisition, difficulty discarding, and clutter generally began in adolescence, onset of moderate symptoms occurred in the early to mid 20s, and onset of severe symptoms occurred in the early to mid 30s. Acquisition problems developed significantly later than difficulty discarding or clutter. Pertusa et al. (2008) reported somewhat later ages of onset of hoarding symptoms among hoarders both with and without OCD, and acquisition difficulties did not develop later than difficulty discarding or clutter. The discrepancy in the findings of these two studies may be due to the method of assessing onset. Pertusa et al. (2008) used a single age of onset for each hoarding symptom. They also noted that compared to hoarders without OCD, hoarders with OCD tended to have an earlier onset of excessive clutter but not acquisition or difficulty discarding.

Some research suggests differing ages of onset for males and females. Winsberg et al. (1999) reported that females had an earlier onset of hoarding than males in a small sample of 20 cases. In a larger sample of OCD cases, Samuels et al. (2008) also found an earlier age at onset of hoarding symptoms in women (13 years old) versus men (17 years old). A number of studies have found OCD patients with hoarding to have earlier onset of OCD than patients without hoarding (Fontenelle, Mendlowicz, Soares, & Versiani, 2004; Millet et al., 2004; Rosario-Campos et al., 2001; Samuels et al., 2002; 2008; Tukel et al., 2005), though a number of studies have failed to replicate this finding (Hassler et al., 2007; Lochner et al., 2005; Mathews et al., 2007; Samuels et al., 2007). Wheaton et al. (2008) found earlier age of onset of OCD, but only among women hoarders.

Factor analyses of children with OCD using the checklist from the Children's Yale-Brown Obsessive-Compulsive Scale (CY-BOCS) have identified hoarding as a separate factor (Stewart et al., 2008), or one combined with checking (Mataix-Cols et al., 2008), or ordering and arranging (McKay et al., 2006). The frequency of hoarding symptoms in children with OCD has varied from 26% (Storch et al., 2007) to 50% for young girls (Mataix-Cols et al., 2008). Hoarding outside the context of OCD has not been well-studied, although hoarding also occurs in Prader-Willi syndrome (Dykens et al., 1996), a genetic disorder that results in mild mental retardation, intense food-seeking behavior, and hoarding. Plimpton, Frost, Abbey, and Dorer (2009) reported childhood hoarding to be associated with little insight, perfectionism, ADHD symptoms, and possible ordering and arranging compulsions manifesting as concerns about others touching or moving possessions. Storch et al. (2007) found more somatic complaints, ordering and arranging compulsions, magical thinking, more externalizing behavior, and less insight in OCD hoarding children than non-hoarding OCD children.

Most studies have found hoarding symptoms to be chronic and relatively unlikely to change (Besiroglu et al., 2007; Grisham et al., 2006; Rufer, Grothusen, MaB, Peter, & Hand, 2005). In studies of OCD, the hoarding symptom factor appears to be more stable than the other subtypes (Besiroglu et al., 2007; Grisham et al., 2005; Mataix-Cols et al., 2002; Rufer et al., 2005). The course of compulsive hoarding in children and adolescents has also been examined in studies of OCD. Delorme et al. (2006) found that the hoarding dimension remained stable across time in a sample of children and adolescents as well.

Demographics

While psychopathology and treatment study samples of compulsive hoarding have tended to be overwhelmingly female, the Samuels et al. (2008) prevalence study found men twice as likely as women to experience hoarding symptoms. Furthermore, males and females may have different clinical characteristics of compulsive hoarding. The magnitude of the association of hoarding with paternal and maternal psychiatric symptoms was significantly stronger in the women versus the men, and hoarding in women was more closely associated with avoidant personality disorder and lifetime alcohol dependence than it was for men. Along this same line, Wheaton et al. (2008) found significant demographic and psychopathology-related differences in female and male participants with hoarding OCD versus nonhoarding OCD. When compared to those female participants with nonhoarding OCD, the female hoarding participants had an earlier age of onset, as well as a higher lifetime prevalence of panic disorder, bipolar I, binge eating disorder, and alcohol abuse disorders. Female hoarders also reported greater rates of contamination, religious, sexual, symmetry, and somatic obsessions, as well as repeating compulsions, than female nonhoarders. Male hoarders reported significantly greater rates of comorbid social phobia, and significantly more symmetry obsessions than male nonhoarders (Wheaton et al., 2008).

Hoarding has been shown to be three times higher in the older adults than younger ones (Samuels, et al., 2008). Echoing this finding, Frost et al. (2000) observed that 40% of all hoarding complaints to local health departments were regarding elders. Hoarding in the elderly has been observed mainly in the form of Diogenes Syndrome, a disorder characterized by extreme self-neglect of personal hygiene, domestic squalor, apathy, social withdrawal, and hoarding of various items (Gannon & O'Boyle, 1992; Shah, 1990).

Kim et al. (2001) conducted one of the only studies focusing specifically on hoarding in the elderly. The study interviewed 36 service providers who work with elderly people, and 8 Board of Health officials, regarding 62 elders (65 and older) who met criteria for compulsive hoarding. The service providers and Board of Health officials had to have observed the home of the elder on at least one occasion in the past year to qualify for the study.

The results showed that the majority of the sample turned out to be elderly white women who lived alone, half of whom had never been married. Elders in the study were likely to live in an apartment or a single-family dwelling in an urban area. The most frequently hoarded items for elders in the sample included paper, containers, clothing, food, books, and other objects from people's trash. Nearly the entire sample had significant clutter in their living rooms, dining rooms, kitchens, and bedrooms and hallways. Stairways and bathrooms were frequently cluttered as well. Nearly two-thirds of the elders in the sample showed difficulty with self-care, with nearly a third of the abovementioned being significantly unkempt. The providers reported that only 10% of their clients' residences were clean, with most homes being moderately or markedly dirty. All but one client experienced at least moderate difficulty moving about the house due to clutter. Nearly 70% of elderly hoarders were unable to use their furniture, and many of the elders' ability to care for their hygiene was impeded by cluttered sinks and showers/tubs. Providers who had frequent contact with their clients estimated that 44% of them had some form of a mental disorder, the most commonly confirmed being unipolar depression. Providers reported that nearly 76% of the sample had no cognitive deficits, contrary to expectations (Kim et al., 2001).

Comorbidity

Hoarding has been reported in a number of Axis I disorders, including schizophrenia (Luchins, Goldman, Lieb, & Hanrahan, 1992), organic mental disorders (Greenberg, Witzum, & Levy, 1990), and eating disorders (Frankenburg, 1984). However, these reports are anecdotal and involve single or very few cases. More systematic reports of hoarding have been reported in dementia (Finkel, et al., 1997; Hwang et al., 1998), brain injury (Anderson et al., 2005), Prader-Willi syndrome (Dykens, Leckman, & Cassidy, 1996), and compulsive buying (Mueller et al., 2007). Most of the research on comorbidity has focused on hoarding in OCD.

One of the most consistent findings has been a high frequency of major depressive disorder in hoarding. In small samples, the frequency of depression in hoarding has varied from 13% (Seedat & Stein, 2002) to 60% (Fontenelle et al., 2004; Grisham, Steketee, & Frost, 2008; Samuels et al., 2002). Larger samples have revealed a high frequency of major depressive disorder (MDD) in hoarding as well. Lochner et al. (2005) found MDD in 75% of their sample of 57 OCD hoarders. Wheaton et al. (2008) reported 67% of 115 hoarders had MDD. Samuels, Bienvenu, Pinto et al. (2007) reported MDD in 68% of 235 hoarders, and in a subsequent study found between 68% and 74% of a sample of 199 hoarders to have MDD (Samuels, Bienvenu, Pinto et al., 2008).

In contrast, several studies report conflicting findings. In two studies, Hasler et al. (2005; 2007) used cluster analyses to generate OCD subtypes (including hoarding) and calculated odds ratios for Axis I comorbidities for each. Both studies failed to find hoarding to be associated with an increased risk for any Axis I disorder. Interestingly, the second of these studies used data that overlapped with the Samuels, Bienvenu, Pinto et al. (2007) paper reporting greater depression in hoarding. Similarly, LaSalle-Ricci et al. (2006) failed to find significant point-biserial correlations between MDD diagnoses and Saving Inventory-Revised total scores, though surprisingly, Beck Depression Inventory scores were one of the significant predictors of SI-R scores in a multiple regression.

All of the above studies of comorbidity in hoarding solicited hoarding participants from samples of people with OCD. Two studies have solicited hoarding participants independent of OCD. Pertusa et al. (2008) found MDD in only 12.5% of OCD hoarders, and even less frequently in hoarders without OCD. In a study that directly solicited people with hoarding problems, Frost, Steketee, and Tolin (under review) found over 50% of 217 hoarders had MDD. This study more carefully defined hoarding patients than others, including interview, self-report, and home visits to verify diagnosis.

Studies of mood state have found depressed moods associated with hoarding. Frost, Steketee, Williams, and Warren (2000) found OCD hoarders to have significantly higher Beck Depression Inventory (BDI) scores than OCD nonhoarders, as well as other anxiety disorder controls. Similarly, several studies have found hoarders with OCD had significantly higher BDI scores than OCD patients without hoarding (Steketee et al., 2003; Wheaton et al., 2008). Others have reported significant and substantial correlations between the BDI and measures of hoarding, or significant differences between hoarders and controls on the BDI (Grisham et al., 2008; LaSalle-Ricci et al., 2006; Thordarson et al., 2004). In contrast to the above studies, Abramowitz, Wheaton, and Storch (2008) found only a small though significant correlation (0.17) between

hoarding and the BDI. Wu and Watson (2005) found significant correlations between a factorially derived hoarding subscale and a similarly derived measure of depression, but found no correlation between the hoarding subscale of the Schedule of Compulsions, Obsessions, and Pathological Impulses (SCOPI) and negative affect. Grisham, Brown, Liverant, and Campbell-Sills (2005) compared hoarders, with and without significant other OCD symptoms, to OCD patients without hoarding. Hoarders with OCD scored significantly higher on the Depression Anxiety and Stress Scale (DASS)-Depression measure than the other two groups, and lower on the Positive Affect Negative Affect Schedule (PANAS) -positive affect. Both the hoarders with OCD and OCD without hoarding scored higher on PANAS-negative affect than the hoarders without OCD.

No studies of hoarding samples have reported elevated frequencies of bipolar disorder. Two studies comparing comorbidities of OCD patients reported opposite results. Maina, Albert, Pessina, and Bogetto (2007) found lower rates of hoarding among OCD patients with bipolar disorder, while Masi et al. (2007) found higher rates of hoarding among bipolar pediatric OCD cases.

Anxiety disorders including social phobia (14%–71%), generalized anxiety disorder (GAD; 23%–47%), panic disorder (10%–41%), agoraphobia (8%–22%), specific phobia (26%–38%), PTSD (7%–16%), and separation anxiety (13%–22%) have also been reported as comorbid conditions in OCD patients with hoarding symptoms (Lochner et al., 2005; Samuels, et al., 2002; Samuels, Bienvenu, Pinto et al., 2008; Wheaton et al., 2008). These studies were limited by recruiting participants with OCD who reported hoarding symptoms, potentially excluding individuals with hoarding behaviors who did not meet criteria for OCD. Tolin, Meunier, Frost, and Steketee (2011) examined hoarding in all patients seeking treatment at an anxiety disorder clinic. Approximately 12%–25% of anxious patients reported significant hoarding symptoms. Twenty-seven percent of patients diagnosed with generalized anxiety disorder and 14% of those with social phobia reported significant hoarding symptoms. Only 16% of the OCD patients had significant hoarding symptoms. Negligible hoarding was found in patients with panic disorder or specific phobias. These findings suggest that hoarding symptoms may be associated with anxiety disorders other than OCD. High frequencies of social phobia and GAD have been found in samples of hoarders solicited solely for their hoarding symptoms independent of OCD (Frost et al., under review; Grisham et al., 2008).

Diagnostic Classification

The classification of compulsive hoarding as a symptom of OCPD had its origins in psychoanalytic theorizing about the anal personality characterized by obstinacy, orderliness, and parsimony (Frost & Steketee, 1998). Hoarding was incorporated into the diagnostic definition of obsessive compulsive personality disorder as "unable to discard worthless objects even when they have no sentimental value (APA, 2004; p. 729)." Research on the validity of hoarding as a diagnostic criterion for OCPD has been inconsistent. While some studies have reported an association between hoarding and OCPD independent of the hoarding criterion (Frost, Steketee, Williams, & Warren, 2000; Mataix-Cols, Baer, Rauch, & Jenike, 2000; Samuels et al., 2002; 2007; 2008), others have not (Frost & Gross, 1993; Frost, Krause, & Steketee, 1996; Pertusa et al., 2008). Furthermore, large-scale factor analyses of the OCPD criteria have consistently found that the hoarding dimension does not load with other OCPD criteria, and has poor predictive value as a criterion (Grilo, 2004a; 2004b; Grilo et al., 2001; Hummelen et al., 2008; Nestadt et al., 2006). This has led some to suggest that hoarding should be removed from the criteria for OCPD (Hummelen et al., 2008; Saxena, 2008). Others have suggested that hoarding, along with perfectionism, may be a special subtype of OCPD that overlaps with OCD (Eisen et al., 2006).

Despite its status as a criterion of OCPD, hoarding has most frequently been associated with obsessive compulsive disorder (Steketee & Frost, 2003). Frequencies of hoarding in clinical OCD samples have ranged anywhere from 13% to 38% (see Bloch, Landeros-Weisenberger, Rosario, Pittenger, & Leckman, 2008), with primary hoarding occurring in approximately 11% (Saxena et al., 2002). Samples of people with compulsive hoarding have been found to have more nonhoarding obsessions and compulsions (Frost & Gross, 1993; Frost, Krause, & Steketee, 1996) and to score higher on general measures of OCD (Frost & Gross, 1993; Frost et al., 1996; Frost, Steketee, Williams, & Warren, 2000). OCD patients with hoarding have also been found to experience more severe OCD symptoms (Samuels et al., 2002). Numerous large-scale factor analyses of OCD symptoms have consistently suggested a multidimensional model with four main

OCD factors (symmetry/ordering, contamination/cleaning, obsessions/checking, and hoarding; see Bloch et al., 2008), which form subtypes of OCD (Mataix-Cols et al., 2005).

Of the four hypothesized subtypes, hoarding has been shown to be particularly distinct (Bloch et al., 2008), and emerging evidence suggests that it should be classified as a separate disorder. Although hoarders appear to have more OCD symptoms than nonhoarders, a relatively small percentage of them would qualify for an OCD diagnosis independent of their hoarding symptoms. Frost et al. (under review) found that fewer than 20% of 217 carefully diagnosed hoarding cases qualified for OCD diagnoses independent of hoarding. Other disorders such as depression (> 50%) and generalized anxiety disorder (> 20%) were more frequent. Other studies have noted the distinctiveness of hoarding in the relatively smaller correlations between hoarding and other OCD subtypes compared to the relatively larger correlations among those nonhoarding subtypes (Abramowitz, Wheaton, & Storch, 2008; Wu & Watson, 2005), though these studies suffer from sampling and measurement problems.

Differences between hoarding and nonhoarding OCD patients have emerged in family and genetic studies. Compulsive hoarding and the risk factors thought to underlie hoarding behaviors appear to run strongly in families (Saxena, 2008; Frost & Gross, 1993). Nearly 84% of those with hoarding report having a first-degree relative who is a "pack-rat," whereas only 37% to 54% report having a family member with a different type of OCD (Frost & Gross, 1993; Saxena, 2008; Winsberg et al., 1999). Relatives of hoarding OCD patients versus nonhoarding OCD patients have been shown to have higher levels of hoarding symptoms, dysthymia and indecisiveness (Samuels et al., 2007; Saxena, 2008; Wheaton et al., 2008). The hoarding symptom appears be strongly familial, and shows an autosomal recessive inheritance pattern (Hasler et al., 2007; Saxena, 2008). Samuels et al. (2007) found a suggestive link between compulsive hoarding and a marker on chromosome 14 in families with early-onset OCD, and a polymorphism on chromosome 22q11 was found to be significantly more prevalent in OCD patients with hoarding symptoms than in nonhoarding OCD patients or controls (Lochner et al., 2005). In the only twin study of compulsive hoarding, Iervolino et al. (2009) found a 50% genetic heritability for compulsive hoarding, with the remaining variance attributed to shared environmental factors and measurement error. These preliminary findings suggest that hoarding may exist as a distinct genetic phenotype.

Recent research on the biological basis of hoarding has suggested separate neural substrates from other OCD symptoms (Mataix-Cols et al., 2004; Saxena, 2008; Tolin et al., 2008). Saxena, Bota and Brody (2001) found that compulsive hoarders had a significantly lower metabolism in the posterior cingulate cortex compared with controls, as opposed to the characteristic hypermetabolism in the obritofrontal cortex (OFC), caudate, and thalamus seen in those with nonhoarding OCD (Saxena et al., 2001). In a follow-up study, Saxena et al. (2004) found lowered metabolism in the ventral and dorsal anterior cingulate cortex for hoarders compared to healthy controls. OCD symptom provocation studies have provided additional evidence for separate neural substrates based on OCD symptom factor. Mataix-Cols et al. (2004) found that hoarding was specifically related to greater activation in the left precentral gyrus and the right OFC. However, this study was limited, in that not all patients with OCD in the study had the symptoms the researchers were trying to provoke, and thus not all of them became anxious during provocation (Mataix-Cols et al., 2004). An et al. (2009) compared hoarding-specific symptom provocation in patients with hoarding and nonhoarding OCD as well as controls, and found that hoarders had greater activation of the bilateral frontal pole and the anterior medial prefrontal cortex mPFC than nonhoarding OCD patients and controls. Tolin et al. (2009) compared fMRI findings of carefully diagnosed hoarders versus healthy controls while they were making decisions about discarding their own versus the experimenter's junk mail. Hoarders displayed more hemodynamic activity in the parahippocampal gyrus and lateral OFC than controls. Greater activation was also observed for decisions regarding their own junk mail compared to the experimenter's.

Differential response to treatment by people who hoard also suggests that hoarding may be distinct from OCD. A number of studies have found that the presence of hoarding predicts poorer response to medication or medication combined with behavior therapy among patients with OCD (Black et al., 1998; Mataix-Cols, Rauch, Manzo, Jenike & Baer, 1999, Matsunaga et al., 2008; Saxena et al., 2001; Stein et al., 2007), though a few studies have failed to find differences in outcomes (see Saxena, 2008). Saxena, Brody, Maidment, and Baxter (2007) conducted the only medication trial that solicited

hoarding patients, rather than using hoarding scores from the Y-BOCS of OCD patients, and the first to use measures designed to specifically assess hoarding. They failed to find differences in response to paroxetine between hoarders and nonhoarding OCD patients, though the response rate among the nonhoarding OCD group was lower than that typically found for paroxetine studies and may have contributed to the lack of significant differences.

Response to standard cognitive-behavior therapy for OCD also appears to be weaker in people with hoarding problems. Mataix-Cols, Marks, Greist, Kobak, and Lee (2002) reported premature dropout and poorer response to treatment among hoarders compared to nonhoarding OCD patients. Rufer, Fricke, Kloss, and Hand (2006) reported that only 37% of hoarding OCD patients responded to cognitive-behavior therapy compared to 63% of nonhoarding OCD patients. Similarly, Abramowitz, Franklin, Schwartz, and Furr (2003) found that the hoarding patients did not improve as much following standard exposure and response prevention as did nonhoarding OCD patients. As with the medication studies, these studies sampled OCD patients rather than soliciting people with hoarding problems. The poor response may be due to comorbidity differences between groups (hoarding plus OCD versus OCD only) rather than hoarding per se.

Treatments tailored for hoarding problems have fared somewhat better. Tolin, Frost, and Steketee (2007) conducted an open treatment trial for 14 individuals with compulsive hoarding. The cognitive-behavioral treatment in this study was an integration of traditional exposure and response prevention with skills-based psychoeducation (e.g. organization, categorization, decision making) designed specifically for those with hoarding. Those in the open trial showed a moderate response to treatment at post-assessment. In a larger controlled trial, hoarding patients showed significantly more benefit after 12 weeks than waitlist controls, with 70% judged to be improved or much improved after 26 weeks of treatment (Steketee, Frost, Tolin, & Rasmussen, 2010).

Aside from these differences, there are important features of hoarding that are absent in people with other OCD subtypes and symptoms. OCD symptoms are universally accompanied by anxiety and distress. In most hoarding cases, however, there is considerable positive affect associated with the acquisition and saving of possessions (Steketee & Frost, 2003). Anxiety and distress typically only accompany attempts to organize or discard possessions (Steketee & Frost, 2003). In this context, hoarding overlaps more with impulse control disorders than with OCD. In fact, higher hoarding scores have been found among pathological gamblers (Frost, Meagher, & Riskind, 2001) and compulsive buyers (Mueller et al., 2007). Hoarding also appears to be more typically characterized by ego-syntonic thoughts surrounding discarding and saving, as opposed to the intrusive ego-dystonic thoughts that are described with OCD. In addition, those with hoarding seem to frequently have less insight or awareness into the nature of the problem as compared to individuals with nonhoarding OCD.

Adding to the hypothesis that compulsive hoarding constitutes a separate diagnosis from OCD are the differences in symptom onset and associated features that have been observed in OCD patients with hoarding versus nonhoarding OCD (Saxena, 2008; Steketee & Frost, 2003). In general, those with hoarding versus nonhoarding OCD report an earlier age for onset, but present later in life for treatment (Saxena et al., 2002). Studies have indicated higher levels of Axis I disorders, such as social phobia, major depression, and generalized anxiety disorder in those hoarding versus nonhoarding OCD patients (Frost, Steketee, Williams, & Warren, 2000; Samuels et al., 2002; Steketee & Frost, 2003). Hoarding patients have been found to have higher levels of avoidant, dependent, and paranoid personality disorder as well (Steketee & Frost, 2003). Hoarding versus nonhoarding OCD patients are less likely to be married, report significantly lower incomes, and have greater family and social disability, as well as lower global functioning (Pertusa et al., 2008; Steketee & Frost, 2003; Tolin et al., 2008). Additionally, those patients with hoarding report a higher incidence of traumatic events and appear to have lower insight than nonhoarding OCD patients (Cromer et al., 2007; Samuels et al., 2002).

A recent study by Pertusa et al. (2008) compared hoarding patients without OCD, those with hoarding plus OCD, those with OCD minus hoarding, patients with another anxiety disorder, and community controls. Patients in the hoarding group were required to have significant symptoms of hoarding (SI-R>40) and patients were only included in the OCD plus hoarding group if they endorsed significant symptoms of OCD outside of hoarding. The study found that individuals in the hoarding minus OCD and the hoarding plus OCD groups were significantly older and more likely to live alone than the comparison groups. The OCD plus hoarding group was less likely to be married than participants in the other groups. The hoarding groups reported an equal frequency of hoarding behaviors after the occurrence of a traumatic event. However, the hoarding minus OCD group reported no other reasons for hoarding besides intrinsic value, in contrast to the hoarding plus OCD group, in which one-fourth of the participants reported other obsessions relating to their hoarding. The hoarding plus OCD group scored higher on the symmetry dimension of the Y-BOCS scale compared to the OCD minus hoarding group. Additionally, the hoarding minus OCD group scored significantly lower on measures of OCD global severity than the OCD plus hoarding and OCD minus hoarding groups, even after removing the hoarding items from the Y-BOCS dimensional scale score. In regard to comorbidity, the two OCD groups were more likely to have generalized anxiety disorder, and the two hoarding groups were more likely to have social phobia than the OCD minus hoarding group. Participants in the two hoarding groups endorsed a significantly higher number of Cluster B personality traits than the two OCD groups, and the OCD plus hoarding group endorsed significantly higher levels of Cluster C traits than OCD minus hoarding and hoarding minus OCD groups. These findings suggest the possibility of 3 distinct types of hoarding: OCD hoarding, hoarding with other OCD symptoms, and hoarding without other OCD symptoms.

Finally, Olatunji, Williams, Haslam, Abramowitz, and Tolin (2008) examined the taxometric structure of latent factors present in OCD. While the washing, checking, neutralizing, obsessing, and ordering subtypes showed a dimensional shape, hoarding appeared to have a distinct taxonic shape. These results, while preliminary, suggest that compulsive hoarding is a distinct categorical construct, most likely separate from OCD.

Although a small number of cases may be considered OCD-based hoarding (Pertusa et al., 2008), the preponderance of evidence suggests that most hoarding is distinct from OCD and may best be considered as a separate disorder. There is some overlap with other OCD symptoms, but also with other disorders such as depression and impulse control disorders. While hoarding traditionally has also been associated with OCPD, it appears that there is little relation apart from overlap in diagnostic item content. Outside of hoarding that occurs secondary to other neurological or psychiatric conditions, the phenomenon seems to be consistent whether in isolation or comorbid with other disorders (Pertusa et al., 2010). All of the recent evidence combined has led to the proposal that compulsive hoarding have its own classification in upcoming editions of the DSM (Mataix-Cols et al., 2010). It has been suggested that hoarding remain under OC spectrum disorders (e.g., body dysmorphic disorder, trichotillomania) as a separate disorder (Pertusa et al., 2010).

Unfortunately, much of the research on hoarding suffers from two substantial limitations. Many studies have drawn their hoarding samples from people diagnosed with OCD based on other (non-hoarding) OCD symptoms. Since the majority of hoarding cases have no other OCD symptoms (Frost et al., under review), they are not well represented in this research, and information drawn from these studies may paint an inaccurate picture of hoarding. The second major limitation is that many of the studies reviewed here rely on measures that have limited validity for assessing hoarding severity. For example, studies using the Y-BOCS checklist items may grossly overestimate hoarding symptoms. In Y-BOCS interviews with community controls, over 30% report hoarding on the Y-BOCS checklist (Frost et al., 1996). Hoarding subscales that are part of more general OCD questionnaires are largely unvalidated for hoarding, and fail to provide information on the critical dimensions. Well validated self-report (Frost et al., 2004), observational (Frost et al., 2008), and interview (Tolin, Frost, & Steketee, 2008) measures have recently become available, and will help to refine our knowledge of this difficult problem in the future.

Conclusion

Hoarding consists of three major features (excessive acquisition, difficulty discarding, disorganization) and several other prominent ones (e.g., indecision, perfectionism). It results in significant impairment in functioning and can pose serious threats to health and safety, and it occurs with a much higher frequency than has been assumed. Information-processing deficits, possibly related to neural substrates, overly emotional attachments to possessions, and rigid beliefs about possessions appear to underlie the disorder. The disorder appears to be distinct from OCD and comorbid with MDD, social phobia, GAD, and specific phobia. Much of the existing research on hoarding suffers from methodological problems having to do with the definition and assessment of hoarding. Newly established diagnostic criteria (Pertusa et al., 2010) and

well-validated measures (Frost et al., 2004; Frost et al., 2008; Tolin, Frost, & Steketee, 2010) will improve the quality of future research on hoarding.

Future Directions

• Replication of existing research with samples drawn from the hoarding population (rather than the OCD population) is needed.

• Research on the overlap of hoarding and impulse control disorders would help to clarify the nature of this construct.

• Investigation into special conditions or subtypes is needed (e.g., animal hoarding; squalid conditions).

Related Chapters

Chapter 22. Treatment of Compulsive Hoarding

References

Abramowitz, J. S., Franklin, M. E., Schwartz, S. A., & Fur, J. M. (2003). Symptom presentation and outcome of cognitive-behavioral therapy for obsessive-compulsive disorder. *Journal of Consulting and Clinical Psychology, 71*, 1049–1057.

Abramowitz, J. S., Wheaton, M. G., & Storch, E. A. (2008). The status of hoarding as a symptom of obsessive-compulsive disorder. *Behavior Research and Therapy, 46*, 1026–1033.

An, S. K., Mataix-Cols, D., Lawrence, N. S., Wooderson, S., Giampietro, V., Speckens, A., Brammer, M. J., and Phillips, M. L. (2009). To discard or not to discard: the neural basis of hoarding symptoms in obsessive compulsive disorder. *Molecular Psychiatry, 14*, 318–331.

Anderson, S. W., Damasio, H., & Damasio, A. R. (2005). A neural basis for collecting behavior in humans. *Brain, 128*, 201–212.

American Psychiatric Association (2004). *Diagnostic and statistical manual of mental heath disorders: Text revision* (4th ed.). Washington, DC: Author.

Bechara, A., Damasio, A. R., Damasio, H., & Anderson, S. W. (1994). Insensitivity to future consequences following damage to human pre-frontal cortex. *Cognition, 50*, 7–15.

Besiroglu, L., Uguz, F., Ozbebit, O., Guler, O., Cilli, A. S., & Askin, R. (2007). Longitudinal assessment of symptom and subtype categories in obsessive-compulsive disorder. *Depression and Anxiety, 24*, 461–466.

Black, D.W., Monahan, P., Gable, J., Blum, N., Clancy, G., & Baker, P. (1998). Hoarding and treatment response in 38 nondepressed subjects with obsessive-compulsive disorder. *Journal of Clinical Psychiatry, 59*, 420–425.

Bloch, M. H., Landeros-Weisenberger, A., Rosario, M. C., Pittenger, C., & Leckman, J. F. (2008). Meta-analysis of the symptom structure of obsessive-compulsive disorder. *American Journal of Psychiatry, 165*, 1532–1542.

Broadbent, D. E., Cooper, P. F., FitzGerald, P., & Parkes, K. R. (1982). The Cognitive Failures Questionnaire (CFQ) and its correlates. *British Journal of Clinical Psychology, 21*, 1–16.

Christensen, D. D. & Greist, J. H. (2001). The challenge of obsessive-compulsive disorder hoarding. *Primary Psychiatry, 8*, 79–86.

Clark, A. N. G., Mankikar, G. O., & Gray, I. (1975). Diogenes syndrome: A clinical study of gross neglect in old age. *The Lancet, 305,* 366–368.

Cromer, K. R., Schmidt, N. B., & Murphy, D. L. (2007). Do traumatic events influence the clinical expression of compulsive hoarding? *Behaviour Research and Therapy, 45,* 2581–2592.

De Berardis, D., Campanelle, D., Gambi, F., Sepede, G., Salini, G., Carano, A., La Rovere R., Pelusi L., Penna L., Cicconetti A., Cotellessa C., Salerno RM., Ferro FM. (2005). Insight and alexithymia in adult outpatients with obsessive-compulsive disorder. *European Archives of Psychiatry and Clinical Neuroscience, 255,* 350–358.

Dykens, E. M., Leckman, J. F., & Cassidy, S. B. (1996). Obsessions and compulsions in Prader-Willi syndrome. *Journal of Child Psychology and Psychiatry, 37,* 995–1002.

Eisen, J. L., Coles, M. E., Shea, T., Pagano, M. E., Stout, R. L., Yen, S., Grilo, C. M., & Rasmussen, S. A. (2006). Clarifying the convergence between obsessive compulsive personality disorder criteria and obsessive compulsive disorder. *Journal of Personality Disorders, 20,* 294–305.

Finkel, S., Costa E Silva, J., Cohen, G., Miller, S., & Sartorius, N. (1997). Behavioral and psychological signs and symptoms of dementia: A consensus statement on current knowledge and implications for research and treatment. *International Journal of Geriatric Psychiatry, 12,* 1060–1061.

Fontenelle, L. F., Mendlowicz, M. V., Soares, I. D., & Versiani, M. (2004). Patients with obsessive-compulsive disorder and hoarding symptoms: A distinctive clinical subtype? *Comprehensive Psychiatry, 45,* 375–383.

Frankenburg, F. R. (1984). Hoarding in anorexia nervosa. *British Journal of Medical Psychology, 57,* 57–60.

Freud, S. (1908). Character and anal eroticism. In *Collected papers* (Vol. II). (pp. 45–51). London: Hogarth Press.

Fromm, E. (1947). *Man against himself: An inquiry into the psychology of ethics.* New York: Rinehart.

Frost, R. O. & Gross, R. C. (1993). The hoarding of possessions. *Behaviour Research and Therapy, 31,* 367–381.

Frost, R. O. & Hartl, T. L. (1996). A cognitive-behavioral model of compulsive hoarding. *Behaviour Research and Therapy, 34,* 341–350.

Frost, R. O., Hartl, T. L., Christian, R., & Williams, N. (1995). The value of possessions in compulsive hoarding: Patterns of use and attachment. *Behaviour Research and Therapy, 33,* 897–902.

Frost, R. O., Kim, H.-J., Morris, C., Bloss, C., Murray-Close, M., & Steketee, G. (1998). Hoarding, compulsive buying and reasons for saving. *Behaviour Research and Therapy, 36,* 657–664.

Frost, R. O., Krause, M. S., & Steketee, G. (1996). Hoarding and obsessive-compulsive symptoms. *Behavior Modification, 20,* 116–132.

Frost, R. O., Kyrios, M., McCarthy, K. D., & Mathews, Y. (2007). Self-ambivalence and attachment to possessions. *Journal of Cognitive Psychotherapy, 21,* 236–247.

Frost, R.O., Meagher, B.M., & Riskind, J.H. (2001). Obsessive-compulsive features in pathological lottery and scratch ticket gamblers. *Journal of Gambling Studies. 17,* 5–19.

Frost, R. O. & Shows, D. L. (1993). The nature and measurement of compulsive indecisiveness. *Behaviour Research and Therapy, 31,* 683–692.

Frost, R. O. & Steketee, G. (1998). Hoarding: Clinical aspects and treatment strategies. In M. Jenike, L. Baer, & J. Minnichelo, (Eds.) *Obsessive compulsive disorder: Practical management* (3rd ed). (pp. 533–554). St. Louis: Mosby.

Frost, R. O., Steketee, G., & Grisham, J. (2004). Measurement of compulsive hoarding: Saving inventory–revised. *Behaviour Research and Therapy, 42,* 1163–1182.

Frost, R. O., Steketee, G., & Tolin, D. F. (under review). *Comorbidity in hoarding disorder.*

Frost, R. O., Steketee, G., Tolin, D. F., & Renaud, S. (2008). Development and validation of the clutter image rating. *Journal of Psychopathology and Behavioral Assessment, 30,* 193–203.

Frost, R. O., Steketee, G., & Williams, L. (2000). Hoarding: A community health problem. *Health and Social Care in the Community, 8,* 229–234.

Frost, R. O., Steketee, G., & Williams, L. (2002). Compulsive buying, compulsive hoarding, and obsessive-compulsive disorder. *Behavior Therapy, 33,* 201–214.

Frost, R. O., Steketee, G., Williams, L. F., & Warren, R. (2000). Mood, personality disorder symptoms and disability in obsessive compulsive hoarders: A comparison with clinical and nonclinical controls. *Behaviour Research and Therapy, 38,* 1071–1081.

Frost, R. O., Steketee, G., Youngren, V. R., & Mallya, G. K. (1999). The threat of the housing inspector: A case of hoarding. *Harvard Review of Psychiatry, 6,* 270–278.

Frost, R. O., Tolin, D. F., Steketee, G., Fitch, K. E., & Selbo-Bruns, A. (2009). Excessive acquisition in hoarding. *Journal of Anxiety Disorders, 23,* 632–639.

Fullana, M. A., Vilagut, G. G., Rojas-Farreras, S. S., Mataix-Cols, D. D., de Graaf, R. R., Demyttenaere, K. K., & Alonso, J. J. (2010). Obsessive–compulsive symptom dimensions in the general population: Results from an epidemiological study in six European countries. *Journal of Affective Disorders, 124,* 291–299.

Gannon, M. & O'Boyle, J. (1992). Diogenes syndrome. *British Medical Journal, 85,* 124.

Gibson, A., Alabiso, J., Steketee, G., & Frost, R.O. (2008, Nov.). *Antecedents of Animal Hoarding Versus Animal Collecting: A Qualitative Analysis.* Paper presented at the annual meeting of the Association for Behavioral and Cognitive Therapy, Orlando, FL.

Greenberg, D. (1987). Compulsive hoarding. *American Journal of Psychotherapy, 41,* 409–416.

Greenberg, D., Witztum, E., & Levy, A. (1990). Hoarding as a psychiatric symptom. *Journal of Clinical Psychiatry, 51,* 417–421.

Grilo, C. M. (2004). Diagnostic efficiency of DSM-IV criteria for obsessive compulsive personality disorder in patients with binge eating disorder. *Behaviour Research and Therapy, 42,* 57–65.

Grilo, C. M., McGlashan T. H., Morey L. C., Gunderson J. G., Skodol A. E., Shea M. T., Sanislow C. A., Zanarini M. C, Bender D., Oldham J. M., Dyck I., & Stout R. L. (2001). Internal consistency, intercriterion overlap and diagnostic efficiency of criteria sets for DSM-IV schizotypal, borderline, avoidant and obsessive-compulsive personality disorders. *Acta Psychiatrica Scandinavica, 104,* 264–272.

Grisham, J. R., Brown, T. A., Liverant, G. I., & Campbell-Sills, L. (2005). The distinctiveness of compulsive hoarding from obsessive-compulsive disorder. *Anxiety Disorders, 19,* 767–779.

Grisham, J. R., Brown, T. A., Savage, C. R., Steketee, G., & Barlow, D. H. (2007). Neuropsychological impairment associated with compulsive hoarding. *Behaviour Research and Therapy, 45,* 1471–1483.

Grisham, J. R., Frost, R. O., Steketee, G., Kim, H.-J., & Hood, S. (2006). Age of onset of compulsive hoarding. *Anxiety Disorders, 20,* 675–686.

Grisham, J. R., Frost, R. O., Steketee, G., Kim, H., Tarkoff, A., & Hood, S. (2009). Formation of attachment to possessions in compulsive hoarding. *Journal of Anxiety Disorders, 23,* 357–361.

Grisham, J. R., Steketee, G., & Frost, R. O. (2008). Interpersonal problems and emotional intelligence in compulsive hoarding. *Depression and Anxiety. 25,* 63–71.

Halliday, G., Banjaree, S., Philpot, M. & MacDonald, A. (2000). Community study of people who live in squalor. *Lancet, 355,* 882–886.

Halliday, G. & Snowdon, J. (2009). The Environmental Cleanliness and Clutter Scale (ECCS). *International Psychogeriatrics, 21,* 1041–1050.

Hartl, T. L., Frost, R. O., Allen, G. J., Deckersbach, T., Steketee, G., Duffany, S. R., & Savage, C. R. (2004). Actual and perceived memory deficits in individuals with compulsive hoarding. *Depression and Anxiety, 20,* 59–69.

Hartl, T. L., Duffany, S. R., Allen, G. J., Steketee, G., & Frost, R. O. (2005). Relationships among compulsive hoarding, trauma, and attention-deficit/hyperactivity disorder. *Behaviour Research and Therapy, 43,* 269–276.

Hasler G., LaSalle-Ricci V. H., Ronquillo J. G., Crawley S. A., Cochran L. W., Kazuba D., Greenberg B. D., & Murphy D. L. (2005). Obsessive-compulsive disorder symptom dimensions show specific relationships to psychiatric comorbidity. *Psychiatry Research, 135,* 121–132.

Hasler G., Pinto A., Greenberg B. D., Samuels J., Fyer A. J., Pauls D., Knowles J. A. McCracken J. T., Piacentini J., Riddle M. A., Rauch S. L., Rasmussen S. A., Willour V. L., Grados M. A., Cullen B., Bienvenu O. J., Shugart Y. Y., Liang K. Y., Hoehn-Saric R., Wang Y., Ronquillo J., Nestadt G., & Murphy D. L.; OCD Collaborative Genetics Study. (2007). Familiality of factor analysis-derived YBOCS dimensions in OCD-affected sibling pairs from the OCD Collaborative Genetics Study. *Biological Psychiatry, 61,* 617–625.

Hoarding of Animals Research Collective (HARC). (2000, April). People who hoard animals. *Psychiatric Times,* 25–29.

Hummelen, B., Wilberg, T., Pedersen, G., & Karterud, S. (2008). The quality of the DSM-IV obsessive-compulsive personality disorder construct as a prototype category. *Journal of Nervous and Mental Disease, 196,* 446–455.

Hwang, J.-P., Tsai, S.-J., Yang, C.-H., Liu, K.-M., & Lirng, J.-F. (1998). Hoarding behavior in dementia: A preliminary report. *American Journal of Geriatric Psychiatry, 6,* 285–289.

Jones, E. (1912). Anal erotic character traits. In *Papers on psychoanalysis* (1938). London: Tindall & Cox.

Kellett, S. & Knight, K. (2003). Does the concept of object-affect fusion refine cognitive-behavioral theories of hoarding? *Behavioural and Cognitive Psychotherapy, 31,* 457–461.

Kessler, R. C., McGonagle, K. A., Zhao, S., Nelson, C. B., Hughes, M., Eshleman, S., Whitchenn, H., et al. (1994). Lifetime and 12-month prevalence of DSM-III-R psychiatric disorders in the United States. Results from the National Comorbidity Survey. *Archives of General Psychiatry, 51,* 8–19.

Kim, H. J., Steketee, G., & Frost, R. O. (2001). Hoarding by elderly people. *Health and Social Work, 26,* 176–184.

Kishore, V. R., Samar, R., Reddy, Y. C. J., Chandrasekhar, C. R., & Thennarasu, K. (2004). Clinical characteristics and treatment response in poor and good insight obsessive-compulsive disorder. *European Psychiatry, 19,* 202–208.

Kyrios, M., Frost, R. O., & Steketee, G. (2004). Cognitions in compulsive buying and acquisition. *Cognitive Therapy and Research, 28,* 241–258.

LaSalle-Ricci, V. H., Arnkoff, D. B., Glass, C. R., Crawley, S. A., Ronquillo, J. G., & Murphy, D. L. (2006). The hoarding dimension of OCD: Psychological comorbidity and the five-factor personality model. *Behaviour Research and Therapy, 44,* 1503–1512.

Lawrence, N. S., Wooderson, S., Mataix-Cols, D., David, R., Speckens, A., & Phillips, M. L. (2006). Decision making and set shifting impairments are associated with distinct symptom dimensions in obsessive-compulsive disorder. *Neuropsychology, 20,* 409–419.

Leonard, H. L., Goldberger, E. L., Rapoport, J. L., Cheslow, D. H., & Swedo, S. E. (1990). Childhood rituals: Normal development or obsessive-compulsive symptoms? *Journal of the American Academy of Child and Adolescent Psychiatry, 29,* 17–23.

Lochner, C., Kinnear, C. J., Hemmings, S. M. J., Seller, C., Niehaus, D. J. H., Knowles, J. A., Daniels W., Moolman-Smook J. C. Seedat S., & Stein D. J. (2005). Hoarding in obsessive-compulsive disorder: Clinical and genetic correlates. *Journal of Clinical Psychiatry, 66,* 1155–1160.

Luchian, S. A., McNally, R. J., & Hooley, J. M. (2007). Cognitive aspects of nonclinical obsessive-compulsive hoarding. *Behaviour Research and Therapy, 45,* 1657–1662.

Luchins, D. J., Goldman, M. B., Lieb, M., & Hanrahan, P. (1992). Repetitive behaviors in chronically institutionalized schizophrenic patients. *Schizophrenia Research, 8,* 119–123.

Maier, T. (2004). On phenomenology and classification of hoarding: a review. *Acta Psychiatrica, 110,* 333–337.

Maina, G., Albert, U., Pessina, E., & Bogetto, F. (2007). Bipolar obsessive-compulsive disorder and personality disorders. *Bipolar Disorders, 9,* 722–729.

Masi, G., Perugi, G., Millepiedi, S., Toni, C., Mucci, M., Pfanner, C., Berloffa, S., Pari, C., & Akiskal, H.S. (2007). Bipolar co-morbidity in pediatric obsessive-compulsive disorder: Clinical and treatment implications. *Journal of Child and Adolescent Psychopharmacology, 17,* 475–486.

Mataix-Cols, D., Baer, L., Rauch, S. L., & Jenike, M. A. (2000). Relation of factor-analyzed symptom dimensions of obsessive-compulsive disorder to personality disorders. *Acta Psychiatrica Scandinavica, 102,* 199–202.

Mataix-Cols, D., Frost, R., Pertusa, A., Clark, L., Saxena, S., Leckman, J., et al. (2010). Hoarding disorder: A new diagnosis for DSM-V? *Depression and Anxiety, 27,* 556–572.

Mataix-Cols, D., Rosario-Campos, M. C., & Leckman, J. F. (2005). A multidimensional model of obsessive-compulsive disorder. *American Journal of Psychiatry, 162,* 228–238.

Mataix-Cols, D., Grayton, L., Bonner, A., Luscombe, C., Taylor, P., & van den Bree, M. B. M. (2008). *Prevalence and correlates of compulsive hoarding in a representative sample of homeless people.* Unpublished manuscript.

Mataix-Cols, D., Marks, I. M., Greist, J. H., Kobak, K. A., & Baer, L. (2002). Obsessive-compulsive symptom dimensions as predictors of compliance with and response to behaviour therapy: Results from a controlled trial. *Psychotherapy and Psychosomatics, 71,* 255–262.

Mataix-Cols, D., Rauch, S. L., Baer, L., Eisen, J. L., Shera, D. M., Goodman, W. K., Steven A. Rasmussen, S.A., & Jenike, M.A. (2002). Symptom stability in adult obsessive-compulsive disorder: Data from a naturalistic two-year follow-up study. *American Journal of Psychiatry, 159*, 263–268.

Mataix-Cols, D., Rauch, S. L., Manzo, P. A., Jenike, M. A., & Baer, L. (1999). Use of factor-analyzed symptom dimensions to predict outcome with serotonin reuptake inhibitors and placebo in the treatment of obsessive-compulsive disorder. *American Journal of Psychiatry, 156*, 1409–1416.

Mataix-Cols, D., Nakatani, E., Micali, N., & Heyman, I. (2008). Structure of obsessive-compulsive symptoms in pediatric OCD. *Journal of the American Academy of Child and Adolescent Psychiatry, 47*, 773–778.

Mataix-Cols, D., Wooderson, S., Lawrence, N., Brammer, M. J., Speckens, A., & Phillips, M. L. (2004). Distinct neural correlates of washing, checking, and hoarding symptom dimensions in obsessive-compulsive disorder. *Archives of General Psychiatry, 61*, 564–576.

Mathews, C. A., Jang, K. L., Herrera, L. D., Lowe, T. L., Budman, C. L., Erenberg, G., Naarden, A., Bruun, R., Schork, N., & Freimer, N. (2007). Tic symptom profiles in subjects with Tourette Syndrome from two genetically isolated populations. *Biological Psychiatry, 61*, 292–300.

Matsunaga, H., Kiriike, N., Matsui, T., Oya, K., Iwasaki, Y., Koshimune, K., Miyata, A., & Stein, D. J. (2002). Obsessive-compulsive disorder with poor insight. *Comprehensive Psychiatry, 43*, 150–157.

Matsunaga, H., Maebayashi, K., Hayashida, K., Okino, K., Matsui, T., Iketani, T., Kiriike, N., & Stein, D. J. (2008). Symptom structure in Japanese patients with obsessive-compulsive disorder. *American Journal of Psychiatry, 165*, 251–253.

McKay, D., Piacentini, J., Greisberg, S., Graae, F., Jaffer, M., & Miller, J. (2006). The structure of childhood obsessions and compulsions: Dimensions in an outpatient sample. *Behaviour Research and Therapy, 44*, 137–146.

Millet, B., Kochman, F., Gallarda, T., Krebs, M. O., Demonfaucon, F., Barrot, I., Bourderl, M.C., Olie, J. P., Loo, H., & Hantouche, E. G.(2004). Phenomenological and comorbid features associated in obsessive-compulsive disorder: Influence of age of onset. *Journal of Affective Disorders, 79*, 241–246.

Moll, G. H., Eysenbach, K., Woerner, W., Banaschewski, T., Schmidt, M. H., & Rothenberger, A. (2000). Quantitative and qualitative aspects of obsessive-compulsive behaviour in children with attention-deficit hyperactivity disorder compared with tic disorder. *Acta Psychiatrica Scandinavica, 101*, 389–394.

Mueller, A., Mitchell, J., Crosby, R., Glaesmer, H., & de Zwaan, M. (2009). The prevalence of compulsive hoarding and its association with compulsive buying in a German population-based sample. *Behaviour Research and Therapy, 47*, 705–709.

Mueller, A., Mueller, U., Albert, P., Mertens, C., Silbermann, A., Mitchell, J. E., & De Zwaan, M. (2007). Hoarding in a compulsive buying sample. *Behaviour Research and Therapy, 45*, 2754–2763.

Nakata, A. C. G., Diniz, J. B., Torres, A. R., de Mathis, M. A., Fossaluza, V., Braganças, C. A., & Ferrão, Y., & Miguel, E. C. (2007). Level of insight and clinical features of

obsessive-compulsive disorder with and without body dysmorphic disorder. *CNS Spectrums, 12*, 295–303.

Nestadt, G., Hus, F.-C., Samuels, J., Bienvenu, O. J., Reti, I., Costa Jr., P. T., & Eaton, W. W. (2006). Latent structure of the *Diagnostic and Statistical Manual of Mental Disorders, Fourth Edition* personality disorder criteria. *Comprehensive Psychiatry, 47*, 54–62.

Oh, M., Frost, R. O., Tolin, D. L., Steketee, G., & Fitch, K. E. (2008, Nov.). Indecisiveness and compulsive hoarding. Paper presented at the annual meeting of the Association for Behavioral and Cognitive Therapy, Orlando, FL.

Olatunji, B. O., Williams, B. J., Haslam, N., Abramowitz, J. S., & Tolin, D. F. (2008). The latent structure of obsessive-compulsive symptoms: A taxometric study. *Depression and Anxiety, 25*, 956–968.

Patronek, G. J. (1999). Hoarding of animals: An under-recognized public health problem in a difficult-to-study population. *Public Health Reports, 114*, 81–90.

Pertusa, A., Frost, R.O., Fullana, M.A., Samuels, J., Steketee, G., Tolin, D., Saxena, S., Leckman, J.F., & Mataix-Cols, D. (2010). Refining the boundaries of compulsive hoarding: a critical review. *Clinical Psychology Review, 30*, 371–386.

Pertusa, A., Fullana, M. A., Singh, S., Alonso, P., Menchón, J. M., & Mataix-Cols, D. (2008). Compulsive hoarding: OCD symptom, distinct clinical syndrome, or both? *American Journal of Psychiatry, 165*, 1289–1298.

Plimpton, E. H., Frost, R. O., Abbey, B. C., & Dorer, W. (2009). Compulsive hoarding in children: 6 case studies. *International Journal of Cognitive Therapy, 2*, 88–104.

Rasmussen, J. L., Steketee, G., Frost, R. O., & Tolin, D. L. (under review). Assessing squalor in compulsive hoarding: The Home Environment Index.

Rosario-Campos, M. C., Leckman, J. F., Mercadante, M. T., Shavitt, R. G., Prado, H.S., Sada, P., Zamignani, D., & Miguel, E. C. (2001). Adults with early-onset obsessive-compulsive disorder. *American Journal of Psychiatry, 158*, 1899–1903.

Rufer, M., Grothusen, A., Maß, R., Peter, H., & Hand, I. (2005). Temporal stability of symptom dimensions in adult patients with obsessive-compulsive disorder. *Journal of Affective Disorders, 88*, 99–102.

Rufer, M., Fricke, S., Moritz, S., Kloss, M., & Hand, I. (2006). Symptom dimensions in obsessive-compulsive disorder: Prediction of cognitive-behavior therapy outcome. *Acta Psychiatrica Scandinavica. 113*, 440–446.

Ruscio, A. M., Stein, D. J., Chiu, W.T., & Kessler, R. C. (2010). The epidemiology of obsessive-compulsive disorder in the National Comorbidity Survey Replication. *Molecular Psychiatry, 15*, 53–63.

Salzman, L. (1973). *The obsessive personality: Origins, dynamics and therapy*. New York: Jason Aronson, Inc.

Samuels, J., Bienvenu, O. J., Grados, M. A., Cullen, B., Riddle, M. A., Liang, K.-Y., Eaton, W.W., & Nestadt, G. (2008). Prevalence and correlates of hoarding behavior in a community-based sample. *Behaviour Research and Therapy, 46*, 836–844.

Samuels, J., Bienvenu, O. J., Pinto, A., Fyer, A. J., McCracken, J. T., Rauch, S. L., Murphy, D. L., Grados, M. A., Greenberg, B. D., Knowles, J. A., Piacentini, J., Cannistraro, P. A., Cullen, B., Riddle, M. A., Rasmussen, S. A., Pauls, D. L., Willour, V. L., Shugart, Y. Y., Liang, K., Hoehn-Saric, R., & Nestadt, G. (2007). Hoarding in obsessive-compulsive disorder: Results from the OCD Collaborative Genetics Study. *Behaviour Research and Therapy, 45,* 673–686.

Samuels, J., Bienvenu, O. J., Pinto, A., Murphy, D. L., Piacentini, J., Rauch, S. L., Fyer, A., Grados, M. A., Greenberg, B. D., Knowles, J. A., McCracken, J. T., Cullen, B., Riddle, M. A., Rasmussen, S. A., Pauls, D. L., Liang, K. Y., Hoehn-Saric, R., Pulver, A. E., & Nestadt, G. (2008). Sex-specific clinical correlates of hoarding in obsessive-compulsive disorder. *Behaviour Research and Therapy, 46,* 1040–1046.

Samuels, J., Bienvenu, O. J., Riddle, M. A., Cullen, B. A. M., Grados, M. A., Liang, K.-Y., Hoehn-Saric, R., & Nestadt, G. (2002). Hoarding in obsessive compulsive disorder: Results from a case-control study. *Behaviour Research and Therapy, 40,* 517–528.

Samuels, J., Shugart, Y. Y., Grados, M. A., Willour, V. L., Bienvenu, O. J., Greenberg, B. D., Knowles, J. A., McCracken, J. T., Rauch, S. L., Murphy, D. L., Want, Y., Pinto, A., Fyer, A. J., Piacentini, J., Pauls, D. L., Cullen, B., Rasmussen, S.A., Hoehn-Saric, R., Valle, D., Liang, K.-Y., Riddle, M. A., & Nestadt, G. (2007). Significant linkage to compulsive hoarding on chromosome 14 in families with obsessive-compulsive disorder: Results from the OCD Collaborative Genetics Study. *American Journal of Psychiatry, 164,* 493–499.

Saxena, S. (2008). Recent advances in compulsive hoarding. *Current Psychiatry Reports, 10,* 297–303.

Saxena, S., Bota, R. G., & Brody, A. L. (2001). Brain-behavior relationships in obsessive-compulsive disorder. *Seminars in Clinical Neuropsychiatry, 6,* 82–101.

Saxena, S., Brody, A. L., Maidment, K. M., & Baxter, L. R. (2007). Paroxetine treatment of compulsive hoarding. *Journal of Psychiatric Research, 41,* 481–487.

Saxena, S., Brody, A. L., Maidment, K. M., Smith, E. C., Zohrabi, N., Katz, E., et al. (2004). Cerebral glucose metabolism in obsessive-compulsive hoarding. *American Journal of Psychiatry, 161,* 1038–1048.

Saxena, S., Maidment, K. M., Vapnik, T., Golden, G., Rishwain, T., Rosen, R. M., Tarlow, G., & Bystritsky, A. (2002). Obsessive-compulsive hoarding: Symptom severity and response to multimodal treatment. *Journal of Clinical Psychiatry, 63,* 21–27.

Shah, A. K. (1990). Senile squalor syndrome: What to expect and how to treat it. *Geriatric Medicine, 20,* 26.

Shaw, P. (1957). The evidence of social breakdown in the elderly. *Journal for the Royal Society for the Promotion of Health: Royal Society of Health Journal, 77,* 823–830.

Seedat, S. & Stein, D. J. (2002). Hoarding in obsessive-compulsive disorder and related disorders: A preliminary report of 15 cases. *Psychiatry and Clinical Neurosciences, 56,* 17–23.

Snowdon, J. (1987). Uncleanliness among persons seen by community health workers. *Hospital and Community Psychiatry, 38,* 491–494.

Snowdon, J., Shah, A., & Halliday, G. (2007). Severe domestic squalor: A review. *International Psychogeriatrics, 19,* 37–51.

Snowdon, J. & Halliday, G. (2009). How and when to intervene in cases of severe squalor. *International Psychogeriatrics, 21,* 996–1002.

Stein, D. J., Anderson, E. W., & Overo, K. F. (2007). Response of symptom dimensions in obsessive-compulsive disorder to treatment with citalopram or placebo. *Revista Brasileira de Psiquiatria, 29,* 303–307.

Steketee, G. & Frost, R. (2003). Compulsive hoarding: Current status of the research. *Clinical Psychology Review, 23,* 905–927.

Steketee, G., Frost, R. O., & Kyrios, M. (2003). Cognitive aspects of compulsive hoarding. *Cognitive Therapy and Research, 27,* 463–479.

Steketee, G., Frost, R. O., Tolin, D. F., Rasmussen, J., & Brown, T. A. (2010). Wait-list controlled trial of cognitive-behavioral therapy for hoarding disorder. *Depression and Anxiety, 27,* 476–484.

Steketee, G., Frost, R. O., Wincze, J., Greene, K. A. I., & Douglass, H. (2000). Group and individual treatment of compulsive hoarding: A pilot study. *Behavioural and Cognitive Psychotherapy, 28,* 259–268.

Stewart, S. E., Rosario, M. C., Baer, L., Carter, A. S., Brown, T. A., Scharf, J. M., Illmann, C., Leckman, J. F., Sukhodolsky, D., Katsovich, L., Rasmussen, S., Goodman, W., Delorme, R., Leboyer, M., Chabane, N., Jenike, M. A., Geller, D. A., & Pauls, D. L. (2008). Four-factor structure of obsessive-compulsive disorder symptoms in children, adolescents, and adults. *Journal of the American Academy of Child and Adolescent Psychiatry, 47,* 763–772.

Storch, E. A., Lack, C. W., Merlo, L. J., Geffken, G. R., Jacob, M. L., Murphy, T. K., & Goodman, W. K. (2007). Clinical features of children and adolescents with obsessive-compulsive disorder and hoarding symptoms. *Comprehensive Psychiatry, 48,* 313–318.

Thordarson, D. S., Radomsky, A. S., Rachman, S., Shafran, R., Sawchuk, C. N., & Hakstian, A. R. (2004). The Vancouver Obsessional Compulsive Inventory (VOCI). *Behaviour Research and Therapy, 42,* 1289–1314.

Tolin, D. F., Brady, R. E., & Hannan, S. (2008). Obsessional beliefs and symptoms of obsessive-compulsive disorder in a clinical sample. *Journal of Psychopathology and Behavioral Assessment, 30,* 31–42.

Tolin, D. L., Frost, R. O., & Steketee, G. (2007). An open trial of cognitive-behavioral therapy for compulsive hoarding. *Behaviour Research and Therapy, 45,* 1461–1470.

Tolin, D. F., Frost, R. O., & Steketee, G. (2010). A brief interview for assessing compulsive hoarding: The Hoarding Rating Scale. *Psychiatry Research, 178(1),* 147–152.

Tolin, D. F., Frost, R. O., Steketee, G., & Fitch, K. E. (2008). Family burden of compulsive hoarding: Results of an internet survey. *Behaviour Research and Therapy, 46,* 334–344.

Tolin, D. F., Frost, R. O., Steketee, G., Gray, K. D., & Fitch, K. E. (2008). The economic and social burden of compulsive hoarding. *Psychiatry Research, 160,* 200–211.

Tolin, D. F., Kiehl, K. A., Worhunsky, G. A., Book, G. A., & Maltby, N. (2009). An exploratory study of the neural mechanisms of decision-making in compulsive hoarding. *Psychological Medicine, 39,* 325–336.

Tolin, D. F., Meunier, S. A., Frost, R. O., & Steketee, G. (2011). Hoarding among patients patients seeking treatment for anxiety disorders. *Journal of Anxiety Disorders, 25,* 43–48.

Tükel, R., Ertekin, E., Batmaz, S., Alyanak, F., Sözen, A., Aslanta, B., Atli, H., & Ozyildirim, I. (2005). Influence of age of onset on clinical features in obsessive-compulsive disorder. *Depression and Anxiety, 21,* 112–117.

Warren, L. W. & Ostrom, J. C. (1988). Pack rats: World-class savers. *Psychology Today, 22,* 58–62.

Wheaton, M., Timpano, K. R., LaSalle-Ricci, V. H., & Murphy, D. (2008). Characterizing the hoarding phenotype in individuals with OCD: Associations with comorbidity, severity, and gender. *Journal of Anxiety Disorders, 22,* 243–252.

Wincze, J. P., Steketee, G., & Frost, R. O. (2007). Categorization in compulsive hoarding. *Behaviour Research and Therapy, 45,* 63–72.

Winsberg, M. E., Cassic, K. S., & Koran, L. M. (1999). Hoarding in obsessive-compulsive disorder: A report of 20 cases. *Journal of Clinical Psychiatry, 60,* 591–597.

Wu, K. D. & Watson, D. (2005). Hoarding and its relation to obsessive-compulsive disorder. *Behaviour Research and Therapy, 43,* 897–921.

Phenomenology and Epidemiology of Tic Disorders and Trichotillomania

Emily J. Ricketts, Douglas W. Woods, Diana Antinoro, *and* Martin E. Franklin

Abstract

This chapter highlights the diagnostic features and clinical characteristics of tic disorders and Tourette syndrome, trichotillomania, and nailbiting, and their diagnostic distinction from OCD and other conditions. Nonclinical forms of these disorders are described. Information on the prevalence and limitations of epidemiological research is provided. The gender ratio, age of onset, longitudinal course, functional impairment, and healthcare utilization are described for each disorder. The cross-cultural features of the disorders are highlighted, and patterns of psychiatric comorbidity are discussed.

Keywords: Tourette syndrome, trichotillomania, nailbiting, nonclinical, differential diagnosis, prevalence, impairment, cross-cultural, comorbidity

Description and Diagnostic Features
Tic Disorders and Tourette Syndrome

Tics are sudden, recurrent, non-rhythmic, stereotyped movements or vocalizations, which can be described as simple or complex, and can occur in all parts of the body (American Psychiatric Association, 2000). Motor tics are repetitive contractions of muscle groups, while vocal tics are repetitive sounds. Simple motor tics are brief, sudden movements, and simple phonic tics are sudden, meaningless sounds. Complex motor tics are longer, sequenced, or more exaggerated movements, and complex vocal tics are longer in duration, more meaningful, and appear purposeful (APA, 2000).

Several diagnostic classifications exist for tic disorders. Chronic motor or vocal tic disorder consists of one or more motor or vocal tics (but not both) lasting longer than 12 months. When tics are present for longer than 4 weeks, but less than 12 months, a diagnosis of transient tic disorder is given. If two or more motor tics and one or more vocal tics are present for over 12 months, a diagnosis of Tourette syndrome (TS) is given. For tic presentations failing to meet the aforementioned criteria, an appropriate diagnosis would be tic disorder not otherwise specified (APA, 2000).

It is common for patients with tic disorders to experience uncomfortable sensations prior to tics. These premonitory urges are described as increasing tension in a certain part of the body, which is temporarily relieved following performance of the tic (Cohen & Leckman, 1992; Kwak, Dat-Vuong, & Jancovic, 2003; Leckman, Walker, & Cohen, 1993; Woods, Piacentini, Himle, & Chang, 2005). The prevalence of these urges is high. Cohen and Leckman found that 82% of child and adult subjects diagnosed with TS experienced premonitory urges preceding motor and vocal tics. Of these subjects, 57% thought the premonitory urges were more bothersome than the tics. In another study of 135 adult and child participants with tic disorders, 93% reported the presence of premonitory urges prior to tics, 84% felt performance of the tic relieved the urges, and 92% of the participants reported that their tics were either completely or partially a voluntary response to urges (Leckman et al., 1993).

Research on children below the age of 10 has shown that while these children experience premonitory urges, they may be inconsistent in their perception or report of the urge (Woods et al., 2005). Research has shown that day-to-day environmental factors can affect tic frequency (Conelea & Woods, 2008). In a study examining the effects of 29 environmental factors on TS symptoms in 14 youth, results indicated that the factors most commonly associated with tic decreases were sleeping, doctor visits, speaking with friends, and reading for pleasure. In contrast, factors primarily associated with an increase in tics included anxiety-provoking situations, emotional trauma, fatigue, watching television, being alone, and social gatherings (Silva, Munoz, Barickman, & Friedhoff, 1995). In another study of 76 adults with chronic tic disorders, intellectual work and socialization were found to be associated with increased tic occurrence. In contrast, study activity and passive attendance were associated with fewer tics (O'Connor, Brisebois, Brault, Robillard, & Loiselle, 2003). Other studies have shown that social attention contingent on tics can maintain tic frequency (Watson & Sterling, 1998), and that vocal tics increase when conversations pertain to tics (Woods, Watson, Wolfe, Twohig, & Friman, 2001).

Trichotillomania

Trichotillomania (TTM) has been defined as the recurrent pulling out of one's hair, resulting in noticeable hair loss, with an increasing sense of tension before pulling followed by a feeling of gratification or relief after the pulling episode (APA, 2000). Although preceding tension and subsequent relief are criteria in the DSM-IV-TR (APA, 2000), research has shown that not all patients who experience pulling-related hair loss report both tension and relief (Christenson, Mackenzie, & Mitchell, 1991). Children, in particular, may not report such experiences (Hanna, 1997; King et al., 1995a; Reeve, Bernstein, & Christenson, 1992; Wright & Holmes, 2003).

Pulling sites vary and include, from most to least common, the scalp, eyelashes, eyebrows, pubic region, face, and body (Cohen et al., 1995; Santhanam, Fairley, & Rogers, 2008; Schlosser, Black, Blum, & Goldstein, 1994). Individuals with TTM generally prefer to pull hairs that feel "coarse," "wiry," or "kinky," and it has been noted that sufferers usually pull out their hairs with their dominant hand. Use of a cosmetic aid, such as tweezers, is also common (Christenson, Mackenzie, et al., 1991; Greenberg & Sarner, 1965; Schlosser et al., 1994).

Many individuals with TTM engage in pre-pulling behaviors including hair touching, twirling or stroking (Casati, Toner, & Yu, 2000; du Toit, van Kradenburg, Niehaus, & Stein, 2001) and post-pulling rituals such as rubbing hair strands across their lips, examining, biting or chewing the root of the hair, and occasionally, tricophagy or hair ingestion (Christenson, Mackenzie, et al., 1991; Schlosser et al., 1994). In some cases, repeated ingestion of hair strands may lead to trichobezoars, which are large masses of hair found in the stomach and digestive tract that can cause several complications including constipation, diarrhea, poor appetite, and impairment in the functioning of the liver and pancreas (O'Sullivan, McGreal, Walsh, & Redmond, 1996; Sharma et al., 2000), and can require surgical intervention (Bouwer & Stein, 1998; Frey, McKee, King, & Martin, 2005).

Patients with TTM may experience a variety of affective states before, during, and following a pulling episode. In a nonclinical sample of 66 college students who engaged in hair pulling, the behavior was associated with decreases in tension, boredom, and sadness over the course of a pulling episode (Stanley, Borden, Mouton, & Breckenridge, 1995). In another study of adults with TTM, participants reported significant decreases in boredom, tension, and anxiety, and significant increases in guilt, relief, sadness, and anger across a pulling episode (Diefenbach, Mouton-Odum, & Stanley, 2002). In children, it has been recently shown that first pulling episodes were associated with both pleasure and pain, while recent episodes were associated with pleasure, suggesting that the punishing quality of hair pulling diminishes over time (Meunier, Tolin, & Franklin, 2009). Although some episodes of pulling are related to emotional variables, this does not appear to be true for all pulling episodes. Recent studies have suggested that there may be multiple styles or functions of pulling. At least two distinct styles have been noted, including focused and automatic hair pulling. Focused pulling usually involves a conscious effort to pull, and includes using pulling to regulate emotion. In contrast, automatic pulling involves a lack of awareness of the pulling, and generally occurs during sedentary activities such as watching television, reading, or driving (Christenson & Crow, 1996; Christenson, Mackenzie, et al., 1991). It is believed that those with TTM exhibit both styles, though they may have a greater tendency toward one or the other (Flessner et al., 2008).

Research on the phenomenological differences between the different pulling styles is limited. In a study examining styles of hair pulling in 47 outpatient chronic hair pullers, findings indicated that participants who were predominantly focused pullers reported pulling from the pubic region at higher rates than automatic pullers (du Toit et al., 2001). Recent findings on phenomenological differences in pulling styles among adults indicated that participants who were high in focused pulling but low in automatic pulling were less likely to pull from the scalp and more likely to pull from the eyebrows, eyelashes, and pubic area, in comparison to those who were low in both focused and automatic pulling. Participants who were high in both focused and automatic pulling were more likely to report eyebrows as the most frequent hair pulling site than those who were low in both focused and automatic hair pulling (Flessner et al., 2008).

Nailbiting

Nailbiting, also known as onychophagia, has not been defined in the DSM-IV-TR (APA, 2000). However, it can be classified as a stereotypic movement disorder and involves repetitive contact between the nails (finger or toe) and the mouth or teeth, in the form of biting and chewing (Leung & Robson, 1990). Individuals engaging in this behavior usually bite the nails of all ten fingers with no selective preference (Malone & Massler, 1952). The degree of severity of nailbiting ranges from mild, in which nails come into contact with the teeth, to a severe form, in which nails are bitten down to the nail bed and may bleed (Leonard, Lenane, Swedo, Rettew, & Rapoport, 1991; Wells, Haines, & Williams, 1998).

Research has suggested a link between various mood states and nailbiting. In a study of 139 men and women, those who regarded their nailbiting as a serious problem had higher manifest anxiety and obsessive compulsive scores than those who regarded their behavior as mild, suggesting that nailbiting is anxiety-related (Joubert, 1993). This link between tension and nailbiting is consistent with the tension reduction model of nailbiting, which posits that individuals bite their nails to reduce tension during times of situational stress (DeFrancesco, Zahner, & Pawelkiewicz, 1989; Wells et al., 1998). Contrary to findings suggesting a link between tension/anxiety and nailbiting, a study of 14 individuals with severe onychophagia, completed by 14 subjects, found that none met current criteria for an affective or anxiety disorder. Additionally, many subjects thought the nailbiting itself was a cause rather than a symptom of their distress, leading the authors to conclude that nailbiting does not stem from underlying anxiety (Leonard et al., 1991).

A few studies have examined the link between other affective states and nailbiting. In an examination of repetitive behaviors in preschool children, findings indicated that increases in habits, including nailbiting, were associated with structured times in the day and negative mood states (Foster, 1998). In another study, activities that were perceived as "inactive" were associated with greater rates of nailbiting (O'Connor et al., 2003). Using a more experimental approach, Williams, Rose, and Chisholm (2007) compared the frequency of nailbiting among 40 undergraduate college students in 4 conditions including: boredom, in which the participant was left alone; frustration, in which the participant solved math problems; contingent attention, in which the participant was reprimanded for nailbiting; and noncontingent attention, in which the participant engaged in continuous conversation. Findings indicated that nailbiting occurred most often in the boredom and frustration conditions. Nailbiting occurred least often when people were engaged in social interaction, or were reprimanded for the behavior (Williams et al., 2007). Although there appears to be a link between negative emotional states and nailbiting, the direction of the relationship is unclear. Nevertheless, one recent study suggests that nailbiting may function to manage tension as measured via psychophysiological recording (Wells, Haines, Williams, & Brain, 1999).

Nonclinical Forms of the Conditions
Tic Disorders and Tourette Syndrome

Tics are common and often benign in childhood, occurring in about 5% to 34% of children (Gadow, Nolan, Sprafkin, & Schwartz, 2002; Khalifa & von Knorring, 2003; Kurlan et al., 2002; Peterson, Pine, Cohen, & Brook, 2001; Stefanoff et al., 2008). Due to their transient nature, these tics often do not result in a formal diagnosis, rarely require medication, and usually improve on their own. Transient tics usually do not cause significant impairment in the individual's academic achievement, social interactions, or daily activities, and may not be audible or noticed by others. In contrast to most psychological disorders in the DSM-IV (APA, 2000), tic disorders do not require clinically significant impairment.

Trichotillomania

Hair manipulation in the form of twirling, stroking, and pulling is quite common, and in several instances it has been associated with habits such as thumb sucking and nailbiting (Byrd, Richards, Hove, & Friman, 2002; Deaver, Miltenberger, & Stricker, 2001; Knell & Moore, 1988; Santhanam et al., 2008; Watson & Allen, 1993). In children, transient hair-pulling episodes are common and often go unreported. Some have suggested that early-onset (i.e., age 2–3 years) hair pulling may be better characterized as a benign habit with a shorter course as opposed to TTM, which usually has a later age of onset (Byrd et al; Santhanam et al; Wright & Holmes, 2003). However, research has not empirically confirmed the differences, either in function or prognosis, between early and later onset pulling.

Nonclinical forms of hair pulling have been studied in college student and community samples, with results generally showing that pulling does not always result in noticeable hair loss, impairment, and distress. Findings from such studies suggest that nonclinical hair pulling might be distinct from TTM (Stanley, Borden, Bell, & Wagner, 1994; Stanley et al., 1995). For example, a study comparing emotion regulation in clinical and nonclinical hair pullers found that during and after a pulling episode, nonclinical hair pullers reported larger increases than the clinical group in happiness, calm feelings, and relief throughout the pulling episode, whereas the clinical group reported larger increases than the nonclinical controls in sadness, guilt, and anger, and larger decreases in boredom (Diefenbach, Tolin, Meunier, & Worhunsky, 2008). More recent findings were generally congruent with the Diefenbach et al. study, showing that more severe pullers experienced affective states at higher frequencies than low-severity pullers (Duke, Keeley, Ricketts, Geffken, & Storch, 2010).

Nailbiting

Nonclinical nailbiting is quite common in children and adults, occurring in up to 51% of the population (Birch, 1955; Deardorff, Finch, & Royall, 1974; Foster, 1998; Odenrick & Brattström, 1985; Teng, Woods, Twohig, & Marcks, 2002). Due to the transient nature of nonclinical nailbiting, it is less likely to result in bleeding or severe damage to the nail bed than more severe forms of the behavior (Wells et al., 1998).

Diagnostic Distinction from OCD and Other Conditions
Tic Disorders and Tourette Syndrome
Complex motor tics associated with TS can be difficult to distinguish from symptoms of obsessive compulsive disorder (OCD). Like compulsions,

complex tics may appear intentional and produce a sense of relief (Mansueto & Keuler, 2005). However, research suggests that there are phenomenological differences in the antecedents to the primary symptoms of the two disorders. Sensory urges and vague somatic tension are associated with TS, while physiological arousal and specific cognitions are linked to obsessive compulsive behavior (Miguel et al., 1995; Miguel et al., 1997; Miguel et al., 2000; Scahill, Leckman, & Marek, 1995; Shapiro & Shapiro, 1992).

Tic disorders also may be confused with hyperkinetic movement disorders (e.g., Huntington's chorea, Parkinson's disease, and hemiballismus; Kompoliti & Goetz, 1998), or with a stereotypic movement disorder, which is defined as repetitive and nonfunctional motor behavior that may interfere with normal activities or result in self-inflicted harm. Stereotypies are more common among children with mental retardation, and may include such movements as head banging, hand waving, body rocking, and twirling objects. However, unlike many tics, stereotypic movements generally appear more rhythmic and intentional (APA, 2000). When working with nonverbal children or adults, identifying the distinction between the positively reinforcing stimulatory behavior and the negatively reinforcing tic behavior is a challenge. Although not part of the diagnostic criteria for tic disorders, recent research suggests that many individuals with TS experience impulsive, aggressive outbursts sometimes called "rage attacks." This feature may be confused with symptoms of oppositional defiant disorder, which is defined as a pattern of hostile, uncooperative, defiant behavior toward people of authority (APA, 2000; Budman, Bruun, Park, Lesser, & Olson, 2000; Wand, Matazow, Shady, Furer, & Staley, 1993).

Trichotillomania
TTM is phenomenologically similar to OCD, because both TTM and OCD patients experience urges that are relieved by engaging in repetitive behaviors (Stein, Simeon, Cohen, & Hollander, 1995). However, while OCD patients tend to have multiple symptoms that can change in focus over time (Besiroglu et al., 2007; Rufer, Grothusen, Maszlig, Peter, & Hand, 2005), patients with TTM usually present with only the symptom of hair pulling, which does not progress into non-self-injurious rituals (Lochner et al., 2005). Additionally, intrusive thoughts are a central feature of OCD, while relatively few TTM patients experience obsessive thoughts as a precursor to hair pulling (Stein et al.,

1995; Swedo & Leonard, 1992). Furthermore, while both the performance of rituals in OCD, and hair-pulling behaviors in trichotillomania, may function to reduce an aversive state, TTM also includes a positively reinforcing component. Further evidence of the distinction between TTM and OCD can be found in results from an analysis of 60 adult chronic hair pullers, in which only 15% of the sample reported being fully aware of their behavior. The majority lacked full awareness of their hair pulling, in contrast to those with OCD, who engage in compulsions that are purposeful in nature (Christenson, Mackenzie, et al., 1991).

Like individuals with TTM, some patients with body dysmorphic disorder (BDD) will remove their body hair in attempt to improve an imagined defect in their appearance. Although patients with BDD may experience hair pulling, individuals with TTM do not typically pull their hair in response to imagined defects in their appearance (APA, 2000).

TTM may also be misdiagnosed as alopecia areata, a medical condition in which hair is lost from areas of the body, most often the scalp (Madani & Shapiro, 2000). In contrast to those with TTM, changes in the appearance of nails can be noticed in patients with alopecia areata including nail thinning, nail pitting, onychomadesis, and severe nail plate surface irregularities (Tosti, Morelli, Bardazzi, & Peluso, 1994). TTM may also be confused with tinea capitis, a disease caused by fungal infection of the scalp, skin, and eyebrows. Distinguishing features of this disease are a scaly scalp, and infected hairs that can be easily extracted from the scalp (Gupta & Summerbell, 2000).

Nailbiting

In certain cases, nailbiting might be a symptom of OCD; however, as a stereotypic movement disorder, it is distinct from OCD. Patients with OCD experience a range of symptoms, but those who engage in nailbiting suffer from one symptom, and generally do not experience associated intrusive thoughts (APA, 2000). In diagnosing an individual with onychophagia, it is important to distinguish associated nail damage from that of childhood nail diseases, including 20-nail dystrophy, lichen planus, onychomycosis, and leukonychia (de Berker, 2006).

Prevalence, and Limitations of Epidemiological Research
Tic Disorders and Tourette Syndrome

Epidemiological research on tic disorders is limited. Due to the varying sample sizes, diagnostic criteria, and age ranges used in studies, prevalence rates have been difficult to ascertain. In a sample of 166 school children ages 13 to 14, 3% met criteria for TS (Mason, Banerjee, Eapen, Zeitlin, & Robertson, 1998). In a community sample of 4475 children, 0.6% had TS, 0.8% had chronic motor tics, 0.5% had chronic vocal tics, and 4.8% had transient tics, yielding a total prevalence rate of 6.6% (Khalifa & von Knorring, 2003). In a study sample comprising 68 primary school children with tic disorders, a prevalence rate of 5.5% was found (Lanzi, et al., 2004). Unfortunately, there is a paucity of research examining the epidemiology of TS in minority populations.

Trichotillomania

Most of the research on the prevalence of TTM has been performed on college student samples. A study examining the prevalence of TTM in college students yielded a rate of 0.6% among the 2534 participants. However, 4.9% of the sample reported hair pulling that resulted in visible hair loss, but that did not meet DSM-III-R (APA, 1987) criteria for TTM (Christenson, Pyle, & Mitchell, 1991). A recent estimate of the prevalence of TTM in college students is slightly higher, at 0.76% (Duke et al., 2010). An examination of the prevalence of TTM in a community sample yielded rates of 0.6% for those meeting diagnostic criteria, and 1.2% for individuals with clinically significant hair pulling (Duke, Bodzin, Tavares, Geffken, & Storch, 2009). Milder forms of hair pulling have prevalence rates generally ranging from 10% to 15.3% in college students (Duke et al., 2010; Rothbaum, Shaw, Morris, & Ninan, 1993; Stanley et al., 1994; Woods, Miltenberger, & Flach, 1996), and 6.5% in a community sample (Duke et al., 2009). Few studies have assessed the prevalence of TTM in children. However, one such study found a prevalence rate of 9.25% among 10 clinically referred infants and toddlers (Wright & Holmes, 2003). TTM prevalence appears similar to populations with disabilities. Researchers surveyed 259 parents and direct care staff and found that 5% of the persons with disabilities had TTM (Long, Miltenberger, & Rapp, 1998). Likewise, in an examination of 457 children and adolescents with mental retardation, TTM was identified in 3.06% of the sample (Dimoski & Duricić, 1991).

Nailbiting

The epidemiological literature on nailbiting has several limitations. Findings on gender ratio and prevalence rates are inconsistent across studies, and the lack of an official operational definition has contributed to these inconsistencies. Likewise, much of the literature on nailbiting is older, and a variety of study designs were employed. Existing studies that have been conducted suggest that nailbiting is common, with prevalence rates ranging from 6% to 51% (Birch, 1955; Ballinger, 1970; Deardorff, Finch, & Royall, 1974; Foster, 1998; Odenrick & Brattström, 1985; Pennington, 1945; Shetty & Munshi, 1998; Teng et al., 2002). When considering severe and problematic nailbiting in children, prevalence rates up to 14% have been reported (Ghanizadeh, 2008; Odenrick & Brattström, 1985).

Demographics
Tic Disorders and Tourette Syndrome
Gender Ratio, Marital and Socioeconomic Status. Research has shown that TS is more common in boys than girls. In various studies, findings have generally shown that at all ages, more males than females have TS, with ratios ranging from 3–9:1 (Burd, Kerbeshian, Wikenheiser, & Fisher, 1986; Caine et al., 1988; Comings & Comings, 1985; Elstner, Selai, Trimble, & Robertson, 2001; Freeman et al., 2000; Khalifa & von Knorring, 2003; Shapiro, Shapiro, & Wayne, 1972). Although few studies have found a significant association between marital status and the presence of tic disorders or TS, one study found that more women with TS were married than men with TS (Shapiro et al., 1972). To date, no studies have found a relationship between TS and socioeconomic status (Khalifa & von Knorring, 2005; Shapiro et al., 1972).

Age of Onset and Longitudinal Course. The mean age of onset for tic symptoms ranges from 5.6 to 7.6 (Comings & Comings, 1985; Freeman et al., 2000; Janik, Kalbarczyk, & Sitek, 2007; Leckman et al., 1998; Lees, Robertson, Trimble, & Murray, 1984). Initial tic symptoms usually occur in the face and head, beginning with eye blinking, nose twitching, or head jerking tics, and then progressing in a rostral caudal manner to the shoulders, midsection, and legs (Coming & Comings, 1985, Leckman, Peterson, Pauls, & Cohen, 1997). Tics are usually performed in short-term bouts or bursts. Over time, tics generally wax and wane, increasing and decreasing in severity (Leckman, Bloch, Scahill, & King, 2006; Peterson & Leckman, 1998). Research shows that tic symptoms reach peak severity at the average age of 10.6. During adolescence, the vast majority of TS patients experience a decrease in tic symptoms, although increased tic severity in childhood is associated with increased tic severity an average of 3.8 to 12.8 years later (Bloch et al., 2006; Bloch & Leckman, 2009). In an investigation of the course of tic severity for 36 patients with TS, researchers found that after onset at a mean of age 5.6, tics progressively worsened until age 10.0, when they reached their most severe period. For 8 patients, the frequency and forcefulness of the tics during this period were severe enough to impede academic functioning. In almost all cases, tics steadily declined following this severe period, and by the age of 18, almost 50% of the sample were tic-free (Leckman et al., 1998).

In contrast to the aforementioned studies, a longitudinal study of 31 adults with TS utilized objective assessment to determine the change in tic severity following an average period of 16.2 years (Pappert, Goetz, Louis, Blasucci, & Leurgans, 2003). Results showed that tics persisted into adulthood for 90% of the sample. However, tic disability and motor tic severity decreased from childhood to adulthood. Interestingly, 50% of adult patients who considered themselves tic-free were incorrect when compared to objective observation. In another longitudinal study of 58 adults with TS diagnosed in childhood, results showed that tics persisted in all patients, with 24% having moderate to severe tics and 76% having mild tics (Goetz, Tanner, Stebbins, Leipziq, & Carr, 1992). Finally, in an evaluation of the course of tics over a 5-year period, researchers found that 65% of the 11–53-year-old sample (n=23) experienced no change in tic severity, 13% experienced an improvement, and 5% experienced a worsening in tic severity, suggesting the stability of tic symptoms over time (de Groot, Bornstein, Spetie, & Burriss, 1994).

Healthcare Utilization. There have been few studies examining healthcare utilization among those with TS. However, in a survey of 763 patients with TS, researchers found that 71.2% of the sample had taken medication for TS during some period of their lives (Bornstein, Stefl, & Hammond, 1990). Haloperidol was the most commonly used medication, with 50.7% of patients reporting this course of treatment. A noteworthy finding was that 28.8% of the participants reported never taking medications for their TS symptoms. Recent findings from independent surveys of 672 adults and 740 parents of children with TS showed that, of those who reported having ever received treatment for tics, 92.7% of the adult sample and 82.9% of the youth sample indicated that they had received medication

(Woods, Conelea, & Himle, 2010). Additionally, 17.2% of the adult sample, and 23.6% of the youth sample reported having received behavioral or cognitive-behavioral treatment. In this study, the main sources of treatment or consultation for tics among adults, from most to least common, were neurologists (35%), primary care physicians (27.5%), psychiatrists (17.2%), psychologists (4.9%), and therapists/counselors (3.2%). Among the youth sample, the first treatment providers contacted were primary care physicians (59.3%), neurologists (40.2%), psychiatrists (20.5%), psychologists (17.2%), and therapists (9.8%).

Trichotillomania

Gender Ratio and Age of Onset. The onset of TTM commonly occurs between the ages of 10.7 and 13 (Christenson, Mackenzie, et al., 1991; Christenson, Mackenzie, & Mitchell, 1994; Cohen et al., 1995), but ranges from the first year of life (Altman, Grahs, & Friman, 1982; Christenson, Mackenzie, et al., 1991) to the beginning of the seventies (Greenberg & Sarner, 1965). In adult samples, TTM predominantly affects females, with ratios ranging from 7.3–9.3: 1 (Christenson, Mackenzie et al., 1991; Cohen et al., 1995; Muller, 1987; Woods et al., 2006). In children, it is unclear if the female to male gender ratio is as pronounced. For example, in 52 preschool children with TTM, almost half (46.2%) were male (Muller, 1987), and among 28 children aged 12 and under, 50% were found to be male (Chang, Lee, Chiang, & Lü, 1991). Nevertheless, some studies have continued to suggest that the gender ratio is heavily skewed toward females, even in young populations. In one study of 21 children with TTM, 71% were girls (Cohen et al., 1995; Oranje, Peereboom-Wynia, & De Raeymaecker, 1986; Reeve et al., 1992; Santhanam et al., 2008).

Reasons for the female to male ratio are unclear, but one possible explanation is that treatment-seeking behavior may be higher in women than in men (Christenson, Mackenzie, et al., 1991; Cohen et al., 1995). Likewise, for men with TTM, hair loss may be attributed to male pattern baldness and therefore perceived as more socially acceptable. Also, men who pull from the beard or mustache can prevent the behavior by shaving these areas (Christenson, Mackenzie, et al., 1991).

Longitudinal Course. Research on the longitudinal course of TTM is limited. However, studies suggest that with an early childhood onset, the duration of the disorder is brief, usually resolving on its own and requiring minimal treatment (Santhanam et al., 2008; Swedo & Leonard, 1992; Winchel, 1992; Wright & Holmes, 2003). One recent study has suggested that if the duration of TTM was less than 6 months, patients were able to easily resolve the behavior. However, if the duration of was greater than 6 months, patients experienced a chronic and treatment-resistant course (Chang et al., 1991).

Healthcare Utilization. Although research on healthcare utilization is limited, a survey among 1697 individuals with TTM showed that pharmacotherapy was the most commonly sought treatment. The second most commonly sought treatment was behavior therapy. Overall, patients perceived treatment as ineffective (Woods et al., 2006). In another study, researchers found that participants with TTM often sought help from multiple healthcare professionals, most commonly psychologists (Wetterneck, Woods, Norberg, & Begotka, 2006).

Nailbiting

Age of Onset, Gender Ratio, and Longitudinal Course. The literature on gender and nailbiting is limited and mixed, with some studies showing a higher preponderance of the behavior in females than males (Bakwin, 1971; Foster, 1998; Shetty & Munshi, 1998), some showing a higher preponderance in males (Ghanizadeh, 2008; Joubert, 1993), and some showing no gender differences (Coleman & McCalley, 1948; Odenrick & Brattström, 1985). Few studies report an age of onset for nailbiting. However, in a recent study of 63 children and adolescents who engaged in nailbiting, the reported mean age of onset was 9.4 years (Ghanizadeh). Research on the longitudinal course of nailbiting is also limited, but a recent study of preschool children found that habits such as nailbiting decreased as age increased (Foster, 1998).

Patterns of Mental Health Comorbidity
Tic Disorders and Tourette Syndrome

Tic disorders can be comorbid with a range of Axis I disorders. Research has shown that the most common comorbid condition is ADHD, with rates ranging from 12% to 60% (Freeman & The Tourette Syndrome International Database Consortium, 2007; Janik et al., 2007; Khalifa & von Knorring, 2006; Robertson, Banerjee, Eapen, & Fox-Hiley, 2002; Termine et al. 2006; Wodrich, Benjamin, & Lachar, 1997). Tic disorders frequently co-occur with OCD, as recent studies have found rates of

OCD in TS samples of 22.3% (Freeman & The Tourette Syndrome International Database Consortium), 30% (King, Leckman, Scahill, & Cohen, 1999), and 41.2% (Termine et al.). TS is also comorbid with anxiety disorders and mood disorders, with respective rates of 16.8% and 16.9% (Freeman & The Tourette Syndrome International Database Consortium). Comorbidity rates as high as 73% have been reported for major depressive disorder (MDD) in particular (Snijders, Robertson, & Orth, 2006; Wodrich et al.).

A significant number of children with TS also experience rage attacks. In an investigation comparing 37 children with TS and rage attacks, and 31 children with TS only, results showed that children with TS and rage attacks were more likely to have comorbid conditions including ADHD, OCD and oppositional defiant disorder (ODD; Budman et al., 2000; Budman, Bruun, Park, & Olson, 1998). This finding is supported by a clinical analysis of 126 cases by Janik et al. (2007) in which results indicated that anger control problems were strongly associated with psychiatric comorbidity. In addition, Comings and Comings (1985) found that 61% of their sample of 250 patients experienced significant discipline problems and problems with anger and violence, and parents most commonly complained that their children often had a short temper and were confrontational. Additionally, autism spectrum disorders are associated with tic disorders and occur more often than by chance. In a study of 105 children and adolescents with autism spectrum disorders, 22% had tic disorders, with 11% having co-occurring TS and 11% having co-occurring chronic motor tics (Canitano & Vivanti, 2007).

Limited research has suggested that TS is also associated with greater risk of Axis II disorders. Schizotypal personality traits are fairly common in people who have TS. In an evaluation of 102 subjects with TS, 15% of the subjects were diagnosed with schizotypal personality disorder (Cavanna, Robertson, & Critchley, 2007).

Trichotillomania

TTM is commonly comorbid with other psychiatric disorders. In a study of 123 hair pullers, 15% had co-occurring anxiety disorders, 14% had comorbid depressive disorders, and 13% had comorbid OCD (Cohen et al., 1995). In a sample of older children, adolescents, and adults with TTM, 39% had comorbid depression, 32% had comorbid generalized anxiety disorder (GAD), 16%

had comorbid OCD, and 15% had comorbid substance abuse (Swedo & Leonard, 1992). In an analysis of 22 chronic hair pullers, Schlosser and colleagues (1994) found that almost two-thirds of the sample met criteria for a major psychiatric disorder, particularly anxiety and mood disorders, and 55% of the subjects met criteria for a personality disorder. Similar findings were noted in a sample of 48 female outpatients with TTM. Researchers found that 42% of the sample met criteria for a personality disorder (Christenson, Chernoff-Clementz, & Clementz, 1992). In a sample of 60 adults with TTM, Christenson, Mackenzie, and Mitchell (1991) found lifetime prevalence rates of 57%, 65%, 20%, and 32% for anxiety disorders, mood disorders, eating disorders, and substance use disorders respectively. Additionally, in a sample of 44 adults diagnosed with TTM, Diefenbach et al. (2002) found that 55% were diagnosed with one or more comorbid anxiety or depressive disorders. Further support for psychiatric comorbidity is provided by a sample of 1697 individuals meeting criteria for TTM showing rates of anxious and depressive symptoms higher than nonpsychiatric controls (Woods et al., 2006).

There is limited research on psychiatric comorbidity in children with TTM. A study of 15 child and adolescent hair pullers found that 47% had comorbid disruptive behavior disorders, 20% had comorbid anxiety disorders including OCD and GAD, and 13% had a chronic tic disorder (King et al., 1995a). In another sample of 10 children, rates of anxiety disorders were higher. Researchers found that 60% had comorbid GAD and 20% had comorbid dysthymia (Reeve et al., 1992). In a recent study assessing hair pulling in 38 children, findings indicated that 40% had a comorbid disorder including separation anxiety, depression, pervasive developmental disorder, adjustment reaction, abuse, and anxiety. However, 60% did not meet criteria for an additional diagnosis (Santhanam et al., 2008). Finally, in a sample of 133 children the most common comorbid disorders were anxiety disorder (24.1%), mood disorder (18.8%), and attention deficit disorder with or without hyperactivity (16.5%; Franklin et al., 2008).

Nailbiting

Several studies have examined the relationship between nailbiting and anxiety, but there have been no known studies analyzing psychiatric comorbidity in adults with nailbiting. The first known study to analyze psychiatric comorbidity among children and adolescents who engaged in nailbiting assessed 63 participants who were referred to a mental healthcare clinic. Nailbiting was found to be comorbid with ADHD (74.6%), ODD (36%), social phobia (20.6%), enuresis (15.6%), tic disorder (12.7%) and OCD (11.1%), MDD (6.7%), mental retardation (9.5%), and pervasive developmental disorder (PDD; 3.2%). The rate of general psychiatric comorbidity was higher in boys than in girls. Additionally, the severity and frequency of nailbiting were not associated with any comorbid psychiatric disorder (Ghanizadeh, 2008).

Functional Impairment
Tic Disorders and Tourette Syndrome
Children and adults with TS often experience impairment in several domains of functioning (i.e., overall quality of life, social, academic, work, family). Research has been conflicted on whether functional impairment is a result of tics in themselves, or common psychiatric comorbidity.

Individuals with TS commonly report impairment in their general quality of life. In an examination of quality of life in 59 children and adolescents with TS, children with tics received lower quality of life scores than healthy controls across multiple domains (i.e., psychosocial, emotional, social, and school) and these scores were moderately and negatively associated with the severity of tic symptoms (Storch et al., 2007b). In another study, youth with TS had significantly lower quality of life than a general sample. Results suggested that the various quality of life domains were influenced by employment status, severity of tics, OCD, depression, and anxiety (Elstner et al., 2001). A more recent study supports previous findings, showing that children with TS experience worse quality of life than healthy controls, and poorer quality of life was associated with higher rates of ADHD and obsessive compulsive symptoms (Cutler, Murphy, Gilmour, & Heyman, 2009). Similarly to studies of quality of life in children, Müller-Vahl and colleagues (2010) found that adults with TS had lower quality of life scores compared to healthy controls, with the most common problems relating to anxious and depressive symptoms, physical pain and discomfort, daily activities, mobility, and self-care.

Beyond broad indices measuring quality of life, research also suggests that individuals with TS commonly experience deficits in social functioning, including difficulties in dating, making and keeping friends, psychosocial stress, peer rejection, negative social perceptions, lower social acceptability, social withdrawal, teasing and low popularity, and aggression (Champion, Fulton, & Shady, 1988; Elstner et al., 2001; Lin et al., 2007; Packer, 2005; Stokes, Bawden, Camfield, Backman, & Dooley, 1991; Marcks, Woods, & Ridosko, 2005; Storch et al., 2007a, 2007c; Woods, Fuqua, & Outman, 1999). Studies have suggested that both the increase in complexity and frequency of tics (Woods et al., 1999) along with the tic topography (motor vs. vocal; Champion et al.) is directly correlated to the increasingly negative impact on social relationships and functioning.

Impairments in academic functioning in those with TS are also commonly reported. For example, a survey of 71 patients/guardians of children with TS found that 50% of the sample reported moderate to significant academic impairment from tics including interference in reading and writing, and avoidance of handwritten work and reading alone or aloud in class (Packer, 2005). Likewise, in a sample of 59 youth with TS, 36% of children were reported as having impairment in academic functioning due to tics, including difficulties in writing during class, doing homework, concentrating on work, and being prepared for class (Storch et al., 2007a).

Few studies have examined occupational impairment among individuals with TS. However, in a sample of 75 patients with TS, results indicated that 25% had difficulty obtaining a job, and 34% had difficulty keeping a job (Jagger et al., 1982). Among patients who were employed full time, 11% reported that their job performance was moderately affected by TS, 15% substantially, and 7% severely. In a survey examining employment in 462 adults with TS, results showed an unemployment rate of 15.5% (Shady, Broder, Staley, Furer, Brezden-Papadopolos, 1995). Approximately 50% of the sample reported that TS influenced their choice of occupation either moderately or greatly. Over 20% reported being fired from their jobs, 17% reported being denied a job, and 12% felt that they did not receive promotions due to TS. Approximately 20% of the sample reported moderate to great job dissatisfaction, and 17% reported mixed feelings. Elstner et al. (2001) provides further support for TS-related occupational impairment, finding an unemployment rate of 32%.

Family functioning can also be negatively affected. Problems have been found with increased caregiver burden, difficulty solving family problems, less family cohesion, and interference with the daily activities of family members (Bawden, Stokes,

Camfield, Camfield, & Salisbury, 1998; Cooper, Robertson, & Livingston, 2003; Hubka, Fulton, Shady, Champion, & Wand, 1988; Storch et al., 2007a).

While research has shown that tics alone can cause impairment in functioning, several studies provide support for the hypothesis that comorbidities, rather than tics, are responsible for resultant psychosocial impairment. In 98 adults with TS, Thibert, Day and Sandor (1995) showed that those with TS and obsessive compulsive symptoms had significantly lower self-concepts and greater social anxiety than subjects with TS alone. Likewise, Wilkinson et al. (2001) showed that families of children with TS and comorbid conditions experienced greater impairment than families having children only diagnosed with TS. Wilkinson, Marshall, and Curtwright (2008) also showed that self-reported stress was higher in parents of children with TS and a comorbid disorder than in parents of children with TS alone. In a study assessing tic persistence and tic-associated impairment in 50 children and adolescents with TS, results showed that from baseline to 2-year follow-up, the percentage of youth meeting criteria for tic persistence remained the same, while the percentage meeting criteria for tic impairment decreased significantly in proportion. This suggests that tic persistence and impairment may not be associated (Coffey et al., 2004).

Several studies have examined the impairment associated with having TS and comorbid ADHD. One such study examined the social and emotional functioning of 16 children with TS, 33 children with TS plus ADHD, and 23 nonpsychiatric controls (Carter et al., 2000). Those with TS and ADHD experienced more externalizing and internalizing behavior problems and poorer social adjustment than children with TS only and controls. Children with TS only were not significantly different than the control group on most measures of externalizing behaviors and social adjustment, although they did have more internalizing symptoms. No relationship was found between tic severity and emotional, social, and behavioral functioning among those with TS. Findings indicate that most of the social and behavioral impairment in children with TS was related to ADHD. In a separate study examining social and emotional functioning in 58 children with a tic disorder, with and without ADHD, results showed that the presence and severity of ADHD was associated with greater social and behavioral difficulties (Hoekstra et al., 2004). In a sample of 45 children with tic disorders, scores on

an ADHD measure accounted for the largest amount of variance in parent ratings on the Impact on Family Scale, suggesting that ADHD symptomatology can have a greater impact on family functioning than tic severity (Woods, Himle, & Osmon, 2005). In a retrospective study of school problems in 138 children with TS, researchers found that among the 108 subjects not diagnosed with a learning disability, ADHD was associated with school problems (Abwender et al., 1996) and tics were not a significant predictor of academic problems in this group. A comparison of children and adolescents with TS only, TS and comorbid ADHD, ADHD only, and controls showed that children with TS only were not different than controls in regard to cognitive functioning and overall maladaptive behavior ratings, but were rated as more delinquent than controls based on parent report. Additionally, ADHD, either alone or comorbid with TS, was associated with greater rates of maladaptive behavior and cognitive impairments than those with TS only; however, the three groups did not differ in terms of anxious and affective symptomatology (Rizzo et al., 2007). In a recent study of quality of life in children with TS, it was found that both ADHD-inattentive and OCD were significantly related with quality of life in children and adolescents with mild to moderate TS, while tic severity was not related (Bernard et al., 2009). Similar findings have been noted in adults, showing that those with TS and ADHD had significantly greater rates of OCD, anxiety, depression, and behavioral difficulties (Haddad, Umoh, Bhatia, & Robertson, 2009).

In summary, it is unclear whether tics themselves or common comorbid conditions are primarily responsible for the negative psychosocial consequences experienced by those with TS. There is evidence to suggest that both factors are responsible. The attribution of functional impairment to either tics or psychiatric comorbidity has implications for assessment and the sequencing of treatment for patients with TS. Future research should continue to separate the independent and interactive contributions of these two factors.

Trichotillomania

Individuals with TTM often have difficulties in several aspects of their lives. Studies indicate that people with TTM experience impairments in social functioning, such as peer relationship difficulties, teasing and social rejection, feelings of isolation, and reluctance to form friendships (Casati et al.,

2000; du Toit et al., 2001; Franklin et al., 2008; King et al., 1995a; Marcks, Woods, & Ridosko, 2005). Individuals with TTM also report difficulty in situations involving intimacy (Casati et al., 2000; Stemberger, Thomas, Mansueto, & Carter, 2000), may experience parental conflict and an increase in family arguments (King et al., 1995a; Stemberger et al.), and many avoid public and social/leisure activities that may cause embarrassment due to visible hair loss (Casati et al., 2000; Franklin et al; King et al, 1995a; Stemberger et al; Wetterneck et al., 2006).

Psychological and emotional distress is common among those with TTM. Individuals commonly report lowered body image, feelings of low self-esteem and unattractiveness, and negative self-evaluations (Casati et al., 2000; Diefenbach, Tolin, Hannan, Crocetto, & Worhunsky, 2005; du Toit et al., 2001; Soriano et al., 1996; Stemberger et al., 2000). Patients may also exhibit negative affect or feelings of depression related to their TTM (Diefenbach et al., 2005; Stemberger et al.). Other commonly reported emotions include feelings of guilt, shame, frustration, fear, anger, irritability, and embarrassment (Casati et al; Stemberger et al.). Additionally, patients may be distracted or experience interference due to the time spent pulling hair (King et al., 1995a; Wetterneck et al., 2006). TTM is also associated with impairment in academic functioning (i.e., school attendance, studying, and performing school work) and occupational functioning (i.e., work duties, job advancement, and attending job interviews; Diefenbach et al., 2005; Franklin et al., 2008; Keuthen et al., 2004; Stemberger et al; Wetterneck et al; Woods et al., 2006).

Demographic and phenomenological variables may also account for differences in functional impairment. A recent study found that women more commonly reported an earlier age of onset, lower rates of comorbidity, and greater rates of impairment than men. Those reporting an increasing sense of tension before pulling and relief following pulling had a more severe course of illness than those who did not meet these criteria. Pulling from the scalp was associated with more functional impairment in several domains, and with greater suicidality, when compared to pulling from other sites. Lastly, those engaging equally in focused and automatic hair pulling reported higher rates of academic, occupational, and global impairment than those engaging in either more focused or more automatic pulling. Findings also showed that the three

groups did not differ significantly in terms of severity of hair pulling (Lochner, Seedat, & Stein, 2009). In contrast, Flessner et al. (2008) found that automatic pulling was associated with a higher severity of hair pulling and increased stress, while focused pulling was associated with increased severity of hair pulling, more stress and depressive symptoms, and greater functional impairment than those low in focused pulling.

Nailbiting

Nailbiting can lead to both social and physical impairment. Nailbiting is considered to be a socially undesirable and repulsive behavior (Silber & Haynes, 1992), which has implications for how individuals with a nailbiting problem view themselves. In two separate surveys, those who bit their nails reported lower self-esteem (Joubert, 1993) and had more negative perceptions of their appearance and health (Hansen, Tishelman, Hawkins, & Doepke, 1990) than those who did not.

Nailbiting can be a factor in several health problems. There is some evidence that nailbiters are at greater risk for infections. For example, one study found that the saliva of children who bit their nails contained higher levels of enterobacteriaceae and escherichia coli bacteria than those who did not (Baydaş, Uslu, Yavuz, Ceylan, & Dağsuyu, 2007). Nailbiting may also result in paronychia, (i.e., a bacterial or fungal infection occurring at the boundaries of the skin and nails where the cuticle is damaged; Leung & Robson, 1990) and longitudinal melanonychia, (i.e., a pigmented stripe of melanin along the length of the nail; Baran, 1990). Additionally, nailbiting may play a role in atypical root resorption (Odenrick & Brattström, 1985).

Cross-cultural Features
Tic Disorders and Tourette Syndrome

Several studies have examined TS cross-culturally, and in general, results have been similar to those from studies conducted with North American and European samples (Staley, Wand, & Shady, 1997). In line with prevalence rates found in the aforementioned studies (Freeman et al., 2000), a sample of 9742 Chinese children and adolescents yielded a TS prevalence rate of 0.43% (Jin et al., 2005). Additionally, studies conducted with Taiwanese, Chinese, and Costa Rican samples have reported mean ages of onset of 9.5 (Chang, Tu, & Wang, 2004), 7.7 (Jin et al., 2005), and 6.1 (Mathews et al., 2001), respectively, which are consistent with those of North American and European samples

(Janik et al., 2007). Findings on the male to female ratio are mixed. In Costa Rican (Mathews et al.) and Iranian (Ghanizadeh & Mossallaei, 2009) samples, the male to female ratios were consistent with findings from studies performed in Western cultures (Comings & Comings, 1985; Freeman et al., 2000). However in the Eastern cultures of Taiwan and China, male to female ratios of 7:1 (Chang et al., 2004) and 10.6:1 (Jin et al.) respectively have been reported, which are higher than what is typically reported in Western cultures (Comings & Comings; Freeman et al.).

Findings on psychiatric comorbidity and behavior problems associated with TS are also similar cross-culturally. Consistent with findings from Western cultures (Freeman & Tourette Syndrome International Database Consortium, 2007), results from cross-cultural studies show that ADHD and OCD are commonly comorbid with TS (Ghanizadeh & Mosallaei, 2009; Mathews et al., 2001). In a study of Chinese patients with TS, tic severity was positively correlated with attention problems, and delinquent, aggressive, and externalizing behaviors on the CBCL (Zhu, Leung, Liu, Zhou, & Su, 2006). Likewise, in a sample of Taiwanese students with TS, tic severity was positively correlated with CBCL scores for internalizing and externalizing behavior problems, and aggressive behavior (Chang et al., 2008). Similar to findings in Western cultures (Wand et al., 1993), rage attacks and aggressive symptoms have been noted in Japanese adolescents (Kano, Ohta, Nagai, Spector, & Budman, 2008).

Cross-cultural research on functional impairment related to TS and tic disorders is mixed. Consistent with findings in Western cultures (Cooper et al., 2003; Packer, 2005), studies conducted in China and Taiwan show that individuals with TS experience academic and social impairment (Lin et al., 2007; Zhu et al., 2006), and that TS symptom severity is associated with parental stress (Lee, Chen, Wang, & Chen, 2007). However, in a Costa Rican sample, several participants reported that their TS caused no distress or impairment, contrary to objective evidence of impairment. Participants and their families commonly perceived the tics as bad habits that should be under voluntary control, rather than as physical symptoms (Mathews et al., 2001).

Trichotillomania

Some research has examined TTM in minority populations and people of other cultures. A few studies have examined the clinical characteristics of TTM in samples of African Americans. In a sample of over 200 African Americans, results indicated that while no one in the sample met criteria for TTM, 6.3% engaged in hair pulling (Mansueto, Thomas, & Brice, 2007), consistent with rates of 10% found in college samples (Rothbaum et al., 1993; Woods et al., 1996). In a study examining the ethnic differences of hair-pulling behavior in 177 African-American students and 422 students of other ethnicities, the prevalence of hair pulling resulting in noticeable hair loss in the total sample was 10.2% (McCarley, Spirrison, & Ceminsky, 2002). However, this rate was higher in African-American women (15.7%), when compared to all other respondents. An interesting finding was that African Americans, especially African-American women, were more likely to report hair pulling due to skin irritation.

Consistent with research on affective correlates in predominantly Caucasian samples, studies have shown that African Americans experience a variety of affective states prior to, during, and following the hair-pulling episode, including boredom, happiness, anxiety, guilt, and relief (Diefenbach et al., 2002; Mansueto et al., 2007; Neal-Barnett & Stadulis, 2006; Stanley et al., 1995). However, in a study examining the ethnic differences of hair pulling in African Americans and people of other ethnicities, African-American women reported higher rates of pleasure or relief associated with hair pulling (McCarley et al., 2002).

Findings on functional impairment due to TTM in African Americans are limited. In one study, secondary reports from hair care professionals with clients who met criteria for TTM revealed that hair pulling caused their customers much embarrassment, leading them to avoid social events (Neal-Barnett, Ward-Brown, Mitchell, & Krownapple, 2000). The avoidance of social situations or potentially embarrassing situations has been observed in several multiethnic samples (Casati et al., 2000; King et al., 1995a; Stemberger et al., 2000; Wetterneck et al., 2006). However, in another study of African Americans, no functional impairment associated with hair pulling was reported; but positive and significant correlations between hair pulling and anxiety were reported (Mansueto et al., 2007).

Research on TTM has also been conducted in Eastern cultures, with results similar to those found in Western cultures. Prevalence rates for subjects in India, Israel, and Singapore, were 1.24%

(Malhotra, Grover, Baweja, & Bhateja, 2008), 1% (King et al., 1995b), and 1% (Fung & Chen, 1999) respectively, consistent with Western prevalence rates (Christenson, Pyle et al., 1991; Rothbaum et al., 1993). Reports of age of onset in Eastern cultures are slightly lower, with 10.1 years in India (Malhotra et al.) and 9.3 years in Singapore (Fung & Chen), compared to the typical age of onset of 12 or 13 years found among Western samples (Christenson, Mackenzie, et al., 1991; Christenson et al., 1994). Findings on the gender ratio in East Indian children (Malhotra et al.) were similar to those of Western cultures, with the majority (85%) of the sample being female. However, an Israeli sample (King et al., 1995b) consisted of slightly more males than females, and a Singaporean sample (Fung & Chen, 1999) had a lower female to male ratio than what is typical in Western cultures (Cohen et al., 1995; Woods et al., 2006). Some differences in hair-pulling topography can be noted in the Eastern samples, including the use of only hands to pluck hair in the East Indian children (Malhotra et al.), and pulling out hair solely in tufts, observed in the Singaporean sample (Fung & Chen, 1999). In studies performed in Western cultures, individuals often use tweezers to pull hair in addition to using their hands, and the majority of individuals pull their hair out in single strands as opposed to tufts (Christenson, Mackenzie, et al., 1991; Schlosser et al., 1994).

Findings on psychiatric comorbidity and habits associated with TTM are similar cross-culturally. Consistent with findings from Western cultures (Santhanam et al., 2008), OCD or obsessive compulsive symptoms, GAD, and MDD were commonly found to be comorbid with TTM in Israeli (King et al., 1995b), East Indian (Malhotra et al., 2008), and Singaporean (Fung & Chen, 1999) samples. Other disorders and habits found to be comorbid with TTM were enuresis, eating disorder, tics, short temper, thumb sucking, and nailbiting (Santhanam et al; Swedo & Leonard, 1992).

Nailbiting

The general literature on nailbiting is quite limited, and few studies have examined nailbiting cross-culturally. One study assessed the prevalence of oral habits among 4,590 children in Mangalore. Findings indicated that nailbiting, with a prevalence rate of 12.7%, was more common among girls and in children ages 13 to 16 years (Shetty, & Munshi, 1998). The first study to examine psychiatric comorbidity in nailbiting was performed in Iran on a sample of children and adolescents. Nailbiting was comorbid with a range of disorders, most commonly ADHD, but additionally, no children had comorbid GAD (Ghanizadeh, 2008). These findings differ from results of studies performed in Western regions that report that nailbiting is a symptom of anxiety (Joubert, 1993; McClanahan, 1995).

Relationship to Psychotic Conditions
Tic Disorders and Tourette Syndrome

The presence of tics has been observed in patients with psychotic conditions following neuroleptic drug treatment. However, these symptoms are likely not due to psychosis (Klawans, Falk, Nausieda, & Weiner, 1978; Kuniyoshi et al., 1992; Lal & AlAnsari, 1986). A few studies have examined patients with TS and comorbid schizophrenia. In a report on the course of TS and schizophrenia in two children, it was noted that both patients first developed TS and then later developed schizophrenia (Kerbeshian & Burd, 1988). This finding was also noted in an analysis of the comorbidity of TS and schizophrenia in five patients, all of whom had severe schizophrenia. The researchers concluded that the disorders may overlap due to a shared pathophysiological pathway (Müller, Riedel, Zawta, Günther, & Straube, 2002).

Trichotillomania

Hair pulling has been observed in those with psychotic conditions. Findings indicate that hair pulling may be caused by delusions or hallucinations involving hair, and associated with mania, or schizophrenia (Slagle & Martin, 1991). Nevertheless, pulling resulting from such variables is unlikely to be classified as TTM.

Nailbiting

In the nailbiting literature, research on the prevalence of nailbiting in psychotic conditions, and the association between nailbiting and psychotic conditions, is limited. Future research would need to be conducted to establish such a link.

Conclusion

Tic disorders, TTM, and nailbiting are body-focused repetitive behavior disorders, associated with rising and decreasing tension or changes in affective states, occurring in certain situations. Research on the phenomenology of these disorders in young children is limited. Nonclinical forms of the disorders have been examined; however, more research is needed to assess whether they lie on a continuum with their diagnostic level counterparts, or if they should be conceptualized as independent from diagnosed disorders. Although these disorders are topographically distinct in nature, their symptoms are often confused with OCD, and other conditions and disorders. Research on the prevalence of these disorders is limited, especially in minority populations. Data on treatment utilization are also limited. These disorders are often comorbid with other conditions, and patients experience deficits in several domains of functioning, causing a challenge for researchers and clinicians attempting to parse out the effects of the primary diagnosis on functional impairment from those of the comorbidities. Research on cross-cultural features of the disorders is limited, with some studies suggesting that symptoms and associated features are similar to that of the general population, and others showing that the symptoms are conceptualized differently. Currently, the research examining the relationship between these disorders and psychotic conditions is too sparse to draw definitive conclusions.

Future Directions

1. Are there distinct subtypes of these disorders that can allow clinicians to predict symptom outcome and severity?

2. Will distinguishing these disorders from OCD offer clues to the etiology of the disorders?

3. Can the age of symptom onset (i.e., early childhood, puberty, and adulthood) be used to predict the type and severity of the longitudinal course of symptoms?

4. How best can we use the findings from upcoming healthcare utilization research to address the issue of dissemination of treatment?

5. Can nonclinical forms of the disorders function as predictors of future disorder at the diagnostic level, or should they be viewed as distinct sets of symptoms?

6. Can we differentiate the contributions to functional impairment of these disorders from that of comorbid conditions, and use these findings to improve overall functioning?

7. Are there cultural differences in the phenomenology of these disorders, yet to be understood, that will increase our understanding of the disorders?

Related Chapters

Chapter 23. Treatment of Tic Disorders and Trichotillomania

References

Abwender, D. A., Como, P.G., Kurlan, R., Parry, K., Fett, K. A., Cui, L., et al. (1996). School problems in Tourette's syndrome. *Archives of Neurology, 53,* 509–511.

Altman, K., Grahs, C., & Friman, P. (1982). Treatment of unobserved trichotillomania by attention-reflection and punishment of an apparent covariant. *Journal of Behavior Therapy and Experimental Psychiatry, 13,* 337–340.

American Psychiatric Association. (1987). *Diagnostic and statistical manual of mental disorders* (3rd ed. Text Revision). Washington, DC: Author.

American Psychiatric Association. (2000). *Diagnostic and statistical manual of mental disorders* (4th ed. Text Revision). Washington, DC: Author.

Bakwin, H. (1971). Nail-biting in twins. *Developmental Medicine and Child Neurology, 13,* 304–307.

Ballinger, B. R. (1970). The prevalence of nail-biting in normal and abnormal populations. *The British Journal of Psychiatry, 117,* 445–446.

Baran, R. (1990). Nail biting and picking as a possible cause of longitudinal melanonychia. A study of 6 cases. *Dermatologica, 181,* 126–128.

Bawden, H. N., Stokes, A., Camfield, C. S., Camfield, P. R., & Salisbury, S. (1998). Peer relationship problems in children with Tourette's disorder or diabetes mellitus. *Journal of Child Psychology and Psychiatry, and Allied Disciplines, 39,* 663–668.

Baydaş, B., Uslu, H., Yavuz, I., Ceylan, I., & Dağsuyu, M. (2007). Effect of a chronic nail-biting habit on the oral carriage of Enterobacteriaceae. *Oral Microbiology and Immunology, 22,* 1–4.

Bernard, B. A., Stebbins, G. T., Siegel, S., Schultz, T. M., Hays, C., Morrissey, M. J., et al. (2009). Determinants of quality of life in children with Gilles de la Tourette syndrome. *Movement Disorders, 24,* 1070–1073.

Besiroglu, L., Uguz, F., Ozbebit, O., Guler, O., Cilli, A. S., & Askin, R. (2007). Longitudinal assessment of symptom and subtype categories in obsessive-compulsive disorder. *Depression and Anxiety, 24,* 461–466.

Birch, L. B. (1955). The incidence of nail biting among school children. *British Journal of Educational Psychology, 25,* 123–128.

Bloch, M. H., & Leckman, J. F. (2009). Clinical course of Tourette syndrome. *Journal of Psychosomatic Research, 67,* 497–501.

Bloch, M. H., Peterson, B. S., Scahill, L., Otka, J., Katsovich, L., Zhang, H., et al. (2006). Adulthood outcome of tic and obsessive-compulsive symptom severity in children with Tourette syndrome. *Archives of Pediatric and Adolescent Medicine, 160,* 65–69.

Bornstein, R. A., Stefl, M. E., & Hammond, L. (1990). A survey of Tourette syndrome patients and their families: The 1987 Ohio Tourette survey. *The Journal of Neuropsychiatry and Clinical Neurosciences, 2,* 275–281.

Bouwer, C., & Stein, D. J. (1998). Trichobezoars in trichotillomania: Case report and literature overview. *Psychosomatic Medicine, 60,* 658–660.

Budman, C. L., Bruun, R. D., Park, K. S., Lesser, M., & Olson, M. (2000). Explosive outburst in children with Tourette's disorder. *Journal of the American Academy of Child and Adolescent Psychiatry, 39,* 1270–1276.

Budman, C. L., Bruun, R. D., Park, K. S., & Olson, M. E. (1998). Rage attacks in children and adolescents with

Tourette's disorder: A pilot study. *The Journal of Clinical Psychiatry, 59,* 576–580.

Burd, L., Kerbeshian, J., Wikenheiser, M., & Fisher, W. (1986). A prevalence study of Gilles de la Tourette syndrome in North Dakota school-age children. *Journal of the American Academy of Child and Adolescent Psychiatry, 25,* 552–553.

Byrd, M. R., Richards, D. F., Hove, G., & Friman, P. C. (2002). Treatment of early onset hair pulling as a simple habit. *Behavior Modification, 26,* 400–411.

Caine, E. D., McBride, M. C., Chiverton, P., Bamford, K. A., Rediess, S., & Shiao, J. (1988). Tourette's syndrome in Monroe County school children. *Neurology, 38,* 472–475.

Canitano, R., & Vivanti, G. (2007). Tics and Tourette syndrome in autism spectrum disorders. *Autism, 11,* 19–28.

Carter, A. S., O'Donnell, D. A., Schultz, R. T., Scahill, L., Leckman, J. F., & Pauls, D. L. (2000). *Journal of Child Psychology, and Psychiatry, and Allied Disciplines, 41,* 215–223.

Casati, J., Toner, B. B., & Yu, B. (2000). Psychosocial issues for women with trichotillomania. *Comprehensive Psychiatry, 41,* 344–351.

Cavanna, A. E., Robertson, M. M., Critchley, H. D. (2007). Schizotypal personality traits in Gilles de la Tourette syndrome. *Acta Neurologica Scandinavia, 116,* 385–391.

Champion, L. M., Fulton, W. A., & Shady, G. A. (1988). Tourette syndrome and social functioning in a Canadian population. *Neuroscience and Biobehavioural Reviews, 12,* 255–257.

Chang, C. H., Lee, M. B., Chiang, Y. C., & Lü, Y. C. (1991). Trichotillomania: A clinical study of 36 patients. *Journal of the Formosan Medical Association, 90,* 176–180.

Chang, H. L., Liang, H. Y., Wang, H. S., Li, C. S., Ko, N. C., & Hsu, Y. P. (2008). Behavioral and emotional problems in adolescent with Tourette syndrome. *Chang Gung Medical Journal, 31,* 145–152.

Chang, H. L., Tu, M. J., & Wang, H. S. (2004). Tourette's syndrome: Psychopathology in adolescents. *Psychiatry and Clinical Neurosciences, 58,* 353–358.

Christenson, G. A., Chernoff-Clementz, E., & Clementz, B. (1992). Personality and clinical characteristics in patients with trichotillomania. *The Journal of Clinical Psychiatry, 53,* 407–413.

Christenson, G. A., & Crow, S. J. (1996). The characterization and treatment of trichotillomania. *The Journal of Clinical Psychiatry, 57,* 42–47.

Christenson, G. A., Mackenzie, T. B., & Mitchell, J. E. (1991). Characteristics of 60 adult chronic hair pullers. *American Journal of Psychiatry, 148,* 365–370.

Christenson, G. A., Mackenzie, T. B., & Mitchell, J. E. (1994). Adult men and women with Trichotillomania. A comparison of male and female characteristics. *Psychosomatics, 35,* 142–149.

Christenson, G. A., Pyle, R. L., & Mitchell, J. E. (1991). Estimated lifetime prevalence of trichotillomania in college students. *The Journal of Clinical Psychiatry, 52,* 415–417.

Coffey, B. J., Biederman, J., Geller, D., Frazier, J., Spencer, T., Doyle, R., et al. (2004). Reexamining tic persistence and tic-associated impairment in Tourette's disorder: Findings from a naturalistic follow-up study. *Journal of Nervous and Mental Disease, 192,* 776–780.

Cohen, A. J., & Leckman, J. F. (1992). Sensory phenomena associated with Gilles de la Tourette's syndrome. *The Journal of Clinical Psychiatry, 53,* 319–323.

Cohen, L. J., Stein, D. J., Simeon, D., Spadaccini, E., Rosen, J., Aronowitz, B., et al. (1995). Clinical profile, comorbidity, and treatment history in 123 hair pullers: A survey study. *Journal of Clinical Psychiatry, 56,* 319–326.

Coleman, J. C., & McCalley, J. E. (1948). Nail-biting among college students. *The Journal of Abnormal and Social Psychology, 43,* 517–525.

Comings, D. E., & Comings, B. G. (1985). Tourette syndrome: Clinical and psychological aspects of 250 cases. *American Journal of Human Genetics, 37,* 435–450.

Conelea, C. A., & Woods, D. W. (2008). Examining the impact of distraction on tic suppression in children and adolescents with Tourette syndrome. *Behavior Research and Therapy, 46,* 1193–1200.

Cooper, C., Robertson, M. M., & Livingston, G. (2003). Psychological morbidity and caregiver burden in parents of children with Tourette's disorder and psychiatric comorbidity. *Journal of the American Academy of Child and Adolescent Psychiatry, 42,* 1370–1375.

Cutler, D., Murphy, T., Gilmour, J., & Heyman, I. (2009). The quality of life of young people with Tourette syndrome. *Child: Care, Health, and Development, 35,* 496–504.

Deardorff, P. A., Finch, A. J., & Royall, L. R. (1974). Manifest anxiety and nail-biting. *Journal of Clinical Psychology, 30,* 378.

Deaver, C. M., Miltenberger, R. G., & Stricker, J. M. (2001). Functional analysis of hair twirling in a young child. *Journal of Applied Behavior Analysis, 34,* 535–538.

de Berker, D. (2006). Childhood nail diseases. *Dermatologic Clinics, 24,* 355–363.

DeFrancesco, J. J., Zahner, G. E. P., & Pawelkiewicz, W. (1989). Childhood nailbiting. *Journal of Social Behaviour and Personality, 4,* 157–161.

de Groot, C. M., Bornstein, R. A., Spetie, L., & Burriss, B. (1994). The course of tics in Tourette syndrome: A 5-year follow-up study. *Annals of Clinical Psychiatry, 6,* 227–233.

Diefenbach, G. J., Mouton-Odom, S., & Stanley, M. A. (2002). Affective correlates of trichotillomania. *Behavior Research and Therapy, 40,* 1305–1315.

Diefenbach, G. J., Tolin, D. F., Hannan, S., Crocetto, J., & Worhunsky, P. (2005). Trichotillomania: Impact on psychosocial functioning and quality of life. *Behaviour Research and Therapy, 43,* 869–884.

Diefenbach, G. J., Tolin, D. F., Meunier, S., & Worhunsky, P. (2008). Emotion regulation and trichotillomania: A comparison of clinical and nonclinical hair pulling. *Journal of Behavior Therapy and Experimental Psychiatry, 39,* 32–41.

Dimoski, A., & Duricić, S. (1991). Dermatitis artefacta, onychophagia and trichotillomania in mentally retarded children and adolescents. *Medicinski Pregled, 44,* 471–472.

Duke, D. C., Bodzin, D. K., Tavares, P., Geffken, G. R., & Storch E. A. (2009). The phenomenology hairpulling in a community sample. *Journal of Anxiety Disorders, 23,* 1118–1125.

Duke, D. C., Keeley, M. L., Ricketts, E. J., Geffken, G. R., & Storch, E. A. (2010). The phenomenology of hairpulling in college students. *The Journal of Psychopathology and Behavioral Assessment, 32,* 281–292.

du Toit, P. L., van Kradenburg, J., Niehaus, D. J. H., & Stein, D. J. (2001). Characteristics and phenomenology of hair pulling: An exploration of subtypes. *Comprehensive Psychiatry, 42,* 247–256.

Elstner, K., Selai, C. E., Trimble, M. R., & Robertson, M. M. (2001). Quality of life (QOL) of patients with Gilles de la

Tourette's syndrome. *Acta Psychiatrica Scandinavica, 103,* 52–59.

Flessner, C. A., Conelea, C. A., Woods, D. W., Franklin, M. E., Keuthen, N. J., & Cashin, S. E. (2008). Styles of pulling in trichotillomania: Exploring differences in symptoms severity, phenomenology, and functional impact. *Behaviour Research and Therapy, 46,* 345–347.

Foster, L. G. (1998). Nervous habits and stereotyped behaviors in preschool children. *Journal of the American Academy of Child and Adolescent Psychiatry, 37,* 711–717.

Franklin, M. E., Flessner, C. A., Woods, D. W., Keuthen, N. J., Piacentini, J. C., Moore, P., et al. (2008). The child and adolescent trichotillomania impact project: Descriptive psychopathology, comorbidity, functional impairment, and treatment utilization. *Journal of Developmental and Behavioral Pediatrics, 29,* 493–500.

Freeman, R. D., Fast D. K., Burd, L., Kerbeshian, J., Robertson, M. M., & Sandor, P. (2000). An international perspective on Tourette syndrome: Selected findings from 3,500 individuals in 22 countries. *Developmental Medicine and Child Neurology, 42,* 436–447.

Freeman, R. D., & Tourette Syndrome International Database Consortium. (2007). Tic disorders and ADHD: Answers from a worldwide clinical dataset. *European Child and Adolescent Psychiatry, 16,* 15–23.

Frey, A. S., McKee, M., King, R. A., & Martin, A. (2005). Hair apparent: Rapunzel syndrome. *The American Journal of Psychiatry, 162,* 242–248.

Fung, D. S., & Chen, Y. (1999). A clinical study of seven cases of trichotillomania in Singapore. *Annals of the Academy of Medicine, Singapore, 28,* 519–524.

Gadow, K. D., Nolan, E. E., Sprafkin, J., & Schwartz, J. (2002). Tics and psychiatric comorbidity in children and adolescents. *Developmental Medicine & Child Neurology, 44,* 380–338.

Ghanizadeh, A. (2008). Association of nail biting and psychiatric disorders in children and their parents in a psychiatrically referred sample of children. *Child and Adolescent Psychiatry and Mental Health, 2,* 13.

Ghanizadeh, A., & Mosallaei, S. (2009). Psychiatric disorders and behavioral problems in children and adolescents with Tourette syndrome. *Brain and Development, 31,* 15–19.

Goetz, C. G., Tanner, C. M., Stebbings, G. T., Leipziq, G., & Carr, W. C. (1992). Adult tics in Gilles de la Tourette's syndrome: Description and risk factors. *Neurology, 42,* 784–788.

Greenberg, H. R., & Sarner, C. A. (1965). Trichotillomania: Symptom and syndrome. *Archives of General Psychiatry, 12,* 482–489.

Gupta, A. K., & Summerbell, R. C. (2000). Tinea capitis. *Medical Mycology: Official Publication of the International Society for Human and Animal Mycology, 38,* 255–287.

Haddad, A. D. M., Umoh, G., Bhatia, V., & Robertson, M. M. (2009). Adults with Tourette's syndrome with and without attention deficit hyperactivity disorder. *Acta Psychiatrica Scandinavica, 120,* 299–307.

Hanna, G. L. (1997). Trichotillomania and related disorders in children and adolescents. *Psychiatry and Human Development, 27,* 255–268.

Hansen, D. J., Tishelman, A. C., Hawkins, R. P., & Doepke, K. J. (1990). Habits with potential as disorders. Prevalence, severity, and other characteristics among college students. *Behavior Modification, 14,* 66–80.

Hoekstra, P. J., Steenhuis, M. P., Troost, P. W., Korf, J., Kallenberg, C. G., & Minderaa, R. B. (2004). Relative contribution of attention-deficit hyperactivity disorder, obsessive-compulsive disorder, and tic severity to social and behavioral problems in tic disorders. *Journal of Behavioral and Developmental Pediatrics, 25,* 272–279.

Hubka, G. B., Fulton, W. A., Shady, G. A., Champion, L. M., & Wand, R. (1988). Tourette syndrome: Impact on Canadian family functioning. *Neuroscience and Biobehavioral Reviews, 12,* 259–261.

Jagger, J., Prusoff, B. A., Cohen, D. J., Kidd, K. K., Carbonari, C. M., & John, K. (1982). The epidemiology of Tourette's syndrome: A pilot study. *Schizophrenia Bulletin, 8,* 267–278.

Janik, P., Kalbarczyk, A., & Sitek, M. (2007). Clinical analysis of Gilles de la Tourette syndrome in 126 cases. *Neurologia I Neurochirurgia Polska, 41,* 381–387.

Jin, R., Zheng, R. Y., Huang, W. W., Xu, H. Q., Shao, B., Chen, H., et al. (2005). Epidemiological survey of Tourette syndrome in children and adolescent in Wenzhou of P.R. China. *European Journal of Epidemiology, 20,* 925–927.

Joubert, C. E. (1993). Relationship of self-esteem, manifest anxiety, and obsessive-compulsiveness to personal habits. *Psychological Reports, 73,* 579–583.

Kano, Y., Ohta, M., Nagai, Y., Spector, I., & Budman, C. (2008). Rage attacks and aggressive symptoms in Japanese adolescents with Tourette syndrome. *CNS Spectrums, 13,* 325–332.

Kerbeshian, J., & Burd, L. (1988). Tourette disorder and schizophrenia in children. *Neuroscience and Biobehavioral Reviews, 12,* 267–270.

Keuthen, N. J., Dougherty, D. D., Franklin, M. E., Bohne, A., Loh, R., Levy, J., et al. (2004). Quality of life and functional impairment in individuals with trichotillomania. *The Journal of Applied Research, 4,* 186–197.

Khalifa, N., & von Knorring, A. L. (2003). Prevalence of tic disorders and Tourette syndrome in a Swedish school population. *Developmental Medicine and Child Neurology, 45,* 315–319.

Khalifa, N., & von Knorring, A. L. (2005). Tourette syndrome and other tic disorders in a total population of children: Clinical assessment and background. *Acta Paediatrica, 45,* 314–319.

Khalifa, N., & von Knorring, A. L. (2006). Psychopathology in a Swedish population of school children with tic disorders. *Journal of the American Academy of Child and Adolescent Psychiatry, 45,* 1346–1353.

King, R.A., Leckman, J.F., Scahill, L., & Cohen, D.J. (1999). Obsessive-compulsive disorder, anxiety, and depression. In J.F. Leckman & D.J. Cohen (Eds.), *Tourette's syndrome - Tics, obsessions, compulsions: Developmental psychopathology and clinical care* (pp. 43–61). New York: Wiley & Sons.

King, R. A., Scahill, L., Vitulano, L. A., Schwab-Stone, M., Tercyak, K., & Riddle, M. (1995a). Childhood Trichotillomania: Clinical phenomenology, comorbidity, and family genetics. *Journal of the American Academy of Child and Adolescent Psychiatry, 34,* 1451–1459.

King, R. A., Zohar, A. H., Ratzoni, G., Binder, M., Kron, S., Dycian, A., et al. (1995b). An epidemiological study of trichotillomania in Israeli adolescents. *Journal of the American Academy of Child and Adolescent Psychiatry, 34,* 1212–1215.

Klawans, H. L., Falk, D. K., Nausieda, P. A., & Weiner, W. J. (1978). Gilles de la Tourette syndrome after long-term chlorpromazine therapy. *Neurology, 28,* 1064–1066.

Knell, S. M., & Moore, D. J. (1988). Childhood trichotillomania treated indirectly by punishing thumb sucking. *Journal of Behavior Therapy and Experimental Psychiatry, 19,* 305–310.

Kompoliti, K., & Goetz, C. G. (1998). Hyperkinetic movement disorders misdiagnosed as tics in Gilles de la Tourette syndrome. *Movement Disorders, 13,* 477–480.

Kuniyoshi, M., Inanaga, K., Arikawa, K., Maeda, Y., Nakamura, J., & Uchimura, N. (1992). A case of tardive Tourette-like syndrome. *The Japanese Journal of Psychiatry and Neurology, 46,* 67–70.

Kurlan, R., Como, P. G., Miller, B., Palumbo, D., Deeley, C., Anderson, E. M., et al. (2002). The behavioral spectrum of tic disorders: A community-based study. *Neurology, 59,* 414–420.

Kwak, C., Dat Vuong, K., & Jankovic, J. (2003). Premonitory sensory phenomenon in Tourette's syndrome. *Movement Disorders, 18,* 1530–1533.

Lal, S., & AlAnsari, E. (1986). Tourette-like syndrome following low dose short-term neuroleptic treatment. *The Canadian Journal of Neurological Sciences, 13,* 125–128.

Lanzi, G., Zambrino, C. A., Termine, C., Palestra, M., Ferrari Ginevra, O., Orcesi, S., et al. (2004). Prevalence of tic disorders among primary school students in the city of Pavia, Italy. *Archives of Disease in Childhood, 89,* 45–47.

Leckman, J. F., Bloch, M. H., Scahill, L., & King, R. A. (2006). Tourette syndrome: The self under siege. *Journal of Child Neurology, 21,* 642–649.

Leckman, J. F., Peterson, B. S., Pauls, D. L., & Cohen, D. J. (1997). Tic disorders. *Psychiatry Clinics of North America, 20,* 839–861.

Leckman, J. F., Walker, D. E., & Cohen, D. J. (1993). Premonitory urges in Tourette's syndrome. *The American Journal of Psychiatry, 150,* 98–102.

Leckman, J. F., Zhang, H., Vitale, A., Lahnin, F., Lynch, K., Bondi, C., et al. (1998). Course of tic severity in Tourette syndrome: The first two decades. *Pediatrics, 102,* 14–19.

Lee, M. Y., Chen, Y. C., Wang, H. S., & Chen, D. R. (2007). Parenting stress and related factors in parents of children with Tourette syndrome. *The Journal of Nursing Research, 15,* 165–174.

Lees, A. J., Robertson, M., Trimble, M. R., & Murray, N. M. (1984). A clinical study of Gilles de la Tourette syndrome in the United Kingdom. *Journal of Neurology, Neurosurgery, and Psychiatry, 47,* 1–8.

Leonard, H. L., Lenane, M. C., Swedo, S. E., Rettew, D. C., & Rapoport, J. L. (1991). A double-blind comparison of clomipramine and desipramine treatment of severe onychophagia (nailbiting). *Archives of General Psychiatry, 48,* 821–827.

Leung, A. K., & Robson, W. L. (1990). Nailbiting. *Clinical Pediatrics, 29,* 690–692.

Lin, H., Katsovich, L., Ghebremichael, M., Findley, D. B., Grantz, H., Lombroso, P. J., et al. (2007). Psychosocial stress predicts future symptom severities in children and adolescents with Tourette syndrome and/or obsessive-compulsive disorder. *Journal of Child Psychology and Psychiatry, and Allied Disciplines, 48,* 157–166.

Lochner, C., Seedat, S., duToit, P. L., Nel, D. G., Niehaus, D. J., Sandler, R., et al. (2005). Obsessive-compulsive disorder and trichotillomania: A phenomenological comparison. *BMC Psychiatry, 5,* 2.

Lochner, C., Seedat, S., & Stein, D. J. (2009). Chronic hair-pulling: Phenomenology-based subtypes. *Journal of Anxiety Disorder, 24,* 196–202.

Long, E. S., Miltenberger, R. G., & Rapp, J. T. (1998). A survey of habit behaviors exhibited by individuals with mental retardation. *Behavioral Interventions, 13,* 79–89.

Madani, S., & Shapiro, J. (2000). Alopecia areata update. *Journal of the American Academy of Dermatology, 42,* 549–566.

Malhotra, S., Grover, S., Baweja, R., & Bhateja, G. (2008). Trichotillomania in children. *Indian Pediatrics, 45,* 403–405.

Malone, A. J., & Massler, M. (1952). Index of nailbiting in children. *Journal of Abnormal Psychology, 47,* 193–202.

Mansueto, C. S., & Keuler, D. J. (2005). Tic or compulsion? It's Tourettic OCD. *Behavior Modification, 29,* 784–799.

Mansueto, C. S., Thomas, A. M., & Brice, L. (2007). Hair pulling and its affective correlates in an African-American university sample. *Journal of Anxiety Disorders, 21,* 590–599.

Marcks, B. A., Woods, D. W., & Ridosko, J. L. (2005). The effects of trichotillomania disclosure on peer perceptions and social acceptability. *Body Image, 2,* 299–306.

Mason, A., Banerjee, S., Eapen, V., Zeitlin, H., & Robertson, M. M. (1998). The prevalence of Tourette syndrome in a mainstream school population. *Developmental Medicine and Child Neurology, 40,* 292–296.

Mathews, C. A., Herrera Amighetti, L. D., Lowe, T. L., van de Wetering, B. J., Freimer, N. B., & Reus, V. I. (2001). Cultural influences on diagnosis and perception of Tourette syndrome in Costa Rica. *Journal of the American Academy of Child and Adolescent Psychiatry, 40,* 456–463.

McCarley, N. G., Spirrison, C. L., & Ceminsky, J. L. (2002). Hair pulling behavior reported by African American and non-African college students. *Journal of Psychopathology and Behavioral Assessment, 24,* 139–144.

McClanahan, T. M. (1995). Operant learning (R-S principles) applied to nail-biting). *Psychological Reports, 77,* 507–514.

Meunier, S. A., Tolin, D. F., & Franklin, M. (2009). Affective and sensory correlates of hair pulling in pediatric trichotillomania. *Behavior Modification, 33,* 396–407.

Miguel, E. C., Baer, L., Coffey, B. J., Rauch, S. L., Savage, C. R., O'Sullivan, R. L., et al. (1997). Phenomenological differences appearing with repetitive behaviours in obsessive-compulsive disorder and Gilles de la Tourette's syndrome. *The British Journal of Psychiatry, 170,* 140–145.

Miguel, E. C., Coffey, B. J., Baer, L., Savage, C. R., Rauch, S. L., & Jenike, M. A. (1995). Phenomenology of intentional repetitive behaviors in obsessive-compulsive disorder and Tourette's disorder. *The Journal of Clinical Psychiatry, 56,* 246–255.

Miguel, E. C., do Rosário-Campos, M. C., Prado, H. S., do Valle, R., Rauch, S. L., Coffey, B. J., et al. (2000). Sensory phenomena in obsessive-compulsive disorder and Tourette's disorder. *The Journal of Clinical Psychiatry, 61,* 150–156.

Müller, N., Riedel, M., Zawta, P., Günther, W., & Straube, A. (2002). Comorbidity of Tourette's syndrome and schizophrenia—biological and physiological parallels. *Progress in Neuro-psychopharmacology and Biological Psychiatry, 26,* 1245–1252.

Muller, S. A. (1987). Trichotillomania. *Dermatologic Clinics, 5,* 595–601.

Müller-Vahl, K., Dodel, I., Müller, N., Münchau, A., Reese, J. P., Balzer-Geldsetzer, M., et al. (2010). Health-related quality of life in patients with Gilles de la Tourette's syndrome. *Movement Disorders, 25,* 309–314.

Neal-Barnett, A., & Stadulis, R. (2006). Affective states and racial identity among African-American women with trichotillomania. *Journal of the National Medical Association, 98,* 753–757.

Neal-Barnett, A. M., Ward-Brown, B. J., Mitchell, M., & Krownapple, M. (2000). Hair pulling African American women—only your hairdresser knows for sure: An exploratory study. *Cultural Diversity & Ethnic Minority Psychology, 6,* 352–362.

O'Connor, K., Brisebois, H., Brault, M., Robillard, S., & Loiselle, J. (2003). Behavioral activity associated with onset in chronic tic and habit disorder. *Behaviour Research and Therapy, 41,* 241–249.

Odenrick, L., & Brattström, V. (1985). Nailbiting: Frequency and association with root resorption during orthodontic treatment. *British Journal of Orthodontics, 12,* 78–81.

Oranje, A. P., Peereboom-Wynia, J. D., & De Raeymaecker, D. M. (1986). Trichotillomania in childhood. *Journal of the American Academy of Dermatology, 15,* 614–619.

O'Sullivan, M. J., McGreal, G., Walsh, J. G., & Redmond, H. P. (1996). Trichobezoar. *Journal of the Royal Society of Medicine, 94,* 68–70.

Packer, L. E. (2005). Tic related school problems: Impact on functioning, accommodations, and interventions. *Behavior Modification, 29,* 876–899.

Pappert, E. J., Goetz, C. G., Louis, E. D., Blassuci, L., & Leurgans, S. (2003). Objective assessments of longitudinal outcomes in Gilles de la Tourette's syndrome. *Neurology, 61,* 936–940.

Pennington, L. A. (1945). The incidence of nail-biting among adults. *American Journal of Psychiatry, 102,* 241–244.

Peterson, B. S., & Leckman, J. F. (1998). The temporal dynamics of tics in Gilles de la Tourette syndrome. *Biological Psychiatry, 44,* 1337–1348.

Peterson, P. S., Pine, D. S., Cohen, P., & Brook, J. S. (2001). Prospective, longitudinal study of tic, obsessive-compulsive, and attention-deficit/hyperactivity disorders in an epidemiological sample. *Journal of the American Academy of Child and Adolescent Psychiatry, 40,* 685–695.

Reeve, E. A., Bernstein, G. A., & Christenson, G. A. (1992). Clinical characteristics and psychiatric comorbidity in children with Trichotillomania. *Journal of the American Academy of Child and Adolescent Psychiatry, 31,* 132–138.

Rizzo, R., Curatolo, P., Gulisano, M., Virzi, M., Arpino, C., & Robertson, M. M. (2007). Disentangling the effects of cognitive and behavioral phenotypes. *Brain and Development, 29,* 413–420.

Robertson, M. M., Banerjee, S., Eapen, V., & Fox-Hiley, P. (2002). Obsessive compulsive behaviour and depressive symptoms in young people with Tourette syndrome. A controlled study. *European Child and Adolescent Psychiatry, 11,* 261–265.

Rothbaum, B. O., Shaw, L., Morris, R., & Ninan, P. T. (1993). Prevalence of trichotillomania in a college freshman population. *Journal of Clinical Psychiatry, 54,* 72.

Rufer, M., Grothusen, A., Maszlig, R., Peter, H., & Hand, I. (2005). Temporal stability of symptom dimensions in adult patients with obsessive-compulsive disorder. *Journal of Affective Disorders, 88,* 99–102.

Santhanan, R., Fairley, M., & Rogers, M. (2008). Is it trichotillomania? Hair pulling in childhood: A developmental perspective. *Clinical Child Psychology and Psychiatry, 13,* 409–418.

Scahill, L. D., Leckman, J. F., & Marek, K. L. (1995). Sensory phenomena in Tourette's syndrome. *Advances in Neurology, 65,* 273–280.

Schlosser, S., Black, D. W., Blum, N., & Goldstein, R. B. (1994). The demography, phenomenology, and family history of 22 persons with compulsive hair pulling. *Annals of Clinical Psychiatry, 6,* 147–152.

Shady, G., Broder, R., Staley, D., Furer, P., & Brezden-Papodopolos, R. (1995). Tourette syndrome and employment: Descriptors, predictors, and problems. *Psychiatric Rehabilitation Journal, 19,* 35–42.

Shapiro, A. K., & Shapiro, E. (1992). Evaluation of the reported association of obsessive-compulsive symptoms or disorder with Tourette's disorder. *Comprehensive Psychiatry, 33,* 152–165.

Shapiro, A. K., Shapiro, E., & Wayne, H. (1972). Birth, developmental, and family histories and demographic information in Tourette's syndrome. *Journal of Nervous and Mental Disease, 115,* 335–344.

Sharma, N. L., Sharma, R. C., Mahajan, V. K., Sharma, R. C., Chauhan, D., & Sharma, A. K. (2000). Trichotillomania and trichophagia leading to trichobezoar. *The Journal of Dermatology, 27,* 24–26.

Shetty, S. R., & Munshi, A. K. (1998). Oral habits in children—A prevalence study. *Journal of the Indian Society of Pedodontics and Preventive Dentistry, 16,* 61–66.

Silber, K. P., & Haynes, C. E. (1992). Treating nailbiting: A comparative analysis of mild aversion and competing response therapies. *Behaviour Research and Therapy, 30,* 15–22.

Silva, R. R., Munoz, D. M., Barickman, J., & Friedhoff, A. J. (1995). Environmental factors and related fluctuation of symptoms in children and adolescents with Tourette's disorder. *Journal of Child Psychology and Psychiatry, and Allied Disciplines, 36,* 305–312.

Slagle, D. A., & Martin, T. A. (1991). Trichotillomania. *American Family Physician, 43,* 2019–2024.

Snijders, A. H., Robertson, M. M., & Orth, M. (2006). Beck Depression Inventory is a useful screening tool for major depressive disorder in Gilles de la Tourette syndrome. *Journal of Neurology, Neurosurgery, and Psychiatry, 77,* 787–789.

Soriano, J. L., O'Sullivan, R. L., Baer, L., Philips, K. A., McNally, R. J., & Jenike, M. A. (1996). Trichotillomania and self-esteem: A survey of 62 hair pullers. *Journal of Clinical Psychiatry, 57,* 77–82.

Staley, D., Wand, R., & Shady, G. (1997). Tourette disorder: A cross-cultural review. *Comprehensive Psychiatry, 38,* 6–16.

Stanley, M. A., Borden, J. W., Bell, G. E., & Wagner, A. L. (1994). Nonclinical hair-pulling: Phenomenology and related psychopathology. *Journal of Anxiety Disorders, 8,* 119–130.

Stanley, M. A., Borden, J. W., Mouton, S. G., & Breckenridge, J. K. (1995). Nonclinical hair-pulling: Affective correlates and comparison with clinical samples. *Behaviour Research and Therapy, 33,* 179–186.

Stefanoff, P., Wolanczyk, T., Gawrys, A., Swirszcz, K., Stefanoff, E., Kaminska, A., et al. (2008). Prevalence of tic disorders among school children in Warsaw, Poland. *European Child and Adolescent Psychiatry, 17,* 171–178.

Stemberger, R. M., Thomas, A. M., Mansueto, C. S., & Carter, J. G. (2000). Personal toll of trichotillomania: Behavioral and interpersonal sequelae. *Journal of Anxiety Disorders, 14,* 97–104.

Stein, D. J., Simeon, D., Cohen, L. J., & Hollander, E. (1995). Trichotillomania and obsessive-compulsive disorder. *The Journal of Clinical Psychiatry, 56,* 28–34.

Stokes, A., Bawden, H. N., Camfield, P. R., Backman, J. E., & Dooley, J. M. (1991). Peer problems in Tourette's disorder. *Pediatrics, 87,* 936–942.

Storch, E. A., Lack, C. W., Simons, L. E., Goodman, W. K., Murphy, T. K., & Geffken, G. R. (2007a). A measure of functional impairment in youth with Tourette's syndrome. *Journal of Pediatric Psychology, 32,* 950–959.

Storch, E. A., Merlo, L. J., Lack, C., Milsom, V. A., Geffken, G. R., Goodman, W. K., et al. (2007b). Quality of life in youth with Tourette's syndrome and chronic tic disorder. *Journal of Clinical Child and Adolescent Psychology, 36,* 217–227.

Storch, E. A., Murphy, T. K., Chase, R. M., Keeley, M., Goodman, W. K., Murray, M., et al. (2007c). Peer victimization in youth with Tourette's syndrome and chronic tic disorder: Relations with tic severity and internalizing symptoms. *Journal of Psychopathology and Behavioral Assessment, 29,* 211–219.

Swedo, S. E., & Leonard, H. L. (1992). Trichotillomania. An obsessive compulsive spectrum disorder? *The Psychiatry Clinics of North America, 15,* 777–790.

Teng, E. J., Woods, D. W., Twohig, M. P., & Marcks, B. A. (2002). Body-focused repetitive behavior problems: Prevalence in a nonreferred population and differences in perceived somatic activity. *Behavior Modification, 26,* 340–360.

Termine, C., Ballotin, U., Rossi, G., Maisano, F., Salini, S., DiNardo, R., et al. (2006). Psychopathology in children and adolescents with Tourette's syndrome: A controlled study. *Brain and Development, 28,* 69–75.

Thibert, A. L., Day, H. I., & Sandor, P. (1995). Self-concept and self-consciousness in adults with Tourette's syndrome. *Canadian Journal of Psychiatry, 40,* 35–39.

Tosti, A., Morelli, R., Bardazzi, F., & Peluso, A. M. (1994). Prevalence of nail abnormalities in children with alopecia areata. *Pediatric Dermatology, 11,* 112–115.

Wand, R. R., Matazow, G. S., Shady, G. A., Furer, P., & Staley, D. (1993). Tourette syndrome: Associated symptoms and most disabling features. *Neuroscience and Biobehavioral Reviews, 17,* 271–275.

Watson, T. S., & Allen, D. K. (1993). Elimination of thumb-sucking as a treatment for severe trichotillomania. *Journal of the American Academy of Child and Adolescent Psychiatry, 32,* 830–834.

Watson, T. S., & Sterling, H. E. (1998). Brief functional analysis and treatment of a vocal tic. *Journal of Applied Behavior Analysis, 3,* 471–474.

Wells, J. H., Haines, J., & Williams, C. L. (1998). Severe morbid onychophagia: The classification of self-mutilation and a proposed model of maintenance. *The Australian and New Zealand Journal of Psychiatry, 32,* 534–545.

Wells, J. H., Haines, J., Williams, C. L., & Brain, K. L. (1999). The self-mutilative nature of severe onychophagia: A comparison with self-cutting. *Canadian Journal of Psychiatry, 44,* 40–47.

Wetterneck, C. T., Woods, D. W., Norberg, M. N., & Begotka, A. M. (2006). The social and economic impact of trichotillomania: Results from two nonreferred samples. *Behavioral Interventions, 21,* 97–109.

Wilkinson, B. J., Marshall, R. M., & Curtwright, B. (2008). Impact of Tourette's disorder on parent reported stress. *Journal of Child and Family Studies, 17,* 582–598.

Wilkinson, B. J., Newman, M. B., Shytle, R. D., Silver, A. A., Sanberg, P. R., & Sheehan, D. (2001). Family impact of Tourette's syndrome. *Journal of Child and Family Studies, 10,* 477–483.

Williams, T. I., Rose, R., & Chisholm, S. (2007). What is the function of nailbiting: An analog assessment study. *Behavior Research and Therapy, 45,* 989–995.

Winchel, R. M. (1992). Trichotillomania: Presentation and treatment. *Psychiatric Annals, 22,* 84–89.

Wodrich, D. L., Benjamin, E., & Lachar, D. (1997). Tourette's syndrome and psychopathology in a child psychiatry setting. *Journal of the American Academy of Child and Adolescent Psychiatry, 36,* 1618–1624.

Woods, D. W., Conelea, C. A., & Himle, M. B. (2010). Behavior therapy for Tourette's Disorder: Utilization in a community sample and an emerging area of practice for psychologists. *Professional Psychology, 41,* 518–525.

Woods, D. W., Flessner, C. A., Franklin, M. E., Keuthen, N. J., Goodwin, R. D., Stein, D. J., et al. (2006). Trichotillomania Learning Center Scientific Advisory Board: The Trichotillomania impact project (TIP): Exploring phenomenology, functional impairment, and treatment utilization. *The Journal of Clinical Psychiatry, 67,* 1877–1888.

Woods, D. W., Fuqua, R. W., & Outman, R. C. (1999). Evaluating the social acceptability of persons with habit disorders: The effects of topography, frequency, and gender manipulation. *Journal of Psychopathology and Behavioral Assessment, 21,* 1–18.

Woods, D. W., Himle, M. B., & Osmon, D. C. (2005). Use of the Impact on Family Scale in children with tic disorders: Descriptive data, validity, and tic severity impact. *Child and Family Behavior Therapy, 27,* 11–21.

Woods, D. W., Miltenberger, R. G., & Flach, A. D. (1996). Habits, tics, and stuttering: Prevalence and relation to anxiety and somatic awareness. *Behavior Modification, 20,* 216–225.

Woods, D. W., Piacentini, J., Himle, M. B., & Chang, S. (2005). Premonitory Urge for Tics Scale (PUTS): Initial psychometric results and examination of the premonitory urge phenomenon in youths with Tic disorders. *Journal of Developmental and Behavioral Pediatrics, 26,* 397–403.

Woods, D. W., Watson, T. S., Wolfe, E., Twohig, M. P., & Friman, P. C. (2001). Analyzing the influence of tic-related talk on vocal and motor tics in children with Tourette's syndrome. *Journal of Applied Behavior Analysis, 34,* 353–356.

Wright, H. H., & Holmes, G. R. (2003). Trichotillomania (hair pulling) in toddlers. *Psychological Reports, 92,* 228–230.

Zhu, Y., Leung, K. M., Liu, P. Z., Zhou, M., & Su, L. Y. (2006). Comorbid behavioural problems in Tourette's syndrome are positively correlated with the severity of tic symptoms. *Australian and New Zealand Journal of Psychiatry, 40,* 67–73.

PART 3

Approaches to Understanding OCD and Spectrum Disorders

Genetic Understanding of OCD and Spectrum Disorders

Jack F. Samuels, Marco A. Grados, Elizabeth Planalp, *and* O. Joseph Bienvenu

Abstract

This chapter reviews the evidence for the genetic etiology of OCD and spectrum conditions. A genetic basis is supported by the familial aggregation of OCD; evidence for involvement of genes of major effect in segregation analyses; and higher concordance for OCD in identical than non-identical twins. Recent studies also support linkage of OCD to specific chromosomal regions and association of OCD with specific genetic polymorphisms. However, specific genes causing OCD have not yet been firmly established. The search for genes is complicated by the clinical and etiologic heterogeneity of OCD, as well as the possibility of gene–gene and gene–environmental interactions. Despite this complexity, developments in molecular and statistical genetics, and further refinement of the phenotype hold promise for further deepening our genetic understanding of OCD and spectrum disorders in the coming decade.

Keywords: obsessive compulsive disorder, genetics, family studies, twin studies, genetic linkage, genetic association, candidate genes

Obsessive compulsive disorder (OCD) is characterized by impairing intrusive, unwanted ideations, images, or urges (obsessions) and/or repetitive, rigid behaviors (compulsions), often occurring in response to obsessions. Although OCD once was thought to be primarily psychogenic in origin (Freud, 1909), there is now compelling evidence that this disorder has a biological basis. First, obsessions and compulsions often occur in the context of several medical conditions, including encephalitis lethargica (von Economo's encephalitis), Parkinson's disease, Huntington's chorea, Sydenham's chorea, certain epilepsies, and insults to specific brain regions due to trauma, ischemia, and tumors (Stein, 2002). Second, serotonin reuptake inhibitors (clomipramine) and selective serotonin reuptake inhibitors (e.g., fluoxetine, fluvoxamine, and sertraline) have demonstrated efficacy in controlling obsessions and compulsions (Koran, Hanna, Hollander, Nestadt, &

Simpson, 2007). Third, results from neuroimaging and pharmacologic studies implicate cortico-striatal-thalamic pathways in the pathophysiology of the disorder (See Chapter 7, Neuroanatomy of Obsessive Compulsive and Related Disorders).

In this chapter, we review the evidence for the genetic etiology of OCD and spectrum conditions. This evidence is provided by over two decades of rigorous research, including family studies, twin studies, genetic linkage studies, and candidate gene studies. These studies have investigated the following questions: Is the prevalence of OCD greater in the relatives of OCD cases than in the relatives of controls (i.e., is there familial aggregation of OCD)? Are other disorders more prevalent in the relatives of OCD cases than the relatives of controls? Are certain clinical subtypes of OCD more likely to be familial? Is the pattern of aggregation of OCD in families consistent with a Mendelian mode of inheritance? Is concordance for OCD greater in identical than nonidentical twins? Are specific chromosomal regions genetically linked to OCD? Is OCD associated with specific candidate genes? Are there specific environmental risk correlates of OCD?

Animal Models

Ethologists have described stereotypical behaviors in animals that appear to be excessive, maladaptive variants of innate, adaptive "fixed action patterns" (Pitman, 1989). The best studied of these stereotypical behaviors is acral lick dermatitis (lick granuloma), which is observed in several species of mammals, including large-breed dogs. It is characterized by excessive licking or biting of the legs, leading to lesions and hair loss. Interestingly, the behavior is responsive to serotonin reuptake inhibitors, including clomipramine and fluoxetine (Veith, 1985). Apparently related disorders include flank-sucking in dogs, tail-sucking and tail-biting in cats, and feather-picking in birds (Korff & Harvey, 2006). "Zoo stereotypies" are sometimes seen in confined or isolated animals; captive primates may demonstrate constant rocking or excessive grooming behaviors, including hair pulling and self-mutilation (Stein, Shoulberg, Helton, Hollander, 1992). Fur and whisker trimming ("barbering") is a common behavior in laboratory mice, with some evidence for genetic influences. Marble burying in rodents, characterized by burying in bedding materials glass marbles introduced into cages, is a possible animal model for hoarding. It has been proposed that evolutionarily conserved neural circuits are important in the detection of threats and avoidance of harm, and that a feedback deficit in these circuits leads to "compulsive" behaviors in animals and humans (Korff & Harvey, 2006).

Researchers also have developed genetically altered mice that exhibit abnormal "compulsive" or "stereotypic" behaviors, and have been proposed as models of OCD. For example, mice with alterations in the dopamine D1 receptor gene exhibit tics, repetitive leaping, and repetitive biting of siblings during grooming. Mice with disruptions of the Hoxb8 gene demonstrate excessive grooming behavior, often leading to hair removal and skin lesions, and mice with disruptions of the dopamine transporter gene exhibit excessive, stereotyped grooming behaviors (Joel, 2006). As discussed in more detail below, mice with deletions of the SAPAP3 gene show compulsive grooming behavior, leading to facial hair loss and skin lesions (Welch et al., 2007).

Twin Studies

Identical (monozygotic) twins are genetically identical, whereas fraternal (dizygotic) twins share, on average, only 50% of their genes. Thus, greater concordance of symptoms in identical than in nonidentical twins supports genetic influence on those symptoms. As reviewed by van Grootheest et al. (2005), concordance of OCD symptoms in identical twins has been reported since 1929. For example, Lewis (1936) described two pairs of identical twins who were concordant for obsessional traits and compulsive features. Since then, there have been several reports of monozygotic twins concordant for obsessive compulsive symptoms (Cryan, Butcher, & Webb, 1992; Marks, Crowe, Drewe, Young, & Dewhurst, 1969; McGuffin & Mawson, 1980; Woodruff & Pitts, 1964), but also reports of monozygous twins discordant for these symptoms (Hoaken & Schnurr, 1980). In a Japanese series, Inouye reported concordance for obsessive compulsive symptoms in 8 of 10 monozygotic twin pairs, as compared to 1 of 4 dizygotic twin pairs (Inouye, 1965). Similar results were reported from the Maudsley Twin Registry; in 15 monozygotic and 15 dizygotic twin pairs, the concordance for "obsessive symptoms or features" were 87% and 47%, respectively (Carey & Gottesman, 1981).

More recently, investigators have evaluated the heritability of obsessive compulsive symptoms assessed dimensionally. Clifford, Murray and Fulker (1984) estimated that the heritability of obsessional symptoms in 419 twin pairs was 47%, whereas unique (i.e., nonshared) environment appeared to explain the remaining 53% of the variation. Jonnal et al. (2000) estimated heritabilities of 33% and 26% for obsessive and compulsive dimensions, respectively, whereas unique environmental influences appeared to account for the remainder (Jonnal, Gardner, Prescott, & Kendler, 2000). In 4,564 four-year-old twin pairs, Eley and colleagues estimated the heritability of obsessive compulsive behaviors at 65%, with the remaining 35% of variance in these behaviors attributed to unshared environmental influences (Eley, Bolton, O'Connor, Perrin, Smith, & Plomin, 2003). In 4,246 child twin pairs, Hudziak and colleagues estimated heritability of 45%–61% for obsessive compulsive symptoms, with unique environmental influences of 42%–55% (Hudziak et al., 2004).

Taken together, the results from these studies suggest that genetic factors strongly contribute to the development of OCD, explaining about 50% of the variance of symptoms. However, unshared environmental factors also explain about 50% of the variance of OC symptoms. An additional strategy for investigating genetic and environmental contributions to OCD would be studies of twins reared apart; however, no such studies have been reported for OCD (van Grootheest et al., 2005).

Family Studies

Clinicians have long observed that many of their patients with OCD have relatives with the disorder, and they have suspected that heredity plays a role in the transmission of the disorder within families. One of the first reports in the English literature was of 50 cases of "obsessional neurosis" treated at the Maudsley Hospital in London. It was found that 37% of the parents of the cases had "pronounced obsessional traits," and 21% of siblings of the cases had "mild or severe obsessional traits" (Lewis, 1936). Other family history studies, which did not directly examine relatives of cases, reported that 4%–8% of relatives of OCD patients themselves had OCD (Brown, 1942), which is higher than the 1%–3% prevalence of OCD in the community (Weissman et al., 1994). Based on these and other early reports of occurrence of the disorder in relatives of patients, Slater concluded that "of all neurotic syndromes, the evidence relating to genetic predisposition is best in the case of obsessional neurosis" (Slater, 1964).

Later family studies which, unlike earlier studies, used explicit diagnostic criteria and directly interviewed relatives, reported that 0%–28% of relatives of adult patients and 7%–15% of relatives of child and adolescent patients had OCD (Bellodi, Sciuto, Diaferia, Ronchi, & Smeraldi, 1992; Chabane et al., 2005; Lenane, et al., 1990; McKeon & Murray, 1987; Riddle et al., 1990; Swedo, Rapoport, Leonard, Lenane, & Cheslow, 1989). However, it is only since 1992 that family studies of OCD have been methodologically rigorous, including use of explicit diagnostic criteria, direct assessment of relatives, structured or semistructured assessment instruments, inclusion of a non-OCD comparison group, and assessment of relatives by interviewers blind to the case or control status of the probands (i.e., the cases through which the families are ascertained).

In the first such study, Black and colleagues (1992) reported that the lifetime prevalence of OCD was similar in 120 adult first-degree relatives of 32 OCD probands (2.5%) and 128 relatives of 33 psychiatrically normal controls (2.3%). The prevalence of "subsyndromal OCD," defined as the presence of obsessions and/or compulsions but without sufficient impairment or distress, also was similar in the two groups of relatives (17.5% vs. 12.5%), as was the prevalence of tics (4% vs. 7%). However, the age-corrected morbid risk of "broadly defined OCD" (OCD plus subsyndromal OCD) was substantially greater in the parents of the OCD probands compared to parents of controls (15.6% vs. 3%). In addition, the lifetime prevalence of generalized anxiety disorder was significantly greater in the relatives of the OCD probands than relatives of controls (22% vs. 12%) (Black, Noyes, Goldstein, & Blum, 1992).

Pauls et al. (1995) reported that the morbid risk of OCD was significantly greater in 466 first-degree relatives of 100 OCD patients, as compared to 113 relatives of 33 psychiatrically normal controls (10.3% vs. 1.9%). The relatives of the OCD probands also had greater morbid risk of subthreshold OCD (7.9% vs. 2.0%), OCD plus subthreshold OCD (18.2% vs. 4%), and tics (4.6% vs. 1.0%). Moreover, the morbid risk of subthreshold OCD was greater in relatives of OCD probands with early onset (age < 19 years) as compared to probands with later onset (9.4% vs. 2.2%), as was the risk of OCD plus subthreshold OCD (20.1% vs. 10.9%; Pauls, Alsobrook, Goodman, Rasmussen, & Leckman, 1995).

In the Johns Hopkins University (JHU) OCD Family Study, Nestadt et al. (2000) reported that the lifetime prevalence of definite OCD was significantly greater in 343 first-degree relatives of 80 adult OCD case probands, compared to 300 relatives of 73 adult control probands (11.7% vs. 2.7%). The lifetime prevalence of definite or probable OCD also was greater in relatives of case probands than in relatives of control probands (16.3% vs. 5.7%). The prevalence of OCD in the relatives of probands with onset of OC symptoms before the age of 18 years was 14%; in contrast, none of the relatives of probands with later age at onset was diagnosed with OCD. In case vs. control relatives, the relative odds of definite OCD was 4.7; of definite compulsions, 3.4; and of definite obsessions, 4.7, suggesting that obsessions are more specific to the inherited phenotype than compulsions. The prevalence of OCD in case relatives was not related to the presence of tics in case probands (Nestadt et al., 2000).

Fyer and colleagues (2000) directly interviewed 179 first-degree relatives of 72 adult OCD probands, and 112 relatives of 32 never mentally ill adult controls. They found that the prevalence of definite

OCD (6.2% vs. 0%), or definite or probable OCD (8.4% vs. 0%), was significantly greater in relatives of case vs. control probands, respectively. They did not find a difference in the prevalence of OCD (5.8% vs. 7.5%) or definite or probable OCD (7.9% vs. 10.0%) in relatives of case probands with onset of OCD before or after 18 years of age, respectively (Fyer, Lipsitz, Mannuzza, Aronowitz, & Chapman, 2005).

More recently, Grabe et al. (2006) reported on the first European family study of OCD, which compared 285 first-degree relatives of 90 OCD patients; 58 relatives of 15 nontreated OCD individuals from the community; and 247 relatives of 70 non-OCD outpatients. They found significantly higher rates of definite OCD in relatives of community probands (10.3%) and in relatives of clinical probands (5.6%) than in relatives of the controls (1.2%). They also found that subclinical OCD, in which obsessions and/or compulsions were present but distress or impairment criteria were not met, was significantly more prevalent in relatives of community probands than in relatives of comparison subjects (15.4% vs. 3.0%). The proband's age at onset of OCD was not found to be related to the risk of OCD in relatives.

Hanna and colleagues (2005) studied the familial aggregation of OCD in relatives of child and adolescent probands (age 10–17 years old). They interviewed 102 case and 39 control relatives. They found that prevalence of definite OCD was substantially greater in the case vs. control relatives (22.5% vs. 2.6%), as was the prevalence of definite+subthreshold OCD (27.4% vs. 2.6%). The prevalence of tic disorders was similar in case and control relatives (7.1% vs. 5.3%). Prevalence of OCD in relatives was not related to proband gender, proband age at onset, or proband tic disorders. However, relatives of case probands with ordering compulsions had a significantly higher rate of definite OCD (33% vs. 17%) and definite+subthreshold OCD (45% vs. 19%) than did relatives of case probands without ordering compulsions (Hanna, Himle, Curtis, & Gillespie, 2005).

In another family study of child and adolescent probands, Rosario-Campos et al. (2005) studied 106 case probands and 325 of their first-degree relatives, compared to 44 community control probands and 140 of their first-degree relatives. They found that the prevalence of OCD was substantially greater in case than control relatives (22.7% vs. 0.9%), as was the prevalence of OCD+subclinical OCD (29.2% vs. 2.4%). In addition, the prevalence of

chronic tics was significantly greater in case than control relatives (11.7% vs. 1.7%). Moreover, the prevalence of OCD was significantly greater in the relatives of case probands with chronic tics (23.8%) than in the relatives of case probands without chronic tics (14.9%).

Additional investigation of the familial phenotypic spectrum of OCD was conducted in the JHU OCD Family Study sample. Nestadt et al. (2001) reported that generalized anxiety disorder, agoraphobia, panic disorder, separation anxiety disorder, and recurrent major depression were significantly more prevalent in case than in control relatives. After controlling for the relative's age, gender, and type of examination (direct or informant-only), presence of OCD, and proband's diagnosis, the odds of generalized anxiety disorder and, on the border of statistical significance, agoraphobia, were greater in relatives of case than control probands, suggesting that these disorders are part of the phenotypic spectrum of OCD in these families. In contrast, other disorders (social phobia, specific phobia, schizophrenia, alcohol dependence, substance dependence, bipolar disorder, or dysthymia) were not more prevalent in the case than control relatives, and not part of the phenotypic spectrum of OCD in these families.

Bienvenu et al. (2000) investigated the familial aggregation of other putative "OCD spectrum" disorders in these families. They found that body dysmorphic disorder and grooming disorders (nailbiting, skin-picking, or trichotillomania) were significantly more prevalent in case than control relatives, suggesting that these disorders are part of the familial OCD phenotypic spectrum in these families. Other disorders, including anorexia, bulimia, kleptomania, pathological gambling, and pyromania did not appear to be part of the OCD phenotypic spectrum; however, the results for these disorders should be interpreted cautiously, given the relatively low prevalence of the disorders and hence low statistical power to detect differences.

Samuels et al. (2000) investigated personality disorders and general personality traits in these families. They found that obsessive compulsive personality disorder was significantly more prevalent in case than control relatives (11.5% vs. 5.8%, respectively). They also found that mean scores on neuroticism were significantly higher in case than control relatives. Moreover, there was a significant relationship between neuroticism score and the prevalence of obsessive compulsive personality disorder in case relatives, but not in control relatives. These findings suggest that high neuroticism also is part of the phenotypic spectrum of OCD in these families.

Grados et al. (2001) reported on the prevalence of tic disorders in the Hopkins OCD Family Study sample. They found that tic disorders were more prevalent in the relatives of OCD probands than in the control relatives, including chronic motor or vocal tic disorder (4.3% vs. 1.4%) and any tic disorder (6.2% vs. 1.7%). Among the case relatives, the prevalence of tic disorders was greater in those with a male than with a female proband (9.1% vs. 3.9%, p=0.05). The prevalence of tic disorders also was greater in case relatives whose proband had early-onset (before 18 years old) compared to later-onset OCD (7.3% vs. 0%, p=0.09).

Thus, of these seven rigorous family studies, all but one found strong evidence for the familial aggregation of OCD. Two of the studies found that the prevalence of OCD was greater in relatives of probands with early age at onset of OCD, while both studies with child and adolescent probands found similar, and very high, prevalences of OCD in case relatives. Three of the studies found that generalized anxiety disorder was significantly more prevalent in the relatives of OCD cases than in controls, suggesting that this disorder is part of the familial phenotypic spectrum in these families. Tic disorders, pathological grooming disorders, body dysmorphic disorder, obsessive compulsive personality disorder, and high neuroticism may also be part of the inherited spectrum of OCD, although these results all come from a single study.

Segregation Analysis

Complex segregation analysis is a statistical approach for determining if transmission of a disorder in families is consistent with a Mendelian model of inheritance. Nicolini et al. (1991) conducted segregation analysis on 24 OCD families ascertained from a child psychiatry clinic. They found that dominant and recessive models had similar "fit" to the data, and neither model could be rejected. Cavallini and colleagues (1999) studied 107 Italian families with an OCD proband. They found that, although the dominant model of transmission of OCD best fit the data, additive or recessive models could not be rejected (Cavallini, Pasquale, Bellodi, & Smeraldi, 1999).

Nestadt et al. (2000) conducted segregation analysis on 153 families (80 case and 73 control families) ascertained in the JHU OCD Family Study. A dominant model best fit the data. In addition, there was evidence of greater penetrance in families with a female proband; in these families, the dominant and codominant models could not be rejected and fit the data almost equally well. In families with a male proband, the data were compatible with Mendelian transmission, but dominant, codominant, and recessive models fit the data almost equally well and could not be rejected.

More recently, Hanna, Fingerlin, Himle, and Boehnke (2005) studied 52 OCD families ascertained through an affected child or adolescent proband. The results were consistent with Mendelian transmission, and the best fit was with the dominant model, but dominant, codominant, and recessive models fit the data almost equally and could not be distinguished.

Alsobrook and colleagues (1999) conducted analyses in 96 OCD probands and 453 first-degree relatives, using dichotomized obsessive compulsive symptom factor scores to characterize probands. They found that, in the families with 2 or more cases of OCD, and in which the proband scored higher on the symmetry and ordering dimension, there was evidence for Mendelian transmission; the best fit was with the recessive model, but dominant and additive models fit the data almost equally well (Alsobrook, Leckman, Goodman, Rasmussen, & Pauls, 1999).

Thus, results from these five published complex segregation analyses suggest that a gene or gene(s) of major effect are involved in the etiology of OCD and is (are) transmitted in a Mendelian fashion. In several of the studies, a dominant or codominant model best fit the data, but the results do not definitively distinguish between models.

Genetic Linkage Studies

The aim of genetic linkage studies in OCD is to identify chromosomal regions containing OCD genes by analyzing the cosegregation of genetic markers with OCD in families. Parametric approaches evaluate genetic recombination events between OCD and genetic markers, and make assumptions about the mode of inheritance. In contrast, nonparametric approaches evaluate the extent to which affected siblings (or other affected relatives) share marker alleles from the same parent (or other ancestor), and explicit assumptions about the mode of inheritance are not required (Lathrop & Weeks, in Bishop & Sham, 2000). If a linkage peak is identified, "fine mapping" is often conducted to narrow the linkage region by including additional genetic markers, either microsatellite markers or single nucleotide polymorphisms (SNPs). In addition, family-based association analyses may be conducted to evaluate associations between specific SNPs within these linkage regions and OCD.

Hanna et al. (2002) conducted a genome scan in 56 individuals from 7 families ascertained through pediatric OCD probands. Parametric linkage analysis under a dominant model identified a suggestive linkage peak on chromosome 9 (chromosomal region 9p24). This region is of interest, because it contains a gene involved in neurotransmission, the glutamate transporter (SLC1A1 and EAAC1), a potential functional candidate gene for OCD. However, a screen for genetic mutations in the 7 pediatric OCD probands did not find coding region mutations leading to amino acid changes in this gene, and there was no association between 2 SNPs in this gene and OCD (Veenstra-VanderWeele, Kim, Gonen, Hanna, Leventhal, & Cook, 2001).

In an attempt to replicate the linkage finding in the chromosome 9p24 linkage region, Willour et al. (2004) conducted linkage analyses in 50 OCD pedigrees, using the same 13 genetic markers in this region used by Hanna et al. (2002). Parametric analyses under a dominant model, as well as nonparametric analyses, found a suggestive linkage peak within the linkage signal previously found by Hanna et al. (2002). Moreover, pedigree-based association analyses identified two markers with modest evidence of association within this region. These findings provide additional evidence for an OCD susceptibility gene in this region. It should be noted that the 9p24 linkage region is wide, spanning 7.5 Mb (i.e., 7.5 million base pairs), and it contains dozens of known and predicted genes that are potential candidate genes for OCD (Willour et al., 2004).

Shugart et al. (2006) conducted another genome-wide linkage study in 219 families with multiple relatives affected with OCD (mostly sibling pairs) ascertained during the OCD Collaborative Genetics Study (OCGS; Samuels et al., 2006). The strongest suggestive linkage signal was found on chromosome 3q27–28; other suggestive linkage signals were found in regions on chromosomes 1, 6, 7, and 15. In addition, there was evidence for stronger linkage on chromosome 1 in families with earlier age at onset, and on chromosome 7 in families with later age at onset, suggesting possible genetic heterogeneity by age at onset of OCD. There was no evidence of linkage in the chromosome 9 region implicated by Hanna et al. (2002) and Willour et al. (2004).

It should be noted, however, that 3 of the 7 pediatric probands in the Hanna study had Tourette syndrome (TS), whereas the OCGS had mostly adult probands and excluded probands with TS. Thus, the Hanna et al. (2002) findings may be more applicable to a tic-related subtype of OCD.

There is substantial evidence that compulsive hoarding constitutes a clinically distinct subtype or factor dimension of OCD (See Chapter 4, Phenomenology and Characteristics of Compulsive Hoarding). In addition, in OCD families, hoarding behavior is more prevalent in relatives of OCD probands with hoarding, compared to relatives of OCD probands without hoarding (Samuels et al., 2007). Therefore, Samuels et al. (2007) examined hoarding in linkage analyses of the 219 multiplex OCD families evaluated for the OCGS. Using compulsive hoarding as the phenotype, there was suggestive linkage at a region on chromosome 14q23–32. Moreover, in families with 2 or more relatives with hoarding, there was significant linkage of OCD to this region of chromosome 14. In contrast, in families with 0 or 1 relative with hoarding, there was suggestive linkage to chromosome 3 but not to chromosome 14. These findings provide support for the genetic heterogeneity of OCD, suggesting a different genetic etiology for hoarding and nonhoarding subtypes.

Additional evidence for the genetic heterogeneity of OCD was provided by linkage analysis of the OCGS families, stratified by proband gender (Wang et al., 2009). There was suggestive linkage to chromosome 11p15 in families with male probands, but not in families with female probands. The linkage signal in the families with male probands became substantially stronger after fine mapping in this region with 632 SNPs. Of 6 SNPs associated with OCD in this region, 4 were significantly associated with OCD in male but not female proband families.

In summary, genetic linkage studies have provided evidence linking specific chromosomal regions to OCD. Results from these studies also support the concept of subtypes of OCD that may be more genetically homogeneous. However, other than the hoarding linkage findings, almost all of the regions identified so far have provided evidence of only "suggestive" linkage and have not met the threshold for "significant" linkage (Kruglyak & Lander, 1995). Additional fine mapping, in larger samples, is required, since the linkage regions so far identified may contain hundreds of potential positional candidate genes, or regulatory regions outside of the protein-coding regions of genes. Linkage analysis may not be sufficiently powerful to identify these genetic variants, which individually may contribute only modestly to OCD vulnerability.

Molecular Genetic Studies

Although the pathological processes underlying core OCD symptoms have not been identified, findings from neuropharmacological, neuroimaging, and neurocognitive research support involvement of cortico-striato-thalamic-cortico (CSTC) circuits in the pathophysiology of OCD (Stein, Goodman, & Rauch, 2000). In theory, neurotransmitter systems within CSTC circuits, individually or via their interactions, may play a role in susceptibility, course, or response to OCD treatment. Therefore, genes affecting the development, connectivity, and neurotransmission in these circuits have been natural foci of interest as potential functional candidates for OCD. The results of candidate gene studies in OCD have been presented in several excellent, recent reviews (Hemmings & Stein, 2006; Grados & Wilcox, 2007).

Serotonergic Genes

Given the therapeutic effect of serotonin reuptake inhibitors in the treatment of OCD, the serotonergic system has been a primary focus of candidate gene studies of OCD. The serotonin transporter gene (SLC6A4) on chromosome 17 is a target for the action of serotonin reuptake inhibitor drugs, which increase the availability of serotonin in synapses by decreasing the action of the gene product. The gene has a functional 44-base pair insertion/deletion polymorphism in the promoter region (5HTTLPR). Several studies have implicated the long (L) allele in OCD. McDougle, Epperson, Price, and Gelernter (1998) reported that the L-allele was transmitted to OCD-affected children significantly more often than the short (S) allele in 34 case-parent trios. In addition, in a population-based association study, Bengel et al. (1999) found that a greater proportion of 75 OCD patients than 397 matched controls carried two copies of the L-allele. However, these findings were not supported by subsequent family-based and population-based association studies in a variety of ethnic groups (Chabane et al., 2004; Kinnear et al., 2000; Meira-Lima et al., 2004Walitza et al., 2004), and other recent studies have implicated the S-allele rather than the L-allele (Lin, 2007; Perez, Brown, Vrshek-Schallhorn, Johnson, & Joiner et al., 2006). Hasler et al. (2006) found that, in 153 OCD cases, the S-allele was associated with a symmetry/ordering factor, whereas Kim et al. (2005) found that, in 124 OCD patients, those with the L-allele had higher scores on a religious/somatic factor (Hasler, Kazuba, & Murphy, 2006; Kim, Lee, & Kim, 2005).

Another variant (I425V) in the serotonin transporter gene was found to be associated with a complex phenotype in two unrelated families; the phenotype included OCD, pervasive developmental disorder, and eating disorders (Ozaki et al., 2003). However, results from subsequent studies suggested that this variant explains, at most, only a very small proportion of cases of OCD (Delorme et al., 2005; Grados et al., 2007; Wendland et al., 2007). More recently, reports have associated OCD with a variable number of tandem repeats polymorphism in intron 2 of the serotonin transporter gene (Baca-Garcia et al., 2007; Saiz et al., 2008).

Animal and pharmacological studies have implicated specific serotonin receptor subtypes in the pathophysiology of OCD, and several of these genes have been investigated as potential functional candidate genes for OCD in family-based and population-based association studies (Hemmings & Stein, 2006). The evidence for the association of these genes to OCD is mixed. For example, the serotonin receptor type 5-HT1Db gene on chromosome 1 was found associated with OCD in some studies (Mundo et al., 2002; Camarena et al., 2004) but not others (Di Bella, Cavallini, & Bellodi, 2002; Walitza et al., 2004). Similarly, the serotonin receptor type 5-HT2A gene on chromosome 13 was found associated with OCD in some studies (Denys, van Nieuwerburgh, Deforce, & Westenberg, 2006; Meira-Lima et al., 2004) but not others (Nicolini et al., 1996).

Dopaminergic Genes

The dopamine receptor 4 (DRD4) gene on chromosome 11 has been extensively investigated as a candidate gene in several psychiatric disorders, including OCD. The gene has a 48-base pair motif that may be repeated 2–10 times (i.e., a variable number of tandem repeats) and affects the functioning of the gene. Several studies have found an association between OCD and specific alleles of the gene, based on the number of repeats (Camarena et al., Loyzaga, Aguilar, Weissbecker, & Nicolini, 2007; Millet et al., 2003). In several of these studies, the magnitude and significance of the association depended on the subphenotype; e.g., comorbid tics, or early onset of OCD (Cruz et al., 1997; Hemmings et al., 2004). Other studies, however, have been negative (Hemmings et al., 2003). The association between OCD and several other dopaminergic genes have been investigated, including dopamine receptor 2 (DRD2), dopamine receptor 3 (DRD3), and the dopamine transporter (DAT or Slc6a3). In general, the results from these studies have been negative (Billet et al., 1998; Catalano et al., 1994; Frisch et al., 2000).

COMT Gene

The catechol-O-methyltransferase (COMT) gene on chromosome 22 codes for an enzyme involved in the inactivation of several important neurotransmitters (norepinephrine, epinephrine, and dopamine) and has been intensively studied as a functional candidate gene for psychiatric diseases, including OCD. A single nucleotide polymorphism (valine-to-methionine substitution) substantially decreases the activity of the enzyme. Karayiorgou et al. (1997) and Karayiorgou et al. (1999) reported an association between OCD and the low activity allele in men but not women, in population-based and family-based studies. In case–control studies, Pooley, Fineberg, and Harrison (2007) also found an association in men but not women. In contrast, Alsobrook et al. (2002) found an association between OCD and the low activity allele in women but not men. Moreover, Schindler et al. (2000) found an association between OCD and homozygosity at the locus which was not gender-specific, whereas Niehaus et al. (2001) found that the heterozygous genotype was more frequent in OCD patients and was not gender-specific. Furthermore, several subsequent studies did not find an association between this polymorphism and OCD (Azzam & Matthews, 2003; Erdal et al., 2003; Meira-Lima et al., 2004; Ohara et al., 1998).

MAO-A Gene

The monoamine oxidase A (MAO-A) gene on the X chromosome codes for a mitochondrial enzyme that degrades several neurotransmitters, including norepinephrine, dopamine, and serotonin. In a family-based association study, Karayiorgou et al. (1999) found an association between a single nucleotide polymorphism in the gene and OCD in men but not women. However, Camarena et al. (2001) found an association between this polymorphism in women but not men, in both family-based and population-based association studies. Moreover, Hemmings et al. (2003) did not find an association between this polymorphism and OCD in Afrikaner cases.

Neurodevelopmental Genes

Other plausible candidates for psychiatric disorders, including OCD, are genes that influence the development of the central nervous system. Brain-derived neurotrophic factor (BDNF) is one of several proteins that affect the growth, differentiation, and maturation of neurons. In 164 trios, Hall, Dhilla, Charalambous, Gogos, and Karayiorgou (2003) found a significant association between OCD and several polymorphisms in the BDNF gene on chromosome 11. However, subsequent family-based and case–control studies did not find an association between these and other SNPs, and OCD (Wendland et al., 2007; Zai et al., 2005).

Another candidate gene for OCD is the oligodendrocyte lineage transcription factor 2 (OLIG2) gene on chromosome 21, which has been reported to be related to the amount of white matter in the brain (Cannistraro et al., 2007). Stewart et al. (2007) reported that, in a family-based association study of 66 OCD families, several haplotypes in this gene were significantly associated with OCD. Another gene, the myelin oligodendrocyte protein (MOG) gene, impacts the amount of myelin in the brain and helps mediate the complement cascade of the immune system. Zai et al. (2004) reported an association between OCD and several polymorphisms in this gene in 160 OCD trios. Additional family-based and population-based studies are needed to replicate these findings, as well as to investigate additional developmental genes, including Hoxb8 on chromosome 17, which has been implicated in grooming behaviors in mice (Greer & Cappechi, 2002).

Glutamatergic Genes

Currently, there is a great deal of excitement about the possible association between a neuronal glutamate transporter gene (SLC1A1) and OCD. As discussed above, the first genome-wide linkage scan of OCD found suggestive linkage of early-onset OCD to a region of chromosome 9p24 that includes this gene (Hanna et al., 2002). A linkage peak very close to this region was subsequently found in in 50 OCD pedigrees, and pedigree-based association analyses identified 2 markers associated with OCD in this region (Willour et al., 2004). Moreover, the gene is expressed in the cortex, striatum, and thalamus, regions of the brain that have been implicated in OCD.

Recently, three research groups reported association findings between OCD and SNPs in the glutamate transporter. Dickel et al (2006) genotyped

9 SNPs in this gene, and reported association with two of them in patients with OCD. Further, they detected a deletion in a flanking region of the gene in a large multigenerational family. In addition, they identified a haplotype comprising two SNPs that was undertransmitted in the entire sample and in the sample of male probands, but not in the sample of female probands. Arnold et al. (2006) found an association between OCD and 3 of SNPs in this gene in patients with OCD. Further, they conducted a haplotype-based association analysis considering two SNPs jointly after stratifying the families by proband gender (97 families with a female proband and 60 families with a male proband). They detected significant evidence of overtransmission to male but not female offspring. Stewart et al. (2007) reported an association between alleles of a 3-SNP haplotype of this gene and OCD in all their families, and in those families with male probands. It is noteworthy that SNPs in this haplotype overlap with those reported by Dickel et al. (2006).

Recently, Welch et al. (2007) reported on mice with a genetic deletion of the SAPAP3 gene. This gene codes for a scaffolding protein at excitatory synapses, and is highly expressed in the striatum. The knockout mice exhibited increased anxiety and compulsive grooming behavior, with facial hair loss and skin lesions. These behaviors were significantly reduced following treatment with the selective serotonin reuptake inhibitor, fluoxetine. The mice had reduced activity in cortico-striatal synapses, which constitute the large majority of glutamatergic synapses in the striatum. When viruses containing the gene were injected into the striatum of the mice with the deletion, the excessive grooming behavior, lesion severity, and anxiety-like behavior were markedly reduced, and cortico-striatal synaptic transmission improved. These findings suggest that defects in glutamatergic excitatory synaptic transmission in the cortico-striatal circuit may contribute to the pathogenesis of grooming disorders, and possibly OCD. Moreover, Bienvenu et al. (2009) recently reported an association between SNPs in the SAPAP3 gene and grooming behavior in OCD families. Thus, although further replication of these findings is required, this gene may be a promising candidate for grooming behaviors and OCD (Leckman & Kim, 2006).

In summary, although there have been many intriguing positive associations between functional candidate genes and OCD, few have been consistently replicated. As noted by Hemmings and Stein (2006), "the preliminary and frequently inconsistent nature of the data represented in the majority of OCD psychiatric genetic-association studies may seem discouraging." There may be differences between study samples that account for this inconsistency, including clinical heterogeneity and underlying genetic differences, as well as methodological differences, including size of the study sample, amount of statistical power, and use of corrections for multiple statistical tests (Hemmings and Stein, 2006). Nevertheless, the consistency of recent linkage, association, and animal findings implicating the glutamatergic system in OCD is striking.

Relative Importance of Genetics and Environment

As presented above, results from twin studies suggest that approximately 50% of individual variation in vulnerability to OCD is due to unique environmental factors not shared by twins. Moreover, family studies have found that a substantial proportion of OCD cases are "sporadic," with no other first-degree relatives affected with OCD. Thus, there is great interest in identifying specific environmental risk factors for OCD.

Clinicians have observed that OCD can emerge following brain injury, including brain trauma, cerebrovascular accident (stroke), brain tumors, and carbon monoxide poisoning (Berthier, Kulisevsky, Gironell, & Lopez, 2001; Childers, Holland, Ryan, & Rupright, 1998; Coetzer, 2004). In addition, β-hemolytic streptococcal infections have been associated with rapid onset of OC symptoms following rheumatic fever, especially in children and adolescents (Murphy, Sajid, & Goodman, 2006; Snider & Swedo, 2004). Moreover, results from a case–control study indicated that a greater proportion of OCD cases than controls reported prenatal or perinatal difficulties, including excessive maternal weight gain during pregnancy, maternal edema during pregnancy, hyperemesis gravidarum, and protracted labor. After statistically controlling for social class, protracted labor (odds ratio=9.3) and maternal edema during pregnancy (odds ratio=7.6) were the perinatal factors most strongly related to the development of OCD (Vasconcelos et al., 2007).

Emotional trauma also has been associated with OCD. There are case reports of OCD emerging after experience of a traumatic event (de Silva & Marks, 1999). Mathews and colleagues reported a significant association between emotional and physical abuse and obsessive compulsive symptoms in college students (Matthews, Kaur, & Stein, 2008). Cromer, Schmidt, and Murphy (2007) reported that, in 265 individuals with OCD, there was a significant relationship between having one or more traumatic life events and severity of OCD, even controlling for severity of depression. Moreover, 2 symptom dimensions (obsessions/checking and symmetry/ordering) were specifically associated with traumatic events, whereas contamination/cleaning and hoarding dimensions were not. Gothelf and colleagues (2004) found that children with OCD had significantly more negative life events in the year before onset than did normal controls. However, children with OCD did not have significantly more negative life events than did children with other anxiety disorders, suggesting that the relationship was not specific for OCD (Gothelf, Aharonovsky, Horesh, Carty, & Apter, 2004). Lochner et al. (2002) found that female patients with OCD or trichotillomania scored significantly higher on a scale of emotional neglect than did normal controls, whereas Wilcox et al. (2008) reported an association between maternal overprotection and OCD. Recently, Cath and colleagues investigated environmental factors in identical twins concordant and discordant for obsessive compulsive symptoms. They found that identical twins who scored high on these symptoms reported more sexual abuse than their co-twin who scored low on these symptoms (Cath, van Grootheest, Willemsen, van Oppen, & Boomsma, 2008).

However, it has been difficult to identify specific environmental risk factors for OCD, as many of these physical and emotional traumas have been associated with the onset of other psychiatric disorders. Furthermore, these retrospective studies have methodological limitations, especially the potential for bias due to selective recall and reliance on the same individual for report of risk factors and OCD symptoms. Thus, confidence in these findings would be greatly enhanced if replicated in prospective studies that measure exposures in individuals without a history of OCD, and follow them forward in time for the development of the disorder (Douglass et al., 1995).

In summary, the relative magnitude of the contribution of genetic and environmental factors to the development of OCD is unclear. We suspect that, as for other complex diseases, there may be interactions between genetic polymorphisms and environmental exposures in the development of OCD. For example, it has been hypothesized that streptococcal infections can lead to OCD, but only in genetically susceptible individuals (Snider & Swedo, 2004). However, potential interactions between other genetic and environmental factors have not been investigated in OCD, given current uncertainties about the relevant candidate susceptibility genes and environmental risk factors. Genetic factors also may correlate with environmental factors; i.e., one's genetic makeup may influence the likelihood of experiencing an adverse event.

Conclusion: Progress and Prospects

As reviewed in this chapter, results from studies conducted over the past two decades strongly support a genetic contribution to the etiology of OCD. First, concordance for OCD is greater in identical than nonidentical twins. Second, OCD aggregates in families, as do other disorders and personality features that may be alternate expressions of the underlying genetic vulnerability. Third, certain clinical features may indicate subtypes that are more likely to be genetic, including early age at onset and hoarding behavior. Fourth, the pattern of OCD in some families is consistent with Mendelian models of transmission. Fifth, several chromosomal regions appear to be linked to OCD.

However, specific genes and genetic variants underlying OCD and spectrum conditions have yet to be convincingly established. We suspect that OCD is genetically complex, with multiple vulnerability genes, each having relatively modest effect; complex interactions between genes, and between genes and environmental factors; and contribution by regulatory and other regions not in the coding regions of genes. Moreover, we suspect that the phenotypic heterogeneity of OCD reflects underlying etiologic heterogeneity, so that specific genes contribute to specific clinical subtypes and dimensions and not to others.

For etiologically complex diseases, in which multiple genetic and environmental factors are thought to contribute, it is crucial to specify clinical phenotypes that most closely reflect the underlying etiology. This is a major challenge for studies of OCD, which is a clinically heterogeneous condition. Obsessions and compulsions are diverse, and there is great variability across affected individuals in the expression of specific symptoms. Other clinical characteristics, including age at onset of symptoms and degree of severity, also vary across individuals with OCD. In addition, affected individuals often have a history of other co-occurring neuropsychiatric disorders, including major depression, anxiety disorders, tic disorders, and grooming disorders, as well as personality disorders and traits (See Chapter 2, Phenomenology and Epidemiology of Obsessive Compulsive Disorder). Progress in elucidating the genetic etiology of OCD will depend on identifying clinical subtypes that are most likely to be transmitted genetically, as well as on identifying the phenotypic spectrum of conditions that may be alternate expressions of an underlying genetic variant.

Nevertheless, despite this complexity, we anticipate substantial progress toward the elucidation of the genetic basis of OCD. First, SNP fine mapping and family-based association analyses are being conducted and should help to significantly narrow the linkage regions (Wang et al., 2009). Second, progress in SNP technology and statistical genetics now makes it possible to conduct genome-wide association studies with thousands of participants and hundreds of thousands of closely-spaced SNP markers distributed throughout the genome, thus greatly increasing the power of finding genes with small effect sizes (Sklar et al., 2008); two large genome-wide association studies of OCD are currently underway. Third, there will be further refinement of OCD phenotypes for genetic investigations, including those based on symptom factors, personality features, and co-occurring psychiatric disorders, as well as newly identified neurocognitive and neuroimaging endophenotypes (that is, phenotypes that lie on the pathogenic pathway between genes and disease) (Menzies et al., 2007; 2008). These developments hold promise for further deepening our genetic understanding of OCD and spectrum disorders in the coming decade.

Future Directions

1. What clinical features should be investigated to characterize potential etiologically distinct subtypes of OCD?

2. How can neurocognition, neuroimaging, and other potential "endophenotypes" be investigated in genetic studies of OCD?

3. What statistical approaches can be applied to investigating gene–gene and gene–environmental interactions in the development of OCD?

4. What statistical approaches are needed to analyze the massive amount of information emerging from genome-wide association studies of OCD?

5. What new genetic approaches (e.g., epigenetics, whole genome sequencing) can be applied to investigating the etiology of OCD?

Related Chapters

Chapter 7. Neuroanatomy of Obsessive Compulsive and Related Disorders

References

Alsobrook, J. P. II, Leckman, J. F., Goodman, W. K., Rasmussen, S. A., & Pauls, D. L. (1999). Segregation analysis of obsessive-compulsive disorder using symptom-based factor scores. *American Journal of Medical Genetics (Neuropsychiatric Genetics), 88,* 669–675.

Alsobrook, J. P., 2nd, Zohar, A. H., Lebover, M., Chabane, N., Ebstein, R. P., & Pauls, D. L. (2002). Association between the COMT locus and obsessive-compulsive disorder in females but not males. *American Journal of Medical Genetics, 114,* 116–120.

Arnold, P. D., Sicard, T., Burroughs, E., Richter, M. A., & Kennedy, J. L. (2006). Glutamate transporter gene SLC1A1 associated with obsessive-compulsive disorder. *Archives of General Psychiatry, 63,* 769–776.

Azzam, A., & Mathews, C. A. (2003). Meta-analysis of the association between the catecholamine-O-methyl-transferase gene and obsessive-compulsive disorder. *American Journal of Medical Genetics Part B (Neuropsychiatric Genetics), 123B,* 64–69.

Baca-Garcia, E., Vaquero-Lorenzo, C., Diaz-Hernandez, M., Rodriguez-Salgado, B., Dolengevich-Segal, H., Arrojo-Romero, M., et al. (2007). Association between obsessive-compulsive disorder and a variable number of tandem repeats polymorphism in intron 2 of the serotonin transporter gene. *Progress in Neuropsychopharmacology and Biological Psychiatry, 30,* 416–420.

Bellodi, L., Sciuto, G., Diaferia, G., Ronchi, P., & Smeraldi, E. (1992). Psychiatric disorders in the families of patients with obsessive-compulsive disorder. *Psychiatry Research, 42,* 111–120.

Bengel, D., Greenberg, B. D., Cora-Locatelli, G., Altemus, M., Heils, A., Li, Q., et al. (1999). Association of the serotonin transporter promoter regulatory region polymorphism and obsessive-compulsive disorder. *Molecular Psychiatry, 4,* 463–466.

Berthier, M. L., Kulisevsky, J., Gironell, A., & Lopez, O. L. (2001). Obsessive-compulsive disorder and traumatic brain injury: behavioral, cognitive, and neuroimaging findings. *Neuropsychiatry, Neuropsychology & Behavioral Neurology, 14,* 23–31.

Bienvenu, O. J., Samuels, J. F., Riddle, M. A., Hoehn-Saric, R., Liang, K.-Y., Cullen, B. A. M., et al. (2000). The relationship of obsessive-compulsive disorder to possible spectrum disorders: results from a family study. *Biological Psychiatry, 48,* 287–293.

Bienvenu, O. J., Wang, Y., Shugart, Y. Y., Welch, J. W., Grados, M. A., Fyer, A. J., et al. (2009). Sapap3 and pathological grooming in humans. *American Journal of Medical Genetics Part B (Neuropsychiatric Genetics), 150B,* 710–720.

Billet, E. A., Richter, M. A., Sam, F., Swinso, R. P., Dai, X.Y., King, N., et al. (1998). Investigation of dopamine system genes in obsessive-compulsive disorder. *Psychiatric Genetics, 8,* 163–169.

Black, D. W., Noyes, R., Jr., Goldstein, R. B., & Blum, N. (1992). A family study of obsessive-compulsive disorder. *Archives of General Psychiatry, 49,* 362–368.

Brown, F. W. (1942). Heredity in the psychoneuroses. *Proceedings of the Royal Society of Medicine, 35,* 785–790.

Camarena, B., Rinetti, G., Cruz, C., Gomez, A., de la Fuente, J. R., & Nicolini, H. (2001). Additional evidence that genetic variation of MAO-A gene supports a gender subtype in obsessive-compulsive disorder. *American Journal of Medical Genetics, 105,* 279–282.

Camarena, B., Aguilar, A., Loyzaga, C., Nicolini, H. (2004). A family-based association study of the 5-HT-1Db receptor gene in obsessive-compulsive disorder. *International Journal of Neuropsychopharmacology, 7,* 49–53.

Camarena, B., Loyzaga, C., Aguilar, A., Weissbecker, K., & Nicolini, H. (2007). Association study between the dopamine receptor D (4) gene and obsessive-compulsive disorder. *European Neuropsychopharmacology, 17,* 406–409.

Cannistraro, P. A., Makris, N., Howard, J. D., Wedig, M. M., Hodge, S. M., Wilhelm, S., et al. (2007). A diffusion tensor imaging study of white matter in obsessive-compulsive disorder. *Depression and Anxiety, 24,* 440–446.

Carey, G., & Gottesman, I. I. (1981). Twin and family studies of anxiety, phobias, and obsessive disorders. In D. F. Klein & J. Rabkin (Eds.), *Anxiety: New Research and Changing Concepts* (pp. 117–136). New York: Raven Press.

Catalano, M., Sciuto, G., Di Bella, D., Novelli, E., Nobile, M., & Bellodi, L. (1994). Lack of association between obsessive-compulsive disorder and the dopamine D3 receptor gene: some preliminary considerations. *American Journal of Medical Genetics, 54,* 253–255.

Cath, D. C., van Grootheest, D. S., Willemsen, G., van Oppen, P., & Boomsma, D. I. (2008). Environmental factors in obsessive-compulsive behavior: evidence from discordant and concordant monozygotic twins. *Behavioral Genetics, 38,* 108–120.

Cavallini, M. C., Pasquale, L., Bellodi, L., & Smeraldi, E. (1999). Complex segregation analysis for obsessive compulsive disorder and related disorders. *American Journal of Medical Genetics (Neuropsychiatric Genetics), 88,* 38–43.

Chabane, N., Delorme, R., Millet, B., Mouren, M.C., Leboyer, M., & Pauls, D. (2005). Early-onset obsessive-compulsive disorder: a subgroup with a specific clinical and familial pattern? *Journal of Child Psychology and Psychiatry, 46,* 881–887.

Chabane, N., Millet, B., Delorme, R., Lichtermann, D., Mathieu, F., Laplanche, J. L., et al. (2004). Lack of evidence for association between serotonin transporter gene (5-HTTLPR) and obsessive-compulsive disorder by case control and family association study in humans. *Neuroscience Letters, 363,* 154–156.

Childers, M. K., Holland, D., Ryan, M. G., & Rupright, J. (1998). Obsessional disorders during recovery from severe head injury: report of four cases. *Brain Injury, 12,* 613–616.

Clifford, C. A., Murray, R. M., & Fulker, D. W. (1984). Genetic and environmental influences on obsessional traits and symptoms. *Psychological Medicine, 14,* 791–800.

Coetzer, B. R. (2004). Obsessive-compulsive disorder following brain injury: a review. *International Journal of Psychiatry in Medicine, 34,* 363–377.

Cromer, K. R., Schmidt, N. B., and Murphy, D. L. (2007). An investigation of traumatic life events and obsessive-compulsive disorder. *Behaviour Research and Therapy, 45,* 1683–1691.

Cruz, C., Camarena, B., King, N., Paez, F., Sidenberg, D., de la Fuente, J. R., & Nicolini, H. (1997). Increased prevalence of the seven-repeat variant of the dopamine D4 receptor gene in patients with obsessive-compulsive disorder with tics. *Neuroscience Letters, 231,* 1–4.

Cryan, E. M., Butcher, G. J., & Webb, M. G. (1992). Obsessive-compulsive disorder and paraphilia in a monozygotic twin pair. *British Journal of Psychiatry, 161,* 694–698.

Delorme, R., Beancur, C., Wagner, M., Krebs, M. O., Gorwood, P., Pearl, P., et al. (2005). Support for the association between the rare functional variant I425V of the serotonin transporter gene and susceptibility to obsessive compulsive disorder. *Molecular Psychiatry, 10,* 1059–1061.

Denys, D., van Nieuwerburgh, F., Deforce, D., & Westenberg, H. G. (2006). Association between serotonergic candidate genes and specific phenotypes of obsessive compulsive disorder. *Journal of Affective Disorders, 91,* 39–44.

De Silva, P., & Marks, M. (1999). The role of traumatic experiences in the genesis of obsessive-compulsive disorder. *Behaviour Research and Therapy, 37,* 941–951.

Di Bella, D., Cavallini, M. C., & Bellodi, L. (2002). No association between obsessive-compulsive disorder and the 5-HT1Db receptor gene. *American Journal of Psychiatry, 159,* 1783–1785.

Dickel, D. E., Veenstra-VanderWeele, J., Cox, N. J., Wu, X., Fischer, D. J., Van Etten-Lee, M., et al. (2006). Association testing of the positional and functional candidate gene SLC1A1/EAAC1 in early-onset obsessive-compulsive disorder. *Archives of General Psychiatry, 63,* 778–785.

Douglass, H. M., Moffitt, T. E., Dar, R., McGee, R., & Silva, P. (1995). Obsessive-compulsive disorder in a birth cohort of 18-year-olds: prevalence and predictors. *Journal of the American Academy of Child and Adolescent Psychiatry, 34,* 1424–1431.

Eley, T. C., Bolton, D., O'Connor, T. G., Perrin, S., Smith, P., & Plomin, R. (2003). A twin study of anxiety-related behaviours in pre-school children. *Journal of Child Psychology and Psychiatry, 44,* 945–960.

Erdal, M. E., Tot, S., Yazici, K., Yazici, A., Herken, H., Erdem, P., et al. (2003). Lack of association of catechol-O-methyltransferase gene polymorphism in obsessive-compulsive disorder. *Depression and Anxiety, 18,* 41–45.

Freud, S. (1909). *Three case histories.* New York: Macmillan.

Frisch, A., Michaelovsky, E., Rockah, R., Amir, I., Hermesh, H., Laor, N., et al. (2000). Association between obsessive-compulsive disorder and polymorphisms of genes encoding components of the serotonergic and dopaminergic pathways. *European Neuropsychopharmacology, 10,* 205–209.

Fyer, A. J., Lipsitz, J. D., Mannuzza, S., Aronowitz, B., & Chapman, T. F. (2005). A direct interview family study of obsessive-compulsive disorder. I. *Psychological Medicine, 35,* 1611–1621.

Gothelf, D., Aharonovsky, O., Horesh, N., Carty, T., and Apter, A. (2004). Life events and personality factors in children and adolescents with obsessive-compulsive disorder and other anxiety disorders. *Comprehensive Psychiatry, 45,* 192–198.

Grabe, H. J., Ruhrmann, S., Ettelt, S., Buhtz, F., Hochrein, A., Schulze-Rauschenbach, S., et al. (2006). Familiality of obsessive-compulsive disorder in nonclinical and clinical subjects. *American Journal of Psychiatry, 163,* 1986–1992.

Grados, M. A., Riddle, M. A., Samuels, J. F., Liang, K.-Y., Hoehn-Saric, R., Bienvenu, O. J., Walkup, J. T., Song, D., & Nestadt, G. (2001). The familial phenotype of obsessive-compulsive disorder in relation to tic disorders: The Hopkins OCD Family Study. *Biological Psychiatry, 50,* 559–565.

Grados, M., & Wilcox, H. C. (2007). Genetics of obsessive-compulsive disorder: a research update. *Expert Review of Neurotherapeutics, 7,* 967–980.

Greer, J. M., & Capecchi, M. R. (2002). Hoxb8 is required for normal grooming behavior in mice. *Neuron, 33,* 23–34.

Hall, D., Dhilla, A., Charalambous, A., Gogos, J. A., Karayiorgou, M. (2003). Sequence variants of the brain-derived neurotrophic factor (BDNF) gene are strongly associated with obsessive-compulsive disorder. *American Journal of Human Genetics, 73,* 370–376.

Hanna, G. L., Fingerlin, T. E., Himle, J. A., & Boehnke, M. (2005). Complex segregation analysis of obsessive-compulsive disorder in families with pediatric probands. *Human Heredity, 60,* 1–9.

Hanna, G. L., Himle, J. A., Curtis, G. C., & Gillespie, B. W. (2005). A family study of obsessive-compulsive disorder with pediatric probands. *American Journal of Medical Genetics Part B (Neuropsychiatric Genetics), 134B,* 13–19.

Hanna, G. L., Veenstra-VanderWeele, J., Cox, N. J., Boehnke, M., Himle, J. A., Curtis, G. C., et al. (2002). Genome-wide linkage analysis of families with obsessive-compulsive disorder ascertained through pediatric probands. *American Journal of Medical Genetics (Neuropsychiatric Genetics), 114,* 541–552.

Hasler, G., Kazuba, D., & Murphy, D. L. (2006). Factor analysis of obsessive-compulsive disorder YBOCS-SC symptoms and association with *5-HTTLPR SERT* polymorphism. *American Journal of Medical Genetics Part B (Neuropsychiatric Genetics), 141,* 403–408.

Hemmings, S. M., Kinnear, C. J., Niehaus, D. J., Moolman-Smook, J. C., Lochner, C., Knowles, J. A., et al. (2003). Investigating the role of dopaminergic and serotonergic candidate genes in obsessive-compulsive disorder. *European Neuropsychopharmacology, 13,* 93–98.

Hemmings, S. M., Kinnear, C. J., Lochner, C., et al. (2004). Early-versus late-onset obsessive-compulsive disorder: investigating genetic and clinical correlates. *Psychiatry Research, 128,* 175–182.

Hemmings, S. M. J., & Stein, D. J. (2006). The current status of association studies in obsessive-compulsive disorder. *Psychiatric Clinics of North America, 29,* 411–444.

Hoaken, P. C., & Schnurr, R. (1980). Genetic factors in obsessive-compulsive neurosis? A rare case of discordant monozygotic twins. *Canadian Journal of Psychiatry, 25,* 167–172.

Hudziak, J. J., van Beijsterveldt, C. E. M., Althoff, R. R., Stanger, C., Rettew, D. C., Nelson, E. C., et al. (2004). Genetic and environmental contributions to the Child Behavior Checklist Obsessive-Compulsive Scale. *Archives of General Psychiatry, 61,* 608–616.

Inouye, E. (1965). Similar and dissimilar manifestations of obsessive-compulsive neuroses in monozygotic twins. *American Journal of Psychiatry, 121,* 1171–1175.

Joel, D. (2006). Current animal models of obsessive compulsive disorder: a critical review. *Progress in Neuro-Psychopharmacology & Biological Psychiatry, 30,* 374–388.

Jonnal, A. H., Gardner, C. O., Prescott, C. A., & Kendler, K. S. (2000). Obsessive and compulsive symptoms in a general population sample of female twins. *American Journal of Medical Genetics Part B (Neuropsychiatric Genetics), 96B,* 791–796.

Karayiorgou, M., Altemus, M., Galke, B. L., Goldman, D., Murphy, D. L., Ott, J., & Gogos, J. A. (1997). Genotype determining low catechol-O-methyltransferase activity as a risk factor for obsessive-compulsive disorder. *Proceedings of the National Academy of Sciences, 94,* 4572–4575.

Karayiorgou, M., Sobin, C., Blundell, M. L., Galke, B. L., Malinova, L., et al. (1999). Family-based association studies support a sexually dimorphic effect of COMT and MAOA on genetic susceptibility to obsessive-compulsive disorder. *Biological Psychiatry, 45,* 1178–1189.

Kim, S. J., Lee, H. S., & Kim, C. H. (2005). Obsessive-compulsive disorder, factor-analyzed symptom dimensions and serotonin transporter polymorphism. *Neuropsychobiology, 52,* 176–182.

Kinnear, C. J., Niehaus, D. J., Moolman-Smock, J. C., du Toit, P. L., van Kradenberg, J., Weyers, J. B., et al. (2000). Obsessive-compulsive disorder and the promoter region polymorphism (5-HTTLPR) in the serotonin transporter gene (SLC6A4): a negative association study in the Afrikaner population. *International Journal of Neuropsychopharmacology, 3,* 327–331.

Koran, L. M., Hanna, G. L., Hollander, E., Nestadt, G., & Simpson, H. B. (2007). Practice guidelines for the treatment of patients with obsessive-compulsive disorder. *American Journal of Psychiatry, 164 (7 Suppl),* 5–53.

Korff, S., & Harvey, B. H. (2006). Animal models of obsessive-compulsive disorder: Rationale to understanding psychobiology and pharmacology. *Psychiatric Clinics of North American, 29,* 371–390.

Kruglyak, L., & Lander, E. S. (1995). High-resolution genetic mapping of complex traits. *American Journal of Human Genetics, 56,* 1212–1223.

Leckman, J. F., & Kim, Y.-S. (2006). A primary candidate gene for obsessive-compulsive disorder. *Archives of General Psychiatry, 63,* 717–720.

Lenane, M.C., Swedo, S. E., Leonard, H., Pauls, D. L., Sceery, W., & Rapoport, J. L. (1990). Psychiatric disorders in first degree relatives of children and adolescents with obsessive compulsive disorder. *Journal of the American Academy of Child and Adolescent Psychiatry, 29,* 407–412.

Lewis, A. (1936). Problems of obsessional illness. *Proceedings of the Royal Society of Medicine, 29,* 325–336.

Lin, P. Y. (2007). Meta-analysis of the association of serotonin transporter gene polymorphism with obsessive-compulsive disorder. *Progress in Neuro-psychopharmacology and Biological Psychiatry, 31,* 683–689.

Lochner, C., du Toit, P. L., Zungru-Dirwayi, N., Marais, A., van Kradenburg, J., Seedata S., et al. (2002). Childhood trauma in obsessive-compulsive disorder, trichotillomania, and controls. *Depression and Anxiety, 15,* 66–68.

Marks, I. M., Crowe, M., Drewe, E., Young, J., & Dewhurst, W. G. (1969). Obsessive compulsive neurosis in identical twins. *British Journal of Psychiatry, 115,* 991–998.

Mathews, C. A., Kaur, N., & Stein, M. B. (2008). Childhood trauma and obsessive-compulsive symptoms. *Depression and Anxiety, 25,* 742–751.

McDougle, C. J., Epperson, C. N., Price, L. H., & Gelernter, J. (1998). Evidence for linkage disequilibrium between serotonin transporter protein gene (SLC6A4) and obsessive compulsive disorder. *Molecular Psychiatry, 3,* 270–273.

McGuffin, P., & Mawson, D. (1980). Obsessive-compulsive neurosis: two identical twin pairs. *British Journal of Psychiatry, 137,* 285–287.

McKeon, P. & Murray, R. (1987). Familial aspects of obsessive-compulsive neurosis. *British Journal of Psychiatry, 151,* 528–534.

Meira-Lima, I., Shavitt, R. G., Miguita, K., Ikenaga, E., Miguel, E. C., & Vallada, H. (2004). Association analysis of the catechol-o-methyltransferase (COMT), serotonin transporter (5-HTT) and serotonin 2A receptor (5HT2A) gene polymorphisms with obsessive-compulsive disorder. *Genes, Brain and Behavior, 3,* 775–779.

Menzies, L., Achard, S., Chamberlain, S. R., Fineberg, N., Chen, C. H., del Campo, N., et al. (2007). *Brain, 130,* 3223–3236.

Menzies, L., Williams, G. B., Chamberlain, S. R., Ooi, C., Fineberg, N., Suckling, J., et al. (2008). White matter abnormalities in patients with obsessive-compulsive disorder and their first-degree relatives. *American Journal of Psychiatry, 165,* 1308–1315.

Millet, B., Chabane, N., Delorme, R., Lebover, M., Leroy, S., Poirier, M. F., et al. (2003). Association between the dopamine receptor D4 (DRD4) gene and obsessive-compulsive disorder. *American Journal of Medical Genetics Part B (Neuropsychiatric Genetics), 116,* 55–59.

Mundo, E., Richter, M. A., Zai, G., Sam, F., McBride, J., Macciardi, F., & Kennedy, J. L. (2002). 5HT1Db receptor gene implicated in the pathogenesis of obsessive-compulsive disorder: further evidence from a family-based association study. *Molecular Psychiatry, 7,* 805–809.

Murphy, T. K., Sajid, M. W., & Goodman, W. K. (2006). Immunology of obsessive-compulsive disorder. *Psychiatric Clinics of North America, 29,* 445–469.

Niehaus, D. J., Kinnear, C. J., Corfield, V. A., du Toit, P. L., van Kradenburg, J., Moolman-Smook, J. C., et al., (2001). Association between a catechol-o-methyltransferase polymorphism and obsessive-compulsive disorder in the Afrikaner population. *Journal of Affective Disorders, 65,* 61–65.

Nestadt, G., Lan, T., Samuels, J., Riddle, M., Bienvenu, O. J. III, Liang, K. Y., et al. (2000). Complex segregation analysis provides compelling evidence for a major gene underlying obsessive-compulsive disorder and for heterogeneity by sex. *American Journal of Human Genetics, 67,* 1611–1616.

Nestadt, G., Samuels, J., Riddle, M. A., Bienvenu O. J. III, Liang, K. Y., LaBuda, M., et al. (2000). A family study of obsessive-compulsive disorder. *Archives of General Psychiatry, 57,* 358–363.

Nestadt, G., Samuels, J., Riddle, M. A., Liang, K.-Y., Bienvenu, O. J., Hoehn-Saric, R., & Cullen, B. (2001). The relationship between obsessive-compulsive disorder and anxiety and affective disorders: results from the Johns Hopkins OCD Family Study. *Psychological Medicine, 31,* 481–487.

Nicolini, H., Hanna, G., Baxter, L., Jr., Schwartz, J., Weissbacker, K., & Spence, M. A. (1991). Segregation analysis of obsessive compulsive and associated disorders: preliminary results. *Ursus Medicus, 1,* 25–28.

Nicolini, H., Cruz, C., Camarena, B., Orozco, B., Kennedy, J. L., King, N., et al. (1996). DRD2, DRD3 and 5HT2A receptor gene polymorphisms in obsessive-compulsive disorder. *Molecular Psychiatry, 1,* 461–465.

Ohara, K., Nagai, M., Suzuki, Y., Ochiai, M., & Ohara, K. (1998). No association between anxiety disorders and catechol-O-methyltransferase polymorphism. *Psychiatry Research, 80,* 145–148.

Ozaki, N., Goldman, D., Kaye, W. H., Poltnicov, K., Greenberg, B. D., Lappalainen, J., et al. (2003). Serotonin transporter missense mutation associated with a complex neuropsychiatric phenotype. *Molecular Psychiatry, 8,* 933–936.

Pauls, D. L., Alsobrook, J. P., Goodman, W. K., Rasmussen, S. A., & Leckman, J. F. (1995). A family study of obsessive compulsive disorder. *American Journal of Psychiatry, 152,* 76–84.

Perez, M., Brown, J. S., Vrshek-Schallhorn, S., Johnson, F., & Joiner, T. E., Jr. (2006). Differentiation of obsessive-compulsive-, panic-, obsessive-compulsive personality-, and non-disordered individuals by variation in the promoter region of the serotonin transporter gene. *Journal of Anxiety Disorders, 20,* 794–806.

Pitman, R. K. (1989). Animal models of compulsive behavior. *Biological Psychiatry, 26,* 189–198.

Pooley, E. C., Fineberg, N., & Harrison, P. J. (2007). The met (158) allele of catechol-O-methyltransferase (COMT) is associated with obsessive-compulsive disorder in men: case-control study and meta-analysis. *Molecular Psychiatry, 12,* 556–561.

Riddle, M. A., Scahill, L., King, R., Hardin, M. T., Towbin, K. E., Ort, S. I., Leckman, J. F., & Cohen, D. J. (1990). Obsessive compulsive disorder in children and adolescents: phenomenology and family history. *Journal of the American Academy of Child and Adolescent Psychiatry, 29,* 766–772.

Rosario-Campos, M. C., Leckman, J. F., Curi, M., Quatrano, S., Katsovitch, L., Miguel, E. C., & Pauls, D. L. (2005). A family study of early-onset obsessive-compulsive disorder. *American Journal of Medical Genetics Part B (Neuropsychiatric Genetics), 136B,* 92–97.

Saiz, P. A., Garcia-Portilla, M. P., Arango, C., Morales, B., Bascaran, M. T., Martinez-Barrondo, S., et al. (2008). Association study between obsessive-compulsive disorder and serotonergic candidate genes. *Progress in Neuropsychopharmacology and Biological Psychiatry, 32,* 765–770.

Samuels, J., Nestadt, G., Bienvenu, O. J., Costa, P. T., Jr., Riddle, M. A., Liang, K. Y., et al. (2000). Personality disorders and normal personality dimensions in obsessive-compulsive disorder: results from the Johns Hopkins OCD Family Study. *British Journal of Psychiatry, 177,* 457-462.

Samuels, J. F., Riddle, M. A., Greenberg, B. D., Fyer, A. J., McCracken, J. T., Rauch, S. L., et al. (2006). The OCD Collaborative Genetics Study: methods and sample description. *American Journal of Medical Genetics Part B (Neuropsychiatric Genetics), 141,* 201–207.

Samuels, J. F., Bienvenu, O. J., Pinto, A., Fyer, A. J., McCracken, J. T., Rauch, S. L., et al. (2007). Hoarding in obsessive-compulsive disorder: results from the OCD Collaborative Genetics Study. *Behaviour Research and Therapy, 43,* 673–686.

Samuels, J., Shugart, Y. Y., Grados, M. A., Willour, V. L., Bienvenu, O. J., Greenberg, B. D., et al. (2007). Significant linkage to compulsive hoarding on chromosome 14 in families with obsessive-compulsive disorder: results from the OCD Collaborative Genetics Study. *American Journal of Psychiatry, 164,* 493–499.

Schindler, K. M., Richter, M. A., Kennedy, J. L., Pato, M. T., & Pato, C. N. (2000). Association between homozygosity at the COMT gene locus and obsessive compulsive disorder. *American Journal of Medical Genetics, 96,* 721–724.

Shugart, Y. Y., Samuels, J., Willour, V. L., Grados, M. A., Greenberg, B. D., Knowles, J. A., et al. (2006). Genomewide linkage scan for obsessive-compulsive disorder: evidence for susceptibility loci on chromosomes 3q, 7p, 1q, 15q, and 6q. *Molecular Psychiatry, 11,* 763–770.

Sklar, P., Smoller, J. W., Fan, J., Ferreira, M. A., Perlis, R. H., Chambert, K., et al. (2008). Whole-genome association study of bipolar disorder. *Molecular Psychiatry, 13,* 558–569.

Slater, E. (1964). Genetical factors in neurosis. *British Journal of Psychology, 55,* 265–269.

Snider, L. A., & Swedo, S. E. (2004). PANDAS: current status and directions for research. *Molecular Psychiatry, 9,* 900–907.

Stein, D. J. (2002). Obsessive-compulsive disorder. *Lancet, 360,* 397–405.

Stein, D. J., Goodman, W. K., & Rauch, S. L. (2000). The cognitive-affective neuroscience of obsessive-compulsive disorder. *Current Psychiatry Reports, 2,* 341–346.

Stein, D. J., Shoulberg, N., Helton, K., & Hollander, E. (1992). The neuroethological approach to obsessive-compulsive disorder. *Comprehensive Psychiatry, 33,* 274–281.

Stewart, S. E., Platko, J., Fagerness, J., Birns, J., Jenike, E., Smoller, J. W., et al. (2007). A genetic family-based association study of OLIG2 in obsessive-compulsive disorder. *Archives of General Psychiatry, 64,* 209–214.

Stewart, S. E., Fagerness, J. A., Platko, J., Smoller, J. W., Scharf, J. M., Illmann, C., et al. (2007). Association of the SLC1A1 glutamate transporter gene and obsessive-compulsive disorder. *American Journal of Medical Genetics Part B (Neuropsychiatric Genetics), 144B,* 1027–1033.

Swedo, S. E., Rapoport, J. L., Leonard, H., Lenane, M., & Cheslow, D. (1989). Obsessive-compulsive disorder in children and adolescents. *Archives of General Psychiatry, 46,* 335–341.

Van Grootheest, D. S., Cath, D. C., Beekman, A. T., & Boomsma, D. I. (2005). Twin studies on obsessive-compulsive disorder: a review. *Twin Research and Human Genetics, 8,* 450–458.

Vasconcelos, M. S., Sampaio, A. S., Hounie, A. G., Akkerman, F., Curi, M., Lopes, A. C., & Miguel, E. C. (2007). Prenatal, perinatal, and postnatal risk factors in obsessive-compulsive disorder. *Biological Psychiatry, 61,* 301–307.

Veenstra-VanderWeele, J., Kim, S.-J., Gonen, D., Hanna, G. L., Leventhal, B. L., & Cook, E. H., Jr. (2001). Genomic organization of the SLC1A1/EAAC1 gene and mutation screening in early-onset obsessive-compulsive disorder. *Molecular Psychiatry, 6,* 160–167.

Veith, L. (1985). Acral lick dermatitis in the dog. *Canine Practice, 13,* 15–22.

Walitza, S., Wewetzer, C., Gerlach, M., Klampfl, K., Geller, F., Barth, N., et al. (2004). Transmission disequilibrium studies in children and adolescents with obsessive-compulsive disorder pertaining to polymorphisms of genes of the serotonergic pathway. *Journal of Neural Transmission, 111,* 817–825.

Wang, Y., Samuels, J. F., Chang, Y. C., Grados, M. A., Greenberg, B. D., Knowles, J. A., et al. (2009). Gender differences in genetic linkage and association on 11p15. In obsessive-compulsive disorder families. *American Journal of Medical Genetics Part B (Neuropsychiatric Genetics), 150B,* 33–40.

Weissman, M. M., Bland, R. C., Canino, G. J., Greenwald, S., Hwu, H-G., Kyoon, C., et al. (1994). The cross national epidemiology of obsessive compulsive disorder. *Journal of Clinical Psychiatry, 55 (Suppl.),* 5–10.

Welch, J. M., Lu, J., Rodriguiz, R. M., Trotta, N. C., Peca, J., Ding, J.-D., et al. (2007). Cortico-striatal synaptic defects and OCD-like behaviours in Sapap3-mutant mice. *Nature, 448,* 894–901.

Wendland, J. R., Kruse, M. R., Cromer, K. R., & Murphy, D. L. (2007). A large case-control study of common functional SLC6A4 and BDNF variants in obsessive-compulsive disorder. *Neuropsychopharmacology, 32,* 2543–2551.

Wilcox, H. C., Grados, M., Samuels, J., Riddle, M. A., Bienvenu, O. J. 3rd, Pinto, A., et al. (2008). The association between parental bonding and obsessive compulsive disorder in offspring at high familial risk. *Journal of Affective Disorders, 111,* 31–39.

Willour, V. L., Shugart, Y. Y., Samuels, J., Grados, M., Cullen, B., Bienvenu, O. J. III, et al. (2004). Replication study supports evidence for linkage to 9p24 in obsessive-compulsive disorder. *American Journal of Human Genetics, 75,* 508–513.

Woodruff, R., & Pitts, F. N., Jr. (1964). Monozygotic twins with obsessional illness. *American Journal of Psychiatry, 120,* 1075–1080.

Zai, G., Bezchlibnyk, Y. B., Richter, M. A., Arnold, P., Burroughs, E., Barr, C. L., & Kennedy, J. L. (2004). Myelin oligodendrocyte glycoprotein (MOG) gene is associated with obsessive-compulsive disorder. *American Journal of Medical Genetics Part B (Neuropsychiatric Genetics), 129B,* 64–68.

Zai, G., Arnold, P., Strauss, J., King, N., Burroughs, E., Richter, M. A., & Kennedy, J. L. (2005). No association between brain-derived neurotrophic factor gene and obsessive-compulsive disorder. *Psychiatric Genetics, 15,* 235.

Neuroanatomy of Obsessive Compulsive and Related Disorders

David Mataix-Cols *and* Odile A. van den Heuvel

Abstract

Obsessive-compulsive disorder (OCD) shares features and often co-occurs with other anxiety disorders, as well as with other psychiatric conditions classified elsewhere in the Diagnostic and Statistical Manual (DSM-IV), the so-called "OCD spectrum disorders." Neurobiologically, it is unclear how all these disorders relate to one another. The picture is further complicated by the clinical heterogeneity of OCD. This chapter will review the literature on the common and distinct neural correlates of OCD vis-à-vis other anxiety and "OCD spectrum" disorders. Furthermore, the question of whether partially distinct neural systems subserve the different symptom dimensions of OCD will be examined. Particular attention will be paid to hoarding, which is emerging as a distinct entity from OCD. Finally, new insights from cognitive and affective neuroscience will be reviewed before concluding with a summary and recommendations for future research.

Keywords: OCD, symptom dimensions, hoarding, anxiety disorders, Tourette's syndrome, trichotillomania, body dysmorphic disorder, neuroimaging, neuroanatomy, brain.

Introduction: The Brain in OCD

Obsessive compulsive disorder (OCD) is a complex and heterogeneous psychiatric disorder characterized by obsessions and compulsions. Obsessions are unwanted ideas, images or impulses that repeatedly enter an individual's mind and are usually experienced as out of character and distressing. Compulsions (also known as "rituals") are repetitive behaviors or mental acts which are often intended to neutralize anxiety provoked by the obsessions. These rituals are often driven by rules that must be applied rigidly (APA, 2000).

Converging lines of evidence suggest that specific brain circuits are involved in mediating the symptoms and cognitive deficits associated with the disorder. These include the presence of OCD symptoms in some neurological conditions (Tourette syndrome, Huntington's disease, Sydenham's chorea, and other basal ganglia disorders), the emergence of OCD-like behaviors in patients with focal brain injury, and the fact that surgical interventions that interrupt these frontal-subcortical circuits improve both mood and OCD symptoms. The advent of modern neuroimaging techniques, which provide a direct window into the OCD brain in vivo, have also contributed to our understanding of the neural systems underlying OCD symptoms. Several excellent recent reviews of this literature exist and will not be duplicated here (Mataix-Cols & van den Heuvel, 2006; Menzies et al., 2008a; Remijnse, van den Heuvel, & Veltman, 2005; Saxena & Rauch, 2000; Whiteside, Port, & Abramowitz, 2004). These converging lines of evidence have led to the development of a widely accepted neuroanatomical model of OCD.

Neuroanatomical Model of OCD

The most widely accepted neuroanatomical model of OCD proposes the involvement of a direct and an indirect cortico-striato-thalamic pathway

(Alexander, DeLong, & Strick, 1986; Cummings, 1993; Groenewegen & Uylings, 2000). In the direct pathway, an excitatory glutamatergic signal projects to the striatum, sending an inhibitory *GABAergic* (gamma-aminobutyric-acid-releasing) signal to the internal part of the globus pallidus. This results in a decreased inhibition (disinhibition) of the thalamus, and thus an increased excitatory effect on the prefrontal cortex (PFC). In the indirect pathway, the striatum projects an inhibitory signal to the external part of the globus pallidus and the subthalamic nucleus, sending an excitatory signal to the internal part of the globus pallidus. The net effect is an increased inhibition of the thalamus and decreased excitation of the prefrontal cortex. It is hypothesized that the direct pathway functions as a self-reinforcing positive feedback loop and contributes to the initiation and continuation of behaviors, whereas the indirect pathway provides a mechanism of negative feedback, which is important for the inhibition of behaviors and in switching between behaviors.

Based on functional neuroimaging results, Saxena and Rauch (2000) described how an imbalance between these frontal-striatal circuits might mediate OCD symptomatology. Focusing on the ventromedial frontal-striatal circuit, they hypothesized an excess tone in the direct relative to the indirect frontal-striatal circuit, resulting in enhanced activation of the orbitofrontal cortex, ventral striatum, and medial-dorsal thalamus. Based on the positive therapeutic effects of selective serotonergic reuptake inhibitors on OCD symptomatology, and the inhibitory effect of serotonin on dopamine, it is suggested that failure of the serotonergic system results in decreased compensation of the dopaminergic influence on the frontal-striatal circuits. In support for this view, a recent positron emission tomography (PET) study found that OCD is associated with a reduction in prefrontal serotonergic (5HT) neurotransmission (shown by reduced $5HT_{2A}$-receptor availability), and increased dopamine release in mainly the ventral striatum (Perani et al., 2008).

Dopamine (D) has a dual role in the balance between the direct and indirect frontal-striatal pathways. In the human brain D_1 receptor expression is prominent in the ventromedial (relative to dorsolateral) prefrontal cortex and ventral (relative to dorsal) striatum (Hurd, Suzuki, & Sedvall, 2001). Functionally, this dopaminergic differentiation implies a stronger D_1 influence on the *direct* pathway of the *ventromedial* frontal-striatal circuit and a stronger D_2 influence on the *indirect* pathway of the *dorsolateral* frontal-striatal circuit, resulting in a hyperactivated ventral and an inhibited dorsal frontal-striatal system (see Figure 7.1). The results of functional neuroimaging studies in OCD broadly support this view, showing increased activation of limbic and ventral frontal-striatal regions at rest and in response to disease-relevant information, and decreased responsiveness of dorsal frontal-striatal regions during executive performance (Remijnse et al., 2006; van den Heuvel et al., 2005a). However, there are also inconsistencies in the literature, and several brain regions that fall outside this circuitry, such as the cerebellum, the parietal cortex, and limbic regions, have also been associated with OCD in several studies (Menzies et al., 2008a).

Structural neuroimaging studies of OCD have also been relatively inconsistent, and relied on the use of the region-of-interest (ROI) approaches to measure the volumes of brain regions defined a priori, therefore preventing the exploration of other brain regions potentially implicated in the disorder. A meta-analysis of such studies found decreased anterior cingulate and orbitofrontal volumes and increased thalamic volumes in OCD, the latter significantly correlating with disease severity (Rotge et al., 2009). Recently developed fully automated, whole-brain, voxel-based morphometry (VBM) methods (Ashburner & Friston, 2000; Ashburner & Friston, 2001; Mechelli, Price, Friston, & Ashburner, 2005), which overcome the limitations of the ROI approach, are more suited to investigate the structural correlates of OCD in an unbiased manner. A recent meta-analysis of all published and unpublished VBM studies in OCD to date found that patients have increased regional gray matter volumes in bilateral lenticular nuclei, and decreased volumes in bilateral dorsal medial frontal (dMFG)/ anterior cingulate (ACG) gyri (Radua & Mataix-Cols, 2009). These results suggest that the basal ganglia and dMFG/ACG may be core nodes in the circuitry that mediates OCD symptoms and that, perhaps, functional alterations in other brain regions may reflect secondary emotional responses or attempts to regulate such responses.

Myths about the OCD Brain

Appealing as it may be, the above model is likely to be overly simplistic, as it is based on several assumptions about the OCD brain and about OCD itself (Mataix-Cols & van den Heuvel, 2006):

1. These brain structures mediate *all types* of OCD symptoms (i.e., OCD is a unitary nosological entity).

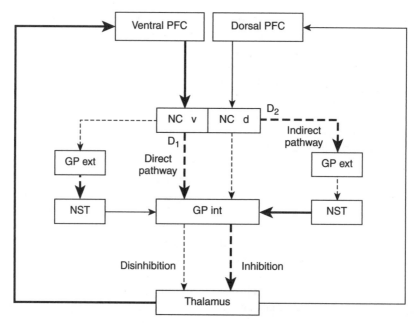

Fig. 7.1. A widely accepted frontal-striatal model of OCD, based on the work of Alexander et al (4), Cummings (5), Saxena & Rauch (1) and Groenewegen & Uylings (6). The direct connections function as a self-reinforcing positive feedback loop and contribute to the initiation and continuation of behaviors, whereas the indirect connections provide a mechanism of negative feedback which is important for the inhibition of behaviors and in switching between behaviors. It is hypothesized that an imbalance between these pathways results in a hyperactivated ventral and an inhibited dorsal frontal-striatal system.
Abbreviations: PFC = prefrontal cortex. NC d = dorsal part of caudate nucleus. NC v = ventral part of caudate nucleus. GP ext = external part of globus pallidus. GP int = internal part of globus pallidus. NST = subthalamic nucleus. D_1 = dopamine type 1. D_2 = dopamine type 2. Dotted lines indicate inhibitory GABAergic projections. Solid lines indicate excitatory glutamatergic projections.
Figure from Mataix-Cols, D. & van den Heuvel, O. A. (2006). Common and distinct neural correlates of obsessive-compulsive and related disorders. *Psychiatric Clinics of North America., 29,* 391–410, with permission.

2. These circuits represent the *unique* neural signature of OCD; i.e., they are not implicated in other disorders.

3. There are *qualitative* differences between the OCD and the healthy brain.

4. Dysfunction in these brain regions *causes* OCD.

Yet, the available literature clearly challenges these views. We shall briefly expand upon each of these points below.

Myth 1. OCD is a unitary nosological entity.
Psychiatric classification systems (DSM-IV-TR and ICD-10) view OCD as a unitary nosological entity, but researchers are currently disputing this view. Although OCD appears to be remarkably consistent throughout the life span, in both sexes and in different cultures, its symptoms are heterogeneous. Two patients with OCD may present with completely non-overlapping symptom profiles. However, more commonly, patients experience multiple types of obsessions and compulsions, which tend to group

in predictable ways (Figure 7.2). Indeed, several factor and cluster analytical studies have identified at least 4 relatively independent and temporally stable symptom dimensions: *(1)* contamination obsessions and washing/cleaning compulsions; *(2)* aggressive, sexual and religious obsessions and related compulsions (often checking); *(3)* obsessions concerning a need for symmetry or exactness, ordering/arranging, repeating and counting compulsions; and *(4)* saving and hoarding obsessions and compulsions (Bloch, Landeros-Weisenberger, Rosario, Pittenger, & Leckman, 2008; Leckman, Rauch, & Mataix-Cols, 2007; Mataix-Cols, Rosario-Campos, & Leckman, 2005).

In fact, although hoarding symptoms consistently emerge as a separate dimension in factor analytical studies, the status of hoarding as a symptom of OCD is also being challenged. It is now clear that many severe hoarders do not meet diagnostic criteria for OCD or other organic, neurological, or psychiatric disorders (Pertusa et al., 2008; Steketee & Frost, 2003). In most cases where hoarding is

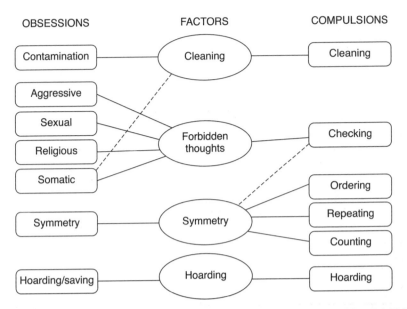

Fig. 7.2. The structure of OCD symptoms. Results of a meta-analysis of 21 factor analytical studies of the Y-BOCS Symptom Checklist across the Lifespan (N=5,124). Factor analysis of studies including adults yielded an identical factor structure compared to the overall meta-analysis. Factor analysis of child-only studies differed, in that checking loaded highest on the Symmetry factor and somatic obsessions on the Cleaning factor (dotted lines).

Adapted from Bloch, M. H., Landeros-Weisenberger, A., Rosario, M. C., Pittenger, C., & Leckman, J. F. (2008). Meta-analysis of the symptom structure of obsessive-compulsive disorder. *American Journal of Psychiatry, 165*, 1532–1542.

comorbid with other conditions, such as OCD, it still appears to be an independent problem (Pertusa et al., 2008). Consequently, several authors have suggested that once other disorders have been ruled out, hoarding should be regarded as a separate disorder with its own separate diagnostic criteria (Abramowitz, Wheaton, & Storch, 2008; Pertusa et al., 2008; Saxena, 2008; Steketee & Frost, 2003) in the next edition of the *Diagnostic and Statistical Manual* (DSM). Tentatively, the proposed name for this new disorder is *hoarding disorder* (Mataix-Cols et al., 2010). Therefore, it is plausible that different symptom dimensions of OCD and hoarding may have distinct neural substrates, and preliminary evidence does indeed support this view.

Myth 2. These circuits represent the unique neural signature of OCD.

OCD (currently classified as an anxiety disorder) shares features and often co-occurs with other anxiety disorders and depression (Rasmussen & Eisen, 1988). OCD also shares characteristics with some of the so-called "OCD spectrum disorders," a broad category that most experts agree should be kept narrow and only include body dysmorphic disorder, tic disorders, trichotillomania and other grooming disorders, hypochondriasis, hoarding disorder, and, potentially, obsessive compulsive personality

disorder (Mataix-Cols, Pertusa, & Leckman, 2007; Phillips et al., 2010). Therefore, one would expect, and the data suggests, a substantial degree of overlap in the neural substrates of all these disorders. Furthermore, other disorders, which like OCD are characterized by difficulties in inhibiting thoughts or behaviors, such as ADHD, may also share neural substrates with OCD.

Myth 3. There are qualitative differences between the OCD brain and the healthy brain.

Another assumption that remains untested is that there are qualitative differences between the OCD brain and healthy brains. However, the few symptom provocation studies that included healthy control groups seem to suggest that the differences could be more quantitative than qualitative. Mataix-Cols and colleagues (2003; 2004) used a symptom provocation procedure consisting of the presentation of symptom-related material to both OCD patients and healthy controls. The results revealed similar patterns of brain activation in both groups, although the degree of activation was, for the most part, significantly higher in the patient group. Clearly, more research on this topic is needed but, if confirmed, the neuroimaging findings could reflect exaggerations of normal emotional responses to personally relevant and highly salient stimuli, rather than fundamentally abnormal neuronal responses.

Myth 4. Dysfunction in these brain regions causes OCD.

Finally, it must be emphasized that differences in brain function between patients and controls do not necessarily indicate that dysfunction in these regions *causes* OCD. Neuroimaging tools should be regarded as correlational techniques that allow researchers to understand the neurophysiological bases of the behaviors under study, but not necessarily their cause. At least 3 possible interpretations of the neuroimaging data are possible: (a) dysfunction in certain brain regions causes OCD; (b) dysfunction in certain brain regions is a consequence of OCD; and (c) another spurious variable causes both phenomena (Whiteside et al., 2004).

Aim of this Review

Keeping these conundrums in mind, this chapter will review the literature on the common and distinct neural correlates of OCD vis-à-vis other anxiety and "spectrum" disorders. Furthermore, we will examine the question of whether partially distinct neural substrates subserve the different symptom dimensions of the disorder. Particular attention will be paid to hoarding, which, as mentioned above, is emerging as a separate entity from OCD. We hope this will contribute to the current debate surrounding the classification of OCD and related disorders in the DSM-V. We will then review some recent contributions to the field from cognitive and affective neuroscience. To conclude, we will offer suggestions for future research.

Relationship between OCD and Other Anxiety Disorders

Because of the strong link between OCD and anxiety (OCD is currently classified as an anxiety disorder and responds to broadly the same treatments as other anxiety disorders), it seems reasonable to expect common underlying neural substrates across these disorders; i.e., predominant involvement of limbic (most notably the amygdala) and paralimbic brain regions. Indeed, OCD and other anxiety disorders share several phenomenological characteristics: anticipatory anxiety, inadequate or enhanced anxiety responses with accompanying arousal, subsequent avoidance behavior, comorbid depressive symptoms, or generalized anxiety. Also, similarities in personality traits seem to be present across anxiety categories; e.g., neuroticism, uncertainty, inhibited temperament.

Important contributions to our understanding of normal and pathological emotional responses in humans come from fear-conditioning studies in animals. The amygdala plays a central role in fear conditioning. LeDoux (1996) described two parallel pathways, the direct pathway and the indirect pathway (see Figure 7.3). In the direct pathway, information about external stimuli reaches the lateral nucleus of the amygdala by direct connections from the thalamus ("thalamic pathway"), bypassing the cortical regions. Because of the lack of cortical processing, it can only provide the amygdala with a crude representation of the external stimulus (LeDoux called it the *"quick and dirty"* processing pathway). It allows the organism to respond to potential danger before we are conscious that we are in danger. The indirect pathway provides the amygdala with more detailed information, and is able to modify the initial effect of the direct pathway. The conditioned stimulus can also be a context. In contextual learning, the hippocampus plays an important role. Fear conditioning is a fast process, with a long-lasting effect. However, repeated exposure to the conditioned stimulus, in the absence of the unconditioned stimulus, can lead to extinction. Extinction reduces the likelihood that the conditioned stimulus elicits the fear response. The medial prefrontal and anterior cingulate cortices have been implicated in extinction learning (Quirk, Likhtik, Pelletier, & Pare, 2003; Quirk, Russo, Barron, & Lebron, 2000; Phelps, Delgado, Nearing, & LeDoux, 2004). Understanding how learned fears are diminished, and how extinction learning is changed in patients with anxiety disorders, might be an important step in translating neurobiological research to diagnosis and treatment of these patients.

Post-Traumatic Stress Disorder

Perhaps the best example of an anxiety disorder that appears to follow the classical fear-conditioning model is PTSD. Using the Eckman and Friesen (1976) face series (a standard set of emotional facial expressions) in patients with PTSD compared with healthy controls, enhanced activation in the amygdala, coupled with attenuated activation of the medial PFC, has frequently been reported (Rauch et al., 2000; Shin et al., 2005). The same reciprocal relationship between medial PFC and amygdala has also been reported in symptom provocation studies (e.g., Shin et al., 2004). Altered brain responses to emotional stimuli are already apparent in the acute phase of PTSD (Armony, Corbo, Clement, &

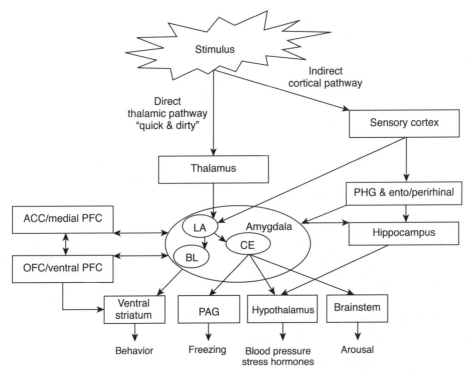

Fig. 7.3. The direct and indirect pathways involved in fear responses (based on LeDoux 1996).
Abbreviations: LA = lateral nucleus of amygdala. CE = central nucleus of amygdala. BL = basolateral nucleus of amygdala. ACC = anterior cingulate cortex. PFC = prefrontal cortex. OFC = orbitofrontal cortex. PHG = parahippocampal gyrus. Ento/perirhinal = entorhinal and perirhinal cortex. PAG = periaquaductal gray.
Figure from Mataix-Cols, D. & van den Heuvel, O. A. (2006). Common and distinct neural correlates of obsessive-compulsive and related disorders. *Psychiatric Clinics of North America., 29,* 391–410, with permission.

Brunet, 2005) and are predictive of cognitive-behavioral treatment response (Bryant et al., 2008). Cognitive activation studies and structural neuroimaging studies have also confirmed the involvement of the amygdala, hippocampus, and medial prefrontal cortex in PTSD (for a review, see Shin, Rauch, & Pitman, 2006).

Phobias

The amygdala and the hippocampus also seem to play a crucial role in the pathophysiology of social phobia. Abnormal activation of these regions has been reported in social phobics both during symptom provocation, i.e., public speaking (Furmark et al., 2002; Lorberbaum et al., 2004; Tillfors, Furmark, Marteinsdottir, & Fredrikson, 2002) and while viewing emotional facial expressions (Birbaumer et al., 1998; Blair et al., 2008; Evans et al., 2008; Phan, Fitzgerald, Nathan, & Tancer, 2006; Schneider et al., 1999; Stein, Goldin, Sareen, Zorrilla, & Brown, 2002).

However, these brain regions may play a smaller or more indirect role in other anxiety disorders,

such generalized anxiety disorder, specific phobias, and OCD (Cannistraro et al., 2004). In a recent comparative study in social phobia and generalized anxiety disorder, Blair et al. (2008) found that the increased amygdala response to fearful faces in social phobia is not present in patients with generalized anxiety disorder, who showed an increased lateral frontal response to angry faces. Symptom provocation and emotional face processing studies in animal phobias have often failed to find amygdala activation (e.g., Rauch et al., 1995; Straube, Mentzel, Glauer, & Miltner, 2004; Wright, Martis, McMullin, Shin, & Rauch, 2003), although there are some exceptions (e.g., Dilger et al., 2003; Larson et al., 2006), or found a nonspecific response in the amygdala (Goossens, Sunaert, Peeters, Griez, & Schruers, 2007; Schienle, Schafer, Walter, Stark, & Vaitl, 2005; Wendt, Lotze, Weike, Hosten, & Hamm, 2008). The lack of amygdala activation in most studies might be explained by fast habituation, since the amygdala response seems to distinguish phobic patients from controls only in the early stages of stimulus processing (Larson et al., 2006), and mainly during automatic (or unconscious) appraisal (Straube, Mentzel, & Miltner, 2006). Taken together, the specific phobia literature suggests a more primary involvement of somatosensory and anterior paralimbic regions, especially the insular cortex. The insular cortex and its adjacent regions have been strongly linked with disgust perception in healthy volunteers (e.g., Phillips et al., 1997; Wicker et al., 2003). These findings are in agreement with the psychological literature linking specific phobias to disgust sensitivity (e.g., Woody, McLean, & Klassen, 2005).

Similarly, most resting-state and symptom provocation studies in OCD found no amygdala activation, although there were some exceptions to this (Breiter et al., 1996; van den Heuvel et al., 2005b; van den Heuvel et al., 2004). A recent face perception study also failed to report amygdala activation (Cannistraro et al., 2004). It is possible that the amygdala is hyperresponsive in OCD only when patients are presented with symptom-specific emotional information, whereas other anxiety disorders, such as panic disorder and generalized anxiety disorder, may be responsive to a broader range of emotional stimuli (van den Heuvel et al., 2005b). Finally, it is also possible that some but not all OCD symptom dimensions are associated with exaggerated amygdala responses.

Perhaps the biggest challenge is a conspicuous lack of studies directly comparing the neural substrates of the anxiety disorders using the same experimental paradigms. Differences in historical background partly explain the limited overlap in the paradigms used. Neuroimaging research in OCD has been dominated for long by a limited, or at least a predominant, focus on the basal ganglia and the ventral prefrontal-striatal circuits. In contrast, neuroimaging work in panic disorder largely consisted of pharmacological challenge studies in order to induce panic attacks, and ligand studies, most of which have addressed the functioning of the GABA-benzodiazepine-receptor complex. In PTSD research, most experiments followed the classical fear-conditioning model, focusing on the amygdala, hippocampus, and medial prefrontal cortex. One study combined data from various symptom provocation studies (OCD, PTSD, and specific phobia) and found that the right inferior frontal cortex, right posterior medial orbitofrontal cortex, bilateral insular cortex, bilateral lenticulate nuclei, and bilateral brain stem may mediate symptoms across the different anxiety disorders including OCD (Rauch, Savage, Alpert, Fischman, & Jenike, 1997).

Using the emotional Stroop task, van den Heuvel et al. (2005b) investigated the disorder-specificity of the neuronal response to disease-specific emotional information in OCD, panic disorder, and hypochondriasis. All patients showed increased distractibility for emotional information associated with frontal-striatal and limbic involvement. However, clear differences were found between OCD patients on the one hand, and panic and hypochondriasis patients on the other. In OCD patients, the response was specific to disease-relevant information (OCD-related words) and correlated mainly with ventral brain regions—mainly the bilateral amygdala and the ventrolateral prefrontal cortex. Patients with panic disorder showed a generalized response to negative stimuli (both OCD and panic-related words), correlating with both ventral and dorsal regions. Also, in patients with panic disorder, the amygdala response was specific to disease-relevant information (panic words). The activation patterns in patients with hypochondriasis were more similar to panic disorder than to OCD.

Structural neuroimaging studies can potentially shed some light on the similarities and differences between OCD and other anxiety disorders, as they are free of the restrictions of specific experimental paradigms. A recent meta-analysis of voxel-based morphometry studies has revealed common (reduced grey matter volume in dorso-medial frontal/anterior cingulate gyri), as well as distinct (increased basal ganglia volume in OCD versus decreased volume in other anxiety disorders) neural substrates in OCD versus other anxiety disorders (Radua, van den Heuvel, Surguladze, & Mataix-Cols, 2010).

To summarize, despite the difficulties integrating and comparing the OCD and anxiety disorder neuroimaging literatures, it appears that these disorders broadly share exaggerated responses in limbic and paralimbic brain regions that are implicated in threat detection and emotion processing. This is particularly obvious when patients are presented with symptom-specific stimuli that are relevant to them. The question is, however, whether these exaggerated emotional responses are primary to OCD, or simply reflect the anxiety that is secondary to the obsessions and compulsions. Studies specifically designed to address this question are needed.

Relationship between OCD and OCD Spectrum Disorders

In its narrowest definition, the group of "OCD spectrum" disorders includes a range of conditions currently classified in different sections of the DSM-IV-TR, such as Tourette syndrome and tics (childhood disorders), BDD and hypochondriasis (somatoform disorders), and trichotillomania (impulse control disorders), all of which are hypothesized to be closely linked with OCD (Hollander, Braun, & Simeon, 2008; Phillips et al., 2010). Unfortunately, there are relatively few neuroimaging studies in these disorders, with the exception of Tourette syndrome (TS).

Tourette Syndrome

Structural MRI studies have consistently reported volumetric abnormalities in the basal ganglia (e.g., Peterson et al., 2003) and related cortical structures (e.g., Peterson et al., 2001) in TS. Sowell et al. (2008) recently reported cortical thinning of sensorimotor cortices (mainly in frontal and parietal lobes), which correlated with tic severity in children with TS. In a longitudinal study of TS, the volumes of the caudate nucleus in childhood predicted tic and OCD symptom severity 7.5 years later (Bloch, Leckman, Zhu, & Peterson, 2005). Functional neuroimaging studies further support the involvement of "sensorimotor" cortico-striato-thalamic loops in TS. For example, one important study (Peterson et al., 1998) used fMRI and a tic suppression paradigm in 22 TS patients, and found significant changes in the basal ganglia (increases in caudate nucleus, decreases in putamen/globus pallidus), thalamus (decreases), and related cortical regions (increases in prefrontal and temporal regions) during tic suppression, compared with spontaneous expression of tics. Another recent study in children with TS has demonstrated altered recruitment of the frontal-striatal circuits during tasks of cognitive control, with increased activation of brain regions involved in the direct pathway (i.e., striatum, globus pallidus–internal part, and thalamus) and compensatory recruitment of the lateral prefrontal regions (Baym, Corbett, Wright, & Bunge, 2008).

Despite the predominant implication of corticostriatal circuits in TS, recent work has also found implication of limbic structures, such as the amygdala and hippocampus. A comparison of 154 patients with TS and 128 healthy controls showed overall increased amygdala and hippocampal volumes in TS (Peterson et al., 2007). The volumes of these limbic structures correlated inversely with age in the patient, but not the healthy control group, perhaps suggesting abnormal neurodevelopment. Moreover, the volumes of these regions correlated inversely with the severity of tic, ADHD, and OCD

symptoms, suggesting that enlargement of the limbic regions may have both a compensatory and neuromodulatory effect on these symptoms.

Trichotillomania

The neuroimaging literature in trichotillomania is sparse. In a morphometric MRI study of 10 female patients and 10 matched controls, O'Sullivan et al. (1997) reported smaller left putamen volumes in the patient group. However, Stein et al. (Stein, Coetzer, Lee, Davids, & Bouwer, 1997) compared caudate nucleus volumes and ventricular-brain ratios in 13 women with OCD, 17 women with trichotillomania, and 12 healthy controls, but found no significant differences between the groups on either variable. Using a semi-automated cortical morphometric method, Grachev (1997) reported volumetric reductions in the right inferior frontal gyrus, and increases in the right cuneus, in 10 female trichotillomania patients compared with controls. A recent voxel-based morphometry study, of 18 trichotillomania patients, found increased grey matter densities in the left striatum, left amygdalohippocampal formation, and multiple (including cingulate, supplementary motor, and frontal) cortical regions bilaterally (Chamberlain et al., 2008b). Using [18F]-fluorodeoxyglucose (FDG) PET, Swedo et al. (1991) found that 10 women with trichotillomania showed increased metabolic rates in bilateral cerebellar and superior parietal cortex, compared with 20 healthy controls. They also found that clomipramine-induced improvement was negatively correlated with anterior cingulate and orbitofrontal metabolism, findings that resemble methodologically comparable studies in OCD. In a single photon emission computed tomography (SPECT) study, Stein et al. (2002) found that the severity of hair pulling correlated with decreased perfusion in the left mid-posterior frontal, parietal, and striatum, and that this pattern of correlations was reversed after treatment with citalopram in 10 patients. Taken together, these preliminary results tentatively suggest involvement of similar sensorimotor cortico-striato-thalamic circuits in TS and in trichotillomania.

Body Dysmorphic Disorder

There have been even fewer neuroimaging studies of BDD. In one morphometric study of 8 women with BDD and 8 matched controls, Rauch et al. (2003) reported overall increased white (but not gray) matter volume in BDD compared with controls. However, they failed to find any between-group regional volume differences. The BDD group did show a significantly different asymmetry of the caudate nucleus, with a leftward shift in the laterality quotient. Using SPECT, Carey et al. (Carey, Seedat, Warwick, van, & Stein, 2004) found widespread perfusion deficits in parieto-occipital, temporal, and frontal regions in 6 patients with BDD. The authors speculated that the involvement of the parieto-occipital cortex might reflect the core feature of disturbed perception of body appearance in BDD. This idea is supported by the only fMRI study to date (Feusner, Townsend, Bystritsky, & Bookheimer, 2007). While viewing other people's faces, patients with BDD (n=12) showed more left-sided activations in the lateral prefrontal cortex and lateral temporal lobe regions, perhaps suggesting detailed encoding and analysis instead of holistic processing of faces. Interestingly, patients with BDD also showed an altered amygdala response compared with controls, suggesting direct or indirect limbic involvement.

Hypochondriasis

Patients with hypochondriasis show perceptual and memory biases for health-related information (Brown, Kosslyn, Delamater, Fama, & Barsky, 1999). To our knowledge, only one neuroimaging study has been published on hypochondriasis (van den Heuvel et al., 2005b). A cognitive and emotional Stroop task, consisting of congruent and incongruent color words, OCD-related, panic-related, and neutral words, was used in 3 patient groups (OCD, panic disorder, and hypochondriasis). Compared with healthy controls, patients with hypochondriasis (n=13) showed increased recruitment of frontal-striatal regions. In contrast to patients with OCD and panic disorder, hypochondriac patients did not show increased activation in the amygdala, although no hypochondriasis-specific (healthy-related) words were employed in this study, thus rendering it inconclusive.

Summary

To summarize, the TS literature strongly suggests a prominent involvement of the sensorimotor cortico-striato-thalamic circuits in the mediation of tics, and a less obvious involvement of limbic/paralimbic regions, possibly reflecting accompanying emotional symptoms. Furthermore, the association between structural brain abnormalities, and both tics and OCD symptoms, in longitudinal studies of TS (Bloch, Leckman, Zhu, & Peterson, 2005) suggests close anatomical proximity between OCD and TS. By contrast, the neuroimaging literature in

other "spectrum" disorders such as trichotillomania, BDD, and hypochondriasis is sparse and plagued with methodological problems (mainly small sample sizes). It is therefore difficult at this stage to draw any firm conclusions about the common and distinct neurobiological substrates of these disorders and how they relate to OCD. Studies that directly compare the neural correlates of OCD and these disorders are needed.

Specific Neural Correlates of the Major Symptom Dimensions of OCD

As mentioned earlier, OCD is clinically heterogeneous, and it is plausible that its symptom dimensions may be subserved by partially distinct neural systems. Because compulsive hoarding is emerging as a sufficiently distinct variant of OCD, or even a separate disorder, this section will review the existing evidence regarding the major symptom dimensions of OCD; that is, contamination/washing, harm/checking, and symmetry/order. The hoarding literature will be reviewed separately in the next section.

In the first study to examine the neural correlates of the major symptom dimensions of OCD, using PET, Rauch et al. (1998) found that checking symptoms correlated with increased, and symmetry/ordering with reduced, regional cerebral blood flow (rCBF) in the striatum, while washing symptoms correlated with increased rCBF in bilateral anterior cingulate and left orbitofrontal cortex. Phillips et al. (2000) compared OCD patients with mainly washing (n=7) or checking (n=7) symptoms, while viewing pictures of either normally disgusting scenes or washer-relevant pictures using fMRI. When viewing washing-related pictures, only washers demonstrated activations in regions implicated in emotion and disgust perception (i.e., visual regions and insular cortex), whereas checkers demonstrated activations in frontal-striatal regions and the thalamus. In a similar study, 8 OCD patients with predominantly washing symptoms demonstrated greater activation than controls in the right insula, ventrolateral prefrontal cortex, and parahippocampal gyrus when viewing disgust-inducing pictures (Shapira et al., 2003). Another study found increased amygdala activation in a group of 11 washers during the presentation of contamination-related pictures (van den Heuvel et al., 2004). Mataix-Cols et al. (2004) and used a symptom provocation paradigm to test the hypothesis that the major symptom dimensions of OCD would be subserved by partially distinct neural systems. Sixteen patients with mixed symptoms and 17 healthy controls participated in 4 fMRI experiments consisting of the provocation of contamination, checking, hoarding and symptom-unrelated anxiety. The results showed that while both patients and controls activated similar brain regions in response to symptom provocation, patients showed greater activations in bilateral ventromedial prefrontal regions and caudate nucleus (washing experiment), putamen/globus pallidus, thalamus, and dorsal cortical areas (checking experiment), left precentral gyrus and right orbitofrontal cortex (hoarding experiment). These results were further supported by correlation analyses within the patient group, which revealed highly specific positive associations between subjective anxiety, symptom measures, and brain activation in each experiment (Mataix-Cols et al., 2004).

Two large structural neuroimaging studies have also examined this question. Pujol et al. (2004) found that, in a sample of 72 mostly medicated patients, those with high scores on the harm/checking dimension had reduced gray matter volume in the right amygdala, compared with other patients and healthy controls. More recently, van den Heuvel et al. (2009) investigated the common and distinct grey matter (GM) and white matter (WM) volume correlates of the three major symptom dimensions of OCD, in a sample of 55 unmedicated patients. Multiple regression analyses controlled for overall symptom severity (Y-BOCS scores), other symptom scores, and excluded cases with comorbid depression. Scores on the contamination/washing dimension were negatively correlated with regional GM volume in bilateral caudate nucleus and WM volume in right parietal region. Scores on the harm/checking dimension were negatively correlated with regional GM and WM volume in bilateral temporal lobes, broadly replicating the previous study by Pujol et al. (2004). Scores on the symmetry/ordering dimension were negatively correlated with *global* GM and WM volumes, and regional GM volume in right motor cortex, left insula, and left parietal cortex, and positively correlated with bilateral temporal GM and WM volume.

Taken together, these preliminary studies suggest that different symptoms may be mediated by distinct, albeit partially overlapping, neural systems, which may be implicated in distinct emotional and cognitive processes. Some symptom dimensions (particularly contamination/washing) resemble anxiety disorders, with predominant involvement of limbic and paralimbic brain regions. Symmetry/ordering symptoms may be neurobiologically closer to tic disorders and trichotillomania, with primary involvement of sensorimotor fronto-striato-thalamic loops. If these preliminary results are replicated and confirmed, the "accepted" neurobiological model of OCD will require revision to accommodate these findings.

Neural Correlates of Hoarding

The neural substrates of hoarding behavior have been well studied in animals that naturally display hoarding behaviors as part of their behavioral repertoire (e.g. rodents, birds), as well as primates. These studies clearly implicate subcortical limbic structures (nucleus accumbens, ventral tegmental area, amygdala, hippocampus, thalamus, hypothalamus) and the ventromedial prefrontal cortex in the mediation of hoarding behavior. For example, electrical stimulation of lateral hypothalamus (a region that also promotes feeding) increases hoarding behavior in rats (Herberg & Blundell, 1967). The animal literature also suggests that the dopaminergic system plays a crucial role in hoarding behavior. For example, neonatal depletion of dopaminergic mesocortical projections decreases hoarding in rats (Kalsbeek, De Bruin, Feenstra, Matthijssen, & Uylings, 1988), and hoarding behavior can be restored to control levels in dopamine-lesion rats by prior treatment with L-dopa (Kelley & Stinus, 1985).

Evidence in humans is available from brain lesion and functional neuroimaging studies. Several case studies and case series of patients who started hoarding after suffering brain lesions suggest that the anterior ventromedial prefrontal and cingulate cortices are somehow implicated in abnormal hoarding behavior (Anderson et al. 2005). Linking the animal and lesion literature, Anderson et al. speculate that "*The evidence suggests that damage to the mesial frontal region disrupts a mechanism which normally modulates subcortically driven predispositions to acquire and collect, and adjusts these predispositions to environmental context*" (p. 201).

Needless to say, the psychological and neural mechanisms involved in "compulsive" hoarding, and hoarding in the context of brain lesions, may be completely different. Only a handful of neuroimaging studies have examined the neural correlates of hoarding in specifically selected samples. Mataix-Cols et al. (2004) did not specifically select hoarders, but recruited a consecutive sample of OCD patients with mixed symptoms; only half of this sample had some hoarding problems and none of the patients in this study were severe hoarders. Two studies selected severe hoarders within samples of patients with OCD; i.e., all hoarders had OCD

(An et al., 2008; Saxena et al., 2004), whereas another study selected hoarding individuals regardless of whether they had OCD (Tolin, Kiehl, Worhunsky, Book, & Maltby, 2009). It is therefore unclear how many of these individuals met criteria for hoarding disorder (Mataix-Cols et al., 2010), as diagnostic criteria were not available at the time. The results of these studies are summarized below.

In their resting-state PET study, Saxena et al. (2004) found that 12 OCD patients with predominantly hoarding symptoms had reduced glucose metabolism in the posterior cingulate cortex (compared with healthy controls) and the dorsal anterior cingulate cortex (compared with nonhoarding OCD), and that severity of hoarding in the whole patient group (n=45) correlated negatively with metabolism in the latter region.

An et al. (2008) recruited 13 OCD patients with prominent hoarding symptoms, 16 patients with no hoarding symptoms, and 21 healthy controls. They employed fMRI and a symptom provocation procedure consisting of audio instructions (e.g. "imagine that these objects belong to you, and you must throw them away forever") and pictures of items commonly hoarded by these patients. Subjective anxiety scores suggested that the procedure was anxiety provoking for the compulsive hoarders, and the severity of hoarding symptoms correlated with the level of provoked anxiety. In response to the hoarding-related (but not symptom-unrelated) anxiety provocation, OCD patients with prominent hoarding symptoms showed greater activation in bilateral anterior ventromedial prefrontal cortex (VMPFC) than patients without hoarding symptoms and healthy controls. In the entire patient group (n=29), provoked anxiety was positively correlated with activation in a frontolimbic network that included the anterior VMPFC, medial temporal structures, thalamus, and sensorimotor cortex. Negative correlations were observed in the left dorsal anterior cingulate gyrus, bilateral temporal cortex, bilateral dorsolateral/medial prefrontal regions, basal ganglia and parieto-occipital regions. These results were independent from the effects of age, sex, level of education, state anxiety, depression, comorbidity, and use of medication.

Finally, Tolin et al. (2009) recruited 12 severe hoarders (2 of whom had OCD) and 12 healthy controls. The participants were scanned (fMRI) while making decisions about whether or not to discard personal paper items (e.g., junk mail) brought to the laboratory, as well as control items

that did not belong to them. Items were either saved or destroyed following each decision. Subjective anxiety scores suggested that the decision-making process was highly anxiety provoking for the compulsive hoarders. When deciding whether to keep or discard personal possessions, compulsive hoarders displayed increased activation in lateral orbitofrontal cortex and parahippocampal gyrus. Among hoarding participants, decisions to keep personal possessions were associated with greater activity in superior temporal gyrus, middle temporal gyrus, medial frontal gyrus, anterior cingulate cortex, precentral gyrus, and cerebellum, than were decisions to discard personal possessions.

To summarize, the results of these preliminary studies implicate frontal-limbic circuits in the mediation of hoarding symptoms, findings that are broadly consistent with the animal and lesion literature. This contrasts with the more likely involvement of frontal-striatal loops in OCD. It is remarkable that similar results were obtained in hoarding samples with (An et al., 2008) and primarily without (Tolin et al., 2009) OCD, indicating that hoarding may indeed be a separate entity from OCD, as is currently being suggested (Abramowitz et al., 2008; Mataix-Cols et al., 2010; Pertusa et al., 2008b; Saxena, 2008; Steketee & Frost, 2003). Because of the key role of these frontal-limbic circuits in decision-making processes (e.g., Bechara, Tranel, & Damasio, 2000), the results of these studies are also consistent with current cognitive-behavioral models, which postulate that decision-making difficulties are landmark features of this condition (Steketee & Frost, 2003). Finally, whether the known involvement of the dopaminergic system in hoarding from the animal literature can explain the poor response of compulsive hoarders to serotonergic agents (e.g., Mataix-Cols, Rauch, Manzo, Jenike, & Baer, 1999) is an attractive hypothesis that remains to be investigated. Ligand studies would be useful to test it.

Recent Insights from Cognitive and Affective Neuroscience

Recent insights from cognitive and affective neuroscience suggest complex interactions between the dorsal and the ventral frontal-striatal circuits in OCD (Figure 7.4).

Dysfunctions in Dorsal Frontal-Striatal Circuits

Dorsal frontal-striatal dysfunctions mainly concern executive processes, such as planning and conflict

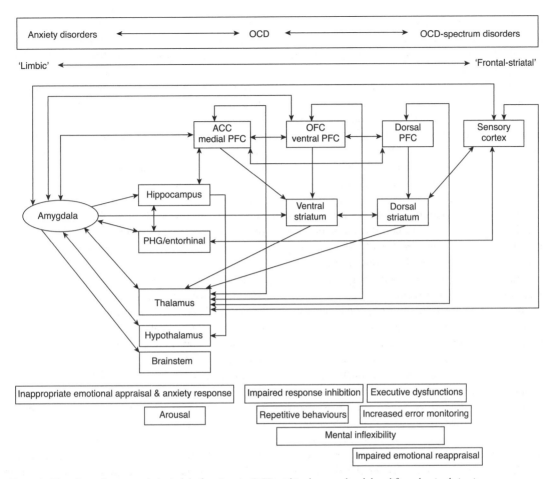

Anxiety disorders ←————————————→ OCD ←————————————→ OCD-spectrum disorders

'Limbic' ←——→ 'Frontal-striatal'

Inappropriate emotional appraisal & anxiety response

Arousal

Impaired response inhibition | Executive dysfunctions

Repetitive behaviours | Increased error monitoring

Mental inflexibility

Impaired emotional reappraisal

Fig. 7.4. Hypothesized neuropsychological dysfunctions in OCD within the ventral and dorsal frontal-striatal circuits.

monitoring, and emotional regulation problems in OCD. Planning strongly relies on an intact dorsal frontal-striatal circuit (premotor and dorsolateral prefrontal cortices, thalamus and basal ganglia) and visuospatial (precuneus and parietal cortices) system. OCD patients show impaired planning performance, correlating with decreased responsiveness of the dorsal frontal-striatal circuit and enhanced recruitment of presumably compensation- and stress-related brain regions, such as the anterior cingulate cortex (van den Heuvel et al., 2005a). Increased activation of the cingulate cortex in OCD seems to reflect enhanced error monitoring processes, both during incorrectly answered trials (Gehring, Himle, & Nisenson, 2000; Ursu, Stenger, Shear, Jones, & Carter, 2003) and correctly answered trials (Maltby, Tolin, Worhunsky, O'Keefe, & Kiehl, 2005; Ursu et al., 2003; van der Wee et al., 2003). This error monitoring phenomenon corresponds to the patients' frequent feeling that "something is wrong" (Aouizerate et al., 2004).

Proper functioning of the dorsal and medial prefrontal regions (e.g., the dorsal part of the anterior cingulate cortex, the medial prefrontal cortex, and the dorsolateral prefrontal cortex) is also important for the regulation of emotional responses (Ochsner & Gross, 2005). Deficits in emotional regulation may not be specific to OCD, but common to a wide range of emotional disorders (Phillips, Drevets, Rauch, & Lane, 2003a; Phillips, Drevets, Rauch, & Lane, 2003b).

Dysfunctions in Ventral Frontal-Striatal Circuits

Ventral frontal-striatal impairment in OCD seems to contribute to the inability to inhibit cognitions and behaviors. In the experimental setting, OCD patients show diminished performance on response inhibition tasks (Chamberlain, Blackwell, Fineberg, Robbins, & Sahakian, 2005) and altered activation of the ventral frontal-striatal circuit (Roth et al., 2007). The loss of normal inhibitory processes is common to most patients with OCD and, according to recent work, even their unaffected first-degree relatives (Chamberlain et al., 2007; Menzies et al., 2007). However, the diagnostic specificity of these findings still remains to be established, as difficulties in inhibitory processes and alterations in the corresponding brain regions may not be exclusive to OCD, but also described in patients with ADHD (Rubia, Smith, Brammer, Toone, & Taylor, 2005; Smith, Taylor, Brammer, Toone, & Rubia, 2006), Tourette syndrome (Muller et al., 2003), pathological gambling (Goudriaan, Oosterlaan, de Beurs, & van den Brink, 2006), and addiction (Hester & Garavan, 2004). It is therefore plausible that these are general vulnerability factors for a number of neuropsychiatric problems including OCD.

The orbitofrontal cortex (OFC) is important for the integration of cognitive and emotional-motivational information. A conventional task to investigate OFC function is the reversal learning task. The paradigm tests cognitive flexibility within an emotional context. OCD patients show cognitive inflexibility correlating with decreased recruitment of both dorsal and ventral frontal-striatal regions (Gu et al., 2008; Remijnse et al., 2006). Chamberlain et al. (2008a) recently showed that altered brain activation during reversal learning processes is also apparent in first-degree relatives of OCD patients.

Discussion and Future Directions

The most widely accepted neurobiological model of OCD suggests that an imbalance between the direct and the indirect fronto-striato-thalamic circuits, both ventral and dorsal, underlies the symptoms and specific cognitive and emotional deficits of these patients. Although this model has esthetical appeal, we have argued that this may be a gross oversimplification. Firstly, because OCD is probably etiologically heterogeneous, different symptom dimensions may be subserved by discrete neural systems. Any viable neurobiological model would need to take account of this heterogeneity.

Secondly, OCD shares features and co-occurs with other anxiety/mood disorders, as well as the so-called OCD "spectrum" disorders. This means that OCD is likely to share neural substrates with these disorders. Indeed, like other anxiety disorders, OCD is characterized by exaggerated neural responses in paralimbic brain regions, particularly when confronted with stimuli that are relevant to them. Also the frontal-striatal dysfunctions, underlying various cognitive deficits in OCD, seem to be rather nonspecific and to overlap with those

described other disorders within the impulsive-compulsive spectrum. As mentioned above, it is of course possible that some symptom dimensions are neuroanatomically closer to the anxiety disorders (e.g., contamination/washing), whereas others may be more similar to other disorders with predominant frontal-striatal dysfunction (e.g., symmetry/ordering). Clearly, research is still needed to delineate the common and distinct neural correlates of OCD, its symptom dimensions, and related disorders. The field will benefit from using identical imaging paradigms across these syndromes to facilitate direct comparisons. This will be a first step toward a pathophysiology-based classification of these disorders.

Thirdly, the current neurobiological model of OCD assumes that there are fundamental qualitative differences between the OCD brain and the healthy brain, yet some research raises the question of whether the differences between OCD patients and controls are more quantitative than qualitative (Mataix-Cols et al., 2003). Furthermore, the brain areas implicated in the model are also implicated in the mediation of "normal" emotional responses in healthy individuals. The multidimensional model of OCD proposes that OCD symptoms are normally distributed in the general population (Mataix-Cols et al., 2005). Research shows that many individuals in the general population experience normal obsessive (intrusive) and compulsive symptoms (compensatory behaviors) at some time, that resemble the form and content of abnormal, pathological phenomena (Muris, Merckelbach, & Clavan, 1997; Rachman & de Silva, 1978). Furthermore, studies involving nonclinical samples have demonstrated that normal individuals with high scores on self-administered scales of obsessions and compulsions show striking similarities to OCD patients regarding clinical and personality characteristics, as well as performance on neuropsychological tests (Gibbs, 1996; Mataix-Cols, Barrios, Sanchez-Turet, Vallejo, & Junque, 1999; Mataix-Cols et al., 1999). Neuroimaging studies comparing healthy individuals with high and low levels of OCD symptoms would provide a more definitive answer to this fundamental question. Eventually, this will shed some light on the categorical versus dimensional nature of OCD and OC-related phenomena.

Fourthly, the widely accepted frontal-striatal model minimizes the role of other brain regions that were not identified in the early studies. For example, the role of the temporal and parietal cortices and the cerebellum is likely to be important, but has been neglected so far (Menzies et al., 2007). Similarly, as discussed above, paralimbic brain regions are likely to play an important role, but have received less attention in the literature. It will be important to further understand the complex interactions between the limbic and the frontal-striatal systems and their relative contribution to all these syndromes. Based on imaging results in OCD, one might hypothesize that altered dorsal frontal-striatal function is responsible for decreased inhibition of ventral frontal-striatal and limbic recruitment, in response to disease-relevant emotional cues. This hypothesis implies a primary failure (*hypo*function) of the *dorsal* frontal-striatal circuit. This dorsal failure could explain the executive dysfunctions displayed by some OCD patients. However, the opposite hypothesis, a primary deficit (*hyper*sensitivity) of the *limbic* or ventral frontal-striatal circuits, might be defended as well. Even in this case, executive impairment may be the consequence, as a result of anxiety-related amygdala influence on the dorsal frontal-striatal circuitry. Although both hypotheses imply direct connections between the amygdala and dorsal frontal-striatal regions, little is known about these complex interactions. Whereas connections of the amygdala with the medial prefrontal and orbitofrontal cortex are robust and bidirectional, connections with lateral prefrontal areas are sparse, unidirectional, and primarily ascending (Amaral & Price, 1984). With regard to the communication between limbic and dorsal frontal-striatal regions, there are at least two important questions: *(1)* which direct and indirect descending connections from the dorsolateral prefrontal cortex (DLPFC) to the amygdala play a role in the presumed top-down control of the amygdala response; and *(2)* in which way can activation of the amygdala directly or indirectly influence executive functioning by the DLPFC? One possible way in which diverse streams of information could guide behavior would be through the rich interconnections between prefrontal areas (Barbas, 2000; Haber, 2008), involving cortico-cortical and cortico-thalamo-cortical connections. Recent developments in non-invasive neuroimaging techniques, e.g., diffusion tension imaging, might contribute to our understanding of functional connectivity within the human brain, and altered connections in patients with psychiatric disorders. Another way to investigate the interactions between limbic and frontal-striatal circuits is by the use of transcranial magnetic stimulation (TMS). The effect of cortical modulation by TMS, both inhibition and stimulation, on

the subcortical and limbic structures can be measured with resting-state MRI and fMRI during cognitive and emotional paradigms, directly after single or repeated TMS treatment.

Useful neuropsychological paradigms to investigate the functional interactions between limbic and frontal-striatal circuits are based on the various strategies for downregulating and/or modulating emotional responses. Ochsner and Gross (2005) described a hypothetical continuum of strategies to *(1)* control attention to, and *(2)* cognitively change the meaning of emotionally evocative stimuli. These processes of attentional control (e.g., attentional bias and attentional distraction) and cognitive modulation (e.g., reappraisal) might be dysfunctional in patients with OCD and related disorders. Cognitive-behavioral techniques both reduce the limbic over-activation (presumably by habituation of the anxiety response during exposure in vivo) and enforce the dorsal top-down control system (perhaps by strengthening the reappraisal processes). Indeed, in a recent study, intensive cognitive-behavioral treatment resulted in increased activation in dorsal prefrontal regions (Saxena et al., 2009).

Future research in this field may benefit from a longitudinal and multimodal approach. Longitudinal studies with appropriate untreated controls are needed to establish which abnormalities are related to the symptomatic state, and which (if any) are trait markers of OCD. The potential of these techniques as clinical tools, e.g., prediction of treatment outcome, is great, but these applications are still in their infancy. Probably the most interesting population for study consists of young children with and without obsessive compulsive and related disorders. Longitudinal follow-up of these children into adolescence and adulthood would enable visualization of the natural history of these disorders, as well as the evaluation of long-term effects of environmental influences and treatment strategies. Multimodal designs, combining volumetric, resting state, functional, and chemical measurements, may contribute to a better differentiation between cause and effect. For instance, altered morphology may be related to an imbalance of interacting neurotransmitter systems, and differences in task related blood oxygenation level-dependent (BOLD) responses may be confounded by early maturation deficits. Another potentially fruitful direction for future research is the combination of brain imaging and genetics. Unaffected first-degree relatives of patients with OCD show similar neuropsychological (Menzies et al., 2007) as well as structural

(Menzies et al., 2008b) and functional (Chamberlain et al., 2008a) brain abnormalities when compared to patients with active symptoms. Whether the endophenotypes derived from such family studies will lead to progress in finding genes for OCD remains to be seen.

To conclude, we propose that the most fruitful research strategy will be to examine the common and distinct neural correlates of OCD, its symptom dimensions, and related disorders, using well-validated methods and comparable paradigms. More insight on the interactions between the limbic and frontal-striatal circuits might contribute to a better understanding of the clinical overlap and differentiation between specific disorders. This ambitious endeavor will require large patient samples and a multimodal, multidisciplinary, and longitudinal approach.

Related Chapters

Chapter 6. Genetic Understanding of OCD and Spectrum Disorders

Reference

Abramowitz, J. S., Wheaton, M. G., & Storch, E. A. (2008). The status of hoarding as a symptom of obsessive-compulsive disorder. *Behaviour Research and Therapy, 46,* 1026–1033.

Alexander, G. E., DeLong, M. R., & Strick, P. L. (1986). Parallel organization of functionally segregated circuits linking basal ganglia and cortex. *Annual Review of Neuroscience, 9,* 357–381.

Amaral, D. G. & Price, J. L. (1984). Amygdalo-cortical projections in the monkey (Macaca fascicularis). *Journal of Comparative Neurology, 230,* 465–496.

American Psychiatric Association. (2000). *Diagnostic and statistical manual of mental disorders* (4th ed. Text Revision). Washington, DC: Author.

An, S. K., Mataix-Cols, D., Lawrence, N. S., Wooderson, S., Giampietro, V., Speckens, A. et al. (2008). To discard or not to discard: the neural basis of hoarding symptoms in obsessive-compulsive disorder. *Molecular Psychiatry, 14,* 318–331.

Anderson, S.W., Damasio, H., Damasio, A.R. (2005). A neural basis for collecting behaviour in humans. *Brain, 128,* 201–212.

Aouizerate, B., Guehl, D., Cuny, E., Rougier, A., Bioulac, B., Tignol, J. et al. (2004). Pathophysiology of obsessive-compulsive disorder: a necessary link between phenomenology, neuropsychology, imagery and physiology. *Progress in Neurobiology, 72,* 195–221.

Armony, J. L., Corbo, V., Clement, M. H., & Brunet, A. (2005). Amygdala response in patients with acute PTSD to masked and unmasked emotional facial expressions. *American Journal of Psychiatry, 162,* 1961–1963.

Ashburner, J. & Friston, K. J. (2001). Why voxel-based morphometry should be used. *Neuroimage, 14,* 1238–1243.

Ashburner, J. & Friston, K. J. (2000). Voxel-based morphometry—the methods. *Neuroimage, 11,* 805–821.

Barbas, H. (2000). Connections underlying the synthesis of cognition, memory, and emotion in primate prefrontal cortices. *Brain Research Bulletin, 52,* 319–330.

Baym, C. L., Corbett, B. A., Wright, S.B., Bunge, S. A. (2008). Neural correlates of tic severity and cognitive control in children with Tourette syndrome. *Brain, 131,* 165–179.

Bechara, A., Tranel, D., & Damasio, H. (2000). Characterization of the decision-making deficit of patients with ventromedial prefrontal cortex lesions. *Brain, 123*(11), 2189–2202.

Birbaumer, N., Grodd, W., Diedrich, O., Klose, U., Erb, M., Lotze, M. et al. (1998). fMRI reveals amygdala activation to human faces in social phobics. *Neuroreport, 9,* 1223–1226.

Blair, K., Shaywitz, J., Smith, B. W., Rhodes, R., Geraci, M., Jones, M. et al. (2008). Response to emotional expressions in generalized social phobia and generalized anxiety disorder: evidence for separate disorders. *American Journal of Psychiatry, 165,* 1193–1202.

Bloch, M. H., Landeros-Weisenberger, A., Rosario, M. C., Pittenger, C., & Leckman, J. F. (2008). Meta-analysis of the symptom structure of obsessive-compulsive disorder. *American Journal of Psychiatry, 165,* 1532–1542.

Bloch, M. H., Leckman, J. F., Zhu, H., & Peterson, B. S. (2005). Caudate volumes in childhood predict symptom severity in adults with Tourette syndrome. *Neurology, 65,* 1253–1258.

Breiter, H. C., Rauch, S. L., Kwong, K. K., Baker, J. R., Weisskoff, R. M., Kennedy, D. N. et al. (1996). Functional magnetic resonance imaging of symptom provocation in obsessive-compulsive disorder. *Archives of General Psychiatry, 53,* 595–606.

Brown, H. D., Kosslyn, S. M., Delamater, B., Fama, J., & Barsky, A. J. (1999). Perceptual and memory biases for health-related information in hypochondriacal individuals. *Journal of Psychosomatic Research, 47,* 67–78.

Bryant, R. A., Felmingham, K., Whitford, T. J., Kemp, A., Hughes, G., Peduto, A. et al. (2008). Rostral anterior cingulate volume predicts treatment response to cognitive-behavioural therapy for posttraumatic stress disorder. *Journal of Psychiatry & Neuroscience, 33,* 142–146.

Cannistraro, P. A., Wright, C. I., Wedig, M. M., Martis, B., Shin, L. M., Wilhelm, S. et al. (2004). Amygdala responses to human faces in obsessive-compulsive disorder. *Biological Psychiatry, 56,* 916–920.

Carey, P., Seedat, S., Warwick, J., van, H. B., & Stein, D. J. (2004). SPECT imaging of body dysmorphic disorder. *Journal of Neuropsychiatry and Clinical Neurosciences, 16,* 357–359.

Chamberlain, S. R., Blackwell, A. D., Fineberg, N. A., Robbins, T. W., & Sahakian, B. J. (2005). The neuropsychology of obsessive compulsive disorder: the importance of failures in cognitive and behavioural inhibition as candidate endophenotypic markers. *Neuroscience and Biobehavioral Reviews, 29,* 399–419.

Chamberlain, S. R., Fineberg, N. A., Menzies, L. A., Blackwell, A. D., Bullmore, E. T., Robbins, T. W. et al. (2007). Impaired cognitive flexibility and motor inhibition in unaffected first-degree relatives of patients with obsessive-compulsive disorder. *American Journal of Psychiatry, 164,* 335–338.

Chamberlain, S. R., Menzies, L., Hampshire, A., Suckling, J., Fineberg, N. A., Del, C. N. et al. (2008a). Orbitofrontal dysfunction in patients with obsessive-compulsive disorder and their unaffected relatives. *Science, 321,* 421–422.

Chamberlain, S. R., Menzies, L. A., Fineberg, N. A., Del, C. N., Suckling, J., Craig, K. et al. (2008b). Grey matter abnormalities in trichotillomania: morphometric magnetic resonance imaging study. *British Journal of Psychiatry, 193,* 216–221.

Cummings, J. L. (1993). Frontal-subcortical circuits and human behavior. *Arch.Neurol., 50,* 873–880.

Dilger, S., Straube, T., Mentzel, H. J., Fitzek, C., Reichenbach, J. R., Hecht, H. et al. (2003). Brain activation to phobia-related pictures in spider phobic humans: an event-related functional magnetic resonance imaging study. *Neuroscience Letters., 348,* 29–32.

Ekman, P., & Friesen, W. V. (1976). Measuring facial movement. *Environmental Psychology and Nonverbal Behavior, 1,* 56–75.

Evans, K. C., Wright, C. I., Wedig, M. M., Gold, A. L., Pollack, M. H., & Rauch, S. L. (2008). A functional MRI study of amygdala responses to angry schematic faces in social anxiety disorder. *Depression and Anxiety, 25,* 496–505.

Feusner, J. D., Townsend, J., Bystritsky, A., & Bookheimer, S. (2007). Visual information processing of faces in body dysmorphic disorder. *Archives of General Psychiatry, 64,* 1417–1425.

Furmark, T., Tillfors, M., Marteinsdottir, I., Fischer, H., Pissiota, A., Langstrom, B. et al. (2002). Common changes in cerebral blood flow in patients with social phobia treated with citalopram or cognitive-behavioral therapy. *Archives of General Psychiatry, 59,* 425–433.

Gehring, W. J., Himle, J., & Nisenson, L. G. (2000). Action-monitoring dysfunction in obsessive-compulsive disorder. *Psychological Science, 11,* 1–6.

Gibbs, N. A. (1996). Nonclinical populations in research on obsessive-compulsive disorder: a critical review. *Clinical Psychology Review, 16,* 729–773.

Goossens, L., Sunaert, S., Peeters, R., Griez, E. J., & Schruers, K. R. (2007). Amygdala hyperfunction in phobic fear normalizes after exposure. *Biological Psychiatry, 62,* 1119–1125.

Goudriaan, A. E., Oosterlaan, J., de Beurs, E., & van den Brink, W. (2006). Neurocognitive functions in pathological gambling: a comparison with alcohol dependence, Tourette syndrome and normal controls. *Addiction, 101,* 534–547.

Grachev, I. D. (1997). MRI-based morphometric topographic parcellation of human neocortex in trichotillomania. *Psychiatry and Clinical Neurosciences., 51,* 315–321.

Groenewegen, H. J. & Uylings, H. B. (2000). The prefrontal cortex and the integration of sensory, limbic and autonomic information. *Progress in Brain Research., 126,* 3–28.

Gu, B. M., Park, J. Y., Kang, D. H., Lee, S. J., Yoo, S. Y., Jo, H. J. et al. (2008). Neural correlates of cognitive inflexibility during task-switching in obsessive-compulsive disorder. *Brain, 131,* 155–164.

Haber, S. N. (2008). The primate basal ganglia: parallel integrative networks. *Journal of Chemical Neuroanatomy, 26,* 317–330.

Herberg, L. J. & Blundell, J. E. (1967). Lateral hypothalamus: hoarding behavior elicited by electrical stimulation. *Science, 155,* 349–350.

Hester, R. & Garavan, H. (2004). Executive dysfunction in cocaine addiction: evidence for discordant frontal, cingulate, and cerebellar activity. *Journal of Neuroscience, 24,* 11017–11022.

Hollander, E., Braun, A., & Simeon, D. (2008). Should OCD leave the anxiety disorders in DSM-V? The case for obsessive compulsive-related disorders. *Depression and Anxiety, 25,* 317–329.

Hurd, Y. L., Suzuki, M., & Sedvall, G. C. (2001). D1 and D2 dopamine receptor mRNA expression in whole hemisphere sections of the human brain. *Journal of Chemical Neuroanatomy, 22,* 127–137.

Kalsbeek, A., De Bruin, J. P., Feenstra, M. G., Matthijssen, M. A., & Uylings, H. B. (1988). Neonatal thermal lesions of the mesolimbocortical dopaminergic projection decrease food-hoarding behavior. *Brain Research, 475,* 80–90.

Kelley, A. E. & Stinus, L. (1985). Disappearance of hoarding behavior after 6-hydroxydopamine lesions of the mesolimbic dopamine neurons and its reinstatement with L-dopa. *Behavioral Neuroscience, 99,* 531–545.

Larson, C. L., Schaefer, H. S., Siegle, G. J., Jackson, C. A., Anderle, M. J., & Davidson, R. J. (2006). Fear is fast in phobic individuals: amygdala activation in response to fear-relevant stimuli. *Biological Psychiatry, 60,* 410–417.

Leckman, J. F., Rauch, S. L., & Mataix-Cols, D. (2007). Symptom dimensions in obsessive-compulsive disorder: implications for the DSM-V. *CNS Spectrums., 12,* 376–87, 400.

LeDoux, J. E. (1996). *The emotional brain: the mysterious underpinnings of emotional life.* New York: Touchstone.

Lorberbaum, J. P., Kose, S., Johnson, M. R., Arana, G. W., Sullivan, L. K., Hamner, M. B. et al. (2004). Neural correlates of speech anticipatory anxiety in generalized social phobia. *Neuroreport, 15,* 2701–2705.

Maltby, N., Tolin, D. F., Worhunsky, P., O'Keefe, T. M., & Kiehl, K. A. (2005). Dysfunctional action monitoring hyperactivates frontal-striatal circuits in obsessive-compulsive disorder: an event-related fMRI study. *Neuroimage, 24,* 495–503.

Mataix-Cols, D., Barrios, M., Sanchez-Turet, M., Vallejo, J., & Junque, C. (1999). Reduced design fluency in subclinical obsessive-compulsive subjects. *Journal of Neuropsychiatry and Clinical Neurosciences, 11,* 395–397.

Mataix-Cols, D., Cullen, S., Lange, K., Zelaya, F., Andrew, C., Amaro, E. et al. (2003). Neural correlates of anxiety associated with obsessive-compulsive symptom dimensions in normal volunteers. *Biological Psychiatry, 53,* 482–493.

Mataix-Cols, D., Frost, R. O., Pertusa, A., Clark, L. A., Leckman, J. F., Saxena, S. et al. (2010). Hoarding disorder: a new diagnosis for DSM-V? *Depression and Anxiety, 27,* 556–572.

Mataix-Cols, D., Junque, C., Sanchez-Turet, M., Vallejo, J., Verger, K., & Barrios, M. (1999). Neuropsychological functioning in a subclinical obsessive-compulsive sample. *Biological Psychiatry, 45,* 898–904.

Mataix-Cols, D., Pertusa, A., & Leckman, J. F. (2007). Issues for DSM-V: how should obsessive-compulsive and related disorders be classified? *American Journal of Psychiatry, 164,* 1313–1314.

Mataix-Cols, D., Rauch, S. L., Manzo, P. A., Jenike, M. A., & Baer, L. (1999). Use of factor-analyzed symptom dimensions to predict outcome with serotonin reuptake inhibitors and placebo in the treatment of obsessive-compulsive disorder. *American Journal of Psychiatry, 156,* 1409–1416.

Mataix-Cols, D., Rosario-Campos, M. C., & Leckman, J. F. (2005). A multidimensional model of obsessive-compulsive disorder. *American Journal of Psychiatry, 162,* 228–238.

Mataix-Cols, D. & van den Heuvel, O. A. (2006). Common and distinct neural correlates of obsessive-compulsive and related disorders. *Psychiatric Clinics of North America, 29,* 391–410.

Mataix-Cols, D., Wooderson, S., Lawrence, N., Brammer, M. J., Speckens, A., & Phillips, M. L. (2004). Distinct neural correlates of washing, checking, and hoarding symptom dimensions in obsessive-compulsive disorder. *Archives of General Psychiatry, 61,* 564–576.

Mechelli, A., Price, C. J., Friston, K. J., & Ashburner, J. (2005). Voxel-based morphometry of the human brain: Methods and applications. *Current Medical Imaging Reviews, 1*, 105–113.

Menzies, L., Achard, S., Chamberlain, S. R., Fineberg, N., Chen, C. H., Del, C. N. et al. (2007). Neurocognitive endophenotypes of obsessive-compulsive disorder. *Brain, 130*, 3223–3236.

Menzies, L., Chamberlain, S. R., Laird, A. R., Thelen, S. M., Sahakian, B. J., & Bullmore, E. T. (2008a). Integrating evidence from neuroimaging and neuropsychological studies of obsessive-compulsive disorder: the orbitofrontal-striatal model revisited. *Neuroscience and Biobehavioral Reviews, 32*, 525–549.

Menzies, L., Williams, G. B., Chamberlain, S. R., Ooi, C., Fineberg, N., Suckling, J. et al. (2008b). White matter abnormalities in patients with obsessive-compulsive disorder and their first-degree relatives. *American Journal of Psychiatry, 165*, 1308–1315.

Muller, S. V., Johannes, S., Wieringa, B., Weber, A., Muller-Vahl, K., Matzke, M. et al. (2003). Disturbed monitoring and response inhibition in patients with Gilles de la Tourette syndrome and co-morbid obsessive compulsive disorder. *Behavioral Neurology, 14*, 29–37.

Muris, P., Merckelbach, H., & Clavan, M. (1997). Abnormal and normal compulsions. *Behaviour Research and Therapy, 35*, 249–252.

O'Sullivan, R. L., Rauch, S. L., Breiter, H. C., Grachev, I. D., Baer, L., Kennedy, D. N. et al. (1997). Reduced basal ganglia volumes in trichotillomania measured via morphometric magnetic resonance imaging. *Biological Psychiatry, 42*, 39–45.

Ochsner, K. N. & Gross, J. J. (2005). The cognitive control of emotion. *Trends in Cognitive Science, 9*, 242–249.

Perani, D., Garibotto, V., Gorini, A., Moresco, R. M., Henin, M., Panzacchi, A. et al. (2008). In vivo PET study of 5HT(2A) serotonin and D(2) dopamine dysfunction in drug-naive obsessive-compulsive disorder. *Neuroimage, 42*, 306–314.

Pertusa, A., Fullana, M. A., Singh, S., Alonso, P., Menchon, J. M., & Mataix-Cols, D. (2008). Compulsive hoarding: OCD symptom, distinct clinical syndrome, or both? *American Journal of Psychiatry, 165*, 1289–1298.

Peterson, B. S., Choi, H. A., Hao, X., Amat, J. A., Zhu, H., Whiteman, R. et al. (2007). Morphologic features of the amygdala and hippocampus in children and adults with Tourette syndrome. *Archives of General Psychiatry, 64*, 1281–1291.

Peterson, B. S., Skudlarski, P., Anderson, A. W., Zhang, H., Gatenby, J. C., Lacadie, C. M. et al. (1998). A functional magnetic resonance imaging study of tic suppression in Tourette syndrome. *Archives of General Psychiatry, 55*, 326–333.

Peterson, B. S., Staib, L., Scahill, L., Zhang, H., Anderson, C., Leckman, J. F. et al. (2001). Regional brain and ventricular volumes in Tourette syndrome. *Archives of General Psychiatry, 58*, 427–440.

Peterson, B. S., Thomas, P., Kane, M. J., Scahill, L., Zhang, H., Bronen, R. et al. (2003). Basal ganglia volumes in patients with Gilles de la Tourette syndrome. *Archives of General Psychiatry, 60*, 415–424.

Phan, K. L., Fitzgerald, D. A., Nathan, P. J., & Tancer, M. E. (2006). Association between amygdala hyperactivity to harsh faces and severity of social anxiety in generalized social phobia. *Biological Psychiatry, 59*, 424–429.

Phelps, E. A., Delgado, M. R., Nearing, K. I., & LeDoux, J. E. (2004). Extinction learning in humans: role of the amygdala and vmPFC. *Neuron, 43*, 897–905.

Phillips, K. A., Stein, D. J., Rauch, S. L., Hollander, E., Fineberg, N., Saxena, S. et al. (2010). Should an obsessive-compulsive spectrum grouping of disorders be included in DSM-V? *Depression and Anxiety, 27*(6), 528–555.

Phillips, M. L., Drevets, W. C., Rauch, S. L., & Lane, R. (2003a). Neurobiology of emotion perception I: The neural basis of normal emotion perception. *Biological Psychiatry, 54*, 504–514.

Phillips, M. L., Drevets, W. C., Rauch, S. L., & Lane, R. (2003b). Neurobiology of emotion perception II: Implications for major psychiatric disorders. *Biological Psychiatry, 54*, 515–528.

Phillips, M. L., Marks, I. M., Senior, C., Lythgoe, D., O'Dwyer, A. M., Meehan, O. et al. (2000). A differential neural response in obsessive-compulsive disorder patients with washing compared with checking symptoms to disgust. *Psychological Medicine, 30*, 1037–1050.

Phillips, M. L., Young, A. W., Senior, C., Brammer, M., Andrew, C., Calder, A. J. et al. (1997). A specific neural substrate for perceiving facial expressions of disgust. *Nature, 389*, 495–498.

Pujol, J., Soriano-Mas, C., Alonso, P., Cardoner, N., Menchon, J. M., Deus, J. et al. (2004). Mapping structural brain alterations in obsessive-compulsive disorder. *Archives of General Psychiatry, 61*, 720–730.

Quirk, G. J., Likhtik, E., Pelletier, J. G., & Pare, D. (2003). Stimulation of medial prefrontal cortex decreases the responsiveness of central amygdala output neurons. *Journal of Neuroscience, 23*, 8800–8807.

Quirk, G. J., Russo, G. K., Barron, J. L., & Lebron, K. (2000). The role of ventromedial prefrontal cortex in the recovery of extinguished fear. *Journal of Neuroscience, 20*, 6225–6231.

Rachman, S. & de Silva, P. (1978). Abnormal and normal obsessions. *Behaviour Research and Therapy, 16*, 233–248.

Radua, J. & Mataix-Cols, D. (2009). Voxel-wise meta-analysis of grey matter changes in obsessive-compulsive disorder. *British Journal of Psychiatry, 195*, 393–402.

Radua, J., van den Heuvel, O. A., Surguladze, S., & Mataix-Cols, D. (2010). Is OCD an anxiety disorder? A meta-analytical comparison of voxel-based morphometry studies in OCD vs. other anxiety disorders. *Archives of General Psychiatry, 67*, 701–711.

Rasmussen, S. A. & Eisen, J. L. (1988). Clinical and epidemiologic findings of significance to neuropharmacologic trials in OCD. *Psychopharmacology Bulletin, 24*, 466–470.

Rauch, S. L., Dougherty, D. D., Shin, L. M., Alpert, N. M., Manzo, P. A., Leahy, L. et al. (1998). Neural correlates of factor-analyzed OCD symptom dimensions: a PET study. *CNS Spectrums, 3*, 37–43.

Rauch, S. L., Phillips, K. A., Segal, E., Makris, N., Shin, L. M., Whalen, P. J. et al. (2003). A preliminary morphometric magnetic resonance imaging study of regional brain volumes in body dysmorphic disorder. *Psychiatry Research, 122*, 13–19.

Rauch, S. L., Savage, C. R., Alpert, N. M., Fischman, A. J., & Jenike, M. A. (1997). The functional neuroanatomy of anxiety: a study of three disorders using positron emission tomography and symptom provocation. *Biological Psychiatry, 42*, 446–452.

Rauch, S. L., Savage, C. R., Alpert, N. M., Miguel, E. C., Baer, L., Breiter, H. C. et al. (1995). A positron emission tomographic study of simple phobic symptom provocation. *Archives of General Psychiatry, 52*, 20–28.

Rauch, S. L., Whalen, P. J., Shin, L. M., McInerney, S. C., Macklin, M. L., Lasko, N. B. et al. (2000). Exaggerated amygdala response to masked facial stimuli in posttraumatic stress disorder: a functional MRI study. *Biological Psychiatry, 47*, 769–776.

Remijnse, P. L., Nielen, M. M., van Balkom, A. J., Cath, D. C., van, O. P., Uylings, H. B. et al. (2006). Reduced orbitofrontal-striatal activity on a reversal learning task in obsessive-compulsive disorder. *Archives of General Psychiatry, 63*, 1225–1236.

Remijnse, P. L., van den Heuvel, O. A., & Veltman, D. J. (2005). Neuroimaging in obsessive-compulsive disorder. *Current Medical Imaging Reviews, 1*, 331–351.

Rotge, J. Y., Guehl, D., Dilharreguy, B., Tignol, J., Bioulac, B., Allard, M. et al. (2009). Meta-analysis of brain volume changes in obsessive-compulsive disorder. *Biological Psychiatry, 65*, 75–83.

Roth, R. M., Saykin, A. J., Flashman, L. A., Pixley, H. S., West, J. D., & Mamourian, A. C. (2007). Event-related functional magnetic resonance imaging of response inhibition in obsessive-compulsive disorder. *Biological Psychiatry, 62*, 901–909.

Rubia, K., Smith, A. B., Brammer, M. J., Toone, B., & Taylor, E. (2005). Abnormal brain activation during inhibition and error detection in medication-naive adolescents with ADHD. *American Journal of Psychiatry, 162*, 1067–1075.

Saxena, S. (2008). Recent advances in compulsive hoarding. *Current Psychiatry Reports, 10*, 297–303.

Saxena, S., Brody, A. L., Maidment, K. M., Smith, E. C., Zohrabi, N., Katz, E. et al. (2004). Cerebral glucose metabolism in obsessive-compulsive hoarding. *American Journal of Psychiatry, 161*, 1038–1048.

Saxena, S., Gorbis, E., O'Neill, J., Baker, S. K., Mandelkern, M. A., Maidment, K. M. et al. (2009). Rapid effects of brief intensive cognitive-behavioral therapy on brain glucose metabolism in obsessive-compulsive disorder. *Molecular Psychiatry, 14*, 197–205.

Saxena, S. & Rauch, S. L. (2000). Functional neuroimaging and the neuroanatomy of obsessive-compulsive disorder. *Psychiatric Clinics of North America, 23*, 563–586.

Schienle, A., Schafer, A., Walter, B., Stark, R., & Vaitl, D. (2005). Brain activation of spider phobics towards disorder-relevant, generally disgust- and fear-inducing pictures. *Neuroscience Letters, 388*, 1–6.

Schneider, F., Weiss, U., Kessler, C., Muller-Gartner, H. W., Posse, S., Salloum, J. B. et al. (1999). Subcortical correlates of differential classical conditioning of aversive emotional reactions in social phobia. *Biological Psychiatry, 45*, 863–871.

Shapira, N. A., Liu, Y., He, A. G., Bradley, M. M., Lessig, M. C., James, G. A. et al. (2003). Brain activation by disgust-inducing pictures in obsessive-compulsive disorder. *Biological Psychiatry, 54*, 751–756.

Shin, L. M., Orr, S. P., Carson, M. A., Rauch, S. L., Macklin, M. L., Lasko, N. B. et al. (2004). Regional cerebral blood flow in the amygdala and medial prefrontal cortex during traumatic imagery in male and female Vietnam veterans with PTSD. *Archives of General Psychiatry, 61*, 168–176.

Shin, L. M., Rauch, S. L., & Pitman, R. K. (2006). Amygdala, medial prefrontal cortex, and hippocampal function in PTSD. *Annals of the New York Academy of Sciences, 1071*, 67–79.

Shin, L. M., Wright, C. I., Cannistraro, P. A., Wedig, M. M., McMullin, K., Martis, B. et al. (2005). A functional magnetic resonance imaging study of amygdala and medial prefrontal cortex responses to overtly presented fearful faces in posttraumatic stress disorder. *Archives of General Psychiatry, 62*, 273–281.

Smith, A. B., Taylor, E., Brammer, M., Toone, B., & Rubia, K. (2006). Task-specific hypoactivation in prefrontal and temporoparietal brain regions during motor inhibition and task switching in medication-naive children and adolescents with attention deficit hyperactivity disorder. *American Journal of Psychiatry, 163*, 1044–1051.

Sowell, E. R., Kan, E., Yoshii, J., Thompson, P. M., Bansal, R., Xu, D. et al. (2008). Thinning of sensorimotor cortices in children with Tourette syndrome. *Nature Neuroscience, 11*, 637–639.

Stein, D. J., Coetzer, R., Lee, M., Davids, B., & Bouwer, C. (1997). Magnetic resonance brain imaging in women with obsessive-compulsive disorder and trichotillomania. *Psychiatry Research, 74*, 177–182.

Stein, D. J., van, H. B., Hugo, C., van, K. J., Warwick, J., Zungu-Dirwayi, N. et al. (2002). Functional brain imaging and pharmacotherapy in trichotillomania. Single photon emission computed tomography before and after treatment with the selective serotonin reuptake inhibitor citalopram. *Progress in Neuro-psychopharmacology, 26*, 885–890.

Stein, M. B., Goldin, P. R., Sareen, J., Zorrilla, L. T., & Brown, G. G. (2002). Increased amygdala activation to angry and contemptuous faces in generalized social phobia. *Archives of General Psychiatry, 59*, 1027–1034.

Steketee, G. & Frost, R. (2003). Compulsive hoarding: current status of the research. *Clinical Psychology Review, 23*, 905–927.

Straube, T., Mentzel, H. J., Glauer, M., & Miltner, W. H. (2004). Brain activation to phobia-related words in phobic subjects. *Neuroscience Letters, 372*, 204–208.

Straube, T., Mentzel, H. J., & Miltner, W. H. (2006). Neural mechanisms of automatic and direct processing of phobogenic stimuli in specific phobia. *Biological Psychiatry, 59*, 162–170.

Swedo, S. E., Rapoport, J. L., Leonard, H. L., Schapiro, M. B., Rapoport, S. I., & Grady, C. L. (1991). Regional cerebral glucose metabolism of women with trichotillomania. *Archives of General Psychiatry, 48*, 828–833.

Tillfors, M., Furmark, T., Marteinsdottir, I., & Fredrikson, M. (2002). Cerebral blood flow during anticipation of public speaking in social phobia: a PET study. *Biological Psychiatry, 52*, 1113–1119.

Tolin, D. F., Kiehl, K. A., Worhunsky, P., Book, G. A., & Maltby, N. (2009). An exploratory study of the neural mechanisms of decision making in compulsive hoarding. *Psychological Medicine, 39*(2), 325–336.

Ursu, S., Stenger, V. A., Shear, M. K., Jones, M. R., & Carter, C. S. (2003). Overactive action monitoring in obsessive-compulsive disorder: evidence from functional magnetic resonance imaging. *Psychological Science, 14*, 347–353.

van den Heuvel, O. A., Remijnse, P. L., Mataix-Cols, D., Vrenken, H., Groenewegen, H. J., Uylings, H. B. et al. (2009). The major symptom dimensions of obsessive-compulsive disorder are mediated by partially distinct neural systems. *Brain, 132*, 853–868.

van den Heuvel, O. A., Veltman, D. J., Groenewegen, H. J., Cath, D. C., van Balkom, A. J., van, H. J. et al. (2005a). Frontal-striatal dysfunction during planning in obsessive-compulsive disorder. *Archives of General Psychiatry, 62,* 301–309.

van den Heuvel, O. A., Veltman, D. J., Groenewegen, H. J., Dolan, R. J., Cath, D. C., Boellaard, R. et al. (2004). Amygdala activity in obsessive-compulsive disorder with contamination fear: a study with oxygen-15 water positron emission tomography. *Psychiatry Research, 132,* 225–237.

van den Heuvel, O. A., Veltman, D. J., Groenewegen, H. J., Witter, M. P., Merkelbach, J., Cath, D. C. et al. (2005b). Disorder-specific neuroanatomical correlates of attentional bias in obsessive-compulsive disorder, panic disorder, and hypochondriasis. *Archives of General Psychiatry, 62,* 922–933.

van der Wee, N. J., Ramsey, N. F., Jansma, J. M., Denys, D. A., van Megen, H. J., Westenberg, H. M. et al. (2003). Spatial working memory deficits in obsessive compulsive disorder are associated with excessive engagement of the medial frontal cortex. *Neuroimage, 20,* 2271–2280.

Wendt, J., Lotze, M., Weike, A. I., Hosten, N., & Hamm, A. O. (2008). Brain activation and defensive response mobilization during sustained exposure to phobia-related and other affective pictures in spider phobia. *Psychophysiology, 45,* 205–215.

Whiteside, S. P., Port, J. D., & Abramowitz, J. S. (2004). A meta-analysis of functional neuroimaging in obsessive-compulsive disorder. *Psychiatry Research, 132,* 69–79.

Wicker, B., Keysers, C., Plailly, J., Royet, J. P., Gallese, V., & Rizzolatti, G. (2003). Both of us disgusted in my insula: the common neural basis of seeing and feeling disgust. *Neuron, 40,* 655–664.

Woody, S. R., McLean, C., & Klassen, T. (2005). Disgust as a motivator of avoidance of spiders. *Journal of Anxiety Disorders, 19,* 461–475.

Wright, C. I., Martis, B., McMullin, K., Shin, L. M., & Rauch, S. L. (2003). Amygdala and insular responses to emotionally valenced human faces in small animal specific phobia. *Biological Psychiatry, 54,* 1067–1076.

Information Processing in Obsessive Compulsive Disorder and Related Problems

Adam S. Radomsky *and* Gillian M. Alcolado

Abstract

Information processing research has become increasingly important in understanding a large number of different disorders, including obsessive compulsive disorder (OCD). This work, which focuses on the factors affecting attention, encoding (learning), and different types of memory, promises not only to improve our knowledge of the psychopathology of OCD and related problems, but also to influence the treatment of these often severe and debilitating conditions. This chapter reviews the history and research associated with aspects of information processing as they relate to both the psychopathology and treatment of OCD, trichotillomania, and body dysmorphic disorder. This includes descriptions of some experimental methodologies used to assess challenging aspects of cognition in OCD. Consistencies and inconsistencies in the literature are highlighted, and an attempt is made to resolve some of them through conceptualizing information-processing studies as either relevant or irrelevant to the experience of OCD. Ideas and questions for future research are proposed.

Keywords: obsessive compulsive disorder, OCD, cognitive processing, information processing, OC spectrum

Introduction: Why is information processing relevant to understanding OCD?

In order to appreciate the reasons why information-processing research is relevant to understanding and treating OCD, a review of the origins of such research is necessary; one must (briefly) go back to a time before investigations of information processing had grown to their current popular and influential status. Prior to the 1980s, modern conceptualizations of, and treatments for, what were then called "neuroses" were largely behavioral in nature. Although not designed to specifically explain OCD, Mowrer's (1947) two-process theory could easily be applied—fear arises from exposure to various triggers (which themselves may have been classically conditioned), and the ensuing compulsion is negatively reinforced by the reduction in fear (operant conditioning). For example, someone who has caught an illness in the past might experience fear at the sight of dirt on their hands. When they wash, their anxiety reduces, thus reinforcing the washing behavior through operant conditioning. Models like these were instrumental in the development of behavioral treatments for neuroses such as those applied by Wolpe (1954, 1958), and more specifically for OCD by Meyer (1966).

In the 1970s, cognitive psychologists began to examine internal processes (rather than only the observable characteristics so important to the behaviorists)—and, building on much earlier work by people such as Ebbinghaus (1913), turned their focus on psychological phenomena such as memory (both its encoding and retrieval) and attention. Some of the factors that promoted enhanced and inhibited memory (e.g., Craik & Lockhart, 1972) were identified and, consistent with the emergence of the information age, research in information processing began to take off. Although behavioral treatments for OCD had been somewhat successful, it was certainly true that a substantial proportion of patients were left unwell—even after receiving a course of exposure and response prevention (ERP). As such, the time was ripe for an integration of cognition and behavior in models of, and treatments for, a number of different psychological problems, including OCD.

Building upon the cognitive (or "rational") therapies of Beck (1979) and Ellis (1962), clinical psychologists began to incorporate cognitive elements into their conceptualizations of and treatments for OCD. This came to a head when Salkovskis (1985) published a cognitive approach to OCD with an emphasis on perceived responsibility (See Chapter 11). But the kinds of cognition described by these clinical approaches were somewhat different from the work of the cognitive scientists engaged in the study of the processing of information (e.g., attention, memory, etc.). Beliefs about responsibility do not seem all that similar to the degree to which individuals remember a number of learned stimuli, for example. Around the same time as Salkovskis's (1985) theory was published, Williams, Watts, MacLeod and Matthews (1988) summarized and proposed ways of applying cognitive science to emotional disorders. This coincided with a surge in interest in the application of cognitive science to the understanding (but not treatment) of mood and anxiety disorders (including OCD), represented by many of the descriptions of specific experiments below.

It became increasing clear that those diagnosed with specific disorders appeared to process information in different ways from nonclinical individuals, and from those diagnosed with different disorders (see Williams et al., 1997). For OCD, this led the way to a large number of fascinating questions: Could particular forms or profiles of information processing be used as diagnostic indicators of OCD and/or related problems? Could they distinguish between OCD and other related disorders? Could they be established as predisposing and/or vulnerability characteristics? Do the ways people process information cause pathology, or result from it? Is OCD associated with particular deficits in information-processing tasks? It is associated with any cognitive strengths? How does emotional state affect the informational aspect of OCD and related problems (in addition to its effects on symptoms)? Does a cognitively based treatment lead to changes in information processing? Do behavioral and pharmacological treatments lead to these changes, as well? Though some of these questions have been addressed (see below), many remain unanswered. In addition, for some of these queries, inconsistent results have emerged—often associated with very different methodologies, as you will read below. In some cases, findings have been quite consistent with models proposed by cognitive scientists, while others appear to be inconsistent with theoretical underpinnings.

Recently, a cognitive model of compulsive checking (Rachman, 2002) incorporated specific elements of cognitive science constructs related to metamemory. This represented a first for OCD, and followed in the footsteps of cognitive-behavioral models for social phobia, which had incorporated an emphasis on self-focused attention (Clark & Wells, 1995; Rapee & Heimberg, 1997), and an approach to post-traumatic stress disorder that stressed the role of encoding and memory processing (Ehlers & Clark, 2000). Given that treatments for other anxiety disorders have begun to incorporate elements more consistent with cognitive science (e.g., attention retraining in social phobia; Clark, Ehlers, Hackmann, McManus et al., 2006), it is likely only a matter of time before this occurs in cognitively based treatments for OCD. For these reasons, an understanding of information processing as it applies to OCD is not only fascinating, but timely. Although still in their early stages, applications of cognitive science to clinical psychology are occurring. Therefore, a better understanding of attentional processes in OCD, explicit and implicit memory processes in OCD, implicit processing in OCD, as well as an examination of these processes in related conditions such as trichotillomania and body dysmorphic disorder, is paramount not only for a better appreciation of the nature of these psychopathologies but also, hopefully, to inform their treatment.

Attentional Processes in OCD

A number of investigators have studied attentional processes in OCD. They postulated that those with OCD attend to information differently than other people, and that symptoms of the disorder can be attributed to the nature of information processing in these individuals (Muller & Roberts, 2005; Summerfeldt & Endler, 1998). For example, those with OCD might be predisposed to have attentional biases toward threatening information, thereby making the development of the disorder much more likely than for a person who processes threatening information less preferentially (Muller & Roberts,

2005; Summerfeldt & Endler, 1998). The literature related to this subject will be reviewed below.

Priming and Attentional Biases in OCD

An attentional bias is a cognitive skew that allows us to concentrate on what is important in our environment by ignoring or downplaying irrelevant information (see May, Kane, & Hasher, 1995, for a review). An interesting consequence of this phenomenon is the negative priming effect: people are slower to respond to items in their environment that they have been previously told to ignore (May et al., 1995). Since difficulties in disregarding unimportant information (for example, seemingly irrelevant thoughts and impulses) are a feature of OCD, one might guess that those diagnosed with OCD would not exhibit the negative priming effect (Enright & Beech, 1993a; Enright & Beech, 1993b). Research on the subject has found mixed results.

Some of the earliest research found evidence for deficits in negative priming in individuals with OCD. Enright and Beech (1993a) asked participants to attend to the red word (the probe) in a series of word pairs, and to name (via key press) its semantic category (out of a set of five previously established categories), while ignoring the distracter word. Anxious control participants exhibited the expected negative priming effect—that is, ignored distracter words that later became the probe words took longer to categorize—whereas participants with OCD did not show this effect. In the semantic negative priming condition, where the ignored distracter word belonged to the same category as the probe word, OCD participants actually exhibited the opposite—positive priming. That is, having seen the probe word previously as a distracter allowed them to respond to it faster, whereas anxious control participants still displayed the typical negative priming effect. This implies that participants with OCD were not able to ignore the irrelevant information, and that by attending to this information they responded faster on subsequent trials. These results were interpreted as evidence of a deficit in unconscious selective attention for individuals with OCD (Enright & Beech, 1993a), and a similar study of theirs replicated these findings (Enright & Beech, 1993b). However, one could reason that they were unable to ignore the irrelevant information because for people with OCD, this information was not actually irrelevant. In fact, a hallmark of OCD is attending to many sources of information, as a way to scan the environment for possible threat.

Other studies using similar negative priming tasks have varied the time between presentation of the distracter stimulus and of the target stimulus (called stimulus onset asynchrony, or SOA). Participants failed to display the typical negative priming effect only at short intervals between the stimuli (Enright, Beech, & Claridge, 1995; McNally, Wilhelm, Buhlmann, & Shin, 2001), and the effect was stronger in OCD checkers than in OCD noncheckers (Enright et al., 1995). Others have found that OCD checkers do not display negative priming at short SOAs, while OCD noncheckers do not display negative priming at long SOAs (Hoenig, Hochrein, Müller, & Wagner, 2002). Some suggest that since the only impairment on negative priming occurred at short SOAs, this is not evidence for biases in selective attention in OCD (if that really is the mechanism tapped by negative priming), but that there is some bias in their preattentive processing (Enright et al., 1995; McNally et al., 2001). They also suggest that attending to many sources of information is part of the profile of an OC checker (i.e., they are perhaps more prone to check things, if they are attending to so many elements in their environment that they can no longer remember what they have done), but is not part of the profile of a nonchecker (Enright et al., 1995). During the time between trials, after they have just made a decision, they are busy verifying their decision and therefore unable to use all the appropriate mental processes to inhibit noticing of a distracter stimulus (Hoenig et al., 2002). Both of these would explain findings of stronger deficits in negative priming in OCD checkers. However, no theory currently explains the preliminary findings of noncheckers not showing negative priming at long SOAs (Hoenig et al., 2002).

A study involving positive priming (i.e., the prime word was sometimes the same as the target word, so that responding should be facilitated, and reaction time faster) found that when personally threatening words were used, participants with OCD failed to display positive priming (Amir, Cobb, & Morrison, 2008). Instead they showed negative priming (slower response when they had previously seen the word, when that previous word should have allowed them to respond to it faster). The rationale for using personally relevant threatening words was that a processing bias in OCD would be present most strongly for words that are related to their concerns (Amir et al., 2008; see also, Radomsky & Rachman, 2004). This study supports the notion that negative priming can be detected in participants with OCD under the right conditions. Whether negative priming is an attentional or memory task is still unclear. However, the authors suggest that the results of this study support the idea that negative priming occurs because participants with OCD assign a "do not respond" tag to threat-related words when they are in the distractor display, and that may be why they take longer to name them when they are presented (Amir et al., 2008).

In contrast, MacDonald, Antony, MacLeod and Swinson (1999) found no evidence for a bias in negative priming in individuals with OCD; they displayed the usual effect that controls do. These results suggest that participants with OCD can ignore irrelevant information, and are not exhibiting biases in this regard. From a theoretical point of view, these results also support the view that negative priming is a memory-retrieval task. In the semantic condition, participants had to look at both words in order to make a decision, and yet still displayed negative priming, making it unlikely that this occurrence is the result of attentional inhibition, and more likely that it stems from a memory-retrieval process (MacDonald et al., 1999). It therefore remains to be seen whether participants with OCD have problems with attentional inhibition, since it has now been proposed that negative priming does not tap into this phenomenon (MacDonald et al., 1999).

Taken together, results from investigations on negative priming suggest that if people with OCD do have some difficulties inhibiting irrelevant information, it is a preattentive process (McNally et al., 2001) present only at short SOAs (Enright et al., 1995). Further, this deficit in negative priming is more characteristic of those who check compulsively than of those with other forms of OCD (Hoenig et al., 2002). Finally, recent evidence would suggest that using personally relevant threatening stimuli is more likely to reveal a deficit in priming (Amir et al., 2008), and may be more useful in general when examining information processes in association with OCD (Radomsky & Rachman, 2004). Methodological inconsistencies likely account for many of the discrepancies, and new research has found that when examined properly, there is no deficit in negative priming as compared to controls (Moritz, Kloss, & Jelinek, 2010); further, one should not necessarily expect a negative priming deficit in OCD, as metacognitive theories may better explain the relationship between OCD and attention.

The Stroop task is a classic tool for assessing cognition (Stroop, 1935), in which participants are slower to name the color ink that the word is printed in, if the word itself is a different color word (i.e., a participant who is asked to name the color of a word, rather than the word itself would be slower to say "blue" if the word RED was blue in color than if the word BLUE was blue in color). This is the classic Stroop interference effect (Stroop, 1935). This tool has been used, with and without modifications, to assess attentional processing in OCD, although it remains unclear exactly into what processes the Stroop test is tapping. The popular theories accounting for it, speed of processing (people are quicker to name words than colors), and automatic processing (words are processed automatically, whereas colors are not, and therefore require extra work) have been found lacking, in that they are unable to account for all the phenomena inherent in the Stroop paradigm (MacLeod, 1991). Therefore, it remains to be seen whether studies are measuring the proposed aspects of attention, and until this is clear, the usefulness and interpretation of the observed performance biases in people with OCD, gleaned from the Stroop task, remains unclear.

Enright and Beech (1993b) compared the performance of individuals with OCD to that of anxious controls on the traditional Stroop task, and found that they displayed less negative priming on the task than controls did. Some work has shown no difference in the latencies to color-name words as compared to controls (Enright et al., 1995), while other work has shown that they are slower to color-name words written in a different color ink (Hartston & Swerdlow, 1999). Foa, Ilai, McCarthy, Shoyer, and Murdock (1993) used a modified Stroop task, wherein participants were told to name the colors of nonwords, neutral words, general threat words, and contamination words (threatening specifically to those with OCD reporting contamination concerns, chosen for their rating by people with OCD in a different study). OC washers were slower to color-name contamination words than neutral words. They were also significantly slower to name contamination words than the control participants. OC nonwashers were slower to name general threat words as compared to neutral words. However, when primed with a threat word, OC washers did not take longer to respond to contamination words. These results support the idea that those with contamination fears show an attentional bias (at least as much as one can conclude this from the Stroop) for information that is relevant to their fears, and this causes interference when they are instructed to ignore it in favor of different information (Foa et al., 1993).

However, a recent study that also used words relevant to participants with OCD (anxiety, depression, responsibility, and conscientious related words as rated by experts) found no difference in latency to name the color ink of the word (Moritz et al., 2004). The authors suggested that using personally relevant words might be more likely to reveal a bias. Comparing reactions of checkers and washers to words that are relevant to their concerns (also as rated by clinicians) did not reveal any differences in reaction times on the Stroop (Moritz et al., 2008). They concluded by suggesting that to observe this attentional bias, researchers need to use stimuli that are stronger than words; perhaps images would be more attention-grabbing, and cause attentional biases to be revealed (Moritz et al.,2008). Incidentally, they later found just that, using an inhibition of return paradigm with images of neutral, anxiety-relevant, checking-relevant, or washing-relevant stimuli (Moritz et al., 2009). Participants with OCD were slower to respond to targets preceded by any OCD-relevant image (regardless of whether their concerns were of checking or washing; Moritz et al., 2009).

One attempt at making this paradigm more attention-grabbing has worked with success. Cohen, Lachenmeyer, and Springer (2003) assessed the effect that reading an anxiety-provoking paragraph or a neutral one would have on one's attention in the Stroop task. Because individuals with OCD are experiencing high levels of anxiety in their own lives while processing information, it is important to test the effects of situational anxiety on information processing in the lab. Previous studies that have used neutral cues or single words to provoke anxiety might not have been as effective at recreating a naturalistic anxious state, and therefore cannot determine the direct role that anxiety plays in information processing. The anxiety-provoking readings involved scenarios of personally relevant OCD cues that participants were told to imagine. OCD participants, as compared to controls, were more anxious after reading about the OCD-related situation, indicating that the anxiety manipulation worked. On the Stroop reading task (involving no colors) participants performed equivalently under the neutral scenario condition and the anxiety-provoking scenario condition. However on the Stroop color-word task, participants with OCD performed worse than controls (i.e., longer reaction times) after

becoming anxious, than in the neutral condition. The authors concluded that this slower reaction time was due to deficits in selective attention, rather than to deficits in general cognitive processes (Cohen et al., 2003).

In conclusion, there have been mixed results for detecting attentional biases using the Stroop task. The pattern that has emerged is that attentional biases are more likely to be detected using anxiety-provoking words or personally relevant information (Foa et al., 1993), as rated by people with OCD (Cohen et al., 2003) rather than clinicians (Moritz et al., 2004). Recent suggestions include moving toward using visual stimuli, to better grab the attention of people with OCD, in order to reveal this probable deficit (Moritz et al., 2008). Of course, all of the above studies are important, but many leave doubts about the true nature of the Stroop task and interpretation of these findings (MacLeod, 1991).

A variety of other tasks have been used to examine priming and attention in OCD. In the visuospatial priming (VSP) task (Hartston & Swerdlow, 1999), participants were asked to press a button in response to the location of the target stimulus "o." During the prime presentations, sometimes the target was in the same place as during the probe display, sometimes it was in a new place, and sometimes the distracter was in the same place where the probe would later appear. Participants with OCD showed more facilitation than did controls, in the condition where the target was in the same position in the prime and the probe trials. (This was especially true for individuals who reported aggressive, violent, or perfectionist obsessions, as well as those with checking compulsions or tics.) That is, they responded faster when the target appeared as a prime in the same location where it was about to appear as a probe, indicating they had been paying attention to the supposedly irrelevant priming information. This finding was expected, as those with OCD are proposed to have difficulty not focusing on irrelevant or previous information, which in this situation actually allows them to be more prepared for the appropriate response (Hartston & Swerdlow, 1999).

Using the dot-probe task (probably a task that more closely measures attention than the Stroop), Tata, Leibowitz, Prunty, Cameron, and Pickering (1996) examined attentional biases in OCD participants. They used contamination-related words and social-threat words (both chosen based on ratings by professionals) to see if there was heightened attentional interference for these emotionally laden words. Participants with OCD had faster reaction times for probe words occurring in the same location where a threat word had just previously appeared (vigilance), when the word was contamination related, as compared to controls. These results support the notion that meaning and personal relevance are important to understanding attentional processes. However, if the target word was in the distracter location in the previous trial, participants had delays in responding (interference) across both groups, for both types of threat words, showing a general threat interference effect. More recent research using this procedure has been mixed, finding either no effect in a clinical population (Harkness et al., 2009), or a bias that habituated over time (which perhaps explains some of the previous mixed results) in a student analog sample (Amir, Najmi, & Morrison, 2009).

The global-local paradigm has also been used by researchers (Moritz & Wendt, 2006) to assess attentional processing in OCD. In this paradigm, hierarchical letters (i.e., where a series of small letters or numbers forms the shape of a larger letter or number) are presented, and participants are typically told to name either the small or large letter or number. The task in this study was to press buttons whenever certain letters appeared, regardless of their local (small letters) or global (shape of large letter) status. They hypothesized that participants with OCD would respond faster to local stimuli than global stimuli, if OCD is characterized by an early attentional bias. They found that OCD participants performed the same as control participants. They therefore concluded that the local bias evident in other tasks, such as the Rey-Osterrieth Complex Figure Test (RCFT), does not occur early in perception and may instead occur in the memory-retrieval stage of information processing (Moritz & Wendt, 2006; also, see below). These results have since been replicated (Moritz, Wendt, et al., 2008) using a more difficult version of the paradigm (i.e., interference was caused by the global image when a response was required about the local target), further supporting their conclusion that there is no bias in early perception.

Attentional biases have also been investigated using a spatial-cueing paradigm (Moritz & von Mühlenen, 2008). In the task, participants respond by pressing a button to indicate the location of a square target on the screen. Its appearance is preceded by a "valid" or "invalid" cue (i.e., in the location the target is about to appear in, or in the

opposite location). Stimuli included neutral words as well as paranoia and checking-related words (chosen by clinicians). There was no evidence for an attentional bias for any word type in any of the groups. These findings are in line with their previous work using the same paradigm but without emotionally laden words (Moritz & von Mühlenen, 2005). Their study was limited, however, by the fact that they did not check to see how personally relevant the checking-related words actually were to the patients (Moritz & von Mühlenen, 2008). A more recent study has used the same task, but with threatening images (that, although not chosen by participants, were rated afterward as more fearful than the neutral words) and did find that people with subclinical levels of contamination fear had significantly greater difficulty disengaging from threatening words than did controls (Cisler & Olatunji, 2010).

Finally, studies using neuropsychological tests have found that compared to anxious controls and healthy participants, OCD participants have greater biases in selective attention, as well as difficulties in attentional switching (Clayton, Edwards, & Richards, 1999). In a study comparing the executive functioning of patients with Tourette syndrome and patients with OCD, participants with OCD were relatively impaired on their ability to shift attention (Watkins et al., 2005).

In summary, it would seem that attentional biases and deficits in OCD do exist, but that these are only evident under stringent experimental conditions. Given evidence of the existence of these attentional biases early in the process of attention, with personally relevant emotional information, we can tentatively conclude that these biases are present in individuals in OCD, and are likely contributors to the occurrence and maintenance of OCD symptoms. They don't allow patients to concentrate on the task at hand, and leave them open instead to an abundance of distracting information that, if threatening, will contribute to their anxiety and increase their OCD symptomatology.

Attention and Memory are not Unrelated
In order to be able to remember events, people must encode them in memory after attending to them (McDonald & McLeod, 1998). Accordingly, links between attention and memory cannot be made until a greater understanding of encoding is achieved. Furthermore, if there are differences in encoding between those diagnosed with OCD and others, findings of memorial differences must be interpreted with caution. Encoding is a necessary

bridge between the world and our memory, and plays an important role in understanding the phenomenology of OCD.

Understanding Encoding Strategies in OCD

Savage et al. (2000) examined strategies used to process visual verbal and nonverbal information in OCD. Their previous research had found evidence for biases in nonverbal strategic processing (Savage et al., 1999). Participants completed the RCFT, in which they had to copy the image from memory immediately after presentation and again 30 minutes later. Participants' scores did not differ between the two recall tasks, suggesting that it was not memory itself that was impaired, but the amount of information that had entered memory storage at the outset (Savage et al., 1999). They assessed the strategy employed by participants during encoding, using a new method whereby they tracked the order in which participants drew "details" versus basic configural elements of the figure (by changing the colored pencil the participants were using every 15 seconds). They also assigned points for each basic element that was drawn in its entirety (Savage et al., 1999).

Savage and his colleagues (2000) again used the RCFT to examine nonverbal memory strategies, and the California Verbal Learning Test (CVLT) to study verbal memory strategies. They hypothesized that by using the CVLT, which is a more complex task requiring strategies for effective memorization, a deficit would be revealed. In the CVLT, participants are presented with 16 words to memorize, but are not told that there are 4 different semantic categories by which they could organize these words. Performance on these two tasks was compared to that of control participants. Results on the RCFT showed that groups did not differ on copy performance, but participants with OCD remembered less of the figure on immediate recall than did control participants, and also had lower copy organization than controls. Results on the CVLT showed no problems with memory retention between the two recall trials in either of the groups, implying OCD participants had no trouble with memory storage (Savage et al., 2000). However, participants with OCD used less semantic clustering than did control participants. Although they remembered less on the free recall task than controls, they performed at par on the recognition tasks. Therefore, the impaired memories on both the verbal and nonverbal memory tasks for OCD participants were mediated by poor encoding strategies. There was no deficit in retrieving memories, but a problem in strategy used to encode the information in the first place (Savage et al., 2000).

Deckersbach et al. (2005) have looked at memory strategies in purely verbal learning tasks, and extended the findings of Savage's earlier work by examining whether participants with OCD (and in this study, bipolar participants as well) can be taught to use better verbal encoding strategies. Participants with OCD, bipolar disorder, and controls completed a word encoding paradigm. Participants listened to lists of words read over audio. In the "spontaneous" encoding condition, subjects were not told that these words could be categorized according to four different semantic categories. In the "directed" encoding condition, however, participants were told about the four existing categories, and told to group the words they heard according to their category. In the "unrelated" encoding condition, participants listened to words from many different categories and were told that they were not related, and to memorize them in any order. In the spontaneous condition, participants with OCD and bipolar disorder clustered words much less than control participants. In the directed condition however, only the bipolar disorder participants displayed less clustering. This suggests that although participants with OCD have difficulties spontaneously implementing encoding strategies, they can use them once they have been taught. As for the number of words recalled, in the directed condition, participants with OCD performed as the controls did, while participants with bipolar disorder remembered fewer words. There was no difference in cued recall or in the recognition task between the groups (Deckersbach et al., 2005).

Taken together, these studies suggest that memory deficits that have been proposed and occasionally detected (see below) in OCD may, in fact, be mediated by encoding deficits due to difficulties in spontaneously using advantageous memorization strategies. It would also seem that with instruction, participants with OCD are able to use and profit from these strategies. Therefore, such strategies appear to be possible candidates for an adjunct to treatment. That is, if those with OCD can be given a better strategy when encoding (during checking, washing, or even cognitive rituals), performance may be improved and doubt consequently reduced.

Memory in OCD
Explicit Memory

Explicit memory (as opposed to implicit memory; see below) refers to memory processes at work when someone is consciously trying to remember something. It can often be measured quite easily, normally in the form of recall and/or recognition tests. A recall test simply involves asking someone to remember something that they have already encoded or learned, and a recognition test involves presenting participants with a variety of stimuli and asking them which ones they have seen before.

MEMORY DEFICITS IN OCD?

Many forms of OCD involve repeated behavior. Patients often claim that they "can't remember whether" something was properly checked, cleaned, counted, etc. Indeed, doubt is a hallmark feature of the disorder (Rachman & Hodgson, 1980). It would therefore be reasonable to hypothesize that those who suffer from OCD—especially those who engage in compulsive checking behavior—would show memory deficits or problems in memory (Tallis, 1997).

An example of an attempt to assess this controversial hypothesis was conducted by Purcell and colleagues (1998). They compared participants diagnosed with OCD against those with depression, panic disorder, and health controls, on a number of neuropsychological tests of memory, and found that the OCD group was impaired on the spatial working memory task on the Stockings of Cambridge test—a test of executive functioning. Purcell and colleagues concluded that OCD was therefore associated with specific deficits in spatial (visual) memory, motor speed (some of the tasks were timed) and executive function. In related studies, both Aronowitz et al. (1994) and Cohen et al. (1996) found that participants with OCD achieved low scores on the Benton Visual Retention Test (BVRT) adding evidence to the claim that OCD is associated with visual memory deficits. Even earlier studies showed that those with high levels of checking behavior performed poorly on tests of memory—in this case, related to complex verbal stimuli (Sher, Mann, & Frost, 1984). In contrast, a number of experiments found no evidence of verbal memory deficits in OCD (e.g., Christensen, Kim, Dyksen & Hoover, 1992; Radomsky & Rachman, 1999). One review of memory in the anxiety disorders cautioned that there was much inconsistency in the literature regarding memory performance in the anxiety disorders in general (Coles & Heimberg, 2002), and another reported that there was some evidence for nonverbal deficits in OCD (Muller & Roberts, 2005; although there is more recent evidence against a nonverbal deficit, see Moritz,

Ruhe, et al., 2009), but also emphasized inconsistencies in the data.

In an attempt to resolve these inconsistencies, Simpson et al. (2006) recently conducted a larger study of neuropsychological deficits in OCD, in which participants with OCD only, participants with OCD plus a comorbid disorder, participants with a history of OCD, and a nonclinical control group were evaluated on neuropsychological tasks of executive functioning, nonverbal memory, and motor speed (all chosen because of previous findings of poor task performance associated with OCD). In general, no reliable deficits were found on neuropsychological tests of memory (or motor speed) associated with a diagnosis of OCD (Simpson et al., 2006). Though the authors called for further study of memory deficits, there may be alternate explanations of previous findings of poor memory functioning in OCD. It should be noted that none of the tests used to assess for memory deficits in OCD bear resemblance to tasks on which those with OCD struggle (e.g., as related to their obsessions or compulsions). Further, if those with OCD use different encoding strategies compared to others (see Savage et al., 1999, 2000, above), memory differences must be interpreted within the context of encoding differences. Finally, under some circumstances, those with OCD have a superior memory compared to controls, and it may therefore be more of a bias in operation in the memories of those with OCD, rather than a deficit.

MEMORY BIASES

Unfortunately, findings of memory deficits are at odds with what patients say in the clinic. Many with OCD are able to recall—often with striking detail—large amounts of information (often quite visual) related to past fears, triggers, and threatening situations (Radomsky & Rachman, 1999). This seems inconsistent with a memory deficit, but could be related to a memory bias. Just as an attentional bias can be defined as a skew in attention, a memory bias can be described as a skew in memory. There are a number of good reasons to suspect a memory bias in association with OCD (and other anxiety disorders).

Two theoretical arguments made in support of information processing biases in general (including both attentional and memorial biases) associated with disorders characterized by emotionality (mood disorders and anxiety disorders, including OCD) were set forth by Kovacs and Beck (1979, initially for depression, but applicable to OCD) and

Bower (1981). Whether one subscribes to the Beckian schema-based approach, or Bower's associative network theory, both approaches propose that there is a structure to our thoughts and ideas. Importantly, this structure incorporates connections between concepts that fluctuate depending on our mood and values. When someone is in a good mood, they should have biased attention, processing, and memory for positive events, concepts, and ideas. That is, someone in a good mood might associate the idea of "birthday party" with "presents," "friends," "cake" and "fun." These associations should be detectable in attention and memory. According to these theories/models, when someone is in a negative mood, they demonstrate biases in favor of negative information—especially information that is consistent with their specific mood state. That is, someone in a negative mood might associate "birthday party" with "aging," "little accomplishment in life," "health problems" and "death"—and again, these cognitive connections should permeate both attention and memory. This implies that, rather than showing *deficits* in processing, those with OCD should show enhanced processing (as they seem to, in attention) for memory related to their specific, OCD-related concerns.

In order to test this approach, a number of different paradigms have been used. In a directed forgetting paradigm (in which participants are asked to forget lists of words they have just learned), Wilhelm, McNally, Baer and Florin (1996) found that participants with OCD were able to recall and recognize more negative-forget words than neutral-forget words; controls did not show this impaired directed forgetting effect. That is, those with OCD had problems forgetting negative information (but not neutral information) compared to controls. In contrast, Foa, Amir, Gershuny, Molnar, and Kozak (1997) used a white noise paradigm in which participants listened to both contamination-related and -unrelated sentences, read over white noise. Interestingly, both participants with and without OCD recognized more contamination-unrelated sentences following encoding, indicating the presence of a memory bias but not one that is specific to OCD. These and other approaches appeared to have a number of features in common with each other: they were producing somewhat inconsistent findings, and they used words as stimuli.

Radomsky and Rachman (1999; 2004) proposed that words may not be ideal stimuli to assess memory biases in OCD, because they may not be emotionally salient enough (compared to more ecologically valid stimuli; see below), and because they may not be appraised as personally significant. That is, although words may draw people's attention (and lend themselves well to research on attentional processes), they may not produce the requisite amount of emotion necessary to be processed, encoded, and retrieved in a biased fashion. Also, though words may serve as a proxy for what is important to someone with OCD, they are almost certainly a weak proxy. Someone who fears harming their children would respond very differently to the word pair "knife-child" than they might respond to being asked to hold a knife while thinking about their child. By extension, their memory of one of these situations will almost certainly be different from their memory for the other.

A study using more ecologically valid stimuli was therefore necessary. Radomsky and Rachman (1999) asked participants to watch as an experimenter held a tissue described as "new and clean, just out of the box" in his right hand and another tissue described as "probably not clean," having been found somewhere in the university hospital, in his rubber-gloved left hand. Participants were asked to watch as the experimenter touched each of 50 objects on a table (they were mostly new office supplies) with the tissues (no object was touched by both tissues) and they were told that they might later have to touch these objects themselves. Following a delay, consisting of a neuropsychological test of memory (see above), participants were asked to recall all of the objects that they had seen on the table. Further, participants were shown the table and were asked, for each object, which had been touched by the clean tissue and which by the contaminated tissue.

Results revealed that OCD participants, who reported contamination fears and/or washing as a primary symptom, remembered similar amounts of threatening (contaminated objects) and nonthreatening (touched, but not contaminated objects) information, as did anxious controls and student controls. But the OCD group also showed a memory bias in favor of threatening information (i.e., they recalled more contaminated objects than noncontaminated objects), whereas controls did not. Further, they found that, though not significant, OCD participants had a better memory than controls for which objects had been contaminated on a source recognition test (Radomsky & Rachman, 1999). In a replication of this study, Ceschi et al. (2003) also detected this bias for source memory. (However, they failed to find the recall bias reported above; this was somewhat surprising, as they used essentially the same paradigm, but may not have screened out objects that might have been perceived as already contaminated by participants at the beginning of the experiment.) Though one study found a bias for contaminated objects, and other for the source of contamination, both studies showed evidence of explicit memory biases in association with contamination-related OCD.

In an extension of the work with contamination-based OCD, Radomsky, Rachman and Hammond (2001) went on to examine memory in compulsive checking, in a home visit study. In this within-participants experiment, manipulations of perceived responsibility (see Lopatka & Rachman, 1995) resulted in conditions of high responsibility, low responsibility, and no responsibility in participants' homes. All participants were tested in each condition, and results revealed that a memory bias in favor of threatening information (e.g., the number of times the stove was touched, the final reading on the thermostat) over nonthreatening information (e.g., the color of the pen in the experimenter's pocket, whether or not the experimenter cleared his throat during the check) was found in the low responsibility condition, as well as the high responsibility condition (in which the bias was amplified), but not in the no responsibility condition (Radomsky et al., 2001). Again, even among participants expected to show memory deficits (i.e., compulsive checkers), a positive memory bias emerged; they showed enhanced memory for threatening information, especially when perceived responsibility was higher.

The above findings are remarkably consistent with an earlier study of memory for actions in OCD (Constans, Foa, Franklin & Mathews, 1995), in which the authors asked participants diagnosed with OCD and controls to either perform an action, or imagine themselves performing an action under conditions of high or low threat. Because of some of the inconsistencies in some of the literature on memory in OCD mentioned above, the researchers predicted that OCD participants would have impaired memory for threatening completed actions, but found the opposite effect. That is, participants with OCD showed superior memory for their last completed action compared to controls, but only if that action produced anxiety (Constans et al., 1995). Perhaps memory biases in OCD may be more easily detected under ecologically valid conditions. That is, when words are used, memory biases may be difficult to detect, whereas when the stimuli are personally relevant to participants, biases are likely present.

Interestingly, in an attempt to assess memory bias as it relates to ordering and arranging, Radomsky and Rachman (2004) found that when the experimental *task* (as opposed to the stimuli) was not specifically related to participants' concerns, a memory bias was not detected. It seems as if participants must perceive both the information and the context as important and significant (something that often happens in the lives of people with OCD) in order for memory biases to occur. These findings have important clinical significance for those who believe that their memories are flawed, as they show that under certain conditions, people with OCD have a superior memory for some types of information—usually the information most important to them (Radomsky & Rachman, 2004).

These findings do leave one mystified, though, about how it is that those with OCD can have superior memories and yet appear as if they do not. Building upon previous work that investigated memory confidence in OCD (e.g., McNally & Kohlbeck, 1993; Sher et al., 1983), Tolin et al. (2001) conducted a study in which participants were asked to rate a series of objects on how safe or unsafe they were. Participants were asked to "learn" or encode objects selected because they were rated as being most safe, most unsafe, or neutral, and were subsequently asked to recall the objects a number of times. Results revealed that although participants with OCD did not show different levels of memory for objects compared to anxious and nonanxious controls, they did show dramatic declines in their confidence in their memories, particularly for unsafe objects. The absence of a memory bias here may be related to the task, rather than to the stimuli, as in Radomsky and Rachman, 2004. That is, although the stimuli were ideal, and idiographic selection of stimuli should have contributed to the ability to detect a bias, the objects themselves were not proposed to be used in a threatening way; that is, the stimuli were ecologically valid, but the task may not have been. As such, perhaps OCD could be characterized by low memory confidence rather than by memory deficits.

In summary, though there are some inconsistencies in these findings, it appears that when experimenters use standardized word lists or other tests of memory, those with OCD either show poor memory or memory that is indistinguishable from controls. However, when the to-be-remembered stimuli are ecologically valid—especially when the task is ecologically valid—a memory bias emerges. This is not only consistent with theories that predict memory biases in psychopathology, and with findings of attentional bias in OCD, but also with what patients say about their experiences of threatening situations and their memories for the details of these experiences.

Implicit Memory

Implicit memory has much to do with how memory is assessed. Contrary to explicit memory in which people are *asked* to remember, implicit memory involves assessing memory without asking people to consciously remember previously learned material. One of the first examples of implicit memory came from Claparède's (1911) landmark observation that there were processes in memory that need not be accessed by conscious means. Working in an asylum, he had the opportunity to observe a patient who had an extremely low capacity in short-term memory; she would forget events that had occurred, even after only a few minutes. Over her five-year stay, she was unable to recall her age, the date, or where she was, despite having been provided with this information on a regular basis. One day, Claparède pricked her hand with a pin and then waited for her to lose all recollective ability of the event. Once it had been forgotten, he moved his hand toward hers, and she pulled her hand away from his, stating that "sometimes there are pins hidden in hands" (Claparède, 1911). Though she did not remember being pricked—and was not asked to remember anything at all—there was an implicit memory of it that emerged only when his hand was close to hers.

Fortunately, this is not commonly used as a test of implicit memory today; more commonly, participants are asked to do some sort of task which, though they do not realize it, is assessing their memory for previously encoded material. This is often done by asking participants to complete word stems or word fragments; experimenters then assess whether they complete these with words they have learned earlier in the experiment (see Roediger, 1990).

Unfortunately, there have been relatively few tests of implicit memory in OCD. In the Foa et al. (1997) study described above, participants in the white noise paradigm were asked to rate the volume of the noise during various parts of the experiment. They rated noise during the reading of contamination-related sentences as louder than the noise during the reading of neutral sentences. What is interesting about this finding is that both those with OCD and nonclinical controls showed this effect,

so, though there was an implicit memory bias for threat, it was not specific to OCD.

In a more recent study of implicit learning, in which participants learn information without being asked to encode it, Deckersbach et al. (2002) examined implicit sequence learning among those diagnosed with OCD and nonclinical controls. In this experiment, participants were asked to respond to visual cues on a computer screen, which came in sequences ending either predictably or unpredictably. In their design, the predictable sequences were repeated so that task improvements representing how well the sequences were encoded and implicitly remembered could be assessed over time. Although these authors found an implicit learning/memory effect among nonclinical controls, those with OCD did not show improvements over time, indicating—in this case—the absence of implicit memory for sequence. A similar study of implicit learning on a serial reaction time task found that those with OCD also failed to show evidence of implicit learning (Goldman et al., 2008), although again, it should be noted that these types of tasks rarely have a close relation to the lives and experiences of those with OCD.

Given the growing interest in implicit memory in general (Roediger, 1990), and in relation to anxiety and mood disorders (Williams, Watts, MacLeod & Mathews, 1997), it is surprising that there isn't more available research on implicit memory in OCD. There is, however, emerging work on implicit processes related to beliefs in OCD (e.g., Teachman & Clerkin, 2007), and we are confident that memory researchers will soon turn their interests to this fascinating and challenging component of memory. Given associative network (Bower, 1981) and schema-based (Kovacs & Beck, 1979) models, one would expect that there should be implicit memory biases in OCD, although based on the above findings—and the paucity of evidence available—this hypothesis cannot be supported at this time.

Metamemory in OCD

Metamemory (literally meaning "about memory") is defined as factors which relate to or describe memory, rather than memory accuracy itself. This could relate to the quality of memory, the nature of memory, feelings about memory, and other aspects related to memory that are not simply reflected by an accuracy score. Interest in metamemory in association with OCD began with McNally and Kohlbeck (1993), who reported that those with

OCD report low confidence in their memories. A number of studies of memory have found similar results (e.g., Hermans et al., 2003; MacDonald et al., 1997; Radomsky et al., 2001; Tolin et al., 2001), and yet only more recently have investigators begun to address the questions of why people with OCD have lower memory confidence, and what other aspects of metamemory might be related to OCD. As you've read above, Tolin et al. (2001) found that with repeated recollections of ideographically selected unsafe objects, participants with OCD reported decreasing levels of confidence in their memories. In the Radomsky et al. (2001) study of memory and checking described above, it was also found that memory confidence was inversely related to perceived responsibility. That is, the more responsible participants with OCD felt, the less confident they were in their memory. Though these types of investigations offer tantalizing hints at some of the mechanisms underlying low memory confidence in OCD, memory confidence was not the primary dependent variable in these studies, and none of them sought to examine metamemory more broadly defined.

Marcel van den Hout and Merel Kindt (2003a, 2003b, 2004) conducted a series of highly novel and important studies in which nonclinical participants were taught how to use a computer mouse to check a series of gas stove rings, and electric light bulb dimmer switches, that appeared on a computer screen. Following this training, all participants completed a pretest check of three stove rings, and were asked about their memory accuracy, their confidence in memory, and the detail in their memory. Participants were then randomly assigned either to complete 20 trials of "relevant" stove checking (in which each trial consisted of turning on, turning off, and checking three stove rings) or 20 trials of "irrelevant" light bulb checking (in which each trial consisted of turning on, turning off, and checking three dimmer switches). All participants were finally asked to complete one trial of stove checking, and were then given a posttest assessment of memory accuracy, confidence, vividness, and detail. Van den Hout and Kindt (2003a, 2003b, 2004) found that memory accuracy (i.e., the number of correct answers to the question, "which stove rings did you check on the last trial?") was nearly perfect for all participants. However, participants who engaged in relevant checking reported significantly reduced memory confidence, memory vividness, and memory detail compared both to their scores at pretest, and to those who completed repeated irrelevant checking, who did not show these declines. It was proposed that as checking continues, processing that was originally perceptual (i.e., more detailed) in nature becomes more semantic—and therefore less salient.

As a replication and extension of this study, Radomsky, Gilchrist, and Dussault (2006) asked nonclinical participants to complete the same experiment, except that instead of checking a virtual stove and light bulbs, participants were asked to check a real stove and a sink/faucet. Results were essentially the same, and showed that repeated checking leads to memory distrust, even if the memory may be quite accurate. Also consistent with van den Hout and Kindt (2003a, 2003b, 2004), those participants who engaged in repeated relevant checking described their memories of the last checking trial much more akin to "knowing" than "remembering" (see Tulving, 1985) compared both to participants who had engaged in irrelevant checking, and to participants at pretest—the majority of whom reported being able to "remember" the last checking trial they completed. That is, after repeated checking, participants reported some familiarity with the sense that they had checked, but could not bring to mind the specific memory of the check itself. This really does represent a degradation in the quality of memory—which is particularly fascinating, since the memory itself was highly accurate.

In order to address the question of how much checking leads to metamemory declines, Coles, Radomsky, and Horng (2006) conducted a study in which participants were randomly assigned to conduct a variety of numbers of checking trials of a real stove between pretest and posttest checks. Results revealed that although significant declines emerged in memory confidence, vividness, and detail after 5 (and before 10) checks, early signs of deterioration of metamemory could be detected after as few as only two checks. It therefore appears that symptoms of OCD (in this case, repeated checking) might actually cause metamemory decreases, which may in turn lead to more checking and other symptoms. The more one checks, the less sure one becomes. This raises the question of whether in treatment clinicians should terminate when patients are at a low level of checking, or at negligible levels of checking.

More recently, investigators have begun to turn their attention to constructs even broader than metamemory in OCD. Because some patients with OCD appear to question their own perceptions and attention (e.g., some with OCD have been known to stare at a light switch that is clearly off and yet still wonder whether or not it is indeed off), and this questioning isn't quite captured by the concept of metamemory, investigators are now beginning to examine how these concerns relate to OCD (van den Hout keynote, Barcelona, 2007). This has been termed *cognitive confidence* (Hermans et al., 2008), and refers to confidence not only in memory, but also in perception, attention, and other cognitive variables. In recent research, scores on the metacognitive variable of cognitive self-consciousness even seem to mediate the relationship between OC symptoms and poor memory (rumination and self-focus about thoughts causes constant divided attention, which is detrimental to memory), which could help forge a link between cognitive and neuropsychological theories of OCD (Exner, Martin, & Rief, 2009; Exner et al., 2009). It is hoped that this expansion will shed more light on why those with OCD have such trouble being satisfied with their compulsions (see also Wahl, Salkovskis & Cotter, 2008).

Attention and Memory in Related Conditions

Trichotillomania (TTM) and Body Dysmorphic Disorder (BDD) are two disorders proposed to be related to OCD, through a highly controversial OCD spectrum (Hollander, 1997; Ravindran, 1999). Though BDD may be somewhat related to OCD because it is often characterized by intrusive thoughts and repetitive behaviors, it differs from OCD in that those suffering from BDD almost always have poor insight into their symptoms (i.e., they do not realize that their thoughts, perceptions, and behaviors are unreasonable; Veale, 2004; for a review see Lochner & Stein, 2006). TTM, by contrast, is different from OCD, in that although it is also characterized by repetitive stereotyped behavior, this behavior seems not to be characterized by anxiety, fear, or beliefs related to negative outcomes (see Lochner & Stein, 2006). As these problems, which are typically very different from OCD, do share different features with OCD, it is useful to review the state of information processing in association with both TTM and BDD.

Trichotillomania

Trichotillomania (TTM) is currently classified as a disorder of impulse control, characterized by hair pulling that is repetitive in nature and results in a significant loss of hair associated with significant distress and/or interference. According to the DSM-IV-TR, People with TTM feel a sense of tension or stress immediately before hair pulling, which is relieved by initiating the act (American Psychiatric Association, 2000). Although this is the current description, there has been (albeit controversial) discussion that TTM should actually be classified as an obsessive compulsive spectrum disorder (Ravindran, 1999; Stein & Lochner, 2006; Jaisoorya, Reddy, & Srinath, 2003) because of similarities between these disorders in levels of anxiety (Ferrão, Almeida, Bedin, Rosa, & Busnello, 2006), brain abnormalities (for a review, see Stein, 2000), behavioral patterns (Chamberlain, Fineberg, Blackwell, Robbins, & Sahakian, 2006), biases on various cognitive tasks (Keuthen et al., 1996, Rettew et al., 1991), genetic and family patterns, and response to therapy (Lochner & Stein, 2006; Bienvenu et al., 2000). This next section reviews the literature on attentional and memory processes in TTM.

Attention. If trichotillomania is in fact related to obsessive compulsive disorder, one would expect that deficits in attentional processing similar to those found in OCD would also be found in TTM (Stanley, Hannay, & Breckenridege, 1997). The mixed results from the handful of studies that have examined this theory are outlined below.

Deficits in inhibiting attention toward irrelevant information, that seem to be a characteristic flaw of people with OCD, are not present in people with TTM (Bohne, Keuthen, Tuschen-Caffier, & Wilhelm, 2005). They found that on a task of cognitive inhibition, TTM participants scored much better than OCD participants. Participants were shown a list of words and then told that they were "just for practice" and to forget them, followed by another list of words that was the "actual" list they needed to remember. Finally, their memory for this second word list was tested. TTM and control participants were able to freely recall more words from the "actual" word list, than from the "practice" word list, indicating the phenomenon of cognitive inhibition was intact (i.e., they could suppress irrelevant information). However, participants with OCD remembered the TTM-relevant words from the "practice list" that they were supposed to forget. This means that TTM participants were able to forget or ignore irrelevant information, while their OCD counterparts could not. These results are particularly interesting in light of the fact that the word lists included some TTM-relevant items (e.g. balding), rather than OCD-relevant ones (Bohne, Keuthen, et al., 2005).

In contrast, Stanley, Hannay, and Breckenridge (1997) did find an attentional bias in individuals with TTM. They found that people with TTM have difficulties specifically with tasks of divided attention, rather than focused attention. They especially had difficulties with the Stroop test (naming the color ink of a word that is itself a color caused a greater amount of interference for them than for the control group, and therefore made their response times slower). These findings are in direct opposition to the findings of Bohne et al. (2005) mentioned above, as they found no deficits in cognitive inhibition. The Stroop task is also a task of cognitive inhibition, where participants must inhibit responding to the word, and respond instead about the color ink that the word is written in. However, the task used by Bohne et al. (2005) has a different structure—in that participants must memorize a list of words, making it more a task of memory inhibition, whereas the Stroop task is (reportedly) a task of attentional inhibition—possibly explaining the difference in results between the two experiments (Stanley et al., 1997).

Bohne, Savage, and colleagues (2005) have found that although both the TTM and OCD individuals have what they termed *deficits on tasks of neuropsychological functioning*, their deficits are different. When running both types of patients through a battery of neuropsychological tests, they found that individuals with OCD were not able to learn from feedback (though this is in contrast with findings above that those with OCD *can* learn if the proper strategy is provided), while individuals with TTM usually had more difficulties when asked to complete tasks that required response flexibility than did the participants with OCD. On all other measures of cognitive ability (visuospatial, memory, problem solving, and planning), all participants were found to be equally as good as healthy controls. The authors believed that the difficulty for participants with TTM in response flexibility is to be expected, as they show similar behavior in their daily lives; namely, once they have begun hair pulling, they have difficulty stopping and choosing another activity (Bohne, Savage, et al., 2005). Results from an earlier neuropsychological study comparing the two disorders have pointed to additional spatial processing biases in people with TTM, but not in people with OCD (Rettew et al., 1991).

Chamberlain, Blackwell, Fineberg, Robbins, and Sahakian (2005) conducted a study that analyzed the effect of cognitive retraining on executive functioning in OCD and TTM. They hypothesized that the participants with OCD would have more trouble than those with TTM, as cognitive inflexibility is more a hallmark of OCD than TTM. Participants had to make as many distinct sequences of 4 computerized blocks as they could. Then they were given training on an effective strategy to maximize the number of sequences they could generate. Their results showed that prior to training, TTM, OCD, and control participants all performed similarly. However, after training, TTM and control participants improved substantially in the number of sequences they were able to generate, but participants with OCD did not (although these results are also in contrast with findings above, that those with OCD *can* learn if the proper strategy is provided).

Although there has not been a wealth of literature on the biases in attention that people with TTM might possess, the work done until now would suggest that people with TTM, unlike people with OCD, do not have deficits in cognitive inhibition in a task involving memorization (Bohne, Savage, et al., 2005), but that they do have difficulties inhibiting attention toward irrelevant information in tasks of attention (Stanley, Hannay, & Breckenridge, 1997). There is also some evidence that they have trouble with spatial processing (Rettew et al., 1991) and response flexibility (Bohne, Savage, et al., 2005). Preliminary research suggests that people with TTM can learn effective cognitive strategies more easily than those with OCD (Chamberlain et al., 2005).

Memory. There do not seem to be memory biases in TTM. As mentioned above, some studies have found that participants with TTM have no memory impairments (Bohne, Savage, et al., 2005; Stanley et al., 1997). Unlike people with OCD (Savage et al., 2000), patients with TTM had intact ability to use such memory strategies as clustering (Bohne, Savage, et al., 2005). However, some memory processes may be different. In another study using a battery of neuropsychological tests, Keuthen et al. (1996) found that patients with TTM were not impaired at all on tasks requiring immediate and verbal memory. They did, however, find that patients with TTM performed worse than controls on tasks that required them to maintain their mental set (an executive functioning task). They proposed that their difficulties with this were due to the fact that they could not use any verbal mediation strategies to help improve their performance. They also had trouble on a task of nonverbal memory functioning where participants with OCD have biases, the RCFT. Both of these findings would suggest a link between TTM and OCD patients, although both are subject to the same limitations as discussed above, in the context of standardized neuropsychological tests of memory in OCD.

Taken together, these results suggest that although verbal memory structures are intact, there may be some biases in nonverbal, specifically spatial, memory in patients with TTM. Current models of TTM do not account for how memory or attentional biases might contribute to the etiology and maintenance of the disorder (Diefenbach, Mouton-Odum, & Stanley, 2002; Mansueto, Stemberger, Thomas, & Golomb, 1997).

Body Dysmorphic Disorder

Body dysmorphic disorder (BDD) is characterized by the erroneous belief that one or more parts of the body are grievously misshapen or abnormal, despite the lack of evidence for this. Worrying over and trying to mask this abnormality interferes with day-to-day functioning (American Psychiatric Association, 2000). As there are known biases in information processing in OCD (for a review see Muller & Roberts, 2005), the possible existence of biases in BDD is explored below.

Attention. Cognitive tasks have been used to assess the presence of attentional biases in BDD, but with mixed results. Using a negative priming task that included BDD-related threatening and nonthreatening items, Wilhelm, Buhlmann, and McNally (2003) found no strong evidence in participants with BDD for a bias in negative priming. The authors concluded that biases in attention for BDD individuals are not best assessed by this task. They also pointed out that OCD patients may show a deficit in negative priming tasks because, as part of their symptomatology, they are constantly trying to inhibit their thoughts, which they recognize as unreasonable. In contrast, BDD patients tend to have poorer insight into the irrationality of their thoughts, and therefore do not spend a lot of time actively trying to suppress them. Therefore, we would not expect them to have difficulty inhibiting information when told to do so (Wilhelm et al., 2003).

However, using a modified Stroop task, Buhlmann, McNally, Wilhelm, & Florin (2002) found that participants with BDD were less able to ignore emotionally charged words, especially those related to BDD, than the participants in the healthy control comparison group. These results suggest

that people with BDD, like people with OCD, have attentional biases toward words that are salient to their worries (Buhlmann et al., 2002). These results are also partially in line with Hanes's (1998) findings that participants with BDD showed attentional biases on the traditional Stroop task.

A study on the processing of faces in BDD revealed that participants with BDD were better able to discriminate differences in appearance between neutral faces than controls (who were other individuals who had either disfiguring or nondisfiguring dermatological conditions; Stangier, Adam-Schwebe, Müller, & Wolter, 2008). Results showed that participants with BDD were much more accurate than either of the control groups at identifying the degree of change between the comparison image and the target image. These results suggest that patients with BDD are more easily able to detect and process minute details and changes in human faces (Stangier et al., 2008).

The results from the facial processing study suggest that people with BDD selectively attend to detail. This could contribute to the development and the maintenance of their disorder, as they are easily able to spot flaws. Results from the Stroop task studies suggest that people with BDD also have trouble ignoring irrelevant information, probably because for them it is quite salient. However, results from a negative priming task suggest the opposite, so future research must continue to address this issue.

Memory. In a study of encoding and memory that compared patients with BDD to healthy controls, Deckersbach et al. (2000) found that BDD patients had problems with verbal and nonverbal memory that was mediated by their poor choice of organizational strategies. This was assessed by examining their semantic clustering on the CVLT, and in how they grouped the elements of the figure when redrawing in the RCFT. In contrast, earlier work by Hanes (1998) found that participants with BDD did not have any problems with nonverbal memory, as assessed using the same tool, the RCFT. Not yet studied is whether these participants can improve their performance when they are taught organizational strategies, an approach that has been used with success for OCD patients (Buhlmann et al., 2006).

One study has looked at the characteristics and quality of memory in participants with BDD compared to controls (Osman, Cooper, Hackmann, & Veale, 2004). They interviewed people about a recent time when they felt anxious or worried about their appearance, and about their appearance-related thoughts in general. Researchers found that individuals with BDD had many more memories that were spontaneous, recurrent, and negative, as compared to controls. These images contained more details, and incorporated more of the sensory modalities than those of controls. Like controls, the most common modality was visual. However, the specific aspects of the images differed. People with BDD saw them from an observer perspective, whereas controls saw them from their own point of view. This difference is very telling, and implies that their memory of what happened is not actually how it occurred, but reflects their inner views of themselves as objects to be criticized (Osman et al., 2004). Furthermore, the specific appearance-related images were associated with stressful childhood experiences. Their thoughts about their appearance tend to be visual in nature, whereas feedback from others about appearance tends to be verbal in nature. This potentially explains why verbal feedback from others is so ineffective at changing erroneous cognitions in these individuals (Osman et al., 2004).

It appears that although the memory bias in BDD presents in different ways from that found in OCD, preliminary evidence suggests differences in processing from that of healthy individuals.

In conclusion, there is some evidence for attentional and memory biases in BDD. Although some of them are similar to those biases evident in OCD, some biases present in OCD are not evident in BDD. The reverse is also true. This suggests partial but not total overlap between the two disorders, which is in keeping with current theories. Recent cognitive behavioral models of BDD predict attentional biases. Attentional biases in these individuals toward the small details, coupled with their perfectionistic attitudes, make them vulnerable to detecting and exaggerating flaws in themselves and becoming overcritical about them (Buhlmann & Wilhelm, 2004).

The Effects of Treatment

There is a wealth of literature on successful treatment studies for OCD using cognitive behavioral therapy (CBT), including some form of exposure and response prevention (ERP; Abramowitz, 2006; Diefenbach, Abramowitz, Norberg, & Tolin, 2007); combinations of CBT, ERP, and medication (Simpson et al., 2004; van Oppen, van Balkom, de Hann, & van Dyck, 2005); and even medication alone, although this is not as effective as ERP (for a review, see McDonough & Kennedy, 2002).

However, few studies have examined the changes in information processing that one would suspect would follow a successful treatment intervention (e.g., Foa & McNally, 1986). If biases in information processing are indeed important factors that contribute to the development and maintenance of OCD (and related problems), and if the current treatments for OCD are effective at reducing or even eliminating these symptoms, it seems likely that treatment has either directly or indirectly corrected the bias(es) in information processing.

Attention in OCD

One of the earliest studies to examine changes in information processing following treatment was conducted by Foa and McNally in 1986. They assessed the tendency of participants with OCD to pay more attention to fear-relevant stimuli than to neutral stimuli, both before and after a three-week intensive course of ERP treatment. To test changes in information processing, they used a dichotic listening task, which consisted of participants simultaneously listening to two passages being read through two different earphones. They were told to repeat aloud (called shadowing) the words that were coming in through only one of their ears. Additionally, they were asked to listen for a target word that would appear *in either ear*. The target word was "pick" for the neutral condition, and a word related to each participant's main concerns for the fear condition. There were no differences between conditions in the number of target words detected in the ear they were shadowing. There was, however, a difference between the number of target words they detected in the ear they were not attending to. Far more fear-relevant stimuli were detected than neutral stimuli in the unattended ear, suggesting a selective attention bias for words that are related to their condition, and that therefore cause fear (Foa & McNally, 1986). Although this bias was present in the dichotic listening task pretreatment, there was no bias in the dichotic listening task posttreatment. They also measured skin-conductance response during the dichotic listening task, and found that participants had an increased response to fear-relevant words before, but not after, treatment (Foa & McNally, 1986). Therefore, fear-relevant stimuli are more salient to people with OCD, because is important for these individuals that they be ready to attend to sources of threat. After ERP treatment, this bias in selective attention was no longer present, suggesting that treatment is very effective at correcting this type of attentional bias that contributes to the maintenance of symptoms in persons with OCD (Foa & McNally, 1986).

An event-related potential study done by Sanz, Molina, Martin-Loeches, Calcedo, and Rubia (2001) showed that attentional biases in cognitive functioning could be improved during treatment with clomipramine. They found that while not on the drug (either pre- or post-treatment, to counterbalance for the learning curve), participants had difficulty shifting their attention, as demonstrated by their performance on the "odd ball" paradigm. This is an auditory task where one presses a button as soon as one hears a different tone (one tone is presented in each ear) from that of the background tone. This cognitive shift represents an attentional ability in which participants with OCD have problems. When not receiving treatment, the event-related potential phenomenon known as the P300 that signals shifting attention was unusual. It spiked later and to a smaller degree than it would in healthy controls. Following treatment, the P300 response more closely resembled that of controls, indicating partial improvement (Sanz et al., 2001). Treatment also allowed participants to better inhibit irrelevant information. Participants needed to refrain from responding to the frequently heard tone (cognitive inhibition), and to only respond when they heard a new and different tone. Because participants with OCD have trouble inhibiting irrelevant information, it might actually have become more difficult to ignore, and therefore to tell the difference between the same old tone and a new tone. The authors believe that when the drugs increased serotonin function, they then increased the amplitude of the P300 wave. This increase in amplitude was indicative of the participants feeling more confident in their ability to tell the difference between the two different tones while receiving treatment. Therefore, treatment increased cognitive confidence and, by extension, patients' abilities to screen out irrelevant information. It should be noted that their results reached a statistical trend, rather than full statistical significance (Sanz et al., 2001).

Although preliminary, results from these two studies suggest that biases in cognition evident in people with OCD can be corrected through therapy, be it behavioral or pharmacological.

Memory in OCD

A recent neuropsychological study found improvements in cognitive functioning after CBT including ERP (Kuelz et al., 2006). Thirty patients and matched controls underwent a battery of neuropsychological tests before and after 12 weeks of treatment. Before treatment, participants with OCD performed worse on tasks requiring attention, cognitive flexibility, and nonverbal memory. After treatment, all participants with OCD who responded to treatment had improved on these tasks, with those who had responded the best to treatment showing more improvement than those who had responded less well. These results were attributed in part to the fact that teaching participants to behave more flexibly in their lives (through CBT) allowed them to apply these strategies in the cognitive tasks, as well (Kuelz et al., 2006). These results are similar to earlier findings on improvement in cognitive flexibility and verbal fluency, following behavior therapy that also improved symptoms (Bolton, Raven, Madronal-Luque, & Marks, 2000). Some of these patients were also receiving drug therapy at the time, but as there were no differences between these participants and nondrugged participants on the Y-BOCS at pretreatment, they were considered one group. This is interesting in and of itself, as it suggests that the drugs were not helping to improve cognitive biases (Bolton et al., 2000).

An earlier neuropsychological study found that pharmacological treatment did not significantly improve performance on a battery of neuropsychological tests (Nielen & Den Boer, 2003). Prior to treatment, participants exhibited biases as compared to control participants in ability to plan, speed of motor response, and spatial memory. They also exhibited biases in focused attention and strategic ability. These biases did not change following a 12-week daily treatment with fluoxetine. This study supported the idea that these impairments in information processing are traits and not symptoms of OCD, and that they are not corrected by at least one type of treatment—in this case, pharmacological (Nielen & Den Boer, 2003). Though the bias was unimproved, the drug therapy did significantly improve their obsessive compulsive symptoms. Similar results were found in a one-year drug therapy treatment study (Roh et al., 2005).

Although not strictly a treatment study, Mataix-Cols, Alonson, Pifarré, Menchón, and Vallejo (2002) did compare the neuropsychological performance of participants with OCD who were on medication (various serotonin reuptake inhibitors [SRIs]) to the performance of participants with OCD who were not on medication. In general, they found that there were no differences between the two groups on a battery of neuropsychological tests meant to assess attention and memory. It should be noted that the purpose of this study was to ensure that there were no deficits caused by the SRIs, not to see whether the SRIs alleviated deficits. Secondly, they did not find any differences on measures of OCD symptomatology between the two groups, implying that the drugs were not effective (Mataix-Cols et al., 2002). Another comparison study found that drug therapy partially alleviated symptoms (although not to subclinical levels), and that it also partially improved biases in nonverbal organizational strategies and focused attention (Kim, Park, Shin, & Kwon, 2002). These results suggest that cognitive biases were not altered completely because the therapy had not worked well enough.

Although not a typical treatment study, Buhlmann et al. (2006) gave OCD and normal controls cognitive training in order to improve their informational organization skills, thereby indirectly impacting their memory skills. Participants initially completed the RCFT. They were then assigned to either receive cognitive training on organization, or to a control group that did not receive any training. Following training, participants once again completed the RCFT. Results showed that all participants who received cognitive retraining improved greatly on this task, both in their copying skills and at redrawing the figure from memory (Buhlmann et al., 2006). Their results highlight that it is not that people with OCD are incapable of using organizational strategies to help improve their memories, but that they are not likely to spontaneously use them. If shown how to properly encode information, participants with OCD should not display any deficits in memory (Buhlmann et al., 2006). A similar study (Park et al., 2006) that defined cognitive retraining more broadly (not only targeting their informational organizational skills, but their life organizational skills) also found improvement in their use of organizational strategies, but additionally also found improvement in OC symptomatology. Results of this study imply not only that cognitive retraining should be considered an adjunct to treatment, but that it may be able to stand alone as a treatment. Further research is needed (Park et al., 2006), especially as some participants were taking SSRIs while enrolled in the study.

In conclusion, the majority of research on cognitive changes in people with OCD following treatment is positive, suggesting that changes in attention and memory are possible with CBT (Foa & McNally, 1986; Kuelz et al., 2006), drug therapy (Sanz et al., 2001), and even cognitive retraining (Park et al., 2006; Buhlmann et al., 2006).

Conclusions/Summary

The above studies show that a diagnosis of OCD certainly indicates the presence of differing information processing phenomena. As far as attention is concerned, it seems that those with OCD may struggle somewhat with disengaging from irrelevant information, particularly at early points in attentional processes, although this trend in the literature must be balanced against methodologies used to assess attention in OCD. Other work in attention in OCD suggests that attentive processes may skew themselves toward personally relevant and/or threatening information, although other studies do not show this effect. Later attentional processes may involve challenges for those with OCD in terms of determining what is relevant to them and what is not. Unfortunately, much of this work lacks ecological validity. More ecologically valid paradigms, perhaps incorporating eye tracking of real-life situations (threatening and/or nonthreatening), may provide more information on the nature of attention in OCD.

As for memory in OCD, some studies show a memory deficit, particularly in association with visuospatial memory, while others do not. None of these studies are high in ecological validity. Studies that are more ecologically valid in design appear to show a memory bias in favor of personally relevant, personally significant, and/or threatening information. There is some evidence that the bias is most detectable when the stimuli *and* the context or paradigm are personally significant and/or important. The finding of memory biases is consistent with clinical reports and with prominent cognitive models of emotional disorders and emotionality.

How is it that those with OCD can have superior memory for threatening information, and yet feel compelled to repeat things over and over again? It appears that although memory accuracy may be quite high, metamemory (including memory confidence) can be quite low. It also seems to be the case that repeated checking causes these decrements in metamemory, such that acts designed to increase certainty, actually prevent it.

Finally, and fascinatingly, problems with information processing appear to diminish or vanish with successful treatment for OCD. If removing the OCD can contribute to the diminution or elimination of problems in attention and/or memory, it leads one to wonder how aspects of information processing relate to the experience of OCD. Rather than viewing them as causing OCD, we may move toward an approach in which they are conceptualized as resulting from OCD. (Of course, one cannot ignore the possibility that specific patterns of information processing and OCD are both caused by some other set of factors, although it can be said with some certainty that there are real associations between them.) Though many studies have tried to address some of the preliminary questions relating to information processing in OCD and related problems, so many questions are left unanswered. New techniques and paradigms will almost certainly prove influential in our understanding of how information and psychopathology interact, and how this interaction might be best used to facilitate treatment.

Future Directions

Though many questions related to information processing in OCD and related problems have been addressed, a number remain, and new ones have evolved from earlier findings. Some of the pertinent questions remaining include:

1. Are findings of poor performance on some standardized neuropsychological tests a cause of OCD, a correlate of OCD, or a consequence of OCD?

2. Can we develop measures of memory (executive function, attention, etc.) that are relevant to the experience of OCD, and which tap into clinically useful constructs?

3. Are attentional biases in OCD related to memory biases in OCD?

4. Can attentional biases in OCD be changed?

5. Is there a place for the development of new encoding strategies in the cognitive treatment of OCD?

6. Can treatment be improved by encouraging those with OCD to stop their compulsions, even when they aren't confident?

7. What is the precise role of cognitive confidence in OCD? How can it be overcome?

8. Can cognitive science inform the treatment of OCD?

9. Will there be a merging of cognitive science and the focus on thoughts, appraisals, and beliefs in OCD?

Related Chapters

Chapter 7. Neuroanatomy of Obsessive Compulsive and Related Disorders

Chapter 12. Cognitive Approaches to Understanding Obsessive Compulsive and Related Disorders

References

Abramowitz, J. S. (2006). The psychological treatment of obsessive-compulsive disorder. *The Canadian Journal of Psychiatry*, 51, 407–416.

American Psychiatric Association. (2000). *Diagnostic and statistical manual of mental disorders* (4th edition. text revision), Washington DC: American Psychiatric Association.

Amir, N., Cobb, M., & Morrison, A. S. (2008). Threat processing in obsessive-compulsive disorder: Evidence from a modified negative priming task. *Behaviour Research and Therapy*, 46, 728–736.

Amir, N., Najmi, S., & Morrison, A. S. (2009). Attenuation of attention bias in obsessive-compulsive disorder. *Behaviour Research and Therapy*, 47, 153–157.

Aronowitz, B. R., Hollander, E., DeCaria, C., Cohen, L., Saoud, J. B., Stein, D., et al. (1994). Neuropsychology of obsessive-compulsive disorder. *Neuropsychiatry, Neuropsychology, and Behavioral Neurology*, 7, 81–86.

Bienvenu, O. J., Samuels, J.F., Riddle, M. A., Hoehn-Saric, R., Liang, K.-Y., Cullen, B. A. M., et al. (2000). The relationship of obsessive-compulsive disorder to possible spectrum disorders: Results from a family study. *Biological Psychiatry*, 48, 287–293.

Bohne, A., Keuthen, N.J., Tuschen-Caffier, B., & Wilhelm, S. (2005). Cognitive inhibition in trichotillomania and obsessive compulsive disorder. *Behaviour Research and Therapy*, 43, 923–942.

Bohne, A., Savage, C. R., Decersbach, T., Keuthen, N. J., Jenike, J. A., Tuschen-Caffier, B., et al. (2005). Visuospatial abilities, memory, and executive functioning in trichotillomania and obsessive-compulsive disorder. *Journal of Clinical and Experimental Neuropsychology*, 27, 385–399.

Bolton, D., Rave, P., Madronal-Luque, & Marks, I. M. (2000). Neurological and neuropsychological signs in obsessive-compulsive disorder: Interactions with behavioral treatment. *Behaviour Research and Therapy*, 38, 695–705.

Bower, G. H. (1981). Mood and memory. *American Psychologist*, 36, 129–148.

Buhlmann, U., Deckersbach, T., Engelhard, I., Cook, L. M., Rauch, S. L., Kathmann, N., et al. (2006). Cognitive retraining for organizational impairment in obsessive-compulsive disorder. *Psychiatry Research*, 144, 109–116.

Buhlmann, U., McNally, R. J., Wilhelm, S., & Florin, I. (2002). Selective processing of emotional information in body dysmorphic disorder. *Anxiety Disorders*, 16, 289–298.

Bulhmann, U., & Wilhelm, S. (2004). Cognitive factors in body dysmorphic disorder. *Psychiatric Annals*, 34, 922–926.

Ceschi, G., der Linden, M. V., Dunker, D., Perroud, A. & Bredart, S. (2003). Further exploration memory bias in compulsive washers. *Behaviour Research and Therapy*, 41, 737–747.

Chamberlain, S. R., Blackwell, A. D., Fineberg, N.A., Robbins, T. W., & Sahakian, B. J. (2005). Strategy implementation in obsessive-compulsive disorder and trichotillomania. *Psychological Medicine*, 36, 91–97.

Chamberlain, S. R., Fineberg, N. A., Blackwell, A. D., Robbins, T. W., & Sahakian, B. J. (2006). Motor inhibition and cognitive flexibility in obsessive-compulsive disorder and trichotillomania. *American Journal of Psychiatry*, 163, 1282–1284.

Christensen, K. J., Kim, S. W., Dyksen, M. W., & Hoover, K. M. (1992). Neuropsychological performance in obsessive-compulsive disorder. *Biological Psychology, 108,* 171–175.

Cisler, J. M., & Olatunji, B. O. (2010). Components of attentional biases in contamination fear : Evidence for difficulty in disengagement. *Behaviour Research and Therapy, 48,* 74–78.

Claparède, M. E. (1911). Recognition et moïïtè. *Archives de Psychologie Geneve, 11,* 79–90.

Clark, D. M., Ehlers, A., Hackmann, A., McManus, F., Fennell, M., Grey, N., Waddington, L., & Wild, J. (2006). Cognitive therapy versus exposure and applied relaxation in Social Phobia: A randomized controlled trial. *Journal of Consulting and Clinical Psychology, 74,* 568–578.

Clark, D. M., & Wells, A. (1995). A cognitive model of social phobia. In R. G. Heimberg, M. R. Liebowitz, D. A. Hope, & F. R. Schneier, *Social phobia: Diagnosis, assessment, and treatment* (pp. 69–93). New York, NY, US: Guilford Press.

Clayton, I. C., Richards, J. C., & Edwards, C. J., (1999). Selective attention in obsessive- compulsive disorder. *Journal of Abnormal Psychology, 108,* 171–175.

Cohen, L. J., Hollander, E., DeCaria, C. M., Stein, D. J. (1996). Specificity of neuropsychological impairment in obsessive-compulsive disorder: A comparison with social phobic and normal control subjects. *Journal of Neuropsychiatry & Clinical Neurosciences, 8,* 82–85.

Cohen, Y., Lachenmeyer, J. R., & Springer, C. (2003). Anxiety and selective attention in obsessive-compulsive disorder. *Behaviour Research and Therapy, 41,* 1311–1323.

Coles, M. E., & Heimberg, R. G. (2002). Memory biases in the anxiety disorders: Current status. *Clinical Psychology Review, 22,* 587–627.

Coles, M. E., Radomsky, A. S., & Horng, B. (2006). Exploring the boundaries of memory distrust from repeated checking: Increasing external validity and examining thresholds. *Behaviour Research and Therapy, 44,* 995–1006.

Constans, J. I., Foa, E. B., Franklin, M. E., & Mathews, A. (1995). Memory for actual and imagined events in OC checkers. *Behaviour Research and Therapy, 33,* 665–671.

Craik, F. I., & Lockhart, R. S. (1972). Levels of processing: A framework for memory research. *Journal of Verbal Learning & Verbal Behavior, 11,* 671–684.

Deckersbach, T., Savage, C.R., Curran, T., Bohne, A., Wilhelm, S., Baer, L., et al. (2002). A study of parallel implicit and explicit information processing in patients with obsessive-compulsive disorder. *American Journal of Psychiatry, 159,* 1780–1782.

Deckersbach, T., Savage, C. R., Dougherty, D. D., Bohne, A., Loh, R., Nierenberg, A., et al. (2005). Spontaneous and directed application of verbal learning strategies in bipolar disorder and obsessive-compulsive disorder. *Bipolar Disorders, 7,* 166–175.

Deckersbach, T., Savage, C. R., Phillips, K. A., Wilhelm, S., Buhlmann, U., Rauch, S. L., et al. (2000). Characteristics of memory dysfunction in body dysmorphic disorder. *Journal of the International Neuropsychology Society, 6,* 673–681.

Diefenbach, G. J., Abramowitz, J.S., Norberg, M. M., & Tolin, D. F. (2007). Changes in quality of life following cognitive-behavioral therapy for obsessive-compulsive disorder. *Behaviour Research and Therapy, 45,* 3060–3068.

Diefenbach, G. J., Mouton-Odum, S., & Stanley, M. A. (2002). Affective correlates of trichotillomania. *Behaviour Research and Therapy, 40,* 1305–1315.

Ebbinghaus, H. (1913). *Memory: A contribution to experimental psychology* (H. A. Ruger & C. E. Bussenius, Trans.). New York: Columbia University, New York Teacher's College. (Original work published 1885)

Ehlers, A., & Clark, D. M. (2000). A cognitive model of posttraumatic stress disorder. *Behaviour Research and Therapy, 38,* 319–345.

Ellis, A. (1962). *Reason and emotion in psychotherapy.* Secaucus, NJ: Citadel.

Enright, S. J., & Beech, A. R. (1993a). Reduced cognitive inhibition in obsessive-compulsive disorder. *British Journal of Clinical Psychology, 32,* 67–74.

Enright, S. J., & Beech, A. R. (1993b). Further evidence of reduced cognitive inhibition in obsessive-compulsive disorder. *Personality and Individual Differences, 14,* 387–395.

Enright, S. J., Beech, A. R., & Claridge, G. S. (1995). A further investigation of cognitive inhibition in obsessive-compulsive disorder and other anxiety disorders. *Personality and Individual Differences, 19,* 532–542.

Exner, C., Kohl, A., Zaudig, M., Langs, G., Lincoln, T. M., & Rief, W. (2009). Metacognition and episodic memory in obsessive-compulsive disorder. *Journal of Anxiety Disorders, 23,* 624–631.

Exner, C., Martin, V., & Rief, W. (2009). Self-focused ruminations and memory deficits in obsessive-compulsive disorder. *Cognitive Therapy and Research, 33,* 163–174.

Ferrão, Y. A., Almeida, V. P., Bedin, N. R., Rosa, R., & Busnello, E. D. (2006). Impulsivity and compulsivity in patients with trichotillomania or skin picking compared with patients with obsessive-compulsive disorder. *Comprehensive Psychiatry, 47,* 282–288.

Foa, E. B., Amir, N., Gershuny, B., Molnar, C., & Kozak, M. J. (1997). Implicit and explicit memory in obsessive-compulsive disorder. *Journal of Anxiety Disorders, 11,* 119–129.

Foa, E. B., Ilai, D., McCarthy, P. R., Shoyer, B., & Murdock, T. (1993). Information processing in Obsessive-Compulsive disorder. *Cognitive Therapy and Research, 17,* 173–189.

Foa, E. B., & McNally, R. J. (1986). Sensitivity to feared stimuli in obsessive-compulsives: A dichotic listening analysis. *Cognitive Therapy and Research, 10,* 477–485.

Goldman, B. L., Martin, E. D., Calamari, J. E., Woodard, J. L., Chik, H. M., Messina, M. G., et al. (2008). Implicit learning, thought-focused attention and obsessive-compulsive disorder: A replication and extension. *Behaviour Research and Therapy, 46,* 48–61.

Hanes, K. R. (1998). Neuropsychological performance in body dysmorphic disorder. *Journal of the International Neuropsychological Society, 4,* 167–171.

Harkness, E., Harris, L. M., Jones, M.K., & Vaccaro, L. (2009). No evidence of attentional bias in obsessive compulsive checking on the dot probe paradigm. *Behaviour Research and Therapy, 47,* 437–443.

Hartston, H. J., & Swerdlow, N. R. (1999). Visuospatial priming and Stroop performance in patients with obsessive compulsive disorder. *Neuropsychology, 13,* 447–457.

Hermans, D., Martens, K., De Cort, K., Pieters, G., & Eelen, P. (2003). Reality monitoring and metacognitive beliefs related to cognitive confidence in obsessive-compulsive disorder. *Behaviour Research and Therapy, 41,* 383–401.

Hermans, D., Engelen, U., Grouwels, L., Joos, E., Lemmens, J., & Pieters, G. (2008). Cognitive confidence in obsessive-compulsive disorder: Distrusting perception, attention and memory. *Behaviour Research and Therapy, 46,* 98–113.

Hoenig, K., Hochrein, A., Müller, D. J., & Wagner, M. (2002). Different negative priming impairments in schizophrenia and subgroups of obsessive-compulsive disorder. *Psychological Medicine, 32*, 459–468.

Hollander, E. (1997). The obsessive-compulsive spectrum disorders. *International Review of Psychiatry, 9*, 99–110.

Jaisoorya, T. S., Reddy, Y. C. J., & Srinath, S. (2003). The relationship of obsessive-compulsive disorder to putative spectrum disorders: Results from an Indian study. *Comprehensive Psychiatry, 44*, 317–323.

Keuthen, N. J., Savage, C.R., O'Sullivan, R. L., Brown, H. D., Shera, D. M., Cyr, P., et al. (1996). Neuropsychological functioning in Trichotillomania. *Biological Psychiatry, 39*, 747–749.

Kim, M.-S., Park, S.-J., Shin, M. S., & Kwon, J. S. (2002). Neuropsychological profile in patients with obsessive-compulsive disorder over a period of 4-month treatment. *Journal of Psychiatric Research, 36*, 257–265.

Kovacs, M., & Beck, A. T. (1979). Cognitive-affective processes in depression. In C. E. Izard (Ed.), *Emotion in personality and psychopathology*(pp. 417-442). New York: Plenum Press.

Kuelz, A. K., Riemann, D., Halsband, U., Vielhaber, K., Unterrainer, J., Kordon, A. et al. (2006). Neuropsychological impairment in obsessive-compulsive disorder–Improvement over the course of cognitive behavioral treatment. *Journal of Clinical and Experimental Neuropsychology, 28*, 1273–1287.

Lochner, C., & Stein, D. J. (2006). Does work on obsessive-compulsive spectrum disorders contribute to understanding the heterogeneity of obsessive-compulsive disorder? *Progress in Neuro-Psychopharmacology & Biological Psychiatry, 30*, 353–361.

Lopatka, C. & Rachman, S. (1995). Perceived responsibility and compulsive checking: An experimental analysis. *Behaviour Research & Therapy, 33*, 673–684.

MacDonald, P. A., Antony, M.M., MacLeod, C. M., & Richter, M. M. (1997). Memory and confidence in memory judgments among individuals with obsessive-compulsive disorder and non-clinical controls. *Behaviour Research and Therapy, 35*, 497–505.

MacDonald, P. A., Antony, M. M., MacLeod, C. M., & Swinson, R. P. (1999). Negative priming for obsessive-compulsive checkers and non-checkers. *Journal of Abnormal Psychology, 108*, 679–686.

MacLeod, C. M. (1991). Half a century of research on the Stroop effect: An integrative review. *Psychological Bulletin, 109*, 163–203.

Mansueto, C. S., Stemberger, R. M. T., Thomas, A. M., & Golomb, R. G. (1997). Trichotillomania: A comprehensive behavioral model. *Clinical Psychology Review, 17*, 567–577.

Mataix-Cols, D., Alonso, P., Pifarré, J., Menchón, J. M., & Vallejo, J. (2002). Neuropsychological performance in medicated vs. unmedicated patients with obsessive-compulsive disorder. *Psychiatry Research, 109*, 255–264.

May, C. P., Kane, M. J., & Hasher, L. (1995). Determinants of negative priming. *Psychological Bulletin, 118*, 35–54.

McDonald, P. A., & McLeod, C. M. (1998). The influence of attention at encoding on direct and indirect remembering. *Acta Psychologica, 98*, 291–310.

McDonough, M., & Kennedy, N. (2002). Pharmacological management of obsessive-compulsive disorder: a review for clinicians. *Harvard Review of Psychiatry, 10*, 127–137.

McNally, R. J., & Kohlbeck, P. A. (1993). Reality monitoring in obsessive-compulsive disorder. *Behaviour Research and Therapy, 31*, 249–253.

McNally, R.J., Wilhelm, S., Buhlmann, U., & Shin, L.M. (2001). Cognitive inhibition in obsessive-compulsive disorder: Application of a valence-based negative priming paradigm. *Behavioural and Cognitive Psychotherapy, 29*, 103–106.

Meyer, V. (1966). Modification of expectations in cases with obsessional rituals. *Behaviour Research and Therapy, 4*, 273–280.

Moritz, S., Fischer, B.-K., Hottenrott, B., Kellner, M., Fricke, S., Randjbar, S., et al., (2008) Words may not be enough! No increased emotional Stroop effect in obsessive-compulsive disorder. *Behaviour Research and Therapy, 46(9)*, 1101–1104.

Moritz, S., Jacobsen, D., Kloss, M., Fricke, S., Rufer, M., & Hand, I. (2004). Examination of emotional Stroop interference in obsessive-compulsive disorder. *Behaviour Research and Therapy, 42*, 671–682.

Moritz, S., Kloss, M., & Jelinek, L. (2010). Negative priming (cognitive inhibition) in obsessive-compulsive disorder (OCD). *Journal of Behavior Therapy and Experimental Psychiatry, 41*, 1–5.

Moritz, S., Ruhe, C., Jelinek, L., & Naber, D. (2009). No deficit in nonverbal memory, metamemory and internal as well as external source memory in obsessive-compulsive disorder. *Behaviour Research and Therapy, 47*, 308–315.

Moritz, S., Von Muhlenen, A., Randjbar, S., Fricke, S., & Jelinek, L. (2009). Evidence for an attentional bias for washing- and checking-relevant stimuli in obsessive-compulsive disorder. *Journal of the International Neuropsychological Society, 15*, 365–371.

Moritz, S., Wendt, M., Jelinek, L., Ruhe, C., & Arzola, G. M. (2008). No disadvantages for the processing of global visual features in obsessive-compulsive disorder. *Journal of the International Neuropsychological Society, 14*, 489–493.

Moritz, S. & von Mühlenen, A. (2005). Inhibition of return in patients with obsessive-compulsive disorder. *Anxiety Disorders, 19*, 117–126.

Moritz, S., & von Mühlenen, A. (2008). Investigation of an attentional bias for fear-related material in obsessive-compulsive checkers. *Depression and Anxiety, 25*, 225–229.

Moritz, S., & Wendt, M. (2006). Processing of local and global visual features in obsessive-compulsive disorder. *Journal of the International Neuropsychological Society, 12*, 566–569.

Mowrer, O. H. (1947). On the dual nature of learning—A reinterpretation of "conditioning" and "problem solving." *Harvard Educational Review, 17*, 102–148.

Muller, J., & Roberts, J. E. (2005). Memory and attention in obsessive-compulsive disorder: A review. *Anxiety Disorders, 19*, 1–28.

Nielen, M. M. A., & Den Boer, J. A. (2003). Neuropsychological performance of OCD patients before and after treatment with fluoxetine: Evidence for persistent cognitive deficits. *Psychological Medicine, 33*, 917–925.

Osman, S., Cooper, M., Hackmann, A., & Veale, D. (2004). Spontaneously occurring images and early memories in people with body dysmorphic disorder. *Memory, 12*, 428–436.

Park, H. S., Shin, Y.-W., Ha, T. H., Shin, M.S., Kim, Y. Y., Lee, Y. H., et al. (2006). Effect of cognitive training focusing on organizational strategies in patients with obsessive-compulsive disorder. *Psychiatry and Clinical Neuroscience, 60*, 718–726.

Purcell, R., Maruff, P., Kyrios, M., & Pantelis, C. (1998). Neuropsychological deficits in obsessive-compulsive disorder : A comparison with unipolar depression, panic disorder. *Archives of General Psychiatry, 55,* 415–423.

Rachman, S. J. (2002). A cognitive theory of compulsive checking. *Behaviour Research and Therapy, 40,* 625–639.

Rachman, S., & Hodgson, R. (1980). *Obsessions and compulsions.* NJ: Prentice-Hall.

Radomsky, A. S., & Rachman, S. (1999). Memory bias in obsessive-compulsive disorder (OCD). *Behaviour Research & Therapy, 37,* 605–618.

Radomsky, A. S., & Rachman, S. (2004). The importance of importance in OCD memory research. *Journal of Behavior Therapy and Experimental Psychiatry, 35,* 137–151.

Radomsky, A. S., Gilchrist, P. T., & Dussault, D. D. (2006). Repeated checking really does cause memory distrust. *Behaviour Research and Therapy, 44,* 305–316.

Radomsky, A. S., Rachman, S. J., & Hammond, D. (2001). Memory bias, confidence and responsibility in compulsive checking. *Behaviour Research & Therapy, 39,* 813–822.

Rapee, R. M., & Heimberg, R. G. (1997). A cognitive-behavioral model of anxiety in social phobia. *Behaviour Research and Therapy, 35,* 741–756.

Ravindran, A. V. (1999). Obsessive-Compulsive Spectrum Disorders. *Journal of Psychiatry and Neuroscience, 24,* 10–12.

Rettew, D. C., Cheslow, D. L., Rapoport, J. L., Leonard, H. L., Lenane, M. C., Black, B., et al. (1991). Neuropsychological test performance in Trichotillomania: A further link with obsessive-compulsive disorder. *Journal of Anxiety Disorders, 5,* 225–235.

Roediger, H. L. (1990). Implicit memory: Retention without remembering. *American Psychologist, 45,* 1043–1056.

Roh, K. S., Shin, M. S., Kim, M.-S., Ha, T.-H., Shin, Y.-W., Lee, K. J., et al. (2005). Persistent cognitive dysfunction in patients with obsessive-compulsive disorder: A naturalistic study. *Psychiatry and Clinical Neurosciences, 59,* 539–545.

Salkovskis, P. M. (1985). Obsessional-compulsive problems: A cognitive-behavioural analysis. *Behaviour Research & Therapy, 23,* 571–583.

Sanz, M., Molina, V., Martin-Loeches, M., Calcedo, A., & Rubia, F.J. (2001). Auditory P300 even related potential and serotonin reuptake inhibitor treatment in obsessive-compulsive disorder patients. *Psychiatry Research, 101,* 75–81.

Savage, C. R., Baer, L., Keuthen, N. J., Brown, H. D., Rauch, S. L., & Jenike M. A. (1999). Organizational strategies mediate nonverbal memory impairment in obsessive compulsive disorder. *Biological Psychiatry, 45,* 905–916.

Savage, C. R., Deckersbach, T., Wilhelm, S., Rauch, S. L., Baer, L., Reid, T., et al. (2000). Strategic processing and episodic memory impairment in obsessive compulsive disorder. *Neuropsychology, 14,* 141–151.

Sher, K. J., Frost, R. O., & Otto, R. (1983). Cognitive deficits in compulsive checkers: An exploratory study. *Behaviour Research and Therapy, 21,* 357–363.

Sher, K.J., Mann, B., & Frost, R.O. (1984). Cognitive dysfunction in compulsive checkers: Further explorations. *Behaviour Research and Therapy, 22,* 493–502.

Simpson, H. B., Liebowitz, M. R., Foa, E. B., Kozak, M. J., Schmidt, A. B., Rowan, V., et al. (2004). Post-treatment effects of exposure therapy and clomipramine in obsessive-compulsive disorder. *Depression and Anxiety, 19,* 225–233.

Simpson, H. B., Rosen, W., Huppert, J. D., Lin, S.-H., Foa, E. B., & Liebowitz, M. R. (2006). Are there reliable neuropsychological deficits in obsessive-compulsive disorder? *Journal of Psychiatric Research, 40,* 247–257.

Stangier, U., Adam-Schwebe, S., Müller, T., & Wolter, M. (2008). Discrimination of facial appearance stimuli in body dysmorphic disorder. *Journal of Abnormal Psychology, 17,* 435–443.

Stanley, M. A., Hannay, H. J., & Breckenridge, J. K. (1997). The neuropsychology of trichotillomania. *Journal of Anxiety Disorders, 11,* 473–488.

Stein, D.J. (2000). Neurobiology of the obsessive-compulsive spectrum disorders. *Biological Psychiatry, 47,* 296–304.

Stein, D. J., & Lochner, C. (2006). Obsessive-compulsive spectrum disorders: A multidimensional approach. *Psychiatric Clinics of North America, 29,* 343–351.

Stroop, J. R. (1935). Studies of interference in serial verbal reactions. *Journal of Experimental Psychology, 18,* 643–662.

Summerfeldt, L.J., Endler, N.S. (1998). Examining the evidence for anxiety-related cognitive biases in Obsessive-Compulsive Disorder. *Journal of Anxiety Disorders, 12,* 579–598.

Tallis, F. (1997). The neuropsychology of obsessive-compulsive disorder: A review and consideration of clinical implications. *British Journal of Clinical Psychology, 36,* 3–20.

Tata, P. R., Leibowitz, J. A., Prunty, M. J., Cameron, M., & Pickering, A. D. (1996). Attentional bias in obsessive-compulsive disorder. *Behaviour Research and Therapy, 34,* 53–60.

Teachmann, B. A., & Clerkin, E. M. (2007). Obsessional beliefs and the implicit and explicit morality of intrusive thought. *Cognition & Emotion, 21,* 999–1024.

Tolin, D. F., Abramowitz, J. S., Brigidi, B. D., Amir, N., Street, G. P., & Foa, E.B. (2001). Memory and memory confidence in obsessive-compulsive disorder. *Behaviour Research and Therapy, 39,* 913–927.

Tulving, E. (1985). Memory and consciousness. *Canadian Psychology, 26,* 1–12.

van Oppen, P., van Balkom, A. J. L. M., de Haan, E., & van Dyck, R. (2005). Cognitive therapy and exposure in vivo alone and in combination with fluvoxamine in obsessive-compulsive disorder: A 5-year follow-up. *Journal of Clinical Psychiatry, 2005,* 1415–1422.

Van den Hout, M. (2007). *Uncertainty in OCD.* Keynote address, World Congress of Behavioural and Cognitive Therapies, Barcelona, Spain.

van den Hout, M., & Kindt, M. (2003a). Repeated checking causes memory distrust. *Behaviour Research and Therapy, 41,* 301–316.

van den Hout, M., & Kindt, M. (2003b). Phenomenological validity of an OCD-memory model and the remember/know distinction. *Behaviour Research and Therapy, 41,* 369–378.

van den Hout, M., & Kindt, M. (2004). Obsessive-compulsive disorder and the paradoxical effects of perseverative behaviour on experienced uncertainty. *Journal of Behavior Therapy and Experimental Psychiatry, 35,* 165–181.

Veale, D. (2004). Advances in a cognitive behavioural model of body dysmorphic disorder. *Body Image, 1,* 113–125.

Wahl, K., Salkovskis, P. M., & Cotter, I. (2008). "I wash until it feels right": The phenomenology of stopping criteria in obsessive–compulsive washing. *Journal of Anxiety Disorders, 22,* 143–161.

Watkins, L. H., Sahakian, B. J., Robertson, M. M., Veale, D. M., Rogers, R. D., Pickard, K. M., et al. (2005). Executive function in Tourette's syndrome and obsessive-compulsive disorder. *Psychological Medicine, 35,* 571–582.

Wilhelm, S., Buhlmann, Y., & McNally, R. J. (2003). Negatve priming for non-threatening information in body dysmorphic disorder. *Acta Neuropschiatrica, 15,* 180–183.

Wilhelm, S., McNally, R. J., Baer, L., & Florin, I. (1996). Directed forgetting compulsive disorder. *Behaviour Research and Therapy, 34,* 633–641.

Williams, J. M. G., Watts, F. N., MacLeod, C., & Mathews, A. (1988). *Cognitive psychology and emotional disorders.* Oxford, England: John Wiley & Sons.

Williams, J. M. G., Watts, F. N., MacLeod, C., & Mathews, A. (1997). *Cognitive psychology and emotional disorders* (2nd ed.). Chichester, UK: Wiley.

Wolpe, J. (1954). Reciprocal inhibition as the main basis of psychotherapeutic effects. *Archives of Neurology and Psychiatry, 72,* 205–226.

Wolpe, J. (1958). *Psychotherapy by reciprocal inhibition.* Stanford: Stanford University Press.

The Role of Family and Social Relationships in OCD and Spectrum Conditions

Keith D. Renshaw, Catherine M. Caska, Camila S. Rodrigues, *and* Rebecca K. Blais

Abstract

Children and adults with obsessive compulsive disorder (OCD) have impairments in social and family functioning, and relatives of those with OCD endorse elevated levels of relationship and psychological distress. The levels of impairments appear equal to or greater than those associated with other disorders. Furthermore, OCD is specifically associated with higher levels of accommodation, or behaviors that facilitate the completion of compulsive rituals, in relatives. Although levels of general social and family impairments do not demonstrate a clear association with treatment response in OCD, higher levels of pretreatment accommodation and hostility in relatives is associated with poorer response to exposure and response prevention (ERP). In contrast, higher levels of nonhostile criticism in relatives may be associated with enhanced response to ERP in patients. Findings are mixed as to whether family-based treatments for OCD, most of which include psychoeducation and attempts to reduce accommodating behaviors in relatives, are associated with enhanced response to ERP.

Keywords: family accommodation, social functioning, family functioning, expressed emotion, obsessive compulsive disorder, OC spectrum disorders, family therapy

As described throughout this book, a wealth of literature has accumulated on neuropsychological, biological, genetic, cognitive, and behavioral influences on OCD and related disorders. The extent of these findings may suggest that there is little need for consideration of interpersonal factors with regard to OCD, but in fact, over the past two decades, empirical evidence regarding the importance of interpersonal variables in OCD has mounted steadily. In this chapter, this evidence is reviewed from the perspective of both individuals with OCD and their relatives, focusing first on general social and family functioning, followed by a discussion of the more specific aspect of accommodation in family members of children and adults with OCD. The chapter concludes with a review of existing family-based interventions for OCD.

OCD and Social Functioning
Children and Adolescents
Although there have been relatively few studies of social functioning in children and adolescents with OCD, existing data suggest that it is significantly impaired. In a study of 151 children and adolescents with OCD, Piacentini, Bergman, Keller, and McCraken (2003) examined both parent- and self-report measures of social functioning via the Child Obsessive Compulsive Impact Scale (COIS; Piacentini & Jaffer, 1999). The researchers found that 19% of children and 33% of parents perceived significant social problems because of children's OCD symptoms, with an additional 35% of children and 42% of parents perceiving at least slight social problems due to OCD symptoms. The likelihood of reporting social problems was significantly greater when symptoms were more severe,

and parent reports of social difficulties were greater than children's self-reports. Although this study suggests significant levels of social impairments, social problems were seen as significantly less severe than problems in school or at home.

Valderhaug and Ivarsson (2005) obtained similar results in a sample of 68 children with OCD (aged 8 to 17 years) in Norway and Sweden. Twenty-five percent of the children and 38% of their parents perceived significant social problems due to OCD symptoms, with an additional 38% of children and 39% of parents perceiving slight social problems. Again, parent ratings of social problems were significantly higher than children's ratings, and both child and parent ratings were significantly and positively correlated with clinician-rated symptom severity. Children's ratings of their own social problems correlated more highly with objective ratings of symptom severity than did parents' ratings. Indeed, parents' ratings were correlated with clinician-rated severity of obsessions only, not with compulsions.

Other studies of children with OCD have yielded similar findings. For instance, Hanna (1995) found that parent ratings of social problems in 31 children and adolescents with OCD were one standard deviation higher than the norm, and parent ratings of children's overall social competence were one standard deviation below the norm. In this sample, however, ratings of social problems were not correlated with clinician-rated symptom severity. Sukhodolsky and colleagues (2005) also found that 56 children with OCD scored significantly lower than 93 healthy controls on interview and parent-rated measures of social functioning, although children with OCD displayed higher levels of social functioning than children with attention deficit hyperactivity disorder (ADHD; n = 95) or children with comorbid OCD and ADHD (n = 43). Bolton, Luckie, and Steinberg (1995) assessed 14 children between 9 and 14 years old, after they had been treated as inpatients or outpatients for OCD. All six individuals who still met criteria for OCD were rated as having significant social impairments, whereas only 2 of the 8 individuals who no longer met criteria for OCD demonstrated any notable social dysfunction. Assessment in this study was not standardized, however, with estimates based on hospital notes, or interviews with the patients or parents, and no information regarding interrater reliability or whether raters were blind to OCD status. Finally, in a case note review of 44 adolescents with OCD, Allsopp and Verduyn (1990) found that 75% of adolescents reported that they had no close friendships; however, the lack of friendships appeared to predate the onset of OCD symptoms in all but 4 cases. Again, measurement of social problems in this study was unstandardized; however, the findings do emphasize the limitations of cross-sectional research in determining whether OCD symptoms themselves lead to social impairment, or if they appear merely as coexisting difficulties.

Adults

Not surprisingly, adults with OCD also endorse elevated levels of social impairment. In fact, in a study comparing social functioning across age groups, Farrell, Barrett, and Piacentini (2006) found that self-reported social impairment in 41 adults (aged 18 to 66) was significantly more extensive than self- or parent-reported social impairment in 40 children (aged 6 to 11). Although no other studies have compared social functioning of individuals with OCD across age groups, multiple groups of investigators have documented social impairments in adults with OCD. For instance, 72% of a sample of 219 Danish individuals with OCD reported that their symptoms negatively impacted their social life (Sorensen, Kirkeby, & Thomsen, 2004). Similarly, in a sample of 197 adults with OCD, Eisen and colleagues (2006) found evidence of significant impairment on multiple self-report and clinician-rated scales of social functioning, relative to population norms. In follow-up analyses, social functioning was negatively related to severity of clinician-rated obsessions and compulsions, but only obsession severity was significant when both were included in a hierarchical regression with other variables. Bobes and colleagues (2001) found similar levels of social impairment in a group of 36 Spanish adults, relative to Spanish norms. Finally, Stengler-Wenzke, Kroll, Matschinger, and Angermeyer (2006a) found that satisfaction with social relationships in a group of 71 German patients with OCD was significantly lower than German population norms.

Researchers have also compared social functioning of adults with OCD to that of adults with other disorders. Lochner and colleagues (2003) found that, on multiple measures of quality of life and functioning, 220 patients with OCD reported similar levels of social impairments as 53 patients with panic disorder (PD). Not surprisingly, both of these groups reported less social impairment than 64 patients with social anxiety disorder (SAD). Within those with OCD, overall functioning (including social, family, school, romantic, and daily living) was significantly and negatively related to clinician-rated symptom severity, and overall functioning was lower in those with comorbid depression, as diagnosed by the Structured Clinical Interview for the DSM-IV (First, Spitzer, Gibbon, & Williams, 1998). In an even larger sample, Rapaport, Clary, Fayyad, and Endicott (2005) examined quality of life in a sample of 521 patients with OCD, 258 patients with SAD, 302 patients with PD, 139 patients with post-traumatic stress disorder (PTSD), 437 patients with premenstrual dysphoric disorder, 315 patients with dysthymia, 366 patients with major depressive disorder (MDD), and 576 patients with chronic/double depression. Those with OCD demonstrated less impairment in overall quality of life than those with most other disorders; however, their impairments in social and family relationships were equivalent to those of all other patient groups, suggesting that OCD affects these specific areas of functioning more than other domains. Interestingly, although the association between symptom severity and overall quality of life was significant in those with OCD, the correlation was lower than that for any other diagnostic group, suggesting that the level of symptoms may not be as important as the simple presence of symptoms. Cramer, Torgersen, and Kringlen (2005) obtained a similar pattern of results in a smaller sample of adults with OCD (n = 33 lifetime diagnosis, n = 14 diagnosis within the last year). They found that, compared to individuals with generalized anxiety or PD, those with OCD had significantly higher ratings of global quality of life, but significantly lower levels of perceived social support when ill.

Three other groups outside the United States have documented similar trends. Torres and colleagues (2006) found that 114 adults with OCD in Great Britain reported significantly more social impairment than 1395 adults with other anxiety or depressive disorders. Also, Bobes and colleagues (2001) found that 36 Spanish adults with OCD reported significantly greater social impairment than did adults with depression or heroin addiction in the United States. Finally, in a unique longitudinal study, Thomsen (1995) followed 47 individuals with childhood OCD and 47 matched participants with other childhood disorders (psychotic disorders, pervasive developmental disorders, and mental retardation were excluded from the comparison group) into adulthood, for a period of 6 to 22 years after their admission to a child psychiatric hospital in Denmark. At the time of follow-up, those with OCD were found to be more likely to be living with their parents in adulthood and less likely to have a romantic partner.

Studies comparing adults with OCD to adults with schizophrenia, a disorder characterized by marked impairments in functioning, have yielded somewhat surprising results. Bystritsky and colleagues (2001) found that objectively rated social skills in 31 patients with OCD were no better than those of 68 patients with schizophrenia, matched on gender and age. After treatment, those with OCD did experience greater improvement on this objective measure, but both groups continued to endorse similarly low levels of quality of life on a self-report measure that included social functioning. Moreover, Bobes and colleagues (2001) found that their sample of Spanish adults with OCD reported significantly poorer social functioning than did a group of adults with schizophrenia in the United States. Similarly, Stengler-Wenzke and colleagues (2006a) found that satisfaction with social relationships in a group of 71 German patients with OCD was significantly lower than that of 243 patients with schizophrenia. These results highlight the clear social dysfunction of those with OCD.

Finally, two groups of investigators have examined differences in social functioning within individuals diagnosed with OCD. In a sample of adults with OCD treated in Brazil, Ferrão and colleagues (2006) found that those with treatment-refractory OCD (defined as less than 25% improvement after at least 3 drug trials and 20 hours of CBT) had significantly lower quality of life with regard to social relationships than did treatment responders (defined as at least 35% improvement). Finally, in the only published study on subtypes of OCD and social functioning, Frost, Steketee, Williams, and Warren (2000) found that 37 adults with the hoarding subtype of OCD reported significantly greater social impairment than 20 adults with other variants of OCD. Those with hoarding also reported greater levels of social impairment than 13 adults with other anxiety disorders, whereas those with non-hoarding variants of OCD reported equivalent levels of social impairment as those with non-OCD anxiety disorders. Although these results are intriguing, no other reports of social functioning across subtypes of OCD have been reported; thus, further research of this type is needed to draw any definitive conclusions about relative social impairments in specific subtypes of OCD.

Conclusion

Overall, there is strong support for the notion that OCD is associated with significant impairments in social functioning in both children and adults. In general, it appears that impairment is worse when symptoms are more severe, although this association was not found in all studies. These impairments appear to be equivalent to (or possibly greater than) the social impairments associated with other disorders, including depression, other anxiety disorders, and even schizophrenia. Furthermore, there is some suggestion that OCD may be more strongly associated with impairments in social functioning than impairments in other domains of functioning (e.g., work). Finally, social impairments have also been documented in adults with OCD outside the United States, for example, in Great Britain, Spain, Germany, and Brazil.

To date, there is little to no information regarding the mechanisms of social impairments and dissatisfaction associated with OCD, or the longitudinal relations between onset of symptoms and social impairments. There has also been little attention to potential differences in the social functioning of individuals with OCD across cultures with individualistic versus collectivist orientations. Finally, there is little research on differential levels of social functioning in different subtypes of OCD. All of these areas represent potential targets for future research in this area.

OCD and General Family Functioning
Parenting

Much of the early literature regarding parenting styles and OCD was somewhat speculative, with theoretical or anecdotal reports of excessive cleanliness or meticulous attention to detail in parents leading to the development of OCD in children (e.g., Hoover & Insel, 1984). More recently, literature on parenting has increasingly recognized the likely transactional nature of associations between parenting styles and OCD symptoms. In this context, a great deal of information has accumulated on parent behaviors and the maintenance or exacerbation of OCD and its symptoms (see next two sections for further detail). However, most of the literature regarding parenting styles and the *development* of OCD remains theoretical, retrospective, and cross-sectional. Given the potential biases of the recollections of adults with OCD, and the impossibility of drawing causal inferences from cross-sectional data, any correlates detected by these types of empirical investigations cannot be viewed as indications that certain parenting styles actually lead to the development of OCD. Furthermore, much of the cross-sectional research with children and parents focuses on children with any anxiety disorder, rather than OCD in particular. Although such research offers a good starting point, it does not provide information specific to OCD. With these caveats in mind, we review theoretical writings, studies of children with OCD and other anxiety disorders, and retrospective studies of adults' reports of their parents' approach to parenting, below.

One of the primary cognitive tendencies observed in those with OCD is an overestimation of responsibility (Obsessive Compulsive Cognitions Working Group, 2005). In a theoretical article, Salkovskis and colleagues (1999) proposed several mechanisms by which such an inflated sense of responsibility might develop as a result of childhood experiences. These included parents' assigning children a level of responsibility that was inappropriate, either developmentally (e.g., the oldest child of a single mother who worked multiple jobs, taking on responsibility for care of younger siblings) or generally (e.g., blaming children for larger problems in family). On the other hand, the authors also speculated that overprotection from any experience with responsibility could lead to problems with responsibility, as could an overly harsh and rigid disciplinary system. Finally, they posited that an inflated sense of responsibility could also spring from an experience in which an actual behavior led, or nearly led, to catastrophic consequences, or in which a specific bad thought was coincidentally followed by an actual related event (e.g., wishing someone dead who then died unexpectedly). These mechanisms are all plausible, theoretically sound, and consistent with anecdotal clinical experience, but have yet to be subject to close empirical scrutiny. In the only identified empirical investigation related to these variables, Jacobi, Calamari, and Woodard (2006) found that the extent of parents' subclinical OCD symptoms was directly related to adolescents' inflated sense of threat and responsibility, which in turn predicted adolescents' own level of subclinical OCD symptoms. Although intriguing, these results have yet to be replicated or studied in a clinical population.

Somewhat in line with Salkovskis and colleagues' (1999) hypotheses, studies of parenting styles in parents of children with anxiety disorders in general do suggest that high parental control and overprotection, and low provision of opportunities for autonomy by parents, are associated with greater anxiety in children (for detailed reviews, see Rapee, 1997; Waters & Barrett, 2000). Similarly, in comparison to nonanxious children, children with anxiety disorders are prone to interpret ambiguous situations as more threatening, and to choose avoidant responses when confronting such situations. Moreover, these tendencies seem to be enhanced by discussions with their parents (Barrett, Rapee, Dadds, & Ryan, 1996; Chorpita, Albano, & Barlow, 1996). As noted above, however, due to lack of differentiation between OCD and other types of anxiety, it is unknown how these findings relate to the development of OCD specifically. Finally, in a study specific to OCD, Black, Gaffney, Schlosser, and Gabel (2003) found that baseline disruptions in affective responsiveness and behavior control by 21 parents with OCD predicted greater likelihood of clinical and subclinical OCD in their 43 children 2 years later. Although this study was prospective, longitudinal, and specific to OCD, the authors did not report on presence or absence of other anxiety disorders. Thus, it is unknown whether these effects were specific to OCD alone.

In perhaps the only study to compare parents of children with OCD to parents of children with other anxiety disorders, Barrett, Shortt, and Healy (2002) compared interactions between 18 children with OCD and their parents to interactions between parents and children with GAD ($n = 78$), separation anxiety disorder ($n = 11$), social phobia ($n = 4$), externalizing disorders ($n = 21$), and no diagnosed disorder ($n = 22$). Mothers and fathers of children with OCD engaged in less positive problem-solving, displayed lower levels of confidence in their children, and were less likely to reward independence in their children than parents in any of the other groups. Interestingly, children with OCD were also less likely to display warmth, confidence, and positive problem-solving behavior during interactions, in comparison to other children. Although informative, there is no evidence that such styles are intrinsically related to the development of OCD, and it is at least equally likely that they are consequences of the symptoms and associated disruptions in family functioning that are associated with OCD (see next section). Despite the cross-sectional nature of this study, it is precisely these types of comparisons of OCD to other anxiety disorders that are needed to gain a greater understanding of potential influences of parenting styles on OCD in children.

Finally, several studies have assessed recollections of parenting styles in adults with clinical OCD or subclinical OC symptoms. Most researchers have utilized the Parental Bonding Instrument (PBI; Parker, Tupling, & Brown, 1979) in this work, although a few have also used checklists of adjectives that respondents mark as either having applied or not applied to their parents during their upbringing. Several of these studies revealed that adults with OCD or subclinical OC symptoms recall their parents as having been more overprotective than norm samples or healthy controls (Ehiobuche, 1988; Frost, Steketee, Cohn, & Griess, 1994; Hafner, 1988; Yoshida, Taga, & Fukui, 2001), although two groups have failed to detect such differences (Alonso et al., 2004; Vogel, Stiles, & Nordahl, 1997). Furthermore, the severity of OC symptoms is typically correlated with the extent to which parents are remembered as overprotective (Cavedo & Parker, 1994; Kimidis, Minas, Ata, & Stuart, 1992).

When those with OCD are compared to individuals with other disorders, however, results are not as clear. Two groups have failed to find any differences between those with OCD and those with PD in their recollection of their parents as overprotective (Chambless, Gillis, Tran, & Steketee, 1996; Merkel, Pollard, Wiener, & Staebler, 1993). Although Merkel and colleagues (1993) found that those with OCD recalled their parents as overprotective more frequently than did those with a depressive disorder, Vogel, Stiles, and Nordahl (1997) failed to detect any such differences between 26 adult outpatients with OCD and 34 adult outpatients with MDD. Finally, Yoshida, Taga, Matsumoto, and Fukui (2005) compared PBI scores of individuals with OCD only, individuals with depression and comorbid severe OCD, individuals with depression and mild or no OC symptoms, and healthy controls. They found that individuals with OCD only, or depression with severe OCD, recalled their fathers as more protective than did individuals with depression and mild OC symptoms and healthy controls, but they only recalled their mothers as more protective than healthy controls. Those with depression and mild OC symptoms did not differ from any group on recollections of mothers' parenting. Given this mixture of findings, it is difficult to conclude that parental overprotection is uniquely linked to the development of OCD, particularly given that all of these findings are based on retrospective report of childhood experiences.

Two groups also have collected self-report ratings of parenting style from parents of adults with OCD. Chambless and colleagues (1996) found that mothers of those with OCD recalled themselves as having been more protective of their children than did mothers of those with PD, but there were no differences detected in fathers' reports. Similarly, Frost and colleagues (1994) collected ratings from two samples of parents of those with subclinical OC symptoms, and parents of those with no such symptoms. Although they detected a handful of differences on personality and parenting measures between parents of those with and without subclinical OC symptoms in each sample, none of the differences replicated across the two samples.

Finally, researchers have reported on other aspects of parenting, such as warmth, perfectionism, and criticism. Although there is some evidence that parents of those with subclinical OC symptoms are recalled as having been more rejecting and less warm than parents of those with no such symptoms (Alonso et al., 2004; Ehiobuche, 1988; Kimidis et al., 1992), all of these studies again involved retrospective recall of adults, and none included comparisons to individuals with other types of symptoms (e.g., depression). Thus, no conclusions can be drawn regarding parental warmth and rejection and the development of OCD.

In sum, despite increased empirical study, the literature on parenting styles and the development of OCD remains primarily theoretical and speculative (in contrast, evidence has grown with regard to parenting behaviors and the maintenance of OCD; see sections below). More research that compares parents of children with OCD to parents of children with other anxiety and other disorders (similar to that conducted by Barrett and colleagues, 2002) is needed. In particular, longitudinal research of this nature is necessary to be able to begin drawing any conclusions with regard to the potential contribution (if any) of parenting styles to the development of OCD. Results based on retrospective recall, cross-sectional designs, and comparisons only to healthy controls runs the risk of blaming parents and confirming widely held beliefs (e.g., parental rigidity leads to OCD) that may be unfounded.

Marital Status

By and large, research examining the family composition of treatment-seeking adults with OCD demonstrates that they are less likely to be married than those in the general population, with estimates from 25% to 50% of those with OCD being married, and males falling in the lower end of that range (Koran, 2000; Lensi, Cassano, Correddu, Ravagli, & Kunovac, 1996; Steketee, 1993; Torres et al., 2006). Torres and colleagues (2006) found that the divorce/separation rate for individuals with OCD was significantly higher than that of a healthy control group, although divorce/separation rates for treatment-seeking patients with OCD, as a whole, range from only 9% to 16% (Eisen et al., 2006; Koran, Thienemann, & Davenport, 1996; Torres et al., 2006). Steketee and Pruyn (1998) reported that up to 25% of treatment-seeking adults continue to live with their parents, and Thomsen and colleagues (1995) observed that individuals who had been hospitalized for OCD as children were more likely than those who had been hospitalized with other diagnoses to still live with their parents once they reached adulthood.

In contrast to these statistics from treatment-seeking samples, findings from the Epidemiological Catchment Area study revealed that 79% of individuals who met criteria for OCD (most of whom were not seeking treatment) were married (Steketee, 1997). Thus, the overall tendency for OCD patients to be single may reflect a greater proclivity of those who are unmarried to seek treatment, or for those who are more severely affected by OCD symptoms to both be single and seek treatment. No significant association has been detected between marital status and treatment response in adults with OCD (e.g., Foa et al., 1983; Hoogduin & Duivenvoorden, 1988), although in a naturalistic study with no control of treatment, Steketee, Eisen, Dyck, Warshaw, and Rasmussen (1999) found that being married predicted greater likelihood of partial remission of OCD over the course of 5 years.

General Impairments in Family Functioning

Similar to reports of social dysfunction, children and adults with OCD, as well as their relatives, report significant impairments in family functioning. In studies focused solely on children and adolescents with OCD, findings generally suggest elevated levels of dysfunction, with some ambiguity. Four groups have detected significant impairments in family functioning as assessed by parent and child reports (Piacentini et al., 2003; Toro, Cervera, & Osejo, 1992; Valderhaug & Ivarsson, 2005; Valleni-Basile et al., 1995), but two groups found no evidence of differential functioning in families of children with and without OCD. Derisley, Libby, Clark, and Reynolds (2005) detected a significant multivariate effect of child's diagnostic status on scores on the Family Assessment Device (FAD; Epstein, Baldwin & Bishop, 1983) in parents of 28 children with OCD, 28 children with other anxiety disorders, and 62 children with no known mental health problems. However, the authors detected no significant differences between any of these groups in follow-up univariate analyses. The lack of univariate differences could be due to lack of power, but because the means and standard deviations for each group were not reported, no inferences regarding the multivariate effect can be made. Sukhodolsky and colleagues (2005) also found no significant differences between parents of children with OCD and parents of healthy control children on the Family Environment Scale (Moos & Moos, 1986). As this scale has not been used in other studies of individuals with OCD, it is possible that the constructs it assesses are different from those assessed by other measures like the FAD, and that these constructs do not differ in families of children with OCD versus families of children without OCD. Further research with this measure would be needed to draw any firm conclusions.

Four groups have examined family functioning in combined samples of children and adults with OCD. Three surveys of patients and relatives (between 400 and 700 respondents each) recruited through the Obsessive Compulsive Foundation revealed that 70% or more report family problems and interference in family relationships (Cooper, 1996; Hollander et al., 1996, 1997). In addition, Shafran, Ralph, and Tallis (1995) found that 90% of a sample of 98 relatives (67.3% spouse/partner, 17.3% parent, 8.2% offspring, 7.2% other) of adolescents and adults with OCD reported at least some interference in their lives due to patients' OCD symptoms, with 20% of the sample rating the interference as extreme. Overall, results of these studies, and those focused solely on children/ adolescents, suggest that families of children with OCD likely experience some significant level of dysfunction.

In addition, multiple researchers have detected elevated family dysfunction in studies focused solely on adults with OCD and their relatives. Livingston-Van Noppen, Rasmussen, Eisen, and McCartney (1990) found that over half of families of 50 outpatients with OCD were classified as unhealthy in at least one domain of functioning on the FAD, with 40% of families classified as unhealthy in global family functioning. Similarly, Black, Gaffney, Schlosser, and Gabel (1998) found that FAD scores of relatives of 19 adults with OCD were significantly lower than those of 20 control subjects on multiple dimensions of family functioning, and the majority of relatives of those with OCD reported significant family conflicts and disruptions in their family/social lives. Finally, Khanna, Rajendra, and Channabasavanna (1988) found that 32 patients with OCD reported significantly lower levels of family and parent functioning on the Social Adjustment Scale–Self-Report (SAS-SR; Weissman & Bothwell, 1976) than 32 control participants matched on age, sex, and marital status.

With regard to marital relationships in particular, more than 60% of the married patients in Black and colleagues' (1998) sample endorsed marital and sexual difficulties, and Cooper (1996) reported that 69% of relatives believed that OCD had led to marital discord in their families. Riggs, Hiss, and Foa (1992) found fairly similar rates of marital distress (47%) on the Marital Adjustment Test (MAT; Locke & Wallace, 1959) in a sample of 54 married patients seeking exposure and response prevention (ERP) for OCD, as did Simmons, Gordon, and Chambless (2005), who reported that 50% of patients with OCD or panic were classified as maritally dissatisfied on the Dyadic Adjustment Scale (Spanier, 1976). Moreover, 40% of the spouses in Simmons and colleagues' sample scored in the maritally distressed range, as well. Thus, it appears that family dysfunction in adults with OCD is present in multiple types of relationships.

Researchers also have found that dysfunction in families of those with OCD is equivalent to or greater than that in families of individuals with other disorders. For example, adults with OCD in Rapaport and colleagues' (2005) sample demonstrated equivalent impairments in family functioning as adults with other anxiety disorders or depressive disorders. In two other studies, adults with OCD demonstrated greater impairments in family functioning than those with other anxiety disorders (Frost et al., 2000; Lochner et al., 2003). Erol, Yazici, and Toprak (2007) found no differences in FAD scores of 15 patients with anorexia nervosa, 13 patients with bulimia nervosa, and 17 patients with OCD, but their sample size provided fairly low power for these comparisons. Finally, as mentioned above, Stengler-Wenzke and colleagues (2006a) found that the adults with OCD in their sample reported even lower overall quality of life with regard to social relationships (which included family relationships) than adults with schizophrenia.

Many of the studies above also have revealed that the severity of family dysfunction is directly correlated with the severity of OCD symptoms (Lochner et al., 2003; Piacentini et al., 2003; Valderhaug & Ivarsson, 2005). Recently, Storch and colleagues

(2007a) reported similar significant associations of clinician-rated OCD symptom severity with parents' report of children's family dysfunction for 57 children and adolescents with OCD, although children's self-report of such dysfunction was not related to symptom severity. This pattern mirrored that detected by Piacentini and colleagues (2003), but contrasts with that observed by Valderhaug and Ivarsson (2005), who found a stronger association using children's own reports of family functioning. These types of discrepancies between parent and child reports are common in research with children and adolescents. Future research that includes other sources of assessment (e.g., observation, sibling reports) may help in resolving them.

Several groups of researchers have examined links between severity of specific symptoms and degree of family dysfunction, with contrasting results. Abbey, Clopton, and Humphreys (2007) found that relationship satisfaction, self-disclosure, and intimacy were all significantly and negatively related to self-reported severity of obsessions in a sample of 64 adults with OCD, but were generally unrelated to self-reported severity of compulsions. In contrast, Khanna and colleagues (1988) found that adults with obsessions only had better family functioning than those with obsessions and compulsions, although they had worse functioning with regard to leisure activities. In yet another contrasting study, Riggs and colleagues (1992) found that marital distress was not related to assessor-rated severity of either obsessions or compulsions, but it was related to severity of assessor-rated avoidance. Thus, to date, there is no clear association of obsessions and compulsions with family dysfunction. Finally, in the only study to compare subtypes of OCD, Frost and colleagues (2000) found that hoarders reported significantly lower family functioning than those with nonhoarding OCD; however, these results have not yet been replicated. Future research investigating the specific associations of symptoms and subtypes of OCD can help clarify which aspects of the disorder (if any) are most strongly linked to family dysfunction.

Finally, researchers also have examined family functioning in the context of treatment. OCD patients with marital distress seem to experience significant improvements in marital satisfaction after individual or partner-assisted ERP (Emmelkamp, de Haan, & Hoogduin, 1990; Riggs et al., 1992), and one study showed that such improvement may, in part, be due to decreases in spouses' demands of and dependence on patients (Riggs et al., 1992).

Trends regarding general family functioning, however, are less clear. Diefenbach, Abramowitz, Norberg, and Tolin (2007) found significant improvements in overall functioning (work, social, and family) in 70 adult outpatients with OCD who received individual ERP-based CBT, with family functioning showing the largest degree of improvement. OCD symptom reduction accounted for 26% of the variance in these improvements (Diefenbach et al., 2007). However, two groups of researchers have found that only patients who participate in family-based ERP experience significant improvements in family functioning (Mehta, 1990; Van Noppen, Steketee, McCorkle, & Pato, 1997). In one of these studies (Van Noppen et al., 1997), OCD symptom reduction in the nonfamily involvement group was lower in magnitude (effect size of 1.01) than is typically observed in studies of individually administered ERP (effect sizes between 1.47 and 3.50; see review by Franklin & Foa, 2002), which may have contributed to the lack of observed improvement in family functioning. However, individuals in both of Mehta's (1990) groups attained large degrees of OCD symptom reduction. In sum, existing evidence suggests that distressed marital relationships routinely improve after ERP for OCD, regardless of whether spouses participate in the treatment, but functioning in other family relationships may improve only if those family members are included in therapy.

Studies of children and adolescents treated for OCD have all involved some form of family-based treatment but, somewhat surprisingly, have revealed no significant improvements in family functioning. Waters, Barrett, and March (2001) and Barrett, Healy-Farrell, and March (2004) found no significant improvements in family functioning immediately following family-based ERP. Further, Thienemann, Martin, Cregger, Thompson, and Dyer-Friedman (2001) found no decreases in parental stress following a pilot study of family-based ERP in 18 adolescents and their parents. As these were the only two identified studies that assessed changes in family functioning, more research in this area is clearly needed before firm conclusions can be drawn.

Lastly, no groups have found that the level of pretreatment marital satisfaction or family functioning predict response to ERP in adults (Emmelkamp et al., 1990; Riggs et al., 1992; Van Noppen et al., 1997), but results regarding treatment of children and adolescents are mixed. Barrett, Farrell, Dadds, and Boulter (2005) reported that higher pretreatment family functioning predicted better outcome in children and adolescents treated with family-based ERP, 18 months after treatment. In a case series, Piacentini, Gitow, Jaffer, Graae, and Whitaker (1994) found that, of three children treated with family-based CBT, the one child who showed the least improvement had high levels of pretreatment family dysfunction. In contrast, Piacentini and colleagues (2002) and Wever and Rey (1997) found that family impairments were not associated with treatment response in children and adolescents treated with family-based versions of ERP. However, Wever and Rey (1997) did find that better family environment was significantly associated with successful weaning from medication in those children treated with a combination of family-based ERP and medication. In sum, the association of family functioning with treatment response is unclear in children, with some evidence indicating that better family functioning predicts better treatment response, but other studies showing no such associations. With regard to adults, there is no evidence to date to suggest that pretreatment family functioning affects treatment response.

Distress in Relatives

In addition to studies of overall family functioning, researchers have examined personal distress in relatives of those with OCD. The findings of such studies must be considered in the context of the strong familiality of OCD. Given that the relatives of those with OCD may be more likely to have OCD or other disorders due to genetic vulnerabilities (see Chapter 6), higher distress in relatives should not automatically be attributed to the effects of living with someone with OCD. Notwithstanding this caveat, Cooper (1993, 1996) found that over 80% of relatives reported distress specifically due to patients' OCD symptoms (particularly compulsive behaviors) and patients' depressive symptoms. Furthermore, 82% of relatives reported disruptions in their own personal lives due to their relatives' OCD symptoms. These rates of personal distress were similar to those detected in Black and colleagues' (1998) small sample of 15 spouses of adults with OCD, nearly all of whom reported some degree of anger, frustration, depression, and fatigue due to their partners' symptoms. Poorer psychological well-being and lower quality of life with regard to mental health have also been detected in German (Stengler-Wenzke et al., 2006b) and Italian (Albert, Salvi, Saracco, Bogetto, & Maina, 2007; Magliano,

Tosni, Guarneri, Marasco, & Catapano, 1996) relatives of adults with OCD.

In a study of children with OCD, Derisley and colleagues (2005) found that patients' parents reported poorer psychological and emotional well-being, greater levels of depression and anxiety, and greater use of avoidant coping than parents of children in a nonclinical group. Also, in the only identified study to examine distress in children of adults with OCD, Black, Gaffney, Schlosser, and Gabel (2003) found that children of adults with OCD were more likely than offspring of control adults to be withdrawn, anxious, and depressed, and to have somatic complaints and social problems, with many of these differences persisting after 2 years. Again, however, it is impossible to know whether these results reflect the stress of living with a parent with OCD, an enhanced predisposition to OCD and related mental health problems in children of those with OCD, or both.

A handful of investigators have also compared personal distress in relatives of those with OCD to relatives of those with other disorders. Renshaw, Chambless, Rodebaugh, and Steketee (2000) found that relatives of adults with OCD and PD endorsed similar levels of general psychological distress on the Symptom Checklist 90–Revised (Derogatis, 1994), but these authors also found that relatives of those with OCD were significantly more likely to express criticism of anxiety-related symptoms than were relatives of those with PD. Also, Magliano and colleagues (1996) found that relatives of 32 Italian adults with OCD endorsed equivalent levels of burden and distress, and more frequent nervous tension, crying, and depressive feelings in comparison to relatives of 26 Italian adults with depression. Finally, Jayakumar, Jagadheesan, and Verma (2002) found that 30 relatives of adults with OCD reported equivalent or greater levels of caregiving burden than 41 relatives of adults with schizophrenia.

In sum, relatives of children and adults with OCD endorse significant levels of psychological distress, often on par with or greater than that endorsed by relatives of individuals with other disorders. The negative experiences of relatives include general psychological distress, depressive symptoms, anxiety symptoms, and caregiver burden. Such distress may, in part, be accounted for by increased genetic vulnerability to OCD and other anxiety or depressive disorders, but studies have also revealed correlations of such distress with the severity of OCD symptoms and associated impairments in the afflicted relatives (Albert et al., 2007; Renshaw et al., 2000).

Surprisingly, in spite of this strong evidence for such distress, we identified only three groups that investigated the distress of relatives following individual or family-based treatment for OCD. Barrett and colleagues (2004, 2005) found no significant improvements in mothers' or fathers' anxiety, depression, or stress after family-based ERP for children and adolescents, at either post-treatment or 18-month follow-up. In contrast, Emmelkamp and colleagues (1990) found significant decreases in psychological distress in partners of adults treated with either individual or partner-assisted ERP at post-treatment and 1-month follow-up. In addition, Grunes and colleagues (2001) found decreases in depression and anxiety in family members of adults treated with individual ERP, with greater decreases detected in relatives who participated in family-only adjunctive groups. Thus, the scant evidence suggests that relatives of adults with OCD experience decreases in distress after patients are treated with ERP, but parents of children with OCD may not experience such decreases. Further research is clearly needed in this area.

OCD and Families: Relatives' Responses to Symptoms

In this section, we review two important aspects of common reactions of family members to the symptoms associated with OCD: criticism/hostility and accommodation. These aspects have been discussed in the past as opposite ends of a continuum (e.g., Livingston-Van Noppen et al., 1990; Renshaw, Steketee, & Chambless, 2005; Van Noppen, Rasmussen, Eisen, & McCartney, 1991). However, as reviewed below, empirical findings suggest that they are, in fact, separate dimensions of behavior that may even be positively rather than negatively correlated. Below, we review the research regarding each aspect of family response and describe an overall model of family response that integrates these findings from a behaviorally-based interpersonal perspective.

Criticism and Hostility

There are many reports in the literature of relatives engaging in angry, hostile behaviors in response to symptoms of OCD (e.g., Allsopp & Verduyn, 1990; Black et al., 1998; Hafner, 1982; Hafner et al., 1981; Tynes, Salins, & Winstead, 1990). Additional data regarding such responses in relatives have been generated through studies of expressed emotion (EE). EE is an index of relatives' expressed attitudes regarding a psychiatric patient, usually generated from objective coding of a semistructured interview with the relative (Leff & Vaughn, 1985). EE includes three primary components: (1) criticism, which is a frequency count of critical comments made during the interview; (2) hostility, which is an overall rating of a relative's global rejection of the patient during the interview; and (3) emotional overinvolvement (EOI), which is an overall rating of excessive emotionality, self-sacrifice, and/or intrusiveness on the part of the relative. Many investigators combine these three components into one overall rating, such that relatives who are high on one or more of these dimensions are considered high EE. In practice, high EE ratings typically reflect high levels of criticism and/or hostility, rather than EOI (Butzlaff & Hooley, 1998). The constructs of criticism and hostility are clearly related, but they are distinguishable, in that criticism represents circumscribed, focused negative comments about the patient (e.g., "I think he could work harder in treatment"), whereas hostility represents a more globalized, harshly rejecting attitude (e.g., "He's lazy and no good").

In one study of 49 children with OCD, Hibbs and colleagues (1991) found that 82% of the sample had at least one parent rated as high EE. In a more fine-grained analysis, Chambless and Steketee (1999) investigated the components of EE separately and found that 40% of relatives of 101 adults with OCD or PD were high in criticism, with an additional 33% high in hostility. Interestingly, many relatives in this and other samples have reported that, when they criticized patients, they did so with the intent of trying to help the patient change his or her behavior (e.g., Chambless, Bryan, Aiken, Steketee, & Hooley, 1999; Tynes et al., 1990). Thus, it may be that circumscribed criticism does not necessarily reflect malicious intent, whereas overt hostility is more strongly tied to anger and resentment in relatives.

As with many disorders (see meta-analysis by Butzlaff & Hooley, 1998), harsh, hostile attitudes in relatives have been linked to poorer treatment response and higher rates of relapse in patients with OCD (Chambless & Steketee, 1999; Emmelkamp, Kloek, & Blaauw, 1992; Leonard et al., 1993; Steketee, 1993). Findings with regard to the effect of relatives' circumscribed criticism, however, are less clear. In the only study to date that investigated the effects of objective ratings of relatives' circumscribed criticism and global hostility separately, Chambless and Steketee (1999) found that, when controlling for hostility, criticism in relatives was actually associated with better response in 60 outpatients with OCD and 41 patients with PD treated with exposure-based therapies. This result was similar to that obtained in a sample of adults with PD (Peter & Hand, 1988), and it was recently replicated in a sample of patients with GAD (Zinbarg, Lee, & Yoon, 2007). Similarly, Mehta (1990, p. 135) noted that "[n]onanxious, firm relatives were more successful than anxious and inconsistent family members" in a trial of family-based ERP for adults with OCD, although there was no formal assessment of these factors in this study.

This pattern is in contrast to that observed in most other disorders, for which criticism in any form is associated with poorer outcomes (Butzlaff & Hooley, 1998), but it can be viewed as consistent with the highly difficult nature of exposure-based therapy. Specifically, focused criticism that is not globally rejecting of the patient may help keep patients motivated for such a difficult treatment, without creating an environment of increased interpersonal stress. Thus, although it is clear that high levels of anger and hostility are detrimental for individuals with OCD, it is plausible that a firm but respectful stance could be more beneficial than simple, unconditional support. Future research that distinguishes between hostile and nonhostile criticism thus has the potential to further our knowledge about the interpersonal environments of those with OCD.

Family Accommodation

Whereas criticism and hostility are seen in relatives of individuals with many disorders, an area of family impairment that appears somewhat unique to OCD (and some other anxiety disorders) is that of accommodation, sometimes referred to as family involvement. In the case of OCD, family accommodation consists of behaviors that facilitate the completion of patients' compulsions. These behaviors may include providing the patient with additional time (e.g., making excuses for patients' lateness) or materials (e.g., cleaning supplies) needed to complete their rituals, taking care of patients' obligations that are left unmet due to obsessions or compulsions, or even participating in rituals, such as checking appliances or helping patients clean. Relatives may engage in such behaviors for a wide variety of reasons. Calvocoressi and colleagues (1999) noted that 57% of relatives of those with OCD reported sometimes engaging in accommodating patients' rituals to reduce patients' distress or anger, while 76% of relatives said that they engaged in accommodation

to reduce time spent on rituals. Accommodating behaviors can be assessed in a number of ways, the most common of which is a 12-item scale of clinician ratings known as the Family Accommodation Scale (FAS; Calvocoressi et al., 1995, 1999).

Studies using the FAS and other measures indicate that between 67% and 100% of relatives of those with OCD engage in some level of accommodating behavior (Allsopp & Verduyn, 1990; Black et al., 1998; Bolton, Collins, & Steinberg, 1983; Calvocoressi et al., 1995, 1999; Cooper, 1993; Shafran et al., 1995; Storch et al., 2007a). Moreover, several family members report actual participation in rituals, with percentages ranging from 50% to 76% of parents of children with OCD (Allsopp & Verduyn, 1990; Cooper, 1996; Storch et al., 2007) and 39% to 67% of relatives of adults with OCD (Black et al., 1998; Calvocoressi et al., 1995, 1999; Cooper, 1996; Shafran et al., 1995). Furthermore, Shafran and colleagues (1995) noted that, when asked directly about participation in rituals, only 2% of relatives of adults in their sample denied ever having engaged in such participation. Preliminary evidence also suggests that accommodation is not limited to parents and spouses, as two studies have documented accommodation in siblings of children with OCD (Barrett, Healy-Farrell, & March, 2004; Barrett, Rasmussen, & Healy, 2000). The degree of relatives' accommodating behaviors is generally correlated with the severity of patients' symptoms and functioning (Calvocoressi et al., 1999; Storch et al., 2007), particularly compulsions (Amir et al., 2000).

Although accommodation is often intended to reduce short-term strain and embarrassment, research indicates that this type of behavior is actually related to higher levels of overall psychological and familial distress in relatives. Cooper (1996) found that 75% of relatives of children and 58% of relatives of adults with OCD reported significant distress as a result of accommodating patients' rituals. Calvocoressi and colleagues found levels of accommodation to be positively correlated with family dysfunction (1999) and general distress in relatives (1995), with over two-thirds of relatives reporting at least mild distress associated with accommodation (1995). Similarly, Amir and colleagues (2000) found that higher levels of accommodation were related to higher levels of both depression and anxiety in 73 relatives of children and adults with OCD. Finally, Albert and colleagues (2007) found that higher accommodation was related to greater impairment in multiple domains of functioning, in 64 Italian relatives of adults with OCD.

Surprisingly, we were unable to identify any studies of the association of accommodation in parents with treatment outcome in children and adolescents, but ample evidence suggests that accommodation in relatives is associated with poorer prognosis for adults with OCD. Amir and colleagues (2000) found that patients improved less in ERP when relatives reported greater modification of their functioning to accommodate patients' symptoms. In this sample, higher pretreatment levels of relatives' participation in rituals also had a medium-sized (Cohen, 1988) association with poorer treatment response, although this association was nonsignificant due to the small sample size. Steketee (1993) found that decreases in significant others' participation in rituals, 6 to 14 months after individual ERP, were associated with better outcomes for patients. Finally, although accommodation is not fully equivalent to EE-related EOI, the two constructs are similar, and Chambless and Steketee (1999) reported that higher rates of EOI in relatives were associated with greater likelihood of dropping out of exposure-based therapy. In a follow-up to this study, Renshaw, Chambless, and Steketee (2006) also found that patients whose relatives attributed patients' problems directly to their OCD had worse treatment outcome than patients whose relatives made no such attributions.

Preliminary evidence suggests that that accommodation is also responsive to treatment. Storch and colleagues (2007b) found that parents who participated in family-based CBT with their children experienced significant decreases in their levels of accommodation, although this improvement deteriorated somewhat by 3-month follow-up. Waters, Barrett, and March (2001) also found significant decreases in parents' accommodation following family-based CBT for 7 children aged 10 to 14 years old; however, they did not report whether these gains were maintained at follow-up. Finally, in a review of family factors in the context of OCD, Maina, Saracco, and Albert (2006) reported that 22 relatives of adults with OCD, who participated in family-only groups that involved psychoeducation about OCD, experienced decreases in accommodation and burden. The authors, however, did not examine these changes in relation to treatment outcome for patients themselves.

Based on these findings, nearly all family-based treatments for OCD include some explicit attempt to reduce accommodation in relatives (e.g., Albert,

Maina, Saracco, & Bogetto, 2006; March & Mulle, 1998; Piacentini, Gitow, Jaffer, Graae, & Whitaker, 1994; Van Noppen, Steketee, McCorkle, & Pato, 1997). Thus, it is surprising that more researchers have not examined changes in accommodation following individual or family-based treatments for OCD. Although more research of this type is clearly needed, it does appear that accommodation, like overt hostility, is highly prevalent in families of individuals with OCD and, moreover, is linked to worse treatment outcome in patients, and greater distress in relatives.

Interpersonal Model of OCD

Although prior reports have proposed that accommodation and antagonistic behaviors lie at opposite ends of a single continuum of family response to OCD symptoms (e.g., Livingston-Van Noppen et al., 1990; Renshaw et al., 2005; Van Noppen et al., 1991), a closer examination of the evidence suggests that these two styles of responding frequently coexist in relatives. Calvocoressi and colleagues (1999) noted that 40% of relatives reported being critical or hostile toward patients when engaging in accommodating behaviors, and relatives' overall levels of accommodation were highly correlated with a measure of their rejection of patients. In an analysis of several variables related to relatives' responses to patients, Chambless, Bryan, Aiken, Steketee, and Hooley (1999) found EOI, criticism, and positivity all formed independent factors, with a very low correlation (−.05) between the EOI and criticism factors. Przeworski and colleagues (1999a, 1999b) also found that parents with higher levels of accommodation displayed higher levels of anger during problem-solving interactions with their children with OCD (as cited in Freeman and colleagues, 2003). Multiple case reports also support an overlap between accommodation and hostility (e.g., Steketee & White, 1990). Thus, it appears that these two types of responding are actually independent dimensions of behavior, and if anything, they are positively rather than negatively related to each other.

Based on this knowledge, and the findings reviewed above, we recently proposed an interpersonal model of OCD that conceptualizes the potential transactions among patients' symptoms and relatives' behaviors from a behavioral perspective of OCD (Renshaw, Steketee, Rodrigues, & Caska, 2010; see Figure 9.1). On the one hand, accommodating patients' rituals may negatively reinforce the anxiety-reducing effect of those rituals, and also prevent patients from learning that feared consequences

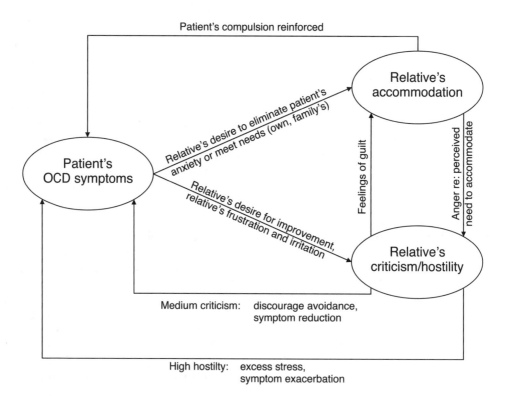

Fig. 9.1. Transactional model of patient's OCD symptoms and relative's accommodating and critical responses.

may not occur even if they do not engage in their compulsions. Also, such behaviors have the potential to undermine patients' beliefs that they can handle their obsessions without ritualizing, and could interfere with exposure assignments that are essential to the successful implementation of ERP for OCD. On the other hand, extreme levels of hostility can create an environment of high interpersonal stress, and greater stress has been associated with exacerbations of OCD symptoms (e.g., Horowitz, 1975). However, a moderate level of circumscribed, non-attacking criticism might provide patients with the necessary motivation to engage in the difficult treatment of ERP, without creating undue interpersonal strain. There is preliminary evidence that such moderate, nonhostile criticism may represent the ideal interpersonal environment for individuals who are undergoing ERP. Moreover, in theory, such an environment could even prove helpful to those with subclinical OC tendencies, by providing them with encouragement to confront feared situations, and thereby learn that anxiety reduces naturally, before serious compulsive behaviors develop.

This model represents a preliminary attempt to integrate the predominant findings regarding interpersonal variables and OCD. However, several questions remain: (1) How can one best assess this type of circumscribed, nonhostile criticism? (2) Are there some patients for whom such criticism is not helpful (e.g., those with comorbid depression)? (3) How can interventions help families attain an interpersonal environment that maximizes the chances for successful response to ERP? (4) Is nonhostile criticism associated with better response to other forms of treatment for OCD, such as SSRIs? These questions represent some of the primary needs for future interpersonally focused research on OCD.

Family-Based Treatment of OCD
Children

Treatment parameters put forth by the American Academy of Child and Adolescent Psychiatry (1998) advocate for the involvement of the family in treatment planning and execution for OCD in children and adolescents. In line with these parameters, nearly all treatment manuals typically consist of some form of ERP-based intervention combined with some level of parental involvement (e.g., Albano, Knox, & Barlow, 1995; Bolton, Collins, & Steinberg, 1983; Franklin et al., 1998; March,

Mulle, & Herbel, 1994; March & Mulle, 1998; Piacentini et al., 1994; Waters, Barrett, & March, 2001; see review by Freeman et al., 2003). Most approaches entail psychoeducation about OCD and ERP for parents, to help them better understand their child's disorder and prepare for the difficult process of ERP (e.g., March & Mulle, 1998; Piacentini et al., 1994; Waters et al., 2001). Such education typically takes place in initial sessions, before exposure begins.

Other approaches also involve parents as coaches or co-therapists, with the child's permission (e.g., March & Mulle, 1998). These activities typically include having parents help plan and enact exposure assignments, while receiving coaching as to how they can best assist the child to carry out exposures and to resist compulsive behaviors, without using emotional or physical force. In this type of approach, parents are usually involved in most, if not all, therapy sessions.

Finally, some approaches include more formalized training for parents in general skills, such as behavioral techniques and communication skills, and in reducing accommodating and/or hostile responses (e.g., March & Mulle, 1998; Waters et al., 2001). At times, this type of training involves separate sessions with parents, but it is often done in the context of family sessions. In addition to variation across manuals, most approaches prescribe flexibility in terms of parental involvement, leaving the extent of parental inclusion to clinical judgment (e.g., March & Mulle, 1998). Thus, there is rarely a standardized level of family involvement in studies of family-based treatment of OCD in children and adolescents.

Several case studies, pilot studies, open trials, and randomly controlled trials of ERP with parent involvement have now been conducted, all of which demonstrate that children and adolescents who receive such treatment have significant improvements in OCD symptoms at post-treatment and follow-up (Barrett, Healy, & March, 2003; Barrett, Healy-Farrell, & March, 2004; Barrett, Farrell, Dadds, & Boulter, 2005; Fischer, Himle, & Hanna, 1998; Franklin et al. 1998; Himle, Fischer, Van Etten, Janeck, & Hanna, 2003; Knox, Albano, & Barlow, 1996; March et al., 1994; Piacentini et al., 2002; Piacentini & Langley, 2004; Scahill, Vitulano, Brenner, Lynch, & King, 1996; Storch et al., 2007; Thienemann, Martin, Cregger, Thompson, & Dyer-Friedman, 2001; Waters et al., 2001; Wever & Rey, 1997). Some of these reports have also noted post-treatment improvements in family functioning,

including decreased levels of accommodation in parents (Piacentini & Langley, 2004; Storch et al., 2007; Waters et al., 2001), but others have failed to detect such improvements (Barrett et al., 2004; Thienemann et al., 2001). Although these studies offer abundant evidence that ERP with family involvement is successful in treating OCD in children, no one has yet systematically investigated the necessity of parental involvement in the treatment. The closest approximation of such an examination is a multiple baseline study of 4 children with OCD, who were treated for 2 weeks with intensive individual ERP, followed by 2 more weeks of intensive ERP with their parents included (Knox et al., 1996). Although there was significantly greater improvement after the second 2-week period of treatment that included parents, it is impossible to know whether this improvement was due to the addition of parents, or the accumulation of treatment effects over time. Thus, as yet, there is no empirical evidence regarding the specific effects of family involvement in the treatment of OCD in children.

Adults

In contrast to the literature on treatment of children and adolescents, there are scores of studies of individually (or group) administered ERP and other treatments for adults with OCD (see Chapters 17–20), but few of these included family members. Emmelkamp and colleagues conducted two studies of patients with OCD and their spouses/romantic partners, in which patients were randomly assigned to either individual ERP or partner-assisted ERP (Emmelkamp, de Haan, & Hoogduin, 1990; Emmelkamp & DeLange, 1983). In the partner-assisted format, partners were included in sessions and instructed to (a) resist providing reassurance to patients regarding their obsessions, and (b) encourage patients to persist when faced with difficult exposure assignments. In the first study, six adults in the partner-assisted condition had significantly greater improvement after treatment than six who received individual therapy, but the differences were no longer significant at 1-month follow-up (Emmelkamp & DeLange, 1983). In a larger study of 50 adults with OCD, no differences between the individual and partner-assisted groups were detected at post-treatment or follow-up (Emmelkamp et al., 1990). Unfortunately, in both of these studies, ERP consisted of only eight or ten 45-minute sessions with no in-session exposures, which is far below the standard recommendations for ERP (e.g., Foa & Kozak, 1996), and the effect sizes (ESs) for treatment response (0.41 and 0.46) were much lower than typically found in studies of standard ERP (1.47 to 3.50; see review by Franklin & Foa, 2002). Thus, it is not clear that these results provide reliable information about the effect of partner inclusion on patients' response to standard ERP.

Van Noppen, Steketee, McCorkle, and Pato (1997) investigated the effect of family involvement for adults with OCD, 17 of whom received standard ERP in a group format, and 19 of whom participated in multifamily groups. These multifamily groups included standard ERP interventions, together with psychoeducation for relatives, discussion of relatives' reactions to symptoms, inclusion of relatives in planning exposure assignments, and establishing communication patterns for dealing with exposure assignments and OCD symptoms. Although treatment response was not significantly different between the two groups, the authors noted that greater percentages of patients in multifamily groups achieved reliable change (74%) and clinically significant improvement (67%), as compared with patients in the standard ERP groups (44% and 57%, respectively). Once again, ESs detected in this study (1.01 at post-test for those in patient-only groups; 1.38 at post-test for those in multifamily groups) were somewhat lower than in studies of traditional individual ERP, which may have been due to the use of group rather than individual format. This difference, coupled with the relatively low sample size, complicates the interpretation of results in terms of the effect of including family members in standard ERP.

Mehta (1990) tested the effects of family inclusion in a sample of 30 adults with OCD in India, using a more standard version of ERP, which included 24 sessions held twice per week. Half of the participants received ERP individually, and the other half received a family-based version of ERP, in which family members were involved as co-therapists, participated in ERP assignments, and were encouraged to avoid accommodation and be supportive. In contrast to the studies with lower-intensity ERP described above, the ESs associated with treatment response in both groups were more similar to those detected in other studies of standard ERP, with an ES of 1.44 for individual ERP and 2.11 for family-based ERP. Patients who received the family-based version of ERP made significantly greater gains than those who received standard individual ERP, a difference that was maintained at 1-month follow-up.

Finally, Grunes, Neziroglu, and McKay (2001) tested the effects of an 8-week family-only group as an adjunct to standard individual ERP for 22 adults and 6 children, with mostly treatment-refractory OCD (the majority of patients had already been in behavior therapy for at least 6 months). Half of the patients' relatives were randomized to the adjunctive groups, and the other half were assigned to receive no additional treatment. The family-only groups included psychoeducation and targeted attempts to reduce accommodating, and harshly critical responses of family members. Analyses revealed that patients whose family members did not participate in the groups showed little treatment response (consistent with their treatment-refractory status), whereas those whose family members participated in the groups had significantly greater improvement in their symptoms at post-treatment and at 1-month follow-up. Interestingly, all family members experienced significant reductions in depression, anxiety, and accommodation after completion of ERP, but those in the family groups experienced significantly greater reductions than those in the control condition. A similar family-only group has been created in Italy (Albert et al., 2006) with similar positive effects for family members, but the authors have not reported on whether such groups result in enhanced treatment response for OCD patients, as well.

Conclusions and Future Directions

Mounting evidence supports the notion that OCD is associated with a variety of interpersonal problems and, in turn, the interpersonal environment of individuals with OCD can affect response to standard treatments like ERP. Children and adults with OCD demonstrate impaired functioning in social and family relationships, and relatives of those with OCD report elevated levels of relationship and psychological distress. Furthermore, relatives' accommodating behaviors and interpersonal hostility, in particular, appear to reduce the effectiveness of ERP for those with OCD. Finally, emerging evidence suggests that some level of nonhostile criticism in relatives may actually enhance patients' response to ERP. Given these findings, future research in this area is needed to: *(1)* further our understanding of nonhostile criticism and its potentially beneficial effects; *(2)* learn how to best integrate family members into ERP for OCD, and whether the extra time and cost of such efforts are justified by the level of improved response (if any); and *(3)* investigate whether interpersonal processes also have an impact on response to other treatments, such as psychotropic medication.

Further research into nonhostile criticism should address how to best define and measure such criticism, whether certain subgroups of individuals with OCD are more or less likely to benefit from it, and what factors in patients and relatives are associated with it. Currently, it is unclear whether nonhostile criticism should be assessed by an outside observer (e.g., objective coder, therapist) or by the individual with OCD. In other words, which is of primary importance: that relatives deliver criticism in a way that would be seen as constructive and non-attacking by an objective observer, or that individuals with OCD perceive a relative as non-hostilely critical? This question also has some bearing on the issue of whether some individuals are more or less likely to benefit from nonhostile criticism. Recent research suggests that people with higher levels of depressive symptoms are less likely to view criticism from others as nonhostile (Renshaw, Blais, & Caska, 2010). Thus, it is possible that individuals with OCD and comorbid depression are less likely to benefit from nonhostile criticism, if a key component of such criticism is the perception of the individual with OCD. Future research in this area that includes multiple methods of assessment of criticism from others, and an assessment of comorbid conditions, can help address these issues. Also, research on individual and relationship-level factors that are associated with nonhostile criticism, in relatives of those with OCD, can help inform us about how to intervene with relatives to facilitate an optimal interpersonal environment.

Findings from the type of research described above can be combined with existing knowledge to help design or refine interventions that incorporate family members into treatment for those with OCD. The small amount of prior research in this area has focused on providing psychoeducation, attempting to alleviate relatives' distress due to patients' OCD, and incorporating relatives as coaches in exposure assignments. Although these methods appear beneficial, the mechanisms by which these interventions serve to enhance treatment response in those with OCD (e.g., possibly by decreasing hostility and/or accommodation) have not yet been established. Future research in this area also should attempt to examine which relatives (and patients) seem to benefit most from which types of procedures. For example, different approaches are likely needed for relatives who are high in hostility and low in accommodation, versus those who are low in hostility and high in accommodation.

Finally, future research that examines whether and how interpersonal processes play a role in response to psychiatric treatment for OCD (e.g., SSRIs) is needed. Although purely biological models of OCD would not necessarily support the existence of a link between interpersonal processes and response to medication, given the wealth of research suggesting that multiple factors influence the development and progression of OCD, it is entirely possible that interpersonal processes might interact with response to biologically driven treatment. Basic research that simply examines associations of the interpersonal environment with response to medication, in those with OCD, could help begin to address this question.

Overall, the importance of interpersonal processes for those with OCD appears clear, and the findings that have emerged are consistent with a behavioral conceptualization of the disorder. Given the preliminary evidence that incorporating relatives into treatment might improve the overall response to ERP (Grunes et al., 2001; Mehta, 1990; Van Noppen et al., 1997), this is an area that deserves greater attention in the future.

Related Chapters

Chapter 14. Assessing Comorbidity, Insight, Family, and Functioning in OCD

References

Abbey, R. D., Clopton, J. R., & Humphreys, J. D. (2007). Obsessive-compulsive disorder and romantic functioning. *Journal of Clinical Psychology, 63,* 1181–1192.

Albano, A. M., Knox, L. S., & Barlow, D. H. (1995). Obsessive-compulsive disorder. In A. Eisen, C. Kearney, & C. Schafer (Eds.), *Clinical handbook of anxiety disorders in children and adolescents* (pp. 282–316). Northvale, NJ: Jason Aaronson.

Albert, U., Maina, G., Saracco, P., & Bogetto, F. (2006). L'intervento psicoeducazionale multifamiliare (IPM) nel disturbo ossessivo-compulsivo: Uno studio pilota. *Epidemiologia e Psichiatria Sociale, 15,* 69–74.

Albert, U., Salvi, V., Saracco, P., Bogetto, F. & Maina, G. (2007). Health-related quality of life among first degree relatives of patients with obsessive-compulsive disorder in Italy. *Psychiatric Services, 58,* 970–976.

Allsopp, M., & Verduyn, C. (1990). Adolescents with obsessive-compulsive disorder: A case note review of consecutive patients referred to a provincial regional adolescent psychiatry unit. *Journal of Adolescence, 13,* 157–169.

Alonso, P., Menchón, J. M., Mataix-Cols, D., Pifarré, J., Urretavizcaya, M., Crespo, J. M., Jiménez, S., Vallejo, G., & Vallejo, J. (2004). Perceived parental rearing style in obsessive-compulsive disorder: Relation to symptom dimensions. *Psychiatry Research, 127,* 267–278.

American Academy of Child and Adolescent Psychiatry (1998). Practice parameters for the assessment and treatment of children and adolescents with obsessive-compulsive disorder.

Journal of the American Academy of Child and Adolescent Psychiatry, 37(Suppl. 10), 27S–45S.

Amir, N., Freshman, M., & Foa, E. B. (2000). Family distress and involvement in relatives of obsessive-compulsive disorder patients. *Journal of Anxiety Disorders, 14,* 209–217.

Barrett, P., Farrell, L., Dadds, M., & Boulter, N. (2005). Cognitive-behavioral family treatment of childhood obsessive-compulsive disorder: Long-term follow-up and predictors of outcome. *Journal of the American Academy of Child and Adolescent Psychiatry, 44,* 1005–1014.

Barrett, P., Healy, L., & March, J. S. (2003). Behavioral avoidance test for childhood obsessive-compulsive disorder: A home-based observation. *American Journal of Psychotherapy, 57,* 80–100.

Barrett, P., Healy-Farrell, L., & March, J. S. (2004). Cognitive-behavioral family treatment of childhood obsessive-compulsive disorder: A controlled trial. *Journal of the American Academy of Child and Adolescent Psychiatry, 43,* 46–62.

Barrett, P. M., Rapee, R. M., Dadds, M. M., & Ryan, S. M. (1996). Family enhancement of cognitive style in anxious and aggressive children. *Journal of Abnormal Child Psychology, 24,* 187–203.

Barrett, P. M., Rasmussen, P. J., & Healy, L. (2000). The effect of obsessive compulsive disorder on sibling relationships in late childhood and early adolescence: Preliminary findings. *Australian Educational and Developmental Psychologist, 17,* 82–102.

Barrett, P., Shortt, A., & Healy, L. (2002). Do parent and child behaviours differentiate families whose children have obsessive-compulsive disorder from other clinic and nonclinic families? *Journal of Child Psychology and Psychiatry, 43,* 597–607.

Black, D. W., Gaffney, G., Schlosser, S., & Gabel, J. (1998). The impact of obsessive-compulsive disorder on the family: Preliminary findings. *Journal of Nervous and Mental Disease, 186,* 440–442.

Black, D. W., Gaffney, G. R., Schlosser, S., & Gabel, J. (2003). Children of parents with obsessive-compulsive disorder–A 2-year follow up study. *Acta Psychiatrica Scandinavica, 107,* 305–313.

Bobes, J., González, M. P., Bascarán, M. T., Arango, C., Sáiz, P. A., & Bousoño, M. (2001). Quality of life and disability in patients with obsessive-compulsive disorder. *European Psychiatry, 16,* 239–245.

Bolton, D., Collins, S., & Steinberg, D. (1983). The treatment of obsessive-compulsive disorder in adolescence–A report of 15 cases. *British Journal of Psychiatry, 142,* 456–464.

Bolton, D., Luckie, M., & Steinberg, D. (1995). Long-term course of obsessive-compulsive disorder treated in adolescence. *Journal of the American Academy of Child and Adolescent Psychiatry, 34,* 1441–1450.

Butzlaff, R. L., & Hooley, J. M. (1998). Expressed emotion and psychiatric relapse: A meta-analysis. *Archives of General Psychiatry, 55,* 547–552.

Bystritsky, A., Liberman, R. P., Hwang, S., Wallace, C. J., Vapnik, T., Maindment, K., & Sexena, S. (2001). Social functioning and quality of life comparisons between obsessive-compulsive and schizophrenic disorders. *Depression and Anxiety, 14,* 214–218.

Calvocoressi, L., Lewis, B., Harris, M., Trufan, S. J., Goodman, W. K., McDougle, C. J., & Price, L. H. (1995). Family accommodation in obsessive-compulsive disorder. *American Journal of Psychiatry, 152,* 441–443.

Calvocoressi, L., Mazure, C. M., Kasl, S. V., Skolnick, J., Fisk, D., Vegso, S. J., Van Noppen, B. L., & Price, L. H. (1999). Reliability and validity of the family accommodation scale for obsessive-compulsive disorder. *Journal of Nervous and Mental Disease, 187,* 636–642.

Cavedo, L. C., & Parker, G. (1994). Parental Bonding Instrument: Exploring links between scores and obsessionality. *Social Psychiatry and Psychiatric Epidemiology, 29,* 78–82.

Chambless, D. L., Bryan, A. D., Aiken, L. S., Steketee, G., & Hooley, J. (1999). The structure of expressed emotion: A three-construct representation. *Psychological Assessment, 11,* 67–76.

Chambless, D. L., Gillis, M. M., Tran, G. Q., & Steketee, G. S. (1996). Parental bonding reports of clients with obsessive-compulsive disorder and agoraphobia. *Clinical Psychology and Psychotherapy, 3,* 77–85.

Chambless, D. L., & Steketee, G. (1999). Expressed emotion and behavior therapy outcome: A prospective study with obsessive-compulsive and agoraphobic outpatients. *Journal of Consulting and Clinical Psychology, 67,* 658–665.

Chorpita, B. F., Albano, A. M., & Barlow, D. H. (1996). Cognitive processing in children: Relation to anxiety and family influences. *Journal of Clinical Child Psychology, 25,* 170–176.

Cohen, J. (1988). *Statistical power analysis for the behavior sciences.* Hillsdale, NJ: Earlbaum.

Cooper, M. (1993). A group for families of obsessive-compulsive persons. *Families in Society, 74,* 301–307.

Cooper, M. (1996). Obsessive-compulsive disorder: Effects on family members. *American Journal of Orthopsychiatry, 66,* 296–304.

Cramer, V., Torgersen, S., & Kringlen, E. (2005). Quality of life and anxiety disorders: A population study. *Journal of Nervous and Mental Disease, 193,* 196–202.

Derisley, J., Libby, S., Clark, S., & Reynolds, S. (2005). Mental health, coping and family-functioning in parents of young people with obsessive-compulsive disorder and with anxiety disorders. *British Journal of Clinical Psychology, 44,* 439–444.

Derogatis, L. R. (1994). *SCL-90-R: Administration, Scoring and Procedures Manual.* National Computer Systems: Minneapolis, MN.

Diefenbach, G. J., Abramowitz, J. S., Norberg, M. M., & Tolin, D. F. (2007). Changes in quality of life following cognitive-behavioral therapy for obsessive compulsive disorder. *Behaviour Research and Therapy, 45,* 3060–3068.

Ehiobuche, I. (1988). Obsessive-compulsive neurosis in relation to parental child-rearing patterns amongst the Greek, Italian, and Anglo-Australian subjects. *Acta Psychiatrica Scandinavica, 78(S344),* 115–120.

Eisen, J. L., Mancebo, M. A., Pinto, A., Coles, M. E., Pagano, M. E., Stout, R., & Rasmussen, S. A. (2006). Impact of obsessive-compulsive disorder on quality of life. *Comprehensive Psychiatry, 47,* 270–275.

Emmelkamp, P. M., de Haan, E., & Hoogduin, C. A. (1990). Marital adjustment and obsessive-compulsive disorder. *British Journal of Psychiatry, 156,* 55–60.

Emmelkamp, P. M., & de Lange, I. (1983). Spouse involvement in the treatment of obsessive-compulsive patients. *Behavior Research and Therapy, 21,* 341–346.

Emmelkamp, P. M. G., Kloek, J., & Blaauw, E. (1992). Obsessive-compulsive disorders in principles and practice of relapse prevention. In P. H. Wilson (Ed.), *Principles and practice of relapse prevention* (pp. 213–234). New York: Guilford.

Epstein, N. B., Baldwin, L., & Bishop, D. S. (1983). The McMaster Family Assessment Device. *Journal of Marital and Family Therapy, 9,* 171–180.

Erol, A., Yazici, F., & Toprak, G. (2007). Family functioning of patients with an eating disorder compared with that of patients with obsessive compulsive disorder. *Comprehensive Psychiatry, 48,* 47–50.

Farrell, L., Barrett, P., & Piacentini, J. (2006). Obsessive-compulsive disorder across the developmental trajectory: Clinical correlates in children, adolescents and adults. *Behaviour Change, 23,* 103–120.

Ferrão, Y. A., Shavitt, R. G., Bedin, N. R., de Mathis, M. E., Lopes, A. C., Fontenelle, L. F., Torres, A. R., & Miguel, E. C. (2006). Clinical features associated to refractory obsessive-compulsive disorder. *Journal of Affective Disorders, 94,* 199–209.

First, M. B., Spitzer, R. L., Gibbon, M., & Williams, J. B. W. (1998). *Structured Clinical Interview for DSM-IV Axis I Disorders–Patient Edition (SCIDI/P, Version 2.0, 8/98 Revision).* New York: Biometric Research, New York State Psychiatric Institute.

Fischer, D., Himle, J., & Hanna, G. (1998). Group behavioral therapy for adolescents with obsessive-compulsive disorder: preliminary outcomes. *Research on Social Work Practice, 8,* 629–636.

Foa, E. B., Grayson, J. B., Steketee, G. S., Doppelt, H. G., Turner, R. M., & Latimer, P. R. (1983). Success and failure in the behavioral treatment of obsessive-compulsives. *Journal of Consulting and Clinical Psychology, 51,* 287–297.

Foa, E. B., & Kozak, M. J. (1996). Psychological treatment for obsessive-compulsive disorder. In M. R. Mavissakalian, & R. F. Prien (Eds.), *Long-term treatment of anxiety disorders* (pp. 285–309). Washington, DC: American Psychiatric Press.

Franklin, M. E., & Foa, E. B. (2002). Cognitive behavioral treatments for obsessive compulsive disorder. In: P. E. Nathan & J. M. Gorman (Eds.), *A guide to treatments that work (2nd ed.)* (pp. 367–386). New York: Oxford University Press.

Franklin, M. E., Kozak, M. J., Cashman, L. A., Coles, M. E., Rheingold, A. A. & Foa, E. B. (1998). Cognitive-behavioral treatment of pediatric obsessive-compulsive disorder: An open clinical trial. *Journal of American Academy of Child and Adolescent Psychiatry, 37,* 412–419.

Freeman, J. B., Garcia, A. M., Fucci, C., Karitani, M., Miller, L., & Leonard, H. L. (2003). Family-based treatment of early-onset obsessive-compulsive disorder. *Journal of Child and Adolescent Psychopharmacology, 13,* S71–S80.

Frost, R. O., Steketee, G., Cohn, L., & Griess, K. (1994). Personality traits in subclinical and non-obsessive compulsive volunteers and their parents. *Behaviour Research and Therapy, 32,* 47–56.

Frost, R. O., Steketee, G., Williams, L. F., & Warren, R. (2000). Mood, personality disorder symptoms and disability in obsessive compulsive hoarders: A comparison with clinical and nonclinical controls. *Behaviour Research and Therapy, 38,* 1071–1081.

Grunes, M. S., Neziroglu, F., & McKay, D. (2001). Family involvement in the behavioral treatment of obsessive-compulsive disorder: A preliminary investigation. *Behavior Therapy, 32,* 803–820.

Hanna, G. L. (1995). Demographic and clinical features of obsessive-compulsive disorder in children and adolescents. *Journal of the American Academy of Child and Adolescent Psychiatry, 34,* 19–27.

Hafner, R. J. (1982). Marital interaction in persisting obsessive-compulsive disorders. *Australian and New Zealand Journal of Psychiatry, 16,* 171–178.

Hafner, R. J. (1988). Obsessive-compulsive disorder: A questionnaire survey of a self-help group. *International Journal of Social Psychiatry, 34,* 310–315.

Hafner, R. J., Gilchrist, P., Bowling, J., & Kahicy, R. (1981). The treatment of obsessional neurosis in a family setting. *Australian and New Zealand Journal of Psychiatry, 15,* 145–151.

Hibbs, E. D., Hamburger, S. D., Lenane, M., Rapoport, J. L., Kruesi, M. J. P., Keysor, C. S., & Goldstein, M. J. (1991). Determinants of expressed emotion in families of disturbed and normal children. *Journal of Child Psychology and Psychiatry, 32,* 757–770.

Himle, J. A., Fischer, D. J., Van Etten, M. L., Janeck, A. S., & Hanna, G. L. (2003). Group behavioral therapy for adolescents with tic-related and non-tic-related obsessive-compulsive disorder. *Depression and Anxiety, 17,* 73–77

Hollander, E., Kwon, J. H., Stein, D. J., Broatch, J., Rowland, C. T., & Himelein, C. A. (1996). Obsessive-compulsive and spectrum disorders: Overview and quality of life issues. *Journal of Clinical Psychiatry, 57(suppl 8),* 3–6.

Hollander, E., Stein, D., Kwon, J., Rowland, C., Wong, C., Broatch, J., & Himelein, C. A. (1997). Psychosocial function and economic costs of obsessive-compulsive disorder. *CNS Spectrums: International Journal of Neuropsychiatric Medicine, 2,* 16–25.

Hoogduin, C. A., & Duivenvoorden, H. J. (1988). A decision model in the treatment of obsessive-compulsive neuroses. *British Journal of Psychiatry, 152,* 516–521.

Hoover, C. F., & Insel, T. R. (1984). Families of origin in obsessive-compulsive disorder. *Journal of Nervous and Mental Disease, 172,* 207–215.

Horowitz, M. (1975). Intrusive and repetitive thoughts after experimental stress. *Archives of General Psychiatry, 32,* 1457–1463.

Jacobi, D. M., Calamari, J. E., & Woodard, J. L. (2006). Obsessive-compulsive disorder beliefs, metacognitive beliefs and obsessional symptoms: Relations between parent beliefs and child symptoms. *Clinical Psychology and Psychotherapy, 13,* 153–162.

Jayakumar, C., Jagadheesan, K., & Verma, A. N. (2002). Caregiver's burden: A comparison between obsessive compulsive disorder and schizophrenia. *Indian Journal of Psychiatry, 44,* 337–342.

Khanna, S., Rajendra, P. N., & Channabasavanna, S. M. (1988). Social adjustment in obsessive compulsive disorder. *The International Journal of Social Psychiatry, 34,* 118–122.

Kimidis, S., Minas, I. H., Ata, A. W., & Stuart, G. W. (1992). Construct validation in adolescents of the brief current form of the Parental Bonding Instrument. *Comprehensive Psychiatry, 33,* 378–383.

Knox, L. S., Albano, A. M., & Barlow, D. H. (1996). Parental involvement in the treatment of childhood obsessive compulsive disorder: a multiple baseline examination incorporating parents. *Behavior Therapy, 27,* 93–115.

Koran, L. M. (2000). Quality of life in obsessive-compulsive disorder. *Psychiatric Clinics of North America, 23,* 509–517.

Koran, L. M., Thienemann, M. L., & Davenport, R. (1996). Quality of life for patients with obsessive-compulsive disorder. *American Journal of Psychiatry, 153,* 783–788.

Leff, J., & Vaughn, C. (1985). *Expressed emotion in families.* New York: Guilford Press.

Lensi, P., Cassano, G. B., Correddu, G., Ravagli, S., & Kunovac, J. J. (1996). Obsessive-compulsive disorder: Familial-developmental history, symptomatology, comorbidity and course with special reference to gender-related differences. *British Journal of Psychiatry, 169,* 101–107.

Leonard, H. L., Swedo, S. E., Lenane, M. C., Rettew, D. C., Hamburger, S. D., Bartko, J. J., & Rapoport, J. L. (1993). A 2- to 7-year follow-up study of 54 obsessive-compulsive children and adolescents. *Archives of General Psychiatry, 50,* 429–439.

Livingston-Van Noppen, B., Rasmussen, S. A., Eisen, J., & McCartney, L. (1990). Family function and treatment in obsessive-compulsive disorder. In M. Jenike, L. Baer, & W. E. Minichiello (Eds.), *Obsessive compulsive disorder: Theory and management (2nd ed.)* (pp. 325–340). Chicago: Year Book Medical Publishers.

Lochner, C., Mogotsi, M., du Toit, P. L., Kaminer, D., Niehaus, D. J., Stein, D. J. (2003). Quality of life in anxiety disorders: A comparison of obsessive-compulsive disorder, social anxiety disorder, and panic disorder. *Psychopathology, 36,* 255–262.

Locke, H. J., & Wallace, K. M. (1959). Short marital-adjustment and prediction tests: Their reliability and validity. *Marriage and Family Living, 21,* 251–255.

Magliano, L., Tosini, P., Guarneri, M., Marasco, C., & Catapano, F. (1996). Burden on the families of patients with obsessive-compulsive disorder: A pilot study. *European Psychiatry, 11*(4),192–197.

Maina, G., Saracco, P., & Albert, U. (2006). Family-focused treatments for obsessive-compulsive disorder. *Clinical Neuropsychiatry, 3,* 382–390.

March, J. S. (1994). *Multidimensional Anxiety Scale for Children (MASC).* Tonawanda, NY: Multi-Health Systems.

March, J. S., & Mulle, K. (1998). *OCD in children and adolescents: A cognitive-behavioral treatment manual.* New York, Guilford Press.

March, J. S., Mulle, K., & Herbel, B. (1994). Behavioral psychotherapy for children and adolescents with obsessive-compulsive disorder: An open trial of a new protocol-driven treatment package. *Journal of the American Academy of Child and Adolescent Psychiatry, 35,* 333–343.

Mehta, M. (1990). A comparative study of family-based and patients-based behavioural management in obsessive-compulsive disorder. *British Journal of Psychiatry, 157,* 133–135.

Merkel, W. T., Pollard, C. A., Wiener, R. L., & Staebler, C. R. (1993). Perceived parental characteristics of patients with obsessive compulsive disorder, depression, and panic disorder. *Child Psychiatry and Human Development, 24,* 49–57.

Moos, R. H. & Moos, B. M. (1986) *Family Environment Scale Manual.* Palo Alto, CA: Consulting Psychologists Press.

Obsessive Compulsive Cognitions Working Group (2005). Psychometric validation of the Obsessive Belief Questionnaire and Interpretation of Intrusions Inventory–Part 2: Factor analyses and testing of a brief version. *Behaviour Research and Therapy, 43,* 1527–1542.

Parker, G., Tupling, H., & Brown, L. B. (1979). A parental bonding instrument. *British Journal of Medical Psychology, 52,* 1–10.

Peter, H., & Hand, I. (1988). Patterns of patient–spouse interaction in agoraphobics: Assessment by Camberwell Family Interview (CFI) and impact on outcome of self-exposure treatment. In I. Hand & H.-U. Wittchen (Eds.), *Panic and phobias: 2. Treatments and variables affecting course and outcome* (pp. 240–251). Berlin, Germany: Springer-Verlag.

Piacentini, J., Bergman, R. L., Jacobs, C., McCracken, J. T., & Kretchman, J. (2002). Open trial of cognitive behavior therapy for childhood obsessive-compulsive disorder. *Anxiety Disorders, 16,* 207–219.

Piacentini, J., Bergman, R. L., Keller, M., & McCracken, J. (2003). Functional impairment in children and adolescents with obsessive-compulsive disorder. *Journal of Child and Adolescent Psychopharmacology, 13 (Suppl.),* S61–S69.

Piacentini, J., Gitow, A., Jaffer, M., Graae, F., & Whitaker, A. (1994). Outpatient behavioral treatment of child and adolescent obsessive-compulsive disorder. *Journal of Anxiety Disorders, 8,* 277–289.

Piacentini, J., & Jaffer, M. (1999). *Measuring functional impairment in youngsters with OCD: Manual for the Child OCD Impact Scale (COIS).* Los Angeles: UCLA Department of Psychiatry.

Piacentini, J., & Langley, A. K. (2004). Cognitive-behavioral therapy for children who have obsessive-compulsive disorder. *Journal of Clinical Psychology/In Session, 60,* 1181–1194.

Przeworski, A., Nelson, A., Zoellner, L., Snyderman, T., Franklin, M. E., March, J., & Foa, E. B. (1999a, November). *Expressed emotion and pediatric OCD.* Poster presented at the 33rd Annual Convention of the Association for Advancement of Behavior Therapy, Toronto, Canada.

Przeworski, A., Sacks, M., Hamlin, C., Zoellner, L., Nelson, A., Foa, E. B., & March, J. (1999b, November): *Family interactions in OCD-relevant and irrelevant situations.* Poster presented at the 33rd Annual Convention of the Association for Advancement of Behavior Therapy, Toronto, Canada.

Rapaport, M. H., Clary, C., Fayyad, R., & Endicott, J. (2005). Quality-of-life impairment in depressive and anxiety disorders. *American Journal of Psychiatry, 162,* 1171–1178.

Rapee, R. M. (1997). Potential role of childrearing practices in the development of anxiety and depression. *Clinical Psychology Review, 17,* 47–67.

Renshaw, K. D., Blais, R. K., & Caska, C. M. (2010). Distinctions between hostile and nonhostile forms of perceived criticism from others. *Behavior Therapy, 41*(3), 364–374.

Renshaw, K. D., Chambless, D. L., Rodebaugh, T. L., & Steketee, G. (2000). Living with severe anxiety disorders: Relatives' distress and reactions to patient behaviors. *Clinical Psychology and Psychotherapy, 7,* 190–200.

Renshaw, K. D., Chambless, D. L., & Steketee, G. (2006). The relationship of relatives' attributions to their expressed emotion and to patients' improvement in treatment for anxiety disorders. *Behavior Therapy, 37,* 159–169.

Renshaw, K. D., Steketee, G., & Chambless, D. L. (2005). Involving family members in the treatment of OCD. *Cognitive Behaviour Therapy, 34,* 164–175.

Renshaw, K. D., Steketee, G., Rodrigues, C. S., & Caska, C. M. (2010). Obsessive compulsive disorder. In J. G. Beck (Ed.), *Interpersonal processes in the anxiety disorders: Implications for understanding psychopathology and treatment* (pp. 153–178). Washington, D.C: American Psychological Association.

Riggs, D. S., Hiss, H., & Foa, E. B. (1992). Marital distress and the treatment of obsessive compulsive disorder. *Behavior Therapy, 23,* 585–597.

Salkovskis, P., Shafran, R., Rachman, S., & Freeston, M. H. (1999). Multiple pathways to inflated responsibility beliefs in obsessional problems: Possible origins and implications for therapy and research. *Behaviour Research and Therapy, 37,* 1055–1072.

Scahill, L., Vitulano, L., Brenner, E., Lynch, K., & King, R. (1996). Behavioral therapy in children and adolescents with obsessive-compulsive disorder: A pilot study. *Journal of Child and Adolescent Psychopharmacology, 6,* 191–202.

Shafran, R., Ralph, J., & Tallis, F. (1995). Obsessive-compulsive symptoms and the family. *Bulletin of the Menninger Clinic, 59,* 472–479.

Simmons, R. A., Gordon, P. C., & Chambless, D. L. (2005). Pronouns in marital interaction: What do "you" and "I" say about mental health? *Psychological Science, 16,* 932–936.

Spanier, G. B. (1976). Measuring dyadic adjustment: New scales for assessing the quality of marriage and similar dyads. *Journal of Marriage & the Family, 38,* 15–28.

Sorensen, C. B., Kirkeby, L., & Thomsen, P. H. (2004). Quality of life with OCD: A self-reported survey among members of the Danish OCD Association. *Nordic Journal of Psychiatry, 58,* 231–236.

Steketee, G. (1993). Social support and treatment outcome of obsessive compulsive disorder at 9-month follow up. *Behavioural Psychotherapy, 21,* 81–95.

Steketee, G. (1997). Disability and family burden in obsessive-compulsive disorder. *Canadian Journal of Psychiatry, 42,* 919–928.

Steketee, G., Eisen, J., Dyck, I., Warshaw, M., & Rasmussen, S. (1999). Predictors of course in obsessive-compulsive disorder. *Psychiatry Research, 89,* 229–238.

Steketee, G., & Pruyn, N. A. (1998). Families of individuals with obsessive-compulsive disorder. In R. P. Swinson, M. M. Antony, S. Rachman, & M. A. Richter (Eds.), *Obsessive-compulsive disorder: Theory, research, and treatment* (pp. 120–140). New York: Guilford Press.

Steketee, G., & White, K. (1990). *When once is not enough: Help for obsessions and compulsions.* Oakland, CA: New Harbinger Press.

Stengler-Wenzke, K., Kroll, M., Matschinger, H., & Angermeyer, M. C. (2006a). Subjective quality of life of patients with obsessive-compulsive disorder. *Social Psychiatry and Psychiatric Epidemiology, 41,* 662–668.

Stengler-Wenzke, K., Kroll, M., Matschinger, H., & Angermeyer, M. C. (2006b). Quality of life of relatives of patients with obsessive compulsive disorder. *Comprehensive Psychiatry, 47,* 523–527.

Storch, E. A., Geffken, G. R., Merlo, L. J., Jacob, M. L., Murphy, T. K., Goodman, W. K., Larson, M. J., Fernandez, M., & Grabill, K. (2007a). Family accommodation in pediatric obsessive-compulsive disorder. *Journal of Clinical Child and Adolescent Psychology, 36,* 207–216.

Storch, E. A., Geffken, G. R., Merlo, L. J., Mann, G., Duke, D., Munson, M., Adkins, J., Grabill, K. M., Murphy, T. K., & Goodman, W. K. (2007b). Family-based cognitive-behavioral therapy for pediatric obsessive-compulsive disorder: Comparison of intensive and weekly approaches. *Journal of the American Academy of Child and Adolescent Psychiatry, 46,* 469–478.

Sukhodolsky, D. G., do Rosario-Campos, M. C., Scahill, L., Katsovich, L., Pauls, D. L., Peterson, B. S., King, R. A., Lombroso, P. J., Findley, D. B., & Leckman, J. F. (2005). Adaptive, emotional, and family functioning of children with obsessive-compulsive disorder and comorbid attention deficit hyperactivity disorder. *American Journal of Psychiatry, 162,* 1125–1132.

Thienemann, M., Martin, J., Cregger, B., Thompson, H. B., & Dyer-Friedman, J. (2001). Manual-driven group cognitive-behavioral therapy for adolescents with obsessive-compulsive disorder: A pilot study. *Journal of the American Academy of Child and Adolescent Psychiatry, 40,* 1254–1260.

Thomsen, P. H. (1995). Obsessive-compulsive disorder in children and adolescents: A 6–22 year follow-up study of social outcome. *European Child & Adolescent Psychiatry, 4,* 112–122.

Toro, J., Cervera, M., & Osejo, E. (1992). Obsessive-compulsive disorder in childhood and adolescence: A clinical study. *Journal of Child Psychology and Psychiatry, 33,* 1025–1037.

Torres, A. R., Prince, M. J., Bebbington, P. E., Bhugra, D., Brugha, T. S., Farrell, Jenkins, R., Lewis, G., Meltzer, H., & Singleton, N. (2006). Obsessive-compulsive disorder: Prevalence, comorbidity, impact, and help-seeking in the British National Psychiatric Morbidity Survey of 2000. *American Journal of Psychiatry, 163,* 1978–1985.

Tynes, L. L., Salins, C., & Winstead, D. K. (1990). Obsessive-compulsive patients: Familial frustration and criticism. *Journal of the Louisiana State Medical Society, 142,* 24–29.

Valderhaug, R., & Ivarsson, T. (2005). Functional impairment in clinical samples of Norwegian and Swedish children and adolescents with obsessive-compulsive disorder. *European Child & Adolescent Psychiatry, 14,* 164–173.

Valleni-Basile, L. A., Garrison, C. Z., Jackson, K. L., Waller, J. L., Mckeown, R. E., Addy, C. L., & Cuffe, S. P. (1995). Family and psychosocial predictors of obsessive compulsive disorder in a community sample of young adolescents. *Journal of Child and Family Studies, 4,* 193–296.

Van Noppen, B. L., Rasmussen, S. A., Eisen, J., & McCartney, L. (1991). A multifamily group approach as an adjunct to treatment of obsessive compulsive disorder. In M. T. Pato, & J. Zohar (Eds.), *Current treatments of obsessive compulsive disorder* (pp. 115–134). Washington, DC: American Psychiatric Press.

Van Noppen, B., Steketee, G., McCorkle, B. H., & Pato, M. (1997). Group and multifamily behavioral treatment for obsessive compulsive disorder: A pilot study. *Journal of Anxiety Disorders, 11,* 431–446.

Vogel, P. A., Stiles, T. C., & Nordahl, H. M. (1997). Recollections of parent-child relationships in OCD out-patients compared to depressed out-patients and healthy controls. *Acta Psychiatrica Scandinavica, 96,* 469–474.

Waters, T. L., & Barrett, P. M. (2000). The role of the family in childhood obsessive-compulsive disorder. *Clinical Child and Family Psychology Review, 3,* 173–184.

Waters, T. L., Barrett, P. M., & March, J. S. (2001). Cognitive-behavioral family treatment of childhood obsessive-compulsive disorder: Preliminary findings. *American Journal of Psychotherapy, 55,* 372–387.

Weissman, M. M., & Bothwell, S. (1976). Assessment of social adjustment by patient self-report. *Archives of General Psychiatry, 33,* 1111–1115.

Wever, C., & Rey, J. M. (1997). Juvenile obsessive-compulsive disorder. *Australian and New Zealand Journal of Psychiatry, 31,* 105–113.

Yoshida, T., Taga, C., & Fukui, K. (2001). Gender difference of parental rearing style of obsessive-compulsive disorder patients: A study using the Parental Bonding Instrument (PBI). *Seisin Igaku, 43,* 951–956.

Yoshida, T., Taga, C., Matsumoto, Y., & Fukui, K. (2005). Paternal overprotection in obsessive-compulsive disorder and depression with obsessive traits. *Psychiatry and Clinical Neurosciences, 59,* 533–538.

Zinbarg, R. E., Lee, J. E., & Yoon, K. L. (2007). Dyadic predictors of outcome in a cognitive-behavioral program for patients with generalized anxiety disorder in committed relationships: A "spoonful of sugar" and a dose of non-hostile criticism may help. *Behaviour Research and Therapy, 45,* 699–713.

Personality Features of OCD and Spectrum Conditions

Anthony Pinto *and* Jane L. Eisen

Abstract

This chapter reviews personality features (comorbid personality disorders, trait dimensions, and related constructs) in obsessive compulsive disorder (OCD) and hypothesized obsessive compulsive spectrum conditions (body dysmorphic disorder, compulsive hoarding, tic disorders, and impulse control disorders). For each disorder, there is a discussion of the impact of personality features on clinical course, including the development and maintenance of symptoms, and treatment outcome. The chapter also includes a review of the longstanding, yet often misunderstood, relationship between OCD and obsessive compulsive personality disorder (OCPD). Understanding the role of personality variables in the psychopathology of OCD and related conditions has important etiological, clinical, and theoretical implications for the study of these disorders.

Keywords: obsessive compulsive disorder, personality disorder, Axis II, trait dimensions, obsessive compulsive personality disorder

Obsessive Compulsive Disorder

Obsessive compulsive disorder (OCD) is characterized by recurrent, intrusive, and distressing thoughts, images, or impulses (obsessions) and repetitive mental or behavioral acts that the individual feels driven to perform (compulsions) to prevent or reduce distress. The disorder produces substantial impairment in social, family, and work functioning (Koran, 2000). This section will cover comorbid personality disorder diagnoses, core trait dimensions, and other personality features associated with OCD, and will include a review of the longstanding, yet often misunderstood, relationship between OCD and obsessive compulsive personality disorder (OCPD). Research on personality aspects of compulsive hoarding will be presented later in this chapter.

Personality Disorder Categories

Personality disorders frequently co-occur in adult patients with OCD, though there is considerable inconsistency in the literature as to rates of specific categories. It can be difficult to compare samples from studies of personality disorders in OCD, due to variability in sample selection and ascertainment, methods of personality disorder assessment (standardized interview versus self-report), unreliability of personality disorder categories, and version of DSM applied, given the substantial changes in diagnostic criteria for many personality disorders across DSM editions. This subsection will review rates of personality disorder categories in OCD, focusing on studies with large (n > 50) clinical samples that apply standardized interviews to assess personality disorder criteria.

A sampling of the literature on Axis II comorbidity in OCD reveals heterogeneity in the personality pathology associated with the disorder. In studies that predate DSM-IV, estimates of the prevalence of comorbid Axis II disorders in OCD range from 36% (Baer, Jenike, Ricciardi, Holland, Seymour, Minichiello, & Buttolph, 1990) to 71% (Horesh, Dolberg, Kirschenbaum-Aviner, & Kotler, 1997).

In a study of 96 OCD patients in which the Structured Interview for the DSM-III Personality Disorders (SIDP) was used, 36% met criteria for one or more DSM-III personality disorders, with dependent (12%), histrionic (9%), and obsessive compulsive (6%) diagnosed most frequently (Baer et al., 1990). In a study of 75 OCD outpatients using the Structured Clinical Interview for DSM-III-R Axis II Personality Disorders (SCID-II), 37% met criteria for one or more Axis II diagnoses, with the most common being the Cluster C disorders, obsessive compulsive (12%), avoidant (11%), and dependent (8%) (Mataix-Cols, Baer, Rauch, & Jenike, 2000). Horesh et al. (1997) reported that 71% of their OCD patient sample (n = 51) had a SCID-II diagnosed personality disorder, including obsessive compulsive (18%), schizotypal (14%), histrionic (14%), dependent (10%), and paranoid (10%). Summerfeldt et al. (1998) observed that half of OCD participants diagnosed with any personality disorder are diagnosed with more than one, typically two to four. While all types of personality disorders have been reported in OCD samples, the most prevalent are those in Cluster C, the "anxious cluster." Other comorbid personality disorders that have emerged with some consistency include histrionic and schizotypal. In contrast, several personality disorders are rarely diagnosed in OCD (less than 5% of cases), including narcissistic, schizoid, and antisocial (Summerfeldt et al., 1998).

Samuels et al. (2000) compared rates of DSM-IV personality disorders, assessed with the Revised SIDP for DSM-IV (SIDP-R), in 72 OCD case probands and 72 community controls. Nearly 45% of case probands had any personality disorder, which was more than four times greater than the 10% prevalence in controls. The most common diagnoses in case probands were obsessive compulsive (32%) and avoidant (15%), both of which were significantly more prevalent in cases than controls. Similar results were reported in a large clinical sample of primary OCD (n = 293), in which 38% met criteria on the SCID-II for at least one DSM-IV personality disorder, with obsessive compulsive (25%) and avoidant (15%) the most common diagnoses (Pinto, Mancebo, Eisen, Pagano, & Rasmussen, 2006).

Relationship between OCPD and OCD

OCPD is a chronic maladaptive pattern of excessive perfectionism, preoccupation with orderliness and detail, and need for control over one's environment that leads to significant distress or impairment, particularly in areas of interpersonal functioning. Individuals with this disorder are often characterized as rigid and overly controlling. They may find it difficult to relax, feel obligated to plan out their activities to the minute, and find unstructured time intolerable (Pinto, Eisen, Mancebo, & Rasmussen, 2007). DSM-IV categorizes OCPD on Axis II within Cluster C, along with avoidant and dependent personality disorders, based on the overarching view that these diagnoses represent enduring and pervasive patterns of behavior characterized by excessive anxiety and fear. The diagnostic criteria for OCPD have undergone substantial changes with each DSM revision, posing obstacles to studying the disorder (Baer & Jenike, 1998). For example, DSM-IV dropped two criteria present in DSM-III-R, restricted expression of affection and indecisiveness, because of their poor specificity (i.e., these traits are commonly found in a variety of personality disorders besides OCPD; Pfohl, 1996).

Interest in the relationship between OCD and OCPD dates back over 100 years. Janet (1904) described the development of frank obsessions and compulsions as being preceded by a period he termed "psychasthenic state," which was characterized by a sense that actions are performed incompletely (and the associated need to do them perfectly), a strong focus on order and uniformity, indecisiveness, and restricted emotional expression (Pitman, 1987). Following Janet's observations, Freud (1908/1963) proposed the construct of the anal character, typified by obstinancy, orderliness, and parsimony. Aspects of Janet's description of the psychasthenic state and Freud's description of the anal character were later integrated into definitions of OCPD (Mancebo, Eisen, Grant, & Rasmussen, 2005). For many years, analysts used the term *obsessive-compulsive neurosis* to describe features of both OCD and OCPD (Angyal, 1965).

Despite longstanding interest in the psychiatric community, the controversial relationship between OCD and OCPD remains unclear. While the presence of comorbid OCPD has been suggested as a possible OCD subtype (Coles, Pinto, Mancebo, Rasmussen, & Eisen, 2008; Garyfallos, Katsigiannopoulos, Adamopoulou, Papazisis, Karastergiou, & Bozikas, 2010), others argue that OCPD should be considered a distinct entity within the OCD spectrum (Bartz, Kaplan, & Hollander, 2007). Underlying etiological similarities and differences have not been adequately studied to date, and the lack of data on OCPD treatment limits any comparison of treatment response between the two disorders.

The overlap in symptom presentations between OCD and OCPD can lead to difficulty differentiating them in clinical practice. For example, while excessive list-making can be viewed as a compulsion if it is repetitive, and time consuming, it can also be viewed as a preoccupation with details characteristic of OCPD. Similarly, a preoccupation with order in one's environment can be considered an OCPD criterion but can be a symptom of OCD when associated with arranging rituals. Similarly, perfectionism is an OCPD criterion and a symptom of OCD if it involves the need for order, symmetry, and arranging. Hoarding is also considered both a compulsion in OCD and a criterion for OCPD see the Hoarding section of this chapter and Chapter 4. In fact, the DSM-IV states that if hoarding is extreme in a patient with OCPD, an additional diagnosis of OCD should be given. The presence of incompleteness, an inner sense of imperfection, or the uncomfortable subjective state that one's actions or experiences are "just not right" (Janet, 1904), is another area of potential overlap (Summerfeldt, 2004), discussed further in the section on perfectionism in this chapter.

Despite similarities between some OCPD criteria, and the obsessions and compulsions of OCD, there are distinct qualitative differences between these disorders. Though the phenotype of OCPD is characterized by excessive cognitive and behavioral inflexibility, it differs phenomenologically from OCD by not having intrusive thoughts or repetitive behaviors. The disorders also differ in the functional aspects of symptoms (i.e., what drives/motivates the individual to do them). In OCD, obsessions are intrusive, distressing, and generally *ego-dystonic*. In contrast, OCPD traits and symptomatic behaviors are considered *ego-syntonic* and are viewed by affected individuals as appropriate and correct. However, the core features of OCPD, perfectionism and rigidity, can still lead to significant distress when the individual's need for control is threatened. While useful, this distinction between the disorders based on ego syntonicity is not absolute, and sometimes clinical presentations defy simple categorization.

There is compelling evidence for a relationship between OCD and OCPD based on comorbidity and familiality. Comorbidity between OCPD and OCD has been reported in numerous studies, most of which have assessed the frequency of OCPD in clinical samples of OCD. (Table 10.1 lists rates of OCPD in OCD clinical samples from studies that used standardized, semistructured diagnostic interviews). Although studies using DSM-III and DSM-III-R criteria for OCPD showed marked variability in prevalence rates of the disorder in subjects with OCD, recent studies using DSM-IV criteria have consistently found elevated rates of OCPD, with estimates ranging from 23% to 32% (Albert, Maina, Forner, & Bogetto, 2004; Garyfallos et al., 2010; Pinto et al., 2006; Samuels et al., 2000) in comparison to rates of 0.9% to 3.0% in community samples (Albert et al., 2004; Samuels, Eaton, Bienvenu, Brown, Costa, & Nestadt, 2002b; Torgersen, Kringlen, & Cramer, 2001). OCPD is the most frequently diagnosed personality disorder in OCD (Garyfallos et al., 2010; Pinto et al., 2006; Samuels et al., 2000). It occurs more frequently in individuals with OCD than in healthy community controls (Albert et al., 2004; Samuels et al., 2000) and individuals with other anxiety disorders (panic disorder, social phobia; Crino & Andrews, 1996; Diaferia, Bianchi, Bianchi, Cavedini, Erzegovesi, & Bellodi, 1997; Skodol, Oldham, Hyler, Stein, Hollander, Gallaher, & Lopez, 1995) or major depressive disorder (Diaferia et al., 1997). However, it is important to note that OCPD is not found in most OCD cases, and is not a prerequisite for OCD.

There is evidence of a familial association between OCPD and OCD. Studies have reported increased frequencies of OCPD traits in the parents of children with OCD (Lenane, Swedo, Leonard, Pauls, Sceery, & Rapoport, 1990; Swedo, Rapoport, Leonard, Lenane, & Cheslow, 1989), and a significantly greater frequency of OCPD in first-degree relatives of OCD probands compared to relatives of control probands (11.5% vs. 5.8%, respectively; Samuels et al., 2000). In fact, OCPD was the only personality disorder to occur more often in the relatives of OCD probands. More recently, Calvo et al. (2009) reported a higher incidence of DSM-IV OCPD in parents of pediatric OCD probands versus the parents of healthy children, even after parents with OCD were excluded. Preoccupation with details, perfectionism, and hoarding were significantly more frequent in parents of OCD children. Counting, ordering, and cleaning compulsions in OCD children predicted elevated odds of perfectionism and rigidity in their parents.

Individuals with both OCD and OCPD present with distinct clinical characteristics, patterns of functioning, and course of OCD. Recent data from 629 individuals with personality disorders indicated that three of the eight DSM-IV OCPD criteria (preoccupation with details, perfectionism, and hoarding) were significantly more frequent in

Table 10.1 Co-Occurrence of OCPD in OCD Clinical Samples

Criteria	Measure	OCD Sample size (N)	OCPD (%)
DSM-III (Baer et al., 1990)	SIDP	96	6
DSM-III (Black, Noyes, Pfohl, Goldstein, & Blum, 1993)	SIDP	32	28
DSM-III (Eisen & Rasmussen, 1991)	SIDP	114	19
DSM-III-R (Baer & Jenike, 1992a)	SIDP-R	55	16
DSM-III-R (Cavedini et al., 1997)	SIDP-R	29	31
DSM-III-R (Crino et al., 1996)	PDE	80	8
DSM-III-R (Diaferia et al., 1997)	SIDP-R	88	31
DSM-III-R (Horesh et al., 1997)	SCID-II	51	18
DSM-III-R (Mataix-Cols et al., 2000)	SCID-II	75	12
DSM-III-R (Matsunaga, Miyata, Iwasaki, Matsui, Fujimoto, & Kiriike, 1999)	SCID-II	16	11
DSM-III-R (Matsunaga, Kiriike, Matsui, Miyata, Iwasaki, Fujimoto, Kasai, & Kojima, 2000)	SCID-II	94	16
DSM-III-R (Sanderson, Wetzler, Beck, & Betz, 1994)	SCID-II	21	5
DSM-III-R (Sciuto, Diaferia, Battaglia, Perna, Gabriele, & Bellodi, 1991)	SIDP-R	30	3
DSM-III-R (Stanley, Turner, & Borden, 1990)	SCID-II	25	28
DSM-III-R (Torres & Del Porto, 1995)	SIDP-R	40	18
DSM-IV (Albert et al., 2004)	SCID-II	109	23
DSM-IV (Samuels et al., 2000)	SIDP-R	72	32
DSM-IV (Pinto et al., 2006)	SCID-II	293	25
DSM-IV (Garyfallos et al., 2010)	IPDE	146	31

Only studies using standardized, semistructured diagnostic interviews are listed. Abbreviations: SIDP = Structured Interview for DSM Personality Disorders. PDE = Personality Disorder Examination. SCID-II = Structured Clinical Interview for (DSM-III-R or DSM-IV) Axis II Personality Disorders. IPDE = International Personality Disorder Examination.

Table adapted with permission from Pinto, A., Eisen, J. L., Mancebo, M. C., & Rasmussen, S. A. (2007). Obsessive compulsive personality disorder. In J. S. Abramowitz, D. McKay & S. Taylor (Eds.), *Obsessive-compulsive disorder: Subtypes and spectrum conditions* (pp. 246–270). New York: Elsevier.

patients with comorbid OCD than in those without OCD (Eisen, Coles, Shea, Pagano, Stout, Yen, Grilo, & Rasmussen, 2006). The relationship between OCD and these three criteria remained significant after controlling for the presence of other anxiety disorders and major depressive disorder, with odds ratios ranging from 2.71 to 2.99. Coles et al. (2008) were the first to systematically examine a range of clinical characteristics in individuals with and without comorbid OCPD, in a primary OCD sample, to evaluate the viability of comorbid OCPD as a potential OCD subtype. As compared to subjects without OCPD, the OCD-plus-OCPD subjects had a significantly younger age at onset of first OC symptoms, as well as poorer psychosocial functioning, even though the groups did not differ in overall severity of OCD symptoms. Individuals with OCD plus OCPD also had higher rates of comorbid anxiety disorders and avoidant personality disorder. They reported higher rates of hoarding and incompleteness-related symptoms (including symmetry obsessions and cleaning, ordering, repeating compulsions), as compared to OCD subjects without OCPD. Those with comorbid OCPD were significantly less likely to partially remit from OCD after two years, as compared to those without comorbid OCPD (Pinto, 2009)—further evidence of a distinct clinical presentation for the putative comorbid OCPD subtype. The findings of Coles et al. (2008) were recently replicated by Garyfallos et al. (2010) in a European sample. OCD subjects with comorbid OCPD have also been shown to have more severe cognitive inflexibility (Fineberg, Sharma, Sivakumaran, Sahakian, & Chamberlain, 2007).

The relationship between OCD and OCPD may be particularly strong for a subgroup of individuals with OCD with symmetry-related symptoms. In a clinical OCD sample, Baer (1994) found that an OCD symptom factor characterized by symmetry, ordering, repeating, counting, and hoarding was most strongly correlated with the preoccupation with details, perfectionism, and hoarding criteria of OCPD. Similarly, Wellen et al. (2007) reported that the ordering and arranging factor of the Leyton Obsessional Inventory was the only one associated with OCPD. Beyond symmetry-related symptoms, Mataix-Cols et al. (2000) reported that, independent of OCD symptom severity, hoarding symptoms predicted a higher probability of having a personality disorder diagnosis, especially OCPD and avoidant.

Personality Dimensions

Considering the variability in results from studies applying personality disorder categories, a dimensional approach to personality, reflecting a comprehensive explanatory model, may be more informative. Determining the nature of the relationship between normal personality traits and OCD may prove helpful in clarifying the disorder's etiology, based on the theoretical view that certain personality traits make individuals vulnerable to the onset of the disorder. Since personality traits are also considered pathoplastic factors that may influence the course and symptom expression of disorders, relating personality dimensions to OCD symptoms may provide a means of identifying more homogeneous phenotypes of the disorder. The psychobiological model of personality and the Five-Factor Model (FFM), are two major conceptualizations of personality that have been studied in OCD.

The psychobiological model of personality (also referred to as the *unified biosocial model* of personality) proposed by Cloninger and colleagues (1986; 1993) reflects a biogenetic understanding of how temperament and character underlie patterns of human behavior. The model has been applied to a range of psychiatric disorders (Cloninger & Svrakic, 1997). According to the theory, there are four temperament dimensions (novelty seeking, harm avoidance, reward dependence, persistence) and three character dimensions (self-directedness, cooperativeness, self-transcendence). Temperament dimensions are defined by individual differences in automatic responses to emotional stimuli (e.g., novelty, danger, reward). They are independently heritable, manifest early in life, and are hypothesized to be related to specific neurotransmitter systems. Character dimensions, on the other hand, refer to response biases that are related to concepts of the self, as well as individual differences in goals and values. They are moderately influenced by sociocultural learning, and mature progressively throughout life.

The components of Cloninger's model are assessed using the Temperament and Character Inventory (TCI; Cloninger, Przybeck, Svrakic, & Wetzel, 1994). The TCI is the successor of the Tridimensional Personality Questionnaire (TPQ; Cloninger, Przybeck, & Svrakic, 1991). Whereas the TPQ only assessed three of the temperament dimensions (novelty seeking, harm avoidance, and reward dependence), the TCI also includes the temperament dimension of persistence in addition to the three character dimensions.

Using the TPQ to evaluate temperament in OCD, Pfohl et al. (1990) found that, compared to healthy controls, OCD subjects had significantly higher scores on harm avoidance and reward dependence, and lower scores on novelty-seeking. Despite a theoretical link between harm avoidance and serotonin-mediated neuropathways, this elevation in the harm avoidance dimension was not associated with a reduction in platelet imipramine binding, a hypothesized indicator of increased serotonergic activity. Richter et al. (1996) also reported that higher scores on the harm avoidance dimension of the TPQ distinguished OCD patients from healthy controls. Within that dimension, the authors noted particular elevations on the lower-order trait of fear of uncertainty, consistent with clinical accounts of obsessional doubt and inability to tolerate ambiguity in OCD (Cloninger, 1986). Bejerot et al. (1998) studied the role of temperament and acquired character in OCD using the TCI. They noted significantly higher scores on harm avoidance (temperament) and lower scores on self-directedness and cooperativeness (character) in OCD subjects versus healthy volunteers. Kusonoki et al. (2000) reported the same profile, compared to healthy controls, in a sample of patients with primary OCD, as well as in a separate sample with major depression. Lower scores on novelty seeking distinguished the OCD group from the depression group, leading the authors to conclude that low novelty seeking may have a specific role in the etiology of OCD. In an OCD patient sample, Lyoo et al. (2001) noted that high harm avoidance and low self-directedness scores predicted greater OCD severity, controlling for age, gender, and level of depression and anxiety. Alonso et al. (2008) reported significantly higher scores on harm avoidance and lower scores on novelty seeking, self-directedness, and cooperativeness than healthy comparison subjects. These results remained even when excluding OCD subjects with comorbid disorders.

The consistent finding of high harm avoidance and low novelty seeking temperament dimensions in OCD is congruent with cognitive theories that point to certain belief domains—such as an inflated sense of responsibility and the overestimation of threat—as having a role in the onset of the disorder (Obsessive Compulsive Cognitions Working Group, 1997). These belief domains explain why individuals with OCD have a tendency to view situations as dangerous unless proven safe, and become vigilant in novel situations. With regard to character dimensions, Bejerot et al. (1998) hypothesized that low scores on self-directedness and cooperativeness observed in OCD subjects, across several of the above studies, reflect the high frequency of personality disorders in OCD, since low scores on these dimensions are key elements of Axis II pathology.

The Five-Factor Model (FFM) has emerged as a robust and comprehensive conceptualization of personality. The FFM proposes that personality is composed of five broad personality trait domains (neuroticism, extraversion, openness to experience, agreeableness, and conscientiousness) that are normally distributed in the general population. As described by Costa and McCrae (1992), neuroticism refers to a tendency toward emotional instability, and the predisposition to experience negative affectivity such as anxiety, depression, anger, guilt, and disgust. Extraversion, a preference for interpersonal interaction and activity, includes sociability, cheerfulness, and liveliness. High levels of neuroticism and low levels of extraversion have been linked to the presence of psychological disorders (Widiger & Trull, 1992). Openness to experience consists of aesthetic sensitivity, intellectual curiosity, and need for variety. Agreeableness incorporates trust, altruism, and sympathy, while conscientiousness includes a strict adherence to principles and a desire to achieve goals. The Revised NEO Personality Inventory (NEO-PI-R) is a widely used, extensive measure of the five trait dimensions (Costa et al., 1992). Each of the five domains contains six separate scales that measure more narrow, lower-order facets of the domains (30 facets in total). Although the domain and facet traits of the FFM were derived from normal, nonclinical samples, the same five domains have been validated in psychiatric patients (Bagby, Bindseil, Schuller, Rector, Young, Cooke, Seeman, McCay, & Joffe, 1997).

The FFM, as assessed by the NEO-PI-R, has been examined in OCD in both community and clinical samples. In an epidemiological study, Samuels et al. (2000) reported that participants with a lifetime diagnosis of OCD scored significantly higher on the neuroticism domain and all its facets, as compared to healthy comparison subjects. They also reported higher scores on two openness facets (openness to fantasy and openness to feelings), and lower scores on two conscientiousness facets (competence and self-discipline). According to the authors, this profile suggests a description of individuals with OCD as "highly neurotic, tender-minded people" who have difficulty carrying tasks to completion. High scores on impulsiveness (a facet of neuroticism) and openness to fantasy may reflect difficulty in resisting intrusive thoughts.

Bienvenu et al. (2004) described normal personality domains and facets in a broad community sample, examined by psychiatrists for lifetime anxiety and depressive disorders. High mean neuroticism was associated with all of the anxiety disorders studied (including OCD) except for simple phobia. In addition, subjects with lifetime OCD reported high openness to experience, consistent with the finding of high openness to fantasy in Samuels et al. (2000). In a clinical sample, Rector et al. (2002) reported that patients with a primary diagnosis of OCD were very high on neuroticism, very low on extraversion, and low on conscientiousness in comparison to normative means. When compared to patients who were presently in a major depressive episode, the OCD subjects scored higher on extraversion and agreeableness, and lower on neuroticism, controlling for depression severity. In a subset of these OCD patients, Rector et al. (2005) examined whether specific FFM facets predict the severity of OCD symptoms. After accounting for depression severity, lower scores on openness to ideas were uniquely associated with greater obsession severity, whereas lower openness to actions was uniquely associated with greater compulsion severity. The authors speculate that while neuroticism may confer a nonspecific vulnerability to the development of OCD, facets of openness may impact the particular expression and severity of OCD symptoms. Further research is needed to replicate these findings, and clarify the mechanisms by which these facets impact OCD severity, especially since the results appear to contradict reports of high scores on several openness facets in the community studies described above.

Little is known about personality dimensions in relatives of patients with OCD. Samuels et al. (2000) compared scores on FFM domains between the first-degree relatives of OCD cases and controls, in order to determine whether specific personality characteristics are part of a familial spectrum of OCD. Case relatives scored significantly higher on neuroticism, but not other domains. At the facet level, case relatives scored significantly lower on excitement seeking and openness to actions, and significantly higher on order. The authors note that this constellation of traits is consistent with a description of obsessionality by Kringlen (1965). Furthermore, neuroticism was associated with the presence of OCPD in case relatives, but not in control relatives. That is, the prevalence of OCPD in case relatives increased at higher levels of neuroticism. This relationship remained even after controlling for the presence of OCD in case relatives. The authors conclude that neuroticism and OCPD may share a common familial etiology with OCD.

Perfectionism

Perfectionism has played a major role in theories and clinical descriptions of OCD. The Obsessive Compulsive Cognitions Working Group (1997) considers perfectionism to be a risk factor for the development of the disorder, while others consider it to be a necessary but insufficient predisposing trait for OCD (Rheaume, Freeston, Dugas, Letarte, & Ladouceur, 1995). The trait has been defined as the tendency to set high standards, and to employ overly critical self-evaluations (Frost & Marten, 1990). Rasmussen and Eisen (1992) describe patients with OCD as being tormented by an inner drive for certainty and perfection, which leads to overwhelming doubt about whether they have performed actions correctly. OCD patients show significantly higher levels of perfectionism than nonclinical controls (Antony, Purdon, Huta, & Swinson, 1998; Frost & Steketee, 1997). Measures of perfectionism, especially with regard to excessive concern over mistakes and doubts about actions, are positively correlated with measures of obsessive compulsive symptoms in both nonclinical (Frost, Steketee, Cohn, & Griess, 1994; Rheaume et al., 1995) and clinical (Ferrari, 1995) samples. In addition, perfectionism has been linked to specific types of OCD symptoms, including ordering (Tolin, Woods, & Abramowitz, 2003), checking (Gershunny & Sher, 1995), cleaning (Tallis, 1996), and hoarding (Frost & Gross, 1993). A recent study by Wu and Cortesi (2009) in a student sample found that perfectionism predicted checking, washing, and ordering symptoms, even after accounting for depression and the cognitive domain of responsibility/threat estimation. In a large eating-disorders sample, perfectionism scores, assessed by the Multidimensional Perfectionism Scale, were highest in individuals with OCPD, whether alone or in combination with OCD (Halmi, Tozzi, Thornton, Crow, Fichter, et al., 2005), suggesting that this trait may be more closely associated with OCPD than OCD.

Studies of perfectionism provide insight into the ways in which this construct may impact the course of and functional impairment in OCD. Recent studies suggest that maladaptive perfectionism, the tendency to feel that any less than perfect performance is unacceptable, is quite stable, and a significant vulnerability factor for later depression (Rice & Aldea, 2006). The presence of perfectionism has been shown to impede the treatment of depression, possibly due to its relationship with rigidity, which may interfere in the therapeutic alliance or make it more difficult to modify core beliefs (Blatt, Quinlan, Pilkonis, & Shea, 1995; Blatt, Zuroff, Bondi, Sanislow, & Pilkonis, 1998). Socially prescribed perfectionism, the belief that others hold unrealistic expectations for one's behaviors, has been uniquely associated with greater likelihood of suicidal ideation (Hewitt, Flett, & Weber, 1994; Hewitt, Newton, Flett, & Callander, 1997) and poorer marital adjustment (for both the individual and the partner; Haring, Hewitt, & Flett, 2003). Further research is needed to explore the potential maladaptive effects of perfectionism, rigidity, and their interaction, on both psychosocial functioning and course of OCD and OCPD.

A strong relationship between aspects of perfectionism and subjective feelings of incompleteness or "not just right experiences" was demonstrated in studies with nonclinical samples (Coles, Frost, Heimberg, & Rheaume, 2003; Pietrefesa & Coles, 2008). Incompleteness often exists in the context of OCD features such as symmetry, counting, repeating, and slowness. In a large clinical OCD sample, Ecker and Gonner (2008) reported that incompleteness was uniquely associated to the symmetry/ordering dimension of OCD. Believed to also underlie obsessive compulsive personality traits, particularly maladaptive perfectionism and indecisiveness, high incompleteness scores in OCD predict meeting criteria for OCPD, and OCD symptoms motivated by feelings of incompleteness are more strongly related to OCPD than OCD symptoms motivated by harm avoidance (Summerfeldt, Antony, & Swinson, 2000). More research is needed to better understand the role of incompleteness in OCD and OCPD.

Role of Personality/Personality Disorders in Course and Treatment

Personality disorders and dimensions have not been systematically examined as predictors of OCD course in prospective longitudinal studies. However, two studies have investigated longitudinal associations between OCD and OCPD, with conflicting results. In a longitudinal study of personality disorders, including OCPD, Shea et al. (2004) found that improvement in OCPD generally did not significantly predict remission from OCD. On the other hand, in a longitudinal study of patients with primary OCD, the presence of OCPD was associated with a poorer course of OCD; those with comorbid OCPD at intake were half as likely to partially remit from OCD after two years, as compared to those without comorbid OCPD at intake (Pinto, 2009). Clearly the association between OCD and OCPD over time is an understudied area, which would shed light on the relationship between these two disorders.

How do comorbid personality disorders impact the outcome of gold standard OCD treatments, serotonin reuptake inhibitors (SRIs) and cognitive behavioral therapy (CBT)? A review of the literature provides evidence for a negative impact, but there are exceptions. Baer et al. (1992b) reported an adverse effect of DSM-III personality disorders on the clomipramine treatment of OCD patients. Specifically, the presence of schizotypal, borderline, and avoidant personality disorders, along with the total number of personality disorders, predicted significantly poorer pharmacotherapy outcome. When examined at the cluster level, results showed that only Cluster A disorders predicted poorer outcome. These findings correspond to reports of greater overall treatment resistance (Jenike, Baer, Minichiello, Schwartz, & Carey, 1986) and poorer behavior therapy outcome (Minichiello, Baer, & Jenike, 1987) among OCD patients with comorbid schizotypal personality disorder. As compared to OCD patients without a comorbid DSM-III-R personality disorder, personality disordered OCD patients had less symptomatic relief following comprehensive behavior therapy, were rated by therapists as more difficult to treat, required more psychiatric hospitalizations during treatment, and were more likely to terminate treatment prematurely (AuBuchon & Malatesta, 1994).

In contrast, a few studies report no negative effect of personality disorders on OCD treatment outcome, or even improvement in personality pathology as a result of such treatment. For example, Steketee (1990) reported that the presence of personality disorders, assessed by the revised Personality Diagnostic Questionnaire (PDQ-R) for DSM-III-R (a self-report measure), at baseline was not associated with outcome of intensive behavior therapy for OCD. Only the presence of passive-aggressive traits predicted treatment failure in this study. Following six months of prospective follow-up, Fricke et al. (2006) noted that most OCD patients in their sample benefited from individually tailored multimodal CBT, regardless of the presence of a comorbid personality disorder. In addition, two studies indicate that abnormal personality traits can improve along with successful OCD response to CBT (McKay, Neziroglu, Todaro, & Yaryura-Tobias, 1996; Ricciardi, Baer, Jenike, Fischer, Sholtz, & Buttolph, 1992).

In a long-term follow-up study of 16 severe and refractory OCD patients who had undergone ventromedial frontal leucotomy in the 1970s, it was noted that 3 patients with comorbid OCPD improved significantly less than the rest, implying that OCPD may be associated with a more refractory form of OCD that might involve different neural pathways (Irle, Exner, Thielen, Weniger, & Ruther, 1998). Given this observation, as well as data reviewed earlier indicating poorer course and functioning for OCD subjects with comorbid OCPD (Coles et al., 2008; Garyfallos et al., 2010; Pinto, 2009), does comorbid OCPD interfere in the clinical efficacy of OCD treatments? The impact of comorbid OCPD on SRI treatment for OCD has been examined in two studies, and results are equivocal. As mentioned previously, in a 12-week study of clomipramine in OCD, only the presence of schizotypal, borderline, and avoidant personality disorders predicted poorer treatment outcome; there was no effect for DSM-III OCPD (Baer et al., 1992b). However, Cavedini et al. (1997) reported a worse outcome for patients with comorbid DSM-III-R OCPD, as compared to those with uncomplicated OCD, after 10 weeks of SRI treatment (either clomipramine or fluvoxamine). The authors concluded that comorbid OCPD may identify a subtype of OCD with a different pattern of SRI response. Only one study has examined the impact of OCPD on exposure and response prevention (ERP) outcome for OCD. Among outpatients with primary OCD, greater OCPD severity (defined as the number of clinically significant DSM-IV OCPD criteria present at baseline) predicted worse ERP outcome (Pinto, Liebowitz, Foa, & Simpson, 2009). Of all the OCPD criteria, the presence of perfectionism was most strongly associated with poor ERP outcome. Further research is needed to systematically evaluate the influence of OCPD and its core components on therapeutic approaches for OCD (pharmacological, behavioral, or a combination).

The relationship between personality disorders and treatment response is complex, and is affected by much more than just interaction between the patient and treatment provider. For instance, higher rates of personality pathology in family members of OCD patients (versus control relatives), as mentioned previously (Calvo et al., 2009; Samuels et al., 2000), may compromise their ability to support and/or participate in the patient's treatment. It is important for clinicians to recognize that pathological personality features in the close relatives of their patients may influence the course of treatment.

Little attention has been focused on change in dimensional traits as predictors of SRI or CBT response in OCD. In one study by Sartory and Grey (1982), OCD patients with high extraversion on the Eysenck Personality Inventory had a better response to clomipramine and/or behavior therapy than patients with low extraversion. An explanation for this finding is that those with high extraversion may have been more engaged with their treatment providers, leading to greater adherence to the intervention. Studies assessing personality dimensions before versus after treatment will further clarify findings by Rector et al. (2005) that point to facets of openness as potentially playing a role in the maintenance of obsessions and compulsions.

Body Dysmorphic Disorder

Body dysmorphic disorder (BDD, see also Chapter 3) is characterized by excessive preoccupation with an imagined or slight defect in appearance that causes clinically significant distress or impairment of functioning (American Psychiatric Association, 2000). It is classified as a somatoform disorder in DSM-IV.

Personality Disorder Categories

Axis II comorbidity has been consistently reported in BDD. In a sample of well-characterized BDD patients, 57% of the subjects interviewed with the SCID-II reported at least one DSM-III-R personality disorder, with avoidant (43%) being most common, followed by dependent (15%), obsessive compulsive (14%), and paranoid (14%; Phillips & McElroy, 2000). In a study of patients with primary BDD evaluated with the SCID-II, 72% met criteria for at least one DSM-III-R personality disorder, with avoidant and paranoid as most common (each present in 38%), followed by obsessive compulsive (28%; Veale, Boocock, Gournay, Dryden, Shah, Willson, & Walburn, 1996). In a study of BDD patients entering a psychopharmacology trial, 87% met criteria for at least one DSM-III-R personality disorder diagnosis, and 53% for more than one (Cohen, Kingston, Bell, Kwon, Aronowitz, & Hollander, 2000). In a separate report of BDD patients entering CBT, all had a DSM-III-R personality disorder, and 77% had four or more (Neziroglu, McKay, Todaro, & Yaryura-Tobias, 1996). In one of the largest clinical samples of BDD (n = 200) to date, Phillips et al. (2005) described a somewhat lower rate of personality disorders as compared to the studies above. They reported that close to 45% of their sample met criteria for at least one DSM-IV personality disorder on the SCID-II, with the most prevalent being avoidant (25%) and obsessive compulsive (13%). In the first study to directly compare samples of primary OCD, primary BDD, and a sample with comorbid OCD and BDD, in a comprehensive and systematic way (Phillips, Pinto, Menard, Eisen, Mancebo, & Rasmussen, 2007), a higher proportion of BDD subjects than OCD subjects had paranoid personality disorder. Contrary to the authors' hypothesis, BDD subjects were not significantly more likely than OCD subjects to have avoidant personality disorder, although the comorbid group was more likely to have the diagnosis than the OCD group. Both the OCD and comorbid groups were more likely than the BDD group to have OCPD, but this finding was at a trend level.

Personality Dimensions

Few studies have systematically examined personality and temperament dimensions in BDD. Cohen et al. (2000) applied the Dimensional Assessment of Personality Impairment (DAPI), a semistructured interview that measures personality using a dimensional rather than categorical approach. The instrument is based on the notion that personality impairment arises from dysregulation of affective, conceptual, and interpersonal functioning. BDD patients scored in the range of moderate impairment on most DAPI scales, with the greatest impairment in the regulation of depression, anxiety, cognitive filtering of distressing information, self-esteem, and self-inhibition. Phillips and McElroy (2000) reported personality dimension scores of BDD patients using the NEO-Five-Factor Inventory (NEO-FFI), a shorter version of the NEO-PI-R that assesses the domains of the FFM without the lower-order facets. Scores were in the very high range for neuroticism, and the low range for extraversion and conscientiousness, similar to findings from a clinical sample of OCD (Rector et al., 2002). Consistent with the low extraversion score and high rates of avoidant personality disorder in these patients, scores on the Rathus Assertiveness Scale, completed by a subset of the sample, indicated a tendency to be unassertive, with women scoring below the 15th percentile and men scoring below the 10th percentile.

Role of Personality/Personality Disorders in Course and Treatment

Based on clinical descriptions and case reports, researchers have hypothesized that particular personality traits, such as perfectionism, self-criticism, insecurity, and sensitivity, may predispose to BDD (Phillips, 1991). On the other hand, to what degree is personality impairment a result of BDD, or of the neurobiological vulnerabilities associated with it? Longitudinal and prospective studies are needed to shed light on these questions.

The presence of comorbid personality disorders appears to increase the morbidity of BDD. In the first naturalistic, prospective study of the course of BDD, having a personality disorder significantly predicted a lower likelihood of remitting from BDD after one year of follow-up (Phillips, Pagano, Menard, Fay, & Stout, 2005). Although personality pathology is expected to play a role in the social impairment noted in BDD, the presence of a personality disorder did not predict psychosocial functioning in this longitudinal study (Phillips,

Quinn, & Stout, 2008). Cohen et al. (2000) reported that the total number of comorbid SCID-II diagnoses in a BDD sample was correlated with depression severity. Compared to BDD subjects without major depressive disorder, BDD subjects with current depression were more likely to have one of the following personality disorders: avoidant, obsessive compulsive, borderline, or depressive (Phillips, Didie, & Menard, 2007). In a sample of depressed outpatients, depressed subjects with BDD had higher rates of avoidant, histrionic, and dependent personality disorder, as compared to depressed subjects without BDD (Nierenberg, Phillips, Petersen, Kelly, Alpert, Worthington, & al, 2002). Finally, in a BDD sample, both suicidal ideation and suicide attempts were associated with the presence of any personality disorder, and particularly borderline personality disorder (Phillips, Coles, Menard, Yen, Fay, & Weisberg, 2005).

There are suggestions in the literature that personality impairment may play a role in BDD treatment response, though the findings are equivocal. Cohen et al. (2000) reported that responders to pharmacotherapy demonstrated less personality impairment, as measured by total DAPI score and number of SCID-II diagnoses, than nonresponders. Phillips and McElroy (2000) found that the number of personality disorders assigned to fluvoxamine responders decreased from study baseline to endpoint. However, in a randomized placebo-controlled trial of fluoxetine in BDD, Phillips et al. (2002) reported that treatment response was independent of the presence of a personality disorder. Furthermore, Neziroglu et al. (1996) found no relationship between Axis II diagnoses and response to intensive CBT in BDD. Studies are needed to investigate whether pharmacotherapy or psychosocial treatments alter personality dimensions associated with BDD, and whether such changes mediate treatment outcome.

Hoarding

Compulsive hoarding is characterized by the acquisition of, and unwillingness or inability to discard, large quantities of seemingly useless objects (Frost et al., 1993; Greenberg, Witztum, & Levy, 1990; see also Chapter 4). The behavior can lead to significantly cluttered living space in the home (rendering parts of the home unusable for their intended purpose), increase the risk of injuries and illnesses, and cause considerable distress and impairment in functioning for individuals and their family members, including occupational impairment, legal citations, and evictions from home by public health authorities (Frost, Steketee, Williams, & Warren, 2000; Tolin, Frost, Steketee, & Fitch, 2008). In sum, compulsive hoarding represents a profound public health burden (Tolin, Frost, Steketee, Gray, & Fitch, 2008).

Hoarding and saving behavior has been observed in several neuropsychiatric disorders, including schizophrenia, dementia, eating disorders, Prader-Willi syndrome, and mental retardation, as well as in nonclinical populations (Saxena & Maidment, 2004). However, this behavior is most commonly found in patients with OCD, with 30%–40% of OCD patients reporting hoarding and 10%–15% citing it as their primary OCD symptom (Steketee & Frost, 2003). Some argue that compulsive hoarding is a clinically distinct subtype of OCD, or even a discrete entity or unique syndrome (possibly an OCD spectrum disorder) based on patterns of treatment response (Abramowitz, Franklin, Schwartz, & Furr, 2003; Mataix-Cols, Marks, Greist, Kobak, & Baer, 2002), functional neuroimaging (Saxena, Brody, Maidment, Smith, Zohrabi, Katz, Baker, & Baxter, 2004), and neurocognitive deficits (Lawrence, Wooderson, Mataix-Cols, David, Speckens, & Phillips, 2006; Steketee et al., 2003) that diverge with nonhoarding OCD. A separate Hoarding Disorder has been proposed for DSM-5.

Personality Disorder Categories

Hoarding is currently listed in DSM-IV as a symptom of OCPD but, as explained by the mixed findings in this subsection, recent evidence suggests that hoarding does not cohere well with other OCPD traits. Of the eight diagnostic criteria of OCPD, the hoarding criterion has the lowest specificity and predictive value, calling into question its utility (Grilo, McGlashan, Morey, Gunderson, Skodol, et al., 2001; Grilo, Skodol, Gunderson, Sanislow, Stout, Shea, et al., 2004). In a factor analysis of all DSM-IV personality disorder criteria, Nestadt et al. (2006) found hoarding to be the OCPD criterion with the least relevance to a compulsive factor, leading them to speculate that this behavior may be better conceptualized as an OCD feature than as a personality disorder trait. Two studies (Frost et al., 1993; Frost, Krause, & Steketee, 1996) failed to find a relationship between hoarding and the OCPD subscale of the Millon Clinical Multiaxial Inventory-II (MCMI-II), a self-report assessment of personality disorders. In Frost et al. (1996), self-identified hoarders did not differ from matched community volunteers on the OCPD subscale of the MCMI-II.

Personality disorders commonly co-occur with hoarding. In an epidemiological study, Samuels et al. (2008) studied correlates of hoarding behavior in the community. They found that the odds of hoarding in community participants increased with the number of DSM-IV symptoms of specific personality disorders, including paranoid, schizotypal, avoidant, and obsessive compulsive. In a study comparing individuals with compulsive hoarding with nonhoarding anxious or depressed patients, and nonclinical community participants, Grisham et al. (2008) reported that the hoarding group endorsed more DSM-IV schizotypal personality disorder symptoms than participants in both comparison groups.

Within OCD, Mataix-Cols et al. (2000) reported that, independent of OCD symptom severity, hoarding symptoms predict a higher probability of having a personality disorder diagnosis, especially obsessive compulsive and avoidant. Frost et al. (2000) compared OCD subjects with hoarding, OCD subjects without hoarding, subjects with anxiety disorders, and community controls, and found that OCD subjects with hoarding had more DSM-IV symptoms of dependent and schizotypal personality disorder than any of the other groups. The fact that the three clinical groups did not differ on the number of nonhoarding OCPD symptoms endorsed, argues against a specific association between hoarding and OCPD. Samuels et al. (2002a) reported that OCPD and several Cluster B disorders (borderline, histrionic, and narcissistic) are more prevalent in hoarding OCD versus nonhoarding OCD. The magnitude of these relationships did not change appreciably after controlling for OCD severity. Among the symptoms of OCPD, perfectionism and preoccupation with details, in addition to the overlapping hoarding symptom, were much more frequent in hoarders. Lochner et al. (2005) noted a higher prevalence of DSM-IV OCPD in hoarding OCD versus nonhoarding OCD. Samuels et al. (2007) found a higher rate of DSM-IV obsessive compulsive and dependent personality disorders in hoarding OCD versus nonhoarding OCD. Results from multivariate analyses indicate that five personality disorder criteria (miserliness and preoccupation with details from OCPD; difficulty making decisions from dependent personality disorder; odd behavior/appearance and magical thinking from schizotypal personality disorder) were strongly and independently related to hoarding in these individuals. Finally, Pertusa et al. (2008) reported that subjects with hoarding OCD endorsed significantly more DSM-IV personality symptoms than subjects with nonhoarding OCD. In this study, the association between hoarding and OCPD was primarily due to overlapping item content. When the hoarding criterion of OCPD was removed, the number of endorsed OCPD criteria was comparable across four patient groups (hoarders with OCD, hoarders without OCD, nonhoarders with OCD, patients with anxiety disorder), evidence that individuals with compulsive hoarding may not be more likely than those with other psychiatric disorders to endorse OCPD. However, these findings conflict with previously mentioned results by Samuels et al. (2002a; 2007) in which several OCPD criteria (besides the hoarding criterion) were strongly associated with hoarding behavior.

Personality Dimensions

Little is known about whether personality dimensions are uniquely associated with hoarding behavior in OCD. Fullana et al. (2004) found that, in a sample of OCD, scores on the hoarding dimension positively correlated with sensitivity to punishment (using the Sensitivity to Punishment and Sensitivity to Reward Questionnaire), and inversely correlated with impulsivity/novelty seeking (as measured by the psychoticism scale of the Eysenck Personality Questionnaire). High sensitivity to punishment and low novelty seeking in OCD hoarders may be an indicator of poor compliance and response to CBT, but further study in a prospective treatment study is required. Alonso et al. (2008) reported a relationship between the hoarding dimension and harm avoidance in an OCD sample. LaSalle-Ricci et al. (2006) used the NEO-PI-R to measure personality in 204 OCD outpatients, and found that the hoarding dimension was positively related to neuroticism and four of its facets (anxiety, self-consciousness, impulsiveness, and vulnerability), and inversely related to conscientiousness and one of its facets, order.

Role of Personality/Personality Disorders in Course and Treatment

There is a need for research on personality predictors of course and treatment outcome in compulsive hoarding. For example, what role does personality pathology play in the consistent finding of poor response to CBT in patients with hoarding (Abramowitz et al., 2003; Mataix-Cols et al., 2002)? Although it is expected that the presence of personality disorder symptoms—particularly those of schizotypal personality disorder and OCPD—and high scores on dimensions such as neuroticism and harm avoidance, may complicate the treatment

and clinical course of hoarding, these assumptions have not yet been empirically tested.

Tic Disorders

Tics are repetitive, involuntary, sudden movements or vocalizations driven by premonitory urges. In contrast, compulsions in OCD are goal-directed and aimed at preventing or reducing distress or a dreaded event. According to DSM-IV, Tourette syndrome (TS) is characterized by both multiple motor and one or more vocal tics (see also Chapter 5).

Personality Disorder Categories

Robertson et al. (1997) were the first to study the associations between personality disorders and adults with TS. They found a high level of personality pathology in this sample, with significantly more TS patients than controls (64% versus 6%) meeting criteria for one or more personality disorders. The most prevalent DSM-III-R personality disorders among the TS patients were depressive, obsessive compulsive, paranoid, passive-aggressive, and borderline. Cavanna et al. (2007) specifically examined the prevalence of DSM-IV schizotypal traits in patients with TS. In their clinical sample, 15% had comorbid schizotypal personality disorder. TS patients with anxious and obsessive compulsive symptomatology were more likely to exhibit schizotypal personality traits, suggesting that the relationship between TS and OCD may play a role in the association between TS and schizotypy. The score on a schizotypy trait measure was positively correlated with number of psychiatric comorbidities.

Personality Dimensions

The association of tic disorders to personality dimensions from leading explanatory models has not been investigated. However, studies show a relationship between TS and the incompleteness phenomenon, mentioned earlier, that has been linked to symmetry-related symptoms in OCD, and aspects of OCPD such as maladaptive perfectionism. Leckman et al. (1994) found that, as compared to TS patients without OCD, patients with both TS and OCD were much more likely to report being aware of a need to perform compulsions until they were "just right," an indicator of incompleteness. Most patients were able to distinguish these "just right" sensations from the premonitory urges associated with tics. Miguel et al. (2000) extended these findings by showing that a need for things to be "just right" was reported in a group of patients with both TS and OCD more frequently than either a group of OCD patients without TS, or a group of TS patients without OCD.

Role of Personality/Personality Disorders in Course and Treatment

Research on the role of personality in the maintenance and treatment of tics is scant. Miguel et al. (2003) noted that the presence of schizotypal personality symptoms predicted poor OCD treatment response in patients with TS, similar to findings in OCD samples (Jenike et al., 1986; Minichiello et al., 1987).

Impulse Control Disorders

DSM-IV defines impulse control disorders as mental disorders characterized by irresistible impulses to perform an act that is harmful to the person or to others. This group of conditions includes: intermittent explosive disorder, kleptomania, pyromania, pathological gambling, trichotillomania (see also Chapter 5), and impulse control disorder not otherwise specified (e.g., skin-picking). Personality research in the impulse control disorders has been quite limited, with most of the available data focusing on comorbidity rates for the personality disorder categories. To our knowledge, the role of personality pathology in the course and treatment of impulse control disorders has not been systematically investigated.

Personality Disorder Categories

Villemarette-Pittman et al. (2004) reported rates of DSM-IV personality disorders in two samples of patients with primary impulsive aggression problems. (It should be noted that these individuals were not specifically evaluated for intermittent explosive disorder.) OCPD was the second most common Axis II diagnosis, after antisocial personality disorder, in a sample of individuals referred to a university aggression clinic from a variety of outpatient settings. In a second, self-referred sample, OCPD was the most common Axis II diagnosis. Regarding the OCPD findings, the authors explained this seemingly contradictory coexistence of compulsive and impulsive symptoms by postulating a compensatory theory of behavioral inhibition, whereby individuals with aggression problems develop compulsivity as a means of controlling impulses.

In the first systematic assessment study of categorical personality disorders, in a sample of DSM-IV kleptomania, 43% met DSM-III-R criteria for at least one personality disorder, with the most common being paranoid, schizoid, and borderline (Grant, 2004). Severity of kleptomania symptoms did not differ among the Axis II comorbidities. In a study of impulsive arsonists (not specifically evaluated for pyromania), 91% met DSM-III-R criteria for either borderline or antisocial personality disorder (Virkkunen, De Jong, Bartko, & Linnoila, 1989).

Findings on the prevalence of DSM-III-R personality disorders in pathological gambling appear to vary depending on assessment method. Using the self-report Personality Diagnostic Questionnaire-Fourth Revision (PDQ-IV), Black and Moyer (1998) reported that 87% of the gamblers in their sample (not seeking treatment) had a personality disorder, with the most common being obsessive compulsive, avoidant, schizotypal, and paranoid. Among subjects admitted to a behavioral treatment program for gambling problems, who completed the PDQ-IV, 93% met diagnostic criteria for at least one personality disorder, with an average of 4.6 personality disorders per subject (Blaszczynski & Steel, 1998). The majority met criteria for Cluster B, with particularly high rates for borderline, histrionic, and narcissistic personality disorders. Patients with either comorbid antisocial or narcissistic personality disorders reported greater severity of problem gambling. In the first study to apply a structured clinical interview of personality disorders (SCID-II) in a sample of treatment-seeking gamblers, Specker et al. (1996) reported at least one Axis II diagnosis in 25% of subjects (5% Cluster A, 7% Cluster B, and 17.5% Cluster C), a much lower rate of personality disorders as compared to prior studies using a self-report instrument. When compared to healthy controls, avoidant personality disorder was the only Axis II diagnosis with elevated rates in pathological gamblers.

Rates of DSM-III-R personality disorders in trichotillomania have ranged from 25% to 55% (Christenson, Chernoff-Clementz, & Clementz, 1992; Schlosser, Black, Blum, & Goldstein, 1994; Stanley, Swann, Bowers, Davis, & Taylor, 1992), with the most frequently comorbid personality disorders being histrionic, borderline, passive-aggressive, and obsessive compulsive (Christenson et al., 1992; Schlosser et al., 1994). However, no one personality disorder is consistently associated with trichotillomania (Christenson et al., 1992). Prevalence estimates of personality disorders are higher than those reported in the general population (Schlosser et al., 1994), but not higher than rates in other psychiatric populations (Christenson et al., 1992).

Personality Dimensions

Grant and Kim (2002) assessed personality dimensions in subjects with kleptomania using the TPQ and reported significantly higher novelty-seeking scores, higher harm-avoidance scores, and lower reward-dependence scores than normal controls. Steel and Blaszczynski (1998) reported elevated traits of impulsivity on the Eysenck Impulsivity Scale among clinic samples of pathological gamblers, compared to normative data. Impulsivity was found to be related to severity of problem gambling. Lochner et al. (2002) reported personality dimensions, also assessed by the TPQ, in samples of trichotillomania and skin-picking. No differences were found between the two groups, with both scoring high on harm avoidance and reward dependence. According to clinical observations by Summerfeldt (2004), incompleteness may be a motivating factor underlying some trichotillomania and skin-picking symptoms, but this assertion has not been empirically tested.

Conclusion

Much of the research on personality pathology in OCD has focused on categorical personality disorders. Although some consistent patterns have emerged with respect to elevated rates of OCPD and other Cluster C personality disorders in OCD, results from studies using categorical Axis II diagnoses have been varied and have had limited impact on advancing our understanding of personality in OCD. In recent years, researchers have increasingly moved away from the notion that personality disorders are distinct, non-overlapping entities, toward a view of these disorders as a constellation of traits on a continuum. In addition, there are many problems with the current categorical classification system. These include diagnostic unreliability when criteria are applied in clinical practice; inadequate coverage of maladaptive personality functioning seen in clinical practice, with overreliance on the diagnosis *personality disorder–not otherwise specified* (PD NOS) as a "wastebasket diagnosis;" heterogeneity within diagnostic categories; arbitrary diagnostic boundaries without a scientific basis; and excessive diagnostic co-occurrence. DSM-5 is expected to incorporate a dimensional conceptualization of personality pathology to address some of these concerns (Skodol et al., 2011).

As documented in this chapter, there has already been substantial progress in research on core personality dimensions in OCD, but there is much work to be done (see next section) to relate these dimensions to OCD symptom dimensions, course, treatment, and etiology. A dimensional view has also been helpful in deconstructing the complex relationship between OCD and OCPD, in that there is now greater appreciation for examining how specific traits of OCPD associate with OCD symptoms (e.g., links between maladaptive perfectionism and incompleteness), and how OCPD traits impact course and treatment of OCD. Research on personality dimensions in the hypothesized obsessive compulsive spectrum conditions is much more limited, but it is hoped that this trend will change, given increased attention to dimensional perspectives in the preparation for DSM-V.

Future Directions

Future research directions are proposed first for the study of personality disorders/dimensions in OCD, and then more specifically for the study of OCPD in OCD. Given the limitations of personality disorder categories, future research should emphasize dimensional constructs of personality. Longitudinal studies will be needed to determine whether dimensional personality traits prospectively predict onset and course of OCD. Prospective studies with clinical samples can also help determine whether personality traits are pathoplastic factors that affect remission from OCD, and whether there are lasting changes in personality related to having had the disorder. Future studies are needed to examine whether there are specific personality vulnerabilities for the development and/or maintenance of specific obsessions and/or compulsions. Along these lines, researchers should consider extending the definitions of personality dimensions to include biological markers. Since previous conflicting findings on the role of personality domains in OCD may at least be partially due to the phenotypic heterogeneity of the disorder, it is recommended that studies look for differential associations between the personality dimensions, and the more homogeneous symptom dimensions, of OCD. This approach would have the added benefit of further validating the multidimensional model of OCD symptoms. With regard to treatment approaches for personality disordered OCD patients, adjunct interventions should be considered as a means of addressing problematic interpersonal functioning and potential ambivalence toward behavior change, both of which can interfere in the patient's engagement in and adherence to ERP.

To progress in our understanding of the relationship between OCPD, OCD, and the hypothesized obsessive compulsive spectrum conditions, several approaches are recommended. First, given recent research linking particular OCPD and OCD symptoms, future studies of OCD course and treatment response should consider the presence of OCPD traits in OCD subjects, rather than just considering the presence of the OCPD category. For instance, it will be important for studies with large samples to examine whether changes in particular OCPD features will predict changes in OCD symptoms over time, and vice versa. Similarly, will changes in specific OCPD features, such as perfectionism, affect OCD treatment response? Second, longitudinal studies would provide information on the temporal relationship between neuroticism, OCPD, and OCD. Investigation of the relationship between neuroticism and OCPD in OCD families is necessary to further understanding of OCD pathogenesis. Third, there is no definitive, empirically validated treatment for OCPD, nor have there been any controlled treatment trials for uncomplicated OCPD. Advances in OCPD treatment would allow for comparisons in treatment response with possibly related disorders, and would inform the treatment of comorbid cases. Fourth, new research endeavors in the area of endophenotypes, unobservable characteristics (e.g., neurophysiological, biochemical, neuropsychological, and cognitive) that mediate the relationship between genes and a given behavioral phenotype (Gottesman & Gould, 2003), may provide insights into the underlying mechanisms and genetic underpinnings of OCD, OCPD, and the obsessive compulsive spectrum.

Related Chapters

Chapter 2. Phenomenology and Epidemiology of Obsessive Compulsive Disorder
Chapter 12. Cognitive Approaches to Understanding Obsessive Compulsive and Related Disorders

Acknowledgments

Supported by NIMH grant K23 MH080221 to Dr. Pinto.

References

Abramowitz, J. S., Franklin, M. E., Schwartz, S. A., & Furr, J. M. (2003). Symptom presentation and outcome of cognitive-behavioral therapy for obsessive-compulsive disorder. *Journal of Consulting and Clinical Psychology, 71*(6), 1049–1057.

Albert, U., Maina, G., Forner, F., & Bogetto, F. (2004). DSM-IV obsessive-compulsive personality disorder: Prevalence in patients with anxiety disorders and in healthy comparison subjects. *Comprehensive Psychiatry, 45*(5), 325–332.

Alonso, P., Menchon, J. M., Jimenez, S., Segalas, J., Mataix-Cols, D., Jaurrieta, N., Labad, J., Vallejo, J., Cardoner, N., & Pujol, J. (2008). Personality dimensions in obsessive-compulsive disorder: relation to clinical variables. *Psychiatry Research, 157*(1–3), 159–168.

American Psychiatric Association. (2000). *Diagnostic and statistical manual of mental disorders, 4th ed., text revision,* Washington, D.C.: Author.

Angyal, A. (1965). *Neurosis and Treatment: A Holistic Theory.* New York: John Wiley and Sons, Inc.

Antony, M. M., Purdon, C. L., Huta, V., & Swinson, R. P. (1998). Dimensions of perfectionism across the anxiety disorders. *Behaviour Research and Therapy, 36*(12), 1143–1154.

AuBuchon, P. G., & Malatesta, V. J. (1994). Obsessive compulsive patients with comorbid personality disorder: associated problems and response to a comprehensive behavior therapy. *Journal of Clinical Psychiatry, 55*(10), 448–453.

Baer, L. (1994). Factor analysis of symptom subtypes of obsessive compulsive disorder and their relation to personality and tic disorders. *Journal of Clinical Psychiatry,* 55 Suppl, 18–23.

Baer, L., & Jenike, M. A. (1992a). Personality disorders in obsessive compulsive disorder. *Psychiatric Clinics of North America, 15*(4), 803–812.

Baer, L., & Jenike, M. A. (1998). Personality disorders in obsessive-compulsive disorder. In M. A. Jenike, L. Baer & W. E. Minichiello (Eds.), *Obsessive Compulsive Disorders: Practical Management* (3rd. ed.) (pp. 65–83). St. Louis, MO: Mosby, Inc.

Baer, L., Jenike, M. A., Black, D. W., Treece, C., Rosenfeld, R., & Greist, J. (1992b). Effect of axis II diagnoses on treatment outcome with clomipramine in 55 patients with obsessive-compulsive disorder. *Archives of General Psychiatry, 49*(11), 862–866.

Baer, L., Jenike, M. A., Ricciardi, J. N., 2nd, Holland, A. D., Seymour, R. J., Minichiello, W. E., & Buttolph, M. L. (1990). Standardized assessment of personality disorders in obsessive-compulsive disorder. *Archives of General Psychiatry, 47*(9), 826–830.

Bagby, R. M., Bindseil, K. D., Schuller, D. R., Rector, N. A., Young, L. T., Cooke, R. G., Seeman, M. V., McCay, E. A., & Joffe, R. T. (1997). Relationship between the five-factor model of personality and unipolar, bipolar and schizophrenic patients. *Psychiatry Research, 70*(2), 83–94.

Bartz, J., Kaplan, A., & Hollander, E. (2007). Obsessive compulsive personality disorder. In W. T. O'Donohue, K. A. Fowler & S. O. Lilienfeld (Eds.), *Personality Disorders: Toward the DSM-V* (pp. 325–351). Los Angeles: Sage Publications.

Bejerot, S., Schlette, P., Ekselius, L., Adolfsson, R., & von Knorring, L. (1998). Personality disorders and relationship to personality dimensions measured by the Temperament and Character Inventory in patients with obsessive-compulsive disorder. *Acta Psychiatrica Scandinavica, 98*(3), 243–249.

Bienvenu, O. J., Samuels, J. F., Costa, P. T., Reti, I. M., Eaton, W. W., & Nestadt, G. (2004). Anxiety and depressive disorders and the five-factor model of personality: a higher- and lower-order personality trait investigation in a community sample. *Depression and Anxiety, 20*(2), 92–97.

Black, D. W., & Moyer, T. (1998). Clinical features and psychiatric comorbidity of subjects with pathological gambling behavior. *Psychiatr Serv, 49*(11), 1434–1439.

Black, D. W., Noyes, R., Jr., Pfohl, B., Goldstein, R. B., & Blum, N. (1993). Personality disorder in obsessive-compulsive volunteers, well comparison subjects, and their first-degree relatives. *American Journal of Psychiatry, 150*(8), 1226–1232.

Blaszczynski, A., & Steel, Z. (1998). Personality Disorders Among Pathological Gamblers. *Journal of Gambling Studies, 14*(1), 51–71.

Blatt, S. J., Quinlan, D. M., Pilkonis, P. A., & Shea, M. T. (1995). Impact of perfectionism and need for approval on the brief treatment of depression: the National Institute of Mental Health Treatment of Depression Collaborative Research Program revisited. *Journal of Consulting and Clinical Psychology, 63*(1), 125–132.

Blatt, S. J., Zuroff, D. C., Bondi, C. M., Sanislow, C. A., 3rd, & Pilkonis, P. A. (1998). When and how perfectionism impedes the brief treatment of depression: further analyses of the National Institute of Mental Health Treatment of Depression Collaborative Research Program. *Journal of Consulting and Clinical Psychology, 66*(2), 423–428.

Calvo, R., Lazaro, L., Castro-Fornieles, J., Font, E., Moreno, E., & Toro, J. (2009). Obsessive-compulsive personality disorder traits and personality dimensions in parents of children with obsessive-compulsive disorder. *European Psychiatry, 24*(3), 201–206.

Cavanna, A. E., Robertson, M. M., & Critchley, H. D. (2007). Schizotypal personality traits in Gilles de la Tourette syndrome. *Acta Neurologica Scandinavica, 116*(6), 385–391.

Cavedini, P., Erzegovesi, S., Ronchi, P., & Bellodi, L. (1997). Predictive value of obsessive-compulsive personality disorder in antiobsessional pharmacological treatment. *European Neuropsychopharmacoly, 7*(1), 45–49.

Christenson, G. A., Chernoff-Clementz, E., & Clementz, B. A. (1992). Personality and clinical characteristics in patients with trichotillomania. *Journal of Clinical Psychiatry, 53*(11), 407–413.

Cloninger, C. R. (1986). A unified biosocial theory of personality and its role in the development of anxiety states. *Psychiatric Developments, 4*(3), 167–226.

Cloninger, C. R., Przybeck, T. R., & Svrakic, D. M. (1991). The Tridimensional Personality Questionnaire: U.S. normative data. *Psychological Reports, 69*(3 Pt 1), 1047–1057.

Cloninger, C. R., Przybeck, T. R., Svrakic, D. M., & Wetzel, R. D. (1994). *The Temperament and Character Inventory (TCI): A Guide to its Development and Use.* St. Louis: Center for Psychobiology of Personality.

Cloninger, C. R., & Svrakic, D. M. (1997). Integrative psychobiological approach to psychiatric assessment and treatment. *Psychiatry, 60*(2), 120–141.

Cloninger, C. R., Svrakic, D. M., & Przybeck, T. R. (1993). A psychobiological model of temperament and character. *Archives of General Psychiatry, 50*(12), 975–990.

Cohen, L., Kingston, P., Bell, A., Kwon, J., Aronowitz, B., & Hollander, E. (2000). Comorbid personality impairment in body dysmorphic disorder. *Comprehensive Psychiatry, 41*, 4–12.

Coles, M. E., Frost, R. O., Heimberg, R. G., & Rheaume, J. (2003). "Not just right experiences": perfectionism, obsessive-compulsive features and general psychopathology. *Behaviour Research and Therapy, 41*(6), 681–700.

Coles, M. E., Pinto, A., Mancebo, M. C., Rasmussen, S. A., & Eisen, J. L. (2008). OCD with comorbid OCPD: A subtype of OCD? *Journal of Psychiatric Research, 42*, 289–296.

Costa, P. T., Jr., & McCrae, R. R. (1992). *Revised NEO Personality Inventory (NEO-PI-R) and NEO Five-Factor Inventory (NEO-FFI) professional manual.* Odessa, FL: Psychological Assessment Resources.

Crino, R. D., & Andrews, G. (1996). Personality disorder in obsessive compulsive disorder: a controlled study. *Journal of Psychiatric Research, 30*(1), 29–38.

Diaferia, G., Bianchi, I., Bianchi, M. L., Cavedini, P., Erzegovesi, S., & Bellodi, L. (1997). Relationship between obsessive-compulsive personality disorder and obsessive-compulsive disorder. *Comprehensive Psychiatry, 38*(1), 38–42.

Ecker, W., & Gonner, S. (2008). Incompleteness and harm avoidance in OCD symptom dimensions. *Behaviour Research and Therapy, 46*(8), 895–904.

Eisen, J. L., Coles, M. E., Shea, M. T., Pagano, M. E., Stout, R. L., Yen, S., Grilo, C. M., & Rasmussen, S. A. (2006). Clarifying the convergence between obsessive compulsive personality disorder criteria and obsessive compulsive disorder. *Journal of Personality Disorders, 20*(3), 294–305.

Eisen, J. L., & Rasmussen, S. A. (1991, May). *OCD and compulsive traits: phenomenology and outcome.* Paper presented at the American Psychiatric Association 144th Annual Meeting, New Orleans, LA.

Ferrari, J. R. (1995). Perfectionism cognitions with nonclinical and clinical samples. *Journal of Social Behavior and Personality, 10*, 143–156.

Freud, S. (1908/1963). Character and anal eroticism. In P. Reiff (Ed.), *Collected papers of Sigmund Freud* (Vol. 10, pp. 45–50). New York: Collier.

Fricke, S., Moritz, S., Andresen, B., Jacobsen, D., Kloss, M., Rufer, M., & Hand, I. (2006). Do personality disorders predict negative treatment outcome in obsessive-compulsive disorders? A prospective 6-month follow-up study. *European Psychiatry, 21*(5), 319–324.

Frost, R., & Marten, P. A. (1990). Perfectionism and evaluative threat. *Cognitive Therapy and Research, 14*, 559–572.

Frost, R. O., & Gross, R. C. (1993). The hoarding of possessions. *Behaviour Research and Therapy, 31*(4), 367–381.

Frost, R. O., Krause, M. S., & Steketee, G. (1996). Hoarding and obsessive-compulsive symptoms. *Behavior Modification, 20*(1), 116–132.

Frost, R. O., & Steketee, G. (1997). Perfectionism in obsessive-compulsive disorder patients. *Behaviour Research and Therapy, 35*(4), 291–296.

Frost, R. O., Steketee, G., Cohn, L., & Griess, K. (1994). Personality traits in subclinical and non-obsessive-compulsive volunteers and their parents. *Behaviour Research and Therapy, 32*(1), 47–56.

Frost, R. O., Steketee, G., Williams, L. F., & Warren, R. (2000). Mood, personality disorder symptoms and disability in obsessive compulsive hoarders: a comparison with clinical and nonclinical controls. *Behaviour Research and Therapy, 38*(11), 1071–1081.

Fullana, M. A., Mataix-Cols, D., Trujillo, J. L., Caseras, X., Serrano, F., Alonso, P., Menchon, J. M., Vallejo, J., & Torrubia, R. (2004). Personality characteristics in obsessive-compulsive disorder and individuals with subclinical obsessive-compulsive problems. *British Journal of Clinical Psychology, 43*(Pt 4), 387–398.

Garyfallos, G., Katsigiannopoulos, K., Adamopoulou, A., Papazisis, G., Karastergiou, A., & Bozikas, V. P. (2010). Comorbidity of obsessive-compulsive disorder with obsessive-compulsive personality disorder: Does it imply a specific subtype of obsessive-compulsive disorder? *Psychiatry Research, 177*(1–2), 156–160.

Gershunny, B., & Sher, K. (1995). Compulsive checking and anxiety in a nonclinical sample: Differences in cognition, behavior, personality, affect. *Journal of Psychopathology and Behavioral Assessment, 17*, 19–38.

Gottesman, II, & Gould, T. D. (2003). The endophenotype concept in psychiatry: etymology and strategic intentions. *American Journal of Psychiatry, 160*(4), 636–645.

Grant, J. E. (2004). Co-occurrence of personality disorders in persons with kleptomania: a preliminary investigation. *Journal of the American Academy of Psychiatry and the Law, 32*(4), 395–398.

Grant, J. E., & Kim, S. W. (2002). Temperament and early environmental influences in kleptomania. *Comprehensive Psychiatry, 43*(3), 223–228.

Greenberg, D., Witztum, E., & Levy, A. (1990). Hoarding as a psychiatric symptom. *Journal of Clinical Psychiatry, 51*(10), 417–421.

Grilo, C. M., McGlashan, T. H., Morey, L. C., Gunderson, J. G., Skodol, A. E., Shea, M. T., Sanislow, C. A., Zanarini, M. C., Bender, D., Oldham, J. M., Dyck, I., & Stout, R. L. (2001). Internal consistency, intercriterion overlap and diagnostic efficiency of criteria sets for DSM-IV schizotypal, borderline, avoidant and obsessive-compulsive personality disorders. *Acta Psychiatrica Scandinavica, 104*(4), 264–272.

Grilo, C. M., Skodol, A. E., Gunderson, J. G., Sanislow, C. A., Stout, R. L., Shea, M. T., Morey, L. C., Zanarini, M. C., Bender, D. S., Yen, S., & McGlashan, T. H. (2004). Longitudinal diagnostic efficiency of DSM-IV criteria for obsessive-compulsive personality disorder: a 2-year prospective study. *Acta Psychiatrica Scandinavica, 110*, 64–68.

Grisham, J. R., Steketee, G., & Frost, R. O. (2008). Interpersonal problems and emotional intelligence in compulsive hoarding. *Depression and Anxiety, 25*(9), 63–71.

Halmi, K. A., Tozzi, F., Thornton, L. M., Crow, S., Fichter, M. M., Kaplan, A. S., Keel, P., Klump, K. L., Lilenfeld, L. R., Mitchell, J. E., Plotnicov, K. H., Pollice, C., Rotondo, A., Strober, M., Woodside, D. B., Berrettini, W. H., Kaye, W. H., & Bulik, C. M. (2005). The relation among perfectionism, obsessive-compulsive personality disorder and obsessive-compulsive disorder in individuals with eating disorders. *International Journal of Eating Disorders, 38*(4), 371–374.

Haring, M., Hewitt, P. L., & Flett, G. L. (2003). Perfectionism, coping, and quality of intimate relationships. *Journal of Marriage and Family, 65*, 143–158.

Hewitt, P. L., Flett, G. L., & Weber, C. (1994). Dimensions of perfectionism and suicide ideation. *Cognitive Therapy and Research, 18*, 439–460.

Hewitt, P. L., Newton, J., Flett, G. L., & Callander, L. (1997). Perfectionism and suicide ideation in adolescent psychiatric patients. *Journal of Abnormal Child Psychology, 25*(2), 95–101.

Horesh, N., Dolberg, O. T., Kirschenbaum-Aviner, N., & Kotler, M. (1997). Personality differences between obsessive-compulsive disorder subtypes: washers versus checkers. *Psychiatry Research, 71*(3), 197–200.

Irle, E., Exner, C., Thielen, K., Weniger, G., & Ruther, E. (1998). Obsessive-compulsive disorder and ventromedial frontal lesions: clinical and neuropsychological findings. *American Journal of Psychiatry, 155*(2), 255–263.

Janet, P. (1904). *Les obsessions et al psychasthenie* (2nd ed.). Paris: Bailliere.

Jenike, M. A., Baer, L., Minichiello, W. E., Schwartz, C. E., & Carey, R. J. (1986). Concomitant obsessive-compulsive disorder and schizotypal personality disorder. *American Journal of Psychiatry, 143*, 530–532.

Koran, L. M. (2000). Quality of life in obsessive-compulsive disorder. *Psychiatric Clinics of North America, 23*(3), 509–517.

Kringlin, E. (1965). Obsessional neurotics: a long-term follow-up. *British Journal of Psychiatry, 111*, 709–722.

Kusunoki, K., Sato, T., Taga, C., Yoshida, T., Komori, K., Narita, T., Hirano, S., Iwata, N., & Ozaki, N. (2000). Low novelty-seeking differentiates obsessive-compulsive disorder from major depression. *Acta Psychiatrica Scandinavica, 101*(5), 403–405.

LaSalle-Ricci, V. H., Arnkoff, D. B., Glass, C. R., Crawley, S. A., Ronquillo, J. G., & Murphy, D. L. (2006). The hoarding dimension of OCD: psychological comorbidity and the five-factor personality model. *Behaviour Research and Therapy, 44*(10), 1503–1512.

Lawrence, N. S., Wooderson, S., Mataix-Cols, D., David, R., Speckens, A., & Phillips, M. L. (2006). Decision making and set shifting impairments are associated with distinct symptom dimensions in obsessive-compulsive disorder. *Neuropsychology, 20*(4), 409–419.

Leckman, J., Walker, D. E., Goodman, W. K., & et al. (1994). "Just right" perceptions associated with compulsive behavior in Tourette's Syndrome. *American Journal of Psychiatry, 151*(5), 675–680.

Lenane, M., Swedo, S. E., Leonard, H. L., Pauls, D. L., Sceery, W., & Rapoport, J. L. (1990). Psychiatric Disorders in first degree relatives of children and adolescents with obsessive-compulsive disorder. *Journal of the American Academy of Child and Adolescent Psychiatry, 29*, 407–412.

Lochner, C., Kinnear, C. J., Hemmings, S. M., Seller, C., Niehaus, D. J., Knowles, J. A., Daniels, W., Moolman-Smook, J. C., Seedat, S., & Stein, D. J. (2005). Hoarding in obsessive-compulsive disorder: clinical and genetic correlates. *Journal of Clinical Psychiatry, 66*(9), 1155–1160.

Lochner, C., Simeon, D., Niehaus, D. J., & Stein, D. J. (2002). Trichotillomania and skin-picking: a phenomenological comparison. *Depression and Anxiety, 15*(2), 83–86.

Lyoo, I. K., Lee, D. W., Kim, Y. S., Kong, S. W., & Kwon, J. S. (2001). Patterns of temperament and character in subjects with obsessive-compulsive disorder. *Journal of Clinical Psychiatry, 62*(8), 637–641.

Mancebo, M. C., Eisen, J. L., Grant, J. E., & Rasmussen, S. A. (2005). Obsessive compulsive personality disorder and obsessive compulsive disorder: clinical characteristics, diagnostic difficulties, and treatment. *Annals of Clinical Psychiatry, 17*(4), 197–204.

Mataix-Cols, D., Baer, L., Rauch, S. L., & Jenike, M. A. (2000). Relation of factor-analyzed symptom dimensions of obsessive-compulsive disorder to personality disorders. *Acta Psychiatrica Scandinavica, 102*(3), 199–202.

Mataix-Cols, D., Marks, I. M., Greist, J. H., Kobak, K. A., & Baer, L. (2002). Obsessive-compulsive symptom dimensions as predictors of compliance with and response to behaviour therapy: results from a controlled trial. *Psychotherapy and Psychosomatics, 71*(5), 255–262.

Matsunaga, H., Kiriike, N., Matsui, T., Miyata, A., Iwasaki, Y., Fujimoto, K., Kasai, S., & Kojima, M. (2000). Gender differences in social and interpersonal features and personality disorders among Japanese patients with obsessive-compulsive disorder. *Comprehensive Psychiatry, 41*(4), 266–272.

Matsunaga, H., Miyata, A., Iwasaki, Y., Matsui, T., Fujimoto, K., & Kiriike, N. (1999). A comparison of clinical features among

Japanese eating-disordered women with obsessive-compulsive disorder. *Comprehensive Psychiatry, 40*(5), 337–342.

McKay, D., Neziroglu, F., Todaro, J., & Yaryura-Tobias, J. A. (1996). Changes in personality disorders following behavior therapy for obsessive-compulsive disorder. *Journal of Anxiety Disorders, 10*(1), 47–57.

Miguel, E. C., do Rosario-Campos, M. C., Prado, H. S., do Valle, R., Rauch, S. L., Coffey, B. J., Baer, L., Savage, C. R., O'Sullivan, R. L., Jenike, M. A., & Leckman, J. F. (2000). Sensory phenomena in obsessive-compulsive disorder and Tourette's disorder. *Journal of Clinical Psychiatry, 61*(2), 150–156.

Miguel, E. C., Shavitt, R. G., Ferrao, Y. A., Brotto, S. A., & Diniz, J. B. (2003). How to treat OCD in patients with Tourette syndrome. *Journal of Psychosomatic Research, 55*(1), 49–57.

Minichiello, W. E., Baer, L., & Jenike, M. A. (1987). Schizotypal personality disorder: a poor prognostic indicator for behavior therapy in the treatment of obsessive compulsive disorder. *Journal of Anxiety Disorders, 1*, 273–276.

Nestadt, G., Hsu, F. C., Samuels, J., Bienvenu, O. J., Reti, I., Costa, P. T., & Eaton, W. W. (2006). Latent structure of the Diagnostic and Statistical Manual of Mental Disorders, Fourth Edition personality disorder criteria. *Comprehensive Psychiatry, 47*(1), 54–62.

Neziroglu, F., McKay, D., Todaro, J., & Yaryura-Tobias, J. A. (1996). Effect of cognitive behavior therapy on persons with body dysmorphic disorder and comorbid Axis II diagnoses. *Behavior Therapy, 27*, 67–77.

Nierenberg, A. A., Phillips, K. A., Petersen, T. J., Kelly, K. E., Alpert, J. E., Worthington, J. J., Tedlow, J. R., Rosenbaum, J. R., & Fava, M. (2002). Body dysmorphic disorder in outpatients with major depression. *Journal of Affective Disorders, 69*, 141–148.

Obsessive Compulsive Cognitions Working Group. (1997). Cognitive assessment of obsessive-compulsive disorder. *Behaviour Research and Therapy, 35*(7), 667–681.

Pertusa, A., Fullana, M. A., Singh, S., Alonso, P., Menchon, J. M., & Mataix-Cols, D. (2008). Compulsive hoarding: OCD symptom, distinct clinical syndrome, or both? *American Journal of Psychiatry, 165*(10), 1289–1298.

Pfohl, B. (1996). Obsessive-compulsive personality disorder. In T. A. Widiger, H. A. Pincus, R. Ross, M. First & W. Wakefield (Eds.), *DSM-IV Sourcebook* (Vol. 2, pp. 777–789). Washington, D.C.: American Psychiatric Association.

Pfohl, B., Black, D., Noyes, R., Jr., Kelley, M., & Blum, N. (1990). A test of the tridimensional personality theory: association with diagnosis and platelet imipramine binding in obsessive-compulsive disorder. *Biological Psychiatry, 28*(1), 41–46.

Phillips, K. A. (1991). Body dysmorphic disorder: the distress of imagined ugliness. *American Journal of Psychiatry, 148*, 1138–1149.

Phillips, K. A., Albertini, R. S., & Rasmussen, S. A. (2002). A randomized placebo-controlled trial of fluoxetine in body dysmorphic disorder. *Archives of General Psychiatry, 59*, 381–388.

Phillips, K. A., Coles, M. E., Menard, W., Yen, S., Fay, C., & Weisberg, R. B. (2005). Suicidal ideation and suicide attempts in body dysmorphic disorder. *Journal of Clinical Psychiatry, 66*(6), 717–725.

Phillips, K. A., Didie, E. R., & Menard, W. (2007). Clinical features and correlates of major depressive disorder in individuals with body dysmorphic disorder. *Journal of Affective Disorders, 97*(1–3), 129–135.

Phillips, K. A., & McElroy, S. L. (2000). Personality disorders and traits in patients with body dysmorphic disorder. *Comprehensive Psychiatry, 41*, 229–236.

Phillips, K. A., Menard, W., Fay, C., & Weisberg, R. (2005). Demographic characteristics, phenomenology, comorbidity, and family history in 200 individuals with body dysmorphic disorder. *Psychosomatics, 46*(4), 317–325.

Phillips, K. A., Pagano, M. E., Menard, W., Fay, C., & Stout, R. L. (2005). Predictors of remission from body dysmorphic disorder: a prospective study. *Journal of Nervous and Mental Disease, 193*(8), 564–567.

Phillips, K. A., Pinto, A., Menard, W., Eisen, J. L., Mancebo, M. C., & Rasmussen, S. A. (2007). Obsessive-compulsive disorder versus body dysmorphic disorder: A comparison study of two possibly related disorders. *Depression and Anxiety, 24*, 399–409.

Phillips, K. A., Quinn, G., & Stout, R. L. (2008). Functional impairment in body dysmorphic disorder: a prospective, follow-up study. *Journal of Psychiatric Research, 42*(9), 701–707.

Pietrefesa, A. S., & Coles, M. E. (2008). Moving beyond an exclusive focus on harm avoidance in obsessive compulsive disorder: considering the role of incompleteness. *Behavior Therapy, 39*(3), 224–231.

Pinto, A. (2009, August). *Understanding obsessive compulsive personality disorder and its impact on obsessive compulsive disorder.* Paper presented at the annual Obsessive Compulsive Foundation Conference, Minneapolis, MN.

Pinto, A., Eisen, J. L., Mancebo, M. C., & Rasmussen, S. A. (2007). Obsessive compulsive personality disorder. In J. S. Abramowitz, D. McKay & S. Taylor (Eds.), *Obsessive-compulsive disorder: Subtypes and spectrum conditions* (pp. 246–270). New York: Elsevier.

Pinto, A., Liebowitz, M. R., Foa, E. B., & Simpson, H. B. (in press). Obsessive compulsive personality disorder as a predictor of exposure and ritual prevention outcome for obsessive compulsive disorder. *Behaviour Research and Therapy.*

Pinto, A., Mancebo, M. C., Eisen, J. L., Pagano, M. E., & Rasmussen, S. A. (2006). The Brown Longitudinal Obsessive Compulsive Study: Clinical features and symptoms of the sample at intake. *Journal of Clinical Psychiatry, 67*, 703–711.

Pitman, R. K. (1987). Pierre Janet on obsessive-compulsive disorder (1903): Review and commentary. *Archives of General Psychiatry, 44*, 226–232.

Rasmussen, S. A., & Eisen, J. (1992). The epidemiology and clinical features of OCD. In M. A. Jenike (Ed.), *Psychiatric Clinics of North America* (Vol. 15, pp. 743–758). Philadelphia, PA: W.B. Saunders Co.

Rector, N. A., Hood, K., Richter, M. A., & Bagby, R. M. (2002). Obsessive-compulsive disorder and the five-factor model of personality: distinction and overlap with major depressive disorder. *Behaviour Research and Therapy, 40*(10), 1205–1219.

Rector, N. A., Richter, M. A., & Bagby, R. M. (2005). The impact of personality on symptom expression in obsessive-compulsive disorder. *Journal of Nervous and Mental Disease, 193*(4), 231–236.

Rheaume, J., Freeston, M. H., Dugas, M. J., Letarte, H., & Ladouceur, R. (1995). Perfectionism, responsibility and obsessive-compulsive symptoms. *Behaviour Research and Therapy, 33*(7), 785–794.

Ricciardi, J. N., Baer, L., Jenike, M. A., Fischer, S. C., Sholtz, D., & Buttolph, M. L. (1992). Changes in DSM-III-R axis II diagnoses following treatment of obsessive-compulsive disorder. *American Journal of Psychiatry, 149*(6), 829–831.

Rice, K. G., & Aldea, M. A. (2006). State dependence and trait stability of perfectionism: A short-term longitudinal study. *Journal of Counseling Psychology, 53*, 205–212.

Richter, M. A., Summerfeldt, L. J., Joffe, R. T., & Swinson, R. P. (1996). The Tridimensional Personality Questionnaire in obsessive-compulsive disorder. *Psychiatry Research, 65*(3), 185–188.

Robertson, M. M., Banerjee, S., Hiley, P. J., & Tannock, C. (1997). Personality disorder and psychopathology in Tourette's syndrome: a controlled study. *British Journal of Psychiatry, 171*, 283–286.

Samuels, J., Bienvenu, O. J., 3rd, Riddle, M. A., Cullen, B. A., Grados, M. A., Liang, K. Y., Hoehn-Saric, R., & Nestadt, G. (2002a). Hoarding in obsessive compulsive disorder: results from a case-control study. *Behaviour Research and Therapy, 40*(5), 517–528.

Samuels, J., Eaton, W. W., Bienvenu, O. J., 3rd, Brown, C. H., Costa, P. T., Jr., & Nestadt, G. (2002b). Prevalence and correlates of personality disorders in a community sample. *British Journal of Psychiatry, 180*, 536–542.

Samuels, J., Nestadt, G., Bienvenu, O. J., Costa, P. T., Jr., Riddle, M. A., Liang, K. Y., Hoehn-Saric, R., Grados, M. A., & Cullen, B. A. (2000). Personality disorders and normal personality dimensions in obsessive-compulsive disorder. *British Journal of Psychiatry, 177*, 457–462.

Samuels, J. F., Bienvenu, O. J., Grados, M. A., Cullen, B., Riddle, M. A., Liang, K. Y., Eaton, W. W., & Nestadt, G. (2008). Prevalence and correlates of hoarding behavior in a community-based sample. *Behaviour Research and Therapy, 46*(7), 836–844.

Samuels, J. F., Bienvenu, O. J., Pinto, A., Fyer, A. J., McCracken, J. T., Rauch, S. L., Murphy, D. L., Grados, M. A., Greenberg, B. D., Knowles, J. A., Piacentini, J., Cannistraro, P. A., Cullen, B., Riddle, M. A., Rasmussen, S. A., Pauls, D. L., Willour, V. L., Shugart, Y. Y., Liang, K., Hoehn-Saric, R., & Nestadt, G. (2007). Hoarding in obsessive compulsive disorder: Results from the OCD Collaborative Genetics Study. *Behaviour Research and Therapy, 45*, 673–686.

Sanderson, W. C., Wetzler, S., Beck, A. T., & Betz, F. (1994). Prevalence of personality disorders among patients with anxiety disorders. *Psychiatry Research, 51*(2), 167–174.

Sartory, G., & Grey, S. J. (1982). Personality and treatment outcome in obsessional-compulsive patients. *Behavioural Psychotherapy, 9*, 34–45.

Saxena, S., Brody, A. L., Maidment, K. M., Smith, E. C., Zohrabi, N., Katz, E., Baker, S. K., & Baxter, L. R., Jr. (2004). Cerebral glucose metabolism in obsessive-compulsive hoarding. *American Journal of Psychiatry, 161*(6), 1038–1048.

Saxena, S., & Maidment, K. M. (2004). Treatment of compulsive hoarding. *Journal of Clinical Psychology, 60*(11), 1143–1154.

Schlosser, S., Black, D. W., Blum, N., & Goldstein, R. B. (1994). The demography, phenomenology, and family history of 22 persons with compulsive hair pulling. *Annals of Clinical Psychiatry, 6*(3), 147–152.

Sciuto, G., Diaferia, G., Battaglia, M., Perna, G., Gabriele, A., & Bellodi, L. (1991). DSM-III-R personality disorders in panic and obsessive-compulsive disorder: a comparison study. *Comprehensive Psychiatry, 32*(5), 450–457.

Shea, M. T., Stout, R. L., Yen, S., Pagano, M. E., Skodol, A. E., Morey, L. C., Gunderson, J. G., McGlashan, T. H., Grilo, C. M., Sanislow, C. A., Bender, D. S., & Zanarini, M. C. (2004). Associations in the course of personality disorders and Axis I disorders over time. *Journal of Abnormal Psychology, 113*(4), 499–508.

Skodol, A. E., Oldham, J. M., Hyler, S. E., Stein, D. J., Hollander, E., Gallaher, P. E., & Lopez, A. E. (1995). Patterns of anxiety and personality disorder comorbidity. *Journal of Psychiatric Research, 5*, 361–374.

Skodol, A. E., Clark, L. A., Bender, D. S., Krueger, R. F., Morey, L. C., Verheul, R., Alarcon, R. D., Bell, C. C., Siever, L. J., Oldham, J. M. (2011). Proposed changes in personality and personality disorder assessment and diagnosis for DSM-5 Part I: Description and rationale. *Personality Disorders: Theory, Research, and Treatment, 2*(1), 4–22.

Specker, S. M., Carlson, G. A., Edmonson, K. M., Johnson, P. E., & Marcotte, M. (1996). Psychopathology in pathological gamblers seeking treatment. *Journal of Gambling Studies, 12*(1), 67–82.

Stanley, M. A., Swann, A. C., Bowers, T. C., Davis, M. L., & Taylor, D. J. (1992). A comparison of clinical features in trichotillomania and obsessive-compulsive disorder. *Behaviour Research and Therapy, 30*(1), 39–44.

Stanley, M. A., Turner, S. M., & Borden, J. W. (1990). Schizotypal features in obsessive-compulsive disorder. *Comprehensive Psychiatry, 31*(6), 511–518.

Steel, Z., & Blaszczynski, A. (1998). Impulsivity, personality disorders and pathological gambling severity. *Addiction, 93*(6), 895–905.

Steketee, G. (1990). Personality traits and disorders in obsessive-compulsives. *Journal of Anxiety Disorders, 4*, 351–364.

Steketee, G., & Frost, R. (2003). Compulsive hoarding: current status of the research. *Clinical Psychology Review, 23*(7), 905–927.

Summerfeldt, L. J. (2004). Understanding and treating incompleteness in obsessive-compulsive disorder. *Journal of Clinical Psychology, 60*(11), 1155–1168.

Summerfeldt, L. J., Antony, M. M., & Swinson, R. P. (2000, November). *Incompleteness: a link between perfectionistic traits and OCD.* Paper presented at the Association for the Advancement of Behavior Therapy meeting, New Orleans, LA.

Summerfeldt, L. J., Huta, V., & Swinson, R. P. (1998). Personality and obsessive-compulsive disorder. In R. P. Swinson, M. M. Antony, S. Rachman & M. A. Richter (Eds.), *Obsessive-compulsive disorder: Theory, research, and treatment* (pp. 79–119). New York: The Guilford Press.

Swedo, S. E., Rapoport, J. L., Leonard, H. L., Lenane, M. C., & Cheslow, D. (1989). Obsessive compulsive disorder in children and adolescents: clinical and phenomenology of 70 consecutive cases. *Archives of General Psychiatry, 46*, 335–341.

Tallis, F. (1996). Compulsive washing in the absence of phobic and illness anxiety. *Behaviour Research and Therapy, 34*(4), 361–362.

Tolin, D. F., Frost, R. O., Steketee, G., & Fitch, K. E. (2008). Family burden of compulsive hoarding: results of an internet survey. *Behaviour Research and Therapy, 46*(3), 334–344.

Tolin, D. F., Frost, R. O., Steketee, G., Gray, K. D., & Fitch, K. E. (2008). The economic and social burden of compulsive hoarding. *Psychiatry Research, 160*(2), 200–211.

Tolin, D. F., Woods, C. M., & Abramowitz, J. S. (2003). Relationship between obsessive beliefs and obsessive-compulsive symptoms. *Cognitive Therapy and Research, 27*(6), 657–669.

Torgersen, S., Kringlen, E., & Cramer, V. (2001). The prevalence of personality disorders in a community sample. *Archives of General Psychiatry, 58*, 590–596.

Torres, A. R., & Del Porto, J. A. (1995). Comorbidity of obsessive-compulsive disorder and personality disorders. *Psychopathology, 28*, 322–329.

Veale, D., Boocock, A., Gournay, K., Dryden, W., Shah, F., Willson, R., & Walburn, J. (1996). Body dysmorphic disorder. A survey of fifty cases. *British Journal of Psychiatry, 169*(2), 196–201.

Villemarette-Pittman, N. R., Stanford, M. S., Greve, K. W., Houston, R. J., & Mathias, C. W. (2004). Obsessive-compulsive personality disorder and behavioral disinhibition. *Journal of Psychology, 138*(1), 5–22.

Virkkunen, M., De Jong, J., Bartko, J., & Linnoila, M. (1989). Psychobiological concomitants of history of suicide attempts among violent offenders and impulsive fire setters. *Archives of General Psychiatry, 46*(7), 604–606.

Wellen, D., Samuels, J., Bienvenu, O. J., Grados, M., Cullen, B., Riddle, M., Liang, K. Y., & Nestadt, G. (2007). Utility of the Leyton Obsessional Inventory to distinguish OCD and OCPD. *Depression and Anxiety, 24*(5), 301–306.

Widiger, T. A., & Trull, T. J. (1992). Personality and psychopathology: an application of the five-factor model. *Journal of Personality, 60*(2), 363–393.

Wu, K. D., & Cortesi, G. T. (2009). Relations between perfectionism and obsessive-compulsive symptoms: examination of specificity among the dimensions. *Journal of Anxiety Disorders, 23*(3), 393–400.

Psychological Models of Obsessive Compulsive and Spectrum Disorders

From Psychoanalytic to Behavioral Conceptualizations

Stephanie E. Cassin *and* Neil A. Rector

Abstract

The current chapter provides an overview of psychoanalytic and behavioral theories of obsessive compulsive disorder and related conditions (i.e., hoarding, hypochondriasis, body dysmorphic disorder, trichotillomania, and tic disorders), and reviews the empirical support for these psychological theories. While Freud correctly ascribed compulsive rituals to an anxiety-reducing role, the more fundamental tenets of his drive model of obsessional development, and the subsequent focus on the role of defense mechanisms, have remained largely untested. In contrast, behavioral theories of obsessive compulsive and spectrum disorders revolutionized the psychological conceptualization and treatment of these disorders, and there is strong evidence accumulated over the past 40 years demonstrating the seminal role of operant conditioning processes in the maintenance of obsessive compulsive and related spectrum disorders. The evidence supporting the role of classical conditioning in symptom development is less clear; however, learning theory has contributed a partial understanding of the etiology of these conditions.

Keywords: obsessive compulsive disorder, hoarding, hypochondriasis, body dysmorphic disorder, trichotillomania, tic disorders, psychological, behavioral, psychoanalytic, conditioning, vulnerability.

Introduction

Comprehensive psychological models of obsessive compulsive disorder (OCD) and related conditions have been proposed over the past century, and have ranged from the early psychoanalytic formulations, to the behavioral models derived from learning theory, to the most recent cognitive models. Important theoretical and empirical advancements, not to mention treatment refinements, over the past 20 years have emerged almost exclusively within cognitive and information processing perspectives, rendering psychoanalytic theory to be of historical importance, and behavioral aspects to be coopted within broader cognitive-behavioral frameworks. While contemporary cognitive modeling of OCD and related conditions will be addressed in Chapter 12, the current chapter aims to provide an overview of psychoanalytic and later psychodynamic theories, followed by early and current behavioral frameworks

of OCD and related conditions. As detailed, while there remains uncertainty as to whether behavioral models can contribute theoretically to the understanding of how normal intrusions reach threshold to convert into distressing clinical obsessions, past and present research highlights the central role of operant conditioning processes in the maintenance of OCD and spectrum disorders, once initiated.

Diagnostic Features of OCD and the Obsessive Compulsive Spectrum

Obsessive compulsive disorder is an anxiety disorder characterized by the presence of recurrent *obsessions* and/or *compulsions* that are time consuming and cause marked distress and/or impairment. Obsessions are persistent thoughts, ideas, and/or images that are regarded by the person as intrusive and/or inappropriate, whereas compulsions are ritualistic behaviors or mental acts that are performed to neutralize the anxiety caused by obsessions, or to prevent a feared event (American Psychiatric Association, 2000). The obsessive compulsive spectrum refers to a number of additional disorders that are thought to have features in common with OCD, and fall along a continuum from compulsive to impulsive (Hollander, Friedberg, Wasserman, Yeh, & Iyengar, 2005). Among the disorders that have received the most attention as potential obsessive compulsive spectrum candidates are hypochondriasis (HC), body dysmorphic disorder (BDD), trichotillomania (TTM), and tic disorders. Hypochondriasis and body dysmorphic disorder are both classified as somatoform disorders, and are characterized by preoccupation with fears of having a serious disease (HC), or with an imagined defect in appearance (BDD; APA, 2000). Trichotillomania is an impulse-control disorder characterized by recurrent hair pulling episodes resulting in noticeable hair loss (APA, 2000). Tic disorders (including transient tic disorder, chronic motor or vocal tic disorder, and Tourette syndrome) are characterized by sudden, rapid, recurrent, non-rhythmic, stereotyped motor movement or vocalizations (APA, 2000). This chapter provides an overview of psychoanalytic and behavioral theories of OCD and the aforementioned spectrum conditions.

Psychodynamic Models of OCD and the Obsessive Compulsive Spectrum
Obsessive Compulsive Disorder

Phenomenological accounts of OCD have existed since the 1860s (Kraepelin, 1915), and while it had been recognized as a clinical entity (Janet, 1903) prior to psychoanalytic formulations of the condition, it was Freud who introduced the clinical term *obsessional neurosis* to distinguish the presence of clinical obsessions from other disorders within the cluster of neurasthenia conditions (Freud, 1896). Freud's earliest accounts of *obsessional ideas* mirrored his general view of the etiology of hysteria, with obsessive compulsive symptoms representing the breaking through of repression of some experience of a sexual act from childhood: "What becomes conscious as obsessional ideas and affects, and takes the place of pathogenic memories so far as conscious life is concerned, are structures in the nature of compromise between the repressed ideas and the repressing ones" (Freud, 1896, p.170). Subsequent accounts of *obsessive compulsive neurosis* limited the role of early childhood sexual experiences and repression of these experiences, and instead focused on the importance of fixation at the anal phase of psychosexual development, with attendant conflicts between aggressive and sexual impulses emerging from the id, followed by swift punishment from a harsh superego (Fenichel, 1945).

The conflict between disorder (id impulses) and order (superego controls) was seen to be a natural component of the anal phase of development. Freud asserted that in *obsessional neuroses* there was a "regressive degradation of the libido" with strongly repressed aggressive impulses, "anal sadism" coupled with an exceptionally severe and "unkind" superego (Freud, 1926). Accordingly, the ego is left to reconcile these extreme forces within the psychic structures of the id and superego, and in so doing is compromised and becomes increasingly reliant upon defense mechanisms to transform the aggressive and sexual impulses. The continued failure of the person with OCD to integrate or balance these opposing aspects in adulthood leads to persistent ambivalent feelings of rage and guilt, as well as love and hate. For instance, in Freud's treatment of the Rat Man (1909), he highlights the importance of ambivalent feelings of love and hate for his father, and the role of repression of hate in this relationship. As such, obsessive compulsive symptoms are hypothesized to represent the compromise between the instinctual drives and the defenses against them—characterized by symptoms of excessive conscientiousness, cleanliness, perfectionism, or some other symbolic disguise (e.g., reaction formation) of the aggressive and sexual impulses (Freud, 1926). The arrival of an unwanted aggressive or sexual intrusion, for example, is assumed to result from the instinctual urge to break through the defense, and compulsive washing is interpreted as an attempt to undo feelings of dirt and contamination that follow from unacceptable sexual urges. More recent psychoanalytic formulations of OCD have afforded a greater role to interpersonal aspects, but nonetheless continue to see ambivalence as the core of the disorder (Kempke & Luyten, 2007).

Despite Freud's writings on OCD that spanned thirty years (1896–1926), continued work by ego analysts on the role of defenses (e.g., Fenichel, 1945a, 1945b; Rado, 1959; Salzman, 1980), and the most recent developments in interpersonal and objects relations perspectives (see Kempke & Luyten, 2007; O'Connor, 2008), psychoanalytic/psychodynamic theories have received little empirical attention, and hence garnered little empirical support for their central tenets. As such, the psychoanalytic perspective of OCD remains largely of historical significance, especially given the current focus on evidence-based treatments. Further, the psychoanalytic treatment approaches, both in their historical beginnings and subsequent revisions within short-term dynamic perspectives (e.g., Sifneos, 1966), have not been shown to be effective and are not part of modern, empirically supported treatment options for the disorder (see National Institute for Health and Clinical Excellence, 2005). However, the rich and detailed accounts of patients with OCD offered by Freud and Fenichel contributed substantially to understanding of the phenomenology of OCD, including the anxiety-reducing role of compulsive rituals. Finally, there has been renewed interest in testing the role of constructs that overlap with psychoanalytic concepts, such as the role of self-ambivalence in OCD (Bhar & Kyrios, 2007) and early attachment processes in compulsive hoarding (Steketee & Frost, 2003).

Obsessive Compulsive Spectrum Disorders

Freud (1908) suggested that stinginess and miserliness resulted from fixation at the anal stage of psychosexual development, and accordingly, the hoarding of money was seen as the symbolic equivalent of fecal retention. In contrast, Freud (1895) originally classified hypochondriasis as an "actual" neurosis (meaning that it had no primary symbolic meaning), resulting from the toxic effects of a dammed-up libido. Other psychodynamically oriented authors have emphasized the importance of anal eroticism, masochism, repression, defense against psychosis, unconscious hostility or guilt, dependency needs, secondary gain, or the combination of the wish to be loved and to suffer, in the etiology of hypochondriasis (Kenyon, 1965, 1976; Lipsett, 1974).

Body dysmorphic disorder had been described in the literature for more than a century under a variety of names, long before it became recognized formally as a psychiatric disorder in DSM-III-R (American Psychiatric Association, 1987). In a review of the historical literature and translated works on BDD, "dysmorphophobia" (Morselli, 1891), and similar syndromes of "imagined ugliness," Phillips (1991) described several psychodynamic accounts of BDD symptoms. According to some psychodynamic models, BDD reflects the unconscious displacement of a sexual or emotional conflict onto an unrelated body part (Cororve & Gleaves, 2001; Phillips, 1991). This process occurs through a variety of putative defense mechanisms, including repression, dissociation, distortion, symbolization, and projection (Sadock, Kaplan, & Sadock, 2007). Body dysmorphic disorder has also been described as reflecting an underlying ego deficit (Phillips, 1991), or "an excuse for deeper personality difficulties" (Oosthuizen & Castle, 1998, p. 768). Other psychodynamic authors have focused heavily on sexual interpretations, and have speculated that the distressing body part may symbolize another body part—for example, a nose symbolizes a phallus, which in turn symbolizes impotence (Biby, 1998; Phillips, 1991). An individual with BDD may also identify their concerning body part with that of another person, such as a parental figure (Phillips, 1991). For example, Freud's description of the Wolf-Man also included an overview of classic BDD features, as he was preoccupied with the appearance of his nose to the exclusion of all other activities (Brunswick, 1928). The psychodynamic interpretation suggested that Wolf-Man's nose represented his penis, and that he wished to be castrated and transformed into a woman. Furthermore, his nose preoccupation was thought to represent identification with his mother, who had recently developed a wart on her nose (Brunswick, 1928).

Relatively little has been written about psychodynamic accounts of trichotillomania and tic disorders. Trichotillomania has been explained by psychodynamic models as a symbolic expression of unconscious conflicts (Greenberg & Sarner, 1965), or a means of working through real or perceived threats of object loss (Krishnan, Davidson, & Guajardo, 1985). In contrast, tics are seen to represent the pathological discharge of erotic and aggressive instinctual impulses (Mahler & Luke, 1946).

Beyond clinical descriptions, there is virtually no empirical evaluation of psychoanalytic or later psychodynamic theories of the obsessive compulsive spectrum disorders. As noted by Frost and Gross (1993), for example, there is no empirical data to support psychoanalytic accounts of hoarding, with the exception of a single early study of questionable reliability and validity, in which children were given a shoebox and informed they could keep any rocks they collected in their box (Heatherington & Brackbill, 1963). Hoarding was operationalized as the number of rocks collected, based on the assumption that rocks are transitional objects representing feces and money. In summary, while Freud and later psychoanalytic theorists were the first to provide a comprehensive account of OCD and select spectrum disorders, there is no empirical support for the proposed role of drives or ego defenses in the development or maintenance of these conditions. Although a number of recent clinical case studies have been presented attempting to demonstrate the effectiveness of a psychoanalytic approach for OCD (Kempke & Luyten, 2007; O'Connor, 2008), the absence of baseline and post-treatment ratings, with a reliable and valid obsessive compulsive symptom measure, severely limits the conclusions that can be drawn regarding the effectiveness of psychoanalytic treatment.

Behavioral Theory of OCD: Conceptualization and Empirical Support
Obsessive Compulsive Disorder

Symptom Development. The origins of behavioral models of OCD derive largely from Mowrer's two-stage model of fear and avoidance behavior (Mowrer, 1939, 1960). Mowrer suggested that fear of stimuli, such as thoughts, images or objects, is acquired through a classical conditioning process. In the first stage of Mowrer's model, neutral stimuli, such as thoughts and images, become conditioned stimuli through pairing with another unconditioned stimulus that naturally provokes fear. As theorized, a traumatic event should represent the catalyst for the activation of obsessive compulsive symptoms. For example, an individual might develop contamination obsessions following a serious illness, or doubting obsessions following a house fire. The emphasis on traumatic life events in the pathogenesis of OCD within learning accounts of the disorder mirror the early accounts of the development of OCD proposed by Freud (1896) and Janet (1903).

Symptom Maintenance. According to the second stage of Mowrer's (1960) model, fear is maintained though operant conditioning processes, notably escape and avoidance behaviors. Learning theory frameworks were extended to account for the range of compulsive rituals observed in OCD. Compulsions were conceptualized as active avoidance strategies that are negatively reinforced and become habitual, given their success in reducing the fear caused by the arrival of the obsession, and the prevention of extinction (Dollard & Miller, 1950). For example, an individual with contamination obsessions might engage in excessive hand washing compulsions, avoid using public restrooms, and exit a room if another person is observed coughing or sneezing, in order to reduce the chance of contamination. An individual with doubting obsessions might check the door locks, stove, and other appliances several times before leaving the house, to ensure safety. This hypothesized functional relationship, between obsessions causing distress and compulsive, escape, and avoidance behaviors reducing obsessional distress, is so widely accepted that it is built into the modern nosologic description of the disorder (APA, 2000).

Beyond classical overt compulsions (such as washing and checking), a broader range of operant conditioning factors have been implicated in the maintenance of OCD. For instance, "safety behaviors," a term referring to a variety of overt or covert strategies that are typically more subtle than compulsions, are often used to avoid or escape a feared outcome (Deacon & Maack, 2008; Salkovskis, 1991). Using a sleeve to open a restroom door, or carrying antibacterial hand sanitizer, are two examples of safety behaviors that might be used by an individual with contamination fears. Similar to compulsions, safety behaviors are negatively reinforced by effectively reducing anxiety in the short term, and have been implicated in the maintenance, and perhaps even exacerbation, of OCD symptoms, because they focus attention on feared stimuli and may be used to justify the non-occurrence of a catastrophe (Deacon & Maack, 2008; Salkovskis, 1991).

Compulsions and safety behaviors are often performed to prevent a feared outcome, but for more than half of individuals with OCD (particularly those with primary symmetry, ordering, repeating, and counting compulsions) these behaviors are motivated by a sense of incompleteness (Ecker & Gonner, 2008; Summerfeldt, 2004; Summerfeldt, 2007). Also known as "not just right experiences" (Coles, Frost, Heimberg, & Rheaume, 2003), incompleteness refers to an inner sense of imperfection, connected with the perception that actions or intentions have not been fully achieved, or have not produced the sought for satisfaction. Viewed as a form of "sensation-based perfection" (Coles et al., 2003, p. 683), "not just right experiences" drive the performance of rituals until the action (e.g., locking the door) or perception (e.g., arranging books on a shelf) conforms to "absolute, yet often inarticulable subjective criteria" (Summerfeldt, Kloosterman, Antony, Richter, & Swinson, 2004, p. 1462). In contrast to harm-avoidant compulsions, which are maintained through negative reinforcement, the rituals performed in response to "not just right experiences" might be maintained through both negative and positive reinforcement. That is, the distress associated with imperfection is reduced, and the satisfying "just right" feeling is achieved.

Empirical Evidence. Although the two-factor model described earlier hypothesizes a traumatic trigger for anxiety, there is little evidence to support the role of traumatic conditioning in OCD (e.g., Emmelkamp, 1982; Mineka & Zinbarg, 2006). However, recent research has demonstrated an association between traumatic incidents, such as sexual abuse or combat, on the subsequent onset of OCD, in addition to post-traumatic stress disorder (PTSD) (De Silva & Marks, 2001; Freeman & Leonard, 2000). Further, epidemiological studies demonstrate the risk for OCD to be 10-fold in persons with PTSD, while the National Vietnam Veterans Readjustment Study found OCD prevalence rates of 5.25% in veterans exposed to high war zone stress compared to 0.3% for veterans in low to moderate war zone stress (Jordan et al., 1991; Sasson et al., 2005). A recent large-scale study examining the role of traumatic and stressful life events in the onset of OCD found that 54% of the sample reported a lifetime traumatic event, and that the range and severity of traumatic events were associated with a more severe expression of OCD, even when depression and other comorbidities were controlled. Subsidiary analyses found specific and robust associations between a history of traumatic life events and harming obsessions/checking compulsions and symmetry/ordering symptom clusters (Cromer, Schmidt, & Murphy, 2007a).

Beyond the role of distinct traumatic events in the development of OCD, a broader literature indicates that general negative life events and life stress are associated with the onset of OCD (Jones & Menzies, 1998). For instance, early research suggested that patients with OCD report experiencing a greater number of negative life events than nonpsychiatric controls (McKeon, Roa, & Mann, 1984). A more recent examination, comparing stressful life events in children and adolescents with OCD to those with non-OCD anxiety disorders and healthy controls, found that negative life events were significantly more common in the year prior to the onset of OCD compared to healthy controls, but not significantly different from children and adolescents with non-OCD anxiety disorders (Gothelf, Aharonovsky, Horesh, Carty, & Apter, 2004). Other research has attempted to demonstrate a direct temporal relationship between negative life events and the onset of OCD symptoms. Horowitz (1975) showed that following exposure to stressful events, people tend to experience intrusive and repetitive thoughts. Similarly, Parkinson and Rachman (1981) found that mothers whose children were to undergo surgery experienced a steep rise in anxiety and a range of unwanted thoughts. Most recent prospective research suggests that particular and paradigmatic

life events, for instance, the birth of a first child, leads to intrusive thoughts and images reflecting OCD themes (i.e., harming, spreading contamination) for the vast majority of people (Abramowitz, Khandker, Nelson, Deacon, & Rygwall, 2006). However, these naturally occurring intrusions can usually be dismissed with little difficulty (Rachman & Hodgson, 1980), and other preexisting vulnerabilities (i.e., cognitive vulnerabilities) are required to account for the transition between the situational activation of nondistressing intrusions, to the development of distressing clinical obsessions.

In summary, recent research supports the potential role of trauma and adverse life events in the development of OCD. However, there remain a number of critical challenges to the role of classical conditioning in the development of OCD. First, the majority of studies examine the role of past traumatic events, and so it remains very difficult to draw any conclusions about trauma and the actual temporal *onset* of OCD. This mirrors the clinical context, where most patients do not report traumatic events as the precipitating factor in the onset of their obsessive compulsive symptoms. Second, there is very little evidence to support the idea that the particular nature of traumatic or negative life events shapes the particular content of the obsessions. Third, and relatedly, while general life stress may be said to potentiate the onset of OCD within a diathesis-stress framework, general life stress (or historical traumatic events) does not represent a discrete, unconditioned stimulus within a classical conditioning framework. Finally, while conditioning of obsessions may also occur via observation and information transmission, little research has examined this question. One possibility is that individuals who are raised by highly perfectionistic parents learn that falling short of standards will lead to punishment, and so they excel and demonstrate perfectionistic behaviors to avoid being punished (see Emmelkamp, 1982 for review). Research has demonstrated that the parents of patients with OCD tend to report elevations on measures of perfectionism and inflated responsibility (Rector, Cassin, Richter, & Burroughs, 2009) suggesting a potentially important role of nontraumatic, observational learning, in conditioning obsessive-compulsive symptoms or vulnerabilities to their subsequent development.

Notwithstanding the uncertainty of the factors that lead to the development of obsessions, there is very strong empirical support to show that once obsessions have developed, their continued occurrence leads to an attendant rise in fear and anxiety, and the compulsive rituals lead to the attenuation of the obsessional anxiety. In a series of early experiments, Rachman and colleagues (see Rachman & Hodgson, 1980 for review), demonstrated that: (a) exposure to obsessional cues was associated with increased anxiety and discomfort, and corresponding urges to perform rituals, based on subjective reports but also pulse rate variability in some of the studies; (b) the engagement of compulsive rituals led to the reduction of anxiety and distress; (c) delaying the compulsive rituals led to a "spontaneous decay" of anxiety and urges to engage in the rituals within 30 minutes; and (d) prevention of the compulsive rituals led to an extinction of anxiety and distress in subsequent exposure to the obsessional cues.

These findings have been replicated in a series of studies examining the effect of covert neutralization on anxiety and distress. Mentally neutralizing obsessive thoughts resulted in short-term reduction in distress, but increased discomfort and stronger urges to neutralize over time (de Silva, Menzies, & Shafran, 2003; Rachman, Shafran, Mitchell, Trant, & Teachman, 1996; Salkovskis, Thorpe, Wahl, Wroe, & Forrester, 2003; Salkovskis, Westbrook, Davis, Jeavons, & Gledhill, 1997). Similar to studies noting spontaneous decay of anxiety following compulsive ritual prevention (Rachman & Hodgson, 1980), anxiety reduced to comparable levels without mentally neutralizing after 20 minutes (Rachman et al., 1996).

Although safety behaviors may be used judiciously in the early stages of treatment (see Rachman, Radomsky, & Shafran, 2008), empirical research suggests that they are negatively reinforced and maintain anxiety over time. The mere availability of safety behaviors has been found to reduce anxiety, regardless of whether they are actually used (Powers, Smits, & Telch, 2004). A recent experimental study found that undergraduates, who were instructed to engage in safety behaviors for one week, reported significant increases in threat overestimation, contamination fear symptoms, and emotional and avoidant responses on behavioral avoidance tasks, regardless of baseline level of contamination fears (Deacon & Maack, 2008). Further, contamination fears remained elevated above baseline levels even after safety behaviors were decreased, suggesting that heightened awareness of contaminants persisted.

The early experimental findings provided the rationale for the development of a behavioral-based treatment, exposure and response prevention, which has led to additional quasi-experimental support for operant conditioning factors in OCD. Exposure and response prevention entails prolonged exposure to obsessional cues that induce discomfort, and strict abstinence from ritualizing behavior until the discomfort abates. Numerous uncontrolled and controlled studies over the past 40 years have demonstrated the efficacy of exposure and response prevention, with between 75%–85% of patients benefiting from the intervention (see Abramowitz, 1997; Eddy, Dutra, Bradley, & Westen, 2004; for reviews). The presumed mechanism of action of exposure and response prevention is that with the prevention of rituals, the patient is exposed to the feared stimuli, thus leading to extinction of the conditioned feared response. While alternative mechanisms could account for the success of exposure and response prevention—for instance, the changes during treatment could occur as a result of reduced negative appraisals and beliefs, rather than habituation and extinction processes—the anxiety-reducing role of rituals, and hence operant conditioning aspects of the behavioral account of OCD, is firmly empirically supported.

Behavioral Theory of Obsessive Compulsive Spectrum Disorders: Conceptualization and Empirical Support
Hoarding
Hoarding refers to the acquisition of, and failure to discard, a large number of possessions that appear to be useless or of limited value, to the point that living spaces are sufficiently cluttered so as to preclude activities for which those spaces were designed (Frost & Hartl, 1996, pg. 341; see also Chapter 4). Hoarding is a not-infrequent symptom constellation in patients diagnosed with primary OCD, and it also occurs as a spectrum condition in those without the diagnosis of OCD (Pertusa et al., 2008). It has been estimated that clinical hoarders only comprise approximately 7% of the total clinical hoarding population. Given this low base rate, and other findings suggesting differences between OCD-based and non-OCD clinical hoarding, in terms of insight levels and patterns of treatment response, there is now broad consensus that clinical hoarding is taxonically distinct from OCD (Rachman, Elliot, Shafran, & Radomsky, 2009).

Hoarders feel compelled to acquire and save possessions (Frost & Gross, 1993), and the excessive doubting, checking, and reassurance seeking that occurs when hoarders attempt to discard their possessions appears related to compulsive rituals (Steketee & Frost, 2003). Hoarders engage in acquiring and saving behaviors to prevent future harm, such as losing important information or being unprepared for a future need (Frost & Gross, 1993). In contrast to obsessions that occur in OCD, hoarding obsessions are thought to be less ego-dystonic and intrusive (Steketee & Frost, 2003). Indeed, some hoarders describe their behavior in positive ways, by emphasizing frugality and environmental consciousness (Frost & Gross, 1993).

A recent study comparing compulsive hoarders with and without OCD, on a number of sociodemographic and psychopathological variables, found that 100% of hoarders without OCD reported hoarding for practical reasons (i.e., fear of needing the item in the future) or sentimental reasons (i.e., strong emotional attachment to possessions), and zero percent experienced obsessional ideas related to hoarding (Pertusa et al., 2008). In contrast, 28% of hoarders with OCD reported obsessional ideas related to hoarding, such as fear of catastrophic consequences, fear of accidentally discarding important items (such as letters or receipts), or need for symmetry/ordering, and 48% reported excessive checking rituals in relation to hoarding.

Symptom Development. Compared to many of the purported OCD subtypes, relatively little has been written about the etiology of hoarding within a behavioral framework (Grisham & Barlow, 2005; Steketee & Frost, 2003). Most behavioral theories of hoarding are actually cognitive-behavioral theories (Frost & Hartl, 1996; Frost & Steketee, 1998) that propose a variety of vulnerability factors, including impaired executive functioning, information processing deficits, maladaptive beliefs about possessions, and family/individual history. With respect to this latter factor, it has been proposed that modeling of hoarding behavior, or experiencing a significant loss or traumatic event, might contribute to the development of hoarding symptoms. Traumatic experiences are hypothesized to leave an individual feeling unsafe, which, in turn, could make them rely more on their personal belongings for comfort and security (Cromer, Schmidt, & Murphy, 2007b; Frost & Hartl, 1996; Hartl, Duffany, Allan, Steketee, & Frost, 2005).

Symptom Maintenance. The behavioral models of hoarding explicitly integrate cognitive aspects in the maintenance of the condition, to arrive at a comprehensive cognitive-behavioral formulation. Hoarding has been conceptualized as an avoidance behavior associated with indecisiveness and perfectionism, which is maintained through both positive and negative reinforcement (Frost & Gross, 1993). Cognitive-behavioral models of hoarding propose that hoarders are overly concerned with making mistakes, and save possessions in order to avoid the mistake of throwing away a needed possession or important information (Frost & Gross, 1993; Frost & Hartl, 1996). When coupled with indecisiveness, such a concern over making mistakes might result in saving possessions that have a low probability of being used in the future (Frost & Gross, 1993). Saving is negatively reinforced by allowing hoarders to avoid the worry associated with making the mistake of prematurely discarding a possession that might be needed in the future. Delaying the decision about whether or not to discard a possession is seen as the "safe" decision. Saving is also negatively reinforced, by allowing hoarders to avoid the feelings of loss associated with discarding a cherished possession (Frost & Gross, 1993; Frost & Hartl, 1996; Frost & Steketee, 1998). Indeed, more recent cognitive accounts of the disorder highlight how some hoarders describe their possessions as being part of the self, and discarding their possessions is comparable to losing a close friend (Frost & Hartl, 1996). Some possessions come to signal a safe environment through their acquired association with comfort and safety (Frost & Hartl, 1996). Buying or acquiring new possessions is thought to be positively reinforced by providing a sense of comfort and safety (Grisham & Barlow, 2005), whereas the thought of discarding possessions violates this feeling of safety and is generally avoided (Frost & Hartl, 1996).

Empirical Evidence. Traumatic events are reported more frequently among hoarders compared to nonhoarders in the community (Hartl et al., 2005; Samuels et al., 2008). Childhood adversities, including sexual abuse, physical abuse, home break-ins, and having had something taken by force, have all been associated with hoarding behavior (Hartl, Duffany, Allan, Steketee, & Frost, 2005; Samuels et al., 2008). There is some evidence that hoarders who experienced a traumatic or stressful life event have significantly greater hoarding severity (specifically with respect to clutter), even when controlling for nonspecific psychological distress such as anxiety, depression, and even broadly based obsessive-compulsive symptomatology, suggesting that traumatic events might influence the clinical expression of hoarding (Cromer et al., 2007b). Individuals with a later age of onset are more likely to report a stressful life event directly prior to the onset of hoarding, compared to individuals with an early age of onset (Grisham, Brown, Liverant, & Campbell-Sills, 2005; Grisham, Frost, Steketee, Kim, & Hood, 2006). This finding has led some to suggest that hoarding behavior develops in response to traumatic or stressful life events for some individuals, whereas it might be a lifelong characterological phenomenon for others (Grisham & Barlow, 2005; Grisham et al., 2006). Research examining the traumatic and stressful life events reported by hoarders is limited by the retrospective collection of data, which could potentially be influenced by current functioning.

In support of the cognitive-behavioral conceptualizations of hoarding, a positive correlation has been demonstrated between hoarding and both indecisiveness and perfectionism (specifically, concern over mistakes and doubts about actions; Frost & Gross, 1993), and between indecisiveness and procrastination (Frost & Shows, 1993). Given their indecisiveness and concern over making mistakes, the task of deciding what to save and what to discard becomes very difficult. The majority of hoarders reported that they purchase extra food, household supplies, and toiletries to ensure they are prepared for future need, and carry "just in case items" in their purses and cars, including pens, paper, books, utensils, makeup, medication, blankets, and footwear (Frost & Gross, 1993). Hoarders also reported greater emotional attachment to their possessions, and derived more comfort from possessing the items (Frost & Gross, 1993; Frost, Hartl, Christian, & Williams, 1995).

Hoarders with and without OCD have been found to make under-inclusive categorizations when asked to sort items of personal relevance. Compared to healthy controls, they required more time to perform the sorting task, created more piles, and experienced greater distress. In addition, hoarding severity was associated with the number of piles created (Wincze, Steketee, & Frost, 2007). Interestingly, group differences were not found when participants sorted nonpersonal household items, suggesting that under-inclusive processing is limited to personally relevant items, and is not a more general feature of their information processing style.

Numerous case studies (Damecour & Charron, 1998; Greenberg, 1987; Greenberg, Witzum, & Levy, 1990; Shafran & Tallis, 1996) have detailed the anxiety-reducing role of compulsive acquisition and saving, indicating that hoarding compulsions function as operant conditioning processes similar to compulsive rituals in OCD. However, numerous randomized controlled trials, testing the efficacy of exposure and response prevention on compulsive hoarding, show reduced efficacy (Abramowitz, Franklin, Schwartz, & Furr, 2003), suggesting potential differences either in the habituation process during exposure exercises, or the presence of other potent factors that interfere with extinction (see the Chapter 12 for an explication of the important cognitive factors that contribute to the persistence of compulsive hoarding).

Hypochondriasis

There are functional parallels in the psychological processes that characterize hypochondriasis and OCD (Abramowitz & Moore, 2007). Although symptoms of hypochondriasis are usually perceived as more ego-syntonic (Bouman, 2008; Warwick & Salkovskis, 1990), both disorders are characterized by compulsive-like behaviors that are performed in response to intrusive thoughts and obsessional fears, but paradoxically maintain anxiety over time (McKay, Abramowitz, & Taylor, 2008). The preoccupation with health is considered akin to obsessional thoughts, and the safety behaviors performed to prevent illness are akin to compulsive rituals (Abramowitz, Schwartz, & Whiteside, 2002; Abramowitz & Moore, 2007; Fallon, Javitch, Hollander, & Liebowitz, 1991).

Despite the functional similarities between hypochondriasis and OCD, behavioral approaches to hypochondriasis have been relatively neglected. Warwick and Salkovskis (1990) attribute this to the fact that early behavioral formulations relied on conditioning theory and the presence of identifiable external stimuli, both of which were difficult to apply to hypochondriasis. Most behavioral theories of hypochondriasis are actually cognitive-behavioral theories that emphasize the central role of dysfunctional beliefs, and persistent misinterpretation of ambiguous or innocuous physical symptoms as personally threatening (Abramowitz et al., 2002; Taylor, Asmundson, & Coons, 2005; Warwick, 1989; Warwick & Salkovskis, 1990).

Symptom Development. A variety of health-related learning experiences are thought to play an important role in the development of hypochondriasis (Taylor, 2004; Taylor & Asmundson, 2004, 2008; Warwick & Salkovskis, 1990). Some potentially formative learning experiences include parental overprotection, parental modeling of illness behavior, previous disappointing healthcare experiences, or learning directly or vicariously that illness is rewarded (e.g., with toys, food, attention, sympathy, special care) or that it excuses one from regular responsibilities such as school, work, or chores (Taylor, 2004; Taylor & Asmundson, 2004; Warwick & Salkovskis, 1990). These learning experiences then contribute to the development of maladaptive health-related beliefs or assumptions (Warwick & Salkovskis, 1990).

Maladaptive beliefs or assumptions may become activated following exposure to health-related triggers (e.g., rashes, headaches, dizziness, muscle soreness) or during periods of heightened stress. Experiencing ambiguous bodily sensations or minor perturbations, visiting a hospital, learning about a friend's recent diagnosis, losing a family member, learning about new diseases through one's work or schooling (e.g., in medical school), and learning about illness-related information in the media (e.g., hearing about the death of a celebrity, AIDS publicity campaigns) are all potential precipitating factors (Abramowitz et al., 2002; Abramowitz & Moore, 2007; Bouman, 2008; Taylor, 2004). These triggers create apprehension, which then increases physiological arousal and preoccupation with the perceived abnormality of physical sensations (Warwick, 1989). Although early learning experiences are thought to play an important role in the development of hypochondriasis, Abramowitz et al. (2002) note that their cognitive-behavioral model of hypochondriasis places "less emphasis on understanding the etiologic process and a higher premium on understanding the persistence of hypochondriasis symptoms" (p. 1325).

Symptom Maintenance. Given the functional similarities between OCD and hypochondriasis, behavioral models propose that hypochondriasis is maintained through processes related to operant conditioning. Exposure to health triggers serves to increase anxiety, which, in turn, prompts the person to engage in a host of safety behaviors to prevent illness or disease. Safety behaviors are negatively reinforced, because they are effective in reducing health-related anxiety more rapidly than would have occurred naturally (Abramowitz & Moore, 2007), but paradoxically maintain health anxiety by preventing the natural extinction of health anxiety and promoting somatic preoccupation with health-related fears (Abramowitz & Moore, 2007; Bouman, 2008; Taylor, 2004; Taylor et al., 2005). Three main types of safety behaviors have been described in the literature: avoidance and escape behavior, checking behavior, and reassurance seeking. In addition to safety behaviors designed to avert feared outcomes, Taylor (2004) notes that individuals with hypochondriasis commonly have several safety "signals," which are stimuli that provide a sense of safety from health threats (e.g., readily accessible prescription medication, proximity to a hospital).

Fear of contracting an illness or disease is typically associated with phobic avoidance. For example, individuals with hypochondriasis may avoid going to the hospital, being close to people who are sick, meeting new people, or engaging in strenuous physical activity, for fear of contracting an illness or disease. They may also try to avoid all anxiety-provoking health-related triggers, such as visiting the doctor or watching the news (Abramowitz et al., 2002; Bouman, 2008; Bouman & Buwalda, 2008; Taylor, 2004; Taylor & Asmundson, 2004, 2008; Warwick, 1989). Although effective in reducing or preventing anxiety, avoidant and escape behaviors maintain health anxiety by preventing the individual from learning that the feared outcome does not occur (Warwick, 1989).

Checking behavior usually involves examining one's physical state or functioning. For example, individuals with hypochondriasis might examine their physical status (e.g., pulse, blood pressure, internal temperature), bodily fluids (e.g., urine, excrement), or bodily functions (e.g., frequent swallowing), feel for cancerous lumps, or examine the size, shape, and appearance of moles and rashes. Although checking behaviors reduce health anxiety in the short term, they can maintain anxiety in a number of ways. Body checking can become so extensive that it directly causes the discomfort or bodily changes that were misinterpreted in the first place, intensifying the fear and catastrophic thoughts. For example, touching an inflamed area, or manipulating a body part repeatedly to see if it still hurts, may actually cause pain and prevent healing (Warwick, 1989; Warwick & Salkovskis, 1990); the pain and inflammation are then misinterpreted as a confirmation of illness (Abramowitz et al., 2002). Checking also serves to maintain focus on particular body parts and health-related fears (Warwick & Salkovskis, 1990). In addition to body checking, individuals with hypochondriasis also tend to repetitively check medical references (e.g., textbooks, Internet websites) for reassurance about their physical state (Bouman, 2008; Bouman & Buwalda, 2008; Taylor, 2004; Taylor & Asmundson, 2004; Warwick, 1989). The reassurance is short-lived, however, as they learn that their symptoms could be attributed to an illness they had not yet considered, or a rare, lethal disease (Taylor, 2004; Taylor & Asmundson, 2004).

Reassurance seeking is considered by some as the defining symptom of hypochondriasis (Abramowitz et al., 2002). In addition to reassuring oneself by frequently examining body symptoms and consulting medical references, individuals with hypochondriasis often turn to others for health-related reassurance. They may request unnecessary medical tests or consultations, and seek reassurance from professionals (e.g., general practitioners, specialists, nurses), family members (e.g., partners, children, parents), or friends (Abramowitz et al., 2002; Bouman, 2008; Bouman & Buwalda, 2008; Taylor, 2004; Taylor & Asmundson, 2004; Warwick, 1989). In addition to frequently visiting their general practitioner, an individual with hypochondriasis might seek out additional physicians, make frequent emergency room visits, and rely on hospital help lines for additional reassurance. Following these interactions, individuals with hypochondriasis often continue to mentally review the reassurance statements, and may press for repeated reassurance regarding the same complaint (Warwick, 1989). Similar to compulsive behaviors, reassurance seeking becomes habitual, and increases in frequency, due to the immediate but short-term reduction in health anxiety (Abramowitz et al., 2002; Salkovskis & Warwick, 1986). Eventually, the individual will come to rely on reassurance to reduce health anxiety (Abramowitz et al., 2002), and the repetitive reassurance seeking maintains hypochondriasis by promoting preoccupation with bodily sensations.

Empirical Evidence. There is some evidence that individuals with elevated hypochondriacal concerns experienced more parental reinforcement and modeling of bodily symptoms during childhood. Anxiety sensitivity, or the fear of anxiety-related symptoms, was found to mediate the relationship between early learning experiences and elevated hypochondriacal concerns later in life (Watt & Stewart, 2000).

Empirical studies have demonstrated that safety behaviors (including checking and reassurance seeking) serve similar functions in both OCD and hypochondriasis. Reassurance has been shown to reduce estimations of negative outcomes (Haenen, de Jong, Schmidt, Stevens, & Visser, 2000), and to produce an immediate but temporary reduction in anxiety, followed by a paradoxical increase in anxiety and urge to seek additional reassurance (Salkovskis & Warwick, 1986). Consistent with a functional view of hypochondriasis, an experimental study demonstrated that personally relevant health-related stimuli triggered anxiety, which was strongly correlated

with the urge to engage in safety behaviors (Abramowitz & Moore, 2007). Participants who were permitted to engage in safety behaviors (e.g., reassurance seeking, taking temperature with an oral thermometer) experienced an immediate reduction in anxiety and urges, whereas those who refrained from using safety behaviors experienced a gradual reduction in anxiety and urges, similar to the spontaneous decay of compulsive urges in OCD (Rachman, de Silva, & Röper, 1976). These findings demonstrate that safety behaviors are negatively reinforced because they reduce health anxiety in the short term; however, they maintain hypochondriasis over time, by preventing the natural extinction of pathological health anxiety. Exposure and response prevention, a behavioral treatment that seeks to eliminate safety behaviors while being exposed to disease-related cues (e.g., visiting hospitals, watching videos about diseases), has been found to be effective in the treatment of hypochondriasis, providing further support for the role of operant processes in the symptom maintenance of this disorder (Visser & Bouman, 2001).

Body Dysmorphic Disorder

Given the functional parallels between BDD and OCD, it is perhaps not surprising that many of the behavioral models that have been proposed to account for the etiology of OCD have also been applied to BDD (Veale, 2004; see also Chapter 3). Although BDD symptoms are experienced as more ego-syntonic compared to OCD symptoms (Eisen, Phillips, Coles, & Rasmussen, 2004; McKay, Gosselin, & Gupta, 2008; Phillips, 1991; Simeon, Hollander, Stein, Cohen, & Aronowitz, 1995), both disorders are characterized by distressing and unwanted thoughts, coupled with irresistible urges to engage in compulsive behaviors aimed at reducing the distress (McKay, Abramowitz, et al., 2008; Neziroglu, Roberts, & Yaryura-Tobias, 2004).

Symptom Development. A comprehensive behavioral model that has been put forth to account for the development and maintenance of BDD (Neziroglu et al., 2004) is based on the two-factor conditioning model of Mowrer (1960). Most people who experience negative body-focused events (e.g., teasing related to appearance) do not develop BDD, and so this diathesis-stress model begins with the assumption that some individuals are at increased risk of developing BDD, due to a biological predisposition in conjunction with early operant conditioning, whereby physical appearance is positively reinforced by others.

According to Neziroglu and colleagues (2004), classical conditioning accounts for the development of BDD symptoms. Individuals with a biological predisposition, who are then exposed to early operant conditioning experiences that reinforce attractiveness, develop a strong belief that physical appearance is of ultimate importance, and is intimately connected with personal identity and self-worth. One's own learning experiences can then be further strengthened through social or vicarious learning (Bandura, 1977), whereby an individual observes another person being either positively reinforced for their attractiveness, or teased for falling short of the societal ideal.

Aversive experiences such as being teased, bullied, or abused, and many common changes in appearance, such as pubertal changes, the development of acne, or thinning hair, can serve as unconditioned stimuli that trigger unconditioned negative emotional responses such as shame, disgust, depression, and anxiety (Neziroglu, Khemlani-Patel, & Yaryura-Tobias, 2006). These unconditioned responses may become conditioned to certain body parts, and continue to trigger the same emotional states even in the absence of the unconditioned stimuli (Neziroglu et al., 2004; Neziroglu, Khemlani-Patel, & Veale, 2008; Veale, 2004). For example, a young woman who is sexually assaulted feels anxious, disgusted, and embarrassed, and is then conditioned to reexperience these emotional states when observing her body. An adolescent boy who is teased about having acne feels ashamed and disgusted, and then continues to feel ashamed and disgusted when observing his face in the mirror, even after his acne has improved and the teasing has stopped. An adolescent boy feels weak and scrawny while being physically bullied by a group of boys at school, and then continues to feel weak and scrawny in the presence of males, even after becoming a body-builder.

Symptom Maintenance. Consistent with Mowrer's (1960) two-factor theory of anxiety, Neziroglu and colleagues (2004) propose that BDD is maintained through operant conditioning processes. When individuals with BDD observe or think about their perceived flaw, their distress level increases. Similar to individuals with OCD, those with BDD develop strategies to reduce distress or avoid it altogether. For example, individuals with BDD are typically considered either "mirror avoiders" or "mirror checkers," and may alternate from one behavior to another over time (Gleaves & Ambwani, 2008; Neziroglu et al., 2004; Phillips,

1991; Veale & Riley, 2001). Mirror avoiders are fearful of observing their perceived "grotesque" image, and so cover all mirrors and reflective surfaces—or, alternatively, restrict looking in mirrors that are considered to be "bad" mirrors that highlight their disavowed features (Veale & Riley, 2001). They may also avoid social and public situations, in an attempt to prevent their appearance concerns and associated negative emotions from being triggered. Mirror checkers, on the other hand, can spend an inordinate amount of time scrutinizing their perceived physical flaws. Moreover, individuals with BDD engage in a host of creative safety behaviors, including camouflaging with makeup or clothing, using excessive skin or hair products, having dermatological and cosmetic procedures, exercising excessively, seeking reassurance, posturing (i.e., positioning themselves to make the defect less apparent), and hiding the perceived defect.

Behavioral models of BDD propose that avoidant, compulsive, and safety behaviors are maintained by negative reinforcement because they serve to temporarily reduce distress regarding appearance. However, they prevent the natural extinction of the conditioned negative emotional response, and are often counterproductive. Mirror checking is reinforced because individuals with BDD occasionally find their appearance acceptable in a "good" mirror or particular lighting (Veale, 2004), and the variable ratio schedule of reinforcement makes mirror checking highly resistant to extinction (Neziroglu et al., 2004; Veale & Riley, 2001). As the individual spends more time looking in the mirror, he or she becomes more self-conscious of the perceived defect, which reinforces the belief that the body part is hideous (Veale, 2004). Consequently, the distress experienced prior to mirror checking can actually be exacerbated (Veale & Riley, 2001), leading to compulsive attempts to correct appearance in order to make the flaw less noticeable. However, these attempts can become counterproductive, because compulsive and safety behaviors often increase self-consciousness and monitoring (e.g., wondering and checking if the camouflage is effective, or muscles appear large enough), draw attention to the perceived flaw, and in some cases, make it objectively worse (e.g., skin-picking). Thus, compulsive and safety behaviors maintain BDD by paradoxically sustaining the individual's preoccupation and distress (Neziroglu, Khemlani-Patel, & Veale, 2008; Veale, 2004).

Individuals with BDD are often concerned with several body parts, either simultaneously or over time (Phillips, 1991), and higher-order conditioning is the mechanism thought to account for this finding (Neziroglu, Khemlani-Patel, & Veale, 2008; Rabinowitz, Neziroglu, & Roberts, 2007). Through higher-order conditioning, a new conditioned stimulus is paired with the original conditioned stimulus, in the absence of the unconditioned stimulus, until the new conditioned stimulus produces the original conditioned response. For example, an adolescent boy who feels ashamed and disgusted, when perceiving acne on his face, shifts his attention to his nose, and then continues to feel ashamed and disgusted by the shape and size of his nose from this point forward. The finding that individuals with BDD typically have one primary concern, and multiple secondary concerns, can be explained by higher-order conditioning, because higher-order conditioned stimuli (e.g., nose) produce a less intense conditioned response compared to the original conditioned stimulus (e.g., skin).

Empirical Evidence. There is some evidence that individuals with BDD received more positive reinforcement for their physical appearance in childhood than for their behavior, intellect, or personality traits (Neziroglu et al., 2004). However, they also report more appearance-based teasing in childhood, and the frequency of childhood teasing has been found to correlate with BDD severity (Buhlmann, Cook, Fama, Wilhelm, 2007). Similarly, bullying victimization has been found to correlate with muscle dysmorphia later in life (Wolke & Sapouna, 2008). Studies of childhood teasing, bullying, and positive reinforcement of appearance are based on retrospective reports, however, and an individual's perception of past events might be influenced by current body concerns. Physical, sexual, and emotional abuse are prevalent among individuals with BDD (Didie et al, 2006; Neziroglu, Khemlani-Patel, & Yaryura-Tobias, 2006); however, abuse is thought to be a nonspecific risk factor for psychopathology, and research has not examined whether early abuse leads to later disturbance in adulthood, in the perception of particular body parts, as predicted from the model (Fallon & Ackard, 2002).

With respect to operant conditioning, it has been demonstrated that individuals with BDD report high levels of distress prior to mirror gazing, and expect that their distress will increase if they resist the urge to look in the mirror. However, in contrast to OCD compulsions, their distress actually increases to a greater extent after checking their appearance in the mirror, than it does after resisting the urge to do so, despite engaging in a series of complex safety behaviors while mirror gazing (Veale & Riley, 2001). Distress was not assessed *during* mirror gazing in the study by Veale and Riley, so it is unclear whether mirror gazing was negatively reinforced. It is possible that distress reduces at the initial glance, but then increases as mirror gazing duration increases. The negative reinforcement experienced during mirror gazing, if any, appears to be very short-lived. Yet, research has demonstrated that individuals with BDD continue to feel compelled to look in the mirror in the hope of looking different, verifying how they appear in public, and camouflaging themselves (Veale & Riley, 2001). Exposure and response prevention, a behavioral treatment which aims to reduce mirror gazing and safety behaviors associated with BDD, has been found to be effective in the treatment of BDD (McKay et al., 1997).

Trichotillomania

Despite apparent similarities in their repetitive behaviors, hair pulling in TTM and compulsive rituals in OCD are functionally dissimilar (Franklin, Tolin, & Diefenbach, 2008; see also Chapter 5). Although both individuals with OCD and TTM experience irresistible urges to engage in repetitive behaviors, and perceive these behaviors as unreasonable (Swedo, 1993), they differ in the extent to which they are aware of their repetitive behaviors (Franklin et al., 2008). In addition, OCD and TTM differ with respect to antecedent events that prompt the repetitive behaviors, as well as the emotions experienced before, during, and after the repetitive behaviors (Franklin et al., 2008; Stanley, Swann, Bowers, & Davis, 1992). Compulsive rituals are performed in response to obsessions to reduce anxiety, whereas hair pulling is often performed in response to boredom or tension, and initially results in feelings of pleasure and gratification (Franklin et al., 2008; Stanley et al., 1992; Woods, Adcock, & Conelea, 2008). Notwithstanding these functional differences, behavioral models have been proposed to account for the development and maintenance of both disorders.

Symptom Development. Most behavioral models of TTM place greater emphasis on the antecedent and consequent variables that perpetuate hair pulling, than on the variables that originally contributed to the development of TTM (Mansueto, Golumb, Thomas, & Stemberger; 1999; Mansueto, Stemberger, Thomas, & Golumb, 1997; Woods et al., 2008). It has been suggested that hair pulling begins as a response to stress or boredom

(Azrin & Nunn, 1973), or as a grooming behavior that is eventually shaped into pulling (Wetterneck & Woods, 2007). According to the behavioral model of TTM proposed by Mansueto and colleagues (1997), an association develops between the original hair pulling cue (conditioned stimulus) and the urge to pull, through classical conditioning. For example, an individual may have started hair pulling when working on a boring task while alone in the office. Over time, an association develops between each of these aspects of hair pulling (e.g., being alone, bored, and/or in the office) and the urge to pull (Mansueto et al., 1997; Wetterneck & Woods, 2007).

Hair pulling becomes a conditioned response to a variety of internal or external cues (Franklin, Tolin, & Diefenbach, 2006; Mansueto et al., 1997, 1999). Internal cues can include positive or negative affective states (e.g., boredom, fatigue, loneliness, indecision, excitement) or sensations (e.g., visual or tactile sensations such as hair color, appearance, or texture; physical sensations such as tingling, pressure, or irritation). These sensations can both result from previous pulling episodes and trigger subsequent episodes, thus creating a vicious cycle. External cues can include settings that trigger the urge to pull (e.g., office, bedroom, bathroom), as well as pulling implements (e.g., mirrors, tweezers). These implements may have initially been used to facilitate pulling, but through classical conditioning, the mere observation of these implements may trigger the urge to pull. Hair pulling cues are thought to differ, depending on whether pulling is focused or non-focused (automatic). Focused pulling is cued by tension, and involves a concerted effort to reduce an aversive internal state, whereas non-focused pulling is cued by low arousal and occurs with little awareness (Woods et al., 2008).

In addition to cues that trigger the urge to pull, other factors (called discriminative stimuli) either facilitate or inhibit the act of pulling (Mansueto et al., 1997). Similar to cues, discriminative stimuli can be internal or external to the individual. Internal facilitators include certain postural stances (e.g., hand resting near scalp) and urges to pull. External facilitators include the presence of pulling implements and the absence of other people.

Symptom Maintenance. Behavioral models propose that TTM functions to modulate emotions, and is maintained through operant conditioning (Franklin et al., 2006, 2008; Mansueto et al., 1997). Both negative and positive reinforcement are thought to perpetuate hair pulling, and urges that are reinforced by pulling will create stronger pulling urges over time (Azrin & Nunn, 1973; Franklin et al., 2008; Mansueto et al., 1997; Wetterneck & Woods, 2007). Hair pulling frequently produces an immediate feeling of pleasure, invigoration, or desired pain. In addition, the sensations derived from self-stimulatory behaviors (e.g., chewing, rubbing, or manipulating the hairs or hair roots) can be experienced as pleasurable and, through repetition, may create cravings for these sensations, which then serve as cues for subsequent pulling urges (Mansueto et al., 1997). The contemporary behavioral model of TTM suggests that pulling urges result from being deprived of a powerful reinforcer for a period of time, in the presence of cues that have previously been associated with hair pulling, and that some individuals have a biological predisposition that makes them more susceptible to specific tactile reinforcers (Wetterneck & Woods, 2007).

According to the emotion regulation hypothesis, the distracting effect of hair pulling can also provide relief from negative affective states (e.g., tension, anxiety, stress, boredom) and sensory discomfort (e.g., pressure or irritation at the pulling site). Contemporary behavioral models of TTM propose that focused hair pulling represents an attempt to avoid or escape from unpleasant private experiences, a concept referred to as "experiential avoidance" (Woods et al., 2008). Finally, the successful removal of particular hairs (e.g., coarse gray hairs) can provide both relief and satisfaction. Hair pulling is typically reinforced on an intermittent schedule (Mansueto et al., 1997), making it highly resistant to extinction. Hair pulling often continues until the episode is interrupted, the goal has been achieved, or the aversive consequences (e.g., negative affective states such as guilt and shame) outweigh the reinforcing effects. However, the negative affective states might serve as internal cues that prompt subsequent pulling episodes, creating a vicious cycle (Diefenbach, Mouton-Odum, & Stanley, 2002; Franklin et al., 2008; Mansueto et al., 1997).

Empirical Evidence. Although behavioral models of TTM say little about symptom development, there is a great deal of empirical support for the purported precipitants of pulling episodes. States of hyperarousal (e.g., feeling rushed, or negative affective states such as anger, anxiety, or frustration) and hypoarousal (e.g., boredom or fatigue, or sedentary activities such as reading and studying) often precipitate hair pulling episodes in individuals with TTM (Christenson, Ristvedt, & Mackenzie, 1993; Mackenzie, Ristvedt,

Christenson, Lebow, & Mitchell, 1995; O'Connor, Brisebois, Brault, Robillard, & Loiselle, 2003), and there is some preliminary evidence that experiential avoidance might mediate the relationship between antecedent private events and pulling (Begotka, Woods, & Wetterneck, 2004). Individuals who frequently engage in focused pulling report more stress, anxiety, and depression than those with TTM who rarely engage in focused pulling, suggesting that focused pulling might function to reduce these negative affective states (Flessner et al., 2008).

Supporting the role of operant conditioning in the maintenance of TTM, empirical research has demonstrated that the vast majority of individuals with TTM experience tension prior to, and gratification or relief following, pulling (Christenson, MacKenzie, & Mitchell, 1991), and a strong positive correlation exists between these two variables (du Toit, van Kradenburg, Niehaus, & Stein, 2001). A study examining the affective correlates of TTM demonstrated that hair pulling decreases boredom, anxiety, and tension across the pulling episode, and increases guilt, sadness, anger, and relief, suggesting that anxiety and tension may serve as both internal stimulus cues and reinforcers, whereas relief may serve as a reinforcer only (Diefenbach et al., 2002). Compared to a nonclinical sample, individuals with TTM reported larger decreases in boredom, sadness, anger, and tension, and larger increases in relief from before to during an experimental hair pulling task (Diefenbach, Tolin, Meunier, & Worhunsky, 2008). However, they also reported larger increases in guilt, sadness, and anger, which could potentially serve as internal cues that prompt subsequent pulling episodes. The authors interpreted their study findings as supporting a tension-reduction-tension hypothesis (Diefenbach et al, 2002), or an emotion regulation hypothesis (Diefenbach et al., 2008) of TTM, but the mechanism by which pulling improves negative affective states is unclear (Wetterneck & Woods, 2007). Individuals with TTM spend as much time manipulating the pulled hair as they do pulling it (Rapp, Miltenberger, Galensky, Ellinson, & Long, 1999), and many have oral self-stimulatory habits associated with pulling (e.g., rubbing hair along lips), suggesting that hair manipulation is positively reinforcing or may be used to self-soothe.

Tic Disorders

Despite superficial similarities in their repetitive behaviors, tics and compulsive rituals have qualitatively different functions (Miguel et al., 1995; see also Chapter 5). Tics and compulsive rituals differ in the extent to which individuals are aware of the repetitive behavior, and compulsive rituals are performed in response to obsessions, whereas tics are triggered by an increase in physical tension (O'Connor & Leclerc, 2008a). The dominant role of neurobiological factors in the etiology of tic disorders is well-accepted (APA, 2000; Leckman & Cohen, 1999); however, multicomponent models of tics, such as the Sensorimotor Regulation Model, have included behavioral factors to account for the maintenance of tics (O'Connor & Leclerc, 2008b). Some etiological models have also implicated behavioral factors in the development of tics.

Symptom Development. The early behavioral models proposed that tics develop as a conditioned response to an aversive event (Azrin & Nunn, 1973). For example, the tic might develop as an adaptive startle reflex (O'Connor & Leclerc, 2008a, 2008b), or as a means of relieving muscle tension (O'Connor, 2002) following a psychological or physical trauma. The tics gradually become incorporated into normal movements, even after the aversive event has passed, and eventually escape awareness (Azrin & Nunn, 1973). Lack of awareness perpetuates the tics, because the tics are repeated under different contingencies. As a result, the tics increase in frequency and become an overlearned, automatic habit that is resistant to extinction (O'Connor & Leclerc, 2008b). In some individuals, tics start off as an infrequent but normal behavior (e.g., throat clearing) that eventually increase in frequency and possibly change form (e.g., from throat clearing to grimacing or head jerking; Azrin & Nunn, 1973). It has also been proposed that tics develop in response to sensorial urges, such as somatic sensations in the bones, joints, or muscles (Evers & van de Wetering, 1994; Miguel et al., 1995).

The types of situations that are considered high risk for eliciting tics are highly variable across individuals. It has been proposed that it is not the situation, per se, that elicit the tics, but rather the emotional state that one experiences while in the situation (e.g., impatience, frustration, dissatisfaction; O'Connor, 2001). With repeated pairings of tics occurring in high-risk situations, eventually the anticipation of a high-risk situation can itself elicit tics.

Symptom Maintenance. The behavioral models propose that tics are maintained through operant conditioning, likely due to tension reduction and/ or social reinforcement (e.g., attention). It has been suggested that tic behaviors resulting from physical or emotional trauma might be socially reinforced in the form of sympathy (Azrin & Nunn, 1973); however, not all individuals develop tics following an aversive event. In these cases, tics are thought to be negatively reinforced by the reduction in muscle tension, or dysphoric feelings evoked by premonitory sensory signals (Azrin & Nunn, 1977; Evers & van de Wetering, 1994; O'Connor & Leclerc, 2008a, 2008b; Woods, Piacentini, Himle, & Chang, 2005). However, similar to compulsions, the relief is temporary and ultimately contributes to the maintenance of the tics (O'Connor, 2002). The tic cycle is a series of tense-release contractions, and by keeping the muscle in a chronic state of preparation, the tension is maintained.

Individuals with tic disorders adopt a variety of behavioral strategies to cope with tics, all of which paradoxically strengthen anticipation of tics, and thus maintain high levels of tension and tic behavior. Common coping strategies have been labeled the 3 Cs–containment, correction, and concealment (O'Connor, 2002). Containment includes strategies aimed at controlling tics, such as tensing, holding in, adopting a posture to control the tics, or contracting the muscle as a competing response. Correction includes incorporating the tics into an action, or changing it into another movement. Concealment includes strategies aimed at hiding the tics (e.g., wearing baggy clothing) or performing a larger action to disguise the tics. These coping strategies are attention-demanding tasks that increase anticipatory anxiety for the next tic, which in turn maintains a high level of tension that needs to be released.

Empirical Evidence. The empirical literature supporting tics as conditioned startle responses is inconclusive (O'Connor & Leclerc, 2008b). Although some tics develop following injury or trauma, this is not true of all tics (O'Connor, 2002).

The observation that tic frequency and intensity vary depending on the situation or context (Jankovic, 1997) suggests that tics are responsive to social and environmental contingencies (Miltenberger, Fugua, & Woods, 1998; O'Connor & LeClerc, 2008a). Tics are frequently elicited in situations appraised as "tense" (O'Connor et al., 2003), and most individuals report that the premonitory urges (e.g., energy, pressure, tension, or feeling that something is not "just right") completely cease following a tic, albeit temporarily (Woods et al., 2005). Functional analytic studies examining the role of reinforcement in tic maintenance have been limited

by small sample size (e.g., single case designs) and have generated mixed results regarding the type of operant maintaining the tics. For example, two studies supported the social-reinforcement function of tics (Carr, Taylor, Wallander, & Reiss, 1996; Watson & Sterling, 1998), whereas others supported a nonsocial function (Anderson, Vu, Derby, Goris, & McLaughlin, 2002; Carr, Sidener, Sidener, & Cummings, 2005; Roane, Piazza, Cercone, & Grados, 2002). In addition, many functional analytic studies examined children with developmental and intellectual disabilities, and it is possible that tics serve a different function in this group compared to typically developing children. For example, tics might actually be a stereotypy maintained by automatic positive (sensory) reinforcement in some individuals with developmental disabilities (Carr et al., 2005). Thus, the type of reinforcement that maintains tics is currently inconclusive.

Tics can be suppressed when instructed to do so (Himle & Woods, 2005; Verdellen, Hoogduin, & Keijsers, 2007), and although it was initially believed that tic suppression would result in a rebound effect during the post-suppression period (O'Connor, 2001), this has generally not been supported in empirical studies (Himle & Woods, 2005; Meidinger, Miltenberger, Himle, Omvig, & Trainor, 2005; Verdellen et al., 2007). Indeed, exposure and response prevention, a behavioral treatment that encourages prolonged tic suppression during exposure to premonitory sensory experiences, has been shown to be effective in the treatment of tics (Verdellen et al., 2007; Verdellen, Keijsers, Cath, & Hoogduin, 2004). Habit reversal, another treatment that developed directly out of the learning model of tics, and aims to weaken the behavioral response chain by practicing an alternative, appropriately reinforced response (Azrin & Nunn, 1973), has also received empirical support in the treatment of tics (see O'Connor, 2001; Verdellen et al., 2004).

Conclusion

While Freud was the first to coin the term *obsessional neurosis*, and correctly ascribed compulsive rituals to an anxiety-reducing role, the more fundamental tenets of his drive model of obsessional development, and the subsequent focus on the role of defense mechanisms, have remained largely untested. Currently, there is little empirical literature supporting psychoanalytic theory or therapy for OCD and related spectrum disorders.

Behavior models have advanced our understanding of OCD and the spectrum disorders by generating hypotheses that can be tested empirically. The role of operant conditioning in the maintenance of OCD and many of the spectrum disorders has been demonstrated through empirical research. It is now widely accepted that compulsive, avoidant, escape, reassurance seeking, and safety behaviors temporarily reduce the distress triggered by obsessive-like fears, but inadvertently function to sustain distress over time. Behavioral therapies for OCD and select spectrum conditions (hoarding, hypochondriasis, body dysmorphic disorder), which developed in response to these empirical findings, aim to weaken the conditioned fear response by exposing individuals to their feared stimuli, and preventing the engagement of these maintenance behaviors, until the discomfort naturally habituates.

In contrast to the strong evidence supporting the role of operant conditioning in symptom maintenance, the evidence supporting the role of classical conditioning in symptom development is relatively sparse. Indeed, some authors explicitly acknowledge that their models place a greater emphasis on symptom maintenance than on symptom development (Abramowitz et al., 2002), and this is also reflected in the substantially greater emphasis placed on maintaining factors in behavioral therapy. Most behavioral models downplay the role of classical conditioning in symptom development, and either attribute onset to operant conditioning (being rewarded/praised for certain behaviors early on) and/or vicarious learning (watching others model the behavior and/or being rewarded). Those models that do discuss the role of classical conditioning, and implicate traumatic or stressful life events in the onset of OCD and the spectrum disorders, have primarily been supported through retrospective research, and even then, for only a subset of individuals with OCD and spectrum conditions. Moreover, these risk factors are not specific to OCD or the spectrum disorders, and do not appear to be contiguous with the onset of conditions in the vast majority of cases.

How, then, do normal intrusions develop into clinical obsessions? The behavioral model has long been known to be unable to offer a comprehensive account of OCD (Rachman & Hodgson, 1980). This would appear even more evident, based on our current understanding of the broad-based heterogeneity of the disorder. Given that some individuals develop psychopathology in the absence of learning factors, and many others experience negative events

without developing psychopathology, it appears that diathesis-stress models are essential to understanding the onset and maintenance of OCD and the spectrum disorders. Biological and/or cognitive factors, when combined with relevant life events, might place some individuals at greater risk of developing OCD or a spectrum disorder. As will be discussed further in the next chapter, cognitive-behavioral theories have been put forth to better understand vulnerability to developing OCD and spectrum disorders. For example, cognitive-behavioral models of OCD discuss the role of inflated responsibility, threat overestimation, perfectionism, intolerance of uncertainty, and the importance of and need to control one's thoughts (Obsessive Compulsive Cognitions Working Group, 1997, 2001, 2003, 2005). Similarly, cognitive-behavioral models of hoarding emphasize the role of beliefs about responsibility, perfectionism, and the importance of possessions (Frost & Hartl, 1996; Frost & Steketee, 1998; Steketee & Frost, 2003). Cognitive-behavioral models of hypochondriasis assign a central role to the threatening appraisal of bodily symptoms (Abramowitz et al., 2002; Taylor et al., 2005; Warwick, 1989; Warwick & Salkovskis, 1990), whereas models of BDD highlight the negative appraisal of body image (Neziroglu, Khemlani-Patel, & Veale, 2008). Behavioral accounts are now incomplete without integration with these cognitive factors—for example, describing health anxiety and the associated reassurance seeking, in the absence of threatening health appraisals. Moreover, cognitive models may also account for apparently behavioral phenomena, such as extinction and habituation in OCD and the spectrum conditions.

Another important question that emerges is whether the behavioral model can help contribute to a better understanding of the phenomenology, clinical course, and outcome of the cluster of disorders belonging together under the umbrella of the "OCD spectrum" (see Table 11.1). Given the functional parallels with OCD symptoms, the strongest arguments for disorders with the greatest overlapping features can be made for hoarding, hypochondriasis, and body dysmorphic disorder. Individuals with these disorders engage in a variety of compulsive, safety, avoidant, and reassurance-seeking behaviors to prevent obsessive-like fears and reduce the associated anxiety, albeit temporarily. In contrast, tics and hair pulling frequently occur outside of awareness, and may be performed to reduce sensory or physical discomfort, or, in the case of hair pulling, to achieve a sense of pleasure or

Table 11.1 Comparison of Maintenance Factors across the OCD Spectrum Disorders

Disorder	Reinforcement	Compulsion	Safety Behaviors	Reassurance	Avoidance
OCD	Negative Positive ("just right" feeling)	**Function:** To prevent feared outcome To achieve "just right" feeling	**Function:** To prevent feared outcome	**Function:** To confirm safety	**Function:** To prevent feared outcome
		Example: Washing Checking	**Example:** Carry hand sanitizer Use paper towel to open door	**Example:** Seeking reassurance from doctors, family, friends	**Example:** Being the last person to leave the house Using public restrooms
Hoarding	Negative Positive	**Function:** To ensure preparation for future need To gain a sense of comfort and safety	**Function:** To ensure preparation for future need	**Function:** To confirm correct decision-making regarding saving and discarding possessions	**Function:** To avoid making a poor decision (discarding a needed possession) To avoid emotional upset (discarding a cherished possession)
		Example: Acquiring possessions Saving possessions	**Example:** Carrying "just in case items" (e.g., medication, pens)	**Example:** Seeking reassurance from family and friends before discarding possessions	**Example:** Making decisions about whether to discard possessions
HC	Negative	**Function:** Provide reassurance Early illness detection in order to prevent feared outcome	**Function:** Provide a sense of safety	**Function:** To confirm health status	**Function:** To avoid becoming ill To avoid health-anxiety triggers
		Example: Body checking Checking medical references	**Example:** Proximity to hospital Carrying medications at all times	**Example:** Unnecessary medical tests and consultations Frequent ER visits and calls to hospital help lines Seeking reassurance from doctors, family, friends	**Example:** Meeting sick people Visiting hospitals Exercising vigorously Watching the news

(Continued)

Table 11.1 Comparison of Maintenance Factors across the OCD Spectrum Disorders (*Continued*)

Disorder	Reinforcement	Compulsion	Safety Behaviors	Reassurance	Avoidance
BDD	Negative	**Function:** To confirm or correct appearance To check if appearance has improved	**Function:** To hide perceived defect	**Function:** To confirm acceptability of appearance	**Function:** To prevent self and others from observing the perceived defect
		Example: Frequent mirror checks Mirror gazing Correcting perceived defect (e.g., skin picking) Excessive exercise	**Example:** Camouflaging perceived defect with makeup or clothes Carrying makeup at all times Posturing to make defect less noticeable	**Example:** Seeking reassurance from friends and family (Note: Individuals with BDD may not want to draw attention to the perceived defect by seeking reassurance)	**Example:** Mirrors Social and public situations
TTM	Negative Positive	**Function:** To modulate emotions (e.g., alleviate anxiety and boredom, provide pleasure and gratification) To reduce sensory discomfort	Unknown	Unknown	Unknown
		Example: Hair pulling			
Tic	Negative	**Function:** To reduce physical tension To stop premonitory urges	**Function:** To control tics To hide or disguise tics	Unknown	Unknown
		Example: Vocal (e.g. grunting, throat clearing) Motor (e.g. blinking, head jerking)	**Example:** Containment (e.g., tense muscles) Correction (e.g., incorporate tic into another movement) Concealment (e.g., hide with clothes)		

gratification. Further, tics and trichotillomania are not associated with prominent reassurance-seeking or avoidance behaviors. Based on similarities in the operant conditioning processes implicated in the maintenance of the disorders, OCD, hoarding, hypochondriasis, and body dysmorphic disorder are the most likely candidates for the obsessive compulsive spectrum.

The conceptualization and treatment of behavioral factors will become clearer as the taxonomic boundaries of the spectrum disorders become better delineated. There also remains a need to examine a greater breadth of behavioral-based constructs, including reassurance-seeking behaviors and the role of "not just right" feelings that frequently prompt behavioral rituals in OCD and spectrum disorders. Finally, future programmatic research is required that aims to integrate contemporary behavioral accounts of OCD and spectrum disorders with the findings emerging from clinical neurosciences.

Summary and Future Directions

The role of operant conditioning in the maintenance of OCD and spectrum conditions has been persuasively demonstrated through empirical research. In contrast, the factors implicated in symptom development are less well understood, in part because much of the research on etiological factors has been limited by retrospective data collection. Prospective research examining the role of early traumatic or stressful events is required to elucidate the role of classical conditioning in the etiology of OCD and the spectrum disorders. The impact of observational learning and informational transmission on the development of OCD and spectrum conditions also warrants additional research.

Obsessive compulsive spectrum conditions have typically been clustered based on the apparent similarities or topography of their symptoms, rather than the function of their symptoms. Ecological momentary assessment methodology could be used to compare precipitants and functions of compulsive, safety, and reassurance-seeking behaviors across the OC spectrum, as well as the operants maintaining the behaviors.

Despite the great success of exposure and response prevention as a behavioral-based treatment of OCD and spectrum conditions, there has been a dearth of investigation into the putative mechanisms of change, and this may represent an optimal arena for the further exploration of behavioral mechanisms in the maintenance of these conditions. Future research should also examine factors that interfere with habituation and extinction, in order to better understand why some OC spectrum conditions, such as hoarding, do not respond as well to exposure and response prevention.

Related Chapters

Chapter 2. Phenomenology and Epidemiology of Obsessive Compulsive Disorder

Chapter 3. Phenomenology and Epidemiology of Body Dysmorphic Disorder

Chapter 4. Phenomenology and Characteristics of Compulsive Hoarding

Chapter 5. Phenomenology and Epidemiology of Tic Disorders and Trichotillomania

Chapter 12. Cognitive Approaches to Understanding Obsessive-Compulsive and Related Disorders

Acknowledgment

The authors would like to thank Beverley Bouffard and Lindsay Dupuis for reviewing and providing comments on the chapter.

References

Abramowitz, J. S. (1997). Effectiveness of psychological and pharmacological treatments for obsessive-compulsive disorder: A quantitative review. *Journal of Consulting and Clinical Psychology, 65,* 44–52.

Abramowitz, J. S., Franklin, M. E., Schwartz, S. A., & Furr, J. M. (2003). Symptom presentation and outcome of cognitive-behavioral therapy for obsessive-compulsive disorder. *Journal of Consulting and Clinical Psychology, 71,* 1049–1057.

Abramowitz, J. S., & Moore, E. L., (2007). An experimental analysis of hypochondriasis. *Behavior Research and Therapy, 45,* 413–424.

Abramowitz, J. S., Khandker, M., Nelson, C. A., Deacon, B. J., & Rygwall, R. (2006). The role of cognitive factors in the pathogenesis of obsessive-compulsive symptoms: A prospective study. *Behavior Research and Therapy, 44,* 1361–1374.

Abramowitz, J. S., Schwartz, S. A., & Whiteside, S. P. (2002). A contemporary conceptual model of hypochondriasis. *Mayo Clinic Proceedings, 77,* 1323–1330.

American Psychiatric Association. (1987). *Diagnostic and statistical manual of mental disorders* (DSM-III-revised). Washington, DC: Author.

American Psychiatric Association. (2000). *Diagnostic and statistical manual of mental disorders* (DSM-IV-text revision). Washington, DC: Author.

Anderson, M. T., Vu, C., Derby, M., Goris, M., & McLaughlin, T. F. (2002). Using functional procedures to monitor medication effects in an outpatient and school setting. *Psychology in the Schools, 39,* 73–76.

Azrin, N. H., & Nunn, R. G. (1973). Habit-reversal: A method of eliminating nervous habits and tics. *Behavior Research and Therapy, 11*, 619–628.

Azrin, N. H. & Nunn, R. G. (1977). *Habit control in a day.* New York, NY: Simon & Schuster.

Bandura, A. (1977). *Social learning theory.* Englewood Cliffs, NJ: Prentice Hall.

Begotka, A. M., Woods, D. W., & Wetterneck, C. T. (2004). The relationship between experiential avoidance and the severity of trichotillomania in a non-referred sample. *Journal of Behavior Therapy and Experimental Psychiatry, 35*, 17–24.

Bhar, S. S., & Kyrios, M. (2007). An investigation of self-ambivalence in obsessive-compulsive disorders. *Behavior Research and Therapy, 45*, 1845–1857.

Biby, E. L. (1998). The relationship between body dysmorphic disorder and depression, self-esteem, somatization, and obsessive–compulsive disorder. *Journal of Clinical Psychology, 54*, 489–499.

Bouman, T. K. (2008). Hypochondriasis. In J. S. Abramowitz, D. McKay, & S. Taylor (Eds.), *Obsessive-compulsive disorder: Subtypes and spectrum conditions* (pp. 196–211). New York, NY: Elsevier.

Bouman, T. K., & Buwalda, F. M. (2008). A psychoeducational approach to hypochondriasis: Background, content, and practice guidelines. *Cognitive and Behavioral Practice, 15*, 231–243.

Brunswick, R. M. (1928). A supplement to Freud's "History of an Infantile Neurosis." *International Journal of Psychoanalysis, 9*, 439–476.

Buhlmann, U., Cook, L. M., Fama, J. M., & Wilhelm, S. (2007). Perceived teasing experiences in body dysmorphic disorder. *Body Image, 4*, 381–385.

Carr, J. E., Sidener, T. M., Sidener, D. W., & Cummings, A. R. (2005). Functional analysis and habit reversal treatment of tics. *Behavioral Interventions, 20*, 185–202.

Carr, J. E., Taylor, C. C., Wallander, R. J., & Reiss, M. L. (1996). A functional-analytic approach to the diagnosis of a transient tic disorder. *Journal of Behavior Therapy and Experimental Psychiatry, 27*, 291–297.

Christenson, G. A., MacKenzie, T. B., & Mitchell, J. E. (1991). Characteristics of 60 adult chronic hair pullers. *American Journal of Psychiatry, 148*, 365–370.

Christenson, G. A., Ristvedt, S. L., & MacKenzie, T. B. (1993). Identification of trichotillomania cue profiles. *Behavior Research and Therapy, 31*, 315–320.

Coles, M. E., Frost, R. O., Heimberg, R. G., & Rheaume, J. (2003). "Not just right experiences": Perfectionism, obsessive-compulsive features and general psychopathology. *Behavior Research and Therapy, 41*, 681–700.

Cororve, M. B., & Gleaves, D. H. (2001). Body dysmorphic disorder: A review of conceptualizations, assessment, and treatment strategies. *Clinical Psychology Review, 21*, 949–970.

Cromer, K. R., Schmidt, N. B., & Murphy, D. L. (2007a). An investigation of traumatic life events and obsessive-compulsive disorder. *Behavior Research and Therapy, 45*, 1683–1691.

Cromer, K. R., Schmidt, N. B., & Murphy, D. L. (2007b). Do traumatic events influence the clinical expression of compulsive hoarding? *Behavior Research and Therapy, 45*, 2581–2592.

Damecour, C. L., & Charron, M. (1998). Hoarding: A symptom, not a syndrome. *Journal of Clinical Psychiatry, 59*, 267–272.

Deacon, B., & Maack, D. J. (2008). The effects of safety behaviors on the fear of contamination: An experimental investigation. *Behavior Research and Therapy, 46*, 537–547.

de Silva, P., & Marks, M. (2001). Traumatic experiences, post-traumatic stress disorder and obsessive-compulsive disorder. *International Review of Psychiatry 13*, 172–180.

de Silva, P., Menzies, R. G., & Shafran, R. (2003). Spontaneous decay of compulsive urges: The case of covert compulsions. *Behavior Research and Therapy, 41*, 129–137.

Didie, E. R., Tortolani, C. C., Pope, C. G., Menard, W., Fay, C., & Philips, K. A. (2006). Childhood abuse and neglect in body dysmorphic disorder. *Child Abuse and Neglect, 30*, 1105–1115.

Diefenbach, G. J., Mouton-Odum, S., & Stanley, M. A. (2002). Affective correlates of trichotillomania. *Behavior Research and Therapy, 40*, 1305–1315.

Diefenbach, G. J., Tolin, D. F., Meunier, S., & Worhunsky, P. (2008). Emotion regulation and trichotillomania: A comparison of clinical and non-clinical hair pulling. *Journal of Behavior Therapy and Experimental Psychiatry, 39*, 32–41.

Dollard, J., & Miller, N. E. (1950). *Personality and psychotherapy: analysis in terms of learning, thinking and culture.* New York: McGraw-Hill.

Du Toit, P. L., van Kradenburg, J., Niehaus, D. J. H., & Stein, D. J. (2001). Characteristics and phenomenology of hair pulling: An exploration of subtypes. *Comprehensive Psychiatry, 42*, 247–256.

Ecker, W., & Gonner, S. (2008). Incompleteness and harm avoidance in OCD symptom dimensions. *Behavior Research and Therapy, 46*, 895–904.

Eddy, K. T., Dutra, L., Bradley, R. & Westen, D. (2004) A multidimensional meta-analysis of psychotherapy and pharmacotherapy for obsessive-compulsive disorder. *Clinical Psychology Review, 24*, 1011–1030.

Eisen, J. L., Phillips, K. A., Coles, M. E., & Rasmussen, S. (2004). Insight in obsessive compulsive disorder and body dysmorphic disorder. *Comprehensive Psychiatry, 45*, 10–15.

Emmelkamp, P. M. G. (1982). *Phobic and obsessive compulsive disorders: Theory, research, and practice.* New York, NY: Plenum Press.

Evers, R. A. F., & van de Wetering, B. J. M. (1994). A treatment model for motor tics based on a specific tension-reduction technique. *Journal of Behavior Therapy and Experimental Psychiatry, 25*, 255–260.

Fallon, P., & Ackard, D. M. (2002). Sexual abuse and body image. In T. F. Cash, & T. Pruzinsky (Eds.), *Body image: A handbook of theory, research, and clinical practice* (pp. 117–124). New York: Guilford Press.

Fallon, B. A., Javitch, J. A., Hollander, E., & Liebowitz, M. R. (1991). Hypochondriasis and obsessive compulsive disorder: Overlaps in diagnosis and treatment. *Journal of Clinical Psychiatry, 52*, 457–460.

Fenichel, O. (1945a). Neurotic acting out. *Psychoanalytic Review, 32*, 197–206.

Fenichel, O. (1945b). *The Psychoanalytic Theory of Neurosis.* New York: Norton.

Flessner, C. A., Conelea, C. A., Woods, D. W., Franklin, M. E., Keuthen, N. J., & Cashin, S. E. (2008). Styles of pulling in trichotillomania: Exploring differences in symptom severity, phenomenology, and functional impact. *Behavior Research and Therapy, 46*, 345–357.

Franklin, M. E., Tolin, D. F., & Diefenbach, D. (2006). Trichotillomania. In E. Hollander & D. J. Stein (Eds.), *Handbook of impulse control disorders* (pp. 149–173). Washington, DC: American Psychiatric Publishing.

Franklin, M. E., Tolin, D. F., & Diefenbach, D. (2008). Trichotillomania. In J. S. Abramowitz, D. McKay, & S. Taylor (Eds.), *Obsessive-compulsive disorder: Subtypes and spectrum conditions* (pp. 139–159). New York, NY: Elsevier.

Freeman, J. B., & Leonard, H. L. (2000) Sexual obsessions in obsessive-compulsive disorder. *Journal of the American Academy of Child and Adolescent Psychiatry, 39*, 141–142.

Freud, S. (1895). On the grounds for detaching a particular syndrome from neurasthenia under the description "anxiety neurosis." In *Standard edition of the complete psychological works of Sigmund Freud* (Vol. 3). London: Hogarth.

Freud, S. (1896). Further remarks on the neuro-psychoses of defence. In *Standard edition* (Vol. 3). London: Hogarth.

Freud, S. (1908). Character and anal erotism. In *Collected papers* (Vol. 10). London: Hogarth.

Freud, S. (1909). Notes upon a case of obsessional neurosis. In *Standard edition* (Vol. 10). London: Hogarth.

Freud., S. (1926). Inhibitions, symptoms and anxiety. In *Standard edition* (Vol. 19). London: Hogarth.

Frost, R. O., & Gross, R. C. (1993). The hoarding of possessions. *Behavior Research and Therapy, 31*, 367–381.

Frost, R. O., & Hartl, T. L. (1996). A cognitive-behavioral model of compulsive hoarding. *Behavior Research and Therapy, 34*, 341–350.

Frost, R. O., Hartl, T. L., Christian, R., & Williams, N. (1995). The value of possessions in compulsive hoarding: Patterns of use and attachment. *Behavior Research and Therapy, 33*, 897–902.

Frost, R., & Shows, D. (1993). The nature and measurement of compulsive indecisiveness. *Behavior Research and Therapy, 31*, 683–692.

Frost, R. O., & Steketee, G. (1998). Hoarding: Clinical aspects and treatment strategies. In M. A. Jenike, L. Baer, & W. E. Minichiello (Eds.), *Obsessive-compulsive disorder: Practical management* (3rd edition, pp. 533–554) St. Louis, MO: Mosby Yearbook Medical.

Gleaves, D. H., & Ambwani, S. (2008). Body dysmorphic disorder. In J. S. Abromowitz, D. McKay, & S. Taylor (Eds.), *Clinical handbook of obsessive-compulsive disorder and related problems* (pp. 288–303). Baltimore, MD: Johns Hopkins University Press.

Gothelf, D., Aharonovsky, O., Horesh, N., Carty, T., & Apter, A. (2004). Life events and personality factors in children and adolescents with obsessive-compulsive disorder and other anxiety disorders. *Comprehensive Psychiatry, 45*, 192–198.

Greenberg, D. (1987). Compulsive hoarding. *American Journal of Psychotherapy, 41*, 409–416.

Greenberg, H. R., & Sarner, C. A. (1965). Trichotillomania: Symptom and syndrome. *Archives of General Psychiatry, 12*, 482–489.

Greenberg, D., Witzum, E., & Levy, A. (1990). Hoarding as a psychiatric symptom. *Journal of Clinical Psychiatry, 51*, 417–421.

Grisham, J. R., & Barlow, D. H. (2005). Compulsive hoarding: Current research and theory. *Journal of Psychopathology and Behavioral Assessment, 27*, 45–52.

Grisham, J. R., Brown, T. A., Liverant, G. I., & Campbell-Sills, L. (2005). The distinctiveness of compulsive hoarding from obsessive–compulsive disorder. *Journal of Anxiety Disorders, 19*, 767–779.

Grisham, J. R., Frost, R. O., Steketee, G., Kim, H. J., & Hood, S. (2006). Age of onset of compulsive hoarding. *Journal of Anxiety Disorders, 20*, 675–686.

Haenen, M. A., de Jong, P. J., Schmidt, A. J. M., Stevens, S., & Visser, L. (2000). Hypochondriacs' estimation of negative outcomes: Domain-specificity and responsiveness to reassuring and alarming information. *Behavior Research and Therapy, 38*, 819–833.

Hartl, T. L., Duffany, S. R., Allen, G. J., Steketee, G., & Frost, R. O. (2005). Relationships among compulsive hoarding, trauma, and attention-deficit/hyperactivity disorder. *Behavior Research and Therapy, 43*, 269–276.

Heatherington. E. M. & Brackbill, Y. (1963). Etiology and covariation of obstinacy, orderliness and parsimony in young children. *Child Development, 34, 919–943.*

Himle, M. B., & Woods, D. W. (2005). An experimental evaluation of tic suppression and the tic rebound effect. *Behavior Research and Therapy, 43*, 1443–1451.

Hollander, E., Friedberg, J., Wasserman, S., Yeh, C., & Iyengar, R. (2005). The case for the OCD spectrum. In J. S. Abramowitz & A. C. Houts (Eds.), *Concepts and controversies in obsessive-compulsive disorder* (pp. 95–118). New York: Springer.

Horowitz, M. J. (1975). Intrusive and repetitive thoughts after experimental stress. *Archives of General Psychiatry, 32*, 1457–1463.

Janet, P. (1903). *Les Obsessions et la Psychasthenie.* Paris: Alcan.

Jankovic, J. (1997). Phenomenology and classification of tics. *Neurologic Clinics of North America, 15*, 267–275.

Jones, M. K., & Menzies, R. G. (1998). Role of perceived danger in the mediation of obsessive- compulsive washing. *Depression and Anxiety, 8*, 121–125.

Jordan, B. K., Schlenger, W. E., Hough, R., Kulka, R. A., Weiss, D., Fairbank, J. A., et al. (1991). Lifetime and current prevalence ofspecific psychiatric disorders among Vietnam veterans and controls. *Archives of General Psychiatry, 48*, 207–215.

Kempke, S., & Luyten, P. (2007). Psychodynamic and cognitive-behavioral approaches of obsessive-compulsive disorder: Is it time to work through our ambivalence? *Bulletin of the Menninger Clinic, 71*, 291–311.

Kenyon, F. E. (1965). Hypochondriasis: a survey of some historical, clinical, and social aspects. British Journal of Medical Psychology, *38*, 117–133.

Kenyon, F. E. (1976). Hypochondriacal states. *British Journal of Psychiatry, 129*, 1–14.

Kraepelin, E. (1915). *Psychiatrie*, Vol 4. Leipzig: Barth.

Krishnan, K. R. R., Davidson, J. R. T., & Guajardo, C. (1985). Trichotillomania: A review. *Comprehensive Psychiatry, 26*, 123–128.

Leckman, J. I., & Cohen, D. J. (1999). Tourette's syndrome: Developmental psychopathology and clinical care. New York, NY: Wiley.

Lipsett, D. R. (1974). Psychodynamic considerations of hypochondriasis. *Psychotherapy and Psychosomatics, 23*, 132–141.

Mackenzie, T. B., Ristvedt, S. L., Christenson, G. A., Lebow, A. S., & Mitchell, J. E. (1995). Identification of cues associated with compulsive, bulimic, & hair pulling symptoms. *Journal of Behavior Therapy and Experimental Psychiatry, 26*, 9–16.

Mahler, M. S., & Luke, J. A. (1946). Outcome of the tic syndrome. *Journal of Nervous and Mental Disease, 103,* 433–445.

Mansueto, C. S. Golumb, R. G., Thomas, A. M., & Stemberger, R. M. T. (1999). A comprehensive model for behavioral treatment of trichotillomania. *Cognitive and Behavioral Practice, 6,* 23–43.

Mansueto, C. S., Stemberger, R. M. T., Thomas, A. M., & Golomb, R. G. (1997). Trichotillomania: A comprehensive behavioral model. *Clinical Psychology Review, 17,* 567–577.

McKay, D., Abramowitz, J. S., & Taylor, S. (2008). Discussion: The obsessive-compulsive spectrum. In J. S. Abramowitz, D. McKay, & S. Taylor (Eds.), *Obsessive-compulsive disorder: Subtypes and spectrum conditions* (pp. 287–300). New York, NY: Elsevier.

McKay, D., Gosselin, J. T., & Gupta, S. (2008). Body dysmorphic disorder. In J. S. Abramowitz, D. McKay, & S. Taylor (Eds.), *Obsessive-compulsive disorder: Subtypes and spectrum conditions* (pp. 177–193). New York: NY: Elsevier.

McKay, D., Todaro, J., Neziroglu, F., Campisi, T., Moritz, E. K., & Yaryura-Tobias, J. A. (1997). Body dysmorphic disorder: A preliminary evaluation of treatment and maintenance using exposure with response prevention. *Behavior Research and Therapy, 35,* 67–70.

McKeon, J., Roa, B., & Mann, A. (1984). Life events and personality traits in obsessive- compulsive neurosis. *British Journal of Psychiatry, 144,* 185–189.

Meidinger, A. L, Miltenberger, R. G., Himle, M., Omvig, M., & Trainor, C. (2005). An investigation of tic suppression and the rebound effect in Tourette's disorder. *Behavior Modification, 29,* 716–745.

Miguel, E., Coffey, B., Baer, L., Savage, C., Rauch, S., & Jenike, M. (1995). Phenomenology of intentional repetitive behaviors in obsessive-compulsive disorder and Tourette's disorder. *Journal of Clinical Psychiatry, 56,* 246–255.

Miltenberger, R. G., Fugua, R. W., & Woods, D. W. (1998). Applying behavior analysis to clinical problems: Review and analysis of habit reversal. *Journal of Applied Behavior Analysis, 31,* 447–469.

Mineka, S., & Zinbarg, R. E. (2006). A contemporary learning theory perspective on the etiology of anxiety disorder: It's not what you thought it was. *American Psychologist, 61,* 10–26.

Morselli, E. (1891). Sulla dismorfofobia e sulla tafefobia. *Bolletinno dello R accademia di Genova, 6,* 110–119.

Mowrer, O. H., (1939). A stimulus-response analysis of anxiety and its role as a reinforcing agent. *Psychological Review, 46,* 553–565.

Mowrer, O. H. (1960). *Learning theory and the symbolic processes.* New York, NY: Wiley.

Neziroglu, F., Khemlani-Patel, S., & Yaryura-Tobias, J. A. (2006). Rates of abuse in body dysmorphic disorder and obsessive-compulsive disorder. *Body Image, 3,* 189–193.

Neziroglu, F., Khemlani-Patel, S., & Veale, D. (2008). Social learning theory and cognitive-behavioral models of body dysmorphic disorder. *Body Image, 5,* 28–38.

Neziroglu, F., Roberts, M., & Yaryura-Tobias, J. A. (2004). A behavioral model for body dysmorphic disorder. *Psychiatric Annals, 34,* 915–920.

National Institute for Health and Clinical Excellence (2005). Obsessive-compulsive disorder: Core interventions in the treatment of obsessive-compulsive disorder and body dysmorphic disorder. London: National Institute for Health and Clinical Excellence.

Obsessive Compulsive Cognitions Working Group (1997). Cognitive assessment of obsessive-compulsive disorder. *Behavior Research and Therapy, 35,* 667–681.

Obsessive Compulsive Cognitions Working Group (2001). Development and initial validation of the obsessive beliefs questionnaire and the interpretations of intrusions inventory. *Behavior Research and Therapy, 39,* 987–1006.

Obsessive Compulsive Cognitions Working Group (2003). Psychometric validation of the obsessional beliefs questionnaire and the interpretations of intrusions inventory. *Behavior Research and Therapy, 41,* 863–878.

Obsessive Compulsive Cognitions Working Group (2005). Psychometric validation of the obsessive beliefs questionnaire and interpretation of intrusions inventory—Part 2: Factor analyses and testing of a brief version. *Behavior Research and Therapy, 43,* 1527–1542.

O'Connor, J. J. (2008). A flaw in the fabric: Toward an interpersonal psychoanalytic understanding of obsessive-compulsive disorder. *Journal of Contemporary Psychotherapy, 38,* 87–96.

O'Connor, K. (2001). Clinical and psychological features distinguishing obsessive-compulsive and chronic tic disorders. *Clinical Psychology Review, 21,* 631–660.

O'Connor, K. (2002). A cognitive-behavioral/psychophysiological model of tic disorders. *Behavior Research and Therapy, 40,* 1113–1142.

O'Connor, K., Brisebois, H., Brault, M., Robillard, S., & Loiselle, J. (2003). Behavioral activity associated with onset in chronic tic and habit disorder. *Behavior Research and Therapy, 41,* 241–249.

O'Connor, K., & Leclerc, J., (2008a). Tic disorders and Tourette syndrome. In J. S. Abramowitz, D. McKay, & S. Taylor (Eds.), *Obsessive-compulsive disorder: Subtypes and spectrum conditions* (pp. 212–229). New York, NY: Elsevier.

O'Connor, K. P., & Leclerc, J. (2008b). Tourette syndrome and chronic tic disorders. In J. S. Abromowitz, D. McKay, & S. Taylor (Eds.), *Clinical handbook of obsessive-compulsive disorder and related problems* (pp. 205–221). Baltimore, MD: Johns Hopkins University Press.

Oosthuizen, P. P., & Castle, D. (1998). Body dysmorphic disorder— a distinct entity? *South African Medical Journal, 88,* 766–769.

Parkinson, L., & Rachman, S. (1981). Part III—Intrusive thoughts: The effects of an uncontrived stress. *Advances in Behaviour Research and Therapy, 3,* 111–118.

Pertusa, A., Fullana, M. A., Singh, S., Alonso, P., Menchon, J. M., & Mataix-Cols, D. (2008). Compulsive hoarding: OCD symptom, distinct clinical syndrome, or both? *American Journal of Psychiatry, 165,* 1289–1298.

Phillips, K. A. (1991). Body dysmorphic disorder: The distress of imagined ugliness. *American Journal of Psychiatry, 148,* 1138–1149.

Powers, M. B., Smits, J. A. J., & Telch, M. J. (2004). Disentangling the effects of safety-behavior utilization and safety-behavior availability during exposure-based treatment: A placebo-controlled trial. *Journal of Consulting and Clinical Psychology, 72,* 448–454.

Rabinowitz, D., Neziroglu, F., & Roberts, M. (2007). Clinical application of a behavioral model for the treatment of body dysmorphic disorder. *Cognitive and Behavioral Practice, 14,* 231–237.

Rachman, S., de Silva, P., & Röper, G. (1976). The spontaneous decay of compulsive urges. *Behavior Research and Therapy, 14,* 445–453.

Rachman, S., Elliot, C. M., Shafran, R., & Radomsky, A.S. (2009). Separating hoarding from OCD. *Behavior Research and Therapy, 47,* 520–522.

Rachman S. J., & Hodgson, R. J. (1980). *Obsessions and compulsions.* Englewood Cliffs, NJ: Prentice-Hall.

Rachman, S., Radomsky, A. S., & Shafran, R. (2008). Safety behavior: A reconsideration. *Behavior Research and Therapy, 46,* 163–173.

Rachman, S., Shafran, R., Mitchell, D., Trant, J., & Teachman, B. (1996). How to remain neutral: An experimental analysis of neutralization. *Behavior Research and Therapy, 34,* 889–898.

Rado, S. (1959). Obsessive behavior. In S. Arieti (Ed.), *American Handbook of Psychiatry* (pp.325–343). New York: Basic Books.

Rapp, J. T., Miltenberger, R. G., Galensky, T. L., Ellingson, S. A., & Long, E. S. (1999). A functional analysis of hair pulling. *Journal of Applied Behavior Analysis, 32,* 329–337.

Rector, N. A., Cassin, S. E., Richter, M. A., & Burroughs, E. (2009). Obsessive beliefs in first-degree relatives of patients with OCD: A test of the cognitive vulnerability model. *Journal of Anxiety Disorders, 23*(1), 145–149.

Roane, H. S., Piazza, C. C., Cercone, J. J., & Grados, M. (2002). Assessment and treatment of vocal tics associated with Tourette's syndrome. *Behavior Modification, 26,* 482–498.

Sadock, B. J., Kaplan, H. I., & Sadock, V. A. (2007). *Kaplan and Sadock's synopsis of psychiatry* (10th edition). Philadelphia, PA: Lippincott Williams & Wilkins.

Salkovskis, P. M. (1991). The importance of behavior in the maintenance of anxiety and panic: A cognitive account. *Behavioral Psychotherapy, 19,* 6–19.

Salkovskis, P. M., Thorpe, S. J., Wahl, K., Wroe, A. L., & Forrester, E. (2003). Neutralizing increases discomfort associated with obsessional thoughts: An experimental study with obsessional patients. *Journal of Abnormal Psychology, 112,* 709–715.

Salkovskis, P. M. & Warwick, H. M. C. (1986). Morbid preoccupations, health anxiety, and reassurance: A cognitive-behavioral approach to hypochondriasis. *Behavior Research and Therapy, 24,* 597–602.

Salkovskis, P. M., Westbrook, D., Davis, J., Jeavons, A., & Gledhill, A. (1997). Effects of neutralizing on intrusive thoughts: An experiment investigating the etiology of obsessive compulsive disorder. *Behavioral Research Therapy, 35,* 211–219.

Salzman, L. (1980). *Treatment of the obsessive personality.* New York: Jason Aronson.

Samuels, J. F., Bienvenu, O. J., Grados, M. A., Cullen, B., Riddle, M. A. Liang, K. Y., et al. (2008). Prevalence and correlates of hoarding behavior in a community-based sample. *Behavior Research and Therapy, 46,* 836–844.

Sasson, Y., Dekel, S., Nacasch, N., Chopra, M., Zinger, Y., Amital, D., et al. (2005). Posttraumatic obsessive-compulsive disorder: A case series. *Psychiatry Research, 135,* 145–152.

Shafran, R., & Tallis, F. (1996). Obsessive-compulsive hoarding: A cognitive-behavioral approach. *Behavioral and Cognitive Psychotherapy, 24,* 209–221.

Sifneos, P. E. (1966). Psychoanalytically-oriented short-term dynamic or anxiety-provoking psychotherapy for mild obsessional neuroses. *Psychiatric Quarterly, 40,* 271–282.

Simeon, D., Hollander, E., Stein, D. J., Cohen, L., & Aronowitz, B. (1995). Body dysmorphic disorder in the DSM-IV field study of obsessive-compulsive disorder. *American Journal of Psychiatry, 152,* 1207–1209.

Stanley, M., Swann, A., Bowers, T., & Davis, M. (1992). A comparison of clinical features in trichotillomania and obsessive-compulsive disorder. *Behavior Research and Therapy, 30,* 39–44.

Steketee, G. & Frost, R. (2003). Compulsive hoarding: Current status of the research. *Clinical Psychology Review, 23,* 905–927.

Summerfeldt, L. J. (2004). Understanding and treating incompleteness in obsessive–compulsive disorder. *Journal of Clinical Psychology, 40,* 1–14.

Summerfeldt, L. J., Kloosterman, P. H., Antony, M. M., Richter, M. A., & Swinson, R. M. (2004). The relationship between miscellaneous symptoms and major symptom factors in obsessive–compulsive disorder. *Behavior Research and Therapy, 42,* 1453–1467.

Summerfeldt, L. J. (2007). Treating incompleteness, ordering, and arranging concerns. In M. M. Antony, C. Purdon, & L. J. Summerfeldt (Eds.), *Psychological treatment of obsessive–compulsive disorder: Fundamentals and beyond* (pp. 187-207). Washington, DC: American Psychological Association.

Swedo, S. E. (1993). Trichotillomania. *Psychiatric Annals, 23,* 402–407.

Taylor, S. (2004). Understanding and treating health anxiety: A cognitive-behavioral approach. *Cognitive and Behavioral Practice, 11,* 112–123.

Taylor, S., & Asmundson, G. (2004). *Treating health anxiety: A cognitive-behavioral approach.* New York: Guilford.

Taylor, S., & Asmundson, G. (2008). Hypochondriasis. In J. S. Abromowitz, D. McKay, & S. Taylor (Eds.), *Clinical handbook of obsessive-compulsive disorder and related problems* (pp. 304–315). Baltimore, MD: Johns Hopkins University Press.

Taylor, S., Asmundson, G. J. G., & Coons, M. J. (2005). Current directions in the treatment of hypochondriasis. *Journal of Cognitive Psychotherapy, 19,* 285–304.

Veale, D. (2004). Advances in a cognitive-behavioral model of body dysmorphic disorder. *Body Image, 1,* 113–125.

Veale, D., & Riley, S. (2001). Mirror, mirror on the wall, who is the ugliest of them all? The psychopathology of mirror gazing in body dysmorphic disorder. *Behavior Research and Therapy, 39,* 1381–1393.

Verdellen, C. W. J., Hoogduin, C. A. L., & Keijsers, G. P. J. (2007). Tic suppression in the treatment of Tourette's Syndrome with exposure therapy: The rebound phenomenon reconsidered. *Movement Disorders, 22,* 1601–1606.

Verdellen, C. W. J., Keijsers, G. P. J., Cath, D. C., & Hoogduin, C. A. L. (2004). Exposure with response prevention versus habit reversal in Tourette's syndrome: A controlled study. *Behavior Research and Therapy, 42,* 501–511.

Visser, S., & Bouman, T. K. (2001). The treatment of hypochondriasis: Exposure plus response prevention versus cognitive therapy. *Behavior Research and Therapy, 39,* 423–442.

Warwick, H. M. C. (1989). A cognitive-behavioral approach to hypochondriasis and health anxiety. *Journal of Psychosomatic Research, 33,* 705–711.

Warwick, H. M. C., & Salkovskis, P. M. (1990). Hypochondriasis. *Behavior Research and Therapy, 28,* 105–117.

Watson, T. S., & Sterling, H. E. (1998). Brief functional analysis and treatment of a vocal tic. *Journal of Applied Behavior Analysis, 31,* 471–474.

Watt, M. C., & Stewart, S. H. (2000). Anxiety sensitivity mediates the relationship between childhood learning experiences and elevated hypochondriacal concerns in young adulthood. *Journal of Psychosomatic Research, 49,* 107–118.

Wetterneck, C. T., & Woods, D. W. (2007). A contemporary behavior analytic model of trichotillomania. In D. W. Woods & J. W. Kanter (Eds.), *Understanding behavior disorders* (pp. 157–180). Reno, NV: Context Press.

Wincze, J. P., Steketee, G., & Frost, R. O. (2007). Categorization in compulsive hoarding. *Behavior Research and Therapy, 45,* 63–72.

Wolke, D., & Sapouna, M. (2008). Big men feeling small: Childhood bullying experience, muscle dysmorphia, and other mental health problems in bodybuilders. *Psychology of Sport and Exercise, 9,* 595–604.

Woods, D. W., Adcock, A. C., & Conelea, C. A. (2008). Trichotillomania. In J. S. Abromowitz, D. McKay, & S. Taylor (Eds.), *Clinical handbook of obsessive-compulsive disorder and related problems* (pp. 205–221). Baltimore, MD: Johns Hopkins University Press.

Woods, D. W., Piacentini, J., Himle, M. B., & Chang, S. (2005). Premonitory urge for tics scale (PUTS): Initial psychometric results and examination of the premonitory urge phenomenon in youths with tic disorders. *Developmental and Behavioral Pediatrics, 26,* 397–403.

Cognitive Approaches to Understanding Obsessive Compulsive and Related Disorders

Steven Taylor, Jonathan S. Abramowitz, Dean McKay, *and* Carrie Cuttler

Abstract

This chapter focuses on cognitive models of obsessive compulsive disorder (OCD) and related disorders. It begins with a historical perspective, in which the antecedents of cognitive models are described. Contemporary cognitive models are then reviewed, predictions derived from the models are identified, and empirical evidence for these predictions is summarized. This is followed by a review of cognitive models of four OC-related disorders: hoarding, hypochondriasis, body dysmorphic disorder, and trichotillomania. Finally, the conceptual problems with cognitive models of OCD and related disorders are identified, suggestions for improvements to the models are made, and potentially fruitful directions for future research are proposed.

Keywords: obsessive compulsive disorder, obsessive compulsive spectrum disorders, cognitive content specificity hypothesis, dysfunctional beliefs and appraisals

Introduction

Epidemiologic surveys and factor analytic studies indicate that obsessive compulsive disorder (OCD) is symptomatically heterogeneous (McKay et al., 2004). The major groups of symptoms identified by factor analyses are: (a) aggressive, sexual, religious, or somatic obsessions and associated checking compulsions; (b) symmetry obsessions and ordering, counting, or repeating compulsions; (c) contamination obsessions and cleaning compulsions; and (d) hoarding-related obsessions and compulsions (McKay et al., 2004). The latter group deserves special mention. Although DSM-IV (American Psychiatric Association, 2000) considers hoarding to be a form of OCD, hoarding is sufficiently different that some researchers consider it to be a separate disorder, which is often described as a "related" or obsessive compulsive (OC) spectrum condition (Frost & Steketee, 2008). This is implied in the very structure of the present volume, in which hoarding is discussed separately from other forms of OCD.

In the present chapter, where we evaluate the evidence for contemporary cognitive models of OCD (which are general models that attempt to account for all varieties of OC symptoms), we will review the research on hoarding symptoms along with other OC symptoms, because researchers have typically examined hoarding in the context of OCD. However, because some cognitive models have been developed specifically to account for hoarding, we will also discuss hoarding separately in a later section on OC-related disorders.

This chapter begins with a brief historical perspective that describes the early behavioral models of OCD, and some of the problems with these models. Contemporary cognitive models, which were developed to deal with these problems, are then described, and their empirical support is examined. This is followed by a review of cognitive models of four disorders that are widely considered to fall within the OCD spectrum: hoarding, hypochondriasis, body dysmorphic disorder, and trichotillomania. The chapter ends with a discussion of future directions, including important conceptual problems that remain to be solved, ways to improve conceptual models, and potentially fruitful directions for further research.

Brief Historical Perspective

In the 1970s and early 1980s, conditioning models were the dominant psychological explanations of OCD, at least among clinical researchers. Based on Mowrer's (1960) two-factor model of fear, conditioning models of OCD (e.g., Rachman & Hodgson, 1980) proposed that obsessional fears were acquired by classical conditioning and maintained by operant conditioning. To illustrate, the obsessional fear of acquiring a serious disease from a public washroom could arise from an aversive learning experience in which the person became severely ill (the unconditioned stimulus) after visiting an unsanitary public convenience (the conditioned stimulus). This purportedly led to classically conditioned obsessional fears (e.g., fear of public washrooms). Such fears were said to be maintained by negative reinforcement—that is, by the reinforcing, distress reducing effects of avoiding public washrooms, or engaging compulsive washing after visiting one.

In terms of treatment implications, the conditioning models were highly fruitful; they led to the development of exposure and response prevention, which remains one of the most effective treatments for OCD. This treatment involves exposure to harmless but fear-evoking stimuli, while delaying or refraining from performing the compulsive rituals (see Chapter 17).

Tests of the mechanisms suggested by conditioning models were not so encouraging (Clark, 2004). Some of the problems with the models include the following: (a) Many OCD patients do not appear to have histories of aversive conditioning experiences that might lead to obsessional fears. In such cases, the conditioning models do not appear to adequately explain the emergence, persistence, and content of obsessions. To illustrate, why would a person suffer from recurrent, repugnant intrusive images of sodomizing a neighbor's pet rabbit, even though he had never engaged in paraphilic activity? (b) The models fail to account for the shifts in OC symptoms that can occur over time (e.g., the patient who had carnal obsessions about a rabbit previously obsessed about inhaling air that had been exhaled by other people, especially by unsavory individuals). Many individuals with OCD show such symptom shifts in the apparent absence of

relevant conditioning experiences. (c) Conditioning models fail to explain why people with OCD display a broad range of insight into the reasonableness of their obsessions and compulsions, as well as why the person's level of insight can fluctuate across time and circumstance. These and other limitations led clinical researchers to consider cognitive explanations of OCD. However, conditioning models were not abandoned in their entirety; elements of these models, particularly mechanisms of operant conditioning, were incorporated into cognitive models.

Contemporary Cognitive Models of OCD
Cognitive Content Specificity Hypothesis

Since the 1980s there has been an increasing emphasis on the role of cognitive factors in OCD. Several cognitive models have been developed as general models of the disorder; that is, as models intended to account for all varieties of OC symptoms. The models fall into two broad classes. The first are the deficit models, which propose that OCD is due to a dysfunction in cognitive processing, which may have its origins in neurobiological dysfunction. These models are discussed elsewhere in this volume (e.g., Chapters 6 and 7). The focus of this chapter is on the second class of models, which propose that OC symptoms arise from particular types of dysfunctional beliefs and appraisals. We will use the term *cognitive models* as convenient shorthand to refer to these formulations. Such models are based on Beck's (1976) cognitive content specificity hypothesis, which proposes that each type of psychopathology is associated with a distinct type or pattern of dysfunctional beliefs. Major depression, for example, is said to arise from beliefs about loss, failure, and self-denigration (e.g., "I'm a defective unit"). Social anxiety disorder is thought to be associated with beliefs about the likelihood or importance of rejection or ridicule by others (e.g., "People think I'm a fool because I'm no good at small talk"). With regard to OCD, particular dysfunctional beliefs have been theoretically linked to particular types of symptoms. Beliefs about inflated personal responsibility, for example, have been conceptually linked to checking symptoms (Salkovskis, 1985). Beliefs about the overimportance of one's thoughts (e.g., "Bad thoughts inevitably lead to bad deeds") have been theoretically linked to obsessions about performing dangerous or inappropriate behaviors (e.g., harming others, committing blasphemy, or engaging in personally repugnant sexual acts; Frost & Steketee, 2002).

Salkovskis' Cognitive Model

Based on the cognitive content specificity hypothesis, several models have been developed that propose that obsessions and compulsions arise from specific sorts of dysfunctional beliefs. According to these models, the content of the beliefs and appraisals influences the types of OC symptoms that the person develops, and the strength of beliefs influences the person's insight into his or her OCD. Among the most sophisticated of these models is Salkovskis' cognitive approach (e.g., Salkovskis, 1985, 1996) and the elaborations of this model (e.g., Frost & Steketee, 2002).

Salkovskis' model begins with the well-established finding that unwanted intrusions (i.e., unwanted thoughts, images, and impulses) are experienced by most people (Gibbs, 1996). These "nonclinical" obsessions, compared to OC symptoms in OCD, tend to be less frequent, shorter in duration, associated with less distress, and more readily removed from consciousness. However, clinical and nonclinical OC symptoms have similar themes, such as violence, contamination, and doubt (Gibbs, 1996). An important task for any model is to explain why almost everyone experiences unwanted intrusions (at least at some point in their lives), yet only a minority of people experience intrusions in the form of clinical obsessions.

Salkovskis argued that intrusions—whether wanted or unwanted—reflect the person's current concerns, which arise from an "idea generator" in the brain. Intrusions are automatically triggered by internal or external reminders of those concerns. For example, intrusive thoughts of being contaminated may be triggered by seeing dirty objects (e.g., trash cans). Salkovskis proposed that intrusions develop into obsessions only when intrusions are evaluated or appraised as posing a threat for which the individual is personally responsible. To illustrate, consider the intrusive image of swerving one's car into oncoming traffic. Most people experiencing such an intrusion would regard it as a meaningless cognitive event, with no harm-related implications (i.e., "mental flotsam"). If, however, the person appraises the intrusion as having serious consequences, for which he or she is personally responsible, the intrusion can develop into a clinical obsession. For example, the following appraisal could lead to clinical obsessions: "Having thoughts about swerving into traffic means that I'm a dangerous person who must take extra care to ensure that I don't lose control." Such appraisals evoke distress and motivate the person to try to suppress or remove the unwanted intrusion, and to attempt to prevent any harmful events associated with the intrusion (e.g., by avoiding driving). Here, compulsions are framed as efforts to remove intrusions and to prevent any perceived harmful consequences.

Why do only some people make harm and responsibility-related appraisals of their intrusive thoughts? Life experiences shape the basic assumptions we hold about ourselves and the world (Beck, 1976), including beliefs about personal responsibility and beliefs about the significance of unwanted thoughts (e.g., beliefs that thoughts are important, and that it is essential to control one's thoughts). Such beliefs may be acquired from a strict moral or religious upbringing, or from other experiences that teach the person to adhere to extreme or rigid codes of conduct and responsibility (Salkovskis, Shafran, Rachman, & Freeston, 1999).

With regard to compulsions, Salkovskis advanced two main reasons why compulsions become persistent and excessive. First, they are reinforced by short-term distress reduction and by temporary removal of the unwanted thought (i.e., negative reinforcement, as in the aforementioned conditioning models). Second, they prevent the person from learning that their appraisals are unrealistic (e.g., the person fails to learn that unwanted harm-related thoughts do not lead to acts of harm). Attempts at distracting oneself from unwanted intrusions may paradoxically increase the frequency of intrusions, possibly because the distracters become reminders of the intrusions. Compulsions can also strengthen one's perceived responsibility. That is, the absence of the feared consequence after performing the compulsion reinforces the belief that the person is responsible for removing the threat.

To summarize, according to the model, when a person appraises intrusions as posing a threat for which he or she is personally responsible, the person becomes distressed and attempts to remove the intrusions and prevent their perceived consequences. This increases the frequency of intrusions. Thus, intrusions become persistent and distressing, and thereby escalate into clinical obsessions. Compulsions prevent the person from evaluating the accuracy of his or her appraisals.

Extending the Cognitive Model

Contemporary cognitive models have extended the work of Salkovskis by expanding the list of dysfunctional beliefs that purportedly contribute to OCD. Although contemporary cognitive models differ from one another in some ways, their similarities generally outweigh the differences. They differ primarily in the relative emphasis that they attach to various dysfunctional beliefs. For example, Salkovskis emphasizes responsibility, whereas Rachman (1998) emphasizes beliefs concerning the personal significance of intrusive thoughts (e.g., "Having this thought means that I'm morally corrupt"). According to Rachman, obsessions arise when the person misinterprets the intrusive thought as implying that he or she is bad, mad, or dangerous. This involves beliefs concerning *thought-action fusion* (Shafran, Thordarson, & Rachman, 1996); that is, beliefs that one's unwanted thoughts will inevitably be translated into actions (e.g., "I can cause an accident simply by thinking about one"), or beliefs that thoughts are the moral equivalent of bad actions (e.g., "Thinking about harming my infant is just as bad as actually doing so").

Building on the work of Salkovskis and others, the most comprehensive contemporary cognitive model of OCD was developed by the Obsessive Compulsive Cognitions Working Group (OCCWG; Frost & Steketee, 2002). This is an international group of over 40 investigators sharing a common interest in understanding the role of cognitive factors in OCD. The group began by developing a consensus regarding the most important beliefs (and associated appraisals) in OCD (OCCWG, 1997). They then identified six belief domains, described in Table 12.1, thought to give rise to dysfunctional appraisals of intrusions. (The table contains acronyms for the six belief domains, which will be used throughout this chapter.) Like the cognitive content

specificity hypothesis, contemporary cognitive models of OCD account for OC symptom heterogeneity by proposing that particular beliefs or patterns of beliefs give rise to specific types of OC symptoms.

Contemporary cognitive models of OCD have led to a promising new cognitive-behavioral therapy. The exposure exercises in this treatment differ from exposure and response prevention, in that they are framed as experiments to test appraisals and beliefs. To illustrate, consider a patient who has recurrent images of terrorist hijackings, and compulsive rituals in which he repeatedly warns airport officials. His belief was that, "Thinking about terrorist hijackings will make them happen." To challenge this belief, the patient and therapist could devise a test that pits this belief against a more realistic belief, such as, "My thoughts have no impact on the occurrence of hijackings." A behavioral experiment might involve deliberately bringing on thoughts of a hijacking and evaluating the consequences (or lack thereof). Cognitive restructuring methods can also be used to challenge OC-related beliefs and appraisals (see Chapter 18).

Cognitive Models of OCD: Empirical Status

A positive feature of the cognitive models is that they are readily falsifiable. Accordingly, they have generated a wealth of research. A list of predictions (albeit not an exhaustive list) derived from these models is presented in Table 12.2, along with a rating of empirical support for each prediction.

Table 12.1 Rationally Derived Domains of Dysfunctional Beliefs Associated with OCD

Belief Domain	Acronym	Description
Inflated responsibility	R	Belief that one has the special power to cause, and/or the duty to prevent, negative outcomes.
Overimportance of thoughts	I	Belief that the mere presence of a thought indicates that the thought is significant. For example, the belief that the thought has ethical or moral ramifications, or that thinking the thought increases the probability of the corresponding behavior or event.
Need to control thoughts	C	Belief that complete control over one's thoughts is possible and necessary.
Overestimation of threat	T	Belief that negative events are especially likely and would be especially awful.
Perfectionism	P	Belief that mistakes and imperfection are intolerable.
Intolerance for uncertainty	U	Belief that it is possible and necessary to be completely certain that negative outcomes will not occur.

Table 12.2 Predictions Derived from the Cognitive (belief and appraisal) Models of OCD

	Prediction	Empirical Support
1.	The belief domains listed in Table 12.1 are distinct from one another, as indicated by factor analysis.	−
2.	OCD patients, as a group, score higher than clinical and nonclinical controls on measures of putatively OC-related beliefs and appraisals.	+/−
3.	Relative to controls, the *majority* of people with OCD have elevated scores on measures of OCD-related dysfunctional beliefs.	−
4.	In cross-sectional studies, the beliefs statistically predict, or are correlated, with OC symptoms.	+
5.	Scores on the beliefs account for a substantial proportion of variance (e.g., a third or more of the variance) in OC symptoms.	−
6.	The beliefs show *patterning*, such that specific beliefs or combinations of beliefs predict specific types of OC symptoms. In other words, specific types of OC symptoms (e.g., checking) are characterized by clearly distinct profiles of dysfunctional beliefs.	+/−
7.	The beliefs interact with one another to statistically predict OC symptoms.	−
8.	Experimental manipulations of appraisals (e.g., manipulations that increase or decrease responsibility appraisals) lead to corresponding changes in OC symptoms.	+
9.	Efforts to suppress unwanted cognitive phenomena (e.g., intrusive thoughts or unwanted doubts) leads to an increase in the frequency of these phenomena.	+/−
10.	Naturally occurring events that increase the strength of beliefs or occurrence of appraisals (e.g., events increasing perceived responsibility such as becoming a new parent) lead to increases in OC symptoms.	+
11.	OCD patients report learning histories that would logically give rise to OC-related beliefs.	?
12.	Treatment-related reductions in OC symptoms are correlated with reductions in the strength of beliefs and frequency of appraisals.	+
13.	Treatments that directly target beliefs and appraisals should be more tolerable for OCD patients (i.e., there should be fewer treatment dropouts).	+
14.	Treatments that directly target beliefs and appraisals (e.g., therapies involving cognitive restructuring) should be more effective than treatments that do not directly target these factors (e.g., exposure and response prevention).	−

Key: + Generally supported by available evidence; +/− Inconclusive or equivocal support; − Mostly not supported; ? Not yet adequately tested.
Note: "beliefs" and "appraisals" refer to OC-related beliefs and appraisals, such as those listed in Table 12.1.

The table shows that cognitive models have received mixed empirical support, with only a limited number of predictions being clearly supported by the data. Details of the findings are summarized below.

Prediction 1

By postulating the various kinds of dysfunctional beliefs listed in Table 12.1, cognitive models of OCD assume that these beliefs are empirically distinguishable from one another. For example, if beliefs about inflated responsibility (R) play a specific role in OCD, then it should be possible to demonstrate that the effects of R are distinct from the effects of beliefs concerning the overimportance of thoughts (I), the need to control thoughts (C), the overestimation of threat (T), perfectionism (P), and intolerance of uncertainty (U).

This prediction has been tested in several factor analytic studies of the 44- and 87-item versions of the Obsessive Beliefs Questionnaire (OBQ; OCCWG,

2001, 2003, 2005). The research uniformly fails to support the prediction, with results suggesting that the OBQ is composed of three or four factors (Julien et al., 2008; Myers, Fisher, & Wells, 2008; OCCWG, 2005; Woods, Tolin, & Abramowitz, 2004). For example, OCCWG (2005) and Julien et al. (2008) obtained three correlated factors: (a) R and T (hereby designated R/T), (b) P and U (P/U), and (c) I and C (I/C). Hierarchical factor analyses indicated that these factors load on a single higher-order factor, which accounted for 22% of the variance in OBQ scores (Taylor, McKay, & Abramowitz, 2005). The three lower-order factors each accounted for an additional 6%–7% of variance. Woods et al. (2004) obtained a 4-factor solution consisting of a general factor, and three smaller factors corresponding to those described above. Although the most stable (replicable) factor structure of the OBQ remains to be identified, the results consistently show that the six types of dysfunctional beliefs listed in Table 12.1 are not distinct from one another. Thus, Prediction 1 is not supported.

Prediction 2

Research provides mixed support for the prediction that OCD patients would tend to score higher than clinical and nonclinical controls on measures of OC-related beliefs and appraisals. Some studies found support for the prediction (e.g., Cougle, Lee, & Salkovskis, 2007; Julien et al., 2008; OCCWG, 2005; Tolin, Worhunsky, & Maltby, 2006). Other studies provided either mixed support or failed altogether to support the prediction. For example, Julien, O'Connor, and Aardema (2007) found that OCD patient and anxious controls did not differ in OBQ scores once general distress was controlled. Anholt et al. (2004) found no differences in scores on OC-related beliefs between OCD patients and those suffering from pathological gambling. Moritz and Pohl (2006) assessed appraisals concerning T, for events that were either washing-related, checking-related, negative, or neutral (e.g., "What percentage of male toilet seats are contaminated with fecal or gangrene agents?"). People with OCD and normal controls did not differ in their threat estimates. In summary, there is mixed support for the prediction that, as a group, OCD patients score higher than clinical and nonclinical controls on measures of OC-related beliefs and appraisals.

Prediction 3

Given the importance that cognitive models place on OC-related dysfunctional beliefs, it is predicted that the *majority* of people with OCD should have elevated scores on measures of such beliefs, compared to control groups. Using cluster analyses of scores on the OBQ, two studies have independently identified clusters of OCD patients who do *not* have elevated scores on the OBQ relative to controls (Calamari et al., 2006; Taylor et al., 2005). In these studies, over 50% of OCD patients were found to have normal scores on the OBQ, thus, Prediction 3 was not supported.

Prediction 4

Several studies, using clinical or nonclinical samples, have examined the correlations between the OBQ subscales—using either the six belief domains identified in Table 12.1, or subscales derived from factor analysis—and particular types of OC symptoms. Such research has usually involved regression analyses in which beliefs are used to statistically predict (in a cross-sectional design) particular types of OC symptoms. Some studies have controlled for general distress, typically measured by general anxiety or depression, in an effort to determine whether the beliefs are specific to OC symptoms or whether they are simply correlates of general distress. There are pros and cons to this approach. On the one hand, it provides a stringent test of the specificity of the belief-symptom relationship. But on the other hand, such analyses would be inappropriate if OC symptoms *cause* general distress. That is, if beliefs cause OC symptoms, which in turn cause general distress, then the statistical relationship between beliefs and OC symptoms will be artifactually attenuated if distress is controlled for.

Several studies have shown that beliefs assessed by the OBQ or similar measures are correlated with, or predict (in cross-sectional regression analyses), OC symptoms (e.g., Julien et al., 2008; Myers et al., 2008; OCCWG, 2005; Tolin, Woods, & Abramowitz, 2003; Wu & Carter, 2008). The strength of this relationship is attenuated when general distress is controlled. An example of these findings, which is based on the largest sample that has been used to date (N = 5015 university students), is presented in Table 12.3 (Taylor et al., 2010), which summarizes results based on structural equation modeling. The table shows that many of the regression weights were statistically significant, although they were not large in magnitude. General distress was not controlled in those analyses. A summary of other regression studies that did control for general distress is presented in Table 12.4. The table shows that in most studies, OC-related beliefs (as assessed

Table 12.3 Predicting OC symptoms from OC-related beliefs, as assessed by the OBQ44, without controlling for general distress

OC Symptom	Adjusted R²	Standardized regression weights (and their standard errors)		
		I/C	P/U	R/T
Checking	.24	.00	.00	.49 (0.02)
Hoarding	.22	.00	.00	.47 (0.02)
Neutralizing	.18	.09 (0.03)	.00	.35 (0.03)
Obsessing	.30	.30 (0.02)	.00	.29 (0.02)
Ordering	.24	.00	.28 (0.02)	.24 (0.02)
Washing	.22	.08 (0.03)	.00	.41 (0.03)

Note: N=3249 university students. All regression weights were significant (p<0.05). Nonsignificant regression weights were set to zero. I/C = importance and control of thoughts; P/U = perfectionism and intolerance of uncertainty; R/T = inflated responsibility and overestimation of threat. OC symptoms were assessed with versions of the Obsessive Compulsive Inventory.
Source: Adapted from Taylor, S., Coles, M. E., Abramowitz, J. S., Wu, K. D., Olatunji, B. O., Timpano, K. R., et al. 2010). How are dysfunctional beliefs related to obsessive-compulsive symptoms? *Journal of Cognitive Psychotherapy, 24*(3), 165–176.

Table 12.4 Significant (p<0.05) beta weights in regression analyses in which OC-related beliefs (measured by either the OBQ44 or OBQ87) were used to predict OC symptoms

OC Symptom	Study				
	Tolin et al. (2003)	OCCWG (2005)	Julien et al. (2006)	Myers et al. (2008)	Tolin et al. (2008)
Checking	T	P/U	P/U	T, I/C	None
Hoarding	None	—	—	T	P/U
Neutralizing	I, T	—	—	T, I/C	R/T
Obsessing	C	—	—	T, I/C	I/C, P/U
Ordering	P	P/U	P/U	T, P/U	P/U
Washing	T	R/T	None	T, P/U	R/T

Note: OBQ87: R = inflated responsibility; T = overestimation of threat; P = perfectionism; U = intolerance of uncertainty; I = importance of thoughts; C = control of thoughts. OBQ44: Combines pairs of scales into 3 factors: R/T, P/C, I/C. OC symptoms were assessed with versions of the Obsessive Compulsive Inventory or the Padua Inventory. Myers et al. was based on slightly modified version of the OBQ44, based on exploratory factor analyses. All studies controlled for general distress, which in most studies was assessed by measures of general anxiety and depression. — = not assessed.

by the OBQ) did predict OC symptoms, although for some studies, particular OC symptoms were not predicted by the beliefs. Overall, the results of these and other studies generally support Prediction 4.

Prediction 5

This prediction states that the OC-related beliefs should account for a substantial proportion of variance in OC symptoms (e.g., a third or more of the variance). This prediction derives from the emphasis that contemporary cognitive models place on the role of OC-related beliefs. The findings generally fail

to support the prediction. This is illustrated by the adjusted R² values in Table 12.3, demonstrating that OC-related beliefs account for only 8%–18% of the variance in OC symptoms. Other studies, such as those cited in Table 12.4, have yielded similar results. Such findings suggest that OC-related beliefs play at most a moderate role in OCD, and additional contributing factors need to be considered.

Prediction 6

Based on the cognitive content specificity hypothesis, cognitive models of OCD propose that particular dysfunctional beliefs are linked to particular types of symptoms. In other words, the major types of OC symptoms (e.g., washing, checking) should be distinguished from one another by their patterns or profiles of OC-related beliefs. For example, checking should be most strongly predicted by beliefs about inflated responsibility, whereas obsessing should be most predicted by beliefs about the overimportance and the need to control thoughts (Frost & Steketee, 2002).

Table 12.3 presents the results of the largest study to examine this issue. Patterning can be assessed by comparing the beta weights within rows and within columns, to see whether the confidence intervals overlap with one another. For example, consider the first column, which provides information on the relative importance (as indicated by the beta weights) of I/C in predicting various types of OC symptoms. Most of the confidence intervals overlap with one another, suggesting that the effects of this belief domain were largely nonspecific in predicting symptoms. The clearest exception is that I/C was particularly important in predicting the tendency to obsess. For the P/U belief domain, Table 12.3 suggests that this domain has nonspecific effects, in that it equally predicted most OC symptoms, with the clearest exception being that P/U was particularly important in predicting OC symptoms to do with ordering (including obsessions and compulsions associated with symmetry and arranging objects). Regarding the belief domain characterized by R/T, Table 12.3 again suggests that the effects of this domain were largely nonspecific in predicting OC symptoms, although R/T was somewhat more important in predicting hoarding than other symptoms.

Row-wise inspection of the confidence intervals also reveals a general lack of patterning. The three belief domains in Table 12.3 did not differ in their relative importance for predicting checking, neutralizing, and washing symptoms. However, row-wise comparisons does reveal that (a) R/T was the most important belief domain for predicting hoarding; (b) I/C was most important for predicting obsessing; and (c) P/C was most important for predicting ordering. The most common types of OC symptoms—checking and washing—were not associated with distinctive patterns of dysfunctional beliefs. To summarize, Table 12.3 reveals some evidence of patterning, but for the most part, the relationship between beliefs and symptoms was nonspecific in nature.

Table 12.4 also provides mixed support for Prediction 6. The table shows that no belief was a consistent predictor of checking or hoarding. Across studies, T consistently predicted neutralizing and washing, I/C consistently predicted obsessing, and P/U consistently predicted ordering. the most consistent finding from comparing Tables 12.3 and 12.4 is that I/C predicted obsessing and P/U predicted ordering. Other studies, using different data analytic procedures, also offer mixed and inconsistent evidence of specificity in the links between beliefs and OC symptoms (Abramowitz, Nelson, Rygwall, & Khandker, 2009; Wu & Carter, 2008). Those studies found that P/U was related to ordering, but did not replicate the finding that the strongest predictor of obsessing is I/C. Finally, research suggests that thought-action fusion (a component of I/C) is not specific to OCD but is also prevalent in other anxiety disorders, mood disorders, and eating disorders (Berle & Starcevic, 2005).

In summary, there is mixed support for Prediction 6. Across studies, there are very few consistent findings about which beliefs are most strongly related to which symptoms. The exception is that P/U has been consistently linked to ordering. The most common OC symptoms—checking and washing—have not been consistently distinguished from one another, or from other OC symptoms, in terms of their profiles of dysfunctional beliefs. This is a serious problem for cognitive models of OCD, because these models are based on the core assumption of cognitive content specificity.

Prediction 7

The cognitive models predict that beliefs (and possibly appraisals) should interact with one another to give rise to obsessions and compulsions. To illustrate the potential interactions, one's sense of personal responsibility could influence the perceived importance of controlling one's thoughts so that harm does not occur. Conversely, beliefs about the importance of one's thoughts could inflate responsibility beliefs (Thordarson & Shafran, 2002). Perfectionism could also interact with other beliefs and appraisals: "Perfectionism is usually defined in terms which suggest more enduring personality-type characteristics, which might be expected to interact with the appraisal of intrusions, particularly when such intrusions concern the completion (or non-completion) of particular actions" (Salkovskis et al., 2000, p. 364). Responsibility might also inflate perfectionism (Salkovskis & Forrester, 2002).

To test these predictions, in a recent study we conducted a series of regression analyses in which the main effects for each belief domain (I/C, P/U, R/T) and their two- and three-way interactions were entered as predictors of OC symptom scores. Main effects were significant predictors, but the interactions were not (Taylor, Abramowitz, & McKay, 2005). The findings therefore fail to support the predicted interaction effects.

Prediction 8

A small number of studies have experimentally manipulated OC-related appraisals, particularly responsibility appraisals, in order to test the prediction that changes in appraisals lead to changes in OC-like symptoms, such as the frequency of checking while performing an experimental task (e.g., Bouchard, Rheaume, & Ladouceur, 1999; Lopatka & Rachman, 1995; Rachman, Shafran, Mitchell, Trant, & Teachman, 1996). Research suggests that checking is more frequent when high responsibility is induced (e.g., by making the participant responsible for ensuring that a stove is turned off), compared to when low responsibility is induced (Arntz, Voncken, & Goosen, 2007; Boschen & Vuksanovic, 2007). Thus, the limited available evidence supports Prediction 8.

Prediction 9

Cognitive models propose that OCD is maintained, in part, by trying too hard to control one's unwanted thoughts, or by trying too hard to allay one's doubts. Consistent with this, experimental evidence suggests that repetitive checking actually increases doubt and uncertainty (van den Hout & Kindt, 2003a, b). Research on attempts to control unwanted thoughts has yielded inconsistent results. Experimental studies of student samples suggests that deliberate attempts to suppress unwanted thoughts often (but not invariably) lead to a paradoxical increase in the frequency of these thoughts (e.g., Wenzlaff & Wegner, 2000; Marcks & Woods, 2007). There is inconsistent evidence for this occurring in OCD. Although research indicates that people with OCD are more likely to try to suppress their unwanted thoughts, there is not necessarily a paradoxical increase in the frequency of these thoughts as a result of attempts at thought suppression (Purdon, 2004). Thus, there is mixed support for Prediction 9.

Prediction 10

Cognitive models suggest that OC-related beliefs may interact with particular types of stressors to influence the onset or exacerbation of OC symptoms. Childbirth, for example, should increase the sense of personal responsibility for both parents,

and therefore should lead to an increase in OC symptoms. Two longitudinal studies of new parents support this prediction. Those studies found that childbirth-related increases in responsibility are followed by an increase in OC-like symptoms (Abramowitz, Khandker, Nelson, Deacon, & Rygwall, 2006; Abramowitz, Nelson, Rygwall, & Khandker, 2007). Most new parents experienced unwanted, intrusive infant-related thoughts, such as thoughts of losing the baby or committing deliberate harm. Compulsive-like behaviors included repetitive checking on the safety of the infant and reassurance seeking. These OC-like symptoms were most prevalent in parents with elevated scores on the OBQ (Abramowitz et al., 2006). Thus, Prediction 10 has received encouraging support.

Prediction 11

Cognitive models emphasize the role of learning experiences that purportedly give rise to OC-related beliefs. This suggests that it should be possible to identify such learning experiences in people with OCD. This prediction has not been systematically investigated, although case reports have described such learning experiences (de Silva & Marks, 2001; Salkovskis, Shafran, Rachman, & Freeston, 1999; Tallis, 1994). Examples include growing up in an environment that encouraged the development of rigid or extreme codes of conduct, and instances in which one's thoughts were followed by serious misfortune (e.g., wishing someone dead and then learning, a short time later, that the person did indeed die from some mishap). Systematic research is needed to determine whether most people with OCD report such experiences, and whether they are more likely to have these experiences than control groups. Thus, Prediction 11 has yet to be adequately tested.

Predictions 12 to 14

The last set of predictions concern the treatment implications of the cognitive models of OCD. These models underscore the importance of OC-related beliefs in maintaining OC symptoms and, as such, predict that interventions that reduce the strength of these beliefs should lead to reductions in OC symptoms. Reducing the strength of these beliefs should also lead patients to be more willing to engage in exposure exercises during treatment, such as exposure to "contaminants" for people with washing-related symptoms. Consistent with the cognitive models, studies have shown that treatments that reduce OC symptoms also reduce the strength of

OC-related beliefs (Bouvard, 2002; Emmelkamp, van Oppen, & van Balkom, 2002; McLean et al., 2001). Thus, Prediction 12 is supported.

Treatments that directly target OC-related beliefs (i.e., those using cognitive restructuring and behavioral experiments) are associated with a lower proportion of dropouts than treatments that do not directly target these beliefs (e.g., exposure and response prevention; Abramowitz, Taylor, & McKay, 2005). Accordingly, there is support for Prediction 13. However, cognitive or cognitive-behavior therapy for OCD is no more effective than exposure and response prevention (Abramowitz et al., 2005), so Prediction 14 is not supported.

Summary

Table 12.2 shows that there is mixed empirical support for contemporary cognitive models of OCD. Of the 14 predictions that were examined, 5 were generally supported, 5 were generally not supported, 3 had equivocal findings, and one has not been adequately tested. The degree of support for the models suggests that they may have some value in accounting for OCD. Accordingly, it may be fruitful to modify these models rather than abandon them. The models may need to be expanded to include other etiologically relevant variables.

Cognitive Models of OC-Related Disorders
Compulsive Hoarding

The central features of compulsive hoarding involve problems with discarding items, compulsive acquisition of items (often in one or more favored categories), and a cluttered environment. Clutter is the component of hoarding that creates the greatest disability (Frost & Steketee, 2008). The items saved by hoarders are similar to those saved by nonhoarders (e.g., magazines, mementos of trips and family events, professional books and journals; Frost & Gross, 1993). However, hoarders accrue these items in greater abundance. Compulsive hoarding is also associated with problems about control over possessions. This is readily observed by therapists who conduct home-based treatment for hoarders. The latter often bristle at the idea of the therapist touching objects, even those that are objectively worthless.

Cognitive Model. A leading cognitive model of hoarding (Frost & Steketee, 2008) implicates problems with information processing, such as problems in deciding which objects to keep or discard. Also implicated are dysfunctional beliefs about the

acquisition and retention of items. Such beliefs often consist of rigidly held reasons for hoarding items. These include unrealistic beliefs about the value of possessions (e.g., "These empty soup cans will come in handy someday") and inflated responsibility regarding possessions, whereby the individual feels that the objects require proper care and oversight. For example, one patient reported that deceased pets required a decent burial, but because the client had trouble finding the time for such a proper funeral, he hoarded many of the dearly departed pets in the home freezer.

Hoarding is also said to be influenced by other factors, such as the person's emotional or sentimental attachment to objects (e.g., "A child gave this drawing to me during my time when I worked as a teacher"), and the intrinsic enjoyment associated with the acquisition of objects, even if they have no value (e.g., collecting all the key chains that one can find; Frost & Steketee, 2008).

Empirical Support. Several studies support the prediction that hoarding is correlated with beliefs about the value of possessions, and with beliefs concerning one's responsibility for taking care of them (Frost & Steketee, 2003). There is also evidence that hoarding is associated with difficulties performing tasks in which the person is required to categorize items, such as organizing items into categories such as "keep this item," "keep it for now, but possibly discard later," and "discard this item." To illustrate, in one study, hoarders, compared to normal controls, found it more stressful to organize items, and organized the items into more categories, thereby leading to greater disorganization (Luchian, McNally, & Hooley, 2007). These results are even more pronounced when hoarders are asked to categorize personally relevant items (Wincze, Steketee, & Frost, 2007).

In summary, there is encouraging support for the cognitive model of hoarding. An issue for further investigation, however, is whether hoarding is associated with a specific pattern or profile of dysfunctional beliefs. As described earlier in this chapter (e.g., Tables 12.2 and 12.3), hoarding is not associated with a consistent pattern of dysfunctional beliefs, as assessed by the OBQ. The beliefs proposed in Frost and Steketee's (2008) cognitive model of hoarding are more specific than those in the OBQ, in that they refer particularly to possessions (e.g., responsibility beliefs specific to the care of one's possessions). It remains to be seen whether such beliefs consistently distinguish hoarding from other types of OC symptoms.

Hypochondriasis

Overlap with OCD. Hypochondriasis is a form of excessive health anxiety characterized by misinterpretations of bodily changes or sensations, which lead to a preoccupation with fears of having, or the idea that one has, a serious disease (American Psychiatric Association, 2000). To be diagnosed with hypochondriasis, the preoccupation must persist despite appropriate medical evaluation and reassurance from physicians. The symptoms must persist for at least six months, and cannot be better accounted for by another disorder. Hypochondriasis is very similar to OCD in terms of phenomenology, etiological models, and treatment. In fact, hypochondriasis can be regarded as a specific variant of OCD in which the person is exclusively concerned with health and disease.

Cognitive Model. A number of theories regarding the etiology of excessive health anxiety have been proposed (Taylor & Asmundson, 2004). However, the cognitive approach (Salkovskis, Warwick, & Deale, 2003), which describes cognitive and behavioral processes underlying health anxiety, has received the most empirical support and has led to effective treatments. According to this model, excessive health anxiety arises from, and is maintained by, dysfunctional beliefs about sickness and health, including beliefs involving the overestimation of the significance and dangerousness of bodily changes and sensations (i.e., a health-specific form of the overestimation of threat).

Bodily sensations (e.g., heart palpitations) are common in healthy people (Pennebaker, 1982) and may be benign physiological perturbations, the result of random noise in proprioceptive perceptual systems, or the effects of minor diseases or stress. People with excessive health anxiety believe that bodily changes and sensations have health-related catastrophic consequences (Warwick & Salkovskis, 1990); for example, chest pain may be interpreted as evidence of poor cardiac health and impending cardiac arrest, or a lump under the skin may be taken as evidence of a life-threatening malignancy. People with excessive health anxiety also typically hold beliefs such as "Good health is indicated by the absence of bodily sensations," "People do not recover from serious diseases," and "Worrying about one's health will keep you safe" (Taylor & Asmundson, 2004). Retrospective studies suggest that these beliefs arise from learning experiences, particularly childhood experiences pertaining to health and disease (Taylor & Asmundson, 2004).

Behaviors performed in order to alleviate health concerns can perpetuate elevated levels of health anxiety. Common maladaptive coping behaviors include persistent reassurance seeking (from physicians or family), other forms of repetitive checking (e.g., bodily checking or searching the Internet for health information), and avoidance of behaviors that evoke bodily sensations (e.g., physical exertion). These maladaptive coping behaviors persist because they are reinforced by short-term reductions in anxiety. In the long term, however, they are not only ineffective in producing lasting reductions in anxiety, but they actually serve to perpetuate health anxiety (Lucock, White, Peake, & Morley, 1998). For example, reassurance seeking can prolong a person's preoccupation with disease, expose them to frightening information about diseases, reduce their sense of independence (e.g., by repeatedly turning to others for help), and lead to iatrogenic effects (i.e., the aversive side effects of unnecessary medical investigations, such as postsurgical scarring) (Taylor & Asmundson, 2004).

Empirical Support. Consistent with the cognitive model, research suggests that relative to nonanxious controls, people with excessive health anxiety tend to misinterpret their bodily sensations as indicative of disease (Haenen, Schmidt, Schoenmakers, & van den Hout, 1998). They are also more likely to overestimate the probability and cost ("badness") of acquiring diseases (Ditto, Jemmott, & Darley, 1988; Easterling & Leventhal, 1989).

Also consistent with the cognitive model, environmental factors account for most of the individual differences in scores on health anxiety (63%–90% of the variance). Genetic factors play a significant but less important role (10%–37% of the variance; Taylor, Thordarson, Jang, & Asmundson, 2006). Environmental factors include early learning experiences (e.g., childhood history of disease or parental reinforcement or special attention when sick; Taylor & Asmundson, 2004). These learning experiences can contribute to dysfunctional beliefs about the dangerousness of bodily sensations, and to beliefs that one's body is weak (Robbins & Kirmayer, 1996; Whitehead et al., 1994).

Body Dysmorphic Disorder

Overlap with OCD. Body dysmorphic disorder (BDD) is classified as a somatoform disorder in DSM-IV. Although affected individuals display a somatic focus, the focus is on imagined or exaggerated concerns about physical defects (e.g., obsessions about the asymmetry of one's face).

Appearance-related preoccupations in BDD are similar to obsessions in OCD because both trigger anxiety or distress. Similarly, avoidance and excessive behaviors to conceal, correct, check, or seek reassurance about the imagined defects among people with BDD serve a similar purpose as compulsive rituals in OCD; namely, to reduce distress. For instance, some individuals with BDD check their appearance for prolonged periods of time; looking in mirrors, windows, and so forth. Others focus their energies on avoiding all reflective surfaces. Additional compulsive behaviors include comparing oneself to others, skin-picking, reading all relevant information on the body part(s) of concern, measuring the "flawed" body part(s), and seeking cures (e.g., dental, dermatological, surgical) for perceived defects (Perugi & Frare, 2005). Due to these similarities, many researchers have regarded BDD to be an OC-related disorder.

Cognitive Model. The best articulated cognitive model of BDD is that proposed by Veale (2004). This model begins with the proposition that episodes of heightened concern with body image in BDD are often precipitated by "external representations" of the individual's appearance (e.g., seeing one's reflection), which triggers a defective mental image. Through selective attention toward appearance-related details, the individual experiences heightened awareness of specific characteristics within the image, and thereby assumes that the perceived defect is clearly apparent to other people. This imagery is associated with heightened self-focused attention, to the extent that in more severe cases of BDD, all of the individuals' attention may be focused on the distorted image and on the negative evaluation of the image.

According to Veale's model, the afflicted person also negatively appraises his or her appearance in the context of dysfunctional beliefs about the importance of physical appearance. The individual may hold beliefs such as, "If I'm unattractive, life isn't worth living." Beliefs regarding inadequacy, worthlessness, abnormality, and rejection are implicated in Veale's model. The individual also compares his or her "defective" features with the ideal, which leads to self-loathing, fear of embarrassment and rejection, depression, and anger at oneself. These emotional responses lead to defensive behaviors such as avoidance, or active escape and concealment of the imagined defect, to prevent the feared outcomes and to reduce distress. Although these defensive behaviors may temporarily alleviate distress, in the long run they maintain the self-conscious

preoccupation with the imagined defect, and negative appraisal of oneself.

Empirical Support. A number of research findings support Veale's model (see Buhlmann & Wilhelm, 2004, for a review). For example, studies show that people with BDD deploy selective attention toward minute details and features, rather than on global figures, which might explain the focus on specific appearance-related details while ignoring more global features. This was demonstrated by a recent study using the emotional Stroop task (Buhlmann, McNally, Wilhelm, & Florin, 2002). Here, BDD patients selectively attended to emotional BDD-related stimuli (both positive and negative), which is consistent with the attentional biases and image-related preoccupations proposed in Veale's model.

Trichotillomania

Overlap with OCD. DSM-IV classifies Trichotillomania (TTM) as an impulse control disorder that involves (a) recurrent hair pulling resulting in noticeable hair loss, (b) heightened tension immediately before pulling, or when attempting to resist pulling, and (c) pleasure, gratification, or relief when pulling out the hair. Thus, TTM, appears to share *some* characteristics with OCD, namely, repetitive compulsion-like behaviors. There are, however, important functional differences between these disorders. First, the intrusive, anxiety-evoking obsessional thoughts that occur in OCD are not present in TTM. Second, the compulsive rituals demonstrated by people with OCD are performed in response to obsessions, and often result in decreased anxiety, whereas hair pulling in TTM is precipitated by feelings of general tension, depression, anger, boredom, frustration, indecision, or fatigue (Christensen, Ristvedt, & Mackenzie, 1993; Stanley & Mouton, 1996). Hair pulling in TTM, unlike compulsive rituals in OCD, leads to pleasurable feelings (Stanley, Swann, Bowers, & Davis, 1992).

Cognitive Model. Most psychological models emphasize the role of learning in TTM. For instance, Azrin and Nun (1973) argued that urges to pull hair become conditioned responses to one or more situations (e.g., being alone), internal sensations (e.g., tension), or activities (e.g., reading). Pulling is followed by feelings of sensory stimulation or gratification that serve as an escape from negative feeling states, thereby reinforcing (both positively and negatively) the pulling behavior (Woods, Adcock, & Conelea, 2008).

The role of cognition has only recently been introduced into models of TTM. Franklin and Tolin (2007) argued that several kinds of dysfunctional beliefs can increase negative emotion in people with TTM, thereby increasing urges to pull. Such beliefs include those pertaining to perfectionism, beliefs about the persistence and controllability of urges to pull (e.g., "The urge will last forever unless I pull"), beliefs about the hair pulling habit itself ("This is an appalling behavior"), and beliefs about negative evaluation from others ("Other people will notice my hair loss and won't want to associate with me"). Episodes of hair pulling may also be exacerbated by beliefs about the positive effects of hair pulling (e.g., "Hair pulling will make me feel better") and facilitative thoughts (e.g., "I'll just pull one more"; Gluhoski, 1995).

Empirical Support. To date, there has been only one study of dysfunctional beliefs in TTM. In this investigation, Norberg, Wetterneck, Woods, and Conelea (2007) assessed, in a self-described sample of people with hair pulling problems, beliefs pertaining to appearance and shame or social rejection in regard to hair pulling. These beliefs were correlated with the severity of the person's hair pulling. Although these findings are consistent with the cognitive model of TTM, it is unclear whether they are a cause or consequence of hair pulling. Further research is needed to test and refine cognitive models of TTM.

Future Directions for Cognitive Models of OCD and Related Disorders

There are several important challenges and research issues for contemporary cognitive models of OCD and related disorders. The failures to find empirical support for several of the predictions derived from contemporary cognitive models of OCD (Table 12.2) suggest that the six domains of OC-related beliefs (as described in Table 12.1) are insufficient for explaining OCD. This situation has arisen despite the fact that the belief domains were identified on the basis of research reviews and the clinical experience of over 40 OCD experts (OCCWG, 1997). It may be necessary to identify and include other types of dysfunctional beliefs into cognitive models of OCD, in order to improve the predictive power of the models (e.g., beliefs about the acquisition of possessions, as discussed earlier). The models of OCD also may need to be expanded to account for important features of OCD that have been hitherto neglected. The phenomena of "not just right" (NJR) experiences and the emotion of disgust are two such features.

"Not Just Right" Experiences

NJR experiences entail problems terminating activities because of a feeling that that the activity has not been properly completed. This can involve arranging objects, walking a precise numbers of steps, or washing a particular number of times until a "just right" experience is attained. Here, the motivation for performing compulsions appears to be the attainment of tension reduction, rather than performing compulsions in order to avert some feared outcome (Leckman, Walker, Goodman, Pauls, & Cohen, 1994). For example, a person might engage in compulsive handwashing until he or she no longer feels distressed, rather than washing with the aim of removing contaminants. Contemporary cognitive models have little to say about the causes of NJR experiences. Perfectionism has been implicated (Coles, Frost, Heimberg, & Rheume, 2003; Moretz & McKay, submitted), although the role that perfectionism plays in NJR experiences is poorly understood. Perfectionism is multidimensional in nature (Hewitt & Flett, 2002), and it is possible that some aspects of perfectionism are more important than others in NJR experiences.

Disgust

Over the past twenty years, there has been a growing emphasis on the importance of disgust in various forms of psychopathology, particularly anxiety disorders (Olatunji & McKay, 2007). In OCD, disgust has been particularly useful in describing contamination fears (McKay & Moretz, 2009). Disgust is a learned, culturally specific emotional state, designed to prevent the ingestion of toxins. A cognitive component of disgust, of relevance to contamination fear, concerns "sympathetic magic" (Rozin & Fallon, 1987). This entails a mechanism whereby otherwise neutral stimuli accrue properties associated with disgust. To illustrate, a pen that comes in momentary contact with feces would become an object of disgust, even if it was cleaned after contact with the contaminant. Sympathetic magic demonstrates the component of disgust where, once a stimulus comes in contact with a disgust-evoking object, it takes on the disgusting properties (called the Law of Contagion). Another feature of sympathetic magic involves the degree that an object resembles stimuli associated with disgust (called the Law of Similarity). For example, reshaping a candy bar to resemble feces would be associated with disgust by virtue of the similar appearance, even without any direct contact with a disgust-evoking stimulus.

Several studies have examined the role of disgust in contamination fear. For instance, a recent study using structural equation modeling showed that contamination fears were associated with disgust, and that this relationship fit the data best when trait anxiety was eliminated from the model as a moderator (Moretz & McKay, 2008). That is, contamination fears appeared to be directly influenced by disgust, independent of trait anxiety. Tolin, Worhunsky, and Maltby (2006) conducted an experiment with individuals diagnosed with OCD, compared to anxious and nonanxious control participants, to examine the degree of sympathetic magic transfer of contaminants. Participants were asked to identify a "contaminated" object, which was then touched with a pencil. Participants then rated the extent that the pencil became contaminated. Following this, a clean pencil was brought into contact with the "contaminated" pencil, and participants again rated the contamination level of the second pencil. This was repeated for a total of 12 pencils. Individuals with OCD, compared to controls, made higher ratings of the degree of contamination of all of the pencils.

Such studies suggest that a deeper understanding of the causes of OCD may be attained by investigating how the cognitive mechanisms associated with sympathetic magic distinguish OCD from controls. Contemporary cognitive models of OCD have placed little if any emphasis on disgust. Such models may provide a more comprehensive account of OC-related phenomena if the models encompass disgust-related cognitive mechanisms.

Testing and Integrating Cognitive Models of OCD and Related Disorders

Cognitive models of OC-related disorders have not been tested as extensively as models of OCD. Given that the cognitive models of the related disorders have been derived from, or are conceptually similar to, the cognitive models of OCD, it is possible that models of OC-related disorders will encounter problems similar to those of OCD models. The models of OCD and related disorders also need to be better integrated with one another, in order to better explain (a) why a person develops one disorder (e.g., OCD) instead of another (e.g., BDD); (b) why OCD and OC-related disorders commonly co-occur with one another at the same time (i.e., current comorbidity, such as the concurrent onset of OCD and TTM); and (c) why a person with one of these disorders is at heightened risk for the developing, at some time in the future, a related disorder

(i.e., lifetime comorbidity; e.g., OCD in childhood followed by hypochondriasis in adulthood; American Psychiatric Association, 2000).

Developmental and Cultural Considerations

Developmental aspects of the cognitive models also require further investigation and elaboration. There is preliminary evidence that the beliefs listed in Table 12.1 can be identified in children as young as 6 years, in adolescents, and in the elderly, and that these beliefs are correlated with OC symptoms in these age groups (e.g., Farrell & Barrett, 2006; Teachman & Clerkin, 2007). However, the cognitive models need to be modified to account for developmental differences across the lifespan. Beliefs about one's thoughts, for example, play less of a role in OCD in young children, particularly in children who have not yet fully developed the capacity to appraise their own thinking (i.e., the child requires a "formal operations" level of cognitive development; Farrell & Barrett, 2006). There is also evidence that responsibility beliefs are less important in childhood OCD compared to OCD in adolescence and adulthood (Farrell & Barrett, 2006). In the elderly, the models may need to be revised to give greater emphasis to beliefs that are more specific to the elderly, such as beliefs relating to cognitive decline (e.g., "I need to keep checking things because my memory is isn't what it used to be"; Teachman, 2007).

Contemporary cognitive models have little to say about cross-cultural differences in OC-related beliefs. There is preliminary evidence that the cognitive models can be applied to different cultures (Sica, Taylor, Arrindell, & Sanavio, 2006; Yorulmaz, Karanci, Bastug, Kista, & Goka, 2008), although more research is needed to account for cultural factors in the development of beliefs associated with OC symptoms.

Dysfunctional Beliefs, Information Processing, and Neuroscience

The cognitive models draw, to some degree, on information processing models (Chapter 8). However, the cognitive models could be more tightly integrated with information processing models and findings. For example, information processing research suggests that implicit (nonconscious) factors play a role in OCD (Chapter 8), and yet the contemporary cognitive models focus almost entirely on conscious factors. A more comprehensive approach would encompass both types of factors in models of OCD and related disorders.

The cognitive models of OCD and related disorders need to be better integrated with research implicating the roles of genetic and neurobiological factors (see Chapters 6 and 7). This may be important not only for understanding mind-brain relationships, but also for identifying possible boundary constraints on cognitive models. That is, the models might only be able to account for a subset of cases. As noted earlier, many OCD patients have essentially normal scores on measures of dysfunctional beliefs, thereby suggesting that such beliefs do not play an etiologic role in all forms of OCD. Some models of OCD do not regard dysfunctional beliefs as playing an important role (see Chapters 6 and 7). Contemporary cognitive models of OCD may be applicable for explaining OC symptoms that arise in the context of particular learning experiences or life stressors, but may be unable to account for OC symptoms that arise as a consequence of biological assaults, such as traumatic brain injury or streptococcal infection.

Summary and Conclusions

Contemporary models of OCD have many of the properties that a good model ought to possess; the models are falsifiable, make clear predictions, are parsimonious, and have treatment relevance. Moreover, the models have led to a rich program of research. Although there is some empirical support for these models, there many ways in which the models might be improved. The models are "works in progress," and will no doubt be refined in the coming years. Cognitive models of related disorders, such as hypochondriasis, are also promising, but more work needs to be done, especially in the area of integrating the models of OCD with models of OC-related disorders.

Perhaps a more important concern is that the cognitive models have been developed in a way that has largely ignored the mounting body of research on the importance of neurobiological factors. A more complete understanding of OCD and related disorders is likely to arise if theorists and researchers are willing to tackle the challenging task of integrating mind and brain; that is, finding a rapprochement between cognitive models and neuroscience. Such efforts may eventually lead to a comprehensive model of OCD.

Another potentially important avenue of research is to extend the conceptual and empirical work on OCD subtypes. It is possible that different theoretical models apply to different subtypes of OCD. Models emphasizing the role of dysfunctional beliefs and appraisals might apply only to a subgroup of cases of OCD, or to particular symptom presentations. Further research is needed to explore this intriguing possibility.

Future Directions

Despite the recent advances in understanding the cognitive factors involved in OCD and related disorders, a number of important questions remain to be addressed, including the following.

1. What is the role of dysfunctional beliefs in the putative OC spectrum disorders, and do dysfunctional beliefs distinguish OCD from these disorders?

2. How are "not just right" feelings explained by cognitive models of OCD?

3. What is the role of disgust in the development and maintenance of OC symptoms?

4. How does the process of cognitive development from childhood to adulthood shape the form and content of dysfunctional beliefs?

5. What is the role of culture in shaping dysfunctional beliefs in OCD?

6. What is the relationship between dysfunctional beliefs and neurobiological correlates of OCD?

7. How are dysfunctional belief related to particular patterns of information processing associated with OCD?

Related Chapters

Chapter 8. Information Processing in Obsessive Compulsive Disorder and Related Problems

Chapter 11. Psychological Models of Obsessive Compulsive and Spectrum Disorders: From Psychoanalytic to Behavioral Conceptualizations

Chapter 18. Cognitive Treatment for OCD

References

Abramowitz, J. S., Khandker, M., Nelson, C. A., Deacon, B. J., & Rygwall, R. (2006). The role of cognitive factors in the pathogenesis of obsessive-compulsive symptoms: A prospective study. *Behaviour Research and Therapy, 44,* 1361–1374.

Abramowitz, J. S., Lackey, G. R., & Wheaton, M. G. (2009). Obsessive-compulsive symptoms: The contribution of obsessional beliefs and experiential avoidance. *Journal of Anxiety Disorders, 23,* 160–166.

Abramowitz. J. S., Nelson, C. A., Rygwall, R. & Khandker, M. (2007). The cognitive mediation of obsessive-compulsive symptoms: A longitudinal study. *Journal of Anxiety Disorders, 21,* 91–104.

Abramowitz, J. S., Taylor, S., & McKay, D. (2005). Potentials and limitations of cognitive therapy for obsessive-compulsive disorder. *Cognitive Behaviour Therapy, 34,* 140–147.

American Psychiatric Association. (2000). *Diagnostic and statistical manual of mental disorders* (4th ed., text rev.). Washington, DC: Author.

Anholt, G. E., Emmelkamp, P. M. G., Cath, D. C., van Oppen, P., Nelissen, H., & Smit, J. H. (2004). Do patients with OCD and pathological gambling have similar dysfunctional cognitions? *Behaviour Research and Therapy, 42*, 529–537.

Arntz, A., Voncken, M., & Goosen, A. C. A. (2007). Responsibility and obsessive-compulsive disorder: An experimental test. *Behaviour Research and Therapy, 45*, 425–435.

Azrin, N. H., & Nunn, R. G. (1973). Habit reversal: A method of eliminating nervous habits and tics. *Behaviour Research and Therapy, 11*, 619–628.

Beck, A. T. (1976). *Cognitive therapy and the emotional disorders.* New York: International Universities Press.

Berle, D., & Starcevic, V. (2005). Thought-action fusion: Review of the literature and future directions. *Clinical Psychology Review, 25*, 263–284.

Boschen, M. J., & Vuksanovic, D. (2007). Deteriorating memory confidence, responsibility perceptions, and repeated checking: Comparisons in OCD and control samples. *Behaviour Research and Therapy, 45*, 2098–2109.

Bouchard, C., Rheaume, J., & Ladouceur, R. (1999). Responsibility and perfectionism in OCD: An experimental study. *Behaviour Research and Therapy, 37*, 239–248.

Bouvard, M. (2002). Cognitive effects of cognitive-behavior therapy for obsessive compulsive disorder. In R. O. Frost & G. S. Steketee (Eds.), *Cognitive approaches to obsessions and compulsions: Theory, assessment, and treatment* (pp. 403–416). Oxford: Elsevier.

Buhlmann, U., McNally, R. J., Wilhelm, S., & Florin, I. (2002). Selective processing of emotional information in body dysmorphic disorder. *Journal of Anxiety Disorders, 16*, 289–298.

Buhlmann, U., & Wilhelm, S. (2004). Cognitive factors in body dysmorphic disorder. *Psychiatric Annals, 34*, 922–926.

Calamari, J. E., Cohen, R. J., Rector, N. A., Szacun-Shimizu, K., Riemann, B. C., & Norberg, M. M. (2006). Dysfunctional belief-based obsessive-compulsive disorder subgroups. *Behaviour Research and Therapy, 44*, 1347–1360.

Christenson, G., Ristvedt, S., & Mackenzie, T. (1993). Identification of trichotillomania cue profiles. *Behaviour Research and Therapy, 31*, 315–320.

Clark, D. A. (2004). *Cognitive-behavioral therapy for OCD.* New York: Guilford.

Coles, M. E., Frost, R. O., Heimberg, R. G., & Rheume, J. (2003). Not just right experiences: Perfectionism, obsessive-compulsive features, and general psychopathology. *Behaviour Research and Therapy, 41*, 681–700.

Cougle, J. R., Lee, H.-J., & Salkovskis, P. M. (2007). Are responsibility beliefs inflated in non-checking OCD patients? *Journal of Anxiety Disorders, 21,* 153–159.

de Silva, P., & Marks, M. (2001). Traumatic experiences, post-traumatic stress disorder and obsessive-compulsive disorder. *International Review of Psychiatry, 13*, 172–180.

Ditto, P. H., Jemmott, J. B., & Darley, J. M. (1988). Appraising the threat of illness: A mental representational approach. *Health Psychology, 7*, 183–201.

Easterling, D. V., & Leventhal, H. (1989). Contribution of concrete cognition to emotion: Neutral symptoms as elicitors of worry about cancer. *Journal of Applied Psychology, 74*, 787–796.

Emmelkamp, P. M. G., van Oppen, P., & van Balkom, A. J. (2002). Cognitive changes in patients with obsessive compulsive rituals treated with exposure in vivo and response

prevention. In R. O. Frost & G. S. Steketee (Eds.), *Cognitive approaches to obsessions and compulsions: Theory, assessment, and treatment* (pp. 391–401). Oxford: Elsevier.

Farrell, L., & Barrett, P. (2006). Obsessive-compulsive disorder across developmental trajectory: Cognitive processing of threat in children, adolescents and adults. *British Journal of Psychology, 97*, 95–114.

Flett, G. L., & Hewitt, P. L. (2002). *Perfectionism: Theory, research, and treatment.* Washington, DC: American Psychological Association Press.

Franklin, M. E., & Tolin, D. F. (2007). *Treating trichotillomania: Cognitive-behavioral therapy of hairpulling and related problems.* New York: Springer Science.

Frost, R. O., & Gross, R. (1993). The hoarding of possessions. *Behaviour Research and Therapy, 31*, 367–382.

Frost, R.O., & Steketee, G. (2002). *Cognitive approaches to obsessions and compulsions: Theory, assessment and treatment.* Oxford: Elsevier.

Frost, R. O., & Steketee, G. (2008). Compulsive hoarding. In J. S. Abramowitz, D. McKay, & S. Taylor (Eds.), *Obsessive-compulsive disorder: Subtypes and spectrum conditions* (pp. 76–93). Amsterdam: Elsevier.

Gibbs, N. (1996). Nonclinical populations in research on obsessive-compulsive disorder. *Clinical Psychology Review, 16*, 729–773.

Gluhoski, V. L. (1995). A cognitive approach for treating trichotillomania. *Journal of Psychotherapy Practice and Research, 4*, 277–285.

Haenen, M. A., Schmidt, A. J. M., Schoenmakers, M., & van den Hout, M. A. (1998). Quantitative and qualitative aspects of cancer knowledge: Comparing hypochondriacal subjects and healthy controls. *Psychology and Health, 13*, 1005–1014.

Julien, D., Careau, Y., O'Connor, K. P., Bouvard, M., Rheaume, J., Langlois, F., et al. (2008). Specificity of belief domains in OCD: Validation of the French version of the Obsessive Beliefs Questionnaire and a comparison across samples. *Journal of Anxiety Disorders, 22*, 1029–1041.

Julien, D., O'Connor, K. P., & Aardema, F. (2007). Intrusive thoughts, obsessions, and appraisals in obsessive-compulsive disorder: A critical review. *Clinical Psychology Review, 27*, 366–383.

Julien, D., O'Connor, K. P., Aardema, F., & Todorov, C. (2006). The specificity of belief domains in obsessive-compulsive symptom subtypes. *Personality and Individual Differences, 41*, 1205–1216.

Leckman, J. F., Walker, D. E., Goodman, W. K., Pauls, D. F., & Cohen, D. J. (1994). "Just right" perceptions associated with compulsive behavior in Tourette's syndrome. *American Journal of Psychiatry, 151*, 675–680.

Lopatka, C., & Rachman, S. (1995). Perceived responsibility and compulsive checking: An experimental analysis. *Behaviour Research and Therapy, 33*, 674–684.

Luchian, S. A., McNally, R. J., & Hooley, J. M. (2007). Cognitive aspects of nonclinical obsessive-compulsive hoarding. *Behaviour Research and Therapy, 45*, 1657–1662.

Lucock, M. P., White, C., Peake, M. D., & Morley, S. (1998). Biased perception and recall of reassurance in medical patients. *British Journal of Health Psychology, 3*, 237–243.

Marcks, B. A., & Woods, D. W. (2007). Role of thought-related beliefs and coping strategies in the escalation of intrusive thoughts: An analog to obsessive-compulsive disorder. *Behaviour Research and Therapy, 45*, 2640–2651.

McKay, D., Abramowitz, J. S., Calamari, J., Kyrios, M., Sookman, D., Taylor, S., et al. (2004). A critical evaluation of obsessive-compulsive disorder subtypes: Symptoms versus mechanisms. *Clinical Psychology Review, 24,* 283–313.

McKay, D., & Moretz, M.W. (2009). The intersection of disgust and contamination fear. In B.O. Olatunji & D. McKay (Eds.), *Disgust and its disorders: Theory, assessment, and treatment implications* (pp. 211–227). Washington, DC: American Psychological Association.

McLean, P. D., Whittal, M. L., Thordarson, D., Taylor, S., Söchting, I., Koch, W. J., et al. (2001). Cognitive versus behavior therapy in the group treatment of obsessive-compulsive disorder. *Journal of Consulting and Clinical Psychology, 69,* 205–214.

Moretz, M. W., & McKay, D. (2008). *The role of perfectionism in obsessive-compulsive symptoms: "Not just right" experiences and checking compulsions.* Paper submitted for publication.

Moritz, S., & Pohl, R. F. (2006). False beliefs maintenance for fear-related information in obsessive-compulsive disorder: An investigation with the hindsight paradigm. *Neuropsychology, 20,* 737–742.

Mowrer, O. H. (1960). *Learning theory and behavior.* New York: Wiley.

Myers, S. G., Fisher, P. L., & Wells, A. (2008). Belief domains of the obsessive beliefs questionnaire-44 (OBQ-44) and their specific relationship with obsessive-compulsive symptoms. *Journal of Anxiety Disorders, 22,* 475–484.

Norberg, M. M., Wetterneck, C. T., Woods, D. W., & Conelea, C.A. (2007). Experiential avoidance as a mediator of relationships between cognitions and hair-pulling severity. *Behavior Modification, 31,* 367–381.

Obsessive Compulsive Cognitions Work Group. (1997). Cognitive assessment of obsessive-compulsive disorder. *Behaviour Research and Therapy, 35,* 667–681.

Obsessive Compulsive Cognitions Working Group. (2001). Development and initial validation of the Obsessive Beliefs Questionnaire and the Interpretation of Intrusions Inventory. *Behaviour Research and Therapy, 39,* 987–1005.

Obsessive Compulsive Cognitions Working Group. (2003). Psychometric validation of the Obsessive Beliefs Questionnaire and the Interpretation of Intrusions Inventory: Part 1. *Behaviour Research and Therapy, 41,* 863–878.

Obsessive Compulsive Cognitions Working Group. (2005). Psychometric validation of the obsessive belief questionnaire and interpretation of intrusions inventory Part 2: Factor analyses and testing of a brief version. *Behaviour Research and Therapy, 43,* 1527–1542.

Olatunji, B. O., & McKay, D. (2007). Disgust and psychiatric illness: Have we remembered? *British Journal of Psychiatry, 190,* 457–459.

Pennebaker, J. W. (1982). *The psychology of physical symptoms.* New York: Springer.

Perugi, G., & Frare, F. (2005). Body dysmorphic disorder. In M. Maj, H.S. Akiskal, J.E. Mezzich, and A. Okasha (Eds.) *Evidence and Experience in Psychiatry* (pp. 191–221) Vol. 9, Chichester: Wiley.

Purdon, C. (2004). Empirical investigations of thought suppression in OCD. *Journal of Behavior Therapy and Experimental Psychiatry, 35,* 121–136.

Rachman, S. (1998). A cognitive theory of obsessions: Elaborations. *Behaviour Research and Therapy, 36,* 385–401.

Rachman, S., & Hodgson, R. J. (1980). *Obsessions and compulsions.* Englewood Cliffs, NJ: Prentice Hall.

Rachman, S., Shafran, R., Mitchell, D., Trant, J., & Teachman, B. (1996). How to remain neutral: An experimental analysis of neutralization. *Behaviour Research and Therapy, 34,* 889–898.

Robbins, J. M., Kirmayer, L. J. (1996). Transient and persistent hypochondriacal worry in primary care. *Psychological Medicine, 26,* 575–589.

Rozin, P. & Fallon, A. E. (1987). A perspective on disgust. *Psychological Review, 94,* 23–41.

Salkovskis, P. M. (1985). Obsessional-compulsive problems: A cognitive-behavioural analysis. *Behaviour Research and Therapy, 25,* 571–583.

Salkovskis, P. M. (1996). Cognitive-behavioral approaches to the understanding of obsessional problems. In R. M. Rapee (Ed.), *Current controversies in the anxiety disorders* (pp. 103–134). New York: Guilford.

Salkovskis, P. M., & Forrester, E. (2002). Responsibility. In R. O. Frost & G. S. Steketee (Eds.), *Cognitive approaches to obsessions and compulsions: Theory, assessment and treatment* (pp. 45–61). Oxford: Elsevier.

Salkovskis, P. M., Shafran, R., Rachman, S., & Freeston, M. H. (1999). Multiple pathways to inflated responsibility in obsessional problems: Possible origins and implications for therapy and research. *Behaviour Research and Therapy, 37,* 1055–1072.

Salkovskis, P. M., Warwick, H. M., & Deale, A. C. (2003). Cognitive-behavioral treatment for severe and persistent health anxiety (hypochondriasis). *Brief Treatment and Crisis Intervention, 3,* 353–367.

Salkovskis, P. M., Wroe, A. L., Gledhill, A., Morrison, N., Forrester, E., Richards, C., et al. (2000). Responsibility attitudes and interpretations are characteristic of obsessive compulsive disorder. *Behaviour Research and Therapy, 38,* 347–372.

Shafran, R., Thordarson, D. S., & Rachman, S. (1996). Thought-action fusion in obsessive-compulsive disorder. *Journal of Anxiety Disorders, 10,* 379–391.

Sica, C., Taylor, S., Arrindell, W. A., & Sanavio, E. (2006). A cross-cultural test of the cognitive theory of obsessions and compulsions: A comparison of Greek, Italian, and American individuals a preliminary study. *Cognitive Therapy and Research, 30,* 585–597.

Stanley, M., & Mouton, S. (1996). Trichotillomania treatment manual. In V. van Hasselt & M. Hersen (Eds.), *Sourcebook of psychological treatment manuals for adult disorders* (pp. 657–687). New York: Plenum.

Stanley, M., Swann, A., Bowers, T., & Davis, M. (1992). A comparison of clinical features in trichotillomania and obsessive-compulsive disorder. *Behaviour Research and Therapy, 30,* 39–44.

Steketee, G., & Frost, R. O. (2003). Compulsive hoarding: Current status of the research. *Clinical Psychology Review, 23,* 905–927.

Tallis, F., (1994). Obsessions, responsibility and guilt: Two case reports suggesting a common and specific aetiology. *Behaviour Research and Therapy, 32,* 143–145.

Taylor, S., Coles, M. E., Abramowitz, J. S., Wu, K. D., Olatunji, B. O., Timpano, K. R., et al. (2010). How are dysfunctional beliefs related to obsessive-compulsive symptoms? *Journal of Cognitive Psychotherapy, 24,* 165–176.

Taylor, S., Abramowitz, J. S., & McKay, D. (2005). Are there interactions among dysfunctional beliefs in obsessive compulsive disorder? *Cognitive Behaviour Therapy, 34,* 89–98.

Taylor, S., Abramowitz, J. S., McKay, D., Calamari, J. E., Sookman, D., Kyrios, M., et al. (2005). Do dysfunctional beliefs play a role in all types of obsessive-compulsive disorder? *Journal of Anxiety Disorders, 20,* 85–97.

Taylor, S., & Asmundson, G. J. G. (2004). *Treating health anxiety: A cognitive-behavioral approach.* New York: Guilford.

Taylor, S., McKay, D., & Abramowitz, J. S. (2005). Hierarchical structure of dysfunctional beliefs in obsessive-compulsive disorder. *Cognitive Behaviour Therapy, 34,* 216–228.

Taylor, S., Thordarson, D. S., Jang, K. L., & Asmundson, G. J. G. (2006). Genetic and environmental origins of health anxiety: A twin study. *World Psychiatry, 5,* 47–50.

Teachman, B. A. (2007). Linking obsessional beliefs to OCD symptoms in older and younger adults. *Behaviour Research and Therapy, 45,* 1671–1681.

Teachman, B. A., & Clerkin, E. M. (2007). Obsessional beliefs and the implicit and explicit morality of intrusive thought. *Cognition & Emotion, 21,* 999–1024.

Thordarson, D. S., & Shafran, R. (2002). Importance of thoughts. In R. O. Frost & G. S. Steketee (Eds.), *Cognitive approaches to obsessions and compulsions: Theory, assessment and treatment* (pp. 15–28). Oxford: Elsevier.

Tolin, D. F., Brady, R. E., & Hannan, S. (2008). Obsessional beliefs and symptoms of obsessive-compulsive disorder in a clinical sample. *Journal of Psychopathology and Behavioral Assessment, 30,* 31–42.

Tolin, D. F., Woods, C. M., & Abramowitz, J. S. (2003). Relationship between obsessive beliefs and obsessive compulsive symptoms. *Cognitive Therapy and Research, 27,* 657–669.

Tolin, D. F., Worhunsky, P., & Maltby, N. (2006). Are "obsessive" beliefs specific to OCD?: A comparison across anxiety disorders. *Behaviour Research and Therapy, 44,* 469–480.

van den Hout, M., & Kindt, M. (2003a). Phenomenological validity of an OCD-memory model and the remember/know distinction. *Behaviour Research and Therapy, 41,* 369–378.

van den Hout, M., & Kindt, M. (2003b). Repeated checking causes memory distrust. *Behaviour Research and Therapy, 41,* 301–316.

Veale, D. (2004). Advances in a cognitive behavioral model of body dysmorphic disorder. *Body Image, 1,* 113–125.

Warwick, H. M., & Salkovskis, P. M. (1990). Hypochondriasis. *Behaviour Research and Therapy, 28,* 105–117.

Wenzlaff, R. M., Wegner, D. M. (2000). Thought suppression. *Annual Review of Psychology, 51,* 59–91.

Whitehead, W. E., Crowell, M. D., Heller, B. R., Robinson, J. C., Schuster, M. M., & Horn, S. (1994). Modeling and reinforcement of the sick role during childhood predicts adult illness behavior. *Psychosomatic Medicine, 56,* 541–550.

Wincze, J. P., Steketee, G., & Frost, R. O. (2007). Categorization in compulsive hoarding. *Behaviour Research and Therapy, 45,* 63–72.

Woods, C. M., Tolin, D. F., & Abramowitz, J. S. (2004). Dimensionality of the obsessive beliefs questionnaire (OBQ). *Journal of Psychopathology and Behavioral Assessment, 26,* 113–125.

Woods, D., Adcock, A., & Conelea, C. (2008). Trichotillomania. In J. S. Abramowitz, D. McKay, & S. Taylor (Eds.), *Clinical handbook of obsessive-compulsive disorder and related problems* (pp. 205–221). Baltimore, MD: Johns Hopkins University Press.

Wu, K., & Carter, S. A. (2008). Further investigation of the Obsessive Beliefs Questionnaire: Factor structure and specificity of relations with OCD symptoms. *Journal of Anxiety Disorders, 22,* 824–836.

Yorulmaz, O., Karanci, A. N., Bastug, B., Kisa, C., Goka, E. (2008). Responsibility, thought-action fusion, and thought suppression in Turkish patients with obsessive-compulsive disorder. *Journal of Clinical Psychology, 64,* 308–317.

PART 4

Assessment of OCD and Spectrum Disorders

Assessing OCD Symptoms and Severity

Nicole M. Dorfan *and* Sheila R. Woody

Abstract

This chapter describes methods and tools for assessing obsessive compulsive disorder (OCD). The chapter outlines the purposes of assessment and discusses special challenges presented by OCD, such as shame associated with socially unacceptable obsessional content. Several types of assessment tools are discussed, including structured diagnostic interviews, semistructured clinician interviews to assess OCD symptom profile and severity, self-report instruments, behavioral assessment and self-monitoring, assessment of appraisals and beliefs relevant to OCD, and functional impairment. The importance of linking assessment findings to an evidence-based treatment plan is discussed.

Keywords: OCD, obsessive compulsive disorder, assessment, Y-BOCS, diagnosis, self-report, cognition, symptoms

Introduction

Anne, a 32-year-old woman who worked in an assisted-living facility for elderly residents, sought treatment for obsessions, compulsions, and depression. Anne reported spending almost all of her waking hours engaged in rituals, although the rituals occurred less frequently while she was at work. During the initial interview, Anne described fairly prototypical obsessions involving harm for which she felt personally responsible (e.g., a fire that would cause property damage and injury to her neighbors) as well as checking compulsions (e.g., checking the stove and appliances). She also revealed a history of trauma (assault and traumatic loss of pregnancy), several past episodes of major depression, and a family history of OCD.

As Anne developed a stronger working alliance with her clinician (a psychologist) in the first few sessions, she began to reveal more details about her symptoms that were relevant for case conceptualization and treatment planning. In addition to the prototypical fear that failing to check the stove

might result in a fire, she also had some obsessions that were functionally, but not logically, connected with rituals. For example, she had persistent thoughts that failing to follow an urge to ritualize (such as aligning her sweaters perfectly, or turning off the DVD player before turning off the television) would cause something bad to happen to someone she loved. In addition, her list of compulsions grew to include rewriting bank checks or emails to be sure she caused no offense, counting squares of toilet paper, repeatedly entering and exiting rooms, turning taps on and off, and applying butter or jam to her toast in a ritualized way. Her main criterion for stopping a ritual was a "just right" feeling or the completion of ritualizing a "good" number of times. At the time of evaluation, her "good" numbers were 7 and 12.

Anne's case demonstrates numerous functions of the assessment process. The initial assessment was, obviously, the first interaction between Anne and her clinician, and they began developing the therapeutic relationship at this time. The psychologist took a collaborative approach to exploring Anne's presenting symptoms, background, current stressors, cultural context, and goals for treatment. The clinician also confirmed that Anne met diagnostic criteria for both OCD and major depressive disorder.

Like most clients with OCD, Anne presented with both obsessions and compulsions. However, the presence of both is not required for a diagnosis of OCD. "Primary obsessions" typically focus on sexual, blasphemous, or aggressive themes, and are usually accompanied by few or no overt compulsions, although detailed questioning often reveals covert, or mental, compulsions. Children, on the other hand, often present primarily with compulsive behavior and may have difficulty articulating obsessive thoughts. While some clients with OCD have concerns that are restricted to a single theme (e.g., contamination fears and washing rituals), many clients report symptoms in a variety of domains, as Anne does. Eliciting a full description of the content and severity of these varied obsessions and compulsions can take some time.

Because of the breadth of Anne's symptoms, understanding them was greatly facilitated by use of a structured symptom checklist, which will be described later in this chapter. Anne's obsessions included doubt about whether things were as they should be in her home, office, car, and relationships. Any stimulus associated with an implicit rule about how it should be (e.g., door locked, parking brake set, butter to edge of bread, cutlery lined up) would evoke doubt about whether she had followed the rule properly, and even whether she could trust her senses (e.g., whether she correctly perceived the stove knob to be in the "off" position). The symptom checklist prompted Anne's psychologist to ask about a wide variety of obsessions and compulsions, which seemed to make it easier for Anne to disclose symptoms about which she felt shame. Anne was surprised by some of the items on the checklist; prior to the evaluation she had thought she was alone in experiencing these symptoms and took them as a sign that she was "crazy."

Compulsions are most typically associated with observable behaviors. In Anne's case, these included checking, rewriting, and repeating behaviors a certain number of times, ordering and arranging her belongings, and reassurance seeking. She frequently stored appliances such as the iron or kettle in the trunk of her car, which helped her to feel more confident that they were indeed unplugged, although she sometimes checked the trunk during the day to

be sure the appliances were actually there. Covert compulsions can be more challenging to assess; these are mental rituals that are used to "undo" an obsessive thought or prevent a dreaded outcome. Anne's covert compulsions included mentally repeating things 7 or 12 times and using repetitive, stereotyped prayers that her loved ones would be all right.

Assessment of OCD also includes inquiry into avoidance behaviors and accommodations made by family members, as well as functional impairment in areas such as work, school, and social life. Anne's life, for example, was extremely restricted, as she used avoidance to help manage the anxiety associated with obsessions and compulsions. Anne found it easier to stay at home on the weekends and evenings rather than endure the anxiety and effort associated with leaving the house. She did go to work, where she had been able to adapt her compulsions to function well enough to keep her job, but she often spent her lunch hour driving back home to check appliances and door locks. Anne's restricted life also caused other problems, including difficulties managing her weight (due to a lack of regular exercise) and depression.

As is normally the case with an initial assessment, it is important to understand the presenting symptoms within the broader context of the client's current life circumstances and historical experiences. As such, it is important to ask about the conditions under which symptoms of OCD first developed, as well as identifying factors that have aggravated or alleviated symptoms in the past. For Anne, symptoms of OCD developed gradually during childhood, and were initially diagnosed by a psychiatrist when she was in her late teens. Although OCD symptoms are typically exacerbated by depression, in Anne's case, her apathy during times of low mood caused her to care less about everything, even her obsessions and compulsions. Trauma triggers, on the other hand, exacerbated her OCD dramatically. Anne had tried numerous types of medications in the past. At the time of initial assessment, she was taking a relatively high dose of fluoxetine, but it was not managing her symptoms sufficiently. Anne had seen numerous counselors to help her recover from the traumatic incidents that she had experienced, but she had never received psychological treatment for her OCD symptoms.

For the initial assessment, Anne's psychologist used a fairly typical set of instruments, including a diagnostic interview and a comprehensive symptom assessment, which in this case was the Yale-Brown

Obsessive Compulsive Scale (Y-BOCS) and the Y-BOCS Symptom Checklist (Goodman, Price, Rasmussen, & Mazure, 1989a). Anne also engaged in self-monitoring of symptoms, and her psychologist used direct observation to assess subtle avoidance and compulsions, as well as to understand the functional relationship between Anne's obsessions and compulsions. In addition, Anne was asked to complete several self-report measures of OCD to elicit further information on the severity of her behavioral and cognitive symptoms. Finally, Anne's husband provided collateral information on the extent of her avoidance behavior at home. These varied forms of assessment will be discussed further in the pages that follow.

After completing the initial assessment, Anne's psychologist integrated the multiple sources of information into a case formulation that succinctly explained Anne's presenting problems, including how the symptoms and problems fit together in functional relationships, as well as hypothesized vulnerability factors, triggering situations, and maintaining factors. A case formulation of this kind should take into account idiosyncratic features of the client's symptoms and problems, the client's level of insight into the excessiveness of his or her behaviors, and the client's apparent degree of motivation for change. In Anne's case, she was highly motivated for treatment but showed fluctuating insight, depending on which symptom she was experiencing and how anxious she felt.

A case conceptualization should lead to an evidence-based treatment plan for the client. Clinicians currently have several choices for evidence-based treatment of OCD (Nathan & Gorman, 2007), including exposure and response prevention, contemporary cognitive approaches to OCD, and medications. The assessment accordingly needs to elicit factors that will guide the choice and pacing of treatment, including the client's view of acceptability of different treatment options, the feasibility of successfully implementing these options, and the client's motivation for change, psychological mindedness, and tolerance for anxiety. Likewise, the treatment plan selected will influence some of the detailed assessment that needs to be done. For example, exposure and response prevention requires a detailed understanding of the degree to which various stimuli evoke anxiety, and the feared consequences associated with these situations, whereas pharmacotherapy does not require this type of detailed assessment. On the other hand, exposure and response prevention does not require a detailed

analysis of beliefs about intrusive thoughts (e.g., importance of controlling them), which would be necessary to implement some cognitively oriented approaches. Following the initial evaluation, ongoing assessment during the course of treatment can guide the clinician's decisions over time, including when to change intervention strategies and when to terminate treatment.

The Initial Interview
Establishing a Trusting Relationship
The clinical interview is typically the primary source of information regarding presenting symptoms, historical information, and contextual factors. Establishing rapport and trust is a basic and critical element of this process for all clients, and this can be particularly important for clients with OCD, as there is often a great deal of shame and fear associated with the content of obsessions. For example, Joe, a devout Catholic, was mortified by intrusive thoughts that he might be gay, even though he was happily married to a woman with whom he had a mutually satisfying sexual relationship. When calm, Joe felt confident that he did not desire sexual relations with other men, but when he became anxious in response to a trigger, he doubted himself. The doubt involved a troubling sense that he could not be one hundred percent sure of his true self. Triggers could include having warm feelings toward one of his longtime male friends, or appraising another man as good-looking (e.g., model in a magazine, television actor). Joe had never spoken to anyone about his thoughts and fears, as he was sure he would be excommunicated and lose his wife if others knew. During the interview, he could not say the word "gay," and simply discussing the concept that other men are attractive was very difficult for him because of his shame and fear of social and spiritual consequences.

Many prototypical OCD symptoms, including washing or checking, do not necessarily evoke the same degree of shame and secrecy, but some obsessions involve content that is personally abhorrent or socially unacceptable. At times, the content of obsessions may be repugnant or even alien to the clinician, yet a warm and accepting tone accompanied by a straightforward manner of asking questions is most useful for helping the client to disclose the content of such obsessions. The clinician may need to focus special attention on establishing trust prior to asking detailed questions about specific OCD symptoms. For most clients, initial discussion of safer topics, such as demographics, social and developmental history, recent life stressors, current living situation, and social support network will allow them to feel more comfortable before discussing difficult content. Some clients may need reassurance about confidentiality, or advance agreements about which details will appear in the clinician's written notes and reports. Even with these efforts, however, some clients will withhold revealing their most disturbing obsessions or compulsions until many sessions into the therapy process. When such content is eventually revealed, the clinician will need to briefly return to assessment mode to gain the necessary understanding of the additional symptoms, in order to add them to the case conceptualization and treatment plan.

Decisions about how to respond to a client's reluctance to disclose information need to be made on the basis of the evolving case conceptualization. For example, Joe's therapist did not initially press him to use the word "gay" during the evaluation, prioritizing instead the development of rapport and trust. She accepted his euphemisms, frequently checking her understanding of his meaning, but she did not shy away from using the word "gay" herself. She agreed not to detail the content of his most disturbing image in her notes. Later in treatment, however, the therapist encouraged Joe to say the word "gay" as part of his exposure hierarchy. Similar situations may arise in the context of assessing and treating obsessions involving topics such as religious beliefs or parenting styles.

Differential Diagnosis

In some cases, a diagnosis of OCD will be well established based on past psychiatric evaluations, and the clinician is more concerned with assessing current symptoms and triggers, recent exacerbations, current stressors, and other details that impact directly on specific treatment planning. If the client is presenting to a mental health professional for the first time, however, ruling out differential diagnoses and assessing comorbid conditions is necessary to arrive at an accurate diagnostic picture and develop an appropriate treatment plan.

Dale, a 30-year-old veteran of the war in Iraq, presented with frequent obsessions about contamination and germs. He spent many hours washing his hands each day, required two hours for his morning showering ritual, and pressured his wife and children to change out of their "dirty" clothing when arriving home from work or school. When asked about the onset of these symptoms, he described being sickened by touching the wound of

another soldier in Iraq who was bleeding to death in his arms. Ever since, the feeling of dirtiness on his skin has triggered traumatic memories, stimulus-bound panic attacks, and strong urges to wash for extended periods of time.

Dale's case highlights an example of a diagnostic challenge that requires careful assessment and thought. Should his treatment be approached from the perspective of OCD, or post-traumatic stress disorder? Alternatively, should the clinician find some way to incorporate both of these perspectives into the treatment plan, and if so, on what basis? Although Dale presents a case where one set of symptoms may be considered in the context of different diagnostic formulations, comorbid diagnoses are also fairly common. Depression often presents alongside OCD, as well as other anxiety disorders and obsessive compulsive spectrum disorders (hypochondriasis, body dysmorphic disorder, trichotillomania, and tic-related disorders).

Structured diagnostic interviews can be a helpful tool for enhancing the reliability of DSM diagnoses. Interviews commonly used in clinical research include the Structured Clinical Interview for DSM-IV (SCID-I; First, Spitzer, Gibbon, & Williams, 1994) and the Anxiety Disorders Interview Schedule for DSM-IV (ADIS-IV; Brown, Di Nardo, & Barlow, 1994). The SCID-I has a streamlined version specifically designed for use in clinical settings (SCID-CV). Both the SCID-CV and ADIS-IV are designed for use by trained professional interviewers. The interviews guide the clinician through diagnostic criteria for anxiety disorders, mood disorders, alcohol and substance use disorders, and provide screening questions for psychotic symptoms. The SCID-I also provides coverage of eating disorders, and full differential diagnosis for all of the anxiety disorders. (The SCID-CV contains abbreviated modules for some anxiety disorders, such as social phobia.) As would be expected of an instrument that focuses on anxiety disorders, the ADIS-IV provides excellent differential diagnosis of all anxiety disorders, as well as hypochondriasis and other somatization disorders. Both diagnostic interviews also query for psychiatric and medical history, prior treatment, age of onset, and other contextual information. The ADIS-IV supplements categorical diagnostic decisions with dimensional ratings of severity, and provides guidance to the clinician in assessing the specific content of feared situations in various anxiety disorders, including OCD.

Both the ADIS-IV and SCID-I require a significant amount of time to administer (approximately

1.5 hours for a skilled interviewer). More time is needed for clients with a complicated symptom picture, and those who are poor historians. Some clients with OCD may require more time to interview, as they feel the need to provide excessive amounts of information or overly precise details for each question. Clinicians can sometimes manage this problem by explaining the structured nature of the interview and the need to interrupt from time to time in order to get through all of the material, as well as providing reassurance that important topics will be revisited numerous times in subsequent sessions. Alternatively, some clinicians may choose to administer only specific modules of interest from one of these interviews. Another option for clinical practice settings is to begin with a brief structured screening interview, such as the MINI International Neuropsychiatric Interview (Sheehan et al., 1998), which takes only 15–20 minutes, and then follow up with detailed questioning about symptom profiles and severity for those disorders that are most relevant for the client.

Symptom Profile and Overall Severity

Obtaining an accurate diagnosis is just the first step in assessment for OCD. Compared with other anxiety disorders, OCD is extremely heterogeneous. Simply knowing that a client meets diagnosis for OCD provides no information regarding the content of the client's concerns. This heterogeneity, coupled with the reluctance of some clients to report their more shameful or bizarre symptoms, makes it especially important to use structured tools to assist in assessing the content of obsessions and compulsions. For behavioral or cognitive therapy, the clinician needs a detailed understanding of obsessions and compulsions in order to develop the case conceptualization that will drive the specifics of the intervention plan. For all treatment approaches, it is important to monitor symptoms over time to ascertain the degree of progress being made, as well as the generalization of symptom reductions across domains. The next few sections of this chapter will describe interview and self-report methods for gathering specific information about symptoms in various domains, including obsessions and compulsions, avoidance behavior, family accommodation of the symptoms, functional impairment, and readiness for change.

Structured Interviews for Monitoring Outcomes

As noted above, the ADIS-IV module for OCD guides a clinician to assess both the presence and severity of different content areas for obsessions and compulsions. Domains of obsessional content in the ADIS-IV include doubting, contamination, nonsensical impulses and thoughts, aggressive impulses, sexual obsessions, religious obsessions, accidental harm to others, and horrific images. Each of these obsessive content areas is rated on two severity scales: persistence and distress associated with the obsession, and level of resistance exerted against the obsession. Compulsion domains in the ADIS-IV include counting, checking, washing, hoarding, mental repetition, and adhering to rules or sequences; the clinician rates each of these domains in terms of the frequency of the compulsions. The ADIS-IV also elicits overall ratings for interference and distress associated with OCD symptoms.

The most widely used measure of OCD symptoms in research settings is the Yale-Brown Obsessive-Compulsive Scale (Y-BOCS; Goodman et al., 1989a; Goodman, Price, Rasmussen, & Mazure, 1989b), a reliable and valid semistructured interview, which is typically administered after identifying the content of particular obsessions and compulsions using the Y-BOCS Symptom Checklist. Both the Y-BOCS and the Y-BOCS Symptom Checklist are included in the Appendix of this book. The Y-BOCS Symptom Checklist assesses current and past occurrence for over 60 types of obsessions and compulsions, which are organized into thematic categories. Categories of obsessions include aggressive/harm, contamination, sexual, hoarding, religious, symmetry or exactness, somatic, and miscellaneous obsessions. Compulsion categories include cleaning and washing, checking, repeating, counting, ordering and arranging, hoarding, and miscellaneous compulsions. Although the Symptom Checklist also includes some symptoms relevant to OCD spectrum disorders (trichotillomania, hypochondriasis, body dysmorphic disorder, and tics), the Y-BOCS lacks discriminant validity (Taylor, 1995) and is not a diagnostic interview. Other instruments or interviews are therefore needed to determine whether symptoms endorsed on the Checklist are best understood within the framework of OCD or another disorder.

The Y-BOCS severity scale consists of 10 items, each rated on a 0–4 scale. Items include time spent on symptoms, degree of interference in daily life, level of distress that the symptoms cause, degree of resistance against the symptoms, and perceived control over symptoms; these questions are asked separately for obsessions and compulsions. Note that the *resistance against obsessions* item presumes that the more the patient tries to resist, the less impaired they are. However, patients who undergo cognitive-behavioral therapy for OCD may learn to stop actively fighting against their thoughts and instead let them "come and go." This intentional strategy for responding to obsessions should be scored as "resistance" on the Y-BOCS.

The Y-BOCS also provides supplemental questions that provide additional clinically relevant information, including level of insight, indecisiveness, pathological responsibility, obsessional slowness, pathological doubting, and, most importantly, degree of avoidance. Together with the symptom checklist, the Y-BOCS takes approximately 45 minutes to administer, but requires only 5–15 minutes on repeated administrations when repetition of the checklist is unnecessary. The Y-BOCS is sensitive to treatment change (Taylor, 1995), making it a potentially useful measure for outcome assessment. The total Y-BOCS score (including both obsessions and compulsions) is typically interpreted as follows: 0–7 = subclinical; 8–15 = mild OCD symptoms; 16–23 = moderate symptoms; 24–31 = severe symptoms; and 32–40 = extreme (Steketee & Neziroglu, 2003). Note, however, that the total score may be lower for those with only obsessions or compulsions (but not both) even if symptoms are quite severe. The Y-BOCS has also been adapted for use with children and adolescents (Scahill, Riddle, McSwiggin-Hardin, & Ort, 1997).

The clinician instructions for the Y-BOCS outline steps for basic assessment, but the Y-BOCS can provide much richer information if the clinician supplements the Y-BOCS interview with detailed probing of symptoms. To illustrate this process, let us reconsider the case of Anne, described at the outset of the chapter. In conducting the Y-BOCS for the first time, Anne's clinician did not simply name the symptoms on the Y-BOCS Symptom Checklist and check off those that Anne endorsed. Instead, she asked questions about each symptom that Anne described. In relation to checking the stove and other electrical appliances in the home, Anne was prompted to describe her compulsions in detail (e.g., how many episodes per day, and how many checks per episode), sometimes even acting them out for the clinician in the office. Anne's clinician also used this opportunity to elicit feared consequences—Anne's thoughts about what might happen if she did not engage in the rituals. During this more detailed questioning, Anne's clinician learned that Anne believed that if she concentrated

hard enough while checking an appliance, then she would feel a satisfying certainty that the appliance was indeed safe.

Note that the Y-BOCS Symptom Checklist simply provides prompts; it does not assess exactly what the client is checking, washing, or ordering. It is up to the clinician to discover these details. In the case of Anne, her psychologist listened carefully for themes and began to ask questions that fit the theme. For example, the threat of fire was a concern that Anne mentioned frequently. Her psychologist began to ask about other appliances that Anne had not mentioned; she discovered that Anne had obsessions and compulsions about all heat-producing appliances, including the iron, hair drier, lamps, clothes dryer, heater, fireplace, dishwasher, and hot water heater. When she was having a very bad day, she would also be concerned about any dormant electrical appliance over which she did not have perfect oversight, such as outdoor flood lights, the home security system, and the garage door opener.

Anne's case presents a good example of the importance of detailed questioning. Some of Anne's symptoms, like those just detailed, had a logical connection to a feared outcome. Most people take precautions to avoid fire, such as not leaving a burning candle unattended; many people without OCD unplug electric kettles or curling irons when not in use. In part, Anne's obsessions represented an exaggeration of normal precautions. With careful questioning, however, Anne's psychologist also learned that Anne had many obsessions that did not have a logical connection to a feared outcome—"magical thinking" with no "normal" version. She had persistent thoughts that failing to perform rituals would cause something bad to happen to someone she loved (e.g., traffic accident, job loss). Even on occasions when Anne was able to convince herself that a particular appliance was not a fire hazard, she had difficulty resisting the urge to ritualize, because of obsessions about loved ones. Understanding these features of Anne's symptoms was essential for her psychologist to proceed with a clear treatment plan.

Using the full clinician interview version of the Y-BOCS is extremely informative, but it may be too time consuming for some purposes. A self-report version of the Y-BOCS Symptom Checklist and the 10-item Y-BOCS severity scale has been developed by Baer, Brown-Beasley, Sorce, and Henriques (1993). Consistent with the interview version, the 10 items are each rated on a 0–4 scale. In a non-clinical sample, all scales showed excellent internal consistency and test–retest reliability (Steketee, Frost, & Bogart, 1996). In a clinical sample, internal consistency was adequate for the total score and compulsion subscale, but less satisfactory for the obsession scale (Steketee et al., 1996). The self-report version of the Y-BOCS total and subscale scores were strongly correlated with the interview version among participants diagnosed with OCD (r's = 0.73–.79), with scores on the interview version being about two points higher than were scores on the self-report (Steketee et al., 1996).

Multisymptom Self-Report Measures

There are numerous self-report measures available for assessing symptom profile and severity of OCD symptoms. These measures can be especially useful for screening purposes and clinical research, but they are probably less useful for ongoing targeted assessment of client outcomes, because they do not adjust to the client's particular symptom profile as do the ADIS-IV and Y-BOCS. The measures discussed below represent psychometrically sound instruments that are frequently used in the literature. Measures focused on beliefs and appraisals associated with OCD will be included in a later section of this chapter. A more comprehensive list of OCD measures can be found elsewhere (Antony, Orsillo, & Roemer, 2001).

The Obsessive Compulsive Inventory-Revised (OCI-R; Foa et al., 2002) is a shortened version of the original OCI (Foa, Kozak, Salkovskis, Coles, & Amir, 1998). The OCI-R consists of 18 items rated on a 5-point distress scale; the measure is divided into six subscales (washing, checking, ordering, obsessing, hoarding, and neutralizing). As the subscale names suggest, this measure focuses more heavily on compulsions than on obsessions. Psychometric properties are strong for the total score and subscales in clinical samples, including good internal consistency and test–retest reliability (Foa et al., 2002). The OCI-R correlates with other OCD measures, although discriminant validity with measures of depression is relatively weak (Foa et al., 2002). Finally, the OCI-R differentiates patients with OCD from anxious and nonanxious control groups (Foa et al., 2002). The OCI-R scale is printed as an appendix in the Foa et al. publication.

The Padua Inventory-Washington State University Revision (PI-WSUR; Burns, Keortge, Formea, & Sternberger, 1996) is a shortened version of the original Padua Inventory (Sanavio, 1988). The PI-WSUR includes 39 items scored on a 5-point scale and includes five subscales (obsessional thoughts about harm to oneself or others, obsessional impulses to harm oneself or others, contamination obsessions and washing compulsions, checking compulsions, and dressing/grooming compulsions). This scale has a stronger focus on obsessions than many of the other OCD self-report instruments. In addition, the PI-WSUR is a more targeted measure of OCD than was the original PI, in which many items tapped worry as opposed to obsessions (Burns et al., 1996). The PI-WSUR total score has adequate test–retest reliability and good internal consistency in a college sample, although the subscales showed lower reliability (Burns et al., 1996). However, more research is needed to assess the utility of the PI-WSUR in clinical samples. An alternate 41-item revision of the PI (van Oppen, Hoekstra, & Emmelkamp, 1995) has demonstrated sound psychometric properties in a clinical sample, and distinguishes individuals with OCD from anxious and normal control groups. The scale items for both revisions of the Padua Inventory are included in the publications cited above.

The Vancouver Obsessional Compulsive Inventory (VOCI; Thordarson et al., 2004) is one of the newer OCD scales, based on a revision of the widely used Maudsley Obsessional Compulsive Inventory (MOCI; Hodgson & Rachman, 1977). The VOCI consists of 55 items rated on a 5-point scale and includes six subscales (contamination, checking, obsessions, hoarding, just right, and indecisiveness). Psychometric properties of the VOCI total score and subscales are good for clinical samples, including excellent test–retest reliability and strong internal consistency. The total score and some subscales differentiate between individuals with OCD and anxious controls. The VOCI demonstrates strong correlations with other self-report measures of OCD, and shows weaker correlations with measures of depression, anxiety, and worry. The VOCI scale items are included in the Thordarson et al. publication.

The Dimensional Obsessive-Compulsive Scale (DOCS; Abramowitz, Deacon, Olatunji, Wheaton, Berman, Losardo et al., 2010) is a new 20-item measure that assesses four dimensions of OCD (contamination obsessions and cleaning compulsions; responsibility for harm and related compulsions; unacceptable obsessions and related neutralizing; symmetry, order, and "just right" obsessions and compulsions). Each symptom area is rated on five 5-point severity scales (time occupied by obsessions and compulsions, avoidance behavior, distress, functional interference, and difficulty disregarding the obsessions or refraining from the compulsions). Psychometric properties are strong for the total score and subscales in clinical and nonclinical samples, including good internal consistency, convergent validity, and discriminant validity. However, test–retest reliability has not yet been established in a clinical sample. The DOCS and its subscales differentiates patients with OCD from anxious and nonanxious control groups, and is sensitive to changes in symptom severity after a course of cognitive-behavioral therapy. The DOCS is printed as an appendix in the Abramowitz et al. publication.

Symptom-Specific Scales for Hoarding

Scales assessing multiple symptom domains of OCD often fail to adequately assess specific symptoms for clinical purposes. Some measures of specific OCD symptoms have been developed; one example is hoarding, which is poorly assessed by multiple symptom self-report rating scales (see also Chapter 4 in this volume). Hoarding severity can be measured by the Saving Inventory-Revised (Frost, Steketee, & Grisham, 2004), a self-report instrument with 23 items each rated on a 5-point scale. The Saving Inventory-Revised includes three subscales: difficulty discarding, compulsive acquisition, and clutter. Both the total score and subscales evidence strong internal consistency, test–retest reliability, known-groups validity, and strong correlations with other measures of hoarding (Frost et al., 2004). The Saving Inventory-Revised is included as an appendix in the Frost et al. publication.

A particularly innovative tool for assessing hoarding symptoms is a visual analog scale called the Clutter Image Rating (CIR; Frost, Steketee, Tolin, & Renaud, 2008). The CIR contains sets of nine color photographs of increasing severity of clutter for each of 3 rooms: living room, kitchen, and bedroom. Clients are asked to select the picture that is the closest to the level of clutter in their own home for the corresponding room. Scores for each room range from 1 to 9, and a composite score is calculated by averaging across the 3 room ratings. The CIR demonstrates good internal consistency, as well as strong convergent and discriminant validity in a sample of hoarders, including strong correlations between client ratings and objective observer CIR ratings (Frost et al., 2008). This tool can be particularly useful for clients who have difficulty articulating the severity of their hoarding symptoms, in part due to differences in how they interpret the word "clutter" (Frost et al., 2008). The CIR is available in conjunction with Steketee and Frost (2007).

Avoidance

Regardless of the client's specific symptom profile, avoidance is a critical area to assess, as it often has a direct impact on functional impairment. Avoidance comes in many varieties, from obvious overt avoidance to more subtle or covert avoidance. More active forms include avoidance of particular people, places, activities, or situations, such as not using public transit due to a fear of contamination, or avoiding young children due to fears that one is dangerous. More passive forms of avoidance include not seeking opportunities for socializing, schooling, or work advancement due to concerns surrounding OCD symptoms. Cognitive avoidance strategies are also common; these include efforts to avoid, suppress, or distract oneself from obsessive thoughts. Clinicians should be on the watch for subtle forms of avoidance during the assessment and subsequent therapy sessions. Some clients may report little distress because they are successfully avoiding OCD triggers, but their lives are very limited as a result of this avoidance. In severe cases, avoidance is so pervasive that individuals become confined to smaller and smaller areas, eventually not being able to leave a portion of their home that they consider safe. Avoidance can also play an important functional role in the symptoms, as clients feel convinced that catastrophe has been averted by avoidance, thereby increasing the probability that the client will avoid again when faced with a similar situation in the future.

Family Accommodation and Functional Impairment

Rachel, a 40 year-old stay-at-home mother, reported constant obsessions regarding accidental harm. Each time she left her home, she worried that she had not locked the doors or closed the windows properly, and she engaged in lengthy checking rituals. While driving, she feared that she may have run over a pedestrian or a cyclist, and would often feel compelled to loop around the block to check for potential victims. In the evening while cooking dinner, Rachel feared she would leave the stove on and cause a fire, causing grave damage to her young children. As Rachel's obsessions intensified and her rituals became more time consuming, mentally exhausting, and embarrassing, she began to avoid all triggering situations. She asked her husband to do a thorough check of the window and door locks before he left for work, and again before bed. She avoided leaving the house during the day, preferring to walk to get groceries rather than risk harming someone while driving. She refused to use the stove; her husband took over the cooking duties, and she would only reheat meals in the microwave when necessary. She became more and more confined in her daily activities and social life. Rachel's relationship with her husband and other social supports became strained.

As Rachel's case illustrates, family members can be keenly aware of the client's overt compulsions and avoidance, often playing an active role in the client's OCD symptoms in an effort to support or soothe the individual. This is especially common among parents of children with OCD, as it is painful to watch a child suffer from the severe anxiety associated with OCD. Family members can be a useful source of collateral information regarding the presence, frequency, and duration of problematic behaviors, especially those that a client is unaware of or is reluctant to discuss fully. In the case of children, parents will be an especially critical source of information, given that children may not find their rituals to be distressing or problematic, whereas parents may be significantly impacted by their child's rigidity.

To elicit information from family members, clinicians may want to use the Family Accommodation Scale for Obsessive-Compulsive Disorder (Calvocoressi et al., 1999), a reliable and valid clinician interview. This measure includes a detailed symptom checklist adapted from the Y-BOCS, followed by a 12-item scale assessing the frequency and severity of a variety of accommodating behaviors: reassurance, avoiding triggering the client, facilitating client avoidance, facilitating or participating in rituals, assisting the client with tasks or decisions, modifying responsibilities or family routine, assuming the client's responsibilities, watching the client complete rituals, waiting for the client, and tolerating aberrant behaviors or conditions in the home. Almost 90% of family members report some type of accommodation to their spouse or child's OCD symptoms (Calvocoressi et al., 1999), suggesting this is a valuable area to assess and address in treatment.

Functional impairment due to OCD can be assessed with the Work and Social Adjustment Scale (Marks, 1986, as cited in Mundt, Marks, Shear, & Greist, 2002). This is a 5-item measure rated on a 9-point scale, which can be completed as a self-report, or by interview in person or via telephone. Items include impairment in relation to work, home management, social leisure activities (done with others), private leisure activities (done alone), and ability to form and maintain close relationships with others. Psychometric properties are strong, including adequate test–retest reliability ($r = 0.73$) and good internal consistency (Mundt et al., 2002). The Work and Social Adjustment Scale correlates with severity on the Y-BOCS ($r = 0.45–.69$) and is sensitive to change across treatment (Mundt et al., 2002).

Readiness for Change

An important aspect of the assessment process is determining how ready the client is to make important life changes. Most clients with OCD will have some ambivalence about beginning a treatment that will bring them into contact with feared material— a natural reaction within the context of the client's fears. In addition to the resistance that fear engenders, some clients with OCD have developed an entire lifestyle around their symptoms. Making changes in their behavior can, in some cases, dramatically alter a client's self-concept, daily rhythms, and habitual ways of relating to family members. As a small example, some clients with more severe symptoms have been spending many hours each day on rituals, sometimes for years. What will the client do with all this free time? Will they need to return to work, or resume other responsibilities at home? Assessing the client's readiness for change is important for setting the pace and scope of the clinician's interventions. Preparing the client for the potential benefits and potential consequences of behavior change is important.

Pollard (2007) recommends exploration of several questions during the assessment phase:

• How well does the client understand OCD and the treatment model?
• How realistic are the client's expectations of the anticipated treatment process and likely outcomes?
• What is the client's level of motivation to change? For example, to what degree is the client conscious of and bothered by the functional interference that OCD is causing?
• What other treatment obstacles need to be addressed? For example, does the clinician observe possible secondary gain, or factors in the client's life context that may motivate resistance to behavioral change?

Assessing readiness should also include ascertaining whether the client can articulate goals (Pollard, 2007), including short-term treatment-oriented goals (e.g., beginning to cook using the stove at home), as well as longer-term life goals (e.g., resuming normal social functioning). Denial or dismissal of the severity of symptoms may be a strong sign that the client is not ready for OCD-specific treatment, and instead needs some preliminary motivational work. Clients with hoarding compulsions may be especially in need of motivational enhancement, as they terminate treatment prematurely more often than those with other types of OCD (Mataix-Cols, Marks, Greist, Kobak, & Baer, 2002 as cited in Pollard, 2007). Furthermore, behaviors such as missing appointments or failure to return assessment questionnaires may indicate a lack of readiness to engage in treatment. This may be especially evident when a client has entered treatment due to external pressures, such as frustration of a family member.

In addition to collecting information on motivation via interview, clinicians and researchers can assess ambivalence with the University of Rhode Island Change Assessment Questionnaire (McConnaughy, DiClemente, Prochaska, & Velicer, 1989; McConnaughy, Prochaska, & Velicer, 1983). This 32-item measure has four subscales (precontemplation, contemplation, action, and maintenance) in addition to an overall readiness for change index. While internal reliability of the subscales has generally been good (McConnaughy et al., 1989; McConnaughy et al., 1983; Pinto, Pinto, Neziroglu, & Yaryura-Tobias, 2007), predictive validity of the scale for treatment outcome of OCD has been mixed (Carter-Sand, 2004; Pinto et al., 2007). Scale items are included as an appendix in McConnaughty et al.'s 1989 publication.

Behavioral Assessment
Self-Monitoring
Self-monitoring often provides a helpful bridge between formal in-session assessment and therapy. Using a diary or column format, clients are asked to monitor their symptoms daily, typically over the course of one or two weeks. Information gathered can include triggers, frequency or duration of specific obsessions and compulsions, as well as avoidance behavior. Monitoring helps the client to become more aware of symptoms as they occur, and to see the links between triggers, obsessions, and resulting behaviors. Monitoring is also one of the best ways to identify internal triggers such as physiological symptoms or worries. These diaries provide the clinician with a snapshot of a client's day, and the level of interference with normal functioning. Monitoring forms also help focus the start of the subsequent therapy session, letting the clinician and client review the most critical events that occurred during the week.

While there is no limit to what one can monitor, it is best to keep these forms brief and manageable, to make adherence more likely. It may be necessary to limit the self-monitoring if it becomes obsessional in quality—sometimes a risk for more perfectionistic clients. Depending on the frequency of symptoms, recording for a designated portion of the day or simply providing estimated ratings each evening will suffice. Table 13.1 shows a sample self-monitoring form used by Dale, the Iraq war veteran described earlier. This form was used early in the assessment process to help Dale observe how much time he spent in various cleaning rituals, and to notice triggers.

Table 13.1   Example Self-Monitoring Form for Dale's Cleaning Compulsions

Date/Time	Trigger	Anxiety (0–100)	Obsessions	Compulsions
10/14 10:15 am	Wife arrives home from errands	40	Her clothes are dirty–she'll bring germs into the house.	Asked wife to remove clothes and do laundry. Wiped door handle 5 times.
10/14 3:30 pm	Driving family car	70	The steering wheel is making my hands feel sticky and grimy.	Used hand sanitizer 3 times. Washed with hot water and soap at home.
10/14 6:00 pm	Watched TV–news of Iraq	95	Traumatic memories of touching a bloody soldier.	Showered for 2 hours. Used full bottle of liquid soap scrubbing hands and body.

Direct Observation

Clinicians can learn a great deal about their client's OCD symptoms by carefully observing them during an interview, home visit, "field trip," or therapy session. Some clients may be reluctant to shake hands, open a door to the office, or touch furniture in the office with their bare hands; these behaviors will be evident as the client avoids activities that would be routine for most office visitors. Other clients may appear distracted and, upon questioning, will describe mental rituals such as counting that have preoccupied them during the conversation.

In addition to noting compulsions that occur spontaneously, it is also useful to create conditions in or near the clinic that trigger a client's most troubling symptoms, so that the client can be assessed in vivo. Although a home visit or "field trip" to a challenging location requires a bigger investment of time, in vivo observations can be invaluable. If it is not practical for the therapist to do this personally, an assistant such as a student can be trained to conduct behavioral assessments and report in detail to the treating clinician. In addition, most OCD symptoms can be observed in and around the clinic with a little creativity or advance planning (e.g., requesting that the client bring relevant objects from home to the clinic).

By using behavioral assessment, the therapist will learn critical information regarding subtle and more overt avoidance behaviors, as well as the quality and intensity of the client's emotional response. In vivo assessments also allow the clinician to assess "hot cognitions" regarding feared consequences of resisting the urge to perform compulsions. This type of assessment can help determine an appropriate starting point for exposure therapy and homework assignments, and can permit the clinician to gauge the client's degree of courage and motivation in the face of anxiety. For example, some clients may try to "bargain" with the therapist during a behavioral assessment (e.g., I'll touch the doorknob, but only if I can then wash for as long as I want), providing a preview of things the therapist will need to consider when planning exposure therapy sessions.

Creating a behavioral assessment involves some creativity, as it should be tailored to the client's idiosyncratic presenting symptoms. The main idea is to set up a relatively standard situation, preferably one that involves behavior that would be part of the client's normal functioning. Part of Anne's behavioral assessment involved going to her car together with the therapist, turning on the car, and using the headlights, radio, and windshield wipers. Then the therapist observed Anne leave the car to return to the office. Anne described the rituals she felt compelled to engage in as she left the car, and the therapist made notes about these rituals, as well as Anne's degree of anxiety and feared consequences about not engaging in the rituals. The therapist also conducted a home visit to observe specific eliciting stimuli in Anne's home.

Within research settings, behavioral assessments of this kind are often referred to as *behavioral avoidance tests* (BATs). During BATs, the clinician or researcher asks for verbal reports of anxiety on a 0–100 or 0–10 scale at critical points in the process. This procedure differs from exposure therapy in that the clinician is observing and learning about the client's symptoms at a given point in time, rather than encouraging the client to go further than she or he feels is acceptable. Outcomes of interest include the degree of approach (e.g., proportion of the task that can be completed without ritualizing), distress level, and degree of correspondence between anticipated distress (when discussing the task in advance) and actual distress once in the situation. Accordingly, as much as possible, the therapist (or assistant) should try to reduce the level of demand characteristics communicated by the instructions, in order to enhance the degree to which the BAT represents how the client would be able to function in a more natural situation. For example, the test should be set up so that responsibility remains with the client (e.g., for correctly checking that a light is off). Prior to the BAT, the therapist should instruct the client to do as much as they feel they can do (e.g., use the opportunity to "test" themselves) but the therapist should not push the client during the actual test.

Designing BATs for clients with contamination fears is relatively straightforward. For instance, Foa's group (Foa, 1984; Foa, Steketee, & Milby, 1980) asked clients to gradually approach their most feared contaminant in discrete steps, the most challenging of which was touching the object with bare hands. Other researchers have used standardized stimuli for all participants, such as a trash can holding a mixture of potting soil, animal hair, raw meat, and food scraps (Jones & Menzies, 1997), or exposure to a used comb, a cookie that had been on the floor, and a bedpan filled with toilet water (Deacon & Olatunji, 2007). However, restricting BATs to exposures that can be completed in the laboratory or clinic may not accurately reflect a client's level of avoidance or distress in natural settings. For clinical purposes, it is probably most informative to construct an idiosyncratic assessment that involves the client's specific feared situations in the real world.

Given the huge heterogeneity of presenting symptoms across clients with OCD, as well as the variety of symptoms any one client may present with, multiple tasks may be necessary to gain sufficient understanding of avoidance behaviors. This approach has been used by several researchers, in which clients are asked to engage in several tasks involving exposure to feared situations without ritualizing (Rachman, Hodgson, & Marks, 1971; Woody, Steketee, & Chambless, 1995a, 1995b). For example, one client with fears of contamination and HIV was asked to sort through household mail (fully touching each envelope) and then touch her own clothes, hair, and face without washing. Another BAT task for this client (a medical professional who was unable to work due to OCD) involved a walk to the nearby hospital with the therapist, and using doors, elevator buttons, and house phones in the hospital without rituals. Finally, this client, with the assistance of her spouse, brought a bag of their household garbage to the clinic. Steps in the BAT involved touching the outside of the bag and gradually immersing her hand in the garbage as though searching for an item she needed to retrieve.

BATs of this kind can be used for initial evaluation of symptoms, and to gather important information the client is unable to report. They can also be repeated over time, as a highly clinically relevant assessment of progress. If used for ongoing monitoring of progress, BATs can be scored most simply as either completed or avoided (Rachman, Cobb, Grey, McDonald, & Mawson, 1979), or with more fine-grained scoring systems that take into account partial avoidance and ritualizing (Barrett, Healy, & March, 2003; Steketee, Chambless, Tran, & Worden, 1996; Woody et al., 1995a). Several BAT indices for OCD have demonstrated convergent and divergent validity, as well as sensitivity to change over the course of treatment for a variety of OCD concerns (Steketee et al., 1996). However, not all OCD symptoms are conducive to BAT assessments. For instance, in the Rachman et al. study (1971), BATs could not be constructed for 2 of the 10 participants. This is often true for clients with no overt rituals or avoidance behavior, although even Joe (described earlier) was able to engage in a BAT that involved tasks of writing the word "gay" on a piece of paper, looking at magazine ads and commenting aloud on attractive features of men in the ads (e.g.,

nice hair, good-looking clothing, great teeth), and reading men-seeking-men personal ads in a local newspaper. When Joe began treatment, he was unable to complete any of these activities, and he experienced extreme anxiety just discussing the tasks.

Assessment of Beliefs and Appraisals

Understanding the core fears and appraisals motivating compulsions is a critical aspect of assessment that influences the case conceptualization. A given compulsion can develop from multiple sources. For instance, excessive handwashing can arise from fear of disease, an inflated sense of responsibility for transferring germs to others, an intolerance of feeling soiled, a need to wash until feeling "just right," or a sense of contempt, disgust, or moral offense. Therefore, it is critical to understand the motivations behind these symptoms, especially if cognitive interventions will be used as the primary basis of treatment.

In the following sections of the chapter, we will describe self-report scales of cognition relevant to OCD, clinical interviewing strategies used to discover and understand beliefs and appraisals that serve to maintain anxiety in OCD, and thought records that can be useful for between-session homework. Several facets of cognition feature in cognitive theories of OCD, and are relevant to case conceptualization and treatment planning.

1) *How does the client appraise tangible stimuli that provoke anxiety?* Magali, a woman with contamination obsessions and washing compulsions, believed germs could jump, crawl, or otherwise move, so they could be transferred without physical contact. This belief was accompanied by visual imagery of germs traveling from a hospital to contaminate sidewalks or other remote objects.

2) *How does the client appraise the occurrence of intrusive thoughts?* Appraisals of thoughts (or thoughts about thoughts) are sometimes referred to as metacognition. Joe, who was described earlier in this chapter, appraised the occurrence of unwanted sexual ideation as being revelatory about his character and his sexuality. He judged the occurrence of the thoughts as indications that, deep down, he wanted the thoughts to come true. Finally, he appraised his lack of control over the thoughts (e.g., they kept occurring despite his efforts not to have them) as an indication that he was personally out of control and could not be trusted.

3) What beliefs does the client have about the value of compulsions? Anne, who was described at the outset of this chapter, believed that if she simply persisted in checking an appliance, she would eventually feel certain that it was switched off and, accordingly, she would feel relaxed. On the flip side, she believed she must feel completely certain in order to rely on a memory of having done something (e.g., stove was turned off). When anxious, she fully accepted her magical thoughts about catastrophes that would occur if she neglected to perform compulsions correctly, although when calm, she acknowledged the absurdity of these thoughts.

Cognitive strategies for treating OCD have been developed and tested in the past 10 years. These interventions rely on cognitive theories of OCD, which suggest that several cognitive constructs contribute to the development and maintenance of obsessions and compulsions. (See Chapters 12 and 18 in this volume for discussion of these theories and treatment approaches.) A large international group of OCD researchers, the Obsessive Compulsive Cognitions Working Group (OCCWG), has worked to identify beliefs and appraisals important to OCD. Their research has demonstrated the relevance of beliefs about the personal significance (importance) of thoughts, inflated perceptions of responsibility, overestimation of threat, thought–action fusion, intolerance of uncertainty, and the importance of maintaining perfect thought control, among others.

Self-Report Scales

The scales described below can be administered repeatedly for a low-cost standardized assessment of beliefs and appraisals relevant to OCD. The scales can also be used as a starting point for discussion if the clinician wishes to follow up on items or subscales that the client endorses particularly strongly. Assessing beliefs and appraisals of thoughts is an important element of preparing to develop a treatment plan, as beliefs and appraisals show the same heterogeneity as other OCD symptoms. In fact, not all clients with OCD endorse maladaptive levels of cognitions in comparison to normal and anxious control groups (Calamari et al., 2006).

The Obsessive Compulsive Cognitions Working Group developed two measures to assist in the systematic assessment of beliefs and appraisals relevant to OCD. The initial versions of these scales were rationally derived (OCCWG; 2003). Subsequent investigation of the psychometric properties of these scales resulted in empirically based scales that have stable factor structures, strong internal consistency, good criterion (i.e., known-groups) validity, and good convergent validity (OCCWG; 2005). Discriminant validity, however, is weaker.

The revised 44-item version of the Obsessional Beliefs Questionnaire (OBQ-44; OCCWG, 2005) has three empirically derived subscales. The 16-item Responsibility/Threat Estimation subscale assesses ideation about preventing harm to oneself or others and responsibility for the occurrence of negative events, including through inaction. Examples of high-loading items include, "For me, not preventing harm is as bad as causing harm" and "Harmful events will happen unless I am very careful." The Perfectionism/Certainty subscale (also 16 items) reflects perfectionism, rigidity, concern over mistakes, and intolerance of uncertainty with items such as, "For me, things are not right if they are not perfect" and "I must be certain of my decisions." Finally, the Importance/Control of Thoughts subscale has 12 items assessing the consequences of having unwanted intrusive thoughts and the need to eliminate such thoughts. High-loading items reflect thought–action fusion and personal significance of unwanted thoughts with content such as, "Having a bad thought is morally no different than doing a bad deed," "Having bad thoughts means I am weird or abnormal," and "Having intrusive thoughts means I am out of control." All items are rated on a 7-point Likert scale. The scale is in the public domain and is available as an appendix to the OCCWG (2005) article.

Unlike the OBQ-44, the Interpretation of Intrusions (III) scale first provides a definition of unwanted intrusive thoughts, and then provides space for respondents to write down two intrusions they have recently experienced. The items of the III are appraisals of these idiographic intrusive thoughts, rated on strength of belief from zero ("I did not believe this idea at all") to 100 ("I was completely convinced this idea was true"). The III was originally designed to have three subscales: Control of Thoughts, Importance of Thoughts, and Responsibility (OCCWG; 2003), but subsequent investigation has shown the scale to have a unifactorial structure (OCCWG; 2005), so a single total score of the 31 items (divided by 10 to facilitate interpretation) is recommended. Items include, "Having this unwanted thought means I will act on it," "Because I've had this thought, I must want it to happen," and "I would be irresponsible if I ignored this intrusive thought." The III is published as an appendix in Frost and Steketee (2002).

There are other scales that could be (and have been) used to assess cognitive constructs relevant to OCD (see OCCWG, 1997 for a summary of these measures); the OBQ-44 and III are presented in detail here because they have been extensively tested by an international group of researchers, and include most of the pertinent content covered by other scales.

Clinical Interviewing

Because of the heterogeneity of OCD, clinical interviewing remains a very important tool for assessing relevant cognition. One good place to begin is to follow up on any items from the self-report scales that a client endorses strongly. Even when conducting the Symptom Checklist portion of the Y-BOCS (described earlier), the clinician can start to establish a sense of the client's feared consequences of coming into contact with stimuli without performing rituals. Similarly, if the clinician is using direct observation to assess obsessions and compulsions, the emotional intensity of this procedure can often allow better access to cognitions that are tightly connected to emotional responses. Another important clue is *stimulus generalization*, a term that describes fear that has generalized from an original anxiety-evoking stimulus (e.g., blood—could carry HIV) to other stimuli (e.g., anything red—could hide blood). Asking what makes the generalized stimulus frightening reveals how the client is thinking about the stimulus.

Note that sometimes the rationale for compulsions will not be logically connected to the stimulus. It is easy to understand washing as a compulsion to remove perceived dirtiness or germs, but sometimes the compulsion serves as an effort to achieve a sense of completeness (e.g., ordering, arranging, checking), or to alleviate a feeling of "not just right." The downward arrow technique is often useful in understanding feared consequences, appraisals, or beliefs that maintain anxiety. The following exchange between Anne and her psychologist illustrates this technique.

Dr. M: You said you get stuck for hours checking certain things in your apartment, such as the stove, fireplace, or clothes dryer. What about those things makes you the most anxious?

Anne: I am afraid they might start a fire.

Dr. M: What about a fire would be the most upsetting to you?

Anne: Someone could get hurt, or the fire could spread to one of my neighbors' houses. If it happened at the right time of year, when it is hot and dry, then the forest near my house might even go up, and all the animals that live there would be hurt or scared or homeless.

Dr. M: That doesn't sound good. This might seem obvious to you, but what part of that would be the worst part for you?

Anne: That it would be my fault. I would be responsible for someone else being inconvenienced or hurt, and I could have prevented it if I were more careful.

Dr. M: What would that mean about you, if you were responsible for something like that?

Anne: It would mean I was thoughtless, insensitive—just an awful person. I don't think I could live with myself if I didn't take care to prevent something like that.

The questioning continues until the client is unable to generate any other responses, refuses to continue, or has repeated the same general content several times. After listing all the feared consequences, it can be useful to have clients rate (perhaps on a 0–100 scale) how bad each consequence would be, how likely each consequence seems to be, and how much influence (control, responsibility) the client feels over the outcome.

A useful tool that provides some structure for assessing the degree to which a client's beliefs are rigid, strongly held, or emotionally overvalued is the Overvalued Ideation Scale (Neziroglu, McKay, Yaryura-Tobias, Stevens, & Todaro, 1999). Although overvalued ideation does not necessarily correlate with overall symptom severity, it appears to predict treatment outcome for both intensive behavior therapy (Neziroglu, Stevens, McKay, & Yaryura-Tobias, 2001) and pharmacotherapy (Neziroglu, Pinto, Yaryura-Tobias, & McKay, 2004). Questions on the Overvalued Ideation Scale include:

• How strongly do you believe that _____ is true? Can your belief be "shaken" if it is challenged by you or someone else?

• How reasonable is your belief? Is the belief logical, justified, rational?

• How accurate or correct is your belief?

• How likely is it that others (in the general population) have the same belief? To what extent do others share your belief?

• To what extent are other people as knowledgeable as you are (have as much information as you do) about the belief?

• How effective are your compulsions in preventing negative outcomes other than anxiety? Do they stop the feared outcome?

Thought Records

Some clients will be able to report their feared consequences, appraisals, and beliefs with relatively little effort. Many, however, have never considered these questions, or are less psychologically minded. In this case, self-monitoring of thoughts can be a useful assessment tool. Thought records are idiographic forms created by the therapist to help answer an assessment question. (Note that thought records are also useful as an element of treatment; see Chapter 18 for discussion.) David, for example, had experienced contamination concerns for several decades, which he "successfully" managed with extensive avoidance strategies. He sought treatment when he began to coach soccer for youngsters ages 5–7. He suddenly became unable to avoid contaminants, as the children often asked for help tying their shoes or adjusting their clothing after using the toilet. The children were also young enough to seek spontaneous hugs from David when they were happy or excited. Because he had avoided triggers for so long, he was unable to spontaneously report what he feared would happen if he did not avoid or engage in washing rituals. He simply knew he did not want to be exposed to possible contamination from the children. His therapist provided him with a thought record with columns to record anxiety-evoking situations, his anxiety rating for each situation, and what he predicted would be the outcome if he did not avoid or ritualize in each situation.

Conclusions

This chapter has outlined numerous tools and methods to assess symptom domains of OCD, including clinician interviews, self-reports, and behavioral observations. As with all assessments, the desire for comprehensive, multi-method approaches must be balanced with time and financial constraints. As such, the selection of assessment tools and the scope of assessment should be driven by the clinical and/or research goals. In most clinical and treatment-outcome research contexts, utilizing the Y-BOCS and the Y-BOCS Symptom Checklist is recommended for optimal assessment of symptom profile and severity ratings. In contexts in which reliable differential diagnosis is essential, we recommend using a structured diagnostic interview such as the ADIS-IV or SCID-I.

For treatment with medication, it may be sufficient to determine an appropriate diagnosis, obtain a general understanding of the presenting obsessions and compulsions, and quantify the severity of the patient's symptoms, in a way that can be repeated to assess changes over time. For cognitive or behavioral treatment strategies, however, much more detailed information is required to be able to construct a case formulation that will drive the details of the intervention. In particular, understanding feared consequences, connections between obsessions and compulsions, and beliefs and avoidance behavior that maintain OCD are important areas to assess. A client who indicates during assessment an unwillingness to directly confront feared stimuli, or who has very low tolerance for anxiety, may be better served initially by cognitive approaches. In this case, the clinician would need to commit greater time to assess the client's core beliefs and appraisals regarding the meaning of their intrusive thoughts, by use of structured questionnaires, the downward arrow interview technique, and thought records. On the other hand, a client with very concrete thinking or language limitations may do better with an exposure-based intervention that is less reliant on language. Here, further assessment time can be devoted to developing a hierarchy of feared situations that can be used to guide treatment, and behavioral assessments may be especially valuable to indicate a starting point for therapeutic exposures.

Evidence-based practice relies on accurate initial diagnosis, ongoing assessment of progress, and, ultimately, measurement of treatment outcome. While this chapter was not intended to provide an exhaustive list of OCD measures, the instruments described represent psychometrically sound tools that can capture a variety of features of OCD in a reliable and valid manner.

Future Directions

1. Can cognition be accurately measured at different levels of specificity (appraisals versus beliefs)?

2. To what degree would it be useful to assess information processing deficits in clinical practice?

3. Should we expect measures of OCD to be independent of depression?

4. Are different subtypes or primary symptom profiles of OCD differentially responsive to various forms of treatment?

5. What assessment data reliably indicate a better prognosis?

Related Chapters

Chapter 2. Phenomenology and Epidemiology of Obsessive Compulsive Disorder

References

Abramowitz, J. S., Deacon, B.J., Olatunji, B.O., Wheaton, M.G., Berman, N.C., Losardo, D. et al. (2010). Assessment of obsessive-compulsive symptom dimensions: Development and evaluation of the Dimensional Obsessive-Compulsive Scale. *Psychological Assessment. 22*, 180–198.

Antony, M. M., Orsillo, S. M., & Roemer, L. (2001). *Practitioner's guide to empirically based measures of anxiety.* Dordrecht, Netherlands: Kluwer Academic Publishers.

Baer, L., Brown-Beasley, M. W., Sorce, J., & Henriques, A. I. (1993). Computer-assisted telephone administration of a structured interview for obsessive compulsive disorder. *American Journal of Psychiatry, 150*, 1737–1738.

Barrett, P., Healy, L., & March, J. S. (2003). Behavioral avoidance test for childhood obsessive-compulsive disorder: A home-based observation. *American Journal of Psychotherapy, 57*, 80–100.

Brown, T. A., Di Nardo, P. A., & Barlow, D. H. (1994). *Anxiety Disorders Interview Schedule for DSM-IV (ADIS-IV).* San Antonio, Texas: Psychological Corporation/Graywind Publications Inc.

Burns, G. L., Keortge, S. G., Formea, G. M., & Sternberger, L. G. (1996). Revision of the Padua Inventory of obsessive compulsive disorder symptoms: Distinctions between worry, obsessions, and compulsions. *Behaviour Research and Therapy, 34*, 163–173.

Calamari, J. E., Cohen, R. J., Rector, N. A., Szacun-Shimizu, K., Riemann, B. C., & Norberg, M. M. (2006). Dysfunctional belief-based obsessive-compulsive disorder subgroups. *Behaviour Research & Therapy, 44*, 1347–1360.

Calvocoressi, L., Mazure, C. M., Kasl, S. V., Skolnick, J., Fisk, D., Vegso, S. J., et al. (1999). Family accommodation of obsessive-compulsive symptoms: Instrument development and assessment of family behavior. *Journal of Nervous and Mental Disease, 187*, 636–642.

Carter-Sand, S. A. (2004). *Examining the utility of the transtheoretical model with psychotherapy for anxiety disorders.*, ProQuest Information & Learning, US.

Deacon, B., & Olatunji, B. O. (2007). Specificity of disgust sensitivity in the prediction of behavioral avoidance in contamination fear. *Behaviour Research and Therapy, 45*, 2110–2120.

First, M. B., Spitzer, R. L., Gibbon, M., & Williams, J. B. W. (1994). *Structured Clinical Interview for DSM–IV Axis I Disorders, Clinician Version.* New York: Biometrics Research.

Foa, E. B. (1984). Deliberate exposure and blocking of obsessive-compulsive rituals: Immediate and long-term effects. *Behavior Therapy, 15*, 450–472.

Foa, E. B., Huppert, J. D., Leiberg, S., Langner, R., Kichic, R., Hajcak, G., et al. (2002). The Obsessive-Compulsive Inventory: Development and validation of a short version. *Psychological Assessment, 14*, 485–495.

Foa, E. B., Kozak, M. J., Salkovskis, P. M., Coles, M. E., & Amir, N. (1998). The validation of a new obsessive-compulsive disorder scale: The Obsessive-Compulsive Inventory. *Psychological Assessment, 10*, 206–214.

Foa, E. B., Steketee, G., & Milby, J. B. (1980). Differential effects of exposure and response prevention in obsessive-compulsive washers. *Journal of Consulting and Clinical Psychology, 48*, 71–79.

Frost, R. O., Steketee, G., & Grisham, J. (2004). Measurement of compulsive hoarding: Saving inventory-revised. *Behaviour Research and Therapy, 42*, 1163–1182.

Frost, R. O., Steketee, G., Tolin, D. F., & Renaud, S. (2008). Development and validation of the clutter image rating. *Journal of Psychopathology and Behavioral Assessment, 30*, 193–203.

Frost, R. O., & Steketee, G. S. (Eds.) (2002). *Cognitive approaches to obsessions and compulsions: Theory, assessment, and treatment.* Amsterdam, Netherlands: Pergamon/Elsevier Science Ltd.

Goodman, W. K., Price, L. H., Rasmussen, S. A., & Mazure, C. (1989a). The Yale-Brown Obsessive Compulsive Scale: I. Development, use, and reliability. *Archives of General Psychiatry, 46*, 1006–1011.

Goodman, W. K., Price, L. H., Rasmussen, S. A., & Mazure, C. (1989b). The Yale-Brown Obsessive Compulsive Scale: II. Validity. *Archives of General Psychiatry, 46*, 1012–1016.

Hodgson, R. J., & Rachman, S. (1977). Obsessional-compulsive complaints. *Behaviour Research & Therapy, 15*, 389–395.

Jones, M. K., & Menzies, R. G. (1997). The cognitive mediation of obsessive-compulsive handwashing. *Behaviour Research & Therapy, 35*, 843–850.

McConnaughy, E. A., DiClemente, C. C., Prochaska, J. O., & Velicer, W. F. (1989). Stages of change in psychotherapy: A follow-up report. *Psychotherapy: Theory, Research, Practice, Training, 26*, 494–503.

McConnaughy, E. A., Prochaska, J. O., & Velicer, W. F. (1983). Stages of change in psychotherapy: Measurement and sample profiles. *Psychotherapy: Theory, Research & Practice, 20*, 368–375.

Mundt, J. C., Marks, I. M., Shear, M. K., & Greist, J. M. (2002). The Work and Social Adjustment Scale: A simple measure of impairment in functioning. *British Journal of Psychiatry, 180*, 461–464.

Nathan, P. E., & Gorman, J. M. (2007). *A guide to treatments that work (3rd ed.).* New York: Oxford University Press.

Neziroglu, F., McKay, D., Yaryura-Tobias, J. A., Stevens, K. P., & Todaro, J. (1999). The overvalued ideas scale: Development, reliability and validity in obsessive-compulsive disorder. *Behaviour Research and Therapy, 37*, 881–902.

Neziroglu, F., Pinto, A., Yaryura-Tobias, J. A., & McKay, D. (2004). Overvalued ideation as a predictor of fluvoxamine response in patients with obsessive-compulsive disorder. *Psychiatry Research, 125*, 53–60.

Neziroglu, F., Stevens, K. P., McKay, D., & Yaryura-Tobias, J. A. (2001). Predictive validity of the Overvalued Ideals Scale: Outcome in obsessive-compulsive and body dysmorphic disorders. *Behaviour Research and Therapy, 39*, 745–756.

Obsessive Compulsive Cognitions Working Group (1997). Cognitive assessment of obsessive-compulsive disorder. *Behaviour Research & Therapy, 35*, 667–681.

Obsessive Compulsive Cognitions Working Group (2003). Psychometric validation of the Obsessive Beliefs

Questionnaire and the Interpretation of Intrusions Inventory: Part I. *Behaviour Research & Therapy, 41*, 863–878.

Obsessive Compulsive Cognitions Working Group (2005). Psychometric validation of the obsessive belief questionnaire and interpretation of intrusions inventory-Part 2, Factor analyses and testing of a brief version. *Behaviour Research & Therapy, 43*, 1527–1542.

Pinto, A., Pinto, A. M., Neziroglu, F., & Yaryura-Tobias, J. A. (2007). Motivation to change as a predictor of treatment response in obsessive compulsive disorder. *Annals of Clinical Psychiatry, 19*, 83–87.

Pollard, C. A. (2007). Treatment readiness, ambivalence, and resistance. In M. M. Antony, L. J. Summerfeldt, M. M. Antony & L. J. Summerfeldt (Eds.), *Psychological treatment of obsessive-compulsive disorder: Fundamentals and beyond.* (pp. 61–77). Washington, DC US: American Psychological Association.

Rachman, S., Cobb, J., Grey, S., McDonald, B., & Mawson, D. (1979). The behavioral treatment of obsessional-compulsive disorders, with and without clomipramine. *Behaviour Research and Therapy, 17*, 467–478.

Rachman, S., Hodgson, R., & Marks, I. M. (1971). The treatment of chronic obsessive-compulsive neurosis. *Behaviour Research and Therapy, 9*, 237–247.

Sanavio, E. (1988). Obsessions and compulsions: The Padua Inventory. *Behaviour Research and Therapy, 26*, 169–177.

Scahill, L., Riddle, M. A., McSwiggin-Hardin, M., & Ort, S. I. (1997). Children's Yale-Brown Obsessive Compulsive Scale: Reliability and validity. *Journal of the American Academy of Child & Adolescent Psychiatry, 36*, 844–852.

Sheehan, D. V., Lecrubier, Y., Sheehan, K. H., Amorim, P., Janavs, J., Weiller, E., et al. (1998). The Mini-International Neuropsychiatric Interview (M.I.N.I): The development and validation of a structured diagnostic psychiatric interview for DSM-IV and ICD-10. *Journal of Clinical Psychiatry, 59*, 22–33.

Steketee, G. S., Frost, R., & Bogart, K. (1996). The Yale-Brown Obsessive Compulsive Scale: interview versus self report. *Behaviour Research & Therapy, 34*, 675–684.

Steketee, G. S., & Frost, R. (2007). *Treatment of compulsive hoarding.* New York: Oxford University Press.

Steketee, G., Chambless, D. L., Tran, G. Q., & Worden, H. (1996). Behavioral Avoidance Test for obsessive compulsive disorder. *Behaviour Research and Therapy, 34*, 73–83.

Steketee, G., & Neziroglu, F. (2003). Assessment of obsessive-compulsive disorder and spectrum disorders. *Brief Treatment and Crisis Intervention, 3*, 169–185.

Taylor, S. (1995). Assessment of obsessions and compulsions: Reliability, validity, and sensitivity to treatment effects. *Clinical Psychology Review, 15*, 261–296.

Thordarson, D. S., Radomsky, A. S., Rachman, S., Shafran, R., Sawchuk, C. N., & Hakstian, A. R. (2004). The Vancouver Obsessional Compulsive Inventory (VOCI). *Behaviour Research & Therapy, 42*, 1289–1314.

van Oppen, P., Hoekstra, R. J., & Emmelkamp, P. M. G. (1995). The structure of obsessive-compulsive symptoms. *Behaviour Research and Therapy, 33*, 15–23.

Woody, S. R., Steketee, G., & Chambless, D. L. (1995a). Reliability and validity of the Yale-Brown Obsessive-Compulsive Scale. *Behaviour Research and Therapy, 33*, 597–605.

Woody, S. R., Steketee, G., & Chambless, D. L. (1995b). The usefulness of the obsessive compulsive scale of the Symptom Checklist-90—Revised. *Behaviour Research and Therapy, 33*, 607–611.

Appendix A

Yale-Brown Obsessive Compulsive Scale (Y-BOCS)

Y-BOCS TOTAL SCORE (add items 1–10) _____

	None	Mild	Moderate	Severe	Extreme
1. Time spent on obsessions	0	1	2	3	4
2. Interference from obsessions	0	1	2	3	4
3. Distress from obsessions	0	1	2	3	4
	Always Resists				Completely Yields
4. Resistance	0	1	2	3	4
	Complete Control	Much Control	Moderate Control	Little Control	No Control
5. Control over obsessions	0	1	2	3	4

Obsession subtotal (add items 1–5) _____

	None	Mild	Moderate	Severe	Extreme
6. Time spent on compulsions	0	1	2	3	4
7. Interference from compulsions	0	1	2	3	4
8. Distress from compulsions	0	1	2	3	4
	Always Resists				Completely Yields

	0	1	2	3	4
9. Resistance					
	Complete Control	Much Control	Moderate Control	Little Control	No Control
10. Control over compulsions	0	1	2	3	4

Compulsion subtotal (add items 1–5) _____

	Excellent				Absent
11. Insight into OC symptoms	0	1	2	3	4

	None	Mild	Moderate	Severe	Extreme
12. Avoidance	0	1	2	3	4
13. Indecisiveness	0	1	2	3	4
14. Pathological Responsibility	0	1	2	3	4
15. Slowness	0	1	2	3	4
16. Pathological Doubting	0	1	2	3	4

			None	Mild	Moderate	Severe	Extreme
17. Global Severity	0	1	2	3	4	5	6
18. Global Improvement	0	1	2	3	4	5	6

19. Reliability	Excellent = 0	Good = 1	Fair = 2	Poor = 3

From Goodman, Price, Rasmussen, Mazure, Fleischmann, et al. (1989). Copyright © 1989 American Medical Association. All rights reserved. Reprinted with permission.

Appendix B

Yale-Brown Obsessive Compulsive Scale (Y-BOCS)

Symptom Checklist

Check all that apply, but clearly mark the principal symptoms with a "P." (Rater must ascertain whether reported behaviors are bona fide symptoms of OCD, and not symptoms of another disorder such as simple phobia or hypochondriasis. Items marked as "*" may or may not be OCD phenomena.)

Current	Past	
		Aggressive obsessions
_____	_____	Fear might harm self
_____	_____	Fear might harm others
_____	_____	Violent or horrific images
_____	_____	Fear of blurting out obscenities or insults
_____	_____	Fear of doing something else embarrassing*
_____	_____	Fear will act on unwanted impulses (e.g., to stab friend)
_____	_____	Fear will steal things
_____	_____	Fear will harm others because not careful enough (e.g., hit/run accident)
_____	_____	Fear will be responsible for something else terrible happening (e.g., fire, burglary)
_____	_____	Other _____
		Contamination obsessions
_____	_____	Concerns or disgust with bodily waste or secretions (e.g., urine, feces, saliva)
_____	_____	Concerns with dirt or germs
_____	_____	Excessive concern with environmental contaminants (e.g., asbestos, radiation, toxic waste)
_____	_____	Excessive concern with household items (e.g., cleansers, solvents)
_____	_____	Excessive concern with animals (e.g., insects)
_____	_____	Bothered by sticky substances or residues
_____	_____	Concerned will get ill because of contaminant
_____	_____	Concerned will get others ill by spreading contaminant (aggressive)
_____	_____	No concern with consequences of contamination other than how it might feel
_____	_____	Other _____
		Sexual obsessions
_____	_____	Forbidden or perverse sexual thoughts, images, or impulses
_____	_____	Content involves children or incest
_____	_____	Content involves homosexuality*
_____	_____	Sexual behavior toward others (aggressive)*
_____	_____	Other _____

Hoarding/saving obsessions
[distinguish from hobbies and concern with objects of monetary or sentimental value]

_____ _____ _____

Religious obsessions (scrupulosity)

_____ _____ Concerned with sacrilege and blasphemy

_____ _____ Excess concern with right/wrong, morality

_____ _____ Other _____

Obsession with need for symmetry or exactness

_____ _____ Accompanied by magical thinking (e.g., concerned that mother will have accident unless things are in the right place)

_____ _____ Not accompanied by magical thinking

Miscellaneous obsessions

_____ _____ Need to know or remember

_____ _____ Fear of saying certain things

_____ _____ Fear of not saying just the right thing*

_____ _____ Fear of losing things

_____ _____ Intrusive (nonviolent) images

_____ _____ Intrusive nonsense sounds, words, or music*

_____ _____ Bothered by certain sounds/noises*

_____ _____ Lucky/unlucky numbers

_____ _____ Colors with special significance

_____ _____ Superstitious fears

_____ _____ Other _____

Somatic obsessions

_____ _____ Concern with illness or disease*

_____ _____ Excessive concern with body part or aspect of appearance (e.g., dysmorphophobia)*

_____ _____ Other _____

Cleaning/washing compulsions

_____ _____ Excessive or ritualized handwashing

_____ _____ Excessive or ritualized showering, bathing, toothbrushing, grooming, or toilet routine

_____ _____ Involves cleaning of household items or other inanimate objects

_____ _____ Other measures to prevent or remove contact with contaminants

_____ _____ Other _____

(Continued)

Current	Past	
		Checking compulsions
_____	_____	Checking locks, stove, appliances, etc.
_____	_____	Checking that did not/will not harm others
_____	_____	Checking that did not/will not harm self
_____	_____	Checking that nothing terrible did/will happen
_____	_____	Checking that did not make mistake
_____	_____	Checking tied to somatic obsessions
_____	_____	Other _____
		Repeating rituals
_____	_____	Rereading or rewriting
_____	_____	Need to repeat routine activities (e.g., in/out door, up/down from chair)
_____	_____	Other _____
		Counting compulsions
_____	_____	_____
		Ordering/arranging compulsions
_____	_____	_____
		Hoarding/collecting compulsions
		[distinguish from hobbies and concern with objects of monetary or sentimental value (e.g., carefully reads junk mail, piles up old newspapers, sorts through garbage, collects useless objects)]
		Miscellaneous compulsions
_____	_____	Mental rituals (other than checking/counting)
_____	_____	Excessive list-making
_____	_____	Need to tell, ask, or confess
_____	_____	Need to touch, tap, or rub*
_____	_____	Rituals involving blinking or staring*
_____	_____	Measures (not checking) to prevent harm to self, harm to others, or terrible consequences
_____	_____	Ritualized eating behaviors*
_____	_____	Superstitious behaviors
_____	_____	Trichotillomania*
_____	_____	Other self-damaging or self-mutilating behaviors*
_____	_____	Other _____

From Goodman, Price, Rasmussen, Mazure, Fleischmann, et al. (1989). Copyright © 1989 American Medical Association. All rights reserved. Printed with permission.

Assessing Comorbidity, Insight, Family and Functioning in OCD

Christine Purdon

Abstract

Obsessive compulsive disorder (OCD) is a complex and debilitating disorder that has a high degree of comorbidity and functional impairment, and significant impact on the family. The purpose of this chapter is to provide a brief overview of comorbidity, family, insight, and quality of life issues, and to review assessment and treatment implications of those issues. Measures for assessing relevant constructs are described.

Keywords: treatment refractory, quality of life, family functioning, comorbidity

Introduction

Obsessive compulsive disorder (OCD) is a complex and debilitating disorder that has a high degree of comorbidity and functional impairment, and significant impact on the family. The purpose of this chapter is to provide a brief overview of comorbidity, family, insight, and quality of life issues, and review assessment and treatment implications. Measures for assessing relevant constructs are described.

Assessment of Mood and Comorbid Conditions in OCD

Obsessive compulsive disorder (OCD) has a high rate of comorbidity with mood disorders and has features in common with several other disorders. The purpose of this section is to review comorbidity, provide recommendations for assessing comorbid conditions, and discuss the implications of comorbidity for diagnosis and treatment.

Mood Disorders

Depression is the most frequent comorbid condition in adults and children with OCD (e.g., Crino & Andrews, 1996; Rasmussen & Tsuang, 1986; Swedo, Rapaport, Leonard, & Cheslow, 1989;

Tükel, Polat, Özdemir, Aksüt, & Türksoy, 2002), with prevalence rates ranging from 30%–80% in clinical and general populations, as determined by DSM-III or III-R criteria. Later studies in which OCD has been diagnosed according to DSM-IV criteria have found relatively high rates of comorbidity as well. In their specialty clinic for treatment of anxiety disorders, Antony, Downie, and Swinson (1998) found that, of the 28% of patients with OCD who had an additional diagnosis, 24% had concurrent major depressive disorder. In a non-Western community sample of 444 individuals with OCD, the lifetime prevalence of major depressive disorder was 14% (the next highest prevalence for a comorbid condition being 10.8% for specific phobia; Mohammadi, Ghanizadeh, & Moini, 2007). Similarly, Denys et al. (2004) found that 27.1% of their large OCD sample had a comorbid mood disorder, with 20.7% presenting with major depressive disorder (single episode). Hong et al. (2004) found that 50% of their clinical sample had recurrent major depressive disorder. The comorbidity rate of OCD with depression is not necessarily different from the comorbidity between other anxiety disorders and depression (Crino & Andrews, 1996).

Angst et al. (2005) assert that OCD is actually most comorbid with "minor bipolar disorders" characterized by low levels of hypomanic symptoms, arguing that the association between depression and OCD found in previous studies is due to the presence of bipolar disorder, as opposed to major depressive disorder. They found that comorbidity with bipolar disorder was more common in men and was associated with greater alcohol abuse/dependence. In their sample, Tükel, Meteris, Koyuncu, Tecer, and Yazici (2006) found that 26 of 117 people with OCD had comorbid bipolar disorder. That group had more symmetry/exactness and ordering/arranging compulsions, a more episodic course of illness, and better insight. Perugi et al. (2002) identified 68 patients with comorbid major depressive episode, and 56% of those had lifetime comorbid bipolar disorder. This was associated with greater substance abuse, but, contrary to Tükel et al. (2006), ordering rituals were less common, as were sexual obsessions, compared to individuals without comorbid bipolar disorder.

The variance in rates of mood disorders likely has much to do with diverse sampling and assessment procedures. What is generally consistent across studies is that OCD has its highest or second-highest rate of comorbidity with depression. In terms of onset and clinical presentation, patients with comorbid depression have an earlier age of onset of OCD, greater symptom severity (Hong et al., 2004; Tükel, Meteris, Koyuncu, Tecer, & Yazici, 2006, but see Denys, Tenney, van Megen, de Geus, & Westenberg, 2004), and greater functional impairment (Abramowitz, Storch, Keeley, & Cordell, 2007). Not surprisingly, depression is one of the few factors identified as a predictor of poorer treatment outcome (Abramowitz & Foa, 2000; Abramowitz, Franklin, Street, Kozak, & Foa, 2000; Steketee, Chambless, & Tran, 2001–but see Steketee, Henninger, & Pollard, 2000). Research on the onset of comorbid OCD and depression suggests that OCD precedes major depressive disorder (e.g., Bellodi, Scioto, Diaferia, Ronchi, & Smiraldi, 1992; Demal, Lenz, Mayrhofer, Zapotoczky, & Zitterl, 1993), and that the depression is alleviated when OCD is successfully treated (Ricciardi & McNally, 1995). There is evidence that negative mood state increases the individual's fear that having the obsession will lead to harm for which the sufferer will be responsible, which in turn leads to greater perseveration of the compulsive ritual (Davey, Startup, Zara, MacDonald, & Field, 2003; MacDonald & Davey, 2005). Furthermore, Abramowitz et al. (2007) found that greater negative appraisal of obsessions was associated with more severe depression.

Taken together, these data suggest that symptoms of depression may complicate treatment of OCD in a number of ways. Depression is, of course, characterized by motivational deficits. It is reasonable to propose that these motivational deficits interfere with treatment engagement and compliance. There is also a considerable body of research suggesting that depression is associated with greater recall of negative memories and with greater accessibility of negative appraisal (e.g., Abramson et al., 2002). Thus, depression is likely to make negative appraisal of the obsession and of the consequences of not performing the compulsion more accessible. Also, as noted by Rachman (1993), the type of negative appraisal one sees in OCD often concerns the implications of the obsession for the person's self-worth, which ties directly into the appraisals and beliefs viewed as central to depression.

Clinicians treating OCD are well advised, then, to ensure that they assess depression both at the outset and periodically throughout treatment. A good diagnostic interview will establish whether there are depressive symptoms, either at the clinical or subclinical level. Determining whether the mood problem or the OCD is primary requires clinical judgment, as well as a good understanding of how the two clusters of symptoms affect the client's functioning. Assessment of depression severity is straightforward, as there are several well-validated self-report symptom measures, including the Beck Depression Inventory (Beck, Steer, & Brown, 1996) and the Depression Anxiety Stress Scale (Lovibond & Lovibond, 1995). The Hamilton Rating Scale for Depression is an interviewer-administered measure with good psychometric properties that is widely used in inpatient and outpatient settings (Schwab, Bialow, & Clemens, 1967).

What may be more important than assessing symptom severity, though, is assessing the types of depressogenic thoughts that interfere with treatment. The obvious include negative predictions about the success of treatment itself, and the success of treatment exercises, such as exposure with response prevention. Depression can also be associated with a self-punitive orientation, such that the person feels he/she does not deserve to get better, or at least feels ambivalent about treatment. Some OCD sufferers with comorbid depression view their symptoms as a form of atonement for past sins, a mental hair shirt, if you will. They may believe that they do not deserve to feel better, or that if they do not continue to atone they or their loved ones will be punished. Patients with superstitious fears (e.g., that something bad might happen if an action is not performed in a precise way) or with perfectionism often conduct their compulsions not only to ensure that nothing bad will happen and to reduce distress, but to protect themselves from self-recrimination later for having caused harm or failed to be perfect. These fears feed directly into the sense of self as a bad, immoral, or deeply flawed person, which is often at the heart of depression. Addressing depressogenic thoughts may be a necessary concomitant to helping individuals view the potential costs of treatment as being less than the potential benefits, and to developing the sense of self-efficacy required to endure exposure exercises.

Comorbid Anxiety Disorders

After major depressive disorder, OCD is most commonly comorbid with anxiety disorders. In their sample of patients with OCD, Tükel et al. (2002) found that comorbidity rates were 26% for specific phobia, 23% for social phobia, 18% for generalized anxiety disorder (GAD), and 14% for panic disorder. In their larger sample, Denys et al. (2004) found that 12.8% had a comorbid anxiety disorder, including social phobia (3.6%), panic disorder with agoraphobia (2.6%), and anxiety disorder not otherwise specified (1.4%). Angst et al. (2005) found that OCD was significantly associated with panic disorder, GAD, and social phobia. In their sample of OCD outpatients treated in a specialty clinic for anxiety disorders, Antony et al. (1998) found that 41.4% met criteria for social phobia, 20.7% specific phobia, 11.5% panic disorder, and 8% GAD. Abramowitz and Foa (1998) found that 20% of their large sample of people with OCD also met criteria for GAD. Again, although the actual rates vary considerably across studies, the trends are relatively consistent, with social phobia, GAD, and panic being the most frequent comorbid anxiety disorders.

Assessment of comorbid anxiety disorders is relatively straightforward. The Anxiety Disorders Interview Schedule for DSM-IV (ADIS; Brown, DiNardo, & Barlow, 1994) is a thorough and comprehensive means of assessing anxiety problems. It assesses more subtle manifestations of these disorders than the Structured Clinical Interview for DSM-IV (First, Spitzer, Gibbon, & Williams, 1995), but it is very lengthy. There are numerous self-report measures of anxiety (for a compendium of measures, see Antony, Orsillo, & Roemer, 2001).

Differential diagnosis between OCD and GAD can sometimes be difficult because people with GAD sometimes exhibit excessive reassurance seeking and checking behaviors (e.g., calling family members to ensure that they are okay) and obsessional preoccupations often take the form, as well as content, of worry (e.g., fears of contracting an illness). However, the checking and reassurance typical of GAD is less frequent and intense than in OCD, and is less ritualized (e.g., Brown et al., 1993).

With respect to differences between obsessions and worry, there are two key distinguishing factors. First, the excessive worry of people with OCD tends to reflect the theme of their primary obsessions as opposed to being generalized across content domains. Second, in OCD the focus of the concern can be odd or extreme and the concern is perceived as having a fairly low probability of occurrence (e.g., the thought of deliberately swerving into the next lane while driving, and killing someone) whereas worry is typically a generation of worst case scenarios that are perceived as being high in probability (e.g., worry that while driving on an unfamiliar narrow country lane, you might hit an animal or get lost, which would make you late for your dinner party, and people will be angry with you and not want to invite you back, etc.; e.g., Turner, Beidel, & Stanley, 1992).

By definition, obsessional thoughts are ego-dystonic, or stand in violation of the person's values and personality and/or sense of what is rational (American Psychiatric Association, 2000). This is certainly the case with repugnant obsessions of causing harm or danger to loved ones or of engaging in behavior contrary to religious principles. However, many kinds of obsessions can be ego-syntonic (Purdon, Cripps, Faull, Joseph, & Rowa, 2007; Rasmussen & Eisen, 1992; Tallis, 1996). A father who is concerned about transmitting contamination to his family may view his obsessions as consistent with his values and his compulsions as important protective actions, even if he acknowledges that the chance of harm is fairly low. The difference between these types of obsessions and worry is in the perceived probability of the event and in the frequency, intensity, and nature of the action taken to ameliorate the distress the concern causes. And, again, if there are multiple concerns crossing many content domains, the concern may be better conceptualized as excessive worry rather than as an obsession.

Comorbid anxiety disorders can complicate assessment. Standard assessment of OCD requires that the sufferer reveal the content of his or her obsessions. We know that this is already a difficult task for sufferers (Newth & Rachman, 2001) but the presence of a comorbid anxiety disorder may complicate disclosure further. For example, social phobia is characterized by the need to make a good impression on others and fears of failing to do so. Revealing the content of obsessions that have anti-social themes or describing compulsive rituals that are odd or excessive may be especially difficult for individuals with comorbid social phobia. Also, people with repugnant obsessions that involve harm to others, especially children, are often concerned that the therapist will be required to report them to the authorities. Such concerns may be more intense in people with comorbid GAD who are quick to generate catastrophic outcomes. It is important to be aware of the ways in which comorbidity may influence disclosure and provide assurances, as well as normalize the content of obsessions. There is substantial evidence that obsessional thoughts are a common phenomenon, with the differences between "normal" obsessions and those symptomatic of OCD being quantitative as opposed to qualitative (e.g., Rachman & de Silva, 1978; Freeston, Ladouceur, Thibodeau, & Gagnon, 1991; Purdon & Clark, 1993, 1994). Purdon and Clark (2005) provide a list of repugnant thoughts reported by people without OCD that can be helpful in normalizing them.

Does comorbidity with anxiety disorders result in greater difficulties engaging in treatment? Purdon, Gifford, Young, and Antony (2005) asked patients with OCD, social phobia, GAD, panic disorder (PD), and anxiety disorder not otherwise specified, to report any fears they had about starting treatment. Their qualitative responses fell into four broad themes: fears that treatment will make the problem worse; fears that treatment will fail (e.g., fears of being a hopeless case); fears that treatment will succeed (e.g., that subsequent expectations will surpass capabilities); and fears of the stigma of seeking treatment. Rowa, Gifford, McCabe, Antony, and Purdon (2011) developed a quantitative measure of treatment fears based on this data. The result was the 30-item Treatment Ambivalence Questionnaire (TAQ). This was administered to 372 outpatients of a specialty anxiety disorders treatment clinic during the process of diagnostic assessment and prior to starting treatment, including 69 individuals with a principal diagnosis of OCD. The items yielded three reliable subscales: (1) fears of the personal consequences of engaging in treatment (e.g., personality change); (2) fears of negative or adverse reactions to treatment (e.g., not getting better); and (3) concerns about the inconvenience of engaging in treatment (e.g., treatment will be time consuming).

There were no differences in TAQ subscale scores between individuals with OCD and those with other diagnoses. The same was true even in comparing those with no comorbidity to those with comorbidity, suggesting that the treatment concerns exhibited by individuals with OCD are neither unique nor related to comorbidity. However, correlations between the TAQ and the Interpretation of Intrusions Inventory (III; OCCWG, 2005)—which assesses overvalued responsibility, need to control thoughts, and importance of thoughts—revealed correlations between the TAQ adverse reactions subscale and the III control of thoughts scale. Thus, greater perceived need to control obsessions was associated with greater fears of having an adverse reaction to treatment. These findings suggest that cognitive therapy directed at appraisal is likely to benefit treatment engagement.

Comorbidity with other anxiety disorders may complicate engagement with treatment, particularly exposure, in other ways. Individuals with comorbid panic disorder are likely to find it difficult to engage in activities that put them at risk for a panic attack, such as doing exposure exercises. It might be necessary to conduct interoceptive exercises to reduce reactivity to physical sensations, in advance of OCD treatment or concomitant to it. Individuals with social anxiety may find it difficult to engage in exposure in front of the therapist, or in any other social setting. People with GAD may worry more about the impact of exposure on their daily functioning (e.g., "what if the obsession stays with me all day and I can't get my work done and I get in trouble") and may see less distinction between worries and obsessions than does the therapist, and thus refer to them interchangeably in session and during between-session exposure (Roth Ledley, Pai, & Franklin, 2007). Steketee et al. (2000) report that in one large study, comorbid GAD was related to more dropout, and poorer outcome at post-treatment follow-up. It is important to be aware of this potential, discuss difficulties with conducting exposure with the patient, and work together to establish feasible exercises. The therapist must establish a climate in which the patient is free to express and discuss treatment concerns and in which the patient is encouraged to treat negative predictions about treatment as hypotheses that can be tested.

Comorbid Axis II Personality Disorders

The relationship of OCD to obsessive compulsive personality disorder (OCPD) has always been of special theoretical and diagnostic interest. The psychoanalytic view was that OCPD was a precursor to OCD, but there is little empirical support for this notion (Black & Noyes, 1997). Diaferia et al. (1997) found that the OCPD criteria of hoarding, inability to delegate, and excessive devotion to work reliably distinguished individuals with OCD from those with a mood disorder or panic. In their large sample of people with OCD, Denys et al. (2004) found that 36% met criteria for a current comorbid personality disorder (PD), the most prevalent being OCPD (9%), followed by dependent PD (7.6%) and PD not otherwise specified (6.6%). Those with comorbid Axis II disorders did not differ from those without, on measures of severity, anxiety, and depression, although they did have lower global axis functioning scores.

Samuels et al. (2000) compared the rate of personality disorders in people with and without OCD, as well as the first-degree relatives of each of those groups. They found that 45% of those with OCD had some personality disorder (compared with 10% of the controls), with avoidant and OCPD being the most common. Furthermore, OCPD was twice as common among relatives of people with OCD than among relatives of people without OCD. Coles, Pinto, Mancebo, Rasmussen, and Eisen (2008) found that 27% of their large (N=238) sample of people with OCD met criteria for OCPD. These individuals exhibited some important differences from those without OCPD, including a younger age of onset of first OCD symptoms, more symptoms of hoarding, more symmetry concerns, and more cleaning, ordering, and repeating compulsions. Furthermore, they had higher rates of OCPD among their first-degree relatives. However, Frost, Steketee, Williams, and Warren (2000) found that their sample of people who had clinically significant hoarding behaviour were more likely to have dependent and schizotypal PD symptoms than did the people with OCD without hoarding symptoms. Wu, Clark, and Watson (2006) identified nearly half of their sample of people with OCD as having a comorbid PD but the most common cluster was avoidant-dependent-schizoid, as opposed to OCPD. Similarly, in their review of epidemiological studies, Steketee et al. (2000) conclude that OCD appears to be most comorbid with avoidant PD.

Summerfeldt, Huta, and Swinson (1998) observe that there is considerable symptom overlap between OCD and personality disorders. For example, reassurance seeking is a common symptom of both OCD and avoidant PD, and both OCD and schizotypal PD can be characterized by cognitive distortions and magical thinking. It is also important to note that OCPD is characterized by perfectionism, hoarding, and rigidity in routines. This introduces the possibility of methodological confounds. Summerfeldt et al. note that OCD has been distinguished from OCPD traits by the degree to which the symptoms are ego-dsytonic. However, as discussed previously, degree of ego-dystonicity may not be universally applicable to OCD symptoms.

With respect to assessing Axis II comorbidity, then, it is important to be sensitive to symptom overlap, and ensure that a specific symptom cluster is not better accounted for by one rather than the other, before making a diagnosis of comorbid PD. This is obviously more easily done in the context of an interview. A commonly used diagnostic interview for personality disorders is the Structured Clinical Interview for Axis II Personality Disorders (SCID-II; First, Gibbon, Spitzer, Williams, & Benjam, 1997), but it is lengthy. There are numerous self-report measures of personality disorders, two prominent ones being the Millon Clinical Multiaxial Inventory–3rd edition (MCMI-III; Millon, Millon, & Davis, 1997) and the Schedule for Nonadaptive and Adaptive Personality (SNAP; Clark, 2006). The latter has the advantage of including behavioral indices of the criteria so requires less insight on the part of the respondent into personality pathology.

What are other implications of Axis II comorbidity for treatment? Fals-Stewart and Lucente (1993) looked at Axis II characteristics and OCD symptoms pretreatment (exposure with response prevention), post-treatment, and at 6-month follow-up. They found that whereas 35% had no elevations, 28% had elevations on the OCPD and dependent PD scales, 21% had elevations on the borderline and histrionic scales, and 15% had elevations on the schizoid, avoidant, dependent, and schizotypal scales. This latter group had the highest treatment refusal rate and the poorest treatment response, which is consistent with Jenike, Baer, Minichiello, Schwartz, and Carey (1986). Otherwise, there were no group differences in treatment compliance or in symptom reduction post-treatment. However, at 6-month follow-up, those with elevations on the borderline and histrionic scales showed symptom increases from post-treatment. Conversely, Steketee et al. (2000) found that personality traits predicted poorer immediate outcome of OCD treatment, but not longer-term outcome. There is some evidence that treatment of an anxiety disorder results in improvement in the personality disorder symptoms (Brandes & Bienvenu, 2009), but that body of work did not include investigation of treatment of OCD on PDs. However, some studies found no impact of comorbid personality disorders on treatment outcome (e.g., Dreesen, Hoekstra, & Arntz, 1997; Steketee et al., 2001). The mixed results suggest that personality disorders may complicate OCD treatment, but not such that the PD needs to be addressed first.

Personality disorders are characterized, of course, by traits that are longstanding. Certain traits may interfere more with treatment than others. In general, the presence of a PD may make it more difficult to establish and maintain rapport, and for the patient to accept the therapist's recommendations on trust. AuBuchon and Malatesta (1994) found that OCD patients with comorbid PD more often dropped out and had more difficulty engaging with treatment. When the personality traits "cross" with the OCD symptoms, it may especially complicate treatment engagement and adherence. For example, people with hoarding symptoms and OCPD may find it very difficult to abandon the pursuit of perfection, and exhibit continued resistance to sorting and discarding items. People with dependent PD and obsessions of harming others may find it difficult to risk upsetting others by failing to perform the protective compulsive act. It is important to ensure that the therapeutic climate allows for open discussion of obstacles to executing the treatment plan, and when a PD is present the therapist may need to devote more time helping the client prepare for change.

Treatment is likely to be most effective if the therapist maximizes the patient's control, choice, and autonomy. Salkovskis sums up the goal of therapy thus: "the patient and therapist to work together to construct and test a new, less threatening explanation of the patient's experience, and then to explicitly examine the validity of the contrasting accounts" (Salkovskis, 1999, p. S36). That is, the therapist is not committed to a particular explanation of the obsessions and compulsions that the patient must be persuaded to adopt; rather, the therapist helps the patient explore contrasting views of the obsessions and compulsions, and facilitates the development of new insights about their meaning. It can be helpful to remind patients that they may always choose their OCD again in the future if they do not like the changes that treatment brings.

Obsessive Compulsive (OC) Spectrum Symptoms

A disorder is considered part of the OC spectrum if the primary symptoms are obsessions, an inability to inhibit repetitive behaviors, and a subjective sense of compulsion to perform them (Angst et al., 2004; Richter, Summerfeldt, Antony, & Swinson, 2003; Steketee & Neziroglu, 2003). OC spectrum disorders are typically said to include body dysmorphic disorder (BDD), hypochondriasis (HC), trichotillomania (TM), skin-picking, and Tourette syndrome (TS). However, it has been argued that other "impulsive" disorders should be counted as OC spectrum disorders as well, such as dissociative disorders, compulsive buying, kleptomania, intermittent explosive disorder, pathological gambling, pyromania, sexual compulsions, and compulsive self-injury which would include skin-picking (du Toit, Kradenburg, Hiehaus, & Stein, 2001; Lochner et al., 2005). OC spectrum disorders are said to be part of the OCD "family" due to similarities in symptomatology, and selective response to specific medications (Richter et al., 2003).

The comorbidity rates obviously vary according to how broadly or narrowly "OC spectrum" is defined. In their study, which had more inclusive criteria for OC spectrum, duToit et al. (2001) found that OCD had its highest overlap with compulsive self-injury, buying, and intermittent explosive disorder. However, other studies have found the highest comorbidity rate with tic disorders, with 28%–63% of those with primary TS meeting criteria for OCD, and 17% of people with OCD meeting criteria for TS (see Radomsky et al., 2007 for a review). Angst et al. (2004) found that OCD and OC spectrum disorders had substantial comorbidity with eating disorders. OCD also has a significant overlap with BDD, with estimates that 34% of BDD sufferers also have OCD, and 8%-37% of those with OCD have BDD (e.g., Philips, 2000). Radomsky et al. (2007) observe a number of areas of criterion overlap between OCD and OC spectrum disorders, particularly with tic disorders, that may inflate comorbidity. They note that the functionality of the symptom is a useful factor that can distinguish between OCD symptoms and OC spectrum symptoms, yet it is not captured on existing diagnostic measures.

Few studies have actually compared the comorbidity of OC spectrum disorders in OCD to the comorbidity of OC spectrum in other anxiety disorders. Richter et al. (2003) compared comorbidity rates in people with OCD, social phobia, and panic disorder, using diagnostic interviews by interviewers blind to the study hypotheses. The OCD group had a higher rate of comorbid OC spectrum conditions, current comorbid OC conditions, and were more likely to have tic disorders than the other groups. There were no group differences in rates of eating disorders, but more people with OCD had comorbid trichotillomania than did those with social phobia, and more people with OCD had comorbid skin-picking than did the panic disorder group.

Diagnostic distinctions between OCD and certain OC spectrum conditions can be subtle. Radomsky, Bohne, and O'Connor (2007) summarize the primary difference as follows: whereas the compulsions symptomatic of OCD are enacted to reduce fear, anxiety, or the perceived likelihood that something awful will happen, *impulsions* reduce tension or discomfort, and can in fact feel pleasurable. Consider people who need to perform a behavior until they get a "just right" feeling. This could be symptomatic of a tic, or of OCD. However, as Radomsky et al. (2007) observe, in the case of OCD, the person is more likely to feel that abandoning the action before getting the "just right" feeling may lead to harm to someone else. In tic disorders, the feeling itself is the goal. Similarly, people with OCD and people with tic disorders may mentally repeat a phrase, prayer, song, etc. but whereas in OCD, the behavior is enacted to prevent a feared outcome, a mental tic is performed to release tension. BDD is characterized by repetitive, time-consuming behavior, but again, the functionality of the symptom is important in distinguishing it from OCD. In BDD the goal is to examine, hide, improve, or seek reassurance about the perceived defect, whereas in OCD it is to prevent harm. People with BDD tend to have poorer insight into the irrationality of their concerns, and indeed are at times delusional (Philips, 2000).

Hoarding can be associated with excessive acquisition, which can look like compulsive buying. When buying occurs in the context of hoarding, it is more likely to be motivated by a fear that the desired item may not be available in the future when it is needed, and/or that the price will have increased and money will therefore be wasted by not having purchased it at a lower price. People with hoarding symptoms may also have an idealized sense of the value and importance of an object, and may anthropomorphize objects such that the idea of not purchasing it would cause dismay (e.g., "If I don't buy this stuffed kitten it will be alone by itself on the shelf and that is too sad!"…"This egg cup will feel much more at home with the others in my collection"…"My set is incomplete without this one, I won't feel whole without it"). The purchases may bring some pleasure because the object is romanticized, idealized, or anthropomorphized, and/or because it helps "complete" a set, but the initial motivation is to avoid discomfort. Compulsive buying outside of OCD is more likely to be motivated by the pursuit of pleasure.

In terms of assessing OC spectrum conditions, a number of interviewer-administered and self-report measures exist. The Yale-Brown Obsessive Compulsive Scale (Y-BOCS) has been adapted to assess BDD (Philips et al., 1997), and the Dysmorphic Concerns Questionnaire is a brief self-report measure of BDD symptoms with strong psychometric properties (Oosthuizen, Lambert, & Castle, 1998). Tics can be assessed with the Yale Global Tic Severity Scale (Leckman et al., 1989) and TM can be assessed with the NIMH Trichotillomania Severity Scale and NIMH Trichotillomania Impairment scale, both of which are also based on the Y-BOCS (Stanley, Breckenridge, Snyder, & Novy, 1999). The Massachusetts General Hospital Hairpulling Scale (Keuthen, O'Sullivan, Ricciardi, Shera, Borgmann, et al., 1995) is a brief self-report instrument with strong reliability. To assess hypochondriasis, Longley, Watson and Noyes (2005) developed the Multidimensional Inventory of Hypochondriacal Traits (MIHT). This 31-item self-report inventory is based on a synthesis of previous theory and research on the constructs underlying HC, and has excellent psychometric properties. Finally, DuToit et al. (2001) developed the Structured Clinical Interview for Obsessive Compulsive Spectrum Disorders (SCID-OCSD), which assesses OC spectrum as widely defined, and report that it has strong interrater reliability.

Comorbid OC spectrum disorders can complicate treatment. Steketee and Neziroglu (2003) note that OCD patients with BDD and HC tend to have greater overvalued ideation than those without such comorbidity. This is likely to make it more difficult for them to consider alternate views of the meaning of their obsessions and to resist their compulsions, so treatment engagement and compliance may be more challenging. With respect to other OC spectrum disorders, Radomsky et al. (2007) advise that tics and OCD can be treated independently and sequentially, in either order. At times, differentiating a tic from a compulsion can be difficult, but fortunately the treatment approach is the same, involving exposure to the urge to complete the act while refraining from doing it.

Assessment of Beliefs and Insight

Individuals with OCD are likely to hold particular beliefs about the meaning or importance of their obsessions and/or compulsions. A group of researchers with expertise in theoretical models of OCD and its treatment have identified several types of beliefs that may be especially important to understanding its development and persistence. Themes include perfectionism, the importance of controlling thoughts, the importance of thoughts, responsibility, intolerance of uncertainty, and overestimation of threat. This group, known as the Obsessive Compulsive Cognitions Working Group (OCCWG), has developed a measure of general beliefs, as well as specific appraisals, of obsessional thoughts. The first is known as the Obsessive Beliefs Questionnaire (OBQ), which is a self-report measure consisting now of 44 items (OCCWG, 2005). The appraisal measure is the Interpretation of Intrusions Inventory, a 31-item self-report measure of importance of thoughts, need to control thoughts and responsibility (OCCWG, 2005). The measures have strong psychometric properties, although the subscale scores within each measure tend to be highly intercorrelated.

Individuals whose beliefs about their obsessions are very strong may have poor insight. The term *insight* refers to "the degree to which the sufferer is aware of the irrationality of their symptoms" (Steketee & Neziroglu, 2003, p. 179). Those with poor insight, then, are extremely certain that the feared consequences of their obsessions are reasonable and warrant the time spent on compulsions, avoidance, etc. As Veale (2007) observes, the term *insight* is often used synonymously with *overvalued ideation* as defined in the DSM-IV-TR. At one end of the continuum is the recognition that the obsessional idea is irrational; at the other, the person holds a delusional belief that it is fully rational. When the latter is the case, the person can be specified as having OCD "with poor insight."

Insight can have important implications for illness onset, course, and response to treatment. Kishore, Samar, Reddy, Chandrasekhar, and Thennarasu (2004) found that 25% of their sample of patients met criteria for poor insight. Poor insight

was associated with earlier age of onset, longer duration of illness, greater symptom severity, higher comorbidity, and poorer response to drug treatment. Several studies found that poor insight was associated with poorer outcome of cognitive-behavior therapy (see Veale, 2007 for a review). Matsunaga et al. (2002) found that OCD sufferers with poor insight had the same degree of functional impairment as OCD sufferers with comorbid schizophrenia.

There are several measures of insight. The Y-BOCS includes an item that assesses insight, and this single item has been used in many studies. However, more comprehensive measures have been developed. The Brown Assessment of Beliefs Scale (Eisen et al., 1998) is a 7-item clinician-administered scale that addresses conviction, perception of others' view of beliefs, fixity of ideas, stability of beliefs, and attempt to disprove beliefs. It has excellent psychometric properties. Neziroglu, McKay, Yaryura-Tobias, Stevens, and Todaro (1999) developed the Overvalued Ideas Scale, which consists of 9 clinician-administered items assessing the reasonableness of obsessions and compulsions, others' perceptions about the necessity of completing compulsions, and whether the symptoms are viewed as unusual. The 9 items can be assessed for up to three beliefs associated with the person's OCD. Neziroglu et al. report that the measure has strong validity and reliability. Veale (2007) notes, though, that neither of these measures assesses abnormal values that may form an important subconstruct of overvalued ideation.

Individuals with poor insight may present a treatment challenge. For treatment purposes, Veale (2007) conceptualizes overvalued ideas as "beliefs that are associated with specific values which have become dominant, idealized and excessively identified with the self" (p. 271). In general, Veale recommends that treatment involve helping the person identify other important values (e.g., being a good mother, being good at one's job) and develop their recognition of how pursuing the value relevant to their OCD compromises these other values, and exploring whether the OCD-relevant value is one they would expect or want their children or other loved ones to hold.

Assessing the Family

People with OCD often involve family members in avoidance or compulsions. For example, they may require family members to be the last to leave the house, or to wash their hands in a highly circumscribed way, and they may insist that family members do not touch certain objects, or they require family members to answer in a specific way when asked particular questions. They may turn to family members for reassurance that something has or has not happened, and they may insist that family members perform certain tasks, such as checking the appliances and locking the house (conversely, they may insist on doing such things themselves). Compliance with such requests can strain relationships, as the family may feel that the sufferer is putting their OCD "first" before the best interests of the family. Noncompliance can also strain relationships, as the sufferer may experience the family as untrustworthy and rather cold for failing to perform an action that would relieve distress. Stengler-Wenzke, Kroll, Matschinger, and Angermeyer (2006) found that relatives of OCD sufferers had substantially lower quality of life than people in the general population.

In their sample of OCD sufferers (N=419), Hollander et al. (1996) found that 73% reported that their illness interfered with family relationships. Cooper (1994) found that 85% of family members reported being bothered by their relatives' rituals, and 75% of relatives of OCD sufferers age 17 and under were drawn into the rituals, as were 58% of relatives of adult sufferers. Shafran, Ralph, and Tallis (1995) similarly found that only 10% of respondents reported that their relatives' OCD did not interfere in their lives, and 60% of the family members of sufferers reported that they were asked to conduct a ritual, observe a ritual, or avoid a feared stimulus. Of those, 40% reported that they complied with the request of the OCD sufferer to conduct a ritual themselves (e.g., washing or checking). Calvocoressi et al. (1995) found that 88% of family members surveyed reported accommodating rituals, and that degree of family accommodation was associated with degree of family dysfunction and stress. In their review, Renshaw, Steketee, and Chambless (2005) found that rates of accommodation of symptoms among family members range from 62% to 100%, and participation from 39% to 75%.

Family members may find it difficult to resist involvement because they find it hard to tolerate the degree of distress it causes the OCD sufferer when they do so. OCD sufferers can feel exceptional anger and a sense of being uncared for when family members do not comply with their rules, even if the noncompliance is not intended to be coercive or is not driven by hostility. Storch et al. (2007) found that 16% of the parents of child sufferers reported that

their children experienced anger and distress on a daily basis in response to parent refusal of accommodation of rituals. However, family members can behave antagonistically toward the sufferer. For example, family members may use compliance or noncompliance coercively (e.g., "I will only recheck the stove for you if you let me go out tonight"), and may exploit sufferers' distress ("If you don't let me use the car, I'm going to go into your room and rub my shoes all over your bed"). Family members may also mock the sufferer for having the symptoms, accusing them of being weak, weird, sick, selfish, or the cause of all family distress. Amir, Freshman and Foa (2000) found that OCD sufferers were more likely to engage in their rituals when their family members made critical comments. They reasoned that the ritual is performed as "punishment" for the criticism, or that the criticism raises anxiety, which in turn leads to more frequent rituals.

Neither compliance nor hostile noncompliance is conducive to overcoming OCD symptoms. Family accommodation of symptoms will interfere with treatment predicated on exposure with response prevention, as it terminates exposure to the distress associated with the obsession and disallows for new learning about the meaning or importance of the obsession. Amir et al. (2000) found that the greater the family accommodation of rituals, the greater the symptom severity at the end of treatment, controlling for pretreatment severity. Storch et al. (2007) found that family accommodation mediated the relationship between symptom severity and functional impairment. The emotional climate in the home can also affect treatment. Steketee (1993) found that the degree of empathy and positive interactions exhibited by the significant others of sufferers was associated with maintenance of treatment gains, whereas criticism, anger, and belief that sufferers could control their symptoms, were associated with relapse.

Chambless and Steketee (1999) examined degree of expressed emotion (EE) in the families of OCD sufferers. The term *EE* refers to the family members' feelings about a patient, including emotional over-involvement, criticism, and hostility. They found that relatives' hostility was a major predictor of treatment dropout, poorer treatment gains, and poorer functioning. However, degree of familial nonhostile criticism was associated with better treatment outcome. In their summation of the relevant literature, Renshaw et al. (2005) concluded that having family who are either overly accommodating of symptoms, or overly antagonistic about symptoms, is associated with poorer treatment outcome.

There are few measures of family accommodation and climate. Calvocoressi et al. (1999) developed a 12-item measure that is administered by a clinician to relatives of the OCD sufferer, and report that it has excellent psychometric properties. The Camberwell Family Interview (Vaughn & Leff, 1976) is an intensive 1–2 hour interview that is taped, and then scored to assess degree of EE. The length of the interview itself, and the scoring process, may render it infeasible in many clinical settings. The Patient Rejection Scale (Kreisman, Simmens, & Joy, 1979) is an 11-item self-report measure of family criticism of, and hostility toward, family members with mental health problems, and has good psychometric properties. The Perceived Criticism Measure (Hooley & Teasdale, 1989) requires patients to rate each adult with whom they live on how critical they are. Chambless and Steketee (1999) express concern about its convergent validity, although reliability across time is strong. The Interpersonal Support Evaluation List is a 40-item true/false questionnaire to assess perceived availability of social support (Cohen, Mermelstein, Kamarck, & Hoberman, 1985).

There are several implications of family accommodation and climate for treatment. First, it may be important to meet with key family members to educate them to the treatment model, and help them brainstorm ways of offering noncritical support without accommodating rituals. Indeed, Grunes, Neziroglu and McKay (2001) found that patients whose family members were randomly assigned to a psychoeducational group had a greater reduction in OCD symptoms and depressed mood, compared with those whose family members did not participate. However, Steketee (1993) makes the important point that the OCD sufferer and the family's attitude are nested; just as criticism by the family can evoke more ritualizing by the sufferer, so can ritualizing put pressure on the family. This issue has important implications for research on family/sufferer dyads, in that statistical analyses must assume a nested design and be performed accordingly. The issue also has implications for treatment of family members; as Steketee notes, one cannot simply direct the family to behave differently without taking their feelings and perspective into account. Van Noppen and Steketee (2003) and Renshaw et al. (2005) advocate for a multifamily behavioral treatment, in which family members are trained in exposure to rituals, contract to improve

communication in the family, and reduce hostile and antagonistic responses to OCD. Each paper provides guidelines for this approach.

Quality of Life in OCD

OCD is recognized as being a major mental illness, and as one in which sufferers experience impaired functioning across domains on par with major physical illnesses. For example, Koran, Thienemann, and Davenport (1996) found that quality of life for those with OCD was substantially poorer than those with diabetes. Eisen et al. (2006) found that one-third of their treatment-seeking sample was unable to work due to their OCD symptoms. Social and family functioning, as well as general well-being and ability to enjoy leisure time, were impaired across the board relative to normative samples, and the degree of impairment in these latter domains was associated in particular with the frequency and intensity of the obsessional concern. The degree of impairment increased dramatically for people whose symptoms were in the moderate or higher level of severity (i.e., Y-BOCS score of 20+). This is consistent with Hollander et al. (1996), who similarly found that individuals with OCD reported substantial disruption in their family relationships and with friends, lowered academic achievement, lowered career aspirations, and substantial work interference. However, there is evidence that symptom alleviation is associated with an improvement in quality of life for OCD sufferers (Bystritsky et al., 1999, 2001; Cordioloi et al., 2003; Tenney et al.; Diefenbach, Abramowitz, Norberg, & Tolin, 2007).

There are many quality of life measures that are commonly used in psychiatric settings. The Range of Impaired Functioning Tool (LIFE-RIFT) is a brief semistructured interview that assesses functioning in four domains, including work, interpersonal relations, recreation, and global satisfaction. It has good validity and reliability (Leon et al., 1999). The Quality of Life Enjoyment and Satisfaction Questionnaire consists of 91 self-report items that address 8 domains (Endicott, Knee, Harrison, & Blumenthal, 1993). The Medical Outcomes Survey 36-item Short-Form Health Survey (McHorney, Ware, & Raczek, 1993) is widely used to assess functioning problems and limitations due to both mental and physical problems. The Lancashire Quality of Life Profile is a self-report measure assessing 9 domains from religion to health to education, etc. (Nieuwenhuizen, Schene, Koeter, & Huxley, 2001). The Sheehan Disability Scale (Sheehan, 1986) has also been widely used, particularly with individuals with anxiety disorders (Mendlowicz & Stein, 2000). Respondents rate the degree to which their symptoms are impairing in 3 domains. All of these self-report measures have strong psychometric properties.

Summary

Obsessive compulsive disorder (OCD) is a problem associated with severe impairment, difficulty functioning, and poorer quality of life, both for the sufferer and the sufferer's immediate family. It is most highly comorbid with mood disorders, social anxiety, and specific phobia. With respect to OC spectrum disorders, OCD is most highly comorbid with tic disorders and with body dysmorphic disorder. Of the Axis II disorders, OCD is most highly comorbid with obsessive compulsive personality disorder, although it is important to note that symptom overlap between the two disorders may artificially inflate comorbidity rates. Comorbid conditions can exacerbate OCD symptoms, as well as influence treatment engagement. Individuals with OCD vary considerably in their insight into the irrationality of their obsessional concerns, and this can affect treatment engagement and outcome. The family environment—particularly, high symptom accommodation and expressed hostility—can have an important impact on symptom severity and treatment outcome. However, it is important to note that symptom severity can evoke accommodation and hostility.

Future Directions

1. What is the relationship of hoarding to OCD, and is it a unique symptom cluster?

2. What is the relationship of OCD to OCPD?

3. How do OCD symptoms, family accommodation, and expressed emotion influence each other?

4. How might family intervention benefit treatment outcome?

Related Chapters

References

Abramowitz, J. S., & Foa, E. B. (2000). Does major depressive disorder influence outcome of exposure and response prevention for OCD? *Behavior Therapy, 31*, 795–800.

Abramowitz, J. S., & Foa, E. B. (1998). Worries and obsession in individuals with obsessive compulsive disorder with and without comorbid generalize anxiety disorder. *Behaviour Research and Therapy, 36*, 695–700.

Abramowitz, J. S., Franklin, M. E., Street, G. P., Kozak, M. J., & Foa, E. B. (2000). Effects of comorbid depression on response to treatment for obsessive-compulsive disorder. *Behavior Therapy, 31*, 517–528.

Abramowitz, J. S., Storch, E. A., Keeley, M., & Cordell, E. (2007). Obsessive-compulsive disorder with comorbid depression: What is the role of cognitive factors? *Behaviour Research and Therapy, 45*, 2257–2267.

Abramson, L. Y, Alloy, L. B., Hankin, B. L., Haeffel, G. J., MacCoon, D. G., & Gibb, B. E. (2002). Cognitive vulnerability-stress models of depression in a self-regulatory and psychobiological context. In I. H. Gotlib and C. L. Hammen (Eds.), *Handbook of Depression* (pp. 268–294). New York: Guilford.

American Psychiatric Association (2000). *The Diagnostic and Statistical Manual of Mental Disorders, Fourth* Edition (Text Revision). Washington, DC: Author.

Amir, N., Freshman, M., & Foa, E. B. (2000). Family distress and involvement in relatives of obsessive-compulsive disorder patients. *Journal of Anxiety Disorders, 14*, 209–217.

Angst, J., Gamma, A., Endrass, J., Hantouche, E., Goodwin, R., Ajdacic, V., Eich, D., & Rossler, W. (2004). Obsessive-compulsive severity spectrum in the community: prevalence, comorbidity, and course. *European Archives of Psychiatry and Clinical Neuroscience, 254*, 156–164.

Angst, J., Gamma, A., Endrass, J., Hantouche, E., Goodwin, R., Ajdacic, V., Eich, D., & Rossler, W. (2005). Obsessive-compulsive syndromes and disorders: significance of bipolar and anxiety syndromes. *European Archives of Psychiatry and Clinical Neuroscience, 255*, 65–71.

Antony, M. M., Downie, F., & Swinson, R. P. (1998). Diagnostic issues and epidemiology in OCD. In R. P. Swinson, M. M. Antony, S. Rachman and M. A. Richter (Eds.), *Obsessive-compulsive disorder: theory, research and treatment* (pp. 3–32). New York: Guilford.

Antony, M. M., Orsillo, S. M., & Roemer, L. (2001). *Practitioner's guide to empirically based measures of anxiety.* New York: Kluwer.

AuBuchon, P. G., & Malatesta, V. J. (1994). Obsessive compulsive patients with co-morbid personality disorders: Associated problems and response to a comprehensive behavior therapy. *Journal of clinical Psychiatry, 5*, 448–452.

Beck, A. T. B., Steer, R. A., & Brown, R. K. (1996). *Manual for the Beck Depression Inventory-II.* San Antonio, Tx: Psychological Corporation.

Bellodi, L., Scioto, G., Diaferia, G., Ronchi, P., & Smiraldi, E. (1992). Psychiatric disorders in families of patients with obsessive-compulsive disorder. *Psychiatry Research, 42*, 111–120.

Black, D. W., & Noyes, R. (1997). Obsessive-compulsive disorder and axis II. *International Review of Psychiatry, 9,* 111–118.

Brandes, M., & Bienvenu, O. J. (2009). Anxiety disorders and personality disorders comorbidity. In M. M. Antony and M. B. Stein (Eds.), *Oxford handbook of anxiety and related disorders* (pp. 587–595). Oxford: Oxford University Press.

Brown, T. A., DiNardo, P. A., & Barlow, D. H. (1994). *Anxiety disorders interview schedule for DSM-IV.* Oxford: Oxford University Press.

Brown, T. A., Moras, K., Zinbarg, R. E., & Barlow, D. H. (1993). Diagnostic and symptom distinguishability of generalized anxiety disorder and obsessive-compulsive disorder. *Behavior Therapy, 24,* 227–240.

Calvocoressi, L., Lewis, B., Harris, M., Trufan, S. J., Goodman, W. K., McDougle, C. J., & Price, L. H. (1995). Family accommodation in obsessive-compulsive disorder. *American Journal of Psychiatry, 152,* 441–443.

Calvocoressi, L., Mazure, C. M., Stanislav, V. K., Skolnick, J., Fisk, D., Vegso, S. J., Van Noppen, B. L., & Price, L. H. (1999). Family accommodation of obsessive-compulsive symptoms: Instrument development and assessment of family behaviour. *The Journal of Nervous and Mental Disease, 187,* 636–642.

Chambless, D. L., & Steketee, G. (1999). Expressed emotion and behaviour therapy outcome: A prospective study with obsessive-compulsive and agoraphobic outpatients. *Journal of Consulting and Clinical Psychology, 67,* 658–665.

Clark, L. A. (1993). *The Schedule for Nonadaptive and Adaptive Personality (SNAP).* Minneapolis, MN: University of Minnesota Press.

Cohen, S., Mermelstein, R., Kamarck, T., & Hoberman, H. (1985). Measuring the functional components of social support. In I. G. Sarason and B. R. Sarason (Eds.), *Social support: theory, research and applications* (pp. 73–94). Dordrecht, Holland: Martines Ujhoff.

Coles, M. E., Pinto, A., Mancebo, M. C., Rasmussen, S. A., & Eisen, J. L. (2008). OCD with comorbid OCPD: A subtype of OCD? *Journal of Psychiatric Research, 42,* 289–296.

Cooper, M. (1994). Report on the findings of a study of OCD family members. *OCD Newsletter, 8,* 1–2.

Cordiolia, A.V., Heldt, E., Bochia, D.B., Margis, R., deSousa, M. B., Tonello, J. F., Manfro, G. G., & Kapczinski, F. (2003). Cognitive-behavioral group therapy in obsessive-compulsive disorder: A randomized clinical trial. *Psychotherapy and Psychosomatics, 72,* 211–216.

Crino, R. D., & Andres, G. (1996). Obsessive-compulsive disorder and Axis I comorbidity. *Journal of Anxiety Disorders, 10,* 37–46.

Davey, G. C. L., Startup, H. M., Zara, A., MacDonald, C. B., & Field, A. P. (2003). The perseveration of checking thoughts and mood-as-input hypothesis. *Journal of Behavior Therapy and Experimental Psychiatry, 34,* 141–160.

Demal, U., Lenz, G., Mayrhofer, A., Zapotoczky, H-G., & Zitterl, W. (1993). Obsessive compulsive disorder and depression: A retrospective study on course and interaction. *Psychopathology, 26,* 145–150.

Denys, D., Tenney, N., van Megen, H. J. G. M., de Geus, F., & Westenberg, H. G. M. (2004). Axis I and II comorbidity in a large sample of patients with obsessive-compulsive disorder. *Journal of Affective Disorders, 80,* 155–162.

Diaferia, G., Bianchi, I., Bianchi, M. L., Cavedini, P., Erzegovesi, S., & Bellodi, L. (1997). Relationship between obsessive-compulsive personality disorder and obsessive-compulsive disorder. *Comprehensive Psychiatry, 38,* 38–42.

Diefenbach, G.J., Abramowitz, J. S., Norberg, M. M., & Tolin, D.F. (2007). Changes in quality of life following cognitive-behavioral therapy for obsessive-compulsive disorder. *Behaviour Research and Therapy, 45,* 3060–3068.

Dreesen, L., Hoekstra, R., & Arntz, A. (1997). Personality disorders do not influence the results of cognitive and behaviour therapy for obsessive compulsive disorder. *Journal of Anxiety Disorders, 11,* 503–521.

duToit, P., van Kradenburg, J., Niehaus, D., & Stein, D. J. (2001). Comparison of obsessive compulsive disorder patients with and without comorbid putative obsessive-compulsive spectrum disorders using a structured clinical interview. *Comprehensive Psychiatry, 42,* 291–300.

Eisen, J. L., Mancebo, M. A., Pinto, A., Coles, M. E., Pagano, M. E., Stout, R., & Rasmussen, S. A. (2006). Impact of obsessive-compulsive disorder on quality of life. *Comprehensive Psychiatry, 47,* 270–275.

Eisen, J. L., Phillips, K. A., Baer, L., Beer, D. A., Atala, K. D., & Rasmussen, S. A. (1998). The Brown Assessment of Beliefs Scale: Reliability and validity. *American Journal of Psychiatry, 155,* 102–108.

Endicott, J., Knee, J., Harrison, W., & Blumenthal, R. (1993). Quality of Life Enjoyment and Satisfaction Questionnaire: a new measure. *Psychopharmacology Bulletin, 29,* 321–326.

Fals-Stewart, W., & Lucente, S. (1993). An MCMI cluster typology of obsessive-compulsives: A measure of personality characteristics and its relationship to treatment participation, compliance and outcome in behavior therapy. *Journal of Psychiatric Research, 27,* 139–154.

First, M. B., Gibbon, M., Spitzer, R. L., Williams, J. B. W., & Benjam, L. S. (1995). *Structured Clinical Interview for DSM-IV Axis I Disorders (SCID-I/P).* New York: Biometrics Press.

First, M. B., Gibbon, M., Spitzer, R. L., Williams, J. B. W., & Benjam, L. S. (1997). *Structured Clinical Interview for DSM-IV Axis II Personality Disorders (SCID-II).* Washington, DC: American Psychiatric Press.

Freeston, M. H., Ladouceur, R., Thibodeau, N., & Gagnon, F. (1991). Cognitive intrusions in a nonclinical population. I. Response style, subjective experience and appraisal. *Behaviour Research and Therapy, 29,* 585–597.

Frost, R. O., Steketee, G., Williams, L. F., & Warren, R. (2000). Mood, personality disorder symptoms and disability in obsessive compulsive hoarders: a comparison with clinical and nonclinical controls. *Behaviour Research and Therapy, 38,* 1071–1081.

Grunes, M. S., Neziroglu, F., & McKay, D. (2001). Family involvement in the behavioral treatment of obsessive-compulsive disorder : A preliminary investigation. *Behavior Therapy, 32,* 803–820.

Hollander, E., Kwon, K., Won, J. H., Stein, D. J., Broatch, J., Rowland, C. T., Himelein, C. A. (1996). Obsessive-compulsive and spectrum disorders: Overview and quality of life issues. *Journal of Clinical Psychiatry, 57(supp. 8),* 3–6.

Hong, J. P., et al. (2004). Clinical correlates of recurrent major depression in obsessive compulsive disorder. *Depression and Anxiety, 20,* 86–91.

Hooley, J. M., & Teasdale, J. D. (1989). Predictors of relapse in unipolar depressives: expressed emotion, marital distress, and perceived criticism. *Journal of Abnormal Psychology, 98,* 229–235.

Jenike, M. A., Baer, L., Minichiello, W. E., Schwartz, C. E., & Carey, R. J. (1986). Concomitant obsessive-compulsive disorder and schizotypal personality disorders. *American Journal of Psychiatry, 143,* 530–532.

Keuthan, N. J., O'Sullivan, R. L., Ricciardi, H. N., Shera, D., Savage, C. R., Borgmann, A. S., et al. (1995). The Massachusetts General Hospital (MGH) Hairpulling Scale : I. Development and factor analyses. *Psychotherapy and Psychosomatics, 64,* 141–145.

Kishore, V. R., Samar, R., Reddy, Y. C. J., Chandrasekhar, C. R., & Thennarasu, K. (2004). Clinical characteristics and treatment response in poor and good insight obsessive-compulsive disorder. *European Psychiatry, 19,* 202–208.

Kreisman, D. E., Simmens, S. J., & Joy, V. D. (1979). Rejecting the patient: preliminary validation of a self-report scale. *Schizophrenia Bulletin, 5,* 220–222.

Leckman, J. F., Riddle, M. A., Hardin, M. T., Ort, S. I., et al. (1989). The Yale Global Tic Severity Scale: Initial testing of a clinician-rated scale of tic severity. *Journal of the American Academy of Child and Adolescent Psychiatry, 28,* 566–573.

Lochner, C., Hemmings, S. M. J., Kinnear, C. J., Niehaus, D. J. H., Nel, D. G., Corfield, V. A., Moolman-Smook, J. C., Seedat, S., & Stein, D. J. (2005). Cluster analysis of obsessive-compulsive spectrum disorders in patients with obsessive-compulsive disorder: clinical and genetic correlates. *Comprehensive Psychiatry, 46,* 14–19.

Longley, S. L., Watson, D., & Noyes, R. (2005). Assessment of the hypochondriasis domain: the Multidimensional Inventory of Hypochondriacal Traits (MIHT). *Psychological Assessment, 17,* 3–14.

Lovibond, S. H., & Lovibond, P. F. (1995). *Manual for the Depression Anxiety Stress Scales, 2nd ed.* Sydney: Psychology Foundation.

MacDonald, B., & Davey, G. C. L. (2005). Inflated responsibility and perseverative checking: The effect of negative mood. *Journal of Abnormal Psychology, 114,* 176–182.

Matsunaga, H., Kiriike, N., Matsui, T., Oya, K., Iwasaki, I., Koshimune, K., Miyata, A., & Stein, D. J. (2002). Obsessive-compulsive disorder with poor insight. *Comprehensive Psychiatry, 43,* 150–157.

McHorney, C. A., Ware, J. E., Raczek, A. E. (1993). The MOS 36-Item Short Form Health Survey (SF-36), II: Psychometric and clinical tests of validity in measuring physical and mental health constructs. *Medical Care, 31,* 247–263.

Mendlowicz, M. V., & Stein, M. B. (2000). Quality of life in individuals with anxiety disorder. *American Journal of Psychiatry, 157,* 669–682.

Millon, T., Millon, C., & Davis, R. (1997). *Millon Clinical Multiaxial Inventory: MCMI-III.* Upper Saddle River, NJ: Pearson Assessments.

Mohammadi, M-R., Ghanizadeh, A., & Moini, R. (2007). Lifetime comorbidity of obsessive compulsive disorder with psychiatrtic disorders in a community sample. *Depression and Anxiety, 24,* 602–607.

Newth, S., & Rachman, S. (2001). The concealment of obsessions. *Behaviour Research and Therapy, 39,* 457–464.

Neziroglu, F., McKay, D., Yaryura-Tobias, J., Stevens, K. P., & Todaro, J. (1999). The overvalued ideas scale: development, reliability and validity in obsessive-compulsive disorder. *Behaviour Research and Therapy, 37,* 881–902.

Obsessive Compulsive Cognitions Working Group. (2005). Psychometric validation of the obsessive belief questionnaire and interpretation of intrusions inventory part 2: Factor analyses and testing of a brief version. *Behaviour Research and Therapy, 43,* 1527–1542.

Oosthuizen, P., Lambert, T., & Castle, D. J. (1998). Dysmorphic concern: Prevalence and associations with clinical variables. *Australian and New Zealand Journal of Psychiatry, 32,* 129–132.

Perugi G., Toni, C., Franco, F., Travierso, M. C., Hantouche, E., & Akiskal, H.S. (2002).Obsessive-compulsive-bipolar comorbidity: A systematic exploration of clinical features and treatment outcome. *Journal of Clinical Psychiatry,63,* 1129–1134.

Philips, K. A. (2000). Connection between obsessive-compulsive disorder and body dysmorphic disorder. In W. K. Goodman, M. V. Rudorfer, and J. D. Maser (Eds.), *Obsessive-compulsive disorder: contemporary issues in treatment* (pp. 23–41). New Jersey: Lawrence Erlbaum.

Philips, K. A., Hollander, E., Rasmussen, S. A., Aronowitz, B. R., DeCaria, C., & Goodman, W. K. (1997). A severity rating scale for body dysmorphic disorder: Development, reliability and validity of a modified version of the Yale-Brown Obsessive-Compulsive Scale. *Psychopharmacology Bulletin, 33,* 17–22.

Purdon, C., & Clark, D. A. (1993). Obsessional intrusive thoughts in nonclinical subjects. Part I: Content and relation with depressive, anxious and obsessional symptoms. *Behaviour Research and Therapy, 31,* 713–720.

Purdon, C., & Clark, D. A. (2005). *Overcoming obsessive thoughts.* Oakland: New Harbinger.

Purdon, C., & Clark, D. A. (1994). Perceived control and appraisal of obsessional intrusive thoughts: A replication and extension. *Behavioural and Cognitive Psychotherapy, 22,* 269–286.

Purdon, C., Cripps, E., Faull, M., Joseph, S., & Rowa, K. (2007). Development of a measure of ego-dystonicity. *Journal of Cognitive Psychotherapy, 21,* 198–216.

Purdon, C., Gifford, S., Young, L., & Antony, M. M. (2005). *Treatment ambivalence in anxiety disorders.* Poster presented at the Association for the Advancement of Behavior and Cognitive Therapies Anxiety Disorders Special Interest Group Poster session, Washington, DC.

Rachman, S. J. (1993). Obsessions, responsibility and guilt. *Behaviour Research and Therapy, 31,* 149–154.

Rachman, S. & de Silva, P. (1978). Abnormal and normal obsessions. *Behaviour Research and Therapy, 16,* 233–248.

Radomsky, A. S., Bohne, A., & O'Connor, K. (2007). Treating co-morbid presentations: obsessive-compulsive disorder and disorders of impulse control. In M. M. Antony, C. Purdon, & L. J. Summerfeldt (Eds.), *Psychological treatment of obsessive-compulsive disorder: fundamentals and beyond* (pp. 295–309). Washington, DC: American Psychological Association Press.

Rasmussen, S. A., & Eisen, J. L. (1992). The epidemiology and clinical features of obsessive compulsive disorder. *Psychiatric Clinics of North America, 15,* 743–758.

Rasmussen, S. A., Twuang, M. T. (1986). Clinical characteristics and family history in DSM-III obsessive-compulsive disorder. *American Journal of Psychiatry, 143,* 317–322.

Renshaw, K. D., Steketee, G., & Chambless, D. L. (2005). Involving family members in the treatment of OCD. *Cognitive Behaviour Therapy, 34,* 164–175.

Ricciardi, J. N., & McNally, R. J. (1995). Depressed mood is related to obsessions, but not to compulsions, in obsessive-compulsive disorder. *Journal of Anxiety Disorders, 9,* 249–256.

Richter, M. A., Summerfeldt, L. J., Antony, M. M., & Swinson, R. P. (2003). Obsessive compulsive spectrum conditions in obsessive-compulsive disorder and other anxiety disorders. *Depression and Anxiety, 18*, 118–127.

Roth Ledley, D., Pai, A., & Franklin, M. E. (2007). Treating comorbid presentations: obsessive compulsive disorder, anxiety disorders, and depression. In M. M. Antony, C. Purdon & L. Summerfeldt (Eds.), *Psychological Treatment of Obsessive Compulsive Disorder: Fundamentals and Beyond* (281–294). Washington, DC: American Psychological Association.

Rowa, K., Gifford, S., McCabe, R., Antony, M. M., & Purdon, C. (2011). *Treatment Fears in anxiety disorders: Development and Validation of the Treatment Ambivalence Questionnaire.* Manuscript submitted.

Salkovskis, P. M. (1999). Understanding and treating obsessive-compulsive disorder. *Behaviour Research and Therapy, 37,* S29–S52.

Samuels, J., Nestadt, G., Bienvenu, O. J., Costa, P. T., Riddle, Jr. M. A., Liang, K-Y., Hoehn Saric, R., Grados, M. A., & Cullen, B. A. M. (2000). Personality disorders and normal personality dimensions in obsessive-compulsive disorder. *British Journal of Psychiatry, 177,* 457–462.

Schwab, J. J., Bialow, M. R., & Clemens, R. S. (1967). Hamilton Rating Scale for Depression with medical in-patients. *British Journal of Psychiatry, 113,* 83–88.

Shafran, R., Ralph, J., & Tallis, F. (1995). Obsessive-compulsive symptoms and the family. *Bulletin of the Menninger Clinic, 59,* 472–478.

Sheehan, D. V. (1986). *The anxiety disease.* New York: Bantam Books.

Stanley, M. A., Breckenridge, J. K., Snyder, A. G., & Novy, D. M. (1999). Clinician-rated measures of hair pulling: A preliminary psychometric evaluation. *Journal of Psychopathology and Behavioral Assessment, 21,* 157–170.

Steketee, G. (1993). Social support and treatment outcome of obsessive compulsive disorder at 9-month follow-up. *Behavioural and Cognitive Psychotherapy, 21,* 81–95.

Steketee, G., Chambless, D. L., Tran, G. Q. (2001). Effects of axis I and II comorbidity on behavior therapy outcome for obsessive-compulsive disorder and agoraphobia. *Comprehensive Psychiatry, 42,* 76–86.

Steketee, G., Henninger, N. J., & Pollard, C. A. (2000). Predicting treatment outcome for obsessive-compulsive disorder: Effects of comorbidity. In W. K. Goodman, M. V. Rudorfer and J. D. Maser (Eds.), *Obsessive-compulsive disorder: Contemporary issues in treatment* (pp. 257–274). New Jersey: Lawrence Erlbaum Associates.

Steketee, G., & Neziroglu, F. (2003). Assessment of obsessive-compulsive disorder and spectrum disorders. *Brief Treatment and Crisis Intervention, 3,* 169–185.

Stengler-Wenzke, K., Kroll, M., Matschinger, H., & Angermeyer, M. C. (2006). Quality of life of relatives of patients with obsessive-compulsive disorder. *Comprehensive Psychiatry, 47,* 523–527.

Storch, E. A., Geffken, G. R., Merlo, L. J., Jacob, M. L., Murphy, T. K., Goodman, W. K., Larson, M. J., Fernandez, M., & Grabill, K. (2007). Family accommodation in pediatric obsessive-compulsive disorder. *Journal of Clinical Child and Adolescent Psychiatry, 36,* 207–216.

Summerfeldt, L. J., Huta, V., & Swinson, R. P. (1998). Personality and obsessive-compulsive disorder. In R. P. Swinson, M. M. Antony, S. Rachman, & M. A. Richter (Eds.), *Obsessive-compulsive disorder: Theory, research and treatment* (pp. 79–119). New York: Guilford.

Swedo, S. E., Rapaport, J. L., Leonard, M., & Cheslow, D. (1989). Obsessive-compulsive disorder in children and adolescents. Clinical phenomenology of 70 consecutive cases. *Archives of General Psychiatry, 46,* 335–341.

Tallis, F. (1996). Compulsive washing in the absence of phobic and illness anxiety. *Behaviour Research and Therapy, 34,* 361–362.

Tükel, R., Meteris, H., Koyuncu, A., Tecer & Yazici, O. (2006). The clinical impact of mood disorder and comorbidity on obsessive-compulsive disorder. *European Archives of Psychiatry and Clinical Neuroscience, 256,* 240–245.

Tükel, R., Polat, A., Özdemir, O., Aksüt, D., & Türksoy, N. (2002). Comorbid conditions in obsessive-compulsive disorder. *Comprehensive Psychiatry, 43,* 204–209.

Turner, S. M., Beidel, D. C., & Stanley, M. A. (1992). Are obsessional thoughts and worry different cognitive phenomena? *Clinical Psychology Review, 12,* 257–270.

Van Nieuwenhuizen, C ., Schene, A. H., Koeter, M. W. J., & Huxley, P. J. (2001). The Lancashire Quality of Life Profile: modification and psychometric evaluation. *Social Psychiatry and Psychiatry Epidemiology, 36,* 36–44.

Van Noppen, B., & Steketee, G. (2003). Family responses and multifamily behavioural treatment for obsessive-compulsive disorder. *Brief Treatment and Crisis Intervention, 3,* 231–247.

Vaughn, C., & Leff, J. (1976). The measurement of expressed emotion in the families of psychiatric patients. *British Journal of Social and Clinical Psychology, 15,* 157–165.

Veale, D. (2007). Treating obsessive-compulsive disorder in people with poor insight and overvalued ideation. In M. M. Antony, C. Purdon, & L. J. Summerfeldt (Eds.), *Psychological treatment of obsessive-compulsive disorder: Fundamentals and beyond* (pp. 267–280). Washington, DC: American Psychological Association.

Wu, K. D., Clark, L. A., & Watson, D. (2006). Relations between Obsessive-Compulsive Disorder and personality: Beyond Axis I-Axis II comorbidity. *Anxiety Disorders, 20,* 695–717.

PART 5

Treatment of OCD

Pharmacological Treatments for Obsessive Compulsive Disorder

Darin D. Dougherty, Scott L. Rauch, *and* Michael A. Jenike

Abstract

Progress in treating OCD has accelerated in recent years. Effective first-line treatments include behavior therapy and medications, with overwhelming evidence supporting the efficacy of serotonergic reuptake inhibitors (SRIs). Second-line medication treatments for OCD include augmentation of SRIs with neuroleptics, clonazepam, or buspirone, with limited support for other strategies at present. Alternative monotherapies (e.g., buspirone, clonazepam, phenelzine) have more limited supporting data and require further study. Behavior therapy, and perhaps cognitive therapy, is as effective as medication and may be superior in risks, costs, and enduring benefits. Future rigorous research is needed to determine which patients respond preferentially to which medications, at what dose, and after what duration. Emerging treatments include new compounds acting via serotonergic, dopaminergic, glutamatergic, and opioid systems.

Keywords: serotonergic reuptake inhibitors, SRI, SSRI, monotherapy, augmentation

It was not until 1967 that the tricyclic antidepressant clomipramine (CMI), the first available serotonergic reuptake inhibitor (SRI), emerged as an effective treatment for OCD (Fernandez & Lopez-Ibor, 1967). Contemporaneously, behavioral therapy for OCD was emerging as a viable treatment modality and the object of formal study (Rachman, Hodgson, & Marks, 1971). The subsequent four decades have seen great development in the assessment and treatment of OCD. Several educational and self-help books written for lay audiences (e.g., Baer, 1991 & 2002; Rapoport, 1980), articles appearing in the general medical literature (Heyman et al., 2006; Jenike, 1989 & 2004), and the birth of an advocacy group (International OCD Foundation, www.ocfoundation.org) all contributed to a growing awareness of OCD. During this same era, the pharmaceutical industry produced a new class of compounds known as *selective serotonergic reuptake inhibitors* (SSRIs) that, like clomipramine (CMI), acted via blockade of serotonergic reuptake sites.

Unlike CMI, however, these new SSRIs had much lower affinities for adrenergic and cholinergic receptors, presumably conferring upon them a more favorable side-effect profile. Investigators in psychopharmacology proceeded to systematically study these new agents, as well as other novel compounds, while their psychotherapist counterparts conducted investigations of cognitive and behavioral treatments. During the 1990s alone, there were more than 1,500 reports published in medical sources about drug treatments and OCD. Moreover, neuroscience advances have brought us closer to understanding the etiology and pathophysiology of OCD and related disorders.

Contemporary Treatment for OCD

Numerous reviews have been written in the last few years regarding pharmacotherapy recommendations for OCD (Dougherty, Rauch, & Jenike, 2004; Jenike, 1998; see Table 15.1). There is broad agreement among experts in the field that first-line treatments for

Table 15.1 Sample Treatment Recommendations for OCD

First Line		
Behavior Therapy		
Exposure & response prevention		at least 20 hrs
Medication: Serial SRI Trials (consider at least 2 SSRI trials and one of CMI)		
CMI	150–250 mg/day	12 wks
fluoxetine	40–80 mg/day	12 wks
sertraline	50–200 mg/day	12 wks
fluvoxamine	200–300 mg/day	12 wks
paroxetine	40–60 mg/day	12 wks
citalopram	40–60 mg/day	12 wks
escitalopram	20–30 mg/day	12 wks
Second Line		
Modifications to Behavior Therapy		
Consider inpatient sessions; home visits or other in situ sessions; or cognitive therapy		
Medication: SRI Augmentation (with controlled data)		
clonazepam	0.5–5 mg/day	4 wks
buspirone	15–60 mg/day	8 wks
neuroleptics		
pimozide	1–3 mg/day	4 wks
haloperidol	0.5–10 mg/day	4 wks
risperidone	0.5–6 mg/day	4 wks
olanzapine	2.5–15 mg/day	4 wks
quetiapine	200–600 mg/day	4 wks
Medication: Alternative Monotherapies		
clonazepam	0.5–5 mg/day	4 wks
buspirone	30–60 mg/day	6 wks
phenelzine	60–90 mg/day	10 wks
venlafaxine	up to 375 mg/day	12 wks
duloxetine	up to 120 mg/day	12 wks
Third Line		
Low-Risk Experimental or Insufficiently Studied Therapies		
Alternative monotherapies without controlled data		
Alternative augmentation strategies without controlled data		
Fourth Line		
Consider Neurosurgery (only if OCD is longstanding, severe, debilitating & unresponsive to an exhaustive array of other treatments)		

OCD include SRIs (CMI or SSRIs) and/or behavior therapy. When these first-line interventions fail, second-line pharmacological approaches include augmentation of SRIs with additional medications, or trials of alternative medications as monotherapies in place of SRIs. Third-line treatments include unproven alternative monotherapies and augmentation therapies. Finally, other nonpharmacological treatments, including neurosurgery and electroconvulsive therapy (ECT), have remained more controversial and are reserved for particular clinical situations, or as treatments of last resort. Although the focus in this chapter is on psychopharmacology, the authors wish to explicitly emphasize that most experts view behavior therapy as a critical and effective first-line treatment for OCD, and that this brand of treatment is all too often overlooked or unavailable.

First-Line Pharmacotherapy: SRIs

Currently, the SRIs are the first-line treatment for OCD (Dougherty & Rauch, 1997; Dougherty, Rauch, & Jenike, 2004; Soomro et al., 2008). There is overwhelming evidence from multiple randomized, double-blind, placebo-controlled studies supporting the efficacy of SRIs in the treatment of OCD (Table 15.2). Specifically, in adults, well-designed and well-controlled trials have demonstrated the relative efficacy of CMI versus placebo, as well as the relative efficacy of SSRIs, including fluoxetine, sertraline, paroxetine, and fluvoxamine, citalopram, and escitalopram versus placebo. Moreover, SRIs have been shown to be significantly more effective than non-SRI tricyclic antidepressants (TCAs) in placebo-controlled (Table 15.2) as well as non-placebo-controlled studies (Table 15.3). In the only

Table 15.2 Placebo-Controlled Trials of SRI Therapy for OCD (Adults)

Treatment Conditions	N	Comments	Study
CMI vs placebo	20	CMI significantly superior to placebo	Karabanow, 1977
CMI vs placebo crossover	14	CMI significantly superior to placebo	Montgomery, 1980
CMI vs nortriptyline vs placebo	24	CMI, but not nortriptyline, superior to placebo	Thoren et al., 1980
CMI vs placebo	12	CMI significantly superior to placebo	Mavissakalian et al., 1985
CMI vs placebo	27	CMI significantly superior to placebo	Jenike et al., 1989*
CMI vs placebo	32	73% improved on CMI; 6% improved on placebo	Greist et al, 1990*
CMI vs placebo	239	38% avg. decrease in symptoms with CMI	CMI collaborative group, 1991
		3% avg. decrease in symptoms with placebo	
CMI vs placebo	281	44% avg. decrease in symptoms with CMI	CMI collaborative group, 1991
		5% avg. decrease in symptoms with placebo	
CMI vs placebo	36	CMI significantly superior to placebo	Foa et al., 2005
CMI vs venlafaxine	47/26	50% CMI responders; 36% venlafaxine responders; no statistically significant difference	Albert et al., 2002
CMI vs fluvoxamine	227	both effective with no statistically significant difference	Mundo et al., 2001
CMI vs fluvoxamine	65/68	both effective with no statistically significant difference	Mundo et al., 2000

(Continued)

Table 15.2 Placebo-Controlled Trials of SRI Therapy for OCD (Adults) (*Continued*)

Treatment Conditions	N	Comments	Study
sertraline vs placebo	87	sertraline significantly superior to placebo	Chouinard et al., 1990
sertraline vs placebo	19	sertraline significantly superior to placebo	Jenike et al., 1990a**
sertraline vs placebo	325	sertraline significantly superior to placebo	Greist, Chouinard, et al., 1995
sertraline vs placebo	167	sertraline significantly superior to placebo	Kronig et al., 1999
sertraline vs fluoxetine	77/73	higher proportion of remission with sertraline	Bergeron et al., 2002
sertraline vs desipramine	166	sertraline significantly superior to desipramine	Hoehn-Saric et al., 2000
fluvoxamine vs placebo	16	fluvoxamine significantly superior to placebo	Perse et al., 1987
fluvoxamine vs placebo	42	fluvoxamine significantly superior to placebo	Goodman et al., 1989
fluvoxamine vs placebo	38	fluvoxamine significantly superior to placebo	Jenike et al., 1990b
fluvoxamine vs placebo	320	fluvoxamine significantly superior to placebo	Rasmussen et al., in press
fluvoxamine vs placebo	160	fluvoxamine significantly superior to placebo	Goodman et al., 1996
fluvoxamine vs BT vs placebo	31	BT>fluvoxamine>placebo	Nakatani et al., 2005
fluvoxamine CR vs placebo	127/126	fluvoxamine CR significantly superior to placebo	Hollander et al., 2003
fluoxetine vs placebo	355	fluoxetine (20, 40, 60 mg) significantly	Tollefson et al., 1994a
fluoxetine vs placebo	217	fluoxetine (40, 60 mg) significantly superior	Montgomery et al., 1993
paroxetine vs placebo	348	paroxetine (40, 60 mg) significantly superior to placebo while 20 mg effects equal to placebo	Wheadon et al., 1993
paroxetine vs venlafaxine	75/75	equally efficacious	Denys et al., 2003
citalopram vs placebo	401	citalopram (20, 40, 60 mg) significantly superior to placebo	Montgomery et al., 2001
escitalopram vs paroxetine vs placebo	466	escitalopram (20 mg, 10 mg) & paroxetine (40 mg) significantly superior tom placebo	Stein et al., 2007

* Included under "The clomipramine collaborative study group, 1991" report above.
** Included under "Chouinard et al, 1990" report above.

Table 15.3 Non-Placebo-Controlled Trials of Drug Therapy for OCD (Adults)

Treatment Conditions	N	Comments	Study
CMI vs amitriptyline	20	CMI significantly superior to amitriptyline	Ananth et al., 1981
CMI vs amitriptyline	39	95% improved on CMI 56% improved on amitriptyline	Zhao, 1991
CMI vs clorgyline	13	CMI effective; clorgyline ineffective	Insel et al., 1983
CMI vs clorgyline	12	CMI superior to clorgyline	Zahn et al., 1984
CMI vs doxepin	32	78% markedly improved on CMI 36% markedly improved on doxepin	Cui, 1986
CMI vs fluvoxamine	6	comparable efficacy	Den Boer et al., 1987
CMI vs fluvoxamine	66	comparable efficacy	Freeman et al., 1994
CMI vs fluvoxamine	79	comparable efficacy	Koran et al., 1996
CMI vs fluvoxamine	26	comparable efficacy	Milanfranchi et al., 1997
CMI vs fluvoxamine	133	comparable efficacy	Mundo et al., 2000
CMI vs fluoxetine	11	comparable efficacy	Pigott et al., 1990
CMI vs fluoxetine	55	comparable efficacy	Lopez-Ibor et al., 1996
CMI vs imipramine	16	CMI superior to imipramine	Volavka et al., 1985
CMI vs imipramine crossover	12	CMI superior to imipramine	Lei, 1986
CMI vs paroxetine	406	comparable efficacy	Zohar et al., 1996
CMI vs sertraline	168	comparable efficacy (fewer dropouts with sertraline)	Bisserbe et al., 1995
fluvoxamine vs desipramine	40	fluvoxamine superior to desipramine	Goodman et al., 1990
fluvoxamine vs paroxetine vs citalopram	30	comparable efficacy	Mundo et al., 1997
citalopram	29	76% improved in 24-week open label trial	Koponen et al., 1997
citalopram	18	14 of 18 showed reduced Y-BOCS score in open label trial	Marazziti et al., 2001
venlafaxine	39	69% improved in open label trial	Hollander et al., 2003

randomized, double-blind, placebo-controlled study involving non-SRI TCAs, nortriptyline was not shown to be significantly more effective than placebo (Thoren, Asberg, Cronholm, Jornestedt, & Traskman, 1980), supporting the view that non-SRI TCAs are not an effective monotherapy for OCD.

Despite a wide range of observed SRI response rates, large-scale studies have generally yielded approximately 40% to 60% responders, with mean improvement in the active treatment group of approximately 20% to 40% (see Greist, Jefferson, Kobak, Chouinard, et al., 1995). In terms of the relative efficacy among SRIs, a large-scale meta-analysis of multicenter trials of SRIs was performed by Greist, Jefferson, Kobak, Katzelnick, and colleagues (1995) in which CMI (*n* = 520), fluoxetine

(n = 355), sertraline (n = 325), and fluvoxamine (n = 320) were all shown to be significantly superior to placebo. This meta-analysis further indicated that CMI might have superior efficacy over SSRIs. Although the meta-analysis of Greist et al. had many strengths, including that all studies used comparable parameters and were conducted at essentially the same centers, the results should be interpreted with caution. Since there was a serial progression in the availability of these agents, and in the performance of these trials, CMI was studied on an SRI-naive population, whereas each successive agent was undoubtedly tried on a cohort comprising a larger subpopulation of patients with histories of past SRI unresponsiveness. Consequently, each successive trial might well have been conducted on a more treatment-resistant population, biasing the efficacy in favor of agents studied in earlier years (i.e., CMI). In fact, a growing number of studies (see Table 15.3) and a comprehensive literature review (Pigott & Seay, 1999), and a recent meta-analysis (Soomro et al., 2008) all suggest that the SRIs all have comparable efficacy. However, despite these group data, any single individual may respond very well to one or two agents of the SRI medications and not the others. Thus, serial trials of each agent may be required to determine which drug is best.

Data regarding duration of treatment, optimal dose, and side effects are also plentiful, but difficult to interpret with confidence because studies often were not designed to specifically answer these questions. The collective wisdom, purportedly supported by the data from the multicenter trials as well as anecdotal clinical experience, has been that response to SRIs is typically delayed such that an adequate trial of an SRI requires at least 10 weeks' duration. Indeed, a meaningful proportion of responders continue to emerge past the 8-week mark in these studies, as well as in anecdotal clinical experience. Experts also suggest that optimal doses of SRIs for OCD may exceed those typically used for major depression (e.g., Montgomery et al., 1993), although the dose-comparison studies of OCD have not always shown significant dose-dependent responses across the OCD study population (e.g., Greist, Chouinard, et al., 1995). As for side effects, although meta-analyses (Greist, Jefferson, Kobak, Katzelnick et al., 1995; Soomro et al., 2008) did not find any significant difference between medication groups regarding dropout rates due to side effects, this is a relatively insensitive measure of side-effect profile. However, as with other TCAs, the risks and side effects mediated by anticholinergic and antiadrenergic

mechanisms (e.g., constipation, cardiac conduction disturbances, orthostatic hypotension) are more commonly associated with CMI than with SSRIs. Furthermore, CMI is believed to pose a significant risk with regard to lowering seizure threshold. All SRIs can pose risks (e.g., serotonergic syndrome) and produce a variety of side effects (e.g., nausea, sleep disturbances, sexual disturbances) attributable to their primary mechanism of action via serotonergic reuptake blockade. There is no substantive evidence that any SRI is significantly superior or inferior to any other, with regard to serotonergically mediated side effects.

Though many clinicians use SRIs as a long-term treatment for OCD, few controlled studies of long-term pharmacotherapy of OCD have been conducted. While most open studies have demonstrated high relapse rates of OCD symptoms within weeks of discontinuation (Thoren et al., 1980; Pato, Zohar-Kaduch, Zohar, & Murphy, 1988), one open-label study of SRI discontinuation found that only 23% of patients relapsed within 1 year (Fontaine & Chouinard, 1989). One randomized, double-blind study incorporating substitution of desipramine for clomipramine in a crossover design found that 89% of patients in the substituted group encountered relapse during a 2-month period (Leonard et al., 1991). More recently, four placebo-controlled relapse prevention studies have been conducted. One study assigned responders to fluoxetine to either continued treatment with fluoxetine (n = 36) or placebo (n = 35) and found 1-year relapse rates of 17.5% and 38%, respectively (Romano, Goodman, Tamura, & Gonzales, 2001). Another study assigned responders to sertraline to either continued treatment with sertraline or placebo and found relapse rates of 21% versus 59%, respectively (Koran, Hackett, Rubin, Wolkow, & Robinson, 2002). One study found that paroxetine responders assigned to continued treatment with paroxetine or placebo exhibited relapse rates of 38% versus 59%, respectively (Hollander, Allen et al., 2003). Lastly, one study found that escitalopram responders assigned to continued treatment with escitalopram or placebo exhibited relapse rates of 23% versus 52%, respectively, at 24 weeks (Fineberg et al., 2007). Some investigators have proposed using lower doses of SRIs for OCD maintenance treatment based on open-label trials (Pato, Hill, & Murphy, 1990; Ravizza, Barzega, Bellino, Bogetto, & Maina, 1996a), and two controlled studies have demonstrated the efficacy of this approach (Mundo, Bareggi, Pirola, Bellodi, & Smeraldi et al., 1997;

Tollefson, Birkett, Koran, & Genduso, 1994). Thus, the data suggest that discontinuation of SRIs in patients with OCD results in a high relapse rate, though there is still some debate regarding maintenance dosages of SRIs.

Second-Line Pharmacotherapy: SRI Augmentation and Alternative Monotherapies

For patients who do not derive satisfactory reduction of symptoms with SRI therapy, second-line pharmacological treatments include SRI augmentation and alternative monotherapies. It is important to appreciate that only a minority of patients with OCD do not respond favorably to SRIs, and that this relatively treatment-resistant group may be quite heterogeneous, including with respect to underlying pathophysiology. Therefore, specific subsequent treatments may be very effective for some subset of this population, while having only modest mean efficacy for the overall cohort. Consequently, some second-line treatment trials have focused on the number or proportion of patients who meet responder criteria, rather than the mean decrease in symptom severity over the entire study population. Moreover, in some instances, attention has been focused on the clinical characteristics that might distinguish responders from nonresponders.

Augmentation of SRIs

Numerous agents have been tried as augmentors in combination with SRIs, for patients who were unresponsive or only partially responsive to SRIs alone. However, few controlled trials of such strategies have been conducted (see Table 15.4). Despite numerous case reports suggesting that lithium might be an effective augmentor in combination with various SRIs, the only two controlled trials of lithium, added to fluvoxamine (McDougle et al., 1991) and CMI (Pigott et al., 1991), respectively, speak against the efficacy of these combinations.

Similarly, the encouraging results from case series and uncontrolled trials of buspirone augmentation were followed by only marginal success in controlled trials. In Pigott, L'Heureux, Hill, and colleagues' 1982 study of buspirone plus CMI, despite a 29% responder rate, there was not significant improvement over the entire cohort with respect to OCD symptoms, and 3 of 14 subjects suffered an exacerbation of more than 25% on measures of depression, for unclear reasons. In Grady and colleagues' (1993) double-blind crossover study of buspirone

augmentation of fluoxetine, only 1 of 14 subjects showed improvement, which may have reflected the brief duration of treatment (only 4 weeks in each phase). Finally, McDougle, Goodman, Leckman, Holzer, and colleagues (1993) found greater improvement with placebo than with buspirone in a double-blind, placebo-controlled study of buspirone augmentation of fluvoxamine for 6 weeks.

Contrary to a small case series reporting unimpressive results (Jenike, 1998), the use of clonazepam as an augmentor with CMI or fluoxetine has been studied in a placebo-controlled fashion, with some studies suggesting significant antiobsessional efficacy, as well as a nonspecific decrease in anxiety measures (Pigott, L'Heureux, Rubenstein, Hill, & Murphy, 1992) and another study finding no significant difference when compared with placebo (Crockett, Churchill, & Davidson, 2004).

The most impressive augmentation data document the benefits of adding low doses of dopamine antagonists (both conventional and atypical neuroleptics) to SRI pharmacotherapy in patients with treatment-refractory OCD (McDougle et al., 1990; McDougle et al., 1994; McDougle et al., 2000). Some data (McDougle, Goodman, Leckman, Barr, et al., 1993) initially suggested that OCD patients with comorbid tics may be less responsive to SRI monotherapy than OCD patients without tics. More recent studies have demonstrated the efficacy of SRI augmentation with neuroleptics in OCD patients with and without comorbid tics (McDougle et al., 2000). Although initial studies demonstrated the efficacy of SRI augmentation with conventional neuroleptics, more recent controlled studies of augmentation with atypical neuroleptics have yielded encouraging results as well. Three controlled trials of risperidone augmentation of an SRI (Hollander, Baldini, Rossi, Sood, & Pallanti, 2003; Li et al., 2005; McDougle et al., 2000) demonstrated efficacy. Of two controlled trials of olanzapine augmentation, one study (Bystritsky et al., 2004) yielded positive results but the other (Shapira et al., 2004) did not. Finally, three controlled studies (Atmaca, Kuloglu, Tezcan, & Gecici, 2002; Denys, de Geus, et al., 2004; Vulink et al., 2009) of quetiapine augmentation yielded positive results, while two studies (Carey et al., 2005; Kordon et al., 2008) did not. It is worth mentioning that, although atypical neuroleptics are efficacious as SRI augmentation agents, they are ineffective when used as monotherapy and may even precipitate or worsen OCD symptoms when used as monotherapy (for review, see Lykouras et al., 2003).

Table 15.4 SRI Augmentation Therapies for OCD: Controlled Trials

Augmenting agent	SRI	N	Trial	Results	Study
lithium	fluvoxamine	30	2-week or 4-week double-blind placebo-controlled	very little improvement	McDougle et al., 1991
lithium	CMI	9	double-blind crossover (with T3)	none	Pigott et al., 1991
L-triiodothyronine (T3)	CMI	9	double-blind crossover (with lithium)	none	Pigott et al., 1991
buspirone	CMI	14	2 wks placebo, then 10 wks buspirone	4/14 (29%) improved ≥ an additional 25% on buspirone; 3/14 (21%) worsened > 25% on depression scores	Pigott et al., 1992
buspirone	fluoxetine	14	double-blind crossover with placebo; 4 wks per treatment condition significantly more with buspirone	1/14 (7%) improved	Grady et al., 1993
haloperidol	fluvoxamine	34	double-blind placebo-controlled, with 17 per group; 4-week trial; after failing fluvoxamine alone	11/17 (65%) responded to haloperidol; 0/17 to placebo; 8/8 with tics responded to haloperidol	McDougle et al., 1994
clonazepam	CMI or fluoxetine	16	placebo-controlled, crossover; 4- week trial; after 20 wks stable dose on CMI or fluoxetine in global anxiety as well	significant improvement in OCD on 1/3 measures for clon. vs placebo; significant improvement	Pigott et al., 1992;
clonazepam	sertraline	37	placebo-controlled, 12-week trial	no significant difference from placebo	Crockett et al., 2004
pindolol	paroxetine	14	double-blind, placebo-controlled; 4-week trial after ~17 weeks stable dose on paroxetine	significant (p<0.01) improvement in Y-BOCS	Dannon et al., 2000

Drug	Adjunct	N	Study design	Results	Reference
risperidone	SRI	36	double-blind, placebo-controlled; 6-week trial after 12 weeks on SRI	50% responders; significant (p<0.001) reduction in Y-BOCS	McDougle et al., 2000
risperidone	SRI	16	double-blind, placebo-controlled; 8-week trial after at least 12 weeks on SRI	40% responders	Hollander et al., 2003
risperidone	SRI	16	double-blind, placebo-controlled; 2 weeks crossover trial with haloperidol	Both risperidone and haloperidol superior to placebo	Li et al., 2005
olanzapine	fluoxetine	44	placebo controlled; 6-week trial after 8 weeks on fluoxetine	no significant difference	Shapira et al., 2004
olanzapine	SRI	26	double-blind, placebo-controlled; 6-week trial	significant improvement of Y-BOCS	Bystritsky et al., 2004
quetiapine	SRI	40	double-blind, placebo-controlled; 8-week trial	quetiapine superior to placebo	Denys et al., 2004
quetiapine	SRI	42	double-blind, placebo-controlled; 6-week trial	no significant difference between quetiapine and placebo	Carey et al., 2005
quetiapine	SRI	27	single-blind, placebo-controlled; 8-week trial improvement with placebo	9/14 in active group had 60% or greater decrease in Y-BOCS score; no	Atmaca et al., 2002
quetiapine	SRI	76	double-blind, placebo-controlled; 10-week trial	quetipiapine superior to placebo	Vulink et al., 2009
quetiapine	SRI	40	double-blind, placebo-controlled; 12-week trial	no significant difference between quetiapine and placebo	Kordon et al., 2008

Numerous other agents have been tried in combination with SRIs, including clonidine, tryptophan, fenfluramine, pindolol, riluzole, trazodone, thyroid hormone, and nortriptyline, as well as other antidepressants (see Dougherty et al., 2004; Jenike, 1998; McDougle & Goodman, 1997, for reviews). The small number of subjects, lack of sufficient controls, and mixed results preclude drawing even preliminary conclusions regarding the potential efficacy of such strategies. If an augmenting agent is indicated for treatment of some comorbid condition (e.g., lithium for bipolar disorder, trazodone for insomnia, or clonidine for TS), and no strong contraindication is present, then a trial of the agent in combination with an SRI is easily rationalized. Anecdotally, these strategies have appeared to be of tremendous benefit in some isolated cases. No studies have sought to establish the optimal dosage or duration of treatment for any of these augmentation strategies. Therefore, current guidelines reflect the parameters used in the reported successful trials, as well as anecdotal experience with OCD and other psychiatric disorders.

Alternative Monotherapies

For patients who fail to derive satisfactory response from trials of SRIs alone, as well as augmentation strategies, the next recommended step is to consider alternative monotherapies in place of SRIs. In addition to uncontrolled data, positive controlled studies lend some support for trials of clonazepam, monoamine oxidase inhibitors (MAOIs), and buspirone (see Table 15.5).

In the case of clonazepam, one placebo-controlled study (Hewlett, Vinogradov, & Agras, 1992) supports its efficacy in OCD, and another placebo-controlled study failed to demonstrate efficacy in OCD (Hollander, Kaplan, & Stahl, 2003). If clonazepam is used as a monotherapy for OCD, recommendations regarding dosage (i.e., 0.5 to 5 mg/day) and duration (i.e., 4 weeks or longer) have no controlled empirical basis and are simply extrapolated from clinical experience with benzodiazepines for other anxiety disorders, and these few reports in OCD.

Non–placebo-controlled studies involving the MAOI clorgyline speak against its efficacy in OCD, showing no significant decrease in OCD severity (Insel et al., 1983) and inferior efficacy in comparison to SRIs (Insel et al., 1983; Zahn, Insel, & Murphy, 1984). While, one non–placebo-controlled study of phenelzine versus CMI suggested significant clinical improvement in both groups, and no significant difference in efficacy between the two agents (Vallejo et al., 1992), a subsequent placebo-controlled trial of phenelzine and fluoxetine demonstrated that patients treated with fluoxetine improved significantly more than those in the placebo or phenelzine groups (Jenike et al., 1997). This study did note that a subgroup of patients with symmetry obsessions did respond to phenelzine, however. Therefore, the efficacy of phenelzine as a monotherapy for OCD should be regarded as provisional. Specific recommendations regarding dosage (i.e., phenelzine 60 to 90 mg/day) have little empirical basis, reflecting extrapolation from clinical

Table 15.5 Alternative Medications as Monotherapies for OCD: Controlled Trials

Treatment Conditions	N	Comments	Study
clorgyline vs CMI	13	clorgyline ineffective; CMI effective	Insel et al., 1983
clorgyline vs CMI	12	clorgyline inferior to CMI	Zahn et al., 1984
phenelzine vs CMI	30	both effective and comparable	Vallejo et al., 1992
clonazepam vs CMI vs clonidine vs active placebo crossover	25	35% avg. decrease with clonazepam; clonazepam comparable to CMI and superior to active placebo	Hewlett et al., 1992
clonazepam vs placebo	27	no significant difference	Hollander et al., 2003
buspirone vs CMI crossover	20	both effective and comparable, > 20% improvement in > 55% in both groups	Pato et al., 1991
fluoxetine vs phenelzine vs placebo	64	fluoxetine group improved significantly more than phenelzine or placebo groups	Jenike et al., 1997
trazodone vs placebo	21	no significant difference	Pigott et al., 1992

practice with MAOIs for major depression and panic disorder; duration of trials (i.e., 10 weeks or longer) mirrors that of SRIs for OCD. In addition to the usual low-tyramine diet, and other precautions typically indicated in the context of an MAOI trial, it is critical to be cautious regarding the transition from serotonergic medications to an MAOI due to the risks of dangerous interactions, including serotonergic crisis. Current guidelines are based primarily on the half-life of the agents involved, rather than direct empirical data related to adverse events per se. Conservative recommendations are washout periods of at least 2 weeks when transitioning from CMI or a short-half-life SSRI to an MAOI, at least 5 weeks when transitioning from fluoxetine to an MAOI, and at least 2 weeks when transitioning from phenelzine to an SRI.

Although one open trial of buspirone did not yield significant antiobsessional benefit (Jenike & Baer, 1988), a controlled trial of buspirone versus CMI suggested that both were comparably effective (Pato, Pigott, Hill, Grover, Bernstein, & Murphy, 1991). The relatively short duration of the trial, the modest power for detecting a difference between treatments, and the absence of a placebo group mitigate against drawing firm conclusions from Pato and colleagues' study. Still, given the excellent tolerability of buspirone, other circumstantial evidence of possible efficacy as an augmentor, and its general efficacy as an anxiolytic, the clinical use of buspirone as an alternative monotherapy for cases of treatment-resistant OCD seems justified pending further information. Specific recommendations regarding dosage (i.e., up to 60 mg/day) and duration of trials (i.e., 6 weeks or longer) have little empirical basis, simply reflecting the protocol adopted in the study by Pato and colleagues.

Because the serotonin-norepinephrine reuptake inhibitors (SNRIs), venlafaxine and duloxetine, have serotonin reuptake inhibition properties, one would expect that the SNRIs might be efficacious in the treatment of OCD. However, no controlled studies of SNRIs for the treatment of OCD have been reported. A recent review of the literature (Dell'Osso et al., 2006) finds that the data that is available suggests that SNRIs seem to be as effective as SSRIs in treating OCD. Nonetheless, controlled trials are needed.

Another exciting target for OCD pharmacology is the glutamatergic system (for review, see Pittenger et al., 2006). Some preliminary findings worthy of mention include small trials of positive results with memantine (Aboujaoude et al., 2009; Feusner et al., 2009), as well as riluzole (Pittenger et al., 2008). Agents targeting opioid receptors have shown promise as well, including a short report of tramadol (Goldsmith, Shapira, & Keck, 1999), as well as a controlled trial suggesting that oral morphine may be effective for treating refractory OCD (Koran et al., 2005). Lastly, controlled trials have failed to demonstrate the efficacy of trazodone (Pigott, L'Heureux, Rubenstein, Bernstein, et al., 1992), clonidine (Hewlett, Vinogradov, & Agras, 1992), and diphenhydramine (Hewlett et al., 1992) as monotherapies for OCD.

Summary

In conclusion, the past 40 years have seen tremendous advances in the treatment and understanding of OCD, with a recent acceleration of progress. It is now appreciated that OCD is a common disorder, and effective treatments including medication and behavior therapy have emerged. There is overwhelming evidence of the most rigorous type supporting the efficacy of SRIs in the treatment of OCD. Along with SRIs, behavior therapy must be considered a viable first-line therapy. The best available data suggest that behavior therapy, and perhaps cognitive therapy, is at least as effective as medication in some instances, and may be superior with respect to risks, costs, and enduring benefits. A variety of second-line medication treatments for OCD have been studied in a controlled or systematic fashion. Augmentation of SRIs with neuroleptics, clonazepam, or buspirone are all recommended based on the available data. Other augmentation strategies find very limited support at present. Alternative monotherapies, including buspirone, clonazepam, and phenelzine, have all been the subject of positive controlled or partially controlled studies. However, the limited quality of these data makes recommendations for these strategies tentative as well, pending additional information. Beyond second-line treatments, the current database is inadequate for making difficult treatment decisions. The future of OCD treatment will hopefully entail rigorous research to more clearly establish the efficacy and safety of preexisting treatment options, as well as a refined sense of which patients might respond preferentially to which interventions, at what dose, and after how long. Furthermore, we can look forward to emerging novel treatment strategies that might include modified cognitive-behavior therapies, and new compounds acting via serotonergic, dopaminergic, glutamatergic, or opioid systems.

Future Directions

• What factors determine when patients receive behavior (and perhaps cognitive) therapy or SRI medications as the first-line treatment? What medication dosages and durations are most effective?

• Do buspirone or clonazepam show additive effects when used to supplement SRIs in well-controlled studies?

• What new compounds acting via serotonergic, dopaminergic, glutamatergic, or opioid systems show the most promise for OCD treatment?

Related Chapters

Chapter 7. Neuroanatomy of Obsessive Compulsive and Related Disorders

Chapter 16. Other Biological Approaches to OCD

This chapter is adapted from Dougherty DD, Rauch SL, Jenike MA. Treatment of Obsessive-Compulsive Disorder. In: Nathan PE, Gorman JM, editors. A Guide to Treatments that Work, Third Edition. New York: Oxford University Press; 2007. pp. 447-473

References

Aboujaoude, E., Barry, J. J., Gamel, N. (2009). Memantine augmentation in treatment-resistant obsessive-compulsive disorder: an open-label trial. *Journal of Clinical Psychopharmacology, 29*, 51–55.

Albert, U., Aguglia, E., Maina, G., & Bogetto, F. (2002). Venlafaxine versus clomipramine in the treatment of obsessive-compulsive disorder: A preliminary single-blind, 12-week, controlled study. *Journal of Clinical Psychiatry, 63*, 1004–1009.

Ananth, J., Pecknold, J. C., van den Steen, N., & Engelsmann, F. (1981). Double-blind comparative study of clomipramine and amitriptyline in obsessive neurosis. *Progress in Neuropsychopharmacology, 5*, 257–262.

Atmaca, M., Kuloglu, M., Tezcan, E., & Gecici, O. (2002). Quetiapine augmentation in patients with treatment resistant obsessive-compulsive disorder: A single-blind, placebo-controlled study. *International Clinical Psychopharmacology, 17*, 115–119.

Baer, L. (1991). *Getting control.* Boston: Little, Brown.

Baer, L. (2002). *The imp of the mind: Exploring the silent epidemic of obsessive bad thoughts.* New York: Penguin.

Bergeron, R., Ravindran, A. V., Chaput, Y. Goldner, E., Swinson, R., van Ameringen, M. A., Austin, C., et al. (2002). Sertraline and fluoxetine treatment of obsessive-compulsive disorder: results of a double-blind, 6-month treatment study. *Journal of Clinical Psychopharmacology, 22*, 148–154.

Bisserbe, J. C., Wiseman, R. L., Goldberg, M. S., and the Franco-Belgian OCD Study Group. (1995). *A double-blind comparison of sertraline and clomipramine in outpatients with obsessive-compulsive disorder.* American Psychiatric Association Annual Meeting, New Research Abstracts 173.

Bystritsky, A., Ackerman, S. L., Rosen, R. M., Vapnik, T., Borbis, E., Maidment, K. M., et al. (2004). Augmentation of serotonin reuptake inhibitors in refractory obsessive-compulsive disorder using adjunctive olanzapine: A placebo-controlled trial. *Journal of Clinical Psychiatry, 65*, 565–568.

Carey, P. D., Vythilingum, B., Seedat, S., Muller, J. E., van Ameringen, M., & Stein, D. J. (2005). Quetiapine augmentation of SRIs in treatment refractory obsessive-compulsive disorder: A double-blind, randomised, placebo-controlled study. *BioMed Central Psychiatry, 5*(1), 5–13.

Chouinard, G., Goodman, W., Greist, J., Jenike, M., Rasmussen, S., White, K., Hackett, E., et al. (1990). Results of a double-blind placebo controlled trial using a new serotonin uptake inhibitor, sertraline, in obsessive-compulsive disorder. *Psychopharmacology Bulletin, 26*, 279–284.

Clomipramine Collaborative Group. (1991). Clomipramine in the treatment of patients with obsessive-compulsive disorder. *Archives of General Psychiatry, 48*, 730–738.

Crockett, B. A., Churchill, E., & Davidson, J. R. (2004). A double-blind combination study of clonazepam with sertraline in obsessive-compulsive disorder. *Annals of Clinical Psychiatry, 16*, 127–132.

Cui, Y. F. (1986). A double-blind trial of chlorimipramine and doxepin in obsessive-compulsive disorder. *Chung Hua Shen Ching Shen Ko Tsa Chih, 19*, 279–281.

Dannon, P. N., Sasson, Y., Hirschmann, S., Iancu, I., Grunhaus, L. J., & Zohar, J.(2000). Pindolol augmentation in treatment-resistant obsessive compulsive disorder: A double-blind placebo controlled trial. *European Neuropsychopharmacology, 10*, 165–169.

Dell'Osso, B., Nestadt, G., Allen, A., Hollander, E. (2006). Serotonin-norepinephrine reuptake inhibitors in the treatment of obsessive-compulsive disorder: a critical review. *Journal of Clinical Psychiatry, 67*, 600–610.

Den Boer, J. A., Westenberg, H. G. M., Kamerbeek, W. D. J., Verhoeven, W. M., & Kahn, R. S. (1987). Effect of serotonin uptake inhibitors in anxiety disorders: A double-blind comparison of clomipramine and fluvoxamine. *International Clinical Psychopharmacology, 2*, 21–32.

Denys, D., de Geus, F., van Megen, H. J., & Westenberg, H. G. (2004). A double-blind, placebo-controlled trial of quetiapine addition in patients with obsessive-compulsive disorder refractory to serotonin reuptake inhibitors. *Journal of Clinical Psychiatry, 65*, 1040–1048.

Denys, D., van der Wee, N., van Megen, H. J., & Westenberg, H. G. (2003). A double- blind comparison of venlafaxine and paroxetine in obsessive-compulsive disorder. *Journal of Clinical Psychopharmacology, 23*, 568–575.

Dougherty, D. D., & Rauch, S. L. (1997). Serotonin-reuptake inhibitors in the treatment of OCD. In E. Hollander & D. J. Stein (Eds.), *Obsessive-compulsive disorders: Diagnosis—etiology—treatment* (pp. 145–160). New York: Marcel Dekker.

Dougherty, D. D., Rauch, S. L., & Jenike, M. A. (2004). Pharmacotherapy for obsessive-compulsive disorder. *Journal of Clinical Psychology, 60*, 1195–1202.

Fernandez, C. E., & Lopez-Ibor, A J. (1967). Monochlorimipramine in the treatment of psychiatric patients resistant to other therapies. *Actas Luso Espanolas de Neurologia, Psiquiatria y Ciencias Afines, 26*, 119–147.

Feusner, J. D., Kerwin, L., Saxena, S., Bystritsky, A. (2009). Differential efficacy of memantine for obsessive-compulsive disorder vs generalized anxiety disorder: an open label trial. *Psychopharmacology Bulletin, 42,* 81–93.

Fineberg, N. A., Tonnoir, B., Lemming, O., Stein, D. J. (2007). Escitalopram prevents relapse of obsessive-compulsive disorder. *European Neuropsychopharmacology, 17,* 430–439.

Foa, E. B., Liebowitz, M. R., Kozak, M. J., Davies, S., Campeas, R., Franklin, M. E., et al. (2005). Randomized, placebo-controlled trial of exposure and ritual prevention, clomipramine, and their combination in the treatment of obsessive-compulsive disorder. *American Journal of Psychiatry, 162,* 151–161.

Fontaine, R., & Chouinard, G. (1989). Fluoxetine in the long-term maintenance treatment of obsessive-compulsive disorder. *Psychiatric Annals, 19,* 88–91.

Fontenelle, L. F., Nascimento, A. L., Mendlowicz, M. V., Shavitt, R. G., Versiani, M. (2007). An update on the pharmacological treatment of obsessive-compulsive disorder. *Expert Opinions in Pharmacotherapy, 8,* 563–583.

Freeman, C. P. L., Trimble, M. R., Deakin, J. F. W., Stokes, T. M., & Ashford, J. J. (1994). Fluvoxamine versus clomipramine in the treatment of obsessive compulsive disorder: A multicenter, randomized, double-blind, parallel group comparison. *Journal of Clinical Psychiatry, 55,* 301–305.

Goldsmith, T. B., Shapira, N. A., &Keck, P. E., Jr. (1999). Rapid remission of OCD with tramadol hydrochloride. *American Journal of Psychiatry, 156,* 660–661.

Goodman, W. K., Kozak, M. J., Liebowitz, M., & White, K. L. (1996). Treatment of obsessive-compulsive disorder with fluvoxamine: A multicentre, double-blind, placebo-controlled trial. *International Clinical Psychopharmacology, 11,* 21–29.

Goodman, W. K., Price, L. H., Delgado, P. L., Palumbo, J., Krystal, J. H., Nagy, L. M., et al. (1990). Specificity of serotonin reuptake inhibitors in the treatment of obsessive compulsive disorder. *Archives of General Psychiatry, 47,* 577–585.

Goodman, W. K., Price, L. H., Rasmussen, S. A., Delgado, P. L., Heninger, G. R., & Charney, D. S. (1989). Efficacy of fluvoxamine in obsessive-compulsive disorder: A double-blind comparison with placebo. *Archives of General Psychiatry, 46,* 36–44.

Grady, T. A., Pigott, T. A., L'Heureux, F., Hill, J. L., Bernstein, S. E., & Murphy, D. L. (1993). A double-blind study of adjuvant buspirone hydrochloride in fluoxetine treated patients with obsessive compulsive disorder. *American Journal of Psychiatry, 150,* 819–821.

Greist, J. H., Chouinard, G., DuBoff, E., Halaris, A., Kim, S. W., Koran, L., et al. (1995). Double-blind comparison of three doses of sertraline and placebo in the treatment of outpatients with obsessive compulsive disorder. *Archives of General Psychiatry, 52,* 289–295.

Greist, J. H., Jefferson, J. W., Kobak, K. A., Chouinard, G., Duboff, E., Halaris, A., et al. (1995). A 1 year double-blind placebo-controlled fixed dose study of sertraline in the treatment of obsessive-compulsive disorder. *International Clinical Psychopharmacology, 10,* 57–65.

Greist, J. H., Jefferson, J. W., Kobak, K. A., Katzelnick, D. J., & Serlin, R. C. (1995). Efficacy and tolerability of serotonin transport inhibitors in obsessive-compulsive disorder: A meta-analysis. *Archives of General Psychiatry, 52,* 53–60.

Greist, J. H., Jefferson, J. W., Rosenfeld, R., Gutzmann, L. D., March, J. S., & Barklage, N. E. (1990). Clomipramine and obsessive-compulsive disorder: A placebo-controlled double-blind study of 32 patients. *Journal of Clinical Psychiatry, 51,* 292–297.

Hewlett, W., Vinogradov, S., & Agras, W. (1992). Clomipramine, clonazepam, and clonidine treatment of obsessive compulsive disorder. *Journal of Clinical Psychopharmacology, 12,* 420–430.

Heyman, I., Mataix-Cols, D., & Fineberg, N. A. (2006). Obsessive-compulsive disorder. *British Medical Journal, 333,* 424–429.

Hoehn-Saric, R., Ninan, P., Black, D. W., Stahl, S., Greist, J. H., Lydiard, B., et al. (2000). Multicenter double-blind comparison of sertraline and desipramine for concurrent obsessive-compulsive disorder and major depressive disorders. *Archives of General Psychiatry, 57,* 76–82.

Hollander, E., Allen, A., Steiner, M., Wheadon, D. E., Oakes, R., Burnham, D. B., et al. (2003). Acute and long-term treatment and prevention of relapse of obsessive-compulsive disorder with paroxetine. *Journal of Clinical Psychiatry, 64,* 1113–1121.

Hollander, E., Baldini Rossi, N., Sood, E., & Pallanti, S. (2003). Risperidone augmentation in treatment-resistant obsessive-compulsive disorder: A double-blind, placebo-controlled study. *The International Journal of Neuropsychopharmacology, 6,* 397–401.

Hollander, E., Friedberg, J., Wasserman, S., Allan, A., Birnbaum, M., & Koran, L. M.(2003). Venlafaxine in treatment-resistant obsessive-compulsive disorder. *Journal of Clinical Psychiatry, 64,* 546–550.

Hollander, E., Kaplan, A., & Stahl, S. M. (2003). A double-blind, placebo-controlled trial of clonazepam in obsessive-compulsive disorder. *The World Journal of Biological Psychiatry, 4,* 30–34.

Hollander, E., Koran, L. M., Goodman, W. K., Greist, J. H., Ninan, P. T., Yang, H., et al. (2003). A double-blind, placebo-controlled study of the efficacy and safety of controlled-release fluvoxamine in patients with obsessive-compulsive disorder. *Journal of Clinical Psychiatry, 64,* 640–647.

Insel, T. R., Murphy, D. L., Cohen, R. M., Alterman, I., Kilts, C. & Linnoila, M. (1983). Obsessive-compulsive disorder: A double-blind trial of clomipramine and clorgyline. *Archives of General Psychiatry, 40,* 605–612.

Jenike, M. A. (1989). Obsessive compulsive and related disorders: A hidden epidemic. *New England Journal of Medicine, 321,* 539–541.

Jenike, M. A. (1998). Drug treatment of obsessive-compulsive disorders. In M. A. Jenike, L. Baer, & W. E. Minichiello (Eds.), *Obsessive-compulsive disorders: Practical management* (3rd ed., pp. 469–532). Boston: Mosby–Year Book.

Jenike, M. A. (2004). Obsessive compulsive disorder. *New England Journal of Medicine, 350,* 259–265.

Jenike, M. A., & Baer, L. (1988). Buspirone in obsessive-compulsive disorder: An open trial. *American Journal of Psychiatry, 145,* 1285–1286.

Jenike, M. A., Baer, L., Minichiello, W. E., Rauch, S. L., & Buttolph, M. L. (1997). Placebo-controlled trial of fluoxetine and phenelzine for obsessive-compulsive disorder. *American Journal of Psychiatry, 154,* 1261–1264.

Jenike, M. A., Baer, L., Summergrad, P., Weilburg, J. B., Holland, A., & Seymour, R. (1989). Obsessive-compulsive disorder: A double-blind, placebo-controlled trial of clomipramine in 27 patients. *American Journal of Psychiatry, 146,* 1328–1330.

Jenike, M. A., Baer, L., Summergrad, P., Minichiello, W. E., Holland, A., & Seymour, R. (1990a). Sertraline in obsessive-compulsive disorder: A double-blind comparison with placebo. *American Journal of Psychiatry, 147,* 923–928.

Jenike, M. A., Hyman, S. E., Baer, L., Holland, A., Minichiello, W. E., Buttolph, L., et al. (1990b). A controlled trial of fluvoxamine for obsessive-compulsive disorder: Implications for a serotonergic theory. *American Journal of Psychiatry, 147,* 1209–1215.

Jenike, M. A. (2004). Clinical practice. Obsessive-compulsive disorder. *New England Journal of Medicine, 350*(3), 259–265.

Karabanow, O. (1977). Double-blind controlled study in phobias and obsessions. *Journal of International Medical Research, 5*(Suppl. 5), 42–48.

Koponen, H., Lepola, U., Leinonen, E., Jokinen, R., Penttinen, J., & Turtonen, J. (1997). Citalopram in the treatment of obsessive-compulsive disorder: An open pilot study. *Acta Psychiatrica Scandinavica, 96,* 343–346.

Koran, L. M., Aboujaoude, E., Bullock, K. D., Franz, B., Gamel, N., & Elliott, M. (2005). Double-blind treatment with oral morphine in treatment-resistant obsessive-compulsive disorder. *Journal of Clinical Psychiatry, 66,* 353–359.

Koran, L. M., Hackett, E., Rubin, A., Wolkow, R., & Robinson, D. (2002). Efficacy of sertraline in the long-term treatment of obsessive-compulsive disorder. *American Journal of Psychiatry, 159,* 88–95.

Koran, L. M., McElroy, S. L., Davidson, J. R. T., Rasmussen, S. A., Hollander, E., & Jenike, M. A.(1996). Fluvoxamine versus clomipramine for obsessive-compulsive disorder: A double-blind comparison. *Journal of Clinical Psychopharmacology, 16,* 121–129.

Kordon, A., Wahl, K., Zurowski, B., Anlauf, M., Vielhaber, K., Kahl, K. G., Broocks, A., Voderholzer, U., Hohagen, F. (2008). Quetiapine addition to serotonin reuptake inhibitors in patients with severe obsessive-compulsive disorder: a double-blind, randomized, placebo-controlled study. *Journal of Clinical Psychopharmacology, 28,* 550–554.

Kronig, M. H., Apter, J., Asnis, G., Bystritsky, A., Curtis, G., Ferguson, J., et al. (1999). Placebo-controlled, multicenter study of sertraline treatment for obsessive-compulsive disorder. *Journal of Clinical Psychopharmacology, 19,* 172–176.

Lei, B. S. (1986). A cross-over treatment of obsessive compulsive neurosis with imipramine and chlorimipramine. *Chung Hua Shen Ching Shen Ko Tsa Chih, 19,* 275–278.

Leonard, H. L., Swedo, S. E., Lenane, M. C., Rettew, D. C., Cheslow, D. L., Hamburger, S. D., & Rapoport, J. L. (1991). A double-blind desipramine substitution during long-term clomipramine treatment in children and adolescents with obsessive compulsive disorder, *Archives of General Psychiatry, 48,* 922–927.

Li, X., May, R. S., Tolbert, L. C., Jackson, W. T., Flournoy, J. M., & Baxter, L. R. (2005). Risperidone and haloperidol augmentation of serotonin reuptake inhibitors in refractory obsessive-compulsive disorder: A crossover study. *Journal of Clinical Psychiatry, 66,* 736–743.

Lopez-Ibor, J. J., Jr., Saiz, J., Cottraux, J., Vinas, R., Bourgeois, M., Hernandez, M., et al. (1996). Double-blind comparison of fluoxetine versus clomipramine in the treatment of obsessive compulsive disorder. *European Neuropsychopharmacology, 6,* 111–118.

Lykouras, L., Alevizos, B., Michalopoulo, P., & Rabavilas, A. (2003). Obsessive-compulsive symptoms induced by atypical antipsychotics: a review of reported cases. *Progress in Neuropsychopharmacology and Biological Psychiatry, 27,* 333–346.

Marazziti, D., Dell'Osso, L., Gemignani, A., Ciapparelli, A., Presta, S., Nasso, E. D., et al. (2001). Citalopram in refractory obsessive-compulsive disorder: An open study. *International Clinical Psychopharmacology, 16,* 215–219.

Mavissakalian, M., Turner, S. M., Michelson, L., & Jacob, R. (1985). Tricyclic antidepressants in obsessive-compulsive disorder: Antiobsessional or antidepressant agents? *American Journal of Psychiatry, 142,* 572–576.

McDougle, C. J., & Goodman, W. K. (1997). Combination pharmacological treatment strategies. In E. Hollander & D. J. Stein (Eds.), *Obsessive compulsive disorders* (pp. 203–224), New York: Marcel Dekker.

McDougle, C. J., Goodman, W. K., Leckman, J. F., Barr, L. C., Heninger, G. R., & Price, L. H. 1993. The efficacy of fluvoxamine in obsessive-compulsive disorder: Effects of comorbid chronic tic disorder. *Journal of Clinical Psychopharmacology, 13,* 354–358.

McDougle, C. J., Goodman, W. K., Leckman, J. F., Holzer, J. C., Barr, L. C., McCance-Katz, E., et al. (1993). Limited therapeutic effect of addition of buspirone in fluvoxamine-refractory obsessive-compulsive disorder. *American Journal of Psychiatry, 150,* 647–649.

McDougle, C. J., Epperson, C. N., Pelton, G. H., Wasylink, S., & Price, L. H. (2000). A double-blind, placebo-controlled study of risperidone addition in serotonin reuptake inhibitor-refractory obsessive-compulsive disorder. *Archives of General Psychiatry, 57,* 794–801.

McDougle, C. J., Goodman, W. K., Leckman, J. F., Lee, N. C., Heninger, G. R., & Price, L. H. (1994). Haloperidol addition in fluvoxamine-refractory obsessive-compulsive disorder: A double-blind, placebo-controlled study in patients with and without tics. *Archives of General Psychiatry, 51,* 302–308.

McDougle, C. J., Goodman, W. K., Price, L. H., Delgado, P. L., Krystal, J. H., Charney, D. S., et al. (1990). Neuroleptic addition in fluvoxamine refractory obsessive compulsive disorder. *American Journal of Psychiatry, 147,* 652–654.

McDougle, C. J., Price, L. H., Goodman, W. K., Charney, D. S., & Heninger, G. R. (1991). A controlled trial of lithium augmentation in fluvoxamine-refractory obsessive compulsive disorder: Lack of efficacy. *Journal of Clinical Psychopharmacology, 11,* 175–184.

Milanfranchi, A., Ravagli, S., Lensi, P., Marazziti, D., & Cassano, G. B. (1997). A double-blind study of fluvoxamine and clomipramine in the treatment of obsessive-compulsive disorder. *International Clinical Psychopharmacology, 12,* 131–136.

Montgomery, S. A. (1980). Clomipramine in obsessional neurosis: A placebo-controlled trial. *Pharmaceutical Medicine, 1,* 189–192.

Montgomery, S. A., Kasper, S., Stein, D. J., Bang Hedegaard, K., & Lemming, O. M. (2001). Citalopram 20 mg, 40 mg and 60 mg are all effective and well tolerated compared with placebo in obsessive compulsive disorder. *International Clinical Psychopharmacology, 16,* 75–86.

Montgomery, S. A., McIntyre, A., Osterheider, M., Sarteschi, P., Zitterl, W., Zohar, J., et al. (1993). A double-blind placebo-controlled study of fluoxetine in patients with *DSM-IIIR* obsessive-compulsive disorder. *European Neuropsychopharmacology, 3,* 143–152.

Mundo, E., Bareggi, S. R., Pirola, R., Bellodi, L., & Smeraldi, E. (1997). Long-term pharmacotherapy of obsessive-compulsive disorder: A double-blind controlled study. *Journal of Clinical Psychopharmacology, 17,* 4–10.

Mundo, E., Bianchi, L., & Bellodi, L. (1997). Efficacy of fluvoxamine, paroxetine, and citalopram in the treatment of obsessive-compulsive disorder: A single-blind study. *Journal of Clinical Psychopharmacology, 17,* 267–271.

Mundo, E., Maina, G., & Uslenghi, C. (2000). Multicentre, double-blind, comparison of fluvoxamine and clomipramine in the treatment of obsessive-compulsive disorder. *International Clinical Psychopharmacology, 15,* 69–76.

Mundo, E., Rouillon, F., Figuera, M. L., & Stigler, M. (2001). Fluvoxamine in obsessive-compulsive disorder: Similar efficacy but superior tolerability in comparison with clomipramine. *Human Psychopharmacology, 16,* 461–468.

Nakatani, E., Nakagawa, A., Nakao, T., Yoshizato, C., Nabeyama, M., Kudo, A., et al. (2005). A randomized controlled trial of Japanese patients with obsessive-compulsive disorder: Effectiveness of behavioral therapy and fluvoxamine. *Psychotherapy and Psychosomatics, 74,* 269–276.

Pato, M. T., Hill, J. L., & Murphy, D. L. (1990). A clomipramine dosage reduction study in the course of long-term treatment of obsessive-compulsive patients. *Psychopharmacology Bulletin, 26,* 211–214.

Pato, M. T., Pigott, T. A., Hill, J. L., Grover, G. N., Bernstein, S., & Murphy, D. L. (1991). Controlled comparison of buspirone and clomipramine in obsessive-compulsive disorder. *American Journal of Psychiatry, 148,* 127–129.

Pato, M. T., Zohar-Kaduch, R., Zohar, J., & Muphy, D. L. (1988). Return of symptoms after discontinuation of clomipramine in patients with obsessive compulsive disorder. *American Journal of Psychiatry, 145,* 1521–1525.

Perse, T. L., Greist, J. H., Jefferson, J. W., Rosenfeld, R., & Dar, R. (1987). Fluvoxamine treatment of obsessive-compulsive disorder. *American Journal of Psychiatry, 144,* 1543–1548.

Pigott, T. A., L'Heureux, F., Hill, J. L., Bihari, K., Bernstien, S. E., & Murphy, D. L. (1982). A double-blind study of adjuvant buspirone hydrochloride in clomipramine-treated patients. *Journal of Clinical Psychopharmacology, 12,* 11–18.

Pigott, T. A., L'Heureux, F., Rubenstein, C. S., Bernstein, S. E., Hill, J. L., & Murphy, D. L. (1992). A double-blind, placebo controlled study of trazodone in patients with obsessive-compulsive disorder. *Journal of Clinical Psychopharmacology, 12,* 156–162.

Pigott, T. A., L'Heureux, F., Rubenstein, C. S., Hill, J. L., & Murphy, D. L. (1992, May). *A controlled trial of clonazepam augmentation in OCD patients treated with clomipramine or fluoxetine.* American Psychiatry Association Annual Meeting, Washington, DC.

Pigott, T. A., Pato, M. T., Bernstein, S. E., Grover, G. N., Hill, J. L., Tolliver, T. J., et al. (1990). Controlled comparisons of clomipramine and fluoxetine in the treatment of obsessive-compulsive disorder. *Archives of General Psychiatry, 47,* 926–932.

Pigott, T. A., Pato, M. T., L'Heureux, F., Hill, J. L., Grover, G. N., Bernstein, S. E., et al. (1991). A controlled comparison of adjuvant lithium carbonate or thyroid hormone in clomipramine-treated patients with obsessive compulsive disorder. *Journal of Clinical Psychopharmacology, 11,* 242–248.

Pigott, T. A., & Seay, S. M. (1999). A review of the efficacy of selective serotonin reuptake inhibitors in obsessive-compulsive disorders. *Journal of Clinical Psychiatry, 60,* 101–106.

Pittenger, C., Krystal, J. H., & Coric, V. (2006). Glutamate-modulating drugs as novel pharmacotherapeutic agents in the treatment of obsessive-compulsive disorder. *NeuroRx: The Journal of the American Society for Experimental Neuro-Therapeutics, 3*(1), 69–81.

Pittenger, C., Kelmendi, B., Waslink, S., Bloch, M. H., & Coric, V. (2008). Riluzole augmentation in treatment-refractory

obsessive-compulsive disorder: a series of 13 cases with long-term follow-up. *Journal of Clinical Psychopharmacology, 28,* 363–367.

Rachman, S., Hodgson, R., & Marks, I. M. (1971). The treatment of chronic obsessive-compulsive neurosis. *Behaviour Research and Therapy, 9,* 237–247.

Rapoport, J. L. (1980). *The boy who couldn't stop washing.* New York: Dutton.

Rasmussen, S. A., Goodman, W. K., Greist, J. H., Jenike, M. A., Kozak, M. J., Liebowitz, M., et al. (in press). Fluvoxamine in the treatment of obsessive compulsive disorder: A multicenter, double-blind placebo-controlled study in outpatients. *American Journal of Psychiatry.*

Ravizza, L., Barzega, G., Bellino, S., Bogetto, F., & Maina, G. (1996). Drug treatment of obsessive-compulsive disorder (OCD): Long-term trial with clomipramine and selective serotonin reuptake inhibitors (SSRIs). *Psychopharmacology Bulletin, 32,* 167–173.

Romano, S., Goodman, W., Tamura, R., & Gonzales, J. (2001). Long-term treatment of obsessive-compulsive disorder after an acute response: A comparison of fluoxetine versus placebo. *Journal of Clinical Psychopharmacology, 21,* 46–52.

Shapira, N. A., Ward, H. E., Mandoki, M., Murphy, T. K., Yang, M. C., Blier, P., et al. (2004). A double-blind, placebo-controlled trial of olanzapine addition in fluoxetine-refractory obsessive-compulsive disorder. *Biological Psychiatry, 55,* 553–555.

Soomro, G. M., Altman, D., Rajaqopal, S., & Oakley-Browne, M. (2008). Selective serotonin reuptake inhibitors (SSRIs) versus placebo for obsessive-compulsive disorder (OCD). *Cochrane Database Systematic Review, 23,* CD001765.

Stein, D. J., Andersen, E. W., Tonnoir, B., & Fineberg, N. (2007). Escitalopram in obsessive-compulsive disorder: a randomized, placebo-controlled, paroxetine-referenced, fixed-dose, 24-week study. *Current Medical Research Opinion, 23,* 701–711.

Thoren, P., Åsberg, M., Cronholm, B., Jornestedt, L., & Traskman, L. (1980). Clomipramine treatment of obsessive compulsive disorder: I. A controlled clinical trial. *Archives of General Psychiatry, 37,* 1281–1285.

Tollefson, G. D., Birkett, M., Koran, L., & Genduso, L. (1994). Continuation treatment of OCD: Double-blind and open-label experience with fluoxetine. *Journal of Clinical Psychiatry, 55*(10, Suppl.), 69–76.

Tollefson, G. D., Rampey, A. H. Jr., Potvin, J. H., Jenike, M. A., Rush, A. J., Dominguez, R. A., et al. (1994). A multicenter investigation of fixed-dose fluoxetine in the treatment of obsessive-compulsive disorder. *Archives of General Psychiatry, 51,* 559–567.

Vallejo, J., Olivares, J., Marcos, T., Bulbena, A., & Menchon, J. (1992). Clomipramine versus phenelzine in obsessive-compulsive disorder: A controlled trial. *British Journal of Psychiatry, 161,* 665–670.

Volavka, J., Neziroglu, F., & Yaryura-Tobias, J. A. (1985). Clomipramine and imipramine in obsessive-compulsive disorder. *Psychiatry Research, 14,* 83–91.

Vulink, N. C., Denys, D., Fluitman, S. B., Meinardi, J. C., & Westenberg, H. G. (2009). Quetiapine augments the effect of citalopram in on-refractory obsessive-compulsive disorder: a randomized, double-blind, placebo-controlled study of 76 patients. *Journal of Clinical Psychiatry, 70*(7), 1001–1008.

Wheadon, D. E., Bushnell, W. D., & Steiner, M. (1993, December). *A fixed dose comparison of 20, 40, or 60 mg of* paroxetine to placebo in the treatment of OCD. Paper presented at the annual meeting of the American College of Neuropsychopharmacology, Honolulu, HI.

Zahn, T. P., Insel, T. R., &Murphy, D. L. (1984). Psychophysiological changes during pharmacological treatment of patients with obsessive-compulsive disorder. *British Journal of Psychiatry, 145,* 39–44.

Zhao, J. P. (1991). A controlled study of clomipramine and amitriptyline for treating obsessive-compulsive disorder. *Chung Hua Shen Ching Shen Ko Tsa Chih, 24,* 68–70.

Zohar, J.,& Judge, R., (1996). Paroxetine versus clomipramine in the treatment of obsessive-compulsive disorder. *British Journal of Psychiatry, 169,* 468–474.

Other Biological Approaches to OCD

Nicole C. R. McLaughlin *and* Benjamin D. Greenberg

Abstract

Interest in psychiatric neurosurgery has waxed and waned since the 1930s. This chapter reviews the history of these methods, with a focus on OCD. This review of lesion procedures and deep brain stimulation includes neuropsychological and neuroimaging research in the context of putative neurocircuitry underlying symptoms and response to treatment. The chapter highlights how an abundance of caution is needed, as well as key issues in long-term management of patients so treated.

Keywords: obsessive compulsive disorder, deep brain stimulation, cingulotomy, capsulotomy, leucotomy, tractotomy, psychiatric neurosurgery

Introduction

Obsessive compulsive disorder (OCD) is the anxiety disorder with the highest percentage (50.6%) of serious cases (Dickel, et al., 2006). Over 20% to 30% of patients with OCD are not responsive to medication or psychological/behavioral therapies (Husted & Shapira, 2004; Jenike, 1998). After other avenues of treatment have been attempted, neurosurgery has been used as a treatment for obsessive compulsive disorder for a very small number with "intractable" OCD, estimated at less than 50 patients per year in the United States. Although neurosurgery for psychiatric disorders has been conducted for decades, current techniques have evolved past the initial, relatively primitive methods. Surgical interventions include lesion procedures, with ablative surgeries requiring craniotomy, and radiosurgery that allows stereotactic lesion placement without craniotomy. Although not completely clear, the pathophysiology of OCD appears to involve abnormal functioning in the medial and orbital-frontal-basal ganglia-thalamic circuits. Lesions and stimulation in the anterior limb of the internal capsule, the anterior cingulate, and/or the subcaudate region, all of which are involved in this circuit, seem to be useful in the treatment of refractory OCD.

Some of the ablative, or lesion techniques that will be discussed, though relatively novel, are, for the most part, considered safe in treating other disorders. For example, gamma knife surgery has been used to treat brain tumors, arteriovenous malformations, and trigeminal neuralgia for many years. The most common ablative procedures include anterior cingulotomy, limbic leucotomy, capsulotomy, thalamotomy, and subcaudate tractotomy.

Deep brain stimulation uses craniotomy to implant electrodes, but is non-ablative and allows for modulation of brain function. In addition, the FDA granted approval to use DBS in essential tremor (1997) and Parkinson's disease (2002/2003). Due to the increased interest in using neurosurgical interventions to treat refractory psychiatric disorders, the use has increased. In February 2009, the FDA approved DBS for a Humanitarian Device Exemption (HDE) for the treatment of OCD. However, with the recognition of the effectiveness of these treatments comes an increased need to exercise caution when utilizing these approaches.

A few other methods will be discussed, including vagus nerve stimulation, transcranial magnetic stimulation, and electroconvulsive therapy, though the research into these methodologies is minimal and outcomes are unclear.

Neurosurgical procedures are carried out only on carefully selected patients who have debilitating illness, methods are strictly regulated, and processes are meticulously followed. There are now centers throughout the world carrying out both systematic prospective studies and controlled trials on these interventions. Long-term data collection for all patients is critical in order for the burdens and benefits of these procedures to be adequately assessed. Data indicate that several ablative or chronic stimulation interventions hold promise for the treatment of otherwise intractable OCD. However, there may be different advantages and disadvantages for contemporary lesion procedures and deep brain stimulation. When using these relatively novel techniques, caution should be exercised with regard to patient selection, procedure implementation, and follow-up care. There is a very strong argument to be made for focusing their use at expert psychiatric neurosurgery centers.

History of Psychiatric Neurosurgery

Neurosurgical interventions for psychiatric disorders have a long history, marked by initial enthusiasm, followed by indiscriminate use, and belated attention to severe adverse effects. The first report of more modern neurosurgical treatment for psychiatric disorders was published in 1891 by Gottlieb Burckhardt, considered by some to be the father of modern psychosurgery. He described the first experimental topectomy (selective removal of parts of the cerebral cortex), with bilateral cortical excisions in aggressive and demented patients. Upon presentation, Burckhardt received a negative response from colleagues and ceased doing psychosurgery.

In 1910, Lodovicus Puusepp (Estonia) sectioned cortex between frontal and parietal lobes in manic depressive and epileptic patients; in 1937, he reported that patients who had later undergone frontal leucotomy had decreased aggressive symptoms (Feldman & Goodrich, 2001). As early as 1932, Ducoste, Marotti, Sciuti, and Ferdiere and Coulloudon (France, Italy) had injected blood from malarial patients, or the patients themselves, into the frontal lobes of psychiatric patients, reporting encouraging results (Valenstein, 1986). Ody (Geneva), and Bagdaser and Constantinesco (Bucharest) had performed frontal leucotomies on schizophrenic patients before 1937, but had not reported results (Valenstein, 1986).

In 1935, Fulton and Jacobsen presented their research on primates who had frontal cortical ablation. The primates showed reduction in "experimental neurosis" and were less fearful, but still able to perform complex tasks. Stimulated by this initial research, Moniz and Lima later extended some of this work to humans, and in 1935 performed a prefrontal leucotomy. This involved injection of alcohol into the centrum ovale of both frontal lobes, through trephine holes in the lateral surfaces of the skull. Moniz chose the centrum ovale for the initial lesions because of the high density of fibers connecting the anterior frontal cortex with the thalamus and other cortical areas, as well as the relative lack of major vasculature in this area. At the time, it appeared that the greatest benefit occurred in patients with predominantly affective symptoms. After these initial forays into surgical interventions, the pair started making lesions in the white matter of the frontal lobes. By the end of 1937, Moniz had coined the term *psychosurgery*, and in 1949, he won the Nobel Prize for his work.

The first surgery for psychiatric disorders completed in the United States was carried out by Freeman and Watts in 1936. Techniques ranged from a "minimal lobotomy" (minimal and anterior) for patients with "affective psychoneurotic disorders" to a "radical lobotomy" (large and posterior) for patients with schizophrenia or those requiring reoperations. Freeman and Watts soon began to realize that specific symptoms responded best to localized lesions, and in 1942, reported on 200 cases. The selection of specific lesion locations was, for many of these early neurosurgeons, influenced by the anatomic base of emotions suggested by Papez in 1937. The classic Papez circuit involves connections from the cingulate gyrus to the hippocampus, fornix, mammillary body, and anterior thalamic nucleus, then to the orbitofrontal cortex and septal nuclei. Current neurosurgical methods target frontolimbic connections (subcaudate tractotomy and capsulotomy), the Papez circuit (anterior cingulotomy) or both areas (limbic leucotomy).

In the 1940s, stereotactic neurosurgery (using internal landmarks) in humans was initiated by Spiegel and Wycis (Gildenberg, 2001); at the time, they reported that dorsomedial thalamotomies decreased OC symptoms. The anterior cingulate was suggested as a target in 1947 (Fodstad, Strandman, Karlsson, & West, 1982; Pribram & Fulton, 1954) because stimulation of the anterior cingulum in monkeys produced autonomic responses of a type associated with emotions, and lesions in this area resulted in less fearful and aggressive animals.

At its peak in the 1940s to early 1950s, lobotomy was being performed on approximately 5,000 patients per year in the United States alone. In 1954, chlorpromazine was launched; with the introduction of this pharmacological intervention, the use of surgical interventions was significantly reduced. Fierce opposition to psychiatric neurosurgery by subsets of the medical community continued, largely based upon the crude operations that had been carried out earlier in the century. In the early 1970s, legislation was passed in several states as a result of this concern. For example, Oregon required approval of a Psychosurgery Review Board, and California required a mandatory judicial review prior to surgery. From 1965 to 1975, two independent scientific teams conducted pilot studies evaluating four different neurosurgical procedures. In the 1970s, the National Commission for the Protection of Human Subjects of Biomedical and Behavioral Research (NCPHS) was convened, and was the first national body established examining bioethics policy. This commission contracted for an evaluation of psychiatric patients who had undergone psychosurgery, led by neuropsychologists Allan Mirsky and Maressa Orzack at Boston University; they also contracted to expand a study already started at the Massachusetts Institute of Technology, led by neuropsychologists Hans-Lukas Teuber and Suzanne Corkin, as well as neurologist Thomas Twitchell. Overall, it was concluded that "(1) more than half of the patients improved significantly following psychosurgery, although a few were worse and some unchanged, and (2) none of the patients experience significant neurological or psychological impairment attributable to the surgery." This was a primary reason was a ban on psychosurgery was not instituted (United States Department of Health, 1978). The report also offered guidelines for the ethical use, continued investigation, and regulation of psychiatric neurosurgery. A favorable report was issued, recommending continued research and the establishment of a national registry documenting techniques and outcomes of neurosurgical procedures for psychiatry, in order to assist the national Psychosurgery Advisory Board in making evaluations regarding the safety and efficacy of specific procedures (United States Department of Health, 1978). It was recommended that data be collected regarding the presenting symptoms and preoperative diagnosis, past medical and social history of the patients, and outcome, requiring that psychosurgery become a "reportable operation." Summary reports would be sent to Congress on a yearly basis. At this point, such a registry has not yet been established. However, leaders in the field have continually emphasized the need for caution, as described below. Media coverage has generally been favorable, and medical professionals have generally been in favor of referring patients for neurosurgical interventions in appropriate situations; a study in Britain indicated that over 75% of psychiatrists in general adult psychiatry would refer patients for a neurosurgical procedure (Snaith, Price, & Wright, 1984).

Scientific Context

Over the years, although there has been some theoretical basis for lesion or stimulation location, given the work of Fulton and Moniz among others, these surgical treatments were developed largely empirically. Psychiatric neurosurgery remains within the era of empirical psychiatry, since the pathophysiological processes involved in major neuropsychiatric disorders have yet to be fully elucidated by ongoing research. Initial studies have been concerned primarily with safety and efficacy, which remain crucial issues. However, research is also beginning to focus on neurophysiological mechanisms that may be involved in the responses to particular procedures.

Procedures and Practices

Neurosurgical interventions are not frequently used to treat any psychiatric disorder, including OCD. This is mainly due to the success of conventional behavioral and medication treatments, and worries about adverse effects following the neurosurgeries of the present, which are dramatically improved compared to those of the mid-twentieth century.

Current recommendations are similar to those developed by the NCPHS, which issued guidelines in its 1977 report for what was then called *psychosurgery*. Those recommendations included rigorous criteria for diagnostic accuracy, illness severity, documentation of an exhaustive array of failed treatments, and a stringent informed consent process. Notably, a very recent study from Belgium found that approximately 28% of patients presenting to a National Advisory Board for case evaluation over the last decade were deemed inappropriate for psychiatric neurosurgery. This was primarily due to apparently inaccurate diagnoses, or lack of sufficient conventional treatment trials before consideration of neurosurgery. Clearly, these and other considerations in patient selection remain crucial (Gabriels, Nuttin, & Cosyns, 2008).

The following procedures are typically followed by expert centers engaged in neurosurgical interventions for OCD. They emphasize a cautious and comprehensive approach to the assessment, treatment, and follow-up of patients. The 2002 OCD-DBS Collaborative Group (OCD-DBS Collaborative Group, 2002), and a 2006 paper by Fins et al. (Fins, Rezai, & Greenberg, 2006) make several key recommendations which are summarized below:

• There should be an ethics committee (e.g., Institutional Review Board [IRB]) with initial and ongoing oversight of the procedures (needed for either investigational use, or under Humanitarian Use approved by the U.S. Food and Drug Administration). In addition to an IRB, ongoing studies also typically have an external data safety monitoring board (DSMB).

• Prospective cases must meet criteria for severe intractable OCD. The severity threshold has varied, but patients must be judged to have "severe" or "extreme" illness. The FDA criterion for Humanitarian Use is a Yale-Brown Obsessive Compulsive Scale (Y-BOCS) severity score of 30 or more despite aggressive and ongoing conventional treatments. This kind of illness will be functionally debilitating.

• Treatment with exposure and ritual (or response) prevention (ERP), generally for 20 or more hours with an experienced therapist, is required. The assessment team should contact previous behavior therapists to ensure that real ERP was delivered, and if not completed, that therapy was interrupted due to marked intolerance of the procedures and not simply minimal to moderate discomfort.

• The patient must have undergone extensive prior treatment, including treatment with several serotonin transporter inhibiting antidepressants (SRIs; usually a trial of clomipramine is required, alone or carefully combined with a more selective SRI), and 2 augmenting agents, at maximally tolerated doses for at least 12 weeks.

• Psychiatric comorbidities should be assessed. OCD should be the primary disorder. These interventions are typically not carried out on individuals who are judged to be imminently or who have recently been suicidal. Bipolar disorder may be a contraindication, especially to DBS, as there is a potential for manic episodes post-surgery.

Patients must also be free of illicit substances. Patients who are of limited intellectual capability are also typically excluded, as there is a need to be able to understand the procedure and consent process, and to be able to actively participate in treatment; preoperative assessment should include an extensive neuropsychological battery, to be used both in ruling out intellectual limitation, and as a baseline measure for comparison of future cognitive skills.

• Medical conditions that increase neurosurgical risks are contraindications, as are patients over 65. Patients under the age of 18 years are also not optimal candidates. EEG and MRI, as well as specific laboratory tests (e.g., PT, INR) are typically included in the preoperative assessment.

• The patient *must* have access to postoperative care. Continued psychiatric and psychotherapeutic treatment is essential after these surgical treatments. In some cases, surgery may enhance the patient's ability to engage in ERP. This continued follow-up is especially important with patients who have had DBS, as they need to be carefully followed for an indefinite period of time. In addition, physicians need to be carefully trained in how to adjust stimulation parameters. Devices may also have to be surgically replaced, an expensive process not always covered by health insurance.

• Patient information is typically reviewed across more than one site, by all investigators and by the DSMB to ensure that all inclusion and exclusion criteria are met. Approval for surgery in our current collaborative National Institute of Mental Health (NIMH)-sponsored trial of DBS for OCD requires that patients be accepted as appropriate for surgery by an independent multidisciplinary group, which reviews each case in detail and typically asks for additional information from referring centers (Butler Hospital, Massachusetts General Hospital, Cleveland Clinic, University of Florida). In Britain and Belgium, a similar function is performed by National Multidisciplinary Boards.

• If independent review deems a patient appropriate, an extensive consent process follows. This process is actively assessed, at collaborating U.S. centers, by independent consent monitors. During this monitoring and throughout the evaluation process, prospective candidates should be assessed for their expectations of improvement after surgery and (in the case of DBS) ongoing stimulation. Patients might have unrealistic expectations of dramatic or rapid improvement in many if not all spheres of their lives after such dramatic interventions. Such expectations, if not elicited and addressed before surgery, might lead a patient to precipitously discontinue needed medications after surgery. Alternatively, a patient, even after marked improvement in their psychiatric illness severity, might commit suicide if his or her psychosocial functioning and quality of life does not improve to match expectations they had before surgery (Abelson, et al., 2005b).

Long-term data collection for all patients undergoing neurosurgery for psychiatric reasons is essential. All of these treatments are developing at an accelerating pace, but optimal targets, device design, and selection criteria have not yet been determined. Systematic data collection across institutions is needed to advance our knowledge of procedure outcomes. To this end, the creation of a national registry for reliable data collection of this information remains a very important goal. This was initially proposed by the National Commission in 1977, but never implemented. A recent statement suggested that such a registry include "1) patient clinical characteristics and past treatment history; 2) adverse events and neuropsychological testing results; 3) clinical outcome as assessed by standardized scales for symptom severity and functioning; 4) target measurements confirmed by postoperative computed tomography; and 5) detailed device settings (e.g., frequency, voltage, and active contact configuration)" (Goodman & Insel, 2009). All centers contemplating such work should, in our view, be willing to contribute such data to a registry once established.

Lesion Procedures/Treatment Outcome

Modern ablative, or lesion, procedures, including those discussed below, are carried out through the use of specialized targeting software and hardware, guided by MRI. Thus, the accuracy of lesion placement has increased, whether the procedure is an "open" procedure, with craniotomy, or "closed," using radiosurgical instruments without craniotomy. Postoperative improvement is typically measured in terms of improvement in OCD severity (typically with the Y-BOCS) and global improvement, by such instruments as the Clinical Global Improvement Scale (CGI), and the Global Assessment of Functioning (GAF). Earlier reports, done prior to the development of modern rating instruments, often used global measures like the Pippard

Postoperative Rating Scale. The majority of published reports have indicated that ratings of *improved* to *much improved* (often noted as a 35% improvement) are indicative of significant improvement. Long-term follow-up data indicate that lesion neurosurgery improves functioning and symptom severity in 40% to 70% of cases (Greenberg et al., 2003). Early indications suggest that effectiveness of ablation and DBS may be similar (Greenberg et al., 2008). However, more definitive conclusions as to relative efficacy will need to await results of controlled trials of DBS [clinicaltrials.gov] and a sham-controlled study of gamma ventral capsulotomy (Lopes et al., 2009). An issue to keep in mind, as this field develops, is that patients receiving lesion procedures versus DBS may not be fully comparable. For example, DBS requires very close and essentially indefinite follow-up, which in turn requires a degree of psychosocial stability and resources that other patients with intractable OCD may not possess.

Subcaudate Tractotomy

Overview. Subcaudate tractotomy was introduced in 1964 (Knight, 1965) as an outgrowth of previous research with restricted orbital undercutting. The intention of this procedure is to interrupt tracts between the orbitofrontal cortex (OFC) and subcortical limbic structures. Subcaudate tractotomy lesions are placed in the substantia innominata, which is ventral to the caudate nucleus. This area contains fiber tracts connecting nodes within ventral fronto-basal-thalamic circuitry, as well as neurons with similar connections to those of the ventral portions of the striatum and ventral globus pallidus. Originally, radioactive yttrium seeds were implanted along a medial to lateral trajectory within the target region. More recent studies have used stereotactically controlled radiofrequency ablation for OCD or depression (Kim, 2008), and a recent study proposed the use of frameless stereotactic surgery (Woerdeman, Willems, Noordmans, Berkelbach, van der Sprenkel, & van Rijen, 2006).

Clinical Outcome. Success rates reported in 1973 for over 650 cases of MDD, OCD, or anxiety were approximately 50% (Knight, 1973). Goktepe, Young, and Bridges (1975) reported significant improvement in 50% of OCD cases. In 1994, a large review of 342 patients (not just restricted to OCD) concluded that subcaudate tractotomy enables 40%–60% of patients to live normal or near normal lives, with a reduction in suicide rate to 1% (Bridges et al., 1994). Another, more recent, comprehensive review including 382 patients showed a 33% to 67% postoperative global improvement (Lopes et al., 2004).

Adverse Effects. There are minimal complications associated with subcaudate tractotomy. The most common complication is transient postoperative disorientation, likely due to postoperative edema (Knight, 1973). Long-term complications include seizure (1.6%–5%; Knight, 1973; Lopes et al., 2004). Fatigue and weight gain are also common (6% and 3%, respectively), and one death was reported due to neurosurgical complication (Lopes et al., 2004). According to a recent review, 5% of patients who received subcaudate tractotomy attempted suicide, and 1.3% completed suicide post-surgery (Lopes et al., 2004).

Anterior Cingulotomy

Overview. In 1947, this target was suggested by Fulton, as lesions in the anterior cingulum resulted in less fearful and aggressive monkeys. In 1948, Sir Hugh Cairns at Oxford performed the first bilateral anterior cingulectomy (Whitty, Duffield, Tov, & Cairns, 1952). The initial aim was to disrupt the Papez circuit at the margin of the cingulum bundle in the anterior cingulate cortex (Papez, 1995). In anterior cingulotomy, lesions are placed within the dorsal anterior cingulate, typically impinging on the cingulum bundle, likely reducing cortical mass and activity within the anterior cingulate cortex (ACC), modifying cingulostriatal projections, and disinhibiting the pregenual ACC. This may influence reciprocal connections between the ACC and other structures, including the OFC, amygdala, hippocampus, and posterior cingulate cortex (Rauch, 2003). Lesions were initially placed using air ventriculography, which allowed for stereotactic ablation through burr holes (Ballantine, Cassidy, Flanagan, & Marino, 1967), but since 1991, this method has largely been replaced by MRI-guided techniques. Ballantine and colleagues (Cosgrove & Ballantine, 1998; Martuza, Chiocca, Jenike, Giriunas, & Ballantine, 1990) developed a method in which thermistor electrodes lesion the cingulum (thermocoagulation). Anterior cingulotomy has been the most widely used neurosurgical method for the treatment of OCD in the United States.

Clinical Outcome. Jenike and colleagues (1991) estimated that between 1965 and 1986, 25% to 30% of patients benefited from cingulotomy, but that sample may have included patients who may have not had adequate pharmacological treatment or therapy. A more recent study with more stringent inclusion/exclusion guidelines indicated that 28% of patients met criteria for improvement (Baer et al., 1995). A comprehensive review has indicated 27% to 57% postoperative global improvement (Lopes et al., 2004). In one study with 44 patients, 32% met criteria for treatment response and 14% were partial responders. The mean improvement on the Y-BOCS at first (6-month) follow-up was 20.4%; at 32 months, improvement on the Y-BOCS was 28.7% (Dougherty et al., 2002). Another study showed a mean Y-BOCS improvement of 36% (Kim et al., 2003).

Adverse Effects. As with the other surgical procedures, complications are relatively minimal. Medication-responsive seizures are evident in 1%–9% of the treated patients, and hemiplegia has been apparent in 0.3%. Suicide has been estimated to occur in approximately 2% to 9% of patients (Ballantine, Bouckoms, Thomas, & Giriunas, 1987; Binder & Iskandar, 2000; Lopes et al., 2004). A comprehensive review showed headache in 1% of patients, transient dizziness in 2.7%, and urinary retention in 2.7% (Lopes et al., 2004). Out of over 1000 cingulotomies performed at Massachusetts General Hospital, there have been no deaths or infections, and two subdural hematomas (Greenberg, Dougherty, & Rauch, 2011).

Limbic Leucotomy

Overview. Limbic leucotomy, introduced in 1973 by Desmond Kelly and colleagues, essentially combined bilateral cingulotomy with subcaudate tractotomy; it was anticipated that this dual lesion technique would produce better functional results than either lesion alone (Kelly & Mitchell-Heggs, 1973; Kelly, et al., 1973). A ventromedial frontal lesion was targeted to interrupt frontolimbic connections, whereas the cingulum lesion was targeted to interrupt the Papez circuit. Limbic leucotomy usually involves the placement of three 6mm lesions in the posterior inferior medial quadrant of the frontal lobes, and two lesions in the cingulate gyrus bilaterally (Cosgrove, 2000).

Clinical Outcome. Early experience with this treatment showed clinical improvement in 87% of the lesioned patients at 6 weeks and 17 months, with 69% being symptom free or very much improved at 17 months (Kelly & Mitchell-Heggs, 1973). In 1993, Hay and colleagues noted a moderate to marked improvement in 38% of individuals with OCD treated with this procedure (Hay et al., 1993). A more recent study indicated that 36% to 50% of OCD and major depression patients were responders at a 26-month follow-up (Montoya et al., 2002), and another reported that 68.8% had a marked response, 18.9% had a possible response, and 12.6% did not improve or became worse (Cho, Lee, & Chen, 2008). A comprehensive review noted 61% to 69% postoperative global improvement (Lopes et al., 2004).

Adverse Effects. Short-term side effects include headache, confusion/delirium, temporary hallucinations, extrapyramidal signs, lethargy, perseveration, local scalp infection, and urinary incontinence, as well as short-term memory deficits (Cho et al., 2008; Greenberg, Dougherty, & Rauch, 2011; Lopes et al., 2004). Although many of these effects are temporary, it is not uncommon for confusion to last several days, and patients often have longer postsurgical hospital stays than is typical in either cingulotomy or subcaudate tractotomy alone (Montoya et al., 2002; Greenberg, Dougherty, & Rauch, 2011; Lopes et al., 2004). The most significant side effects are seizure (approximately 3%) and enduring lethargy (Greenberg, Dougherty, & Rauch, 2011; Lopes et al., 2004). According to a recent review, suicide attempts were made in 2.7% of individuals with OCD after limbic leucotomy, and 3.2% completed suicide (Lopes et al., 2004).

Anterior Capsulotomy

Overview. Anterior capsulotomy was first introduced by Talairach and colleagues, and was later further developed by Leksell and colleagues in Sweden. Portions of the anterior arm of the internal capsule are lesioned, and fibers connecting the dorsomedial thalamus to the prefrontal cortex and subgenual anterior cingulate are sectioned (Rauch, 2003). This is conducted either with thermolesion by radiofrequency, or stereotactic radiosurgery using a gamma knife. Gamma capsulotomy lesions are usually smaller than those induced with thermolesions, and remain within the ventral capsule and impinge on the adjacent ventral striatum; thus, the term *gamma ventral capsulotomy* is increasingly being used.

Clinical Outcome. Early research completed by Leksell in the 1950s indicated favorable responses in 50% of OCD patients who had undergone capsulotomy. Waziri (1990) reviewed 253 cases of anterior capsulotomy for OCD, and reported satisfactory outcomes in 67%. A recent review noted an overall 56% to 100% postoperative global improvement with capsulotomy (Lopes et al., 2004). Leksell, using thermocapsulotomy, reported a favorable response in 50% of individuals with OCD (Herner, 1961).

Research from China (thermolesions) has indicated that, 6 months post-surgery, 57% of patients became symptom free (as represented by a Y-BOCS decline of 80%–100%), 29% experienced improvement, and 14% experienced no significant improvement (Liu et al., 2008). Data from Sweden (using thermolesions and gamma knife) have shown a Y-BOCS decrease of 16 points (34 to 18) over 10 years in a sample of 25 patients who underwent the procedure in the 1980s and 1990s, with lasting improvement in 48% of patients and with no significant difference between procedures (Ruck et al., 2008). In a pilot prospective study, therapeutic response (35% improvement in Y-BOCS) has been noted in three of five OCD patients who underwent gamma ventral capsulotomy (Lopes et al., 2009), which has prompted a larger sham-controlled trial of this procedure. That ongoing work represents the first randomized controlled trial of a lesion procedure in psychiatry. The estimate of a 60% response rate after this gamma procedure is consistent with that in an ongoing open series of patients studied at Butler Hospital and Brown University (Noren et al., 2002).

Adverse Effects. Short-term side effects of thermocapsulotomy, in which the lesions are made immediately, include transient headache or incontinence, transient postoperative confusion, fatigue, and weight gain. With gamma knife capsulotomy, there is typically less discomfort and a swifter recovery because there is no need to open the skull, and the development of radiation-induced lesions is much more gradual. Previous reports have indicated that peak volume of necrotic lesions following gamma capsulotomy in other populations occurs at 6–9 months (Kihlstrom et al., 1997). There is also variability in eventual lesion size, which may not be completely consistent with the initial mapped lesions (i.e., lesions on MRI may be absent in a small subset of patients, or of lesser or greater extent than those initially targeted, due to idiosyncratic variation in tissue susceptibility to radiation). Radiosurgical edema, delayed in onset post-surgery, may require a longer period of time to resolve. In 1.6%– 3.6% of patients undergoing gamma knife surgery for arteriovenous malformations, delayed formation of cysts has been reported (Pan, Sheehan, Stroila, Steiner, & Steiner, 2005); the incidence of cyst formation after gamma ventral capsulotomy is unclear. In the research completed at Butler Hospital/Brown University, brain cysts developed after a long delay (3-5 years post radiosurgery) in three of a total of 55 patients after gamma ventral capsulotomy. Two patients were asymptomatic. In the third, neurological symptoms including headache, dizziness, and visual changes required surgical cyst drainage, on two occasions. All three cysts occurred after double-shot radiosurgery with a newer-generation gamma knife; the group is currently working to modify the ventral capsulotomy method to minimize the chance of cyst development going forward. Post-radiosurgical edema can be addressed through steroid treatment. Gamma knife capsulotomy may also cause small, asymptomatic caudate infarctions (Lopes et al., 2004) and possible exacerbation of mania. The latter, on clinical observation, appears to be manageable with mood stabilizer medications in patients who adhere to such treatment.

Neuromodulation
Deep Brain Stimulation
Overview. Although much earlier in development than ablative procedures, deep brain stimulation has been of interest for many decades; in 1948, Poole implanted an electrode in the caudate nucleus to treat depression and anorexia (Poole, 1954). Nearly a half-century later, Nuttin and colleagues reported on OCD cases treated with DBS on an anterior capsulotomy target (Nuttin, Cosyns, Demeulemeester, Gybels, & Meyerson, 1999). In this application of deep brain stimulation for OCD, electrodes are placed (via burr holes in the skull) into the anterior limb of the internal capsule and adjacent ventral striatum, and are connected to a pacemaker-like device. The electrodes typically deliver high-frequency stimulation to a defined brain target site. Lead placement is usually bilateral and is guided by imaging and targeting platforms. A neurostimulator is placed subdermally, for example in the upper chest wall, and is connected to the brain leads through wires under the skin. Neurostimulation can be independently adjusted in several important ways, including the number of active contacts on a lead, and via stimulation polarity, intensity, and frequency. Patients may opt for deep brain stimulation over lesion procedures because DBS may be considered reversible. For example, stimulation may be modified to optimize benefit, or changed or stopped to improve DBS-induced side effects. However, the procedure is not innocuous (potential risks are described below). More recently, several groups have been involved in DBS research for otherwise intractable OCD: Leuven/Antwerp, Butler Hospital/Brown University, Cleveland Clinic, Massachusetts General Hospital, and University of Florida.

Clinical Outcome. Patients treated with VC/VS DBS have shown decreased Y-BOCS scores along with improvement in GAF, with improvements in self-care, independent living, and work, school, and social functioning (Greenberg et al., 2008). Twenty-six participants showed a 35% or more improvement on the Y-BOCS in the initial group, with over 70% response rate in the second and third patient cohorts, potentially because of refinement of implantation site to a more posterior location (Greenberg et al., 2008).

Adverse Effects. Although DBS for OCD generally appears to be well-tolerated, complications have included asymptomatic hemorrhage, one instance of a single seizure, superficial infection, and hypomanic/manic symptoms. In addition, battery depletion may lead to worsened depression and OCD (Greenberg et al., 2006). Stimulation may cause transient sensorimotor effects, such as paresthesias, muscle contraction, dysarthria, and diplopia. Adverse effects have ranged from transient psychiatric symptom exacerbations (Greenberg et al., 2008) to permanent neurological sequelae (Mallet, et al., 2008) or, on longer-term follow-up, suicide in the context of psychosocial stress (Abelson, et al., 2005a). But, as is also the case for efficacy, only quite tentative conclusions about safety can be drawn given the data available.

Transcranial Magnetic Stimulation
Transcranial magnetic stimulation (TMS) creates a pulsed magnetic field over the scalp, causing electric current induction in the cortex of the brain that leads either to net stimulation or disruption of the neurons in the given brain region. The first TMS for OCD study was not actually a treatment trial, but used the technique as an anatomical probe of prefrontal regions that may be involved in OCD symptoms. Using an anatomical control (occipital cortex), there was a decrease in compulsive urges (but not obsessions) after repeated stimulation of the right lateral prefrontal cortex (Greenberg et al., 1997). With TMS, there appears to be a significant improvement in OCD, anxiety, and depression symptomology (Mantovani et al., 2006; Sachdev et al., 2001). However, studies (stimulating the dorsolateral prefrontal cortex (DLPFC)) have indicated that, after controlling for depression, there may not be a significant difference in OC symptoms between those receiving sham TMS and those who had already received rTMS (Alonso et al., 2001; Prasko et al., 2006; Sachdev, Loo, Mitchell, McFarquhar, & Malhi, 2007). One recent randomized controlled

study of rTMS over the right DLPFC showed no therapeutic effect on OC symptoms (Kang, Kim, Namkoong, Lee, & Kim, 2009). Adverse effects may include transient headache, localized scalp pain during session, facial nerve stimulation during session, feeling dizzy/faint, and weepiness (Mantovani et al., 2006).

Vagus Nerve Stimulation

The vagus nerve, the 10th cranial nerve, has reciprocal influences on the limbic system and higher cortical activity. Vagus cell bodies convey information centrally to the nucleus tractus solitarius that then project to the brain through three pathways: autonomic feedback loop, direct projections to the medullary reticular formation, and ascending projections to the forebrain. Ascending projections have connections to the locus coeruleus, parabrachial nucleus, thalamus, hypothalamus, amygdala, stria terminalis. Vagus nerve stimulation (VNS) uses an implanted stimulator that uses a bipolar pulse generator to send electrical impulses to the vagus nerve. VNS is FDA approved for partial-onset epilepsy and depression, but there is minimal information regarding the use of VNS in OCD. However, one study found that using VNS, at 3 and 6 months, 43% of treated patients met response criteria for the Y-BOCS (>25% reduction). Five of the seven treated patients remained in the study for two years, and showed some benefit, though not as robust a benefit as shown with DBS for OCD (George, 2008).

Electroconvulsive Therapy

Although electroconvulsive therapy has been used for many years to treat depression, there is little information regarding its potential use in treating OCD, though some groups have indicated that it may help OCD symptoms (Maletzky, McFarland, & Burt, 1994). There are a number of case reports in the literature (Mellman & Gorman, 1984; Strassnig, Riedel, & Muller, 2004), but many of the studied patients had comorbid depression that also improved (Casey & Davis, 1994). The current consensus appears to be that ECT for OCD is generally ineffective in treating primary OC symptoms, though it may improve OC symptoms that are secondary to depression.

Exercise

Preliminary research has indicated that exercise may lower symptoms of OCD (Brown, et al., 2007, Shannahoff-Khalsa, 1999; Shannahoff-Khalsa et al.,

1999). In one pilot study, 15 patients who had received pharmacotherapy and/or behavioral therapy but continued to have significant OCD symptoms completed a 12-week moderate intensity exercise program. There were reductions in OCD symptomology, as well as an increase in overall sense of well-being after the intervention, and reductions in OCD remained 6 months later. Another small study (N=14) examining yoga in participants with OCD, who were on stable pharmacotherapy, demonstrated a decrease of 38% on the Y-BOCS in the group who practiced yoga daily (as compared to a 14% decrease for a control group).

Surgical Procedures in the Context of OCD Brain Circuit Models

As techniques become more specific, researchers are beginning to develop more specific hypotheses regarding discrete neuroanatomic regions and their effects on cognition and behavior. Individuals with OCD most likely have dysfunction in frontal-subcortical circuitry, especially between the OFC/cingulate and the thalamus and/or basal ganglia (Graybiel & Rauch, 2000). OCD patients in a resting state have an increase in metabolic activity of the orbitofrontal circuit, cingulate, and caudate nucleus (Rauch, 2003). There is normalization of this activity after drug or behavioral therapy in responsive participants (Graybiel & Rauch, 2000). Neurosurgical approaches target one or more areas in these tracts.

Neuropsychological assessments are routinely conducted pre- and post-surgery. We think this is highly desirable, though is not universally done. Initially, these assessments were mainly conducted for safety purposes, because of the possibility that neurosurgical interventions may cause a decline in cognitive abilities. Although evaluations continue to be conducted to monitor safety, research has extended into the assessment of effects on neurocircuitry. Traditionally, assessments have examined all cognitive domains with neuropsychological tests commonly used in the clinical setting. Experimental tasks may be added to these batteries in an attempt to increase the sensitivity and specificity of these evaluations. Given the small number of expert centers throughout the world that carry out neurosurgical procedures for OCD, data regarding neuropsychological outcomes are limited.

Note that the same generic name of a procedure, e.g., "capsulotomy," may obscure large differences in lesion techniques, including rapidity of lesion formation (immediate for thermocapsulotomy versus delayed, as in gamma knife radiosurgery) and in ultimate lesion volume. Patients judged to have poor therapeutic outcomes might receive repeated procedures, raising the risk of adverse effects in multiple domains. Another issue to keep in mind is that data have primarily been reported on a group basis. Thus, declines on neuropsychological measures in individual cases might be obscured when data are reported by group. More recent reports are emphasized in the following information, as data collection and reporting is easier to interpret.

Overall Intelligence. Global measures of intellectual ability include the Wechsler scales. The majority of studies have indicated average intellectual abilities prior to surgery, with no significant change, and even a minor improvement in scores post-surgery. Early data indicated that treatment with cingulotomy caused no decline in cognition or emotional regulation, and that there may actually be minor improvement in Wechsler Quotient (IQ) scores (Corkin, 1979). Short- and long-term (2-year) follow-up of the patients who had undergone anterior cingulotomy showed no significant adverse cognitive effects, including in overall intelligence (Jung, et al., 2006). Other early research indicated that overall intelligence was not affected by leucotomy (Kelly & Mitchell-Heggs, 1973), with an improvement 6 weeks post-surgery in performance and full scale IQ, and improvements on the information, block design, and picture arrangement subtests of the Wechsler Adult Intelligence Scale (WAIS); however, only 16 of the 30 patients had "obsessional neurosis," and the other patients had various psychiatric disorders. A group in Spain has reported no decline in cognition (WAIS) after capsulotomy (Oliver, et al., 2003). Taub et al. (2009) reported slight improvement in intelligence compared to baseline in a small group (N=5) of patients one year post–gamma ventral capsulotomy. Preliminary case studies have not shown any change in cognitive functioning or personality after DBS (Aouizerate et al., 2004; Gabriels, Cosyns, Nuttin, Demeulemeester, & Gybels, 2003).

Attention/Executive Functioning. A large review indicated a potential decrease in concentration after subcaudate tractotomy and "mental slowness" after limbic leucotomy. Although not fully clear in the published literature, these appear to be statements of primarily clinical observations (Lopes et al., 2004). Transient attention problems have also been reported after cingulotomy, though these difficulties do not persist (Dougherty et al., 2002; Kim et al., 2003). Taub et al. (2009) reported improvement in 4 of 5 patients one year post–gamma ventral capsulotomy for sustained attention (Trails A), with a decline in divided attention for 3 of 5 patients (Trails B).

Executive functions refer to "higher order" cognitive abilities, such as planning, organization, abstraction, and set shifting. Most studies examining cognitive deficits in OCD indicate primary executive functioning deficits, consistent with frontal-subcortical dysfunction (Lawrence, et al., 2006; Penades, Catalan, Andres, Salamero, & Gasto, 2005; Purcell, Maruff, Kyrios, & Pantelis, 1998; Rao, Reddy, Kumar, Kandavel, & Chandrashekar, 2008; Savage et al., 1999). Initial follow-up (12 months) of patients who had undergone cingulotomy showed no significant cognitive dysfunction, with improvement in total errors and perseverative errors on a set shifting/concept formation task (Wisconsin Card Sorting Test / WCST; Kim et al., 2003). Long-term follow-up (24 months) of the same group showed no significant adverse cognitive effects; consistent with initial research, there was a decrease in total number of errors, perseverative errors, and perseverative responses on a set shifting/concept formation task (WCST). In addition, there was no change in phonemic fluency, or in rapidly retrieving and verbalizing words beginning with a certain letter (Jung et al., 2006). A group in Spain has reported no decline in cognition after capsulotomy, including on a test of executive functioning (TMT; Oliver et al., 2003). As compared to a control OCD group, OCD patients who had undergone capsulotomy did not show long-lasting impairments in neuropsychological performance; dysfunction involving the frontal lobes was evident in the immediate postoperative period, but this seemed to resolve with time (Nyman, Andreewitch, Lundback, & Mindus, 2001). In notable contrast, long-term results (approximately 10 years post-surgery) from a subset of these patients indicated decline in performance on the WCST in 6 of 7 patients, with more variable results for digit span (Ruck, et al., 2008). They also reported elevated ratings on an execution, apathy, and disinhibition scale (with no comparison to baseline). Other neuropsychological test scores (with no comparison to baseline; N=22–23) were generally in the average to borderline range (phonemic fluency, visual and verbal working memory). These patients in the Ruck et al. series typically received more than one procedure, and larger lesions than those used currently. The authors suggested that lesions with more medial and posterior extension, particularly in the right hemisphere, were more prone to these adverse effects.

Visuospatial Function. Research has variably implicated visuospatial dysfunction in OCD (Purcell, et al., 1998; van der Wee et al., 2003; van der Wee, et al., 2007). A recent review reported visuospatial impairments in patients undergoing limbic leucotomy (Lopes et al., 2004). A group in Spain has reported no decline in cognition after capsulotomy, including on a visuospatial task (Kohs' cubes; Oliver et al., 2003). There has been shown to be no change in visuospatial reasoning one year post–gamma ventral capsulotomy (Matrix Reasoning, Block Design; Taub et al., 2009).

Memory. Transient memory problems have been demonstrated post-cingulotomy, but typically do not persist (Dougherty et al., 2002; Kim et al., 2003). Initial (12-month) and long-term (24-month) follow-up of cingulotomy patients showed no significant adverse cognitive effects, including in nonverbal and verbal memory (Jung et al., 2006). One study mentioned that 24% of the participants who had undergone limbic leucotomy had difficulties with "short-term memory" but there were no testing results available (Montoya et al., 2002). A group in Spain has reported no decline in visual memory after capsulotomy (Oliver et al., 2003). One-year follow-up of patients who had undergone gamma ventral capsulotomy showed an improvement of story recall (Logical Memory) in 2 of 5 patients. Total words recalled on a word list task in this same group showed an improvement in 2 patients, decline in 1 patient, and no change in 2 of 5 patients (Taub et al., 2009).

Personality. A recent review indicated an increase in irritability after subcaudate tractotomy in 3% of patients, as well as apathy, aggressiveness, and impulsivity post-leucotomy (Lopes et al., 2004). Post-capsulotomy, individuals show higher monotony avoidance and lower guilt scores on personality testing (Mindus, 1991). Research has indicated that there is a decrease in neuroticism on the Eysenck Personality Inventory after either orbitomedial or cingulate lesions (Hay et al., 1993).

Neuroimaging

There are few neuroimaging studies in this population. Those that have been reported show changes in the neurocircuitry implicated in OCD. There was reduced volume in the caudate nucleus and posterior cingulate cortex 6–12 months following anterior cingulotomy (Rauch et al., 2000; Rauch, Makris, et al., 2001). The size of the lesion in the anterior cingulate appeared to be associated with volume reduction, primarily in the head of the caudate bilaterally. In contrast, volume on morphometric MRI was not reduced in the amygdala, thalamus, lenticular nuclei, or hippocampus. In terms of potential predictors of surgical effectiveness, patients who responded to cingulotomy (defined as a 35% reduction in Y-BOCS OCD severity plus a clinical global impression of *much* or *very much improved*) had higher metabolism (on FDG-PET) in the right posterior cingulate cortex before surgery (Rauch, Dougherty, et al., 2001).

Five to 12 months after subcaudate capsulotomy there was a reduction in volume bilaterally in the anterior limb of the internal capsule, head of the caudate, and thalamus (Taren, Curtis, & Gebarski, 1994). An increased volume of the third ventricle was also seen, reflecting thalamic/caudate atrophy. The result that some areas were distant to the lesion sites suggested an effect on neurocircuits as a whole. Another study reported that OCD patients with better postoperative outcome had lesions in a relatively specific territory of the right anterior limb of the internal capsule; those with poor postoperative outcomes had more anterior lesions (Lippitz et al., 1997). However, the Lippitz et al. study is limited by the fact that lesion locations were measured by an investigator who was not masked to outcomes.

In contrast to the volume reductions after lesion procedures that were made at once (using thermolytic techniques), a small pilot study (N=5) of gamma ventral capsulotomy, using voxel-based morphometry, found that gray matter increased after surgery in the right inferior frontal cortex (Brodmann area 47) when comparing all patients preoperatively and postoperatively (Cecconi et al., 2008). Other pilot studies have found decreased metabolism on FDG-PET in the anterior cingulate, orbitofrontal cortex, and caudate nucleus after bilateral capsulotomy, bringing metabolism to levels comparable with controls (Liu et al., 2008). Research has shown decreased PET-FDG metabolism in the frontal cortex after months of ventral capsule DBS (Nuttin et al., 2003). There is also activation of the OFC, anterior cingulate cortex, striatum, pallidum, and thalamus on perfusion PET during acute stimulation at the VC/VS site compared to sham and/or low frequency (5Hz) DBS (Rauch et al., 2006).

Conclusion and Future Directions

The initial forays into neurosurgery for psychiatric disorders were over a century ago. The mid twentieth century had the indiscriminate and frequently disastrous use of a crude freehand procedure, prefrontal lobotomy, in an era of otherwise pervasive therapeutic nihilism. Especially in the last decade, this area has been the focus of renewed interest and a more rigorous approach to research. The state of knowledge, however, remains quite incomplete. While the safety of the procedures in current use has improved very substantially, the potential for serious adverse effects remains for both lesion procedures and deep brain stimulation. We remain in the early stages of determining the degree of clinical effectiveness of these procedures, their associated burdens, and the mechanisms that may underlie their actions. An understanding of mechanisms of therapeutic benefit is not, however, a prerequisite for careful clinical use of the safest procedures at expert centers. There, the key questions are:

1) Do the procedures help some otherwise untreatable people?

2) Are their adverse effect profiles acceptable in the context of the probable benefit?

Improving neurosurgery for OCD will depend on a better understanding of the mediating mechanisms at the anatomical, pharmacological, and behavioral levels. In the realm of behavior, it will be important to further explore the strong clinical impressions that behavior therapy for OCD is facilitated by neurosurgery in this group of patients who, by definition, were not helped by rigorous behavioral approaches before surgery. Additional knowledge on all these levels, gained in continuing clinical and translational research, should enable us to determine the best candidates for these and other procedures in development. In our opinion, a registry of clinical and neurosurgical data for all patients receiving neurosurgery for psychiatric conditions will be central to progress in the decades ahead (Goodman & Insel, 2009).

Related Chapters

Chapter 2. Phenomenology and Epidemiology of Obsessive Compulsive Disorder

Chapter 7. Neuroanatomy of Obsessive Compulsive and Related Disorders

Chapter 8. Information Processing in Obsessive Compulsive Disorder and Related Problems

Chapter 11. Psychological Models of Obsessive Compulsive and Spectrum Disorders: From Psychoanalytic to Behavioral Conceptualizations

Chapter 12. Cognitive Approaches to Understanding Obsessive Compulsive and Related Disorders

Chapter 27. Future Research on Obsessive Compulsive and Spectrum Conditions

Further Reading

Greenberg, B. D., Gabriels, L. A., Malone, D. A., Jr., Rezai, A. R., Friehs, G. M., Okun, M. S., et al. (2008). Deep brain stimulation of the ventral internal capsule/ventral striatum for obsessive-compulsive disorder: worldwide experience. *Molecular Psychiatry*, 15(1), 64–79.

Greenberg, B. D., Rauch, S. L., & Haber, S. N. (2010). Invasive circuitry-based neurotherapeutics: stereotactic ablation and deep brain stimulation for OCD. *Neuropsychopharmacology*, 35(1), 317–36.

Lopes, A. C., de Mathis, M. E., Canteras, M. M., Salvajoli, J. V., Del Porto, J. A., & Miguel, E. C. (2004). [Update on neurosurgical treatment for obsessive compulsive disorder]. *Revista Brasileira de Psiquiatria*, 26(1), 62–66.

United States Department of Health, Education, and Welfare (1978). Determination of the Secretary regarding the recommendations on psychosurgery of the National Commission for the Protection of Human Subjects of Biomedical and Behavioral Research.

Valenstein, E. S. (1986). *Great and Desparate Cures: The Rise and Decline of Psychosurgery and Other Radical Treatments for Mental Illness*. New York: Basic Books, Inc.

References

Abelson, J. L., Curtis, G. C., Sagher, O., Albucher, R. C., Harrigan, M., Taylor, S. F., et al. (2005a). Deep brain stimulation for refractory obsessive-compulsive disorder. *Biological Psychiatry*, 57(5), 510–516.

Abelson, J. L., Curtis, G. C., Sagher, O., Albucher, R. C., Harrigan, M., Taylor, S. F., et al. (2005b). Deep brain stimulation for refractory obsessive-compulsive disorder. *Biological Psychiatry*, 57(5), 510–516.

Alonso, P., Pujol, J., Cardoner, N., Benlloch, L., Deus, J., Menchon, J. M., et al. (2001). Right prefrontal repetitive transcranial magnetic stimulation in obsessive-compulsive disorder: a double-blind, placebo-controlled study. *American Journal Psychiatry*, 158(7), 1143–1145.

Aouizerate, B., Guehl, D., Cuny, E., Rougier, A., Bioulac, B., Tignol, J., et al. (2004). Pathophysiology of obsessive-compulsive disorder: a necessary link between phenomenology, neuropsychology, imagery and physiology. *Progress in Neurobiology*, 72(3), 195–221.

Baer, L., Rauch, S. L., Ballantine, H. T., Jr., Martuza, R., Cosgrove, R., Cassem, E., et al. (1995). Cingulotomy for intractable obsessive-compulsive disorder. Prospective long-term follow-up of 18 patients. *Archives of General Psychiatry*, 52(5), 384–392.

Ballantine, H. T. Jr., Bouckoms, A. J., Thomas, E. K., & Giriunas, I. E. (1987). Treatment of psychiatric illness by stereotactic cingulotomy. *Biological Psychiatry*, 22(7), 807–819.

Ballantine, H. T. Jr., Cassidy, W. L., Flanagan, N. B., & Marino, R. Jr. (1967). Stereotaxic anterior cingulotomy for neuropsychiatric illness and intractable pain. *Journal of Neurosurgery*, 26(5), 488–495.

Binder, D. K., & Iskandar, B. J. (2000). Modern neurosurgery for psychiatric disorders. *Neurosurgery*, 47(1), 9–21.

Bridges, P. K., Bartlett, J. R., Hale, A. S., Poynton, A. M., Malizia, A. L., & Hodgkiss, A. D. (1994). Psychosurgery: stereotactic subcaudate tractomy. An indispensable treatment. *British Journal of Psychiatry*, 165(5), 599–611.

Brown, R. A., Abrantes, A. M., Strong, D. R., Mancebo, M. C., Menard, J., Rasmussen, S. A., et al. (2007). A pilot study of moderate-intensity aerobic exercise for obsessive compulsive disorder. *Journal of Nervous and Mental Disease, 195*(6), 514–520.

Casey, D. A., & Davis, M. H. (1994). Obsessive-compulsive disorder responsive to electroconvulsive therapy in an elderly woman. *Southern Medical Journal, 87*(8), 862–864.

Cecconi, J. P., Lopes, A. C., Duran, F. L., Santos, L. C., Hoexter, M. Q., Gentil, A. F., et al. (2008). Gamma ventral capsulotomy for treatment of resistant obsessive-compulsive disorder: a structural MRI pilot prospective study. *Neuroscience Letter, 447*(2–3), 138–142.

Cho, D. Y., Lee, W. Y., & Chen, C. C. (2008). Limbic leukotomy for intractable major affective disorders: a 7-year follow-up study using nine comprehensive psychiatric test evaluations. *Journal of Clinical Neuroscience, 15*(2), 138–142.

Corkin, S. (1979). Hidden-figures-test performance: lasting effects of unilateral penetrating head injury and transient effects of bilateral cingulotomy. *Neuropsychologia, 17*(6), 585–605.

Cosgrove, G. R. (2000). Surgery for psychiatric disorders. *CNS Spectrum, 5*(10), 43–52.

Cosgrove, G. R., & Ballantine, H. T. (1998). Cingulotomy in psychosurgery. In P. L. T. Gildenberg, R.R. (Ed.), *Textbook of stereotactic and functional neurosurgery.* (pp. 1965–1970). New York: McGraw-Hill.

Dickel, D. E., Veenstra-VanderWeele, J., Cox, N. J., Wu, X., Fischer, D. J., Van Etten-Lee, M., et al. (2006). Association testing of the positional and functional candidate gene SLC1A1/EAAC1 in early-onset obsessive-compulsive disorder. *Archives of General Psychiatry, 63*(7), 778–785.

Dougherty, D. D., Baer, L., Cosgrove, G. R., Cassem, E. H., Price, B. H., Nierenberg, A. A., et al. (2002). Prospective long-term follow-up of 44 patients who received cingulotomy for treatment-refractory obsessive-compulsive disorder. *American Journal Psychiatry, 159*(2), 269–275.

Feldman, R. P., & Goodrich, J. T. (2001). Psychosurgery: a historical overview. *Neurosurgery, 48*(3), 647–657.

Fins, J. J., Rezai, A. R., & Greenberg, B. D. (2006). Psychosurgery: avoiding an ethical redux while advancing a therapeutic future. *Neurosurgery, 59*(4), 713–716.

Fodstad, H., Strandman, E., Karlsson, B., & West, K. A. (1982). Treatment of chronic obsessive compulsive states with stereotactic anterior capsulotomy or cingulotomy. *Acta Neurochirurgica (Wien), 62*(1–2), 1–23.

Gabriels, L., Cosyns, P., Nuttin, B., Demeulemeester, H., & Gybels, J. (2003). Deep brain stimulation for treatment-refractory obsessive-compulsive disorder: psychopathological and neuropsychological outcome in three cases. *Acta Psychiatrica Scandanavica, 107*(4), 275–282.

Gabriels, L., Nuttin, B., & Cosyns, P. (2008). Applicants for stereotactic neurosurgery for psychiatric disorders: role of the Flemish advisory board. *Acta Psychiatrica Scandanavica, 117*(5), 381–389.

George, M. S. (2008). A pilot study of vagus nerve stimulation (VNS) for treatment-resistant anxiety disorders. *Brain Stimulation, 1,* 112–121.

Gildenberg, P. L. (2001). Spiegel and Wycis—the early years. *Stereotactic Functional Neurosurgery, 77*(1–4), 11–16.

Goktepe, E. O., Young, L. B., & Bridges, P. K. (1975). A further review of the results of sterotactic subcaudate tractotomy. *British Journal of Psychiatry, 126,* 270–280.

Goodman, W. K., & Insel, T. R. (2009). Deep brain stimulation in psychiatry: concentrating on the road ahead. *Biological Psychiatry, 65*(4), 263–266.

Graybiel, A. M., & Rauch, S. L. (2000). Toward a neurobiology of obsessive-compulsive disorder. *Neuron, 28*(2), 343–347.

Greenberg, B. D., Dougherty, D., & Rauch, S. L. (2011). Neurosurgical Treatments: Lesion Procedures and Deep Brain Stimulation. In B. J. Sadock, V.A. Sadock, & P. Ruiz (Eds.), *Kaplan & Sadock's Comprehensive Textbook of Psychiatry,* 9e (pp. 3314–3322). Baltimore, MD: Lippincott Williams & Wilkins.

Greenberg, B. D., Gabriels, L. A., Malone, D. A., Jr., Rezai, A. R., Friehs, G. M., Okun, M. S., et al. (2008). Deep brain stimulation of the ventral internal capsule/ventral striatum for obsessive-compulsive disorder: worldwide experience. *Molecular Psychiatry, 15*(1), 64–79.

Greenberg, B. D., George, M. S., Martin, J. D., Benjamin, J., Schlaepfer, T. E., Altemus, M., et al. (1997). Effect of prefrontal repetitive transcranial magnetic stimulation in obsessive-compulsive disorder: a preliminary study. *American Journal Psychiatry, 154*(6), 867–869.

Greenberg, B. D., Malone, D. A., Friehs, G. M., Rezai, A. R., Kubu, C. S., Malloy, P. F., et al. (2006). Three-year outcomes in deep brain stimulation for highly resistant obsessive-compulsive disorder. *Neuropsychopharmacology, 31*(11), 2384–2393.

Greenberg, B. D., Price, L. H., Rauch, S. L., Friehs, G., Noren, G., Malone, D., et al. (2003). Neurosurgery for intractable obsessive-compulsive disorder and depression: critical issues. *Neurosurgery of Clinical North America, 14*(2), 199–212.

Hay, P., Sachdev, P., Cumming, S., Smith, J. S., Lee, T., Kitchener, P., et al. (1993). Treatment of obsessive-compulsive disorder by psychosurgery. *Acta Psychiatrica Scandanavica, 87*(3), 197–207.

Herner, T. (1961). Treatment of mental disorders with frontal stereotaxic thermal lesions: a follow-up study of 116 cases. *Acta Psychiatrica Neurologica Scandanavica 36,* 1–140.

Husted, D. S., & Shapira, N. A. (2004). A review of the treatment for refractory obsessive-compulsive disorder: from medicine to deep brain stimulation. *CNS Spectrum, 9*(11), 833–847.

Jenike, M. A. (1998). Neurosurgical treatment of obsessive-compulsive disorder. *British Journal of Psychiatry, Supplement* (35), 79–90.

Jenike, M. A., Baer, L., Ballantine, T., Martuza, R. L., Tynes, S., Giriunas, I., et al. (1991). Cingulotomy for refractory obsessive-compulsive disorder. A long-term follow-up of 33 patients. *Archives of General Psychiatry, 48*(6), 548–555.

Jung, H. H., Kim, C. H., Chang, J. H., Park, Y. G., Chung, S. S., & Chang, J. W. (2006). Bilateral anterior cingulotomy for refractory obsessive-compulsive disorder: Long-term follow-up results. *Stereotactic Functional Neurosurgery, 84*(4), 184–189.

Kang, J. I., Kim, C. H., Namkoong, K., Lee, C. I., & Kim, S. J. (2009). A randomized controlled study of sequentially applied repetitive transcranial magnetic stimulation in obsessive-compulsive disorder. *Journal of Clinical Psychiatry, 70*(12), 1645–1651.

Kelly, D., & Mitchell-Heggs, N. (1973). Stereotactic limbic leucotomy—a follow-up study of thirty patients. *Postgraduate Medical Journal, 49*(578), 865–882.

Kelly, D., Richardson, A., Mitchell-Heggs, N., Greenup, J., Chen, C., & Hafner, R. J. (1973). Stereotactic limbic leucotomy: a preliminary report on forty patients. *British Journal of Psychiatry, 123*(573), 141–148.

Kihlstrom, L., Hindmarsh, T., Lax, I., Lippitz, B., Mindus, P., & Lindquist, C. (1997). Radiosurgical lesions in the normal human brain 17 years after gamma knife capsulotomy. *Neurosurgery, 41*(2), 396–401.

Kim, C. H., Chang, J. W., Koo, M. S., Kim, J. W., Suh, H. S., Park, I. H., et al. (2003). Anterior cingulotomy for refractory obsessive-compulsive disorder. *Acta Psychiatrica Scandanavica, 107*(4), 283–290.

Kim, M. C. L. T. (2008). Stereotactic lesioning for mental illness. *Acta Neurochirurgica Supplementum, 101*, 39–43.

Knight, G. (1965). Stereotactic Tractotomy In The Surgical Treatment Of Mental Illness. *Journal of Neurological and Neurosurgical Psychiatry, 28*, 304–310.

Knight, G. (1973). Further observations from an experience of 660 cases of stereotactic tractotomy. *Postgraduate Medical Journal, 49*(578), 845–854.

Lawrence, N. S., Wooderson, S., Mataix-Cols, D., David, R., Speckens, A., & Phillips, M. L. (2006). Decision making and set shifting impairments are associated with distinct symptom dimensions in obsessive-compulsive disorder. *Neuropsychology, 20*(4), 409–419.

Lippitz, B., Mindus, P., Meyerson, B.A., Kihlstrom, L., Lindquist, C. (1997). Obsessive compulsive disorder and the right hemisphere: topographic analysis of lesions after anterior capsulotomy performed with thermocoagulation. *Acta Neurochir (Wien), 68*, 61–63.

Liu, K., Zhang, H., Liu, C., Guan, Y., Lang, L., Cheng, Y., et al. (2008). Stereotactic treatment of refractory obsessive compulsive disorder by bilateral capsulotomy with 3 years follow-up. *Journal of Clinical Neuroscience, 15*(6), 622–629.

Lopes, A. C., de Mathis, M. E., Canteras, M. M., Salvajoli, J. V., Del Porto, J. A., & Miguel, E. C. (2004). [Update on neurosurgical treatment for obsessive compulsive disorder]. *Revista Brasileira Psiquiatria, 26*(1), 62–66.

Lopes, A. C., Greenberg, B. D., Noren, G., Canteras, M. M., Busatto, G. F., de Mathis, M. E., et al. (2009). Treatment of resistant obsessive-compulsive disorder with ventral capsular/ventral striatal gamma capsulotomy: a pilot prospective study. *Journal of Neuropsychiatry Clinical Neuroscience, 21*(4), 381–392.

Maletzky, B., McFarland, B., & Burt, A. (1994). Refractory obsessive compulsive disorder and ECT. *Convulsive Therapy, 10*(1), 34–42.

Mallet, L., Polosan, M., Jaafari, N., Baup, N., Welter, M. L., Fontaine, D., et al. (2008). Subthalamic nucleus stimulation in severe obsessive-compulsive disorder. *New England Journal of Medicine, 359*(20), 2121–2134.

Mantovani, A., Lisanby, S. H., Pieraccini, F., Ulivelli, M., Castrogiovanni, P., & Rossi, S. (2006). Repetitive transcranial magnetic stimulation (rTMS) in the treatment of obsessive-compulsive disorder (OCD) and Tourette's syndrome (TS). *International Journal of Neuropsychopharmacology, 9*(1), 95–100.

Martuza, R. L., Chiocca, E. A., Jenike, M. A., Giriunas, I. E., & Ballantine, H. T. (1990). Stereotactic radiofrequency thermal cingulotomy for obsessive compulsive disorder. *Journal of Neuropsychiatry Clinical Neuroscience, 2*(3), 331–336.

Mellman, L. A., & Gorman, J. M. (1984). Successful treatment of obsessive-compulsive disorder with ECT. *American Journal Psychiatry, 141*(4), 596–597.

Mindus, P., Nyman, H. (1991). Normalization of personality characteristics in patients with incapacitating anxiety disorders after capsulotomy. *Acta Psychiatrica Scandanavica, 83*(4), 283–291.

Montoya, A., Weiss, A. P., Price, B. H., Cassem, E. H., Dougherty, D. D., Nierenberg, A. A., et al. (2002). Magnetic resonance imaging-guided stereotactic limbic leukotomy for treatment of intractable psychiatric disease. *Neurosurgery, 50*(5), 1043–1049; discussion 1049–1052.

Noren, G., Lindquist, C., Rasmussen, S. A., Greenberg, B. D., Friehs, G., Chougule, P. B., et al. (2002). Gamma Knife capsulotomy for obsessive-compulsive disorder [abstract]. *Journal of Neurosurgery, 96*(2), 414–415.

Nuttin, B., Cosyns, P., Demeulemeester, H., Gybels, J., & Meyerson, B. (1999). Electrical stimulation in anterior limbs of internal capsules in patients with obsessive-compulsive disorder. *Lancet, 354*(9189), 1526.

Nuttin, B. J., Gabriels, L. A., Cosyns, P. R., Meyerson, B. A., Andreewitch, S., Sunaert, S. G., et al. (2003). Long-term electrical capsular stimulation in patients with obsessive-compulsive disorder. *Neurosurgery, 52*(6), 1263–1272.

Nyman, H., Andreewitch, S., Lundback, E., & Mindus, P. (2001). Executive and cognitive functions in patients with extreme obsessive-compulsive disorder treated by capsulotomy. *Applied Neuropsychology, 8*(2), 91–98.

OCD-DBS Collaborative Group. (2002). Deep brain stimulation for psychiatric disorders. *Neurosurgery, 51*(2), 519.

Oliver, B., Gascon, J., Aparicio, A., Ayats, E., Rodriguez, R., Maestro De Leon, J. L., et al. (2003). Bilateral anterior capsulotomy for refractory obsessive-compulsive disorders. *Stereotactic Functional Neurosurgery, 81*(1–4), 90–95.

Pan, H. C., Sheehan, J., Stroila, M., Steiner, M., & Steiner, L. (2005). Late cyst formation following gamma knife surgery of arteriovenous malformations. *Journal of Neurosurgery, 102* Suppl, 124–127.

Papez, J. W. (1995). A proposed mechanism of emotion. 1937. *Journal of Neuropsychiatry Clinical Neuroscience, 7*(1), 103–112.

Penades, R., Catalan, R., Andres, S., Salamero, M., & Gasto, C. (2005). Executive function and nonverbal memory in obsessive-compulsive disorder. *Psychiatry Research, 133*(1), 81–90.

Poole, J. L. (1954). Psychosurgery of older people. *Journal of the Geriatric Association, 2*, 456–465.

Prasko, J., Paskova, B., Zalesky, R., Novak, T., Kopecek, M., Bares, M., et al. (2006). The effect of repetitive transcranial magnetic stimulation (rTMS) on symptoms in obsessive compulsive disorder. A randomized, double blind, sham controlled study. *Neurology and Endocrinology Letters, 27*(3), 327–332.

Pribram, K. H., & Fulton, J. F. (1954). An experimental critique of the effects of anterior cingulate ablations in monkey. *Brain, 77*(1), 34–44.

Purcell, R., Maruff, P., Kyrios, M., & Pantelis, C. (1998). Cognitive deficits in obsessive-compulsive disorder on tests of frontal-striatal function. *Biological Psychiatry, 43*(5), 348–357.

Rao, N. P., Reddy, Y. C., Kumar, K. J., Kandavel, T., & Chandrashekar, C. R. (2008). Are neuropsychological deficits trait markers in OCD? Progress in *Neuropsychopharmacology and Biological Psychiatry, 32*(6), 1574–1579.

Rauch, S. L. (2003). Neuroimaging and neurocircuitry models pertaining to the neurosurgical treatment of psychiatric disorders. *Neurosurgery in Clinical North America, 14*(2), 213–223, vii–viii.

Rauch, S. L., Dougherty, D. D., Cosgrove, G. R., Cassem, E. H., Alpert, N. M., Price, B. H., et al. (2001). Cerebral metabolic correlates as potential predictors of response to anterior cingulotomy for obsessive compulsive disorder. *Biological Psychiatry, 50*(9), 659–667.

Rauch, S. L., Dougherty, D. D., Malone, D., Rezai, A., Friehs, G., Fischman, A. J., et al. (2006). A functional neuroimaging investigation of deep brain stimulation in patients with obsessive-compulsive disorder. *Journal of Neurosurgery, 104*(4), 558–565.

Rauch, S. L., Kim, H., Makris, N., Cosgrove, G. R., Cassem, E. H., Savage, C. R., et al. (2000). Volume reduction in the caudate nucleus following stereotactic placement of lesions in the anterior cingulate cortex in humans: a morphometric magnetic resonance imaging study. *Journal of Neurosurgery, 93*(6), 1019–1025.

Rauch, S. L., Makris, N., Cosgrove, G. R., Kim, H., Cassem, E. H., Price, B. H., et al. (2001). A magnetic resonance imaging study of regional cortical volumes following stereotactic anterior cingulotomy. *CNS Spectrum, 6*(3), 214–222.

Ruck, C., Karlsson, A., Steele, J. D., Edman, G., Meyerson, B. A., Ericson, K., et al. (2008). Capsulotomy for obsessive-compulsive disorder: long-term follow-up of 25 patients. *Archives of General Psychiatry, 65*(8), 914–921.

Sachdev, P. S., Loo, C. K., Mitchell, P. B., McFarquhar, T. F., & Malhi, G. S. (2007). Repetitive transcranial magnetic stimulation for the treatment of obsessive compulsive disorder: a double-blind controlled investigation. *Psychological Medicine, 37*(11), 1645–1649.

Sachdev, P. S., McBride, R., Loo, C. K., Mitchell, P. B., Malhi, G. S., & Croker, V. M. (2001). Right versus left prefrontal transcranial magnetic stimulation for obsessive-compulsive disorder: a preliminary investigation. *Journal of Clinical Psychiatry, 62*(12), 981–984.

Savage, C. R., Baer, L., Keuthen, N. J., Brown, H. D., Rauch, S. L., & Jenike, M. A. (1999). Organizational strategies mediate nonverbal memory impairment in obsessive-compulsive disorder. *Biological Psychiatry, 45*(7), 905–916.

Shannahoff-Khalsa, D. S., Ray, L. E., Levine, S., Gallen, C. C., Schwartz, B. J., & Sidorowich, J. J. (1999). Randomized controlled trial of yogic meditation techniques for patients with obsessive-compulsive disorder. *CNS Spectrum, 4*(12), 34–47.

Snaith, R. P., Price, D. J., & Wright, J. F. (1984). Psychiatrists' attitudes to psychosurgery: Proposals for the organization of a psychosurgical service in Yorkshire. *British Journal of Psychiatry, 144*, 293–297.

Strassnig, M., Riedel, M., & Muller, N. (2004). Electroconvulsive therapy in a patient with Tourette's syndrome and co-morbid Obsessive Compulsive Disorder. *World Journal of Biological Psychiatry, 5*(3), 164–166.

Taren, J. A., Curtis, G. C., & Gebarski, S. S. (1994). Late local and remote structural changes after capsulotomy for obsessive compulsive disorder. *Stereotactic Functional Neurosurgery, 63*(1–4), 1–6.

Taub, A., Lopes, A. C., Fuentes, D., D'Alcante, C. C., de Mathis, M. E., Canteras, M. M., et al. (2009). Neuropsychological outcome of ventral capsular/ventral striatal gamma capsulotomy for refractory obsessive-compulsive disorder: a pilot study. *Journal of Neuropsychiatry Clinical Neuroscience, 21*(4), 393–397.

United States Department of Health, Education, and Welfare (1978). Determination of the Secretary regarding the recommendations on psychosurgery of the National Commission for the Protection of Human Subjects of Biomedical and Behavioral Research.

Valenstein, E. S. (1986). *Great and desparate cures: The rise and decline of psychosurgery and other radical treatments for mental illness.* New York: Basic Books, Inc.

van der Wee, N. J., Ramsey, N. F., Jansma, J. M., Denys, D. A., van Megen, H. J., Westenberg, H. M., et al. (2003). Spatial working memory deficits in obsessive compulsive disorder are associated with excessive engagement of the medial frontal cortex. *Neuroimage, 20*(4), 2271–2280.

van der Wee, N. J., Ramsey, N. F., van Megen, H. J., Denys, D., Westenberg, H. G., & Kahn, R. S. (2007). Spatial working memory in obsessive-compulsive disorder improves with clinical response: A functional MRI study. *European Neuropsychopharmacology, 17*(1), 16–23.

Waziri, R. (1990). Psychosurgery for anxiety and obsessive-compulsive disorders. In R. Noyes, M. Roth, & G. Burrows (Eds.), *Handbook of Anxiety: The treatment of anxiety.* (pp. 519–535) Amsterdam: Elsevier.

Whitty, C. W., Duffield, J. E., Tov, P. M., & Cairns, H. (1952). Anterior cingulectomy in the treatment of mental disease. *Lancet, 1*(6706), 475–481.

Woerdeman, P. A., Willems, P. W., Noordmans, H. J., Berkelbach van der Sprenkel, J. W., & van Rijen, P. C. (2006). Frameless stereotactic subcaudate tractotomy for intractable obsessive-compulsive disorder. *Acta Neurochir (Wien), 148*(6), 633–637; discussion 637.

Exposure-Based Treatment for Obsessive Compulsive Disorder

Jonathan S. Abramowitz, Steven Taylor, *and* Dean McKay

Abstract

Exposure and response prevention (ERP) is one of the oldest and most effective treatments for obsessive compulsive disorder. The present chapter describes the empirical foundations, development, delivery, and latest research on ERP. Commonly used methods and procedural variants of ERP are described, along with findings concerning the underlying mechanisms of action. The efficacy of ERP in relation to other treatments is discussed, in addition to research on the long-term effects of ERP and its effects in non-research settings. Pretreatment predictors of the outcome of treatments using ERP are also considered. Efforts to improve treatment outcome are discussed, including research into the benefits of combining ERP with other psychosocial interventions such as cognitive therapy, or with particular medications. The chapter concludes by considering important future research directions for improving the outcome of treatment packages that include ERP.

Keywords: cognitive therapy, D-cycloserine, emotional processing, exposure and response prevention, fear extinction, obsessive compulsive disorder, serotonin reuptake inhibitors.

Introduction

Obsessive compulsive disorder (OCD) involves excessive fear and anxiety that the person tries to control or remove by using strategies that paradoxically maintain the fear and anxiety. The anxiety in OCD is triggered by *obsessions*; that is, recurrent, unwanted, and seemingly bizarre thoughts, impulses, or doubts (e.g., the thought that one might have struck a pedestrian with an automobile). The anxiety-reduction strategies are typically repetitive (compulsive) behavioral or mental *rituals* (e.g., constantly checking the rearview mirror for injured persons). Obsessional fears tend to concern issues related to uncertainty about personal safety or the safety of others, and can take various forms and be concerned with numerous themes (e.g., contamination, violence, religion). Rituals are deliberately performed to reduce this uncertainty. The chapters in Part 1 of this volume address the heterogeneity of OCD.

Although many OCD sufferers recognize (at least at some point during the course of their disorder) that their obsessional fears and rituals are senseless and excessive, others strongly believe that their rituals serve to prevent the occurrence of disastrous consequences; that is, they have "poor insight" (Foa et al., 1995). The patient's degree of insight can vary over time, as well as across symptom categories. For example, one patient evaluated in our clinic realized that her fears of being contaminated by mercury if she changed a fluorescent light bulb were unrealistic (although she avoided fluorescent bulbs *just to be on the safe side*), yet she was strongly convinced that if she didn't wash her hands after handling pieces of mail sent by her father with hepatitis, she would develop this disease as well.

The lifetime prevalence rate of OCD in adults is two to three percent (American Psychiatric Association, 2000). Although symptoms typically wax and wane as a function of general life stress, a chronic and deteriorating course is the norm if adequate treatment is not sought. Fortunately, there are effective psychological treatments for OCD that have been developed from empirical research on the nature of this problem. The best studied treatment involves two procedures known as exposure and response prevention (ERP). The aim of the present chapter is to provide an overview of the development and delivery of this therapy, and to review the latest treatment-related research.

History of Exposure-Based Treatments for OCD

Prior to the 1960s, treatment for OCD consisted largely of supportive therapy, or psychodynamic psychotherapy derived from psychoanalytic ideas of unconscious motivation. The general consensus of clinicians of that time was that OCD was an unmanageable condition with a very poor prognosis, with some suggesting no treatment at all, as the interventions of the time only worsened the disorder (Kringlen, 1965). This characterization shows with clarity the degree of confidence (or perhaps the lack thereof) clinicians had in psychodynamic treatments for OCD. Indeed, the available anecdotal reports suggest that the effects of the psychodynamic approach were neither robust nor durable. The few reports that included outcome data suggested that psychodynamic approaches worsened the condition (Christensen, et al., 1987).

By the last quarter of the twentieth century, however, the prognostic picture for OCD had improved dramatically. This was due in large part to the work of Victor Meyer (1966), and other behaviorally oriented clinicians and researchers, who adapted animal laboratory research on fear reduction, conducted in the first half of the century for treating human anxiety problems. From this early experimental work, the behaviorists carefully derived behaviorally-based therapy for OCD. We will next discuss this historical event in some detail, as it represents a model for the derivation of a treatment from existing experimental findings.

Early Laboratory Research

The work of Richard Solomon and his colleagues (Solomon, Kamin, & Wynne, 1953) provided an elegant, yet often overlooked animal behavior model of what we now refer to as OCD. This model of compulsive behavior, and its reduction through behavioral methods, is probably the closest theoretical and practical antecedent to contemporary exposure-based therapy for OCD. Solomon et al. worked with dogs in shuttle boxes (small rooms divided in two by a hurdle over which the animal could jump). Each half of the shuttle box was separately furnished with an electric floor grating, which could be independently electrified to give the dog an electric shock. In addition, there was a flickering light that served as a conditioned stimulus. The procedure for producing a compulsive, ritual-like behavior was to pair the flickering light with an electric shock (the shock occurred 10 seconds after the light was turned on). The dog soon learned to jump into the other compartment of the shuttle box, which was not electrified, once he had received the shock. After several trials, the dog learned to successfully avoid the shock by jumping to the non-electrified compartment in response to the flickering light (i.e., within 10 seconds). In other words, the experimenter had produced a conditioned response to the light; namely, jumping from one compartment of the box to the other.

Once this conditioned response was established, the electricity was disconnected and the dog never received another shock. Nevertheless, the animal continued to jump across the hurdle each time the conditioned stimulus (i.e., the light) was turned on, as if shock was imminent. This continued for hundreds (and in some cases, thousands) of trials, despite no actual risk of shock. Apparently, the dog had acquired an obsessive compulsive habit—jumping across the hurdle—that was maintained by negative reinforcement (i.e., avoidance of pain and emotional distress). This serves as an animal analogue to human OCD, where compulsive behavior is triggered by fear that is associated with situations or stimuli such as toilets, floors, and obsessional thoughts (conditioned stimuli) that pose little or no objective risk of harm. This fear is reduced by avoidance and compulsive rituals (e.g., washing) which provide an escape from distress, and in doing so are negatively reinforced (i.e., they become habitual).

Solomon's work provided experimental evidence for Mowrer's (1947, 1960) two-factor theory of the acquisition and maintenance of fear and avoidance behavior, which was adapted by Dollard and Miller (1950) to explain OCD from a human learning perspective. The first stage of this model (acquisition) involves classical conditioning: a neutral stimulus or event (e.g., leaving the house) comes to evoke obsessional fear by being paired with another stimulus that, by its nature, provokes discomfort or anxiety (e.g., the idea that a house fire could occur while no one is home). In the second stage (maintenance), active avoidance (e.g., unplugging electrical appliances) or passive avoidance (e.g., not using any appliances) is used to reduce the anxiety or discomfort associated with the conditioned stimulus—in this case, leaving the house. The avoidance behavior is negatively reinforced because it provides an immediate reduction in anxiety (operant conditioning). Thus, the avoidance becomes habitual.

Dollard and Miller (1950) explained the development of compulsive rituals by arguing that many obsessional stimuli, such as using the bathroom and leaving the house, as well as intrusive obsessional thoughts themselves, cannot be easily avoided because of their ubiquitous nature. Thus, compulsive rituals (e.g., washing, checking, neutralizing unacceptable thoughts) develop as active avoidance strategies to cope with anxiety and restore a sense of safety. These rituals are therefore also maintained (negatively reinforced) because of their success in reducing obsessional fear. Although rituals provide a temporary respite from obsessional fear, they prevent the natural extinction of obsessional anxiety, thereby perpetuating the fear.

An Animal Model of Exposure-Based Therapy

Solomon and his colleagues also attempted to reduce the compulsive jumping behavior of their "obsessive compulsive" dogs using various techniques, the most effective of which involved a combination of procedures we would now call ERP. Specifically, the experimenter turned on the conditioned stimulus (light; an in vivo exposure technique), and increased the height of the hurdle in the shuttle box so that the dog was unable to jump (response prevention). When this was done, the dog immediately showed signs of a strong fear response: running around the chamber, jumping on the walls, defecating, urinating, and yelping. Gradually, however, this emotional reaction subsided until, finally, the dog displayed calmness without the slightest hint of distress. In behavioral terms, this experimental paradigm produced fear *extinction*. After several "extinction trials," the entire emotional response was extinguished, such that even when the light was turned on and the height of the hurdle was lowered, the dog did not attempt to jump.

Translational Research: From the Lab to the Clinic

During the 1960s and 1970s, behaviorally oriented researchers became interested in adapting similar treatment paradigms to human beings with OCD (for a review, see Rachman & Hodgson, 1980). Of course, no electric shocks were used, but the adaptation was as follows. OCD patients with hand-washing rituals, after providing informed consent, were seated at a table with a container of dirt and miscellaneous garbage. The experimenter, after placing his own hands in the mixture, asked the patient to do the same and explained that he or she would not be permitted to wash his or her hands for some length of time. When the patient began the procedure, an increase in anxiety, fear, and urges to wash his or her hands, was (of course) observed. This increase in distress was conceptualized as akin to the dogs' response once the light was turned on and hurdle had been increased in height, making jumping impossible. However, like the dogs, the patients eventually evidenced a substantial reduction in fear and urge to wash, thus demonstrating therapeutic extinction. This procedure was repeated on subsequent days, with behavioral theory predicting that after some time, extinction would be complete and the OCD symptoms would be reduced.

Victor Meyer (1966) was the first to apply this approach in the treatment of OCD, and articulated the rationale for doing so from a cognitive-behavioral perspective quite eloquently:

> Learning theories take into account the mediation of responses by goal expectancies, developed from previously reinforcing situations. When these expectations are not fulfilled, new expectancies may evolve, which, in turn, may mediate new behavior. Thus, if the obsessional is persuaded or forced to remain in feared situations and prevented from carrying out the rituals, he may discover that the feared consequences no longer take place. Such modification of expectations should result in the cessation of ritualistic behaviour (Meyer, 1966, p. 275).

Essentially, Meyer argued that when a patient with OCD confronts his or her obsessional fear, without performing rituals, estimates of the probability and costs of feared outcomes are able to be corrected, leading to the reduction of obsessive fear and ritualistic behavior. These procedures form the backbone of ERP.

In Meyer's (1966) initial report using ERP, his patients deliberately confronted, for two hours each day, obsessional situations and stimuli they usually avoided (e.g., floors, bathrooms), while also refraining from compulsive rituals (e.g., no washing or checking). Most of these individuals demonstrated at least partial improvement at posttreatment, and very few relapsed at follow-up (Meyer, Levy, & Schnurer, 1974). The interest generated by these initial findings led to additional studies in centers around the world, using more advanced methodology in both inpatient and outpatient settings. Research conducted in the United Kingdom (Hodgson, Rachman, & Marks, 1972), Holland (Emmelkamp & Kraanen, 1977), Greece (Rabavilas, Boulougouris, & Stefanis, 1976), and the United States (Foa & Goldstein, 1978), with hundreds of patients and many therapists, affirmed the beneficial effects and generalizability of exposure-based treatment for OCD. By the end of the 1980s, ERP was widely considered the psychosocial treatment of choice for obsessions and compulsions.

Contemporary Exposure-Based Treatment

Contemporary ERP entails therapist-guided, systematic, repeated, and prolonged exposure to situations that provoke obsessional fear. During these exposure trials the patient is encouraged to refrain from performing compulsive behaviors. This might take the form of repeated actual confrontation with feared low-risk situations (i.e., in vivo exposure), or take the form of imaginal confrontation with the feared disastrous consequences of confronting the low-risk situations (imaginal exposure). For example, an individual who fears getting herpes from touching bathroom doors, and that she will die if she encounters the color black, would practice touching bathroom doors and imagining being diagnosed with herpes, and wearing black clothes and imagining her own death.

Refraining from performing compulsive rituals (response prevention) is a vital component of treatment, because the performance of such rituals to reduce obsessional anxiety would prematurely discontinue exposure and rob the patient of learning that (a) the obsessional situation is not truly dangerous, and (b) anxiety subsides on its own, even if the ritual is not performed. Thus, successful ERP requires that the patient remain in the exposure situation until the obsessional distress decreases spontaneously, without attempting to reduce the distress by withdrawing from the situation, or by performing compulsive rituals or neutralizing strategies. For the individual described above, response prevention would entail refraining from handwashing after touching the bathroom door, and refraining from any rituals designed to prevent death from exposure to the color black.

At the start of exposure tasks (situational and imaginal), the patient typically experiences a rapid elevation in subjective anxiety and physiological arousal. In fact, patients are told that they must engage in the exposure task fully, until such experiences are evoked. During the course of an exposure session, however, the subjective distress (and associated physiological responding) subsides, even if the individual remains exposed to the feared stimulus. Furthermore, extinction occurs more rapidly with repeated exposure to the same stimulus over subsequent sessions, and the obsessional fear progressively abates.

Implementation of ERP

Contemporary ERP can be delivered in a number of ways. One highly successful format is a few hours of assessment and treatment planning, followed by 16 twice-weekly treatment sessions, lasting about 90–120 minutes each, spaced over about 8 weeks (Abramowitz, Foa, & Franklin, 2003). Generally, the therapist supervises the patient when conducting exposure during the therapy sessions, and assigns self-exposure practice to be completed by the patient between appointments. Depending on the patient's symptom presentation and the practicality of confronting actual feared situations, treatment sessions might involve varying amounts of actual and imaginal exposure practice. It might also involve leaving the therapist's office to confront stimuli for exposure (e.g., items in a grocery store).

A course of ERP typically begins with the assessment of (a) obsessional thoughts, ideas, impulses; (b) stimuli that trigger the obsessions; (c) rituals and avoidance behavior; and (d) the anticipated harmful consequences of confronting feared situations without performing rituals. Before actual treatment commences, the therapist uses psychoeducational techniques to socialize the patient to a psychological model of OCD that is based on the principles of learning and emotion (e.g., Salkovskis, 1996). The patient is also given a clear rationale for how ERP is expected to be helpful in reducing OCD. Conveying this information to the patient clearly and effectively is a critical step in therapy, because it helps the patient develop the motivation to endure the distress that typically accompanies carrying out in vivo and imaginal exposure exercises. A helpful rationale includes information about how ERP involves the temporary provocation and eventual reduction of distress during prolonged exposure. Information gathered during the assessment sessions is then used to plan, collaboratively with the patient, the specific exposure exercises that will be practiced.

In addition to explaining and planning a hierarchy of exposure exercises, the educational stage of ERP must also acquaint the patient with response prevention procedures. Importantly, the term "response prevention" does not imply that the therapist actively restrains the patient from performing rituals. Instead, the therapist must convince the patient to make the difficult decision to resist, on his or her own, even strong urges to perform rituals. Self-monitoring of rituals is often used in support of this goal.

In vivo Exposure. The exposure exercises themselves typically begin with the patient confronting moderately distressing situations and stimuli. Stimuli that trigger low levels of anxiety are left out of the treatment plan, since these would not teach the patient how to manage obsessional anxiety. The treatment plan is arranged so that gradually, the patient practices confronting more and more difficult situations until the most distressing situations are presented. Beginning with less anxiety-evoking exposure tasks increases the likelihood that the patient will learn to manage their distress and complete the exposure exercise successfully. Moreover, having success with initial exposures increases confidence in the treatment, and helps motivate the patient to persevere during later, more difficult, exercises. The most feared items must be confronted in treatment to allow the patient to learn that even these stimuli are manageable and not dangerous.

Imaginal Exposure. In contrast to situational fear cues—which are often concrete, obsessional thoughts, ideas, and images are intangible, and therefore can be elusive targets when designing exposure. Although in vivo exposure often evokes obsessional thoughts, imaginal exposure provides a more systematic way of exposing the patient to the key fear-evoking elements of their obsessions. The recommended methods for conducting imaginal exposure include (a) using digital voice recorders or audiocassette tapes (continuous loop tapes work especially well), or (b) written scripts containing the anxiety-evoking material (Freeston & Ladouceur, 1999). Both of these media allow the therapist to prolong the patient's confrontation with an otherwise covert event and, if necessary, manipulate the content of the stimulus. The use of a digital voice recorder or audio tape further ensures that unsupervised (homework) exposure will include confrontation with the correct stimuli.

Abramowitz (2006) described three types of imaginal exposure that can be used, based on the specifics of the patient's symptoms. *Primary imaginal exposure* is, essentially, situational exposure to unwanted thoughts. It involves directly confronting spontaneously occurring repugnant thoughts, images, and urges (i.e., violent, sexual, or blasphemous obsessions) via methods such as loop tapes. *Secondary imaginal exposure* is used when situational exposure evokes fears of disastrous consequences. In such instances, imaginal exposure is begun during or after situational exposure, and should involve visualizing the feared outcomes, or focusing on uncertainty associated with the risk of feared outcomes. Finally, *preliminary imaginal exposure* entails imagining confronting a feared stimulus as a preliminary step in preparing for situational exposures. For example, a patient might vividly *imagine* touching the bathroom floor before actually engaging in situational exposure to the bathroom floor. This type of exposure might be used as an intermediate step in preparing the patient to confront a situation of which they are extremely fearful.

Response Prevention. Response prevention, which is a necessary accessory to exposure in the treatment of OCD, entails resisting the urge to perform compulsive rituals and other safety-seeking or neutralizing behaviors that serve as an escape from obsessive fear (e.g., no handwashing after exposure to touching the floor). This allows for prolonged exposure, and facilitates the extinction of obsessional anxiety. If the patient engages in compulsive rituals in an effort to reduce anxiety during exposure, habituation cannot occur, and the patient cannot learn that his or her anxiety would have eventually diminished without the ritual.

At the end of each treatment session, the therapist instructs the patient to continue exposure for several hours, and in different environmental contexts, without the therapist. Response prevention is also used during treatment, so that no rituals are occurring. Any violations of response prevention rules are recorded by the patient on self-monitoring forms, and discussed with the therapist as areas in need of additional work.

Exposure to the most anxiety-evoking situations is not left to the end of the treatment, but rather is practiced about midway through the schedule of treatment sessions. This allows the patient ample opportunity to repeat exposure to the most difficult situations in different contexts, to allow for generalization of treatment effects. During the later treatment sessions, the therapist emphasizes the importance of the patient continuing to apply the ERP procedures after treatment is complete.

Procedural Variations of Exposure-Based Therapy

A wide range of methods of conducting exposure have been developed. Most OCD symptoms may be treated with any of the various methods of implementation; some approaches, however, are more effective in producing change for specific types of obsessions and rituals.

In-session versus Homework Exposure. In some ERP programs, therapy session time is used for practicing exposure under the supervision of the therapist. In addition to this "therapist-supervised exposure," homework exposure—usually involving repeating the same tasks practiced in session—is assigned for each day between sessions. In other programs, session time is devoted only to planning and discussing exposure assignments, which are carried out exclusively as homework assignments (self-directed exposure). There are advantages of therapy programs using exclusively self-directed exposure, including reduced therapist time. Self-directed exposure also circumvents the problem of generalizing the effects of therapy from the treatment session to the patient's everyday environment. That is, the therapist's presence during exposure can serve as a safety signal and prevent the evocation of anxiety. For example, OCD patients with compulsive checking rituals experience fewer obsessional doubts (e.g., of hitting pedestrians while driving) and urges to check (e.g., the roadside) when accompanied by the therapist during exposures (e.g., to driving through a business district), as compared to when they conduct such exposures on their own (Abramowitz, 2006; Tolin & Hannan, 2005).

On the other hand, confronting extremely frightening stimuli and resisting the urge to carry out rituals is a demanding task that requires no small degree of courage. It is to be expected that patients will, at some point, cut corners to avoid facing the most frightening aspects of their exposure assignments. They might also prematurely terminate the exposure if it becomes highly anxiety provoking, rather than remaining in the situation until habituation occurs. Although these behaviors might not represent a deliberate attempt to undermine the therapy, they can dilute the integrity of exposure and lead to attenuated outcome. Thus, it is important that therapist supervision of exposure occur, at least to some degree, to ensure the authenticity of exposure.

Perhaps the optimal approach is to use a fading procedure, in which the patient first practices and learns how to conduct exposure correctly, under the therapist's careful supervision. Then, the therapist gradually fades himself or herself from involvement in these exercises. The patient learns to decide on exposure tasks, arrange them, and execute them sufficiently. In our clinics, we use both therapist-supervised and self-directed exposure. Specifically, patients receive therapist-supervised exposure during most treatment sessions, and the therapist assigns for homework the repetition of what was practiced during the session. This allows the patient an opportunity to generalize what was learned in session, by affording him or her with the opportunity to practice exposure in varied contexts.

Full versus Partial Response Prevention. Another common variant of ERP is the way in which response prevention is used. While some therapists insist that patients stop all ritualizing during the entire time that they are in treatment, others use a partial response prevention approach, in which rituals are stopped during exposure sessions and, perhaps, for a specific period of time afterward. Given the relationship between response prevention, and eventual reduction of the frequency and intensity of OCD symptoms, it would seem important to encourage patients to target complete ritual abstinence early on in treatment. At times, however, this goal may be inconsistent with that of systematic, gradual exposure using a hierarchy. Indeed, patients may have chance encounters with frightening stimuli that evoke high urges to ritualize, but that have not yet been practiced in session. A related difficulty is that patients could become demoralized if they feel overwhelmed, or think that they cannot achieve complete ritual abstinence immediately. An alternative to full response prevention is a *graded* approach, in which instructions for stopping rituals parallel the progress up the exposure hierarchy, with the goal being complete ritual abstinence midway into treatment. The box text on page 328 illustrates the use of this approach for a patient with severe washing and cleaning rituals, who likely would have discontinued treatment had the therapist insisted upon complete response prevention from the start of therapy.

The gradual nature of this response prevention schedule delayed accidental exposures to Mandy's worst fears, which were not planned for exposure practice right away. At the end of treatment, Mandy told her therapist that she was prepared to drop out of treatment after the first session upon hearing about the goal of complete and immediate ritual abstinence, and had come to the second session only

Mandy was contamination-fearful, had clinically significant OCD since high school, and had experienced a gradual worsening of her symptoms over the last five years, such that her general functioning was largely impaired, especially in non-work domains. To make matters worse, Mandy worked in a medical context, in which handwashing between patients was required, and she had ready access to Betadine, an abrasive cleanser that she used with great frequency both at home and at work. She managed to function at work by wearing triple gloves, which went unchallenged by coworkers. Unlike most OCD patients with contamination fears, who worry about contamination from the environment, the source of contamination for Mandy was herself: she feared contaminating others with her "negative essence" that was especially concentrated in the lower half of her body. As a medical professional she recognized that this concern was illogical and unfounded, yet she was so fearful of the possibility of harming others that she was entirely unwilling to take such a risk. The extent of avoidance and rituals was remarkable. At intake, Mandy reported that she had not touched the lower half of her body in five years without some sort of barrier (e.g., glove) to prevent direct contact with her skin.

When the rationale for voluntary ritual abstinence was presented in the first treatment session, Mandy immediately burst into tears, saying, "There's just no way that I can possibly do that." The therapist assured her that many people feel this way before beginning the therapy, and that gradual exposure to feared situations and thoughts would allow for titration of anxiety; yet this information was only mildly helpful. Mandy correctly pointed out that once her use of barriers was eliminated, complete flooding would ensue, and she would then have to wipe herself after urinating or defecating, scratch itches, and dress herself without any protection against contaminating the upper half of her body and then contaminating other people. Additional discussion with the therapist further underscored the distance between her current functioning and the desired ritual abstinence. Even at home, she was using abrasive cleaners, triple gloves, and engaging in an extensive laundry ritual that reduced her fears of becoming contaminated by the lower half of her body and spreading contamination with her hands.

The therapist believed that this patient was correct in her assessment, and would be unable to negotiate this dramatic adjustment in her ritualized routine without becoming overwhelmed. Thus, a revised response prevention plan was contrived. According to this plan, she would eliminate the third set of gloves in the home environment after the first session, and eliminate the second pair of gloves at home and the third set of gloves at work, after session two. Gradual removal of rituals and avoidance would continue until she was wearing no gloves and doing no washing in her home or work environment. Additionally, it was acceptable for Mandy to use single gloves after defecating and urinating until such time as these items were confronted on the exposure hierarchy. Only after she had virtually refrained from rituals for two consecutive weeks were exposures to directly contacting skin on the lower half of her body implemented.

as a courtesy. Upon hearing that this treatment goal could indeed be shifted, she engaged fully in the treatment; she was highly compliant with in-session exposure, completed exposure homework faithfully, and was diligent in adhering to the revised response prevention program.

Using Cognitive Therapy Techniques in ERP

One of the less explicit components of exposure-based therapy for OCD is the use of more or less informal cognitive therapy techniques during the exposure sessions. The therapist should take an active role in facilitating cognitive change during exposure, by helping the patient challenge dysfunctional beliefs about feared stimuli and feared consequences relevant to the exposure exercise. Commonly, such discussions turn to risk-taking and the importance of learning how to manage acceptable (everyday) degrees of uncertainty. Rather than provide reassurance, or argue with patients about the exact probabilities of their most feared consequences, it is useful to emphasize the practicalities of taking the low-level risks presented during exposure. That is, learning to live with a reasonable amount of risk and uncertainty is preferable to the consequences of trying to demand absolute certainty and eliminate all risk (i.e., avoidance), or performing compulsive rituals in order to secure an absolute guarantee of safety—which is not feasible. Importantly, it is counterproductive to try to convince the patient that exposure situations are "not dangerous." This is for the patient to discover for himself or herself through experience. Risk levels are best described as "acceptably low" rather than "zero" (see Chapter 18 for a discussion of cognitive therapy for OCD).

Managing Symptom Accommodation by Significant Others

Many patients involve the people around them in OCD symptoms, such as asking a partner to carry out checking rituals or provide reassurance to decrease obsessive doubts, or demanding that family members take off their contaminated shoes as they enter the house. In many instances, such symptom accommodation becomes a way of life for a couple, or an entire family, in which one member has OCD. An obvious short-term advantage of this sort of behavior is that it provides relief from the sufferer's obsessive compulsive symptoms. Sometimes, the family accommodates because this seems easier (at least in the short term) than putting up with the sufferer's fear or anger responses when accommodation does not occur. Over the long term, however, this behavior maintains OCD symptoms, since it has the same effect as if the patient were performing the ritual or avoidance behavior himself or herself.

Because symptom accommodation is counterproductive to ERP, significant others must be educated about the nature of OCD and its treatment, and taught more productive ways of managing the patient's obsessional distress and requests for help with rituals. Within a couples context, both partners can be taught more productive methods of sharing their thoughts and feelings with one another, as well as strategies for resolving conflicts and working through anxious moments together as a team (as opposed to simply trying to avoid anxiety). They can also be helped to structure their relationship within the context of exposure and response prevention (i.e., going toward the anxiety), as opposed to accommodating OCD (i.e., always running away from anxiety). Family members and friends who accommodate OCD symptoms can be taught to change their behavior by refusing to respond to requests for rituals (e.g., "I know you feel very anxious right now, but I'm not supposed to do that ritual for you anymore. How can I help you get through this without reinforcing your OCD symptoms?").

Mechanisms Underlying the Effects of Exposure-Based Therapy

Several theoretical accounts have been proposed to explain the mechanism of action of exposure-based therapy for fear-related problems such as OCD.

While these models all propose that exposure-based therapy leads to *learning* in one form or another, what exactly is learned, and how it is learned, differs across models. We will describe the three leading theoretical models here.

Extinction

From a behavioral perspective, exposure-based therapy is thought to reduce obsessional fear by the process of *extinction*. As we described earlier, classical behavioral models of OCD propose that obsessional anxiety is a classically conditioned fear response to a previously neutral (conditioned) stimulus. The purpose of exposure therapy from this perspective, therefore, is to extinguish the conditioned fear response by prolonged and repeated confrontation with the feared (but nondangerous) stimulus. Recent analyses have led to a conceptualization of extinction as an active process of inhibiting the previously learned fear, following repeated exposure (Craske & Mystkowski, 2006). With this sort of exposure, the patient's anxiety decreases. Response prevention fosters extinction by blocking the performance of anxiety-reducing rituals, which would foil the extinction process. This affords the patient an opportunity to repeatedly be in the presence of the fear trigger (conditioned stimulus) absent the anxiety response (conditioned response), thereby inhibiting the anxiety response (extinction). When the once-feared obsessional stimulus is repeatedly paired with this *reduction* of anxiety, extinction is thought to occur, as the person now learns to associate this stimulus with anxiety reduction. The active inhibition of previously feared stimuli has also been suggested to play a role in incomplete extinction, or symptom reemergence even after seemingly complete extinction. For example, certain contexts associated with the fear, that were not the object of exposure during treatment, can lead to the return of anxiety following otherwise successful treatment (see Bouton, 1993).

Neurobiological (animal) research has extended the extinction model in many important ways, thereby illustrating another example of translational research, in which basic animal science leads to important research findings with humans. For example, animal research indicates that fear reduction is most enduring when exposure is conducted across multiple stimuli and contexts (Bouton, 2002). This translates into an empirical basis to the clinical wisdom, cited earlier in this chapter, that ERP should be conducted in multiple situations in order to reduce OCD.

Neurobiologically informed extinction research also indicates that conditioned fears are not unlearned or forgotten. Instead, extinction learning leads to the development of competing associations, whereby one set of associations (e.g., the association between "touching a trash can" and intense fear) is replaced by another association ("touching a trash can" and little or no discomfort). In other words, conditioned fear reduction persists until there is some adverse event (e.g., getting sick after touching a trash can) that reactivates the original learned association (LeDoux, 2000). Thus, contemporary neurobiologically based versions of the extinction model provide an explanation of relapse after ERP.

Emotional Processing Theory

Foa and Kozak (1986) attempted to explain the mechanisms of exposure therapy by building on the work of Rachman (1980) and Lang (1977), who proposed that fear is represented in memory as a network comprising (a) *stimulus propositions* that express information about feared cues; (b) *response propositions* that express information about behavioral and physiologic responses to these cues; and (c) *meaning propositions* that elaborate on the significance of other elements in the fear structure. Foa and Kozak likened this fear network to a computer program for avoiding threat, in which pathological fear amounted to "bugs" in the program characterized by excessive response elements, resistance to change, and impairments in processing certain types of information about danger and safety. Exposure therapy, they proposed, amounted to reprogramming the computer to diminish fear, by providing information incompatible with pathological aspects of the program.

Activating the fear network and incorporating incompatible information is referred to as *emotional processing*. Foa and Kozak proposed that emotional processing requires a close match between the feared stimulus, and elements in the fear network. That is, the extent to which an exposure situation or image matches elements of the fear structure determines how accessible the fear program is for modification. They also asserted that successful exposure therapy depends on the patient attending to the feared stimulus. Cognitive avoidance (i.e., distraction), on the other hand, would prevent activation of the fear structure and prevent new, nonfearful information from being incorporated.

Foa and Kozak also delineated three indicators of emotional processing: (a) activation of the fear network as evinced by an increase in fear; (b) decreases

in the fear response during an exposure session (i.e., *within-session* habituation); and (c) a gradual decline in the peak anxiety level across exposure sessions (*between-sessions* habituation). Further, they proposed that as emotional processing occurs, habituation of fear weakens associations between feared stimuli and fear responses, and diminishes subjective estimates of the probability and severity of harm arising from feared stimulus.

Although an advancement over the aforementioned extinction model, because of its emphasis on cognitive factors (such as expectancies, originally identified as important in OCD by Victor Meyer), Foa and Kozak's (1986) emotional processing explanation is not without limitations. First, as McNally (2007) has pointed out, the propositional network characterization of fear appears to be circular, in that it merely rephrases the phenomenon it's designed to explain. For example, Foa and Kozak propose that *response propositions* regarding intrusive obsessional images are linked in the fear network with *meaning propositions* regarding danger. But this simply reiterates what astute clinicians already know: that people with OCD respond fearfully to their own intrusive thoughts and images, often misinterpreting them as threatening and as having implications for causing or preventing harm (e.g., Salkovskis, 1996). To assert that individuals with anxiety disorders (such as OCD) are characterized by fear networks, in which propositions about feared stimuli (e.g., intrusive thoughts) are linked to propositions about danger, seems merely to restate clinical observations using a different terminology.

Second, although early research suggested that cognitive avoidance (i.e., distraction) during exposure practice would limit activation of the fear network and impede emotional processing (e.g., Grayson, Foa, & Steketee, 1982), more recent work has indicated that distraction during exposure can *facilitate* fear reduction. For example, studying spider phobics, Johnstone and Page (2004) found that phobic-stimulus-irrelevant conversation with the patient during exposure hastened successful fear reduction, and this was especially true for those phobics with the highest initial baseline level of fear. Considering this and related studies, Foa et al. (2006) revised the initial emotional processing model, and argued that whether distraction helps or hinders emotional processing may depend on the specific type of fear being modified. For example, distraction might hinder progress in exposure for agoraphobic avoidance, whereas it might facilitate it in specific phobia and certain forms of OCD, such as contamination fears. Another interpretation of these discrepant results on distraction's effect on outcome is potentially consistent with Foa and Kozak's original formulation (McNally, 2007). That is, the effect of distraction may vary as a function of the degree of fear. If fear is above an optimal level for emotional processing to occur, distraction may titrate it, thereby enhancing outcome.

Cognitive Models

Other models of fear reduction have been proposed, although their advantages over the emotional processing and extinction models have yet to be convincingly demonstrated. Clark (1999), for example, proposed that exposure therapy is effective because it corrects dysfunctional beliefs that underlie fear, such as overestimations of threat, pathologic interpretations of intrusive thoughts, and the intolerance of risk or uncertainty. Belief change is thought to occur because exposure presents the patient with information that disconfirms the anxiogenic dysfunctional beliefs. For example, when a patient confronts feared situations and refrains from rituals, he or she finds out that (a) obsessional fear declines naturally (habituation), and (b) feared negative consequences are unlikely to occur. This evidence is processed and incorporated into the patient's belief system. Thus, fear is reduced and the compulsive rituals, once used to reduce anxiety and prevent feared disasters, become unnecessary (redundant). Exposure therapy might also help patients gain more positive feelings about themselves and their ability to cope with feared situations and stimuli, by helping them to master their fears without having to rely on avoidance or compulsive rituals. The importance of this sense of mastery is an often overlooked effect of exposure-based treatment.

Summary and Synthesis

None of these models provide completely satisfactory accounts of the mechanisms of exposure-based therapies. Space limitations preclude a detailed discussion. The extinction model, while being the simplest, is the most closely tied to animal research on the neurobiology of fear reduction. It has the advantages of providing an account of the conditions under which ERP will be most effective (e.g., under multiple exposure contexts), and also describes the conditions under which relapse is most likely to occur (i.e., when the initial conditioned responses are reinforced or "reinstated"). But on the other hand, the extinction model has little to say about the importance of meaning and expectations in fear reduction. From the perspective of cognitive models, for example, we can understand the success of the treatment of Mandy, discussed earlier, because cognitive models emphasize the role of expectations in fear reduction. Mandy, for example, would not have engaged in ERP assignments if she expected to have no control in determining the intensity of fear-evoking stimuli that she was to encounter. A limitation of the cognitive models is that they suggest that learned fears are unlearned, whereas the animal research suggests that such learning is suppressed by new learning, and learned fears can be later reactivated. It may be that some hybrid of the models described in this section might ultimately provide the best explanation of fear reduction, as it occurs during ERP.

Efficacy and Effectiveness of ERP
Dismantling Studies

Dismantling studies, which examine the effects of individual treatment procedures in multicomponent therapy programs, have addressed three questions with respect to ERP: (a) What are the differential effects of exposure and response prevention? (b) How do these individual treatment components compare to the complete ERP package? (c) Is adding exposure in imagination to situational (in vivo) exposure superior to situational exposure alone?

Differential Effects of Exposure and Response Prevention. The two studies that have examined the separate effects of exposure and response prevention have found similar results (Foa, Steketee, Grayson, Turner, & Lattimer, 1984; Foa, Steketee, & Milby, 1980). Using a sample of individuals with contamination fear, Foa, Steketee, and Milby (1980) randomly assigned participants to exposure only (E) or response prevention only (RP). They found that RP reduced rituals to a greater extent than it reduced anxiety, while E produced the converse effects. Foa et al. (1984) randomly assigned another group of contamination phobic OCD "washers" to one of three treatment groups: Exposure only (E), response prevention (RP) only, or the combination (ERP). At post-treatment, patients who received only E evidenced greater reductions in contamination fears than did those who received only RP. In contrast, RP was superior to E in reducing washing rituals. These results suggest that exposure and response prevention have differential effects on OCD symptoms: response prevention is superior to exposure in decreasing compulsive rituals, and exposure is superior to response prevention for decreasing obsessional fear.

Foa et al.'s (1984) study also addressed the question of whether there is an additive effect of combining E and RP. As these authors hypothesized, ERP was indeed more effective than either of its individual components, and this combination led to the greatest short-term and long-term reduction of anxiety (i.e., contamination fear) and urges to ritualize. To explain this finding, Foa et al. (1984) proposed that response prevention helps render information learned during exposure more incompatible with the patient's expectations. For example, without response prevention, a patient who repeatedly practices exposure to touching garbage cans, yet does not become very sick, may attribute his or her good health to compulsive washing. In this case, the maladaptive beliefs that garbage cans are dangerous, and washing rituals prevent illness, will persist. If, however, response prevention is implemented along with exposure, good health cannot be attributed to washing rituals, and thus the patient's overestimations of danger can be corrected.

Imaginal and Situational Exposure. Most individuals with OCD experience intrusive anxiety-evoking thoughts, images, ideas, or impulses that elicit excessive anxiety and therefore must also be dealt with in therapy. Whereas confrontation with tangible fear cues, such as dirt or unlucky numbers, can be accomplished through situational exposure, confrontation with imagined disasters—the feared consequences of confronting feared situations without performing rituals—obviously cannot. A woman afraid of causing fires, and therefore constantly checking light switches, can conduct situational exposure by leaving her house lights on and her iron plugged in; yet she *cannot* be exposed to actually causing a fire as a result of not checking carefully enough. Confrontation with such situations must, therefore, be conducted in imagination. It follows from Foa and Kozak's (1986) proposition, regarding the importance of matching the exposure stimulus with the patient's fear, that obsessional fears of disastrous consequences should improve when imaginal exposure is added to in vivo exposure.

To examine the additive effect of imagined exposure, Foa, Steketee, Turner, and Fischer (1980) assigned 15 OCD patients with checking compulsions to either 10 daily sessions of ERP with only situational exposure, or a similar regimen of ERP that incorporated both situational and imaginal exposure. Imaginal exposure consisted of repeated and prolonged confrontation with thoughts of anxiety-evoking scenes, related to particular obsessional fears. For example, a woman who performed rituals in order to protect her family from death, purposely imaged that her husband died as a result of her failure to perform her rituals. At post-treatment, both groups of patients improved substantially, but did not differ significantly from one another. However, at follow-up (3 months to 2.5 years), the group that received both imaginal and situational exposure better maintained their improvements relative to the group that had received only situational exposure. Thus, imaginal exposure to the consequences of not ritualizing appears to be an important adjunct to situational exposure, when stimuli that match patients' obsessional fears cannot be directly reproduced in the context of situational exposure.

Summary of Dismantling Studies. In summary, the findings of dismantling studies on ERP reveal that: (a) exposure techniques are more effective than response prevention when it comes to reducing obsessional fear; (b) response prevention is more effective than exposure in reducing compulsive urges; (c) the combination of exposure and response prevention is more effective than either component by itself, for reducing both obsessional fear and compulsive rituals; and (d) imaginal exposure adds to the effectiveness of situational exposure, especially when the patient's obsessional fears focus on imagined disasters that cannot be confronted in situational exposure.

Short-Term and Long-Term Effects of ERP

Expert consensus and practice guidelines state that ERP is the first-line psychosocial intervention for OCD (American Psychiatric Association, 2007; March, Frances, Carpenter & Kahn, 1997). In this section, we review meta-analytic and controlled studies on the short-term and long-term outcome of ERP.

Meta-analytic Findings. Data from a large number of controlled and uncontrolled outcome trials consistently indicate that ERP is extremely helpful in reducing OCD symptoms. A meta-analysis of this literature (Abramowitz 1996) that included 24 studies conducted between 1975 and 1995 (and involving over 800 patients) revealed very large treatment effect sizes of 1.16 (on self-report measures) and 1.41 (interview measures) at posttest, and 1.10 (for self-report measures) and 1.57 (for interview measures) at follow-up. Using a different meta-analytic approach, Foa and Kozak (1996) calculated the percent of patients in each study that were "responders" (usually defined as achieving a pretreatment to post-treatment improvement of at least 30%). They found that across 13 ERP studies, 83% of patients were responders at post-treatment, and across 16 studies, 76% were responders at follow-up (mean follow-up was 29 months). In concert, these findings suggest that the majority of OCD patients who undergo treatment with ERP evidence substantial short-term and long-term benefit. More recent meta-analytic studies have found results consistent with those reported above (e.g., Eddy, Dutra, Bradey, & Weston, 2004).

Randomized Controlled Trials. The Yale-Brown Obsessive Compulsive Scale (Y-BOCS; Goodman et al., 1989a, 1989b), a 10-item semistructured clinical interview, is considered the gold standard measure of OCD severity. Due to its respectable psychometric properties (Taylor 1995), the Y-BOCS is widely utilized in OCD treatment outcome research, providing an excellent "measuring stick" by which to compare results across studies. When administering the Y-BOCS, the interviewer rates the following parameters of obsessions (items 1–5) and compulsions (items 6–10) on a scale from 0 (no symptoms) to 4 (extreme): time, interference with functioning, distress, resistance, and control. The total score is the sum of the 10 items, and therefore ranges from 0 to 40. Y-BOCS scores of 0–7 tend to indicate subclinical OCD symptoms, 8–15 = mild symptoms, 16–25 = moderate symptoms, 26–35 = severe symptoms, and 36–40 = extreme severity. Table 17.1 summarizes the results of the five published randomized controlled trials (RCTs) that examined the efficacy of ERP using the Y-BOCS as an outcome measure.

Two studies have compared ERP to credible psychotherapy placebos (Lindsay, Crino, & Andrews, 1997; Fals-Stewart, Marks, & Schafer, 1993). In the study by Fals-Stewart et al., patients were randomly assigned to receive 24 sessions of individual ERP, group ERP, or progressive relaxation treatment, which was not expected to produce OCD symptom reduction. All treatments were delivered over 12 weeks with twice-weekly sessions. Although both ERP treatments were superior to relaxation, there was no effect of ERP format (i.e., group and individual treatment produced similar outcomes). The average improvement across the two ERP groups was 41% on the Y-BOCS, and post-treatment scores fell to within the mild range of severity.

In the study by Lindsay et al. (1997), patients were assigned to receive either ERP or anxiety management training (AMT), which consisted of breathing retraining, relaxation, and training in the use of problem-solving skills. Both treatments were intensive: 15 daily sessions conducted over a 3-week period. On average, patients receiving ERP improved almost 62% from pretreatment to post-treatment on the Y-BOCS, with posttest scores ending up in the mild range. In contrast, there was no improvement with AMT.

The clear superiority of ERP over credible psychotherapy placebos, such as relaxation and AMT, indicates that improvement in OCD symptoms can

Table 17.1 Results of Randomized Controlled Trials Examining the Efficacy of Exposure and Response Prevention for OCD

Study	Control condition	ERP group			Control group		
		n	Pre	Post	n	Pre	Post
Fals-Stewart et al. (1993)[1]	Relaxation	31	20.2	12.1	32	19.9	18.1
Lindsay et al. (1997)	Anxiety management	9	28.7 (4.6)	11.0 (3.8)	9	24.4 (7.0)	25.9 (5.8)
Van Balkom et al. (1998)	Waiting list	19	25.0 (7.9)	17.1 (8.4)	18	26.8 (6.4)	26.4 (6.8)
Foa et al. (2005)	Pill placebo	29	24.6 (4.8)	11.0 (7.9)	26	25.0 (4.0)	22.2 (6.4)
Nakatani et al. (2005)	Pill placebo	10	29.9 (3.1)	12.9 (4.9)	8	30.5 (3.7)	28.4 (5.5)

Mean (SD) Y-BOCS total score (header spanning ERP group and Control group)

Y-BOCS = Yale-Brown Obsessive Compulsive Scale.
[1] Standard deviation not reported.

be attributed to the ERP procedures themselves, over and above any nonspecific factors such as time, attention, or expectancy of positive outcome. Just as importantly, the findings described above clearly show that despite the intuitive appeal of using strategies such as relaxation, deep breathing, and problem solving, with individuals suffering from obsessional anxiety and persistent rituals, these techniques do not work in the treatment of OCD.

In their study on the relative efficacy of various combinations of ERP, cognitive therapy, and fluvoxamine, van Balkom et al. (1998) included a waiting-list control group, affording a somewhat less rigorous test of the efficacy of ERP as compared to the studies reviewed directly above. In this study, ERP fared somewhat less well than in other RCTs. One explanation for the mere 32% symptom reduction is that the ERP protocol in van Balkom et al.'s study was less than optimal. First, all exposure was conducted as homework assignments rather than in session under the therapist's supervision. Second, therapists did not discuss expectations of disastrous consequences during the first eight weeks of ERP, because this would have overlapped substantially with cognitive therapy. As we discussed earlier in this chapter, however, such discussions are a necessary part of ERP. Still, patients who received this self-directed and disadvantaged version of ERP fared significantly better than those in the waiting-list condition.

Foa et al. (2005) examined the relative efficacy of (a) intensive (15 daily sessions) ERP (including in-session exposure); (b) the serotonin and norepinephrine reuptake inhibitor, clomipramine; (c) combined treatment (ERP + clomipramine); and (d) pill placebo. Intensive ERP produced a 50% Y-BOCS reduction, which was far superior to the effects of pill placebo, as can be seen in Table 17.1. Moreover, endpoint Y-BOCS scores fell within the mild range of OCD severity.

In a study conducted in Japan, Nakatani and colleagues (2005) randomly assigned patients to receive weekly ERP sessions, fluvoxamine, or pill placebo. The ERP group evinced a mean Y-BOCS reduction of nearly 60%, which was superior to that reported for the placebo group (7%). Moreover, at posttest, the ERP group's Y-BOCS scores were again within the mild range of symptoms.

Overall, the findings from RCTs suggest that ERP—even when delivered in a suboptimal fashion—produces substantial and clinically meaningful improvement in OCD symptoms. There is also consistent evidence from these studies that symptom reduction is due to the specific techniques used in ERP (i.e., exposure to fear-provoking stimuli, while refraining from rituals) over and above the nonspecific (e.g., expectations, attention) that are common to all psychological treatments.

ERP for Mental Ritualizers. Traditionally, it was thought that individuals with OCD who had severe obsessions without overt rituals such as washing, checking, ordering, and repeating, were resistant to ERP (e.g., Baer 1994). This belief was predicated on the erroneous (as it turns out) notion that such patients don't have rituals that could be resisted as part of response prevention; thus, the maintenance of their obsessional fear was less understood. A clearer recognition of the phenomenology and function of *mental rituals* (often mistaken for obsessions because they are not visibly apparent behaviors) and other subtle anxiety-reduction strategies that are present among patients without overt rituals (e.g., Freeston et al., 1997; Rachman, 1993), however, gave way to the adaptation of ERP for this presentation of OCD.

Specifically, Freeston and colleagues (1997) obtained excellent results with a treatment package that entailed (a) psychoeducation about intrusive thoughts and their development into obsessions (see Chapter 18 of this volume); (b) ERP consisting of in-session and homework exposure, in which the patient repeatedly writes out the unwanted obsessional thought, says it aloud, or records it on a continuous-loop audiotape and then plays it back repeatedly on a portable audiocassette player, while refraining from covert rituals and mental compulsions; and (c) cognitive therapy targeting exaggerated responsibility, inappropriate interpretations of intrusive thoughts, and inflated estimates of the probability and severity of negative outcomes. Compared to a waitlist control group, treated patients achieved substantial improvement: among all patients (*n* = 28), Y-BOCS scores improved from 23.9 to 9.8, after an average of 25.7 sessions over 19.2 weeks. Moreover, patients retained their gains at 6-months follow-up (mean Y-BOCS score = 10.8). This study demonstrated that ERP can be successfully adapted for the management of a presentation of OCD that had previously been considered resistant to psychological treatment. In a later study, Abramowitz, Franklin, Schwartz, and Furr (2003) found that ERP was no less effective for such patients than it was for OCD patients displaying primarily overt washing, checking, and arranging/ordering rituals.

Group ERP

In most of the studies reviewed above, treatment was delivered on an individual basis. Group OCD treatment programs emphasizing ERP, however, have been found to be effective in reducing OCD symptoms (Anderson & Rees, 2007; Cordioli et al., 2003; McLean et al., 2001). In one study, 12 weeks of group ERP was more effective than group therapy emphasizing cognitive techniques; and both programs were more effective than waitlist (McLean et al., 2001). In another investigation, group ERP resulted in significant improvement relative to waiting list, and patients continued to improve at 3-month follow-up (Cordioli et al., 2003). In the only study directly comparing individual and group therapy for OCD, Anderson and Rees (2007) found that 10 weeks of either treatment format was more effective than waitlist, but there were no differences between treatments. Therapy included ERP and cognitive therapy techniques, and the average posttest and follow-up Y-BOCS scores were in the 16–18 range (indicating mild symptom severity). Strengths of a group approach to the treatment of OCD include the support and cohesion that are nonspecific effects of group therapy. Potential disadvantages, however, include the relative lack of attention to each individual's particular symptom presentation, particularly given the heterogeneity of OCD.

Home-Based versus Office-Based Treatment

Rowa et al. (2007) examined whether the effects of ERP differ depending whether treatment was delivered exclusively in the therapist's office versus in the patient's home or other natural environments where symptoms tend to occur (e.g., at work, in public places, in the car, etc.). These authors randomly assigned 28 individuals with OCD to the aforementioned treatment conditions. Patients received fourteen 90-minute sessions of ERP with an individual therapist. Results suggested that participants improved significantly, regardless of where treatment occurred. Post-treatment Y-BOCS reductions were 44% for office-based, and 48% for home-based treatment. At 6-month follow-up, reductions were 39% and 48% respectively. Although the home-based group appeared to show greater symptom reduction, the differences in improvement rates were not statistically significant—probably due to the relatively small sample size (14 patients per group).

Although Rowa et al. (2007) found that home-based ERP was no more effective than office-based ERP, it is possible that home-based ERP is beneficial and useful for certain individuals with particular symptom presentations. For example, those whose symptoms cannot be replicated in any meaningful way within an office setting, or who are unable to try ERP on their own, may find home-based ERP especially effective—for example, individuals with fears of disasters in the home (e.g., fires and burglaries), and checking rituals whose symptoms are very difficult to replicate in an office setting, due to the decrease in perceived responsibility. Clinical observations suggest that home-based treatment may also be helpful for patients who have not benefited from previous office-based ERP.

Relapse Prevention

Hiss and colleagues (1994) reported encouraging results of a relapse prevention program following ERP treatment of OCD. Eighteen patients were treated with 3 weeks of intensive ERP, and then randomly assigned to either a relapse prevention condition (consisting of four 90-minute sessions over 1 week) or a control condition (consisting of relaxation training and associative therapy). Based on a 50% improvement on the Y-BOCS as the criterion for treatment response, 75% of the patients assigned to the relapse prevention condition were responders after initial treatment, and 75% were responders at 6-month follow-up. However, 70% of the patients assigned to the control condition were responders after initial treatment, but only 33% were responders at 6-month follow-up. Although there were few statistically significant results because of the small sample size, this study suggested that a brief relapse prevention program, including brief telephone contacts, may help prevent relapse, at least in cleaning and checking rituals.

Comparisons between ERP and Cognitive Therapy

A number of investigators have attempted to determine the relative efficacy of ERP and cognitive therapy (CT) by directly comparing variants of the two therapies. In two early investigations, Emmelkamp and colleagues compared rational emotive therapy (RET; which is a form of CT) to ERP (Emmelkamp, Visser, Hoekstra, 1988; Emmelkamp & Beens, 1991). RET (Ellis, 1962) involved identifying anxiety-evoking thoughts (e.g., "not washing my hands would be 100% awful"), challenging the basis of these thoughts, and replacing them with alternative beliefs and assumptions that do not lead to anxiety; however, no behavioral experiments were performed.

Exposure in the ERP condition was completely *self-directed*, meaning patients completed all exposure practice on their own as homework assignments. In both studies, RET and self-directed ERP produced roughly similar results. Limitations of these studies included the relatively small sample sizes, and use of an ERP format that was less than optimal (no therapist-supervised exposure). In addition, these investigations were conducted before the Y-BOCS was available. Given the problems with these studies, it is difficult to draw from them firm conclusions regarding the relative efficacy of ERP and RET.

Four additional studies that used the Y-BOCS compared contemporary cognitive interventions, similar to van Oppen and Arntz's (1994) program, to variations of ERP. The results of these investigations are summarized is Table 17.2 and discussed below. Van Oppen et al. (1995) randomly assigned patients to either 16 sessions of CT or 16 sessions of self-directed ERP. Both treatments led to an improvement in OCD symptoms, and CT was more effective than ERP (Y-BOCS reductions of 53% and 43% respectively). Importantly, the brief and infrequent therapist contact (weekly 45-minute sessions), along with reliance upon patients to manage all exposure practice on their own, likely accounted for the relatively modest effects of ERP in this study. Moreover, CT involved behavioral experiments that resembled exposure, which blurred the distinction between the two study treatments. Only after behavioral experiments were introduced (at the 6th session) did symptom reduction in the CT group approach that of ERP. Thus, it is possible that the exposure component of behavioral experiments is key to the efficacy of CT. Using a sample that overlapped with van Oppen et al's, van Balkom et al. (1998) found no significant difference between CT with behavioral experiments and self-directed ERP.

Cottraux et al's. (2001) study seems to provide the fairest comparison between CT and an adequate ERP regimen. Both treatments involved 20 hours of therapist contact over 16 weeks. CT was based on Salkovskis' (1996) cognitive model of OCD, and included psychoeducation, modification of unrealistic interpretations of intrusive thoughts (i.e., cognitive restructuring), and behavioral experiments to test dysfunctional assumptions (both in session and for homework). ERP involved therapist-supervised and homework exposure, and complete response prevention. As is shown in Table 17.2, the two programs produced comparable outcomes at post-treatment (Y-BOCS reductions = 42%–44%). Interestingly, ERP resulted in changes in cognitions (e.g., thought-action fusion) that were not explicitly addressed in therapy. At 1-year follow-up, patients treated with ERP had continued to improve from their post-treatment status (follow-up mean Y-BOCS = 11.1), whereas this was not the case with CT (follow-up mean Y-BOCS = 15.0). Finally, McLean et al. (2001) compared the two treatment approaches as conducted in group settings. Patients received 12 weekly 2.5 hour group sessions (6 to 8 participants per group) of either CT (similar to the program used by Cottraux et al.'s 2001 study) or ERP involving in-session and homework exposures. Both treatments were more effective than a waitlist control condition, and ERP was associated with greater improvement than CT at both post-treatment

Table 17.2 Comparisons between Cognitive Therapy and Exposure and Response Prevention (ERP)

		Y-BOCS total score					
		Cognitive therapy group			ERP group		
Study	Comments	n	Pre	Post	n	Pre	Post
van Oppen et al. (1995)	No therapist-supervised ERP	28	24.1 (5.5)	13.3 (8.5)	29	31.4 (5.0)	17.9 (9.0)
Van Balkom et al. (1998)	Sample overlapped with van Oppen et al. (1995)	25	25.3 (6.6)	13.5 (9.7)	22	25.0 (7.9)	17.1 (8.4)
Cottraux et al. (2001)	Both treatments included exposure-like procedures	30	28.6 (5.1)	16.1 (8.2)	30	28.5 (4.9)	16.4 (7.8)
McLean et al. (2001)	All treatment in groups	31	21.9 (5.8)	16.1 (6.7)	32	21.8 (4.6)	13.2 (7.2)

Y-BOCS = Yale-Brown Obsessive Compulsive Scale.

(40% and 27% Y-BOCS reductions, respectively) and follow-up (41% and 2% Y-BOCS reductions).

Although the results of several comparison studies suggest that ERP and CT are of similar efficacy for OCD, one should not conclude that well-executed ERP is only as effective as CT. Particularly, in the earlier studies, both ERP and CT yielded minimal improvements in OCD symptoms. The efficacy of ERP was likely attenuated by the use of suboptimal procedures, such as the lack of therapist-supervised exposure. Moreover, CT programs were likely enhanced by behavioral experiments, which probably have similar effects to supervised exposure. Using meta-analytic methods, we found that behavioral experiments improve the efficacy of CT for OCD (Abramowitz, Franklin, & Foa, 2002). Thus, CT may have been systematically advantaged, and ERP systematically disadvantaged, in these investigations.

Comparisons between ERP and Medication

Numerous double-blind, randomized, placebo-controlled trials have established the efficacy of pharmacotherapy using serotonin reuptake inhibitors (SRIs; e.g., fluvoxamine) for OCD (e.g., Montgomery et al., 1993). The exact mechanisms by which they reduce OCD symptoms have not yet been well elucidated. However, one theory is that they change aspects of the serotonin system that some hypothesize to be involved in the production of OCD symptoms (e.g., Zohar & Insel, 1987). Given that the two effective treatments for OCD appear to have such different proposed mechanisms of action, clinicians and researchers alike have been interested in determining their relative efficacy.

Surprisingly, however, there are very few direct head-to-head comparisons between ERP and medication for OCD. A number of early studies (e.g., Rachman, Hodgson, & Marks, 1971) attempted to compare these two interventions, but the designs of these studies were highly complex, the sample sizes were small, and the researchers did not use psychometrically sound assessment instruments such as the Y-BOCS. Because the results of such investigations are difficult to interpret with clarity, we focus on two recent randomized, controlled trials, Foa et al. (2005) and Nakatani et al. (2005), which permitted clear comparisons between ERP and SRI medications.

Foa et al. (2005) compared 12 weeks of ERP and 12 weeks of clomipramine. At post-treatment, both treatments were superior to placebo, and ERP (mean 50% Y-BOCS reduction) was superior to clomipramine (mean 35% Y-BOCS reduction). One might question whether this finding is influenced by investigator allegiance. After all, Foa is well known for her research on exposure-based therapies for anxiety problems. This study, however, was conducted at two locations: the University of Pennsylvania—a cognitive-behavior oriented OCD clinic—and Columbia University—a pharmacology-oriented clinic under the direction of Michael Liebowitz, MD. The fact that ERP maintained superiority to clomipramine at both sites strongly suggests that this effect is stronger than any researcher allegiance. It is, however, important to note a caveat of this study: patients who received ERP had an *intensive* version of this treatment that included 15 daily therapy sessions (Monday through Friday) over three weeks. Thus, this treatment regimen is not necessarily representative of typical clinical practice.

Nakatani et al.'s (2005) randomized, controlled trial included a comparison between ERP and fluvoxamine. The ERP program consisted of 12 weekly treatment sessions in which exposure exercises were planned for practice between sessions. Thus, most of the ERP work was conducted by the patient alone, rather than as supervised by a therapist. Even so, the 58% Y-BOCS reduction from ERP was significantly greater than the 29% reduction observed in the fluvoxamine group. Thus, even in its patient-directed format, which is inferior to therapist-directed treatment (Abramowitz, 1996), ERP is a more effective treatment than pharmacotherapy by fluvoxamine. Taken together, these two studies support the view that ERP should be the overall first-line treatment for OCD.

Combining ERP with Medication

The aforementioned studies examining the differential efficacy of ERP compared to medication have helped delineate the relative superiority of ERP as a psychosocial intervention. Office treatment of individuals with OCD, however, often includes both medication and ERP. Although the concurrent use of medication and psychological treatment seems intuitive, and is commonly advocated in clinical practice, relatively few studies have empirically examined whether combining ERP with medication is more beneficial than monotherapy (e.g., ERP alone).

Traditional Antidepressant and Antianxiety Medications. There are three possible outcomes when one combines treatments for OCD. First, one might expect a synergistic effect, in which combining ERP and SRIs is more effective than either treatment alone. It is also possible that medication and ERP add little to each other—for instance, if either therapy is sufficiently powerful, then the other has little additional to contribute. We must also face the third possibility—that one treatment *undermines* from the efficacy of the other—for example, if patients improve with ERP, but attribute their gains to medication and subsequently fail to comply with ERP procedures. There are indeed examples of medications, such as benzodiazepines, attenuating the effects of exposure-based treatments for anxiety (for a review see Abramowitz, Deacon, & Whiteside, 2011). Specifically, because benzodiazepines reduce anxious arousal more quickly than would have occurred naturally, the use of these medications during exposure can serve as a safety signal, and prevent the anxious patient from learning that fear declines naturally even if the medicine is not used.

Studies conducted to date generally support the view that simultaneous treatment with ERP and SRIs yields superior outcome compared to SRI monotherapy, *but not compared to ERP alone* (Cottraux et al., 1990; Foa et al., 2005; O'Connor et al., 1999; van Balkom et al., 1998). One exception was reported by Hohagen et al. (1998), who found that combined ERP and fluvoxamine offered an advantage over ERP monotherapy, although this finding was among severely depressed OCD patients. We note, however, that many of the studies cited above have limitations that preclude definitive conclusions. Most important is the fact that patients with severe comorbid disorders—perhaps the very patients that would show the greatest benefit from combined treatment—were often excluded from these outcome studies.

D-Cycloserine. A relatively recent approach to combining exposure-based treatments with medication involves the search for pharmacologic agents that facilitate the extinction of fear responses. Animal research suggests that the N-methyl-D-aspartate (NMDA) glutamatergic receptors in the basolateral amygdala receptors are important for the expression of conditioned fears (Walker, Ressler, Lu, & Davis, 2002). Because NMDA receptors in the amygdala are critical for excitatory fear conditioning, and because extinction, like fear acquisition, is a form of learning, researchers have investigated the possibility that NMDA receptors in the amygdala might also be involved in extinction. In fact, research indicates that NMDA receptors in the amygdala play an important role in conditioned fear extinction.

These findings raise the possibility that NMDA agonists, administered before exposure therapy, might facilitate extinction.

One such compound is D-cycloserine (DCS), which has been used for years in humans to treat tuberculosis and is not associated with significant side effects. Animal research has shown that this compound facilitates extinction after either systemic administration or intra-amygdala infusion (Walker et al., 2002). Research on humans suffering from either animal phobia or social anxiety disorder provides preliminary evidence that DCS, administered shortly before an exposure session, can facilitate (i.e., speed up) fear extinction (Hofmann et al., 2006; Ressler et al., 2004). With regard to OCD, two studies found that DCS facilitated the effects of ERP (Kushner et al., 2007; Wilhelm et al., 2008), whereas one study did not (Storch et al., 2007). Further research is needed to understand the reasons for the discrepant results, such as research into the optimal dose of the drug and timing for administration prior to the therapy session, the skill of the therapist in administering ERP, and the way in which treatment progress and outcome is assessed (the benefits of the drug are most apparent in the early sessions of treatment).

ERP as an Adjunct to Medication

Medications are easy to obtain, and do not involve confronting frightening stimuli without resorting to rituals. Accordingly, these are the most commonly used treatments for OCD. Yet, in studies on the effects of SRIs, average post-treatment Y-BOCS scores are in the 15–20 range (e.g., Greist et al., 1995), indicating that even adequate trials of these drugs leave patients with clinically significant OCD symptoms. As a result, researchers have examined whether adding ERP improves outcome following one or more adequate trials of an SRI. Simpson, Gorfinkle, and Liebowitz (1999), for example, offered ERP to six patients who had shown minimal response to adequate trials of SRIs. At the completion of ERP, scores on the Y-BOCS were substantially further reduced, indicating that ERP augments the effects of SRIs in medication-resistant patients. Similar results were reported by Kampman et al. (2002), who provided ERP to 14 patients who had shown less than 25% symptom reduction after 12 weeks on fluoxetine. Tolin and colleagues (2004) studied a sample of 20 patients with high rates of comorbid conditions, who had not responded sufficiently to adequate medication trials. After a 1-month waitlist period, these patients received

15 sessions of ERP. Results indicated a statistically significant drop in OCD symptoms following ERP, and those who completed the study maintained their gains as far out as 6 months after the end of treatment (follow-up mean Y-BOCS score = 19).

Two controlled augmentation studies with large patient samples have since been conducted. In the first, Tenneij et al. (2005) randomly assigned 96 OCD patients on adequate medication trials to receive either 6 additional months of their medication, or ERP. Those who received ERP showed greater improvement on the Y-BOCS (19% improvement) compared to those who continued on medication alone (21% worsening; i.e., an increase in Y-BOCS scores). Analysis of individual patient data showed that even medication *responders* benefitted further from adjunctive ERP. In the second study, Simpson et al. (2008) randomly assigned 108 OCD patients with Y-BOCS scores of 16 or greater, despite a therapeutic SRI dose for at least 12 weeks, to receive either 17 sessions of ERP or stress management training, while continuing SRI pharmacotherapy. They found that ERP was superior to stress management training in reducing OCD symptoms. At week 8, significantly more patients receiving ERP than those receiving stress management training had a decrease of at least 25% on the Y-BOCS, and achieved Y-BOCS scores of 12 or less. Taken together, the controlled and uncontrolled studies reviewed in this section show that augmentation of SRI pharmacotherapy with ERP is an effective strategy for further reducing residual OCD symptoms. The clinical implications of these finding are important, because medication is the most widely available and most widely used form of treatment for OCD, yet it typically produces only modest improvement.

Effectiveness of ERP in Non-Research Settings

Whereas randomized trials substantiate the *efficacy* of ERP, by demonstrating that this treatment leads to significantly more OCD symptom reduction relative to control treatments and other active therapies (e.g., SRI medication), some authors (e.g., Silberschatz in Persons & Silberschatz, 1998) have criticized such studies as not being relevant to "real world" clinical settings. Specifically, fault is found with the fact that most randomized trials are conducted under highly controlled conditions (e.g., expert supervision, use of treatment manuals) and using rarified samples (e.g., highly selective inclusion and exclusion criteria often rule out "complicated"

cases) that are not typical of usual clinical practice. Thus, an important question concerns whether the beneficial effects of this treatment extend beyond randomized trials, to more typical service delivery environments and representative patient populations.

To address this issue, Franklin et al. (2000) examined outcome for 110 consecutively referred individuals with OCD, who received 15 sessions of intensive ERP on an outpatient fee-for-service basis. Half of this sample had comorbid Axis I or Axis II diagnoses, and patients were only denied ERP if they were actively psychotic, abusing substances, or suicidal (conditions under which ERP could be contraindicated). Mean Y-BOCS scores for this highly representative sample improved from 27 to 12 (60% reduction in OCD symptoms). Moreover, only 10 patients dropped out of treatment prematurely. Warren and Thomas (2001) replicated these results in a smaller study (N = 26) conducted within a private practice setting. They reported improvement in Y-BOCS scores from 23 at pretest to 12 at posttest—a 48% reduction. In a multicultural naturalistic study, Friedman and colleagues (2003) found that whereas treatment was effective in reducing OCD and depressive symptoms, many patients reported significant residual symptoms after therapy: mean Y-BOCS scores for African American patients were 24 (pretreatment) and 17 (post-treatment; 27% reduction), and for Caucasians were 26 (pre) and 18 (post; 23% reduction). There were no between-group differences in treatment outcome. Taken together, the findings from these naturalistic studies indicate that the effects of ERP for OCD are transportable from highly controlled research settings to typical clinical settings that serve more heterogeneous patient populations.

Predictors of Response to Exposure-Based Treatment

Given the fact that not all individuals with OCD respond uniformly well to ERP, investigators have been interested in determining the predictors of success and failure. A number of prognostic factors have been identified, most of which can be grouped into three broad categories: (a) ERP procedural variations, (b) patient-related characteristics, and (c) supportive factors.

ERP Procedural Variations

Abramowitz (1996), in a meta-analysis of many treatment studies, examined the relationship between short-term and long-term treatment outcome and the manner in which ERP is delivered. The results from this study can be summarized as follows. First, across the literature, ERP programs that involved more in-session, therapist-supervised exposure practice produced greater short-term and long-term improvements, compared to programs in which all exposure was performed by the patient as home-work assignments. Second, combining in vivo and imaginal exposure was superior to in vivo exposure *alone* in reducing anxiety symptoms. Third, pro-grams in which patients refrained completely from ritualizing during the treatment period (i.e., total response prevention) produced superior immediate and long-term effects, compared to those that involved only partial response prevention.

If in-session exposure practice is an important component of ERP, what is the optimal session fre-quency? To examine whether the robust effects of intensive (daily) therapy are substantially compro-mised by reducing the session frequency, Abramowitz, Foa, and Franklin (2003) compared 15 sessions of intensive (daily) ERP to 15 sessions of ERP delivered on a twice-weekly basis. Whereas intensive therapy was minimally superior to the twice-weekly regimen immediately following treatment (post-treatment Y-BOCS scores were 10 for intensive ERP and 13 for twice-weekly ERP), this difference disappeared at 3-month follow-up (Y-BOCS = 13 for intensive and 14 for twice-weekly). The results of this study suggest that a twice-weekly therapy schedule pro-vides clinicians with a more pragmatic, yet equally effective, alternative to the highly demanding and often impractical intensive protocol.

There also appears to be a relationship between adherence with ERP instructions and treatment outcome (Abramowitz, Franklin, Zoellner, & DiBernardo, 2002; Lax, Basoglu, & Marks, 1992). For example, Abramowitz et al. (2002) found that better outcomes were associated with understand-ing the rationale for ERP techniques, and adhering to the therapist's instructions for exposure practice (both in-session and homework assignments). These findings suggest that it is important for clinicians to provide a compelling explanation for using ERP procedures, and to elicit the patient's input when developing an exposure plan.

Patient Characteristics

A number of patient characteristics have been iden-tified as predictors of poorer treatment response. These include the presence of extremely poor insight into the senselessness of obsessions and compulsions (Foa, 1979; Foa, Abramowitz, Franklin, & Kozak,

1999), severe depression (Abramowitz & Foa, 2000; Abramowitz, Franklin, Kozak, Street, & Foa, 2000; Steketee, Chambless, & Tran, 2001), generalized anxiety disorder (Steketee et al., 2001), extreme emotional reactivity during exposure (Foa et al., 1983), and severe borderline personality traits (Steketee et al., 2001). Whereas some studies have reported that more severe OCD symptoms pre-dicted poorer outcome (e.g., Franklin et al., 2000), others have not (e.g., Foa et al., 1983). However, consistent evidence is emerging to suggest that patients who present with primarily hoarding symp-toms respond less well to traditional exposure-based treatments for OCD (Abramowitz et al., 2003; Mataix-Cols et al., 2002).

Supportive Factors

Hostility from romantic partners and relatives toward the individual with OCD is predictive of premature dropout from ERP, and poor response among patients who complete treatment (Chambless & Steketee, 1999). Interestingly, when partners and relatives express dissatisfaction with patients' *symp-toms*, but do not express personal rejection, such constructive criticism may have motivational prop-erties that enhance treatment response (Chambless & Steketee, 1999).

Conclusions

Prior to the advent of ERP, clinicians were pessimistic about their ability to help people suffering from OCD. Since the pioneering work of the 1960s, ERP has emerged as one of the most effective treatments for OCD. Several types of empirically supported ERP protocols have been developed, with some being more effective than others. Despite the initial prom-ise of multicomponent interventions for OCD, the incorporation of cognitive therapy into ERP pro-grams has not greatly improved treatment outcome (see Chapter 18 in this volume). Further research is required to determine how, if at all, treatment out-come can be augmented by combining ERP with other interventions such as cognitive interventions. Similarly, further research is required to determine whether treatment outcome can be improved by augmenting ERP with SRI medications. Treatment outcome is improved when ERP is added to SRIs. However, the converse has yet to be demonstrated; that is, it has yet to be clearly shown that the effects of ERP are augmented when SRIs are added. One of the most promising options for augmenting ERP is D-cycloserine, but even here, the initial findings have been mixed and more research is required.

Translational research has long been important in developing exposure-based treatments for OCD, beginning with the application of animal behavioral models to humans (Dollard & Miller, 1950), which led to the development of ERP. Later translational research on fear extinction has also informed the refinement of ERP, such as animal research suggesting that ERP will be most effective when conducted under multiple exposure contexts (Bouton, 2002). If the promise of D-cycloserine is fulfilled, then this will be another translational milestone, in which animal research on an "exposure enhancer" (D-cycloserine) has led to treatment advances in humans.

Future Directions

1. The efficacy of ERP has been demonstrated in a wide range of symptom presentations. However, there remain significant subgroups of sufferers for whom ERP has limited efficacy. Research into how ERP may be modified to address the needs of specific subgroups (i.e., individuals with higher overvalued ideas) is warranted.

2. Medications to augment exposure per se (such as DCS) appear to hold promise for the treatment of a wide range of anxiety problems. While the early research on DCS in conjunction with ERP for OCD has been mixed, there are a number of important factors that require investigation in order to clarify its efficacy. For example, will this treatment combination be optionally effective for OCD patients with poor insight?

3. There are several fundamental symptoms of OCD (such as "not just right" experiences) that have not received careful empirical scrutiny using ERP that warrant investigation.

Related Chapters

Chapter 15. Pharmacological Treatments for Obsessive Compulsive Disorder

Chapter 18. Cognitive Treatment for OCD

Chapter 19. Combining Pharmacotherapy and Psychological Treatments for OCD

Chapter 20. Additive and Alternative Approaches to Treating Obsessive Compulsive Disorder

References

Abramowitz, J. S. (1996). Variants of exposure and response prevention in the treatment of obsessive-compulsive disorder: a meta-analysis. *Behavior Therapy, 27*, 583–600.

Abramowitz, J. S. (2006). *Understanding and treating obsessive-compulsive disorder: A cognitive-behavioral approach.* Mahwah, NJ: Erlbaum.

Abramowitz, J. S., Deacon, B. J., & Whiteside, S. P. (2011). *Exposure therapy for anxiety: Principles and practice.* New York: Guilford.

Abramowitz, J. S., & Foa, E. (2000). Does comorbid major depressive disorder influence outcome of exposure and response prevention for OCD? *Behavior Therapy, 31*, 795–800.

Abramowitz, J. S., Foa, E. B., & Franklin, M. E. (2003). Exposure and ritual prevention for obsessive-compulsive disorder: effects of intensive versus twice-weekly sessions. *Journal of Consulting and Clinical Psychology, 71*, 394–398.

Abramowitz, J. S., Franklin, M. E., & Foa, E. B. (2002). Empirical status of cognitive-behavioral therapy for obsessive-compulsive disorder: a meta-analytic review. *Romanian Journal of Cognitive and Behavioral Psychotherapies, 2*, 89–104.

Abramowitz, J. S., Franklin, M. E., Schwartz, S. A., & Furr, J. M. (2003). Symptom presentation and outcome of cognitive-behavioral therapy for obsessive-compulsive disorder. *Journal of Consulting and Clinical Psychology, 71*, 1049–1057.

Abramowitz, J. S., Franklin, M. E., Street, G. P., Kozak, M. J., & Foa, E. B. (2000). Effects of comorbid depression on response to treatment for obsessive-compulsive disorder. *Behavior Therapy, 31*, 517–528.

Abramowitz, J. S., Franklin, M., Zoellner, L., & DiBernardo, C. (2002). Treatment compliance and outcome in obsessive-compulsive disorder. *Behavior Modification, 26*, 447–463.

American Psychiatric Association. (2000). *Diagnostic and statistical manual of mental disorders (4th ed., Text revision) (DSM-IV-TR).* Washington, DC: Author.

Anderson, R. A. & Rees, C. S. (2007) Group versus individual cognitive-behavioural treatment for obsessive-compulsive disorder: A controlled trial. *Behaviour Research and Therapy, 45*, 123–137

American Psychiatric Association. (2007). *Practice guidelines: Treatment of patients with obsessive-compulsive disorder.* Author. Available at: http://www.psychiatryonline.com/pracGuide/pracGuideTopic_10.aspx.

Baer, L. (1994). Factor analysis of symptom subtypes of obsessive compulsive disorder and their relation to personality and tic disorders. *Journal of Clinical Psychiatry, 55*, 18–23.

Bouton, M. E. (1993). Context, time, and memory retrieval in the interference paradigms of Pavlovian learning. *Psychological Bulletin, 114*, 90–99.

Bouton, M. E. (2002). Context, ambiguity, and unlearning: Sources of relapse after behavioral extinction. *Biological Psychiatry, 52*, 976–986.

Chambless, D. L., & Steketee, G. (1999). Expressed emotion and behavior therapy outcome: A prospective study with obsessive-compulsive and agoraphobic outpatients. *Journal of Consulting and Clinical Psychology, 67*, 658–665.

Christensen, H., Hadzi-Pavlovic, D., Andrews, G., & Mattick, R. (1987). Behavior therapy and tricyclic medication in the treatment of obsessive-compulsive disorder: A quantitative review. *Journal of Consulting and Clinical Psychology, 55*, 701–711.

Clark, D. M. (1999). Anxiety disorders: why they persist and how to treat them. *Behaviour Research & Therapy, 37*, S5–S27.

Cordioli, V., Heldt, A., Braga, E., Bochi, D., Margis, R., Basso de Sousa, M., Fonseca Tonello, J., Gus Manfro, G., & Kapczinski, F. (2003). Cognitive-behavioral group therapy in obsessive-compulsive disorder: A randomized clinical trial. *Psychotherapy and Psychosomatics, 72*, 211–216.

Cottraux, J., Mollard, E., Bouvard, M., Marks, I., Sluys, M., Nury, A., Douge, R., & Ciadella, P. (1990). A controlled study of fluvoxamine and exposure in obsessive compulsive disorder. *International Journal of Clinical Psychopharmacology, 5*, 17–30.

Cottraux, J., Note, I., Yao, S. N., Lafont, S., Note, B., Mollard, E., Bouvard, M., Sauteraud, A., Bourgeois, M., & Dartigues, J.-F. (2001). A randomized controlled trial of cognitive therapy versus intensive behavior therapy in obsessive compulsive disorder. *Psychotherapy and Psychosomatics, 70*, 288–297.

Craske, M. G. & Mystkowski, J. L. (2006). Exposure therapy and extinction: Clinical studies. In M.G. Craske, D. Hermans, & D. Vansteenwegen (Eds.), *Fear and learning: From basic processes to clinical implications (pp. 217–233)*. Washington, DC: American Psychological Association.

Dollard, J., & Miller, N. E. (1950). *Personality and psychotherapy: An analysis in terms of learning, thinking, and culture.* New York: McGraw-Hill.

Eddy, K., Dutra, L., Bradley, R., & Weston, D. (2004). A multidimensional meta-analysis of psychotherapy and pharmacotherapy for obsessive-compulsive disorder. *Clinical Psychology Review, 24*, 1011–1030.

Ellis, A. (1962). *Reason and emotion in psychotherapy.* Secaucus NJ: Lyle Stuart.

Emmelkamp, P. M. G., & Beens, H. (1991). Cognitive therapy with obsessive-compulsive disorder: A comparative evaluation. *Behaviour Research and Therapy, 29*, 293–300.

Emmelkamp, P. M. G., & Kraanen, J. (1977). Therapist-controlled exposure *in vivo* versus self-controlled exposure *in vivo*: a comparison with obsessive-compulsive patients. *Behaviour Research and Therapy, 15*, 491–195.

Emmelkamp, P. M. G., Visser, B., & Hoekstra, R. J. (1988). Cognitive therapy vs. exposure in vivo in the treatment of obsessive-compulsives. *Cognitive Therapy and Research, 12*, 103–114.

Fals-Stewart, W., Marks, A. P., & Schafer, J. (1993). A comparison of behavioral group therapy and individual behavior therapy in treating obsessive-compulsive disorder. *The Journal of Nervous and Mental Disease, 181*(3), 189–193.

Foa, E. B. (1979). Failure in treating obsessive-compulsives. *Behaviour Research and Therapy, 17*, 169–176.

Foa, E. B., Abramowitz, J. S., Franklin, M. E., & Kozak, M. J. (1999). Feared consequences, fixity of belief, and treatment outcome in patients with obsessive-compulsive disorder. *Behavior Therapy, 30*, 717–724.

Foa, E. B., Huppert, J. & Cahill, S. (2006). Emotional processing theory: An update. In: B.O. Rothbaum (Ed.). *Pathological anxiety: Emotional processing in etiology and treatment* (3–24). Guilford, New York.

Foa, E. B., & Goldstein, A. (1978). Continuous exposure and complete response prevention in the treatment of obsessive-compulsive neurosis. *Behavior Therapy, 9*, 821–829.

Foa, E. B., Grayson, J. B., Steketee, G. S., Doppelt, H. G., Turner, R. M., & Latimer, P. R. (1983). Success and failure in the behavioral treatment of obsessive-compulsives. *Journal of Consulting and Clinical Psychology, 51*, 287–297.

Foa, E. B., & Kozak, M. J. (1986). Emotional processing of fear: Exposure to corrective information. *Psychological Bulletin, 99*, 20–35.

Foa, E. B., & Kozak, M. J. (1995). DSM-IV field trial: Obsessive-compulsive disorder. *American Journal of Psychiatry, 152*(1), 90–96.

Foa, E. B., & Kozak, M. J. (1996). Psychological treatment for obsessive-compulsive disorder. In M. R. Mavissakalian & R. F. Prien (Eds.), *Long-term treatments of anxiety disorders* (pp. 285–309). Washington, DC: American Psychiatric Press, Inc.

Foa, E., Liebowitz, M. R., Kozak, M. J., Davies, S., Campeas, R., Franklin, M. E., et al. (2005). Randomized, placebo-controlled trial of exposure and ritual prevention, clomipramine, and their combination in the treatment of obsessive-compulsive disorder. *American Journal of Psychiatry, 162*, 151–161.

Foa, E. B., Steketee, G, Grayson, J., Turner, R., & Lattimer, P. (1984). Deliberate exposure and blocking of obsessive-compulsive rituals: Immediate and long-term effects. *Behavior Therapy, 15*, 450–472.

Foa, E. B., Steketee, G., & Milby, J. (1980). Differential effects of exposure and response prevention in obsessive-compulsive washers. *Journal of Consulting and Clinical Psychology, 48*, 71–79.

Foa, E. B., Steketee, G., Turner, R. M., & Fischer, S. C. (1980). Effects of imaginal exposure to feared disasters in obsessive-compulsive checkers. *Behaviour Research and Therapy, 18*, 449–455.

Franklin, M. E., Abramowitz, J. S., Foa, E. B., Kozak, M. J., & Levitt, J. T. (2000). Effectiveness of exposure and ritual prevention for obsessive-compulsive disorder: randomized compared with nonrandomized samples. *Journal of Consulting and Clinical Psychology, 68*(4), 594–602.

Freeston, M. H., & Ladouceur, R. (1999). Exposure and response prevention for obsessive thoughts. *Cognitive & Behavioral Practice, 6*, 362–383.

Freeston, M. H., Ladouceur, R., Gagnon, F., Thibodeau, N., Rheaume, J., Letarte, H., et al. (1997). Cognitive-behavioral treatment of obsessive thoughts: a controlled study. *Journal of Consulting and Clinical Psychology, 65*, 405–413.

Friedman, S., Smith, L. C., Halpern, B., Levine, C., Paradis, C., Viswanathan, R., et al. (2003). Obsessive-compulsive disorder in a multi-ethnic urban outpatient clinic: initial presentation and treatment outcome with exposure and ritual prevention. *Behavior Therapy, 34*, 397–410.

Goodman, W. K., Price, L. H., Rasmussen, S. A., Mazure, C., Delgado, P., Heninger, G. R., & Charney, D. S. (1989). The Yale-Brown Obsessive Compulsive Scale: validity. *Archives of General Psychiatry, 46*, 1012–1016.

Goodman, W. K., Price, L. H., Rasmussen, S. A., Mazure, C., Fleischmann, R. L., Hill, C. L., Heninger, G. R., & Charney, D. S. (1989). The Yale-Brown Obsessive Compulsive Scale: development, use, and reliability. *Archives of General Psychiatry, 46*, 1006–1011.

Grayson, J. B., Foa, E. B., & Steketee, G. (1982). Habituation during exposure treatment: Distraction vs attention-focusing. *Behaviour Research and Therapy, 20*, 323–328.

Greist, J. H., Jefferson, J. W., Kobak, K. A., Katzelnick, D. J., & Serlin, R. C. (1995). Efficacy and tolerability of serotonin transport inhibitors in obsessive compulsive disorder: A meta-analysis. *Archives of General Psychiatry, 52*, 53–60.

Hiss, H., Foa, E. B., & Kozak, M. J. (1994). Relapse prevention program for treatment of obsessive-compulsive disorder. *Journal of Consulting and Clinical Psychology, 62*, 801–808.

Hodgson, R., Rachman, S., & Marks, I. (1972). The treatment of chronic obsessive-compulsive neurosis: follow-up and further findings. *Behaviour Research and Therapy, 10*, 181–189.

Hofmann, S.G., Meuret, A.E., Smits, J.A., Simon, N.M., Pollack, M.H., Eisenmenger, K., et al. (2006): Augmentation of exposure therapy with D-Cycloserine for social anxiety disorder. *Archives of General Psychiatry*, 63, 298–304.

Hohagen, F., Winkelmann, G., Rasche-Rauchle, H., Hand, I., Konig, A., Munchau, N., Hiss, H., Geiger-Kabisch, C., Kappler, C., Schramm, P., Rey, E., Aldenhoff, J., & Berger, M. (1998). Combination of behaviour therapy with fluvoxamine in comparison with behaviour therapy and placebo. *British Journal of Psychiatry*, 173, 71–78.

Johnstone, J. & Page, A. (2004). Attention to phobic stimuli during exposure: The effect of distraction on anxiety reduction, self-efficacy and perceived control, *Behaviour Research and Therapy*, 42, 249–275.

Kampman, M., Keijsers, G. P. J., Hoogduin, C. A. L., & Verbank, M. J. P. M. (2002). Addition of cognitive-behavior therapy for obsessive-compulsive disorder patients non-responding to fluoxetine. *ACTA Psychiatrica Scandinavica*, 106, 314–319.

Kringlen, E. (1965). Obsessional neurotics: A long-term follow-up. *British Journal of Psychiatry*, 111, 709–722.

Kushner, M. G., Kim, S. W., Donahue, C., Thuras, P., Kotlyar, M., et al. (2007). D-cycloserine augmented exposure therapy for obsessive-compulsive disorder. *Biological Psychiatry*, 62, 835–838.

Kushner, M. G., Kim, S-W., Donahue, C., Thuras, P., Adson, D., Kvtlyar, M., McCabe, J., Peterson, J., & Foa, E. (2007). D-cycloserine augmented exposure therapy for obsessive-compulsive disorder. *Biological Psychiatry*, 62, 835–838.

Lang, P. (1977). Imagery in therapy: An information processing analysis of fear, *Behavior Therapy*, 8, 862–886.

Lax, T., Basoglu, M., & Marks, I. M. (1992). Expectancy and compliance as predictors of outcome in obsessive-compulsive disorder. *Behavioural Psychotherapy*, 20, 257–266.

LeDoux, J. E. (2000). Emotion circuits in the brain. *Annual Review of Neuroscience, 23*, 155–184.

Lindsay, M., Crino, R., & Andrews, G. (1997). Controlled trial of exposure and response prevention in obsessive-compulsive disorder. *British Journal of Psychiatry, 171*, 135–139.

March, J. S., Frances, A., Carpenter, D., Kahn, D. (1997). The expert consensus guidelines series: Treatment of obsessive-compulsive disorder. *Journal of Clinical Psychiatry*, 58 (Suppl. 4).

Mataix-Cols, D., Marks, I. M., Greist, J. H., Kobak, K. A., & Baer, L. (2002). Obsessive-compulsive symptom dimensions as predictors of compliance with and response to behaviour therapy: results from a controlled trial. *Psychotherapy and Psychosomatics*, 71, 255–262.

McLean, P. D., Whittal, M. L., Thordarson, D. S., Taylor, S., Sochting, I., Koch, W. J., Paterson, R., & Anderson, K. W. (2001). Cognitive versus behavior therapy in the group treatment of obsessive-compulsive disorder. *Journal of Consulting and Clinical Psychology*, 69, 205–214.

McNally, R. J. (2007). Mechanisms of exposure therapy: How neuroscience can improve psychological treatments for anxiety disorders. *Clinical Psychology Review*, 27, 750–759.

Meyer, V. (1966). Modification of expectations in cases with obsessional rituals. *Behaviour Research and Therapy*, 4, 273–280.

Meyer, V., Levy, R., & Schnurer, A. (1974). The behavioral treatment of obsessive-compulsive disorders. In H. R. Beech (Ed.), *Obsessional states* (pp. 233–258). London: Methuen.

Montgomery, S. A., McIntyre, A., Ostenheider, M., Sarteschi, P., Zitterl, W., Zohar, J., Birkett, M., & Wood, A. J. (1993). A double-blind placebo-controlled study of fluoxetine in patients with DSM-III-R obsessive-compulsive disorder. *European Neuropsychopharmacology, 3*, 142–152.

Mowrer, O. (1960). *Learning theory and behavior.* New York: Wiley.

Nakatani, E., Nakagawa, A., Nakao, T., Yoshizato, C., Nabeyama, M., Kudo, A., Isomura, K., Kato, N., Yoshioka, K., & Kawamoto, M. (2005). A randomized trial of Japanese patients with obsessive-compulsive disorder: effectiveness of behavior therapy and fluvoxamine. *Psychotherapy and Psychosomatics, 74*, 269–276.

O'Connor, K., Todorov, C., Robillard, S., Borgeat, F., & Brault, M. (1999). Cognitive-behaviour therapy and medication in the treatment of obsessive-compulsive disorder: A controlled study. *Canadian Journal of Psychiatry, 44*, 64–71.

Persons, J. B., & Silberschatz, G. (1998). Are results of randomized controlled trials useful to psychotherapists? *Journal of Consulting and Clinical Psychology, 66*, 126–135.

Rachman, S. (1980) Emotional processing. *Behaviour Research and Therapy, 18*, 51–60.

Rachman, S. (1993). Obsessions, responsibility and guilt. *Behaviour Research and Therapy, 31*, 149–154.

Rachman, S., Hodgson, R., & Marks, I. (1971). The treatment of chronic obsessive-compulsive neurosis. *Behaviour Research and Therapy, 9*, 237–247.

Rabavilas, A., Boulougouris, J., & Stefanis, C. (1976). Duration of flooding sessions in the treatment of obsessive-compulsive patients. *Behaviour Research and Therapy, 14*, 349–355.

Ressler, K. J., Rothbaum, B. O., Tannenbaum, L., Anderson, P., Graap, K., Zimand, E., et al. (2004). Cognitive enhancers as adjuncts to psychotherapy: Use of D-cycloserine in phobics to facilitate extinction of fear. *Archives of General Psychiatry, 61*, 1136–1144.

Rowa, K., Antony, M. M., Summerfeldt, L. J., Purdon, C., Young, L. & Swinson, R. P. (2007). Office-based vs. home-based behavioral treatment for obsessive compulsive disorder: A preliminary study. *Behaviour Research and Therapy, 45*, 1883–1892.

Salkovskis, P. M. (1996). Cognitive-behavioral approaches to the understanding of obsessional problems. In R. Rapee (Ed.), *Current controversies in the anxiety disorders* (pp. 103–133). New York: Guilford.

Simpson, H. B., Foa, E., Liebowitz, M., Ledley, D., Huppert, J., Cahill, S., Vermes, D., Schmidt, A., Hembree, E., Franklin, M., Campeas, R., & Hahn, C. (2008). A randomized controlled trial of cognitive-behavior therapy for augmenting pharmacotherapy in obsessive-compulsive disorder. *American Journal of Psychiatry, 165*, 621–630.

Simpson, H. B., Gorfinkle, K. S., & Liebowitz, M. R. (1999). Cognitive-behavioral therapy as an adjunct to serotonin reuptake inhibitors in obsessive-compulsive disorder: an open trial. *Journal of Clinical Psychiatry, 60*, 584–590.

Solomon, R. L., Kamin, L. J., & Wynne, L. C. (1953). Traumatic avoidance learning: The outcomes of several extinction procedures with dogs. *Journal of Abnormal Social Psychology, 48*, 291–302.

Steketee, G. S., Chambless, D. L., & Tran, G. Q. (2001). Effects of Axis I and II comorbidity on behavior therapy outcome for obsessive-compulsive disorder and agoraphobia. *Comprehensive Psychiatry, 42*, 76–86.

Storch, E. A., Merlo, L. J., Bengtson, M., Murphy, T. K., Lewis, M. H., Yang, M. C., et al. (2007). D-cycloserine does not enhance exposure-response prevention therapy in obsessive-compulsive disorder. *International Clinical Psychopharmacology, 22*, 230–237.

Taylor, S. (1995). Assessment of obsessions and compulsions: reliability, validity, and sensitivity to treatment effects. *Clinical Psychology Review, 15*, 261–296.

Tenneij, N., van Megen, H., Denys, D., & Westenberg, H. (2005). Behavior therapy augments response of patients with obsessive-compulsive disorder responding to drug treatment. *Journal of Clinical Psychiatry, 66*, 1169–1175.

Tolin, D. F. & Hannan, S. (2005). The role of the therapist in behavior therapy for OCD. In J. S. Abramowitz & A. C. Houts (Eds.), *Concepts and controversies in obsessive-compulsive disorders* (pp. 317–332). New York: Springer.

Tolin, D. F., Maltby, N., Diefenbach, G. J., Hannan, S. E., & Worhunsky, P. (2004). Cognitive-behavioral therapy for medication nonresponders with obsessive-compulsive disorder: A wait-list controlled open trial. *Journal of Clinical Psychiatry, 65*, 922–931.

Van Balkom, A. J. L. M., De Haan, E., Van Oppen, P., Spinhoven, P., Hoogduin, K. A. L., & Van Dyck, R. (1998). Cognitive and behavioral therapies alone versus in combination with fluvoxamine in the treatment of obsessive compulsive disorder. *The Journal of Nervous and Mental Disorders, 186*(8), 492–499.

Van Oppen, P., & Arntz, A. (1994). Cognitive therapy for obsessive-compulsive disorder. *Behaviour Research and Therapy, 32*, 79–87.

Van Oppen, P., De Haan, E., Van Balkom, A. J. L. M., Spinhoven, P., Hoogduin, K., & Van Dyck, R. (1995). Cognitive therapy and exposure *in vivo* in the treatment of obsessive compulsive disorder. *Behaviour Research and Therapy, 33*, 379–390.

Walker, D. L., Ressler, K. J., Lu, K.-T., & Davis, M. (2002). Facilitation of conditioned fear extinction by systemic administration or intra-amygdala infusions of D-cycloserine as assessed with fear-potentiated startle in rats. *Journal of Neuroscience, 22*, 2343–2351.

Warren, R. & Thomas, J. C. (2001). Cognitive-behavior therapy of obsessive-compulsive disorder in private practice: an effectiveness study. *Journal of Anxiety Disorders, 15*, 277–285.

Wilhelm, S., Buhlmann, U., Tolin, D. F., Meunier, S. A., Pearlson, G. D., Reese, H. E., et al. (2008). Augmentation of behavior therapy with D-cycloserine for obsessive-compulsive disorder. *American Journal of Psychiatry, 165*, 335–341.

Zohar, J. & Insel, T. R. (1987). Obsessive-compulsive disorder: Psychobiological approaches to diagnosis, treatment, and pathophysiology. *Biological Psychiatry, 22*, 667–687.

Cognitive Treatment for OCD

Maureen L. Whittal *and* Melisa Robichaud

Abstract

The cornerstone of cognitive treatment (CT) for OCD is based upon the knowledge that unwanted intrusions are essentially a universal experience. As such, it is not the presence of the intrusion that is problematic but rather the associated meaning or interpretation. Treatment is flexible, depending upon the nature of the appraisals and beliefs, but can include strategies focused on inflated responsibility and overestimation of threat, importance and control of thoughts, and the need for perfectionism and certainty. The role of concealment and the relationship to personal values are important maintaining and etiological factors. The short-term and long-term treatment outcome is reviewed, along with predictors of treatment response and mechanisms of action, and the chapter concludes with future directions regarding CT for OCD.

Keywords: cognitive treatment, OCD, treatment outcome, mediators, prediction

The treatment of obsessive compulsive disorder (OCD) has seen great advancement in the past 40 years, shifting from a view of OCD as highly treatment-resistant to that of good treatment efficacy using empirically supported psychotherapies. A relatively recent treatment that has shown promise is cognitively focused therapy for OCD. In the present chapter, we will review the evolution from behavior therapy to cognitive therapy for OCD, as well as provide a detailed description of the OCD cognitive treatment protocol, using clinical case examples. In addition, a thorough review of research on the short-term and long-term efficacy of cognitive therapy, both in isolation and in combination with exposure and response prevention, will be presented. Finally, mediating variables underlying the effectiveness of the treatment, as well as predictors of treatment outcome, will be discussed.

The Evolution of Cognitive Therapy for OCD

The introduction of behavioral conceptualizations to the understanding of anxiety disorders led to great strides in the treatment for OCD. Previously viewed as an intractable disorder when psychoanalytic theories were applied, the two-stage theory of fear acquisition (Dollard & Miller, 1950; Mowrer, 1939) provided the first behavioral foray into a model for the development and maintenance of OCD (see Chapter 11 for more detail on behavioral theories of OCD). The resultant psychosocial treatment, exposure and response prevention (ERP), is currently the treatment of choice for OCD. In isolation, it is considered efficacious for mild to moderate forms of the disorder, and in more severe forms of the disorder, a combination of medication and ERP is the recommendation (March, Frances, Carpenter, & Kahn, 1997). Moreover, a number of clinical trials conducted throughout the world identified significant treatment gains when ERP was the assigned treatment: in a recent meta-analysis, Yale-Brown Obsessive Compulsive Scale (Y-BOCS) scores showed an average decline of 43.5% following ERP, and an aggregate effect size (ES) of $d=1.50$ for ERP was found (Abramowitz, Franklin & Foa, 2002).

It is clear that ERP is a highly efficacious treatment for OCD, and that significant gains result, both in the short and long term (see Chapter 17 for more detail on treatment outcome with behavior therapy).

Despite the obvious benefits of ERP, it also has some limitations that dampen its salutary effects, largely due to the nature of the intervention itself. In brief, ERP involves repeated exposure to feared situations, and the suspension of compulsive responses. For example, an individual with contamination obsessions and associated washing rituals might be asked to touch a bathroom door handle and resist the compulsion to wash their hands. Repeated exposure to a feared situation and blocking of the compulsive response is posited to provide disconfirming evidence about the dangerousness of the situation, and to allow for habituation (Foa & Kozak, 1986). Although ERP is typically conducted in a graduated fashion, wherein moderate fears are addressed prior to facing more severe fears, individuals are nonetheless required to approach situations that are perceived as threatening, that cause marked anxiety, and that typically have been avoided. As a result, a significant minority of OCD patients has been found to either refuse or drop out of treatment. Up to 25% of patients refuse ERP treatment, and 3% to 12% drop out of treatment early (Foa, Steketee, Grayson, & Doppelt, 1983; Kobak et al., 1998; van Oppen, et al., 1995). Although ERP remains an efficacious treatment for OCD, Stanley and Turner (1995) found that the benefits were attenuated when a conservative estimate of 30% was used to account for individuals who refuse or drop out of treatment. Of note, only 63% of OCD patients will display at least a moderate reduction in symptoms at post-treatment. Moreover, research suggests that 10% to 33% of OCD patients fail either to show any benefits from ERP, to meet criteria for improvement, or to maintain their treatment gains (Foa, Steketee, & Ozarow, 1985; Foa & Kozak, 1996; Steketee, Henninger, & Pollard, 2000).

The efficacy of ERP may also be impacted by the particular symptom presentation of OCD patients. Compulsions are highly varied and idiographic, ranging from behavioral rituals such as washing, checking, or ordering/arranging, to mental rituals and neutralizations such as the mental repetition of prayers or specific words or sentences. In a review of treatment outcome studies, Ball, Baer, and Otto (1996) concluded that although ERP has established benefits for OCD patients presenting with washing and checking compulsions, its effectiveness for other OCD subtypes was less clear. In particular, ERP alone is viewed as inadequate for the treatment of pure obsessionals and ruminators, primary obsessional slowness, clinical hoarding, and symmetry/ordering rituals (Clark, 2005; Frost & Steketee, 1998; Rachman, 1985, 2003; Salkovskis & Westbrook, 1989).

Despite the obvious efficacy of ERP in treating many OCD symptoms, there clearly remain significant limitations such that alternative treatment options are warranted. Since the seminal article by Salkovskis (1985) elucidating the role of cognitive factors in the maintenance of OCD, researchers have identified a number of dysfunctional beliefs linked to OCD, including overimportance of thoughts, exaggerated responsibility, the need to control thoughts, and overestimation of threat (see Obsessive Compulsive Cognitions Working Group [OCCWG], 1997 for a review). To date, a number of contemporary cognitive theories and associated treatments have been developed (e.g., Clark & Purdon, 1993; Rachman, 1997, 1998). The underlying principle of the current cognitive conceptualizations of OCD is that unwanted intrusions are a universal and normal experience, and it is the individual's appraisal of the intrusion, and resultant response to that appraisal, that leads to the development and maintenance of OCD (see Chapter 12 for a discussion of cognitive models of OCD). Inherent in cognitive theory is the development of an idiographic model for OCD, such that treatment is tailored to a patient's particular symptom presentation and dysfunctional beliefs. Given the limitations of ERP in addressing certain OCD subtypes, as well as the difficulty for a number of patients in tolerating exposure, cognitive therapy may prove a viable alternative to ERP and a complement to existing behavioral interventions.

Treatment
Psychoeducation

Subsequent to assessment, cognitive treatment begins with presentation of an idiographic cognitive model for the maintenance of OCD. The goals of the educational sessions are to discuss the ubiquity of unwanted intrusions (e.g., Rachman & de Silva, 1978) and to identify the importance of the appraisal process. Appraisals are differentiated from feared consequences, and are identified as the meaning to the individual if the feared consequence were to occur. For example, upon leaving the house, a typical person with doubting and checking symptoms may have an intrusive thought of the stove being on. An appraisal typically associated with this intrusion is related to responsibility (e.g., "it will be my fault if there is a fire; I'm careless"). Depending upon the content of the intrusion, some appraisals are more easily accessible than others. Obsessionals with ego-dystonic repugnant intrusions typically have little trouble in identifying appraisals (e.g., "I'm evil. I'm dangerous"), whereas others may have more difficulty. Given that unwanted intrusions are essentially universal, treatment does not directly target obsessions. However, as appraisals tend to differentiate clinical from nonclinical presentations, treatment is focused on identifying, challenging, and testing existing interpretations.

To illustrate the importance of the appraisal process, patients are provided a list of intrusions experienced by people without OCD (Rachman & de Silva, 1978). Using this list, patients are asked to identify infrequent intrusions that are associated with little to no distress. The appraisals of the frequent and infrequent intrusions can be graphically illustrated side by side, using a whiteboard. Figure 18.1 illustrates the idiographic cognitive model. The right-hand side of the figure reflects the appraisal process experienced by a doubter/checker, whereas the left-hand side of Figure 18.1 illustrates a typical but relatively nondistressing intrusion. The difference between the appraisals is clear. The OCD appraisals on the right-hand side of Figure 18.1 are characterized by negative, personally relevant meaning, whereas the appraisals of the infrequent intrusions on the left-hand side of Figure 18.1 tend to be neutral in meaning and nonthreatening. As treatment is focused on the appraisals, initial assignments involve increasing familiarity with the cognitive model by identifying appraisals while experiencing an obsession. Patients are provided self-monitoring forms, and are asked to track a variety of situations in which intrusions and associated appraisals are experienced.

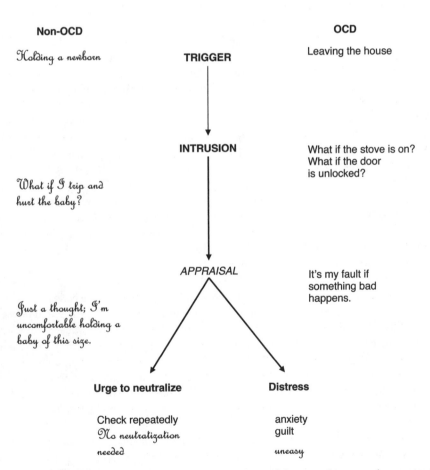

Fig. 18.1. The CT model for maintenance of OCD illustrating the importance of the appraisal process and contrasting it with appraisals of intrusions experienced by people without *OCD*.

The universality of unwanted intrusions is the foundation from which treatment is based. As such, this information is emphasized throughout treatment. For some patients, the ubiquity of unwanted intrusions comes as a surprise and a relief. Others may question or not believe that everyone experiences unwanted intrusions. Regardless of preexisting knowledge, patients are asked to share the list of intrusions experienced by nonclinical individuals with friends and family members. For those patients who have concealed their OCD, this task is placed later in treatment. Alternatively, if available, clinicians can ask their coworkers to anonymously complete a survey regarding their own experience of unwanted intrusions. The goal with these surveys is to normalize the presence of intrusions, and for patients to have explicit knowledge that people they know also experience unwanted intrusions that are not that different in content from their own. Part of the exercise is to also make enquiries regarding how others appraise their intrusions. The latter is another opportunity for patients to distinguish the threatening appraisals that characterize their OCD from those experienced by people with infrequent intrusions. If the therapists are comfortable in sharing their own experiences with infrequent intrusions, it would be appropriate to do so at this stage of treatment, as it aids in the normalization process.

The Cognitive Approach to OCD

Given the heterogeneous presentation of OCD, the direction of treatment is dependent upon the characteristics of the appraisals. Self-monitoring and self-report questionnaires (e.g., the Obsessional Belief Questionnaire (OBQ) Interpretations of Intrusions Inventory (III)) are helpful tools to ascertain the relative importance of cognitive domains. The approaches suggested herein are discussed according to cognitive domain but how they are put together in the course of treatment is idiographic. The existing published treatment manuals (e.g., Rachman, 2003, Wilhelm & Steketee, 2006) are also reflective of this flexible approach to treatment. Despite the varying presentations and treatment strategies, the overarching goal remains the same for each patient; to help them construct a less threatening explanation based upon their own experience that accounts for the development and maintenance of the intrusions.

Importance and Control of Thoughts

This cognitive domain reflects the tendency to view the mere presence of a thought as suggestive of its importance, as well as the belief that one should be able to control one's thoughts. It is likely to be a central one for obsessionals and those with OCD themes that include ego-dystonic, repugnant thoughts, images, and impulses. Thought-action fusion (TAF) and the self-propelling nature of thought characterize overimportance of thoughts. If a thought is considered important, a common response is to dwell on that thought, which ultimately strengthens the belief in its importance. In dwelling on thoughts, patients often wonder why such an unusual thought is present, that it must mean something if it has occurred. Using ex-consequential reasoning (Arntz, Rauner, & van den Hout, 1995), the anxiety that typically accompanies these thoughts may also provide evidence that the thought is important (i.e., "if I'm anxious, it must be dangerous").

TAF (Shafran, Thordarson & Rachman, 1996), as the name suggests, is the belief that thought and outcome or action are linked. Factor analysis supports a two-factor solution, *likelihood TAF* and *moral TAF*. Likelihood TAF reflects the belief that a thought (e.g., family member involved in a motor vehicle accident) increases the probability of that event. Moral TAF involves the judgment that thought and actions are morally equivalent (e.g., an unwanted thought of stabbing the family dog is as bad as stabbing the dog).

To the extent that a thought is appraised as foreshadowing the future (i.e., likelihood TAF) or being morally equivalent to engaging in the action (moral TAF), it follows that the thought is likely to be considered important. Challenging the power and independence of thought (i.e., a thought does not start a chain reaction resulting in the feared consequence) can be accomplished through thought experiments. Patients are asked to think about an untoward event happening to an individual who is a routine part of the patient's life. Often, the clinician is the "target" of these initial thought experiments, which can also include family and friends. The untoward event is meant to be something that is observable to the patient and uncommon, but not rare. If a low (e.g., getting typhoid) or high (e.g., stomach flu in January) base rate event is chosen, it provides no information on the power or independence of thought.

The strength of belief in TAF lies on a continuum. For those who hold strong TAF beliefs, Freeston, Rhéume and Ladouceur (1996) suggest using inanimate objects (e.g., thinking about a reliable appliance breaking) for initial thought experiments. Interestingly, likelihood TAF almost always focuses on negative outcomes. In the absence of a thought disorder, TAF for positive events (e.g., thinking about winning the lottery increases the likelihood) is rare. However, when the latter is present, positive TAF experiments (e.g., purchasing inexpensive scratch tickets and thinking about winning) can be instituted. Thought experiments about adverse events continue throughout treatment, with the severity of the outcome increasing (e.g., mild ankle sprain, broken bone, coma, death). All experiments are debriefed according to what they reveal about the ability of thought to produce outcome, and the independence of thought and action.

Using a continuum can be a helpful strategy to challenge moral TAF. Depending upon the intent of the exercise, the continuum can take several forms. In one version, the continuum is anchored at each extreme with "best and worst person." The people chosen in these extremes are either public figures or individuals personally known to the patient. In the context of the best and worst anchors, the patient places him/herself on the continuum. Individuals experiencing ego-dystonic obsessions often place themselves near to or at the worst end of the continuum. Situations varying in intentionality are put forward, as well as those that are differentiated by thought and action. Examples include thoughts of cheating on your taxes versus actually doing so, using your vehicle as a weapon to murder another person, accidentally killing someone (manslaughter), and killing an individual who committed suicide by jumping in front of the car. Typically, patients have no trouble rating the relative goodness/badness of the person, despite the brief descriptions, perhaps secondary to a tendency to engage in black and white thinking. A double standard often becomes apparent, where patients are able to separate thought from action for others, but not for themselves. Investigating the origin and challenging the utility of the double standard, as well as exploring the feared consequences associated with eradicating it, can result in a reassessment of themselves in a more positive light.

A different type of continuum may be helpful for individuals with a strong moral code, or the belief that being a responsible person is a positive personality trait. Anchors similar to the previous continuum are used, and the patient provides names of people that s/he personally knows at each of the anchors. Relative "goodness" and "badness" is emphasized during this exercise, as patients often do not personally know people who are "truly bad" but merely "bad" relative to the other people in their lives. Once these anchors are identified, the patient once again places him/herself on the continuum. The patient and therapist collaborate on the adjectives that would describe each of the people at the anchors (e.g., kind, caring, responsible, selfish, insensitive, etc.) and the percentage of time the person displays this characteristic. The clinician endeavors to ensure that the patient has realistic percentages, as opposed to those that may reflect black and white thinking. The patient is then asked to rate the percentage of time they display the same behaviors (e.g., "how often do you show others that you care?" "How often are you selfish?"). The goal of this type of continuum is twofold. An initial goal is to have patients recognize that they do not have access to the same information in judging themselves as other people. In judging themselves, they have access to their thoughts as well as their behaviors, whereas for others, judgments of worth/value/responsibility are based exclusively upon on observable behaviors. Clinicians emphasize that we only see what others want to show us, and we cannot know the thoughts of other people. More importantly, how we judge others, and how others judge us, is based upon our actions, not on our thoughts.

If a thought is appraised as important and likely to start a chain reaction of events terminating in catastrophe, it follows that the intrusion should be controlled by either quick removal or efforts to prevent its initial appearance. Mental control strategies include thought suppression, distraction, and mental rituals (e.g., changing the word "kill" into "kiss"). Mental control strategies, paradoxically, serve to increase the frequency of intrusions, likely due in part to the heightened focus of attention on the thought process. Attention experiments can illustrate this process. A meaningless target is identified (e.g., "for sale" signs, flags) and patients are asked to recall instances of seeing the target item in the previous week. Patients are then assigned to look for and record sightings of the target item. Not surprisingly, attention toward a stimulus increases the frequency with which it is seen and remembered, particularly when it has meaning. Other examples of the latter include buying a new vehicle and seeing it with increasing frequency on the street. Couples who are pregnant also commonly report seeing a higher frequency of pregnant women, compared to the months prior to contemplation of starting a family. These numerous examples provide an alternate explanation for the increased frequency of the thoughts—that they seem more frequent because of the importance and meaning attributed to them, and because of the increased attention paid to these thoughts.

In another technique, being "on duty" or hypervigilant for intrusions is contrasted with being "off duty" regarding thoughts in an alternating day experiment (Rachman, 2003). At the end of each day, patients are asked to record the severity of their OCD, anxiety, responsibility, and percentage of the day they were able to complete the strategy of the day (i.e., being off duty/letting thoughts come and go, versus being on duty/hypervigilant for intrusions). Contrary to their predictions, patients who are able to be off duty often experience less OCD, anxiety, and responsibility. Using the conclusions reached with these alternating-day experiments, patients are encouraged to let thoughts in, and decrease reliance on efforts to block or get rid of thoughts.

Inflated Responsibility and Overestimation of Threat

Salkovskis (1985) highlighted responsibility interpretations in his cognitive model of OCD, and subsequently suggested that appraisals of responsibility are associated with increased awareness of intrusions and associated triggers, and attempts to discharge responsibility that include overt and covert neutralizing (Salkovskis, 1999). Inflated responsibility potentially plays a role in all OCD presentations, but is particularly evident among individuals with contamination concerns and doubting/checking (e.g., "it will be my fault if something bad happens to my family"). Pie charting is a central strategy for challenging responsibility. Ratings of subjective probability for either a hypothetical (e.g., if there were a house fire tomorrow) or actual event (e.g., a child

falls and scrapes his knee) can be used to illustrate this strategy. The patient and therapist collaborate regarding the other people or situations that contribute to the event under investigation. The patient is included in this list, but is only considered after others are given consideration. Relative proportions of responsibility are graphically assigned, again with the patient's portion assigned at the end. Logical estimates of responsibility, once other factors are considered, are often much lower compared to subjective responsibility estimates. For some, responsibility is seen as absolute (i.e., they are either responsible or not). The goal with pie charting is viewing responsibility as a shared phenomenon. Figure 18.2 demonstrates a pie chart with an individual concerned about contaminating a person who broke into her car. She initially assumed high amounts of responsibility, but after considering the other people and factors involved, the amount of responsibility she assumed was notably lower.

Responsibility transfers can be useful if the patient cannot delegate tasks to others (e.g., the spouse that must retire for the evening prior to the patient's nighttime checking routine). It is, however, not helpful if patients are purposely avoiding responsibility (e.g., the patient who quickly exits the house, leaving the spouse to lock the door). Using the example of a checker, the patient's spouse or family member who lives in the same house is asked to assume physical and psychological responsibility for the safety and security of the household. If helpful, a contract that both parties sign can be written up to reflect the agreement. The spouse then assumes the checking duties, if they so wish, as the choice to check now belongs to

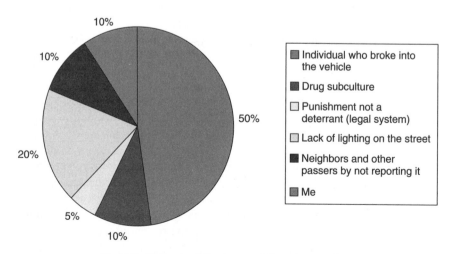

Fig. 18.2. Challenging inflated responsibility using a pie chart.

the spouse. The patient refrains from overseeing the process or seeking reassurance regarding completion of the activities. A slight variation of this exercise includes an alternating-day experiment that also addresses overestimation of threat. The spouse is asked to check on some nights but not others, and to keep track of each condition. Each morning the patient is asked to review the safety and security of the household. The goal of this behavioral experiment is twofold: allowing the sharing of responsibility, and assessing the lack of catastrophe associated with not checking.

As suggested above, overestimation of threat is closely related to inflated responsibility. Perhaps the failure to account for all the steps that would need to occur prior to the final feared consequence leads to threat overestimation. For example, leaving a stove burner on is often a direct line to an uncontrollable fire. Table 18.1 lists the other necessary steps prior to the final feared consequence. Probabilities associated with each step are estimated. The logical probability of the final feared event is the multiplicative product of the steps before it. For example if there are three steps, each with a 1 in 10 chance of occurrence, the overall probability is 1/1000.

Perfectionism and Certainty

The need to have order, and to do things in a particular way, is a characteristic feature of people with OCD. For some it is associated with magical thinking, and the compulsions involve efforts to keep others safe, likely reflecting appraisals of overimportance of thoughts and inflated responsibility. For others, the need to have things in a particular place or done in a particular way reflects personal preference, and avoidance of tension and anxiety should it not be completed to the individual's satisfaction. There is often an ego-syntonic foundation to the behaviors (e.g., they like to have things clean). What is distressing is the amount of time it takes to achieve an acceptable standard. Challenging this perfectionism involves identifying the feared consequences, beyond anxiety/tension, associated with not being perfect. Once the function of the perfectionism is identified, designing a behavioral experiment to test these beliefs is the main thrust of treatment. As is typical in other behavioral experiments, it becomes important to construct experiments with observable and measurable effects (i.e., an increase in anxiety is not sufficient, but testing the consequences of high anxiety may be the focus of the experiment). Outcomes that are concrete and observable allow for maximal disconfirmation.

The need for certainty is closely related to perfectionism. With the exception of the need to know (e.g., people who have difficulty driving secondary to looping back to read billboards), the need for certainty likely plays a role in many other OCD presentations (e.g., certainty that the door is locked, that something is clean, and that danger is removed). If uncertainty exists, then it is possible that a mistake is looming; not knowing for certain is often equated with the possibility that it isn't correct. Normalizing uncertainty is helpful, which can be done through surveys. A typical example includes surveying the number of non-OCD people who remember locking their door, and contrast it with the individual's level of certainty that it is locked. It is quite common for people to not recall locking their door, yet they "know" that it is locked. The contrast between these positions can be surprising, as it is often not the case with an OCD individual.

Table 18.1 Subjective probability of the feared consequence = 70%

Event		Probability
1.	Leaving stove burner on	1/100
2.	Something flammable on or near stove	10/100
3.	Catches fire	50/100
4.	Smoke alarm doesn't go off	1/1000
5.	Goes unnoticed by occupants of the house	10/100
6.	House engulfed in flames Probability of that final step is	

$$\frac{1 \times 10 \times 50 \times 1 \times 10 = 5000}{100 \times 100 \times 100 \times 1000} = \frac{000005\%}{100,000,000,000}$$

The goal with these surveys is to come to the conclusion that just because something isn't recalled, doesn't mean that it wasn't done correctly. Not knowing for sure, or not remembering, is a normal part of the human experience, as many overlearned activities are not encoded as meaningful secondary to the frequency of their occurrence.

Relationships between Values, Beliefs, and Intrusions

Although the experience of unwanted intrusions is essentially universal, the content of the intrusions is often a reflection of the individual's values. Using a nonclinical sample, Rowa and Purdon (2003) reported that participants who were asked questions regarding their most upsetting thought believed the thought contradicted valued aspects of self, more so compared to participants reporting on a least upsetting thought. People tend to not have intrusions about individuals who are confident and strong, but rather those who are perceived as weak and vulnerable (e.g., children or the elderly). Moreover, intrusions tend also to focus on people or groups that are particularly important to the individual (e.g., a new mother who experiences intrusions regarding her infant).

Personal values likely also play an important role in the development of repetitive intrusions. For a thought to be noticed and recalled, it must be memorable in some way; for example, one that runs counter to existing values. For something to be appraised as "bad" or inappropriate, there must be a framework to identify it as such, and it must be distinguished from "right" or acceptable. For instance, it is impossible for an atheist to experience an intrusion perceived as blasphemous. If an individual with a history of violence has a thought about harming another person, it would be considered consistent with the existing value system and would not raise internal alarm bells regarding the possibility of losing control. On the other hand, a pacifist who has a violent thought would be more likely to react and remember that thought, due to its inconsistency with the preexisting value system.

The above relationship between values, beliefs, and intrusions is explained to patients, and a tentative reinterpretation is put forward. As discussed earlier, the person often believes that the intrusion is evidence that they are evil and untrustworthy. Alternatively, the therapist suggests that intrusions became repetitive *because* they are so different from the fundamental nature of the individual. Further, the person reacted with horror *because* they are especially kind, caring, and sensitive. Although this interchange is typically presented after several sessions, patients may respond with skepticism. If so, they are encouraged to not reject the reinterpretation but rather let it remain as a possibility. Patients are then asked to "build their case" that they are indeed a kind, caring and sensitive person. This exercise is idiographic, but can include categorizing everyday behaviors (e.g., giving up a seat on a crowded bus to an elderly person) as reflective of someone who is kind or insensitive.

The Maintaining Role of Concealment

It is not uncommon for people with OCD to conceal their unwanted thoughts and compulsive behaviors from others. As Newth and Rachman (2001) discuss, there are a variety of reasons for concealment. However, the central fear that promotes concealment is a concern that others will think about the OCD individual the way they think of themselves (i.e., mad, bad, or dangerous) and abandon or reject the person (e.g., "if my spouse knew about my violent thoughts toward her, she would be scared of me and leave the home"). If concealment is an issue as treatment progresses, decreasing it becomes a therapeutic target, provided there is a trusted person in the patient's life.

Dropping concealment is typically introduced in the latter third of treatment, for two primary reasons. It is often a very difficult task for patients, and is quite anxiety provoking. It also provides therapists the time to get to know the patient, establish trust and rapport, and become informed regarding the people in their lives. It is recommended that only those close to the patient, who know the individual well, be considered as potential people with whom to reveal information. A close friend or family member, who has the benefit of knowing the person in a variety of situations, is in a better position to offer an opinion compared to a casual acquaintance.

Concealment is particularly common among people with ego-dystonic obsessions. The goal of revealing obsessions is a disconfirmation, showing that others do not believe the obsessional to be a danger, and that they will not be rejected. That the information is coming from an individual who knows the patient well in a variety of settings, or has longevity in the relationship, strengthens the conclusion. Alternatively, if the obsessional person is surrounded by critical people who have little understanding of psychological disorders, or by only casual acquaintances, this exercise has a high likelihood of failure and is not initiated.

Treatment Outcome Literature Review
Cognitive Treatments Alone compared to Waitlist or ERP

The difficulty in separating cognitive from behavioral treatments is broadly acknowledged. As pointed out by Abramowitz, Taylor & McKay (2005) behavioral treatments contain cognitive elements, and cognitive treatments contain exposure. However, the thrust of each type of treatment does differ and is distinguishable. Cognitive treatments, as described in the preceding section, focus on reappraising the meaning of intrusions, and testing the veracity of these reappraisals through behavioral experiments. Behavioral treatments emphasize prolonged and repetitive exposure to the intrusions, combined with refraining from engaging in the compulsive behavior (see Abramowitz et al., Chapter 17 of the current volume), with the goal of extinguishing the fear response. Within the context of exposure, it is common to discuss cognitive concepts such as threat overestimation and responsibility, although they are not central to the treatment. Although there are definite overlaps between these two types of treatment, the therapeutic techniques are quite different. The subsequent paragraphs will describe the outcomes of cognitively focused treatments, followed by those combined with traditional exposure plus response prevention.

Emmelkamp and colleagues completed the first randomized trials of a cognitive method using rational emotive therapy (RET). In the first of these studies, participants were randomly assigned to RET or ERP (Emmelkamp, Visser, & Hoekstra, 1988). Treatment consisted of 10 individual 60-minute sessions over 8 weeks. In the RET condition, irrational beliefs were identified and challenged in session, with encouragement to continue challenging these beliefs between sessions. Participants in the ERP group selected items from their fear hierarchy to complete at home each week, but in-session ERP was not conducted. Treatment resulted in significant decreases in ratings of anxiety/discomfort, severity of OCD symptoms, self-rated depression, and social anxiety. There were, however, no significant between-group differences.

Van Oppen et al. (1995) completed the first randomized controlled trial (RCT) with contemporary cognitive treatments comparing it to ERP, using 71 patients randomized to either individual CT or ERP. Sessions duration was 50–60 minutes. In the first 6 sessions, CT was completed without behavioral experiments, and ERP without a discussion of feared consequences. The groups were equivalent on

all measures at the end of session six. An additional 10 sessions were completed that included behavioral experiments for the CT group, and a discussion of feared consequences for the ERP group. Seven patients from each condition dropped out of treatment. The following results are based upon the 57 patients who completed treatment. Although there were no between-group differences on any dependent measures, significantly more patients treated with CT improved to a clinically significant degree (50%) compared to those treated behaviorally (28%). There is a suggestion that the self-directed ERP used by van Oppen et al (1995) was less effective than that used in other studies, and that the relatively high post-treatment Y-BOCS score of the exposure group (17.3) made the CT group look relatively strong (Foa, Franklin, & Kozak, 1998; Steketee et al., 1998).

Jones and Menzies (1998) conducted a small RCT with a subgroup of OCD individuals. Twenty-three patients with contamination fears were randomized to either waitlist or active treatment focused on reducing the perception of danger associated with potential contaminants. Danger Ideation Reduction Therapy (DIRT), primarily a cognitive intervention, consisted of restructuring contamination thoughts, normalizing information from people who worked with potential contaminants (e.g., cleaners, bank tellers, and medical personnel), corrective information regarding illness and disease, logical probabilities, attentional focusing, and a discussion of the results of microbiological experiments. In the latter, the authors "contaminated" one hand using a variety of stimuli (e.g., petting a cat, shaking multiple hands, touching public toilet doors). The control hand, which did not come into contact with the stimuli, was compared to the "contaminated" hand regarding the number of microorganisms present. In no case did the microbiologist detect differences between the control and experimental hand. Treatment consisted of eight 60-minute sessions in groups of 5 to 6 participants over 9 weeks. Assessments were completed at pretreatment and post-treatment, and 3-month follow-up. Using a number of self-report OCD measures and depression, the patients who completed DIRT (n=11) reported significantly lower scores compared to waitlist participants (n=10). Gains were maintained through a 3-month follow-up, but there was no further decline in symptoms.

Cottraux et al. (2001) randomized 65 participants to either CT or intensive ERP. Each group received 20 hours of individual treatment. Treatment in the CT group occurred weekly over 16 weeks. Participants in the ERP group received 16 hours of treatment in the first 4 weeks, and the remaining 4 hours of maintenance occurred over 12 weeks. Improvement was defined as a 25% reduction in Y-BOCS total scores from pretreatment to post-treatment. Nonclinical status was defined as 50% Y-BOCS reduction, and a final post-treatment Y-BOCS score of < 8. The numbers of participants that reported improvement and reached nonclinical status at post-treatment and through a 1-year follow-up did not differ between groups. Cottraux et al. (2001) concluded that the treatments had largely equivalent effects on OCD symptoms, but that CT showed a broader change in other variables including depression, interpretations of obsessions, and general fear.

McLean et al. (2001) used group treatment to compare CT and ERP with 63 patients. Sessions were conducted over 12 consecutive weeks. Group treatment was 150 minutes in duration and completed with 2 therapists and 6–8 patients per group. The cognitive treatment involved challenging appraisals of overimportance of thoughts, inflated responsibility, and overestimation of threat. Behavioral experiments were utilized to test reappraisals. Repetitive and prolonged exposure for the purpose of extinction was not used in the CT group. ERP consisted of in-session and home-based exposure, modeled by the therapist and completed according to hierarchies collaboratively developed during assessment. Any discussion of cognitive factors initiated by the patients was redirected by the therapists in favor of an extinction explanation to account for change. At post-treatment there was a slight advantage for the ERP group that was retained through a 3-month follow-up. Significantly more patients treated with ERP reached a clinically significant improvement (45%) criterion compared to only 13% in the CT group. The group format was thought to favor exposure-based treatments, whereas the more idiographic cognitive treatment was hypothesized to be better suited to individual treatment.

Whittal, Thordarson and McLean (2005) randomized 59 patients to individual treatment using the same protocol as McLean et al. (2001). Both treatments resulted in significant symptom decreases from pretreatment, but Y-BOCS scores at post-treatment (10.6 for the CT group and 10.4 for the ERP group) and 3-month follow-up (9.7 for the CT group and 10.6 for the ERP group) were equivalent between CT and ERP. There was also no difference between groups on the percentages of patients who made clinically significant changes. At post-treatment, 67% of the CT patients were classified as recovered compared to 58% of those who received ERP.

Wilson and Chambless (2005) used a multiple baseline design to treat 6 OCD patients using a modular treatment protocol that allowed tailoring of treatment to a wide variety of automatic thoughts and underlying schemas. Behavioral experiments were minimized to allow for a more stringent test of cognitive restructuring. Treatment was delivered in 10–18 one-hour sessions. Termination was flexible and according to improvement. Using a reliable change index, 2 of 6 patients were considered recovered. Although the effect size for OCD symptoms was large, the magnitude of change compared to other studies was notably lower. The average post-treatment Y-BOCS for the 6 participants was 14.0. Wilson and Chambless (2005) speculated that perhaps the relatively pure cognitive treatment that deemphasized behavioral experiments was associated with the smaller change.

Wilhelm et al. (2005) treated 15 participants using a modular CT protocol based on the Beckian principles of Socratic dialogue and the identification of cognitive errors. Five participants were ERP treatment failures, and the remainder had not received ERP. Treatment entailed 14 weekly individual sessions of 50–60 minutes in duration. Treatment modules were selected according to patient presentation. Behavioral experiments were used to test and correct a belief, but the exposure was not repetitive or prolonged. Y-BOCS total scores declined significantly (post-treatment Y-BOCS was 13.5). Although ERP refractory patients also demonstrated significant declines, the magnitude of change was smaller compared to ERP naïve patients. However, caution is needed in interpreting these results, as only four ERP refractory patients completed treatment.

Whittal, Woody, McLean, Rachman and Robichaud (2010) used a CT protocol with obsessionals who had few to no overt compulsions, and compared it to an active control of stress management (SMT) and a waitlist control. Patients were provided 12 individual sessions. Treatment consisted of reappraising the personally relevant and threatening meaning of intrusions, using a variety of strategies focused on overimportance and the need to control thoughts as well as "off duty" experiments. When compared to waitlist, the CT group had substantially lower Y-BOCS scores, as well as lower scores on OCD-related cognitions. Using an intent-to-treat sample (n=73), both CT and SMT showed large equivalent effects on Y-BOCS that persisted through a 12-month follow-up. The strong treatment effect of SMT was surprising, but not unwelcome. The broad and enduring results of both treatments counter the longstanding belief that obsessions are resistant to treatment.

In sum, the clinical trials conducted to assess the treatment outcome of cognitive protocols for OCD suggest that CT produces significant reductions in OCD symptoms. When compared to the gold standard ERP, CT is at least as efficacious as BT. With slight variations across treatment studies, equivalent gains tend to emerge for both treatment modalities, although it appears that CT is less beneficial for patients receiving group treatment, given the idiographic nature of cognitive interventions. Not surprisingly, a number of clinical trials have also been conducted to determine the efficacy of CBT for OCD, wherein both cognitive and behavioral interventions are combined in treatment. The following section will review the treatment outcome findings on the efficacy of combining BT and CT.

Combined Cognitive and Behavioral Treatment

Emmelkamp and Beens (1991) compared a combined treatment of RET plus ERP to the standalone effects of ERP. The combined treatment included 6 sessions of RET followed by 6 sessions of combined RET/ERP, compared to 12 sessions of ERP. The treatment was individual, and each session was 60 minutes in duration. The exposure was self-directed and exclusively conducted at home between sessions. A break of 4 weeks was inserted for both treatments after 6 sessions. Anxiety reduction associated with the main OCD problem from pretreatment to post-treatment was significant. The magnitude of the decline was similar between the groups at mid-treatment and post-treatment, and there were no between-group differences.

Freeston et al. (1997) completed a randomized trial using primary obsessionals with no overt compulsions. Treatment consisted of cognitive strategies combined with the use of loop tapes to repeatedly expose patients to their obsessions. The cognitive strategies included challenging overimportance of thoughts and magical thinking, exaggerated responsibility, perfectionistic expectations regarding control and uncertainty, overestimations of threat, and severity of consequences associated with feared events. In cases where the patient would have otherwise refused exposure, cognitive restructuring occurred first. In other cases, the cognitive challenging and imaginal exposure occurred in parallel. Sessions were 90 minutes twice a week for the first two-thirds of treatment. Therapy was terminated when the patient felt that s/he made sufficient clinical improvement, or a maximum of 40 sessions was reached. Follow-up sessions were conducted at 1, 2, 3, and 6 months. Treatment completers attended an average of 26 sessions and 3 follow-up sessions, or approximately 41 hours of therapy. Compared to waitlist, the combined treatment resulted in significantly lower Y-BOCS scores at post-treatment (mean Y-BOCS at post-treatment for the 22 completers was 7.2 [sd=5.2]). Among those who completed treatment, 77% showed clinically significant change at post-treatment, but this declined to 59% at 6-month follow-up.

Cordioli et al. (2003) completed a randomized trial suggesting that adding prolonged and repetitive exposure to cognitive treatment improves immediate outcomes compared to CT without prolonged exposure. Specifically, using a group treatment format following 12 two-hour weekly sessions, the 23 completers reported a remarkable average post-treatment Y-BOCS score of 15.1 (43.4% decline from pretreatment). This result is an improvement over McLean et al.'s group CT condition (26.5% decline pre to post) and similar to the ERP group (39.4%).

Vogel, Stiles, and Götestam (2004) randomized 35 participants to a standard ERP treatment that was either augmented with cognitive or relaxation strategies, or to a 6-week waitlist. The first phase of treatment entailed twice weekly 2-hour sessions for 6 weeks. A habituation model was presented and hierarchies developed. For those in the cognitive group, the addition of cognitive strategies was framed as an aid to increase motivation for the completion of exposure, and to prevent dropout and relapse by addressing comorbid problems. Relaxation was framed as making stressful exposures easier to tolerate, and potentially helpful for comorbid anxiety and depression problems. Traditional ERP was carried out for both treatment groups, according to predetermined hierarchies, over 10 sessions. Participants were offered monthly 15-minute telephone follow-ups to address relapse prevention and to provide support. Additionally, 60-minute supportive follow-up sessions were offered at 3, 6, 9, and 12 months. Significantly more participants dropped out of the relaxation condition (n=7) compared to the CT condition (n=1). Both groups reported significantly lower Y-BOCS scores at post-treatment compared to waitlist, but there were no between-group differences among the active treatments (ERP/CT and ERP/relaxation post-treatment Y-BOCS scores were 16.7 and 16.1, respectively). These results were retained in an intent-to-treat analysis. Likewise, there were no group differences in the number of participants who made clinically significant changes after acute treatment or during the follow-up.

O'Connor et al. (2005) randomized 26 obsessionals with no or minimal overt compulsions to either group or individual combined treatment. Refusal to be randomized was high (38%), primarily because of a hesitation to share obsessional content in a group setting. The final sample only consisted of two groups and 9 treatment completers. Seventeen participants completed individual treatment. Treatment included explaining the role of beliefs in maintaining cognitive biases associated with faulty appraisals of threat. Participants were taught to identify key beliefs that were Socratically challenged. ERP was introduced approximately one-third into treatment, and was conceptualized as a method to disconfirm beliefs by reality testing. ERP was completed using loop tape or in vivo exposure, and linked to the cognitive biases identified earlier in treatment. Follow-ups were completed at 3-week intervals for 3 months after treatment. Each participant received 20 hours of therapy. Not surprisingly, individual treatment (mean = 8.0, sd = 2.8) resulted in a significantly lower Y-BOCS total score compared to group treatment (mean = 10.8, sd = 6.8). Participants in individual treatment reported an average decline of 68% on the Y-BOCS from pretreatment to post-treatment, compared to 38% in the group treatment. Gains were maintained at 6-month follow-up and continued to demonstrate superiority for individual treatment.

Fineberg, Hughes, Gale, and Roberts (2005) allocated 48 patients to either CBT or a relaxation therapy (RT) control. Patients were not randomized to type of treatment, but rather were placed in the group that was next to be conducted, alternating between CBT and RT. Treatment sessions were conducted on 12 consecutive weeks for two hours each. The CBT condition consisted of home-based ERP, challenging automatic thoughts with the goal of developing less threatening alternatives, refraining from seeking reassurance, a cost-benefit analysis of OCD, and relapse prevention. Assessments were completed pretreatment and post-treatment, and at 3-month follow-up. Fineberg et al. (2005) reported that participants in both groups "tended toward improvement" during acute treatment, but there was no significant difference between the groups on Y-BOCS or any of the secondary outcome measures at post-treatment or 3-month follow-up.

Anderson and Rees (2007) randomized 63 participants to a combined cognitive and behavioral treatment completed either individually or in group. Treatment involved 10 two-hour (group) or one-hour (individual) sessions. Cognitive challenging, using logical analysis and hypothesis testing, augmented specific cognitive strategies to target overestimations of danger, inflated responsibility, and thought-action fusion. Exposure exercises were introduced as a method of testing beliefs and as an opportunity to habituate to anxiety. When compared to waitlist, participants in group and individual treatment reported significantly lower Y-BOCS scores. There were no significant Y-BOCS differences between the two active treatments among treatment completers, or in an intent-to-treat analysis. There were also no between-group differences in the clinical improvement or recovery rates. Although the results of this study are initially encouraging from the standpoint of treatment efficiency, it appears that the magnitude of change in the individual treatment was less (30.4%) than the average of 51% as reported by Eddy et al. (2004). As such, it remains an empirical question if group and individual treatment are equally effective.

To date, not a single study has compared a combined ERP and CT protocol with either of these singular approaches. However, it appears from the studies summarized in the preceding paragraphs that cognitive and behavioral treatments are equivalent at least in the short term. With the results of only one small study available (Cordioli et al., 2003), it is premature to conclude that combined CT and ERP treatment is superior compared to either of the singular approaches. Perhaps the commonality between the treatments (i.e., behavioral experiments in CT, and discussions of risk and responsibility in ERP) is one of the reasons for the equivalent effects. Regardless, that practitioners have additional strategies that are equally effective to the gold standard treatment is positive.

Another strategy to measure the utility of a treatment is to examine the durability of the treatment over a long-term follow-up. Although the numbers of studies that reported follow-ups of one year or longer and examined them in detail are few in number, they are discussed in the subsequent paragraphs.

Long-term Follow-up

Whereas the long-term follow-up results of ERP have been extensively evaluated (e.g., Foa & Kozak, 1996), given the relatively recent development of cognitive approaches for OCD, the literature on long-term follow-up is scant. A number of the previously described studies included either no follow-up or only a short-term follow-up (e.g., Anderson & Rees, 2007; McLean et al., 2001; Whittal et al., 2005; Wilhelm et al., 2005; Wilson & Chambless, 2005). Other studies reported a 12-month follow-up (e.g., Vogel et al., 2004; Cottraux et al., 2001; Freeston et al., 1997; Whittal et al., 2010), but results were generally limited to listing the primary and secondary dependent measures, as opposed to a detailed examination of treatment durability. Eddy et al. (2004) indicated that there were too few studies with a follow-up of at least 12 months to calculate an aggregate effect size for ERP or CT studies. Since the publication of the Eddy et al. meta-analysis, three additional long-term follow-up studies have been conducted, and will be described.

Van Oppen and colleagues (2005) reported a 5-year follow-up study of 2 randomized trials comparing CT and ERP to each other (van Oppen et al., 1995), or in combination with fluvoxamine (van Balkom et al., 1998). Given the focus of the current chapter, the reporting of results will be limited to the comparison of the CT and ERP groups and will not include the medication group. Of the 71 patients randomized in van Oppen et al.'s (1995) study, follow-up data are available for 62, and included patients who dropped out of the initial study. This 87% retention rate is remarkable, particularly given the length of the follow-up. The Y-BOCS total scores at five years (CT=12.3 and ERP=15.1) were significantly lower compared to pretreatment, with most change occurring between pretreatment and post-treatment. There were no significant Y-BOCS changes between post-treatment and follow-up. An increase of 7 points on the Y-BOCS was considered to be a reliable change, and if it was combined with a final Y-BOCS score of 12 or less, the patient was considered clinically recovered. In the CT group, 53% were considered recovered compared to 40% in the ERP group, which was not a significant difference. Moreover, only 19% (n=6) of the CT patients and 33% (n=10) of the ERP patients were using antidepressants at follow-up. Initially, this percentage of patients on medication appears surprisingly low. However, it should be noted that these patients were not on any medication when they were randomized to the original 1995 study (i.e., exclusion criterion was use of antidepressant medication). Higher numbers of patients did receive additional psychotherapy for unstated reasons during the follow-up (53% of the CT sample and 63% of the ERP sample).

Braga, Cordioli, Niederauer, and Manfro (2005) reported on the 1-year follow-up from Cordioli et al. (2003). Results are based on 42 patients (95% retention) who completed group CBT. Improvement was arbitrarily defined as a minimum decline of 35% on the Y-BOCS. Full remission equated to a Y-BOCS total score of less than 8, plus a clinical global impression score (CGI, range from 1=minimal symptoms to 7= very severe symptoms) of 2 or less. Partial remission was given when the decline was at least 35% compared to pretreatment, but the final Y-BOCS total score was above 8 and a CGI of 2. The significant Y-BOCS decline achieved during acute treatment was maintained through follow-up (Y-BOCS of 13.2 at post-treatment, and 11.6 at 12-month follow-up). At 12-month follow-up, 16 patients (38%) met criteria for full remission and 16 for partial remission. Of the 31 patients who improved during acute treatment, 35.5% relapsed during the 12-month follow-up.

Whittal, Robichaud, Thordarson, and McLean (2008) reported on the 2-year follow-up from McLean et al. (2001) group treatment, and the Whittal et al. (2005) individual treatment. Among treatment completers (n=41; 69.5% retention), Y-BOCS total scores for individual CT (10.3) and ERP (11.2) were not significantly different over the 2-year follow-up. However, for those patients treated in groups (n=45; 71.4% retention), ERP (12.9) resulted in lower Y-BOCS scores over time compared to group CT (14.2). Less than 10% of treatment completers relapsed in each of the treatment trials, and there was no difference according to type of treatment. Patients who scored 11 or below on the Y-BOCS, and experienced a minimal decline of 6 points compared to pretreatment, were considered recovered. Among patients given individual treatment, 61% met criteria for recovery with 51.2% maintaining this status from post-treatment to follow-up, and 9.7% (4 patients) achieved recovery during the follow-up. There was no significant difference in recovery status according to type of treatment at 2-year follow-up (68.4% of CT patients and 54.5% of ERP patients were recovered). At their follow-up assessment, 25 patients (61%) reported taking medication, with approximately 50% maintaining their medications during follow-up.

Five patients (12.2%) discontinued medication, and four (9.7%) started medication. Fourteen patients (34%) sought out additional psychological treatment for the OCD. However, additional treatment did not lead to further improvements in recovery status.

Among patients who received treatment in groups, 40% were recovered at follow-up with 20% maintaining this status from post-treatment and 20% achieving recovery during the follow-up. Recovery status did not differ according to type of treatment received (33.3% of CT patients were recovered, and 47.6% of ERP patients). At 2-year follow-up, 25 participants reported being on medication, with 44.5% continuing their medication from post-treatment. Three patients (6.7%) discontinued medication, and five (11.1%) began medication. During the follow-up, 21 patients (46.7%) sought out additional psychological treatment for OCD. Similar to the individual study, additional treatment did not result in a change in recovery status.

In sum, it appears that the findings from the few long-term outcome studies that the efficacy of CT for OCD echo the results of short-term outcome. CT is equally beneficial in reducing symptoms as BT, although it seems that BT consistently outperforms CT when treatment is conducted in a group format. Taken together, and contrary to initial expectation, research suggests that CT does not provide any incremental benefits above and beyond that seen with BT. However, as noted by Clark (2005), there are still too few studies comparing behavioral and cognitive interventions to allow for any definitive conclusions about CT's utility. In addition, it is noteworthy that most clinical trials include OCD patients with varied symptom presentations, and it has been posited that CT may be most suitable for specific OCD subtypes, such as primary obsessionals and ruminators. In fact, treatments studies for pure obsessionals that included either CT (Whittal et al., 2010) or a combined CBT protocol (Freeston et al., 1997) were highly efficacious. Given that pure behavioral interventions for this OCD subtype have shown poor treatment outcomes (see Rachman, 2003 for discussion), these results are encouraging and point to the need for more controlled research studies on the efficacy of CT.

Treatment efficacy is one strategy by which to measure the utility of a treatment. Intent-to-treat analyses are meant to account for the impact of dropouts, and those who refuse treatment. However, there are other indicators of a treatment's efficacy; for example, the number of people who are retained is an alternate marker of a treatment's utility. Although the numbers of studies that directly compare ERP and CT within the same study are small, there is a suggestion that cognitively focused treatment results in fewer dropouts. Whittal et al. (2008) tentatively reported that 9.8% of participants randomized to CT dropped out, compared to 26.2% in the ERP conditions, a significant difference. Abramowitz et al. (2005) reported a similar finding in comparing the dropout rates in four studies that used CT and ERP in the same study. Specifically, across the four studies, 18.6% of ERP participants dropped out compared to 10.2% in CT/CBT conditions.

Although they are indirect measures, and likely confounded by other factors, medication use and additional psychotherapy sessions in the months and years following treatment offer another indicator of treatment utility. The few studies listing these statistics suggest that the long-term functioning of the participants who complete acute treatment and receive benefit may not be as promising as initially suggested by measures of OCD symptoms, such as the Y-BOCS. Although the majority of people who complete treatment experience on average over a 50% decline in the intensity, severity, and duration of their OCD, long-term follow-ups suggest that over half either stay on medications or seek out additional psychological treatment, for OCD or perhaps related conditions.

Moreover, treatment effectiveness has reached a plateau in the past 20 years. As reported by Rachman (2006), it appears that "improvement rates are not improving" (p.8), a statement based upon a comparison of the results obtained by Rachman et al., (1979) and Foa et al. (2005). The plateau in response rates becomes more evident when using the same dependent measure to compare studies. In the first reported psychological treatment study using the Y-BOCS, Fals-Stewart, Marks and Schafer (1993) reported post treatment Y-BOCS scores of 12.0 and 12.1, respectively, for group and individual treatment. The percent decline from pretreatment Y-BOCS scores was 45% for group participants and 40% for individuals, using 48 (group) or 24 (individual) therapist hours. Foa et al. (2005) used an intensive individual treatment protocol, with 2 months of weekly maintenance sessions and approximately 38 hours of therapist time. They reported a post-treatment Y-BOCS score of 11.0, which represents a decline of 55% from pretreatment.

Although the initial treatment gains with the Foa study were greater than those of Fals-Stewart et al., they also used more therapist time when comparing the individual treatment conditions.

Perhaps an in-depth exploration of predictors and mediators of treatment response will provide clues to what is helpful and what is not, which will ultimately allow us to develop treatments that have a deeper, broader, and more durable impact. Although it is early in the natural history of cognitive treatment of OCD, the subsequent paragraphs will explore what is known about predictors of treatment response and mediators of change.

Prediction of Treatment Response

It is only within the last fifteen years that clinical trials have been undertaken to investigate the efficacy of CT for OCD. As a consequence, there is a paucity of research on variables that might predict success in treatment using CT. Within the literature on prediction of treatment outcome with ERP, notable obstacles to success include severe depression (Steketee & Shapiro, 1995; Steketee et al., 2000) and, as noted previously, symptom presentations that do not include overt behavioral compulsions. It is postulated that CT might address these limitations, as its idiographic nature lends itself to varying symptom subtypes, and cognitive restructuring could be used to reduce depressive mood (Salkovskis & Warwick, 1988).

To date, only one large-scale study has directly evaluated predictors of treatment success using cognitively based treatments. Wilhelm, Steketee and Yovel (2006) amassed data from 9 treatment centers around the world. Four-hundred and one patients (after accounting for dropouts and missing data) with a primary diagnosis of OCD were treated individually with either CT, behavior therapy (BT), or a combination thereof (CBT). Consistent with prior findings, severe pretreatment depression predicted worse outcome for patients receiving BT. Depression scores did not impact treatment success for those receiving CBT, and although patient response to CT was negatively impacted by depression, this effect was weaker than that seen with BT. Educational status had a positive relationship to treatment success; however, only for patients receiving CT. Finally, analyses with OCD subtypes yielded interesting results. BT and CT were equally effective for patients with washing compulsions; however, patients without washing compulsions received greater benefits from CT than BT. In addition, irrespective of treatment modality, less symptom reduction was observed for patients with hoarding compulsions, although CT, BT, and CBT yielded equivalent reductions in OCD symptoms when subtypes were not considered.

In a 1-year follow-up study of patients receiving CBT for OCD in a group format, predictors of relapse were evaluated (Braga et al., 2005). As with Wilhelm et al.'s (2006) findings, depression scores did not predict a return of symptoms for patients receiving CBT. Moreover, the presence or absence of comorbidity, pretreatment OCD severity, and the intensity of overvalued ideas also did not impact relapse rates. Of note, patients who exhibited full remission at post-treatment, as well as those who displayed more intense improvement (i.e., greater than 54% reduction in Y-BOCS scores), were less likely to relapse at 1-year follow-up.

Hansen, Vogel, Stiles and Götestam (2007) researched potential predictors of treatment outcome in the Vogel et al. (2004) clinical trial, where participants received either ERP+CT or ERP+REL (relaxation). The authors reported that comorbid diagnoses of panic disorder or generalized anxiety disorder led to poorer treatment outcome for both conditions; however, patients who received the combined treatment that included CT displayed more treatment gains than the ERP+REL condition (when intent-to-treat criteria were used). However, patients with comorbid Cluster A or B personality disorders displayed poorer treatment outcomes irrespective of the treatment modality.

Kempe et al. (2007) investigated predictors of course across 5 years for patients in the clinical trials led by van Oppen and colleagues (1995, 2005). Results suggested that patients with more severe OCD symptoms, longer duration of symptoms, and comorbid personality or Axis I disorders were less likely to experience remission, although the authors noted that predictors of remission differ according to the time period in which patients are measured (e.g., 2 months vs. 5 years). These results should nevertheless be interpreted with caution, as patients in both the CT and BT trials were combined for the assessment of predictors, and, as such, no general conclusions about CT predictors can be made.

It is clear that more clinical trials of CT and CBT for OCD need to be conducted, to better understand both the efficacy of cognitive interventions and the predictors of favorable treatment response. Clark (2005) noted that to date, CT does not appear to adequately address the issues of treatment nonresponse, poor homework compliance, or treatment dropout or refusals that occur when ERP is used. However, some of the preliminary findings suggest that the picture of treatment response with CT and BT is more complex than previously believed. For example, it appears that severe comorbid depression has a notably deleterious impact on treatment response for those receiving BT, and that this negative effect is either dampened or eliminated using CT or CBT. Moreover, cognitive interventions appear to show a differential benefit according to the particular OCD subtype, with non-washers exhibiting a greater treatment response with CT than BT. It therefore appears that favorable treatment outcome might be case-dependent, with BT, CT, and CBT each having particular benefits according to the patient's idiographic presentation. More research is needed into the impact of cognitive and behavioral interventions on the various OCD subtypes, in the hope of ultimately best tailoring treatment to the individual.

Mechanisms of Action

In the natural history of testing the utility of a treatment, the early focus is on efficacy. Does the treatment work better than nothing (i.e., is it better than waitlist)? How does it compare to the gold standard treatment? Do modifications to the standard treatment increase efficacy? Examples of the latter include involving family in treatment, the use of booster sessions, varying the intensity of treatment, etc. Once these questions are answered, then the focus often turns to mediators of treatment response. However, testing mediation requires changes in methodology. Process measures, in addition to the traditional focus on pre, post, and follow-up, need to be included to address mediation, and preferably be measured at least weekly if not daily. As many of the above-described CT studies focused on efficacy and pre/post changes, mediation taking into account the temporality of change was not addressed.

However, with the pre/post focus, a number of CT and ERP studies report largely equivalent amounts of cognitive change (e.g., Cottraux et al., 2001; McLean et al., 2001; Whittal et al., 2005), but there is no indication regarding the direction or timing of change. In an early effort, Rhéaume and Ladouceur (2000) examined individual cognitive change in a group of 6 checkers treated with a "pure" CT protocol devoid of behavioral experiments or ERP. Using multivariate time series analysis Rhéaume and Ladouceur (2000) reported that for most of the patients treated with either CT or ERP, some cognitive change precedes change in checking.

However, the reverse was also reported, in that for many patients, behavioral changes were noted prior to cognitive changes. Perhaps not surprisingly, these researchers concluded that cognitive change clearly occurs in OCD, but that behavioral strategies appeared to be the most efficacious way to produce this change.

Woody, Whittal and McLean (under review) tested mediation using data from a recent RCT of primary obsessions. Given the multiple measures of the mediator (i.e., cognition) and the outcome variable (i.e., obsession severity), it was possible to test the dynamic relationship between change in cognition and change in obsessions. Using a traditional mediation analysis, change in cognition mediated change in obsession severity but the direction of the change was called into question with subsequent analyses. Specifically, using a bivariate dual change analysis with data collected weekly, it was illustrated that prior obsession severity is a leading indicator of subsequent change in appraisals, rather than the reverse. Similar to Rhéaume and Ladouceur (2000), it appears that behavior change precedes cognitive change, at least in these early mediation studies.

Despite the paucity of outcome studies examining mediation, experimental studies testing cognitive theory may shed light on the variables that will ultimately bear mediational fruit. Following cognitive theory, it seems reasonable that factors posited as etiologically significant in the development of OCD should be explored as potential mediators (e.g., responsibility, overimportance of thoughts, overestimation of threat, etc.). Using an analogue sample, Valentiner and Smith (2008) reported that the relationship between obsessions and compulsions was stronger for those participants with a propensity to experience shame and moral TAF. Interestingly, these authors found no support regarding the role of guilt and likelihood TAF in the development of OCD. Alternatively, Rassin, Merckelbach, Muris and Spaan (1999) experimentally induced TAF and reported that it was associated with more intrusions, discomfort, and resistance.

Lopatka and Rachman (1995) experimentally manipulated responsibility using a group of OCD checkers or washers. Decreases in perceived responsibility were associated with decreases in discomfort, urge to check, severity and probability of harm, and the duration spent checking. Experimentally manipulated increases in responsibility had generally weaker effects on distress, anticipated harm, and urges to check.

Abramowitz et al. (2006) conducted a prospective study with a group of new mothers and fathers, as it is a time where the majority experience occasional unwanted intrusions regarding harm to their infant. OBQ scores obtained during the prenatal period predicted scores on the Obsessive Compulsive Inventory (OCI) three months postpartum, after controlling for preexisting OCD symptoms, anxiety, and depression. Additionally, the OBQ predicted a subset of OCI subscales (washing, checking obsessions) and not others (neutralizing, hoarding, and ordering), suggesting that dysfunctional beliefs may contribute to the development of some forms of OCD. Abramowitz et al. (2007) extend the previous results to a second sample of new parents. Although there is some confusion between the mediator (the III) and the predictor (the OBQ), it was reported that III scores at one month postpartum mediated the relationship between pre-birth OCD beliefs (as measured by the OBQ) and OCD symptoms.

Thought suppression and its relationship to OCD is complex. The literature is inconclusive regarding the association between suppression and thought frequency. However, as reviewed by Purdon (2004), suppression is most consistently associated with negative interpretations of the intrusion and more OCD symptoms. Moreover, the failure of thought control predicts increases in negative mood and anxiety over the thought reoccurrence. Despite this relationship, it is not clear if thought suppression is the cause of intrusions, or the result of experiencing unwanted and distressing intrusions.

Conclusion

The number of outcome studies in OCD increased notably in the past 15 years, perhaps due to interest in testing cognitive theory and treatment. Nine studies testing either CT alone compared to wait-list, or compared to ERP, were reviewed, as well as seven studies that tested a combined cognitive and behavioral treatment. Based upon this review, it appears as if CT is equally effective as the gold standard ERP, at least when delivered on an individual basis. CT may be better tolerated compared to ERP, resulting in less dropouts and overall greater effectiveness. For those who complete treatment, the prospect of maintaining gains is promising, although it may be secondary to occasional appointments with mental health providers. The substantial numbers of people who remain on medication or seek out additional psychological treatments suggest that

perhaps we have more work to do in helping people remain emotionally healthy, broadly defined.

Future Directions

As CT for OCD is in its infancy, relatively little is available on predictors of treatment response or mechanisms of action. At this early stage, it appears that severe comorbidity and the presence of hoarding are poor prognostic indicators. Treating people to full remission may be protective against relapse. The latter, however, remains an empirical question.

With the plateau in treatment outcomes in the past 20 years, it is clear that additional work needs to be done. It is hoped that the results of mediational studies will suggest additional future directions. However, it seems that we must look at complementary types of treatment protocols. Examples include extended maintenance sessions, similar to Hiss, Foa and Kozak, (1994), involving family to a greater degree, so that they are not inadvertently supporting OCD behaviors, working with patients longer, and aiming for a broader treatment response that includes medication discontinuation (i.e., is it possible that some patients continue on medication because that's what they have always done?).

Lastly, the impact of comorbidity requires additional consideration. Although, for example, most depression is secondary to OCD, this does not mean that it is not important in the long-term functioning of those who present for OCD treatment. Cognitive approaches have value in many areas, and perhaps a treatment that is focused on the individual patient and ALL the difficulties they bring to the table, as opposed to treating what is the primary problem, will produce a broad and durable response.

Related Chapters

References

Abramowitz, J. S., Franklin, M. E., & Foa, E. B. (2002). Empirical status of cognitive-behavioral therapy for obsessive-compulsive disorder: A meta-analytic review. *Romanian Journal of Cognitive and Behavioral Psychotherapies, 2,* 89–104.
Abramowitz, J. S., Khandker, M., Nelson, C. A., Beacon, B. J., & Rygwall, R. (2006). The role of cognitive factors in the pathogenesis of obsessive-compulsive symptoms: A prospective study. *Behaviour Research and Therapy, 44,* 1361–1374.

Abramowitz, J. S., Taylor, S., & McKay, D. (2005). Potentials and limitations of cognitive treatments for obsessive-compulsive disorder. *Cognitive Behaviour Therapy, 34,* 140–147.

Abramowitz, J. S., Nelson, C. A., Rygall, R., & Khandker, M. (2007). The cognitive mediation of obsessive-compulsive symptoms: A longitudinal study. *Journal of Anxiety Disorders, 21,* 91–104.

Anderson, R. A., & Rees, C. S. (2007). Group versus individual cognitive-behavioural treatment for obsessive-compulsive disorder: A controlled trial. *Behaviour Research and Therapy, 45,* 123–138.

Arntz, A., Rauner, M., & van den Hout, M. (1995). "If I feel anxious, there must be danger": ex-consequential reasoning in inferring danger in anxiety disorders. *Behaviour Research and Therapy, 33,* 917–925.

Ball, S. G., Baer, L., & Otto, M. W. (1996). Symptom subtypes of obsessive-compulsive disorder in behavioral treatment studies: A quantitative review. *Behaviour Research and Therapy, 34,* 47–51.

Braga, D. T., Cordioli, A. V., Niederauer, K., Manfro, G. G. (2005). Cognitive-behavioral group therapy for obsessive-compulsive disorder: a 1-year follow-up. *Acta Psychiatry Scandinavia, 112,* 180–186.

Clark, D. A. (2005). Focus on "cognition" in cognitive behavior therapy for OCD: Is it really necessary? *Cognitive Behaviour Therapy, 34,* 131–139.

Clark, D. A., & Purdon, C. (1993). New perspectives for a cognitive theory of obsessions. *Australian Psychologist, 28,* 161–167.

Cordioli, A. V., Heldt, E., Bochi, D. B., Margis, R., de Sousa, M. B., Tonello, J. F., Manfro, G. G., & Kapczinski, F. (2003). Cognitive-behavioral group therapy in obsessive-compulsive disorder: A randomized clinical trial. *Psychotherapy and Psychosomatics, 72,* 211–216.

Cottraux, J., Note, I., Yao, S.N., Lafont, S., Note, B., Mollard, E., Bouvard, M., Sauteraud, A., Bourgeois, M., & Dartigues, J. F. (2001). A randomized controlled trial of cognitive therapy versus intensive behavior therapy in obsessive compulsive disorder. *Psychotherapy and Psychosomatics, 70,* 288–297.

Dollard, J., & Miller, N. L. (1950). *Personality and psychotherapy: An analysis in terms of learning, thinking and culture.* New York: McGraw-Hill.

Eddy, K. T., Dutra, L., Bradley, R., & Westen, D. (2004). A multidimensional meta-analysis of psychotherapy and pharmacotherapy for obsessive-compulsive disorder. *Clinical Psychology Review, 24,* 1011–1030.

Emmelkamp, P. M. G., & Beens, H. (1991). Cognitive therapy with obsessive-compulsive disorder: A comparative evaluation. *Behaviour Research and Therapy, 29,* 293–300.

Emmelkamp, P. M. G., Visser, S., & Hoekstra, R. J. (1988). Cognitive therapy vs. exposure in vivo in the treatment of obsessive-compulsives. *Cognitive Therapy and Research, 12,* 103–114.

Fals-Stewart, W., Marks, A. P., & Schafer, J. (1993). A comparison of behavioral group therapy and individual behavior therapy in treating obsessive-compulsive disorder. *Journal of Nervous and Mental Disease, 181,* 189–193.

Fineberg, N. A., Hughes, A., Gale, T. M., & Roberts, A. (2005). Group cognitive behaviour therapy in obsessive-compulsive disorder (OCD): a controlled study. *International Journal of Psychiatry in Clinical Practice, 9,* 257–263.

Foa, E. B., Franklin, M. E., & Kozak, M. J. (1998). Psychosocial treatment for obsessive-compulsive disorder. In R. P. Swinson, M. M. Antony, S. J. Rachman & M. A. Richter (Eds.). *Obsessive-compulsive disorder: Theory, research and treatment* (pp. 258–276). New York: Guilford.

Foa, E. B., & Kozak, M. J. (1986). Emotional processing of fear: Exposure to corrective information. *Psychological Bulletin, 99,* 20–35.

Foa, E. B., & Kozak, M. J. (1996). Psychological treatment for obsessive-compulsive disorder. In M. R. Mavissakalian & R. F. Prien (Eds.), *Long-term treatments of anxiety disorders* (pp. 285–309). Washington, DC: American Psychiatric Press.

Foa, E. B., Liebowitz, M. R., Kozak, M. J., Davies, S., Campeas, R., Franklin, M. E., Huppert, J. D., Kjernisted, K., Rowan, V., Schmidt, A. B., Simpson, H. B., & Tu, X. (2005). Randomized, placebo-controlled trials of exposure and ritual prevention, clomipramine, and their combination in the treatment of obsessive-compulsive disorder. *American Journal of Psychiatry, 162,* 151–161.

Foa, E. B., Steketee, G. S., & Ozarow, B. J. (1985). Behavior therapy with obsessive-compulsives: From theory to treatment. In M. Mavissakalian, S. M. Turner, & L. Michelson (Eds.), *Obsessive-compulsive disorder: Psychological and pharmacological treatment* (pp. 49–129). New York: Plenum Press.

Foa, E. B., Steketee, G., Grayson, J. B., & Doppelt, H. G. (1983). Treatment of obsessive-compulsives: When do we fail? In E. B. Foa & P. M. G. Emmelkamp (Eds.), *Failures in behavior therapy* (pp. 10–34). New York: Wiley.

Freeston, M. H., Ladouceur, R., Gagnon, F., Thibodeau, Rhéaume, J., Letarte, H., & Bujold, A. (1997). Cognitive-behavioral treatment of obsessive thoughts: A controlled study. *Journal of Consulting and Clinical Psychology, 65,* 405–413.

Freeston, M. H. Rhéume, J., & Ladouceur, R. (1996). Correcting faulty appraisals of obsessional thoughts. *Behaviour Research and Therapy, 34,* 433–446.

Frost, R. O., & Steketee, G. (1998). Hoarding: Clinical aspects and treatment strategies. In M. A. Jenike, L. Baer, & W. E. Minichiello (Eds.), *Obsessive-compulsive disorder: Practical Management (3rd ed.)* (pp. 533–554). St Louis: Mosby Press.

Hansen, B., Vogel, P. A., Stiles, T. C., & Götestam, K. G. (2007). Influence of co-morbid generalized anxiety disorder, panic disorder and personality disorders on the outcome of cognitive behavioural treatment of obsessive-compulsive disorder. *Cognitive Behaviour Therapy, 36,* 145–155.

Hiss, H. Foa, E. B., & Kozak, M. J. (1994). Relapse prevention program for treatment of obsessive-compulsive disorder. *Journal of Consulting and Clinical Psychology, 62,* 801–808.

Jones, M. K., Menzies, R. G. (1998). Danger ideation reduction therapy, (DIRT) for obsessive-compulsive washers. A controlled trial. *Behaviour Research and Therapy, 36,* 959–970.

Kempe, P. T., van Oppen, P., de Haan, E., Twisk, J. W. R., Sluis, A., Smit, J. H., van Dyck, R., van Balkom, A. J. L. M. (2007). Predictors of course in obsessive-compulsive disorder: Logistic regression versus Cox regression for recurrent events. *Acta Psychiatrica Scandinavica, 116,* 201–210.

Kobak, K. A., Greist, J. H., Jefferson, J. W., Katzelnick, D. J., & Henk, H. J. (1998). Behavioral versus pharmacological treatments of obsessive compulsive disorder: A meta-analysis. *Psychopharmacology, 136,* 205–216.

March, J., Frances, A., Carpenter, D., & Kahn, D. (1997). The expert consensus guideline series: Treatment of obsessive-compulsive disorder. *Journal of Clinical Psychiatry, 58* (Suppl. 4), 1–16.

McLean, P. D., Whittal, M. L., Thordarson, D. S., Taylor, S., Sochting, I., Koch, W. J., Paterson, R., & Anderson K.W. (2001). Cognitive versus behavior therapy in the group treatment of obsessive-compulsive disorder. *Journal of Consulting and Clinical Psychology, 69,* 205–214.

Mowrer, O. H. (1939). A stimulus-response analysis of anxiety and its role as a reinforcing agent. *Psychological Review, 46,* 553–565.

Newth, S., & Rachman, S. (2001). The concealment of obsessions. *Behaviour Research and Therapy, 39,* 457–464.

Obsessive Compulsive Cognitions Working Group (OCCWG) (1997). Cognitive assessment of obsessive-compulsive disorder. *Behaviour Research and Therapy, 35,* 667–681.

O'Connor, K., Freeston, M. H., Gareau, D., Careau, Y, Dufour, M. J., Aardema, F., & Todorov, C. (2005). Group versus individual treatment in obsessions without compulsions. *Clinical Psychology and Psychotherapy, 12,* 87–96.

Purdon, C. (2004) Empirical investigations of thought suppression in OCD. *Journal of Behavior Therapy and Experimental Psychiatry, 35,* 121–136.

Rachman, S. J. (1985). An overview of clinical and research issues in obsessional-compulsive disorder. In M. Mavissakalian, S. M. Turner, & L. Michelson (Eds.), *Obsessive-compulsive disorder: Psychological and pharmacological treatment* (pp. 1–47). New York: Plenum.

Rachman, S. (1997). A cognitive theory of obsessions. *Behaviour Research and Therapy, 35,* 793–802.

Rachman, S. (1998). A cognitive theory of obsessions: Elaborations. *Behaviour Research and Therapy, 36,* 385–401.

Rachman, S. J. (2003). *The treatment of obsessions.* Oxford: Oxford University Press.

Rachman, S. (2006). *Fear of contamination: Assessment and treatment.* Oxford: Oxford University Press (p.8).

Rachman, S., Cobb, C., Grey, S., McDonald, B., & Sartory, G. (1979). Behavioural treatment of obsessional compulsive disorder, with and without clomipramine. *Behaviour Research and Therapy, 17,* 467–478.

Rachman, S., & de Silva, P. (1978). Abnormal and normal obsessions. *Behaviour Research and Therapy, 16,* 233–248.

Rassin, E., Merckelbach, H., Muris, P. & Spaan, V. (1999). Thought-action fusion as a causal factor in the development of intrusions. *Behaviour Research and Therapy, 37,* 231–237.

Rhéaume, J., & Ladouceur, R. (2000). Cognitive and behavioural treatments of checking behaviours: An examination of individual cognitive change. *Clinical Psychology and Psychotherapy, 7,* 118–127.

Rowa, K., & Purdon, C. (2003). Why are certain intrusive thoughts more upsetting than others? *Behavioural and Cognitive Psychotherapy, 31,* 1–11.

Salkovskis, P. M. (1985). Obsessional-compulsive problems: a cognitive-behavioural analysis. *Behaviour Research and Therapy, 23,* 571–583.

Salkovskis, P. M. (1999). Understand and treating obsessive-compulsive disorder. *Behaviour Research and Therapy, 37,* S29–S52.

Salkovskis, P. M., & Warwick, H. M. C. (1988). Cognitive therapy of obsessive-compulsive disorder. In C. Perris, I. M. Blackburn, & H. Perris (Eds.), *Cognitive psychotherapy: Theory and practice* (pp. 376–395). Berlin: Springer-Verlag.

Salkovskis, P. M., & Westbrook, D. (1989). Behaviour therapy and obsessional ruminations: Can failure be turned into success? *Behaviour Research and Therapy, 27,* 211–219.

Shafran, R., Thordarson, D. S., & Rachman, S. (1996). Thought-action fusion in obsessive compulsive disorder. *Journal of Anxiety Disorders, 10,* 379–391.

Steketee, G. S., Frost, R. O., Rheaume, J., & Wilhelm, S. (1998). Cognitive theory and treatment of obsessive-compulsive disorder. In M. A. Jenike, L. Baer, & W. E. Minichiello (Eds.). *Obsessive-compulsive disorder: Practical management* (pp. 368–399). St. Louis: Mosby.

Steketee, G. S., Henninger, N. J., & Pollard, C. A. (2000). Predicting treatment outcome for obsessive-compulsive disorder: Effects of comorbidity. In W. K. Goodman, M. V. Rudorfor, & J. D. Maser (Eds.), *Obsessive-compulsive disorder: Contemporary issues in treatment* (pp. 257–274). Mahwah, NJ: Lawrence Erlbaum Associates.

Steketee, G. S., & Shapiro, L. J. (1995). Predicting behavioral treatment outcome for agoraphobia and obsessive compulsive disorder. *Clinical Psychology Review, 15,* 317–346.

Stanley, M. A., & Turner, S. M. (1995). Current status of pharmacological and behavioral treatment of obsessive-compulsive disorder. *Behavior Therapy, 26,* 163–186.

Valentiner, D. P., Smith, S. A. (2008). Believing that intrusive thoughts can be immoral moderates the relationship between obsessions and compulsions for shame-prone individuals. *Cognitive Therapy and Research, 32,* 714–720.

van Balkom, A. J., de Haan, E., van Oppen, P. Spinhoven, P., Hoogduin, K. A. L., & van Dyck, R (1998). Cognitive and behavioral therapies alone versus in combination with fluvoxamine in the treatment of obsessive compulsive disorder. *Journal of Nervous and Mental Disease, 186,* 492–499.

van Oppen, P., de Haan, E., van Balkom, A. J. L. M., Spinhoven, P, Hoogduin, K., & van Dyck, R. (1995). Cognitive therapy and exposure in vivo in the treatment of obsessive compulsive disorder. *Behaviour Research and Therapy, 33,* 379–390.

van Oppen, P., van Balkom, A. J. L. M., de Haan, E., & van Dyck, R. (2005). Cognitive therapy and exposure in vivo alone and in combination with fluvoxamine in obsessive-compulsive disorder: A 5-year follow-up. *Journal of Clinical Psychiatry, 66,* 1415–1422.

Vogel, P. A., Stiles, T. C., & Götestam, K. G. (2004). Adding cognitive therapy elements to exposure therapy for obsessive compulsive disorder: A controlled study. *Behavioural and Cognitive Psychotherapy, 32,* 275–290.

Whittal, M. L, Thordarson, D., & McLean, P. (2005). Treatment of obsessive-compulsive disorder: Cognitive behavior therapy vs. exposure and response prevention. *Behaviour Research and Therapy, 43,* 1559–1576.

Whittal, M. L., Robichaud, M., Thordarson, D. S., & McLean, P. D. (2008). Group and individual treatment of OCD using cognitive therapy and exposure plus response prevention: A two-year follow-up of 2 randomized trials. *Journal of Consulting and Clinical Psychology, 76,* 1003–1014.

Whittal, M. L., Woody, S. R., McLean, P. D., Rachman, S. J. & Robichaud, M. (2010). Treatment of Obsessions: A Randomized Controlled Trial, *Behaviour Research and Therapy, 48,* 295–303.

Wilhelm S., & Steketee, G. S. (2006). Cognitive therapy for obsessive-compulsive disorder: A guide for professionals. Oakland, CA: New Harbinger Press.

Wilhelm S., Steketee, G., Reilly-Harrington, N. A., Deckersbach, T., Buhlmann, U., & Baer, L. (2005). Effectiveness of cognitive therapy for obsessive-compulsive disorder: An open trial. *Journal of Cognitive Psychotherapy, 19*, 173–179.

Wilhelm, S., Steketee, G., & Yovel, I. (2006, November). *Mega-analysis of predictors of treatment outcome of OCD*. Symposium presented at the annual meeting of the Association of Behavioral and Cognitive Therapy. Chicago, IL.

Wilson, K. A., & Chambless, D.L. (2005). Cognitive therapy for obsessive-compulsive disorder. *Behaviour Research and Therapy, 43*, 1645–1654.

Woody, S. R., Whittal, M. L., & McLean, P.D. (under review). *Mechanisms of symptom reduction in treatment of obsessions*.

Combining Pharmacotherapy and Psychological Treatments for OCD

David F. Tolin

Abstract

This chapter reviews the outcome literature on the efficacy of combined pharmacotherapy and cognitive-behavioral therapy (CBT) for obsessive compulsive disorder (OCD). Quantitative review of randomized studies, in which treatments were combined simultaneously, indicated that combined therapy shows a small but significant advantage over exposure and response prevention (ERP) monotherapy, and a moderate advantage over serotonin reuptake inhibitor (SRI) monotherapy. Studies of sequential treatment combination, in which CBT was added after a trial of SRI monotherapy, suggest a significant incremental benefit of CBT, including for patients who show minimal response to SRI monotherapy. The chapter concludes by discussing new possibilities for combined therapy, including the use of pharmacologic strategies explicitly intended to potentiate the mechanisms of CBT.

Keywords: obsessive compulsive disorder, medications, antidepressants, SSRI, cognitive-behavioral therapy, exposure and response prevention, behavior therapy, combination therapy

Introduction

As discussed in Chapter 17 of this volume, cognitive-behavioral therapy (CBT) incorporating exposure and response prevention (ERP) shows clear and robust evidence of efficacy in the treatment of obsessive compulsive disorder (OCD) in adults and children. In addition, as indicated in Chapter 15, serotonin reuptake inhibitor (SRI) medications have also been shown to be effective in adults and children. Over 10 years ago, an expert consensus panel (March, Frances, Carpenter, & Kahn, 1997) recommended that for more severe cases of adult OCD, CBT should be combined with SRI medication. The implication, therefore, was that ERP plus SRI should be more efficacious than is ERP alone. A later practice guideline by the American Psychiatric Association (APA), however, recommended a different course of treatment, with SRI medications prescribed only after failure to respond to ERP monotherapy, or for patients who are "too depressed, anxious, or severely ill to cooperate with this treatment modality" (Koran, Hanna, Hollander, Nestadt, & Simpson, 2007, p. 9). Thus, expert opinion appears to have shifted somewhat, with greater emphasis on ERP monotherapy and decreased claims of the superiority of combined treatment. This chapter will review the extant literature on the efficacy of combined pharmacotherapy and CBT for OCD, and suggest directions for future research.

Simultaneous Psychological and Pharmacologic Treatments

To date, 5 randomized studies have been published examining the efficacy of CBT, SRIs, and their simultaneous combination for OCD patients. Results are depicted in Figures 19.1 and 19.2: Figure 19.1 indicates the degree of symptom remission from baseline to post-treatment on standardized measures of OCD severity, and Figure 19.2 shows rates of clinical response (variously defined across studies) at post-treatment. In the first of these

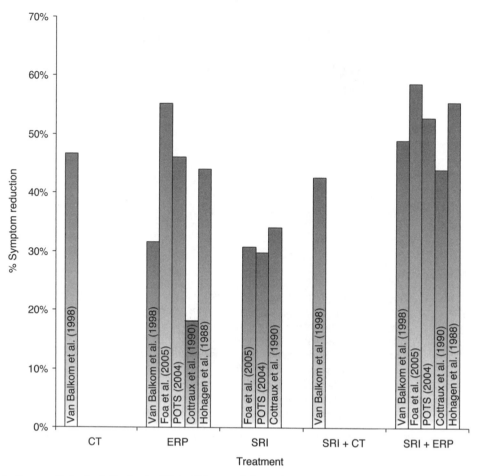

Fig. 19.1. Symptom Reduction in Randomized Trials of Cognitive-Behavioral Therapies, Serotonergic Medications, and Their Combination for Obsessive-Compulsive Disorder Patients. CT = Cognitive therapy. ERP = Exposure and response prevention. SRI = Serotonin reuptake inhibitor. The Yale-Brown Obsessive-Compulsive Scale (Y-BOCS) or Child Y-BOCS was the outcome measure in all but the Cottraux et al. study, which used the Compulsive Activity Checklist.

studies, Cottraux et al. (1990) randomly assigned 60 adult OCD patients to receive 24 weeks of ERP + fluvoxamine (FLV), ERP + pill placebo (PBO), and FLV plus "anti-exposure" (instructions "to avoid any kind of exposure to feared situations," p. 19). ERP sessions were delivered approximately weekly. Symptom severity was assessed using the Compulsive Activity Checklist (CAC; Cottraux, Bouvard, Defayolle, & Messy, 1988), and clinical response was defined as a 30% or greater reduction in duration of compulsive behavior (Foa & Emmelkamp, 1983). Figure 19.1 shows that ERP + FLV yielded a 44% reduction in CAC scores, which represents an improvement over ERP + PBO (18% reduction) and FLV + anti-exposure (34% reduction). Figure 19.2 shows that at post-treatment, 69% of ERP + FLV patients were considered responders, compared to 40% of ERP + PBO patients and 54% of SRI

patients. At 6-month follow-up (during which ERP was discontinued and FLV was tapered off), the ERP + FLV group showed a 55% reduction from baseline, compared to 23% and 24% for the ERP + PBO and FLV + anti-exposure groups, respectively (not shown). Global improvement was observed in 64% of ERP + FLV patients, compared to 50% of ERP + PBO patients and 45% of FLV + anti-exposure patients. At 1-year follow-up, the ERP + FLV group showed a 40% reduction from baseline, compared to 16% and 37% for the ERP + PBO and FLV + anti-exposure groups, respectively (not shown; Cottraux, Mollard, Bouvard, & Marks, 1993).

In a second study (Hohagen et al., 1998), 49 inpatients were randomly assigned to receive 4 weeks of ERP + PBO or ERP + FLV. ERP was delivered 3 times per week for 2 weeks; the remainder of

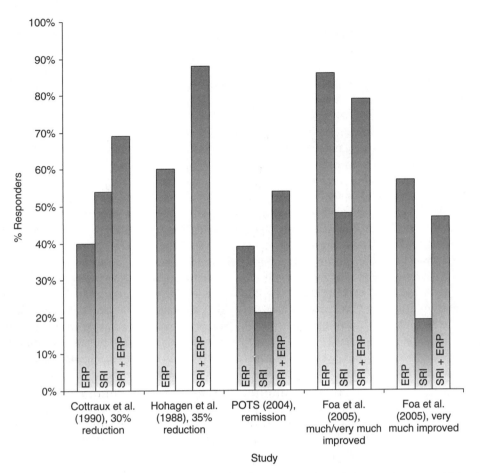

Fig. 19.2. Response Rates (Variously Defined) in Randomized Trials of Cognitive-Behavioral Therapies, Serotonergic Medications, and Their Combination for Obsessive-Compulsive Disorder Patients. ERP = Exposure and response prevention. SRI = Serotonin reuptake inhibitor.

the ERP consisted of daily self-administered treatment. Symptom severity was assessed using the Yale-Brown Obsessive Compulsive Scale (Y-BOCS; Goodman et al., 1989), and response to treatment was defined as a Y-BOCS reduction of 35% or more. As shown in Figure 19.1, ERP + FLV patients showed a 56% decrease in symptom severity, compared to a 44% decrease for ERP + PBO patients. Figure 19.2 shows that response to treatment was observed in 88% of ERP + FLV patients, compared to 60% of ERP + PBO patients.

A larger study (van Balkom et al., 1998) randomly assigned 117 outpatients to one of 5 conditions: cognitive therapy (CT), ERP, CT + FLV, ERP + FLV, and waitlist (WL). CT and ERP consisted of 16 therapy sessions over 16 weeks. ERP was described as "self-controlled" in this study (p. 493). As shown in Figure 19.1, Y-BOCS scores decreased by 32% and 47% in the ERP and CT groups,

respectively. When FLV was added, decreases were 49% and 43%, respectively. Response rates were not reported.

The Pediatric OCD Treatment Study Team (POTS; 2004) randomly assigned 112 outpatient children age 7–17 to ERP (with some elements of CT), sertraline (SERT), ERP + SERT, or PBO. Treatment lasted for 12 weeks, with ERP visits occurring weekly. Symptom severity was assessed using the Children's Y-BOCS (CY-BOCS; Scahill et al., 1997), and clinical response was defined as a CY-BOCS score of 10 or less (remission). Figure 19.1 shows that symptom severity decreased by 53% for ERP + SERT patients, compared to 46% and 30% for patients receiving ERP and SERT monotherapy, respectively. Remission was observed in 54% of ERP + SERT patients, compared to 39% and 21% of ERP and SERT monotherapy patients, respectively.

In the largest study to date on the topic (Foa et al., 2005), 149 outpatients (122 who actually entered treatment) were randomly assigned to ERP, clomipramine (CMI), ERP + CMI, or PBO. Treatment lasted 12 weeks, with ERP administered twice weekly with additional twice-weekly telephone contacts. Symptom severity was assessed using the Y-BOCS. Response was assessed using the Clinical Global Impression scale (CGI; Guy, 1976) in two ways: "response" was defined as a rating of "much improved" or "very much improved" on the CGI. "Excellent response" was defined as a rating of "very much improved" on the CGI. As shown in Figure 19.1, Y-BOCS scores decreased by 59% for the ERP + CMI group, compared to 55% for the ERP group and 31% for the CMI group. As Figure 19.2 shows, 79% of ERP + CMI patients were rated as responders, compared to 86% of ERP patients and 48% of CMI patients. Forty-seven percent of ERP + CMI patients were labeled "excellent responders," compared to 57% of ERP patients and 19% of CMI patients. After treatment discontinuation (not shown), treatment responders were followed for an additional 12 weeks (Simpson et al., 2004). Relapse rates were 11% for ERP and 14% for ERP + CMI, but 45% for CMI monotherapy.

As Figures 19.1 and 19.2 depict, there is a fair amount of discrepancy across studies (e.g., ERP appeared much less effective in the Cottraux et al. study than in the Foa et al., study, which also found the least advantage for combined treatment). To examine trends across these reports, random-effects model meta-analytic strategies (Glass, McGaw, & Smith, 1981) were employed. For each comparison of ERP +SRI vs. ERP or SRI monotherapy, Cohen's d (weighted by sample size) was calculated at post-treatment; d values of 0.2, 0.5, and 0.8 are conventionally accepted to represent small, medium, and large effects, respectively (Cohen, 1988). Differences between effect size estimates were examined by calculating the mixed-effects between-group heterogeneity (Q). To test the file drawer effect (the probability that unpublished null results would eliminate the obtained results), for each result the fail-safe N (FSN), or the number of null results that would be needed to overturn a significant result, was calculated. Generally, if the FSN is greater than or equal to 5 times the number of studies in the analysis plus 10, the obtained results are considered robust against the file drawer effect (Rosenthal, 1991). Results indicated that ERP + SRI combined therapy was associated with significantly lower symptom severity at post-treatment than was ERP monotherapy ($d = 0.38$, $p = 0.006$) or SRI monotherapy ($d = 0.69$, $p < .001$). Of note, neither finding was robust against the file drawer effect. The advantage of combined therapy was statistically equivalent for ERP vs. SRI monotherapy, Q (1) = 1.77, $p = 0.183$, although it is noted that the advantage is in the small range for combined therapy over ERP monotherapy, and in the moderate range for combined therapy over SRI monotherapy.

Thus, across studies, combined therapy appears to have a small but significant advantage over ERP monotherapy, and a moderate advantage over SRI monotherapy. However, these impressions must be considered tentative for several reasons. First, the number of studies is relatively small (only 5 comparisons of combination treatment vs. ERP, and only 3 comparisons of combination treatment vs. SRI), and therefore none of the findings can be considered robust against the file drawer effect. Second, substantial variability in treatment administration is noted (e.g., Hohagen et al.'s self-administered ERP vs. Foa et al.'s more intensive version of the treatment). Third, the long-term outcome of these treatments following discontinuation is unclear. As noted previously, Cottraux et al. (who had the worst-performing ERP treatment) reported that the advantage of combined treatment was maintained over monotherapy at 1-year follow-up. However, examining Foa et al.'s treatment responders at 3-month follow-up, Simpson et al. found that patients who did not receive ERP (with or without CMI) were significantly more likely to have relapsed. Fourth, patients in these studies were generally selected for the absence of certain comorbid conditions such as psychosis, substance abuse, suicidality, or developmental disorders, although other conditions such as depression and personality disorders were usually allowed. It could be argued, based on the available research (Foa, Kozak, Steketee, & McCarthy, 1992; Hohagen, et al., 1998), that some comorbid conditions such as severe depression might indicate the use of medications, particularly when such comorbidity makes OCD treatment difficult or impossible (for example, a depressed patient who is unable to get out of bed and come to therapy reliably). Finally, studies that randomly assign patients to treatment conditions might fail to account for the potentially large impact of patients' preference for one treatment over the other (TenHave, Coyne, Salzer, & Katz, 2003). There are several ways that patient preference may impact treatment outcome, including enrollment and attrition, homework and medication compliance, and expectancy for improvement.

Sequential Treatment with CBT and Serotonin Reuptake Inhibitors

Rather than applying two treatments simultaneously, an alternative clinical strategy is to apply one treatment first, reserving the second treatment only for patients who fail to respond adequately to the initial treatment. To date, no studies have been published in which CBT was administered first. However, 7 studies point to the efficacy of adding CBT after an initial trial of SRI medication. In three of those studies, a sequential treatment program was followed regardless of patients' response to the initial intervention. In the first of these, Marks et al. (1980) administered CMI to 40 patients for 8 months. After 4 weeks of CMI monotherapy, patients were randomly assigned to receive 15 sessions of ERP or relaxation training. Results at the end of these 15 sessions indicated that ERP (compared to relaxation) yielded significantly greater improvement on a behavioral avoidance task, as well as ratings of time spent performing compulsions. Foa et al. (1992) classified 38 OCD patients as highly or mildly depressed (although none met criteria for major depressive disorder), and assigned patients to receive the tricyclic antidepressant imipramine (IMI) or PBO for 6 weeks. Following the IMI/PBO lead-in, all patients received 15 sessions of ERP over 3 weeks, followed by 12 weekly sessions of supportive psychotherapy. Whereas only 1 patient (3%) was rated as "highly" improved after IMI/PBO treatment, 17 (45%) received this designation following ERP. IMI monotherapy did not yield a reduction in OCD symptoms (although it did reduce depressive symptoms among the highly depressed group), nor did it potentiate the effects of subsequent ERP (which proved effective for OCD symptoms, regardless of medication status). Neziroglu et al. (2000) administered FLV to 10 pediatric OCD patients. After 10 weeks of FLV treatment, patients were randomly assigned to receive ERP (20 sessions over 33 weeks), or no additional treatment while FLV was continued for 1 year. Patients who received FLV + ERP showed significantly greater improvement on the CY-BOCS than did those who received FLV only; these results were maintained at 2-year follow-up. Tenneij et al. (2005) randomly assigned 96 patients who had responded to venlafaxine (VEN) or paroxetine (PAR) to either receive the addition of ERP (18 45-minute sessions) or to continue drug

monotherapy for an additional 6 months. Those who received ERP immediately after drug response showed a greater improvement in symptoms than did those who continued on drug treatment alone. Significantly more patients in the ERP group achieved remission (defined as Y-BOCS score of 8 or less) relative to drug treatment alone.

The remaining three sequential-treatment trials specifically investigated the addition of CBT for patients who fail to respond adequately to SRI medication. Simpson et al. (1999) selected 6 patients who had received an adequate trial (defined as 12 weeks or more at a therapeutic dose) of SRI medications, had experienced some symptom reduction (assessed by verbal report), but remained significantly symptomatic (as evidenced by Y-BOCS score of 16 or higher). All patients received 17 twice-weekly sessions of ERP. Average Y-BOCS scores decreased by 49% following ERP, and 5 (83%) were rated "much improved" (defined as a Y-BOCS reduction of 6 or more points) at follow-up (between 6 and 12 months). Kampman et al. (2002) selected 14 patients who had failed to respond adequately (defined as less than 25% Y-BOCS reduction) to 60 mg fluoxetine (FLU) over 12 weeks under experimental conditions. All patients received 12 weekly sessions of ERP + CT while continuing FLU. Nine patients completed this phase of the study (36% attrition). Patients exhibited an average 41% reduction in Y-BOCS scores following ERP + CT. Tolin et al. (2004) selected 20 patients who had had received an adequate trial (defined as 10 weeks or more at a therapeutic dose) of at least 2 SRI medications (mean = 4.6 medication trials) but remained significantly symptomatic (as evidenced by Y-BOCS score of 16 or higher). After a 1-month waitlist condition, all patients received 15 sessions of ERP using a flexible-dose schedule from 1–5 visits per week. Average Y-BOCS scores decreased by less than 1% after waitlist, and by 37% after ERP. At 1-month, 3-month, and 6-month follow-up, Y-BOCS scores remained 32%, 28%, and 26% below pretreatment levels. Clinically significant change (Jacobson & Truax, 1991) was observed in 53%, 29%, 29%, and 40% of treatment completers at post-treatment and 1-, 3-, and 6-month follow-up, respectively.

From Addition to Interaction: New Medication Possibilities

The CBT + SRI combined treatments described above consist of an additive strategy, in which two known monotherapies are applied, either simultaneously or sequentially. The expectation underlying this strategy is that if CBT produces *x* benefit, and SRIs produce *y* benefit, then the benefit of CBT + SRI should approximate *x* + *y*. This is clearly not the case, however. At best (with numerous caveats described previously), combined treatment offers a small advantage over ERP monotherapy, although the advantage over SRI monotherapy is perhaps more substantial in both simultaneous and sequential intervention protocols.

The search for new psychotherapy/pharmacotherapy combinations might be aided by a reexamination of the mechanisms underlying the efficacy of psychotherapy. The most well-studied psychotherapy for OCD, ERP, is based on the principle of *extinction*, in which repeated presentations of a conditioned stimulus (CS, e.g., dirt), outside the presence of an unconditioned stimulus (US, e.g., illness), eventually leads to reductions in the conditioned response (CR, e.g., fear). Extinction does not imply that the patient forgets the original CS–US association; rather, extinction is thought to represent the learning of new associations (e.g., the CS becomes associated with stimuli other than the US) that eventually inhibit the original association (Bouton, 1993). Cognitive theorists have modified the model slightly, by suggesting that through repeated benign experiences with the feared stimulus, the person learns that the stimulus is not dangerous or harmful; e.g., that touching "dirty" objects does not lead to fatal illness (Beck, Emery, & Greenberg, 1985; Foa & Kozak, 1986; Williams, Watts, MacLeod, & Mathews, 1997). In both of these models, however, the therapy process is viewed as a form of new learning.

At the neural level, learning (including extinction learning) reflects a synaptic association between two or more neurons. During extinction, the neural association is not broken (as would be the case in "unlearning"); rather, new neural associations are formed that eventually predominate. Extinction of fear appears to be mediated by the N-methyl-D-aspartic acid (NMDA) subtype of glutamate receptor within the basolateral amygdala (Baker & Azorlosa, 1996; Cox & Westbrook, 1994; Davis, 2002; Davis & Myers, 2002; Fanselow & LeDoux, 1999; Goosens & Maren, 2002; Rogan, Staubli, & LeDoux, 1997; Royer & Pare, 2002).

NMDA receptor antagonists seem to block the extinction of learned fear associations in rats and in humans (Santini, Muller, & Quirk, 2001). In contrast, NMDA receptor agonists (drugs that facilitate NMDA activity) may accentuate extinction effects. In one study by Walker et al. (2002), rats were conditioned to exhibit a startle reflex toward a light after the light was repeatedly paired with a foot shock. The rats were then given the NMDA partial agonist d-cycloserine (DCS) and underwent extinction training, in which the light was presented repeatedly without the accompanying shock. Rats receiving DCS in addition to extinction training showed significantly less startle at post-treatment than did rats receiving extinction alone. Interestingly, rats receiving DCS without extinction training did not benefit, suggesting that the impact of DCS on extinction training is interactive, rather than additive: although DCS has no apparent value as a monotherapy for fear, when combined with extinction it appears to potentiate the underlying mechanisms of extinction training.

Could the facilitative effects of DCS + extinction also apply to fearful humans receiving exposure therapy? In the first test of DCS augmentation of exposure therapy in anxiety-disordered humans, Ressler et al. (2004) randomly assigned acrophobic patients to receive DCS or PBO 2–4 hours prior to two sessions of virtual reality-based exposure therapy. Consistent with the animal findings, there was no effect of DCS on baseline fear level, but patients receiving DCS benefited more from exposure therapy than did those receiving PBO. At post-treatment, approximately 60% of patients who received exposure + DCS, vs. approximately 20% of those receiving exposure + placebo, rated themselves "much improved" or "very much improved" at post-treatment. Subsequent studies have yielded similar findings among patients with social phobia (Guastella et al., 2008; Hofmann et al., 2006) and panic disorder (Otto et al., 2010). Meta-analysis of all studies in which DCS was compared to PBO in addition to exposure or extinction training has revealed that DCS enhances extinction effects in both animals and anxiety-disordered humans, with gains generally maintained at follow-up. Unlike SRI medications, which are taken daily over a long period of time, DCS was most effective when administered a limited number of times (e.g., 5 doses), and when given immediately preceding or following extinction training/exposure therapy (Norberg, Krystal, & Tolin, 2008).

Three preliminary studies to date have examined the effect of adding DCS to ERP for patients with OCD. Kushner et al. (2007) randomly assigned 25 patients to receive either DCS 125 mg or PBO 2 hours before each of up to 10 twice-weekly sessions of ERP. Results revealed no significant difference between the two groups at post-treatment or

3-month follow up in OCD severity on the Y-BOCS. However, after four sessions, patients in the DCS group reported significantly greater decreases in subjective units of distress (SUDS) toward obsession-related stimuli compared to the PBO group. Storch et al. (2007) randomly assigned 24 patients to receive DCS 250 mg or PBO 4 hours before each of 12 weekly ERP sessions. No significant group differences were found across outcome variables, with Y-BOCS scores decreasing equally for both groups. However, more detailed analysis revealed that DCS might have led to greater improvements than did PBO from week 4 to week 6 ($p = 0.16$). DCS and PBO patients were equally likely to meet criteria for clinically significant change at mid-treatment, post-treatment, and follow-up. Wilhelm et al. (2008) randomly assigned 23 patients to receive DCS 100 mg 1 hour prior to each of 10 ERP sessions. Results indicated that the DCS group had significantly lower Y-BOCS scores at mid-treatment than did the placebo group, with a large effect size. No significant group differences were detected at post-treatment and 1-month follow-up, although effect sizes were in the moderate range at each time point. At mid-treatment, 70% of DCS patients, compared to 8% of PBO patients, met remission criteria (Y-BOCS score of 12 or lower). At post-treatment, 70% of DCS vs. 42% of PBO patients met this criterion.

Figure 19.3 depicts the effect sizes (d) for each of these three studies at mid-treatment and post-treatment. The pattern of results is highly similar across the studies, with the strongest effects shown at mid-treatment and a diminishing rate of return at post-treatment. The Storch et al. study, while showing the same general pattern as the other two studies, failed to demonstrate any facilitative effect of DCS. The meta-analysis described above (Norberg et al., 2008) provides several clues that might explain this discrepancy. Storch et al. administered DCS 4 hours prior to each session, rather than the 1–2 hours used in most other human studies. Although DCS reaches peak plasma levels 4–8 hours after oral administration, the augmenting effects of DCS appear to take place during the period of memory consolidation that occurs several hours *after* training (Ledgerwood, Richardson, & Cranney, 2003; Santini, et al., 2001). Storch et al. also administered DCS + ERP over a longer period of time (12 weeks, compared to 5 weeks in the Wilhelm et al. study); treatment length was inversely related to the efficacy of DCS, which might be attributable to desensitization of the NMDA receptor following prolonged exposure to DCS (Boje, Wong, & Skolnick, 1993) and might help explain the general failure of DCS in the long-term treatment of conditions such as schizophrenia and Alzheimer's disease (Duncan et al., 2004; Fakouhi et al., 1995; Goff et al., 2005;

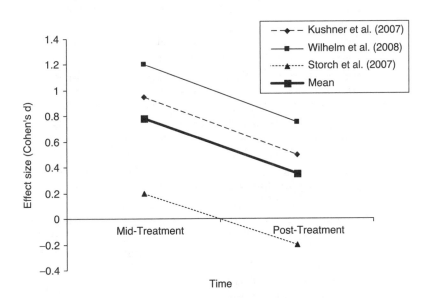

Figure 19.3. Effect sizes at mid-treatment and post-treatment for three studies of DCS augmentation of behavior therapy for obsessive-compulsive disorder.
Adapted from *Biological Psychiatry*, *63*(12), Norberg, M. M., Krystal, J. H., & Tolin, D. F., A meta-analysis of D-cycloserine and the facilitation of fear extinction and exposure therapy, 1118–1126, Copyright 2008, with permission from Elsevier.

Laake & Oeksengaard, 2002; Tuominen, Tiihonen, & Wahlbeck, 2005). Thus, DCS administration over a shorter time period may be critical for augmenting exposure-based treatment. Finally, ceiling effects cannot be ruled out in the Storch study. Dr. Storch obtained a Y-BOCS reduction of over 70% in the ERP + PBO group, substantially greater than in the other studies, and potentially obscuring any effect of DCS.

Thus, the available evidence suggests that DCS may augment the effects of CBT by speeding up the extinction process, although it is not clear whether longer-term outcomes are affected significantly. This line of research is noteworthy for two primary reasons. First, with 70% of DCS patients in remission status after only 5 sessions (Wilhelm, et al., 2008), it is likely that the more rapid response would translate to decreased attrition, decreased direct (e.g., therapy, medications) and indirect (e.g., forgone earnings) costs of illness, decreased suffering (e.g., fear and impairment) and increased caseload capacity for clinicians. Second, and perhaps more critical, research on DCS provides proof of concept that pharmacotherapy aimed at enhancing the neural underpinnings of psychotherapy can influence outcomes. This represents an interactive approach, rather than an additive one in which two known monotherapies are applied simultaneously, and a significant success of translational research from basic science to practice.

Research on DCS, in some ways, recalls attempts to augment psychotherapy with lysergic acid diethylamide-25 (LSD), a line of research that gained steam in the 1960s and 1970s (for a review see Neill, 1987) and continues to the present time (Multidisciplinary Association for Psychedelic Studies, 2008). Although the neural mechanisms of LSD and psychotherapy were not well understood at the time, the initial rationale for LSD-augmented psychotherapy was that the drug would facilitate the retrieval of childhood memories, enrich associative capacity, increase emotional expressiveness, reduce ego defenses, and increase suggestibility, thus enabling the patient to benefit more fully from therapy (Busch & Johnson, 1950; Holzinger, 1964; Mechaneck, Feldstein, Dahlberg, & Jaffe, 1968). Most of the literature on "psychedelic therapy" is limited to case reports, although a small number of controlled reports have been published. In one, LSD-augmented psychotherapy appeared to yield greater reductions in global psychiatric symptoms among narcotic addicts (Ludwig & Levine, 1965). In another study, however, LSD did not add to the effects of psychotherapy in a group of psychosomatic patients, and indeed, at follow-up the group receiving psychotherapy plus placebo was described as more emotionally stable (Soskin, 1973). These mixed results, as well as concerns about the long-term effects of psychedelic drug use, have, and will likely continue to, dampen enthusiasm for this line of research (Arnone & Schifano, 2006). As a side note, recently LSD and other hallucinogens (e.g., psilocybin) have been explored in the treatment of OCD and related disorders, due to these drugs' facilitative effects on the 5-HT$_{2A}$ receptor (for a review see Delgado & Moreno, 1998), and some uncontrolled case reports suggest that hallucinogens might indeed diminish obsessions and compulsions (Hanes, 1996; Leonard & Rapoport, 1987; Moreno & Delgado, 1997; Moreno, Wiegand, Taitano, & Delgado, 2006). In these cases, however, the hallucinogenic drugs are discussed as monotherapies, rather than as adjuncts to psychotherapy or behavior therapy.

Conclusion

Both SRI medications and CBT have proven effective as monotherapies for OCD as described in Chapters 16, 17 and 18 in this volume. Intuitively, it might be expected that their combination would be more effective than either treatment alone. However, controlled research affirms this hypothesis only partially. When two treatments are applied simultaneously, combined therapy shows a distinct advantage over pharmacotherapy. However, combined therapy offers only a small advantage over CBT monotherapy, and the potential side effects of medication might tip the cost/benefit ratio to CBT monotherapy as the first-line treatment of choice. Thus, the available data are more consistent with the APA's practice guidelines (Koran et al., 2007), in which CBT monotherapy was recommended as an initial treatment for all patients who could comply with this prescription, than with the previous Expert Consensus Guidelines (March et al., 1997) in which combined treatment was recommended for the more severe OCD cases.

The APA practice guidelines recommend that SRI medications be prescribed when patients have failed to respond to an adequate trial of CBT monotherapy. No published data speak to the efficacy of CBT + SRI for CBT nonresponders or partial responders. The idea seems intuitively reasonable, although (as has been discussed previously in this chapter), many intuitively reasonable hypotheses end up being incorrect. Given the greater availability of pharmacotherapy, and the likelihood that many OCD patients will not seek CBT until after at least one failed medication trial, it is encouraging that CBT appears reasonably effective even for these patients. Recently, research has investigated an entirely different approach to combined treatment: instead of applying two known monotherapies, compounds are being investigated that potentiate the neural mechanisms thought to underline successful CBT. In the first development of this line of research, the NMDA receptor agonist d-cycloserine appears to augment the neural mechanisms of extinction learning, resulting in more rapid response to CBT. Ongoing basic research in neuroplasticity is hoped to lead to increasingly refined methods.

Future Directions

1. How do non-SRI medications (e.g., benzodiazepines, atypical antipsychotics) augment or attenuate the effects of CBT?

2. How effective are SRI medications for CBT nonresponders or partial responders?

3. What are the economic costs and benefits of combined therapy vs. monotherapy?

4. To what extent does the efficacy of monotherapy vs. combined therapy depend on patient variables such as severity of illness, previous treatment history, or depressive or other comorbidity?

5. To what extent do under-studied variants of OCD (e.g., compulsive hoarding) benefit from combined therapy?

6. To what extent can other cognitive enhancers or other neuroplasticity compounds impact the effects of CBT?

Related Chapters

Chapter 15. Pharmacological Treatments for Obsessive Compulsive Disorder

Chapter 17. Exposure-Based Treatments for Obsessive Compulsive Disorder

Chapter 20. Additive and Alternative Approaches to Treating Obsessive Compulsive Disorder

References

Arnone, D., & Schifano, F. (2006). Psychedelics in psychiatry. *British Journal of Psychiatry, 188*, 88; author reply 89.

Baker, J. D., & Azorlosa, J. L. (1996). The NMDA antagonist MK-801 blocks the extinction of Pavlovian fear conditioning. *Behavioral Neuroscience, 110*(3), 618–620.

Beck, A. T., Emery, G., & Greenberg, R. L. (1985). *Anxiety disorders and phobias: A cognitive perspective.* New York: Basic Books.

Boje, K. M., Wong, G., & Skolnick, P. (1993). Desensitization of the NMDA receptor complex by glycinergic ligands in cerebellar granule cell cultures. *Brain Research, 603*(2), 207–214.

Bouton, M. E. (1993). Context, time, and memory retrieval in the interference paradigms of Pavlovian learning. *Psychological Bulletin, 114*(1), 80–99.

Busch, A. K., & Johnson, W. C. (1950). L.S.D. 25 as an aid in psychotherapy; preliminary report of a new drug. *Diseases of the Nervous System, 11*(8), 241–243.

Cohen, J. (1988). *Statistical power analysis for the behavioral sciences* (2 ed.). Hillsdale, NJ: Lawrence Erlbaum Associates.

Cottraux, J., Bouvard, M., Defayolle, M., & Messy, P. (1988). Validity and factorial structure study of the compulsive activity checklist. *Behavior Therapy, 19*, 45–53.

Cottraux, J., Mollard, E., Bouvard, M., Marks, I., Sluys, M., Nury, A. M., et al. (1990). A controlled study of fluvoxamine and exposure in obsessive-compulsive disorder. *International Clinical Psychopharmacology, 5*(1), 17–30.

Cottraux, J., Mollard, E., Bouvard, M., & Marks, I. (1993). Exposure therapy, fluvoxamine, or combination treatment in obsessive-compulsive disorder: one-year followup. *Psychiatry Research, 49*(1), 63–75.

Cox, J., & Westbrook, R. F. (1994). The NMDA receptor antagonist MK-801 blocks acquisition and extinction of conditioned hypoalgesic responses in the rat. *Quarterly Journal of Experimental Psychology B, 47*(2), 187–210.

Davis, M. (2002). Role of NMDA receptors and MAP kinase in the amygdala in extinction of fear: clinical implications for exposure therapy. *The European Journal Of Neuroscience, 16*(3), 395–398.

Davis, M., & Myers, K. M. (2002). The role of glutamate and gamma-aminobutyric acid in fear extinction: clinical implications for exposure therapy. *Biological Psychiatry, 52*(10), 998–1007.

Delgado, P. L., & Moreno, F. A. (1998). Different roles for serotonin in anti-obsessional drug action and the pathophysiology of obsessive-compulsive disorder. *British Journal of Psychiatry (Suppl.)*(35), 21–25.

Duncan, E. J., Szilagyi, S., Schwartz, M. P., Bugarski-Kirola, D., Kunzova, A., Negi, S., et al. (2004). Effects of D-cycloserine on negative symptoms in schizophrenia. *Schizophrenia Research, 71*(2–3), 239–248.

Fakouhi, T. D., Jhee, S. S., Sramek, J. J., Benes, C., Schwartz, P., Hantsburger, G., et al. (1995). Evaluation of cycloserine in the treatment of Alzheimer's disease. *Journal of Geriatric Psychiatry and Neurology, 8*(4), 226–230.

Fanselow, M. S., & LeDoux, J. E. (1999). Why we think plasticity underlying Pavlovian fear conditioning occurs in the basolateral amygdala. *Neuron, 23*(2), 229–232.

Foa, E. B., & Emmelkamp, P. M. (1983). *Failures in behavior therapy.* New York: Wiley.

Foa, E. B., & Kozak, M. J. (1986). Emotional processing of fear: Exposure to corrective information. *Psychological Bulletin, 99*(1), 20–35.

Foa, E. B., Kozak, M. J., Steketee, G., & McCarthy, P. R. (1992). Treatment of depressive and obsessive-compulsive symptoms in OCD by imipramine and behaviour therapy. *British Journal of Clinical Psychology, 31* (Pt 3), 279–292.

Foa, E. B., Liebowitz, M. R., Kozak, M. J., Davies, S., Campeas, R., Franklin, M. E., et al. (2005). Randomized, placebo-controlled trial of exposure and ritual prevention, clomipramine, and their combination in the treatment of obsessive-compulsive disorder. *American Journal of Psychiatry,* *162*(1), 151–161.

Glass, G. V., McGaw, B., & Smith, M. L. (1981). *Meta-analysis in social research.* London: Sage Publications.

Goff, D. C., Herz, L., Posever, T., Shih, V., Tsai, G., Henderson, D. C., et al. (2005). A six-month, placebo-controlled trial of D-cycloserine co-administered with conventional antipsychotics in schizophrenia patients. *Psychopharmacology (Berl),* *179*(1), 144–150.

Goodman, W. K., Price, L. H., Rasmussen, S. A., Mazure, C., Fleischmann, R. L., Hill, C. L., et al. (1989). The Yale-Brown Obsessive Compulsive Scale. I. Development, use, and reliability. *Archives of General Psychiatry, 46*(11), 1006–1011.

Goosens, K. A., & Maren, S. (2002). Long-term potentiation as a substrate for memory: evidence from studies of amygdaloid plasticity and Pavlovian fear conditioning. *Hippocampus, 12*(5), 592–599.

Guastella, A. J., Richardson, R., Lovibond, P. F., Rapee, R. M., Gaston, J. E., Mitchell, P., et al. (2008). A randomized controlled trial of D-cycloserine enhancement of exposure therapy for social anxiety disorder. *Biological Psychiatry, 63*(6), 544–549.

Guy, W. (1976). *Assessment manual for psychopharmacology.* Washington, DC: U.S. Government Printing Office.

Hanes, K. R. (1996). Serotonin, psilocybin, and body dysmorphic disorder: a case report. *Journal of Clinical Psychopharmacology, 16*(2), 188–189.

Hofmann, S. G., Meuret, A. E., Smits, J. A., Simon, N. M., Pollack, M. H., Eisenmenger, K., et al. (2006). Augmentation of exposure therapy with D-cycloserine for social anxiety disorder. *Archives of General Psychiatry, 63*(3), 298–304.

Hohagen, F., Winkelmann, G., Rasche-Ruchle, H., Hand, I., Konig, A., Munchau, N., et al. (1998). Combination of behaviour therapy with fluvoxamine in comparison with behaviour therapy and placebo. Results of a multicentre study. *British Journal of Psychiatry, 35,* 71–78.

Holzinger, R. (1964). Lsd-25, a Tool in Psychotherapy. *Journal of General Psychology, 71,* 9–20.

Jacobson, N. S., & Truax, P. (1991). Clinical significance: A statistical approach to defining meaningful change in psychotherapy research. *Journal of Consulting and Clinical Psychology, 59*(1), 12–19.

Kampman, M., Keijsers, G. P., Hoogduin, C. A., & Verbraak, M. J. (2002). Addition of cognitive-behaviour therapy f or obsessive-compulsive disorder patients non-responding to fluoxetine. *Acta Psychiatrica Scandinavica, 106*(4), 314–319.

Koran, L. M., Hanna, G. L., Hollander, E., Nestadt, G., & Simpson, H. B. (2007). Practice guideline for the treatment of patients with obsessive-compulsive disorder. *American Journal of Psychiatry, 164*(7 Suppl), 5–53.

Kushner, M. G., Kim, S. W., Donahue, C., Thuras, P., Adson, D., Kotlyar, M., et al. (2007). D-cycloserine augmented exposure therapy for obsessive-compulsive disorder. *Biological Psychiatry, 62*(8), 835–838.

Laake, K., & Oeksengaard, A. R. (2002). D-cycloserine for Alzheimer's disease. *Cochrane Database of Systematic Reviews* (2), CD003153.

Ledgerwood, L., Richardson, R., & Cranney, J. (2003). Effects of D-cycloserine on extinction of conditioned freezing. *Behavioral Neuroscience, 117*(2), 341–349.

Leonard, H. L., & Rapoport, J. L. (1987). Relief of obsessive-compulsive symptoms by LSD and psilocin. *American Journal of Psychiatry, 144*(9), 1239–1240.

Ludwig, A. M., & Levine, J. (1965). A controlled comparison of five brief treatment techniques employing LSD, hypnosis, and psychotherapy. *American Journal of Psychotherapy, 19,* 417–435.

March, J. S., Frances, A., Carpenter, D., & Kahn, D. A. (1997). The expert consensus guideline series: Treatment of obsessive-compulsive disorder. *Journal of Clinical Psychiatry, 58* (Suppl. 4).

Marks, I. M., Stern, R. S., Mawson, D., Cobb, J., & McDonald, R. (1980). Clomipramine and exposure for obsessive-compulsive rituals: i. *British Journal of Psychiatry, 136,* 1–25.

Mechaneck, R., Feldstein, S., Dahlberg, C. C., & Jaffe, J. (1968). Experimental investigation of LSD as a psychotherapeutic adjunct. *Comprehensive Psychiatry, 9*(5), 490–498.

Moreno, F. A., & Delgado, P. L. (1997). Hallucinogen-induced relief of obsessions and compulsions. *American Journal of Psychiatry, 154*(7), 1037–1038.

Moreno, F. A., Wiegand, C. B., Taitano, E. K., & Delgado, P. L. (2006). Safety, tolerability, and efficacy of psilocybin in 9 patients with obsessive-compulsive disorder. *Journal of Clinical Psychiatry, 67*(11), 1735–1740.

Multidisciplinary Association for Psychedelic Studies. (2008). LSD and psilocybin research Retrieved September 1, 2008, from http://www.maps.org/research/cluster/psilo-lsd/

Neill, J. R. (1987). "More than medical significance": LSD and American psychiatry 1953 to 1966. *Journal of Psychoactive Drugs, 19*(1), 39–45.

Neziroglu, F., Yaryura-Tobias, J. A., Walz, J., & McKay, D. (2000). The effect of fluvoxamine and behavior therapy on children and adolescents with obsessive-compulsive disorder. *Journal of Child and Adolescent Psychopharmacology, 10*(4), 295–306.

Norberg, M. M., Krystal, J. H., & Tolin, D. F. (2008). A meta-analysis of D-cycloserine and the facilitation of fear extinction and exposure therapy. *Biological Psychiatry, 63*(12), 1118–1126.

Otto, M. W., Tolin, D. F., Simon, N. M., Pearlson, G. D., Basden, S., Meunier, S. A., et al. (2010). Efficacy of d-cycloserine for enhancing response to cognitive-behavior therapy for panic disorder. *Biological Psychiatry, 67*(4), 365–370.

Pediatric OCD Treatment Study Team. (2004). Cognitive-behavior therapy, sertraline, and their combination for children and adolescents with obsessive-compulsive disorder: the Pediatric OCD Treatment Study (POTS) randomized controlled trial. *Journal of the American Medical Association, 292*(16), 1969–1976.

Ressler, K. J., Rothbaum, B. O., Tannenbaum, L., Anderson, P., Graap, K., Zimand, E., et al. (2004). Cognitive enhancers as adjuncts to psychotherapy: use of D-cycloserine in phobic individuals to facilitate extinction of fear. *Archives of General Psychiatry, 61*(11), 1136–1144.

Rogan, M. T., Staubli, U. V., & LeDoux, J. E. (1997). Fear conditioning induces associative long-term potentiation in the amygdala. *Nature, 390*(6660), 604–607.

Rosenthal, R. (1991). *Meta-analytic procedures for social research.* London: Sage Publications.

Royer, S., & Pare, D. (2002). Bidirectional synaptic plasticity in intercalated amygdala neurons and the extinction of conditioned fear responses. *Neuroscience, 115*(2), 455–462.

Santini, E., Muller, R. U., & Quirk, G. J. (2001). Consolidation of extinction learning involves transfer from NMDA-independent to NMDA-dependent memory. *Journal of Neuroscience, 21*(22), 9009–9017.

Scahill, L., Riddle, M. A., McSwiggin-Hardin, M., Ort, S. I., King, R. A., Goodman, W. K., et al. (1997). Children's

Yale-Brown Obsessive Compulsive Scale: reliability and validity. *Journal of the American Academy of Child and Adolescent Psychiatry, 36*(6), 844–852.

Simpson, H. B., Gorfinkle, K. S., & Liebowitz, M. R. (1999). Cognitive-behavioral therapy as an adjunct to serotonin reuptake inhibitors in obsessive-compulsive disorder: an open trial. *Journal of Clinical Psychiatry, 60*(9), 584–590.

Simpson, H. B., Liebowitz, M. R., Foa, E. B., Kozak, M. J., Schmidt, A. B., Rowan, V., et al. (2004). Post-treatment effects of exposure therapy and clomipramine in obsessive-compulsive disorder. *Depression and Anxiety, 19*(4), 225–233.

Soskin, R. A. (1973). The use of LSD in time-limited psychotherapy. *Journal of Nervous and Mental Disease, 157*(6), 410–419.

Storch, E. A., Merlo, L. J., Bengtson, M., Murphy, T. K., Lewis, M. H., Yang, M. C., et al. (2007). D-cycloserine does not enhance exposure-response prevention therapy in obsessive-compulsive disorder. *International Clinical Psychopharmacology, 22*(4), 230–237.

TenHave, T. R., Coyne, J., Salzer, M., & Katz, I. (2003). Research to improve the quality of care for depression: alternatives to the simple randomized clinical trial. *General Hospital Psychiatry, 25*(2), 115–123.

Tenneij, N. H., van Megen, H. J., Denys, D. A., & Westenberg, H. G. (2005). Behavior therapy augments response of patients with obsessive-compulsive disorder responding to drug treatment. *Journal of Clinical Psychiatry, 66*(9), 1169–1175.

Tolin, D. F., Maltby, N., Diefenbach, G. J., Hannan, S. E., & Worhunsky, P. (2004). Cognitive-behavioral therapy for medication nonresponders with obsessive-compulsive disorder: A wait-list-controlled open trial. *Journal of Clinical Psychiatry, 65*(7), 922–931.

Tuominen, H. J., Tiihonen, J., & Wahlbeck, K. (2005). Glutamatergic drugs for schizophrenia: a systematic review and meta-analysis. *Schizophrenia Research, 72*(2–3), 225–234.

van Balkom, A. J., de Haan, E., van Oppen, P., Spinhoven, P., Hoogduin, K. A., & van Dyck, R. (1998). Cognitive and behavioral therapies alone versus in combination with fluvoxamine in the treatment of obsessive compulsive disorder. *Journal of Nervous and Mental Disease, 186*(8), 492–499.

Walker, D. L., Ressler, K. J., Lu, K. T., & Davis, M. (2002). Facilitation of conditioned fear extinction by systemic administration or intra-amygdala infusions of D-cycloserine as assessed with fear-potentiated startle in rats. *Journal of Neuroscience, 22*(6), 2343–2351.

Wilhelm, S., Buhlmann, U., Tolin, D. F., Meunier, S. A., Pearlson, G. D., Reese, H. E., et al. (2008). Augmentation of behavior therapy with D-cycloserine for obsessive-compulsive disorder. *American Journal of Psychiatry, 165*(3), 335–341.

Williams, J. M. G., Watts, F. N., MacLeod, C., & Mathews, A. (1997). *Cognitive psychology and emotional disorders* (2nd ed.). New York: John Wiley & Sons.

Additive and Alternative Approaches to Treating Obsessive Compulsive Disorder

Jordana Muroff, Abigail Ross, *and* Joseph Rothfarb

Abstract

While cognitive-behavioral therapy (CBT) and pharmacotherapy are "gold standard" treatments for obsessive-compulsive disorder (OCD), complementary and alternative treatments are frequently sought for anxiety disorders. The purpose of this chapter is to review and discuss the available research on the application, efficacy and effectiveness of complementary and alternative methods for treating OCD. The first section identifies and reviews studies focusing on specific alternative and complementary treatments that are independent from, or work in conjunction with CBT, such as yoga, herbal remedies, motivational strategies, and bibliotherapy. The second section discusses alternative and complementary methods of more mainstream CBT and related techniques, with a particular focus on technology-supported approaches. The chapter concludes with a discussion of the methodological issues in the existing research on complementary and alternative methods in the treatment of OCD, questions for future research, and implications for providers.

Keywords: alternative, complementary, treatment, obsessive compulsive disorder, ACT, meditation, motivational interviewing, self-help, herbal, technology

Introduction

Obsessive-compulsive disorder (OCD) is a disabling mental disorder characterized by time-consuming and distress-inducing obsessions and compulsions associated with significant social, functional, and economic impairment. The lifetime prevalence rate of OCD is estimated to be approximately two to three percent in the general population of the United States (Weissman et al., 1994). Pharmacological and cognitive-behavioral treatments (CBT) are currently viewed as "gold standard" for both adult and pediatric OCD (Franklin & Foa, 1998; March, Frances, Carpenter, & Kahn, 1997; Stein, Ipser, Baldwin, & Bandelow, 2007). The majority of people who receive CBT seem to benefit from it; however, an estimated 30% do not demonstrate sufficient improvement from the first-line treatment of choice (Rasmussen, Eisen, &

Pato, 1993; Schruers, Koning, Luermans, Haack, & Griez, 2005).

Additionally, only a small proportion of people receive CBT. There is also a dearth of practitioners trained to provide manualized CBT for OCD (Nakagawa et al., 2000), and those with training tend to be concentrated in U.S. urban areas. Furthermore, people with OCD tend not to seek specialized mental health services where CBT generally is delivered; in the Epidemiological Catchment Area Survey (Leon, Portera, & Weissman, 1995), only 7% of males and 12% of females were found to utilize such services for their OCD. Moreover, approximately 25% do not wish to pursue CBT, and another 20% drop out of treatment (Greist, 1992; Schruers et al., 2005). Thus, it is important to consider complementary or alternative treatments for OCD, given the stress and impairment associated with the disorder, the fact that one-third of OCD sufferers do not adequately respond to conventional treatments, the barriers to accessing well-trained CBT providers, and preferences for nontraditional methods.

The use of complementary and alternative methods (CAM), functionally defined as interventions that are neither taught widely in medical schools nor generally available in U.S. hospitals (Eisenberg et al., 1993), has increased substantially since 1990 in the United States among the general population (Eisenberg et al., 1998). The public reports positive attitudes about complementary and alternative methods (Jorm et al., 2004). In fact, people perceive that complementary and alternative methods are equally as helpful as traditional standard treatments (e.g., CBT; Kessler, Davis et al., 2001). The distressing nature of traditional exposure and response prevention (ERP) exercises may account for both the high dropout and treatment refusal rates of individuals with OCD (Abramowitz, Taylor, & McKay, 2005) as well as the increased frequency of complementary and alternative methods use that is evident in individuals with anxiety symptoms or disorders (Kessler, Soukup et al., 2001; Wahlstrom et al., 2008). Approximately 57% of people with anxiety attacks report using complementary and alternative methods, and about 66% use these methods in conjunction with their CBT treatment (Kessler, Davis et al., 2001).

Despite the prevalence of use and positive perceptions associated with CAM in the treatment of anxiety, research on these methods is quite limited. Though reviews of complementary and alternative treatment methods for anxiety and related disorders do exist (Jorm et al., 2004; Saeed, Bloch, & Antonacci, 2007), to date, there has been no comprehensive review of complementary and alternative treatments for OCD. The purpose of this chapter is to review and discuss the available research on the application, efficacy and effectiveness of complementary and alternative methods and delivery mechanisms for treating OCD.

Part I: Alternative and Complementary Treatments Unrelated to CBT Methods
Herbal Treatment/Dietary Augmentation

Although research on herbal treatment and dietary augmentation for psychological disorders is widespread, the literature with respect to the use of such treatments for OCD is limited. To date, very few trials have evaluated the efficacy of herbal treatment specifically for OCD (Bootsani, Paksheresht, & Malayeri, 2010; Greenberg et al., 2009; Kobak et al., 2005; Kushner et al., 2007; Taylor & Kobak, 2000; Wilhelm et al., 2008). In a double-blind randomized trial, 35 adult outpatients were randomly assigned to receive either 600 mg/day of Silybum marianum (L.) Gaertn, a medicinal plant commonly known as milk thistle found in the Mediterranean area, or fluoxetine (30 mg/day) of a period of eight weeks (Sayyah et al., 2010). Results revealed significant reductions on Yale-Brown Obsessive Compulsive Scale (Y-BOCS) scores from pre-to post-test in both groups, and no statistical differences between groups at post-test, indicating that Silybum marianum (L.) Gaertn may be as effective as 30 mg/day of fluoxetine in obsessive-compulsive symptom reduction (Sayyah et al., 2010).

Results of an open trial of St. John's wort (*Hypericum perforatum*), in which participants ingested a fixed dose of 450 mg of 0.3% hypericum, an active compound found in St. John's wort, revealed significant improvement in Y-BOCS scores at post-test (Taylor & Kobak, 2000). Kobak and colleagues (2005) later conducted a controlled trial in which 60 participants were randomized to 12 weeks of treatment with St. John's wort (flexible dose of 600–1800 mg/daily) or placebo control. No significant changes were observed in Y-BOCS scores in the controlled trial, though agitation was reported significantly more often in participants randomized to the St. John's wort condition (Kobak et al., 2005). Thus, results on the effectiveness of St. John's wort as a treatment for OCD are relatively inconclusive. Greenberg and colleagues (2009) evaluated SSRI augmentation with the amino acid glycine (60g/day) through a double-blind randomized placebo-controlled trial. Results revealed no significant differences between glycine and placebo groups; notably, the study was plagued by high dropout rates due to side effects of nausea and dissatisfaction with the taste (Greenberg et al., 2009).

Other herbal treatments, including kava (*Piper methysticum*) and passionflower (*Passiflora*), have been used in the treatment of anxiety and have yielded mixed results, but have yet to be evaluated for OCD treatment specifically (Akhondzadeh et al., 2001; Andreatini, Sartori, Seabra, & Leite, 2002; Leathwood & Chauffard, 1985; Lehmann, Kinzler, & Friedemann, 1996; Lehmann, Klieser, Klimke, Krach, & Spatz, 1989; Malsch & Kieser, 2001; Pittler & Ernst, 2000, 2003; Volz & Kieser, 1997).

5-hydroxytryptophan (5-HTP), an amino acid generated naturally by the human body and also available as a plant extract, may have implications for the treatment of OCD (Jorm et al., 2004). When combined with L-tryptophan, 5-HTP results in the production of 5-hydroxytryptamine, also known as serotonin. The hypothesis that a deficiency in 5-HTP transmission may account for the treatment-refractory nature of some OCD patients has provided rationale for neurosurgery as a possibility for treatment-refractory OCD patients (McDougle, 1997). Neuroanatomy and other biological treatments are discussed in further detail in Chapters 7 and 16 of this volume, respectively. Though no controlled trials have evaluated the use of 5-HTP augmentation in the treatment of OCD exclusively to date, results from a single open trial with five treatment-refractory OCD participants indicates that patients showed no improvement after 5-HTP was added to the existing SSRI and pindolol treatment regimen (Blier & Bergeron, 1996).

It is well documented that selective serotonergic reuptake inhibitors (SSRIs) are effective in treating OCD symptoms (Dell'Osso et al., 2008; Fineberg, 1996; Greist, Jefferson, Kobak, Katzelnick, & Serlin, 1995; Piccinelli, Pini, Bellantuono, & Wilkinson, 1995) and are reviewed in Chapter 15 of this volume. Myo-inositol, an isomer of glucose found in the regular human diet, is also involved in the second-messenger systems of some serotonin and noradrenalin receptors (Benjamin et al., 1995). In the treatment of OCD, effects of 18 mg/day of myo-inositol were found to be superior to placebo control in participants who were not concurrently prescribed SSRIs (Fux, Benjamin, & Belmaker, 1999; Seedat & Stein, 1999). No significant changes in Y-BOCS scores were evident in later studies, in which participants augmented SSRI prescription dosage with the same 18 mg/day dosage of myo-inositol tested in the previous study (Fux et al., 1999; Seedat & Stein, 1999). However, a small number of treatment-refractory individuals (n=3) did report a clinically significant response on the Clinical Global Improvement (CGI) scale (Seedat & Stein, 1999). Case studies also indicate that treatment-refractory adults may benefit from augmenting SSRIs with either N-acetylcysteine (NAC), the N-acetyl derivative of cysteine (Lafleur et al., 2006), or glycine (Cleveland et al., 2009).

Surprisingly, the only research trials that have examined the utility of non-SSRI ingestibles in conjunction with behavior therapy for OCD have done so with D-cycloserine (DCS), an NMDA partial agonist (Kushner et al., 2007; Wilhelm et al., 2008).

Both studies utilized a single dose of the D-cycloserine administered 1-2 hours prior to commencing each session of behavior therapy treatment regimen (10 and 11 sessions each, respectively). Findings from Kushner et al (2007) indicate promise for the utility of DCS in reducing dropout rates and accelerated extinction of obsession-related stress in OCD; scores on the Y-BOCS were significantly lower in the DCS group compared to the placebo group at ERP session 4, but no significant differences between groups were found at post-test or 3 month follow up. Similar findings were revealed by Wilhelm and colleagues (2008), in which only the DCS group showed significant reductions in mid-treatment Y-BOCS scores, but no significant between-group differences were evident at either post-test or follow up in OCD symptoms. Notably, the DCS group in Wilhelm's sample showed significant improvement in depressive symptoms at post-test, whereas the placebo group did not.

The body of literature addressing the efficacy and effectiveness of herbal treatments for OCD is sparse compared to that available for depression and other anxiety disorders. The few studies that do provide empirical evidence of efficacy of herbal treatment indicate that herbal treatments are best conceptualized as alternative treatments to be used independently of SSRIs, as opposed to integrative or adjunctive. Findings from a number of studies suggest that long-term consumption of St. John's wort may in fact reduce the clinical effectiveness or increase dosage requirements for CYP 3A4 substrates, which represent approximately 50% of all prescription medications (Markowitz & DeVane, 2001; Markowitz et al., 2003; Zhou & Lai, 2008). Cases have also been reported where the combination of St. John's wort and SSRIs has induced serotonin syndrome (Dannawi, 2002; Gordon, 1998; Lantz, Buchalter, & Giambanco, 1999), a serious condition characterized by alterations in cognitive, behavioral, and autonomic nervous system levels of functioning due to increased brainstem serotonin activity (Mills, 1995). 5-HTP also presents safety concerns; it has been associated with eosinophilia-myalgia syndrome (Cauffield & Forbes, 1999). Though the temporary ban of serotonin precursors from the U.S. market has been lifted, speculation regarding the association between consumption of 5-HTP and the potential for serious adverse side effects remains (Saeed et al., 2007). Results from the few studies exploring the use of myo-inositol suggest that it may have positive effects when used in treating OCD independent of SSRI use only

(Fux et al., 1999; Fux, Levine, Aviv, & Belmaker, 1996; Saeed et al., 2007). It is possible that herbal treatments may be adjunctive or integrative with noningestible treatments, but only a single randomized controlled trial has been conducted to date and important safety precautions must be taken.

Exercise and Yoga

Although no studies to date have exclusively evaluated the effect of exercise as a standalone treatment for OCD or any OC-related spectrum disorder, three recent studies indicate that aerobic exercise may be associated with reductions in OCD symptoms (Abrantes et al., 2009; Brown et al., 2007; Lancer, Motta, & Lancer, 2007). Findings from Brown et al. (2007) suggest that exercise regimens (i.e., a 12-week exercise intervention) may be used effectively as an adjunctive or integrative component to empirically supported OCD interventions, such as pharmacotherapy and behavior therapy, with gains maintained at 6-month follow-up. Participants in the same sample (N=15) reported acute reductions in OCD symptoms, anxiety, and negative mood upon completion of the exercise regimen when compared to measurements reported at baseline (Abrantes et al., 2009). Additionally, results from Lancer and colleagues (2007) showed reductions in OCD symptoms among an OCD sample (N=11 completers) participating in a 6-week exercise intervention; however, there was a reduction in treatment gains during the one-month follow-up period after the exercise ceased. CBT may be a particularly opportune treatment modality for the inclusion of exercise since it involves completion of assigned tasks, or homework, outside of treatment sessions (Stathopoulou, Powers, Berry, Smits, & Otto, 2006). Exercise has been shown to reduce anxiety and depressive symptoms that commonly co-occur with OCD (Broman-Fulks, Berman, Rabian, & Webster, 2004; Broocks et al., 1998; Lancer et al., 2007); thus, future studies may continue to examine the effects of exercise on OCD.

Yoga, a nonaerobic form of exercise, has also been employed in the treatment of OCD. Although only one randomized controlled trial exists to date, yoga was found to significantly improve OCD symptoms (Shannahoff-Khalsa et al., 1999). Participants (n=20) were randomized to either kundalini yoga meditation or relaxation response plus mindful meditation conditions. A comparison of Y-BOCS questionnaires administered at baseline and at 3 months demonstrated a significant decrease in scores among the kundalini yoga group and a nonsignificant decrease in scores among relaxation response plus mindfulness group.

Clinical case reports also indicate that yoga may improve symptoms of OCD (Shannahoff-Khalsa & Beckett, 1996). Though yoga has yet to be evaluated as an adjunctive component of more empirically supported OCD treatments, future studies may test the effectiveness of combined yoga and CBT (or pharmacotherapy) for OCD.

Access to yoga interventions may be restricted by the availability of qualified practitioners, or the individual's own financial resources (as yoga and meditation do not generally receive third-party reimbursement). Once educated on the proper method of yoga practice, however, such interventions do not necessitate a practitioner (Arias, Steinberg, Banga, & Trestman, 2006).

Mindfulness

An integral aspect of meditation is "thoughtless awareness," or mindfulness (Arias et al., 2006, p. 820). Mindfulness has been incorporated into the framework of both traditional and alternative anxiety disorder treatments, though it has not yet received extensive clinical attention as a standalone treatment modality for OCD. Based upon principles of nonjudgment, attention to bodily sensations, and anchoring in the present, mindfulness provides the clinical practitioner with resources to increase awareness of anxiety sensitivity and response—a factor that has been shown to be salient in the treatment of anxiety disorders (Tory, 2004).

The use of mindfulness-based techniques for the treatment of OCD is evidenced by a small but growing body of literature. A controlled pilot trial of individuals with OCD symptoms (N=15) received either mindfulness training (n=8) or were assigned to a waitlist control group (n=9). The mindfulness training intervention had a significant and large effect on OCD symptoms and thought–action fusion at post-test (TAF; Hanstede, Gidron, & Nyklicek, 2008). These reductions in OCD symptoms seemed to be mediated by enhanced ability in "letting go." Case studies also provide additional accounts of the utility of mindfulness-based interventions in significantly reducing symptoms of OCD in both clinical OCD and treatment refractory populations (Patel, Carmody, & Simpson, 2007; Singh, Wahler, Winton, & Adkins, 2004). In the case of a 25-year-old female with contamination OCD, pharmacotherapy and psychotherapy proved minimally effective, though Y-BOCS scores demonstrated significant improvement over the 16-week course of treatment, dropping from 35 to 5 after completing a mindfulness intervention derived from Buddhist principles (Singh et al., 2004). In a single-subject experimental trial, detached mindfulness techniques resulted in a decrease in Y-BOCS score from 36 to 12 from pre-test to post-test, as well as significant reductions in worry and punishment subscales on the Thought Control Questionnaire (TCQ). Treatment gains were maintained at follow-up (Firouzabadi & Shareh, 2009).

Mindfulness and acceptance-based treatments encourage nonjudgment, which may reduce the likelihood of the client becoming frustrated with treatment, and enhance client retention and recovery (Twohig, Hayes, & Masuda, 2006a). Mindfulness is generally not used in isolation, but rather as a way to render traditional therapies more "user-friendly" (Hannan & Tolin, 2005, p.271). Mindfulness interventions have not been shown to independently reduce OCD symptoms, but rather, to allow CBT techniques to be implemented with greater ease (Fairfax, 2008). Mindfulness-based interventions used in conjunction with other traditional treatments, such as CBT, may facilitate a more holistic treatment approach that extends treatment beyond primary OCD symptoms to include other domains (Didonna, 2009). This is especially important for OCD, given its disabling impact on so many areas of an individual's life.

The benefit of mindfulness-based techniques is that they can be practiced at home after they have been properly elucidated by the practitioner. As of yet, mindfulness-based therapy may not receive third-party reimbursement, thus limiting access to an extent (Singh et al., 2004). Widely available are guided meditation and mindfulness recordings that participants may use, although individuals are encouraged to consult their mental health provider to ensure that these techniques are applied properly.

Acceptance and Commitment Therapy (ACT)

Acceptance and commitment therapy (ACT) is a recently developed alternative psychotherapy approach that incorporates mindfulness-based techniques of awareness and acceptance into a broader network of interwoven principles. Theoretical underpinnings of ACT are rooted in the idea that psychological inflexibility can be counteracted by building client skills in six areas: "acceptance of experience, cognitive diffusion, being present, self as

context, values, and committed action" (Hayes, Luoma, Bond, Masuda, & Lillis, 2006, pp.8–9). One of the core principles of ACT directly addresses emotional avoidance, which is hypothesized to contribute to OCD. Although recent research indicates that "emotional avoidance" is too general to explain specific manifestations of OC symptoms (Abramowitz, Lackey, & Wheaton, 2009), ACT has garnered a growing clinical reputation in the treatment of anxiety disorders, including OCD, OC spectrum disorders, and treatment refractory populations (Twohig, Plumb, Mukherjee, & Hayes, 2010).

To date, only one randomized controlled trial has evaluated the efficacy of ACT for OCD (Twohig et al., 2010). Seventy-nine adults were randomly assigned to receive 8 sessions of either ACT or progressive relaxation training (PRT) that involved no in-session ERP. Greater reductions in Y-BOCS scores were evident in the ACT group at post-test and follow-up when compared to the PRT group. Moreover, clinically significant change in symptom severity occurred in 46-66% of ACT group participants compared to 13%-18% in the PRT group (Twohig et al., 2010). In a non-concurrent multiple-baseline across-participant study, 4 participants were offered ACT as a treatment protocol for OCD (Twohig, 2008). The protocol was composed of 8 weekly treatment sessions that addressed, in the following order, the nature of obsessions and compulsions, the problematic nature of attempting to control obsessions, reconceptualization of obsessions as unremarkable rather than pernicious features, contact with the present moment, self-as-context, and commitment to values. A comparison of pre- and post-treatment Obsessive Compulsive Inventory (OCI) self-reports showed that scores improved 68% across participants. This improvement percentage increased to 81% when pretreatment and follow-up scores were compared.

Multiple case studies add further clinical evidence to these findings (Twohig et al., 2006a). Additionally, ACT has been successful in the treatment of other OC spectrum disorders, such as compulsive skin-picking (Twohig, Hayes, & Masuda, 2006b). In combination with other therapeutic interventions, ACT has provided symptom reduction along the OC spectrum. A randomized trial of ACT and habit reversal (ACT/HR) significantly reduced hair pulling in trichotillomania (Woods, Wetterneck, & Flessner, 2006). Further evidence from a pilot study lends support to the use of acceptance enhanced behavior therapy (AEBT) in effectively treating both trichotillomania and compulsive skin-picking (Flessner, Busch, Heideman, & Woods, 2008).

Control-based strategies such as thought-stopping are generally not effective components of OCD treatment (Hannan & Tolin, 2005). Both mindfulness and acceptance-based techniques differ from control strategies, in that the emphasis is not on "doing away with" the thought, but rather "sitting with hot thoughts" (Fairfax, 2008, p.56). ACT, for instance, deemphasizes control in its treatment of OCD symptoms. For treatment refractory OCD clients, interventions that stress nonjudgment and acceptance can reduce the client's frustration with the treatment process, as well as quell the inner struggle for control (Twohig et al., 2006a).

Though ACT is intended to deemphasize control, it differentiates itself from other therapies, such as CBT and ERP, which involve techniques designed to help the individual gain control over obsessions and compulsions. Yet, at the most basic level, all three treatment modalities share a common objective to increase an individual's ability to pursue a valued lifestyle irrespective of feared stimuli. As this concept is at the heart of both CBT and ERP, the difference between ACT and its predecessors may be essentially a theoretical one (Twohig et al., 2006a).

Yoga and meditation techniques, along with ACT, have been used primarily as standalone treatments for OCD in lieu of traditional treatments such as CBT/ERP (DeBerry, Davis, & Reinhard, 1989; Forman, Herbert, Moitra, Yeomans, & Geller, 2007; Koszycki, Benger, Shlik, & Bradwejn, 2007; Shannahoff-Khalsa et al., 1999; Twohig, 2008). As previously discussed, a small but growing body of research demonstrates that these modalities exhibit a significant level of efficacy independent of traditional methods. The future of alternative OCD treatment would benefit, however, from clinical trials evaluating yoga/meditation, ACT, and CBT/ERP as treatment modalities independent of one another. Research of this nature would provide more conclusive evidence regarding efficacy and effectiveness of specific traditional and alternative treatments.

Religion and Spirituality

ACT may be representative of a new series of therapeutic interventions known as the *third wave* (Andersson, 2006). These therapies "emphasize contextual and experiential change strategies in addition to more direct and didactic ones" (Hayes, 2004, p. 658; as cited in Hayes et al., 2006). This treatment perspective encourages consideration of a myriad of sociocultural phenomena. Religion and spirituality, as examples of such phenomena, may inform third-generation therapies in a critical manner, inasmuch as they provide added contextual and experiential texture to the clinician–client therapeutic interaction. Please see Chapter 26 for a discussion of cultural issues involved in understanding and treating OCD.

The use of religion and spirituality in the treatment of OCD is not well established, though a number of studies have documented the relationship between OCD symptoms/cognitions and religiosity (Abramowitz, Deacon, Woods, & Tolin, 2004; Nelson, Abramowitz, Whiteside, & Deacon, 2006; Steketee, Quay, & White, 1991; Yorulmaz, Gençöz, & Woody, 2009), including positive correlations between thought–action fusion (TAF) in morality and degree of religious involvement (Nelson et al., 2006; Rassin & Koster, 2003). At present, the clinical application of these techniques is limited to case studies (Bonchek & Greenberg, 2009; Gangdev, 1998). The benefit of religious and spiritual techniques in OCD treatment has yet to be significantly substantiated clinically (Heberling, 2005; Kennemer, 2007; Olson, 2003; Osborn, 2008).

For religious individuals, religious and spiritual psychotherapies can replace negative automatic thoughts (obsessions) with positive ones, without using cognitive restructuring. This is exemplified by the case of the woman who felt assured that Jesus would safeguard her from harm, resulting in the complete and rapid resolution of her OCD symptoms (Gangdev, 1998). The operationalization of religious interventions for OCD, thus, may be framed in terms of cognitive restructuring of negative automatic thoughts. The rationale, in this instance, is identical for both cognitive therapy and religious intervention, although religious intervention harnesses positive thoughts inveterate to the individual's cognitive framework.

Similarly, access to religious interventions may be easier because individuals might already know the religious rituals they are to perform as treatment, or can learn them from religious leaders. The rekindling of religious faith, implicated in a clinically documented resolution of OCD (Gangdev, 1998), may be facilitated by weekly attendance at temple, mosque, or church. In the case of religious psychotherapy, access may become more complicated because mental health practitioners must be familiar with the particular tenets of a client's religion (Razali, Hasanah, Aminah, & Subramaniam, 1998), as OCD symptom manifestation may differ depending upon one's religion. For example, one study found that TAF was related to religiosity among Christians, but not among Jews (Siev & Cohen, 2007).

A client's obsessions and compulsions may also be rooted in religiosity (Bonchek & Greenberg, 2009; Trenholm, Trent, & Compton, 1998; Yorulmaz et al., 2009). Examples of obsessive-compulsive religiosity have been found among Orthodox Jewish clients (Bonchek & Greenberg, 2009; Greenberg & Shefler, 2002; Gross-Isseroff & Weiszman, 2006), as well as within other religious traditions (Osborn, 2008; Yorulmaz et al., 2009). The argument has been made that OCD and other anxiety disorders can and should be treated by the religions from which they originally derived (Heberling, 2005; Jackson, 1975; Osborn, 2008; Yorulmaz et al., 2009). While this debate is ongoing, mental health practitioners should assess the relationship between OCD and religiosity before considering religious psychotherapy as an alternative treatment for the disorder.

Hypnosis

The use of hypnosis in OCD treatment has been advocated by some researchers (Wester & Sugarman, 2007; Wolberg, 1948). Despite this optimism, it is clear that a broader base of evidence, including randomized controlled trials, is required to substantiate the effectiveness of hypnotherapy (Frederick, 2007). Thus far, hypnosis has only been shown to reduce OCD symptoms in case studies where it was used adjunctively and not as the sole treatment (Scrignar, 1981). In addition, people with OCD may be less receptive to hypnosis in comparison to others (see Lynn, Kirsch, Barabasz, Cardena, & Patterson, 2000, p. 253; Spinhoven, Van Dyck, Hoogduin, & Schaap, 1991). However, hypnosis has demonstrated symptom improvement for other OC spectrum disorders, such as trichotillomania (Robiner, Edwards, Christenson, Stein, & Hollander, 1999; Zalsman, Hermesh, & Sever, 2001), and has been associated with decreases in anxiety symptoms (Benson, 1978; Hart, 1994).

Hypnosis is also argued to be an important additive to treatment for OCD and other anxiety disorders (Kraft & Kraft, 2006). Typically, an OCD or OC spectrum intervention involving hypnosis is short-term. Whether implemented as an adjunct or as a standalone treatment, the duration of hypnosis interventions is typically a maximum of six sessions (Moore, 1991; Zalsman et al., 2001), although longer-term treatment has been employed as well (Frederick, 2007). The short-term usage of hypnosis may be due to its utility in enriching imagined "flooding" exposures, interventions that are performed, typically, in a limited number of sessions (Scrignar, 1981). Case studies suggest that hypnosis may be a useful adjunct to CBT for OCD (Kellerman, 1981). Hypnotically-induced exposure may enhance traditional ERP methods, making exposure a more easily performed and more effective, technique.

Acupuncture and Tai Chi

Neither acupuncture nor tai chi has been evaluated specifically for the treatment of OCD. There are virtually no studies examining the use of acupuncture in the treatment of OCD (Pilkington, Kirkwood, Rampes, Cummings, & Richardson, 2007). Earlier studies show that acupuncture was associated with a poor treatment response for obsessional symptoms (Shuaib & Haq, 1977). A study from Japan reported that transcutaneous electrical stimulation was used in conjunction with exposure and response prevention for people with OCD, by applying low levels of electrical stimuli to specific points after negative mood has been evoked via in vivo or imagined exposure. The technique demonstrated positive effects (Yamashita, Fujimoto, Aoi, Shimura, & Kubo, 1991).

Despite these findings, research evidence is not sufficient to attest to the efficacy of acupuncture to treat specific anxiety disorders, including OCD (Pilkington et al., 2007; Samuels, Gropp, Singer, & Oberbaum, 2008). Problematic methodology, including small sample sizes (Chao-Ying, 2003; Liu, Zang, Guo, & Liu, 1998) and inclusion of herbs and multiple types of acupuncture (Zhang, Zeng, & Deng, 2003), complicates interpretations of findings.

The majority of studies that have evaluated the efficacy of tai chi have focused on health outcomes and well-being in elderly populations (Kuramoto, 2006). Results from a number of studies indicate that tai chi may improve symptom management and health-related quality of life in populations affected by a number of clinical conditions, including osteoporosis (Murphy et al., 2005), and fibromyalgia (Taggart, Arslanian, Bae, & Singh, 2003). To date, no studies have explored the efficacy or the effectiveness of tai chi in the treatment of OCD, OC spectrum, or other anxiety disorders.

Part II: Alternative and Complementary Methods Related to CBT
Motivational Interviewing

A strategy that has been used additively to treat OCD is motivational interviewing (Franklin & Foa, 1998; Maltby & Tolin, 2005; Simpson, Zuckoff, Page, Franklin, & Foa, 2008). Widely used in treating psychological problems such as addictions (Arkowitz, Westra, Miller, & Rollnick, 2008), motivational interviewing (MI) is a client-centered, directive method of engaging intrinsic motivation to change clients' behaviors through the exploration (and resolution) of ambivalence (Miller & Rollnick, 2002). The expression of empathy, developing discrepancy, supporting one's self-efficacy, and the ability to roll with resistance are also core principles that guide the conduct of MI (Miller & Rollnick, 2002). To date, no published studies utilize a "pure" MI approach to treat OCD or any other psychological disorder (Hettema, Steele, & Miller, 2005).

The three studies that document the use of MI in treating OCD in adult populations have addressed specific treatment-related issues of refusal (Maltby & Tolin, 2005) and resistance (Simpson et al., 2008; 2010). The majority of randomized controlled trials for OCD in which MI has been used have involved adjunctive use of MI as either a 4-session readiness intervention for ERP-refusing adult patients (Maltby & Tolin, 2005), additional individual sessions in conjunction with thought mapping within a group cognitive-behavioral protocol (Meyer et al., 2010) or an additional component to family-based CBT for pediatric patients (Merlo et al.,2010). Only one randomized controlled trial has integrated MI into ERP treatment (Simpson et al., 2010). In the study by Maltby and colleagues (2005), 12 participants meeting DSM-IV criteria for OCD, who had initially refused ERP treatment, were randomly assigned to either a readiness intervention (RI) or a waitlist (WL) control group. The 4-session readiness intervention involved a psychoeducation component that included explanations of the neurobiological and behavioral models of OCD, and a review of the efficacy of ERP as a treatment for OCD; a fear-reduction component that involved viewing a videotape of a simulated ERP session; the construction of a sample exposure hierarchy with therapist assistance; and a telephone conversation with a successful ERP completer. Although nonconfrontational and collaborative therapist–client interactions guided the assumptions of the readiness intervention, explicit use of MI procedures was included in only 2 of the 4 sessions.

Results revealed that reductions in OCD symptoms occurred in neither the RI nor the WL conditions, suggesting that the RI intervention may not be effective in direct treatment of OCD symptoms. Although, a significantly greater proportion of RI participants agreed to enroll in ERP treatment, 50% dropped out of treatment prematurely. Of the ERP completers, RI participants on average exhibited improvement rates in OCD symptoms comparable to those of OCD patients who were not initially ERP treatment refusers (Foa et al., 2005), whereas the single waitlisted ERP completer did not respond to ERP.

A randomized controlled trial (N=16) of 6- to 17-year-olds found that receiving 4 sessions of family-based CBT for OCD plus MI resulted in significantly lower Children's Yale-Brown Obsessive Compulsive Scale (CY-BOCS) scores than family-based CBT plus psychoeducation (PE); however, this improvement apparently decreased over time, as there were no significant differences at post-test. Additionally, participants in the CBT plus MI group completed treatment approximately 3 sessions sooner than the CBT plus PE group, suggesting that MI may be useful in facilitating a brief treatment model (Merlo et al., 2010). Results from the randomized controlled trial by Meyer and colleagues (2010) in which 93 patients were randomized to either 12 weeks of manualized group cognitive behavioral therapy (GCBT) or GCBT with 2 individual sessions of thought mapping (TM) and MI revealed significant symptom reductions in both groups; however, symptom reduction was significantly greater in the GCBT MI +TM group than in the GCBT alone group. Further symptom improvement was evident in the GCBT MI + TM group only at 3 month follow-up, indicating that 2 additional individual sessions of MI and TM prior to beginning GCBT may enhance treatment outcomes (Meyer et al., 2010).

In addition to enhancing treatment refusers' entry into standard ERP and expediting brief treatment, MI has also been used to treat OCD in a more integrative manner with ERP in adults. Simpson et al. (2008) pilot tested and later conducted a randomized controlled trial (Simpson et al., 2010) of a manualized treatment for OCD, in which three introductory information-gathering/ motivational enhancement sessions were combined with 15 exposure and ritual prevention sessions. The three introductory sessions involved psychoeducation, development of discrepancy, construction of a sample exposure hierarchy, and collaborative self-efficacy building. During the ERP sessions, MI techniques were used when patient resistance became evident. An optional MI module, which included further exploration of ambivalence with a focus on client-directed change, was also used as needed upon completion of the third session. The integrative MI/ERP approach resulted in improved outcomes, as evidenced by decreases in Y-BOCS scores and increases in quality of life reports for 5 of 6 patients. Notably, the one patient who did not indicate improvement in OCD symptoms dropped out of the study after the fourth session. In a later open trial (Simpson & Zuckoff, 2011), MI also appeared to enhance treatment outcomes. Conversely, results of the randomized controlled trial revealed no significant differences between MI/ERP and standard ERP groups in symptom outcomes or adherence. This suggests that adherence to ERP may be either unrelated to ambivalence about change, a larger dose of MI than that provided in the protocol may be required, or that use of MI may be less effective in reducing OCD symptoms when it is integrated throughout treatment, as opposed to a precursor to standard ERP (Simpson et al., 2010). Preliminary research indicates that MI shows promise as an adjunctive treatment for OCD and other anxiety disorders when used as a precursor to both individual and group CBT, especially with treatment-refusing or treatment refractory populations (Maltby & Tolin, 2005; Meyer et al., 2010; Westra & Dozois, 2006; Westra & Phoenix, 2003).

MI utilizes a more empathetic, collaborative therapeutic approach, whereas ERP relies on a more directive, structured and didactic therapeutic approach. The directive and didactic approach may contribute, in part, to the estimated 25% of OCD patients who refuse ERP in the general population (Franklin et al., 1998). ERP treatment resistance may also be a reflection of ambivalence about change (Engle & Arkowitz, 2006). A number of case studies (Westra, 2004) demonstrate favorable treatment outcomes resulting from the integration of MI techniques such as generating discrepancy, exploring ambivalence, and expressing empathy. These are contingent upon the various stages of change (Prochaska & DiClemente, 1992) the client is experiencing. Although positive response to the MI interventions may result from other factors, such as previous exposure to CBT, the passage of time, or increased client awareness of contextual variables, the favorable outcomes suggest that MI may be an effective adjunctive treatment for managing resistance and ambivalence at various stages during CBT

(Westra, 2004). Future research recommendations include: developing randomized controlled trials of MI in conjunction with psychopharmacological treatment; testing the effectiveness of MI as an adjunctive treatment within certain subtypes of OCD; and continued exploration of the optimal MI dosage at various time points during both traditional and alternative OCD interventions.

Self-Help and Technology Methods

Another area of alternative or complementary treatment for OCD includes the integration of adjunctive or additive methods, such as self-help and self-administered treatments, as well as technology supported approaches. Self-help materials and technology supports may be components of a stepped care approach used independently and/or in combination with CBT methods. Self-help interventions for OCD may include books, as well as audio, video, and computer aids (Baer, Minichiello, & Jenike, 1987; Kirkby et al., 2000) and automated and interactive telephone systems (Greist et al., 2002; Mains & Scogin, 2003). Some of these interventions are home-based, whereas others are clinic-based and/or clinician-guided. The level of therapist involvement may also vary along a continuum: from no contact to minimal contact without treatment delivery, to regular therapeutic contact. Self-help may be fully self-administered therapy, mainly self-help (i.e., therapist assesses, provides initial rationale, and teaches clients how to use the self-help book), minimal contact therapy (i.e., active therapist involvement, but less than traditional therapy), or therapist-administered (i.e., regular contact with therapist in conjunction with self-help materials; Andersson, Bergstrom, Carlbring, & Lindefors, 2005).

Self-Help for OCD

Several studies show that self-help interventions for OCD may be associated with some improvement in symptoms. A randomized controlled trial of 41 adult outpatients with OCD comparing self-administered versus therapist-administered ERP found that both groups demonstrated significant improvement in symptoms over time. Therapist-administered ERP, however, was associated with a greater reduction of OCD symptoms and functional impairment (Tolin et al., 2007). A study of 14 OCD patients in home-based treatment found that self-directed ERP was as effective as therapist-controlled ERP for OCD (Emmelkamp, van Linden van den Heuvell, Ruphan, & Sanderman, 1989). In a double-blind controlled study, self-exposure homework plus clomipramine resulted in better improvement than homework and placebo, but these gains disappeared over time. Systematic self-exposure homework led to greater improvement in OCD symptoms than did therapist-assisted exposure (Marks et al., 1988). At 2-year follow-up, patients' gains from one year were maintained and showed significant improvement compared to their baseline symptoms in the self-exposure group only (Marks et al., 1988). In another study evaluating self-directed non-traditional treatments of OCD, 70 participants were randomly assigned to receive a self-help manual for OCD either in conjunction with a video explanation of progressive muscle relaxation (PMR) or meridian tapping (MT), a body-focused therapeutic technique. Though participant self-reports indicated MT was more helpful than PMR at the 4 week post-test (39% versus 19%) Y-BOCS self-reports did not significantly change across time for either group (Moritz et al., 2011).

Bibliotherapy

Bibliotherapy is a form of self-help with guided or unguided reading of materials that are relevant to the circumstances of the client. Bibliotherapy for other anxiety (e.g., specific phobias) and mood disorders has been shown to be more effective than placebos or waiting lists with regard to symptom reduction (see meta-analysis by den Boer, Wiersma, & Van den Bosch, 2004; Jorm et al., 2004; from Mataix-Cols & Marks, 2006). There has been limited study of bibliotherapy for OCD. One small open trial showed improvement among all 9 OCD patients using a self-help book (Steketee & White, 1990) plus self-exposure exercises and 5 face-to-face sessions with a therapist to check comprehension of the materials (Fritzler, Hecker, & Losee, 1997). Three of the participants reached clinically significant levels of improvement. In a larger study by Moritz and colleagues (2010), 86 patients meeting criteria for OCD were randomly assigned to receive a self-help manual entitled "My Metacognitive Training for OCD" (myMCT) designed to raise awareness about cognitive biases that may exacerbate OCD symptoms or a waitlist control condition. At the four week time-point, significantly greater improvement on Y-BOCS scores, especially obsessions, was evident in the my MCT group compared to the waitlist group (Moritz, Jelinek, Hauschildt & Naber, 2010).

Another pilot study illustrated a stepped-care approach to OCD treatment by measuring treatment response at each level of intervention (Tolin, Diefenbach, Maltby, & Hannan, 2005). Among 11 adults who completed bibliotherapy ERP treatment for their OCD, 20% were considered responders (Tolin et al., 2005). Therapists met with the nonresponders to deliver education and advice on OCD and ERP but did not engage in ERP exercises with the clients. Of those clients who completed this intervention, 29% were considered responders. Among nonresponders who went on to complete therapist-administered ERP, 67% became responders.

Self-Help Groups

No controlled trials have tested the efficacy of self-help groups for OCD, although such groups have been described as useful (Black & Blum, 1992; Broatch, 1996; from Mataix-Cols & Marks, 2006; Tynes, Salins, Skiba, & Winstead, 1992). In a recent study of an online self-help group for people with OCD and compulsive hoarding using CBT skills, participants reported modest improvement in their hoarding symptoms (Muroff, Steketee, Himle, & Frost, 2010).

Generally, self-administered interventions for OCD are associated with positive outcomes for only approximately 50% of participants, due to problems with low motivation, more severe OCD symptoms, considerable disability and impairment, and poor adherence to self-help treatment (Mains & Scogin, 2003). Future research may help determine the optimal level of therapist involvement and the further development of technological enhancements.

Use of newer technologies, such as the telephone, computers, Internet, and other technology supports are currently being tested in self-help interventions for OCD.

Telephone Interventions

There is some evidence to suggest that self-help in conjunction with clinician-guided therapy may reduce OCD symptoms. A pilot study of brief telephone treatment for OCD included two face-to-face sessions (one at the beginning and one at the end) and 8 weekly 15-minute telephone calls. Of 4 participants, 3 improved substantially and 1 improved a marginally (Lovell, Fullalove, & Garvey, 2000). A randomized controlled non-inferiority trial with 72 OCD patients showed that telephone-delivered CBT was equally as effective as face-to-face treatment at post-treatment and at 6-month follow-up. Both treatments led to similar satisfaction levels, as well (Lovell et al., 2006). Two open trials demonstrated the effectiveness of 12 weeks of 45-minute telephone-administered sessions of CBT with ERP using a supplemental self-help book (Schwartz, 1996), with a total of 33 OCD (nondepressed) patients (Taylor et al., 2003). Treatment gains were maintained at a 12-month follow-up and effect sizes of telephone-based OCD treatment were similar to those of face-to-face ERP treatment.

Computer-Assisted Therapy

There is also evidence to suggest that computer-assisted treatment for OCD may be effective (see Lack & Storch, 2008 for a review). Two case studies included the use of a computer program, OC-CHECK, aimed to manage and decrease OCD-related checking (Baer et al., 1987; Baer, Minichiello, Jenike, & Holland, 1988). The program requests the patient to refrain from acquiescing to the OCD urge to check, but instead to watch the clock on the computer countdown for 3 minutes while being told that no negative consequences will occur as a result of not checking. Participants used laptops at home and handheld devices when outside the home. The case studies found that the program was associated with substantial reductions in checking behavior. However, the OCD symptoms returned when the clients discontinued their use of the palm computers, suggesting that this method is helpful for controlling symptoms but not for long-term change (Baer et al., 1988).

OCD therapy that is exclusively self-assisted, such as an interactive computer program CAVE (computer-aided vicarious exposure) designed to provide ERP for handwashing, has resulted in minimal clinical improvement (Clark, Kirkby, Daniels, & Marks, 1998; Kirkby et al., 2000). This pilot study included 13 OCD patients with washing and checking symptoms who participated in 3 weekly 45-minute sessions using CAVE. The program teaches participants about ERP and has the patient guide an animation (a person on screen) through ERP exercises, such as vicarious exposure to dirt. Those with washing symptoms showed more improvement than those with checking behaviors, and those with checking behaviors experienced more improvement with depression symptoms. Thus, vicarious exposure may complement face-to-face behavior therapy.

A number of studies have employed BTSTEPS, featuring a self-help manual and a computer-driven touchtone telephone interactive voice response system (IVR), used for assessment and treatment. BTSTEPS includes a 4-step self-assessment module and 5-step self-treatment module (see Greist et al., 1998; Marks et al., 1998). These studies included

minimal therapist involvement restricted to assessment, self-tool instruction, and occasional check-ins (not therapist-administered CBT) with both therapist and computer feedback provided.

Uncontrolled open trials examining BTSTEPS (Bachofen et al., 1999; Greist et al., 1998; Marks et al., 1998) found that participants who completed the self-assessment and at least 2 self-administered ERP sessions showed significant improvement with their OCD, mood, and work and social adjustment symptoms. Another 12-week open trial in the United States and the United Kingdom (London) demonstrated that patients using BTSTEPS showed significant improvement on OCD measures (Greist et al., 1998), equivalent to that demonstrated by trials using SSRIs (Greist et al., 1995). A further pilot study found that 21 patients using a self-administered manual and BTSTEPS for a minimum of 3 weeks showed similar improvement to those in treatment with a behavioral therapist (Nakagawa et al., 2000).

A large multisite randomized controlled trial compared three 10-week treatments for OCD: BTSTEPS, clinician-guided behavior therapy, and a systematic relaxation control condition (audiotape and manual). Findings showed that BTSTEPS was effective, clinician-guided therapy was more effective, and the relaxation condition was not effective. BTSTEPS was as efficacious as therapist-guided CBT for those who completed at least one ERP session. In both conditions, those who completed more than one ERP session showed significant improvement compared to those who did not. Greist and colleagues (2002) concluded that BTSTEPS may be an initial method to treat OCD patients. Finally, a smaller randomized controlled trial of BTSTEPS with brief scheduled clinician support calls (compared to requested calls) led to less dropout, more self-ERP homework completion, and greater improvement in OCD symptoms (Kenwright, Marks, Graham, Franses, & Mataix-Cols, 2005).

The National Institute for Clinical Excellence (NICE) has approved and now recommends a number of computer-aided CBT systems including *FearFighter* for panic and phobic disorders, and *Beating the Blues* for depression. NICE has recently granted approval regarding the "absolute clinical efficacy of BTSTEPS for OCD" (see Baer, Greist, & Marks, 2007; National Institute for Health and Clinical Excellence, 2004).

Although virtual reality (VR) has been used as an effective treatment tool for other psychological disorders (see Powers & Emmelkamp, 2008 for a meta-analysis), its utility within OCD treatment as anxiety provocation (Kim et al., 2008) and behavioral assessment (Kim et al., 2009) tools have only begun to be explored within OCD patient populations.

Internet and Telephone Treatment

The Internet is another way to disseminate self-help treatment and provide support. There are no studies of Internet treatment for OCD specifically, other than the previously mentioned observational study of a web-based support group for OCD hoarding subtype (Muroff, Steketee, Himle, & Frost, 2007). Evidence suggests that Internet-based interventions are more helpful if participants are screened, have a password, and receive brief occasional therapist support via phone, email, or face-to-face, as intervention websites that are open and unmonitored tend to have much higher rates of dropout (Baer et al., 2007; Christensen, Griffiths, & Jorm, 2004; I. Marks, Cavanagh, & Gega, 2007).

Videoconferencing Methods

Cognitive-behavioral therapy delivered via videoconferencing is another alternative method to standard face-to-face CBT treatment for OCD. CBT delivered through videoconferencing appears to be as effective as CBT delivered face-to-face (Bouchard et al., 2004; Christensen et al., 2004; Day & Schneider, 2002; Griffiths, Blignault, & Yellowlees, 2006). A pilot study demonstrated that CBT for OCD can be successfully treated through videoconferencing (Himle et al., 2006). Several other case studies and an uncontrolled study have demonstrated that videoconferencing-based CBT may be effective for treating anxiety and mood symptoms (Cowain, 2001; Griffiths et al., 2006; Manchanda & McLaren, 1998).

Methodological Concerns for Self-help and Technology Treatments

Reviews of technology-supported psychological treatments discuss the methodological problems of these studies (Bessell et al., 2002; see Carlbring, Ekselius, & Andersson, 2003; Nguyen, Carrieri-Kohlman, Rankin, Slaughter, & Stulbarg, 2004). However, more recent studies are showing more promise. Dropout rates vary for self-help and technology-supported studies. Observational studies tended to have higher dropout rates, as demonstrated by two such studies of BTSTEPS with reported total dropout rates of 52% (Bachofen et al., 1999) and 57.5% (Greist et al., 1998).

In contrast, dropout was much less problematic in the controlled trial of BTSTEPS, with a total discontinued reported rate of 19.3% (Greist et al., 2002).

Dropout rates tend to be somewhat higher for web-based than face-to-face interventions (Emmelkamp, 2005). While dropout rates are reportedly higher in open and unguided websites (Spek et al., 2007), defining dropouts among this population is a challenge. Attrition rates with Internet-based CBT seem to be improving (Andersson, Bergstrom, Carlbring et al., 2005). Scheduled phone contact with a therapist also may reduce attrition rates associated with computer-aided treatments for OCD, and may enhance homework completion (Kenwright et al., 2005).

In addition, concerns around technology (e.g., Internet, videoconferencing interface) as a functional barrier to the development of the therapeutic alliance have not been substantiated (Lange et al., 2003). In fact, clients have reported high ratings of therapeutic alliance when engaging in videoconferencing-based treatment for OCD (Himle et al., 2006).

While a stepped care approach to OCD treatment has been recommended (Mataix-Cols & Marks, 2006), the level of therapist involvement and most effective mediums of self-help interventions, with and without technology enhancements, have not been determined. Dosages with respect to the optimal frequency and nature of contact with a therapist or self-help materials also warrant examination. Tolin and colleagues' (2005) approach to treatment that begins first with bibliotherapy, followed by therapist-administered psychoeducation for nonresponders, and, finally, therapist administered ERP, may be helpful in identifying the optimal dosage, or the minimum level of therapist involvement necessary to produce a clinical response.

In order to determine the relationship between dose and response in computer-administered behavior treatment on OCD outcomes, some have proposed using human–computer interactions (HCIs) as an objective process measure (Kirkby et al., 2000). For example, Kirkby and colleagues (2000) found that the number of vicarious exposure enactments correlated with outcome. Participant characteristics and other treatment factors may be explored, as well.

Findings regarding self-help and technology-supported treatments may not be applicable or relevant across OCD subtypes. Study samples did not necessarily include the full range of OCD subtypes. For example, some researchers specifically note that their BTSTEPS sample mostly had problems with checking and cleaning (obsessions and compulsions; Greist et al., 2002); therefore, the intervention may or may not be effective for people with other principal OCD symptoms. Findings from Fritzler and colleagues (1997) also suggest that self-administered ERP with minimal therapist involvement may not be sufficient in the treatment of hoarding, another OCD subtype; instead, more intensive treatment may be required to treat hoarding (Frost & Hartl, 1996).

Perhaps relevant to the previous discussion about the client's level of motivation, the question remains regarding which therapeutic tasks could be delegated to a book, computer program, etc., and which need to be administered by a therapist. Self-help materials such as bibliotherapy may be utilized either as a substitution for, or as a complement to standard CBT treatment. In the case of OCD, there is limited evidence to support a recommendation for the exclusive use of bibliotherapy or Internet-based treatments (Marks et al., 2007; Mataix-Cols & Marks, 2006). Tolin and colleagues (2005; 2007) did show that approximately one-fifth of patients experience reductions in OCD symptoms during the course of using a self-help book alone; however, this was not compared with a no-treatment control group. Most of the research that has focused on self-administered interventions for OCD includes some therapist contact, even though the therapist does not administer the actual ERP exercises (Tolin et al., 2005).

Technologically supported methods may be an alternative to standard face-to-face care (e.g., phone-based instead of in-person sessions; see Taylor et al., 2003) or an adjunctive enhancement (e.g., phone contact in addition to in-person sessions). In the former, the phone-based intervention is the primary mode of treatment delivery, in contrast to the latter, where the phone contact is supplementary. In both cases, therapist involvement and time is quite substantial (Baer et al., 2007).

In some computer-aided CBT treatments for OCD (i.e., BTSTEPS), most of the treatment tasks are allocated to the computer, which is the primary therapeutic mechanism, with therapists assuming an adjunctive supportive role (requiring less of their time and involvement). The structure of CBT facilitates its conversion to manual or software materials (Selmi, Klein, Greist, Sorrell, & Erdman, 1990).

Future research is needed to address these issues in a programmatic way, by systematically testing varying levels and nature of therapist contact and role of self-help tools (Newman, Erickson, Przeworski, & Dzus, 2003). For example, the same treatment was tested in manualized versus video form to compare whether medium of delivery revealed differences in effectiveness of treatment (Ost, Stridh, & Wolf, 1998). Such methods may extend access to CBT treatment and save resources for those who require more intensive (i.e., face-to-face) treatment. Additionally, engaging in specific elements of treatment, or progressing through a specific series of steps, may enhance outcomes substantially. For example, completing at least 2 ERP sessions with BTSTEPS was associated with significant improvement (Bachofen et al., 1999; Griest et al., 1998; Newman et al., 2003).

Concerns have also been raised regarding the influence of self-help care upon subsequent care; for example, whether engaging in self-help treatment first may reduce effectiveness of subsequent face-to-face treatment (Andersson, Bergstrom, Hollandare et al., 2005). Thus, the interactive effect of stepped care models may be examined. In addition, there are concerns that dropping out of self-help CBT may reduce the likelihood of engaging in face-to-face CBT because of the perception that CBT "does not work" (Cuijpers & Schuurmans, 2007). Such issues need to be explored with people with OCD specifically.

A number of regulatory, safety, and ethical issues also surround the use of technology-supported methods and stepped care models. Those who use technology as adjunctive to regular practice, or as a principal treatment method (e-mail, web-based, etc.) must seriously consider and address specific liability and risk issues (see Banach & Bernat, 2000), especially when employing or encouraging use of self-administered interventions (Step 1 of the stepped-care model; Tolin et al., 2005). Internet-based and other self-help materials must be updated regularly to ensure quality control of information (Andersson, Bergstrom, Carlbring et al., 2005). Inappropriate or outdated information may put users at risk (Cuijpers & Schuurmans, 2007). Additionally, the provision of treatment across U.S. state lines has implications for licensure, reimbursement, and liability (Banach & Bernat, 2000). Specific professional guidelines in social work and psychology for Internet-based and technology-supported therapy are needed (Wells, Mitchell, Finkelhor, & Becker-Blease, 2007).

Other ethical issues include consideration of the fit between symptom severity and intensity level of treatment. People who experience dissociative states, psychotic episodes, and/or suicidal symptoms require more intensive levels of treatment on the stepped care model; thus, technology supported treatments are likely not appropriate (Emmelkamp, 2005). In addition, individuals with personality disorders, emotional avoidance, and interpersonal challenges may benefit more from face-to-face treatment than self-help interventions (Mains & Scogin, 2003). Conversely, if complexity level of the case is low (e.g., problems with symptoms, insight, comorbidity, and motivation are not severe), then self-help with limited therapist support may be appropriate (Mataix-Cols & Marks, 2006). Regardless of whether treatment follows a standard face-to-face format or utilizes alternative mediums, therapists have the duty to conduct thorough assessments, deliver quality care, and be appropriately supervised (Banach & Bernat, 2000; Cuijpers & Schuurmans, 2007).

Among those necessitating intensive treatment and direct therapist contact, many people do not have access to or choose not to seek formal CBT therapy, either due to financial, logistical or geographic barriers (Marques, LeBlanc, Weingarden, Timpano, Jenike & Wilhelm, 2010). Research suggests that some alternative and complementary delivery methods may be more cost effective when treating anxiety (Tolin et al., 2005), and therefore there is a clear need to determine cost-effectiveness of the most promising alternative treatments and technology delivery methods. A compelling analysis has been presented to illustrate how computer aided therapy (i.e., BTSTEPS) is a cost-effective alternative in the treatment of OCD, costing 264% less than face-to-face treatment for each unit of reduction on the Yale-Brown Obsessive Compulsive Scale (see McCrone et al., 2007).

In addition, self-help and computer-assisted therapy programs may be "therapist extenders" (Heimberg & Coles, 1999, p.259). Self-help and technology-assisted CBT methods extend access to CBT resources and the limited number of CBT experts in OCD, and appeal to people who would not seek formal mental health services. For example, computer programs, such as BTSTEPS, expand access to effective care without the burden of needing to train more therapists in CBT (Bachofen et al., 1999). Computer-based interventions can be accessed any time of day. The importance and appeal of being able to access help at any time of day is illustrated by the fact that more than half of the calls made to the BTSTEPS IVR system were made outside of regular office hours. Moreover, people may prefer to use computer-assisted CBT in their homes instead of visiting the clinic because they perceived it as more private, confidential, affordable, less stigmatized, and requiring less travel time (Baer et al., 2007).

General Methodological Issues

While the previous section focused on methodological concerns specific to self-help and technology-supported interventions, this section addresses the broader scope of alternative and complementary treatments and methods. The studies presented in this chapter offer a range of evidence regarding the efficacy and effectiveness of various alternative and complementary treatments. One of the prevailing methodological problems common across many of the studies examining complementary and alternative treatments for OCD is the issue of small sample size. Overall, small sample sizes have led to limited power and inconclusive results for a number of alternative treatments for OCD.

A number of the studies presented in the areas of technology-supported self-help (Greist et al., 1998), herbal remedies (Taylor et al., 2003), and religion (Yorulmaz et al., 2009) were also either uncontrolled or did not include a comparison group; thus, effect sizes could not be determined. In addition, some studies were not randomized trials (e.g., Zhang et al., 2003), limiting the generalizability of results. It is also unclear whether the self-report ratings used in many of the self-help studies (Bachofen et al., 1999; Greist et al., 1998), correspond with clinician ratings of improvement. Moreover, case studies must be interpreted with caution, as those published often present "successful" cases, whereas unsuccessful ones are rarely published. Finally, some studies included intent-to-treat analyses (e.g., Bachofen et al., 1999; Moritz et al., 2011) whereas others included only completers (Greenberg, et al., 2009).

Another concern is client retention and dropout. Individuals diagnosed with OCD are disproportionately affected by attrition rates compared to those with other anxiety disorders (Franklin et al., 1998). Retention may be a special issue for studies of complementary and alternative treatments because of their small sample sizes. For some methods, such as acupuncture studies, attrition rates were not reported (Pilkington et al., 2007), whereas other methods, such as MI, were designed in part to address attrition and dropout rates (Maltby & Tolin, 2005; Simpson et al., 2008).

It is imperative, therefore, that future trials address these methodological issues by recruiting larger sample sizes, randomizing participants to condition, and including a control or comparison condition, blinding, and self and other ratings, in order to reach more robust conclusions.

Conclusions and Future Directions

As noted previously, the use of complementary and alternative methods to CBT for anxiety disorders is on the rise; these methods are perceived as comparable in effectiveness to conventional treatments (Kessler, Davis et al., 2001). The purpose of this chapter was to review and discuss the available evidence surrounding the use of complementary and alternative methods for OCD treatment and delivery that might assist clinicians and consumers in their clinical decision-making processes. A number of questions may help guide future research.

- *Which complementary and alternative treatment methods are optimal, and for whom?*

Given the substantial number of individuals who do not respond, do not have access to standard treatment for OCD at their disposal, or have other preferences, it is important to consider other methods that show promise. As reviewed, there have been some positive findings for yoga (Shannahoff-Khalsa et al., 1999), motivational interviewing (Maltby & Tolin, 2005; Simpson et al., 2008), and BTSTEPS (Greist et al., 1998, 2002) as alternative and/or complementary treatments for OCD. A number of studies have revealed inconsistencies in findings or inconclusive results. More rigorous studies, including randomized controlled trials, are needed to demonstrate clinical efficacy. As Jorm and colleagues (2004) remind us, demonstrating effectiveness is not enough; the "quality of the evidence" (p. S30) also must be robust.

- *Given that RCTs may not be feasible to test some complementary and alternative treatments, what methodologies may determine level of efficacy?*

Given recent increases in popularity and utilization, more rigorous investigations that determine and maximize the efficacy of such methods are warranted. While RCTs tend to be the gold standard, alternative and complementary treatments do not always fit well with this methodology, and suitable placebos may be a challenge to find (van der Watt, Laugharne, & Janca, 2008). The personalization and individualization of specific methods (e.g.,

acupuncture, motivational interviewing), may not fit with a randomized controlled trial methodology, whereby methods are standardized across clients. Ironically, however, the emphasis on evidence-based practice methods may in part contribute to the increasing openness toward complementary medicine. If empirical data show that complementary alternative methods improve outcomes, then such results may trump theory. In this case, the search for underlying mechanisms to explain why a treatment works begins after the therapy has been shown to be associated with positive outcomes (Vickers, 2000).

Prompted by the National Center for Complementary and Integrative Medicine, the Institute of Medicine Committee was developed. The Committee subsequently established that complementary/alternative and standard/traditional methods must achieve the "same standards and principles" in order to demonstrate treatment effectiveness (Bondurant & Sox, 2005, p.149; from Samuels et al., 2008, p.59). The aim of this evidence-based "integrated approach to disease and health management" is to increase the availability of standard and alternative treatments associated with positive outcomes to clients/consumers (Mamtani & Cimino, 2002, p.373).

- *Will the use of alternative and complementary methods extend access to effective treatments for OCD either independently or in conjunction with traditional standard treatments?*

Complementary and alternative treatments may appeal to people with anxiety disorders for a number of reasons (Wahlstrom et al., 2008). *(1)* People with anxiety disorders may use complementary and alternative methods to address their physical symptoms exacerbated by their mental health issues. *(2)* Those with anxiety disorders with greater somatic symptoms (e.g., panic and GAD) tend to use complementary and alternative methods more. It has been suggested that OCD has a somatic subtype, "characterized by excessive concerns about health or appearance" (Lochner & Stein, 2006, p.28; Wahlstrom et al., 2008). *(3)* Complementary and alternative methods are associated with a more holistic approach (i.e., "the importance of body, mind and spirit together to health"), that may especially appeal to people with mental disorders, and there are many methods from which to select (Wahlstrom et al., 2008, p.79). *(4)* Complementary and alternative methods providers may be perceived as providing more time, companionship, hope, and healing, as compared to rushed physicians (Machleidt, 2007).

Interest in complementary and alternative methods may also vary by culture. (Please see Chapter 26 for a more in-depth review of the role of culture in the treatment of OCD). Limited data suggests that Blacks are less likely to seek formal mental health services for their OCD (Goodwin, Koenen, Hellman, Guardino, & Struening, 2002), even though African-American and Caribbean Blacks have similar rates of OCD compared to Whites (Himle et al., 2008). Results from studies that have explored service utilization reveal that racial and ethnic minorities access specialty mental health services less than whites (Atkinson & Gim, 1989; Brondino et al., 1997; Goodwin et al., 2002). Lack of access and stigma may explain some of these disparities. In addition, African-Americans, Asian Americans, and Latinos were found to report greater utilization rates of complementary and alternative treatments than Whites/Caucasians (Barnes, Powell-Griner, McFann, & Nahin, 2004; Snowden & Yamada, 2005). However, other studies did not reach the same conclusion (e.g., Cherniack, Senzel, & Pan, 2001; Mackenzie, Taylor, Bloom, Hufford, & Johnson, 2003). It seems that rates varied depending on the specific methods considered as alternative or complementary in each study (Snowden & Yamada, 2005) and by specific cultural groups (Hsiao et al., 2006). Though it is possible that non-White groups substitute standard OCD treatment (e.g., CBT) with alternative and complementary techniques, there is not sufficient evidence to support such conclusions (Snowden & Yamada, 2005). Additionally, future studies may examine the role of culture in the use and utility of alternative and complementary treatments.

Implications for Providers

Although complementary and alternative methods are frequently applied, such use is often not discussed with mental health providers and general practitioners (Elkins, Rajab, & Marcus, 2005). It is critical that mental health and general practitioners inquire about client use of complementary and alternative treatments for OCD, in order to enhance treatment decisions (e.g., address medication interactions) and minimize risk (Jorm et al., 2004).

While there are concerns that complementary and alternative methods, self-help, and technological supports may displace health professionals, this is unlikely to occur. Instead, such treatments may expand upon ways in which therapists are able to assist people with OCD, broadening access to care and appropriate resources (Heimberg & Coles, 1999).

This chapter has focused on reviewing OCD-specific interventions and delivery methods; however, future studies may also investigate the use of alternative and complementary methods (e.g., Internet-based interventions) for prevention of anxiety disorders (Kenardy, McCafferty, & Rosa, 2003). Early access to computer-assisted CBT, for example, may reduce individual, family, and societal burden (Baer et al., 2007).

Complementary and alternative treatments are likely to continue to increase in use. With growing evidence of effectiveness, such techniques may begin to be covered by insurance, which will likely increase rates of treatment utilization further (Kessler, Davis et al., 2001). Much of the research on complementary and alternative treatments for OCD is inconclusive. Future research will, hopefully, provide more answers about its effectiveness in order to advance clinical decision-making processes and recommendations.

Related Chapters

Chapter 7. Neuroanatomy, Neuroimaging and Neuroendocrinology in OCD and Spectrum Conditions

Chapter 15. Pharmacological Treatments for OCD

Chapter 16. Other Biological Treatments for OCD

Chapter 26. Cultural Issues in Understanding and Treating Obsessive Compulsive and Spectrum Conditions

References

Abramowitz, J. S., Deacon, B. J., Woods, C. M., & Tolin, D. F. (2004). Association between Protestant religiosity and obsessive-compulsive symptoms and cognitions. *Depression and Anxiety, 20,* 70–76.

Abramowitz, J. S., Lackey, G. R., & Wheaton, M. G. (2009). Obsessive-compulsive symptoms: the contribution of obsessional beliefs and experiential avoidance. *Journal of Anxiety Disorders, 23,* 160–166.

Abramowitz, J. S., Taylor, S., & McKay, D. (2005). Potentials and limitations of cognitive treatments for obsessive-compulsive disorder. *Cognitive Behaviour Therapy, 34,* 140–147.

Abrantes, A. M., Strong, D. R., Cohn, A., Cameron, A. Y., Greenberg, B. D., Mancebo, M. C. et al. (2009). Acute changes in obsessions and compulsions following moderate-intensity aerobic exercise among patients with obsessive-compulsive disorder. *Journal of Anxiety Disorders, 23,* 923–927.

Akhondzadeh, S., Naghavi, H. R., Vazirian, M., Shayeganpour, A., Rashidi, H., & Khani, M. (2001). Passionflower in the treatment of generalized anxiety: a pilot double-blind randomized controlled trial with oxazepam. *Journal of Clinical Pharmacy and Therapeutics, 26,* 363–367.

Andersson, G. (2006). CBT and religion. *Cognitive Behaviour Therapy, 35*, 1–2.

Andersson, G., Bergstrom, J., Carlbring, P., & Lindefors, N. (2005). The use of the internet in the treatment of anxiety disorders. *Current Opinion in Psychiatry, 18*, 73–77.

Andersson, G., Bergstrom, J., Hollandare, F., Carlbring, P., Kaldo, V., & Ekselius, L. (2005). Internet-based self-help for depression: Randomised controlled trial. *British Journal of Psychiatry, 187*, 456–461.

Andreatini, R., Sartori, V. A., Seabra, M. L., & Leite, J. R. (2002). Effect of valepotriates (valerian extract) in generalized anxiety disorder: A randomized placebo-controlled pilot study. *Phytotherapy Research, 16*, 650–654.

Arias, A. J., Steinberg, K., Banga, A., & Trestman, R. L. (2006). systematic review of the efficacy of meditation techniques as treatments for medical illness. *The Journal of Alternative and Complementary Medicine, 12*, 817–832.

Arkowitz, H., Westra, H., Miller, W., & Rollnick, S. (2008). *Motivational interviewing in the treatment of psychological problems.* New York, NY: The Guilford Press.

Atkinson, D. R., & Gim, R. H. (1989). Asian-American cultural identity and attitudes toward mental health services. *Journal of Counseling Psychology, 36*, 209–212.

Bachofen, M., Nakagawa, A., Marks, I. M., Park, J. M., Greist, J. H., Baer, L. et al. (1999). Home self-assessment and self-treatment of obsessive-compulsive disorder using a manual and a computer-conducted telephone interview: Replication of a UK-US study. *Journal of Clinical Psychiatry, 60*, 545–549.

Baer, L., Greist, J., & Marks, I. M. (2007). Computer-aided cognitive behaviour therapy. *Psychotherapy and Psychosomatics, 76*, 193–195.

Baer, L., Minichiello, W. E., & Jenike, M. A. (1987). Use of a portable-computer program in behavioral treatment of obsessive-compulsive disorder. *American Journal of Psychiatry, 144*(8), 1101.

Baer, L., Minichiello, W. E., Jenike, M. A., & Holland, A. (1988). Use of a portable computer program to assist behavioral treatment in a case of obsessive compulsive disorder. *Journal of Behavior Therapy and Experimental Psychiatry, 19*, 237–240.

Banach, M., & Bernat, P. (2000). Liability and the internet: Risks and recommendations for social work practice. *Journal of Technology in Human Services, 17*, 153–171.

Barnes, P. M., Powell-Griner, E., McFann, K., & Nahin, R. L. (2004). *Complementary and alternative medicine use among adults: United States, 2002.* Hyattsville, MD: National Center for Health Statistics.

Benjamin, J., Agam, G., Levine, J., Bersudsky, Y., Kofman, O., & Belmaker, R. H. (1995). Inositol treatment in psychiatry. *Psychopharmacology Bulletin, 31*, 167–175.

Benson, H. (1978). Treatment of anxiety: A comparison of the usefulness of self-hypnosis and a meditational relaxation technique: An overview. *Psychotherapy and Psychosomatics, 30*, 229–242.

Bessell, T. L., McDonald, S., Silagy, C. A., Anderson, J. N., Hiller, J. E., & Sansom, L. N. (2002). Do Internet interventions for consumers cause more harm than good? A systematic review. *Health Expectations, 5*, 28–37.

Black, D. W., & Blum, N. S. (1992). Obsessive-compulsive disorder support groups: the Iowa model. *Comprehensive Psychiatry, 33*, 65–71.

Blier, P., & Bergeron, R. (1996). Sequential administration of augmentation strategies in treatment-resistant obsessive-compulsive

disorder: preliminary findings. *International Clinical Psychopharmacology, 11*, 37–44.

Bonchek, A., & Greenberg, D. (2009). Compulsive prayer and its management. *Journal of Clinical Psychology, 65*, 396–405.

Bondurant, S., & Sox, H. C. (2005). Mainstream and alternative medicine: converging paths require common standards. *Annals of Internal Medicine, 142*, 149–150.

Bouchard, S., Paquin, B., Payeur, R., Allard, M., Rivard, V., Fournier, T. et al. (2004). Delivering cognitive-behavior therapy for panic disorder with agoraphobia in videoconference. *Telemedicine Journal and E-Health, 10*, 13–25.

Broatch, J. W. (1996). Obsessive-compulsive disorder: adding value to treatment through patient support groups. *International Clinical Psychopharmacology, 11* Suppl 5, 89–94.

Broman-Fulks, J. J., Berman, M. E., Rabian, B. A., & Webster, M. J. (2004). Effects of aerobic exercise on anxiety sensitivity. *Behaviour Research and Therapy, 42*, 125–136.

Brondino, M. J., Henggeler, S. W., Rowland, M. D., Pickrel, S. G., Cunningham, P. B., & Schoenwald, S. K. (1997). Culturally responsive and clinically effective. In D. K. Wilson, J. R. Rodrigue & T. W.C. (Eds.), *Health-Promoting and Health Compromising Behaviors Among Minority Adolescents* (pp. 229–250). Washington, DC: APA Books.

Broocks, A., Bandelow, B., Pekrun, G., George, A., Meyer, T., Bartmann, U. et al. (1998). Comparison of aerobic exercise, clomipramine, and placebo in the treatment of panic disorder. *American Journal of Psychiatry, 155*, 603–609.

Brown, R. A., Abrantes, A. M., Strong, D. R., Mancebo, M. C., Menard, J., Rasmussen, S. A. et al. (2007). A pilot study of moderate-intensity aerobic exercise for obsessive compulsive disorder. *Journal of Nervous and Mental Disease, 195*, 514–520.

Carlbring, P., Ekselius, L., & Andersson, G. (2003). Treatment of panic disorder via the Internet: a randomized trial of CBT vs. applied relaxation. *Journal of Behavior Therapy and Experimental Psychiatry, 34*, 129–140.

Cauffield, J. S., & Forbes, H. J. (1999). Dietary supplements used in the treatment of depression, anxiety, and sleep disorders. *Lippincott's Primary Care Practice, 3*, 290–304.

Chao-Ying, W. (2003). The electroacupuncture treatment of 20 cases of anxiety disorder. [Anxiety Disorder & Electroacupuncture. Blue Poppy Press]. *Hunan Journal of Chinese Medicine, 3*, 26 (abstracted and translated by Wolfe, HL.).

Cherniack, E. P., Senzel, R. S., & Pan, C. X. (2001). Correlates of use of alternative medicine by the elderly in an urban population. *Journal of Alternative and Complementary Medicine, 7*, 277–280.

Christensen, H., Griffiths, K. M., & Jorm, A. F. (2004). Delivering interventions for depression by using the internet: randomised controlled trial. *British Medical Journal, 328*, 265.

Clark, A., Kirkby, K. C., Daniels, B. A., & Marks, I. M. (1998). A pilot study of computer-aided vicarious exposure for obsessive-compulsive disorder. *Australian and New Zealand Journal of Psychiatry, 32*, 268–275.

Cleveland, W. L., DeLaPaz R. L., Fawwaz, R. A., Challop, R. S. (2009). High-dose glycine treatment of refractory obsessive-compulsive disorder and body dysmorphic disorder in a 5-year period. *Neural Plast* 2009:768398768398

Cowain, T. (2001). Cognitive-behavioural therapy via videoconferencing to a rural area. *Australian and New Zealand Journal of Psychiatry, 35*, 62–64.

Cuijpers, P., & Schuurmans, J. (2007). Self-help interventions for anxiety disorders: an overview. *Current Psychiatry Reports, 9*, 284–290.

Dannawi, M. (2002). Possible serotonin syndrome after combination of buspirone and St John's Wort. *Journal of Psychopharmacology, 16*(4), 401.

Day, S., & Schneider, P. (2002). Psychotherapy using distance technology: A comparison of face-to-face, video and audio treatment. *Journal of Counseling Psychology, 49*, 499–503.

DeBerry, S., Davis, S., & Reinhard, K. E. (1989). A comparison of meditation-relaxation and cognitive/behavioral techniques for reducing anxiety and depression in a geriatric population. *Journal of Geriatric Psychiatry, 22*, 231–247.

Dell'Osso, B., Hadley, S., Allen, A., Baker, B., Chaplin, W. F., & Hollander, E. (2008). Escitalopram in the treatment of impulsive-compulsive internet usage disorder: an open-label trial followed by a double-blind discontinuation phase. *Journal of Clinical Psychiatry, 69*, 452–456.

den Boer, P. C., Wiersma, D., & Van den Bosch, R. J. (2004). Why is self-help neglected in the treatment of emotional disorders? A meta-analysis. *Psychological Medicine, 34*, 959–971.

Didonna, F. (2009). Mindfulness and obsessive-compulsive disorder: Developing a way to trust and validate one's internal experience. In F. Didonna (Ed.), *Clinical handbook of mindfulness* (pp. 189–219). New York, NY: Springer Science + Business Media.

Eisenberg, D. M., Davis, R. B., Ettner, S. L., Appel, S., Wilkey, S., Van Rompay, M. et al. (1998). Trends in alternative medicine use in the United States, 1990-1997: results of a follow-up national survey. *The Journal of the American Medical Association, 280*, 1569–1575.

Eisenberg, D. M., Kessler, R. C., Foster, C., Norlock, F. E., Calkins, D. R., & Delbanco, T. L. (1993). Unconventional medicine in the United States. Prevalence, costs, and patterns of use. *New England Journal of Medicine, 328*, 246–252.

Elkins, G., Rajab, M. H., & Marcus, J. (2005). Complementary and alternative medicine use by psychiatric inpatients. *Psychological Reports, 96*, 163–166.

Emmelkamp, P. M. (2005). Technological innovations in clinical assessment and psychotherapy. *Psychotherapy and Psychosomatics, 74*, 336–343.

Emmelkamp, P. M., van Linden van den Heuvell, C., Ruphan, M., & Sanderman, R. (1989). Home-based treatment of obsessive-compulsive patients: intersession interval and therapist involvement. *Behaviour Research and Therapy, 27*, 89–93.

Engle, D. E., & Arkowitz, H. (2006). *Ambivalence in psychotherapy: Facilitating readiness to change.* New York: Guilford Press.

Fairfax, H. (2008). The use of mindfulness in obsessive-compulsive disorder: Suggestions for its application and integration into existing treatment. *Clinical Psychology and Psychotherapy 15*, 53–59.

Fineberg, N. (1996). Refining treatment approaches in obsessive-compulsive disorder. *International Clinical Psychopharmacology, 11 Suppl 5*, 13–22.

Firouzabadi, A., & Shareh, H. (2009). Mindfulness. *Advances in Cognitive Science, 11*, 1–7.

Flessner, C. A., Busch, A. M., Heideman, P. W., & Woods, D. W. (2008). Acceptance-enhanced behavior therapy (AEBT) for trichotillomania and chronic skin picking: exploring the effects of component sequencing. *Behavior Modification, 32*, 579–594.

Foa, E. B., Liebowitz, M. R., Kozak, M. J., Davies, S., Campeas, R., Franklin, M. E. et al. (2005). Randomized, placebo-controlled trial of exposure and ritual prevention, clomipramine, and their combination in the treatment of obsessive-compulsive disorder. *American Journal of Psychiatry, 162*, 151–161.

Forman, E. M., Herbert, J. D., Moitra, E., Yeomans, P. D., & Geller, P. A. (2007). A randomized controlled effectiveness trial of acceptance and commitment therapy and cognitive therapy for anxiety and depression. *Behavior Modification, 31*, 772–799.

Franklin, M. E., & Foa, E. B. (1998). Cognitive-behavioral treatments for obsessive-compulsive disorder. In J. M. Gorman (Ed.), *A guide to treatments that work* (pp. 339–357). New York, NY: Oxford University Press.

Franklin, M. E., Kozak, M. J., Cashman, L. A., Coles, M. E., Rheingold, A. A., & Foa, E. B. (1998). Cognitive-behavioral treatment of pediatric obsessive-compulsive disorder: an open clinical trial. *Journal of the American Academy of Child and Adolescent Psychiatry, 37*, 412–419.

Frederick, C. (2007). Hypnotically facilitated treatment of obsessive-compulsive disorder: can it be evidence-based? *International Journal of Clinical and Experimental Hypnosis, 55*, 189–206.

Fritzler, B. K., Hecker, J. E., & Losee, M. C. (1997). Self-directed treatment with minimal therapist contact: preliminary findings for obsessive-compulsive disorder. *Behaviour Research and Therapy, 35*, 627–631.

Frost, R. O., & Hartl, T. L. (1996). A cognitive-behavioral model of compulsive hoarding. *Behaviour Research and Therapy, 34*, 341–350.

Fux, M., Benjamin, J., & Belmaker, R. H. (1999). Inositol versus placebo augmentation of serotonin reuptake inhibitors in the treatment of obsessive-compulsive disorder: A double-blind cross-over study. *International Journal of Neuropsychopharmacology, 2*, 193–195.

Fux, M., Levine, J., Aviv, A., & Belmaker, R. H. (1996). Inositol treatment of obsessive-compulsive disorder. *American Journal of Psychiatry, 153*, 1219–1221.

Gangdev, P. S. (1998). Faith-assisted cognitive therapy of obsessive-compulsive disorder. *Australian and New Zealand Journal of Psychiatry, 32*, 575–578.

Goodwin, R., Koenen, K. C., Hellman, F., Guardino, M., & Struening, E. (2002). Helpseeking and access to mental health treatment for obsessive-compulsive disorder. *Acta Psychiatrica Scandinavica, 106*, 143–149.

Gordon, J. B. (1998). SSRIs and St. John's Wort: Possible toxicity? *American Family Physician, 57*, 950–953.

Greenberg, W. M., Benedict, M. M., Doerfer, J., Perrin, M., Panek, L., Cleveland, W. L., et al. (2009). Adjunctive glycine in the treatment of obsessive–compulsive disorder in adults. *Journal of Psychiatric Research, 43*, 664–70.

Greenberg, D., & Shefler, G. (2002). Obsessive compulsive disorder in ultra-orthodox Jewish patients: a comparison of religious and non-religious symptoms. *Psychology and Psychotherapy, 75*, 123–130.

Greist, J. H. (1992). An integrated approach to treatment of obsessive compulsive disorder. *Journal of Clinical Psychiatry, 53 Suppl*, 38–41.

Greist, J. H., Jefferson, J. W., Kobak, K. A., Katzelnick, D. J., & Serlin, R. C. (1995). Efficacy and tolerability of serotonin transport inhibitors in obsessive-compulsive disorder. A meta-analysis. *Archives of General Psychiatry, 52,* 53–60.

Greist, J. H., Marks, I. M., Baer, L., Kobak, K. A., Wenzel, K. W., Hirsch, M. J. et al. (2002). Behavior therapy for obsessive-compulsive disorder guided by a computer or by a clinician compared with relaxation as a control. *Journal of Clinical Psychiatry, 63,* 138–145.

Greist, J. H., Marks, I. M., Baer, L., Parkin, J. R., Manzo, P. A., Mantle, J. M. et al. (1998). Self-treatment for obsessive compulsive disorder using a manual and a computerized telephone interview: A U.S.-U.K. study. *MD Computing, 15,* 149–157.

Griffiths, L., Blignault, I., & Yellowlees, P. (2006). Telemedicine as a means of delivering cognitive-behavioural therapy to rural and remote mental health clients. *Journal of Telemedicine and Telecare, 12,* 136–140.

Gross-Isseroff, R., & Weiszman, A. (2006). *Obsessive compulsive disorder and comorbidity.* New York: Nova Science Publishers, Inc.

Hannan, S. E. &Tolin, D. F. (2005). *Acceptance and Mindfulness-Based Behavior Therapy for Obsessive-Compulsive Disorder* In S. M. Orsillo & L. Roemer (Eds.), Acceptance and mindfulness-based approaches to anxiety: Conceptualization and treatment. (pp. 271–299). New York: Springer Science + Business Media.

Hanstede, M., Gidron, Y., & Nyklicek, I. (2008). The effects of a mindfulness intervention on obsessive-compulsive symptoms in a non-clinical student population. *Journal of Nervous and Mental Disease, 196,* 776–779.

Hart, B. B. (1994). Hypnotizability and type of suggestion in the hypnotic treatment of generalized anxiety. *Contemporary Hypnosis, 11,* 55–65.

Hayes, S. C. (2004). Acceptance and commitment therapy, relational frame theory, and the third wave of behavior therapy. *Behavior Therapy, 35,* 639–665.

Hayes, S. C., Luoma, J. B., Bond, F. W., Masuda, A., & Lillis, J. (2006). Acceptance and commitment therapy: model, processes and outcomes. *Behaviour Research and Therapy, 44,* 1–25.

Heberling, K. L. (2005). *Religious problems require religious solutions.* 66, ProQuest Information & Learning, US. Retrieved from http://search.ebscohost.com/login.aspx?direct=true&-db=psyh&AN=2005-99020-226&site=ehost-live&scope=site

Heimberg, R., & Coles, M. (1999). Reflections on innovations in cognitive behavioral treatment of anxiety disorders. *Cognitive and Behavioral Practice, 6,* 258–263.

Hettema, J., Steele, J., & Miller, W. R. (2005). Motivational interviewing. *Annual Review of Clinical Psychology, 1,* 91–111.

Himle, J. A., Fischer, D. J., Muroff, J. R., Van Etten, M. L., Lokers, L. M., Abelson, J. L. et al. (2006). Videoconferencing-based cognitive-behavioral therapy for obsessive-compulsive disorder. *Behaviour Research and Therapy, 44,* 1821–1829.

Himle, J. A., Muroff, J. R., Taylor, R. J., Baser, R. E., Abelson, J. M., Hanna, G. L. et al. (2008). Obsessive-compulsive disorder among African Americans and blacks of Caribbean descent: results from the National Survey of American Life. *Depression and Anxiety, 25,* 993–1005.

Hsiao, A. F., Wong, M. D., Goldstein, M. S., Yu, H. J., Andersen, R. M., Brown, E. R. et al. (2006). Variation in complementary and alternative medicine (CAM) use across racial/ethnic groups and the development of ethnic-specific measures of CAM use. *Journal of Alternative and Complementary Medicine, 12,* 281–290.

Jackson, G. E. (1975). Anxiety and the church's role. *Journal of Religion and Health, 14,* 231–241.

Jorm, A. F., Christensen, H., Griffiths, K. M., Parslow, R. A., Rodgers, B., & Blewitt, K. A. (2004). Effectiveness of complementary and self-help treatments for anxiety disorders. *Medical Journal of Australia, 181,* S29–46.

Kellerman, J. (1981). Hypnosis as an adjunct to thought-stopping and covert reinforcement in the treatment of homicidal obsessions in a twelve-year-old boy. *International Journal of Clinical and Experimental Hypnosis, 29,* 128–135.

Kenardy, J., McCafferty, K., & Rosa, V. (2003). Internet-delivered indicated prevention for anxiety disorders: A randomized controlled trial. *Behavioural and Cognitive Psychotherapy, 31,* 279–289.

Kennemer, D. L. (2007). Pastoral theory and practice in the team approach to treatment of scrupulosity as a component of obsessive compulsive disorder. *The Journal of Pastoral Care & Counseling, 61,* 319–327.

Kenwright, M., Marks, I., Graham, C., Franses, A., & Mataix-Cols, D. (2005). Brief scheduled phone support from a clinician to enhance computer-aided self-help for obsessive-compulsive disorder: randomized controlled trial. *Journal of Clinical Psychology, 61,* 1499–1508.

Kessler, R. C., Davis, R. B., Foster, D. F., Van Rompay, M. I., Walters, E. E., Wilkey, S. A. et al. (2001). Long-term trends in the use of complementary and alternative medical therapies in the United States. *Annals of Internal Medicine, 135,* 262–268.

Kessler, R. C., Soukup, J., Davis, R. B., Foster, D. F., Wilkey, S. A., Van Rompay, M. M. et al. (2001). The use of complementary and alternative therapies to treat anxiety and depression in the United States. *American Journal of Psychiatry, 158,* 289–294.

Kim, K., Kim, S. I., Cha, K. R., Park, J., Rosenthal, M. Z., Kim, J. J., et al. (2009). Development of a computer-based behavioral assessment of checking behavior in obsessive-compulsive disorder. *Compr Psychiatry.* doi: 10.1016/j.comppsych.2008.12.001.

Kim, K., Kim, C. H., Cha, K. R., Park, J., Han, K., Kim, Y. K., et al. (2008). Anxiety provocation and measurement using virtual reality in patients with obsessive-compulsive disorder. *Cyberpsychol Behav., 11,* 637–641.

Kirkby, K. C., Berrios, G. E., Daniels, B. A., Menzies, R. G., Clark, A., & Romano, A. (2000). Process-outcome analysis in computer-aided treatment of obsessive-compulsive disorder. *Comprehensive Psychiatry, 41,* 259–265.

Kobak, K. A., Taylor, L. V., Bystritsky, A., Kohlenberg, C. J., Greist, J. H., Tucker, P. et al. (2005). St John's wort versus placebo in obsessive-compulsive disorder: results from a double-blind study. *International Clinical Psychopharmacology, 20,* 299–304.

Koszycki, D., Benger, M., Shlik, J., & Bradwejn, J. (2007). Randomized trial of a meditation-based stress reduction program and cognitive behavior therapy in generalized social anxiety disorder. *Behaviour Research and Therapy, 45,* 2518–2526.

Kraft, T., & Kraft, D. (2006). The place of hypnosis in psychiatry: Its applications in treating anxiety disorders and sleep disturbances. *Australian Journal of Clinical & Experimental Hypnosis, 34,* 187–203.

Kuramoto, A. M. (2006). Therapeutic benefits of Tai Chi exercise: research review. *Wisconsin Medical Journal, 105,* 42–46.

Kushner, M. G., Kim, S. W., Donahue, C., Thuras, P., Adson, D., Kotlyar, M., McCabe, J., Peterson, J., Foa E. B. (2007). D-cycloserine augmented exposure therapy for obsessive compulsive Disorder. *Biological Psychiatry, 62*, 835–838.

Lack, C. W., & Storch, E. A. (2008). The use of computers in the assessment and treatment of obsessive-compulsive disorder. *Computers in Human Behavior, 24*, 917–929.

Lancer, R., Motta, R., & Lancer, D. (2007). The effect of aerobic exercise on obsessive compulsive disorder, anxiety, and depression: a preliminary investigation. *The Behavior Therapist, 30*, 53–42.

Lange, A., Rietdijk, D., Hudcovicova, M., van de Ven, J. P., Schrieken, B., & Emmelkamp, P. M. (2003). Interapy: a controlled randomized trial of the standardized treatment of posttraumatic stress through the internet. *Journal of Consulting and Clinical Psychology, 71*, 901–909.

Lantz, M. S., Buchalter, E., & Giambanco, V. (1999). St. John's wort and antidepressant drug interactions in the elderly. *Journal of Geriatric Psychiatry and Neurology, 12*, 7–10.

Leathwood, P. D., & Chauffard, F. (1985). Aqueous extract of valerian reduces latency to fall asleep in man. *Planta Medica, 51*, 144–148.

Lehmann, E., Kinzler, E., & Friedemann, J. (1996). Efficacy of a special kava extract (Piper methysticum) in patients with states of anxiety, tension and excitedness of non-mental origin: a double-blind placebo-controlled study of four weeks treatment. *Phytomedicine, 3*, 113–119.

Lehmann, E., Klieser, E., Klimke, A., Krach, H., & Spatz, R. (1989). The efficacy of Cavain in patients suffering from anxiety. *Pharmacopsychiatry, 22*, 258–262.

Leon, A. C., Portera, L., & Weissman, M. M. (1995). The social costs of anxiety disorders. *British Journal of Psychiatry, 166* (Suppl. 27) 19–22.

Liu, G. Z., Zang, Y. J., Guo, L. X., & Liu, A. Z. (1998). Comparative study on acupuncture combined with behavioural desensitisation for treatment of anxiety neuroses. *American Journal of Acupuncture, 26*, 2–3.

Lochner, C., & Stein, D. J. (2006). Obsessive-compulsive disorder: Comorbidity with obsessive-compulsive spectrum disorders. In R. Gross-Isseroff & A. Weiszman (Eds.), *Obsessive Compulsive Disorder and Comorbidity* (pp.17-33). New York: Nova Science Publishers, Inc.

Lovell, K., Cox, D., Haddock, G., Jones, C., Raines, D., Garvey, R. et al. (2006). Telephone administered cognitive behaviour therapy for treatment of obsessive compulsive disorder: randomised controlled non-inferiority trial. *British Medical Journal (Clinical Research Edition), 333*, 883.

Lovell, K., Fullalove, L., & Garvey, R. (2000). Telephone treatment of obsessive-compulsive disorder. *Behavioural and Cognitive Psychotherapy, 28*, 87–91.

Lynn, S. J., Kirsch, I., Barabasz, A., Cardena, E., & Patterson, D. (2000). Hypnosis as an empirically supported clinical intervention: The state of the evidence and a look to the future. *International Journal of Clinical and Experimental Hypnosis, 48*, 239–259.

Machleidt, W. (2007). Unconventional and alternative methods parallel to a professional psychiatric treatment. *Acta Psychiatrica Scandinavica, 116*, 161–164.

Mackenzie, E. R., Taylor, L., Bloom, B. S., Hufford, D. J., & Johnson, J. C. (2003). Ethnic minority use of complementary and alternative medicine (CAM): a national probability survey of CAM utilizers. *Alternative Therapies in Health and Medicine, 9*, 50–56.

Mains, J. A., & Scogin, F. R. (2003). The effectiveness of self-administered treatments: a practice-friendly review of the research. *Journal of Clinical Psychology, 59*, 237–246.

Malsch, U., & Kieser, M. (2001). Efficacy of kava-kava in the treatment of non-psychotic anxiety, following pretreatment with benzodiazepines. *Psychopharmacology, 157*, 277–283.

Maltby, N., & Tolin, D. F. (2005). A brief motivational intervention for treatment-refusing OCD patients. *Cognitive Behaviour Therapy, 34*, 176–184.

Mamtani, R., & Cimino, A. (2002). A primer of complementary and alternative medicine and its relevance in the treatment of mental health problems. *Psychiatric Quarterly, 73*, 367–381.

Manchanda, M., & McLaren, P. (1998). Cognitive behaviour therapy via interactive video. *Journal of Telemedicine and Telecare, 4*, 53–55.

March, J., Frances, A., Carpenter, D., & Kahn, D. (1997). The expert consensus guidelines series: Treatment of obsessive-compulsive disorder. *Journal of Clinical Psychiatry, 58*, 3–72.

Markowitz, J. S., & DeVane, C. L. (2001). The emerging recognition of herb-drug interactions with a focus on St. John's wort (Hypericum perforatum). *Psychopharmacology Bulletin, 35*, 53–64.

Markowitz, J. S., Donovan, J. L., DeVane, C. L., Taylor, R. M., Ruan, Y., Wang, J. S. et al. (2003). Effect of St John's wort on drug metabolism by induction of cytochrome P450 3A4 enzyme. *Journal of the American Medical Association, 290*, 1500–1504.

Marks, I., Cavanagh, K., & Gega, L. (2007). *Hands-on help. Computer aided psychotherapy, Maudsley Monograph No 49.* London, UK: Psychology Press, Routledge, London.

Marks, I. M., Baer, L., Greist, J. H., Park, J. M., Bachofen, M., Nakagawa, A. et al. (1998). Home self-assessment of obsessive-compulsive disorder. Use of a manual and a computer-conducted telephone interview: two UK-US studies. *British Journal of Psychiatry, 172*, 406–412.

Marks, I. M., Lelliott, P., Basoglu, M., Noshirvani, H., Monteiro, W., Cohen, D. et al. (1988). Clomipramine, self-exposure and therapist-aided exposure for obsessive-compulsive rituals. *British Journal of Psychiatry, 152*, 522–534.

Mataix-Cols, D., & Marks, I. (2006). Self-help for obsessive-compulsive disorder: How much therapist contact is necessary? *Clinical Neuropsychiatry: Journal of Treatment Evaluation, 3*, 404–409.

Mataix-Cols, D., & Marks, I. M. (2006). Self-help with minimal therapist contact for obsessive-compulsive disorder: a review. *European Psychiatry, 21*, 75–80.

McCrone, P., Marks, I. M., Greist, J. H., Baer, L., Kobak, K. A., Wenzel, K. W. et al. (2007). Cost-effectiveness of computer-aided behaviour therapy for obsessive-compulsive disorder. *Psychotherapy and Psychosomatics, 76*, 249–250.

McDougle, C. J. (1997). Update on pharmacologic management of OCD: agents and augmentation. *Journal of Clinical Psychiatry, 58*, 11–17.

Merlo, L. J., Storch, E. A., Lehmkuhl, H. D., Jacob, M. L., Murphy, T. K., Goodman, W. K. et al. (2010). Cognitive behavioral therapy plus motivational interviewing improves outcome for pediatric obsessive-compulsive disorder: a preliminary study. *Cognitive Behaviour Therapy, 39*, 24–27.

Meyer, E., Souza, F., Heldt, E., Knapp, P., Cordioli, A., Shavitt, R.G., Leukefeld, C. (2010). A randomized clinical trial to examine enhancing cognitive-behavioral group therapy for obsessive-compulsive disorder with motivational interviewing and thought mapping. *Behavioral and Cognitive Psychotherapy, 38*, 319–36.

Miller, W., & Rollnick, S. (2002). *Motivational interviewing: preparing people for change* (Second Edition ed.). New York, NY: The Guilford Press.

Mills, K. C. (1995). Serotonin syndrome. *American Family Physician, 52*, 1475–1482.

Moore, K. A., & Burrows, G. D. (1991). Hypnosis in the treatment of obsessive-compulsive disorder. *Australian Journal of Clinical Hypnotherapy, 19*, 63–75.

Moritz, S., Aravena, S.C., Guczka, S.R., Schilling, L., Eichenberg, C., Raubart, G., Seebeck, A., Jelinek, L. (2011). Knock, and it will be opened to you? An evaluation of meridian-tapping in obsessive-compulsive disorder (OCD). *Journal of Behavior Therapy and Experimental Psychiatry, 42*, 81–88.

Moritz, S., Jelinek, L., Hauschildt, M., Naber, D. (2010). How to treat the untreated: effectiveness of a self-help metacognitive training program (myMCT) for obsessive-compulsive disorder. *Dialogues of Clinical Neuroscience, 12*, 209–220.

Muroff, J., Steketee, G., Himle, J., & Frost, R. (2009) Delivery of internet treatment for compulsive hoarding (D.I.T.C.H.). *Behaviour Research and Therapy, 48*, 79–85.

Muroff, J. R., Steketee, G., Himle, J. A., & Frost, R. (2007). *Delivery of Internet Treatment for Compulsive Hoarding (DITCH): Empirical findings from a longitudinal study.* Paper presented at the 42nd Annual Convention for the Association for Behavioral and Cognitive Therapies, Orlando, Florida.

Murphy, L., Riley, D., Rodgers, J., Plank, S., Lehman, S., & Duryea, B. (2005). Effects of tai chi on balance, mobility, and strength among older persons participating in an osteoporosis prevention and education program. *Explore (NY), 1*, 192–193.

Nakagawa, A., Marks, I. M., Park, J. M., Bachofen, M., Baer, L., Dottl, S. L. et al. (2000). Self-treatment of obsessive-compulsive disorder guided by manual and computer-conducted telephone interview. *Journal of Telemedicine and Telecare, 6*, 22–26.

National Institute for Health and Clinical Excellence. (2004). Anxiety: management of anxiety (panic disorder, with or without agoraphobia, and generalised anxiety disorder) in adults in primary, secondary and community care. Clinical Guideline 22 (CG022). Retrieved May 8, 2006

Nelson, E. A., Abramowitz, J. S., Whiteside, S. P., & Deacon, B. J. (2006). Scrupulosity in patients with obsessive-compulsive disorder: relationship to clinical and cognitive phenomena. *Journal of Anxiety Disorders, 20*, 1071–1086.

Newman, M. G., Erickson, T., Przeworski, A., & Dzus, E. (2003). Self-help and minimal-contact therapies for anxiety disorders: Is human contact necessary for therapeutic efficacy? *Journal of Clinical Psychology, 59*, 251–274.

Nguyen, H. Q., Carrieri-Kohlman, V., Rankin, S. H., Slaughter, R., & Stulbarg, M. S. (2004). Internet-based patient education and support interventions: a review of evaluation studies and directions for future research. *Computers in Biology and Medicine, 34*, 95–112.

Olson, T. (2003). Buddhism, behavior change, and OCD. *Journal of Holistic Nursing, 21*, 149–162.

Osborn, I. (2008). *Can Christianity cure obsessive-compulsive disorder? A psychiatrist explores the role of faith in treatment.* Ada, MI: Brazos Press/Baker Publishing Group.

Ost, L. G., Stridh, B. M., & Wolf, M. (1998). A clinical study of spider phobia: prediction of outcome after self-help and therapist-directed treatments. *Behaviour Research and Therapy, 36*, 17–35.

Patel, S. R., Carmody, J., & Simpson, H. B. (2007). Adapting mindfulness-based stress reduction for the treatment of obsessive-compulsive disorder: A case report. *Cognitive and Behavioral Practice, 14*, 375–380.

Piccinelli, M., Pini, S., Bellantuono, C., & Wilkinson, G. (1995). Efficacy of drug treatment in obsessive-compulsive disorder. A meta-analytic review. *British Journal of Psychiatry, 166*, 424–443.

Pilkington, K., Kirkwood, G., Rampes, H., Cummings, M., & Richardson, J. (2007). Acupuncture for anxiety and anxiety disorders a systematic literature review. *Acupuncture in Medicine, 25*, 1–10.

Pittler, M. H., & Ernst, E. (2000). Efficacy of kava extract for treating anxiety: systematic review and meta-analysis. *Journal of Clinical Psychopharmacology, 20*, 84–89.

Pittler, M. H., & Ernst, E. (2003). Kava extract for treating anxiety. *Cochrane Database of Systematic Reviews, 1*, CD003383.

Prochaska, J. O., & DiClemente, C. C. (1992). Stages of change in the modification of problem behaviors. *Progress in Behavior Modification, 28*, 183–218.

Rasmussen, S. A., Eisen, J. L., & Pato, M. T. (1993). Current issues in the pharmacologic management of obsessive compulsive disorder. *Journal of Clinical Psychiatry, 54*, 4–9.

Rassin, E., & Koster, E. (2003). The correlation between thought-action fusion and religiosity in a normal sample. *Behaviour Research and Therapy, 41*, 361–368.

Razali, S. M., Hasanah, C. I., Aminah, K., & Subramaniam, M. (1998). Religious-sociocultural psychotherapy in patients with anxiety and depression. *Australian and New Zealand Journal of Psychiatry, 32*, 867–872.

Robiner, W. N., Edwards, P. E., Christenson, G. A., Stein, D. J., & Hollander, E. (1999). Hypnosis in the treatment of trichotillomania *Trichotillomania*. (pp. 167–199). Washington, DC US: American Psychiatric Association.

Saeed, S. A., Bloch, R. M., & Antonacci, D. J. (2007). Herbal and dietary supplements for treatment of anxiety disorders. *American Family Physician, 76*, 549–556.

Samuels, N., Gropp, C., Singer, S. R., & Oberbaum, M. (2008). Acupuncture for psychiatric illness: a literature review. *Behavioral Medicine, 34*, 55–64.

Sayyah, M., Boostani, H., Pakseresht, S., Malayeri, A. (2010). Comparison of Silybum marianum (L.) Gaertn. with fluoxetine in the treatment of Obsessive-Compulsive Disorder. *Progress in Neuropsychopharmacology and Biological Psychiatry, 34*, 362–365.

Schruers, K., Koning, K., Luermans, J., Haack, M. J., & Griez, E. (2005). Obsessive-compulsive disorder: a critical review of therapeutic perspectives. *Acta Psychiatrica Scandinavica, 111*, 261–271.

Schwartz, J. (1996). *Brain Lock: Free yourself from obsessive-compulsive disorder.* New York: HarperCollins Publishers.

Scrignar, C. B. (1981). Rapid treatment of contamination phobia with hand-washing compulsion by flooding with hypnosis. *American Journal of Clinical Hypnosis, 23*, 252–257.

Seedat, S., & Stein, D. J. (1999). Inositol augmentation of serotonin reuptake inhibitors in treatment-refractory obsessive-compulsive disorder: an open trial. *International Clinical Psychopharmacology, 14*, 353–356.

Selmi, P. M., Klein, M. H., Greist, J. H., Sorrell, S. P., & Erdman, H. P. (1990). Computer-administered cognitive-behavioral therapy for depression. *American Journal of Psychiatry, 147*, 51–56.

Shannahoff-Khalsa, D. S., & Beckett, L. R. (1996). Clinical case report: efficacy of yogic techniques in the treatment of obsessive compulsive disorders. *International Journal of Neuroscience, 85,* 1–17.

Shannahoff-Khalsa, D. S., Ray, L. E., Levine, S., Gallen, C. C., Schwartz, B. J., & Sidorowich, J. J. (1999). Randomized controlled trial of yogic meditation techniques for patients with obsessive-compulsive disorder. *CNS Spectrums, 4,* 34–47.

Shuaib, B. M., & Haq, M. F. (1977). Electro-acupuncture treatment in psychiatry. *The American Journal of Chinese Medicine, 5,* 85–90.

Siev, J., & Cohen, A. B. (2007). Is thought-action fusion related to religiosity? Differences between Christians and Jews. *Behaviour Research and Therapy, 45,* 829–837.

Simpson, H. B., & Zuckoff, A. M. (2011). Using motivational interviewing to enhance treatment outcome in people with OCD. *Cognitive and Behavioural Practice, 18,* 28–37.

Simpson, H. B., Zuckoff, A. M., Maher, M. J., Page, J. R., Franklin, M. E., Foa, E. B., Schmidt, A. B., Wang, Y. (2010). Challenges using motivational interviewing as an adjunct to exposure therapy for obsessive-compulsive disorder. *Behaviour Research and Therapy, 48,* 941–948.

Simpson, H. B., Zuckoff, A., Page, J. R., Franklin, M. E., & Foa, E. B. (2008). Adding motivational interviewing to exposure and ritual prevention for obsessive-compulsive disorder: an open pilot trial. *Cognitive Behaviour Therapy, 37,* 38–49.

Singh, N. N., Wahler, R. G., Winton, A. S. W., & Adkins, A. D. (2004). A Mindfulness-Based Treatment of Obsessive-Compulsive Disorder. *Clinical Case Studies, 3,* 275–287.

Snowden, L. R., & Yamada, A. M. (2005). Cultural differences in access to care. *Annual Review of Clinical Psychology, 1,* 143–166.

Spek, V., Cuijpers, P., Nyklicek, I., Riper, H., Keyzer, J., & Pop, V. (2007). Internet-based cognitive behaviour therapy for symptoms of depression and anxiety: a meta-analysis. *Psychological Medicine, 37,* 319–328.

Spinhoven, P., Van Dyck, R., Hoogduin, K., & Schaap, C. (1991). Differences in hypnotizability of Dutch psychiatric outpatients according to two difference scales. *Australian Journal of Clinical and Experimental Hypnosis, 19,* 107–116.

Stathopoulou, G., Powers, M. B., Berry, A. C., Smits, J. A. J., & Otto, M. W. (2006). Exercise Interventions for Mental Health: A Quantitative and Qualitative Review. *Clinical Psychology: Science and Practice, 13,* 179–193.

Stein, D. J., Ipser, J. C., Baldwin, D. S., & Bandelow, B. (2007). Treatment of obsessive-compulsive disorder. *CNS Spectrums, 12,* 28–35.

Steketee, G., Quay, S., & White, K. (1991). Religion and guilt in OCD patients. *Journal of Anxiety Disorders, 5*(4), 359–367.

Steketee, G., & White, K. (1990). *When Once is Not Enough: Help for Obsessive Compulsives.* Oakland, CA: Harbinger Publications.

Taggart, H. M., Arslanian, C. L., Bae, S., & Singh, K. (2003). Effects of T'ai Chi exercise on fibromyalgia symptoms and health-related quality of life. *Orthopaedic Nursing, 22,* 353–360.

Taylor, L. H., & Kobak, K. A. (2000). An open-label trial of St. John's Wort (Hypericum perforatum) in obsessive-compulsive disorder. *Journal of Clinical Psychiatry, 61,* 575–578.

Taylor, S., Thordarson, D. S., Spring, T., Yeh, A. H., Corcoran, K. M., Eugster, K. et al. (2003). Telephone-administered cognitive behavior therapy for obsessive-compulsive disorder. *Cognitive Behaviour Therapy, 32,* 13–25.

Tolin, D. F., Diefenbach, G., Maltby, N., & Hannan, S. (2005). Stepped care for obsessive-compulsive disorder: A pilot study. *Cognitive and Behavioral Practice, 12,* 403–414.

Tolin, D. F., Hannan, S., Maltby, N., Diefenbach, G. J., Worhunsky, P., & Brady, R. E. (2007). A randomized controlled trial of self-directed versus therapist-directed cognitive-behavioral therapy for obsessive-compulsive disorder patients with prior medication trials. *Behavior Therapy, 38,* 179–191.

Tory, P. B. (2004). *A mindfulness-based stress reduction program for the treatment of anxiety.* Hofstra University, Hempstead, N.Y.

Trenholm, P., Trent, J., & Compton, W. C. (1998). Negative religious conflict as a predictor of panic disorder. *Journal of Clinical Psychology, 54,* 59–65.

Twohig, M. P. (2008). A randomized clinical trial of acceptance and commitment therapy versus progressive relaxation training in the treatment of obsessive compulsive disorder. *Dissertation Abstracts International 68,* 4850.

Twohig, M. P., Hayes, S. C., & Masuda, A. (2006a). Increasing willingness to experience obsessions: acceptance and commitment therapy as a treatment for obsessive-compulsive disorder. *Behavior Therapy, 37,* 3–13.

Twohig, M. P., Hayes, S. C., & Masuda, A. (2006b). A preliminary investigation of acceptance and commitment therapy as a treatment for chronic skin picking. *Behaviour Research and Therapy, 44,* 1513–1522.

Twohig, M. P., Hayes, S. C., Plumb, J. C., Pruitt, L. D., Collins, A. B., Hazlett-Stevens, H., Woidneck, M. R. (2010). A randomized clinical trial of acceptance and commitment therapy versus progressive relaxation training for obsessive-compulsive disorder. *Journal of Consulting and Clinical Psychology, 78,* 705–716.

Twohig, M. P., Plumb, J. C., Mukherjee, D., & Hayes, S. C. (2010). Suggestions from acceptance and commitment therapy for dealing with treatment-resistant obsessive-compulsive disorder. In D. Sookman & R. Leahy (Eds.), *Treatment resistant anxiety disorders: Resolving impasses to symptom remission* (pp. 255–289). New York, NY: Routledge/Taylor & Francis.

Tynes, L. L., Salins, C., Skiba, W., & Winstead, D. K. (1992). A psychoeducational and support group for obsessive-compulsive disorder patients and their significant others. *Comprehensive Psychiatry, 33,* 197–201.

van der Watt, G., Laugharne, J., & Janca, A. (2008). Complementary and alternative medicine in the treatment of anxiety and depression. *Current Opinion in Psychiatry, 21,* 37–42.

Vickers, A. (2000). Recent advances: complementary medicine. *British Medical Journal (Clinical Research Ed.), 321,* 683–686.

Volz, H. P., & Kieser, M. (1997). Kava-kava extract WS 1490 versus placebo in anxiety disorders—a randomized placebo-controlled 25-week outpatient trial. *Pharmacopsychiatry, 30,* 1–5.

Wahlstrom, M., Sihvo, S., Haukkala, A., Kiviruusu, O., Pirkola, S., & Isometsa, E. (2008). Use of mental health services and complementary and alternative medicine in persons with common mental disorders. *Acta Psychiatrica Scandinavica, 118,* 73–80.

Weissman, M. M., Bland, R. C., Canino, G. J., Greenwald, S., Hwu, H. G., Lee, C. K. et al. (1994). The cross national epidemiology of obsessive compulsive disorder. The Cross National Collaborative Group. *Journal of Clinical Psychiatry, 55,* 5–10.

Wells, M., Mitchell, K. J., Finkelhor, D., & Becker-Blease, K. A. (2007). Online mental health treatment: concerns and considerations. *Cyberpsychology and Behavior*, *10*, 453–459.

Wester, W. C., II, & Sugarman, L. I. (2007). Hypnotic Treatment of Anxiety in Children *Therapeutic hypnosis with children and adolescents*. (pp. 199–215). Norwalk, CT, US: Crown House Publishing Limited.

Westra, H. (2004). Managing resistance in cognitive behavioural therapy: the application of motivational interviewing in mixed anxiety and depression. *Cognitive Behaviour Therapy*, *33*, 161–175.

Westra, H., & Dozois, D. (2006). Preparing Clients for Cognitive Behavioral Therapy: A Randomized Pilot Study of Motivational Interviewing for Anxiety. *Cognitive Therapy and Research*, *30*, 481–498.

Westra, H. A., & Phoenix, E. (2003). Motivational enhancement therapy in two cases of anxiety disorder. *Clinical Case Studies*, *2*, 306–322.

Wilhelm, S., Buhlmann, U., Tolin, D. F., Meunier, S. A., Pearlson, G. D., Reese, H. E., Cannistraro, P., Jenike, M. A., Rauch, S. L. (2008) Augmentation of behavior therapy with D-cycloserine for obsessive-compulsive disorder. *American Journal of Psychiatry*, *165*, 335–41

Wolberg, L. R. (1948). Hypnosis in compulsion neurosis *Medical hypnosis. Volume I: The principles of hypnotherapy*. (pp. 240–259). New York, NY: Grune & Stratton.

Woods, D. W., Wetterneck, C. T., & Flessner, C. A. (2006). A controlled evaluation of acceptance and commitment therapy plus habit reversal for trichotillomania. *Behaviour Research and Therapy*, *44*, 639–656.

Yamashita, T., Fujimoto, K., Aoi, K., Shimura, E., & Kubo, K. (1991). [A study of psychopathology in phobia and obsessive-compulsive disorder: through the treatment of exposure and response prevention by transcutaneous electrical stimulation]. *Seishin Shinkeigaku Zasshi (Psychiatria et Neurologia Japonica)*, *93*, 645–673.

Yorulmaz, O., Gençöz, T., & Woody, S. (2009). OCD cognitions and symptoms in different religious contexts. *Journal of Anxiety Disorders*, *23*(3), 401–406.

Zalsman, G., Hermesh, H., & Sever, J. (2001). Hypnotherapy in adolescents with trichotillomania: Three cases. *American Journal of Clinical Hypnosis*, *44*, 63–68.

Zhang, H., Zeng, Z., & Deng, H. (2003). Acupuncture treatment for 157 cases of anxiety neurosis. *Journal of Traditional Chinese Medicine*, *23*, 55–56.

Zhou, S. F., & Lai, X. (2008). An update on clinical drug interactions with the herbal antidepressant St. John's wort. *Current Drug Metabolism*, *9*, 394–409.

PART 6

Treatment of OC Spectrum Conditions

Treatment of Body Dysmorphic Disorder

Jennifer L. Greenberg, Anne Chosak, Angela Fang, *and* Sabine Wilhelm

Abstract

Body dysmorphic disorder (BDD) is characterized by an excessive preoccupation with an imagined or slight defect in one's appearance. BDD is a severe and common disorder associated with high levels of functional impairment and high rates of suicidality. Interventions, including cognitive-behavioral therapy and pharmacotherapy, are effective for BDD. This chapter outlines the cognitive-behavioral model and therapy of BDD. The chapter reviews pharmacotherapy of BDD, and discusses the role of combination therapy. The chapter also addresses ineffective approaches for the treatment of BDD, including the role of cosmetic procedures. Early recognition and intervention are critical, and limit its chronicity and subsequent morbidity.

Keywords: BDD, body dysmorphic disorder, cognitive-behavioral therapy, pharmacotherapy, empirically supported treatment

Introduction

Julia, a 24-year-old Asian-American woman, was brought in by her husband for the treatment of BDD. Julia reported that as a child she received a lot of attention based on her "button nose" and "silky" hair. However, during puberty, around age 13, Julia experienced a growth spurt, her facial features became more pronounced, and her smooth, silky hair developed a coarse, wavy texture. Julia combed her hair each morning and night, first for 10–15 minutes, and soon for up to 1 hour at a time in an effort to smooth out her tresses. She spent hundreds of dollars on styling products intended to improve the texture of her hair. Julia found it increasingly difficult to be around friends in school or in social situations, because she would become completely caught up in comparing their hair or noses to her own. She frequently touched her hair and checked the mirror to see whether her hair or nose had grown or changed in any way. When she sat in class or interacted with peers, she used her hands or her hair

to cover her nose so that nobody would notice the "lumpy mound" in the middle of her face.

Julia frequently surfed the Internet and magazines looking for "perfect" noses and for cosmetic surgeons who specialized in rhinoplasty. By the time she was 22, Julia had sought consultations from 12 plastic surgeons and had received 2 rhinoplasty procedures. She had been devastated with the results of the first procedure, after which she described feeling regret for having undergone the surgery ("I looked better before"). Julia had the second procedure to correct the first one, but felt "the surgeon messed up and made [her nose] look even worse." Although Julia's husband and friends told her she looked fine, Julia found it difficult to leave the house for fear that others would see and judge her based on her "disfigured nose." When Julia did leave the house, it was only following an extensive 2–3 hour routine involving camouflaging (e.g., with makeup, clothing, sunglasses, hat) and checking. Julia took precautions to only attend situations in which she knew there would be few people and dim lighting. She rarely returned phone calls from friends, because it triggered such intense anxiety about having to leave the house. When Julia's husband brought her in for treatment, she was convinced that a third surgery was her only solution.

Description of the Disorder

Many people experience some degree of concern or discontent about their appearance. However, some individuals are so distressed about the way they look that it interferes with their daily life. Concerns similar to those experienced by Julia reflect a diagnosis of BDD, a severe disorder characterized by an often-delusional preoccupation with an imagined or slight defect in appearance (American Psychiatric Association, 2000). BDD is common, and associated with significant public health sequelae, thus underscoring the need for the development and dissemination of effective treatments. BDD is associated with functional impairment (i.e., social, academic, and work), compromised quality of life, and significant morbidity, including hospitalization and suicide (Phillips, 2000; Phillips, Coles, et al., 2005; Phillips & Menard, 2006; Phillips, Menard, Fay & Pagano, 2005; Phillips, Quinn, & Stout, 2008). Individuals with BDD frequently spend several hours per day worrying about their appearance.

Common areas of concern involve the skin, hair, nose, eyes, or teeth (Phillips & Diaz, 1997; Phillips, Didie et al., 2006; Phillips, Menard, Fay & Weisberg, 2005); however, any body part may be the focus of concern, including the ears, hips, butt, bone structure, breasts, and genitals (Cansever, Uzun, Donmez, & Ozsahin, 2003; Phillips, 2005; Veale, Boocock, Gournay, & Dryden, 1996). In *muscle dysmorphia*, a subtype of BDD, the primary concern focuses on muscle shape and size (Pope, Gruber et al., 1997; Pope, Pope et al., 2005). The number of concerns can progress and shift focus over time (Phillips, 2005; Phillips, McElroy, Keck, Pope, & et al., 1993), with patients averaging a preoccupation with 5–7 body areas over the course of their illness (Phillips, Menard, Fay, & Weisberg, 2005). Perceived appearance imperfections and delusions of reference (e.g., the conviction that others are laughing or staring at the perceived flaw) cause strong emotional reactions, including anxiety, and disgust. Feelings of shame, and a fear of social rejection based on perceived appearance flaws, often lead individuals to become withdrawn, socially isolated, and at times housebound (Phillips, McElroy et al., 1993).

Patients often go to great lengths to try to reduce their distress or fix perceived defects. This includes seeking and receiving costly surgical, dermatologic, and other medical treatments, which are usually ineffective and can worsen BDD symptoms. Other rituals have the potential for causing real physical damage. For example, more than one-third of individuals with BDD engage in skin-picking (Grant, Menard, & Phillips, 2006; Phillips & Taub, 1995). Skin-picking may involve the use of sharp tools (e.g., razor blades) and can cause noticeable skin damage or infection (Grant et al., 2006; Phillips & Taub, 1995). Other individuals engage in "do it yourself" surgeries, such as breaking one's own nose (Phillips, 2005; Veale, Boocock et al., 1996).

BDD affects an estimated 0.7%–2.4% of the population (Bienvenu et al., 2000; Buhlmann et al., 2010; Koran et al., 2008; Otto et al., 2001 Rief, et al., 2006). Onset typically occurs in early adolescence. Left untreated, BDD is associated with a chronic course and severe lifetime morbidity. Yet, despite being a common, severe disorder, with substantial psychosocial impact, BDD remains largely under-recognized (Phillips, Pagano, Menard, & Stout, 2006; also, see Chapter 3).

Several factors contribute to the underreporting of BDD. BDD may be under-recognized in part because patients are reluctant to seek psychiatric help. Individuals with BDD often experience shame or embarrassment due to appearance concerns; unless appearance concerns are specifically asked about, patients are reluctant to disclose BDD symptoms to providers, even when such symptoms are their primary concern (Conroy et al., 2008; Grant, Kim, & Crow, 2001). Thus, it is critical that health providers query the existence of appearance-related concerns. When BDD goes unnoticed, individuals may not receive appropriate treatment. Indeed, BDD patients are most likely to seek and receive nonpsychiatric medical treatment, or psychiatric treatment for a similar or comorbid disorder. This may be due in part to shame or embarrassment about appearance-related symptoms. Additionally, many individuals with BDD have poor insight into the disorder and may have frank delusions about their appearance concerns; consequently, individuals seek help from dermatologists and cosmetic surgeons, convinced that their appearance concerns are physical, rather than psychological, in origin (Crerand, Phillips, Menard, & Fay, 2005; Phillips, Grant, Siniscalchi, & Albertini, 2001; Phillips, Menard, Fay, & Weisberg, 2005; Sarwer & Crerand, 2008). Indeed, in an examination of 200 BDD patients,

71% sought and 64% received nonpsychiatric (e.g., dermatologic and surgical) medical treatment (Crerand et al., 2005). Alternatively, individuals with BDD may seek treatment for a comorbid psychiatric condition.See Chapter 3 for more detail on the phenomenology and epidemiology of BDD.

Etiology

Although its etiology remains elusive, biological, psychological and socio-environmental factors likely play a role in the development and maintenance of BDD. Additional research is needed to fully elucidate the contribution and interaction of these factors.

BIOLOGICAL FACTORS

Most of the biological research in BDD has focused on the role of serotonin (5-HT) dysfunction although abnormalities in dopaminergic (DA) circuitry have also been proposed (Hadley, Newcorn, & Hollander, 2002). Psychopharmacologic treatment studies provide support for the role of 5-HT dysfunction in BDD; patients with nondelusional and delusional variants of BDD demonstrate a selective therapeutic response to high-dose SRIs. Additional evidence for the role of the 5-HT system comes from exacerbation of BDD symptoms following depletion of tryptophan, a 5-HT precursor amino acid, (Barr, Goodman, & Price, 1992) and administration of m-chlorophenylpiperazine (mCPP), a 5-HT agonist (Hollander & Wong, 1995). Dysregulation of 5-HT and DA systems may contribute to the dysregulated attention, inhibition, and mood states observed in individuals with BDD (Feusner, Yaryura-Tobias & Saxena, 2008; Saxena & Feusner, 2006. Data from neuroimaging and neuropsychological studies also suggest a role for hemispheric imbalance and fronto-striatal cortical circuitry dysfunction in the pathophysiology of BDD.

Emotions and body image are largely processed in the right hemisphere, and new onset of BDD has been described subsequent to inflammatory medical illness (Gabbay, O'Dowd, Weiss, Asnis, 2002; Mathew, 2001; Salib, 1988) and right temporal lobe lesions (Gabbay et al., 2003; Naga, Devinsky, & Barr, 2004). Secondary psychotic symptoms, including somatic delusions, have also been associated with right hemispheric lesions. Increased left hemispheric activation (involving the prefrontal and lateral temporal regions) may contribute to early-stage visual processing biases observed in BDD patients (Feusner et al., 2007).

Evidence of frontal striatal circuitry dysfunction comes from clinical and neurobiological findings.

However, research into the pathophysiology or neurobiology of BDD is still nascent. In neuropsychological studies, individuals with BDD demonstrate a tendency to overfocus on small details in lieu of the configural whole (Deckersbach et al., 2000). In a structural morphometric magnetic resonance imaging study of eight women with BDD, BDD subjects had a leftward shift in caudate asymmetry, and greater overall white matter compared with controls (Rauch et al., 2003). A small, uncontrolled functional imaging study of six BDD patients using single photon emission computed tomography (SPECT) yielded a wide range of discrepant findings, including parietal involvement and relative occipital and temporal perfusion deficits (Carey et al., 2004).

More recently, in studies using fMRI to examine visual processing in individuals with BDD compared with healthy controls, individuals with BDD exhibited aberrant visual processing when viewing high, low, and normal spatial frequency faces of others (Feusner et al. 2007) and of themselves (Feusner et al., 2010). High spatial frequencies (HSF) are used for perceiving details (e.g., eyes and lips), whereas low spatial frequencies (LSF) convey configural aspects of faces (e.g., general shape of face); normal spatial frequency images are unaltered. When viewing faces of others, individuals with BDD demonstrated overactivation of the left hemisphere, which suggests a tendency for BDD patients to utilize local (detail-oriented) rather than global (holistic) processing (Feusner et al., 2007). Specifically, BDD patients demonstrated increased activation in the inferior frontal gyrus and lateral temporal parietal regions compared to controls, as well as abnormal amygdala activity (right greater than left; Feusner et al., 2007). When viewing their own faces, BDD subjects showed hypoactivity in the primary and secondary visual processing regions (left occipital cortex) for LSF faces and hyperactivity in the frontostriatal system (left orbitofrontal cortex and bilateral head of the caudate) for NSF faces (Feusner et al., 2010). More neuroimaging research is needed to fully elucidate the neurobiological basis of BDD and how these regions function together. Furthermore, functional neuroimaging data may be used to predict treatment response and examine neural correlates of treatment response.

Lastly, genetic factors may play a role in the etiology of BDD. BDD appears to have a strong heritable component. In family studies, between 5.8%–8% of BDD patients report BDD among first-degree relatives (Bienvenu et al., 2000; Phillips,

Gunderson, Mallya, McElroy, & Carter, 1998; Phillips, Menard, Fay & Weisberg, 2005; Saxena & Feusner, 2006). Similarly, the presence of OCD in one's immediate family has also been associated with increased risk for the development of BDD, OCD, and other obsessive compulsive spectrum disorders. In the only published, preliminary genetic association study, Richter et al. (2004) found an association between gamma-aminobutyric acid (GABA) A-γ2 gene and BDD, and comorbid BDD and OCD (but not OCD alone); a trend was observed toward an association with the serotonin transporter promoter polymorphism (5-HTTPRL) short allele. Direct investigations into the genetics of BDD are scarce. Such studies are needed to inform our understanding of the neurophysiology of BDD and to determine potential linkage peaks.

PSYCHOLOGICAL FACTORS

Psychodynamic Theories. Psychodynamic theories of BDD focus on unconscious sexual or emotional conflict, feelings of inferiority, guilt, or poor self-image that are thought to have been displaced onto the body part(s) of concern. Deeply rooted problems are conceptualized as being displaced onto appearance, so as to make the underlying problem less threatening (Phillips, 2005). For example, in a case of a young woman with concerns around breast size, the hypothesized core issue was ambivalence about growing up (i.e., becoming a woman) and sexuality (Horowitz, Gorfinkle, Lewis, & Phillips 2002). In another case, a woman's "abnormal looking, ugly, and deformed" eyebrows were conceptualized as stemming from low self-esteem and a sense of hopelessness about heterosexual relationships (Bloch, & Glue, 1988). Psychodynamic theorists suggest that problems are rooted in childhood experiences, and the body part onto which concerns are displaced (e.g., the nose, mouth) are frequently more palatable representations of other, more emotionally threatening body parts (e.g., the penis). The goal of dynamic psychotherapy is to aid the patient to resolve his or her unconscious conflicts, which in turn should be expected to resolve the BDD symptoms. While therapies driven by psychodynamic theories may be helpful in resolving general life difficulties, they are not adequate in explaining the etiology of BDD, nor has there been any empirical support for psychodynamic treatment of BDD (Phillips, 2005).

Cognitive-Behavioral Theories. Cognitive-behavioral theories of BDD maintain a diathesis-stress model, by which an individual biologically predisposed to BDD develops onset of symptoms subsequent to an environmental stressor. As BDD typically develops around adolescence, the hormonal, psychological, and social changes that occur during puberty have been proposed as proximal stressors. Stressors may also include socio-environmental factors, such as appearance-based reinforcement (teasing or praise). Subsequently, individuals can develop maladaptive beliefs about their appearance and the importance of appearance; for instance, believing that self-worth and social acceptance are based in appearance, and that in order to be loved or accepted, one must look perfect. Situations that trigger maladaptive beliefs induce feelings of shame, disgust, anxiety, and depression.

Cognitive factors, including selective attention, likely contribute to a vulnerability to, and maintenance of, this vicious cycle. In neuropsychological tests of verbal and nonverbal memory, BDD patients tend to focus on the small details and features, rather than on the global framework (Deckersbach et al., 2000). This is consistent with clinical observation of BDD patients selectively attending to certain details of their appearance while ignoring global physical appearance. In addition to demonstrating selective attention to appearance-based stimuli relative to healthy controls, individuals with BDD tend to overestimate the physical attractiveness of others and underestimate their own physical attractiveness (Buhlmann, Etcoff, & Wilhelm, 2008). Thus, individuals with BDD focus only on self-perceived imperfections (i.e., aspects of their appearance with which they are dissatisfied). Selective attention to perceived flaws contributes to an increase in distress, which prompts individuals to engage in compulsive or escape (avoidant) behavior designed to reduce distress or enhance appearance. Negative reinforcement occurs when safety behaviors provide temporary relief from distress; however, such behaviors preclude learning of adaptive responses, and subsequently increase the frequency of and distress associated with intrusive appearance-related cognitions and behaviors over time.

SOCIO-ENVIRONMENTAL FACTORS

Contemporary Western culture has placed a remarkable emphasis on appearance and the importance of attaining the ideal appearance. Billions of industry dollars are spent each year advertising implicit and explicit messages about the importance of attractiveness, and encouraging people of all ages to spend their disposable income on products, clothing, and services designed to reach this unattainable standard

(Wilhelm, 2006). There is no seeming end to the pursuit of ideal beauty; one's teeth can always be a little straighter or whiter; after one has lost weight, there could be improvements in muscle tone, or removal of excess skin; there are always refinements and changes to be made to hair and makeup, to increasing muscularity, to decreasing body fat.

With this omnipresent pressure to look good, even perfect, it is not surprising that some individuals take these messages personally and to an extreme. The fact that many plastic surgeons provide multiple surgeries for the same patient, on the same body part, suggests that even the medical community may inadvertently collude with societal pressures. Thus, socio-environmental factors likely contribute to the development and maintenance of BDD; however, BDD is not exclusively an American, nor Western phenomenon. BDD has been reported across cultures, even in countries with minimal advertising and with different standards of beauty (Faravelli, Salvatori, Galassi, & Aiazzi, 1997; Fontenelle et al., 2006; Hitzeroth, Wessels, Zungu-Dirwayi, Oosthuizen, & Stein, 2001; Suzuki, Takei, Kawai, Minabe, & Mori, 2003; Tignol, Biraben-Gotzamanis, Martin-Guehl, Grabot, & Aouizerate, 2007). While the most common areas of concern involve the face, nose, hair, and skin, the significance or meanings of these body areas may vary cross-culturally. Culture may influence the body part of concern (Marques et al., 2011), as well patients' access and attitude to mental health treatment. However, in the only cross-cultural study of BDD, Bohne et al. (2002) found similar prevalence rates in nonclinical samples of American (4%, n=101) and German (5.3%, n=133) students. Thus, it is unlikely that socio-environmental emphasis on appearance is a necessary or sufficient cause of BDD.

COGNITIVE BEHAVIORAL MODEL

The cognitive-behavioral model of BDD (e.g., Veale, Gournay et al., 1996; Wilhelm, Buhlmann, Cook, Greenberg, & Dimaite, 2010) acknowledges the role of psychological, biological, and socio-environmental factors in the etiology and maintenance of an individual's BDD. For instance, a trigger situation, such as seeing one's reflection in the mirror, may set off a cycle of BDD thoughts and behaviors. A cognitive (selective attention) bias may make individuals with BDD vulnerable to attend to minor appearance concerns. For example, individuals with BDD have a tendency to pay attention only to certain (perceived flawed) details within the reflected image, rather than experiencing the holistic image in the mirror (e.g., attending to a minor blemish or a small patch of hair rather than on the rest of one's face or overall appearance). Next, the individual experiences negative thoughts, based on his or her existing values and assumptions about appearance standards and the importance of physical appearance.

BDD patients tend to attach undue significance to appearance as related to their self-worth and social acceptance. For example, the individual might experience thoughts such as, "my hair is limp," followed by the subsequent interpretation, "If my hair is limp, I look defective; no one will want to date me." Beliefs that "I have to be perfect to be loved" and "appearance is the most important thing" are common in BDD. This type of negative thinking is typically followed by negative emotions, including anxiety, shame, disgust, guilt, and sadness. Anyone might see a mirror and think, "oh, my hair looks limp today," but the level of importance placed on appearance in determining one's self-worth will determine how much of an impact it will have on one's emotional state. Thus, any perceived imperfection becomes cause for severe distress, and BDD patients are compelled to try to ameliorate their distress by engaging in rituals (e.g., excessive grooming or camouflaging, reassurance seeking, mirror checking, skin-picking) or avoidance (e.g., of bright lighting, mirrors, social situations) in order to improve their perceived flaw or to prevent distress. Paradoxically, while BDD-related behaviors may provide some short-term relief, attending to appearance concerns via rituals and avoidance can worsen the perceived flaw (e.g., picking at perceived acne can cause reddening and infection of the skin), and increases preoccupation and distress over time.

Assessment

CLASSIFICATION

BDD is defined by a preoccupation with an imagined defect in appearance, which causes clinically significant distress or impairment and is not better accounted for by another disorder (American Psychiatric Association [APA], 2000). Notably, the behavioral symptoms typically associated with BDD (i.e., rituals and avoidance) are not featured under the current nosology; however, maladaptive behaviors are an important target for assessment and treatment. BDD is currently classified as a somatoform disorder with other soma- (i.e., body) focused disorders, including hypochondriasis, somatization disorder, conversion disorder, and pain disorder. However, the appropriate placement of BDD within the *Diagnostic and Statistical Manual of Mental*

Disorders (DSM) has been the source of recent debate. Moreover, symptom overlap between BDD and other disorders (e.g., social phobia, OCD, eating disorders) can make the diagnostic process challenging.

COMORBIDITY AND DIFFERENTIAL DIAGNOSIS

Many researchers (e.g., Chosak et al., 2008; Hadley et al., 2002; Hollander, 2005; Neziroglu & Khemlani Patel, 2005; Phillips, McElroy et al., 1993) have suggested that BDD may be better conceptualized as part of a putative obsessive compulsive spectrum, based on its similarities to obsessive compulsive disorder with regard to phenomenology (repetitive thought and behavior), family history, biological correlates, and treatment response. Based on its considerable comorbidity with depression, it has also been suggested that BDD be grouped under an affective spectrum, which would include other Axis I disorders, such as major depressive disorder, anxiety disorders (e.g., OCD, GAD, panic disorder), and bulimia (Phillips, McElroy, Hudson, & Pope, 1995; Phillips & Stout, 2006).

BDD frequently co-occurs with other Axis I disorders, including major depressive disorder (82%), social phobia (38%), obsessive compulsive disorder (30%), and substance use disorders (36%; Gunstad & Phillips, 2003; Phillips & Diaz, 1997); therefore, a structured clinical interview (e.g., SCID; First, Spitzer, Gibbon & Williams, 2002) should be used to assess, and to help differentiate between, DSM-IV diagnoses.

In addition, insight is often very limited and should be assessed; the appearance-related beliefs of nearly half of patients are delusional (Phillips, 2004; Phillips, McElroy, et al., 1994). In a recent survey of adults with BDD (N=164), current delusionality was reported in 33.1%, with lifetime rates as high as 75.6% (Phillips, Didie et al., 2006). Almost half of Phillips et al.'s sample (45.7%, N= 75) reported delusional ideas of reference, for example being convinced that others are laughing about or staring at their perceived imperfection (Phillips, Didie et al. 2006). In cases where the concern is delusional, a diagnosis of delusional disorder, somatic subtype, may be warranted; however, it has been argued that delusional and nondelusional forms of BDD represent a single disorder with a continuum of insight (Phillips, McElroy et al., 1994). Insight often varies over the course of the disorder, and individuals with delusional and nondelusional BDD are largely comparable with regard to demographic and clinical

features. Moreover, both variants respond preferentially to serotonin reuptake inhibitor (SRI) treatment. It is also important to distinguish delusions associated with BDD from other delusional symptomatology. Patients with schizophrenia or other psychotic disorders may also experience concerns about their appearance; however, these tend to be bizarre or unusual and are accompanied by other symptoms typical of the disorder, which are not found in BDD. Conversely, BDD delusions are restricted to somatic concerns, and do not respond well to antipsychotic medication (Phillips & Hollander, 2008).

BDD preoccupations and behaviors may resemble the time-consuming obsessions and rituals of OCD; however, the content of BDD concerns is focused on appearance. Similarly, individuals with eating disorders and hypochondriasis may also experience time-consuming thoughts and behaviors related to their bodies. The pervasive concern with shape and size, and perceptual distortions that characterize anorexia nervosa, may present similarly to BDD. Moreover, shape/weight concerns and dietary compulsions may be present in both disorders (Kittler, Menard, & Phillips, 2007). However, in the absence of other non–weight related concerns, weight-related symptoms and a pursuit of thinness (rather than to become normal in appearance) may be more indicative of primary eating pathology (Phillips, 2005). In hypochondriasis, patients may be overly concerned about perceived imperfections or irregularities in their appearance; however, whereas an individual with BDD would be concerned with the unattractiveness and social ramifications of a blemish, an individual with hypochondriasis would be worried that the blemish indicates the presence of a serious illness, such as cancer. As noted, individuals with BDD are often preoccupied by a fear of being negatively evaluated based on their perceived imperfections, which leads to significant social anxiety and avoidance. When fear of negative evaluation and social avoidance occur exclusively within the context of feared rejection based on appearance, social anxiety may be better conceptualized under a patient's BDD.

Finally, comorbid depression is very common. More than 60% of patients with BDD experience concurrent depression, and individuals with BDD are at high risk of suicide (Gunstad & Phillips, 2003; Phillips & Menard, 2006). A recent 4-year prospective study of BDD patients (n=185) (Phillips & Menard, 2006) found annual rates of suicidal ideation (57.8%), attempts (2.6%) and completions (0.3%) to be markedly high in BDD patients; the annual suicide rate in BDD (0.3%) patients is approximately 45 times higher than in the general U.S. population when controlling for age, gender, and geographic region (Phillips & Menard, 2006). These figures underscore the critical nature of early assessment and intervention for BDD and related depressive symptoms.

ASSESSMENT OF BDD SYMPTOMS

BDD is a disorder associated with secrecy and shame. Most people will not volunteer information about their symptoms, due to embarrassment or fear of being considered vain. Individuals may be afraid of drawing additional attention to their perceived imperfection by talking about it. Thus, when assessing BDD and related symptomatology, it is important to inquire about areas of concern, appearance-related thoughts, behaviors, distress, and impairment. As already noted, preoccupation with perceived appearance flaws manifests in time-consuming (e.g., more than 1 hour and often 3–8 hours per day) thoughts and behaviors, including excessive mirror checking, camouflaging to hide the flaw, grooming, reassurance seeking, scrutinizing or comparing with others' appearance, changing clothes, touching or measuring body parts, dieting, and tanning (Phillips, Didie et al., 2006; Phillips, Menard, Fay & Weisberg, 2005).

Oftentimes, these behaviors are compulsive in nature; patients feel compelled to repeatedly check, hide, or improve the perceived imperfection in order to reduce or prevent distress. However, patients also avoid people and situations that might exacerbate their appearance concerns. It is important to ask about situations that patients may be avoiding, or that they endure under great duress and with the use of rituals or neutralizing behaviors. For example, patients may alternate between checking and avoiding mirrors and other reflective surfaces (e.g., storefront windows). They may avoid activities or situations they believe would accentuate their flaws (e.g., bright lighting) or that would require revealing areas of concern (e.g., intimate sexual encounters, going to the beach or pool). Patients avoid social engagements, such as parties or dating, that they feel would lead to rejection based on their appearance, and they may stop going to work or school altogether. A majority of individuals with BDD are either single or divorced, which suggests difficulty forming and maintaining intimate relationships (Phillips, Pagano, Menard, et al., 2006).

The following assessment tools can be used to screen, diagnose, and assess for the severity of BDD.

The *Body Dysmorphic Disorder Questionnaire* (BDDQ; Phillips, 1996) is a brief self-report measure of appearance concerns, distress, and functional impairment. A perceived appearance flaw (not solely accounted for by weight or shape concerns) and at least moderate distress and/or functional impairment are required to meet criteria for a positive screen. The BDDQ is a screening tool and not indicated for use as a diagnostic instrument.

BDD Diagnostic Module. The BDD Diagnostic Module (*BDD-DM*) is a brief, semistructured module based on DSM-IV criteria used to diagnose BDD. The BDD-DM has yielded excellent interrater reliability (kappa = 0.96; Phillips, Atala & Pope, 1995).

The *Yale-Brown Obsessive Compulsive Scale Modified for BDD (BDD-YBOCS;* Phillips, Hollander, Rasmussen, & Aronowitz, 1997) is a reliable and valid 12-item semistructured clinician-administered scale, adapted from the Y-BOCS (Goodman, Price, Rasmussen, Mazure, & et al., 1989), that rates current severity of BDD symptoms. The BDD-YBOCS is easily administered, and is considered to be the gold standard for measuring BDD severity and change. It has strong interrater and test–retest reliability (ICC for total score = 0.99 and 0.88, respectively), internal consistency (Cronbach's α = 0.80), and convergent validity (Phillips et al., 1997). Scores range from 0 to 48. Although there are no empirically derived cutoff scores, a score of 20 or greater generally indicates moderate BDD.

The *Body Dysmorphic Disorder Examination (BDDE;* Rosen & Reiter, 1996) is a measure of BDD symptoms and body image disturbance available in both clinician-administered and self-report formats. Responses to each of the 34 items are rated on a 6-point scale, and scores range from 0 to 168 with higher scores indicating more severe symptoms. The BDDE has good test–retest reliability (r = 0.94), internal consistency (α = 0.95), and concurrent validity with other body image questionnaires (r = 0.68 to 0.83). The BDDE takes approximately 15–30 minutes to administer. Sensitivity to change in moderate to severely ill BDD patients has not been well established.

BDD Symptom Scale (BDD-SS; Wilhelm, 2006). This self-report scale identifies and rates the severity of specific BDD symptoms. The scale organizes symptoms into similar clusters of problem behaviors, such as checking and comparing; fixing and correcting appearance; avoiding and hiding; weight and shape concerns; accepting compliments; skin-picking and hair pulling; and seeking cosmetic surgery.

The scale also assesses problematic beliefs and attitudes about appearance.

The *Brown Assessment of Beliefs Scale (BABS;* Eisen et al., 1998) is a reliable and valid 7-item semistructured clinician-administered interview, designed to assess current delusionality and degree of insight into appearance beliefs. The BABS provides a dimensional score of insight from 0 to 24, with higher scores reflecting greater delusionality (Eisen et al., 1998). It also provides a categorical measure of insight, whereby delusionality is defined as a total score ≥ 18 and a score of 4 on item 1 (conviction). It has good interrater and test–retest reliability (ICC = 0.96 and 0.95), internal consistency (Cronbach's α = 0.87), convergent validity (r's = 0.56–0.85 with measures of delusionality), and divergent validity (r = 0.20 with the BDD-Y-BOCS (Eisen et al., 1998).

Treatment

Effective treatments are available for BDD. Cognitive behavioral therapy (CBT) and pharmacotherapy with serotonin reuptake inhibitors (SRIs) are considered the first-line treatments for BDD.

Although many patients seek cosmetic treatment, these procedures typically offer little relief, and often worsen BDD symptoms (Crerand et al., 2005; Phillips, Grant, Siniscalchi, & Albertini 2001; Sarwer & Crerand, 2008). Of the minority of patients who experience an improvement in BDD symptoms following cosmetic procedures, benefits tend to be short term, and some patients become preoccupied by worries about how long the improvement will last (Crerand et al., 2005). More commonly, patients become increasingly distraught following surgery, and may blame themselves for electing a procedure they feel caused them disfigurement. In addition to turning against the self, extreme dissatisfaction following cosmetic procedures has resulted in threats, lawsuits, and homicides against physicians who performed the procedures (Sarwer & Crerand, 2008).

COGNITIVE-BEHAVIORAL THERAPY

Cognitive-behavioral therapy (CBT) is the most studied and empirically supported psychosocial treatment for BDD. Cognitive-behavioral treatments are based on the CBT model of BDD, and aim to improve functioning and quality of life by identifying and modifying maladaptive thought and behavior patterns. CBT for BDD also addresses current mood and life events as they influence BDD symptoms. Most studies have combined cognitive

and behavioral methods, although cognitive-behavioral therapy, cognitive therapy (cognitive restructuring alone), and behavior therapy (exposure and response prevention alone) have all been found to be effective in treating BDD, and can be delivered successfully in group (Rosen, 1995; Wilhelm, Otto, Lohr, & Deckersbach, 1999) and individual formats (McKay, 1999; McKay, Todaro, Neziroglu, & Campisi, 1997; Neziroglu, McKay, Todaro, & Yaryura-Tobias, 1996; Veale, Gournay et al., 1996). Comprehensive treatments generally include psychoeducation, self-monitoring, exposure with response prevention, cognitive restructuring, and relapse prevention; treatment may also include mindfulness/attention retraining, habit reversal, and activity scheduling.

CBT for BDD was first studied systematically by Rosen and colleagues (1995), who developed a group CBT protocol. Rosen et al. used cognitive techniques to modify dysfunctional thoughts, and behavioral techniques to reduce rituals and behavioral avoidance, over eight 2-hour sessions of group CBT. Compared to a no-treatment control group, 82% of the CBT group responded to treatment and reported a significant reduction in BDD symptoms. In addition, Rosen and colleagues found that treatment gains were maintained in 77% of the CBT group at 4.5-month follow-up. The generalizability of this well-designed study, however, is limited by its sample, which included females with primary body shape and weight concerns, whose BDD symptoms were milder and insight greater relative to typical BDD symptoms. Wilhelm and colleagues (1999) also reported significant reductions in mean BDD-Y-BOCS scores following a group treatment protocol: BDD-YBOCS scores decreased a mean of 9.6 points from 29.9 to 20.3 ($t(10)= 3.94$, p < . 01). Wilhelm et al.'s sample was characterized by BDD patients more similar to those typically described in the literature; patients in the Wilhelm et al. sample were severely ill, with substantial comorbidity and a high degree of functional and social impairment, as evidenced by rates of unemployment (39% vs. 22%) and marriage (0% vs. 52%) relative to Rosen et al.'s sample.

Veale and colleagues (1996) reported significantly greater reductions in mean BDD-YBOCS scores for patients treated with individual CBT relative to wait list control. Following 12 weeks of individual CBT, 7 of 9 treated patients were rated as recovered (BDD symptoms were rated as absent or subclinical), whereas all patients on the waiting list met clinical BDD diagnosis at the end of the trial

(Veale, Gournay et al., 1996). In the CBT group, BDD-YBOCS scores decreased a mean of 11.25 points (from 22.00 to 10.25). However, delusional and suicidal patients were excluded from this study, and the sample comprised 90% women, thereby limiting the generalizability of the results.

Patients have reported reduction in depressive symptoms, in addition to improvement in BDD symptoms, following CBT (Veale et al., 1996, Wilhelm et al., 1999). Empirical research is still needed to determine the optimal length and frequency of treatment. It has been suggested (Rosen, 1995; Veale, Gournay et al., 1996) that 18–22 sessions may be optimal. Spacing apart of final sessions and the use of booster sessions may help to reinforce a patient's independent use of skills (Wilhelm et al., 2010). In addition, modular psychological treatments are promising (e.g., Eifert, Schulte, Zvolensky, Lejuez & Lau, 1997; Wilhelm et al., 2010; Wilhelm, Fama, et al., in press) and allow for a flexible, individualized approach to treatment. For example, a modular manual for BDD (Wilhelm, Phillips, & Steketee in press) offers specific modules to address skin-picking, muscle dysmorphia (e.g., weight/shape concerns), and the desire to pursue cosmetic surgery. Therapists administer measures that assess specific symptomatology, and subsequently use only the available modules as appropriate (Wilhelm, Fama, et al., in press).

Assessment and Psychoeducation. CBT begins with a careful assessment of BDD and related symptoms. Clinicians should inquire about BDD-related areas of concern, thoughts, behaviors, and impairment. An assessment of motivation is helpful to determine potential barriers to treatment—for example, resistance to a psychological treatment is common when insight is poor. The treatment rationale and CBT approach to BDD should be discussed. Review with patients that the goal of CBT is to elicit and modify maladaptive beliefs and behaviors maintaining their symptoms. Each session begins with a review of symptoms and homework, and an agenda is set to determine which strategies to cover during the session; agendas are determined collaboratively between therapist and patient. Each session ends with a review and discussion of an assignment to be completed during the week. The importance of between-session homework should be stressed. The session review allows for patient feedback, and for the therapist to address any questions or concerns about the session or homework. The patient is asked to refrain from engaging in surgical or dermatological procedures during the course of CBT, as this

type of intervention is contraindicated with CBT treatment goals and outcome. If the patient is ready to engage in treatment, it can be useful to set and sign a treatment contract agreeing to the treatment goals and plan.

Following a thorough assessment, the first phase of active treatment includes psychoeducation and assessment of motivation. The therapist provides information about BDD and the CBT model. The therapist and patient review factors that may have contributed to the development and maintenance of the patient's BDD. As described above, the CBT model of BDD acknowledges the impact of biological and socio-environmental factors, but focuses treatment strategies on the specific beliefs and behavior patterns currently contributing to the maintenance of symptoms. The model highlights how patients' appearance-related distress is an understandable consequence of their beliefs, but that beliefs are often the inaccurate and/or unhelpful result of a cognitive bias. Moreover, maladaptive thoughts are upsetting, and thus lead to drastic behaviors intended to alleviate distress. Patients learn that ritualistic and avoidant behavior may provide short-term relief or accommodation, but paradoxically worsen BDD beliefs, maladaptive behavioral tendencies, and distress in the long run.

In the context of individualizing the model for each patient, details about the patient's BDD, including course, family history, daily routine, past treatments, and co-occurring disorders should be discussed. More specifically, the clinician inquires about dissatisfaction with each part of the face or body, beliefs about appearance ("I need to look perfect to leave the house"), related maladaptive behaviors (excessive body checking, grooming, makeup, camouflage, exercise, etc.), and avoided situations (people, places, situations).

Motivational Enhancement. In addition to assessment of motivation, the first phase of treatment often includes motivational enhancement strategies (Miller & Rollnick, 2002). Many BDD patients are ambivalent about receiving therapy for their disorder, and may see a considerable downside to giving up maladaptive beliefs and behaviors. It is important for clinicians to maintain a nonjudgmental stance to allow for a candid discussion of pros/cons of change, and the impact BDD has had on a patient's life. Avoid the trap of trying to persuade the patient that the BDD concerns are irrational, or, worse still, to reassure him or her about any appearance issues. For instance, rather than argue with the patient that he or she shouldn't pursue another cosmetic surgery procedure, the therapist may use Socratic questioning regarding the pros and cons of further surgery. It is helpful to provide the patient with psychoeducation about the outcome of BDD patients who have undergone cosmetic surgery, and have the patient integrate in any data he or she may have from prior surgeries. Most patients can agree that appearance has had a severe impact on their life and functioning; thus, coming to a common goal of improving functioning and quality of life can be an effective approach.

Increased symptom severity and poor insight may require a slower pace through treatment. Moving quickly through treatment may be tempting with very ill patients; however, patients may still be ambivalent about engaging in CBT and thus resist (overtly or covertly) using CBT strategies. Assigning homework, such as symptom monitoring, from the very beginning of treatment helps to socialize the patient to this central expectation of CBT for BDD, and allows the therapist to help the patient problem-solve barriers to homework as needed.

Cognitive Strategies. The second active phase of CBT for BDD involves cognitive evaluation and restructuring. Cognitive restructuring helps to increase insight into maladaptive beliefs about appearance concerns. It is helpful to review common cognitive distortions, errors in thinking that affect how we feel about certain situations, particularly as they relate to BDD. Typical cognitive distortions associated with BDD include jumping to conclusions ("if I go to the party, nobody will talk to me"); mindreading ("that man didn't make eye contact; that must mean he thinks I look hideous and deformed"); and all-or-nothing thinking ("this pimple makes me disgusting"). Homework during this phase of treatment involves using thought records to monitor the frequency and impact of BDD-related thinking errors as they come up in daily life.

After the patient has learned to identify problematic BDD thoughts, he or she practices generating alternative ways of thinking by developing and evaluating rational responses to the distorted beliefs ("that man didn't make eye contact, maybe because he was thinking about something else, or maybe he is shy"). Cognitive restructuring exercises are guided by the use of thought record and restructuring forms. Homework would involve having the patient fill out restructuring forms when he or she notices their anxiety or distress building, and/or before engaging in a maladaptive BDD behavior.

Behavioral Strategies. Once a patient has successfully learned and practiced using cognitive restructuring

skills, behavioral strategies may be initiated. A thorough assessment will have helped identify maladaptive behaviors to be discussed and targeted for change. Reviewing the role of rituals and avoidance in the maintenance of the patient's BDD reinforces the rationale for exposure and response prevention (ERP): the patient's gradual exposure to anxiety-provoking situations without the use of rituals or safety behaviors. It is helpful to remind patients that while rituals and avoidance may provide short-term relief, these behaviors typically worsen distress in the long run. The therapist will help the patient to develop a list of anxiety-provoking and avoided situations (hierarchy) that he or she is encouraged to gradually reenter (exposure) without the use of rituals or safety behaviors (response prevention). Initial exposure tasks are mild-to-moderately challenging, and likely to produce a mastery experience for the patient—for example, going to the supermarket without styling one's hair, and without touching it or checking it in the store or car mirror reflection. Over time, patients embark on more difficult tasks, such as meeting friends at a busy restaurant or bar without having styled one's hair, and refraining from touching or checking. Increasing normal activities can sometimes function as an exposure/response prevention assignment (e.g., going through the day without the typical camouflage such as loose clothing, hat, or sunglasses). Activities are repeated until the patient has had the opportunity to habituate to the anxiety and can perform the activity without the use of any safety or neutralizing behaviors. Avoidance of daily activities, or activities that would require showing off one's body, is common. For example, patients may avoid shopping (i.e., changing and observing themselves in a dressing room), swimming or going to the beach, intimate sexual encounters, going to work or class, or accepting social invitations, for fear of social rejection. In this case, situations aimed at broadening overall social experiences are included in the exposure hierarchy. For example, instead of avoiding friends on days when she thought her nose or hair looked really "awful," a patient is encouraged to go out twice per week with friends for lunch or dinner.

Exposure and response prevention exercises can be set up as behavioral experiments, with the goal of information gathering to test a particular hypothesis: "if I don't wear that long-sleeved shirt, someone will comment on my hairy arms." In a behavioral experiment, patients are asked to record specific observable predictions about the outcome of designated tasks, and then reevaluate their beliefs based on the actual outcome. Finally, behavioral change tasks can be assigned with the purpose of behavioral activation and enhancing a holistic sense of self-for instance, when encouraging a patient to hone a new skill or hobby in order to increase their mood, self-efficacy, and expand their vision of self-worth beyond appearance.

A perceptual retraining task known as *mirror retraining* is a behavioral strategy unique to the treatment of BDD and other body image disorders (Delinsky & Wilson, 2006; Wilhelm, 2006; Wilhelm, Phillips, et al., in press). As described above, individuals with BDD often have a conflicted relationship with mirrors and other reflective surfaces. A patient may alternate between spending hours in front of the mirror inspecting, grooming, prodding, or picking, and extraordinary efforts to avoid catching any glimpse of their reflection. Perceptual retraining in the mirror helps patients to see "the big picture" rather than hone in on perceived "hot spots" and problem areas, by teaching the patient to observe and describe his or her body in *objective, nonjudgmental* terms. For example, patients learn to modify negative self-talk so that "frizzy, wiry, muddy" hair is described as "shoulder length, dark brown, wavy." As part of this exercise, patients typically stand in front of a full-length mirror and describe the whole body, starting with the hair and ending with the feet. Patients are instructed to refrain from negative labeling, and to avoid ritual and safety behaviors (e.g., touching or measuring flaws, closing eyes). It is helpful for the therapist to demonstrate the task first. Initially, this can be a very challenging and emotionally charged task for patients, but after repeated trials, most patients report mirror retraining to be one of the most powerful experiences during CBT.

Advanced Cognitive Strategies. After some cognitive and behavioral progress has been made, treatment targets the patient's core beliefs. Core beliefs are the deeply rooted beliefs individuals hold about themselves, the future, and the world. Whereas a healthy person might endorse the statement, "I'm a good enough person" or "I'm attractive enough," a person with BDD is more likely to hold core beliefs such as, "I'm inadequate," "I'm worthless," or "I'm unlovable" (Veale, Boocock et al., 1996). These core beliefs filter a patient's experiences, are self-maintaining, and if not addressed, are likely to impede CBT progress and long-term maintenance of gains. Oftentimes a patient's core beliefs will have manifested during the course of the therapy. However, the therapist can help to elicit core beliefs by using the downward arrow technique. Using this approach, the therapist acts as a broken record, continuing to ask a patient to elaborate on the worst consequences of their beliefs (e.g., "and if that were true, what would that mean?") until the patient reaches his/her core belief. Once the maladaptive core belief is elicited, distorted core beliefs can be tested through cognitive restructuring records, behavioral experiments, and strategies such as the cognitive continuum. Patients are encouraged to take a more objective approach by evaluating beliefs as if they were detectives or scientists, judging the accuracy and utility of beliefs based on evidence and pros and cons of holding the belief. For example, for a core belief of being unlovable, a patient could be asked to generate a continuum of "lovability" from 0 ("completely and universally hated") to 100 ("completely and universally loved"). The patient would first assign himself or herself a rating on the scale, and then anchor the continuum by providing examples of behavior for each of the extremes (0 and 100) and for the middle of the scale (50). Patients should also be asked to consider situational factors that may impact one's score on the continuum. Once a patient has acquired this data, he or she will re-rank himself or herself on the revised scale, and generate a more neutral, adaptive belief based on the new evidence.

Relapse Prevention. Finally, a relapse prevention plan is essential to helping patients maintain treatment gains. Aspects of relapse prevention for BDD may include developing a formal list of strategies, encouraging self-therapy sessions, recognizing triggers for increased BDD concerns, and differentiating a lapse (short-term increase in symptoms) from a relapse (return of full disorder). If the patient holds maladaptive beliefs about ending therapy, these are elicited and evaluated before ending the treatment. Therapy sessions may be spaced out toward the end of treatment, so that the patient becomes more independent of the therapist and more accustomed to selecting and implementing strategies for themselves. For a more detailed description of CBT for BDD, we refer the reader to Wilhelm et al (2010). CBT for BDD is now being developed for adolescents; for a more detailed description of CBT for adolescent BDD, the reader is referred to Greenberg et al. (2010).

PHARMACOLOGICAL TREATMENT

Available data indicate appropriate pharmacotherapy improves BDD and associated symptoms, such as depression (Ipser, Sander, & Stein, 2009). No medications are FDA approved for BDD. However, serotonin reuptake inhibitors (SRIs) have been the most extensively studied pharmacotherapy for BDD, and are considered the first-line medication treatment (Ipser et al., 2009; National Institute for Clinical Excellence, 2005). Early case reports (Brady, Austin, & Lydiard, 1990; Hollander, Liebowitz, Winchel, Klumker, & Klein, 1989; Phillips, 1991) first suggested the effectiveness of fluoxetine and clomipramine for BDD, and prompted subsequent, larger clinical series and open label trials. Two randomized controlled studies have been done. Taken together, BDD symptoms significantly improved with SRI treatment, with a response rate of 53%–73% (intention-to-treat analyses, all published SRI data; see Ipser et al., 2009).

The first controlled medication study for BDD compared clomipramine to desipramine in a double-blind cross-over design (Hollander et al., 1999). Subjects (n=29) were randomized to 8 weeks of each medication. Clomipramine was more effective than the non-SRI antidepressant desipramine in reducing BDD symptom severity (Hollander et al., 1999). Furthermore, these data underscore the importance of specifically treating BDD symptoms, and not just depression, in patients with BDD (Hollander et al., 1999; Phillips & Hollander, 2008).

In a double-blind placebo controlled trial, subjects (n=67) were randomized to 12 weeks of treatment with fluoxetine or placebo (Phillips, Albertini, & Rasmussen, 2002). Fluoxetine was significantly more efficacious than placebo; more than half (53%) of subjects responded to fluoxetine compared to 18% to placebo. Moreover, a retrospective analysis of this cohort demonstrated a protective effect against worsening of suicidal symptoms in the fluoxetine group relative to the placebo group (Phillips and Kelly, 2009).

In both controlled trials, SRIs were efficacious in treating individuals with delusional BDD as well as those with the nondelusional variant. Of note, clomipramine was even more effective for delusional patients than nondelusional ones (Hollander et al., 1999).

Open label studies have also been done with other SRIs. A 16-week open label trial of fluvoxamine significantly reduced BDD severity in 63% of subjects (n=30; Phillips, Dwight, & McElroy, 1998). In a 10-week open trial of fluvoxamine, 10 of 15 subjects were much or very much improved on the CGI, and 10 of 12 who completed treatment were responders (Perugi et al., 1996). Open label studies of citalopram (n=15) and escitalopram (n=15) are also promising; patients show improvement in BDD symptoms, functioning, and quality of life in about 73% of participants (Phillips, 2006; Phillips & Najar, 2003).

SRIs are potentially efficacious for children and adolescents with BDD; however, data are limited to case reports and one case series (Albertini, Phillips, & Guvremont, 1996; Phillips, Atala, & Albertini, 1995). In a case series of 33 children and adolescents, 53% (n=19) of subjects treated with an SRI demonstrated significant improvement in BDD symptoms (Albertini & Phillips, 1999). Of note, SRIs are already indicated for the treatment of similar pediatric disorders, including OCD and depression.

It is recommended that SRIs be administered at their optimal dose (i.e., highest tolerated dose) and duration (e.g., at least 12–16 weeks) before trying other medications or augmentation strategies. Phillips and colleagues (2006) recently examined the characteristics of pharmacotherapy (i.e., frequency, type, dose, and adequacy) received by 151 individuals with BDD (Phillips, Pagano, & Menard, 2006). While nearly three-quarters (72.9%) of the sample had received pharmacotherapy (mean number of medications= 5, SD=4.5), most commonly SRIs, SRI trials were not adequate. Thus, most patients had not received medication at the dose or duration associated with BDD symptom improvement. When prescribed appropriately for BDD, most SRIs work. In a chart review of 90 patients, 63% (n=55) of adequate SRI trials led to clinically significant improvement in BDD symptoms (Phillips, Albertini, Siniscalchi, Khan, & Robinson, 2001).

Successful SRI treatment can reduce BDD symptoms, including preoccupation with appearance and related behaviors. Insight and depression may also improve over the course of treatment. Following successful pharmacotherapy, patients may report a change in the distress associated with appearance, although they think they look the same. Conversely, some patients do report a belief that their appearance has improved over the course of SRI treatment. For patients who would like or need to discontinue medication, gradual tapering is recommended to mitigate the rate of relapse. Combining SRI discontinuation with CBT may also help reduce the risk of relapse; however, this approach requires empirical investigation.

Non-SRI medications have not been well studied as monotherapy for BDD. Venlafaxine, a serotonin-norepinephrine reuptake inhibitor (SNRI), was found to be effective in improving BDD symptoms in a small open trial (n=11; Allen et al., 2008). Until larger, controlled studies are completed, SRIs are the first-line medication treatment.

No research has directly compared the efficacy of SRIs for BDD. In a chart review study, 43% of patients who did not respond to an initial SRI responded to at least one subsequent SRI trial (Phillips, Albertini, et al., 2001). Patients who respond initially to an SRI, but who need to switch (e.g., due to side effects, insurance coverage), fare even more favorably with subsequent SRI trials, with 92% of subsequent trials resulting in response (Phillips, Albertini, et al., 2001). Thus, if a patient has not responded to an adequate SRI trial (high dose, 12–16 weeks), another SRI may be tried.

Augmentation strategies may be warranted if patients do not respond to an adequate SRI trial(s) (Phillips & Hollander, 2008). A small double-blind controlled trial examined pimozide versus placebo augmentation to fluoxetine (n=28); pimozide was not more efficacious than placebo (Phillips. 2005). Buspirone augmentation has been shown to provide improvement in patients who had not responded, or only partially responded, to SRI treatment (Phillips, Albertini, et al., 2001).

Combining cognitive behavioral therapy with an SRI may be helpful for some patients; however, empirical research is needed to investigate the efficacy of combined approaches.

TREATMENT SELECTION

A meta-analysis comparing medications to CBT, BT, and CT found that all approaches led to improvements in BDD symptoms and depression (Williams et al., 2006). Large effect sizes were found both for case series and RCTs, with significantly larger effect sizes for CBT (M_d = +1.78, $Q_{W3}(6)$ = 6.10, p>0.05) than for pharmacotherapy (M_d = +0.92, $Q_{W1}(7)$ = 12.32, p>0.05) (χ^2 (1) = 15.65, p <0.01). No significant differences emerged between CBT and BT, or between BT and pharmacotherapy.

Although CBT and SRIs are effective monotherapies, no studies have examined their combined efficacy in treating BDD. Existing research in OCD may be helpful in understanding the role for combined treatment in specific clinical BDD situations. For example, both ERP (e.g., Foa et al., 2005), CT (e.g., Wilhelm et al., 2005) and SRI (e.g., Koran et al., 2007) monotherapies have been found effective in reducing OCD severity. In studies exploring combined treatment of OCD, both ERP and combined therapies fare better than medication alone (Foa et al., 2005). However, combined treatment (SRI + ERP) may be more effective for some patients, including patients with more severe symptoms, comorbid depression (Cottraux et al., 1990;

Hohagen et al., 1998), or with dominant obsessions (Hohagen et al., 1998).

In the absence of data on combined treatments in BDD, an adequate trial of SRI or CBT monotherapy may be administered before augmenting treatment in cases of mild to moderate BDD. However, patient factors, including symptom severity, delusionality, comorbidity, treatment adherence, and partial response to an adequate monotherapy should be considered when determining the best combination or sequencing of therapies (for review see Simpson and Leibowitz, 2005). For example, even after an adequate trial SRI therapy, many patients continue to be symptomatic. CBT can be used to taper patients from medication or, when used concurrently, to continue to reduce symptom severity and improve both functioning and quality of life (Simpson et al., 2008). Conversely, if, following an adequate trial of CBT, a patient's BDD symptoms, BDD-related delusions, or clinically significant depression are unremitting, augmentation with an SRI may be considered.

Finally, the empirical literature should be taken together with patient's preference for treatment. In the absence of empirical support for combination therapy in BDD, it is important to consider the financial and psychological burden of adding unnecessary treatment. Making sure the patient is an active participant in his or her treatment can increase motivation and treatment compliance, both of which are positively associated with outcome. This is of particular importance in CBT, where the goal of treatment is to enhance accurate attributions and self-efficacy. When a patient simultaneously begins two treatments—for example, a psychological and pharmacological intervention—the patient may be prone to attribute effects of change to medication rather than to active changes they have made to their thought and behavior patterns. Enhancing a patient's ability to make personal attributions regarding treatment gains is important to achieving and maintaining maximum outcome in CBT.

Case Vignette

Julia, who was described at the beginning of this chapter, was 24 years old when she presented for treatment. Her decision to seek treatment was not due to her own body image concerns, but rather a way to assuage her husband's concerns about her. They had already had numerous fights about surgeries and Julia's seemingly irrational concerns regarding her nose and hair. At intake, the strong conviction with which Julia held her beliefs about her perceived imperfections became apparent. During the assessment, the therapist asked about BDD and related symptoms. The therapist used a SCID to assess for Axis I diagnostic disorders, the BDD-Diagnostic Module to diagnosis BDD and a BDD-YBOCS and BDD-SS to further explore the details and severity of Julia's appearance-related concerns. Julia met diagnostic criteria for severe BDD (with poor but not delusional insight; BDD-YBOCS = 35) and major depression. Julia described how her depression worsened and her withdrawal increased after her second rhinoplasty procedure one year ago. She feared that "others would be scared off when they saw her disfigured nose."

For the past few months, Julia reported leaving the house only a handful of times, and following time-intensive camouflaging and checking rituals. Her depression started subsequent to, and only in the context of, her BDD symptoms. Although Julia was resistant to psychiatric treatment, she felt strongly about improving the quality of her life and helping to ease the distress her concerns had caused her husband. Julia voiced her skepticism about improving without changing her appearance; however, after reviewing the evidence (i.e., her dissatisfaction following previous surgeries), she agreed it was worth trying something new. Julia was not amenable to pharmacotherapy. Had she been amenable, SRI monotherapy would have also been an appropriate consideration, given her poor insight and depressive symptoms. However, given Julia's preference, she and the therapist agreed to begin CBT for BDD; having Julia's husband sign on as part of the treatment team (i.e., offering help and support with homework assignments) facilitated the decision to pursue CBT.

Following the initial evaluation and assessment of symptoms, motivational issues around treatment were discussed. The therapist used Socratic questioning to elicit the pros/cons of Julia's current beliefs and behaviors. Julia was able to agree that some aspect of her beliefs and behaviors were maladaptive, in so far as they were time consuming, expensive, and causing her and her husband to become upset. After Julia was on board with treatment, they discussed the individual factors that contributed to the development and maintenance of Julia's BDD. For instance, as a first-generation American, Julia recalled the pressures she felt as a child to fit in. She remembered feeling as though she "didn't fit in anywhere because [she] wasn't as white as [her] friends, or as Chinese as [her] parents or cousins." Growing up in a mostly Caucasian,

upper middle-class neighborhood, Julia reported that her friends would frequently play with and comment on her "stick straight, silky hair" or petite nose. When Julia began experiencing physical and psychological changes during puberty, she remembered thinking, "There's something wrong with me" and "It's not okay for me to have a problem, I will disgrace my family," which caused her to keep her appearance concerns bottled up inside of her. Julia felt very ashamed about her appearance, and ashamed that she worried so much about her appearance. She never sought help from a mental health professional for her concerns.

During the initial stages of treatment, Julia was taught how to identify her current maladaptive thoughts and evaluate them more objectively. For example, Julia was avoiding leaving the house because of feared negative social evaluation based on her nose. The therapist helped Julia to monitor her negative thoughts in trigger situations using thought records. Next, the therapist helped Julia to identify cognitive distortions (mindreading, jumping to conclusions) and used Socratic questioning ("Has anyone commented negatively on your nose?" "What have people said to you?") to evaluate her beliefs more objectively, and generate a more accurate belief. Another useful strategy was developing and modifying a self-esteem pie chart, in which various components of self-esteem were identified and targeted for development. For example, Julia was able to recognize that by basing her self-esteem solely on her appearance, she was neglecting many positive qualities that made her feel good about herself, including her intelligence, creativity, strong family relationships, and personality characteristics (e.g., being a kind, loyal, and compassionate wife, daughter, and friend).

As Julia became more adept at cognitive restructuring, a hierarchy was developed to address anxiety-provoking and avoided situations (phone calls, bright lighting, social activities). Items from the hierarchy were worked on, in and out of session, to gradually introduce Julia to anxiety-provoking situations without the use of rituals or safety behaviors. For example, the therapist first asked Julia to attend sessions with makeup but without her sunglasses, and over time worked up to more difficult assignments until Julia was able to tolerate each experience. Perceptual (i.e., mirror) retraining was used to help Julia perceive the big picture. She learned how to use a mirror without focusing selectively on "hot spots" like her nose or hair. Julia was reminded that anyone who spends a significant time staring at their least favorite feature could be expected to become discouraged about their appearance. Finally, Julia's core beliefs (e.g., "I'm unacceptable") were addressed and modified using cognitive strategies, such as the cognitive continuum, so that she could develop more adaptive and accurate beliefs (e.g., "Nobody is perfect, but I'm good enough and have friends, family, and a husband who cares about me."), as well as an exploration of Julia's beliefs within their cultural context. She and the therapist discussed how acculturation stress contributed to Julia's sense that she did not fit in; they discussed within-group intergenerational conflicts that Julia experienced within her own family as a first-generation Asian American, as well the conflict Julia felt between fitting in at home versus within her peer group.

Julia's treatment lasted 22 sessions, with the 2 last sessions tapered over 2-week periods. The final sessions were spent identifying and planning for future challenges (e.g., her brother's wedding, applying for jobs). By the end of treatment, Julia was reasonably independent at applying all of her skills and managing BDD triggering situations. Her BDD-YBOCS had decreased from a 35 (severe) to an 10 (subclinical), and the prospect of further surgery was no longer appealing to Julia after treatment. Although Julia still experienced some negative beliefs about her appearance, they were less frequent, intense, and meaningful to her. As Julia's symptoms improved, she was able to take classes and work toward a career in graphic design. Julia no longer avoided phone calls or social invitations, and by the end of treatment, Julia was going out on a date night with her husband and having lunch with at least one friend on a weekly basis. A more detailed description of the treatment strategies can be found in Wilhelm and colleagues (2010; in press).

Troubleshooting: Clinical Considerations and Challenges

Several factors can complicate the treatment of individuals suffering with BDD. As noted, persons with BDD often elude accurate diagnosis because they are not likely to seek treatment for BDD symptoms. Shame and embarrassment may preclude individuals from seeking treatment for "issues of vanity," and those who seek treatment often seek physical (i.e., medical and nonmedical cosmetic) treatment for psychological concerns.

AMBIVALENCE AND MOTIVATION

Ambivalence around treatment is common, and may stem in part from a patient's level of insight into the disorder. Of patients who present for psychiatric or psychological services, many have done so at the urging of loved ones (e.g., spouses or parents). In addition to ambivalence due to poor or wavering insight, patients may also report uneasiness associated with treatment. For example, patients may describe a negative association to being on a medication, or the difficulty associated with intentional exposure to previously avoided situations (i.e., CBT). Thus, motivation to change may be low. Moreover, many patients have poor insight into their symptoms and mistakenly believe that cosmetic procedures are their only hope, which can make them afraid to commit to a treatment focused on psychological rather than physical change. Motivational enhancement strategies (e.g., Miller and Rollnick's Motivational Interviewing, 2002) can be used to resolve ambivalence and increase a patient's readiness to engage in treatment. Motivation can be assessed using the University of Rhode Island Change Assessment Questionnaire (URICA; DiClemente & Hughes, 1990), a 32-item self-report questionnaire that measures 4 stages of change: pre-contemplation, contemplation, action, and maintenance. Motivation will likely wax and wane over the course of treatment; thus, motivational enhancement strategies should be used throughout the course of treatment as needed. In addition, a clear treatment rationale and gradual, collaborative approach to treatment can help patients feel more comfortable, and thus more engaged in the treatment.

DELUSIONAL BDD

Level of insight may affect treatment, and considerations should be made when working with patients with fixed beliefs (delusional BDD). Patients who are convinced that their problems are physically based may be difficult to engage in a psychosocial treatment aimed at reducing psychological distress. In such cases, a more gradual approach is recommended, with a focus on evaluating the utility and associated distress of self-defeating beliefs, rather than refuting the accuracy of such beliefs (Wilhelm et al., 2010). Concurrent or sequential pharmacotherapy with CBT may also be indicated for patients with delusional BDD. As noted, patients with delusional BDD fare as well as those with the nondelusional variant in response to SRI treatment.

DEPRESSION AND SUICIDALITY

Depressive symptoms (e.g., lethargy, anhedonia, impaired concentration) can make it difficult for patients to participate effectively in treatment.

Thoroughly assessing the nature and impairment of depressive symptoms can help inform a decision about treatment focus and sequencing. For example, when depression seems primary, or interferes with a patient's ability to engage in CBT, a decision may be made to target the depression directly through CBT (focused on depressive symptoms) or pharmacotherapy. Due to the markedly high rates of suicidality associated with BDD, depressive symptoms, including suicidality, should be monitored closely throughout treatment. Acute suicidality may warrant a higher level of care.

SKILLS DEFICITS AND QUALITY OF LIFE

A successful treatment involves increasing a patient's functioning and quality of life; usually this is achieved via symptom reduction. However, other quality of life factors may need to be addressed, including skills deficits and psychosocial stressors. Because of its early onset, BDD can interrupt typical skills acquisition, such as social and problem-solving skills, and the ability to tolerate and cope with distressing emotions. Areas for skills building should be identified throughout the course of treatment. Similarly, patients with BDD, particularly those with severe symptoms, may have limited financial, occupational, and social resources. In addition, many patients have spent so much time engaged in BDD-related thoughts and rituals, they have given up other daily activities or hobbies. Thus, a comprehensive treatment should focus on helping patients to rebuild activity across the various dimensions of their life, increasing social networks, hobbies, and occupational activity.

SPECIAL POPULATIONS

Adolescents. Adolescence combines a period of substantial physical, psychological, emotional, and social changes with an increased value placed on body image (Levine & Smolak, 2002). Taken together, it is no wonder that adolescents are so concerned with and often dismayed by their own appearance. BDD typically onsets during adolescence when appearance concerns are common and often normalized as something one ought to "tough out" or will "grow out of." However, adolescents with BDD spend excessive periods of time (i.e., more than one hour, often 3–8 hours) thinking about imagined or minor imperfections. The concern is so upsetting that these teens often spend hours trying to fix or hide the perceived defect by checking their appearance repeatedly in the mirror, excessive grooming and camouflaging (e.g., with makeup, hair products, hats, tanning), and

frequent reassurance seeking. Rituals can take the place of homework, classes, and social gatherings with peers. Due to appearance-related thoughts and behaviors, adolescents with BDD may end up falling behind in school, refuse to go to classes, and become socially isolated. Concurrently, during adolescence, teens are faced with a number of developmental challenges, including identity formation and increasing dependence on peer groups for identification and approval (Levine & Smolak, 2002). These developmental processes are interrupted by BDD, which can lead to deficits in social skills, emotion regulation, and developing a stable sense of self. Thus, treatment with adolescents, and adults who developed symptoms during adolescence, should identify and modify skills deficits. For a description of the assessment and cognitive behavioral treatment of adolescent BDD see Greenberg et al., (2010).

Ethnic Minorities. Although general body dissatisfaction is more prevalent in Western cultures, where physical attractiveness is highly valued, the prevalence of clinically significant BDD seems relatively consistent across cultures. Culture and ethnic identity development may have an important influence on the body area of concern, as well as patients' access and attitude to mental health treatment (Marques et al., 2011). Cross-cultural studies are still needed to examine clinical features in clinical samples. Research is also needed to explore the relationship between BDD and its cultural variants, including *taijin kyofusho*, a Japanese phobia in which individuals are afraid of offending others by their "deformed body"(Suzuki et al., 2003), and *koro* or *suo yang*, an Asian genital retraction syndrome in which individuals are preoccupied by penile (labia, nipples, or breasts in women) shrinking or retraction into the body resulting in death (Chowdhury, 1996). Clinicians should inquire about cultural considerations, including acculturation and ethnic identity development, as part of their assessment, and address cultural factors as needed in treatment.

Conclusion

There is a growing clinical and research interest in BDD. However, BDD treatment outcome research is still scarce relative to other disorders, and individuals struggling with BDD remain reluctant to seek treatment.

While BDD patients share common core features, such as preoccupation with an imagined or slight appearance flaw and compensatory (ritualistic and avoidant) behaviors, the heterogeneity of BDD symptomatology has not been fully elucidated. Small and biased samples make it difficult to draw meaningful conclusions about the impact of psychological (e.g., comorbidity, insight), epidemiological (e.g., age, gender, culture), and other patient factors (e.g., motivation for change).

Controlled studies are needed, including systematic comparisons of CBT to other types of psychosocial therapies (e.g., nondirective supportive psychotherapy) and SRIs, in order to adequately determine the relative efficacy for existing treatments. Studies of combined and sequential pharmacotherapy and CBT are also necessary to help address patients who do not respond adequately to SRI or CBT monotherapy.

BDD is a severe disorder with substantial psychosocial impact. Shame and poor insight often preclude individuals from seeking treatment for BDD symptoms, or from disclosing appearance-related concerns unless specifically queried. Thus, while patients may seek treatment for comorbid disorders, such as anxiety or depression, their struggles with BDD frequently go undetected and untreated. Health providers need to be aware of the disorder and of the need to specifically screen patients for BDD. Given the early onset of BDD, it is particularly important to screen for BDD in adolescents. Increased awareness of this disorder may help to promote early detection and treatment. Early diagnosis and treatment may help reduce the personal and public health sequelae typically associated with BDD, including functional impairment, reduced quality of life, hospitalization, and morbidity.

This chapter is intended to explicate the nature of this disorder and to offer some useful tools for the assessment and treatment of BDD. Effective psychosocial and pharmacologic treatments are available for the treatment of adult BDD, and more research is underway to enhance and broaden the quality of care for BDD patients.

Future Directions

1. Treatment outcome research in BDD is nascent relative to other disorders. Nevertheless, effective treatments are available. BDD is more than a matter of vanity; it can be severely debilitating, and, if left untreated, is associated with the development of additional psychopathology and morbidity. Dissemination of treatment strategies is necessary in order to effectively reduce the substantial personal and public health burdens associated with this severe disorder.

2. The interplay of biological, psychological, and socio-environmental factors in the development, presentation, and treatment of BDD underscores the need for more comprehensive intervention and prevention approaches. New data from treatment, neurobiological, and imaging studies are promising and, taken together, can help inform the most effective methods for conceptualizing and treating BDD. Learning more about the neurobiological basis and neural correlates of BDD can help us to predict treatment response, and may help to identify modifiable risk factors.

3. Appearance-related concerns are common during adolescence. However, providers need to specifically query youth about potential body image concerns. Measures of time, distress, and avoidance can be indicative of pathological concern. Treatments are currently being developed for adolescents with BDD. In addition, future research should focus on prevention and early intervention efforts, which could provide education and skills to buffer against the internalization of unrealistic sociocultural standards of beauty, and the accompanying pressures adolescents and young adults face in trying to attain this ideal.

Related Chapters

Chapter 3. Phenomenology and Epidemiology of Body Dysmorphic Disorder

Recommended Reading

Phillips, K. A. (2005). *The broken mirror: Understanding and treating body dysmorphic disorder (revised and expanded edition)*. New York, NY: Oxford University Press.

Wilhelm, S. (2006). *Feeling good about the way you look: A program for overcoming body image problems*. New York, NY: Guilford Press.

Wilhelm, S., Phillips, K. A., & Steketee, S. (in press). *A modular treatment manual for body dysmorphic disorder*. New York, NY: Guilford Press.

References

Albertini, R., & Phillips, K. (1999). Thirty-three cases of body dysmorphic disorder in children and adolescents. *Journal of the American Academy of Child & Adolescent Psychiatry, 38(4)*, 453–459.

Albertini, R., Phillips, K. A., & Guvremont, D. (1996). Body dysmorphic disorder in a young child (letter). *Journal of the American Academy of Child and Adolescent Psychiatry, 35*, 1425–1426.

Allen, A., Hadley, S. J., Kaplan, A., Simeon, D., Friedberg, J., Priday, L., Baker, B. R., Greenberg, J. L., & Hollander, E. (2008). An open-label trial of venlafaxine in body dysmorphic disorder. *CNS Spectrums, 13*,138–144.

American Psychiatric Association. (2000). *Diagnostic and Statistical Manual of Mental Disorders: DSM-IV*, ed. 4 Washington: American Psychiatric Association.

Barr, L. C., Goodman, W. K., & Price, L. H. (1992). Acute exacerbation of body dysmorphic disorder during tryptophan depletion. *American Journal of Psychiatry, 149*, 1406–1407.

Bienvenu, O., Samuels, J. F., Riddle, M. A., Hoehn-Saric, R., Liang, K.-Y., Cullen, B. A., et al. (2000). The relationship of obsessive-compulsive disorder to possible spectrum disorders: Results from a family study. *Biological Psychiatry, 48(4)*, 287–293.

Bloch, S., & Glue, P. (1988). Psychotherapy and dysmorphophobia: A case report. *British Journal of Psychiatry, 152*, 271–274.

Bohne, A., Keuthen, N. J., Wilhelm, S., Deckersback, T., & Jenike, M. A. (2002). Prevalence of symptoms of body dysmorphic disorder and its correlates: A cross-cultural comparison. *Psychosomatics: Journal of Consultation Liaison Psychiatry, 43(6)*, 486–490.

Brady, K. T., Austin, L., & Lydiard, R. B. (1990). Body dysmorphic disorder: the relationship to obsessive-compulsive disorder. *Journal of Nervous and Mental Disease, 178(8)*, 538–540.

Buhlmann, U., Glaesmer, H., Mewes, R., Fama, J.M., Wilhelm, S., Brähler, E., & Rief, W. (2010). Updates on the prevalence of body dysmorphic disorder: A population-based survey. *Psychiatry Research, 178*, 171–175.

Buhlmann, U., Etcoff, N. L., & Wilhelm, S. (2008). Facial attractiveness ratings and perfectionism in body dysmorphic disorder and obsessive-compulsive disorder. *Journal of Anxiety Disorders, 22(3)*, 540–547.

Cansever, A., Uzun, O., Donmez, E., & Ozsahin, A. (2003). The prevalence and clinical features of body dysmorphic disorder in college students: A study in a Turkish sample. *Comprehensive Psychiatry, 44(1)*, 60–64.

Carey, P., Seedat, S., Warwick, J., et al. (2004). SPECT imaging of body dysmorphic disorder. *Journal of Neuropsychiatry and Clinical Neuroscience, 16*, 357–359.

Chosak, A., Marques, L. M., Greenberg, J. L., Jenike, E., Dougherty, D. D., & Wilhelm, S. (2008). Body dysmorphic disorder and obsessive compulsive disorder: similarities, differences, and the classification debate. *Expert Review of Neurotherapeutics, 8(8)*, 1209–1218.

Chowdhury, A. N. (1996). The definition and classification of Koro. *Culture, Medicine and Psychiatry, 20(1)*, 41–65.

Conroy, M., Menard, W., Fleming-Ives, K., Modha, P., Cerullo, H., & Phillips, K. A. (2008). Prevalence and clinical characteristics of body dysmorphic disorder in an adult inpatient setting. *General Hospital Psychiatry, 30(1)*, 67–72.

Cottraux, J., Mollard, E., Bouvard, M., & Marks, I. (1990, January). A controlled study of fluvoxamine and exposure in obsessive-compulsive disorder. *International Clinical Psychopharmacology, 5(1)*, 17–30.

Crerand, C. E., Phillips, K. A., Menard, W., & Fay, C. (2005). Nonpsychiatric medical treatment of body dysmorphic disorder. *Psychosomatics: Journal of Consultation Liaison Psychiatry, 46(6)*, 549–555.

Deckersbach, T., Savage, C. R., Phillips, K. A., Wilhelm, S., Buhlmann, U., Rauch, S. L., et al. (2000). Characteristics of memory dysfunction in body dysmorphic disorder. *Journal of the International Neuropsychological Society, 6(6)*, 673–681.

Delinsky, S. S., & Wilson, G. T. (2006). Mirror exposure for the treatment of body image disturbance. *International Journal of Eating Disorders, 39(2)*, 108–116.

DiClemente, C. C. & Hughes, S. O. (1990). Stages of change profiles in alcoholism treatment. *Journal of Substance Abuse, 2*, 217–235.

Eifert, G. H., Schulte, D., Zvolensky, M. J., Lejuez, C. W., Lau, A.W. (1997). Manualized behavior therapy: Merits and challenges. *Behavior Therapy, 28(4)*, 499–509.

Eisen, J. L., Phillips, K. A., Baer, L., Beer, D. A., Atala, K. D., & Rasmussen, S. A. (1998). The Brown Assessment of Beliefs Scale: Reliability and validity. *American Journal of Psychiatry, 155(1)*, 102–108.

Faravelli, C., Salvatori, S., Galassi, F., & Aiazzi, L. (1997). Epidemiology of somatoform disorders: A community survey in Florence. *Social Psychiatry and Psychiatric Epidemiology, 32(1)*, 24–29.

Feusner, J. D., Moody, T., Hembacher, E., Townsend, J., McKinley, M., Moller, H., et al. (2010). Abnormalities of visual processing and frontostriatal systems in body dysmorphic disorder. *Archives of General Psychiatry, 67*, 197–205.

Feusner, J. D., Townsend, J., Bystritsky, A., & Bookheimer, S. (2007). Visual information processing of faces in body dysmorphic disorder. *Archives of General Psychiatry, 64*, 1417–1425.

Feusner, J. D., Yaryura-Tobias, J., Saxena, S., (2008). The pathophysiology of body dysmorphic disorder. *Body Image, 5(1)*, 3–12.

First, M. B, Spitzer, R. L, Gibbon, M., & Williams, J.B. (2002). *Structured Clinical Interview for DSM-IV-TR Axis I Disorders, Research Version, Patient Edition. (SCID-I/P)* New York: Biometrics Research, New York State Psychiatric Institute.

Foa, E., Liebowitz, M., Kozak, M., Davies, S., Campeas, R., Franklin, M., et al. (2005). Randomized, placebo-controlled trial of exposure and ritual prevention, clomipramine, and their combination in the treatment of obsessive-compulsive disorder. *American Journal of Psychiatry, 162(1)*, 151–161.

Fontenelle, L. F., Telles, L. L., Nazar, B. P., De Menezes, G. B., Do Nascimento, A. L., Mendlowicz, M. V., et al. (2006). A sociodemographic, phenomenological, and long-term follow-up study of patients with body dysmorphic disorder in Brazil. *International Journal of Psychiatry in Medicine, 36(2)*, 243–259.

Gabbay, V., Asnis, G. M., Bello, J. A., Alonso, C. M., Serras, S. J., & O'Dowd, M. A. (2003). New onset of body dysmorphic disorder following fronto-temporal lesion. *Neurology, 61*, 123–125.

Gabbay, V., O'Dowd, M. A., Weiss, A. J., & Asnis, G. M. (2002). Body dysmorphic disorder triggered by medical illness? *American Journal of Psychiatry, 159*, 493.

Goodman, W. K., Price, L. H., Rasmussen, S. A., Mazure, C., & et al. (1989). The Yale-Brown Obsessive Compulsive Scale: II. Validity. *Archives of General Psychiatry, 46(11)*, 1012–1016.

Grant, J. E., Kim, S. W., & Crow, S. J. (2001). Prevalence and clinical features of body dysmorphic disorder in adolescent and adult psychiatric inpatients. *Journal of Clinical Psychiatry, 62(7)*, 517–522.

Grant, J. E., Menard, W., & Phillips, K. A. (2006). Pathological skin picking in individuals with body dysmorphic disorder. *General Hospital Psychiatry, 28(6)*, 487–493.

Greenberg, J. L., Markowitz, S., Petronko, M. R., Taylor, C. E., Wilhelm, S., & Wilson, G. T. (2010). Cognitive-behavioral therapy for adolescent body dysmorphic disorder. *Cognitive and Behavioral Practice, 17(3)*, 248–258.

Gunstad, J., & Phillips, K. A. (2003). Axis I comorbidity in body dysmorphic disorder. *Comprehensive Psychiatry, 44(4)*, 270–276.

Hadley, S. J., Newcorn, J. H., & Hollander, E. (2002). The neurobiology and psychopharmacology of body dysmorphic disorder. In D. J. Castle & K. A. Phillips (Eds.), *Disorders of body image* (pp. 139–155). Petersfield, UK: Wrightson Biomedical Publishing.

Hitzeroth, V., Wessels, C., Zungu-Dirwayi, N., Oosthuizen, P., & Stein, D. J. (2001). Muscle dysmorphia: A South African sample. *Psychiatry and Clinical Neurosciences, 55*(5), 521–523.

Hohagen, F., Winkelmann, G., Rasche-Räuchle, H., Hand, I., König, A., Münchau, N., et al. (1998). Combination of behaviour therapy with fluvoxamine in comparison with behaviour therapy and placebo: Results of a multicentre study. *British Journal of Psychiatry, 173(35),* 71–78.

Hollander, E. (2005). Obsessive-compulsive disorder and spectrum across the life span. *International Journal of Psychiatry in Clinical Practice, 9(2),* 79–86.

Hollander, E., Allen, A., Kwon, J., Aronowitz, B., Schmeidler, J., Wong, C., & Simeon, D. (1999). Clomipramine vs desipramine crossover trial in body dysmorphic disorder: selective efficacy of a serotonin reuptake inhibitor in imagined ugliness. *Archives of General Psychiatry, 56,* 1033–1039.

Hollander, E., Liebowitz, M. R., Winchel, R., Klumker, A., & Klein, D. F. (1989). Treatment of body-dysmorphic disorder with serotonin reuptake blockers. *American Journal of Psychiatry, 146*(6), 768–770.

Hollander, E., & Wong, C. M. (1995). Body dysmorphic disorder, pathological gambling, and sexual compulsions. *Journal of Clinical Psychiatry, 56 (Suppl 4),* 7–12.

Horowitz, K., Gorfinkle, K., Lewis, O., Phillips, K. A. (2002). Body dysmorphic disorder in an adolescent girl. *Journal of the American Academy of Child & Adolescent Psychiatry, 41(12),* 1503–1509.

Ipser, J., Sander, C., & Stein, D. (2009). Pharmacotherapy and psychotherapy for body dysmorphic disorder. *Cochrane Database of Systematic Reviews, Jan 21*(1), CD005332.

Kittler, J. E., Menard, W., & Phillips, K. A. (2007). Weight concerns in individuals with body dysmorphic disorder. *Eating Behaviors, 8*(1), 115–120.

Koran, L. M., Abujaoude, E., Large, M. D., & Serpe, R. T. (2008). The prevalence of body dysmorphic disorder in the United States adult population. *CNS Spectrums, 13*(4), 316–322.

Koran, L. M., Hanna, G. L., Hollander, E., Nestadt, G., Simpson, H. B.; American Psychiatric Association. (2007). Practice guideline for the treatment of patients with obsessive-compulsive disorder. *American Journal of Psychiatry, 164* (7Suppl), 5–53.

Levine, M. P., & Smolak, M. (2002). Body image development in adolescence. In T.F. Cash and T. Pruzinsky (Eds.). *Body Image: A Handbook of Theory, Research, and Clinical Practice,* (pp. 74–82). New York: Guilford.

Marques, L., LeBlanc, N., Weingarden H., Greenberg, J. L., Traeger, L. N., Keshaviah, A., & Wilhelm, S. (2011). Body dysmorphic symptoms: phenomenology and ethnicity. *Body Image, 8*(2), 163-167.

Mathew, S. J. (2001). PANDAS variant and body dysmorphic disorder. *American Journal of Psychiatry, 158*(6), 963.

McKay, D. (1999). Two-year follow-up of behavioral treatment and maintenance for body dysmorphic disorder. *Behavior Modification, 23*(4), 620–629.

McKay, D., Todaro, J., Neziroglu, F., & Campisi, T. (1997). Body dysmorphic disorder: A preliminary evaluation of treatment and maintenance using exposure with response prevention. *Behaviour Research and Therapy, 35*(1), 67–70.

Miller, W. R., & Rollnick, S. (2002). Motivational interviewing: Preparing people for change. Book Review. *Journal of Studies on Alcohol, 63*(6), 776–777.

Naga, A. A., Devinsky, O., & Barr, W. B. (2004). Somatoform disorders after temporal lobectomy. *Cognitive Behavioral Neurology, 17(2),* 57–61.

National Institute for Clinical Excellence. (2005). *Obsessive-compulsive disorder: Core interventions in the treatment of obsessive-compulsive disorder and body dysmorphic disorder.* London: HMSO.

Neziroglu, F., & Khemlani-Patel, S. (2005). Overlap of body dysmorphic disorder and hypochondriasis with OCD. In J. S. Abramowitz & A. C. Houts (Eds.), *Concepts and controversies in obsessive-compulsive disorder* (pp. 163–175). New York, NY: Springer Science + Business Media.

Neziroglu, F., McKay, D., Todaro, J., & Yaryura-Tobias, J. A. (1996). Effect of cognitive behavior therapy on persons with body dysmorphic disorder and comorbid Axis II diagnosis. *Behavior Therapy, 27*(1), 67–77.

Otto, M. W., Wilhelm, S., Cohen, L. S., & Harlow, B. L. (2001). Prevalence of body dysmorphic disorder in a community sample of women. *American Journal of Psychiatry, 158(12),* 2061–2063.

Perugi, G., Giannotti, D., Di Vaio, S., Frare, F., Saettoni, M., & Cassano, G. B. (1996). Fluvoxamine in the treatment of body dysmorphic disorder (dysmorphophobia). *International Clinical Psychopharmacology, 11*(4), 247–254.

Phillips, K. A. (1991). Body dysmorphic disorder: The distress of imagined ugliness. *American Journal of Psychiatry, 148*(9), 1138–1149.

Phillips, K. A. (1996). *The broken mirror: Understanding and treating body dysmorphic disorder.* New York, NY: Oxford.

Phillips, K. A. (2000). Quality of life for patients with body dysmorphic disorder. *Journal of Nervous and Mental Diseases, 188,* 170–175.

Phillips, K. A. (2004). Psychosis in body dysmorphic disorder. *Journal of Psychiatric Research, 38,* 63–72.

Phillips, K. A. (2005). *The broken mirror: Understanding and treating body dysmorphic disorder (rev. & exp ed.).* New York, NY: Oxford.

Phillips, K. A. (2006). An open-label study of escitalopram in body dysmorphic disorder. *International Clinical Psychopharmacology, 21*(3), 177–179.

Phillips, K. A., Albertini, R. S., & Rasmussen, S. A. (2002). A randomized placebo-controlled trial of fluoxetine in body dysmorphic disorder. *Archives of General Psychiatry, 59*(4), 381–388.

Phillips, K. A., Albertini, R. S., Siniscalchi, J. M., Khan, A., & Robinson, M. (2001). Effectiveness of pharmacotherapy for body dysmorphic disorder: A chart-review study. *Journal of Clinical Psychiatry, 62*(9), 721–727.

Phillips, K. A., Atala, K. D., Albertini, R. S. (1995). Case study: body dysmorphic disorder in adolescents. *Journal of the American Academy of Child and Adolescent Psychiatry. 34,* 1216–1220.

Phillips, K., Atala, K., & Pope, H. (1995, May). *Diagnostic instruments for body dysmorphic disorder.* In New Research Program and Abstracts from the 148th Annual Meeting of the American Psychiatric Association, Miami, FL.

Phillips, K. A., Coles, M., Menard, W., Yen, S., Fay, C., & Weisberg, R. B. (2005). Suicidal ideation and suicide attempts in body dysmorphic disorder. *Journal of Clinical Psychiatry, 66,* 717–725.

Phillips, K. A., & Diaz, S. F. (1997). Gender differences in body dysmorphic disorder. *Journal of Nervous and Mental Disease*, *185*(9), 570–577.

Phillips, K. A., Didie, E. R., Menard, W., Pagano, M. E., Fay, C., & Weisberg, R. B. (2006). Clinical features of body dysmorphic disorder in adolescents and adults. *Psychiatry Research*, *141*(3), 305–314.

Phillips, K. A., Dwight, M. M., & McElroy, S. L. (1998). Efficacy and safety of fluvoxamine in body dysmorphic disorder. *Journal of Clinical Psychiatry*, *59*(4), 165–171.

Phillips, K. A., Grant, J., Siniscalchi, J., & Albertini, R. S. (2001). Surgical and nonpsychiatric medical treatment of patients with body dysmorphic disorder. *Psychosomatics: Journal of Consultation Liaison Psychiatry*, *42*(6), 504–510.

Phillips, K. A., Gunderson, C. G., Mallya, G., et al. (1998). A comparison study of body dysmorphic disorder and obsessive-compulsive disorder. *Journal of Clinical Psychiatry*, *59*, 568–575.

Phillips, K. A., & Hollander, E. (2008). Treating body dysmorphic disorder with medication: Evidence, misconceptions, and a suggested approach. *Body Image*, *5*(1), 13–27.

Phillips, K. A., Hollander, E., Rasmussen, S. A., Aronowitz, B. R., DeCaria, C., & Goodman, W. K. (1997). A severity rating scale for body dysmorphic disorder: Development, reliability, and validity of a modified version of the Yale-Brown Obsessive Compulsive Scale. *Psychopharmacology Bulletin*, *33*(1), 17–22.

Phillips, K. A., & Kelly, M. M. (2009). Suicidality in a placebo-controlled fluoxetine study of body dysmorphic disorder. *International Clinical Psychopharmacology*, *24(1)*, 26–28.

Phillips, K. A., McElroy, S. L., Hudson, J. I., & Pope, H. G. (1995). Body dysmorphic disorder: An obsessive-compulsive spectrum disorder, a form of affective spectrum disorder, or both? *Journal of Clinical Psychiatry*, *56* (Suppl 4), 41–51.

Phillips, K. A., McElroy, S. L., Keck, P. E., Pope, H. G., Hudson, J. I. (1994). A comparison of delusional and nondelusional body dysmorphic disorder in 100 cases. *Psychopharmacology Bulletin*, *30*, 179–186

Phillips, K. A., McElroy, S. L., Keck, P. E., Pope, H. G., & et al. (1993). Body dysmorphic disorder: 30 cases of imagined ugliness. *American Journal of Psychiatry*, *150*(2), 302–308.

Phillips, K. A., & Menard, W. (2006). Suicidality in Body Dysmorphic Disorder: A Prospective Study. *American Journal of Psychiatry*, *163*(7), 1280–1282.

Phillips, K. A., Menard, W., Fay, C., & Pagano, M. E. (2005). Psychosocial functioning and quality of life in body dysmorphic disorder. *Comprehensive Psychiatry*, *46*(4), 254–260.

Phillips, K. A., Menard, W., Fay, C., & Weisberg, R. (2005). Demographic Characteristics, Phenomenology, Comorbidity, and Family History in 200 Individuals With Body Dysmorphic Disorder. *Psychosomatics: Journal of Consultation Liaison Psychiatry*, *46*(4), 317–325.

Phillips, K. A., & Najar, F. (2003). An open-label study of citalopram in body dysmorphic disorder. *Journal of Clinical Psychiatry*, *64*(6), 715–720.

Phillips, K. A., Pagano, M. E., & Menard, W. (2006). Pharmacotherapy for body dysmorphic disorder: Treatment received and illness severity. *Annals of Clinical Psychiatry*, *18*(4), 251–257.

Phillips, K. A., Pagano, M. E., Menard, W., & Stout, R. L. (2006). A 12-month follow-up study of the course of body dysmorphic disorder. *American Journal of Psychiatry*, *163*(5), 907–912.

Phillips, K. A., & Stout, R. L. (2006). Associations in the longitudinal course of body dysmorphic disorder with major depression, obsessive-compulsive disorder, and social phobia. *Journal of Psychiatric Research*, *40*(4), 360–369.

Phillips, K. A., & Taub, S. L. (1995). Skin picking as a symptom of body dysmorphic disorder. *Psychopharmacology Bulletin*, *31*(2), 279–288.

Phillips, K. A., Quinn, G., & Stout, R. L. (2008). Functional impairment in body dysmorphic disorder: A prospective, follow-up study. *Journal of Psychiatric Research*, *42*, 701–707.

Pope, H. G. Jr., Gruber, A. J., Choi, P., Olivardia, R., Phillips, K. A. (1997). Muscle dysmorphia: An underrecognized form of body dysmorphic disorder. *Psychosomatics: Journal of Consultation Liaison Psychiatry*, *38*(6), 548–557.

Pope, C. G., Pope, H. G. Jr., Menard, W., Fay, C., Olivardia, R. & Phillips, K. A. (2005). Clinical features of muscle dysmorphia among males with body dysmorphic disorder. *Body Image*, *2*(4), 395–400.

Rauch, S. L., Phillips, K. A., Segal, E., Makris, N., Shin, L. M., Whalen, P. J., et al. (2003). A preliminary morphometric magnetic resonance imaging study of regional brain volumes in body dysmorphic disorder. *Psychiatry Research*, *122*, 13–19.

Richter, M., Tharmalingam, S., Burroughs, E., King, N., Menard, W., Kennedy, J., et al. (2004). A preliminary genetic investigation of the relationship between body dysmorphic disorder and OCD. Paper presented at the American College of Neuropsychopharmacology Annual Meeting, San Juan, Puerto Rico.

Rief, W., Buhlmann, U., Wilhelm, S., Borkenhagen, A., & Brahler, E. (2006). The prevalence of body dysmorphic disorder: A population-based survey. *Psychological Medicine*, *36*(6), 877–885.

Rosen, J. C., & Reiter, J. (1996). Development of the body dysmorphic disorder examination. *Behaviour Research and Therapy*, *34*(9), 755–766.

Rosen, J. C., Reiter, J., & Orosan, P. (1995). Cognitive-behavioral body image therapy for body dysmorphic disorder. *Journal of Consulting and Clinical Psychology*, *63*(2), 263–269.

Salib, E. A. (1988). Subacute sclerosing panencephalitis (SSPE) presenting at the age of 21 as a schizophrenia-like state with bizarre dysmorphophobic features. *British Journal of Psychiatry*, *152*, 709–710.

Sarwer, D. B., & Crerand, C. E. (2008). Body dysmorphic disorder and appearance enhancing medical treatments. *Body Image*, *5*(1), 50–58.

Saxena, S., Feusner, J. D. (2006). Toward a neurobiology of body dysmorphic disorder. *Primary Psychiatry*, *13*(7), 41–48.

Simpson, H. B., Foa, E. B., Liebowitz, M. R., Ledley, D. R., Huppert, J. D., et al. (2008). A randomized, controlled trial of cognitive-behavioral therapy for augmenting pharmacotherapy in obsessive-compulsive disorder. *American Journal of Psychiatry*, *165*(5), 621–630.

Simpson, H., & Liebowitz, M. (2005). Combining pharmacotherapy and cognitive-behavioral therapy in the treatment of OCD. *Concepts and controversies in obsessive-compulsive disorder* (pp. 359–376). New York, NY: Springer

Suzuki, K., Takei, N., Kawai, M., Minabe, Y., & Mori, N. (2003). Is *taijin kyofusho* a culture-bound syndrome? *American Journal of Psychiatry*, *160*(7), 1358.

Tignol, J., Biraben-Gotzamanis, L., Martin-Guehl, C., Grabot, D., & Aouizerate, B. (2007). Body dysmorphic disorder and cosmetic surgery: Evolution of 24 subjects with a minimal defect in appearance 5 years after their request for cosmetic surgery. *European Psychiatry, 22*(8), 520–524.

Veale, D., Boocock, A., Gournay, K., & Dryden, W. (1996). Body dysmorphic disorder: A survey of fifty cases. *British Journal of Psychiatry, 169*(2), 196–201.

Veale, D., Gournay, K., Dryden, W., Boocock, A., Shah, F., Willson, R., et al. (1996). Body dysmorphic disorder: A cognitive behavioural model and pilot randomised controlled trial. *Behaviour Research and Therapy, 34*(9), 717–279.

Wilhelm, S., Buhlmann U., Cook, L. M. Greenberg, J. L, & Dimaite, R. A. (2010). Cognitive-behavioral treatment approach for body dysmorphic disorder. *Cognitive and Behavioral Practice, 17*(3), 241–247.

Wilhelm, S., Fama, J.M., Greenberg, J.L., Phillips, K.A., & Steketee, G. (in press). Modular cognitive-behavioral therapy for body dysmorphic disorder. *Behavior Therapy.*

Wilhelm, S., Otto, M. W., Lohr, B., & Deckersbach, T. (1999). Cognitive behavior group therapy for body dysmorphic disorder: A case series. *Behaviour Research and Therapy, 37*(1), 71–75.

Wilhelm, S., Phillips, K. A., & Steketee, S. (in press). *A modular treatment for body dysmorphic disorder.* New York, NY: Guilford Press.

Wilhelm, S., Steketee, G., Reilly-Harrington, N. A., Deckersbach, T., Buhlmann, U., & Baer, L. (2005). Effectiveness of cognitive therapy for obsessive-compulsive disorder: An open trial. *Journal of Cognitive Psychotherapy, 19*(2), 173–179.

Williams, J., Hadjistavropoulos, T., & Sharpe, D. (2006). A meta-analysis of psychological and pharmacological treatments for body dysmorphic disorder. *Behaviour Research and Therapy, 44*, 99–111.

Treatment of Compulsive Hoarding

Jessica R. Grisham, Melissa M. Norberg, *and* Sarah P. Certoma

Abstract

Compulsive hoarding is a prevalent and chronic problem that is associated with a profound public health burden. Individuals with hoarding symptoms who have been included in OCD treatment outcome trials have responded poorly to standard pharmacological and psychological treatments. Interventions based on a cognitive-behavioral model specific to compulsive hoarding have shown more promise, according to recent studies. This chapter reviews assessment practices, current evidence regarding biological and psychological treatments for hoarding, and challenges associated with treating hoarding. The cognitive-behavioral treatment for hoarding developed by Steketee and Frost (2007) is described, followed by research questions regarding how to improve treatment outcomes for hoarding.

Keywords: hoarding, saving, collecting, clutter, obsessive compulsive disorder, cognitive-behavior therapy, pharmacotherapy.

Introduction

The development, evaluation, and dissemination of effective treatments for compulsive hoarding is an urgent public health priority. Compulsive hoarding is more prevalent than previously estimated (4%; Samuels et al., 2008), and is associated with a profound public health burden (Tolin, Frost, Steketee, Gray, & Fitch, 2008). There also is evidence that without intervention, hoarding is a chronic disorder that worsens with age (Grisham, Frost, Steketee, Kim, & Hood, 2006). Although hoarding appears to be associated with obsessive compulsive disorder (OCD; Frost & Gross, 1993; Frost, Krause, & Steketee, 1996), it is not clear whether it is accurately conceptualized as an OCD subtype (Wu & Watson, 2005). Nevertheless, individuals with hoarding symptoms have often been included in OCD treatment outcome trials. In these studies, individuals with compulsive hoarding have responded poorly to standard pharmacological and psychological treatments (Abramowitz, Franklin,

Schwartz, & Furr, 2003; Black et al., 1998; Christenson & Greist, 2001). Interventions based on a cognitive-behavioral model specific to compulsive hoarding have shown more promise (Cermele, Melendez-Pallitto, & Pandina, 2001; Hartl & Frost, 1999; Saxena et al., 2002; Steketee, Frost, Wincze, Greene, & Douglass, 2000; Tolin, Frost, & Steketee, 2007b).

This chapter begins with a brief history of assessment practices for compulsive hoarding, so that readers will be able to understand the limitations of the findings from treatment outcome research. We then review the current evidence for biological and psychological treatments for compulsive hoarding, as well as some of the challenges associated with treating hoarding patients. We also describe the structure and strategies of the cognitive-behavioral treatment for hoarding developed by Steketee and Frost (2007). The chapter concludes with research questions pertaining to improving treatment outcome for compulsive hoarding.

Treatment Outcome Studies
Assessment

OCD Self-Report Measures. The majority of treatment outcome studies for compulsive hoarding has relied on using measures that were developed originally for OCD. Several of these measures include hoarding subscales, such as the Yale-Brown Obsessive Compulsive Scale Checklist (Y-BOCS; Goodman et al., 1989), the Obsessive Compulsive Inventory (OCI; Foa, Kozak, Salkovskis, Coles, & Amir, 1998) and the OCI–Revised (OCI-R; Foa et al., 2002). The Y-BOCS Checklist hoarding subscale comprises two categorical items that pertain to hoarding obsessions and compulsions, while the 3-item hoarding subscales of the OCI and OCI-R assess acquisition, clutter, and difficulty discarding.

Although the OCI and OCI-R are somewhat better than the Y-BOCS Checklist at indexing hoarding symptoms, all of these measures are limited in their ability to assess the multiple facets of compulsive hoarding (Steketee & Frost, 2003). In addition, the hoarding subscale of the OCI failed to distinguish pathological hoarding from ordinary collecting (Foa et al., 1998), demonstrated weak internal consistency (Hajcak, Huppert, Simons, & Foa, 2004), and correlated weakly with the other OCI subscales (Abramowitz & Deacon, 2006). The lack of specificity of OCD measures in indexing hoarding symptoms raises concerns about the appropriateness of utilizing such measures to assess compulsive hoarding in both clinical and research contexts.

Hoarding-Specific Self-Report Measures. The Hoarding Scale (HS; Frost & Gross, 1993) represents the first systematic attempt to develop a scale solely to measure hoarding symptoms. This 21-item questionnaire was designed to measure key aspects of hoarding, including emotional reactions to discarding items, indecision regarding when to discard items, concerns over future necessity of discarded items, and sentimental attachment to possessions. Although the HS has excellent internal reliability, and a number of studies have established its validity in college, clinical, and community samples (Frost & Gross, 1993; Frost et al., 1996; Frost, Steketee, Williams, & Warren, 2000), the scale fails to assess all of the symptoms that are known to play a role in compulsive hoarding (Frost, Steketee, & Grisham, 2004).

The Saving Inventory-Revised (SI-R; Frost et al., 2004) and the Saving Cognitions Inventory (SCI; Steketee, Frost, & Kyrios, 2003) were developed to overcome the limitations of the HS. The SI-R assesses excessive acquisition of purchased and free items, saving and discarding behaviors, and excessive clutter as a result of these behaviors, while the SCI assesses emotional attachment to possessions, beliefs about objects as memory aids, responsibility for possessions, and the desire for control over possessions. Although both self-reports reflect the multidimensional nature of hoarding, and demonstrate adequate psychometric properties (Coles, Frost, Heimberg, & Steketee, 2003; Frost et al., 2004; Steketee et al., 2003; Tolin et al., 2007b), poor insight and the tendency among self-identified compulsive hoarders to underestimate or overestimate symptom severity raises concerns about the validity of these inventories (Steketee & Frost, 2003).

Pictorial Assessment. In order to address validity concerns, Frost, Steketee, Tolin, and Renaud (2008) developed the Clutter Image Rating (CIR), a pictorial index of the extent of clutter within kitchens, living rooms, and bedrooms. Each room contains nine different pictures that vary in rating from no clutter to severe clutter. For each room, respondents select the picture that most closely matches the patient's actual room. The CIR has demonstrated good internal consistency, test-retest reliability, and interrater reliability, as well as good convergent validity with other questionnaire and interview measures of clutter (Frost et al., 2008).

In sum, assessment of compulsive hoarding has improved in recent years. In the beginning, assessment relied heavily on OCD-based measures and narrowly focused hoarding self-report instruments, limiting the interpretability of early treatment outcome research. Recent advances in the conceptualization of hoarding have led to the development of multidimensional measures and the use of multimethod assessment. Ideally, future treatment outcome studies will include an in-home assessment of hoarding severity, and several hoarding specific-measures, such as the CIR, SI-R, and SCI.

Biological Treatment Outcome Research

In OCD serotonergic medication trials, the presence of hoarding symptoms is typically a negative treatment predictor (Black et al., 1998; Mataix-Cols, Rauch, Manzo, Jenike, & Baer, 1999; Winsberg, Cassic, & Koran, 1999). For example, an open trial of paroxetine and cognitive behavioral treatment (CBT) for non-depressed individuals with OCD found that nonresponders had significantly higher baseline scores on the hoarding subscale of the Y-BOCS Checklist than treatment responders (Black et al., 1998). Specifically, only 18% of those who reported hoarding symptoms responded to treatment, whereas 67% of patients without prominent hoarding symptoms responded to treatment. Likewise, Mataix-Cols et al. (1999) found that hoarding was the only factor on the Y-BOCS Checklist to predict poor SRI treatment outcome, after controlling for baseline symptom severity, across 6 placebo-controlled treatment trials.

Winsberg et al. (1999) examined the treatment response of 20 individuals with both OCD and compulsive hoarding. Of the 18 individuals who received an adequate trial with a selective serotonin reuptake inhibitor (SRI), only half showed an improvement by at least 25% on the Y-BOCS, and only one individual showed a marked response. Individuals who received cognitive-behavioral therapy for hoarding, in addition to an SRI, evidenced greater improvements than those who received medication alone. Given that all participants reported OCD symptoms, it is not possible to determine whether these changes reflect improvement in hoarding symptoms or nonhoarding OCD symptoms.

Although the presence of hoarding symptoms usually predicts poor pharmacological treatment response for OCD, Saxena, Brody, Maidment, and Baxter (2007) demonstrated that individuals with hoarding symptoms can respond as well to SRIs as those without hoarding symptoms. In this study, 79 individuals with OCD were treated openly with the SRI paroxetine. Those with hoarding symptoms showed a reduction of 23% on the Y-BOCS, while nonhoarding patients showed a 24% reduction in symptoms. Although these findings provide some support for the use of serotenergic medications for hoarding symptoms, there are a number of limitations. First, the treatment response of both groups was suboptimal. Second, individuals with hoarding symptoms were on paroxetine for a significantly greater number of days than individuals without hoarding symptoms. Third, it is not possible to determine whether treatment actually targeted hoarding symptoms, given that a measure specific to hoarding symptoms was not utilized.

Psychological Treatment Outcome Research

As with pharmacological approaches, hoarding symptoms are a negative predictor of cognitive-behavioral treatment outcome (e.g., Abramowitz et al., 2003; Mataix-Cols, Marks, Greist, Kobak, & Baer, 2002). For example, a review of the literature demonstrates that 46%–76% of nonhoarders with OCD exhibit a clinically significant response to exposure and response prevention, whereas only 31% of OCD hoarders demonstrate clinically significant improvement (Abramowitz et al., 2003). It has been suggested that poor treatment response among those with hoarding problems may be associated with treatment refusal and/or lack of motivation to engage due to poor insight (Christenson & Greist, 2001). For instance, it is usually a family member or spouse that pressures the hoarder to seek treatment. Kozak and Foa (1997) suggest that traditional treatments for obsessive compulsive disorder may be less effective because hoarders often display perfectionistic thinking and magical ideas that interfere with the treatment components.

Several recent studies have investigated a psychological treatment for compulsive hoarding that is based on Frost and Hartl's (1996) cognitive-behavioral model. This multifaceted model conceptualizes manifestations of hoarding behavior (i.e., acquisition, saving, and difficulty discarding) as involving four primary problem areas: information processing deficits, excessive emotional attachment to possessions, behavioral avoidance, and erroneous beliefs about the nature of saving and possessions. These treatment techniques will be described in detail in a subsequent section of this chapter.

Based on their model, Hartl and Frost (1999) treated a 53-year-old female who had a longstanding hoarding problem. At pretreatment, cluttered possessions took up approximately 70% of the living space in her house, and with the exception of the bathroom, none of the rooms could be easily used for their intended purpose. Treatment progressed room by room, and comprised training in decision making, exposure and habituation to discarding, and cognitive restructuring. The treatment strategies were delivered in weekly 2-hour sessions, combined with regular and detailed homework assignments. After 9 months of treatment, there was a reduction in indecisiveness, hoarding symptoms, and nonhoarding OCD symptoms. After 18 months (approximately 45 sessions), the targeted living spaces were almost completely free of clutter, while clutter ratios remained stable for a room that was used as a baseline control (i.e., no intervention).

Steketee et al. (2000) used a revised version of the CBT applied by Hartl and Frost (1999) to treat 7 individuals who reported hoarding symptoms as their only symptoms of OCD. Six of the participants attended 15 group treatment sessions over a 20-week period plus individual home treatment sessions, while the seventh received 20 weekly sessions of individual home treatment only. Outcome was assessed using the Y-BOCS, modified to assess only hoarding symptoms, as well as self-ratings of percent improvement in target areas. After 20 weeks (15 sessions), Y-BOCS scores showed a 16% improvement. In addition, self-ratings indicated reduced acquisition of hoarded items (47% improvement), increased awareness of irrational reasons for saving (37%), greater ability to organize possessions (31%), and improved decision-making skills (30%). Clutter was slowest to improve (18%). For those participants who continued fortnightly treatment for one year, further improvements in scores on the modified Y-BOCS, as well as self-report measures, were noted. Importantly, participants who also received SRI medication fared no better than those who did not. Steketee et al. (2000) note that, consistent with other reports, problems with motivation and homework adherence may have limited the effectiveness of the treatment protocol.

Using a combined approach, Saxena et al. (2002) examined a 6-week daily multimodal treatment involving SRI medications, CBT, and psychosocial rehabilitation in individuals with OCD with and without hoarding symptoms. CBT for the hoarders was based on Frost and Hartl's (1996) model, whereas CBT for the nonhoarders consisted of exposure and response prevention targeting the patient's individual symptoms, as well as cognitive restructuring. Post-treatment scores on the Y-BOCS showed improvement for both the hoarding (N = 20) and nonhoarding (N = 170) groups. However, the improvement was less marked for the hoarding group (35% improvement) than the nonhoarding group (46%). Improvements in mood and psychosocial functioning were similar for both groups. Although the above studies show promise for CBT specific to hoarding, their findings are limited in that they utilized obsessive compulsive measures to index symptom severity and change.

Utilizing hoarding-specific measures, Tolin, Frost, and Steketee (2007b) examined outcomes based on Steketee and Frost's (2007) cognitive-behavioral treatment manual for compulsive hoarding. Fourteen individuals (10 treatment completers), who reported compulsive hoarding as their primary complaint, received 26 individual sessions, including in-office sessions and at least one home visit per month, over a 7- to 12-month period. Post-treatment measures on the CIR and SI-R indicated reductions in hoarding behaviors including clutter, excessive acquisition, and difficulty discarding.

Following this open trial, Steketee, Frost, Tolin, Rassmussen, and Brown (Steketee et al., 2010) made minor modifications to the treatment and examined its efficacy in the first randomized controlled trial for compulsive hoarding. In this trial, hoarding participants were assigned to CBT (n=23) or to a waitlist condition (n=23). Participants in both groups were assessed before treatment and after 12 weeks. Participants in the CBT group were also assessed after 26 sessions. Findings indicated that improvements in hoarding symptoms were greater after receiving 12 sessions of CBT than after waiting for a comparable period. CBT was associated with significantly more improvement on most hoarding measures, with moderately large effect sizes. The mean score on the SI-R for the CBT group decreased an average of 10 points (15%) from a baseline of 63.4 to 53.7. Participants assigned to the waitlist showed almost no reduction in hoarding symptoms. This study demonstrated that CBT for hoarding provides benefits beyond the passage of time and repeated assessment. Overall, research findings indicate that compulsive hoarders do respond to CBT, although improvements are moderate in comparison with gains observed in non-hoarders with obsessive compulsive disorder.

Given that changes are slow to occur during the treatment of compulsive hoarding, researchers have recently examined alternative delivery models in the hope of increasing the cost-effectiveness of treatment. Using a multiple cohort pretest-posttest design, Muroff and colleagues examined the effectiveness of group CBT using Steketee and Frost's treatment manual (Muroff, Steketee, Rasmussen et al., 2009). After 16–20 sessions and two home visits, patients evidenced a mean reduction of 8.6 points on the Saving Inventory-Revised (SI-R), which is less than that produced from individual treatment using the same manual (18.7 or 16.9; Steketee et al., 2010; Tolin et al., 2007b). After the investigators modified their research procedures to more thoroughly screen group members, and utilized a more detailed and structured manual for the group, the mean SI-R reduction in the final group was 14.25.

Because access to clinicians trained in CBT for compulsive hoarding is sometimes limited, a web-based CBT group intervention has also been examined for its effectiveness (Muroff, Steketee, Himle, & Frost, 2010). This web-based treatment also was modeled on Steketee and Frost's manual (Steketee & Frost, 2007), and required individuals to take active steps to reducing their hoarding behavior within 2 months of membership. After 6 months of membership, SI-R scores decreased by an average of 6 points. Internet treatment approaches are important because they have the potential to expand significantly the number of individuals with hoarding who receive treatment;thus, ways to improve outcomes achieved from Internet-delivered therapy are much needed. New research also suggests possibilities for other treatment delivery strategies for hoarding, including a home-based webcam trial (Muroff, Steketee, & Frost, 2009) and a bibliotherapy-based self-help group (Pekareva-Kochergina & Frost, 2009). These types of interventions may provide promising alternatives that will extend treatment access to a more geographically diverse group.

Challenges to Hoarding Treatment

Despite advances in the treatment of compulsive hoarding over the past decade, treatment response remains suboptimal. Several clinical characteristics common to hoarding patients, including comorbid psychiatric disorders, impaired cognitive functioning, and poor insight and motivation for treatment, contribute to the unique challenge of developing and implementing efficacious treatment for this population.

Comorbid Axis I Psychopathology

When compared to nonhoarding OCD, hoarding has been found to be associated with higher rates of comorbid mood and anxiety disorders, including social phobia, generalized anxiety disorder, and depression (Frost, Steketee, Williams et al., 2000; Samuels et al., 2002), as well as higher rates of alcohol dependence (Samuels et al., 2008). Comorbid psychiatric issues may significantly impede treatment progress for hoarding patients. For example, depression symptoms may erode a hoarding patient's confidence and motivation, while social phobia may influence one's ability to engage in treatment, particularly group therapy. In some cases, hoarding beliefs and behaviors may serve to facilitate social avoidance, if an individual uses their cluttered home as a rationale for withdrawing and isolating themselves from others. These beliefs and maintaining factors must be directly addressed and challenged within compulsive hoarding treatment.

Comorbid OCD symptoms also may complicate the clinical picture for a hoarding client and interfere with treatment. For example, a patient in one of our compulsive hoarding treatment groups reported severe, lifelong OCD symptoms related to contamination, in addition to her collecting and saving behavior. When she participated in sorting and discarding tasks during therapy and as homework, her contamination concerns made her anxious about handling certain items. She had developed rituals related to these concerns, which included wearing rubber gloves and performing a series of elaborate cleaning procedures before and after each sorting task. These OCD-related behaviors considerably impaired her ability to effectively reduce the clutter in her home. Depending on the specific factors involved, it may be advantageous for some individuals with hoarding difficulties to pursue treatment for depression, comorbid OCD symptoms, or other comorbid anxiety issues prior to participating in hoarding treatment. This decision must be based on clinical judgment regarding which of the client's disorders is currently more interfering and distressing.

Interpersonal Difficulties and Personality Pathology

Hoarding patients are less likely to be married (Frost & Gross, 1993; Samuels et al., 2002), and may report beliefs indicating a lack of emotional connection with other people (Steketee et al., 2003). Moreover, anecdotal clinical evidence suggests that these individuals often present with a disorganized, tangential, or detached style of interaction, and have difficulty with perspective-taking. Research has also found that hoarding is associated with higher levels of personality disorders, including OCPD, avoidant, dependent, paranoid, and schizotypal, although the specific disorders have been inconsistent across studies (Frost, Steketee, Williams et al., 2000; Mataix-Cols, Baer, Rauch, & Jenike, 2000; Samuels et al., 2007; Samuels et al., 2008). Despite the association between hoarding and Axis II disorders (Frost, Steketee, Williams et al., 2000; Mataix-Cols et al., 2000; Samuels et al., 2002), a recent study found that hoarding patients did not report more interpersonal difficulties than nonhoarding anxiety patients (Grisham, Steketee, & Frost, 2008). This study was limited, however, by its reliance upon patient self-report, and requires replication with more objective measures of social difficulty.

Recently, hoarding was found to be associated with increased family conflict. Tolin and colleagues (Tolin, Frost, Steketee, & Fitch, 2008) administered the Patient Rejection Scale to assess rejecting or hostile attitudes toward hoarding patients among their families. The findings suggested a high degree of patient rejection attitudes among families, comparable to family members of patients hospitalized for schizophrenia. Dysfunction and conflict within the families of hoarding patients may serve as a barrier to treatment success. Clinicians treating hoarding patients may find it helpful to incorporate the family within treatment, and educate family members about the harmful effects of negative attitudes. For example, the therapist could focus on improving coping within the family and use cognitive techniques to encourage family members to attribute the patient's behavior to the disorder, rather than interpreting it as malicious (Steketee & Van Noppen, 2003).

Neurocognitive Impairment and Information Processing Deficits

The neuropsychological problems that can accompany compulsive hoarding behavior present another important challenge in hoarding treatment. Several neuropsychological studies of compulsive hoarding support the notion that there are cognitive deficits associated with this syndrome. In a recent study, hoarding group participants had intact verbal intelligence and working memory, but were impaired on measures of attention and nonverbal intelligence compared to a mixed clinical group and a community control group (Grisham, Brown, Savage, Steketee, & Barlow, 2007). Hoarding patients were slow to initiate responses, and had difficulty inhibiting impulsive responses. Similarly, Hartl and colleagues (Hartl, Duffany, Allen, Steketee, & Frost, 2005) found that hoarding participants displayed symptoms consistent with attention-deficit/hyperactivity disorder (ADHD) in adults on a self-report measure. Other studies have found evidence for indecisiveness (Frost & Shows, 1993) and deficits in verbal and nonverbal memory (Hartl et al., 2004). Finally, hoarding behavior appears to be associated with specific deficits in organizing and categorizing common objects, tasks that are central to hoarding treatment (Luchian, McNally, & Hooley, 2007; Wincze, Steketee, & Frost, 2007).

Weaknesses in these neuropsychological domains may interfere with psychological treatments for hoarding by limiting patients' ability to sustain attention during tasks (e.g., when deciding what possessions to save or discard) and to organize their possessions. In addition, memory and attention difficulties may contribute to problems with treatment compliance for psychological and biological treatments for hoarding (Saxena & Maidment, 2004). Hoarding patients may have difficulty attending therapy appointments and taking their medication at the correct time. They may also lose their homework assignments, therapy materials or medications, or forget to renew prescriptions.

In current cognitive-behavioral therapy for hoarding (Steketee & Frost, 2007), some of the specific deficits, such as impaired categorization and organization, are included as skills to be developed within treatment. For example, hoarding patients are taught strategies for organizing their possessions, such as identifying specific places to save stored items and setting deadlines by which the items will be stored. An under-inclusive categorization style also may be targeted. Specific techniques will be described in the following section. In addition to these strategies, it may also be helpful in some cases to consider the addition of the cognitive remediation therapy focused on general cognitive deficits with organization, attentional focus, and planning. Cognitive-behavioral treatments that have been found to be efficacious for adult ADHD (Safren, 2006) also could be incorporated into therapy for hoarding.

In addition to psychological strategies, recent data has suggested that compulsive hoarders have a unique pattern of brain activity, distinct from non-hoarding OCD patients and normal controls (Saxena et al., 2004). Diminished activity in certain regions, particularly the cingulate cortex, may contribute to the poor treatment response associated with hoarding. Future pharamacological approaches, such as cognitive enhancers and stimulant medications, might directly target brain dysfunction associated with hoarding. These medications may be an important way to address comorbid ADHD symptoms (Saxena & Maidment, 2004).

Insight and Motivation

Limited insight and motivation among hoarding patients can be a daunting obstacle for clinicians. Many hoarding patients have poor insight into the disorder and seem unaware of how much it has negatively impacted their lives. Further, unlike most OCD obsessions and compulsions, hoarding tends to be ego-syntonic (Grisham, Brown, Liverant, & Campbell, 2005). Many individuals have a positive attitude toward their possessions and their hoarding behavior, and are reluctant to engage in treatment. Frost and Gross (1993) found that many hoarding participants thought that their behavior was not problematic, or only sometimes found it problematic. The authors noted that these participants described their hoarding as an integral part of their identity, and some even characterized their hoarding behavior positively. Consistent with family member reports in Tolin et al. (2008), however, most of relatives found the hoarding patient's behavior problematic (Frost & Gross, 1993).

An associated problem is that hoarding patients often have poor motivation to engage in treatment, reflected by high dropout rates and poorer treatment outcomes for compulsive hoarding. Christenson and Greist (2001) concluded that many clients with compulsive hoarding display passive resistance to treatment. Often, hoarding patients are pressured by family members into seeking treatment and are prone to skipping sessions, arriving late, and not doing homework. Individuals with hoarding problems might be ambivalent about participating in treatment, or simply refuse to seek treatment at all. For example, many patients report that they do not have a problem with compulsive hoarding, but simply do not have enough storage space and need a larger home. Another factor that may intermittently impact upon a hoarding patient's motivation to engage in treatment is the sheer volume of clutter he or she may have accumulated. Sometimes there is so much clutter that organizing and discarding all of the possessions has become an enormous task that would be overwhelming even for someone without hoarding difficulties. Approaches to address these motivation issues will be described in a later section.

Health and Safety Problems

Clinicians who treat hoarding patients often encounter specific ethical dilemmas related to the physical condition of the patient's home environment. The accumulation of clutter can lead to unhealthy and unsafe living environments (Frost, Steketee, & Williams, 2000; Snowdon, Shah, & Halliday, 2007; Steketee, Frost, & Kim, 2001). For example, a staircase filled with objects creates a risk of falling, a heater surrounded by objects is a fire hazard, and an excessively unkempt house leads to exposure to dust pollen and bacteria, which can have deleterious health effects. In addition, the accumulation of urine and feces from animal hoarding poses risks for the animals themselves, and can damage the structure of home, threatening the health and safety of the individual and those living nearby (Patronek, 1999). When there is a health concern, it is essential for the therapist to discuss health and safety issues with clients.

Clutter, and in particular squalor, can lead to violations of local health, housing, and sanitation laws. Occasionally, clients are mandated by the courts to seek treatment for hoarding. Sometimes health and safety officials issue an order to enter the person's home. It is usually best to avoid forced interventions whenever possible, as they are usually very traumatic and reduce the likelihood of future cooperation. In addition, health violations may become apparent during the assessment process, especially when completing home visits for discarding exposures. Depending on the local laws, therapists will be required to intervene to protect the individual and those living nearby. Occasionally, children are involved and issues of mandatory reporting of neglect arise. Such breaches of confidentially can potentially damage the therapeutic relationship, especially since only half of hoarders acknowledge the lack of sanitation in their homes (Tolin, Frost, Steketee, Gray et al., 2008). Therefore, it is essential that therapists be open and direct with patients about the limitations of confidentially during the informed consent process.

Cognitive-Behavioral Treatment Strategies for Hoarding

As mentioned previously, compulsive hoarding does not respond well to treatments that were developed originally to manage OCD (Steketee & Frost, 2003). Furthermore, compulsive hoarding often occurs in the absence of other OCD symptoms and in the presence of a variety of other psychiatric disorders (e.g., Meunier, Tolin, Frost, Steketee, & Brady, 2006). These findings have led researchers to develop a cognitive-behavioral model specifically to guide treatment for compulsive hoarding. This model characterizes compulsive hoarding as a multifaceted problem that results from information processing deficits, problems with emotional attachment, rigid beliefs about possessions and saving, and behavioral avoidance (Frost & Hartl, 1996). Steketee and Frost (Steketee & Frost, 2007) have developed a novel treatment that highlights these areas, as well as the low motivation that individuals with compulsive hoarding so often display (Christenson & Greist, 2001). CBT for compulsive hoarding is structured around five general themes: motivation, skills training, imaginal and in vivo exposure, cognitive strategies, and relapse prevention (Steketee & Frost, 2007). Typically, sessions occur weekly for the first three months, and then taper over the next six months. Depending on the setting, sessions last from one to two hours. Much longer sessions can be held during home visits.

Psychoeducation

Treatment begins with psychoeducation. During the first session, patients are provided with information about the cognitive-behavioral model. The model is presented in simplistic terms, and a few references for empirical findings are given to increase patients' sense of trust in the treatment. If family members are unable to attend this session, then the therapist should have provided them with a handout on compulsive hoarding. Providing family members with education facilitates treatment by decreasing the chances that loved ones will help in maladaptive ways (e.g., cleaning out a patient's house without permission). In addition to teaching patients and their family members about compulsive hoarding, psychoeducation serves to frame the expectations of patients regarding the frequency, intensity, and rules of treatment.

Clinicians may find it helpful to be very clear about treatment rules and have patients sign behavioral contracts attesting to their knowledge and acceptance of these rules. For example, individuals with compulsive hoarding have a tendency to show up late for appointments, cancel appointments, and forget homework assignments. Therefore, setting conditions such as not holding sessions if patients are more than 15 minutes late and terminating therapy if patients cancel more than two consecutive sessions may assist in increasing treatment adherence. In order to set a collaborative atmosphere, the therapist also must adhere to rules, such as not touching any items without explicit permission and letting the patient make all decisions regarding their possessions.

As part of the psychoeducation process, the therapist will work collaboratively with patients to develop functional-analytic models of hoarding that are relevant to each individual. Thus, these models are idiosyncratic in that they only include features of the cognitive-behavioral model that serve to maintain hoarding behaviors for the current patient. As patients are likely to view only certain behaviors as problematic, model building allows the therapist to demonstrate how multiple behaviors contribute to hoarding. By exploring how their clutter developed and how it is maintained, patients may be more likely to consider changing their beliefs and behaviors. These functional-analytic models are used throughout therapy, and can be revised as more information is gained. What follows is a brief description of the specific strategies outlined in Steketee and Frost's (2007) CBT for compulsive hoarding. Not all strategies will be needed, and they can be applied in any order, depending on a particular patient's functional analytic model.

Motivation

As previously mentioned, individuals with hoarding problems often fail to see their behavior as problematic (Frost, Steketee, & Williams, 2002; Grisham et al., 2006). Thus, many patients enter treatment under the demands of friends and family members (Steketee et al., 2000). Even when patients do present on their own volition, they often report that they only need help with organizing their possessions. As individuals are unlikely to change their behavior unless they decide changes are necessary, cognitive-behavioral treatment for compulsive hoarding utilizes the principles of motivational interviewing (Miller & Rollnick, 2002). Motivational interviewing often is used formally at the beginning of treatment to develop a collaborative relationship and resolve initial ambivalence, and then later in therapy when motivation fades in response to discarding tasks.

Motivational interviewing attempts to increase patients' awareness of the consequences experienced and the risks faced as a result of hoarding, while helping patients to imagine a better future, so that they become more motivated to achieve a clutter-free life. In essence, the semi-directive approach attempts to get patients to consider what might be gained through discarding. The key principles of motivational interviewing are to express empathy, develop discrepancy, roll with resistance, and support self-efficacy (Miller & Rollnick, 2002). These principles can be obtained using a variety of strategies, such as imagery, goal setting, and the decisional balance exercise.

The clutter visualization task can be helpful in understanding a patient's motivation for change. This task requires patients to visualize a cluttered room in their house and determine how much discomfort they feel as a result of that clutter and their associated thoughts (Steketee & Frost, 2007). To perform this task, patients close their eyes and imagine turning around in the middle of their chosen room. Patients use a scale from 0 (no discomfort) to 100 (the most discomfort imaginable) to describe their discomfort. This task can be followed by the unclutter visualization task, in which patients visualize the same room devoid of clutter. A review of the information presented during these tasks can lead to discussions of potential treatment barriers and goal setting.

Goal setting can be a useful tool for increasing patients' motivation when combined with an assessment of reasons for change. In the self-help manual, *Buried in Treasures*, Tolin, Frost, and Steketee (2007a) encourage patients to write out their goals, along with why these goals are important to them. Patients are asked to reflect why they want to work on hoarding, what will happen if they are successful, and what will happen if they do not change. Patients are asked to remember these goals when treatment becomes difficult. Thus, goal setting can serve as a motivator early in treatment, and later on when patients are confronted with decisions to discard.

One way to expose the ambivalence that patients feel about working on clutter is by using the decisional balance exercise (Miller & Rollnick, 2002). A *decisional balance* is a metaphor for a scale that weighs the pros and cons of discarding. In this exercise, patients are asked to list all of their motivators to discard on one side of the scale, and all of their motivators for acquiring and saving on the other side of the scale. *Benefits of discarding* and *costs of acquiring and saving* make up *motivators to discard*, while *benefits of acquiring and saving* and *costs of discarding* form *motivators to acquire and save*. If ambivalence is demonstrated, patients can be asked to "tip the scale" in favor of discarding by increasing the number of items on the *benefits of discarding* side. This can be done by asking their friends, family, group members, and therapist for additional reasons to discard. Another way to "tip the scale" is to decrease the weight of "motivators to acquire and save." To do so, patients write down a benefit of acquiring and saving, and then write a list of problems and costs associated with that benefit. Next, they write down a positive nonhoarding alternative, followed by a list of reasons why that positive alternative is better. These steps are repeated for each motivator to save and acquire. The decisional balance scale can not only increase motivation, but it also can serve to increase patients' insight and to improve their problem-solving skills.

Skills Training

Individuals with hoarding problems often display skills deficits, such as difficulties with problem solving, time management, and categorization (Frost & Gross, 1993; Steketee et al., 2003; Wincze et al., 2007). When patients demonstrate difficulties generating solutions to problems, other than avoidance, they may need problem-solving training. This involves teaching patients to follow six simple steps: *(1)* identify the problem; *(2)* brainstorm solutions; *(3)* evaluate the pros and cons of each solution; *(4)* pick a solution based on the evaluation; *(5)* implement the solution; and *(6)* evaluate the outcome.

A common obstacle observed in hoarding treatment is that patients seem to be unable to complete their homework assignments (Steketee & Frost, 2007). Sometimes patients report to the therapist that they forget that they had a homework assignment, and other times they report not having enough time to complete it. If the former occurs, the therapist may have patients use the problem-solving steps to generate solutions; however, if the latter occurs, the therapist may find it necessary to implement time-management training. This training may include encouraging patients to write down all of their appointments and tasks in a daily planner. Patients also may need to be instructed to set aside a specific time of day to plan out their activities, and to write them into their planners. Other time-management training may include making lists, breaking complex tasks down into smaller, more manageable tasks, prioritizing tasks, getting rid of distractions, and identifying and eliminating "time stealers."

Individuals with compulsive hoarding often require organizational training when they evidence problems with creating categories. Typically, hoarders create too many categories when sorting because they identify each of their possessions as unique (Luchian et al., 2007; Wincze et al., 2007). Organizational training begins by having patients prepare for sorting by scheduling times to work on sorting, obtaining storage containers and labels, and researching where items will go inside and outside of their homes. Information needs to be collected on recycling agencies, charitable organizations, and trash collection. Skills training for sorting involves creating an organizational plan that lists categories of saved items (e.g., mail, photos, clothing, etc.), locations to store these saved items, and rules for letting go.

Usually, patients are advised to follow the rule of three and the "only handle it once" rule (OHIO). The rule of three requires patients to discard an item if they have more than three of the same item, and OHIO specifies that items should not be sorted more than once. Organizational training also provides patients with information regarding the usual length of time that different paper products should be saved. For example, credit card receipts are saved for one month, whereas tax returns are kept indefinitely. Often, patients with compulsive hoarding are unaware of how long nonhoarding individuals save items. Once patients have been trained in organization and sorting, they can begin discarding exposures.

Imaginal and In Vivo Exposure

Exposures are aimed at reducing the avoidance associated with fears about making wrong decisions, losing information, having a poor memory, loss, and embarrassment. Therefore, therapists should review with their patients how avoidance serves to maintain their hoarding behaviors, and explain how exposure works to lessen their fears through the process of habituation and hypothesis testing. Exposure assignments should be tailored to target the patients' specific avoidance behaviors. For example, if a patient avoids noticing the clutter in their home so that they can maintain a positive mood, a relevant exposure would be for her to go home and examine the clutter. On the other hand, if a patient keeps possessions in sight so that she does not forget about them, a relevant exposure would be for her to put things out of sight and check in periodically to see if she still remembers the items.

When conducting discarding exposures, the number of outcomes should be limited to two: save or discard. Once a decision has been made, the item should be placed where it belongs according to the organizational plan that was developed. Because the decision-making process is typically the hardest part of an exposure, discarding exposures usually are carried out as behavioral experiments. This means that exposures are conducted to test out the beliefs that support patients' hoarding, rather than to experience habituation. To conduct a behavioral experiment, patients write down the context of the situation, their specific hypothesis of what will happen from discarding, and their anticipatory discomfort. Patients then conduct the experiment and write down what actually happened and their actual discomfort. They then state whether or not their hypothesis was supported.

Therapists can assist in discarding exposures by asking challenging questions, such as "Do you really need it?"; "If you do not keep this, will you suffer financially or physically?"; "Do you have a specific plan for this item, and will you use it within a reasonable time frame?"; and "Will getting rid of this help you solve your hoarding problem?" After a few exposures have been completed, patients are asked to identify which questions facilitated their decision making, and to write them down on a note card to be used when completing discarding exposures as homework. As therapy progresses, patients are encouraged to abandon the note card and to generate the questions from memory.

In addition to increasing motivation (i.e., clutter and unclutter visualization tasks), imaginal exposures can be used when patients are too fearful to begin sorting and discarding. During imaginal exposures, patients are asked to close their eyes and imagine their feared situation. Patients describe the situation in the first person and provide sensory and visual details to make the image as clear as possible. Therapists should inquire about the thoughts and feelings associated with the situation, and encourage the patient to think about the worst possible aspect of the situation. Discomfort ratings can be taken every 5 to 10 minutes until patients' peak discomfort has decreased by half. When this occurs, the imaginal exposure can be discontinued and then a plan to conduct an in vivo exposure can be made.

Reducing clutter is achieved by both discarding and by not acquiring. Nonacquisition exposures are used to lessen patients' urges to acquire. In order to generate nonacquisition exposure assignments, patients must identify places in which they have experienced difficulties resisting urges to acquire. Nonacquiring exposures usually progress from "Drive-by Nonshopping," to "Walk-by Nonshopping," to "Walk Through Nonshopping," and then to "Browsing and Picking-up Nonshopping" (Frost & Steketee, 1999). When possible, nonacquiring exposures that are expected to be extremely challenging for patients should be done in the presence of therapist. In the early stages of the non-acquiring exposures, patients should leave their money at home; however, when patients gain experience they should incorporate bringing money into the exposures.

Cognitive Strategies

Erroneous beliefs about control, responsibility, and memory are thought to contribute to compulsive hoarding (Steketee et al., 2003). Consequently, Steketee and Frost (2007) recommend that therapists are experienced in the application of cognitive therapy. Many different strategies can be used to identify and challenge maladaptive thoughts; therapists should choose strategies based upon what they think will be most useful given the current situation. Some of the more common techniques are psychoeducation about problematic thoughts, thought records, the downward arrow, and needs-versus-wants scales.

Psychoeducation about thoughts involves reviewing a list of problematic thinking styles associated with compulsive hoarding, such as all-or-nothing thinking, overgeneralization, and jumping to conclusions. Automatic thoughts that represent such thinking styles include, "If I can't figure out the perfect place for this, I should just leave it here."… "I will never find this if I move it."… and "My sister only offered to help me clean up because she thinks I'm inadequate, and plans to throw away everything I own." Thought records help patients identify the connection between triggering events, automatic thoughts, emotions, and behavior. To create a thought record, four columns can be drawn down a paper and labeled "Situation – Emotions – Automatic Thoughts – Behavior." Once patients become adept and noticing their automatic thoughts and resultant emotions and behaviors, they can then be instructed to challenge their thoughts by adding a fifth column labeled "Alternative Beliefs." Alternative beliefs can be generated by asking a series of questions that cause patients to look at the evidence for and against an automatic thought.

Another way to train patients in how to challenge their beliefs is by using the downward arrow technique. The downward arrow method involves the use of Socratic questioning to explore catastrophic fears associated with hoarding. The purpose of this technique is to identify core beliefs that may underlie hoarding behaviors. Typical questions asked during the technique include, "In thinking about getting rid of this item, what thoughts occur to you?" … "If you got rid of this item, what do you think would happen? … "If this were true, why would it be so upsetting?" … "If that were true, what's so bad about that?" … "What's the worst part about that?" … and finally, "What does that mean about *you*?" Once core beliefs are discovered, they can be examined and challenged.

The thinking styles of overgeneralization and emotional reasoning can strengthen the importance of possessions to such a point that it seems essential to save them. In order for patients to determine the true value of a possession, they must distinguish between what they truly need from what they simply want. The Need versus Want Scale (Steketee & Frost, 2007) can assist in making this decision. The form initially asks patients to rate their need and desire for a specific item. Patients are then asked a series of questions to reflect on the importance and need for the item. Such questions include, "Would you die without the item?" and "Do you have to have this for your work?" Patients are then asked to rerate their need for the item. Patients are then asked a second series of questions that target want, such as "Are you keeping this item for sentimental reasons?" and "Is this the best way to remember?" Patients are asked for a final rating of their need for an item, and then instructed to reflect on what they learned from the exercise.

Relapse Prevention

Relapse prevention is designed to help patients continue to make progress, and to manage current and future stressors without reverting to hoarding behaviors. Relapse prevention begins with a review of the cognitive-behavioral model of compulsive hoarding, followed by a review of the various skills that have been enhanced throughout the course of treatment. Those skills that have been most helpful for a particular patient are emphasized. In order to foster self-efficacy, patients' accomplishments are highlighted. Taking "after" photos of the areas of the home in which patients have worked can facilitate this purpose (Saxena & Maidment, 2004). If "before" pictures were taken during the assessment phase, patients can appreciate the improvement they have made, and be reminded about the benefit of their hard work.

Finally, a review of the ups and downs of treatment can assist patients in developing realistic expectations of what the future might entail. This can lead to a discussion of patients' strengths and weaknesses. Patients can be asked to generate their own strategies to overcome any weaknesses by using the 6 problem-solving steps that were learned during therapy. Therapists should also ask patients to reflect over the entire course of therapy and to describe what they have learned, what they still need to work on, and their new goals.

Conclusion

While compulsive hoarding is notoriously treatment-resistant to psychological and biological treatment approaches for OCD, recent cognitive-behavioral treatment approaches tailored specifically to hoarding have shown some efficacy. Nonetheless, treatment of a hoarding patient generally involves many challenges related to clinical characteristics, practical, and ethical concerns. The most promising treatment approach is CBT specifically adapted for compulsive hoarding (Steketee & Frost, 2007). This treatment is derived from the cognitive-behavioral model and focuses on five general areas: education about hoarding, improving decision-making skills, development of an organizational system for possessions, graded exposure to avoidance behaviors (e.g., exposure to making decisions, to the emotional distress associated with discarding, and to putting possessions out of sight in order to provoke fears about memory and loss), and cognitive restructuring regarding beliefs about possessions (Frost & Steketee, 1999). An initial motivational interviewing module (Miller & Rollnick, 2002) may also be added to the treatment protocol (Frost, Steketee, & Greene, 2003; Tolin et al., 2007b). Some of the strategies directly target specific challenges common to hoarding patients, such as motivational interviewing to address difficulties with treatment refusal, lack of motivation, and poor insight into hoarding-related problems. Despite some promising recent findings, there is ample opportunity to further evaluate and improve treatment for compulsive hoarding.

Future Directions

The following questions represent future directions for research on hoarding.

1. What behavioral, cognitive remediational, and pharmacological approaches might help to address neurocognitive deficits found in a significant portion of compulsive hoarding patients?

2. Are there additive benefits of combining cognitive-behavioral and biological treatments for compulsive hoarding?

3. What may be the benefits of intensive hoarding treatment relative to weekly outpatient therapy?

4. Do motivational interviewing approaches improve treatment outcome for compulsive hoarding?

5. How might CBT for compulsive hoarding be tailored to address different subtypes of hoarding patients, such as those with and without comorbid OCD symptoms?

Related Chapters

Chapter 4. Phenomenology and Characteristics of Compulsive Hoarding

Chapter 11. Psychological Models of Obsessive Compulsive and OC Spectrum Disorders: From Psychoanalytic to Behavioral Conceptualizations

Chapter 27. Future Research on Obsessive Compulsive and Spectrum Conditions

Further Reading

Pertusa, A., Frost, R.O., Fullana, M.A., Samuels, J., Steketee, G., Tolin, D., Saxena, S., Leckman, J.F., & Mataix-Cols, D. (2010). Refining the diagnostic boundaries of compulsive hoarding: a critical review. *Clinical Psychology Review, 30,* 371–386.

Steketee, G., Frost, R. O. (2007). *Compulsive hoarding and acquiring: Therapist guide.* New York: Oxford University Press.

References

Abramowitz, J. S., & Deacon, B. J. (2006). Psychometric properties and construct validity of the Obsessive-Compulsive Inventory-Revised: Replication and extension with a clinical sample. *Journal of Anxiety Disorders, 20,* 1016–1035.

Abramowitz, J. S., Franklin, M. E., Schwartz, S. A., & Furr, J. M. (2003). Symptom presentation and outcome of cognitive-behavioral therapy for obsessive-compulsive disorder. *Journal of Consulting and Clinical Psychology, 71,* 1049–1057.

Black, D. W., Monahan, P., Gable, J., Blum, N., Clancy, G., & Baker, P. (1998). Hoarding and treatment response in 38 nondepressed subjects with obsessive-compulsive disorder. *Journal of Clinical Psychiatry, 59,* 420–425.

Cermele, J. A., Melendez-Pallitto, L., & Pandina, G. J. (2001). Intervention in compulsive hoarding: A case study. *Behavior Modification, 25,* 214–232.

Christenson, D. D., & Greist, J. H. (2001). The challenge of obsessive-compulsive disorder hoarding. *Primary Psychiatry, 8,* 79–86.

Coles, M. E., Frost, R. O., Heimberg, R. G., & Steketee, G. (2003). Hoarding behaviors in a large college sample. *Behaviour Research and Therapy, 41,* 179–194.

Foa, E. B., Huppert, J. D., Leiberg, S., Langner, R., Kichic, R., Hajcak, G., et al. (2002). The Obsessive-Compulsive Inventory: development and validation of a short version. *Psychological Assessment, 14,* 485–496.

Foa, E. B., Kozak, M. J., Salkovskis, P. M., Coles, M. E., & Amir, N. (1998). The validation of a new obsessive-compulsive disorder scale: The Obsessive-Compulsive Inventory. *Psychological Assessment, 10,* 206–221.

Frost, R. O., & Gross, R. C. (1993). The hoarding of possessions. *Behaviour Research and Therapy, 31,* 367–381.

Frost, R. O., & Hartl, T. (1996). A cognitive-behavioral model of compulsive hoarding. *Behaviour Research and Therapy, 34,* 341–350.

Frost, R. O., Krause, M. S., & Steketee, G. (1996). Hoarding and obsessive-compulsive symptoms. *Behavior Modification, 20,* 116–132.

Frost, R. O., & Shows, D. L. (1993). The nature and measurement of compulsive indecisiveness. *Behaviour Research and Therapy, 31,* 683–692.

Frost, R. O., & Steketee, G. (1999). Issues in the treatment of compulsive hoarding. *Cognitive and Behavioral Practice, 6,* 397–407.

Frost, R. O., Steketee, G., & Greene, K. A. (2003). Interventions for compulsive hoarding. *Journal of Brief Treatment and Crisis Intervention, 25,* 323–337.

Frost, R. O., Steketee, G., & Grisham, J. R. (2004). Measurement of compulsive hoarding: Saving Inventory Revised. *Behaviour Research and Therapy, 42,* 1163–1182.

Frost, R. O., Steketee, G., Tolin, D. F., & Renaud, S. (2008). Development and validation of the Clutter Image Rating. *Journal of Psychopathology and Behavior Assessment, 30,* 193–203.

Frost, R. O., Steketee, G., & Williams, L. (2002). Compulsive buying, compulsive hoarding, and obsessive-compulsive disorder. *Behavior Therapy, 33,* 201–214.

Frost, R. O., Steketee, G., & Williams, L. F. (2000). Hoarding: A community health problem. *Health and Social Care in the Community, 8,* 229–234.

Frost, R. O., Steketee, G., Williams, L. F., & Warren, R. (2000). Mood, personality disorder symptoms, and disability in obsessive-compulsive hoarders: A comparison with clinical and nonclinical controls. *Behaviour Research and Therapy, 38,* 1071–1081.

Goodman, W. K., Price, L. H., Rasmussen, S. A., Mazure, C., Fleischmann, R. L., Hill, C. L., et al. (1989). The Yale–Brown

Obsessive–Compulsive Scale. I. Development, use and reliability. *Archives of General Psychiatry, 46*, 1006–1011.

Grisham, J. R., Brown, T. A., Liverant, G., & Campbell, L. A. (2005). The distinctiveness of hoarding from other dimensions of obsessive-compulsive disorder. *Journal of Anxiety Disorders, 19*, 767–769.

Grisham, J. R., Brown, T. A., Savage, C. R., Steketee, G., & Barlow, D. H. (2007). Neuropsychological impairment associated with compulsive hoarding. *Behaviour Research and Therapy, 45*, 1471–1483.

Grisham, J. R., Frost, R. O., Steketee, G., Kim, H. J., & Hood, S. (2006). Age of onset of compulsive hoarding. *Journal of Anxiety Disorders, 20*, 675–686.

Grisham, J. R., Steketee, G., & Frost, R. O. (2008). Interpersonal problems and emotional intelligence in compulsive hoarding. *Depression and Anxiety, 25*, E63–71.

Hajcak, G., Huppert, J., Simons, R., & Foa, E. (2004). Psychometric properties of the OCI-R in a college sample. *Behaviour Research and Therapy 42*, 115–123.

Hartl, T. L., Duffany, S. R., Allen, G. J., Steketee, G., & Frost, R. O. (2005). Relationships among compulsive hoarding, trauma, and attention-deficit/hyperactivity disorder. *Behaviour Research and Therapy, 43*, 269–276.

Hartl, T. L., & Frost, R. O. (1999). Cognitive-behavioral treatment of compulsive hoarding: a multiple baseline experimental case study. *Behaviour Research and Therapy, 37*, 451–461.

Hartl, T. L., Frost, R. O., Allen, G. J., Deckersbach, T., Steketee, G., Duffany, S. R., et al. (2004). Actual and perceived memory deficits in individuals with compulsive hoarding. *Depression and Anxiety, 20*, 59–69.

Kozak, M. J., & Foa, E. B. (1997). *Mastery of obsessive-compulsive disorder: A cognitive-behavioral approach. [Therapist Guide].* San Antonio: Psychological Corporation.

Luchian, S. A., McNally, R. J., & Hooley, J. M. (2007). Cognitive aspects of nonclinical obsessive-compulsive hoarding *Behaviour Research and Therapy, 45*, 1657–1662.

Mataix-Cols, D., Baer, L., Rauch, S., & Jenike, M. A. (2000). Relation to factor analyzed symptom dimensions of obsessive-compulsive disorder to personality disorders. *Acta Psychiatrica Scandinavica, 102*, 199–202.

Mataix-Cols, D., Marks, I. M., Greist, J. H., Kobak, K. A., & Baer, L. (2002). Obsessive-compulsive symptom dimensions as predictors of compliance with and response to behaviour therapy: Results from a controlled trial. *Psychotherapy and Psychosomatics, 71*, 255–262.

Mataix-Cols, D., Rauch, S., Manzo, P., Jenike, M., & Baer, L. (1999). Use of factor-analyzed symptom dimensions to predict outcome with serotonin reuptake inhibitors and placebo in the treatment of obsessive-compulsive disorder. *American Journal of Psychiatry, 156*, 1409–1416.

Meunier, S. A., Tolin, D. F., Frost, R. O., Steketee, G., & Brady, R. E. (2006). *Prevalence of hoarding symptoms across the anxiety disorders.* Paper presented at the Annual Meeting of the Anxiety Disorders Association of America.

Miller, W. R., & Rollnick, S. (2002). *Motivational Interviewing: Preparing people for change* (2nd ed.). New York: Guilford.

Muroff, J., Steketee, G., & Frost, R. (2009). *Cognitive behavioral treatment delivered via webcam.* Paper presented at the Association for Behavioral and Cognitive Therapies.

Muroff, J., Steketee, G., Himle, J., & Frost, R. (2010). Delivery of internet treatment for compulsive hoarding (D.I.T.C.H.). *Behaviour Research and Therapy, 48*(1), 79–85.

Muroff, J., Steketee, G., Rasmussen, J., Gibson, A., Bratiotis, C., & Sorrentino, C. (2009). Group cognitive and behavioral treatment for compulsive hoarding: a preliminary trial. *Depression and Anxiety, 26*(7), 634–640.

Patronek, G. J. (1999). Hoarding of animals: an under-recognized public health problem in a difficult-to-study population. *Public Health Reports, 114*, 81–87.

Pekareva-Kochergina, A., & Frost, R. O. (2009). *The Effects of a biblio-based self-help program for compulsive hoarding.* Paper presented at the Association of Behavioral and Cognitive Therapies.

Safren, S. A. (2006). Cognitive-behavioral approaches to ADHD treatment in adulthood. *Journal of Clinical Psychiatry, 67*, 46–50.

Samuels, J., Bienvenu III, O. J., Riddle, M. A., Cullen, B. A. M., Grados, M. A., Liang, K. Y., et al. (2002). Hoarding in obsessive-compulsive disorder: Results from a case-control study. *Behaviour Research and Therapy, 40*, 517–528

Samuels, J. F., Bienvenu Iii, O. J., Pinto, A., Fyer, A. J., McCracken, J. T., Rauch, S. L., et al. (2007). Hoarding in obsessive-compulsive disorder: Results from the OCD Collaborative Genetics Study. *Behaviour Research and Therapy, 45*, 673–686.

Samuels, J. F., Bienvenu, O. J., Grados, M. A., Cullen, B., Riddle, M. A., Liang, K. Y., et al. (2008). Prevalence and correlates of hoarding behavior in a community-based sample. *Behaviour Research and Therapy, 46*, 836–844.

Saxena, S., Brody, A. L., Maidment, K. M., & Baxter, L. R. J. (2007). Paroxetine treatment of compulsive hoarding. *Journal of Psychiatry Research, 41*, 481–487.

Saxena, S., Brody, A. L., Maidment, K. M., Smith, E. C., Zohrabi, N., Katz, E., et al. (2004). Cerebral glucose metabolism in obsessive-compulsive hoarding. *American Journal of Psychiatry, 161*, 1038–1048.

Saxena, S., & Maidment, K. M. (2004). Treatment of compulsive hoarding. *Journal of Clinical Psychology, 60*, 1143–1154.

Saxena, S., Maidment, K. M. V, Vapnik, T., Golden, G., Rishwain, T., Rosen, R., et al. (2002). Obsessive-compulsive hoarding: Symptom severity and response to multimodal treatment. *Journal of Clinical Psychiatry, 63*, 21–27.

Snowdon, J., Shah, A., & Halliday, G. (2007). Severe domestic squalor: a review. *International Psychogeriatrics, 19*, 37–51.

Steketee, G., & Frost, R. O. (2003). Compulsive hoarding: Current status of the research. *Clinical Psychology Review, 23*, 905–927.

Steketee, G., & Frost, R. O. (2007). *Compulsive hoarding and acquiring: Therapist guide.* New York, NY: Oxford University Press.

Steketee, G., Frost, R. O., & Kim, H. J. (2001). Hoarding by elderly people. *Health and Social Work, 26*, 176–184

Steketee, G., Frost, R. O., & Kyrios, M. (2003). Cognitive aspects of compulsive hoarding. *Cognitive Therapy and Research, 27*, 463–479.

Steketee, G., Frost, R. O., Wincze, J., Greene, K., & Douglass, H. (2000). Group and individual treatment of compulsive hoarding: A pilot study. *Behavioural and Cognitive Psychotherapy, 28*, 259–268.

Steketee, G., & Van Noppen, B. (2003). Family approaches to treatment for obsessive compulsive disorder. *Revista Brasileira de Psiquiatria, 25*, 43–50.

Steketee, G., Frost, R. O., Tolin, D. F., Rasmussen, J, & Brown, T (2010). Waitlist-controlled trial of cognitive behavior therapy for hoarding disorder. *Depression and Anxiety, 27*(5), 476–484.

Tolin, D. F., Frost, R. O., & Steketee, G. (2007a). *Buried in Treasures: Help for Compulsive Acquiring, Saving, and Hoarding*: Oxford; University Press.

Tolin, D. F., Frost, R. O., & Steketee, G. (2007b). An open trial of cognitive-behavioral therapy for compulsive hoarding. *Behaviour Research and Therapy, 45*, 1461–1470.

Tolin, D. F., Frost, R. O., Steketee, G., & Fitch, K. E. (2008). Family burden of compulsive hoarding: Results of an internet survey. *Behaviour Research and Therapy, 46*, 334–344.

Tolin, D. F., Frost, R. O., Steketee, G., Gray, K. D., & Fitch, K. E. (2008). The economic and social burden of compulsive hoarding. *Psychiatry Research, 160*, 200–211.

Wincze, J. P., Steketee, G., & Frost, R. O. (2007). Categorization in compulsive hoarding. *Behaviour Research and Therapy, 45*, 63–72.

Winsberg, M. E., Cassic, K. S., & Koran, L. M. (1999). Hoarding in obsessive-compulsive disorder: A report of 20 cases. *Journal of Clinical Psychiatry, 60*, 591–597.

Wu, K. D., & Watson, D. (2005). Hoarding and its relation to obsessive-compulsive disorder. *Behaviour Research and Therapy, 43*, 897–921.

Treatment of Tic Disorders and Trichotillomania

Martin E. Franklin, Diana Antinoro, Emily J. Ricketts, *and* Douglas W. Woods

Abstract

This chapter briefly describes tic disorders and trichotillomania (TTM) and reviews the pharmacotherapy and psychosocial treatment outcome literature for each of these conditions. In contrast to anxiety or depression, distorted or maladaptive cognitions do not appear to play a central role in the etiology or maintenance of tic disorders and TTM, and therefore cognitive therapy is not emphasized in the psychosocial treatments studied to date. Treatment protocols are best characterized as "behavioral," although some include ancillary cognitive interventions. Behavioral treatments that include habit reversal training (HRT) appear to hold the greatest promise for each of these conditions, and these are described in some detail. Future directions in treatment research are suggested.

Keywords: tic disorders, trichotillomania, Tourette syndrome, habit reversal training, behavior therapy

Introduction

The current chapter briefly describes tic disorders and trichotillomania (TTM), then provides a review of the pharmacotherapy and psychosocial treatment outcome literature separately for each of these conditions. Notably, in contrast to anxiety or depression, the psychopathology literatures on tic disorders and TTM indicate that distorted or maladaptive cognitions do not play a central role in the etiology or maintenance of these conditions (e.g., Mansueto, Golomb, Thomas, & Stemberger, 1999; Miguel et al., 1995). Accordingly, cognitive therapy techniques are not typically emphasized in the psychosocial treatments that have been studied thus far. These protocols are more accurately characterized as "behavioral," even though some do include some ancillary cognitive interventions (e.g., Franklin & Tolin, 2007; O'Connor et al., 2001), and therefore the section headings in our chapter will be labeled as such. The literature review also reveals that the application of behavioral treatments, specifically those including habit reversal training

(HRT), appear to hold the greatest promise for each of these conditions. We then describe the application of HRT in some detail, and conclude with a section on future directions in treatment research.

Tic Disorders
Phenomenology and Implications for Treatment

Tics are sudden, recurrent, non-rhythmic, stereotyped movements or vocalizations, which can be described as simple or complex and can occur in all parts of the body (American Psychiatric Association; APA, 2000). Tics can be either repetitive contractions of muscle groups known as *motor tics*, or repetitive sounds known as *vocal tics*; many patients have both. Patients often report experiencing uncomfortable sensations prior to engaging in tics; these sensations are often more prominent as tic complexity increases. These sensations, which are known as *premonitory urges*, are often described as an increasing tension in a certain part of the body. The temporary relief of these sensations following performance of the tic also appears to be common (Leckman, Walker, & Cohen, 1993; Woods, Piacentini, Himle, & Chang, 2005) and, as will be discussed later, this negative reinforcement process is critically important in the conceptual model of behavioral treatments for the tics themselves. In addition to these internal sensations, external environmental factors (e.g., settings or social reactions to tics) can also influence tic frequency (Conelea & Woods, 2008) and therefore need to be considered in treatment planning.

Pharmacotherapy

The acknowledged neurobiological nature of tics (e.g., Mink, 2001) has led to an emphasis on psychopharmacological approaches to reduce tics and associated comorbid symptoms (e.g., obsessions, compulsions, inattention, hyperactivity, and impulsivity) acutely. Specifically, medications including clonidine (Leckman et al., 1991), and the typical/atypical neuroleptics of pimozide (Shapiro et al., 1989), haloperidol (Sallee, Nesbitt, Jackson, Sine, & Sethuraman, 1997), and risperidone (Scahill, Leckman, Schultz, Katsovich, & Peterson, 2003) have been found efficacious in reducing symptoms of chronic tic disorders (CTDs) relative to placebo, at least in the short run. On the whole, however, the pharmacotherapy outcome data also indicate that (1) the mean response to active treatment is typically partial; (2) a subset of patients do not improve or worsen on active medication; (3) a substantial proportion of patients experience dose-limiting side effects or cannot tolerate the medications at all; and (4) some patients decline pharmacotherapy altogether. Long-term outcome studies for pharmacotherapies are also lacking, and few double-blind discontinuation studies are available to inform clinical practice. This is especially unfortunate in light of the side-effect profile for neuroleptics (e.g., weight gain, sedation), and thus patients and physicians are left in the difficult position to decide without empirical guidance whether, when, and how best to conduct medication taper. It is also clear from the recently completed Comprehensive Behavioral Intervention for Tics Study (CBITS) for youth (Piacentini et al., 2008), and from recent reviews of psychosocial interventions (e.g., Cook & Blacher, 2007), that concomitant pharmacotherapy does not interfere with response to psychosocial treatments, and thus medication and psychosocial interventions do not have to be considered to be mutually exclusive.

Behavioral Approaches

HABIT REVERSAL TRAINING

Overview. As noted above, although CTDs clearly have a strong neurobiological component; environmental factors have also been found to influence tic frequency, severity, expression, and associated impairment (O'Connor, 2002). Specifically, it has been posited that tic severity is influenced by both positive and negative reinforcement processes. Positive reinforcement processes operate on tic frequency by directly reinforcing tic expression (e.g., peers praise a child for doing particular tics), making tics more likely in those situations that predict such reinforcement. Likewise, tic suppression is rewarded (e.g., child suppresses tics to avoid teasing), and tics are thus less likely to occur in similar situations. Negative reinforcement also functions as a potential tic-maintaining process. Tics can result in the removal from or avoidance of potentially stressful situations (e.g., child is asked to leave a difficult class due to disruptive tics), and perhaps of greatest importance in tic maintenance, tics have repeatedly been found to temporarily reduce the aversive premonitory urge, thus reinforcing tic occurrence when the urge appears. This latter process is similar to behavioral theories of OCD, such as the two-factor theory (Mowrer, 1960), in which obsessions are theorized to give rise to anxiety, and compulsions reduce the obsessional distress, thereby reinforcing this behavioral response to obsessions.

Behavioral treatments for tics have been developed to focus on these core maintaining behavioral processes, and include both function-based interventions and habit reversal (Woods et al., 2008). Function-based interventions are designed to identify and systematically implement individualized interventions to modify environmental variables that may be maintaining tics. Habit reversal training involves awareness training and competing response training, both of which are designed to weaken the negative reinforcement cycle of temporary urge reduction. In HRT, competing responses are initiated in response to awareness of the premonitory urges themselves, or when in environmental situations found to increase ticking. By doing so, the patient refrains from providing negative reinforcement for tics, and with repeated practice, the urges to engage in tics in response to premonitory sensations are weakened, presumably as a function of habituation. Additional behavioral techniques, such as contingency management and relaxation training, can also be included in HRT to reduce negative mood states (anger, anxiety, stress) that may influence the frequency of the premonitory tic urges/sensations themselves, or to enhance motivation and utilization of these core techniques (Piacentini & Chang, 2005).

Outcome Research. A variety of behavioral interventions for CTDs have been studied in open trials, small case series, or single-subject experimental designs, but thus far only HRT and exposure and response prevention therapy (ERP) have been examined in randomized controlled trials (RCTs) (see Cook & Blacher, 2007; Piacentini & Chang, 2005; Woods et al., 2008). The four published randomized trials involving HRT that have included a comparison condition of some kind have consistently yielded superior outcome for HRT (Azrin & Peterson, 1990; Deckersbach, Rauch, Buhlmann, & Wilhelm, 2006; O'Connor et al., 2001; Wilhelm et al., 2003). Azrin and Peterson (1990) published the first RCT describing HRT as a treatment for tics, and found substantial reduction of motor and vocal tics both at home and in the clinic for patients treated with HRT, whereas massed practice was associated with little change. The sample was quite small (10), and afforded little opportunity to examine predictors of response or developmental factors, since the study included both adults and children. O'Connor and colleagues (2001) were the next group to publish a randomized trial involving HRT, employing a larger sample (n = 69 w/a CTD). They used a waitlist (WL) control comparison to a cognitive-behavioral treatment package that included awareness training, HRT, and more general cognitive restructuring of anticipations linked to ticking. The behavioral package yielded significant and clinically meaningful reductions in tics, perceived control over tics, as well as secondary outcome measures such as self-esteem, anxiety, and depression. Gains appeared to be largely maintained at follow-up for the group treated behaviorally.

Although these two trials provided preliminary evidence for the efficacy of HRT relative to no treatment, studies equating therapist contact time and controlling for other nonspecific effects associated with being in treatment were still needed. To meet this scientific aim, Wilhelm and colleagues (2003) randomized 32 adult patients with Tourette syndrome (TS) to receive either HRT or a supportive psychotherapy (SP) intervention. Results indicated an advantage for HRT over SP in reducing tic severity at post-treatment; HRT patients also remained improved over the course of a 10-month follow-up period. This same research group replicated and extended these findings for HRT over SP in a second

sample of 30 adults with TS (Deckersbach et al., 2006). A fifth study, comparing HRT and ERP in 43 patients with TS, found that both treatments yielded similar reductions in tics and in tic urges (Verdellen, Keijsers, Cath, & Hoodguin, 2004), and will be discussed below in the ERP section.

Data from the treatment trials reviewed above now provide a sufficient evidence base from which to draw broader conclusions about the efficacy of HRT in particular. In light of these studies' fairly consistent findings, HRT is now considered a well-established treatment for CTDs (Cook & Blacher, 2007). Accordingly, the next stage of treatment development in CTDs may well be to determine how best to disseminate HRT more broadly so that most CTD patients can have access to this efficacious form of treatment.

Exposure Plus Response Prevention

Overview. As alluded to above, Mowrer's two-factor theory (1960) explains the maintenance of pathology in OCD by suggesting that intrusive, spontaneous, and involuntary obsessions give rise to anxiety, and that compulsions are executed responses designed specifically to reduce it. The neurobiology of the obsessional process, and changes in glucose metabolism in implicated brain regions following behavioral treatment designed to intentionally confront situations that evoke obsessional distress and eliminate compulsions (ERP), has been established (Baxter et al., 1992). An analogous application in CTDs has been posited: in the case of CTDs, the unpleasant premonitory urges are also intrusive, unwanted, and involuntary, and clearly have their origins in neurobiological dysfunction (e.g., Mink, 2001). That said, completion of the tics themselves can be considered according to the two-factor theory to be semi-volitional, in that although the premonitory sensation or prompt is clearly involuntary, the tics themselves are executed responses designed to reduce these premonitory sensations (Bliss, 1980; Himle et al., 2007; Leckman et al., 1993). By extension, then, ERP may also be applicable in CTD treatment, in that it also interrupts the stimulus-response associations between premonitory urges and tics, just as it has been used for this same purpose with respect to obsessions and compulsions. According to this theory, the use of proscribed competing responses in the presence of urges to complete tics, central to the treatment of CTDs using HRT, may be at best superfluous.

Outcome Research. The efficacy of ERP for OCD is already well established (see Abramowitz,

Whiteside, & Deacon, 2005; Franklin & Foa, 2008), and there is no evidence that teaching a proscribed competing response is necessary in OCD to promote successful implementation of response prevention; moreover, habituation to urges to engage in compulsions occurs over time, and subsequent reductions in the frequency and intensity of obsessions and urges to ritualize are consistently observed (Himle & Franklin, 2009). Empirical study of this theoretical approach, and the behavioral procedures emanating from this theory, is relatively new in CTDs, but there is now empirical evidence for ERP's efficacy for CTDs (Hoogduin, Verdellen, & Cath, 1997; Verdellen et al., 2004). The second of these studies was a direct, randomized comparison of HRT versus ERP in 43 patients with TS. Both treatments resulted in statistically significant improvement on all three measures of tic frequency and/or severity. No significant differences between the two conditions emerged, although trends tended to favor ERP.

The absence of a no-treatment group in this study does leave unanswered the question of whether this particular sample would have responded to nonspecific interventions, the passage of time, or repeated assessment. Further, the ERP treatment sessions were twice as long as the HRT sessions, which also may potentially explain the trends toward better outcomes in ERP. Future studies are needed to replicate these potentially important findings, examine patient preferences, and to determine whether HRT or ERP will be easier to disseminate into community settings where most patients with CTDs will likely be able to access clinical services.

Review of a Typical HRT Protocol

Overview. Given that the preponderance of the evidence from RCTs supports the use of HRT for CTDs, and that HRT now meets the criteria for an empirically supported treatment for CTDs (Cook & Blacher, 2007), we will expand upon its description here. Consistent with expert recommendations and with the behavior therapy protocol (which relied heavily on HRT procedures) used in the recently completed CBITS trial (Woods et al., 2008), the protocol that we employ in our respective clinical settings typically involves 8 sessions delivered over 10 weeks, with the first six sessions delivered weekly, and sessions 7 and 8 delivered biweekly. To promote maintenance of gains and based on recommendations by CTD treatment experts, we also include booster sessions at weeks 14 and 18.

Session 1 begins with the therapist providing psychoeducation about tics, presenting a neurobehavioral model of tics (described above) and providing a rationale for treatment that flows directly from the model. The therapist and patient form a collaborative relationship and create a tic hierarchy to guide treatment planning, and review instructions in self-monitoring of tics. In the case where the patient is a child or adolescent, parents are actively involved in this first session, so that the psychoeducation that is presented is consistent, and in order to explicate the parents' ancillary role in treatment.

Session 2 focuses on awareness training, and the development of a specific competing response for one tic from the tic hierarchy. Notably, treatment initially focuses on the tic rated on the hierarchy as most bothersome, with gradual progression down the hierarchy in subsequent sessions (i.e., 1 tic per session) to address less bothersome tics. Awareness training involves describing the tic, and the sensations and behaviors that precede the tic, identifying tic simulations by the therapist, and then acknowledging the actual or simulated tic exhibited by the participant. Competing response training involves teaching the patient to engage in a behavior that is physically incompatible with the tic, or makes the tic difficult to occur. The competing response is done contingent on the tic or the emergence of the urge, for one minute or until the urge diminishes substantially. An inconvenience review is also conducted in Session 2, and this list of problems caused by the tics is used in subsequent sessions as a motivational tool (i.e., as the tic-related hassles diminish with symptom reduction, patients are motivated).

Sessions 3 and 4 involve continued awareness and competing response training, along with self-monitoring instructions for other tics on the hierarchy. In the fourth session, deep-breathing training is introduced.

Session 5 involves the therapist and patient continuing to work on all treatment elements described earlier, and initiating progressive muscle relaxation.

Session 6, the last of the weekly sessions, involves ongoing review and continuation of previous treatment elements, as well as relapse prevention.

Sessions 7 and 8, which are typically delivered biweekly, continue work on relapse prevention training. In these sessions, continuing difficulties with tics and with implementing treatment procedures are discussed.

Booster sessions typically are conducted monthly for 2 to 3 months, and then as needed by the patient.

During these sessions, the therapist and patient review emergent symptoms and treatment strategies, and discuss how to address factors likely to predict increases in urges and in tic severity and intensity (e.g., stress).

Trichotillomania
Phenomenology & Implications for Treatment

Trichotillomania (TTM) has been defined as the recurrent pulling out of one's hair, resulting in hair loss with an increasing sense of tension before pulling, followed by a feeling of gratification or relief after the pulling episode (APA, 2000). Although preceding tension and subsequent relief are criteria in the DSM-IV-TR (APA, 2000), research has shown that not all patients who experience pulling-related hair loss report both tension and relief (Christenson, Mackenzie, & Mitchell, 1991; Woods et al., 2006a). Children, in particular, may not report such experiences (Franklin et al., 2008; Hanna, 1997; King et al., 1995; Reeve, Bernstein, & Christenson, 1992; Tolin, Franklin, Diefenbach, Anderson, & Meunier, 2007; Wright & Holmes, 2003).

Pulling sites vary and include, from most to least common, the scalp, eyelashes, eyebrows, pubic region, face, and body (Cohen et al., 1995; Franklin et al., 2008; Santhanam, Fairley, & Rogers, 2008; Schlosser, Black, Blum & Goldstein, 1994; Tolin et al., 2007). Many individuals with TTM engage in pre-pulling behaviors including hair touching, twirling, or stroking (Casati, Toner, & Yu, 2000; du Toit, van Kradenburg, Niehaus, & Stein, 2001) and post-pulling rituals such as rubbing hair strands across their lips, examining, biting or chewing the root of the hair, and occasionally, tricophagy or hair ingestion (Christenson et al., 1991; Schlosser et al.). At least two distinct styles have been noted, including focused and automatic hair pulling. Focused pulling usually involves a conscious effort to pull, and includes using pulling to regulate emotion. Automatic pulling, in contrast, involves a lack of awareness of the pulling, and generally occurs during sedentary activities such as watching television, reading, or driving (Christenson & Crow, 1996; Christenson et al., 1991). It is believed that those with TTM often exhibit both styles, though they may have a greater tendency toward one or the other (Flessner et al., 2008); the treatment implications of these styles have yet to be confirmed, although clinically it would appear that HRT might be ideally suited for the more automatic episodes,

whereas other augmentative strategies to assist with affect management may be needed to address focused pulling.

Pharmacotherapy

Studies examining the efficacy of pharmacotherapy for TTM in adults have focused primarily on treatment with medications with established serotonergic properties, which may in part reflect the previously prevailing view that TTM is a variant of OCD, and thus ought to be responsive to the same medications proven efficacious for OCD. In the first of these studies, Swedo et al. (1989) found the tricyclic antidepressant clomipramine (CMI) superior to desipramine at post-treatment in a double-blind crossover study; long-term response to CMI varied widely, with an overall 40% reduction in symptoms maintained at 4-year follow-up (Swedo, Lenane, & Leonard, 1993). However, Christenson et al. (1991) failed to find an advantage for the selective serotonin reuptake inhibitor (SSRI) fluoxetine (FLU) over placebo (PBO) in another double-blind crossover study, and Streichenwein and Thornby (1995) failed to detect an effect for FLU compared to PBO despite having increased the maximum FLU dose to 80 mg. Similarly, Ninan, Rothbaum, Marsteller, Knight, and Eccard (2000) found an advantage for cognitive behavioral therapy (CBT) involving HRT over both CMI and PBO, which did not differ significantly from each other. Another RCT found HRT superior to both FLU and WL, but failed to find a significant effect for FLU compared to WL (van Minnen, Hoogduin, Keijsers, Hellenbrand, & Hendriks, 2003). With respect to combined treatment approaches, Dougherty and colleagues (2006) found an advantage for BT plus the SSRI fluvoxamine (FLV) over either treatment alone, suggesting the need for further examination of this approach.

As is evident from the above review, the TTM pharmacotherapy literature to date is both underdeveloped and equivocal. Perhaps, as discussed above, important differences in the mechanisms that underlie OCD and TTM are responsible for their differential responses to medications that affect serotonin. Intriguingly, in an unpublished study, naltrexone, an opioid blocking compound thought to decrease positive reinforcement by preventing the binding of endogenous opiates to relevant receptor sites in the brain, was found superior to PBO in reducing TTM symptoms (Christenson, Crow & Mackenzie, 1994). Several case studies have indicated that augmentation of SSRIs with atypical neuroleptics may be beneficial (e.g., Epperson, Fasula, Wasylink, Price, & McDougle, 1999), and a recent open trial suggested that olanzapine may be efficacious as a monotherapy for TTM (Stewart & Nejtek, 2003). These developments notwithstanding, there is as yet no clear pharmacotherapy candidate for future study or for direct comparison to alternative treatments (e.g., BT) in TTM.

The absence of a single RCT in pediatric TTM severely restricts recommendations that can be made to parents whose children suffer from this disorder, and also has clear implications for proposing controlled studies directly comparing BT and pharmacotherapy for pediatric TTM. Clinically, we have seen a wide array of pharmacotherapy options attempted for TTM, including SRIs, psychostimulants, mood stabilizers, atypical neuroleptics, and naltrexone, yet the empirical literature has not been developed sufficiently as yet to support the use of pharmacotherapy for pediatric TTM per se.

Habit Reversal Therapy

Overview. A wide array of behavioral and cognitive-behavioral treatments and treatment packages has been applied to TTM, involving components such as self-monitoring, aversion, covert sensitization, negative practice, relaxation training, competing response training, cognitive restructuring, and over-correction. Of these, the package that has received the most attention thus far for TTM and other habit/impulse control disorders is HRT (Azrin & Nunn, 1973) which, as applied to TTM, typically includes awareness training/self-monitoring procedures and instructions to engage in a competing response using the same muscle groups involved in pulling (e.g., fist clenching), when the urge to pull is present or when pulling is present.

Outcome Research. The vast majority of the outcome literature consists of uncontrolled case reports or small case series (Woods et al., 2006b). In the first RCT examining BT for TTM (Azrin, Nunn, & Frantz, 1980), HRT was superior to negative practice, with patients in the HRT group reporting a 99% reduction in number of hair pulling episodes compared to a 58% reduction for patients in the negative practice group. The HRT group maintained their gains at 22-month follow-up, with patients reporting 87% reduction compared to pretreatment. However, the generalizability of these findings was limited by the absence of a formal treatment protocol, exclusive reliance on self-reports as the sole outcome measure, and by limited patient participation in the follow-up phase.

Since then, several more RCTs have indicated that treatments involving HRT are efficacious. In a small trial, Ninan et al. (2000) found a CBT package emphasizing HRT superior to CMI and PBO at post-treatment; CMI and PBO failed to separate from one another. Van Minnen et al. (2003) randomized 43 patients with TTM to receive either behavior therapy (BT), fluoxetine (FLU), or waitlist (WL) for 12 weeks. Patients in the BT group experienced a greater reduction in their TTM symptoms than did patients in the FLU or WL groups. Woods et al. (2006c) found a combination of Acceptance and Commitment Therapy (ACT) plus HRT superior to WL, although the study design did not allow for conclusions about the separate contributions of ACT and habit reversal, respectively. Dougherty et al.'s study (2006), reviewed above, suggested an additive effect for sertraline (SER) compared to HRT alone.

Randomized and open studies of behavioral therapy (BT) or CBT that have included follow-up data suggest problems with relapse in adults. Lerner, Franklin, Meadows, Hembree, and Foa (1998), Keuthen et al. (2001), Mouton and Stanley (1996), and Keijsers et al. (2006) indicated that relapse was common, whereas Azrin et al. (1980) and Woods et al. (2006c) reported maintenance of gains. A recently completed open study of HRT for children and adolescents found better maintenance of gains over time than typically reported in adult studies (Tolin et al., 2007). Despite these contrasting findings, several TTM treatment experts (e.g., Christenson & Mackenzie, 1994; Vitulano, King, Scahill, & Cohen, 1992) have observed that clinically, patients often experience a recurrence of hair pulling after treatment, especially in response to external stressors. Mouton and Stanley (1996) suggested that additional attention might need to be given to extending awareness training and the use of competing responses to maximize long-term outcome.

Review of a Typical HRT Protocol

Overview. Similar to the protocol designed for CTDs, the HRT program typically delivered in our clinic settings involves weekly sessions followed by a maintenance phase. In the case of HRT for TTM, the first 8 sessions are conducted weekly in hour-long sessions, which are usually followed by 4 sessions conducted biweekly to promote maintenance of gains. Booster sessions can then be employed as needed to ensure continued use of techniques, management of emergent symptoms using techniques used in acute treatment, and provision of continuing support.

Session 1 begins with the therapist and patient trying to determine whether the patient is aware of his/her pulling, whether he/she can identify early warning signs of pulling, and whether the pulling occurs in many different settings or only in one or two (e.g., upstairs bathroom). The rationale for and details of self-monitoring of hair pulling is introduced during this session. If the patient cannot successfully monitor pulling for developmental reasons, parents are enlisted to assist. Psychoeducation is also included in this session, as patients and their families may have received misinformation or no information about TTM prior to contact with our clinic. The therapist uses clinical examples, epidemiological information, and analogies to more common nervous habits such as nailbiting, in order to begin the process of destigmatizing patients. The therapist explains that TTM appears to be responsive to stress, and associated with internal and external cues such as places where pulling occurs, physical sensations, sedentary activities such as talking on the phone, and emotional states such as boredom. The therapist shares with the patient typical patterns of pulling, describes differences among pullers with respect to what they do with pulled hair, and generally tries to convey knowledge and acceptance to the child or adolescent. The importance of improving awareness of urges to pull is emphasized with age-appropriate metaphors and analogies (e.g., "It's hard to know how to outsmart TTM if we don't know when it's likely to come and bug you. . ."), as increased awareness is critical for successful implementation of stimulus control and habit reversal. The patient is sent home with instructions to begin monitoring pulling using self-monitoring forms available in the BT manual.

Session 2 involves the introduction of stimulus control (SC) techniques. Following review of self-monitoring data, the therapist explains the rationale for SC, in which patients are taught to interfere with pulling by wearing band-aids on fingers in high-risk situations, avoid touching their face or scalp with bare hands, looking into mirrors in well-lit areas such as bathrooms, and placing signs that have meaning to the patient in places associated with pulling (e.g., telephone). The patient and the therapist consider specific stimulus control methods to be employed during the week; suggestions are tailored to the specifics of the patients' pulling behaviors.

Session 3 involves the introduction of competing response/habit reversal procedures. This session begins with review of self-monitoring data, discussion of progress in identifying high-risk situations, and in using stimulus control methods to prevent pulling behavior or to stop pulling earlier in an episode sooner than he/she has been able to do previously. Instruction in habit reversal also begins, in which the therapist helps the patient identify how to interrupt the chain of pulling movements, preferably with a physically competing response. Competing responses that are often used include playing with clay, shelling peanuts, and making tight fists and holding for several minutes. Patients are instructed to implement the HRT procedures with competing responses at the first sign of pulling urges. Therapists bring with them to the session several objects or "manipulatives" that can be used for competing response training in order to allow the patient to try out some of the possibilities. Arrangements are made for the patient to either borrow one of these objects from the therapist, or to purchase during the week.

Sessions 4–6 involve continuation of SC and HRT. These sessions begin with inspection of self-monitoring data, review of high-risk situations, and use of treatment procedures during the previous week. Positive reinforcement of effort is emphasized, as is the analogy of "acting like a detective to outsmart your TTM." Therapists work with patients to identify times when the treatment procedures have proven easy to implement and useful, as well as times when they have not; patient and therapist together troubleshoot for those times and places when BT procedures have not been effective or have not been put in place. Involvement of family in treatment efforts during the previous week is also reviewed, with helpful efforts acknowledged and reinforced, and less helpful efforts discussed.

Session 7 involves the introduction of *relapse prevention*. In addition to reviewing self-monitoring data and use of treatment procedures as described above, therapists introduce the concept of relapse prevention for patients who have made at least some progress in BT. Patients are taught to imagine coping effectively with stressful situations, instead of returning to pulling as a means to cope. Discussion of relapse prevention begins early on in treatment, yet is emphasized particularly in Sessions 7 and 8, as well as during the maintenance phase. Techniques include focusing on how to control setbacks, to differentiate "lapses" from "relapses" and to teach the patient that occasional setbacks are a natural occurrence rather than an uncontrollable catastrophe. Typically, when a patient has experienced ups and downs during treatment, discussion focuses on how the patient got him/herself back on track during the active treatment phase when a lapse was encountered. Patients are also reminded that they are better equipped to deal with future lapses because of what they have learned in treatment. Patients and therapists also design a written list of procedures that the patient can use if he/she senses a return to previous functioning; calling the therapist for assistance is typically included on this list. Identified triggers for pulling, and effective responses to these triggers, are reviewed with family members to ensure that they are sufficiently aware of the patient's high-risk situations and affective states. Families are advised on how to help the patient cope with occasional setbacks, as clinically we have observed that strong negative responses to lapses can demoralize the patient to the point where he/she chooses not to intervene.

Sesssion 8 includes further discussion of relapse prevention and wrapping up of acute treatment. Self-monitoring data and use of techniques are reviewed, relapse prevention methods are discussed further, and the session focuses particularly on preparing for the reduction of session frequency. Patients are reminded that they have learned the core skills needed to "fight back" against TTM, and their efforts during the treatment are reviewed and praised. The patient is encouraged to discuss any concerns about ending the acute phase of treatment, and parent(s) are brought into the last half of this session to hear a summary of progress and future efforts from the patient's perspective. For younger patients, these sessions can be conducted as a "graduation ceremony," complete with a certificate of achievement and reminder lists of how to stay on track in the "battle against TTM."

Maintenance Sessions. We typically include 4 in-person sessions conducted over an 8-week period to promote maintenance of gains in TTM; this is informed by the data on relapse discussed above. Therapists first ask patients whether they have experienced any increases in urges, or in actual pulling behavior, in the time since the previous contact. In the event that the patient does report any of these changes, the therapist normalizes these increases, contextualizes them as challenges to be faced rather than as failures on the part of the patient or of the therapy, asks if there were any contributing factors that might have led to these increases (e.g., academic challenges, interpersonal stressors), and helps to develop an effective "battle plan" to deal with the hair pulling itself, and with managing the

precipitating events without relying on pulling. For patients who report no change in their pulling symptoms or urges, therapists pose hypothetical situations (e.g., "let's say that it's the week before finals and your TTM is starting to bug you again at night—how would you deal with that?") and ask patients to elaborate on how they would manage these situations. All patients are encouraged to contact the therapist prior to the next scheduled appointment, in cases where a crisis develops.

Habit Reversal Training: What's in a Name?

Psychology's use of the term *habit reversal* originated in the 1970s during the height of behavioral psychology. Originally coined to refer to treatment of nervous habits and tics (Azrin & Nunn, 1973), this treatment has been shown to be effective with many other psychological and behavioral difficulties, such as stuttering, alcohol abuse, enuresis and behavior problems (Azrin & Foxx, 1971; Azrin & Nunn, 1974; Azrin et al., 1980; Foxx & Azrin, 1972; Hunt & Azrin, 1973). The word *habit* connotes a "behavior that requires little or no thought and is learned," (www.brittanica.com). Based on this definition and the colloquial use of the term, one may therefore assume that the target behavior could be prevented simply through awareness and rewards or motivation. This conceptualization includes some components of habit reversal (awareness training and motivational plans to reinforce compliance), but it does not encompass the entire treatment. In fact, the use of the word *habit* prohibits the full understanding of the distress, impairment, and dysfunction associated with these disorders. Additionally, it may insinuate that the patient is to blame for "not stopping" the symptoms. Furthermore, it minimizes the need for a more formal, systematic approach such as the one we advocate above. Overall, the effects of using such a term to describe treatment may well result in increased stigma for patients, and potentially decreased utilization of treatment, which may inadvertently discourage treatment dissemination.

Summary and Future Directions

Pharmacotherapy Treatment Development. Although we do not have, as yet, an extremely effective, safe, and durable medication for CTDs, some progress has been achieved in the last 15 years, in that several medications generally appear to be efficacious. Pharmacotherapy research for TTM, however, has largely stagnated in that same period. This lack of progress plays out in the clinical realm with unfortunate consequences: despite a pharmacotherapy outcome literature that can only be described as discouraging, TTM continues to be treated medically, largely with SSRIs (Franklin et al., 2008; Woods et al., 2006a). This may well be an artifact of TTM's topographic similarity to OCD, and a function of the lack of basic research in TTM that may distinguish its more specific neurobiological and neuroanatomical pathways. Despite its similarity to OCD in the form of repetitive behavior, TTM's response to SSRIs is far less robust or consistent than has been seen in OCD (Christenson et al., 1991; Stanley, Breckenridge, & Swann, 1997; Streichenwein & Thornby, 1995), with multiple double-blind experiments yielding limited results. Recent discussions in the literature of TTM's addictive qualities (e.g., Grant, Odlaug, & Potenza, 2007) may promote further investigation of the use of compounds found efficacious for these disorders.

Pharmacotherapy treatment development for CTDs and for TTM will likely be informed by NIMH's increasing focus on neurobiological variables and mechanisms, and the relationship between these factors and the development of novel interventions. Recent efforts have suggested that opioid blockers may be more appropriate for TTM, shifting focus to the dopamine system and the concept of pleasure-seeking (positive reinforcement) found in TTM (Grant et al., 2007), as opposed to the negative reinforcement observed in OCD, and likely in the maintenance of tics as well. In addition to discriminating between diagnoses, it is essential to identify which types of medication are most effective in treating the different subtypes of each disorder. For instance, depending on the types of tics (motor vs. vocal, complex vs. simple) and the types of hair pulling (focused vs. automatic), different areas of the brain may be over- or understimulated, and thus warrant distinct medications. Psychiatry will greatly benefit from further identification of these essential and unique aspects of the disorders that direct pharmaceutical intervention. In order to push past treatment plateaus that we appear to have reached, a return to our basic science roots may well be needed to stimulate new ideas. With regard to the available pharmacotherapies for both TTM and CTDs, it is essential to improve our knowledge regarding both the efficacy and safety of long-term use, maximum dose-response ratios, and clinical management of side effects.

Behavior therapy, too, may benefit from an improved understanding of the etiological and maintaining variables at play in TTM. As mentioned above, various emotional and cognitive events may evoke pulling. Research has primarily focused on negative states such as anxiety, tension, urges, or cravings (Grant et al., 2007), but has also implicated emotional states, such as loneliness, fatigue, guilt, anger, indecision, frustration, and excitement (Mansueto et al., 1997). Diefenbach et al. (2002) examined the occurrence and intensity of different emotional states reported by those with TTM prior to, during, and after pulling episodes. Some of these aversive states decreased in intensity (i.e., anxiety and tension) after pulling, whereas others, such as sadness and guilt, increased in salience after pulling. Likewise, some individuals with TTM report intense pleasure while engaged in pulling (Grant et al., 2007), though it is unclear if the pleasure is derived from the removal of the tension, or is a specific consequence of the pulling itself. Research from our lab also demonstrated that physical symptoms of anxiety (i.e., accelerated heart rate, tingling feelings), bodily sensations (i.e., general tension, sensations localized to specific areas), or general discomfort (i.e., vague urges, inner pressure, or feeling not "just right") preceded a majority of hair pulling episodes in a nonreferred sample of pullers (Wetterneck et al., 2004).

Interestingly, there is growing evidence that the relationship between specific emotional states and TTM severity may be moderated by an individual's history of escaping or avoiding unpleasant emotions or cognitions. This response tendency, dubbed *experiential avoidance* (Hayes et al., 1996), may be particularly important in the analysis of TTM. Begotka et al. (2003) first demonstrated a significant relationship between pulling severity (as measured by the MGH-HS) and experiential avoidance (as measured by the Acceptance and Action Questionnaire; AAQ; Hayes et al., 2004), and a follow-up study found that worry and/or physiological arousal prior to pulling were significantly correlated with higher TTM severity. However, these relationships were moderated by experiential avoidance (Wetterneck et al., 2004), as they were stronger for those who were higher in experiential avoidance.

In addition to vague sensory and emotional experiences, specific cognitions may also come to control pulling. For example, seeing a coarse or gray hair in the mirror may evoke thoughts that lead to the removal of the hair (e.g., "My eyebrows should be symmetrical" or "Gray hairs are bad, and I need to remove them."). Research in those with TTM suggests that dysfunctional beliefs about appearance, thoughts of shame, and fears about being evaluated in a negative manner are significantly and positively correlated with hair pulling severity (i.e., greater endorsement of these thoughts correlated with higher levels of hair pulling). However, these relationships diminished or disappeared when controlling for experiential avoidance (Norberg et al., 2007). Combined, these results suggest that components of TTM treatment, addressing the cognitive or emotional factors contributing to pulling, should consider addressing the individual's general tendency to escape from or avoid these events.

It is also important to consider how the effects of cognitive/emotional/sensory variables differ according to a specific pulling style. As stated above, at least two styles of pulling have been empirically identified (i.e., automatic and focused pulling). Existing research suggests that each style predicts a differential relationship between pulling and emotional-cognitive-sensory phenomena. For example, correlations between the MIST-A *automatic* scale and the depression, anxiety, and stress subscales of the DASS-21 (Lovibond & Lovibond, 1995) have been found to be very weak (r's=0.05, 0.12, & 0.15 respectively). In contrast, the MIST-A *focused* scale has been found to be significantly and moderately correlated with the DASS-21 depression, anxiety, and stress subscales (r's=0.32, 0.32, & 0.36 respectively). Research also suggests that the different pulling processes are differentially related to experiential avoidance, thus lending additional validity to the focused/automatic distinction. Begotka et al. found that self-reported levels of focused, but not automatic pulling, were significantly positively correlated with experiential avoidance (Begotka et al., 2003).

In another study, those with primarily focused pulling, primarily automatic pulling, and mixed focused and automatic pulling (as measured by the MIST-A) were compared on the DASS-21 subscales after controlling for TTM severity (Flessner et al., 2006). Results suggested that those with primarily automatic pulling experienced less depressive, anxiety, and stress symptoms than those with primarily focused or mixed patterns. Likewise, those with mixed pulling experienced more depressive, anxious, and stress symptoms than those with either focused or automatic pulling. These results demonstrate that those who exhibit focused pulling are experiencing more negative emotion symptoms that are unrelated to TTM severity, and leave open the possibility that focused pulling may be occurring to regulate such emotions.

Psychosocial Treatment Development. Behavior therapy (i.e., HRT+SC) may be a useful tool in the treatment of TTM, but there are gaps in its evaluation and in its effectiveness that have yet to be addressed. First, there is no evidence that HRT alone impacts co-occurring psychiatric symptoms (van Minnen et al., 2003) which, given the virtual ubiquity of comorbidity in adults with TTM, is a significant issue to study further and to address in the context of treatment development. Second, HRT does not appear to explicitly address the emotional/cognitive regulatory functions associated with focused pulling (van Minnen et al., 2003). To address this issue, two specific treatment components may be useful. Traditionally, cognitive therapy procedures (e.g., cognitive restructuring) have been used to reduce the frequency or intensity of maladaptive thinking associated with negative emotions. Clearly, some researchers have incorporated cognitive-therapy-based procedures into traditional behavior therapy (i.e., HRT + SC procedures) for TTM (e.g., Ninan et al., 2000). More recently, acceptance/mindfulness-based strategies, which have begun to be employed in the treatment of a variety of different disorders including OCD (Twohig, Hayes, & Masuda, 2006a), skin-picking (Twohig, Hayes, & Masuda, 2006b), and psychotic behavior (Bach & Hayes, 2002), have also been integrated with traditional behavior therapy procedures (Twohig & Woods, 2004; Woods et al., 2006c). The rationale for including such procedures is based on the finding that focused pulling and global TTM severity have been linked to experiential avoidance, and it is experiential avoidance that is specifically targeted in acceptance/mindfulness-based therapies. As evidence accrues on the efficacy of interventions that include an acceptance-based component, data are beginning to demonstrate clearly that such procedures decrease experiential avoidance, and that this decrease was strongly correlated with pulling reductions (Twohig & Woods, 2004; Woods, Wetterneck & Flessner, 2006c).

Dissemination. Across the randomized studies of psychosocial interventions for CTDs and TTM reviewed above, data are convergent in suggesting the "efficacy" of HRT for CTDs and TTM and the "probable efficacy" of ERP for CTDs. What remains to be discovered is whether these treatments can be readily disseminated into the clinical and medical settings where most CTD patients would be likely to access care. Given that establishment of a treatment's efficacy requires design elements that emphasize internal validity at the cost of external validity, and that efficacy studies logically precede examination of treatment effectiveness (e.g., Franklin, 2005; Franklin, Cahill, & Compton, 2006), all of the RCTs discussed above were conducted in centers with a significant amount of technical and clinical expertise. Coupled with the data from Marcks, Woods, and Ridosko (2004) suggesting widespread misunderstanding of behavioral treatments of TS and CTDs, it is imperative to determine which of these treatments can be taught most easily to patients, their families, and clinicians, and to examine the effectiveness of these interventions as delivered in community clinical settings as opposed to within the "ivory tower" of academic settings.

There are a number of dissemination models that now warrant testing, including one that was used with great success in pediatric OCD in recent years. The efficacy of CBT for pediatric OCD is now well established (Abramowitz et al., 2005; Barrett, Farrell, Pina, Peris, & Piacentini, 2008), and a recent study examined the effectiveness of a "supervision of supervisors" model wherein masters level clinicians in middle Norway provided manualized CBT to pediatric patients presenting for treatment of OCD, as part of their regular case flow. The clinicians employed Piacentini and colleagues' manualized treatment (Piacentini et al., 2008) under the supervision of psychologists who were very familiar with CBT for OCD; these supervisors were provided regular access to the manual's creator, Dr. Piacentini, as part of the study. Findings from their open trial are extremely encouraging: the outcomes achieved both at end of acute treatment and at follow-up were comparable to what had been found in pediatric OCD RCTs, and in open studies conducted in centers that developed the CBT protocol for pediatric OCD (e.g., Franklin et al., 1998; March et al., 1994). Now that the efficacy of HRT for CTDs and TTM has been established in RCTs, this same dissemination model should now be applied to the treatment of CTDs and TTM to promote better access to empirically supported treatment for those families who do not live within commuting distance of these kinds of subspecialty settings.

Advocacy and Public Education. One of the issues facing the field is the influence of stigma on patients' and families' willingness to seek and accept assistance for their child, or for themselves, when CTD and TTM symptoms emerge. Unfortunately, findings suggest that individuals with CTD and TTM are viewed by their peers as less socially acceptable than those without these behaviors

(Boudjouk, Woods, Miltenberger, & Long, 2000; Stokes, Bawden, Camfield, Backman, & Dooley, 1991), and due to the shame and stigma surrounding CTD and TTM, it is common for patients with these disorders to not disclose their condition to others (Stemberger, Mansueto, Thomas, & Carter, 2000).

Efforts to overcome this social stigma have been undertaken. For example, studies have shown that preventative disclosure and peer education about CTD is associated with the formation of more positive attitudes toward individuals with tics, suggesting that educational interventions may result in the reduction of stigma (Marcks, Berlin, Woods, Davies, 2007; Woods, 2002; Woods, Koch, & Miltenberger, 2003). Patient advocacy groups have also played a part in improving the lives of persons with tics and trichotillomania. Over the last decade, the Tourette Syndrome Association (TSA) has garnered resources from both the private and public sectors to mount aggressive educational campaigns to combat misperceptions about CTDs. These efforts have yielded significant gains within the professional communities who encounter individuals with CTDs as part of their work, and TSA has developed materials for use in educational settings to assist school personnel in better understanding and responding to the needs of youth with CTDs in the academic context.

In addition, the Trichotillomania Learning Center has more recently taken up this same cause with respect to TTM and other body-focused repetitive behaviors, and TLC's advocacy efforts with the NIMH director set the stage for an NIMH-sponsored conference in November 2004 bringing together leaders in the scientific community to identify and address gaps in the knowledge base about TTM's phenomenology, neurobiology, and treatment (http://www.nimh.nih.gov/scientificmeetings/trichotillomania.pdf). Discussions at this conference, and the collaborations that ensued among the scientists present, led to a great increase in research attention to TTM in the last four years that is helping to address the problems noted by the conference attendees.

Related Chapter

Chapter 5. Phenomenology and Epidemiology of Tic Disorders and Trichotillomania

References

Abramowitz, J. S., Whiteside, S. P., & Deacon, R. J. (2005). The effectiveness of treatment for pediatric obsessive-compulsive disorder: A meta-analysis. *Behavior Therapy, 36*, 55–63.

American Psychiatric Association. (2000). *Diagnostic and statistical manual of mental disorders* (4th ed. Text Revision). Washington, DC: Author.

Azrin, N. H., & Foxx, R. (1971). A rapid method of toilet training the institutionalized retarded. *Journal of Applied Behavior Analysis, 2*, 323–334.

Azrin, N. H., & Nunn, R.G. (1973). Habit-reversal: a method of eliminating nervous habits and tics. *Behaviour Research and Therapy, 11*, 619–628.

Azrin, N. H., & Nunn, R. G. (1974). A rapid method of eliminating stuttering by a regulated breathing approach. *Behaviour Research and Therapy, 12*, 279–286.

Azrin, N. H., Nunn, R. G., & Frantz, S. E. (1980). Treatment of hair pulling (trichotillomania):A comparative study of habit reversal and negative practice training. *Journal of Behavior Therapy and Experimental Psychiatry, 11*, 13–20.

Azrin, N. H., & Peterson, A. L. (1990). Treatment of Tourette syndrome by habit reversal: A waiting-list control group comparison. *Behavior Therapy, 21*, 305–318.

Bach, P., & Hayes, S. C. (2002). The use of acceptance and commitment therapy to prevent the rehospitalization of psychotic patients: A randomized controlled trial. *Journal of Consulting and Clinical Psychology, 70*, 1129–1139.

Barrett, P. M., Farrell, L., Pina, A. A., Peris, T. S., & Piacentini, J. (2008). Evidence-based psychosocial treatments for child and adolescent obsessive-compulsive disorder. *Journal of Clinical Child and Adolescent Psychology, 37*, 131–155.

Baxter, L. J., Schwartz, J. M., Bergman, K. S., Szuba, M. P., Guze, B. H., Mazziotta, J. C., et al. (1992). Caudate glucose metabolic rate change with both drug and behavior therapy for obsessive-compulsive disorder. *Archives of General Psychiatry, 49*, 681–689.

Begotka, A. M., Woods, D. W., & Wetterneck, C. T. (2003, November). The relationship between experiential avoidance and the severity of trichotillomania in a nonreferred sample. In M. E. Franklin & N. J. Keuthen (Chairs), *New Developments in Trichotillomania Research.* Symposium conducted at the meeting of the Association for the Advancement of Behavior Therapy, Boston, MA.

Bliss, J. (1980). Sensory experiences of Gilles de la Tourette syndrome. *Archives of General Psychiatry, 37*, 1343–1347.

Boudjouk, P. J., Woods, D. W., Miltenberger, R. G., & Long, E. S. (2000). Negative peer evaluation in adolescents: Effects of tic disorders and trichotillomania. *Child and Family Behavior Therapy, 22*, 17–28.

Casati, J., Toner, B. B., & Yu, B. (2000). Psychosocial issues for women with Trichotillomania. *Comprehensive Psychiatry, 41*, 344–351.

Christenson, G. A., & Crow, S. J. (1996). The characterization and treatment of trichotillomania. *The Journal of Clinical Psychiatry, 57*, 42–47.

Christenson, G. A., Crow, S. J., & Mackenzie, T. B. (1994, May). A placebo controlled double blind study of naltrexone for trichotillomania. *New Research Program and Abstracts of the 150th Annual Meeting of the American Psychiatric Association*, Philadelphia, PA, NR597.

Christenson, G. A., Mackenzie, T. B., & Mitchell, J. E. (1991). Characteristics of 60 adult chronic hair pullers. *American Journal of Psychiatry, 148*, 365–370.

Christenson, G. A., & Mackenzie, T. B. (1994). Trichotillomania. In M. Hersen & R. T. Ammerman (Eds.), *Handbook of prescriptive treatments for adults* (pp. 217–235). New York: Plenum.

Cohen, L. J., Stein, D. J., Simeon, D., Spadaccini, E., Rosen, J., Aronowitz, B., et al. (1995). Clinical profile, comorbidity, and treatment history in 123 hair pullers: A survey study. *Journal of Clinical Psychiatry, 56*, 319–326.

Conelea, C. A., & Woods, D. W. (2008). The influence of contextual factors on tic expression in Tourette's syndrome: A review. *Journal of Psychosomatic Research, 65*, 487–496.

Cook, C. R., & Blacher, J. (2007). Evidence-based psychosocial treatments for tic disorder. *Clinical Psychology: Science and Practice, 14*, 252–267.

Deckersbach, T., Rauch, S., Buhlmann, U., & Wilhelm, S. (2006). Habit reversal versus supportive psychotherapy in Tourette's Disorder: A randomized controlled trial and predictors of treatment response. *Behaviour Research & Therapy, 44*, 1079–1090.

Diefenbach, G. J., Mouton-Odum, S., & Stanley, M. A. (2002). Affective correlates of trichotillomania. *Behavior Therapy and Research, 40*, 1305–1315.

Dougherty, D. D., Loh, R., Jenike, M. A., & Keuthen, N. J. (2006). Single modality versus dual modality treatment for trichotillomania: sertraline, behavioral therapy, or both? *Journal of Clinical Psychiatry, 67*, 1086–1092.

du Toit, P. L., van Kradenburg, J., Niehaus, D. J. H., & Stein, D. J. (2001). Characteristics and phenomenology of hair pulling: An exploration of subtypes. *Comprehensive Psychiatry, 42*, 247–256.

Epperson, N. C., Fasula, D., Wasylink, S., Price, L. H., & McDougle, C. J. (1999). Risperidone addition in serotonin reuptake inhibitor-resistant trichotillomania: Three cases. *Journal of Child and Adolescent Psychopharmacology, 9*, 43–49.

Flessner, C. A., Conelea, C. A., Woods, D. W., Franklin, M. E., Keuthen, N. J., & Cashin, S. E. (2008). Styles of pulling in Trichotillomania: Exploring differences in symptoms severity, phenomenology, and functional impact. *Behaviour Research and Therapy, 46*, 345–347.

Flessner, C. A., Conelea, C. A., Woods, D. W., Franklin, M. E., Keuthen, N. J., & TLC-Scientific Advisory Board. (2006, November). Do those with different styles of trichotillomania differ? An investigation of focused, automatic, and combined subtypes. In D.W. Woods & M.E. Franklin (Chairs). *The Trichotillomania Impact Project: Assessing the Phenomenology, Functional Impairment, and Psychopathology of Adults with Trichotillomania.* Symposium conducted at the meeting of the Association for Behavioral and Cognitive Therapies, Chicago, IL.

Foxx, R. M., & Azrin, N. H. (1972). Restitution: a method of eliminating aggressive-disruptive behavior of retarded and brain damaged patients. *Behaviour Research and Therapy, 10*, 15–27.

Franklin, M. E. (2005). Seeing the complexities: A comment on "Combined psychotherapy and pharmacotherapy for mood and anxiety disorders: Review and analysis." *Clinical Psychology: Science & Practice, 12*, 151–161.

Franklin, M., Cahill, S. P., & Compton, S. N. (2006). What is the question? A comment on "Investigating treatment mediators when simple random assignment to a control group is not possible." *Clinical Psychology: Science and Practice, 13*, 337–341.

Franklin, M. E., Flessner, C. A., Woods, D. W., Keuthen, N. J., Piacentini, J. C., Moore, P. S., et al. (2008). The Child and Adolescent Trichotillomania Impact Project (CA-TIP): Exploring descriptive psychopathology, functional impairment, comorbidity, and treatment utilization. *Journal of Developmental and Behavioral Pediatrics*, 29, 493–500.

Franklin, M. E., & Foa, E. B. (2008). Obsessive compulsive disorder. In D. H. Barlow (Ed.), *Clinical handbook of psychological disorders* (4th edition, pp. 164–215). New York: Guilford Press.

Franklin, M. E., Kozak, M. J., Cashman, L., Coles, M., Rheingold, A., & Foa, E. B. (1998). Cognitive behavioral treatment of pediatric obsessive compulsive disorder: An open clinical trial. *Journal of the American Academy of Child and Adolescent Psychiatry*, 37, 412–419.

Franklin, M. E., & Tolin, D. F. (Eds.). (2007). *Treating trichotillomania: Cognitive behavioral therapy for hair pulling and related problems.* New York: Springer Science and Business Media.

Grant, J. E., Odlaug, B.L., & Potenza, M. N. (2007). Addicted to hair pulling? How an alternate model of trichotillomania may improve outcome. *Harvard Review of Psychiatry*, 15, 80–85.

Habit. (2009). In *Encyclopædia Britannica.* Retrieved January 14, 2009, from Encyclopædia Britannica Online: http://www.britannica.com/EBchecked/topic/250806/habit

Hanna, G. L. (1997). Trichotillomania and related disorders in children and adolescents. *Psychiatry and Human Development*, 27, 255–268.

Hayes, S. C., Bissett, R. T., Strosahl, K., Wilson, K., Pistorello, J., Toarmina, M., Polusny, M. A., Batten, S. V., Dykstra, T. A., Stewart, S. H., Zvolensky, M. J., Eifert, G. H., Bergan, J., & Follette, W. C. (2004). Measuring experiential avoidance: A preliminary test of a working model. *The Psychological Record*, 54, 553–578.

Hayes, S. C., Wilson, K. G., Gifford, E. V., Follette, V. M., Strosahl, K. D. (1996). Experiential avoidance and behavioral disorders: A functional dimensional approach to diagnosis and treatment. *Journal of Consulting and Clinical Psychology*, 64, 1152–1168.

Himle, M., Chang, S., Woods, D., Bunaciu, L., Pearlman, A., Buzzella, B., & Piacentini, J. (2007). Evaluating the contributions of ADHD, OCD, and tic symptoms in predicting functional competence in children with tic disorders. *Journal of Physical and Developmental Disabilities*, 19, 503–512.

Himle, M. B., & Franklin, M. E. (2009). The more you do it, the easier it gets: Exposure and response prevention for OCD. *Cognitive and Behavioral Practice*, 16(1), 29–39.

Hoogduin, C. A. L., Verdellen, C. W. J., & Cath, D. C. (1997). Exposure and response prevention in the treatment of Gilles de la Tourette's syndrome: Four case studies. *Clinical Psychology and Psychotherapy*, 4, 125–137.

Hunt, G. M., & Azrin, N. H. (1973). A community reinforcement approach to alcoholism. *Behaviour Research and Therapy*, 11, 91–104.

Keijsers, G. P., van Minnen, A., Hoogduin, C. A., Klaassen, B. N., Hendriks, M. J., & Tanis-Jacobs, J. (2006). Behavioural treatment of trichotillomania: Two-year followup results. *Behaviour Research and Therapy*, 44, 359–370.

Keuthen, N. J., Fraim, C., Deckersbach, T., Dougherty, D. D., Baer, L., & Jenike, M. A. (2001). Longitudinal follow-up of naturalistic treatment outcome in patients with trichotillomania. *Journal of Clinical Psychiatry*, 62, 101–107.

King, R. A., Scahill, L., Vitulano, L. A., Schwab-Stone, M., Tercyak, K., & Riddle, M. (1995). Childhood Trichotillomania: Clinical phenomenology, comorbidity, and family genetics. *Journal of the American Academy of Child and Adolescent Psychiatry*, 34, 1451–1459.

Leckman, J. F., Hardin, M. T., Riddle, M. A., Stevenson, J., Ort, S. I., & Cohen, D. J. (1991). Clonidine treatment of Gilles de la Tourette's syndrome. *Archives of General Psychiatry*, 48, 324–328.

Leckman, J. F., Walker, D. E., & Cohen, D. J. (1993). Premonitory urges in Tourette's syndrome. *The American Journal of Psychiatry*, 150, 98–102.

Lerner, J., Franklin, M. E., Meadows, E. A., Hembree, E., & Foa, E. B. (1998). Effectiveness of a cognitive-behavioral treatment program for trichotillomania: An uncontrolled evaluation. *Behavior Therapy*, 29, 157–171.

Lovibond, S. H. & Lovibond, P. F. (1995). *Manual for the Depression and Anxiety Stress Scales (2nd Ed.).* Sydney, Australia: Psychological Foundation of Australia.

Mansueto, C. S., Golomb, R. G., Thomas, A. M., & Stemberger, R. M. (1999). A comprehensive model for behavioral treatment of Trichotillomania. *Cognitive and Behavioral Practice*, 6, 23–43.

Mansueto, C. S., Townsley-Stemberger, R. M., McCombs-Thomas, A., & Goldfinger-Golomb, R. (1997). Trichotillomania: A comprehensive behavioral model. *Clinical Psychology Review*, 17, 567–577.

March, J. S., Mulle, K., & Herbel, B. (1994). Behavioral psychotherapy for children and adolescents with obsessive-compulsive disorder: An open trial of a new protocol-driven treatment package. *Journal of the American Academy of Child & Adolescent Psychiatry*, 33, 333–341.

Marcks, B. A., Berlin, K. S., Woods, D. W., & Davies, W. H. (2007). Impact of Tourette syndrome: A preliminary investigation of the effects of disclosure on peer perceptions and social functioning. *Psychiatry*, 70, 59–67.

Marcks, B. A., Woods, D. W., & Ridosko, J. L. (2004). The effects of trichotillomania disclosure on peer perceptions and social acceptability. *Body Image*, 2, 299–306.

Miguel, E. C., Coffey, B. J., Baier, L., Savage, C. R., Rauch, S. L., & Jenike, M. A. (1995). Phenomenology of intentional repetitive behaviors in obsessive-compulsive disorder and Tourette's disorder. *Journal of Clinical Psychiatry*, 56, 246–255.

Mink, J. W. (2001). Neurobiology of basal ganglia circuits in Tourette syndrome: faulty inhibition of unwanted motor patterns? *Advances in Neurology*, 85, 113–122.

Mouton, S. G., & Stanley, M. A. (1996). Habit reversal training for trichotillomania: A group approach. *Cognitive and Behavioral Practice*, 3, 159–182.

Mowrer, O. H. (1960). *Learning theory and behavior.* New York: Wiley.

Ninan, P. T., Rothbaum, B. O., Marsteller, F. A., Knight, B. T. & Eccard, M. B. (2000). A placebo-controlled trial of cognitive–behavioral therapy and clomipramine in trichotillomania. *Journal of Clinical Psychiatry* 61, 47–50.

Norberg, M. M., Woods, D. W., & Wetterneck, C. T. (2007). Experiential avoidance as a mediator of relationships between cognitions and hair-pulling severity. *Behavior Modification*, 31, 367–381.

O'Connor, K. (2002). A cognitive behavioral/psychophysiological model of tic disorders. *Behaviour Research and Therapy*, 40, 1113–1142.

O'Connor, K., Brault, M., Robillard, S., Loiselle, J., Borgeat, F., & Stip, E. (2001). Evaluation of a cognitive-behavioural program for the management of chronic tic and habit disorders. *Behaviour Research and Therapy*, 39, 667–681.

Piacentini, J., & Chang, S. (2005). Habit reversal training for tic disorders in children and adolescents. *Behavior Modification*, *29*, 803–822.

Piacentini, J., Sherrill, J., Walkup, J., Scahill, L., Ginsburg, G., Himle, M., et al. (2008). *Behavior therapy for child and adolescent tic disorder: The NIMH CBITS Study*. Symposium presented at the annual meeting of the Association for Behavioral and Cognitive Therapies, Orlando, FL.

Reeve, E. A., Bernstein, G. A., & Christenson, G. A. (1992). Clinical characteristics and psychiatric comorbidity in children with trichotillomania. *Journal of the American Academy of Child and Adolescent Psychiatry*, *31*, 132–138.

Sallee, F. R., Nesbitt, L., Jackson, C., Sine, L., & Sethuraman, G. (1997). Relative efficacy of haloperidol and pimozide in children and adolescents with Tourette's disorder. *American Journal of Psychiatry*, *154*, 1057–1062.

Santhanan, R., Fairley, M., & Rogers, M. (2008). Is it trichotillomania? Hair pulling in childhood: A developmental perspective. *Clinical Child Psychology and Psychiatry*, *13*, 409–418.

Scahill, L., Leckman, J. F., Schultz, R. T., Katsovich, L., & Peterson, B. S. (2003). A placebo-controlled trial of risperidone in Tourette syndrome. *Neurology*, *60*, 1130–1135.

Schlosser, S., Black, D. W., Blum, N., & Goldstein, R. B. (1994). The demography, phenomenology, and family history of 22 persons with compulsive hair pulling. *Annals of Clinical Psychiatry*, *6*, 147–152.

Shapiro, E., Shapiro, A. K., Fulop, G., Hubbard, M., Mandeli, J., Nordlie, J., et al. (1989). Controlled study of haloperidol, pimozide and placebo for the treatment of Gilles de la Tourette's syndrome. *Archives of General Psychiatry*, *46*, 722–730.

Stanley, M. A., Breckenridge, J. K., & Swann, A. C. (1997). Fluvoxamine treatment of trichotillomania. *Journal of Clinical Psychopharmacology*, *17*, 278–283.

Stemberger, R. M., Thomas, A. M., Mansueto, C. S., & Carter, J. G. (2000). Personal toll of trichotillomania: Behavioral and interpersonal sequelae. *Journal of Anxiety Disorders*, *14*, 97–104.

Stewart, R. S., & Nejtek, V. A. (2003). An open-label, flexible-dose study of olanzapine in the treatment of trichotillomania. *Journal of Clinical Psychiatry*, *64*, 49–52.

Streichenwein, S. M., & Thornby J. I., (1995). A long-term, double-blind, placebo-controlled crossover trial of the efficacy of fluoxetine for trichotillomania. *American Journal of Psychiatry*, *152*, 1192–1196.

Stokes, A., Bawden, H. N., Camfield, P. R., Backman, J. E., & Dooley, J. M. (1991). Peer problems in Tourette's disorder. *Pediatrics*, *87*, 936–941.

Swedo, S. E., Lenane, M. C., & Leonard, H. L. (1993). Long-term treatment of trichotillomania (hair pulling) [Letter to the editor]. *The New England Journal of Medicine*, *329*, 141–142.

Swedo, S. E., Leonard, H. L., Rapoport, J. L., Lenane, M. C., Goldberger, E. L., & Cheslow, D. L. (1989). A double-blind comparison of clomipramine and desipramine in the treatment of trichotillomania (hair pulling). *The New England Journal of Medicine*, *321*, 497–501.

Tolin, D. F., Franklin, M. E., Diefenbach, G. J., Anderson, E., & Meunier, S. A. (2007). Pediatric trichotillomania: Descriptive psychopathology and an open trial of cognitive-behavioral therapy. *Cognitive Behaviour Therapy*, *36*, 129–144.

Twohig, M. P., Hayes, S. C., & Masuda, A. (2006a). Increasing willingness to experience obsessions: Acceptance and Commitment Therapy as a treatment for obsessive compulsive disorder. *Behavior Therapy*, *37*, 3–13.

Twohig, M. P., Hayes, S. C., & Masuda, A. (2006b). A preliminary investigation of Acceptance and Commitment Therapy as a treatment for chronic skin picking. *Behaviour Research and Therapy*, *44*, 1513–1522.

Twohig, M. P. & Woods, D. W. (2004). A preliminary investigation of Acceptance and Commitment Therapy and habit reversal as a treatment for trichotillomania. *Behavior Therapy*, *35*, 803–820.

van Minnen, A., Hoogduin, K. A., Keijsers, G. P., Hellenbrand, I., & Hendriks, G. (2003). Treatment of trichotillomania with behavioral therapy or fluoxetine. *Archives of General Psychiatry*, *60*, 517–522.

Verdellen, C. W., Keijsers, G. P., Cath, D. C., & Hoogduin, C. A. (2004). Exposure with response prevention versus habit reversal in Tourette's syndrome: A controlled study. *Behaviour Research and Therapy*, *42*, 501–511.

Vitulano, L. A., King, R. A., Scahill, L., & Cohen, D. J. (1992). Behavioral treatment of children and adolescents with trichotillomania. *Journal of American Academic Child and Adolescent Psychiatry*, *31*, 139–146.

Wilhelm, S., Deckersbach, T., Coffey, B. J., Bohne, A., Peterson, A. L., & Baer, L. (2003). Habit reversal versus supportive psychotherapy for Tourette's disorder: A randomized controlled trial. *American Journal of Psychiatry*, *160*, 1175–1177.

Woods, D. W. (2002). The effect of video-based peer education on the social acceptability of adults with Tourette's syndrome. *Journal of Developmental and Physical Disabilities*, *14*, 51–62.

Woods, D. W., Flessner, C. A., Franklin, M. E., Keuthen, N. J., Goodwin, R. D., Stein, D. J., et al. (2006a). The Trichotillomania impact project (TIP): Exploring phenomenology, functional impairment, and treatment utilization. *The Journal of Clinical Psychiatry*, *67*, 1877–1888.

Woods, D. W., Flessner, C. A., Franklin, M. E., Wetterneck, C. T. Walther, M., Anderson, E., & Cardona, D. (2006b). Understanding and treating trichotillomania: What we know and what we don't know. *Psychiatric Clinics of North America*, *29*, 487–501.

Woods, D. W., Koch, M., & Miltenberger, R. G. (2003). The impact of tic severity on the effects of peer education about tourette's syndrome. *Journal of Developmental and Physical Disabilities*, *15*, 67–78.

Woods, D. W., Piacentini, J., Himle, M. B., & Chang, S. (2005). Premonitory urge for tics scale (PUTS): Initial psychometric results and examination of the premonitory urge phenomenon in youths with tic disorders. *Journal of Developmental & Behavioral Pediatrics*, *26*, 397–403.

Woods, D. W., Piacentini, J. C., Chang, S., Deckersbach, T., Ginsburg, G., Peterson, A. L., et al. (2008). *Managing Tourette syndrome: A behavioral intervention for children and adults (therapist guide)*. New York: Oxford University Press.

Woods, D. W., Wetterneck, C. T., & Flessner, C. A. (2006c). A controlled evaluation of acceptance and commitment therapy plus habit reversal for trichotillomania. *Behaviour Research and Therapy*, *44*, 639–656.

Wright, H. H., & Holmes, G. R. (2003). Trichotillomania (hair pulling) in toddlers. *Psychological Reports*, *92*, 228–230.

PART 7

OC Spectrum Conditions in Special Populations

OCD and Spectrum Conditions in Older Adults

Cheryl N. Carmin, John E. Calamari, *and* Raymond L. Ownby

Abstract

Despite its chronic and unremitting nature and impact on quality of life, unlike other of the anxiety disorders, surprisingly little attention has been paid to the epidemiology, descriptive psychopathology, and treatment of OCD and related spectrum conditions in late life. ERP remains the mainstay of evidence-based psychological treatment, as is the use of SRIs for pharmacological management. The need to evaluate older adults and design treatment interventions, taking individual medical and cognitive limitations into account, is discussed. Recent statistical modeling approaches using older adult samples suggest that addressing the role of beliefs about intrusive thoughts, cognitive decline, and aging in general may be important additions to a cognitive approach to OCD treatment that is unique to older adults.

Keywords: late-life OCD, OCD treatment, hoarding, neurological and medical comorbidity

Over the course of a lifetime, anxiety disorders as a general category of mental health conditions affect more than one in four adults in the United States (Kessler et al., 2005). A study conducted almost a decade ago that was based on prevalence data, with the exception of OCD, indicated that the economic burden of these conditions approximated $42.3 billion annually (Greenberg et al., 1999). Given the increase in healthcare costs, inflation, and taking OCD into consideration, this figure is undoubtedly an underestimate of the burden placed on society, especially in light of the chronic and unremitting nature of these conditions if they are left untreated. Despite the compelling nature of these data, and a greater proportion of our population entering into late life, surprisingly little attention has been paid to the epidemiology, descriptive psychopathology, or treatment of anxiety disorders in older adults. Even more surprising is that anxiety disorders are more prevalent than mood disorders (Beck & Stanley, 1997; Kessler et al., 2005), which are given considerably more attention in the older segment of the population. While some of the anxiety disorders (e.g, generalized anxiety disorder) which persist into late life have received limited attention, this is not the case for obsessive compulsive disorder (OCD), and even more so for OC spectrum conditions. It is the purpose of this chapter to review the current state of knowledge regarding OCD and spectrum conditions in older adults.

Prevalence

In other publications, we have summarized early studies describing the epidemiology of OCD in later life (see Calamari, Janeck, & Deer, 2002); Pollard, Carmin, & Ownby, 1997). In these early studies, the prevalence of OCD in older adults was reported to range from 0.6% to 1.9% (Bland, Newman, & Orn, 1988; Blazer, George, & Hughes, 1991; Junginger, Phelan, Cherry, & Levy, 1993; Kolada, Bland, & Newman, 1994; Myers et al., 1984; Robins et al., 1984).

In the recent replication of the National Comorbidity Survey (NCS-R), Kessler et al. (2005)

included OCD, a diagnosis which was omitted in the original study. In addition, they examined prevalence at various points across adult life. Throughout adulthood, these authors reported that the lifetime prevalence of OCD is 1.6%, making it among the least commonly occurring of the anxiety disorders.

There appears to be a trend for the prevalence of OCD to decrease over the adult lifespan. Kessler et al. (2005) divided their sample into adult age-based cohorts. The prevalence of OCD in younger groups aged 18–29 and 30–44 was 2.0% and 2.3%, respectively. OCD was found to occur in 1.3% of adults in the 45–59 years age group, and 0.7% in the 60 and older age group. Similar results (i.e., 0.61%) were found by the authors of the National Survey of American Life (NASL; Ford et al., 2007) which is the first survey of African American adults from age 55 to 93. Thus, while the disorder is present, OCD is far less common in older adults than in younger adult samples.

One noteworthy limitation of both the NCS-R and NSAL reports is that these studies utilized a face-to-face interview procedure involving community-dwelling adults. Prevalence rates may be influenced by whether those sampled are community dwelling, compared to those who reside in nursing homes or other institutional settings. It is likely that the prevalence of OCD is considerably higher for older adults residing in noncommunity settings (Bland et al., 1988; Junginger et al., 1993).

Beekman and colleagues (1998) conducted an epidemiological study in Amsterdam. This was a 10-year study of predictors and consequences of changes in well-being and autonomy of older adults living in the Netherlands. The sample was stratified for age and sex. The number of males and females were weighted using projected survival rates, and thus the older old were heavily oversampled. Individuals older than 85 years were excluded due to the expected high attrition rate over the course of the study. Limiting the generalizability of the study is its use of DSM-III diagnostic criteria, and that results are based on 6-month prevalence rates, which are typically lower than the lifetime rates. Overall prevalence of anxiety disorders was estimated at 10.2% (N = 3056) with women suffering about twice as often as men. OCD was estimated at 0.6%, making it rare in this European sample but comparable to the prevalence rates reported in studies conducted in the United States (Ford et al., 2007; Kessler et al., 2005).

Based on large-scale epidemiological studies that have been conducted over the last two decades, the rates of OCD in the elderly have appeared to be remarkably consistent at approximately 0.6% to 0.7% for individuals living in the community. This figure holds for studies conducted in both North America and Europe, as well as for African American samples.

While there is limited information with respect to the epidemiology of OCD in older adults, even less information is available on OC spectrum conditions. A notable exception is hoarding (see also Chapter 4). Samuels and colleagues (Samuels, Bienvenu, Grados, Cullen, Riddle, et al., 2008) found that the weighted prevalence of hoarding in their sample was 5.3%. Unlike OCD, which the NCS-R study reported decreased with age, the opposite appears to be true for hoarding. The prevalence in adults 34–44 years was 2.3%, in those 45–54 years it was 2.9%, and in older adults age 55–94, the prevalence of hoarding was 6.2% (Samuels et al., 2008). Based on retrospective report, Steketee, Dierberger, DeNoble, and Frost (personal communication) found that when comparing an elderly sample of hoarders to controls, approximately one-third of their subjects began their hoarding behaviors before the age of 20, and 40% began before the age of 30. A large group, 38.5%, began to hoard after the age of 50.

Hoarding was also frequently comorbid with other anxiety disorders (i.e., social anxiety disorder, generalized anxiety disorder) as well as conditions that are considered OC spectrum (i.e., body dysmorphic disorder, tics), although Samuels et al. (2008) did not indicate if this is the case specifically in the elderly patients they sampled. In contrast, Steketee et al. (personal communication) found that when comparing an older sample of both hoarders and controls (age range from 58–90 years), OCD was not highly comorbid, occurring in only 4% of their sample. This latter finding is in contrast with earlier reports, which indicate that hoarding symptoms occur in approximately one-third of OCD patients (Frost, Krause, & Steketee, 1996).

Hoarding has also been examined in the context of dementia. Of 133 patients who were being treated on an inpatient geropsychiatric ward in Taiwan, 30 (22.6%) were found to have hoarding behaviors (Hwang, Tsai, Yang, Liu, & Lirng, 1998). In contrast, when hoarding was the primary diagnostic concern, only 10% of elderly hoarders were believed to have moderate to severe memory problems (Steketee, Frost, & Kim, 2001).

Using an innovative method for characterizing elderly hoarders, Steketee, Frost and Kim (2001) systematically interviewed providers of services to older adults in the Boston area who had hoarders assigned to their caseloads. Most of the hoarders were Caucasian women who lived alone, half of whom had never married. Over 90% of the subjects had received services from social service agencies, although only 11% received mental health services. Only a scant 3% of those suffering with hoarding were self-referred for services, with the majority of individuals coming to the attention of the service providers as a result of referral from other agencies or complaints from neighbors, friends, or anonymous sources. Hoarding posed a threat (e.g., creating a fire hazard, risk for falling, inability of emergency service providers to gain access, unsanitary conditions due to infestations, feces, or rotten food), to the physical health of 81% of the clients, with greater threat related to increased amounts of clutter. This study, while limited by the use of reports by service providers rather than from the hoarders themselves, still illustrates the impact of this condition on quality of life and public health.

Age of Onset

Like with other anxiety disorders, the course of OCD appears to be chronic. Despite this chronicity, there are only a few studies that systematically examine age of onset (see Chapter 2 of this volume for a comprehensive review of this issue). Grant and colleagues (Grant, Mancebo, Pinto, Williams, Eisen, & Rasmussen, 2007) noted that there is variability in the definition of age of onset. Onset has been described as when OCD symptoms begin, the age at which the person displays significant distress or impairment, or when the person first meets diagnostic criteria for OCD. There also appears to be a trend in recent studies focusing on age of onset, to cluster OCD patients into "early" versus "late" onset categories (e.g., Fontenelle, Mendlowicz, Marques, & Versiani, 2003; Pinto, Mancebo, Eisen, Pagano, & Rasmussen, 2006; Tükel et al., 2005). The term *late onset* is, however, misleading. For example, Grant et al. (2007) noted that in their late-onset OCD group, subjects reported the onset of their symptoms on or after age 30 (mean = 38.9, +/- 9.7; range 30–62), and in other publications, the "late-onset" group is considerably younger.

With respect to the onset of this disorder in older adults, fewer than 15% of cases of OCD develop in adults after the age of 35 (Rasmussen & Eisen, 1992), making onset in those in late life a rare event. As reported elsewhere in this volume (see Chapter 2), studies examining age of onset that were drawn from general OCD samples demonstrate a bimodal distribution, with one peak at 12–14 years and another in the early adult years (i.e.,18–22) (Burke, Burke, Regier, & Rae, 1990; Pinto, Mancebo, Eisen, Pagano, & Rasmussen, 2006; Rasmussen & Tsuang, 1986).

OCD was once believed to have a uniform onset in early adulthood (e.g., Antony et al., 1998), which may have contributed to the lack of clarity in the use of the "early" and "late" onset terminology. In more recent investigations, an early-onset subtype of the disorder has been identified by several investigators (e.g., Delorme et al., 2005; Geller et al., 2001; do Rosario-Campos et al., 2001). In a relatively recent review, Calamari, Janeck, and Deer (2002) posited that OCD onset might be more variable and include a very late onset subgroup that experiences OCD symptoms for the first time in the sixth decade of life or later. Calamari et al. (Calamari et al., 2002) suggested that available research, although limited, indicated several onset variations for older adults with OCD. Some older adults diagnosed with OCD in late life will have had a typical onset in their early adult years, unremitting symptoms, or waxing and waning symptoms throughout their lives, and for them OCD continues after age 60 and beyond. If older adults with earlier onset OCD are not diagnosed until late life, this situation reflects the often-reported long delays between OCD onset and proper diagnosis and treatment (e.g., Piggott, 2004). For other older adults, obsessional symptoms have been present for many years, but the condition has remained subclinical until affected by the sometimes severe stressors of late life (e.g., death of a spouse, significant medical problems) or by the neurobiological changes that characterize aging. For these older adults, the challenges of late life push their obsessional symptoms across a threshold, resulting in significant life interference and OCD. Lastly, for another group of older adults, OCD symptoms have been absent throughout their earlier years, and the condition appears for the first time in late life, sometimes in association with severe stressors, neurologic events (e.g., infarct; Carmin, Wiegartz, Yunus, & Gillock, 2002) or neurologic disorder (e.g., Huntington's disease; Scicutella, 2000).

Identification of a subgroup of older adults who experience OCD for the first time late in life might have important implications for understanding late-life psychopathology broadly, and OCD specifically. The identification of such a subgroup would suggest that the late-life developmental period should be one of several foci for OCD etiology researchers.

Further, it also suggests that the distinct psychosocial or neurobiological processes of late life can be important to the development of the disorder. Calamari et al. (2002) argued that determination of the age at onset for an occurrence of late-life OCD connects cases to a specific developmental context, which might prove important for assessment and treatment planning. Disorder onset at different developmental stages might result from different etiologic processes, and the factors maintaining the disorder might also differ. Even if few cases of OCD onset after age 60 are identified, the unique characteristics of late life might prove useful for elucidating OCD etiology broadly. The sometimes extreme stressors of late life, or the neurologic changes that occur more often in seniors, might present opportunities to model etiologic processes that have implications for the development of OCD in any age group. We critically examine Calamari et al.'s (2002) conclusions on the age at onset issue, after considering more recent literature on the descriptive psychopathology of late-life OCD.

Descriptive Psychopathology

Recent research on OCD symptom heterogeneity has identified a broad range of symptom subtypes (e.g., Abramowitz, Schwartz, Moore, & Luenzmann, 2003; Calamari et al., 2004). These symptom differences have been related to different neuropathology (e.g., Saxena et al., 2004), different disorder-related dysfunctional beliefs (e.g., Calamari et al., 2006; Taylor et al., 2006), and to a diminished response to treatment (e.g., Abramowitz et al., 2003). In this section, we evaluate whether specific symptoms, or clusters of symptoms, characterize the obsessional concerns or compulsive behavior of older adults diagnosed with OCD. We focus our evaluation on the rapidly developing literature on hoarding. Finally, we evaluate new developments in risk factor and mechanism research designed to elucidate processes that might precipitate or maintain obsessional disorders in late life.

Age of Onset in Late-Life OCD. In much of the contemporary age at onset research on OCD, an early-onset group of children is identified, a group that is predominantly male (e.g., Geller et al., 1998) and who may experience a more severe form of the disorder (e.g., Fontenelle et al., 2003). When analyses are structured to identify early and later onset age ranges (Delorme et al., 2005), an older child (*M* age = 11.1; *SD* = 4.1), and a young adult (*M* age = 23.5; *SD*=11.1) subgroup emerged. Support for the existence of a much later onset OCD subgroup (age

60 or later) continues to predominantly come from the clinical case report literature.

In some case reports, the origins of the individuals' OCD are largely unknown, while in an increasing number of case studies, an association with neurological injuries or disorders is found. Petrikis, Andreou, Pitsavas and Garyfallos (2004) described a 68-year-old married man seeking mental health treatment with symptom onset at age 66. Obsessional concerns focused on fears of infection. A neurologic evaluation that included computed tomography and magnetic resonance imaging (MRI) did not reveal any central nervous system infections or abnormalities. In a similar case, the patient was an 80-year-old, well-educated man with a reported onset of OCD at approximately age 65. Again, MRI studies of the brain were normal, although the patient had a son with OCD with onset during adolescence (Bhattacharyya & Khanna, 2004).

In other case reports, a neurological abnormality is associated with symptom onset. Kim and Lee (2002) reported a case of OCD onset in a 66-year-old man with an infarct in the left orbitofrontal region. The infarct was visible on MRI, and the authors posited that disinhibition caused by damage to the left orbitofrontal cortex, especially the medial portion, may have produced obsessive compulsive symptoms. Carmin et al. (2002) reported a similar late-onset case in a 78-year-old man where onset of OCD followed basal ganglia infarcts. Scicutella (2000) described a late-onset OCD case in a 72-year-old man associated with Huntington's disease, suggesting commonalities in basal ganglia pathophysiology for OCD and Huntington's. Lastly, Serby (2003) reported a case of methylphenidate-induced OCD in an 82-year-old man with treatment-resistant depression and Alzheimer's disease.

While Kessler et al. (2005) report on OCD in adults over the age of 60, there is no indication whether this is a new onset, or the reflection of the unremitting nature of OCD that began earlier in life. Nestadt and colleagues' study continues to provide the strongest support for an OCD subtype with first onset of the disorder after age 60 (Nestadt, Bienvenu, Cai, Samuels, & Eaton, 1998). The authors reevaluated participants in the Epidemiologic Catchment Area Study in the Baltimore cohort. Study participants were re-interviewed using the Diagnostic Interview Schedule (Robins, Helzer, Croughan, & Ratcliff, 1981), and the diagnostic criteria of the *Statistical Manual of Mental Disorders-III-Revised* (DSM-III-R; American Psychiatric Association, 1987) were used to define OCD. A large group (*N* = 1,920) was re-interviewed and a high rate of new cases of OCD in elderly women was found. The authors suggested there were two peak onsets of OCD for women over the life span, both of which occur later in women than men. Based on their data, Nestadt et al. suggested that the second peak onset for women occurred after age 64.

The presence of a late-onset subtype of OCD (i.e., first incidence after the age of 60) continues to be largely under-studied, despite there being at least some indication that adults falling into this subtype differ from younger persons. Case reports of late-onset OCD, often in association with neurological problems, persist. These reports and Nestadt et al.'s (1998) results suggest that systematic evaluation of the issue is warranted. Additional epidemiologic studies are needed. Prospective studies of older adults at risk (e.g., positive family history for OCD, female gender) might also elucidate onset and processes that might precipitate OCD for the first time late in life.

OCD Symptoms. Although the very limited study of late-life OCD prevents definitive conclusions, there is no objective information to suggest that Pollard, Carmin, and Ownby's (1997) conclusion is incorrect, that there was no convincing evidence that a particular constellation of OCD symptoms was unique to older adults. Descriptions of symptoms for this age group are, in general, comparable to other age groups; for example, moral and religious scrupulosity (Calamari & Cassiday, 1999; Fallon et al., 1990); harming and checking (Calamari, Faber, Hitsman, & Poppe, 1994); and contamination and illness (Petrikis et al., 2004). Nevertheless, there are indications in the literature that some cases of late-life obsessional disorders connect more so to stage-of-life concerns (e.g., bowel functioning, Hatch, 1997; Ramchandani, 1990).

Hoarding. Although hoarding obsessions and related compulsions are seen in many age groups (e.g., Grisham, Frost, Steketee, Kim, & Hood, 2006), there is growing evidence that this important OC spectrum condition might often manifest in older adults (see Chapter 4 for an extended review of hoarding). As McKay's review suggests, hoarding symptoms emerge as a distinct OCD subtype in most analyses of OCD symptom heterogeneity (McKay et al., 2004). In severe form, the disorder is characterized by the excessive accumulation and failure to discard often useless items, to the point where significant life interference or distress results (e.g., Tolin, Frost, Steketee, & Fitch, 2008). Although a lack of insight characterizes individuals with predominant hoarding symptoms generally,

Steketee and her colleagues (Steketee et al., 2001) suggested this might more so be the case with elderly hoarders.

Case reports of older adult hoarding have appeared in the literature for some time (e.g., Hwang et al., 1998) and these reports continue to be published. In several case reports, the hoarding symptoms seen in elderly adults are described as a component of Diogenes syndrome, a disorder sometimes associated with dementing disorders, and characterized by self-neglect, poor personal hygiene, poor housekeeping, and the hoarding of rubbish (Clark, Mankikar, & Gray, 1975). The overlap between reports of Diogenes syndrome cases and clinical hoarding is unclear. Ngeh (2000) described a 79-year-old woman who experienced a stroke that had exacerbated her dementia. The woman covertly hoarded rubbish so that her living space was significantly limited. Not all cases of Diogenes syndrome have been associated with hoarding symptoms, though. Fontenelle (2008) described a patient with Diogenes syndrome, based on clinical interview and self-report, who had longstanding OCD and Tourette syndrome in the absence of hoarding symptoms.

Steketee, Sorrentino, Dierberger, DeNobel, and Frost (personal communication) directly surveyed older adults with clinically significant hoarding problems and compared the scoring of this group on multiple measures to other older adults without hoarding or other psychiatric disorders. Between-group analyses revealed that groups did not differ on depression, and both groups scored, on average, in the nonclinical range. Only one participant from each group met diagnostic criteria for OCD, suggesting that OCD did not occur more often among the hoarding sample. Lower rates of OCD comorbidity might have resulted from the relatively mild hoarding symptoms of this elderly sample. Steketee et al. reported that the mean age of onset of hoarding symptoms for the hoarding group was 37 years, although the age at onset was highly variable (0 to 77 years of age), similar to Samuels et al.'s (2007) study. Steketee et al. (personal communication) suggested that age at onset for hoarding was bimodal, with more than one-third beginning to hoard before age 20 and another group starting to hoard after age 50.

Conclusions about late-life hoarding can only be based on the limited study of hoarding in general, and the few evaluations of older adults with hoarding symptoms in particular. With those limitations in mind, we conclude that there is a connection between hoarding and late-life OCD, although it remains unclear if this disorder begins for some seniors late in life, or simply becomes more severe during this developmental period. Steketee et al. (personal communication) suggested that late-life stressors or neurologic changes could make hoarding symptomatology worse in later life. Importantly, they point out the inherent problems in attempting to study hoarding in a group that does not seek help for their problem, or participate in disorder-related research, because of their awareness of the social consequences of this behavior. In some situations, hoarding difficulties and the related disability will cause family members to force older adults to accept placement in supported living settings, a move perceived as demeaning or freedom-limiting by many older adults. Steketee, Frost and colleagues (personal communication) called for the development of strategies, including working with many types of community agencies, to identify older adults with hoarding problems.

Risk Factors for Late-Life Obsessive Compulsive Disorder. Although specific psychological characteristics are assumed related to anxiety proneness, information about vulnerability for adults in general is scarce (McNally, 2001). Information on risk factors for late-life anxiety disorders broadly, or OCD specifically, is even more limited. Several demographic factors have correlated with specific types of late-life anxiety or depression symptoms. Christensen et al. (2000) found that lower levels of depression and anxiety were associated with being older, being male, and being married, while higher levels of anxiety and depression were associated with financial hardship. Beekman et al. (1998) reported that late-life anxiety disorders were associated with female gender, lower levels of education, traumatic experiences during World War II, and late-life stressors (e.g., loss of a spouse). Research on psychological risk factors for late-life OCD has only recently begun.

Teachman (2007) evaluated a variation of Calamari et al.'s (2002) developmental stage hypervigilance hypothesis. She suggests that subjective cognitive complaints may help explain how obsessional beliefs contribute to OCD symptoms in older adults, and predicted that subjective cognitive concerns would partially mediate the relationship between obsessional beliefs and OCD symptoms. Teachman hypothesized that individuals who believe that thoughts are important and need to be controlled, and who have other OCD-related dysfunctional beliefs (see Steketee & Frost, 2001), might be especially likely to become concerned about their cognitive functioning as they age and to

be hypervigilant for even normal changes due to aging. She hypothesized that as a result, older adults would become more distressed in response to normal unwanted, intrusive thoughts.

Using structural equation modeling, Teachman (2007) found that the relationship between obsessional beliefs and OCD symptoms was partially mediated by subjective cognitive concerns, a latent variable consisting of questions developed by the author about cognitive functioning and the general functioning question from the Memory Functioning Questionnaire (MFQ; Gilewski, Zelinski, & Schaie, 1990). The MFQ is a measure of an individual's perceptions of their memory functioning. Evaluation of a younger comparison group revealed that the model fit their data equally well. Teachman concluded that relationships among subjective cognitive concerns, obsessional beliefs, and OCD symptoms were invariant for younger and older adults.

Messina (2008) evaluated the metacognitive construct cognitive self-consciousness (CSC), which was defined as excessive thought-focused attention, as a risk factor for OCD in late life. In prior research, higher scores on the CSC subscale of the Metacognitions Questionnaire differentiated obsessional patients from patients with generalized anxiety disorders (Cartwright-Hatton & Wells, 1997). Further, CSC score on a related measure predicted OCD group membership, even after controlling for scores on dysfunctional OCD-related beliefs (Janeck, Calamari, Riemann, & Heffelfinger, 2003). Messina (2008) evaluated whether late-life developmental concerns about cognitive functioning (scoring on the Memory Functioning Questionnaire; Gilewski, et al., 1990) mediated the relation between CSC and OCD symptoms. He compared a CSC model to two equivalent models: a general cognitive risk factor model, with a measure of mental incapacitation concerns (a subscale of the Anxiety Sensitivity Index; Peterson & Reiss, 1993), substituted as the independent variable; and a general negative affectivity model, with a measure of negative affect substituted as the independent variable in the mediator model. Participants were 165 community-dwelling elderly (age 65 and older) volunteers. The partial mediation model, testing CSC as a predictor of obsessional symptoms through developmental cognitive dysfunction concerns, received stronger support than comparison models. Messina's results indicate that CSC affects OCD symptoms directly and through developmental level concerns (e.g., perceptions of memory decline). Both Messina's (2008) and Teachman's

(2007) earlier study were limited by their cross-sectional designs.

Information on risk and protective factors for late-life anxiety disorders and OCD is surprisingly limited, given the magnitude of the problem and the importance of the issue to public health. Teachman (2007) and Messina's (2008) initial efforts to model the development of late-life OCD are promising. Such investigations and other types of risk-factor studies might function to elucidate processes responsible for the development or continuation of OCD in late life. Methods for reducing risk or preventing disorder development could result, and prospective studies are needed.

Relationship to Neurological Illnesses

As already noted, symptoms of obsessive compulsive disorders may appear as part of several neurological illnesses. These include Huntington's disease, Parkinson's disease, and several dementing illnesses including Alzheimer's disease and frontotemporal dementia. OCD symptoms have been reported in patients with Alzheimer's disease (AD), and the significance of OCD-like behaviors may be obscured by patients' cognitive impairments. Repetitive and meaningless behaviors may be the manifestations of anxiety in cognitively impaired patients, and are generally considered aspects of the ill-defined construct "agitation" rather than obsessions or compulsions. It is thus possible that obsessive compulsive symptoms may be more common in persons with dementing illnesses due to their presentation in the context of cognitive impairment.

When authors have focused on compulsive behaviors in patients with AD, they have noted that standard treatments may be useful. Fluoxetine may be useful in treatment of OCD symptoms in patients with AD (Marksteiner, Walch, Bodner, Gurka, & Donnemiller, 2003). In one instance, clomipramine was tolerated and resulted in substantial treatment response in a 93-year-old patient with AD who could not take fluoxetine (Trappler, 1999).

Obsessive compulsive symptoms are more frequent in patients with Parkinson's disease than in similar persons without the disease (Alegret et al., 2001; Maia, Pinto, Barbosa, Menezes, & Miguel, 2003). These authors speculate that the apparent increased prevalence of symptoms results from the same neural structures being involved in both OCD and Parkinson's disease. Interestingly, several studies suggest an increased prevalence of obsessive compulsive symptoms in individuals with asymmetric motor symptoms (Levin, Tomer, & Rey, 1992; Maia et al.,

2003). This connection is strengthened by the observation that obsessive compulsive disorder or symptoms can arise in late life after a stroke that affects the area of the basal ganglia (Carmin, Wiegartz, Yunus, & Gillock, 2002; Lopez-Rodriguez, Gunay, & Glaser, 1997). Obsessive compulsive symptoms may also arise in Huntington's disease, another condition known to affect the basal ganglia (Scicutella, 2000).

No readily identifiable study has reported on treatment response of obsessive compulsive symptoms in patients with Parkinson's disease. A report of a series of cases (Philpot & Bannerjee, 1998) suggested that serotonergic antidepressant treatment may be useful for patients with basal ganglia stroke-related OCD. Carmin et al. (2002) note that exposure and response prevention were effective in a patient with stroke-related OCD, even when serotonergic medication was not. Behavioral therapies may be especially useful in patients with Parkinson's disease, as the treatment of their Parkinson's disease may require the use of several medications that make pharmacologic treatment of OCD symptoms difficult due to drug interactions.

Other Spectrum Disorders in Late Life

Obsessive compulsive disorder, hoarding, and tic disorders may occur in the context of several neurological disorders that are more common in late life. Although clinical symptomatology may be similar, and the same areas of the brain may be affected, these disorders should be considered as distinct from the same disorders that arise earlier in life or in the absence of other known neuropathology.

Tics. Tics occur in a number of disorders occurring in late life, A common thread appears to be a relation to basal ganglia dysfunction, as can be seen after stroke (Gomis, Puente, Pont-Sunyer, Oliveras, & Roquer, 2008), Parkinson's disease, or immune dysfunction causing basal ganglia dysfunction (Edwards et al., 2004).

Hoarding. Although generally considered an obsessive compulsive spectrum disorder, some studies on the phenomenological, neurobiological, neuroimaging, and genetic aspects of hoarding suggest that it may be a distinct syndrome (An et al., 2008; Olatunji, Williams, Haslam, Abramowitz, & Tolin, 2007; Pertusa et al., 2008; Saxena, 2007). Because a key clinical aspect of hoarding is affected individuals' uncertainty about throwing away objects that have little or no worth, hoarding appears to be related to other spectrum disorders in which uncertainty is central (Steketee & Frost, 2003).

As noted above, hoarding behavior in the elderly has been related to a putative symptom cluster of hoarding and self-neglect called Diogenes syndrome (Clark, Mankikar, & Gray, 1975). The relation of hoarding to cognitive changes in Diogenes syndrome is not clear. Although it may be related to dementing illnesses, one case report provided information on a 5-year follow-up of a patient who did not show evidence of cognitive decline (Greve, Curtis, & Bianchini, 2007). Another clinician reported that Diogenes syndrome can be present in a patient with OCD but without hoarding (Fontenelle, 2008). Limited information is also available on treatment. One investigator reported on the use of valproic acid and quetiapine in treating Diogenes syndrome associated with frontotemporal dementia and mania (Galvez-Andres et al., 2007).

Hoarding is often listed as a behavioral characteristic of frontotemporal dementia, or FTD (Neary et al., 1998). Hoarding may present as the first symptom of FTD (Nakaaki et al., 2007) so that clinicians working with the elderly may find it useful to screen individuals with hoarding for cognitive dysfunction. Hoarding is not specific for FTD, however, and has been reported in other dementias, as well as in cognitively unimpaired elders (Marx & Cohen-Mansfield, 2003). Diogenes syndrome has been reported in older persons with OCD who do not have symptoms (Fontenelle, 2008).

Psychological Treatment

Few demographic variables, including age, have been examined in light of OCD treatment outcome (Keeley, Storch, Merlo, & Geffken, 2008). This is true for both the pediatric as well as the adult OCD literature. Across a number of adult studies, age does not appear to influence treatment response (Franklin, Abramowitz, Kozak, Levin & Foa, 2000; Carmin, Pollard, & Ownby, 1998; Hoogduin & Duivenvoorden, 1988; McLean et al., 2001; Moritz et al., 2004) with treatment protocols highlighting the need for sensitivity to developmental considerations in elderly patients (Carmin, Pollard, & Ownby, 1999). The only exception in the adult literature is one early study that found younger age was predictive of better outcome at post-treatment and follow-up (Foa et al., 1983).

Consistent with our earlier reviews (Calamari et al., 1994; Pollard et al., 1997), the general consensus appears that, much as with younger adults, cognitive behavior therapy (CBT) in the form of exposure and response/ritual prevention (ERP) is the treatment of choice for older adults. Only one study (Carmin et al., 1998) has compared treatment outcome of younger with older (mean age 68) OCD patients. In this naturalistic study, younger and older adults admitted to an inpatient behavioral treatment program were matched based on gender and severity of depression. All subjects received ERP, and most were also prescribed medication. Despite the older adult group being symptomatic for over twice the length of time as the younger cohort, there were no differences in either self-rated improvement or being classified as a treatment responder (i.e., a 50% reduction in symptoms). The authors concluded that ERP was equally effective for older and younger adults, in spite of the durability of OCD in the older group.

The study reported by Carmin et al. (1998) is preliminary, insofar as there have been no randomized controlled trials of OCD treatment in older adults. In the decade since this study was published, the prevailing methodology reported in the literature continues to be case studies (Calamari & Cassiday, 1999; Carmin & Wiegartz, 2000; Carmin et al., 2002; Hirsh et al., 2006; Philpot & Banerjee, 1998), with the studies by Carmin and colleagues (2002) being among the few that have utilized a multiple baseline approach.

As the chapters in this text authored by Taylor et al. on cognitive models (Chapter 12) and Whittal et al. on cognitive therapy for OCD (Chapter 18) would suggest, OCD-related dysfunctional beliefs, and reactivity to intrusive thoughts resulting from maladaptive interpretations of these common experiences, are important elements to be addressed in treatment. However, as Teachman (2007) suggests, it is not clear whether the existing cognitive therapy models apply to older populations, due to the changes in older persons' cognitive functioning that accompany normal aging. In addition, existing treatment models typically assume that beliefs about the importance of thoughts develop early in life, which makes it difficult to understand why obsessional thinking would not be evident until much later in life. While Teachman's comments are well taken, the onset of OCD in late life appears to be relatively infrequent, methodological issues notwithstanding. OCD that has appeared during earlier stages of childhood or adulthood, especially if untreated, does appear to persist into old age. Further, as our research has demonstrated (Carmin et al., 1998; Carmin & Wiegartz, 2000; Carmin et al., 2002), in situations where OCD begins prior to or during later life, ERP including a cognitive component can be successful.

Teachman's (2007) structural model described above examined whether subjective cognitive concerns were instrumental to linking obsessional beliefs to OCD symptoms in an older adult sample. Her results indicated that subjective cognitive complaints do partially mediate how obsessional beliefs, such as the importance of thoughts, predicted OCD symptoms. Interestingly, age invariance was mostly supported, with no differences in the model between adults over or under age 65 in the number of factors, associated indicators, and pattern of relationships. However, older adults did report relatively greater levels of subjective cognitive concerns. Teachman noted that her results provide support for cognitive models of obsessions. Further, obsessional beliefs that have been validated in younger adult samples are also important for older adults, insofar as obsessional belief domains and OCD symptom clusters were similar across age groups. Finally, there was age variance with respect to elevated levels of subjective cognitive concerns among persons over age 65. This finding suggests that while the partial mediating role of subjective cognitive concerns seems to operate in similar ways across adulthood, cognitive concerns related to the importance of thoughts may occur with greater frequency in older populations. The finding of a significant difference in subjective cognitive concerns, but comparable associations with obsessional beliefs and OCD symptoms across age groups, suggests that complaints about general cognitive abilities may have important implications for OCD treatment regardless of age (Teachman, 2007).

Older adults experience a number of challenges that are unique to the aging process. In order to develop an adequate case formulation and treatment plan, both assessment and intervention processes may need to be modified in order to take the concerns of geriatric patients into account (Carmin et al., 1999). A bidirectional interaction between anxiety/OCD symptoms and medical illness can be present, wherein either can mimic and/or exacerbate the other. Accordingly, careful attention needs to be given to ascertain whether OCD, a medical problem, or both, may be present. Sensitivity to generational norms with regard to discussing what can be considered delicate, or even inappropriate issues (e.g., intrusive thoughts about sex, scrupulosity), is also important, as some elderly patients may be too embarrassed to openly discuss these concerns despite how much distress these thoughts may be causing. It is also crucial to determine whether there is a legitimate physical impairment present that is misidentified as an OCD ritual or, conversely, if the ritual is present but misrepresented as due to a disability. As we reported elsewhere, one of our OCD patients attributed his reassurance seeking (i.e., asking to have information repeated) as due to a hearing loss which, upon audiological assessment, was not found to be a legitimate impairment (Carmin & Wiegartz, 2000).

Differentiating between an adaptive response to a physical limitation and OCD is a necessary component of the assessment process. Using direct observation or therapist-directed exposure can facilitate a better understanding of what may be a ritual, or what may be an adaptation. For example, an elderly patient with balance or mobility concerns or medical problems may be quite emphatic about the placement of a cane or walker, or certain medications. In some cases, this may be a placement ritual. For other individuals, this may be a matter of needing to reliably know where ambulation assistance devices are located, to avoid the risk of falling. Likewise, for an OCD patient who can have an unexpected and acute exacerbation of medical symptoms, as in the case of emphysema or angina, having immediate access to inhalers or antianginal medication is essential. However, these placement concerns can exist simultaneously with OCD-bound rituals, making these distinctions important to assess.

ERP with older adults appears to be successful. However, just as the assessment process must be individualized, attention needs to be paid to the physical and cognitive abilities of each elderly patient. This is not to say that every adult over the age of 60 will have physical infirmities, or suffer from memory decline or dementia. It is, however, important to design a treatment strategy that takes these issues, should they be present, into account. In addition, clinicians need to be attentive to designing homework that does not require more physical stamina than the patient can manage.

An important concern for late-life OCD is the disorder's impact on patients' families. As with both pediatric and younger adult groups, family members may want to be involved in treatment. In the case of older adults, this may mean that their children wish to be included, and thereby raises issues regarding confidentiality. While family involvement may be an asset to treatment (see Carmin, Wiegartz, & Wu, 2005), family members may also bear the burden of years of dealing with someone suffering with OCD, or of having been involved in the OCD sufferer's rituals. Thus, not all family caregivers are willing to be a part of treatment, nor do all family members have the patience to provide coaching or play an appropriately supportive role in the treatment process (Carmin & Wiegartz, 2000). This consideration may be especially important if the affected individual has other impairments that require ongoing support from a caregiver. As behavioral problems are among the most difficult issues for caregivers to cope with, and may be related to caregivers' health and the patients' likelihood of institutionalization (Schulz et al., 2000; Schulz & Martire, 2004), implementing effective treatments is critically important. Although a number of studies have documented the relation between patient behavior problems and caregiver stress, no readily identifiable study has examined the effect of OCD on caregivers of cognitively impaired patients.

Just as ERP needs to be adapted to developmental issues, so does the cognitive component of therapy. Teachman (2007) noted that defining the role of beliefs may be an important first step to adapting cognitive treatments for late-life OCD. She suggests that determining both the nature of older adults' beliefs about their intrusive thoughts, and the role that aging processes, including subjective cognitive decline, play in their beliefs, is necessary. The interplay between escalating, anxiety-producing beliefs about deteriorating cognitive function and the exacerbation of OCD symptoms may need to be addressed, and may be an important target for cognitive therapy intervention.

Information about the psychological treatment of OC spectrum conditions in older adults is almost nonexistent. As noted earlier in this chapter, hoarding is an OC spectrum condition, which is more readily found in an aging population. As hoarding and its treatment are discussed in detail in Chapters 4 and 22, respectively, that information will not be duplicated here. The psychological treatment of other spectrum conditions in elderly adults has received no attention.

Pharmacologic Treatment

The mainstay of pharmacologic treatment for late-life OCD is treatment with serotonin-reuptake inhibitor antidepressants (SRIs). Since the early studies of clomipramine in OCD showed that the symptoms of OCD could be reduced with pharmacologic treatments (Clomipramine Study Group, 1991), serotonergic medications have constituted one of the most important agents in treating OCD Agarwal, Biswas, & Sadhu, 2008). SRIs are first-line treatments in OCD in older persons as well,

although little information is available about their effectiveness. Consistent with studies of SRIs in younger persons with OCD, older adults may require treatment with higher doses of SRIs for longer periods than those used to treat depression or anxiety. Since some studies have suggested that older adults with depression may respond more slowly to antidepressant treatment than do younger persons, it is reasonable to speculate that older persons treated with antidepressants for OCD may similarly require even longer periods of treatment to show evidence of response.

Single-agent treatments have been shown to produce significant decreases in OCD symptoms (Jenike, 2004), but complete resolution of OCD symptoms with single-agent treatments is unusual (Pallanti & Quercioli, 2006). The distinction between partial response and treatment resistance is not always made in the clinical literature, but partial response to pharmacologic treatments for OCD is so common that a clear definition of true treatment resistance in OCD might be quite difficult to create. At the clinical level, it is important to note that single-agent SRI treatment may not adequately resolve OCD symptoms for many persons, and that additional pharmacologic strategies may have to be used in many, if not most, patients (Pallanti & Quercioli, 2006).

Augmentation or combination strategies are thus quite often employed in treatment of OCD. Many of these strategies are likely to be as effective in older persons as they are in younger persons, but several may be associated with adverse effects that are more important to consider in older persons. Augmenting SRI treatment of OCD with the benzodiazepine clonazepam may be effective. This strategy has been shown to be effective in several studies (Kaplan & Hollander, 2003), although treatment with clonazepam alone may be ineffective (Hollander, Kaplan, & Stahl, 2003). While benzodiazepines are typically well tolerated in younger adults, they are associated with a number of adverse effects in older persons that should be considered by any clinician. Benzodiazepine use in older persons has been associated with an increased risk for falls (Ray, Griffin, & Downey, 1989). Benzodiazepines may also cause memory impairment in older persons (Salzman, 1985), a side effect that is troubling and may actually increase patients' anxiety.

Atypical antipsychotics may also be useful as adjuncts in treating older adults as they are in younger persons (Skapinakis, Papatheodorou, & Mavreas, 2007). As with younger persons, these agents have been associated with weight gain and increased risk of metabolic syndrome and diabetes. Use of atypical antipsychotics has been associated with an increased risk for death in older patients with dementia, and even the older, or typical, antipsychotics may be associated with similar risks (Kuehn, 2010). As with benzodiazepines, atypical antipsychotics may cause memory impairments in older persons, as they are more likely to be susceptible to the anticholinergic effects of these and other medications.

Although lithium is a well-established augmenting agent in depression and has been helpful in OCD, controlled trials of lithium in OCD did not provide convincing results of effectiveness (Jenike, 2004). Lithium might be helpful for residual depression in patients with OCD, but several issues arise in using it with older persons. These include increased risk for sedation and cognitive impairment, and the need for careful blood level monitoring in persons whose renal function may be reduced (Juurlink et al., 2004).

A novel recent approach to the pharmacologic treatment of OCD is to augment the behavioral treatment of the disorder using D-cycloserine. This drug is most often used as an antibiotic treatment for tuberculosis, but has activity at glutamate receptors (Rothbaum, 2008) and improved extinction of learned fear in animal models (Davis, Ressler, Rothbaum, & Richardson, 2006). The ability of D-cycloserine was thus tested in a human model of extinction of anxiety during treatment of phobias and was found useful (Ressler et al., 2004). This approach was subsequently tested in treating persons with OCD and found useful, as well (Wilhelm et al., 2008). The mean age of the treatment group in this study was 40 years with a standard deviation of 13.3, showing that at least some of the individuals in the treatment group were probably at least 50 years or older. This pharmacologic approach to augmenting the effect of exposure and response prevention may be a promising strategy that may work with older as well as younger individuals. As with other medications, concerns arise about possible drug interactions in use with all individuals, and these concerns may be especially relevant in treating older persons.

Finally, direct brain interventions in treating OCD in all individuals have become more sophisticated in recent years. While psychosurgery for intractable OCD may be effective, recent interest has focused on deep brain stimulation (DBS). DBS has the advantage of being less invasive, reversible, and allowing more precise control of stimuli applied to the brain. DBS may be useful in late-life OCD (Larson, 2008).

Conclusions

In the decade since we last reviewed the epidemiology and treatment of OCD in older adults, our knowledge has grown, albeit slowly. Unfortunately, this is not the case with regard to OC spectrum conditions. The only area that has received any consistent attention in older samples is hoarding.

While anxiety disorders have the highest prevalence of the diagnostic categories, the prevalence of OCD is relatively low. This is especially the case for geriatric presentations of the disorder. There have been two large-scale epidemiological studies in the United States, and one in Europe, that have consistently documented that the prevalence of OCD in the later stages of life is less than one percent. As with many of the anxiety disorders, the prevalence of OCD decreases with age. However, this is not the case with hoarding, which appears to increase over the course of adulthood.

Methodological issues with regard to sampling of the elderly in epidemiological studies have not changed to any great degree. Despite authors noting that prevalence rates are apt to be higher in institutional settings, the two most recent studies that included older adults with OCD only sampled individuals residing in the community. It is likely to be a more complex study that would take non-community-dwelling elderly into account. Despite the complexity and cost, there is a need for such a study if we are to have a clearer understanding with regard to age of onset and the enduring nature of OCD in late life.

The issue of age of onset is one which we have given considerable attention in this chapter, and is an issue that merits further consideration. Much of the recent literature discusses early-onset and late-onset OCD, with the latter being a misnomer, at least with regard to the onset of OCD in older adults. There is increasing evidence suggesting that a subtype of OCD, which embraces the phenomenological differences in older adults compared to younger groups, may be warranted. Additional research addressing this question is needed.

There have not been any striking advances in the OCD treatment literature as it pertains to older groups. ERP remains the mainstay of evidence-based psychological treatment, as is the use of SRIs for pharmacological management. We continue to underscore the need to evaluate older adults, and design their treatment interventions taking individual medical and cognitive limitations into account. These limitations may be as minor as physical stamina, or reflect serious comorbid medical conditions and the potential for drug interactions. In the adult OCD treatment literature, cognitive therapy is receiving positive attention. Recent statistical modeling approaches using older adult samples suggest that addressing the role of beliefs about intrusive thoughts, cognitive decline, and aging in general may be important additions to a cognitive approach to OCD treatment that is unique to older adults. Similarly, augmenting ERP and/or cognitive therapy with D-cycloserine poses an innovative and potentially beneficial approach, drug interactions and physical limitations notwithstanding.

The area of OCD in the elderly is wide open to systematic research. More investigations into issues related to prevalence, age of onset, the features of descriptive psychopathology, and treatment that are unique to aging adults will benefit our understanding of how OCD evolves over the lifespan. There is an even greater need for research in the area of OC spectrum conditions in older adults. At this juncture, we do not know for certain if disorders such as trichotillomania, body dysmorphic disorder, or conditions other than hoarding persist into old age, let alone if there is any data indicating that there are new onsets of these conditions in the later stages of adulthood.

Future Directions

As summarized above, there are several critical questions that researchers must address to advance knowledge about late-life OCD. Prevalence estimates for late-life OCD based on epidemiologic studies are consistently low. These findings imply that research designed to elucidate the etiologic processes important to the development of OCD should be conducted with younger age groups. Further, the very low prevalence estimates might suggest that the limited public health resources available to understand mechanisms and refine treatment interventions for psychiatric disorders be directed toward other late-life anxiety disorders with much higher prevalence estimates. Therefore, it is important that several issues identified in our review, important to better understanding prevalence, be addressed in future studies.

The psychometric properties of OCD-related measures have not been evaluated in older adult samples, and this basic work is essential for determining disorder prevalence, as well as for clinical

evaluation (see Carmin & Ownby, 2010). Effective assessment strategies for differentiating seniors' OCD symptoms from the symptoms of other anxiety disorders and mood disorders must be more fully articulated and tested. Similarly, strategies for distinguishing the emotional sequelae of deteriorating health, or cognitive functioning changes, from the characteristics of late-life psychiatric disorders, must also be developed and evaluated. Additionally, because initial evaluations of older adults living in supported environments (e.g., retirement communities, nursing homes) suggest the prevalence of OCD might be significantly higher in this group, researchers must develop strategies for evaluating seniors who live in these settings. This work will be particularly challenging, as many of these older adults will have significant cognitive impairment, major general health problems, or several co-occurring psychiatric disorders.

Although the obsessions and compulsions experienced by older adults appear to be very similar to symptoms experienced by other age groups, preliminary evaluations suggest clinical hoarding might occur frequently with seniors. Clinical hoarding is an importantly distinct syndrome, currently conceptualized as an important OCD subtype or as an OCD spectrum condition. Because individuals with this condition rarely seek treatment from mental health professionals, the prevalence of the condition is likely broadly underestimated, including its occurrence with older adults. Researchers must determine if the syndrome does indeed concentrate in older adults, and if this is the case, begin to identify the processes responsible. This work will be essential to the refinement of recently developed treatments for clinical hoarding for this age group.

Related Chapters

References

American Psychiatric Association. (1987). Diagnostic and Statistical Manual of Mental Disorders: DSM-III-R. Washington, DC: American Psychiatric Association.

Abramowitz, J. S., Schwartz, S. A., Moore, K. M., & Luenzmann, K. R. (2003). Obsessive-compulsive symptoms in pregnancy and the puerperium: a review of the literature. *Journal of Anxiety Disorders, 17*(4), 461–478.

Agarwal, A., Biswas, D., & Sadhu, R. (2008). Treatment for late-onset obsessive-compulsive disorder with parkinsonism. *Journal of Neuropsychiatry and Clinical Neurosciences, 20,* 331–336.

Alegret, M., Junque, C., Valldeoriola, F., Vendrell, P., Pilleri, M., Rumia, J. et al. (2001). Effects of bilateral subthalamic stimulation on cognitive function in Parkinson disease. *Archives of Neurology, 58,* 1223–1227.

An, S. K., Mataix-Cols, D., Lawrence, N. S., Wooderson, S., Giampietro, V., Speckens, A. et al. (2009). To discard or not to discard: the neural basis of hoarding symptoms in obsessive-compulsive disorder. *Molecular Psychiatry, 14,* 318–331.

Antony, M. M., Downie, F., & Swinson, R. P. (1998). Diagnostic issues and epidemiology in obsessive-compulsive disorder. In R. P. Swinson, M. M. Antony, S. Rachman, & M. A. Richter (Eds.) *Obsessive-compulsive disorder: Theory, research and treatment* (pp. 3–32). NY: Guilford.

Beck, J. G., & Stanley, M. A. (1997). Anxiety disorders in the elderly: The emerging role of behavior therapy. *Behavior Therapy, 28*(1), 83–100.

Beekman, A. T. F., Bremmer, M. A., Deeg, D. J. H., Van Balkom, A. J. L. M., Smit, J. H., De Beurs, E., et al. (1998). Anxiety disorders in later life: A report from the Longitudinal Aging Study Amsterdam. *International Journal of Geriatric Psychiatry, 13*(10), 717–726.

Bhattacharyya, S., & Khanna, S. (2004). Late onset OCD. *Australian and New Zealand Journal of Psychiatry, 38*(6), 477–478.

Bland, R. C., Newman, S. C., & Orn, H. (1988). Prevalence of psychiatric disorders in the elderly in Edmonton. *Acta Psychiatrica Scandinavica. Supplementum, 338,* 57–63.

Blazer, D., George, L., & Hughes, D. (1991). The epidemiology of anxiety disorders: An age comparison. In C. Saltzman & B. Lebowitz (Eds.), *Anxiety in the elderly: Treatment and research* (pp. 17–30). N.Y.: Springer.

Burke, K. C., Burke, J. D., Regier, D. A., & Rae, D. S. (1990). Age of onset of selected mental disorders in five community populations. *Archives of General Psychiatry, 47,* 511–518.

Calamari, J. E., & Cassiday, K. (1999). Treating obsessive-compulsive disorder in older adults: A review of strategies. In M. Duffy (Ed.), *Handbook of counseling & psychotherapy in older adults* (pp. 526–538). New York: Wiley.

Calamari, J. E., Faber, S. D., Hitsman, B. L., & Poppe, C. J. (1994). Treatment of obsessive compulsive disorder in the elderly: a review and case example. *Journal of Behavior Therapy and Experimental Psychiatry, 25*(2), 95–104.

Calamari, J., Janeck, A., & Deer, T. (2002). Cognitive processes and obsessive compulsive disorder in older adults. In R. O. Frost & G. Steketee (Eds.), *Cognitive approaches to obsessions and compulsions: Theory, assessment & treatment* (pp. 315–336). New York: Elsevier.

Calamari, J. E., Wiegartz, P. S., Riemann, B. C., Cohen, R. J., Greer, A., Jacobi, D. M., et al. (2004). Obsessive-compulsive disorder subtypes: an attempted replication and extension of a symptom-based taxonomy. *Behaviour Research and Therapy, 42*(6), 647–670.

Calamari, J. E., Cohen, R. J., Rector, N. A., Szacun-Shimizu, K., Riemann, B. C., & Norberg, M. M. (2006). Dysfunctional belief-based obsessive-compulsive disorder subgroups. *Behaviour Research and Therapy, 44*(9), 1347–1360.

Carmin, C. N. & Ownby, R. L. (2010). Assessment of anxiety in older adults. In P. A. Lichtenberg, *Handbook of assessment in clinical gerontology* (2nd ed.) (pp. 45–60), New York: Elsevier.

Carmin, C. N., Pollard, C. A., & Ownby, R. L. (1998). Cognitive behavioral treatment of older versus younger adults with OCD. *Clinical Gerontologist, 19,* 81–88.

Carmin, C. N., Wiegartz, P., & Wu, K. (2005). Self-directed exposure in the treatment of obsessive-compulsive disorder. In J. S. Abramowitz & A. Houts (Eds.), *Concepts and controversies in obsessive-compulsive disorder* (pp. 333–346). New York: Kluwer.

Carmin, C., Pollard, C. A., & Ownby, R. L. (1999). Cognitive behavioral treatment of older adults with obsessive-compulsive disorder. *Cognitive and Behavioral Practice, 6*(2), 110–119.

Carmin, C. N., & Wiegartz, P. S. (2000). Successful and Unsuccessful Treatment of Obsessive-Compulsive Disorder in Older Adults. *Journal of Contemporary Psychotherapy, 30*(2), 181–193.

Carmin, C. N., Wiegartz, P. S., Yunus, U., & Gillock, K. L. (2002). Treatment of late-onset OCD following basal ganglia infarct. *Depression & Anxiety, 15*(3), 87–90.

Cartwright-Hatton, S., & Wells, A. (1997). Beliefs about worry and intrusions: the Meta-Cognitions Questionnaire and its correlates. *Journal of Anxiety Disorders, 11*(3), 279–296.

Christensen, H., Jorm, A. F., MacKinnon, A. J., Korten, A. E., Jacomb, P. A., Henderson, A., et al. (2000). Age differences in depression and anxiety symptoms: A structural equation modelling analysis of data from a general population sample. *Psychological Medicine, 29*(02), 325–339.

Clark, A., Mankikar, G., & Gray, I. (1975). Diogenes syndrome: A clinical study of gross neglect in old age. *The Lancet, 305*(7903), 366–368.

Clomipramine Collaborative Study Group (1991). Clomipramine in the treatment of patients with obsessive-compulsive disorder. *Archives of General Psychiatry, 48,* 730-738.

Davis, M., Ressler, K., Rothbaum, B. O., & Richardson, R. (2006). Effects of D-cycloserine on extinction: translation from preclinical to clinical work. *Biological Psychiatry, 60,* 369–375.

Delorme, R., Golmard, J., Chabane, N., Millet, B., Krebs, M., Mouren-simeoni, M. C., et al. (2005). Admixture analysis of age at onset in obsessive–compulsive disorder. *Psychological Medicine, 35*(02), 237–243.

Edwards, M. J., Dale, R. C., Church, A. J., Trikouli, E., Quinn, N. P., Lees, A. J. et al. (2004). Adult-onset tic disorder, motor stereotypies, and behavioural disturbance associated with antibasal ganglia antibodies. *Movement Disorders, 19,* 1190–1196.

Fallon, B., Leibowitz, M., Hollander, E., Schneier, F., Campeas, R., Fairbanks, J., et al. (1990). The pharmacotherapy of moral or religious scrupulosity. *Journal of Clinical Psychiatry, 51,* 517–521.

Foa, E. B., Grayson, J. B., Steketee, G. S., Doppelt, H. G., Turner, R. M., & Latimer, P. R. (1983). Success and failure in the behavioral treatment of obsessive-compulsives. *Journal of Consulting and Clinical Psychology, 51*(2), 287–297.

Fontenelle, L. F. (2008). Diogenes syndrome in a patient with obsessive-compulsive disorder without hoarding. *General Hospital Psychiatry, 30*(3), 288–290.

Fontenelle, L. F., Mendlowicz, M. V., Marques, C., & Versiani, M. (2003). Early- and late-onset obsessive–compulsive disorder in adult patients: an exploratory clinical and therapeutic study. *Journal of Psychiatric Research, 37*(2), 127–133.

Ford, B. C., Bullard, K. M., Taylor, R. J., Toler, A. K., Neighbors, H. W., & Jackson, J. S. (2007). Lifetime and 12-month prevalence of Diagnostic and Statistical Manual of Mental Disorders, Fourth Edition disorders among older African Americans: findings from the National Survey of American Life. *American Journal of Geriatric Psychiatry, 15*(8), 652–659.

Franklin, M.E., Abramowitz, J.S., Kozak, M.J., Levitt, J.T., & Foa, E.B. (2000). Effectiveness of exposure and ritual prevention for obsessive-compulsive disorder: Randomized compared with nonrandomized samples. Journal of Consulting and Clinical Psychology, 68, 594-602.

Frost, R. O., Krause, M., & Steketee, G. (1996). Hoarding and obsessive-compulsive symptoms. *Behavior Modification, 29*, 116–132.

Galvez-Andres, A., Blasco-Fontecilla, H., Gonzalez-Parra, S., Molina, J. D., Padin, J. M., & Rodriguez, R. H. (2007). Secondary bipolar disorder and Diogenes syndrome in frontotemporal dementia: behavioral improvement with quetiapine and sodium valproate. *Journal of Clinical Psychopharmacology., 27*, 722–723.

Geller, D. A., Biederman, J., Faraone, S., Agranat, A., Cradock, K., Hagermoser, L., et al. (2001). Developmental aspects of obsessive compulsive disorder: findings in children, adolescents, and adults. *The Journal of Nervous and Mental Disease, 189*(7), 471–477.

Geller, D., Biederman, J., Jones, J., Park, K., Schwartz, S., Shapiro, S., et al. (1998). Is juvenile obsessive-compulsive disorder a developmental subtype of the disorder? A review of the pediatric literature. *Journal of the American Academy of Child and Adolescent Psychiatry, 37*(4), 420–427.

Gilewski, M. J., Zelinski, E. M., & Schaie, K. W. (1990). The Memory Functioning Questionnaire for assessment of memory complaints in adulthood and old age. *Psychology and Aging, 5*(4), 482–490.

Gomis, M., Puente, V., Pont-Sunyer, C., Oliveras, C., & Roquer, J. (2008). Adult onset simple phonic tic after caudate stroke. *Movement Disorders, 23*, 765–766.

Grant, J. E., Mancebo, M. C., Pinto, A., Williams, K. A., Eisen, J. L., & Rasmussen, S. A. (2007). Late-onset obsessive compulsive disorder: Clinical characteristics and psychiatric comorbidity. *Psychiatry Research, 152*(1), 21–27.

Greve, K. W., Curtis, K. L., & Bianchini, K. J. (2007). Diogenes Syndrome: a five-year follow-up. *International Journal of Geriatric Psychiatry, 22*, 1166-1167.

Greenberg, P. E., Sisitsky, T., Kessler, R. C., Finkelstein, S. N., Berndt, E. R., Davidson, J. R., et al. (1999). The economic burden of anxiety disorders in the 1990s. *The Journal of Clinical Psychiatry, 60*(7), 427–435.

Grisham, J. R., Frost, R. O., Steketee, G., Kim, H., & Hood, S. (2006). Age of onset of compulsive hoarding. *Journal of Anxiety Disorders, 20*(5), 675–686.

Hatch, M. (1997). Conceptualization and treatment of bowel obsessions: Two case reports. *Behaviour Research and Therapy, 35*(3), 253–257.

Hirsh, A., O'Brien, K., Geffken, G., Adkins, J., Goodman, W., & Storch, E. (2006). Cognitive-behavioral treatment for obsessive-compulsive disorder in an elderly man with concurrent medical constraints. *American Journal of Geriatric Psychiatry, 14*(4), 380–381.

Hollander, E., Kaplan, A., & Stahl, S. M. (2003). A double-blind, placebo-controlled trial of clonazepam in obsessive-compulsive disorder. *World Journal of Biological Psychiatry, 4*, 30–34.

Hoogduin, C. A. L. & Duivenvoorden, H. J. (1988). A decision model in the treatment of obsessive-compulsive neuroses. *British Journal of Psychiatry, 152*, 516–521.

Hwang, J., Tsai, S., Yang, C., Liu, K., & Lirng, J. (1998). Hoarding behavior in dementia: A preliminary report. *American Journal of Geriatric Psychiatry, 6*(4), 285–289.

Janeck, A. S., Calamari, J. E., Riemann, B. C., & Heffelfinger, S. K. (2003). Too much thinking about thinking?: Metacognitive differences in obsessive-compulsive disorder. *Journal of Anxiety Disorders, 17*(2), 181–195.

Jenike, M. A. (2004). Clinical practice: Obsessive-compulsive disorder. *New England Journal of Medicine, 350*, 259–265.

Junginger, J., Phelan, E., Cherry, K., & Levy, J. (1993). Prevalence of psychopathology in elderly persons in nursing homes and in the community. *Hospital & Community Psychiatry, 44*(4), 381–383.

Juurlink, D. N., Mamdani, M. M., Kopp, A., Rochon, P. A., Shulman, K. I., & Redelmeier, D. A. (2004). Drug-induced lithium toxicity in the elderly: a population-based study. *Journal of the American Geriatrics Society, 52*, 794–798.

Kaplan, A. & Hollander, E. (2003). A review of pharmacologic treatments for obsessive-compulsive disorder. *Psychiatric Services, 54*, 1111–1118.

Keeley, M. L., Storch, E. A., Merlo, L. J., & Geffken, G. R. (2008). Clinical predictors of response to cognitive-behavioral therapy for obsessive-compulsive disorder. *Clinical Psychology Review, 28*(1), 118–130.

Kessler, R., Berglund, P., Demler, O., Jin, R., Merikangas, K. R., & Walters, E. E. (2005). Lifetime prevalence and age-of-onset distributions of DSM-IV disorders in the National Comorbidity Survey Replication. *Archives of General Psychiatry, 62*(6), 593–602.

Kim, K., & Lee, D. (2002). Obsessive-compulsive disorder associated with a left orbitofrontal infarct. *Journal of Neuropsychiatry and Clinical Neurosciences, 14*(1), 88–89.

Kolada, J. L., Bland, R. C., & Newman, S. C. (1994). Epidemiology of psychiatric disorders in Edmonton. Obsessive-compulsive disorder. *Acta Psychiatrica Scandinavica. Supplementum, 376*, 24–35.

Kuehn, B. M. (2010). Questionable antipsychotic prescribing remains common, despite serious risks. *Journal of the American Medical Association, 303*, 1582–1584.

Larson, P. S. (2008). Deep brain stimulation for psychiatric disorders. *Neurotherapeutics., 5*, 50–58.

Levin, B. E., Tomer, R., & Rey, G. J. (1992). Cognitive impairments in Parkinson's disease. *Neurology Clinics, 10*, 471–485.

Lopez-Rodriguez, F., Gunay, I., & Glaser, N. (1997). Obsessive compulsive disorder in a woman with left basal ganglia infarct:A case report. *Behavioural Neurology, 10*, 101–103.

Maia, A. F., Pinto, A. S., Barbosa, E. R., Menezes, P. R., & Miguel, E. C. (2003). Obsessive-compulsive symptoms, obsessive-compulsive disorder, and related disorders in Parkinson's disease. *Journal of Neuropsychiatry and Clinical Neurosciences, 15*, 371–374.

Marksteiner, J., Walch, T., Bodner, T., Gurka, P., & Donnemiller, E. (2003). Fluoxetine in Alzheimer's disease with severe obsessive compulsive symptoms and a low density of serotonin transporter sites. *Pharmacopsychiatry, 36,* 207–209.

Marx, M. S. & Cohen-Mansfield, J. (2003). Hoarding behavior in the elderly: a comparison between community-dwelling persons and nursing home residents. *International Psychogeriatrics, 15,* 289–306.

McKay, D., Abramowitz, J. S., Calamari, J. E., Kyrios, M., Radomsky, A., Sookman, D., et al. (2004). A critical evaluation of obsessive-compulsive disorder subtypes: Symptoms versus mechanisms. *Clinical Psychology Review, 24*(3), 283–313.

McLean, P., Whittal, M., Thordarson, D., Taylor, S., Sochting, I. & Koch, W., et al. (2001). Cognitive versus behavior therapy in the group treatment of Obsessive-Compulsive disorder. *Journal of Consulting and Clinical Psychology, 69,* 205–221.

McNally, R. (2001). Vulnerability to anxiety disorders in adulthood. In R. Ingram & J. Prince (Eds.), *Vulnerability to Psychopathology: Risk across the Lifespan* (pp. 305–325). New York: Guilford.

Messina, M. (2008). Cognitive self-consciousness and hypervigilance for cognitive functioning: An evaluation of risk factors for obsessive-compulsive symptoms in the elderly. Unpublished doctoral dissertation, Rosalind Franklin University of Medicine and Sciences. North Chicago, IL.

Moritz, S. Fricke, D. Jacobsen, M. Kloss, C. Wein and M. Rufer et al. (2004). Positive schizotypal symptoms predict treatment outcome in obsessive–compulsive disorder. *Behavior Research and Therapy, 42,* 217–227.

Myers, J. K., Weissman, M. M., Tischler, G. L., Holzer, C. E., Leaf, P. J., Orvaschel, H., et al. (1984). Six-month prevalence of psychiatric disorders in three communities 1980 to 1982. *Archives of General Psychiatry, 41*(10), 959–967.

Nakaaki, S., Murata, Y., Shinagawa, Y., Hongo, J., Furukawa, T. A., Sato, J. et al. (2007). A case of late-onset obsessive compulsive disorder developing frontotemporal lobar degeneration. *Journal of Neuropsychiatry and Clinical Neurosciences, 19,* 487–488.

Neary, D., Snowden, J. S., Gustafson, L., Passant, U., Stuss, D., Black, S. et al. (1998). Frontotemporal lobar degeneration: a consensus on clinical diagnostic criteria. *Neurology, 51,* 1546–1554.

Nestadt, G., Bienvenu, O. J., Cai, G., Samuels, J., & Eaton, W. W. (1998). Incidence of Obsessive-Compulsive Disorder in Adults. *Journal of Nervous & Mental Disease, 186*(7), 401–406.

Ngeh, J. K. T. (2000). Diogenes syndrome presenting with a stroke in an elderly, bereaved woman. *International Journal of Geriatric Psychiatry, 15*(5), 468–469.

Olatunji, B. O., Williams, B. J., Haslam, N., Abramowitz, J. S., & Tolin, D. F. (2008). The latent structure of obsessive-compulsive symptoms: a taxometric study. *Depression and Anxiety, 25,* 956–968.

Pallanti, S. & Quercioli, L. (2006). Treatment-refractory obsessive-compulsive disorder: methodological issues, operational definitions and therapeutic lines. *Progress in Neuropsychopharmacology and Biological Psychiatry, 30,* 400–412.

Pertusa, A., Fullana, M. A., Singh, S., Alonso, P., Menchon, J. M., & Mataix-Cols, D. (2008). Compulsive hoarding: OCD symptom, distinct clinical syndrome, or both? *American Journal of Psychiatry, 165,* 1289–1298.

Peterson, R., & Reiss, S. (1993). *Anxiety Sensitivity Index-Revised Test Manual.* Worthington, OH: IDF.

Petrikis, P., Andreou, C., Pitsavas, A., & Garyfallos, G. (2004). Late-onset obsessive-compulsive disorder without evidence of focal cerebral lesions: A case report. *Journal of Neuropsychiatry and Clinical Neuroscience, 16*(1), 116–117.

Philpot, M. P., & Banerjee, S. (1998). Obsessive-compulsive disorder in the elderly. *Behavioural Neurology, 11*(2), 117–121.

Piggott, T. (2004). OCD. *CNS Spectrum, 9,* 14–16.

Pinto, A., Mancebo, M. C., Eisen, J. L., Pagano, M. E., & Rasmussen, S. A. (2006). The Brown Longitudinal Obsessive Compulsive Study: clinical features and symptoms of the sample at intake. *The Journal of Clinical Psychiatry, 67*(5), 703–711.

Pollard, C. A., Carmin, C. N., & Ownby, R. (1997). Obsessive-compulsive disorder in later life. In M. Pato & G. Steketee (Eds.), *Review of Psychiatry* (Vol. 16, pp. III-57–III-72). Washington, DC: American Psychiatric Press.

Ramchandani, D. (1990). Trazadone for bowel obsession. *American Journal of Psychiatry, 147,* 124–125.

Rasmussen, S., & Eisen, J. L. (1992). The epidemiology and clinical features of obsessive compulsive disorder. *Child and Adolescent Psychiatric Clinics of North America, 15,* 743–758.

Rasmussen, S., & Tsuang, M. (1986). Epidemiologic and clinical findings of significance to the design of neuropharmacologic studies of obsessive-compulsive disorder. *Psychopharmacology Bulletin, 22,* 723–729.

Ray, W. A., Griffin, M. R., & Downey, W. (1989). Benzodiazepines of long and short elimination half-life and the risk of hip fracture. *Journal of the American Medical Association, 262,* 3303–3307.

Ressler, K. J., Rothbaum, B. O., Tannenbaum, L., Anderson, P., Graap, K., Zimand, E. et al. (2004). Cognitive enhancers as adjuncts to psychotherapy: use of D-cycloserine in phobic individuals to facilitate extinction of fear. *Archives of General Psychiatry, 61,* 1136–1144.

Robins, L. N., Helzer, J. E., Croughan, J., & Ratcliff, K. S. (1981). National Institute of Mental Health Diagnostic Interview Schedule. Its history, characteristics, and validity. *Archives of General Psychiatry, 38*(4), 381–389.

Robins, L. N., Helzer, J. E., Weissman, M. M., Orvaschel, H., Gruenberg, E., Burke, J. D., et al. (1984). Lifetime prevalence of specific psychiatric disorders in three sites. *Archives of General Psychiatry, 41*(10), 949–958.

Rothbaum, B. O. (2008). Critical parameters for D-cycloserine enhancement of cognitive-behaviorial therapy for obsessive-compulsive disorder. *American Journal of Psychiatry, 165,* 293–296.

Rosario-Campos, M. C., Leckman, J. F., Mercadante, M. T., Shavitt, R. G., Prado, H. D. S., Sada, P., et al. (2001). Adults With Early-Onset Obsessive-Compulsive Disorder. *American Journal of Psychiatry, 158*(11), 1899–1903.

Salzman, C. (1985). Geriatric psychopharmacology. *Annual Review of Medicine, 36,* 217–228.

Samuels, J. F., Bienvenu III, O. J., Pinto, A., Fyer, A. J., McCracken, J. T., Rauch, S. L., et al. (2007). Hoarding in obsessive-compulsive disorder: Results from the OCD Collaborative Genetics Study. *Behaviour Research and Therapy, 45*(4), 673–686.

Samuels, J. F., Bienvenu, O. J., Grados, M. A., Cullen, B., Riddle, M. A., Liang, K., et al. (2008). Prevalence and correlates of hoarding behavior in a community-based sample. *Behaviour Research and Therapy, 46*(7), 836–844.

Saxena, S. (2007). Is compulsive hoarding a genetically and neurobiologically discrete syndrome? Implications for diagnostic classification. *American Journal of Psychiatry, 164,* 380–384.

Saxena, S., Brody, A., Maidment, K., Smith, E., Zohrabi, N., Katz, E., et al. (2004). Cerebral glucose metabolism in obsessive-compulsive hoarding. *American Journal of Psychiatry*, *161*(6), 1038–1048.

Schulz, R., & Martire, L.M., (2004). Family caregiving of persons with dementia: Prevalence, health effects and support strategies. *American Journal of Geriatric Psychiatry*, *12*, 240–249.

Schulz, R., Beach, S.R., Ives, D.G., Martire, L.M., Ariyo, A.A., & Kop, W.J. (2000). Association between depression and mortality in older adults: The cardiovascular health study. *Archives of Internal Medicine*, *160*(12), 1761–1768.

Scicutella, A. (2000). Late-life obsessive-compulsive disorder and Huntington's disease. *Journal of Neuropsychiatry and Clinical Neurosciences*, *12*(2), 288–289.

Serby, M. (2003). Methylphenidate-induced -induced obsessive-compulsive symptoms in an elderly man. *CNS Spectrums*, *8*(8), 612–613.

Skapinakis, P., Papatheodorou, T., & Mavreas, V. (2007). Antipsychotic augmentation of serotonergic antidepressants in treatment-resistant obsessive-compulsive disorder: a meta-analysis of the randomized controlled trials. *European Neuro-psychopharmacology*, *17*, 79–93.

Steketee, G., & Frost, R. O. (2001). *Cognitive approaches to obsessions and compulsions: Theory, assessment & treatment*. New York: Elsevier.

Steketee, G. & Frost, R. (2003). Compulsive hoarding: current status of the research. *Clinical Psychology Review*, *23*, 905–927.

Steketee, G., Frost, R. O., & Kim, H. (2001). Hoarding by elderly people. *Health & Social Work*, *26*(3), 176–184.

Taylor, S., Abramowitz, J. S., McKay, D., Calamari, J. E., Sookman, D., Kyrios, M., et al. (2006). Do dysfunctional beliefs play a role in all types of obsessive-compulsive disorder? *Journal of Anxiety Disorders*, *20*(1), 85–97.

Teachman, B. A. (2007). Linking obsessional beliefs to OCD symptoms in older and younger adults. *Behaviour Research and Therapy*, *45*(7), 1671–1681.

Tolin, D., Frost, R. O., Steketee, G., & Fitch, E. (2008). Family burden of compulsive hoarding: Results of an internet survey. *Behaviour Research and Therapy*, *46*(1), 334–344.

Tomer, R., Levin, B. E., & Weiner, W. J. (1993). Side of onset of motor symptoms influences cognition in Parkinson's disease. *Annals of Neurology*, *34*, 579–584.

Trappler, B. (1999). Treatment of obsessive-compulsive disorder using clomipramine in a very old patient. *Annals of Pharmacotherapy*, *33*, 686–690.

Tükel, R., Ertekin, E., Batmaz, S., Alyanak, F., Sözen, A., Aslanta, B., et al. (2005). Influence of age of onset on clinical features in obsessive-compulsive disorder. *Depression & Anxiety (1091–4269)*, *21*(3), 112–117.

Wilhelm, S., Buhlmann, U., Tolin, D. F., Meunier, S. A., Pearlson, G. D., Reese, H. E. et al. (2008). Augmentation of behavior therapy with D-cycloserine for obsessive-compulsive disorder. *American Journal of Psychiatry*, *165*, 335–341.

Obsessive Compulsive Spectrum Disorders in Children and Adolescents

Eric A. Storch, Omar Rahman, Mirela A. Aldea, Jeannette M. Reid, Danielle Bodzin, *and* Tanya K. Murphy

Abstract

This chapter reviews the literature on obsessive compulsive spectrum disorders (i.e., obsessive compulsive disorder, body dysmorphic disorder, trichotillomania, Tourette syndrome, and varied body-focused repetitive behaviors) in children and adolescents. For each disorder, data on phenomenology, associated clinical characteristics, etiology, and treatment are reviewed. The chapter concludes with a discussion of future research and clinical directions, such as novel augmentation strategies, diagnostic classification of obsessive compulsive spectrum disorders, and methods of maximizing treatment outcome.

Keywords: obsessive compulsive disorder, children, adolescents, body dysmorphic disorder, Tourette syndrome, tic disorders, trichotillomania, treatment, cognitive-behavioral therapy

The obsessive compulsive spectrum is generally considered to comprise disorders closely linked to obsessive compulsive disorder (OCD); namely, body dysmorphic disorder (BDD), trichotillomania, Tourette syndrome, and varied body-focused repetitive behaviors (BFRB) such as nailbiting or stereotypies. These disorders have been linked by a variety of shared phenomenological characteristics, including similarity in presentation (e.g., repetitive behaviors characterize each), in family history and comorbid diagnoses, in psychological and psychiatric treatment approaches, and in both brain circuitry and neurotransmitter/peptide abnormalities.

As with many psychiatric disorders, much of the available information is extrapolated from adult studies downward to children. Accordingly, relatively less data exist on children with obsessive compulsive spectrum disorders, particularly disorders such as trichotillomania, BDD, and BFRBs. With this in mind, the purpose of the present chapter is to review the literature on obsessive compulsive spectrum disorders in children and adolescents. For each disorder, the phenomenology, etiology, and treatment data are reviewed, with the hope that the synthesis of information will foster additional scholarship and understanding of these conditions.

Obsessive Compulsive Disorder

Obsessive compulsive disorder during childhood and adolescence is one of the most common psychiatric disorders among youth. Among adults, OCD is ranked 10th internationally as a leading cause of disability; among the 1%–3% of affected children (Rapoport et al., 2000; Zohar, 1999), functional impairments across a variety of domains are substantial (e.g., Piacentini, Bergman, Keller, & McCracken, 2003; Piacentini, Peris, Bergman, Chang, & Jafer, 2007). For example, in 151 youth with OCD (Piacentini et al., 2003), 90% endorsed at least one functional domain as being significantly impacted by their symptoms, and over 50% endorsed impairment in all three areas—social, academic, and familial functioning. Originating during childhood for up to 80% of cases (Pauls, Alsobrook, Goodman, Rasmussen, & Leckman, 1995), and running a chronic course in the absence of appropriate treatment, childhood-onset

OCD is associated with increased impairment in adulthood (cf. Ulloa, Nicolini, Avila, & Fernandez-Guasti, 2007).

Symptom Phenomenology

Currently classified as an anxiety disorder, OCD is defined by the presence of obsessions (persistent and intrusive thoughts, ideas, impulses, or images that result in anxiety) and/or compulsions (repetitive or ritualistic behaviors or mental acts that reduce or prevent anxiety in response to the obsessive thought[s]) that are distressing, time consuming, and/or interfering with day-to-day functioning (American Psychiatric Association [APA], 2000). Obsessions and compulsions have a functional relationship, in that obsessional fear/anxiety evokes rituals that serve to reduce anxiety (Turner, 2006), and this anxiety reduction further motivates future ritual engagement.

Symptom expression in children is quite similar to that seen in adults, with common obsessions including contamination fears, aggressive/sexual/religious obsessions, symmetry concerns, and saving obsessions; common compulsions include cleaning rituals, checking, reassurance seeking/confessing, ordering and repeating rituals, and hoarding behaviors (Gallant et al., 2008); Swedo, Rapoport, Leonard, Lenane, & Cheslow, 1989). Indeed, factor analytic studies of the Children's Yale-Brown Obsessive Compulsive Scale Symptom Checklist (Scahill et al., 1997) produced similar results to those of adults, indicating symptom similarity across ages (e.g., Stewart, Rosario et al., 2007). Despite phenomenological similarities between childhood and adult OCD, children are not required to have insight into their symptoms, whereas adults are. Also, though it is common among both adults and children, family accommodation is especially prevalent in families with children (Peris et al., 2008; Storch, Geffken et al., 2007), for whom there exists a negative association between family accommodation and treatment outcome (Merlo, Lehmkuhl, Geffken, & Storch, 2009).

Comorbidity

Comorbid conditions are commonly present in pediatric OCD, affecting up to 74% of youth (Storch, Merlo, Larson, Geffken et al., 2008). Although there is some variation in results, high rates of comorbid major depression (10%–73%), anxiety disorders (26%–70%), tic disorders (17%–59%), disruptive behavior (10%–53%), attention deficit hyperactivity disorder (ADHD; 10%–50%), and mania (27%) exist (Geller, Biederman, Griffin, Jones, & Lefkowitz, 1996; Geller, Biederman et al., 2001; Hanna, Yuwiler, & Coates, 1995; Riddle et al., 1990; Swedo, Rapoport et al., 1989). Notably, the presence of a comorbid condition often plays an interactive role with the primary obsessive compulsive symptoms, reducing functional impairment above and beyond the OCD diagnosis (Geller, Biederman, Stewart, Mullin, Farrel et al., 2003; Masi et al., 2004; Masi et al., 2006; Sukhodolsky et al., 2005).

In addition to adverse effects on the clinical presentation, comorbidity negatively affects pharmacological and psychological treatment response. Storch, Merlo, Larson, Geffken et al. (2008), for example, showed that participants with one or more comorbid diagnoses responded to CBT at lower frequencies than did those without a comorbid diagnosis. In particular, the presence of disruptive behavior disorders, ADHD, and major depression was linked to worse outcome. In 193 pediatric OCD patients treated with paroxetine, Geller, Biederman, Stewart, Mullin, Farrel et al. (2003) showed that youth with ADHD, tics, and oppositional defiant disorder responded significantly less frequently than did the sample as a whole (56%, 53%, and 39%, versus 71%). Others have found attenuated pharmacological treatment response (but not CBT response; March et al., 2007) in the presence of comorbid tics (Leonard et al., 1993; McDougle et al., 1993).

Etiology

Multiple factors, including biological, behavioral, and cognitive factors, likely contribute to the etiology and maintenance of OCD. Further, interactions between such variables are presumed. Each etiological variable is briefly reviewed below.

Biological. A number of lines of evidence point to biological determinants of OCD. Chapter 7 in this volume addresses this topic; here, we highlight specific areas relevant to childhood OCD. Neurochemical models highlight the role of serotonin in symptom expression (Barr, Goodman, Price, McDougle, & Charney, 1992; Gilbert, Moore et al., 2000). Through the modulation of serotonin neurotransmission within regions of the frontal cortex and thalamocortical circuits (Baxter et al., 1996), serotonergic medications (e.g., clomipramine, fluoxetine) have been shown to effectively decrease orbitofrontal regional cerebral glucose metabolism among those with childhood-onset OCD (Swedo et al., 1992). In addition, treatment with another serotonergic medication, paroxetine, has been shown to decrease thalamic volumes in pediatric

OCD, as evidenced through volumetric MRI (Gilbert, Moore et al., 2000). The dopaminergic system has also been implicated in the pathophysiology of OCD (Goodman et al., 1990). Most notably, abnormalities in dopamine binding patterns within the caudate and putamen (regions important in the production and regulation of dopamine) have been evidenced in adults with OCD (Denys, de Geus, van Megan, & Westenberg, 2004; van der Wee et al., 2004). In addition, a number of clinical trials support the efficacy of atypical antipsychotics in treatment resistant adult patients (see Bloch et al., 2006 for a review). Finally, the glutamate system has received recent attention, given reduced glutamate concentrations in the anterior cingulate of those with OCD (Rosenberg et al., 2004); treatment efficacy of glutamate antagonists (e.g., riluzole; Grant, Lougee, Hirschtritt, & Swedo, 2007); and evidence of altered glutamatergic neurotransmission in OCD (e.g., Arnold, Sicard, Burroughs, Richter, & Kennedy, 2006; Stewart, Fagerness et al., 2007).

In addition to neurotransmitter dysregulation, OCD is associated with neuroanatomical abnormalities. For example, relative to healthy controls, adults with OCD evidence increased gray matter of the anterior cingulate gyrus (Rosenberg & Keshavan, 1998; Szeszko et al., 2004), increased volume of the thalamus (Gilbert, Moore et al., 2000), and decreased volume of the globus pallidus (within the basal ganglia; Szeszko et al., 2004). These findings support a fundamental dysfunction of frontal-striatal circuitry in OCD (Saxena & Rauch, 2000), such that feedback loops involving the orbitofrontal cortex, thalamus, and striatum (within the basal ganglia) are hypothesized to mediate intrusive thoughts and repetitive behaviors (Saxena, Brody, Schwartz, & Baxter, 1998; Szeszko et al., 2004), resulting in the characteristic obsessive compulsive symptoms.

Cognitive-Behavioral. Cognitive-behavioral theory provides an empirically based, well-established framework for understanding the acquisition and maintenance of obsessive compulsive symptoms. Central to the behavioral framework is Mowrer's (1939; 1960) two-factor theory, which states that the acquisition of fears is based on classical conditioning, and maintained by operant principles (i.e., negative reinforcement) associated with safety behaviors/rituals. In the conditioning process, a neutral stimulus (e.g., physical object, cognition) becomes associated with a feared stimulus and thereby produces distress. To reduce this distress, the person develops a repertoire of behaviors or

rituals. If successful, the individual may effectively create a negative reinforcement loop—such that the likelihood of engaging in the chosen repertoire of behaviors or rituals is increased during future periods of distress.

Cognitive theorists, on the other hand, highlight the beliefs or appraisals that people have regarding intrusive thoughts, images, and impulses (Frost & Steketee, 2002; Salkovskis, 1999) rather than the actual occurrence of such thoughts. As opposed to intrusive thoughts common in typical development, those of OCD are associated with multiple cognitive errors—namely, an exaggerated importance attributed to the thoughts, inflated concern about the importance of being able to control these thoughts, inability to tolerate ambiguity/uncertainty, and a need for perfectionism (Barrett & Healy, 2003; Comer, Kendall, Franklin, Hudson, & Pimentel, 2004; Obsessive Compulsive Cognitions Working Group, 1997). Integrating the cognitive and behavioral models provides a cyclical pattern of thoughts and behaviors, whereby cognitive misattributions result in anxiety/distress, which results in anxiety-reducing (in the short term) rituals and, finally, the increased likelihood of intrusive thoughts and performance of associated rituals (Turner, 2006). Notably, the cycle prevents adaptive learning from taking place, as the individual performs routines and rituals rather than facing the possibility of feared consequences and learning about the likelihood of his or her fears occurring and/or their associated consequences.

PANDAS. Pediatric Autoimmune Neuropsychiatric Disorders Associated with Streptococcus (PANDAS), first described by Swedo et al. (1998), describes the abrupt onset and progression of neuropsychiatric disorders such as OCD and Tourette's disorder, secondary to an autoimmune reaction to Group A ß-hemolytic streptococcus (GAS). Onset of neuropsychiatric symptoms associated with PANDAS must be prepubertal, and the course and severity of these symptoms are episodic (Murphy & Pichichero, 2002; Swedo et al., 1998). In addition, neurological abnormalities (e.g., hyperactivity, frequent urination, deterioration in handwriting) are often present, and many youth also experience an onset of separation anxiety. On a neuroanatomical level, some have hypothesized that basal ganglia inflammation mediates the association between GAS and neuropsychiatric symptoms (Leonard & Swedo, 2001; Murphy et al., 2004), similar to what is seen in Sydenham's chorea (Kotby, el Badawy, el Sokkary, Moawad, & el Shawarby, 1998). Although the exact prevalence of PANDAS remains unknown, practice recommendations suggest appropriate antibiotic treatment for the infection, and standard psychological and pharmacological therapies for the presenting symptoms (Storch et al., 2006). Some preliminary data suggest the possibility of increased incidence of side effects associated with SSRI use in youth with OCD of the PANDAS phenotype (Murphy, Storch, & Strawser, 2006).

Treatment

The past two decades have seen a tremendous expansion in knowledge about efficacious treatments for pediatric OCD. As described in Chapters 15, 17, 18 and 19, both cognitive-behavioral therapy (CBT) with exposure and response prevention (ERP), and serotonin reuptake inhibitors (SRIs) have shown efficacy in methodologically rigorous clinical trials. Although two direct comparison trials (de Haan et al., 1998; Pediatric OCD Study (POTS) Team, 2004) and a recent meta-analysis (Abramowitz, Whiteside, & Deacon, 2005) indicate that CBT with ERP is a superior monotherapy to medication alone, the majority of affected adults and children initially receive medication treatment, either alone or with a non-CBT form of psychotherapy (Blanco et al., 2006). Thus, increasing patient access to effective psychological care remains a tremendous challenge to be addressed. What follows is a review of the extant data in support of both pharmacological and psychological treatments.

Pharmacotherapy

Pharmacological treatment for OCD is an effective, relatively safe, and readily available treatment modality. Currently, there are four medications approved by the FDA for use in pediatric populations with OCD—a tricyclic, clomipramine, prescribed down to 10 years of age (DeVeaugh-Geiss et al., 1992), and three selective serotonin reuptake inhibitors (SSRIs): fluoxetine, down to 7 years of age (Geller, Hoog et al., 2001); fluvoxamine, down to 8 years of age (Riddle et al., 2001); and sertraline, down to 6 years of age (March et al., 1998; POTS, 2004). The efficacy of clomipramine has been shown to rival (or even surpass) that of SSRIs (Geller, Biederman, Stewart, Mullin, Martin et al., 2003); however, this agent is not typically used as a first-line medication, given the greater number of associated side effects (e.g., antiadrenergic and anticholinergic) as well as required monitoring of the heart (via EKG) and blood. While the SSRIs are associated with some modest side effects among

youth (Goodman, Murphy, & Storch, 2007), they are generally well tolerated and considered safe (see Murphy, Segerra, Storch, & Goodman, 2008 for a review). Recently, some concerns related to "activation syndrome" have received considerable attention (Goodman, Murphy, & Storch, 2007). More specifically, increased risk of suicidality and other adverse side effects (e.g., irritability, restlessness, emotional lability) have been linked to SSRI initiation and/or dosage increases. As a result, the FDA adopted a "black box" warning to remind prescribers and consumers about the importance of closely monitoring SSRI-related adverse effects.

With regard to treatment efficacy, findings have been consistently positive. For instance, in a 12-week randomized, double blind, placebo-controlled trial of youth ages 13 to 17 years, March et al. (1998) found that 42% of sertraline-treated patients and 26% of placebo-treated patients were considered responders. In a similarly randomized, double blinded and placebo-controlled 12-week trial of youth ages 6 to 12 years, Cook et al. (2001) again reported significantly greater efficacy with sertraline than with placebo. A total of 72% of children and 61% of adolescents treated with sertraline were treatment responders. In their 11-week study of fluoxetine in youth ages 7 to 17 years, Geller, Hoog et al. (2001) found that 49% of fluoxetine-treated pediatric patients responded relative to 25% of those receiving placebo. Although encouraging, it is fair to note that treatment response is moderate and symptom remission is relatively rare. For example, in the POTS (2004) trial, only 21% of youth achieved symptom remission after taking sertraline.

Antipsychotics. As noted, complete remission is infrequent on medication alone, requiring additional interventions to augment initial treatment efforts. To date, very little on augmentation has been published on pediatric OCD patients, and applied practice tends to rely on off-label use that is based on data extrapolated from adults with OCD. Antipsychotic augmentation has shown modest efficacy among treatment-resistant adults (i.e., those who have not found significant symptom reduction with SRIs), with approximately one-third of individuals responding (see Bloch et al., 2006 for review). Unfortunately, side effects associated with atypical antipsychotic use are common, notably weight gain and metabolic syndrome (Correll & Carlson, 2006; Kane et al., 2004). In children, there is considerably less data. Thomsen (2004) reported on 17 SRI treatment-resistant adolescents (15 to 19 years of age) with OCD in an open-label trial of risperidone augmentation. Statistically significant reductions in CY-BOCS/Y-BOCS symptoms were found at 12 weeks. In addition, Storch, Lehmkuhl, Geffken, Touchton, and Murphy (2008) reported on successful aripiprazole augmentation of CBT and SSRI treatment for OCD in a 13-year-old male. Fitzgerald, Stewart, Tawile, & Rosenberg (1999) reported on successful risperidone augmentation of 4 pediatric SRI nonresponders in a non-blinded open trial that did not use quantitative measures. Lombroso et al. (1995) investigated the short-term (11 weeks) safety and efficacy of risperidone in the treatment of chronic tic disorders in 7 youth, 3 of whom had comorbid OCD. Each of the children with comorbid OCD had a partial response to an SSRI that they remained on during the trial. One child with comorbid OCD showed substantial improvement (100% symptom reduction); the two others had Y-BOCS reductions of 16% and 22%, respectively. Overall Y-BOCS reduction for the 3 youth was 58%. Finally, in an 8-week, double blind study of 21 youth with Tourette syndrome, Gaffney et al. (2002) examined the efficacy and tolerability of risperidone relative to clonidine. A Y-BOCS change of 6.3 ± 5.1 was found for the risperidone group at post-treatment, versus only 2.8 ± 5.5 for clonidine. Although this finding is informative, youngsters in the sample did not have a primary OCD diagnosis, evidenced symptoms that may have been more a function of tics, were generally of mild severity (Baseline Y-BOCS = 15.1), and did not necessarily have a history of limited response to past treatments.

Cognitive-Behavioral Therapy

Cognitive-behavioral therapy with exposure and response prevention differs from other forms of psychotherapy in its structured incorporation of set skills for symptom management. There are three primary components to CBT with ERP; namely, *(1)* exposure (confronting situations that elicit obsessional anxiety); *(2)* response prevention (deterring the ritualistic or compulsive behaviors that serve to reduce or avoid anxiety); and *(3)* teaching the child methods of coping with anxiety-provoking cognitions. Briefly, in exposure and response prevention, the patient is exposed to fear-producing stimuli and prohibited from engaging in rituals that might typically be used to alleviate anxiety. Anxiety will naturally habituate after extended exposure. Further, continued exposures to the feared stimulus without ritual engagement will produce less extreme anxiety elevations, as well as more rapid attenuation

of distress (March, Franklin, Nelsom, & Foa, 2001). As noted above, this framework is based on the assumption that compulsions temporarily reduce anxiety/distress, thereby motivating future ritual engagement vis-à-vis negative reinforcement. In the cognitive component of CBT with ERP, skills are developed to contend with anxious thoughts that are presumably motivating the compulsive behaviors (Barrett, Farrell, Pina, Peris, & Piacentini, 2008), as well as inaccurate appraisals (e.g., of associated danger, responsibility, or probability) therein (Abramowitz, Khandker, Nelson, Deacon, & Rygwall, 2006). With regard to childhood OCD, there are three primary techniques for countering anxious thoughts: constructive self-talk, cognitive restructuring, and cultivating detachment (March & Mulle, 1998). In constructive self-talk, the child is taught how to identify problematic self-statements (e.g., "OCD will always be in control") and to respond in a positive (yet accurate) and forceful manner (e.g., "OCD can't boss me around"). In cognitive restructuring, children are taught, in an age-appropriate manner, to challenge the validity of anxious thoughts and to replace such cognitions with more accurate beliefs. Finally, detachment from obsessions is cultivated; instead of suppressing intrusive thoughts, the child learns to regard them as "brain hiccups" that need not be attended. Cognitive-behavioral therapy has been demonstrated in several studies to be superior to SRI monotherapy, waitlist control conditions, and attention control conditions. Overall, response and remission rates in controlled trials are quite high, with up to 90% of youth being classified as responders and 82% as achieving clinical remission following treatment. Among the extant published trials to date, several stand out as particularly notable.

In the first study comparing the effects of ERP and clomipramine in pediatric OCD, de Haan et al. (1998) reported on 23 individuals between the ages of 8 and 18 years. Treatments were given over a 12-week period, and participants were randomly assigned to one of the two treatment conditions. Both ERP and clomipramine resulted in significant symptom reductions on the Child Yale-Brown Obsessive Compulsive Scale (CY-BOCS), a measure of obsessive compulsive symptom severity. Between the two treatments, though, ERP proved more effective—a nearly 60% reduction on the CY-BOCS was found in the ERP arm versus a 33% reduction for those youth randomized to clomipramine. The rate of improvement was more rapid for those receiving ERP relative to those receiving clomipramine.

The Pediatric OCD Treatment Study (POTS, 2004), the gold standard of pediatric OCD clinical trials to date, randomized 112 youth with OCD (ages 7–17 years) into groups receiving CBT alone, sertraline alone, a combination of CBT and sertraline, or placebo. All three therapies proved significantly more effective than did placebo in symptom reduction on the CY-BOCS. Further, whereas the efficacy of CBT alone did not differ significantly from that of sertraline alone, symptom improvement was significantly greater under the combined condition than under either individual therapy. Effect sizes (Cohen's d) relative to placebo for treatments were as follows: combined treatment = 1.4; CBT alone = 0.97; and sertraline alone = 0.67. Approximately 54% of children who received combined treatment experienced symptom remission, compared to 39% for CBT alone and 21% for sertraline alone. Rates of remission did not differ between those who received CBT alone or sertraline alone. Interestingly, a site difference existed, with one site showing very large effect sizes for CBT alone, whereas the other site found only a moderate effect size for CBT alone. Based on these data, the authors concluded that youth with OCD should be treated with the combination of CBT plus SSRI, or with CBT alone.

The POTS (2004) and de Haan et al. (1998) studies are consistent with adult data (e.g., Foa et al., 2005) indicating that CBT monotherapy is superior to SRI monotherapy. However, a particularly relevant question pertaining to working with children is how to include parents and family members in treatment, particularly given the high rates of family accommodation found in this population (Peris et al., in press; Storch, Geffken et al., 2007). In this vein, Barrett, Healy-Farrell, and March (2004) developed a family-based CBT program to incorporate parents and siblings into treatment, with the goal of reducing accommodating behaviors and teaching parents to be their child's at-home coach/therapist. In their trial, Barrett et al. (2004) randomly assigned 77 youth with OCD into 14-week sessions of individual family-based CBT (CBFT); group CBFT; or a 4–6 week waitlist. At post-treatment, 65% and 61% CY-BOCS reductions were found for individual and group CBFT arms, respectively. Further, 82% of individual CBFT completers and 76% of group CBFT completers had achieved clinical remission. At 6-month follow-up, 65% of individual CBFT and 87% of group CBFT participants were considered remitted. And an 18-month follow-up study showed that gains had largely been maintained, with 70% of individual CBFT and 84% of group CBFT participants remitted (Barrett, Farrell, Dadds, & Boulter, 2005).

Subsequently, Storch, Geffken et al. (2007) compared the efficacies of intensive and weekly family-based CBT in 40 youth with OCD (ages 7–17 years). Participants all received 14 sessions of CBFT, and were randomly assigned to have either daily (i.e., intensive) sessions for 3 weeks, or weekly sessions across 14 weeks. At post-treatment, both CBFT groups evidenced significant decreases in obsessive compulsive symptoms. However, no significant differences were found between those treated with intensive CBT and those treated with weekly CBT. Post-treatment, 90% of the intensive group and 65% of the weekly group were treatment responders, and 75% of the intensive group and 50% of the weekly group had achieved clinical remission.

Finally, to address the absence of treatment approaches and data in young children with OCD, Freeman et al. (2008) examined family-based CBT relative to family-based relaxation training, in 42 youth with OCD, between the ages of 5 and 8 years. At post-treatment, there was a significant group difference, such that those in the family-based CBT group evidenced a significantly greater reduction in CY-BOCS scores than did those in the family-based relaxation training group. Effect sizes in favor of CBT were moderate for the intent-to-treat sample (Cohen's d = 0.53), and large for the completer sample (Cohen's d = 0.85). Sixty-nine percent of CBT completers achieved clinical remission versus only 20% of those who received relaxation training.

From the above data, it is clear that CBT has a strong evidence base, and thus therapists should be encouraged to become trained in, and implement, such practices. On the other hand, some other forms of psychotherapy, such as play, supportive, and psychoanalytic therapies, have not been studied and therefore have not demonstrated efficacy in the treatment of OCD.

Body Dysmorphic Disorder
Phenomenology
Body dysmorphic disorder (BDD) has been described in the literature for several decades (see Chapters 3 and 21 of this volume). Janet (1903) referred to "obsession de la hontu de corps," an obsession or distressing fear of being perceived as ridiculous or ugly. Approximately two decades earlier, Morselli (1886) coined the term *dysmorphophobia*, meaning "fear of ugliness." However, it was not until 1987 that BDD was formally recognized as a

psychiatric disorder in the *Diagnostic and Statistical Manual of Mental Disorders–III* (APA, 1987). The suffix "phobia" was removed, though, as the disorder involves an irrational fear of already being ugly or deformed, rather than a fear of *becoming* as such. Thus, the core characteristic of BDD is a preoccupation with an imagined or minor defect in appearance. Although any area of the body can be the focus of concern, and preoccupation with multiple body areas is not uncommon, concerns are most frequently centered on head areas or skin (Phillips, 1996). For example, patients may perceive that they have conspicuous blemishes and acne, their head is too large, their ears are too large or misshapen, their hair is thinning, or their nose is deformed (Hollander, Cohen, & Simeon, 1993; Phillips, McElroy, Keck, Pope, & Hudson, 1993; Veale et al., 1996). Most patients spend an excessive amount of time worrying about their professed flaws, and engaging in compensatory ritualistic behaviors such as mirror checking, hiding the defects with makeup, hats, or sun glasses, grooming (e.g., applying makeup, tweezing, styling, or cutting hair), camouflaging, skin-picking, and seeking reassurance that they look adequate (Neziroglu & Yaryura-Tobias, 1993; Veale et al., 1996). These behaviors are often described as "compulsive" in the sense that the urge to perform them is strong and difficult to resist. Body dysmorphic disorder is associated with substantial distress, impairment in everyday functioning, and poor quality of life (Phillips, 2000; Phillips et al., 2006).

A German nationwide survey of 2552 individuals between the ages of 14 and 99 years found that 1.7% had symptoms indicative of clinical BDD (Rief, Buhlmann, Wilhelm, Borkenhagen, & Brahler, 2006). Retrospective studies of adults have indicated that BDD usually begins during the early to middle teenage years. For instance, two large studies found that the mean age of onset of BDD symptoms was 16.0 years (range 4–43 years, mode 13 years), with symptoms starting before age 18 years in 70% of cases (Gunstad & Phillips, 2003; Phillips & Diaz, 1997). Reports on the prevalence in pediatric populations are scarce (Phillips, 2001), but one study of a large high school sample (*n* = 566) of ethnically diverse adolescents reported that 2.2% met DSM-IV criteria for BDD (Mayville, Katz, Gipson, & Cabral, 1999).

The prevalence of BDD among psychiatric inpatient samples is vastly greater. For instance, a study of 122 adults and adolescents (composed of 101 and 21, respectively) indicated that 13.1% of the sample met criteria for BDD (Grant, Kim, & Crow, 2001). A study of 208 adolescent inpatients reported that 6.7% "definitely" met criteria or "probably" met criteria for BDD (Dyl, Kittler, Phillips, & Hunt, 2006).

With regard to symptom presentation, the very few existing studies of pediatric BDD suggest that it is similar across adolescence and adulthood (Albertini & Phillips, 1999; Dyl et al., 2006; Phillips et al., 2006). A case series of 33 children and adolescents (mean age=14.9; age range=6–17 years) found that the most frequent bodily concerns were centered on skin (61%), hair (55%), face (39%), and teeth (30%; Albertini & Phillips, 1999). Participants also presented with associated compulsive behaviors including camouflaging with clothes, makeup, or a hat (94%), comparing to others (87%), checking in mirrors (85%), and seeking reassurance (73%). Most participants engaged in more than one BDD-related compulsion (mean=4.5) and many (25%) carried out such behaviors for more than 8 hours a day. Two other studies, based on smaller samples, found similar results (Dyl et al., 2006; Phillips et al., 2006).

As with adult BDD, pediatric BDD is associated with considerable distress and significantly impaired psychosocial functioning. More specifically, poor grades (Phillips, McElroy, Hudson, & Pope, 1995), social withdrawal (el-Khatib & Dickey, 1995), and dropping out of school (Albertini & Phillips, 1999) are common in youth with BDD. Further, one study (Phillips et al. 2006) reported that 80.6% of adolescents had a history of suicidal ideation and 44.4% had attempted suicide. Another study reported that 39% of their participants had a history of psychiatric hospitalizations (at least one), and 21% had made a suicide attempt (Albertini & Phillips, 1999). In a study of inpatient adolescents, Dyl et al. (2006) found that—as compared to those with other psychiatric disorders—patients who had a body image disorder displayed more psychopathology; in particular, adolescents with BDD exhibited higher levels of depression, anxiety, and suicidality. Thus, the limited available evidence points to the potential for considerable and concerning morbidity in children and adolescents with BDD, although further study is required.

Although youth and adults with BDD are comparable on most clinical variables, the extant literature delineates a few noteworthy distinctions. Relatively fewer youth seek nonpsychiatric treatment such as body modifications for their perceived dysmorphia (e.g., 41.0% versus 76.4% of adults; Phillips, Grant, Siniscalchi, & Albertini, 2001). Rather than indicating gradations in severity, this difference may be a function of external variables (e.g., parental restrictions). Also, as opposed to their adult counterparts, adolescents with BDD have more delusional beliefs and may have a higher lifetime rate of suicide attempts.

Etiology

Despite its seriousness, very little is known about the etiology of BDD, and no single theoretical model of BDD etiology is broadly accepted. Different models of BDD implicate biological, psychosocial, and cultural factors. As with OCD, biological theories of BDD focus on (1) the dysregulation of the serotonin system (Phillips et al., 1995) and (2) neurological disturbances that have been proposed to constitute a common genetic basis for disorders of the obsessive compulsive spectrum (Allen & Hollander, 2004; Rauch et al., 2003). In a comprehensive review of the pathophysiology of BDD, Feusner, Yaryura-Tobias, and Saxena (2008), based on neuroimaging studies and studies of brain-damaged patients, concluded that

> "a combination of frontal-striatal circuit dysfunction, hemispheric imbalances (perhaps involving the right PHG, dorsal occipital cortex, IPL, fusiform gyrus, IFG, and greater left prefrontal and temporal activation for processing faces), and hyper responsiveness of the amygdala and insula may be involved in mediating the symptoms and neuropsychological deficits of BDD." (p. 10)

Cognitive-behavioral models take into consideration cognitive, affective, and behavioral components of BDD, and include aspects such as biological predispositions, childhood experiences, and cultural factors. These theories are analogous to anxiety disorder models, and propose that both biased information processing and dysfunctional behavioral strategies are involved in the etiology and maintenance of BDD (Buhlmann, McNally, Etcoff, Tuschen-Caffier, & Wilhelm, 2004; Neziroglu, Khemlani-Patel, & Veale, 2008; Neziroglu, Roberts, & Yaryura-Tobias, 2004). For instance, Buhlmann et al. (2004) suggest that individuals with BDD perceive, process, and recall information in a biased way. This may affect the way life experiences are processed, resulting, in turn, in negative cognitive, emotional, and behavioral patterns. In support of this hypothesis, studies have found that BDD patients, in contrast to healthy controls, selectively attended to BDD-related words such as "attractive" or "ugly" (Buhlmann, McNally, Wilhelm, & Florin, 2002), tended to interpret ambiguous situations as threatening (Buhlmann et al., 2002), had difficulty identifying emotions in others' facial expressions, and often misinterpreted expressions in a negative valence (Buhlmann et al., 2004; Buhlmann, Etcoff, & Wilhelm, 2006).

Veale (2004; Veale et al., 1996) and Neziroglu (Neziroglu et al., 2004) base their BDD etiological theories on Cash's (2002; 2008) model of body image disturbance. Broadly speaking, the model proposes that factors such as cultural socialization, interpersonal experiences, physical characteristics, and personality attributes result in body image perceptions and attitudes leading to certain beliefs and emotions; associated behaviors may be implemented, and subsequently maintained through negative reinforcement. For example, being bullied, teased, or criticized about a physical characteristic might convince an individual to view the characteristic as flawed. This negative interpretation may lead to a subjective feeling of anxiety, performance of ritualistic behaviors (e.g., grooming) in an attempt to neutralize this feeling, and/or avoidance of social interactions in an attempt to reduce attention directed toward the perceived flaw. Because ritualistic behaviors and avoidance result in a temporary lessening of anxiety, they are negatively reinforced, and thus contribute to the maintenance of BDD symptoms.

Comorbidity and Assessment

Comorbid conditions are common in pediatric BDD. The constant self-scrutiny and unhappiness with one's appearance are often associated with depressive symptoms. Other disorders, such as social phobia, OCD, eating disorders, and substance use disorders, are also common (Gunstand & Phillips, 2003). For instance, Phillips et al. (1998) reported that about 70% of 33 adolescents with BDD had comorbid major depression, 36% had OCD, and 30% had social phobia. As these comorbid disorders share many phenomenological features with BDD (e.g., intrusive thoughts in BDD and OCD; fears of negative social evaluations in BDD and social phobia), and BDD remains relatively unknown and under-studied, it is thought that BDD is largely underdiagnosed or misdiagnosed (Phillips, 2000; Phillips & Hollander, 2008). In fact, a study of 122 adult and adolescent psychiatric inpatients found that none of 16 patients who met criteria for BDD had been diagnosed by their original treating clinician (Grant et al., 2001). When diagnosing, clinicians must clearly ascertain whether presenting complaints relate specifically to physical appearance

(Buhmann et al., 2008). This may prove difficult, as some patients are reluctant to share their appearance concerns due to embarrassment or shame (Phillips, 1996; De Wall, Arnold, Eekhof, & Van Hemert, 2004); thus, explicit BDD-related questions and/or standardized measures are advised.

With regard to assessment, the choices are limited, especially for pediatric BDD. The most commonly used adult BDD assessment is the Yale-Brown Obsessive Compulsive Scale modified to measure obsessions and compulsions specific to BDD (BDD-Y-BOCS; Phillips, 1993; Phillips et al., 1997). For assessing BDD severity in children and adolescents, studies (e.g., Philips et al., 2006) have used a slightly modified version based on the adult BDD-Y-BOCS and the CY-BOCS (Scahill et al., 1997). Similarly, other measures designed for adults have been used in pediatric BDD studies, such as the Body Dysmorphic Disorder Examination (BDDE; Rosen & Reiter, 1996) and the Brown Assessment of Beliefs Scale (BABS; Eisen et al., 1998). Although these measures have acceptable psychometric properties, they have been designed for adults and should be used with caution for pediatric BDD patients.

Treatment

Unfortunately, many individuals with BDD seek and receive costly nonpsychiatric surgical, dermatologic, or dental treatments, but such treatments are usually unsuccessful, as the worked-upon flaw tends to be imagined (Phillips, Grant et al., 2001). On the other hand, the extant data suggests efficacy of both pharmacological and psychological treatments. Pharmacological trials have mainly investigated SRIs among adults with BDD: for example, clomipramine (Hollander et al., 1999), fluvoxamine (Perugi et al., 1996; Phillips, Dwight, & McElroy, 1998; Phillips, McElroy, Dwight, Eisen, & Rasmussen, 2001), fluoxetine (Phillips, Albertini, & Rasmussen, 2002) and citalopram (Phillips & Najjar, 2003) were superior to placebo in treating BDD symptoms among adults. However, a meta-analysis of adult studies suggested greater efficacy with cognitive and behavioral therapies as compared to medication (d=1.78 versus d=0.92, respectively; Williams, Hadjistavropoulos, & Sharpe, 2006). Investigations specific to children and adolescents have been scarce, but preliminary data suggest response to psychological and pharmacological treatments (e.g., Phillips, Atala, & Albertini, 1995).

Cognitive-behavioral therapy has received the most attention of any psychotherapy in the literature. Several methodologically rigorous controlled trials of CBT in adults have been reported, as well as a number of positive case series and case studies. These positive findings are not surprising, given the success of CBT with OCD and other anxiety disorders that have phenomenological similarities to BDD. Rosen, Reiter, and Orosan (1995) developed a group CBT protocol for the treatment of adult BDD patients. Fifty-four individuals with BDD were randomly assigned to either the treatment or placebo group and, following 8 two-hour sessions, those who participated in group CBT evidenced significantly greater symptom reductions than did those in the placebo group. In another controlled study (Veale et al., 1996), 19 adults with BDD were randomly assigned either to 12 weekly CBT sessions or to an equivalent waitlist control. Patients in the CBT condition scored significantly lower than did the patients in the control group on measures of BDD, as well as on measures of depression post-treatment, and the symptoms for 7 out of 9 treated patients had either dropped to subclinical or were in remission. In addition to these studies, findings from several case reports and uncontrolled studies suggest that CBT is effective in reducing BDD symptoms in adults (Marks & Mishan, 1988; McKay et al., 1997; Neziroglu & Yayura-Tobias, 1993; Wilhelm, Otto, Lohr, & Deckersbach, 1999).

Although the efficacy of CBT with adult BDD has been demonstrated, information on CBT with pediatric BDD is limited and secondary to the exploration of clinical features (Albertini & Phillips, 1999; Phillips et al., 1995). For instance, of the four cases presented by Phillips et al. (1995), one underwent CBT and showed a positive response. In light of the phenomenological similarities between adult and pediatric BDD, and the encouraging results of CBT in the treatment of adult BDD, it is reasonable to expect that BDD in children and adolescents would respond well to CBT. Nevertheless, an examination of this treatment tailored specifically to pediatric BDD is warranted. In addition, future studies should investigate potential differential effectiveness of various CBT techniques (e.g., cognitive versus behavioral interventions), develop other psychotherapy approaches, compare SSRIs to CBT, and examine augmentation of these approaches with each other.

Studies aimed at potential moderating variables in treatment response (e.g., age of onset, family constellation, degree of delusionality, motivation for treatment, comorbid diagnoses) are critical. Additionally, clinical strategies are needed to maximize pediatric treatment engagement, as is the development of sound assessment instruments specific to this age group. As with any disorder, elucidating its underlying etiology and maintaining factors may allow for more targeted and effective treatments and, thus, future studies that empirically test existing models and propose new theories for understanding BDD are warranted.

Tic Disorders

Phenomenology

Gilles de la Tourette's syndrome, or Tourette's disorder, is named after French neurologist Georges Gilles de la Tourette, who, in 1885, described 9 patients with childhood-onset motor and vocal tics (Jankovich, 2001). As noted in Chapter 5, Tourette syndrome is characterized by multiple motor tics and at least one vocal tic occurring several times a day, almost every day, for at least a year. These tics are involuntary, sudden, and rhythmic (APA, 2000). Tourette's disorder is considered by some to be a more severe form of chronic tic disorder, in which either motor or vocal tics, but not both, are present for at least a year (Spencer, Biederman, Harding, Wilens, & Faraone, 1995). If symptoms persist for less than one year, the appropriate diagnosis is transient tic disorder. In this chapter—as with the DSM-IV-TR (APA, 2000)—the term "tic disorders" will refer to Tourette syndrome, chronic tic disorder, and transient tic disorder. The focus of the ensuing review will be childhood presentation.

The presentation of tics differs substantially across children. Examples of motor tics include rapid blinking, squeezing eyes shut, grimacing, smacking lips, opening the jaw, shrugging shoulders, and making other odd facial or muscular gestures (Leckman, 2002; Alsobrook & Pauls, 2002). Common vocal tics include throat clearing, coughing, grunting, repeating words, or saying random words. The socially unacceptable nature of some more severe tics, such as biting and hitting oneself, or cursing loudly in public, may augment an individual's level of impairment even further (Leckman, 2002).

Before performing a tic, many individuals with a tic disorder describe having an urge to do so, known as a *premonitory urge* (Leckman, Walker, & Cohen, 1993). For instance, a child may feel an itch or a scratchy sensation that necessitates a clearing of the throat or a cough. According to Woods, Piacentini, Himle, and Chang (2005), the prevalence of the premonitory urge depends on the operational definition of the construct. Although studies have reported the range anywhere from 8.7% to 96%, more systematic studies have suggested that between 77% and 93% experience a premonitory urge (Woods et al., 2005). In some instances, children may be able to suppress tics, or find a mentally or physically exerting task to be sufficiently distracting (Jankovic, 2001). Although some have suggested that tic suppression (e.g., while in school, due to embarrassment) is often followed by a period of increased tic frequency (e.g., Jankovich, 1997), empirical research has not consistently supported this (Himle & Woods, 2005). In any case, whether an effort to suppress has been made or not, the individual experiences an immediate drop in tension upon performing the tic (Verdellen, Keijsers, Cath, & Hoogduin, 2004).

Children with tic disorders tend to experience motor or vocal tics in several high-frequency periods each day, with a relative paucity of tic behaviors in between those periods (Leckman, 2002). Although the time between individual tics can vary, it is usually short, typically a second or less (Peterson & Leckman, 1998). A child's tics can be precipitated by stress, anxiety, boredom, or a variety of auditory or visual cues specific to the individual. Symptoms of Tourette syndrome and other tic disorders usually wax and wane in severity as the child matures; in fact, even weeks or months may go by with relatively few high-frequency episodes (Robertson, 2000).

In general, children and adolescents with Tourette syndrome and chronic tic disorder experience significant impairment because of their symptoms— either directly due to the tics, or indirectly due to associated embarrassment or comorbid conditions (Kadesjo & Gillberg, 2000; Storch, Lack et al., 2007; Sukhodolsky et al., 2003). Among youth, impairment can include interruption of activities (e.g., concentrating at school), social withdrawal, depression, and diminished self-esteem. Storch, Lack et al. (2007) found that, in a sample of 59 children and adolescents with Tourette's disorder or chronic tic disorder, tics impaired functioning particularly in school-related activities, such as writing, doing homework, concentrating, and being prepared for class. Children also experienced problems with being teased and making new friends. Similarly, Storch, Merlo, Lack et al. (2007) found that children and adolescents experienced a significantly lower quality of life than did healthy children in a number of facets, including emotional, social, and school functioning, as well as psychosocial health. Childhood tics have also been associated with impairments in daily functioning (Ernberg, Cruse, & Rothner,

1987), parent–child interaction, and family functioning (Cohen, Ort, Leckman, Riddle, & Hardin, 1988; Wilkinson et al., 2001).

Prevalence

Tourette syndrome and other tic disorders are typically diagnosed in childhood. Most often, motor tics are first apparent, preceding the phonic tics by several years. While tic disorders, in general, have appeared in children as young as 3 years of age (Leckman, Peterson, Pauls, & Cohen, 1997), the average age of onset is approximately 7 years (Hebebrand et al., 1997; Robertson, 2000). Reports suggest an overall childhood prevalence of 0.6% to 3% (Comings, Hines, & Comings, 1990; Kurlan, Whitmore, Irvine, McDermott, & Como, 1994; Mason, Banarjee, Eapen, Zeitlin, & Robertson, 1998); however, rates of Tourette syndrome among psychiatric samples and special education students may be as high as 10% and 25%, respectively (Kurlan et al., 1994; Sverd, Curley, Jandorf, & Volkersz, 1988). A diagnosis of either Tourette syndrome or chronic tic disorder is three to five times more likely in boys than in girls (Comings et al., 1990; Kadesjo & Gillberg, 2000; Mason et al., 1998).

Comorbidity

In children, Tourette's disorder displays a high comorbidity rate with other psychiatric disorders, including attention deficit hyperactivity disorder (ADHD), obsessive compulsive disorder (OCD), disruptive behavior disorders, anxiety, and depressive disorders (Gadow, Nolan, Sprafkin & Schwartz, 2002). Comorbidity with ADHD has been reported from 20% to 70% (Robertson, Banarjee, Eapen, & Fox-Hiley, 2002). Hebebrand et al. (1997) found that approximately 16% of individuals with Tourette syndrome aged 2 to 13 years had comorbid OCD, with other studies suggesting a greater prevalence as the adolescent years progress (Cohen & Leckman, 1994; Pauls et al., 1995; Robertson et al., 2002). Comorbidity with disruptive behavior disorders ranges from 20% to 90% (Kadesjo & Gillberg, 2000; Spencer, Biederman, & Wilens, 1999; Spencer et al., 2001; Sukhodolsky et al., 2003; Walkup et al., 1999; Wodrich, Benjamin, & Lachar, 1997). Comorbidity with depression ranges from 14% to 73% (Ghanizadeh & Mosallaei, 2009; Kurlan et al., 2002; Robertson et al., 2002; Wodrich et al., 1997). Comorbidity with anxiety disorders has been reported between 40% and 50% (Ghanizadeh & Mosallaei, 2009, Wodrich et al., 1997).

Etiology

Multiple lines of evidence have pointed to a neurobiological theory of etiology for Tourette syndrome. Family studies have identified prevalence rates among first-degree relatives to be several times the rate in the general population (Hebebrand et al., 1997; Pauls, Raymond, Stevenson, & Leckman, 1991; Pauls et al., 1995), suggesting a possible genetic link. Further, the high comorbidity with other disorders such as OCD and ADHD suggests a common genetic vulnerability or biological mechanism. Although the current neurobiological mechanism for tics is unknown, studies have implicated the basal ganglia and thalamus, as well as cortical and subcortical regions involved in behavioral inhibition (Berardelli, Currà, Fabbrini, Gilio, & Manfredi, 2003; Mink, 2003). Several genetic studies, investigating factors such as candidate genes, autosomal dominance, dopamine pathways, and molecular level associations have been conducted, but no specific factors have been identified (Robertson & Stern, 1998).

An immunological link between tics and group A streptococcal infections (PANDAS) has also been implicated (Church, Dale, Lees, Giovannoni, & Robertson, 2003; Murphy et al., 2004; Swedo et al., 1998). In a case-control study of 202 children, Mell, Davis, and Owens (2005) found that those diagnosed with OCD or a tic disorder (or both) were more likely than were controls to have had a streptococcal infection within the 3 months prior to diagnosis. Additionally, Mell et al. (2005) found that having had multiple streptococcal infections within the last 12 months significantly increased the risk of Tourette's disorder.

In the maintenance, exacerbation, and attenuation of tics, behavioral factors may play a role (Himle, Woods, Conelea, Bauer, & Rice, 2007; Piacentini et al., 2006). Specifically, as tics reduce the premonitory urge, they are more likely to be performed when this urge occurs in the future. Thus, tic expression may be maintained through negative reinforcement. External stress may also serve to exacerbate symptoms (Lin et al., 2007). Many parents, for example, note that their child's tics augment in the presence of daily stressors (e.g., Surwillo, Shafii, & Barrett, 1978).

Assessment

Assessment of Tourette syndrome is generally done via clinical interview and behavioral observation. One of the major issues in this work is differentiating tic disorders from other movement disorders.

Sanger (2007) puts forth three criteria as being unique to tic disorders: (1) suppressibility, i.e., the individual should be able to suppress or delay the tic at least some of the time (Jankovic, 2001); (2) suggestibility, i.e., discussion or mimicry of the tic will increase the likelihood of it occurring; and (3) predictability, i.e., the patient knows, at least some of the time, when the behavior is about to occur. The Tourette Syndrome Classification Study Group (1993) identified additional diagnostic criteria: tic performance must change in location, severity, complexity, number, and frequency over time; tics must be present before 21 years of age; the tics must be observed by others; and they cannot be explained by medical conditions. High comorbidity rates with other psychiatric disorders indicate the importance of simple, and widely practiced, screening for tic disorders.

The most widely used tic rating scale is the Yale Global Tic Severity Scale (YGTSS; Leckman et al., 1989), a semistructured clinician-rated scale that assesses for motor and vocal tics in the past week. On this measure, the clinician is to rate the presence and severity of tics based on observation, parent report, and child report. The clinician also rates tic-related impairment in interpersonal, academic, and occupational functioning. The YGTSS has demonstrated good internal consistency, interrater reliability, test–retest reliability, and correlation with parent-rated tic severity when used on children with Tourette syndrome (Leckman et al., 1989; Walkup, Rosenberg, Brown, & Singer, 1992; Storch et al., 2005). Other commonly used scales to assess tic symptoms among pediatric patients include the 15-item parent- and clinician-rated Tourette's Disorder Scale (TODS; Shytle et al., 2003), which shows good reliability and validity for ages above 10; and the Premonitory Urge for Tics Scale (PUTS; Woods et al., 2005), which has demonstrated good psychometric properties in children and youth aged 10–17.

Treatment

Pharmacology. The most common pharmacological treatment for tic disorders involves the use of antipsychotic medications using dopamine antagonists (Sandor, 2003). Although traditional antipsychotics such as haloperidol and pimozide have been effective in treating tics in children (cf., Salee, Nesbitt, Jackson, Sine, & Sethuraman, 1997), associated adverse effects (e.g., extrapyramidal effects; Gaffney et al., 2002) often limit their use as a first line of treatment. In addition, the significant side effects

with traditional antipsychotics often lead to nonadherence or medication discontinuation (Leckman, 2002). A newer class of medications, atypical antipsychotics, which differ somewhat in their mechanism from traditional antipsychotics (Meltzer, 2004), have shown comparable or superior efficacy paired with fewer side effects (Gaffney et al., 2002; Budman, Gayer, Lesser, Shi, & Bruun, 2001; Chappell, Scahill, & Leckman, 1997).

Other medications have also been used to treat tics in children with Tourette syndrome—including clonidine, which is an adrenergic agonist (e.g., Lichter & Jackson, 1996); peroglide, a dopamine agonist (Gilbert, Sethuraman, Sine, Peters, & Sallee, 2000); and selegiline, a selective MAO-B inhibitor that is typically used in Parkinson's but has shown promise in the treatment of tics (Feigin et al., 1996). In a study of 41 children and adolescents with chronic tics, Spencer et al. (2002) found that the tricyclic antidepressant desipramine reduced tics and was well tolerated.

There are several matters to consider in using pharmacological treatment for pediatric Tourette syndrome. First, side effects may be significant, and result in limited compliance and high rates of treatment attrition. For example, common side effects of atypical antipsychotics include weight gain and sedation (e.g., Gaffney et al., 2002). Second, because of the significant psychiatric comorbidity associated with Tourette syndrome, medication response can be difficult to predict. Accordingly, pharmacological treatment of tics should be considered only when the tics, themselves, are causing significant impairment. Third, the presence of tics may moderate the efficacy of various medications for other disorders (March et al., 2007). For instance, use of medication to reduce tics in comorbid ADHD and Tourette's disorder may limit the efficacy of stimulant medication, just as stimulants may exacerbate or induce tics (Sverd, Gadow, & Paolicelli, 1989). Finally, because of the waxing and waning nature of tics, medication response may be difficult to differentiate from the normal abatement of symptoms, something which is also true of response to behavioral treatments.

Behavioral Therapy. Azrin and Nunn (1973) developed one of the first effective behavioral treatments for tics, known as habit reversal training (HRT). Habit reversal training focuses first on increasing awareness of each tic, and identifying situational factors that influence these behaviors. Thereafter, the clinician and patient develop a competing response, or an alternative behavior that is incompatible with the tic and can be maintained for several minutes (e.g., holding the chin slightly towards the chest to prevent an upward jerk of the head). Finally, the patient practices resisting the tic by using this competing response. In patients with multiple tics, the steps of HRT are systematically applied to each tic, starting with the most problematic one. Several case studies have demonstrated the efficacy of HRT in children with tic disorders (Finney, Rapoff, Hall, & Christopherson, 1983; Woods, Miltenberger, & Lunley, 1996; Woods & Twohig, 2002; Woods, Twohig, Flessner, & Roloff, 2003). A large multisite trial funded by the National Institutes of Health was recently published investigating a HRT protocol – named Comprehensive Behavioral Intervention for Tics (CBIT) - among youth with tic disorders (Piacentini et al., 2010). In this trial, 126 youth with a tic disorder were randomly assigned to 8 sessions during 10 weeks of treatment or a psychosocial control treatment consisting of supportive therapy and education. The CBIT intervention was associated with a significantly greater decrease in tic symptom severity relative to the control condition (effect size = .68). More youth receiving the CBIT protocol were considered treatment responders relative to the control group (52.5% vs. 18.5%).

In addition to HRT, both exposure and response prevention (ERP) and tic suppression have shown efficacy in adults and children with Tourette syndrome (Himle et al., 2007; Verdellen et al., 2004; Woods et al., 2008). In ERP, a patient is exposed to situations or stimuli that are likely to induce or increase tics, and is asked to suppress the tics. Tic suppression is a similar procedure, but without the intentional exposure to tic-inducing stimuli. As compared to pharmacological therapy, behavioral techniques offer a milder side effect profile; however, a thorough evaluation of their overall efficacy awaits publication from the Piacentini trial.

Trichotillomania

Trichotillomania is a disorder in which an individual engages in the pulling out of one's own hair (see also Chapter 5). The DSM-IV-TR (APA, 2000) diagnostic criteria specify that the hair pulling be preceded by an increase in tension; be paired with a sense of relief or gratification; be recurrent; and result in noticeable hair loss. In the DSM-IV-TR, the disorder is classified under impulse-control disorders not classified elsewhere. In both children and adults, trichotillomania can result in significant impairment as a function of related embarrassment,

social isolation and avoidance behaviors, and comorbid pathology (e.g., Tolin et al., 2008).

Phenomenology

Trichotillomania typically starts in childhood, with the average age of onset approximately 11 years (Cohen et al., 1995; Tay, Levy, & Metry, 2004). Cohen et al. (1995) also reported that the most common age of onset was in middle childhood, and the least common before age 6 years. The nature of hair pulling behaviors varies widely across trichotillomania patients. Most commonly, hair is pulled from the scalp individually, although some patients may display a tendency to pull hair in clumps (Krishnan, Davidson, & Guajardo, 1985; Mansueto, Stemberger, Thomas, & Golomb, 1997), which can result in more serious physical damage. Although generally limited to one or two sites (Chamberlain, Menzies, Sahakian, & Fineberg, 2007), hair pulling can occur at any site on the body, the most common being the scalp—followed by eyelashes, eyebrows, and the pubic area (Christenson, Pyle, & Mitchell, 1991; Tay et al., 2004). Hair pulling can occur at other, less common sites, such as the beard, legs, mustache, sideburns, arms, and underarms (Stemberger, Stein, & Mansueto, 2003). In a minority of cases, and most noted among children, individuals may pull hair from someone else, such as a parent, spouse, or pet.

Hair pulling behavior can vary in the extent to which it is either automatic or focused. Automatic hair pulling usually occurs outside the awareness of the patient, whereas focused hair pulling is more intentional and is often done to relieve stress or tension (Flessner et al., 2007). Flessner et al. (2007), in a study with 168 youth aged 10–17 years, found that individuals who tended to pull automatically were more likely to have depressive symptoms, whereas those who tended to pull in a focused manner had more severe pulling symptoms. The researchers also found, however, that most youth with trichotillomania engaged in both styles of pulling. Behaviors that commonly proceed hair pulling include playing with or twirling the hair, feeling the hair between the fingers, and scratching the scalp (Christenson, Pyle et al., 1991; du Toit, van Kradenburg, Niehaus, & Stein, 2001). After pulling the hair out, individuals often play with the hair, examine it, feel its texture, or run the hair over their face or lips. In many cases, individuals engage in some variant of oral behavior with the hair, such as eating, chewing, biting the root, or swallowing the hair. These oral behaviors can sometimes lead to serious medical complications such as trichobezoars or dental erosion. Trichotillomania can also result in repetitive motion injuries or infection at the site from which the hair is pulled. Persons with trichotillomania sometimes display particular preferences in deciding which hair to pull, such as texture (Diefenbach, Reitman, & Williamson, 2000).

The pattern of individual hair pulling episodes can vary significantly between patients, and even within the same individual. Episodes may occur infrequently, but last up to several hours when they do present; or hair pulling may occur throughout the day, in several episodes of short duration. In either case, episodes are commonly precipitated by anxiety or boredom. The resulting hair loss varies from being barely noticeable to complete baldness (Frey, McKee, King, & Martin, 2005; Diefenbach et al., 2000).

In addition to associated medical complications, trichotillomania can lead to significant impairment in daily functioning. Often, affected individuals attempt to hide their hair loss by grooming or styling the hair to cover it up, or by wearing wigs or hats. Individuals with trichotillomania frequently experience shame, embarrassment, low self-esteem, depression, and anxiety; many sufferers also avoid social contact and public activities (Stemberger, Stein, Mansueto, Thomas, & Carter, 1999). Using a combined Internet and clinic sample of 154 children and 173 parents, in a test of a new pediatric trichotillomania measure (The Trichotillomania Scale for Children), Tolin et al. (2008) found that symptom severity was associated positively with interferences in social life, making new friends/getting closer to friends, and school/school work. Trichotillomania symptoms can also increase isolation and exacerbate or induce depressive symptoms. Indeed, Stemberger et al. (1999) reported that 80% of patients in their study felt depressed or unattractive due to hair pulling; almost half experienced conflicts with loved ones about hair pulling; approximately 75% attempted to hide their hair pulling from their loved ones; and over a third of the subjects avoided sexual intimacy due to embarrassment. Cohen et al. (1995) found that trichotillomania patients sometimes even avoided going for a medical appointment.

Prevalence

The prevalence rate of trichotillomania in the general population has been estimated to range from 0.6% to 3% (Christenson, Pyle, et al., 1991; Rothbaum, Shaw, Morris, & Ninan, 1993; Malhotra, Grover, Baweja, & Bhateja, 2008). By some estimates, females comprise 75% to 90% of the sufferers (Christenson, Pyle et al., 1991; Rothbaum et al., 1993; Chamberlain, Menzies, Sahakian, & Fineberg, 2007; Flessner et al., 2007). Some have suggested that this gender difference may not be a true difference in the population but, rather, may reflect either a greater reluctance for men to seek treatment or a greater tendency to blame hair loss on naturally occurring baldness (Christenson, Pyle et al., 1991). Among children, there is less available data. The findings of one study with children suggested a relatively equal prevalence rate across the genders (Mueller, 1990). Hair pulling in young children may be more likely to be a temporary behavior, whereas in adolescents and adults, it typically runs a chronic course (Christenson, Pyle et al., 1991; Rothbaum et al., 1993). In general, it is important to note that the majority of the prevalence studies on trichotillomania have been conducted with college students, limiting generalizability to the pediatric population.

Comorbidity

Researchers have identified high rates of comorbid affective and anxiety disorders (e.g., Christenson, 1995; Hanna, 1997) as well as personality disorders (Christenson, Chernoff-Clementz, & Clementz, 1992; Schlosser, Black, & Blum 1994; Swedo & Leonard, 1992) among adults and children with trichotillomania. For instance, Lochner et al. (2005) found that, among 49 adults with trichotillomania, 55% had a lifetime prevalence of an anxiety disorder; 51%, a mood disorder; 21%, a personality disorder; 18%, an eating disorder; and 8%, a tic disorder. In addition, several researchers have found the rate of OCD in persons with trichotillomania to be much higher than in the general population (Swedo & Leonard, 1992; Cohen et al., 1995; Christenson et al., 1995; Schlosser et al., 1994). Among a pediatric sample of 164 child–parent dyads, Flessner et al. (2008) found that 40.9% had been diagnosed with at least one comorbid psychiatric disorder, the most frequent being mood disorders, anxiety disorders, and ADHD. King et al. (1995) found that, compared to a general child psychiatry clinic sample, girls with trichotillomania (n = 15) had higher internalizing and externalizing symptoms. Corroborating a high pediatric comorbidity with depression, Tolin et al. (2008) reported that children and youth with trichotillomania were more likely to endorse depressive symptoms.

Of interest, a recent study of 112 10–14-year-old children with autism found that 3.9% met the

3-month point prevalence criteria for trichotillomania—a significantly higher rate than is found in the general population (Simonoff et al., 2008).

Etiology

A complete review of etiological features is beyond the scope of this chapter. Briefly, there is some evidence that family members of patients with trichotillomania have a higher rate of the disorder than does the general population (Swedo & Leonard, 1994; Cohen et al., 1995; Schlosser et al., 1994), suggesting a genetic linkage that is likely influenced by multiple genes (Cohen et al., 1995). However, specific genetic or neurological abnormalities have not been directly linked to trichotillomania thus far (Cohen et al., 1995), and recent genetic investigations (e.g., Hemmings et al., 2006; Zuchner et al., 2006), although promising, require further study, application to humans, and replication.

The neurotransmitter serotonin has also been implicated in trichotillomania. There seems to be an association between serotonergic neurons and repetitive motor behaviors. As noted earlier, dysfunction in serotonergic systems has been implicated in other obsessive compulsive spectrum disorders, such as OCD and BDD; and, some studies on trichotillomania have shown positive treatment outcomes with serotonin reuptake inhibitors (SRI; Stein, Bouwer, & Maud, 1997). Behaviorally, trichotillomania is often stress-related (Chamberlain, Menzies, Sahakian, & Fineberg, 2007), and the pulling behavior often leads to relief of a premonitory urge (Woods et al., 2005). However, whether stress plays an etiological role or simply exacerbates symptoms is unclear. Habitual hair pulling has also been conceptualized as a reinforcement mechanism, in which the relief in tension due to pulling reinforces the pulling behavior, similar to OCD in which a compulsion temporarily relieves the anxiety caused by an obsession (Stein, Chamberlain, & Fineberg, 2006). However, this model does not capture the many cases where hair pulling occurs at a time of boredom or relaxation, and functions as a self-stimulatory behavior, rather than as an anxiety-relieving one. Other perspectives include the view that hair pulling is a neurological impulse control problem, in which the patient is unable to successfully inhibit a particular behavior (Chamberlain, Blackwell, Fineberg, Robbins, & Sahakian, 2005).

Assessment

Assessment methods include the clinical interview, rating scales, report by others, and self-monitoring.

A thorough clinical interview is probably the most comprehensive single method for assessing symptom presence and severity. However, a child may be hesitant to report symptoms due to embarrassment, and may be particularly reluctant to report hair pulling from more "private" regions such as the pubic area.

There are several rating scales for trichotillomania that have been applied for use with children. The most widely used is the Massachusetts General Hospital Hairpulling Scale (MGH-HPS; Keuthen et al., 1995), adapted from the Yale-Brown Obsessive Compulsive Scale (Goodman et al., 1989). The MGH-HPS is a 7-item self-report scale that assesses the frequency, intensity, and control related to hair pulling. The measure has demonstrated good internal consistency, test–retest reliability, and convergent and discriminant validity (Keuthen et al., 1995; O'Sullivan et al., 1995).

Other rating scales for trichotillomania include the NIMH Trichotillomania Severity and Impairment Scales (Swedo, Rapoport et al., 1989), which consist of a clinical interview and global trichotillomania severity rating, and the Psychiatric Institute Trichotillomania Scale (PITS; Winchel et al., 1992), a 6-item clinician-rated measure. Tolin et al. (2008) have developed the Trichotillomania Scale for Children (TSC), a measure completed by children and/or parents. Their validation study with 113 children revealed two factors, severity and distress/impairment. Although the TSC had good psychometric properties overall, it had modest parent–child agreement for part of the sample. Flessner et al. (2007) developed the Milwaukee Inventory for Styles of Trichotillomania-Child Version, which assesses automatic and focused styles of hair pulling.

Self–monitoring—using methods such as the recording of hair pulling behavior in charts, or counting pulled hairs—can help to identify patterns of pulling, situational factors, and reinforcement contingencies influencing the behavior, as well as to measure treatment progress. Saving hairs pulled is also useful in this regard. With children, particularly younger ones, rating scales and self-monitoring may have limited utility because children may have low insight, be unable or unwilling to monitor symptoms, and/or struggle to report on internal states. In such cases, using parent reports and having parents monitor hair pulling may be necessary, particularly since parents are integral in treatment implementation (Tolin, Franklin, Diefenbach, Anderson, & Meunier, 2007).

Treatment

Pharmacological Treatment. Findings on the efficacy of tricyclic antidepressant clomipramine have been arguably equivocal. Initially, Swedo, Leonard et al. (1989) found support for the effectiveness of the tricyclic antidepressant clomipramine. In a 10-week double-blind crossover study comparing clomipramine and desipramine (a standard tricyclic antidepressant at the time of study) in 12 women, physician-rated improvement of both trichotillomania symptoms and related impairment were significantly greater among the clomipramine group than among those taking desipramine. In contrast, Ninan et al. (2000), in a study of 16 adults, found no statistical separation between clomipramine and placebo at post-treatment. Overall, however, a meta-analysis by Bloch et al. (2007) demonstrated a modest effect size favoring clomipramine over placebo ($d = 0.68$).

Selective serotonin reuptake inhibitors have been evaluated for the treatment of trichotillomania in four placebo-controlled trials (Christenson, MacKenzie, Mitchell, & Callies, 1991, $n = 15$; Streichenwein & Thornby, 1995, $n = 16$; van Minnen, Hoogduin, Keijsers, Hellenbrand, & Hendriks, 2003, $n = 40$; Dougherty, Loh, Jenike, & Keuthen, 2006, $n = 15$). Of these trials, only one (Dougherty et al., 2006) found a statistical difference between the effects of SSRI and placebo. In a meta-analysis of the above four studies, Bloch et al. (2007) found no overall effect of SSRIs ($d = 0.02$). Although controlled trials have shown mixed results, findings are more promising with open trials. In a 12-week open-label trial with 14 adults, Stein, Bouwer, and Maud (1997) found a positive effect for citalopram. Ninan et al. (1998), in a 12-week open trial with 12 adults, found that venlafaxine, a serotonin-norepinephrine reuptake inhibitor, was effective in reducing symptoms. The results of these studies should be interpreted with their limitations in mind. Most had small sample sizes and, most relevant to this chapter, none involved children.

Treatment effects have been found for non-SSRI medications. De Souza (2008), in a 12-month open-label pilot study with 14 children, found that 8 showed improvement with naltrexone, an opioid receptor antagonist. Stewert and Nejtek (2003), in a study of 17 adult women, found that the antipsychotic olanzapine was effective in reducing the severity of trichotillomania. Of the 12 women who completed treatment, 8 maintained treatment gains at one-month follow-up. Similar effects were found by Lochner, Seedat, Niehaus, and Stein (2006)

among those who completed treatment with the anticonvulsant topiramate; however, due to significant side effects, 5 of 9 patients in the study dropped out prematurely.

Behavioral Therapy. Habit reversal training (described earlier in this chapter) has been successfully applied to trichotillomania. Azrin and Nunn (1973) first randomized 34 trichotillomania patients (including 4 children) to either HRT or to a technique called "individual negative practice," consisting of an hourly practice of hair pulling motions without the individual pulling the hair. Overall, the effects of HRT were significantly greater than were those of individual negative practice, with gains being maintained at 4-week follow-up. Several studies since have also demonstrated the efficacy of HRT (e.g., Woods, Wetterneck, & Flessner, 2006; Lerner, Franklin, Meadows, Hembree, & Foa, 1998; van Minnen et al., 2003). Often, HRT is combined with other behavioral techniques focused on managing contingencies, learning to relax, managing emotions, and improving self-efficacy. In studies directly comparing evidence-based psychotherapies to medication, CBT including HRT has been more effective than clomipramine (Ninan et al., 2000), and HRT has been more effective than fluoxetine (van Minnen et al., 2003). Finally, in 24 adults, Dougherty et al. (2006) found that conjoint treatment with HRT and sertraline was associated with greater improvement than with either behavior therapy or sertraline alone.

In children, only one systematic investigation of behavior therapy for trichotillomania has been conducted to date. In an open trial of cognitive-behavioral therapy with 22 children and adolescents, Tolin et al. (2007) found a significant reduction in symptom severity at post-treatment. Treatment, based on a recently published manual (Franklin & Tolin, 2007), included habit reversal with an emphasis on relapse prevention. A meta-analysis by Bloch et al. (2007), with 59 subjects across three studies, found that HRT significantly improved symptoms of trichotillomania (effect size = 1.14).

Treatment options for trichotillomania in youth are, at present, lacking. Case studies have reported success with pharmacologic treatment via paroxetine (Block, West, & Baharoglu, 1998) and olanzapine augmentation (Pathak, Danielyan, & Kowatch, 2004). However, a large survey (of 133 youth aged 10 to 17 years) found that only 17% of those who had received treatment for their condition were rated as being either "very much improved" or "much improved" upon completion (Franklin et al., 2008). We contend that the literature would benefit from combination studies of behavior and pharmacological treatments, studies for treating specific comorbid disorders, and studies that investigate the role of parents in treatment. Chapter 23 discusses more completely the extant treatment outcome data among youth with trichotillomania.

Body-Focused Repetitive Behaviors

Though prevalent in development, body-focused repetitive behaviors (BFRB) have been largely overlooked in the literature, and often confused with such diagnoses as autism and tic disorder (Mahone, Bridges, Prahme, & Singer, 2004). A review of the literature finds nailbiting to be common throughout youth—with an estimated 28%–33% of children ages 7 to 10 years engaging in this behavior, and approximately 45% of adolescents biting their nails (Leung & Robson, 1992). Also prevalent are stereotypies, which are defined as repetitive and purposeless movements that are predictable in their presentation (Tan, Salgado, & Fahn, 1997). Examples of behavioral presentation include hand or arm flapping, tensing movements, hand/arm/trunk shaking, and rituals such as repetitive bending of the body or pacing. Mahone et al. (2004) found these behaviors in 48%, 38%, 28%, and 13%, respectively, in a review of 40 individuals with complex motor stereotypies, aged 9 months to 17 years. However, other BFRB have been noted, such as body rocking, leg shaking, eye blinking, and involuntary noisemaking (Tan et al., 1997). While stereotypies occurred daily, or even more frequently, in 90% of a pediatric sample aged 9 months to 17 years, the duration of individual "episodes" tended to be short: fewer than 10 seconds in 30%; between 10 and 30 seconds (inclusive) in 30%; between 31 and 60 seconds (inclusive) in 10%; and greater than 60 seconds in 30% (Mahone et al., 2004). Though stereotypies are associated with excitement and stress (as well as with boredom and fatigue), they differ from tics in a number of important ways—they lack a premonitory urge, are predictable and rhythmic, and typically abate when the individual is cued to their immediate presentation (Mahone et al., 2004). Of import, the review of stereotypies among youth aged 9 months to 17 years reported that only 5% evidenced complete resolution of their symptoms within a year (whereas 32.5% improved; 50% persisted unchanged; and 12.5% worsened). Investigation into the daily, social, and school functioning of those with BFRB is clearly warranted—as, potentially, may be a study of evidence-based treatments among this population.

Future Directions and Issues

HOW TO CLASSIFY OCD IN THE DSM-V?

Recently, the classification of OCD as an anxiety disorder has come under some debate. Clinicians and researchers differ widely in their stances (e.g., Mataix-Cols, Pertusa, & Leckman, 2007), with various groups advocating for (1) the separation of OCD from anxiety and other spectrum disorders (i.e., marking the disorder as utterly unique); (2) the grouping of OCD with several closely related disorders (e.g., tics, body dysmorphic disorder); (3) the implementation of a large spectrum of disorders characterized by the commonality of repetitive behavior; or (4) the status quo. Data have been presented in support of the third classification (i.e., a spectrum of repetitive behavior/obsessive compulsive disorders) due to similarities in phenomenology, etiology, family history, neurocircuitry, and treatment response (Bartz & Hollander, 2006; Stein & Lochner, 2006). However, others have argued that there is inadequate empirical support for this conceptual and nosological shift (Storch, Abramowitz, & Goodman, 2008), and that incorrect conclusions have been drawn from existing data. A critical review of the research regarding proposed diagnostic shifts is beyond the scope of this review; clearly, though, further research into the diagnostic alignment of OCD, with the integration of child data, is needed.

NOVEL AUGMENTATION STRATEGIES

D-cycloserine (DCS) has received considerable attention of late, as it lacks the undesirable side effects that often accompany atypical antipsychotic use, and thus may prove a safe augmenting strategy to enhance the efficacy of CBT (see Chapter 20). The presumed efficacy of DCS is based upon evidence suggesting that the N-methyl-D-aspartate (NMDA) system plays a primary role in the neural processes underlying learned associations and fear extinction, which are core theoretical underpinnings of ERP. Since NMDA receptor antagonists block or inhibit extinction (Walker, Ressler, Lu, & Davis, 2002), DCS, a partial agonist that acts at the strychnine-insensitive glycine-recognition site of the NMDA receptor complex, may enhance the acquisition and/or consolidation processes that occur during associative learning (Ledgerwood, Richardson, & Cranney, 2003). And, as the extinction training inherent to ERP therapy is a form of associative learning, pharmacological agents like DCS that enhance extinction learning may improve behavioral therapies.

Following the accumulation of a large body of data in nonhuman animals (Ledgerwood et al., 2003; Ledgerwood, Richardson, & Cranney, 2004; Ledgerwood, Richardson, & Cranney, 2005; Walker et al., 2002), several trials in adult humans have supported DCS augmentation among adults with varied anxiety disorders (e.g., Hofmann et al., 2006; Ressler et al., 2004), including OCD (Kushner et al., 2007; Storch et al., 2007; Wilhelm et al., 2008). Recently, the first author completed a double blind placebo-controlled trial of DCS augmentation in youth with OCD. Children (n = 30) received either 25mg or 50mg DCS/placebo (depending on weight) one hour prior to each of seven ERP sessions. Although not significantly different, compared to the ERP+Placebo group, youth in the ERP+DCS arm showed small-to-moderate treatment effects (effect size = .31 to .47 on primary outcomes). Overall, these findings complement results in adult OCD and non-OCD anxiety disorders and provide initial support for a more extensive study of DCS augmentation of CBT among youth with OCD.

WHICH TREATMENT AND HOW TO AUGMENT?

The treatment literature in pediatric obsessive compulsive spectrum disorders is variable and rather limited, with the most data on OCD and TS, and a clear paucity of published treatment work on BDD and trichotillomania. Further, data applied to clinical work with children has typically been extrapolated from adult studies, and thus, clinicians are not provided with the necessary tools to meet the unique needs of the child, such as how to integrate families into treatment, adapt therapeutic skills for varying cognitive levels, address comorbidities, and understand medication-related issues (e.g., titration, side effects, pharmacodynamics, etc.). The efficacy of various treatment augmentations in youth remains largely unstudied as well, and marks an area in which future research endeavors are greatly needed. Currently, there are several important trials underway. For instance, the team from POTS (2004) is conducting a sequential trial to examine the relative efficacies of "gold standard" CBT (i.e., provided by highly trained psychologists); diluted CBT (i.e., a brief form of psychotherapy provided by the prescribing psychiatrist that encourages cognitive-behavioral skills such as exposure); and continued sertraline treatment in youth who have been partial responders to 8 weeks of sertraline. And, along the

vein of prior work by Freeman et al. (2008), Franklin et al. have initiated a randomized trial examining CBFT adapted for young children, ages 5–8 years (see Chapter 23 for a complete review). Clearly, however, large gaps in the knowledge base remain requiring considerable future research efforts.

Related Chapters

Chapter 1. Phenomenology and Epidemiology of Obsessive Compulsive Disorder

Chapter 3. Phenomenology and Epidemiology of Body Dysmorphic Disorder

Chapter 5. Phenomenology and Epidemiology of Tic Disorders and Trichotillomania

Chapter 6. Genetic Understanding of OCD and Spectrum Disorders

Chapter 7. Neuroanatomy of Obsessive Compulsive and Related Disorders

Chapter 9. The Role of Family and Social Relationships in OCD and Spectrum Conditions

Chapter 11. Psychological and Behavioral Models for Understanding Obsessive Compulsive and OC Spectrum Disorders

Chapter 13. Assessing OCD Symptoms and Severity

Chapter 15. Pharmacological Treatments for Obsessive Compulsive Disorder

Chapter 17. Exposure-Based Treatments for OCD

Chapter 18. Cognitive Treatment for OCD

Chapter 19. Combining Pharmacotherapy and Psychological Treatments for OCD

Chapter 21. Treatment of Body Dysmorphic Disorder

Chapter 23. Treatment of Tic Disorders and Trichotillomania

References

Abramowitz, J. S., Khandker, M., Nelson, C. A., Deacon, B. J., & Rygwall, R. (2006). The role of cognitive factors in the pathogenesis of obsessive compulsive symptoms: A prospective study. *Behaviour Research and Therapy, 44,* 1361–1374.

Abramowitz, J. S., Whiteside, S. P., & Deacon, B. J. (2005). The effectiveness of treatment for pediatric obsessive compulsive disorder: A meta-analysis. *Behavior Therapy, 36,* 55–63.

Albertini, R. S. & Phillips, K. A. (1999). Thirty-three cases of body dysmorphic disorder in children and adolescents. *Journal of the American Academy of Child and Adolescent Psychiatry, 38,* 452–459.

Allen, A. & Hollander, E. (2004). Similarities and differences between body dysmorphic disorder and other disorders. *Psychiatric Annals, 34,* 927–933.

Alsobrook, J. P. 2nd & Pauls, D. L. (2002). A factor analysis of tic symptoms in Gilles de la Tourette's syndrome. *American Journal of Psychiatry, 159,* 291–296.

American Psychiatric Association (1987). *Diagnostic and Statistical Manual of Mental Disorders*. 3rd Edition. Washington, DC: Author.

American Psychiatric Association (2000). *Diagnostic and Statistical Manual of Mental Disorders*. 4th Edition Text Revision. Washington, DC: Author

Arnold, P. D., Sicard, T., Burroughs, E., Richter, M. A., & Kennedy, J. L. (2006). Glutamate transporter gene SLC1A1 associated with obsessive compulsive disorder. *Archives of General Psychiatry*, 63, 769–776.

Azrin, N. H. & Nunn, R. G. (1973). Habit-reversal: A method of eliminating nervous habits and tics. *Behavioral Research and Therapy*, 11, 619–628.

Barr, L. C., Goodman, W. K., Price, L. H., McDougle, C. J., & Charney, D. S. (1992). The serotonin hypothesis of obsessive compulsive disorder: Implications of pharmacologic challenge studies. *Journal of Clinical Psychiatry*, 53, S17–28.

Barrett, P. M. & Healy, L. J. (2003). An examination of the cognitive processes involved in childhood obsessive compulsive disorder. *Behaviour Research and Therapy*, 41, 285–299.

Barrett, P., Farrell, L., Dadds, M., & Boulter, N. (2005). Cognitive behavioral family treatment of childhood obsessive compulsive disorder: Long-term follow-up and predictors of outcome. *Journal of the American Academy of Child and Adolescent Psychiatry*, 44, 1005–1014.

Barrett, P. M., Farrell, L., Pina, A. A., Peris, T. S., & Piacentini, J. (2008). Evidence-based psychosocial treatments for child and adolescent obsessive compulsive disorder. *Journal of Clinical Child and Adolescent Psychology*, 37, 131–155.

Barrett, P., Healy-Farrell, L., & March, J. S. (2004). Cognitive behavioral family treatment of childhood obsessive compulsive disorder: A controlled trial. *Journal of the American Academy of Child and Adolescent Psychiatry*, 43, 46–62.

Bartz, J. A. & Hollander, E. (2006). Is obsessive compulsive disorder an anxiety disorder? *Progress in Neuro-Psychopharmacology and Biological Psychiatry*, 30, 338–352.

Baxter, L. R. Jr., Saxena, S., Brody, A. L., Ackermann, R. F., Colgan, M., Schwartz, J. M., et al. (1996). Brain mediation of obsessive compulsive disorder symptoms: Evidence from functional brain imaging studies in the human and nonhuman primate. *Seminars in Clinical Neuropsychiatry*, 1, 32–47.

Berardelli, A., Curra, A., Fabbrini, G., Gilio, F., & Manfredi, M. (2003). Pathophysiology of tics and Tourette syndrome. *Journal of Neurology*, 250, 781–787.

Blanco, C., Olfsom, N., Stein, D. J., Simpson, H. B., Gameroff, M. J., & Narrow, W. H. (2006). Treatment of obsessive compulsive disorder by U.S. psychiatrists. *Journal of Clinical Psychiatry*, 67, 946–951.

Bloch, M. H., Landeros-Weisenberger, A., Dombrowski, P., Kelmendi, B., Wegner, R., Nudel, J., et al. (2007). Systematic review: Pharmacological and behavioral treatment for trichotillomania. *Biological Psychiatry*, 62, 839–846.

Bloch, M. H., Landeros-Weisenberger, A., Kelmendi, B., Coric, V., Bracken, M. B., & Leckman, J. F. (2006). A systematic review: Antipsychotic augmentation with treatment refractory obsessive compulsive disorder. *Molecular Psychiatry*, 11, 622–632.

Block, C., West, S. A., & Baharoglu, B. (1998). Paroxetine treatment of trichotillomania in an adolescent. *Journal of Child and Adolescent Psychopharmacology*, 8, 69–71.

Budman, C. L., Gayer, A., Lesser, M., Shi, Q., & Bruun, R. D. (2001). An open-label study of the treatment efficacy of olanzapine for Tourette's disorder. *Journal of Clinical Psychiatry*, 62, 290–294.

Buhlmann, U., Etcoff, N. L., Wilhelm, S. (2006). Emotion recognition bias for contempt and anger in body dysmorphic disorder. *Journal of Psychiatric Research*, 40, 105–111.

Buhlmann, U., McNally, R. J., Etcoff, N. L., Tuschen-Caffier, B., & Wilhelm, S. (2004). Emotion recognition deficits in body dysmorphic disorder. *Journal of Psychiatric Research*, 38, 201–206.

Buhlmann, U., McNally, R. J., Wilhelm, S., & Florin, I. (2002). Selective processing of emotional information in body dysmorphic disorder. *Journal of Anxiety Disorders*, 16, 289–298.

Buhlmann, U., Reese, H. E., Reneud, S., & Wilhelm, S. (2008). Clinical considerations for the treatment of body dysmorphic disorder with cognitive behavioral therapy. *Body Image*, 5, 39–49.

Buhlmann, U., Wilhelm, S., McNally, R. J., Tuschen-Caffier, B., Baer, L., & Jenike, M. A. (2002). Interpretive biases for ambiguous information in body dysmorphic disorder. *CNS Spectrums: International Journal of Neuropsychiatric Medicine*, 7, 435–443.

Cash, T. F. (2002). Cognitive behavioral perspectives on body image. In T. F. Cash & T. Pruzinsky (Eds.), *Body image: A handbook of theory, research, and clinical practice* (pp. 14–38). New York: Guilford Press.

Cash, T. F. (2008). *The body image workbook*. Oakland, CA: New Harbinger Publications.

Chamberlain, S. R., Blackwell, A. D., Fineberg, N. A., Robbins, T. W., & Sahakian, B. J. (2005). The neuropsychology of obsessive compulsive disorder: The importance of failures in cognitive and behavioral inhibition as candidate endophenotypic markers. *Neuroscience and Biobehavioral Reviews*, 23, 399–419.

Chamberlain, S. R., Menzies, L., Sahakian, B. J., & Fineberg, N. A. (2007). Lifting the veil on trichotillomania. *American Journal of Psychiatry*, 164, 568–574.

Chappell, P. B., Scahill, L. D., & Leckman, J. F. (1997). Future therapies of Tourette syndrome. *Neurologic Clinics*, 15, 429–450.

Christenson, G. A., Chernoff-Clementz, E., & Clementz, B. (1992). Personality and clinical characteristics in patients with trichotillomania. *Journal of Clinical Psychiatry*, 53, 407–413.

Christenson, G. A., MacKenzie, T. B., & Mitchell, G. E. (1995). Characteristics of 60 adult chronic hair pullers. *American Journal of Psychiatry*, 148, 365–370.

Christenson, G. A., Pyle, R. L., & Mitchell, G. E. (1991). Estimated lifetime prevalence of trichotillomania in college students. *Journal of Clinical Psychiatry*, 52, 415–417.

Church, A. J., Dale, R. C., Lees, A. J., Giovannoni, G., & Robertson, M. M. (2003). Tourette's syndrome: A cross sectional study to examine the PANDAS hypothesis. *Journal of Neurology, Neurosurgery, and Psychiatry*, 74, 602–607.

Cohen, D. J. & Leckman, J. F. (1994). Developmental psychopathology and neurobiology of Tourette's syndrome. *Journal of the American Academy of Child and Adolescent Psychiatry*, 33, 2–15.

Cohen, D. J., Ort, S. I., Leckman, J. F., Riddle, M. A., & Hardin, M. T. (1988). Family functioning and Tourette's syndrome. In D. Cohen, R. Brunn, & J. Leckman (Eds.), *Tourette's syndrome and tic disorders* (pp. 170–196). New York, NY: Wiley.

Cohen, L. J., Stein, D. J., Simeon, D., Spadaccini, E., Rosen, J., Aronowitz, B., et al. (1995). Clinical profile, comorbidity, and treatment history in 123 hair pullers: A survey study. *Journal of Clinical Psychiatry*, 56, 319–326.

Comer, J. S., Kendall, P. C., Franklin, M. E., Hudson, J. L., & Pimentel, S. S. (2004). Obsessing/worrying about the overlap between obsessive compulsive disorder and generalized anxiety disorder in youth. *Clinical Psychology Review*, 24, 663–683.

Comings, D. E., Himes, J. A., & Comings, B. G. (1990). An epidemiological study of Tourette's syndrome in a single school district. *Journal of Clinical Psychiatry, 11*, 463–469.

Cook, E. H., Wagner, K. D., March, J. S., Biederman, J., Landau, P., Wolkow, R., et al. (2001). Long-term sertraline treatment of children and adolescents with obsessive compulsive disorder. *Journal of the American Academy of Child and Adolescent Psychiatry, 40*, 1175–1181.

Correll, C.U., & Carlson, H.E. (2006). Endocrine and metabolic adverse effects of psychotropic medications in children and adolescents. *Journal of the American Academy of Child and Adolescent Psychiatry, 45(7)*, 771–91.

de Haan, E., Hoogduin, K. A., Buitelaar, J. K., & Keijsers, G. P. (1998). Behavior therapy versus clomipramine for the treatment of obsessive compulsive disorder in children and adolescents. *Journal of the American Academy of Child and Adolescent Psychiatry, 37*, 1022–1029.

Denys, D., de Geus, F., van Megen, H.J.,& Westenberg, H.G. (2004). Use of factor analysis to detect potential phenotypes in obsessive-compulsive disorder. *Psychiatry Research, 128*, 273–280.

De Souza, A. (2008). An open-label pilot study of naltrexone in childhood-onset trichotillomania. *Journal of Child and Adolescent Psychopharmacology, 18*, 30–33.

de Wall, M. W. M., Arnold, I. A., Eekhof, J. A., & van Hemert, A. M. (2004). Somatoform disorders in general practice: Prevalence, functional impairment, and comorbidity with anxiety and depressive disorders. *British Journal of Psychiatry, 184*, 470–476.

DeVeaugh-Geiss, J., Moroz, G., Biederman, J., Cantwell, D., Fontaine, R., Greist, J.H., et al. (1992). Clomipramine hydrochloride in childhood and adolescent obsessive compulsive disorder—a multicenter trial. *Journal of the American Academy of Child and Adolescent Psychiatry, 31*, 45–49.

Diefenbach, G. J., Reitman, D., & Williamson, D. A. (2000). Trichotillomania: A challenge to research and practice. *American Journal of Psychiatry, 148*, 365–370.

Dougherty, D. D., Loh, R., Jenike, M. A., & Keuthen, N. J. (2006). Single modality versus dual modality treatment for trichotillomania: sertraline, behavioral therapy, or both? *Journal of Clinical Psychiatry, 67*, 1086–1092.

du Toit, P. L., van Kradenburg, J., Niehaus, D., & Stein, D. J. (2001). Characteristics and phenomenology or hair pulling: An exploration of subtypes. *Comparative Psychiatry, 42*, 247–256.

Dyl, J., Kittler, J., Phillips, K. A., & Hunt, J. I. (2006). Body dysmorphic disorder and other clinically significant body image concerns in adolescent psychiatric inpatients: Prevalence and clinical characteristics. *Child Psychiatry and Human Development, 36*, 369–382.

Eisen, J. L., Phillips, K. A., Baer, L., Beer, D. A., Atakala, K. D., & Rasmussen, S. A. (1998). The Brown Assessment of Beliefs Scale: Reliability and validity. *American Journal of Psychiatry, 155*, 102–108.

el-Khatib, H. E., & Dickey, T. O. 3rd (1995). Sertraline for body dysmorphic disorder. *Journal of the American Academy of Child and Adolescent Psychiatry, 34*, 1404–1405.

Ernberg, G., Cruse, R. P., & Rothner, D. A. (1987). The natural history of Tourette's syndrome: A follow-up study. *Annals of Neurology, 22*, 383–385.

Feigin, A., Kurlan, R., McDermott, M. P., Beach, J., Dimitsopulos, T., Brower, C. A., et al. (1996). A controlled trial of deprenyl in children with Tourette's syndrome and attention deficit hyperactivity disorder. *Neurology, 46*, 965–968.

Feusner, J. D., Yaryura-Tobias, J., & Saxena, S. (2008). The pathophysiology of body dysmorphic disorder. *Body Image, 5*, 3–12.

Finney, J. W., Rapoff, M. A., Hall, C. L. & Christopherson, E. R. (1983). Replication and social validation of habit reversal treatment for tics. *Behavior Therapy, 14*, 116–126.

Fitzgerald, K. D., Stewart, C. M., Tawile, V., & Rosenberg, D. R. (1999). Risperidone augmentation of serotonin reuptake inhibitor treatment of pediatric obsessive compulsive disorder. *Journal of Child and Adolescent Psychopharmacology, 9*, 115–123.

Flessner, C.A., Conelea, C.A., Woods, D.W., Franklin, M.E., Keuthen, N.J., & Cashin, S.E. (2008). Styles of pulling in trichotillomania: exploring differences in symptom severity, phenomenology, and functional impact. *Behaviour Research and Therapy, 46(3)*, 345-357.

Flessner, C. A., Woods, D. W., Franklin, M. E., Keuthen, N. J., Piacentini, J., Cashin, S. E., et al. (2007). The Milwaukee Inventory for Styles of Trichotillomania-Child Version: Initial development and psychometric properties. *Behavior Modification, 31*, 896–918.

Foa, E. B., Liebowitz, M. R., Kozak, M. J., Davies, S., Campeas, R., Franklin, M. E., et al. (2005). Randomized, placebo-controlled trial of exposure and ritual prevention, clomipramine, and their combination in the treatment of obsessive compulsive disorder. *American Journal of Psychiatry, 162*, 151–161.

Franklin, M. E., Flessner, C. A., Woods, D. W., Keuthen, N. J., Piacentini, J. C., Moore, P. et al. (2008). The child and adolescent trichotillomania impact project: Descriptive psychopathology, comorbidity, functional impairment, and treatment utilization. *Journal of Developmental and Behavioral Pediatrics, 29*, 493–500.

Franklin, M. E. & Tolin, D. F. (2007). *Treating trichotillomania: Cognitive behavioral therapy for hairpulling and related problems.* New York: Springer-Verlag.

Freeman, J. B., Garcia, A. M., Coyne, L., Ale, C., Przeworski, A., Himle, M., et al. (2008). Early childhood OCD: Preliminary findings from a family-based cognitive behavioral approach. *Journal of the American Academy of Child and Adolescent Psychiatry, 47*, 593–602.

Frey, A. S., McKee, M., King, R. A., & Martin, A. (2005). Hair apparent: Rapunzel syndrome (clinical case conference). *American Journal of Psychiatry, 162*, 242–248.

Frost, R. & Steketee, G. (2002). *Cognitive approaches to obsessions and compulsions: Theory, assessment, and treatment.* Oxford: Elsevier.

Gadow, K. D., Nolan, E. E., Sprafkin, J., & Schwartz, J. (2002). Tics and psychiatric comorbidity in children and adolescents. *Developmental Medicine and Child Neurology, 44*, 330–338.

Gaffney, G. R., Perry, P. J., Lund, B. C., Bever-Stille, K. A., Arndt, S., & Kuperman, S. (2002). Risperidone versus clonidine in the treatment of children and adolescents with Tourette's syndrome. *Journal of the American Academy of Child and Adolescent Psychiatry, 41*, 330–336.

Gallant, J., Storch, E. A., Merlo, L. J., Ricketts, E. D., Geffken, G. R., Goodman, W. K., et al. (2008). Convergent and discriminant validity of the Children's Yale-Brown Obsessive Compulsive Scale–Symptom Checklist. *Journal of Anxiety Disorders, 22(8)*, 136–176.

Geller, D. A., Biederman, J., Faraone, S., Agranat, A., Cradock, K., Hagermoser, L., et al. (2001). Developmental aspects of obsessive compulsive disorder: Findings in children, adolescents, and adults. *Journal of Nervous and Mental Disease, 189,* 471–477.

Geller, D. A., Biederman, J., Griffin, S., Jones, J., & Lefkowitz, T. R. (1996). Comorbidity of juvenile obsessive compulsive disorder with disruptive behaviour disorders. *Journal of the American Academy of Child and Adolescent Psychiatry, 35,* 1637–1646.

Geller, D. A., Biederman, J., Stewart S. E., Mullin, B., Martin, A., Spencer, T., et al. (2003). Which SSRI? A meta-analysis of pharmacotherapy trials in pediatric obsessive compulsive disorder. *American Journal of Psychiatry, 160,* 1919–1928.

Geller, D. A., Biederman, J., Stewart, S. E., Mullin, B., Farrel, C., Wagner, K. D., et al. (2003). Impact of comorbidity on treatment response to paroxetine in pediatric obsessive compulsive disorder: Is the use of exclusion criteria empirically supported in randomized clinical trials? *Journal of Child and Adolescent Psychopharmacology, 13,* S19–29.

Geller, D. A., Hoog, S. L., Heiligenstein, J. H., Ricardi, R. K., Tamura, R., Kluszynski, S., et al. (2001). Fluoxetine treatment for obsessive compulsive disorder in children and adolescents: A placebo-controlled clinical trial. *Journal of the American Academy of Child and Adolescent Psychiatry, 40,* 773–779.

Ghanizadeh, A. & Mosallaei, S. (2009). Psychiatric disorders and behavioral problems in children and adolescents with Tourette syndrome. *Brain and Development, 31(1),* 15–19.

Gilbert, A. R., Moore, G. J., Keshavan, M. S., Paulson, L. A., Narula, V., Master, F. P., et al. (2000). Decrease in thalamic volumes of pediatric patients with obsessive compulsive disorder who are taking paroxetine. *Archives of General Psychiatry, 57,* 449–456.

Gilbert, D. L., Sethuraman, G., Sine, L., Peters, S., & Sallee, F. R. (2000). Tourette's syndrome improvement with pergolide in a randomized double blind, crossover trial. *Neurology, 28,* 1310–1315.

Goodman, W. K., McDougle, C. J., Price, L. H., Riddle, M. A., Pauls, D. L., & Leckman, J. F. (1990). Beyond the serotonin hypothesis: A role for dopamine in some forms of obsessive compulsive disorder? *Journal of Clinical Psychiatry, 51,* S36–43.

Goodman, W. K., Murphy, T. K., & Storch, E. A. (2007). Risk of adverse behavioral effects with pediatric use of antidepressants. *Psychopharmacology, 191,* 87–96.

Goodman, W.K., Price, L.H., Rasmussen, S.A., Mazure, C., Fleischmann, R.L., Hill, C.L., Heninger, G.R., & Charney, D.S. (1989). The Yale-Brown Obsessive Compulsive Scale. I. Development, use, and reliability. *Archives of General Psychiatry, 46(11),* 1006–11.

Grant, J. E., Kim, S. W., & Crow, S. J. (2001). Prevalence and clinical features of body dysmorphic disorder in adolescent and adult psychiatric inpatients. *Journal of Clinical Psychiatry, 62,* 517–522.

Grant, P., Lougee, L., Hirschtritt, M., & Swedo, S. E. (2007). An open-label trial of riluzole, a glutamate antagonist, in children with treatment-resistant obsessive compulsive disorder. *Journal of Child Adolescent Psychopharmacology, 17,* 761–767.

Gunstad, J., & Phillips, K. A. (2003). Axis I comorbidity in body dysmorphic disorder. *Comprehensive Psychiatry, 44,* 270–276.

Hanna, G. L. (1997). Trichotillomania and related disorders in children and adolescents. *Child Psychiatry and Human Development, 27,* 255–268.

Hanna, G. L., Yuwiler, A., & Coates, J. K. (1995). Whole blood serotonin and disruptive behaviors in juvenile obsessive compulsive disorder. *Journal of the American Academy of Child and Adolescent Psychiatry, 34,* 28–35.

Hebebrand, J., Klug, B., Fimmers, R., Sechter, S. A., Wettke-Schafer, R., Deget, F., et al. (1997). Rates for tic disorders and obsessive compulsive symptomatology in families of children and adolescents with Gilles de la Tourette Syndrome. *Journal of Psychiatry Research, 31,* 519–530.

Hemmings, S. M., Kinnear, C. J., Lochner, C., Seedat, S., Corfield, V. A., Moolman-Smook, J. C., et al. (2006). Genetic correlates in trichotillomania–A case-control assocation study in the South African Caucasian population. *The Israel Journal of Psychiatry and Related Sciences, 43,* 93–101.

Himle, M. B., & Woods, D. W. (2005). An experimental evaluation of tic suppression and the tic rebound effect. *Behaviour Research and Therapy, 43,* 1443–1451.

Himle, M. B., Woods, D. W., Conelea, C. A., Bauer, C. C., & Rice, K. A. (2007). Investigating the effects of tic suppression on premonitory urge ratings in children and adolescents with Tourette's syndrome. *Behaviour Research and Therapy, 45,* 2964–2976.

Hofmann, S. G., Meuret, A. E., Smits, J. A., Simon, N. M., Pollack M. H., & Eisenmenger, K. (2006): Augmentation of exposure therapy for social anxiety disorder with D-Cycloserine. *Archives of General Psychiatry, 63,* 298–304.

Hollander, E., Allen, A., Kwon, J., Aronowitz, B., Schmeidler, J., Wong, C., et al. (1999). Clomipramine vs desipramine crossover trial in body dysmorphic disorder: Selective efficacy of a serotonin reuptake inhibitor in imagined ugliness. *Archives of General Psychiatry, 56,* 1033–1039.

Hollander, E., Cohen, L. J., & Simeon, D. (1993). Body dysmorphic disorder. *Psychiatric Annals, 23,* 359–364.

Janet, P. (1903). *Les obsessions and la psychastenine.* Paris: Felix Alcan.

Jankovic, J. (1997). Phenomenology and classification of tics. *Neurologic Clinics of North America, 15,* 267–275.

Jankovic, J. (2001). Tourette's syndrome. *New England Journal of Medicine, 345,* 1184–1192.

Kadesjo, B. & Gillberg, C. (2000). Tourette's disorder: Epidemiology and comorbidity in primary school children. *Journal of Psychosomatic Research, 55,* 3–6.

Kane, J.M., Barrett, E.J., Casey, D.E., Correll, C.U., Gelenberg, A.J., Klein, S., & Newcomer, J.W. (2004). Metabolic effects of treatment with atypical antipsychotics. *Journal of Clinical Psychiatry, 65(11),* 1447–55.

Keuthen, N. J., O'Sullivan, R. L., Ricciardi, J. A., Shera, D., Savage, C. R., Borgmann, A. S., et al (1995). The Massachusetts General Hospital hair pulling scale: Development and factor analyses. *Psychotherapy and Psychosomatics, 64,* 141–145.

King, R. A., Scahill, L., Vitulano, L. A., Schwab-Stone, M., Tercyak, K. P. Jr., & Riddle, M. A. (1995). Childhood trichotillomania: Clinical phenomenology, comorbidity, and family genetics. *Journal of the American Academy of Child and Adolescent Psychiatry, 34,* 1451–1459.

Kotby, A. A., el Badawy, N., el Sokkary, S., Moawad, H., & el Shawarby, M. (1998). Antineuronal antibodies in rheumatic chorea. *Clinical and Diagnostic Laboratory Immunology, 5,* 836–839.

Krishnan, K. R. R., Davidson, J. R. T., Guahardo, C. (1985). Trichotillomania: A review. *Comprehensive Psychiatry, 23,* 123–128.

Kurlan, R., Como, P. G., Miller, B., Palumbo, D., Deeley, C., Andresen, E. M., et al. (2002). The behavioral spectrum of tic disorders: A community based study. *Neurology, 59,* 414–420.

Kurlan, R., Whitmore, D., Irvine, C., McDermott, M. P., & Como, P. G. (1994). Tourette's syndrome in a special education population: A pilot study involving a single school district. *Neurology, 44,* 699–702.

Kushner M. G., Kim, S. W., Donahue, C., Thuras, P., Adson, D., Kotlyar, M., et al. (2007). D-cycloserine augmented exposure therapy for obsessive compulsive disorder. *Biological Psychiatry, 62,* 835–838.

Leckman, J. F. (2002). Tourette's syndrome. *Lancet, 360,* 1577–1586.

Leckman, J. F., Peterson, B. S., Pauls, D. L., & Cohen, D. J. (1997). Tic disorders. *Psychiatric Clinics of North America, 20,* 839–861.

Leckman, J. F., Riddle, M. A., Hardin, M. T., Ort, S. I., Swartz, K. L., Stevenson, J., et al. (1989). The Yale Global Tic Severity Scale: Initial testing of a clinician-rated scale of tic severity. *Journal of the American Academy of Child and Adolescent Psychiatry, 28,* 566–573.

Leckman, J. F., Walker, D. E., & Cohen, D. J. (1993). Premonitory urges in Tourette's syndrome. *American Journal of Psychiatry, 150,* 98–102.

Ledgerwood, L., Richardson, R., & Cranney, J. (2003). Effects of d-cycloserine on the extinction of conditioned freezing. *Behavioral Neuroscience, 117,* 341–349.

Ledgerwood, L., Richardson, R., & Cranney, J. (2004). D-cycloserine and the facilitation of extinction of conditioned fear: Consequences for reinstatement. *Behavioral Neuroscience, 118,* 505–513.

Ledgerwood, L., Richardson, R., & Cranney, J. (2005). D-cycloserine facilitates extinction of learned fear: Effects on reacquisition and generalized extinction. *Biological Psychiatry, 57,* 841–847.

Leonard, H. L. & Swedo, S. E. (2001). Paediatric autoimmune neuropsychiatric disorders associated with streptococcal infection. *The International Journal of Neuropsychopharmacology, 4,* 191–198.

Leonard, H. L., Swedo, S. E., Lenane, M. C., Rettew, D. C., Hamburger, S. D., Bartko, J. J., et al. (1993). A 2- to 7-year follow-up study of 54 obsessive compulsive children and adolescents. *Archives of General Psychiatry, 50,* 429–439.

Lerner, J., Franklin, M. E., Meadows, E. A., Hembree, E. & Foa, E. B. (1998). Effectiveness of a cognitive behavioral treatment program for trichotillomania: An uncontrolled evaluation. *Behavior Therapy, 29,* 157–171.

Leung, A. K. & Robson, W. L. (1992). Nailbiting. *Clinical Pediatrics, 29,* 690–692.

Lichter, D. G. & Jackson, L. A. (1996). Predictors of clonidine response in Tourette syndrome: implications and inferences. *Journal of Child Neurology, 11,* 93–97.

Lin, H., Katsovich, L., Ghebremichael, M., Findley, D. B., Grantz, H., Lombroso, P. J., et al. (2007). Psychosocial stress predicts future symptom severities in children and adolescents with Tourette syndrome and/or obsessive compulsive disorder. *Journal of Child Psychology and Psychiatry, 48,* 157–166.

Lochner, C., Seedat, S., du Toit, P. L., Nel, D. G., Niehaus, D. J. H., Sandler, R., et al. (2005). Obsessive compulsive disorder and trichotillomania: A phenomenological comparison. *BMC Psychiatry, 5,* 2.

Lochner, C., Seedat, S., Niehaus, D.J., & Stein, D.J. (2006) Topiramate in the treatment of trichotillomania: an open-label pilot study. *International Clinical Psychopharmacology, 21(5),* 255-9.

Lombroso, P. J., Scahill, L., King, R. A., Lynch, K. A., Chappell, P. B., Peterson, B. S., et al. (1995). Risperidone treatment of children and adolescents with chronic tic disorders: A preliminary report. *Journal of the American Academy of Child and Adolescent Psychiatry, 34,* 1147–1152.

Mahone, E. M., Bridges, D., Prahme, C., & Singer, H. S. (2004). Repetitive arm and hand movements (complex motor stereotypies) in children. *Journal of Pediatrics, 145,* 391–395.

Malhotra, S., Grober, S., Baweja, R., & Bhateja, G. (2008). Trichotillomania in children. *Indian Pediatrics, 45,* 403–405.

Mansueto, C. S., Stemberger, R. M., Thomas A. M., & Golomb, R. G. (1997). Trichotillomania: A comprehensive behavioral model. *Clinical Psychology Review, 17,* 567–577.

March, J. S. & Mulle, K. (1998). *OCD in children and adolescents: A cognitive behavioral treatment manual.* Guilford Press, New York.

March, J. S., Biederman, J., Wolkow, R., Safferman, A., Mardekian, J., Cook, E. H., et al. (1998). Sertraline in children and adolescents with obsessive compulsive disorder: A multicenter randomized control trial. *Journal of the American Medical Association, 280,* 1752–1756.

March, J. S., Franklin M., Nelson A., & Foa, E. (2001). Cognitive behavioral psychotherapy for pediatric obsessive compulsive disorder. *Journal of Clinical Child Psychology, 30,* 8–18.

March, J. S., Franklin, M. E., Leonard, H., Garcia, A., Moore, P., Freeman, J., et al. (2007). Tics moderate treatment outcome with sertraline but not cognitive behavior therapy in pediatric obsessive compulsive disorder. *Biological Psychiatry, 61,* 344–347.

Marks, I. & Mishan, J. (1988). Dysmorphophobic avoidance with disturbed bodily perception. A pilot study of exposure therapy. *British Journal of Psychiatry, 152,* 674–678.

Masi, G., Millepiedi, S., Mucci, M., Bertini, N., Pfanner, C., & Arcangeli, F. (2006). Comorbidity of obsessive compulsive disorder and attention-deficit/hyperactivity disorder in referred children and adolescents. *Comprehensive Psychiatry, 46,* 42–47.

Masi, G., Perugi, G., Toni, C., Millepiedi, S., Mucci, M., Bertini, N., et al. (2004). Obsessive compulsive bipolar comorbidity: Focus on children and adolescents. *Journal of Affective Disorders, 78,* 175–183.

Mason, A., Banarjee, S., Eapen, V., Zeitlin, H., & Robertson, M. M. (1998). The prevalence of Tourette's syndrome in a mainstream school population. *Developmental Medicine and Child Neurology, 40,* 292–296.

Mataix-Cols, D., Pertusa, A., & Leckman, J. F. (2007). Issues for DSM-V: How should obsessive compulsive and related disorders be classified? *American Journal of Psychiatry, 164,* 1313–1314.

Mayville, S., Katz, R. C., Gipson, M. T. & Cabral, K. (1999). Assessing the prevalence of body dysmorphic disorder in an ethnically diverse group of adolescents. *Journal of Child and Family Studies, 8,* 357–362.

McDougle, C. J., Goodman, W. K., Leckman, J. F., Barr, L. C., Heninger, G. R., & Price, L. H. (1993). The efficacy of fluvoxamine in obsessive compulsive disorder: Effects of comorbid chronic tic disorder. *Journal of Clinical Psychopharmacology, 15,* 354–358.

McKay, D., Todaro, J., Neziroglu, R., Campisi, T., Moritz, E. K., & Yaryura-Tobias, J. A. (1997). Body dysmorphic disorder: A preliminary evaluation of treatment and maintenance using exposure with response prevention. *Behaviour Research and Therapy, 35,* 67–70.

Mell, L. K., Davis, R. L., & Owens, D. (2005). Association between streptococcal infection and obsessive compulsive disorder, Tourette's syndrome, and tic disorder. *Pediatrics, 116,* 56–60.

Meltzer, H. Y. (2004). What's atypical about atypical antipsychotic drugs? *Current Opinion in Pharmacology, 4,* 53–57.

Merlo, L. J., Lehmkuhl, H., Geffken, G. R., & Storch, E. A. (2009). Decrease in family accommodation is associated with improved cognitive behavioral therapy outcome in pediatric obsessive compulsive disorder. *Journal of Consulting and Clinical Psychology, 77*(2), 355–360.

Mink, J. W. (2003). The basal ganglia and involuntary movements: Impaired inhibition of competing motor patterns. *Archives of Neurology, 60,* 1365–1368.

Morselli, E. (1886). Sulla dismorfofobia e sulla tafefobia, *Bolletinno della R Accademia di Genova, 6,* 110–119 [translated by Jerome L., 2001]. *History of Psychiatry, 12,* 103–114.

Mowrer, O. H. (1939). A stimulus-response analysis and its role as a reinforcing agent. *Psychological Review, 46,* 553–565.

Mowrer, O. H. (1960). Basic research methods, statistics, and decision theory. *American Journal of Occupational Therapy, 14,* 199–205.

Mueller, S. A. (1990). Trichotillomania: A histopathological study in sixty-six patients. *Journal of the American Academy of Dermatology, 23,* 56–62.

Murphy, M. L. & Pichichero, M. E. (2002). Prospective identification and treatment of children with pediatric autoimmune neuropsychiatric disorder associated with group A streptococcal infection (PANDAS). *Archives of Pediatrics and Adolescent Medicine, 156,* 356–361.

Murphy, T. K., Sajid, M., Soto, O., Shapira, N., Edge, P., Yang, M., et al. (2004). Detecting pediatric autoimmune neuropsychiatric disorders associated with streptococcus in children with obsessive compulsive disorder and tics. *Biological Psychiatry, 55,* 61–68.

Murphy, T. K., Segarra, A., Storch, E. A., & Goodman, W. K. (2008). SSRIs-adverse events: How to monitor and manage. *International Review of Psychiatry, 20,* 203–208.

Murphy, T. K., Storch, E. A., & Strawser, M. (2006). SSRI-induced behavioral activation in the PANDAS subtype. *Primary Psychiatry, 13*(8), 87–89.

Neziroglu, F., Khemlani-Patel, S., & Veale, D. (2008). Social learning theory and cognitive behavioral models of body dysmorphic disorder. *Body Image, 5,* 28–38.

Neziroglu, F. & Yaryura-Tobias, J. A. (1993). Body dysmorphic disorder: Phenomenology and case descriptions. *Behavioral Psychotherapy, 21,* 27–36.

Neziroglu, F., Roberts, M., & Yaryura-Tobias, J. A. (2004). A behavioral model for body dysmorphic disorder. *Psychiatric Annals, 34,* 915–920

Ninan, P. T., Knight, B., Kirk, L., Rothbaum, B. O., Kelsey, J., & Nemeroff, C. B. (1998). A controlled trial of venaflexine in trichotillomania: Interim phase I results. *Psychopharmacology Bulletin, 34,* 221–224.

Ninan, P. T., Rothbaum, B. O., Marsteller, F. A., Knight, B. T., & Eccard, M. B. (2000). A placebo-controlled trial of cognitive behavioral therapy and clomipramine in trichotillomania. *Journal of Clinical Psychiatry, 61,* 47–50.

Obsessive Compulsive Cognitions Working Group (1997). Cognitive assessment of obsessive compulsive disorder, *Behaviour Research and Therapy, 35,* 667–681.

O'Sullivan, R. L., Keuthen, N. J., Hayday, C. F., Ricciardi, J. N., Buttolph, M. L., Jenike, M. A., et al. (1995) The Massasuchets General Hospital (MGH) Hairpulling Scale: 2. Reliability and validity. *Psychotherapy and Psychosomatics, 64,* 146–148.

Pathak, S., Danielyan, A., & Kowatch, R. A. (2004). Successful treatment of trichotillomania with olanzapine augmentation in an adolescent. *Journal of Child and Adolescent Psychopharmacology, 14,* 153–154.

Pauls, D. L., Alsobrook, J. P. 2nd, Goodman, W., Rasmussen, S., & Leckman, J. F. (1995). A family study of obsessive compulsive disorder. *American Journal of Psychiatry, 152,* 76–84.

Pauls, D. L., Raymond, C. L., Stevenson, J. M., & Leckman, J. F. (1991). A family study of Gilles de la Tourette's syndrome. *American Journal of Human Genetics, 48,* 154–163.

Pediatric OCD Treatment Study (POTS) Team (2004). Cognitive behavior therapy, sertraline, and their combination for children and adolescents with obsessive compulsive disorder: The Pediatric OCD Treatment Study randomized controlled trial. *Journal of the American Medical Association, 292,* 1969–1976.

Peris, T. S., Bergman, R. L., Langley, A., Chang, S., McCracken, J. R., & Piacentini, J. (2008). Correlates of accommodation of pediatric obsessive compulsive disorder: Parent, child, and family characteristics. *Journal of the American Academy of Child and Adolescent Psychiatry, 47*(10), 1173–1181.

Perugi, G., Giannotti, D., Di Vaio, S., Frare, F., Saettoni, M., & Cassano, G. B. (1996). Fluvoxamine in the treatment of body dysmorphic disorder. *International Clinical Psychopharmacology, 11,* 247–254.

Peterson, B. S. & Leckman, J. F. (1998). Temporal characterization of tics in Gilles de la Tourette's syndrome. *Biological Psychiatry, 44,* 1337–1348.

Phillips, K. A. & Diaz, S. F. (1997). Gender differences in body dysmorphic disorder. *Journal of Nervous and Mental Disorders, 185,* 570–577.

Phillips, K. A. (2001). Body dysmorphic disorder. In J. M. Oldham, M. B. Riba (Series Eds.), K. A. Phillips (Vol. Ed.), *Somatoform and factitious disorders: Review of psychiatry* (pp. 219–223). Washington, DC: American Psychiatric Publishing.

Phillips, K. A. (1996). Body dysmorphic disorder: Diagnosis and treatment of imagined ugliness. *Journal of Clinical Psychiatry, 57,* S61–S64.

Phillips, K. A. (2000). Quality of life for patients with body dysmorphic disorder. *Journal of Nervous and Mental Disease, 188,* 170–175.

Phillips, K. A., Albertini, R. S., & Rasmussen, S. A. (2002). A randomized placebo-controlled trial of fluoxetine in body dysmorphic disorder. *Archives of General Psychiatry, 59,* 381–388.

Phillips, K. A., Atala, K. D., & Albertini, R. S. (1995). Case study: Body dysmorphic disorder in adolescents. *Journal of the American Academy of Child and Adolescent Psychiatry, 34,* 1216–1220.

Phillips, K. A., Didie, E. R., Menard, W., Pagano, M. E., Fay, C., & Weisberg, R. B. (2006). Clinical features of body dysmorphic disorder in adolescents and adults. *Psychiatry Research, 141,* 305–314.

Phillips, K. A., Dwight, M. M., & McElroy, S. L. (1998). Efficacy and safety of fluvoxamine in body dysmorphic disorder. *Journal of Clinical Psychiatry, 59,* 165–171.

Phillips, K. A., Grant, J., Siniscalchi, J., & Albertini, R. S. (2001). Surgical and nonpsychiatric medical treatment of patients with body dysmorphic disorder. *Psychosomatics, 42,* 504–510.

Phillips, K. A. & Hollander, E. (2008). Treating body dysmorphic disorder with medication: Evidence, misconceptions, and a suggested approach. *Body Image, 5,* 13–27.

Phillips, K. A., Hollander, E., Rasmussen, S. A., Aronowitz, B. R., DeCaria, C., & Goodman, W. K. (1997). A severity rating scale for body dysmorphic disorder: Development, reliability, and validity of a modified version of the Yale-Brown Obsessive Compulsive Scale. *Psychopharmacology Bulletin, 33,* 17–22.

Phillips, K. A., McElroy, S. L., Dwight, M. M., Eisen, J. L., & Rasmussen, S. A. (2001). Delusionality and response to open-label fluvoxamine in body dysmorphic disorder. *Journal of Clinical Psychiatry, 62,* 87–91.

Phillips, K. A., McElroy, S. L., Hudson, J. I., & Pope, H. G. Jr. (1995). Body dysmorphic disorder: An obsessive compulsive spectrum disorder, a form of affective spectrum disorder, or both? *Journal of Clinical Psychiatry, 56,* S41–S51.

Phillips, K. A., McElroy, S. L., Keck, P. E., Jr., Pope, H. G., Jr., & Hudson, J. I. (1993). Body dysmorphic disorder: 30 cases of imagined ugliness. *American Journal of Psychiatry, 150,* 302–308.

Phillips, K. A. & Naijar, F. (2003). An open-label study of citalopram in body dysmorphic disorder. *Journal of Clinical Psychiatry, 64,* 715–720.

Piacentini, J., Bergman, R.L., Keller, M., & McCracken, J. (2003). Functional impairment in children and adolescents with obsessive compulsive disorder. *Journal of Child and Adolescent Psychopharmacology, 13,* S61–69.

Piacentini, J., Himle, M. B., Chang, S., Baruch, D. E., Pearlman, A., Buzzella, B., et al. (2006). Reactivity of tic observation procedures to situation and setting: A multi-site study. *Journal of Abnormal Child Psychology, 34,* 647–656.

Piacentini, J., Peris, T. S., Bergman, L., Chang, S., & Jafer, M. (2007). Functional impairment in childhood OCD: Development and psychometric properties of the Child Obsessive Compulsive Impact Scale—Revised. *Journal of Clinical Child and Adolescent Psychology, 36,* 645–653.

Rapoport, J. L., Inoff-Germain, G., Weissman, M. M., Greenwald, S., Narrow, W. E., Jensen, P. S., et al. (2000). Childhood obsessive compulsive disorder in the NIMH MECA study: Parent versus child identification of cases. Methods for the epidemiology of child and adolescent mental disorders. *Journal of Anxiety Disorders, 14,* 535–548.

Rauch, S. L., Phillips, K. A., Segal, E., Makris, N., Shin, L. M., Whalen, P. J., et al. (2003). A preliminary morphometric magnetic resonance imaging study of regional brain volumes in body dysmorphic disorder. *Psychiatry Research, 122,* 13–19.

Ressler, K. J., Rothbaum, B. O., Tannenbaum, L., Anderson, P. Graap, K., Zimand, E., et al. (2004). Cognitive enhancers as adjuncts to psychotherapy: Use of D-cycloserine in phobic individuals to facilitate extinction of fear. *Archives of General Psychiatry, 61,* 1136–1144.

Riddle, M. A., Scahill, L., King, R. Hardin, M. T., Towbin, K. E., Ort, S. I., et al. (1990). Obsessive compulsive disorder in children and adolescents: Phenomenology and family history. *Journal of the American Academy of Child and Adolescent Psychiatry, 29,* 766–772.

Riddle, M. A., Reeve, E. A., Yaryura-Tobias, J. A., Yang, H. M., Claghorn, J. L., Gaffney, G., et al. (2001). Fluvoxamine for children and adolescents with obsessive compulsive disorder: A randomized, controlled, multicenter trial. *Journal of the American Academy of Child and Adolescent Psychiatry, 40,* 222–229.

Rief W, Buhlmann U, Wilhelm S, Borkenhagen A, & Brähler E. (2006). The prevalence of body dysmorphic disorder: A population-based survey. *Psychological Medicine, 36,* 877–885.

Robertson, M. M. & Stern, J. S. (1998). Tic disorders: New developments in Tourette syndrome and related disorders. *Movement Disorders, 11,* 373–380.

Robertson, M. M. (2000). Tourette syndrome, associated conditions and the complexities of treatment. *Brain, 123,* 425–462.

Robertson, M. M., Banerjee, S., Eapen, V., & Fox-Hiley, P. (2002). Obsessive compulsive behaviour and depressive symptoms in young people with Tourette syndrome: A controlled study. *European Child and Adolescent Psychiatry, 11,* 261–265.

Rosen, J. C. & Reiter, J. (1996). Development of the body dysmorphic disorder examination. *Behaviour Research and Therapy, 34,* 755–766.

Rosen, J. C., Reiter, J., & Orosan, P. (1995). Cognitive behavioral body image therapy for body dysmorphic disorder. *Journal of Consulting and Clinical Psychology, 63,* 263–269.

Rosenberg, D. R. & Keshavan, M. S. (1998). A.E. Bennett Research Award. Toward a neurodevelopmental model of obsessive compulsive disorder. *Biological Psychiatry, 43,* 623–640.

Rosenberg, D. R., Mirza, Y., Russell, A., Tang, J., Smith, J., Banerjee, S., et al. (2004). Reduced anterior cingulate glutamatergic concentrations in childhood OCD and major depression versus healthy controls. *Journal of the American Academy of Child and Adolescent Psychiatry, 43,* 1146–1153.

Rothbaum, B. O., Shaw, L., Morris, R., & Ninan, P. T. (1993). Prevalance of trichotillomania in a college freshman population. *Journal of Clinical Psychiatry, 52,* 72.

Salkovskis, P. M. (1999). Understanding and treating obsessive compulsive disorder. *Behavioral Research and Therapy, 37,* S29–S52.

Sallee, F. R., Newbitt, L., Jackson, C., Sine, L., & Sethuraman, G. (1997). Relative efficacy of haloperidol and pimozide in children and adolescents with Tourettes disorder. *American Journal of Psychiatry, 154,* 1057–1062.

Sandor, P. (2003). Pharmacological management of tics in patients with TS. *Journal of Psychosomatic Research, 55,* 41–48.

Sanger, T. D. (2007). Tic disorders and Tourette syndrome. *Continuum: Lifelong Learning in Neurology, 13,* 139–153.

Saxena, S. & Rauch, S. L. (2000). Functional neuroimaging and the neuroanatomy of obsessive compulsive disorder. *Psychiatric Clinics of North America, 23,* 563–586.

Saxena, S., Brody, A. L., Schwartz, J. M., & Baxter, L. R. (1998). Neuroimaging and frontal-subcortical circuitry in obsessive compulsive disorder. *British Journal of Psychiatry, 35,* S26–S37.

Scahill, L., Riddle, M. A., McSwiggin-Hardin, M., Ort, S.L., King, R. A., Goodman, W. K., Cicchetti, D., & Leckman, J. F. (1997). Children's Yale-Brown Obsessive Compulsive Scale: Reliability and validity. *Journal of the American Academy of Child and Adolescent Psychiatry, 36,* 844–852.

Schlosser, S., Black, D. W., & Blum, N. (1994). The demography, phenomenology, and family history of 22 persons with compulsive hair pulling. *Annals of Clinical Psychiatry, 6,* 147–152.

Shytle, R. D., Silver, A. A., Sheehan, K. H., Wilkinson, B. J., Newman, M., Sanberg, P. R., et al. (2003). The Tourette's Disorder Scale development, reliability, and validity. *Assessment, 10,* 273–287.

Simonoff, E., Pickles, A., Charman, T., Chandler, S., Loucas, T., & Baird, G. (2008). Psychiatric disorders in children with autism spectrum disorders: Prevalence, comorbidity, and associated factors in a population-derived sample. *Journal of the American Academy of Child and Adolescent Psychiatry, 47,* 921–929.

Spencer, T, Biederman, J., Harding, M., Wilens, T., & Faraone, S. (1995). The relationship between tic disorders and Tourette's syndrome revisited. *Journal of the American Academy of Child and Adolescent Psychiatry, 34,* 1133–1139.

Spencer, T., Biederman, J., Coffey, B., Geller, D., Crawford, M., Bearman, S. K., et al. (2002). A double-blind comparison of desipramine and placebo in children and adolescents with chronic tic disorder and comorbid attention-deficit/hyperactivity disorder. *Archives of General Psychiatry, 59,* 649–656.

Spencer, T., Biederman, J., Coffey, B., Geller, D., Faraone, S., & Wilens, T. (2001). Tourette disorder and ADHD. *Advances in Neurology, 85,* 57–77.

Spencer, T., Biederman, J., Wilens, T. (1999). Attention-deficit/hyperactivity disorder and comorbidity. *Pediatric Clinics of North America, 46,* 915–927.

Stein, D.J., Bouwer, C., & Maud, C.M. (1997). Use of the selective serotonin reuptake inhibitor citalopram in treatment of trichotillomania. *European Archives of Psychiatry and Clinical Neuroscience, 247(4),* 234-6.

Stein, D. J., Chamberlain, S. R., & Fineberg, N. (2006). An A-B-C model of habit disorders: Hair-pulling, skin-picking, and other stereotypic conditions. *CNS Spectrum, 11,* 824–827.

Stein, D. J. & Lochner, C. (2006). Obsessive compulsive spectrum disorders: A multidimensional approach. *Psychiatric Clinics of North America, 29,* 343–351.

Stemberger, R. M., Thomas, A. M., Mansueto, C. S., & Carter, J.G. (1999). Personal toll of trichotillomania: Behavioral and interpersonal sequelae. *Journal of Anxiety Disorders, 14,* 97–104.

Stemberger, R. M. T., Stein, D. J. & Mansueto, C. S. (2003) Behavioral and pharmacological treatment of trichotillomania. *Brief Treatment and Crisis Intervention, 3,* 339–352.

Stewart, S. E., Fagerness, J. A., Platko, J., Smoller, J. W., Illmann, C., Jenike, E., et al. (2007). Association of the SLC1A1 glutamate transporter gene and obsessive compulsive disorder. *The American Journal of Medical Genetics. Part B, Neuropsychiatric Genetics: The Official Publication of the International Society of Psychiatric Genetics, 144B,* 1027–1033.

Stewart, S. E., Rosario, M. C., Brown, T. A., Carter, A. S., Leckman, J. F., Sukhodolsky, D., et al. (2007). Principal components analysis of obsessive compulsive disorder symptoms in children and adolescents. *Biological Psychiatry, 61,* 285–291.

Stewert, R. S. & Nejtek, V. A. (2003). An open-label, flexible-dose study of olanzapine in the treatment of trichotillomania. *Journal of Clinical Psychiatry, 64,* 49–52.

Storch, E. A., Abramowitz, J., & Goodman, W. K. (2008). Where does obsessive compulsive disorder belong in DSM-V? *Depression and Anxiety, 25,* 336–347.

Storch, E. A., Geffken, G. R., Merlo, L. J., Jacob, M. J., Murphy, T. K., Goodman, W. K., et al. (2007). Family accommodation in pediatric obsessive compulsive disorder. *Journal of Clinical Child and Adolescent Psychology, 36,* 207–216.

Storch, E. A., Lack, C. W., Simons, L. E., Goodman, W. K., Murphy, T. K., & Geffken, G. R. (2007). A measure of functional impairment in youth with Tourette's syndrome. *Journal of Pediatric Psychology, 32,* 950–959.

Storch, E. A., Lehmkuhl, H., Geffken, G. R., Touchton, A., & Murphy, T. K. (2008). Aripiprazole augmentation of incomplete treatment response in an adolescent male with obsessive compulsive disorder. *Depression and Anxiety, 25,* 172–174.

Storch, E. A., Merlo, L. J., Bengtson, M., Murphy, T. K., Lewis, M. H., Yang, M. C., et al. (2007). D-cycloserine does not enhance exposure-response prevention therapy in obsessive compulsive disorder. *International Clinical Psychopharmacology, 22,* 230–237.

Storch, E. A., Merlo, L. J., Larson, M. J., Bloss, C. S., Geffken, G. R., Jacob, M. L., et al. (2008). Symptom dimensions and cognitive behavioural therapy outcome for pediatric obsessive compulsive disorder. *Acta Psychiatrica Scandinavica, 117,* 67–75.

Storch, E. A., Merlo, L. J., Larson, M. J., Geffken, G. R., Lehmkuhl, H. D., Jacob, M. L., et al. (2008). Impact of comorbidity on cognitive behavioral therapy response in pediatric obsessive compulsive disorder. *Journal of the American Academy of Child and Adolescent Psychiatry, 47,* 583–592.

Storch, E. A., Murphy, T. K., Geffken, G. R., Sajid, M., Allen, P., Roberti, J. W., et al. (2005). Reliability and validity of the Yale Global Tic Severity Scale. *Psychological Assessment, 17,* 486–491.

Storch, E. A., Merlo, L. J., Lack, C., Milsom, V. A., Geffken, G. R.; Goodman, W. K., et al. (2007). Quality of life in youth with Tourette's syndrome and chronic tic disorder. *Journal of the American Academy of Child and Adolescent Psychiatry, 36,* 217–227.

Streichenwein, S. M. & Thornby, J. I. (1995). A long-term, double-blind, placebo-controlled crossover trial of the efficacy of fluoxetine for trichotillomania. *American Journal of Psychiatry, 152,* 1192–1196.

Sukhodolsky, D. G., do Rosario-Campos, M. C., Scahill, L., Katsovich, L., Pauls, D. L., Peterson, B. S., et al. (2005). Adaptive, emotional, and family functioning of children with obsessive compulsive disorder and comorbid attention deficit hyperactivity disorder. *American Journal of Psychiatry, 162,* 1125–1132.

Sukhodolsky, D. G., Scahill, L., Zhang, H., Peterson, B. S., King, R. A., Lombroso, P. J., et al. (2003). Disruptive behavior in children with Tourette's syndrome: Association with ADHD comorbidity, tic severity, and functional impairment. *Journal of the American Academy of Child and Adolescent Psychiatry, 42,* 98–105.

Surwillo, W. W., Shafii, M., & Barrett, C. L. (1978). Gilles do la Tourette syndrome: A 20-month study of the effects of stressful life events and haloperidol on symptom frequency. *The Journal of Nervous and Mental Disease, 166,* 812–816.

Sverd, J., Curley, A. D., Jandorf, L., & Volkersz, L. (1988). Behavior disorders and attention deficit in boys with Tourette's syndrome. *Journal of the American Academy of Child and Adolescent Psychiatry, 27,* 413–417.

Sverd, J., Gadow, K. D., & Paolicelli, L. M. (1989). Methylphenidate treatment of attention-deficit hyperactivity disorder in boys with Tourette's syndrome. *Journal of the American Academy of Child andAdolescent Psychiatry, 28,* 574–579.

Swedo, S. E. & Leonard, H. L. (1994). Childhood movement disorders and obsessive compulsive disorder. *Journal of Clinical Psychiatry, 55,* S32–S37.

Swedo, S. E. & Leonard, H. L. (1992). Trichotillomania: An obsessive compulsive spectrum disorder? *Psychiatric Clinics of North America, 15,* 777–790.

Swedo, S. E., Leonard, H. L., Garvey, M., Mittleman, B., Allen, A. J., Perlmutter, S., et al. (1998). Pediatric autoimmune neuropsychiatric disorders associated with streptococcal infections: Clinical description of the first 50 cases. *American Journal of Psychiatry, 155,* 264–271.

Swedo, S. E., Leonard, H. L., Rapoport, J. L., Lenane, M. C., Goldberger, E. L., & Cheslow, D. L. (1989). A double-blind comparison of clomipramine and desipramine in the treatment of trichotillomania. *New England Journal of Medicine, 321,* 497–501.

Swedo, S. E., Pietrini, P., Leonard, H. L., Schapiro, M. B., Rettew, D. C., Goldberger, E. L., et al. (1992). Cerebral glucose metabolism in childhood-onset obsessive compulsive disorder: Revisualization during pharmacotherapy. *Archives of General Psychiatry, 49,* 690–694.

Swedo, S. E., Rapoport, J. L., Leonard, H. Lenane, M. & Cheslow, D. (1989). Obsessive compulsive disorder in children and adolescents. Clinical phenomenology of 70 consecutive cases. *Archives of General Psychiatry, 46,* 335–341.

Szeszko, P. R., MacMillan, S., McMeniman, M., Chen, S., Baribault, K., Lim, K. O., et al. (2004). Brain structural abnormalities in psychotropic drug-naive pediatric patients with obsessive compulsive disorder. *American Journal of Psychiatry, 161,* 1049–1056.

Tan, A., Salgado, M., & Fahn, S. (1997). The characterization and outcome of stereotypical movements in non-autistic children. *Movement Disorders, 12,* 47–52.

Tay, Y. K., Levy, M. L., & Metry, D. W. (2004). Trichotillomania in childhood: Case series and review. *Pediatrics, 113,* e494–498.

Thomsen, P. H. (2004). Risperidone augmentation in the treatment of severe adolescent OCD in SSRI-refractory cases: A case-series. *Annals of Clinical Psychiatry, 16,* 201–207.

Tolin, D. F., Franklin, M. E., Diefenbach, G. J., Anderson, E., & Meunier, S. A. (2007). Pediatric trichotillomania: Descriptive psychopathology and an open trial of cognitive behavioral therapy. *Cognitive Behaviour Therapy, 36,* 129–144.

Tolin, D. F., Diefenbach, G. J., Flessner, C. A., Franklin, M. E., Keuthen, N. J., Moore, P., et al. (2008). The trichotillomania scale for children: Development and validation. *Child Psychiatry and Human Development, 39,* 331–349.

Tourette Syndrome Classification Study Group. (1993). Definitions and classification of tic disorders. *Archives of Neurology, 50,* 1013–1016.

Tourette's Syndrome Study Group. (2002). Treatment of ADHD in children with tics: A randomized controlled trial. *Neurology, 58,* 527–536.

Turner, C. M. (2006). Cognitive behavioural theory and therapy for obsessive compulsive disorder in children and adolescents: Current status and future directions. *Clinical Psychology Review, 26,* 912–938.

Ulloa, R. E., Nicolini, H., Avila, M., & Fernandez-Guasti, A. (2007). Age onset subtypes of obsessive compulsive disorder: Differences in clinical response to treatment with clomipramine. *Journal of Child and Adolescent Psychopharmacology, 17,* 85–96.

van der Wee, N. J., Stevens, H., Hardeman, J. A., Mandl, R. C., Denys, D. A., van Megan, H. J., et al. (2004). Enhanced dopamine transporter density in psychotropic-naive patients with obsessive compulsive disorder shown by–CIT SPECT. *American Journal of Psychiatry, 161,* 2201–2206.

van Minnen, A., Hoogduin, K. A., Keijsers, G. P., Hellenbrand, I., & Hendriks, G. J. (2003). Treatment of trichotillomania with behavioral therapy or fluoxetine: A randomized, waiting-list controlled study. *Archives of General Psychiatry, 60,* 517–522.

Veale, D. (2004). Advances in a cognitive behavioural model of body dysmorphic disorder. *Body Image, 1,* 113–125.

Veale, D., Boocock, A., Gournay, K., Dryden, W., Shah, F., Willson, R., et al. (1996). Body dysmorphic disorder: A survey of fifty cases. *British Journal of Psychiatry, 169,* 196–201.

Verdellen, C. W., Keijsers, G. P., Cath, D. C., & Hoogduin, C. A. (2004). Exposure and response prevention versus habit reversal in Tourette's syndrome: A controlled study. *Behavioral Research and Theory, 42,* 501–511.

Walker, D. L., Ressler, K. J., Lu, K. T., & Davis, M. (2002). Facilitation of conditioned fear extinction by systemic administration or intra-amygdala infusions of D-cycloserine as assessed with fear-potentiated startle in rats. *Journal of Neuroscience, 22,* 2343–2351.

Walkup, J. T., Khan, S., Schuerholz, L., Paik, Y., Leckman, J. F., & Cohen, D. J. (1999). Phenomenology and natural history of tic-related ADHD and learning disabilities. In: J. F. Leckman, D. J. Cohen (Eds.), *Tourette's syndrome: Developmental psychopathology and clinical care* (pp. 63–79). New York, NY: Wiley.

Walkup, J. T., Rosenberg, L. A., Brown, J., & Singer, H. S. (1992). The validity of instruments measuring tic severity in Tourette's syndrome. *Journal of the American Academy of Child and Adolescent Psychiatry, 31,* 472–477.

Wilhelm, S., Buhlmann, U., Tolin, D. F., Meunier, S. A., Pearlson, G. D., Reese, H. E., et al. (2008). Augmentation of behavior therapy with D-cycloserine for obsessive compulsive disorder. *American Journal of Psychiatry, 165,* 335–341.

Wilhelm, S., Otto, M. W., Lohr, B., & Deckersbach, T. (1999). Cognitive behavior group therapy for body dysmorphic disorder: A case series. *Behaviour Research and Therapy, 37,* 71–75.

Wilkinson, B. J., Newman, M. B., Shytle, R. D., Silver, A. A., Sanberg, P. R., & Sheehan, D. (2001). Family impact of Tourette's syndrome. *Journal of Child and Family Studies, 10,* 477–483.

Williams, J., Hadjistavropoulos, T., & Sharpe, D. (2006). A meta-analysis of psychological and pharmacological treatments for Body Dysmorphic Disorder. *Behaviour Research and Therapy, 44,* 99–111.

Winchel, R. M., Jones, J. S., Molcho, A., Parsons, B., Stanley, B., & Stanley, M. (1992). The Psychiatric Institute Trichotillomania Scale. *Psychopharmacology Bulletin, 28,* 463–476.

Wodrich, D. L., Benjamin, E., & Lachar, D. (1997). Tourette's syndrome and psychopathology in a child psychiatry setting. *Journal of the American Academy of Child and Adolescent Psychiatry, 36,* 1618–1624.

Woods, D. W. & Twohig, M. P. (2002). Using habit reversal to treat chronic vocal tic disorder in children. *Behavioral Interventions, 17,* 159–168.

Woods, D. W., Himle, M. B., Miltenberger, R. G., Carr, J. E., Osmon, D. C., Karsten, A. M., et al. (2008). Durability, negative impact, and neuropsychological predictors of tic suppression in children with chronic tic disorder. *Journal of Abnormal Child Psychology, 36*, 237–245.

Woods, D. W., Miltenberger, R. G., & Lumley, V. A. (1996). Sequential application of major habit-reversal components to treat motor tics in children. *Journal of Applied Behavioral Analysis, 29*, 483–493.

Woods, D. W., Piacentini, J., Himle, M. B., & Chang, S. (2005). Premonitory Urge for Tics Scale: Initial psychometric results and examination of the premonitory urge phenomenon in youths with tic disorders. *Journal of Developmental and Behavioral Pediatrics, 26*, 397–403.

Woods, D. W., Twohig, M. P., Flessner, C. A., & Roloff, T. J. (2003). Treatment of vocal tics in children with Tourette syndrome: Investigating the efficacy of habit reversal. *Journal of Applied Behavioral Analysis, 36*, 109–112.

Woods, D. W., Wetterneck, C. T., & Flessner, C. A. (2006). A controlled evaluation of acceptance and commitment therapy plus habit reversal for trichotillomania. *Behavioral Research and Therapy, 44*, 639–656.

Zohar, A. H. (1999). The epidemiology of obsessive compulsive disorder in children and adolescents. *Child and Adolescent Psychiatry Clinics of North America, 8*, 445–460.

Zuchner, S., Cuccaro, M. L., Tran-Viet, K. N., Cope, H., Krishnan, R. R., Pericak-Vance, M. A., et al. (2006). SLITRK1 mutations in trichotillomania. *Molecular Psychiatry, 11*, 887–889.

Cultural Issues in Understanding and Treating Obsessive Compulsive and Spectrum Disorders

Maja Nedeljkovic, Richard Moulding, Elham Foroughi, Michael Kyrios, *and* Guy Doron

Abstract

This chapter discusses the cross-cultural understanding of the obsessive compulsive and spectrum disorders. Epidemiological studies suggest a reasonably consistent prevalence of OCD around the world. The role of other culturally influenced factors in the presentation of OCD is also considered (i.e., religiosity, superstition, and beliefs), with religion considered particularly important in the presentation of OCD, although not in its prevalence per se. Treatment effect sizes across countries and within minority cultures from Western countries are outlined. The influence of cultural factors on help-seeking behaviors, assessment, misdiagnosis, and treatment are considered. Limitations of the literature base are discussed, particularly the lack of non-Western studies of treatment effects, and the low evidence base for the spectrum disorders.

Keywords: cross-cultural psychology, cross-cultural treatment, epidemiology, obsessive compulsive disorder, body dysmorphic disorder, cognition.

Introduction

It is well recognized that all psychological phenomena are embedded in specific social and cultural contexts. According to Betancourt and Lopez (1993), culture is defined by the values, beliefs, and practices that pertain to a given ethnocultural group and are transmitted from generation to generation. Cultural factors greatly influence the way we think, behave, and the responses we receive to our behaviors, thus often determining, encouraging, or sanctioning specific actions and behaviors. Researchers have emphasized the importance of understanding the way in which culture shapes mental illness (Draguns, 1980; Kleinman, 1977; Marsella, 1980;). For example, according to Tseng (1997), culture can exert its influence on the perceptions of psychopathology (i.e., what defines a disorder), its phenomenology (i.e., the specific symptom content), the development or prevention of psychopathology (e.g., supports, demands), and the individual's perception and description of the specific disorders.

All of these factors could have significant implications for the etiology and treatment of psychological disorders.

The obsessive compulsive spectrum disorders (OCSDs) constitutes a collection of debilitating mental disorders with obsessive compulsive disorder (OCD) at their center, and including other related disorders, such as body dysmorphic disorder (BDD), Tourette syndrome (TS), and trichotillomania. While the spectrum construct has been the subject of equivocation (Castle & Phillips, 2006), it remains a useful way to identify a heterogeneous group of disorders with some common features. For instance, the OCSDs share features such as persistent, recurrent thoughts, images, impulses, or doubts that are sometimes seen by the individuals as morally unacceptable, physically repugnant, anxiety provoking, or uncontrollable (e.g., blasphemous thoughts, thoughts about harm, thoughts about physical disfigurement, unwanted impulses to yell obscenities, pull one's hair), and various repetitive or ritualistic behaviors that are conducted to alleviate the distress caused by the obsessions (e.g., checking, repetitive mirror inspection). Descriptions of OCD-like behaviors were recorded as early as 2500 years ago in early Buddhist texts, with descriptions continuing to occur throughout history and across various cultural settings (de Silva, 2006). It is now well accepted that the occurrence of OCD, and most likely other OCSDs, is not restricted to a specific culture or particular era. Clinical and epidemiological data from a range of geographic and ethnic settings have shown a remarkable consistency in the presence and main characteristics of OCD and the OCSDs. Nevertheless, this does not mean that this group of disorders is immune to cultural influence.

Variations in culture imply that there are important differences in meaning construction between ethnocultural groups. Cultural factors influence how one perceives oneself, one's body, and one's health, along with how one defines constructs such as disorder and normality, and how one conducts social interactions (e.g., Fabrega, 1989; Marsella & Yamada, 2000; Marsella, Kaplan, & Suarez, 2002). This may be of particular importance in the OCSDs, as the construction of meaning and interpretations of common intrusive phenomena have been suggested to play a major role in the development and maintenance of specific obsessive and compulsive symptoms associated with these disorders.

Current cognitive-behavioral models of OCD and related disorders suggest that the variety of obsessional and compulsive symptoms develop as a result of misinterpretation and reaction to normal intrusive experiences. This is corroborated by numerous findings demonstrating that intrusive thoughts and experiences are experienced by the majority of the population (e.g., Rachman & de Silva, 1978; Salkovskis & Harrison, 1984; cf. Rassin & Muris, 2007). Similarly, repetitive and ritualized behaviors are common in the nonclinical population (Muris, Merckelbach, & Clavan, 1997), and are apparent within culturally prescribed religious practices. Thus compulsions in and of themselves, are not indicators of OCD, unless they are performed in ways inconsistent with shared cultural norms accepted by the individual.

Rachman (1997; 1998) emphasized the importance of intrusive thought content in the development of obsessions, suggesting that obsessions encompassing themes from the major moral systems (e.g., sex, aggression, blasphemy) are more likely to be misinterpreted as significant, personally revealing, or threatening. Logically it follows that, as religious concerns differ across cultures with consequent differences in systems of morality, the obsessions that are most ego-dystonic would differ across cultures also. Studies examining the impact of religious and superstitious beliefs on contamination and scrupulosity concerns have provided probably the strongest support for the role of culture in shaping OCD symptoms. In addition, people within a particular culture at a particular time are likely to share a common history, and specific social and environmental concerns, which would be reflected in the nature of their preoccupations. For example, HIV/AIDS or asbestos-related concerns have become more prominent among contamination/cleaning symptoms over the past decades, particularly within Western countries.

In sum, culture could potentially influence the manifestation of symptoms (i.e., the specific themes of obsessions, preoccupations), as well as the course of the disorder and, therefore, its assessment and treatment. This chapter will attempt to review the epidemiology and phenomenology of the OCSDs across various geographical and cultural settings. It will also examine the influence of culture-specific factors on the phenomenology and treatment of these disorders, and discuss the implications for their assessment and treatment; although the literature pertaining to many of these issues is not comprehensive in these fields. Nonetheless, such an examination of the culture-specific influences on symptoms can also give us important insights into the mechanisms involved in the development and maintenance of these disorders within a culture, and better inform our approaches to assessment and treatment.

Prevalence across Cultures

Increases in our knowledge of the OCSDs, and the development of more objective, comprehensive and reliable assessment methods, has led to a growing interest in the epidemiology of these disorders worldwide. The first comprehensive epidemiological account of OCD came with the results of the National Epidemiological Catchment Area (ECA) Survey, conducted across various regions in the United States in 1984. The study used a structured diagnostic interview, the Diagnostic Interview Schedule (DIS; Robins, Helzer, Croughan, & Ratkliff, 1981) administered in a face-to-face manner by lay interviewers trained in its administration, to examine the prevalence of a range of psychiatric disorders in a large community-based sample from various regions in the United States in accordance with the DSM-III (and later, DSM-III-R) criteria.

The results from the study placed OCD as the fourth most common psychiatric disorder after phobias, substance use disorders, and major depression, with a 6-month point prevalence of 1.6% and a lifetime prevalence of 2.5%. Six other international studies using similar methodology, conducted in Puerto Rico, Canada, Germany, Taiwan, New Zealand, and Korea, found annual prevalence rates ranging from 1.1% to 1.8% and lifetime prevalence rates from 1.9%–2.5% (see Table 26.1). The exception was Taiwan, which recorded a lower prevalence rate, but also reported lower rates of psychiatric disorders more generally. It is unclear whether this difference in prevalence is due to differences in reporting of psychiatric diagnosis. It has been suggested that in Asian cultures, there is a greater reluctance to disclose psychological problems and seek treatment, and a greater tendency to keep problems in the family (Cheung, 1991; Staley & Wand, 1995). Alternatively, prevalence rates may reflect specific environmental and/or cultural factors that act as protective factors.

Several other international studies have since used the DIS on populations from Germany, Hong Kong, Iceland, and Hungary, with lifetime prevalence rates ranging from 1.1% in Hong Kong to 2.7% in Hungary. Again, there seems to be some consistency in the rates across various geographical regions, with perhaps the exception of the Far East, which recorded the lowest rates, supporting the need for further cross-cultural research in this region.

Epidemiological studies using other structured interview schedules have also been conducted (see Table 26.1). For example, studies using the Composite International Diagnostic Instrument (CIDI) and DSM-IV and/or IDC-10 criteria, conducted in Canada, Netherlands, Germany, Australia, Brazil and Turkey, show lifetime prevalence rates from 0.5% to 2%, although the differences may reflect the criteria used. Similarly, studies using the Schedule for Affective Disorders and Schizophrenia (SADS), based on the Research Diagnostic Criteria and the DSM, show some variability in the prevalence rates, depending on the criteria used to arrive at a diagnosis. Earlier studies employing the RDC show very low prevalence due to the use of a diagnostic hierarchy that virtually excludes the diagnosis of OCD in the presence of depression, TS, schizophrenia, and other organic disorders. Considering the high rates of comorbidity between OCD and some of these disorders, the rates reported by these studies are likely to grossly underestimate the prevalence of OCD. Consistent with this, a more recent study of OCD prevalence in Iran, employing DSM-IV criteria, reported estimates closer to those observed in other studies using different instruments. In contrast to the relatively low rates in some parts of Asia, Morocco was the other exception, with considerably higher overall prevalence (6.4%) relative to all other sites. This site also recorded the greatest gender bias, with the majority of affected individuals being women. The reasons for this difference are unclear in the absence of further data from this region.

In terms of demographic characteristics, there seems to be a slightly higher prevalence in females across studies, with these differences being statistically significant in three studies from Germany, New Zealand, and Iran, although another Germany study recorded slightly higher lifetime prevalence among males. The notable exception to the slightly higher ratio of females in samples is the substantially higher prevalence among females in Morocco. In general, there is a tendency for an earlier age of onset among males across the various regions, with the average age of onset ranging from mid/late twenties and early thirties across various sites (for review see Matsunaga & Seedat, 2007; Staley & Wand, 1995). Considerable comorbidity with depression and other anxiety disorders was also consistently found across countries and sites.

In addition to epidemiological data, studies examining OCD in psychiatric populations have provided further support for the consistency in prevalence and core characteristics of OCD across various regions (for review see Fontenelle, Mendlowicz, Marques, & Versiani, 2004; Staley & Wand, 1995). Themes of dirt/contamination, harm/aggression, symmetry, religion/morality/sex, and somatic concerns are present across various cultures, although there appears to be some variation in the predominance of specific themes across different cultural and ethnic groups. These are discussed in more detail in later sections. The gender ratios remain similar, with only a few exceptions, including higher prevalence of males in psychiatric samples in Egypt and India (Jaisoorya, Reddy, Srinath, & Thennarasu, 2008; Khanna et al., 1986; Okasha, Saad, Khalil, El-Dawla, & Yehia, 1994). These are likely to reflect sociocultural factors related to differential access to psychiatric services, and different patterns of referrals for the two genders in these cultures. Gender differences in presentation have also shown remarkable consistency across various

Table 26.1 Comparisons of Epidemiological Data across Various Geographical Regions

Disorder	Region	Sites	Studies	Assessment material used	Prevalence (point)	Prevalence (lifetime)	Gender ratio (lifetime)
OCD	North America and Europe	ECA/USA (various cities)	Burnam et al., 1987; Myers et al., 1984; Blazer et al., 1985; Karno et al., 1987; Robins et al., 1984	DIS, lay interviewers	0.7–2.1 (6mo.)	1.9–3.1	1.2–2.7
		Canada (Edmonton)	Bland et al., 1988	DIS, lay interviewers	1.6 (6mo.)	3.0	1.1
		Italy (urban)	Faravelli et al., 1989	SADS, psychiatry interns	6 (point)	0.7	1
		Germany	Wittchen et al., 1992; Grabe et al., 2001	DIS/CIDI	0.4	0.5–2.0	5.7
		UK	Jenkins et al., 1997; Torres et al., 2006	CIS-R	1.1 (1mo.)	—	1.4–1.7
		Netherlands	Bijl et al., 1998	CIDI,	0.5 (1yr.)	0.9	0.9
		Hungary	Németh et al., 1997	DIS, lay interviewers	1.9 (1mo.)	2.7	1.2
	Australia/NZ	Australia (urban and rural)	Slade et al. (2009)	CIDI, lay interviewers	1.9 (1yr.)	—	—
		New Zealand	Oakley-Browne et al., 1989; Wells et al., 1989; Douglass et al., 1995	DIS	1.1–4.0 (1yr.)	2.2	3.4
	Middle East	Iran	Mohammadi et al., 2004	SADS, Clinical psychologists		1.8	4
		Turkey	Çilli et al., 2004	CIDI, psychiatry interns	3.0 (1yr.)	—	1.3
	Asia	Taiwan (urban & rural)	Hwu et al., 1989	DIS	0.1–0.3	0.3–0.9	1.3–1.9
		Hong Kong	Chen et al., 1993	DIS	—	1.0	—
		Korea (urban & rural)	Lee et al., 1987	DIS	—	2.3	—
	Africa	Morocco	Kadri et al., 2007	MINI, GPs	—	6.1	15
	Central and South America	Puerto Rico	Canino et al., 1987	DIS	1.8	3.2	0.9
		São Paulo, Brazil	Andrade et al., 2002	CIDI, lay interviewers	0.3 (1 mo.)	0.3	1.6
BDD	North America	Boston, US	Otto et al., 2001	SCID (women only)	0.7	—	—
	Europe	Florence, Italy	Faravelli, et al., 1997	SADS-L, doctors/psychiatric trainees	0.7	—	100% female

cultures, with sexual, symmetry, and harm themes more common presentations among men, and contamination/dirt obsessions and cleaning compulsions more common among females. These trends have been found across Brazil, India, Iran, Italy, Spain, Taiwan, Japan, and Turkey (Fontenelle, Marques, & Versiani, 2002; Ghassemzadeh et al., 2002; Jaisoorya, Reddy, Srinath, & Thennarasu, 2008; Juang & Liu, 2001; Karadaĝ, Oguzhanoglu, Ozdel, Ateşci, & Amuk, 2006; Labad et al., 2008; Lensi, Cassano, Correddu, Ravagli, Kunovac, & Akiskal, 1996; Matsunaga et al., 2000; Tükel, Polat, Geng, Bozkurt, & Atla, 2004; Torresan et al., 2008).

Cross-cultural data regarding other OCSDs is generally limited to clinical populations, with very little epidemiological data available. The two studies examining the prevalence of BDD in Florence, Italy, and in a community sample of women in Boston, U.S., showed equivalent rates of 0.7 (Faravelli et al., 1997; Otto, Wilhelm, Cohen, Harlow, 2001). Remarkably consistent, albeit higher, rates (4%–5.3%) have been noted using self-report measures in student populations in Germany, the United States, and Turkey (Bohne, Keuthen, Wilhelm, Deckersbach, & Jenike, 2002; Cansever, Uzun, Dönmez, & Özşahin, 2003). It has been suggested, however, that cross-cultural differences may be present at a subclinical symptom level (e.g., body concerns were more prevalent among American relative to German students; Bohne et al., 2002) or in the aspects of the body representing the focus of concern (see Cansever et al., 2003; Phillips, McElroy, Keck, Pope, & Hudson, 1993). Earlier studies suggested that the disorder affected mainly women, or the studies were conducted on exclusively female samples. However, in their student sample, Bohne et al. recorded a 1:1 female to male ratio, which may reflect sociocultural and gender role influences on reporting of BDD concerns, with males more likely to disclose such concerns on a self-report measures. Further research is also required to establish the cross-cultural prevalence of the other OCSDs.

Overall, irrespective of the assessment instruments or methods used, the available cross-cultural epidemiological research suggests only slight variability across various geographic regions in the world, with somewhat lower prevalence rates in Far East Asia. However, there are considerable limitations in terms of variability in methodology (assessment tools, interviewers, mode of assessment), availability of reliable data from specific regions (Central Asia, Eastern Europe, Africa), or on specific disorders (e.g., BDD, TS, trichotillomania). The use of different

methodologies across studies makes comparisons difficult. For example, the use of lay interviewers has been suggested to inflate prevalence data due to overestimation of distress, and misinterpretation of concerns and worries as obsessions by the interviewers (Crino et al., 2005; Fontenelle, Mendlowicz, & Versiani, 2006). In a prevalence study using the CIDI administered by lay telephone interviewers, Stein and colleagues recorded the 1-month prevalence of OCD at 3.1%, relative to a much lower figure of 0.6% found after face-to-face interviews with professionals. In contrast, several studies employing the CIDI and lay interviewers have reported lower than general rates (e.g., Bijl et al., 1998; Grabe et el., 2001; Andrade, 2002), indicating that other factors may also play a role in influencing the prevalence estimations from such surveys.

In addition, a majority of the assessment measures have been developed in the English-speaking western countries (United States, United Kingdom) and may be culturally or linguistically inappropriate in other cultural contexts. For example, using the DIS and a design comparable to that in the ECA, a Puerto Rican study found a lifetime prevalence for OCD of 3%. However, this rate dropped to 1.1% in a subsequent study using a version of the DIS modified to account for cultural and linguistic factors, and including a more detailed examination of the differences between OCD symptoms and obsessive personality (Canino et al., 1987). The role of the diagnostic criteria employed is particularly pertinent, with studies using ICD criteria or specific hierarchical approaches (RDC) arriving at lower estimates of prevalence.

Therefore, the establishment and use of specific, standardized, internationally valid assessment methods are necessary to improve the validity and reliability of cross-cultural data regarding the OCSDs. Further, the paucity or absence of cross-cultural epidemiological data on some of the disorders in this group, including BDD, TS and trichotillomania, highlights the need for further studies using standardized international assessment methods. For those disorders where some data is available, such as in OCD, it is predominantly Western-centric, with little data for Central and South East Asia, Eastern and Southern Europe, and Africa. In addition, a large proportion of the available data is from metropolitan areas, which are more likely to be subject to globalization, thus minimizing culture-specific influences. The very few studies that have included rural samples suggest lower prevalence in these areas relative to urban areas (e.g., 0.3% in rural areas versus 0.9% in metropolitan areas in Taiwan; 2.2% versus 3.7% in Puerto Rico). Interestingly, the trend seems consistent across several geographic regions—possibly suggesting that urban versus rural factors may play a role in the prevalence of the disorders, or at least in the tendency to report them.

Similarly, only a few studies have examined differences between cultural groups within specific geographic regions. The ECA study reported slightly lower rates for OCD among Hispanics (1.8%) than Caucasians (2.4%) or African Americans (2.5%; Hollander, et al., 1998). A study examining only the Los Angeles site indicated that the prevalence seemed to increase with length of stay in United States, with U.S.-born Mexican Americans recording higher lifetime prevalence (2.4%) than Mexican immigrants (1.6%) but still lower than Caucasians (3.2%), suggesting a possible influence of cultural and environmental factors on prevalence. While the differences were nonsignificant, this line of research is important, as it provides a more fine-grained analysis of the role of specific cultural and environmental factors and their interaction in determining the prevalence of OCD.

Phenomenology across Cultures

While research on the prevalence of OCD across cultures shows some consistency, there is limited data about the influence of cultural factors on the form and content of OCD symptoms across cultures (Greenberg & Witztum, 1994). While Matsunaga et al. (2008) supported the transcultural stability in OCD symptom structure when examining 343 Japanese patients, there is a need for more such research across a range of cultures. As noted by de Silva (2006), the content of obsessions and compulsions may reflect common concerns within a culture. For example, contamination fears about asbestos in OCD patients in the United Kingdom, two to three decades ago, have been replaced in recent years by more contemporary concerns and contamination fears related to the theme of HIV/AIDS. Similarly, concerns in BDD tend to reflect sociocultural beauty and appearance ideals; so, for example, in an Australian sample, females with BDD were concerned with the appearance of their chest, waist, and legs, whereas males were concerned with thinning hair (Mancuso, Knoesen, & Castle, 2010). In contrast, in TD, a recent review concluded that Western presentations were relatively similar to those found in reports from Asia, the Far East, the Middle East, and Eastern Europe (Staley, Wand, & Shady, 1997). The investigation of the

interaction between culture and psychopathology may advance the understanding of the factors affecting nosological entities and their validity across cultures. In the area of OCSDs, and OCD in particular, cross-cultural research has focused on the interaction between religion, superstition, and specific belief/value systems. This research is reviewed in the following section.

Religion

To date, several empirical studies in specific cultural settings, investigating both clinical and nonclinical samples, have reported a link between the presentation of OCD and religion (Greenberg, 1984; Steketee et al., 1991). The epidemiology of OCD appears to be stable across many cultures (see above), and phenomenological studies of OCD also indicate that the core features of OCD (obsessions and compulsions) appear to be similar across cultures. However, some notable differences in the prevailing themes of obsessions and compulsions have been reported. For example, the prevalence rate of religious themes varies widely across different cultural settings. Religious OCD symptoms, often referred to as *scrupulosity*, are characterized by excessive concern about minor and trivial aspects of the religion, often to the exclusion of more important issues (Nelson et al., 2006). Obsessions may take the form of persistent doubts and fear about sin, blasphemy, and punishment from God, while compulsions may revolve around excessive religious behavior such as repeated praying and seeking reassurance about religious issues (Hepworth et al., 2010).

The prevalence of religious obsessions in clinical populations with OCD from the West, India, and Far East is reported to be 10% in the United States (Eisen et al., 1999), 5% in England (Dowson, 1977), 11% in India (Akhtar et al., 1975), and 7% in both Singapore (Chia, 1996) and Japan (Matsunaga et al., 2000). In contrast, a much higher rate is reported in studies from Muslim and Jewish cultures, with 60% of individuals with OCD having religious obsessions in Egypt (Okasha et al., 1994), 50% in Saudi Arabia (Mahgoub & Abdel-Hafeiz, 1991), 50% in Israel (Greenberg, 1984), and 40% in Bahrain (Shooka et al., 1998).

A number of cross-cultural studies seem to provide empirical evidence that supports the proposed link between religion and OCD. For example, Greenberg and Witzum (1994) reported that in their investigation of OC symptoms in 34 Israeli patients, 13 of the 19 ultra-orthodox patients exhibited symptoms related to religious practices, while such symptoms were reported in only one of the 15 non-ultra-orthodox subjects. The authors reported four main preoccupations of the religious symptoms: prayer, dietary practices, menstrual practices, and cleanliness before prayer.

In Egypt, Okasha et al. (1994) found that both obsessions and compulsions showed the influence of Islamic culture. The authors reported that in the 90 Egyptian patients studied, the most commonly occurring obsessions were religious and contamination obsessions (60%) and somatic obsessions (49%), and the most commonly occurring compulsions were repeating rituals (68%), cleaning and washing compulsions (63%), and checking compulsions (58%). The investigators compared the phenomenology of OCD in their Egyptian sample with that of 82 Indian, 45 English, and ten Israeli OCD patients. While the themes of obsessions in the Egyptian and Israeli patients were predominately concerned with religious matters related to cleanliness and hygiene, in the Indian and British samples, common themes were related to orderliness and aggressive issues. Similarly, in Saudi Arabia, also considered to be a conservative Muslim country, themes of obsessions are also frequently linked to religious practices (Mahgoub & Abdel-Hafeiz, 1991).

Ghassemzadeh et al. (2002) examined the content of symptoms in a sample of OCD patients in Iran. In their sample of 135 patients, recruited from three treatment settings, doubts and indecisiveness were found to be the most common obsessions, reported by 85% of patients, followed by obsessional slowness, reported by 69% of patients. The third and fourth most common obsessions in this sample were fear of impurity (62%) and fear of contamination (60%). Obsessions with self-impurity content were more common in women, whereas blasphemous thoughts and orderliness compulsions were found to be more common in men. The most common compulsions in the sample were washing (73%), which was almost twice as common in females as in their male counterparts (82% vs. 45%), and checking (78%). A similar pattern has been reported from Bahrain, another Middle Eastern country, where 43% of women compared to 23% of men had dirt and contamination obsessions and 46% of women compared to 31% of men had cleaning and washing compulsions (Shooka et al., 1998). Preliminary results from our ongoing study in Iran also support the importance of investigating religiosity and OCD symptom presentation in this population (Foroughi & Kyrios, in preparation).

Turkey, a secular state, with its geographical location spanning Eastern Europe and the Middle East, consists of both a liberal Muslim population as well as a more conservative and traditional group. Studies conducted in Turkey have reported contradictory results; for example, one study in western Turkey reported prevalence rates of religious themes similar to those found in Western studies (5%), despite the influence of Muslim culture (Egrilmez, Gulseren, Gulseren, & Kultur, 1997). Karadağ and colleagues (2006) also reported the presence of religious obsessions in only 20% of their sample of OCD patients from Denizli in western Turkey. On the other hand, Tek and Ulug (2001) examined a sample of Turkish OCD patients in Turkey's capital city, Ankara, and reported that 42% of the patients experienced religious obsessions. Although the highly religious patients tended to report more religious obsessions, there were no significant differences in the overall symptom severity of the obsessions and compulsions across the groups of patients with and without religious obsessions. In an earlier study in Ankara, Tek and colleagues again reported a high frequency of OCD patients (48%) suffering from religious obsessions (see Tek & Ulug, 2001). Finally, in Eastern Turkey, 34% of participants reported religious obsessions—the second most common obsessive theme after dirt and contamination (Tezkan & Millet, 1997; cited in Tek & Ulug, 2001). It should also be noted that some dirt and contamination obsessions may reflect religious concerns related to issues of purity within the Muslim culture. Karadağ et al. (2006) propose that the discrepancy in the reported prevalence rates of religious obsessions in Turkish studies may be due to the influence of diverse sociocultural factors in various sites of the studies, suggesting that the prevalence rate may increase as you travel eastward, reflecting the more conservative and religious society in eastern Turkey.

A preponderance of OCD symptoms with contamination and cleaning themes have been reported in Hindu patients in clinical studies from India; such findings are seen as being congruent with the emphasis that the Hindu religion places on issues of purity and cleanliness, and the presence of a variety of purification rituals in that religion (Chaturvedi, 1993; Khanna & Channabasavanna, 1988). Similarly, in Nepal, a predominantly Hindu nation, themes of obsessions are often related to religious practices (Sharma, 1968). In contrast, Chia (1996) examined a large clinical sample consisting of a Chinese majority in Singapore, and found that there was no association between religiosity and symptom severity or presentation in these individuals diagnosed with OCD.

Studies have also revealed that in religions emphasizing rituals, OC symptoms more often take the form of rituals, whereas in religions where purity of thought and the equation of thought and action is inferred, OC symptoms take a more cognitive form, and revolve around intrusive blasphemous obsessions. For example, Jewish religious teachings and practices are markedly ritualistic in nature. Everyday life is governed by a large number of laws, as stipulated in the Jewish Code of Law, or *Shulchan Aruch* (Haggai, Masser-Kavitzky, & Gross-Isseroff, 2003). The Jewish religious law emphasizes cleanliness, personal hygiene, exactness, and allows for repetition, providing the individual with OCD with another potential arena for the expression of their symptoms (Greenberg & Witztum, 1994). Islam is also a very ritualistic religion; contamination themes and cleaning rituals are also dominant in Islamic practice, where each prayer is preceded by a ritualistic cleansing process (*El woodoo* or ablution), which requires several parts of the body to be washed in a fixed order, and for a specific number of times. Therefore, while the rituals revolve around contamination and cleaning themes, they are tangled with issues of religious contamination and purity, which usually manifest as a fear of spiritual impurity. Okasha et al. (1994) also noted that there were similarities between the contents of obsessions in Muslim and Jewish samples. Thus, the content of OCD symptoms may be influenced by the more salient aspects of the religious teachings (i.e., observance of rules, hygiene) emphasized in each religion, regardless of the patient's religious affiliation.

In addition, religion has been linked to maladaptive beliefs and appraisals relevant to OCD, as well as OCD symptom presentation (Abramowtiz et al., 2004; Nelson et al., 2006). According to Rachman (1997); "people who are taught, or learn, that all their value-laden thoughts are of significance will be more prone to obsessions—as in particular types of religious beliefs and instructions" (p. 798). Recent studies have suggested that, perhaps due to the differences in religious doctrines and teachings, the relationship between religiosity and OC-related cognitions might differ among various religions, or even across different religious denominations. For example, Protestant Christianity places greater importance on the individual's beliefs, intentions, or motivations, than on the observance of rituals. Therefore, it would be plausible to suggest that increased concern about the importance of thoughts, thought control, and morality related thought–action fusion (the belief that bad thoughts are morally equivalent to bad actions), would play a greater role in the religious cognitive world of a Christian (Zohar et al., 2005). Rassin and Koster (2003) found that Protestants showed a greater tendency to believe that their thoughts were morally equivalent to actions (i.e., moral thought–action fusion) compared to Catholics, atheists, and members of other religions. Moreover, this cognitive bias was more strongly related to OCD symptoms among Protestants than among other religious groups. Similarly, Siev and Cohen (2007) reported that religiosity was associated with TAF in their Christian sample. This association was not replicated in their Jewish sample, which showed lower levels of morality-related TAF in comparison to their Christian counterparts.

Partial support for this premise is also provided by Abramowitz et al. (2002), who developed an inventory of religious OC symptoms (scrupulosity) and administered it to a sample of American college students. They found that highly devout participants scored higher on the two scales of the inventory, fear of sin and fear of God's punishment. However, highly devout Christians obtained higher scores on both scale scores than highly devout Jews, suggesting that the components of obsessive religiosity examined by the inventory may be culture-specific.

In addition, Sica et al. (2002a) found that Italian Catholics with a high or moderate degree of religiosity showed higher scores on measures of obsessionality and OCD-related cognitions, such as overimportance of thoughts, control of thoughts, perfectionism, and responsibility, relative to less religious Catholics. Measures of control of thoughts and the overimportance of thoughts were associated with OCD symptoms only in religious subjects. However, it has been noted that the mean OCD score in the highly religious group in this study was lower than normative data for nonclinical groups reported in other studies (Huppert, Siev, & Kushner, 2007). Therefore, overall, these studies indicate that both religious affiliations and strength of devotion are associated with the presentation of obsessive compulsive symptoms, as well as beliefs and assumptions presumed to underlie the development and maintenance of these symptoms in cognitive models (e.g., thought–action fusion, importance of thoughts).

In a recent cross-cultural study, Yorulmaz and colleagues (2009) compared the relationship between religiosity and OC symptoms and cognitions in

Muslim and Christian student samples from Turkey and Canada. The results indicated that overall, the Muslim participants obtained higher scores on OCD symptoms, and more strongly endorsed beliefs about the importance of and need to control intrusive thoughts. However, regardless of religious affiliation, highly religious participants evidenced more obsessional thoughts and checking, reported more concern about the importance of thoughts and the need for controlling them, as well as endorsing more thought–action fusion in the morality domain. The participants' degree of religiosity was found to contribute to a significant difference on morality-related thought–action fusion in the Christian sample only. As with previous findings, highly religious Christians were more likely to engage in moral thought–action fusion, in comparison to less religious Christians. Based on these findings, the authors concluded that religiosity is a relevant issue for OCD in both Islam and Christianity, although the characteristics of the religion may mediate the nature of this association.

In another study from a Muslim country, Naziry et al. (2005) examined the association of nonadaptive religious beliefs (pertaining to cleansing and hygiene codes) with the severity of OCD symptoms, in an Iranian sample of 43 OCD patients with predominately washing compulsions. The authors reported a significant positive association between these nonadaptive religious beliefs and the severity of the OCD symptoms. In addition, the nonadaptive religious beliefs measure was a better predictor of the severity of OCD symptoms than other variables, such as OC-related cognitive beliefs as measured by the Beliefs Inventory (BI), and guilt feelings. Furthermore, the researchers did not find any significant association between the individual's level of religious commitment (e.g., participation in religious ceremonies) and the severity of the OCD symptoms. The authors argued that the individual with OCD is influenced by their faulty or ill-informed preconceived ideas about religious hygiene and washing codes, rather than their level of religious commitment. Naziry et al. (2005) strongly recommended the inclusion of religion as an important cultural factor in OCD research, and suggested that the identification of the patient's dysfunctional beliefs about religion and its codes of conduct need to be incorporated in the formulation of treatment plans.

Although there is an emerging body of research that supports a link between religiosity and OCD, the need for data from a greater number of countries, along with the relatively small sample sizes in many of the studies and differences in the assessment tools and measures used, all make it difficult to draw unequivocal conclusions about the nature of the relationship between religiosity and OCD (Sica, Novara, Sanavio, Dorz, & Coradeschi, 2002b). To date, there is little support for the notion that religiosity increases rates of OCD per se, though the converging evidence suggests that the presentation of OCD symptoms and OCD-related cognitions may be influenced by religion.

Superstition

In addition to religion, another cultural factor that may play a role in OCD is superstition. Superstitious beliefs and behaviors have been found in a diverse range of cultures for thousands of years (Jahoda, 1969), and surveys show that these beliefs continue to flourish in modern times, even among educated people in Western countries. In fact, in some societies, superstition is a widespread and accepted attitude in mainstream culture (de Silva, 2006). We can see similar beliefs reflected in Western cultures, such as in the popularity of herbal supplements taken in order to avoid illness, despite no evidence for the effectiveness of many of the products (Aeschleman, Rosen & Williams, 2003). Superstitious beliefs are a form of magical thinking, and may serve to increase the individual's sense of control or feelings of self-efficacy where no other avenue exists. Magical thinking has been defined as (a) the belief that thoughts, words, or actions can serve to control situations through rules that are outside of normal cultural concepts of scientific effect or transfer of information (see Bolton, Dearsley, Madronal-Luque, & Baron-Cohen, 2002; Zusne & Jones, 1989); or (b) the transfer of energy or information between physical systems solely because of their similarity or contiguity in time and space (Zusne & Jones, 1989).

Superstition is regarded as a maladaptive coping strategy, and has been reported to be associated with various forms of maladjustment. For example, positive correlations have been reported between superstitiousness and general psychopathology (Dag, 1999; Tobacyk, Backman, & Maija, 1992), between an external locus of control and decreased levels of self-efficacy (Tobacyk & Shrader, 1991; Tobacyk, Nagot, & Miller, 1988), and between trait-anxiety and dissociative experiences (Wolfradt, 1997). Due to the similarity between some superstitious manifestations and OCD phenomena (e.g. rituals, magical thinking, the belief that specific thoughts can directly influence the relevant external event), studies have examined the connections between superstition and OCD (for discussion, see Moulding & Kyrios, 2006).

Leonard et al. (1990) conducted semistructured interviews with a group of 38 OCD patients (children) and their matched controls. They reported no differences between OCD and normal control groups in the frequency of childhood superstitions, and the authors concluded superstition did not show any etiological significance in the development of OCD. However, a recent experimental study in Israel found that individuals high in OC symptoms are more likely than individuals with low OC symptoms to develop the illusion that they can control an objectively uncontrollable experimental task, with similar differences between OCD and non-OCD samples (Reuven-Magril, Dar, & Liberman, 2008). Frost et al. (1993) administered a measure of both superstitious beliefs and behaviors, and measures of obsessive and compulsive symptom and OC- related cognitions (perfectionism and responsibility) to a sample of U.S. female college students. They found that superstition measures were correlated with total compulsiveness, compulsive checking, and with both perfectionism and responsibility, but not with compulsive cleaning/washing. Furthermore, the correlations between superstition and cognitive measures (i.e., perfectionism and responsibility) were larger than the correlations between superstition and OC symptoms, suggesting that superstition might be more closely associated with obsessional thoughts than compulsive behaviors.

Zebb and Moore (2003) replicated and extended these findings in their sample of 191 U.S. undergraduate students. The authors found additional evidence for a relationship between measures of superstition and obsessive compulsive symptoms in nonclinical individuals. However, they indicated that this relationship was not exclusive; superstition was also significantly associated with other forms of psychopathology, such as general psychological distress, and measures corresponding to other anxiety disorders, such as agoraphobia and social phobia. An interesting finding of this study was that this pattern of relationship was exclusive to females, suggesting the need to further investigate gender differences in this area.

In a recent Italian study by Sica et al. (2002b), 258 students completed a series of measures assessing superstition, obsessive compulsive cognitions and symptoms, depression, anxiety, and worry. After controlling for anxiety and depression, highly superstitious participants scored higher than the low-superstitious group on measures of overestimation of threat, impaired mental control, contamination, and worry. A logistic regression analysis revealed that two cognitive domains, as measured by the Obsessive Beliefs Questionnaire (OBQ) (i.e., overestimation of threat and perfectionism), discriminated high from low superstitious participants over and above anxiety and depression. The authors concluded that superstition seemed to play a role in OCD phenomenology, in particular with obsessional symptoms.

Due to the limited number of studies in this area, the influence of superstition on OCD etiology requires further examination. More research is needed in order to obtain a better understanding of the influence of superstition on OC symptoms and cognitions, in both clinical and nonclinical samples across various cultures. It has been hypothesized that some OCD behaviors (e.g., behavioral or mental rituals) may cause less distress in cultures where they are considered culturally congruent or acceptable (Sica et al., 2002c). However, given the stability of prevalence across cultures, the increased acceptance of superstition in certain cultures does not seem to lead to increased overall rates of OCD, although it may be that superstition is present but only in more subtle forms in some Western countries.

Beliefs

An implicit assumption underlying current cognitive models is that OCD and the OCSDs are influenced by the same cognitions across different cultures, although most cognitive research has been undertaken in Western, English-speaking cultures. If there is consistency across cultures in the interrelationship between cognitions and OCD/OCSD symptoms, there would be greater confidence in the applicability to non-English settings of cognitive-behavior therapy that was developed in the West (Kyrios, Sanavio, Bhar & Liguori, 2001). However, it is to be expected that culture may differentially influence the form of the beliefs that are thought to be relevant to the OCSDs and OCD (see Sica, et al., 2002b). Even within Western cultures, obsessional beliefs are not always reported by all OCD patients (Taylor et al., 2006).

The evidence that beliefs in the OCD model will relate similarly to symptoms in non-English-speaking samples is fairly limited (see also the previous discussion of the relationship between religiosity and OCD-related cognitions). Julien et al. (2008) investigated the factor structure of the 44-item version of the OBQ in a French-speaking sample

(Montreal and Quebec City, Canada; Lyon, France). The OBQ is an instrument developed to measure the belief domains theorized to be relevant to OCD (importance and control of thoughts; responsibility and threat; perfectionism and the need for certainty). While the original three-factor model did not fit adequately using confirmatory methods, they found a similar structure of the questionnaire to the English-speaking version, using an exploratory factor analysis. The total scale, and two of three subscales, differentiated OCD participants from anxiety and nonclinical controls, with all scales differentiating the OCD and nonclinical controls over and above depression. The scales also correlated highly with self-report OCD symptoms measured on the Padua Inventory, with correlations between subscales ranging from 0.14 (perfectionism with impulse phobia) to 0.52 (responsibility/threat with rumination).

In an earlier study, Kyrios et al. (2001) examined the interrelationships between OCD symptoms and three cognition and affect-related measures assessing responsibility, perfectionism, and guilt, in university student samples in Italy and Australia. They found similar factor structures for the measures across the cultures. Supporting the cross-cultural generalizability of the OCD model, there were little differences in the pattern of interrelationships between symptoms and affect/cognitions (responsibility, perfectionism, guilt) across the cohorts. The few notable differences included the higher-magnitude associations between self-oriented perfectionism and symptoms in the Australian sample, and relatively stronger relationships between OCD urges/worries and affective/cognitive variables in the Australian sample. The authors suggested that self-oriented perfectionism may play a greater role in the more individualized Australian culture, while urges/impulses may be seen as less problematic in the Italian context due to greater levels of acceptance within the Italian culture.

Sica, Taylor, Arrindell and Sanavio (2006) examined the original 87-item version of the OBQ in 46 Greek students, 348 Italian students. and 73 U.S. students. While beliefs were correlated with symptoms in all three groups, there were differences in the patterns of association. In all three groups, the correlation between the OBQ scales and obsessionality (PI impaired control) was large, while correlations between the OBQ scales and PI urges scale were medium. However, the relationship of beliefs to checking and contamination changed by sample, being unrelated in the Greek sample,

moderately related in the Italian sample, and highly related in the U.S. sample. Although limited by the small sample size of Greek students, the authors interpreted these results as indicating some cultural specificity regarding the relationship between pathological belief and OCD symptoms. For example, they suggest that a high level of uncertainty avoidance (and associated powerlessness) characterizes the Greek participants, and may attenuate the relationship between the beliefs and symptoms. They further suggested that, while results generally supported the cognitive model, some culture-specific modifications may be necessary.

In a clinical study, Sica et al. (2004) examined the original 6-domain version of the Obsessive Beliefs Questionnaire in groups with OCD, GAD, and nonclinical controls in Italy. They found that intolerance of uncertainty, control of thoughts, and perfectionism differentiated all three groups, whereas threat did not differentiate the GAD and OCD groups, and the importance of thoughts and perfectionism were not higher in the GAD group versus the student controls. They suggest that the cognitive construct of responsibility "appears to have less relevance in non–Anglo-Saxon or Anglo-Celtic cultures" (p. 305), while the importance of thoughts may be relevant only in a subgroup with particular features, such as religious obsessions (Sica et al., 2004).

Findings from studies investigating the relevance of the proposed belief systems in the Middle East have returned conflicting findings. In two studies investigating the factor structure and specificity of OBQ to OCD patients, Shams et al. (2004; 2007) found support for the three subscales, although only the importance/control of thoughts subscale was specific to OCD, with no significant differences between OCD patients and anxiety controls on responsibility/threat estimation and perfectionism/intolerance of uncertainty. In their sample of OCD patients with predominately cleaning and washing symptoms, Naziry et al. (2005) reported a negative association between dysfunctional cognitive beliefs, as measured by the Beliefs Inventory (BI), and OC symptoms. Ghassemzadeh et al. (2005) found significant differences between OCD patients and anxiety and healthy controls on the Responsibility Attitudes Scale (RAS) and Responsibility Interpretation Questionnaire (RIQ). The authors suggested that the findings indicate the need to consider the inclusion of responsibility in theoretical formulations and treatment programs of OCD in Iran. Foroughi, Shams, and Kyrios (2007) examined the psychometric properties and cross-cultural utility of a Thought–Action Fusion (TAF) scale in Iranian OCD and nonclinical samples, and found remarkable similarities in the factor structure and psychometric properties with previous research in Western samples. Pourfaraj et al. (2008) also reported a positive correlation between the TAF construct and OC symptoms in a large sample of university students in Iran. However, other studies have suggested that there may be cross-cultural differences in the pattern of correlations between TAF factors and the OCD symptoms, with cultural features such as religious affiliation contributing to some of the differences (Yorulmaz, Yilmaz, & Gencoz, 2004; Yorulmaz, Gencoz, & Woody, 2009).

In sum, there has only been a limited investigation of the differential importance of OCD beliefs across cultures. However, that which exists, perhaps not surprisingly, suggests that the belief domains may have differential importance within different settings and with different patients. Furthermore, some domains may be more influenced by cultural context than others, particularly domains that are more greatly related to social context (responsibility) and to religious perceptions (importance and control of thoughts).

There is even less research on the cross-cultural relevance of beliefs highlighted in models of other disorders. However, it is likely that similar limitations apply, and similar considerations should be attempted as with OCD when transporting Western models to other settings. For example, current cognitive models of BDD highlight sociocultural norms as crucial in the pathology; the individual perceives himself or herself to be unattractive or inadequate relative to the societal ideal, with self-worth being dependent upon their perceptions of their own attractiveness (Rosen, Reiter & Orosan, 1995; Veale, 2001). Such ideals of physical attractiveness would differ across cultures and subcultures (e.g., Cogan, Bhalla, Sefa-Dedeh, & Rothblum, 1996), with possible differences resulting in levels of preoccupation with deficits and types of perceived deficits. For example, Bohne et al. (2002) found that body image concerns and preoccupations were higher in a small sample of U.S. versus German students, although levels of "probable BDD" remained the same. It is plausible that, given the cultural dependency of aspects of the models of BDD, some alteration to fit alternative cultures may be warranted.

In sum, what is missing from the literature is a substantial understanding of cross-cultural differences in the processes leading from the experience of common intrusive phenomena, to obsessional and compulsive symptoms. There appear to be cross-cultural differences in the associations between specific beliefs and specific symptoms, but there is little understanding of cultural influences in what constitutes an unwanted intrusion, reactions that occur in response to the unwanted intrusions, and the functional value of such responses. Just as cognitive therapists need to be sensitive to the variable importance of beliefs and responses in individuals, they should also be aware of cultural influences on the associations between such variables.

Treatment Outcomes across Cultures

Little direct research has compared treatment outcomes for OCSDs across cultures. Regarding OCD, most controlled treatment trials have been conducted in the United States and United Kingdom, mostly with white adults. For example, Rosa-Alcázar et al. (2008) recently conducted a meta-analysis of controlled psychological treatment trials for adult OCD, where articles were published in English, Spanish, or French (see Table 26.2). Of the 19 trials included, 10 were in the United States or Canada, three in the United Kingdom; two in Australia, and one each in the Netherlands, Norway, Brazil, and Japan (Rosa-Alcázar, Sánchez-Meca, Gómez-Conesa & Marín-Martínez, 2008). It is of note that those treatment trials outside the U.K./U.S. do appear to demonstrate large effect sizes, although that could be biased by the relatively small sample sizes in such studies. Nakatani et al. (2005) conducted one of the few randomized controlled trials of behavior therapy in a non-Western country, treating 31 OCD patients in Japan. Patients were assigned to behavior therapy and pill placebo, fluvoxamine plus "autogenic training" (relaxation training serving as psychological placebo), or autogenic training and pill placebo (control group). The two active groups showed more improvement than the control group, while the behavior therapy was superior to medication alone. Patients with lower baseline symptoms, past major depression, and no cleaning compulsions improved more with fluvoxamine.

There have been fewer examinations still of the treatment effects in OCD patients from minority cultures. However, case reports and smaller studies are promising. For example, Huppert et al. (2007) report that, from their caseload of 12 ultra-orthodox Jews in the United States, 9 were considered improved or very much improved, while only 2 had dropped out of treatment. Similarly, Freidman et al. (2003)

Table 26.2 Psychological treatment trials for OCD included in Rosa-Alcázar et al.'s (2008) meta-analysis

Study	Treatment	d (SE)	N^c	Location	Ethnicity
Black et al. (1998)	ERP + CR	1.425 (0.530)	18	Iowa, US	Not Stated
Cordioli et al. (2003)	ERP + CR	1.068 (0.319)	45	Brazil	Not stated
Fals-Stewart et al. (1993)	ERP	0.924 (0.270)	61	US	Not stated
	ERP	0.909 (0.269)			
Fineberg et al. (2005)	ERP + CR	0.281 (0.368)	34	UK	Not stated
Foa et al. (2005)	ERP	1.646 (0.362)	41	Philadelphia & NY, US	84% Caucasian 4% Asian
				Winnipeg, Canada	4% Latino 3% African American 4% Not known
Freeston et al. (1997)	ERP + CR	1.007 (0.394)	29	Quebec, Canada	100% French speaking Caucasian
Greist et al. (2002)	ERP	0.996 (0.193)	121	US and Canada	Not stated
	ERP	0.731 (0.188)	121		
Jones & Menzies (1998)	CR	1.882 (0.525)	21	Sydney, Australia	Not stated
Kozak, Liebowitz, & Foa (2000)	ERP	1.082 (0.399)	29	US	77% White 3% African American 4% Hispanic 2% Asian 4% Native American 9% Unavailable
Lindsay et al. (1997)	ERP	2.326 (0.610)	18	Sydney, Australia	Not stated
Lovell et al. (1994)	ERP	-0.229 (.579)	12	UK	Not stated
Marks et al. (1980)	ERP	0.191 (0.448)	20	UK	Not stated
McLean et al. (2001)	CR	0.980 (0.309)	51	Canada	78% European Canadian 17% Asian 2% First Nations 2% Other
	ERP	1.620 (0.346)	49		
Nakatani et al. (2005)	ERP	2.997 (0.689)	18	Japan	Not stated
O'Connor et al. (1999)	ERP + CR	0.860 (0.603)	12	Quebec, Canada	Not stated
O'Connor et al. (2006)	ERP + CR	1.494 (0.506)	20	Quebec, Canada	Not stated
Taylor et al. (2003)	ERP + CR	0.597 (0.405)	26	British Columbia, Canada	91% Caucasian 9% Other
Van Balkom et al. (1998)a	CR	0.674 (0.349)	35	Netherlands	Not stated
	ERP	0.490 (0.344)	35		
Vogel et al. (2004)	ERP	3.780 (0.868)	15	Norway	Not stated
	ERP + CR	1.590 (0.527)	19		

Note: N^c is number in comparison of psychological therapy versus control group. Demographic percentages may reflect total sample in study rather than those in specific comparison. Where not stated in article, location derived from author affiliations. ERP=Exposure and Response prevention; CR=cognitive restructuring. d = Cohen's d; SE = standard error. Treatment information, number of participants in comparison, and effect size sourced from the respective study. See Rosa-Alcázar et al. (2008) for more information.

report a naturalistic trial with 62 outpatients with OCD in Brooklyn, including 15 African American and 11 Caribbean American patients. They found that the black participants were more likely to be female and to have been initially diagnosed with panic disorder only, relative to the white participants, despite the use of OCD screening questions in a structured interview at intake. At post-treatment, both groups improved moderately and significantly, with no effect of ethnicity.

Help-Seeking Behaviors and Misdiagnosis in Minority Groups

One issue of note is that help-seeking behaviors, and the reliability of diagnosis of OCD, may differ across cultures, and even with respect to minority cultures within Western countries. For example, Williams et al. (1998) cite more general research suggesting that in the United States, African Americans are less likely to seek treatment in psychiatric settings, rather preferring to see a minister or a physician, or to visit the emergency room in a crisis situation. Individuals may also present to alternative settings for treatment. For instance, Neal-Barnett et al. (2000) interviewed a sample of 39 African American hair care professionals in the United States. On the basis of their reports and records, they suggested that 21 of their customers appeared to meet general criteria for trichotillomania. Friedman et al. (1993) found that in a sample of African American dermatology patients, 15% met diagnosis of OCD, a significantly higher rate than expected in a general medical population (2%–3%).

With respect to help-seeking behavior, Goodwin et al. (2002) report on U.S. participants who were screened in the 1996 National Anxiety Disorders Screening Day. On this day, participants presented for screening following advertisements in various media outlets. They viewed a video that dramatized the symptoms of a number of disorders, including OCD, before completing a questionnaire and seeing a mental health professional for final diagnosis. They note that of the 15,606 participants presenting for screening, about one-fifth (3,069) met criteria for OCD. Participants with OCD were likely to be younger, male and white, and less likely to be married. They found that access to some form of mental health treatment for OCD was heavily influenced by age (older), gender (female) and race (Caucasian). Thus, "while readiness for treatment was a consistent and significant predictor of treatment, race and age are just as powerful determinants of access to care." (p. 148)

Even when presenting for treatment, individuals with OCD from minority groups may be misdiagnosed. Friedman et al. (2003) reported that, of 62 outpatients with OCD at an inner-city clinic in Brooklyn, 39% of African Americans versus 14% of Caucasian participants received an initial (mis)diagnosis of panic disorder. Hatch, Friedman and Paradis (1996) suggest that, as African Americans with affective disorders are more often misdiagnosed with schizophrenia, those with OCD in this population may be particularly susceptible to this misdiagnosis due to the often bizarre rituals within the disorder.

Treatment and Assessment Issues
Culture and Assessment

During assessment, it is important to note that cultural differences can also influence the responses of patients to questionnaire assessments. Kyrios et al. (1996) commented on the range of mean scores on the Padua Inventory, a 60-item inventory of OCD (Sanavio, 1988), across Australian, U.S., Dutch, and Italian nonclinical cohorts. They argued that a range of cultural factors could influence responses on questionnaire measures of OCD, including response styles, the distress caused by obsessive compulsive phenomena, and social perceptions of obsessive compulsive symptoms. They also cautioned against the use of assessment inventories with cohorts where normative data is not available.

Indeed, most self-report instruments have not been normed on ethnic minority samples, and this may influence the responses that are given. Thomas et al. (2000) found that black U.S. university students (N=214) scored almost one standard deviation higher than white students (N=1633) on the Maudsley Obsessional Compulsive Inventory (MOCI), a 30-item true/false self-report measure of OCD symptoms. However, while high scores on the measure were associated with greater diagnoses of OCD in the white population (obtained by interview methods), this was not the case in the black population. That is, while the black population endorsed more MOCI items, this was not associated with greater levels of OCD.

More recently, responses of black (N=105) and white (N=582) participants were compared on an online version of the Padua Inventory (Williams, Turkheimer, Schimdt, & Oltmanns, 2005). In this study, there were no overall differences between the samples on mean responses, but the black participants were more likely to endorse the contamination subscale. Specific item-level differences were also found, over and above mean scale differences. For example, black participants were more likely to endorse items that they feel are dirty after touching an animal, that they return home to check doors/windows, that they check letters before posting, that they feel the need to read passages more than once, that they are late because they keep on doing things more often than necessary, and that unwanted obscene words come into their minds and are hard to dismiss. White participants over-endorsed feeling dirty after touching money, and impulses to tear their clothes off in public.

The authors speculate that differences in cultural norms may underlie such differences; for example, they suggest that black individuals are less likely to own pets than white participants (Williams, Turkheimer, Magee, & Guterbock, 2008). In addition, differences may be due to a self-presentation bias, where black individuals may over-endorse certain items to counter negative stereotypes. Studies have found that priming racial salience through administering a measure of identification with ethnic background increases the Padua-contamination scores of black, but not white, participants (Williams et al., 2008).

In sum, overall levels of endorsement of OCD symptom levels on screening instruments and questionnaires is likely to be affected by cultural factors. Furthermore, differential endorsement of particular items and subscales within such measures may also be influenced by cultural schemas, and the accessibility of those schemas. Such differences are likely to be emphasized in situations where racial identity is an issue, for example, when a majority-culture therapist treats a minority-culture client.

Religious Factors in Treatment

While the role of religion as a factor in the form or prevalence of OCD has not been fully ascertained (see above), that religious beliefs can influence cognitive behavioral treatment is beyond question. OCD is a disorder where repugnant or immoral thoughts are a salient issue, with the perceptions about immorality influenced by religious beliefs. Furthermore, religious issues may also affect factors such as the therapeutic relationship, what is and is not permissible in terms of behavioral strategies within treatment, and judgments about responsibility for treatment outcome.

Within treatment, it is important for the therapeutic relationship that, rather than blame a client's religious beliefs for their OCD, the therapist be cognizant of how a client's religious beliefs influence the manifestation of OCD. Consistent with recent theories about the importance of sensitivity to particular intrusive phenomena on the basis of individual's beliefs and experiences (Doron & Kyrios, 2005; Doron, Kyrios & Moulding, 2007; Doron, Moulding, Kyrios & Nedeljkovic, 2008), it is likely that OCD manifests itself in the most important areas of an individual's life (Purdon, 2004; Huppert et al., 2007) and, in many instances, religion defines an individual's construction of their experiences and their behavioral motivations. For instance, orthodox Jews may particularly fear experiencing repugnant obsessions on Yom Kippur, as this may preclude them gaining atonement and therefore from entering the "book of life" for the coming year (Paradis, Friedman, Hatch & Ackerman, 1996).

Difficulties in treating highly religious patients with OCD lie in framing therapy so that the client does not feel he or she is being asked to commit a sin. For example, asking a patient with sexual intrusive thoughts to expose themselves to these thoughts may be taken as asking them to defy their religious principles. In such cases, it is important to work with the patient to understand the limits of religiously acceptable behavior—so as to "create situations that violate OCD law, but not religious law" (Huppert et al., 2007; p. 932). It is also important that the patient clearly understands the rationale for treatment, and the therapist works to enhance motivation for undergoing exposure. It is not that the therapist is trying to eliminate religion; indeed, OCD can be framed as a barrier to the patient having a positive spiritual life—however, patients may excessively rely on rituals and rules rather than trusting their knowledge and soul (Huppert et al., 2007). Involvement of the client's spiritual leader can be important in establishing the acceptable guidelines for religious practice, for instance in ascertaining the normal frequency of praying (de Silva, 2006; Purdon, 2004) and in teaching the client and therapist the correct interpretation of religious laws related to the patient's rituals and to therapy (Paradis et al., 1996). Involvement can also serve to prevent the religious leader from unintentionally becoming a source of (obsessive) reassurance for the patient (Huppert et al., 2007).

Purdon (2004) noted that the difference between religious observance and religious obsession lies in the sense of certainty; if one is uncertain that one has committed a sin, then one cannot be held as responsible for that sin. In therapy, Purdon suggested prohibiting the client from questioning reality on the basis of doubt—the intrusion "Maybe I have committed a sin" cannot be allowed to lead to the question "Am I certain I did not sin?" Conversely, rituals can be framed within the certainty spectrum—one is not asking the patient to sin, but to tolerate a *small possibility that they may* sin (Huppert et al., 2007). Thus, techniques that put the behavior in perspective may be useful. For instance, where would the feared accidental violation lie, relative to deliberate violations of religious law (e.g., buying a bacon cheeseburger from a fast-food restaurant, for those religions that prohibit eating of meat/bacon; Huppert et al., 2007).

Greenberg and Witztum (2001) note additional factors that may assist in the discrimination between religion and obsession. First, compulsive law exceeds and may disregard the requirement of religious law. Second, compulsive behavior usually concentrates on specific areas and does not reflect an overall concern for religious practice. Third, the choice of obsessional area reflects general symptom themes within OCD, such as cleaning and checking. Fourth, the patient may neglect other areas of life as they focus specifically on one area, for example, having to omit sections of prayers due to the time spent washing. Finally, the patient repeats rituals because of doubt alone, whereas religious codes often prohibit or discourage the repetition of rituals.

Other Culture-Related Factors in Treatment

Discussion of issues in the treatment of nonwhite patients has been limited. With respect to the treatment of minority cultures, Williams et al. (1998) present two cases of African American individuals that attended a behavioral treatment in Washington, D.C. While many issues were common to the white and black clients, culture did affect treatment presentation. For example, one client with washing obsessions also believed that if she touched a spot that had been touched by another, that person would gain the power to "put the root" (or cast a spell) on her. While such beliefs were common to the particular cultural group, they could potentially lead to misdiagnosis of psychosis when the therapist is from a different culture and unknowledgeable about the patient group.

In addition, the minority culture clients were more sensitive to judgments about having the disorder, experiencing greater shame due to symptoms (Williams et al., 1998). Such reactions led to difficulties in treatment, as the clients were reluctant to undergo exposure in public, and even to reveal their problems. The patients also felt more isolated as individuals with OCD *and* as members of a minority

culture. Hatch et al. (1996) report similar increased reluctance among black compared to white clients attending treatment, with the patients taking much longer even to admit to OCD symptoms. Hatch et al. recommend using a structured interview during psychiatric intake to help overcome reticence by patients in reporting symptoms.

Due to such secrecy, Hatch et al. (1996) found that patients with OCD were extremely reluctant to involve their family in treatment, and their families were also less likely to be drawn into assisting patients with their compulsions. They suggested coaching the client on how to convey such information, rather than the therapist seeking meetings. However, when the family is involved, they may be extremely tolerant of the patient's OCD activities. They suggested that the therapist should expect resistance when broaching family involvement, consider abandoning such ideas if the resistance is too strong, and to perhaps involve a friend or neighbor instead of a family member so as to lower such resistance.

A further issue in therapy pertains to patient–therapist matching in terms of ethnic background. For example, will ethnic minorities disclose symptoms to therapists from the majority ethnic background? Will different backgrounds lead to a poorer therapeutic alliance? Finally, will therapists misinterpret symptoms reported by clients from different backgrounds? Karlsson (2005) conducted a recent review of the more general literature on ethnic matching. He noted that while archival studies of hospital records suggested greater dropouts and shorter length of treatment when client and therapist were of dissimilar ethnicity, due to the nature of the studies it is difficult to establish the reason for this. In contrast, actual studies of psychotherapy found no effect on outcome due to ethnic matching. Based on clinical experience, Hatch et al. (1996) suggested that the issue of culture or race may need to be discussed when therapists from the majority culture work with clients from minority cultures. They consider it the therapist's responsibility to raise the issue of cultural and ethnic incongruity, in order to enhance the therapeutic alliance and uncover any destructive beliefs that the client may hold about the relationship (e.g., "You can't understand what it's like to be on public assistance"; p. 313).

Conclusion

This chapter has reviewed evidence relevant to the cross-cultural aspects of the OCSDs, with a particular focus upon OCD. It discussed cross-national prevalence rates, as well as difficulties pertaining to such assessments in terms of variability in methods of assessment and diagnostic criteria across studies. Differences in phenomenology were discussed, including the importance of various culturally specific constructs in the disorder. These included the influence of religion on the presentation of OCD, and the acceptability of superstition across cultures in relationship to OCD. The under-researched issue of whether beliefs theorized to be relevant to the disorders are constant across cultures was broached. The chapter discussed the dearth of research on the relationship between culture and treatment outcomes. In the final part of the chapter, the relevance of cultural factors to the treatment setting was discussed, with an emphasis on the treatment of minority cultures. This included issues such as the relationship between minority group membership and decreased help-seeking behavior, as well as increased misdiagnosis. We discussed the importance of taking culture into account when utilizing assessment instruments, and when treating highly religious clients or clients with religious obsessions. Broader issues were also discussed, such as the importance of the therapist being culturally knowledgeable, and the issue of therapist–client matching.

Future Directions

Questions for further study include the following:

• Which cultural factors influence responses on measures of OCD and OCSD symptoms, and how can we attain a more reliable assessment of diagnosis and severity across cultures?

• Is the structure of OCD consistent across cultures? For instance, are the various OCD subtypes seen across all cultures?

• What cultural factors can supplement the cognitive-behavioral model of OCD? The literature requires a more substantial understanding of cross-cultural differences in the processes leading from the experience of common intrusive phenomena to obsessional and compulsive symptoms. Are there cross-cultural differences in the definition and experience of unwanted intrusions? How do cultural factors influence the experience of and responses to unwanted intrusions, and the functional significance of such responses?

• If subtle or even substantial revisions need to be made to the cognitive-behavioral model of OCD, how can this be reflected in adaptations to evidence-based treatments? What effects will such adaptations to CBT have on treatment outcomes cross-culturally?

Related Chapters

Chapter 2. Phenomenology and Epidemiology of Obsessive Compulsive Disorder

Chapter 3. Phenomenology and Epidemiology of Body Dysmorphic Disorder

Chapter 4. Phenomenology and Characteristics of Compulsive Hoarding

Chapter 5. Phenomenology and Epidemiology of Tic Disorder and Trichotillomania

Further Reading

Hatch, M. L., Friedman, S., Paradis, C. M. (1996). Behavioral treatment of obsessive-compulsive disorder in African Americans. *Cognitive and Behavioral Practice*, 3, 303–315.

Purdon, C. (2004). Cognitive-behavioral treatment of repugnant obsessions. *Journal of Clinical Psychology–In Session*, 60, 1169–1180.

Sica, C., Novara, C., Sanavio, E., Dorz, S., & Coradeschi, D. (2002b). Obsessive compulsive disorder cognition across cultures. In R. O. Frost & G. Steketee (Eds.), *Cognitive approaches to obsessions and compulsions: theory, assessment and treatment* (pp. 372–384). Oxford: Elsevier

Staley, D., Wand, R. (1995). Obsessive compulsive disorder: A review of the cross-cultural epidemiological literature. *Transcultural Psychiatry*, 32, 103–136.

Staley, D., Wand, R., & Shady, G. (1997). Tourette Disorder: A cross-cultural review. *Comprehensive Psychiatry*, 38, 6–16.

References

Abramowitz, J., Huppert, J. D., Cohen, A. B., Tolin, D. F., & Cahil, S. P. (2002). Religious obsessions and compulsions in a non-clinical sample: the Penn Inventory of Scrupulosity (PIOS). *Behaviour Research and Therapy*, 40, 825–838.

Abramowitz, J. S., Deaconi, B. J., Woods, C. M., & Tollin, D. F. (2004). Association between Protestant religiosity and obsessive-compulsive symptoms and cognitions. *Depression & Anxiety*, 20, 70–76.

Aeschleman, S. R., Rosen, C. C., & Williams, M. R. (2003). The effect of non-contingent negative and positive reinforcement operations on the acquisition of superstitious behaviors. *Behavioural Processes*, 61, 37–45.

Akhtar, S., Wig, N. N., Varma, V. K., Pershad, D., & Verma, S. K. (1975). A phenomenological analysis of symptoms in obsessive-compulsive neurosis. *British Journal of Psychiatry*, 127, 342–348.

Andrade, L., Walters, E. E., Gentil, V., & Laurenti, R. (2002). Prevalence of ICD-10 mental disorders in a catchment area in the city of São Paulo, Brazil. *Social Psychiatry and Psychiatric Epidemiology*, 37, 316–325.

Betancourt, H., & Lopez, S. R. (1993). The study of culture, ethnicity, and race in American psychology. *American Psychologist*, 48, 629–637.

Bijl, R. V., Ravelli, A., & van Zessen, G. (1998). Prevalence of psychiatric disorder in the general population: results of The Netherlands Mental Health Survey and Incidence Study (NEMESIS). *Social Psychiatry and Psychiatric Epidemiology*, 33, 587–595.

Black, D., Monahan, P., Gable, J., Blue, N., Clancy, G., & Baker, P. (1998). Hoarding and treatment response in 38 nondepressed subjects with obsessive–compulsive disorder. *Journal of Clinical Psychiatry*, 59, 420–425.

Bland, R. C., Om, H., & Newman, S. C. (1988). Lifetime prevalence of psychiatric disorders in Edmonton. *Acta Psychiatrica Scandinavica, 77 (Suppl. 388),* 24–32.

Blazer, D., George, L. K., Landerman, R., Pennybacker, M., Melville, M. L., Woodbury, M., et al. (1985). Psychiatric disorders: a rural/urban comparison. *Archives of General Psychiatry, 42,* 651–656

Bohne, A., Keuthen, N. J., Wilhelm, S., Deckersbach, T., & Jenike, M. A. (2002). Prevalence of body dysmorphic disorder and its correlates: A cross-cultural comparison. *Psychosomatics, 43,* 486–490.

Bolton, D., Dearsley, P., Madronal-Luque, R., & Baron-Cohen, S. (2002). Magical thinking in childhood and adolescence: Development and relation to obsessive compulsion. *British Journal of Developmental Psychology, 20,* 479–494.

Burnham, M. A., Hough, R. L., Escobar J. I., Karno, M., Timbers, D. M., Telles, C. A., et al. (1987). Six month prevalence of specific psychiatric disorders among Mexican Americans and non-Hispanic whites in Los Angeles. *Archives of General Psychiatry, 44,* 687–694.

Canino, G. J., Bird, H. R., Shrout, P. E., Rubio-Stipec, M., Bravo, M., Martinez, R., et al. (1987). The prevalence of specific psychiatric disorders in Puerto Rico. *Archives of General Psychiatry, 44,* 727–735.

Cansever, A., Uzun, Ö., Dönmez, E., & Özşahin, A. (2003). The prevalence and clinical features of body dysmorphic disorder in college students: A study in a Turkish sample. *Comprehensive Psychiatry, 44,* 60–64.

Castle, D. J. & Phillips, K. A. (2006). Obsessive-compulsive spectrum of disorders: A defensible construct? *Australian and New Zealand Journal of Psychiatry, 40,* 114–120.

Chaturvedi, S. K. (1993). Neurosis across cultures. *International Review of Psychiatry, 5,* 179–191.

Chen, C.-N., Wong, J., Lee, N., Chan-Ho, M.-W., Lau, J. T., & Fung, M. (1993). The Shatin community mental health survey in Hong Kong: II. Major findings. *Archives of General Psychiatry, 50,* 125–133.

Cheung, P. (1991). Adult psychiatric epidemiology in China in the 80s. *Culture, Medicine and Psychiatry, 15,* 479–496.

Chia, B. H. (1996). A Singapore study of obsessive compulsive disorder. *Singapore Medical Journal, 37,* 402–406.

Cordioli, A. V., Heldt, E., Bochi, D. B., Margis, R., de Sousa, M. B., Tonello, J. F., et al. (2003). Cognitive-behavioral group therapy in obsessive–compulsive disorder: A randomized clinical trial. *Psychotherapy and Psychosomatics, 72,* 211–216.

Crino, R., Slade, T., & Andrews, G. (2005). The changing prevalence and severity of obsessive compulsive disorder criteria from DSM-III to DSM-IV. *American Journal of Psychiatry, 162,* 876–882.

Çilli, A. S., Telcioğlu, M., Aşkın, R., Kaya, N., Bodur, S., & Kucur, R. (2004). Twelve-month prevalence of obsessive-compulsive disorder in Konya, Turkey. *Comprehensive Psychiatry, 45,* 367–374.

Cogan, J. C., Bhalla, S. K., Sefa-Dedeh, A., & Rothblum, E. D. (1996). A comparison study of United States and African students on perceptions of obesity and thinness. *Journal of Cross-Cultural Psychology, 27,* 98–113

Dag, I. (1999). The relationships among paranormal beliefs, locus of control and psychopathology in a Turkish college sample. *Personality and Individual Differences, 26,* 723–737.

de Silva, P. (2006). Culture and obsessive-compulsive disorder. *Psychiatry, 5,* 402–405

Doron, G., & Kyrios, M. (2005). Obsessive compulsive disorder: A review of possible specific internal representations within a broader cognitive theory. *Clinical Psychology Review, 25,* 415–432.

Doron, G., Kyrios, M., & Moulding, R. (2007). Sensitive domains of self-concept in obsessive-compulsive disorder: Further evidence for a multidimensional model of OCD. *Journal of Anxiety Disorders, 21,* 433–444.

Doron, G., Moulding, R., Kyrios, M., & Nedeljkovic, M. (2008). Sensitivity of self-beliefs in obsessive compulsive disorder (OCD). *Depression and Anxiety, 25,* 874–884.

Dowson, J. H. (1977). The phenomenology of severe obsessive-compulsive neurosis. *British Journal of Psychiatry, 131,* 75–78.

Douglass, H. M., Moffitt, T. E., Dar, R., McGee, R., de Silva, P. (1995). Obsessive-compulsive disorder in a birth cohort of 18-year-olds: Prevalence and predictors. *Journal of the American Academy of Child & Adolescent Psychiatry, 34,* 1424–1431.

Draguns, J. G. (1980). Psychological disorders of clinical severity. In H. C. Triandis & J. G. Draguns (Eds.), *Handbook of cross-cultural psychology Vol. 6: Psychopathology* (pp. 99–174). Boston: Allyn and Bacon.

Egrilmez, A., Gulseren, L., Gulseren, S., Kultur, S., (1997). Phenomenology of obsessions in a Turkish series of OCD patients. *Psychopathology, 30,* 106–110.

Eisen, J. L., Goodman, W. K., Keller, M. B., Warshaw, M. G., DeMarco, L. M., Luce, D. D., et al. (1999). Patterns of remission and relapse in obsessive-compulsive disorder: A 2-year prospective study. *Journal of Clinical Psychiatry, 60,* 346–351.

Fabrega, H. (1989). Cultural relativism and psychiatric illness. *Journal of Nervous and Mental Disease, 77,* 415–425.

Fals-Stewart, W., Marks, A. P., & Schafer, J. (1993). A comparison of behavioral group therapy and individual behavior therapy in treating obsessive–compulsive disorder. *Journal of Nervous and Mental Disease, 181,* 189–193.

Faravelli, C., Degl'Innocenti, B. G., & Biardinelli, L. (1989). Epidemiology of anxiety disorders in Florence. *Acta Psychiatrica Scandinavica, 79,* 308–312.

Faravelli, C., Salvatori, S., Galassi, F., Aiazzi, L., Drei, C., & Cabras, P. (1997). Epidemiology of somatoform disorders: A community survey in Florence. *Social Psychiatry and Psychiatric Epidemiology, 32,* 24–29.

Fineberg, N. Hughes, A. Gale, T., & Roberts, A. (2005). Group cognitive behaviour therapy in obsessive-compulsive disorder (OCD): A controlled study. *International Journal of Psychiatry in Clinical Practice, 9,* 257–263.

Foa, E. B., Liebowitz, M. R., Kozak, M. J., Davies, S., Campeas, R., Franklin, M. E., et al. (2005). Randomized, placebo-controlled trial of exposure and ritual prevention, clomipramine, and their combination in the treatment of obsessive–compulsive disorder. *American Journal of Psychiatry, 162,* 151–161.

Fontenelle, L. F., Mendlowicz, M. V., Marques, C., & Versiani, M. (2004). Trans-cultural aspects of obsessive-compulsive disorder: A description of a Brazilian sample and a systematic review of international clinical studies. *Journal of Psychiatric Research, 38,* 403–411.

Fontenelle, L. F., Mendlowicz, M. V., & Versiani, M. (2002). The effect of gender on the clinical features and therapeutic response in obsessive-compulsive disorder. *Revista Brasileira de Psiquiatria, 24,* 7–11.

Fontenelle, L. F., Mendlowicz, M. V., & Versiani, M. (2006). The descriptive epidemiology of obsessive-compulsive disorder. *Progress in Neuro-psychopharmacology and Biological Psychiatry, 30*, 327–337.

Foroughi, E. & Kyrios, M. (In preparation). An investigation of the role of cultural factors in obsessive-compulsive disorder in Iranian clinical and non-clinical cohorts.

Foroughi, E., Shams, G., & Kyrios, M. (2007, July).*Psychometric Validation of the Thought-Action Fusion Scale in an Iranian Sample.* Poster presented at the 5th World Congress of Behavioural & Cognitive Therapies, Barcelona.

Freeston, M. H., Ladouceur, R., Gagnon, F., Thibodeau, N., Rhéaume, J., Letarte, H., et al. (1997). Cognitive-behavioral treatment of obsessive thoughts: A controlled study. *Journal of Consulting and Clinical Psychology, 65*, 405–413.

Friedman, S., Hatch, M. L., Paradis, C., Popkin, M., Shalita, A. R. (1993). Obsessive compulsive disorder in two Black ethnic groups: Incidence in an urban dermatology clinic. *Journal of Anxiety Disorders, 7*, 343–348.

Friedman, S., Smith, L. C., Halpern, B., Levine, C., Paradis, C., Viswanathan, R., et al. (2003). Obsessive-compulsive disorder in a multi-ethnic urban outpatient clinic: Initial presentation and treatment response with Exposure and Response Prevention. *Behavior Therapy, 34*, 397–410.

Frost, R. O., Krause, M. S., McMahon, M. J., Peppe, J., Evans, M., McPhee, A. E., et al. (1993). Compulsivity and superstitiousness. *Behaviour Research and Therapy, 31*, 423–425.

Ghassemzadeh, H., Mojtabai, R., Khamseh, A., Ebrahimkhani, N., Issazadegan, A., & Saif-Nobakht, Z. (2002). Symptoms of obsessive-compulsive disorder in a sample of Iranian patients. *International Journal of Social Psychiatry, 48*, 220–228.

Ghassemzadeh, H., Bolhari, J., Birashk, B., & Salavati, M. (2005). Responsibility attitude in a sample of Iranian obsessive-compulsive patients. *International Journal of Social Psychiatry, 51*(1), 13–22.

Goodwin, R, Koenen, K. C., Hellman, F., Guardino, M., & Struening, E. (2002). Helpseeking and access to mental health treatment for obsessive-compulsive disorder. *Acta Psychiatrica Scandinavica, 106*, 143–149.

Grabe, H. J., Meyer, C., Hapke, U., Rumpf, H.-J., Freyberger, H. J., Dilling, H., et al. (2001). Lifetime-comorbidity of obsessive-compulsive disorder and sublinincal obsessive-compulsive disorder in northern Germany. *European Archives of Psychiatry and Clinical Neuroscience, 251*, 130–135.

Greenberg, D. (1984). Are religious compulsions religious or compulsive: A phenomenological study. *American Journal of Psychotherapy, 38*, 524–532.

Greenberg, D., & Witztum, E. (1994). Cultural aspects of obsessive compulsive disorder. In. E. Hollander, D. Zohar, D. Marazzati, B. Olivier (eds*). Current insights in obsessive compulsive disorder*, (pp. 11–21). Chichester: Wiley.

Greenberg, D., & Witztum, E. (2001). Treatment of strictly religious patients. In. M. T. Pato, J. Zohar (eds*). Current treatments of obsessive compulsive disorder*, (p.173–191). Washington DC: American Psychiatric Publishing.

Greist, J. H., Marks, I. M., Baer, L., Kobak, K. A., Wenzel, K. W., Hirsch, M. J., et al. (2002). Behavior therapy for obsessive–compulsive disorder guided by a computer or by a clinician compared with relaxation as a control. *Journal of Clinical Psychiatry, 63*, 138–145.

Haggai, H., Masser-Kavitzky, R., & Gross-Isseroff, R. (2003). Obsessive-compulsive disorder and Jewish religiosity. *The Journal of Nervous and Mental Disease, 191*, 201–203.

Hatch, M. L., Friedman, S., & Paradis, C. M. (1996). Behavioral treatment of obsessive-compulsive disorder in African Americans. *Cognitive and Behavioral Practice, 3*, 303–315.

Hepworth, M., Simonds, L. M., & Marsh., R. (2010). Catholic priests' conceptualisation of scrupulosity: a grounded theory analysis. *Mental Health, Religion & Culture, 13(1)*, 1–16.

Huppert, J. D., Siev, J., & Kushner, E. S. (2007). When religion and obsessive-compulsive disorder collide: Treating scrupulosity in ultra-orthodox Jews. *Journal of Clinical Psychology, 63*, 925–941.

Hwu, H.-G., Yeh, E.-K., & Chang, L.-Y. (1989). Prevalence of psychiatric disorders in Taiwan defined by the Chinese Diagnostic Interview Schedule. *Acta Psychiatrica Scandinavica, 79*, 136–147.

Jahoda, G. (1969). *The psychology of superstition*. London: Penguin.

Jaisoorya, T. S., Reddy, Y. C. J., Srinath, S., & Thennarasu, K. (2008). Sex differences in Indian patients with obsessive-compulsive disorder. *Comprehensive Psychiatry, 50*, 70–75.

Jenkins, R., Lewis, G., Bebbington, P., Brugha, T., Farrell, M., Gill, B., et al. (1997). The National Psychiatric Morbidity Surveys of Great Britain - initial findings from the Household Survey. *Psychological Medicine, 27*, 775–789.

Jones, M. K., & Menzies, R. G. (1998). Danger ideation reduction therapy (DIRT) for obsessive–compulsive washers: A controlled trial. *Behaviour Research and Therapy, 36*, 959–970.

Juang, Y.-Y., & Liu, C.-I. (2001). Phenomenology of obsessive-compulsive disorder in Taiwan. *Psychiatry and Clinical Neurosciences, 55*, 623–627.

Julien, D., Careau, Y., O'Connor, K. P., Bouvard, M., Rheaume, J., Langlois, F., et al. (2008). Specificity of belief domains in OCD: Validation of the French version of the Obsessive Beliefs Questionnaire and a comparison across samples. *Journal of Anxiety Disorders, 22*, 1029–1041.

Kadri, N., Agoub, M., el Gnaoui, S., Berrada, S., & Moussaoui, D. (2007). Prevalence of anxiety disorders: a population-based epidemiological study in metropolitan area of Casablanca, Morocco. *Annals of General Psychiatry, 10*, 6.

Karadaĝ, F., Oguzhanoglu, N. K., Ozdel, O., Ateşci, F. C., & Amuk, T. (2006). OCD symptoms in a sample of Turkish patients: A phenomenological picture. *Depression and Anxiety, 23*, 145–152.

Karlsson, R. (2005). Ethnic matching between therapist and patient in psychotherapy: An overview of findings, together with methodological and conceptual issues. *Cultural Diversity and Ethnic Minority Psychology, 11*, 113–129.

Karno, M., Hough, R. L., Burnham, M. A., Escobar, J. I., Timbers, D. M., Santana, F., et al. (1987) Lifetime prevalence of specific psychiatric disorders among Mexican Americans and non-Hispanic whites in Los Angeles. *Archives of General Psychiatry, 44*, 695–701

Khanna, S., & Channabasavanna, S. M (1988). Phenomenology of obsessions in obsessive-compulsive neurosis. *Psychopathology, 20*, 23–28.

Khanna, S., Rejendra, P. N., & Channabasavanna, S. M. (1986). Socio-demographic variables in obsessive compulsive disorder in India. *International Journal of Social Psychiatry, 32*, 47–54.

Kleinman, A. (1977). Depression, somatization and the new "cross-cultural psychiatry." *Social Science and Medicine, 11*, 3–10.

Kozak, M., Liebowitz, M., & Foa, E. B. (2000). Cognitive behavior therapy and pharmacotherapy for obsessive–compulsive disorder: The NIMH-Sponsored collaborative study.

In W. K. Goodman (Ed.), *Obsessive–compulsive disorder* (pp. 501–530). Mahwah: Erlbaum.

Kyrios, M., Bhar, S., & Wade, D. (1996). The assessment of obsessive-compulsive phenomena: Psychometric and normative data on the Padua Inventory from an Australian nonclinical sample. *Behaviour Research and Therapy, 34*, 85–95.

Kyrios, M., Sanavio, E., Bhar, S., & Liguori, L. (2001). Associations between obsessive-compulsive phenomena, affect and beliefs: Cross-cultural comparisons of Australian and Italian data. *Behavioral and Cognitive Psychotherapy, 29*, 409–422.

Labad, J., Menchon, J. M., Alonso, P., Segalas, C., Jimenez, S., Jaurrieta, N., et al. (2008). Gender differences in obsessive-compulsive symptom dimensions. *Depression and Anxiety, 25*, 832–838.

Lee, C. K., Han, J. H., & Choi, J. O. (1987). The epidemiological study of mental disorders in Korea (IX): Alcoholism, anxiety, and depression. *Seoul Journal of Psychiatry, 12*, 183–191.

Lensi, P., Cassano, G. B., Correddu, G., Ravagli, S., Kunovac, J. L., & Akisal, H. S. (1996). Obsessive-compulsive disorder: Familial-developmental history, symptomatology, comorbidity and course with special reference to gender-related differences. *British Journal of Psychiatry, 169*, 101–107.

Leonard, H. L., Goldberger, E. L., Rapoport, J. L., Cheslow, D., & Swedo, S. (1990). Childhood rituals: Normal development or obsessive-compulsive symptoms. *Journal of the American Academy of Child and Adolescent Psychiatry, 29*, 17–23.

Lindsay, M., Crino, R., & Andrews, G. (1997). Controlled trial of exposure and response prevention in obsessive–compulsive disorder. *British Journal of Psychiatry, 171*, 135–139.

Lovell, K., Marks, I. M., Noshirvani, H., & O'Sullivan, G. (1994). Should treatment distinguish anxiogenic from anxiolytic obsessive–compulsive ruminations? *Psychotherapy and Psychosomatics, 61*, 150–155.

Mahgoub, O. M & Abedel-Hafeiz, H. B. (1991). Patterns of obsessive-compulsive disorder in eastern Saudi Arabia. *British Journal of Psychiatry, 158*, 840–842.

Marks, I. M., Stern, D. M., Cobb, J., & McDonald, R. (1980). Clomipramine and exposure for obsessive–compulsive rituals: I. *British Journal of Psychiatry, 136*, 1–25.

Mancuso, S. G., Knoesen, N. P., Castle, D. J. (2010). Delusional versus nondelusional body dysmorphic disorder patients. *Comprehensive Psychiatry, 51*, 177–182.

Marsella, A. J. (1980). Depressive experience and disorder across cultures. In H. Triandis & J. Draguns (Eds.) *Handbook of cross-cultural psychology: Volume 6–Psychopathology* (pp. 237–289). Boston: Allyn & Bacon.

Marsella, A. J., & Yamada, A. (2000). Culture and mental health: An introduction and overview of foundations, concepts, and issues. In I. Cuellar & Paniagua, F. (Eds.) *The handbook of multicultural mental health: Assessment and treatment of diverse populations* (pp. 3–24). New York: Academic Press.

Marsella, A. J., Kaplan, A., & Suarez, E. (2002). Cultural considerations for understanding, assessing, and treating depressive experience and disorder. In M. Reinecke & M. Davison (Eds.) *Comparative treatments of depression* (pp. 47–78). NewYork: Springer

Matsunaga, H., Kiriike, N., Matsui, T., Miyata, A., Iwasaki, Y., Fujimoto, K., et al. (2000). Gender difference in social and interpersonal features and personality disorders among Japanese patients with obsessive-compulsive disorder. *Comprehensive Psychiatry, 41*, 266–272.

Matsunaga, H., & Seedat, S. (2007). Obsessive-compulsive spectrum disorders: Cross-national and ethnic issues. *CNS Spectrums, 12*, 392–400.

Matsunaga, H., Maebayashi, K., Hayashida, K., Okino, K., Matsui, T., Iketani, T., et al. (2008). Symptom structure in Japanese patients with obsessive-compulsive disorder. *American Journal of Psychiatry, 165*, 251–253.

McLean, P. D., Whittal, M. L., Söchting, I., Koch, W. J., Paterson, R., Thordarson, et al. (2001). Cognitive versus behavior therapy in the group treatment of obsessive–compulsive disorder. *Journal of Consulting and Clinical Psychology, 69*, 205–214.

Mohammadi, M. R., Ghanizadeh, A., Rahgozar, M., Noorbala, A. A., Davidian, H., Afzali, H. M., et al. (2004). Prevalence of obsessive-compulsive disorder in Iran. *BMC Psychiatry, 4*, 2. (doi:10.1186/1471–244X-4–2).

Moulding, R., & Kyrios, M. (2006). Anxiety disorders and control related beliefs: The exemplar of obsessive-compulsive disorder (OCD). *Clinical Psychology Review, 26*, 573–583.

Muris, P., Merckelbach, H., & Clavan, M. (1997). Abnormal and normal compulsions. *Behaviour Research and Therapy, 35*, 249–252.

Myers, J. K., Weissman, M. M., Tischler, G. L., Holzer, C. E., Leaf, P. J., Orvaschel, H., et al. (1984). Six month prevalence of psychiatric disorders in three communities: 1980–1982. *Archives of General Psychiatry, 41*, 959–967

Nakatani, E., Nakagawa, A., Nakao, T., Yoshizato, C., Nabeyama, M., Kudo, A., et al. (2005). A randomized controlled trial of Japanese patients with obsessive-compulsive disorder effectiveness of behavior therapy and fluvoxamine. *Psychotherapy and Psychosomatics, 74*, 269–276.

Naziry, G., Dadfar, M., & Karimi Keisami, I. (2005). The role of religious commitment, non-adaptive religious beliefs, guilt feelings and non-adaptive cognitive beliefs in the severity of obsessive- compulsive symptoms. *Iranian Journal of Psychiatry and Clinical Psychology (Andisheh Va Raftar), 11*(3), 283–289.

Neal-Barnett, A. M., Ward-Brown, B. J., Mitchell, M., & Krownapple, M. (2000). Hair pulling in African Americans— Only your hairdresser knows for sure: An exploratory study. *Cultural Diversity and Ethnic Minority Psychology, 6*, 352–362.

Nelson, E. A., Abramowitz, J. S., Whiteside, S. P., & Deacon, B. J. (2006). Scrupulosity in patients with obsessive-compulsive disorder: relationship to clinical and cognitive phenomena. *Journal of Anxiety Disorders, 20*, 1071–1086.

Németh, A., Szádóczky, E., Treuer, T., Vandlik, E., & Papp, Z. S. (1997). Epidemiology of OCD in Hungary. *European Neuropsychopharmacology, 7*(Suppl. 2), 234.

Oakley-Browne, M. A., Joyce, P. R., Wells, J. E., Bushnell, J. A., & Hornblow, A. R. (1989). Christchurch psychiatric epidemiology study, part II: Six month and other period prevalences of specific psychiatric disorders. *Australian and New Zealand Journal of Psychiatry, 23*, 327–340.

O'Connor, K., Aardema, F., Robillard, S., Guay, S., Pélissier, M.-C., Todorov, C., et al. (2006). Cognitive behaviour therapy and medication in the treatment of obsessive–compulsive disorder. *Acta Psychiatrica Scandinavica, 113*, 408–419.

O'Connor, K., Todorov, C., Robillard, S., Borgeat, F., & Brault, M. (1999). Cognitive-behaviour therapy and medication in the treatment of obsessive–compulsive disorder: A controlled study. *Canadian Journal of Psychiatry, 44*, 64–71.

Okasha, A., Saad, A., Khalil, A., El-Dawla, A., & Yehia, N. (1994). Phenomenology of obsessive-compulsive disorder: A transcultural study. *Comprehensive Psychiatry, 35*, 191–197.

Otto, M. W., Wilhelm, S., Cohen, L. S., & Harlow, B. L. (2001). Prevalence of body dysmorphic disorder in a community sample of women. *American Journal of Psychiatry, 158*, 2061–2063.

Paradis, C. M., Friedman, S., Hatch, M. L., & Ackerman, R. (1996). Cognitive behavioral treatment of anxiety disorders in Orthodox Jews. *Cognitive and Behavioral Practice, 3*, 271–288.

Phillips, K. A., McElroy, S. L., Keck, P. E., Pope, H. G., & Hudson, J. I. (1993). Body dysmorphic disorder: 30 Cases of imagined ugliness. *American Journal of Psychiatry, 150*, 302–308.

Pourfaraj, M., Mohammadi, N., & Taghavi, M. (2008). Psychometric properties of revised thought-action fusion questionnaire (TAF-R) in an Iranian population. *Journal of Behavior Therapy and Experimental Psychiatry, 39*, 600–609.

Purdon, C. (2004). Cognitive-behavioral treatment of repugnant obsessions. *Journal of Clinical Psychology–In Session, 60*, 1169–1180.

Rachman, S. (1997). A cognitive theory of obsessions. *Behaviour Research and Therapy, 35*, 793–802.

Rachman, S. (1998). A cognitive theory of obsessions: Elaborations. *Behaviour Research and Therapy, 36*, 385–401

Rachman, S., & de Silva, P. (1978). Abnormal and normal obsessions. *Behaviour Research and Therapy, 16*, 233–248.

Rassin, E., & Koster, E. (2003). The correlation between thought-action fusion and religiosity in a normal sample. *Behaviour Research and Therapy, 41*, 361–368.

Rassin, E., & Muris, P. (2007). Abnormal and normal obsessions: A reconsideration. *Behaviour Research and Therapy, 45*, 1065–1070.

Reuven-Magril, O., Dar, R., & Liberman, N. (2008). Illusion of control and behavioral control attempts in obsessive-compulsive disorder. *Journal of Abnormal Psychology, 117*, 334–341.

Rosa-Alcázar, A. I., Sánchez-Meca, J., Gómez-Conesa, A., & Marín-Martínez, F. (2008). Psychological treatment of obsessive-compulsive disorder: A meta-analysis. *Clinical Psychology Review, 28*, 1310–1325.

Rosen, J. C., Reiter, J., & Orosan, P. (1995). Cognitive-behavioral image therapy for body dysmorphic disorder. *Journal of Consulting and Clinical Psychology, 63*, 263–269.

Robins, L. N., Helzer, J. E., Croughan, J., Ratcliff, K. S. (1981). National institute of Mental Health Diagnostic Interview Schedule. *Archives of General Psychiatry, 38*, 381–390.

Robins, L. N., Helzer J. E., Weissman, M. M., Orvaschel, H., Gruenberg, E., Burke, J. D., et al. (1984) Lifetime prevalence of specific disorders in three sites. *Archives of General Psychiatry, 41*, 949–958.

Salkovskis, P. M., & Harrison, J. (1984). Abnormal and normal obsessions: A replication. *Behaviour Research and Therapy, 22*, 549–552.

Sanavio, E. (1988). Obsessions and compulsions: The Padua Inventory. *Behaviour Research and Therapy, 26*, 169–177.

Shams, G., Karamghadiri, N., Esmaili Torkanbori, Y., & Ebrahimkhani, N. (2004). Validation and reliability assessment of Persian version of Obsessive Beliefs Questionnaire-44. *Advances in Cognitive Science, 6*, 23–37.

Shams, G., Shams, G., Karamghadiri, N., Esmaili Torkanbori, Y., Rahiminejad, F., & Ebrahimkhani, N. (2006). Obsessional beliefs in patients with obsessive-compulsive disorder and other anxiety disorders as compared to the control group. *Advances in Cognitive Science, 2*, 83–90.

Sharma, B. P. (1968). Obsessive compulsive neurosis in Nepal. *Transcultural Psychiatry Research Review, 5*, 38–41.

Shooka, A., Al-Haddad, M. K & Raees, A. (1998). OCD in Bahrain: A phenomenological profile. *International Journal of Social Psychiatry, 44*, 147–154.

Sica, C., Novara, C., & Sanavio, E. (2002a). Religiousness and obsessive compulsive cognitions and symptoms in an Italian population. *Behaviour Research and Therapy, 40*, 813–823.

Sica, C., Novara, C., Sanavio, E., Dorz, S., & Coradeschi, D. (2002b). Obsessive compulsive disorder cognition across cultures. In R. O. Frost & G. Steketee (Eds.), *Cognitive approaches to obsessions and compulsions: theory, assessment and treatment* (pp. 372–384). Oxford: Elsevier.

Sica, C., Novara, C., & Sanavio, E. (2002c). Culture and psychopathology: superstition and obsessive-compulsive cognitions and symptoms in a non-clinical Italian sample. *Personality and Individual Differences, 32*, 1001–1012.

Sica, C., Coradeschi, D., Sanavio, E., Dorz, S., Manchisi, D., & Novara, C. (2004). A study of the psychometric properties of the Obsessive Beliefs Inventory and Interpretation of Intrusions Inventory on clinical Italian individuals. *Journal of Anxiety Disorders, 18*, 291–307.

Sica, C., Taylor, S., Arrindell, W. A., & Sanavio, E. (2006). A cross-cultural test of the cognitive theory of obsessions and compulsions: A comparison of Greek, Italian and American individuals–A preliminary study. *Cognitive Therapy and Research, 30*, 585–597.

Siev, J., & Cohen, A. B. (2007). Is thought-action fusion related to religiosity? Differences between Christians and Jews. *Behaviour Research and Therapy, 40*, 813–823.

Slade, T., Johnston, A., Teesson, M., Whiteford, H., Burgess, P., Pirkis, J., et al. (2009). *The mental health of Australians 2: Report on the 2007 National Survey of Health and Wellbeing.* Department of Health and Ageing: Canberra.

Staley, D., & Wand, R. (1995). Obsessive compulsive disorder: A review of the cross-cultural epidemiological literature. *Transcultural Psychiatry, 32*, 103–136.

Staley, D., Wand, R., & Shady, G. (1997). Tourette Disorder: A cross-cultural review. *Comprehensive Psychiatry, 38*, 6–16.

Steketee, G., Quay, S., & White, K. (1991). Religion and guilt in OCD patients. *Journal of Anxiety Disorders, 5*, 359–367.

Taylor, S., Abramowitz, J. S., McKay, D., Calamari, J. E., Sookman, D., Kyrios, M., et al. (2006). Do dysfunctional beliefs play a role in all types of obsessive-compulsive disorder? *Journal of Anxiety Disorders, 20*, 85–97.

Taylor, S., Thordarson, D. S., Spring, T., Yeh, A. H., Corcoran, K. M., Eugster, K., et al. (2003). Telephone-administered cognitive behavior therapy for obsessive-compulsive disorder. *Cognitive and Behavioral Therapy, 32*, 13–25.

Tek, C., & Ulug, B. (2001). Religiosity and religious obsessions in obsessive-compulsive disorder. *Psychiatry Research, 104*, 99–108.

Tezcan, E., & Millet, B. (1997). Phenomenology of obsessive-Compulsive disorders: Forms and characteristics of obsessions and compulsions in East Turkey. *Encephale, 23*, 342–350

Thomas, J., Turkheimer, E., & Oltmanns, T. F. (2000). Psychometric analyses of racial differences on the Maudsley Obsessional Compulsive Inventory. *Assessment, 7*, 247–258.

Tobacyk, J. J., Backman, P., & Maija, A. (1992). Paranormal beliefs and their implications in university students from Finland and the United States. *Journal of Cross-Cultural Psychology, 23*, 59–71.

Tobacyk, J. J., Nagot, E., & Miller, M. (1988). Paranormal beliefs and locus of control: A multidimensional examination. *Journal of Personality Assessment, 52*, 241–246.

Tobacyk, J. J., & Shrader, D. (1991). Superstition and self-efficacy. *Psychological Reports, 68*, 1387–1388.

Torres, A. R., Prince, M. J., Bebbington, P. E., Bhugra, D., Brugha, D., Farrell, M., et al. (2006). Obsessive-compulsive disorder: Prevalence, comorbidity, impact and help-seeking in the British National Psychiatric Morbidity Survey of 2000. *American Journal of Psychiatry, 163*, 1978–1985.

Torresan, R., de Abreu Ramos-Cerqueira, A., de Mathis, M., Diniz, J., Ferrão, Y., Miguel, E., et al. (2008). Sex differences in the phenotypic expression of obsessive-compulsive disorder: an exploratory study from Brazil. *Comprehensive Psychiatry, 50*, 63–69.

Tseng, W. S. (1997). Overview: Culture and Psychopathology. In W. S. Tseng & J. Streitzer (Eds.). *Culture and psychopathology: A guide to clinical assessment* (pp. 1–27). New York: Psychology Press.

Tükel, R., Polat, A., Geng, A., Bozkurt, O., & Atla, H. (2004). Gender-related differences among Turkish patients with obsessive-compulsive disorder, *Comprehensive Psychiatry, 45*, 362–366.

van Balkom, J. L. M., de Haan, E., van Oppen, P., Spinhoven, P., Hoogduin, K. A. L., & van Dyck, R. (1998). Cognitive and behavioral therapies alone versus in combination with fluvoxamine in the treatment of obsessive–compulsive disorder. *Journal of Nervous and Mental Disease, 186*, 492–499.

Veale, D. (2001). Cognitive-behavioural therapy for body dysmorphic disorder. *Advances in Psychiatric Treatment, 7*, 125–132.

Vogel, P. A., Stiles, T. C., & Götesman, K. G. (2004). Adding cognitive therapy elements to exposure therapy for obsessive-compulsive disorder: A controlled study. *Behavioural and Cognitive Psychotherapy, 32*, 275–290.

Wells, J. E., Bushnell, J. A., Hornblow, A. R., Joyce, P. R., & Oakley-Browne, M. A. (1989). Christchurch Psychiatric Epidemiology Study, Part I: Methodology and lifetime prevalence for specific psychiatric disorders. *Australian and New Zealand Journal of Psychiatry, 23*, 315–326

Williams, K. E., Chambless, D. L., & Steketee, G. (1998). Behavioral treatment of obsessive-compulsive disorder in African Americans: Clinical issues. *Journal of Behaviour Therapy and Experimental Psychiatry, 29*, 163–170.

Williams, M. T., Turkheimer, E., Schimdt, K. M., & Oltmanns, T. F. (2005). Ethnic identification biases responses to the Padua Inventory for obsessive-compulsive disorder. *Assessment, 12*, 174–185.

Williams, M. T., Turkheimer, E., Magee, E., & Guterbock, T. (2008). The effects of racial priming on self-report of contamination anxiety. *Personality and Individual Differences, 44*, 746–757.

Wittchen, H.-U., Essau, C. A., von Zerssen, D., Krieg, J.-C., & Zaudig, M. (1992). Lifetime and six month prevalence of mental disorders in the Munich follow-up study. *European Archives of Psychiatry and Clinical Neuroscience, 241*, 247–258.

Wolfradt, U. (1997). Dissociative experiences, trait anxiety and paranormal beliefs. *Personality and Individual Differences, 23*, 15–19.

Yorulmaz, O., Yilmaz, E., & Gencöz, T. (2004). Psychometric properties of the Thought-Action Fusion Scale in a Turkish sample. *Behaviour Research and Therapy, 42*, 1203–1214.

Yorulmaz, O., Gencöz, T., & Woody, S. (2009). OCD cognitions and symptoms in different religious contexts. *Journal of Anxiety Disorders, 23*, 401–406.

Zebb, B. J., Moore, M. C. (2003). Superstitious and perceived anxiety control as predictors of psychological distress. *Journal of Anxiety Disorders, 17*, 115–130.

Zohar, A. J., Goldman, E., Calamary, R., & Mashiah, M. (2005). Religiosity and obsessive-compulsive behavior in Israeli Jews. *Behaviour Research & Therapy, 43*, 857–868.

Zusne, L., & Jones, W. H. (1989). *Anomalistic psychology: A study of magical thinking* (2nd ed.). Hilsdale: Lawrence Erlbaum.

PART 8

Conclusions and Future Directions

Future Research on Obsessive Compulsive and Spectrum Conditions

Gail Steketee *and* Brian H. McCorkle

Abstract

This chapter reviews comments raised by authors of 25 chapters of the *Handbook of Obsessive Compulsive and Spectrum Disorders*. Among the challenges raised are those within the areas of diagnosis and features of the several OC spectrum conditions, including revisions to the diagnostic nomenclature for DSM-V under consideration, especially with regard to the possible addition of hoarding disorder to distinguish this more clearly from OCD. Research on clinical versus nonclinical samples, and controversies regarding possible subtypes of OCD and of some of its spectrum conditions like BDD and hoarding, are examined. Relationships among OCD and the spectrum conditions are examined with attention to the general lack of information about this issue. Several authors in the handbook comment on personality features and their association with outcomes following treatment, with a general consensus that assessing features rather than disorders will be most useful. The impact of culture on expression of OC spectrum conditions is clearly under-studied. Causes and mechanisms underlying OCD and spectrum conditions are examined, including neurological and genetic underpinnings, information processing, beliefs and cognitive models, as well as social and familial factors. Concerns about assessment are raised with regard to OCD and its expression in older adults, in hoarding and in BDD, and the impact of culture on assessment. With regard to treatment, chapters focus on research needs concerning mechanisms of action and predictors of change, and the need to improve treatments to enhance their effects. Improvement of outcomes in a variety of areas (e.g., hoarding, children, culturally sensitive treatments) is noted, including outcomes for medications and combined CBT plus medication regimens. Special issues are raised with regard to BDD, tic disorders, and trichotillomania.

Keywords: obsessive compulsive disorder, OCD, OC spectrum, research, body dysmorphic disorder, trichotillomania, tics, hoarding

The chapters in this book cover the current knowledge about obsessive compulsive disorder (OCD) and its spectrum conditions. Although we certainly know a great deal more about these problems than we did many years ago, it is also clear that we still know too little. This is most evident in the research on interventions, especially for the obsessive compulsive (OC) spectrum conditions, where our knowledge depends on our understanding of the phenomenology, psychopathology, and biology of these problems, as well as our ability to synthesize this information into sensible theories that guide treatments. Below, we review chapter authors' highlights of the inadequacies and remaining challenges in understanding these disorders, with the goal of pointing toward future research that will help answer the many remaining questions in the field. Our review is organized around the following topics: diagnosis and epidemiology, causes and mechanisms, assessment concerns, treatment, and special concerns. We hope that this discussion will point the way to important collaborative research efforts to move the study of OCD and OC spectrum conditions forward.

Diagnosis and Phenomenology

A number of challenges with regard to diagnosis and phenomenology of OC spectrum conditions are apparent from the research summaries in this book. Below, we describe concerns raised in several areas, including: revisions to diagnostic systems along dimensional versus categorical lines; the value of nonclinical samples in studying the features of OC spectrum conditions; the validity of subtyping of OCD, and possibly its related disorders; the relationship among OC spectrum conditions; and personality features and cultural factors, especially as these inform our understanding of the etiology of these disorders. Our goal is not to answer these concerns, but to deliberately raise questions and point to areas needing further study.

Revising the Diagnostic System

Calamari, Chik, Pontarelli and DeJong (Chapter 2) point to the evident need to elucidate the phenomenology of OCD before attempting to revise the diagnostic system toward the 5th edition of the Diagnostic and Statistical Manual (DSM-V), on which the American Psychiatric Association has begun to work. At the present time in 2010, the DSM 5 work group is recommending that OCD be included under a grouping of "Anxiety and Obsessive-Compulsive Spectrum Disorders," responding in part to some suggestions that OCD may be less clearly an anxiety disorder than has been assumed in the past. The work group is also considering adding *avoidance* to define obsessions, as well as indicating the need to distinguish OCD from hoarding disorder and from skin-picking disorder (if these are added to the DSM as separate conditions).

A major concern here is the validity and utility of identifying OCD subtypes. While research on subtypes has advanced, it is not yet clear that distinguishing among those that most clinicians and researchers agree are common (such as washing, checking, ordering, repeating) will prove helpful in advancing the field toward effective interventions. Among the concerns here is whether our natural human tendency to collect symptoms into categories, rather than dimensions, best serves the understanding of the meaning and associations among these features. However, the separation of hoarding symptoms into an independent diagnostic category separate from OCD, now in the works for DSM-V, is clearly an advance, given the substantial differences

between the two in symptom patterns as well as a variety of behavioral, emotional, cognitive, and biological features (see Frost & Rasmussen, Chapter 4).

Another major problem that may be impeding progress is a tendency across OC spectrum conditions to develop diagnostic criteria for children as scaled-down interpolations of adult diagnoses. Because most information is based on data gathered from adults, the field often falls short in understanding the child and adolescent manifestations of OCD and of OC spectrum conditions, such as body dysmorphic disorder (BDD) and hoarding. This is partly because it is easier to conduct research on adults—participant access, IRB approval, and informed consent is more difficult with legal minors—and we often lack the longitudinal studies that follow children well into adulthood to determine how symptoms evolve over time. In a related vein, Ricketts, Woods, Antinoro and Franklin (Chapter 5) raise the question of whether age of onset might predict the type and/or severity of the longitudinal course of OCD symptoms. As Storch and colleagues (Chapter 25) suggest, it may be time to revise the OCD diagnostic scheme by integrating data about children.

Clinical Versus Nonclinical Samples

The debate about whether findings from nonclinical research can be generalized to the understanding of clinical phenomena continues to this day, but in fact, considerable information has accumulated in the past three decades from research on students and on those with subclinical levels of OCD. Calamari et al. (Chapter 2) point to the commonalities and the differences between clinical and nonclinical obsessions, as do Kelly and Phillips (Chapter 3) for delusional and nondelusional body dysmorphic disorder (BDD) obsessions and behaviors. In a similar vein, Ricketts et al. (Chapter 5) raise the question of whether nonclinical forms of tics, Tourette syndrome, and trichotillomania actually predict future onset of the full blown disorder, or instead are distinct and stable traits. Nonetheless, the potential benefits of conducting research into not-yet-clinical symptoms of any of these conditions seem substantial. This is perhaps well underscored by reliably reproduced findings that the precursors to obsessive thoughts, images, and impulses—"intrusions"—are actually very common among ordinary people (e.g., Rachman & de Silva, 1978; Salkovskis & Harrison, 1984), but such intrusions appear to require vulnerability factors to advance to clinical symptoms that spiral into a serious disorder (see Taylor, Abramowitz, McKay and Cuttler's Chapter 12 in this volume).

This observation has led to important theoretical advances that seem to benefit the field with regard to explaining symptom onset and expanding treatment options.

Subtypes

Virtually all of the authors in this volume have pointed out the clinical heterogeneity of OCD itself, as well as the heterogeneity within each of the spectrum disorders (see especially Calamari et al., Chapter 2, and Taylor, Abramowitz, McKay, and Cuttler, Chapter 12). Even the newest disorder, hoarding, might be subtyped into object hoarding versus animal hoarding, as well as hoarding with and without squalid conditions in the home (Frost & Rasmussen, Chapter 4). The challenge is to determine what falls inside and outside of the diagnostic category, even as we try to better understand the dimensions on which syndromes or disorders vary. As geneticists Samuels, Bienvenu, Planalp, and Grados (Chapter 6) suggest, the field needs clarity on phenotypes (clinical subtypes) to determine how they are genetically similar or different. Likewise, Mataix-Cols and van den Heuvel (Chapter 7) express concern that clinical heterogeneity makes it more difficult to interpret findings from neuroscience studies of OCD. Similar arguments can be made for examining other features, such as severity, comorbidity, cognitive processing, and so forth.

Within this discussion of subtypes, one challenge put forward by Cassin and Rector (Chapter 11) is to examine similarities and differences not only in how symptoms appear, but also in the functions they serve. This important distinction between appearance and function yielded an especially helpful understanding of OCD decades ago when it became clear that obsessions provoke discomfort, whereas compulsions are intended to reduce this discomfort (see Rachman & Hodgson, 1980; Foa, Steketee, & Milby, 1980). This understanding further clarified that rituals might take either a behavioral or mental form (e.g., undoing a bad image with a good image, or with a ritual behavior), and therefore effective behavioral treatment requires identifying not only the form but the function, to apply the appropriate corrective experience. Although as Cassin and Rector have noted, the behavioral model described more than 30 years ago by Rachman and Hodgson (1980) is not sufficient to account for the complexity and heterogeneity of OCD, it nonetheless provided an important window that advanced understanding and treatment of OCD. Perhaps novel ways of examining subtypes will result in new, and perhaps more meaningful, clusters that differ in responsiveness to different treatments (see also Dorfan & Woody, Chapter 13). This has begun to yield fruit in the case of hoarding. When separated from OCD, so that recruitment does not bias samples toward the presence of obsessions and compulsions, a better understanding of the features and functions of difficulty discarding and clutter begin to emerge (see Frost & Rasmussen, Chapter 4, and Purdon, Chapter 14). Working from the other direction, responses to treatment may also guide our understanding of the phenotype. So, for example, a better understanding of the clinical response to neurosurgery might guide the understanding of OCD symptoms (McLaughlin & Greenberg, Chapter 10).

Relationships among OC Spectrum Disorders

It is not at all clear that the somewhat disparate conditions known as OC spectrum disorders share an underlying pathology. This issue has been hotly debated (see Abramowitz & Houts, 2005) and it will not likely be resolved anytime soon. Ricketts et al. (Chapter 5) raise the question of whether efforts to distinguish tics from Tourette syndrome from trichotillomania and from OCD will help clarify the etiology of these conditions. Nor is it clear that the functional impairment associated with the first three of these conditions can be separated from the functional impairment from their non-OC spectrum co-occurring conditions. Further, would doing so usefully inform efforts to improve overall functioning? A similar concern arises in BDD, the recognizable obsessive and compulsive symptoms of which seem a more severe and highly specialized form of OCD; in surface symptoms, BDD seems more similar to OCD than do tic disorders and trichotillomania. However, both BDD and OCD are highly comorbid with other anxiety and mood disorders, raising the question of whether it is equally important to examine the similarities and differences of these conditions with social anxiety, panic, and depression, as well as with each other (see comments by Kelly and Phillips in Chapter 3). In the same vein, hoarding bears similarities to impulse control disorders and addictive conditions such as gambling and compulsive buying, but is also highly comorbid with mood and anxiety disorders (social phobia, generalized anxiety disorder; see Frost & Rasmussen, Chapter 4).

Studying the shared features (phenomenology) among like disorders may be more important for understanding phenotype than examining comorbid conditions that could be simply a consequence or side effect of the problem (e.g., excessive clutter impairs functioning, which gives rise to depressed mood). However, might an underlying problem give rise to both conditions in either case? For example, BDD and hoarding share substantial social phobia comorbidity; might all three arise from some basic source of low self-esteem, leading to feelings of social inadequacy and isolation? On the other hand, both BDD and hoarding also share unusually high rates of major depression (although suicidal ideation and intent seem to characterize BDD more than hoarding). Is depression merely a side effect of the debilitation that stems from both conditions (and therefore less interesting as an explanatory factor), or is it a central feature and, again, somehow a driving force for the symptoms themselves? For example, are depressed people more likely to develop hoarding and/or BDD? Clearly, understanding both the central and secondary features of these conditions could hold clues to explaining their etiology.

Personality

Just as concerns about categorical classification versus dimensions arises for OC spectrum disorders, so it does for the associated personality disorders detailed in DSM-III and DSM-IV. Pinto and Eisen (Chapter 10) suggest that research on obsessive compulsive personality disorder (OCPD), in particular, underlies much of our understanding of OCD, beset as personality diagnoses are by serious problems with validity, reliability, and excessive overlap between diagnoses. They suggest, and many agree, that research using dimensional approaches to personality seems more promising, especially in teasing apart the complex relationship between OCD and OCPD. Interestingly, for example, it seems likely that the revised DSM-V will at least remove the hoarding criteria from OCPD, given its low loading (dimensionally) with other features of OCPD, which are more strongly related to each other. Specifically, Pinto and Eisen recommend assessing people with OCD for the dimensional strength of individual OCPD traits, rather than for the presence or absence of an overall OCPD diagnosis. This suggestion follows recent studies of predictors of therapy outcome, in which individual personality disorder categories are rarely prevalent enough to study, and often do not predict outcome even in large samples (e.g., Steketee & Shapiro, 1995; Steketee, Chambless & Tran, 2001). In contrast, researchers are more likely to study whether the number of personality disorders or traits

are predictive. Similarly, longitudinal studies may examine whether certain traits (rather than full blown OCPD) predict onset, course, or treatment response, as well as whether certain traits change in response to successful treatment. Pinto and Eisen also suggest that biological processes (neurophysiological, biochemical, neuropsychological) are likely to underlie personality differences between people with OCD, and that these basic features may help us find endophenotypes that could mediate the relationship between genes and behavioral manifestations/phenotypes (Gottesman & Gould, 2003).

Culture

Considerable research points to similarities in the expression of OCD symptoms across cultures, although the source of the obsessive content can be idiosyncratic to the specific culture (e.g., de Silva, 2006). Surprisingly little research has been done on OC spectrum conditions in this regard, perhaps simply because they are somewhat less prevalent than OCD. Kelly and Phillips (Chapter 3) raise the question of how BDD might manifest in different cultural contexts. Similarly, Nedeljkovic, Moulding, Foroughi, and Kyrios (Chapter 26) call for more research to understand the similarities and differences in OCD presentation across cultures—for example, to determine whether various subtypes of OCD are similar in structure and frequency across cultures. Interestingly, Ricketts et al. (Chapter 5) wonder whether cultural differences in the phenomenology of tics, Tourette's Syndrome, and trichotillomania might increase our understanding of those conditions. Their interest lies not merely in understanding the expression of these disorders and the effects of treatment, but also in understanding the mechanisms of action/underlying processes. This seems a particularly promising avenue of study, to take the next step whenever possible beyond mere descriptive studies to examining mechanisms, a natural segue into our next section.

Causes and Mechanisms

Just as the previous paragraph pointed to the importance of understanding the mechanisms of action behind the symptoms described in our OC spectrum conditions, here we examine possible ways to do so. Below are comments and discussions of possible neurological and genetic underpinnings, research on information processing, and potential cognitive factors that might influence onset and maintenance of OCD and some spectrum disorders.

Neurological and Genetic Underpinnings

An important goal of understanding and modeling these disorders is to improve treatment efforts and outcomes, and possibly even prevent the development of the disorder (see Kelly and Phillips discussion of BDD in Chapter 3). Samuels et al. (Chapter 6) point to some of the major challenges of genetics research with regard to the possibility of gene–gene and gene–environmental interactions, and the involvement of multiple genes and regions to map different subtypes with different genetic inheritance patterns. The challenge here is the need to identify different clinical subtypes or phenotypes. As they note, developments in molecular and statistical genetics will, hopefully, enable researchers to examine the entire genome for thousands of participants, looking for much narrower linkage areas using newer SNP markers. It is clear that very large samples are needed to boost power to detect small regions with more subtle effects, and that the statistical approaches must be sophisticated to do this work across multiple sites. Such research has been undertaken by large groups of genetics researchers, supported by the International OC Foundation (IOCDF, www.ocfoundation.org) and by the federal government. New developments in genetic research (such as epigenetics and genome sequencing) are being applied to this topic and seem likely to bear fruit.

In another biological arena, Mataix-Cols and van den Heuvel (Chapter 7) point out that the widely accepted neurobiological model of OCD involving the fronto-striato-thalamic circuits may be an oversimplification of the true situation, given the extensive heterogeneity of OCD. As noted earlier, the overlap of OCD with various anxiety and mood disorders will require a neurobiological model that includes an understanding of these conditions and how they might interface with OCD and OC spectrum conditions. This will require research that compares OCD with other anxiety and mood disorders, either directly within single studies or by using identical imaging protocols in different studies (cross-study comparisons). According to these authors, the current model proposes qualitative differences in the brains of those with and without clinical OCD. One challenge, however, is that some brain regions identified in recent OCD studies are also involved in "normal" emotional responses of healthy brains, suggesting differences in quantity rather than quality. This seems to support neuroimaging research on subclinical OCD, and also favors a dimensional diagnostic approach over a categorical one.

Mataix-Cols and van den Heuvel (Chapter 7) further note that recent studies implicate additional brain regions that were not included in the early studies on which the "standard model" (fronto-striato-thalamic circuits) was based. These include the temporal and parietal cortices, the cerebellum and paralimbic regions. They suggest the importance of examining complex cortical/limbic interactions (see Chapter 7 for more details about suggested areas of study), and of doing so using longitudinal studies that include untreated control groups. For example, longitudinal studies might follow children with and without OCD into adulthood, allowing study of the natural history of OCD using multimodel designs that combine imaging studies with chemical assays, or with genetic research. They propose that a particularly fruitful strategy will be to examine the overlapping and distinct neural correlates of OCD, of symptom dimensions/subtypes, and of related disorders, using well-validated and comparable paradigms. The goal of this work is to gain insight into the interactions between a wider purview of specific circuits, in order to better understand the clinical overlap and differentiation among OC spectrum disorders. This is challenging research because it requires combining research groups with disparate areas of expertise, retention of large patient samples over time, and a multimodal, multidisciplinary, longitudinal approach. Certainly it will benefit from a planned program of research that can rarely be accomplished by individual investigators.

Following upon this ambitious suggestion is McLaughlin and Greenberg's argument for a better understanding of anatomical, pharmacological, and behavioral underpinnings, especially the mediating mechanisms, in order to improve neurosurgery for OCD (Chapter 10). They note the need to verify empirically the clinical impression of a number of researchers that at least some patients who are unresponsive to rigorous behavioral treatment do, in fact, benefit from neurosurgery. Identifying what distinguishes these individuals is an especially important part of the discovery effort, with regard to determining who qualifies for this more radical treatment when all else fails. These authors also propose that a registry be maintained of all patients who have received neurosurgery for psychiatric conditions, including both surgical and clinical data. This seems likely to help identify the characteristics of the most appropriate candidates for future surgeries (Goodman & Insel, 2009).

Information Processing

Radomsky and Alcolado (Chapter 8) argue that the clinical presentation of OCD clearly indicates a difference from the general population in information processing, but that many studies have lacked ecological validity to demonstrate this. One problem is that information-processing problems reduce or disappear, following successful treatment for the symptoms of OCD, making it difficult to determine whether these problems cause OCD, are a parallel problem with the same cause as OCD, or result from OCD. To adequately study information processing, the measures must be highly clinically relevant (ecologically valid) in order to facilitate an understanding of the nature, course, and interrelationship of attentional and memory biases and executive functioning in OCD. For example, studies can examine processing in vivo during real-life threatening and nonthreatening situations.

One clear need Radomsky and Alcolado identify is for measures or assessment strategies that are clinically relevant. This improved assessment is a prerequisite to the better understanding of the nature of the attentional biases, memory biases, and difficulties in executive functioning in OCD, both in their development courses and their interrelationships. This gap is highlighted by the as yet unexplained finding that information processing problems lessen or disappear when treatment for OCD is successful. Do information-processing problems lead to OCD, or does OCD lead to information-processing problems? In general, it remains to be seen what contributions cognitive science can make to understanding and treating OCD, but the gap between laboratory assessments in controlled conditions, and the fluid real-world settings in which OCD manifests, remains a barrier at this time. In this regard, it is unclear what contributions cognitive science can make to understanding and treating OCD, and much remains to be done in research on information processing.

In a similar vein, Radomsky and Alcolado point out that it is still not clear how best to address OC spectrum clients' information-processing problems. For example, many clients who hoard show neurocognitive deficits in attention, memory, and executive functioning (e.g., organizing information). Similarly, Taylor et al. (Chapter 12) point to recent studies of the emotional components of abstract decision making (for example, in doing math problems) that may be part of the information-processing challenges faced by people with OCD and related disorders. However, as yet, we know little about what behavioral, cognitive remediational, and/or pharmacological approaches might help improve these skills (see Grisham, Norberg, and Certoma, Chapter 22). Training in skills for organizing and managing attention problems (akin to those used for adults with attention deficit hyperactivity disorder) have been applied as part of a multicomponent cognitive and behavioral treatment (Steketee et al., 2010), but have not been assessed separately to determine their specific impact on cognitive processing problems. Dismantling designs that examine the specific effects of treatment components may be helpful in this regard, but it seems likely that additional targeted treatments of information processing may be needed for hoarding, and perhaps for other OC spectrum conditions. For example, Amir and colleagues (Najmi, S., & Amir, N., 2010) have shown benefits of information-processing training for people with subclinical OCD. Further development of these or similar cognitive training methods may prove helpful in resolving this aspect of OC spectrum disorders.

Pertinent to this topic, another area of interest is to determine the effects of neurosurgeries on neurocognitive processing, as well as on OCD symptoms. However, this goal must be embedded in the larger question of whether the risks associated with various types of neurosurgeries are acceptable in comparison to the benefits in OCD symptoms and in quality of life (see McLaughlin & Greenberg, Chapter 10).

Beliefs

Considerable research activity in recent decades has focused on the types of beliefs evident in OCD patients, and the role of such beliefs in the development and maintenance of OCD symptoms. As Taylor and colleagues point out in Chapter 12, it is possible that the subset of beliefs adopted by a research working group (OCCWG, 1997) may not have included all of the relevant belief patterns. For example, many OCD patients report having "not just right" experiences, in which they have difficulty ending an activity because of a feeling that the action has not been completed fully or adequately. As these authors note, this uncomfortable sensation leads to rituals aimed at reducing internal tension, rather than avoiding any specific feared outcomes. Likewise, the sympathetic magic involving disgust reactions may account for contamination fears better than trait anxiety about contamination (e.g., Moretz & McKay, 2008). Inclusion of not just right experiences and disgust in a more comprehensive model of obsessive compulsive phenomena seems an important next step.

Cognitive models of OC spectrum disorders (e.g., BDD, hoarding) remain inadequately tested at this time. In general, these have been modeled after cognitive theories of OCD, and thus are likely to suffer from some of the same limitations being discovered in those models; for example, incomplete articulation of the types, sources, and impact of various beliefs. As Taylor and colleagues propose (Chapter 12), the models of OCD and of OC spectrum disorders also require more integration and fine-tuning to account for why individuals develop one rather than another condition, why some disorders are more likely to be comorbid than others, and why the presence of one disorder increases risk for another in the future. Further, cognitive models need to account for developmental differences across the lifespan. These include differences in cognitive development, especially from childhood through adolescence and into adulthood, as well as changes in salient content of obsessions. For example, what matters to a child in school can be quite different from what matters to an elderly person in retirement. An important unanswered question is whether cognitive development over the lifespan shapes the form and content of dysfunctional OC beliefs.

Further, as Taylor and colleagues indicate in Chapter 12, such models have not yet been integrated with regard to findings from information processing research, neuroscience, and genetics, especially with regard to identifying subtypes of OCD for which various cognitive models, or parts of models, have more or less salience. Unfortunately, these models were developed largely independently of (and therefore uninformed by) neurobiological research. This serious omission in the literature leaves questions about whether certain dysfunctional beliefs are based on specific neurobiological correlates, or particular patterns of information-processing problems.

In addition, current cognitive models are undeveloped with regard to accounting for cross-cultural differences in both beliefs and the focus of concerns in spectrum conditions such as BDD and hoarding. As Nedeljkovic et al. suggest in Chapter 26, elucidation of cultural factors and how these affect symptomatic expression may require substantial revision of the cognitive-behavioral therapy (CBT) models of OCD and spectrum conditions. For example, Cassin and Rector (Chapter 11) ask, might early traumas and stressful events have different impacts on beliefs and manifestations of OC spectrum conditions across cultures?

Social and Family Factors

Also under-studied are the social and familial factors that affect the development and expression of OCD and OC spectrum conditions. As Renshaw, Caska, Rodriues, and Blais note in Chapter 9, people with OCD who are treated with hostility from family members experience a well-demonstrated negative impact on treatment outcomes, leading to the clear conclusion that hostility in the living environment is problematic and should be corrected whenever possible. However, many questions remain understudied. For example, is hostility an important contributing factor to the anxiety and often negative self-esteem that generates OCD, as well as BDD and hoarding? Given that nonhostile criticism did not confer the same serious negative treatment outcomes (e.g., Chambless & Steketee, 1999), might it actually be beneficial as a motivator (see Renshaw et al., Chapter 9)? Further, Purdon (Chapter 14) raises questions about possible reciprocal influences of OCD symptoms, family accommodation, and expressed emotion (criticism, hostility, emotional overinvolvement). For example, do excessive overinvolvement and/or family accommodation produce more or less tolerance among relatives to OCD symptoms? What impact does this have on symptoms of OCD or OC spectrum disorders? Nedeljkovic, Moulding, Foroughi and Kyrios (Chapter 26) also raise the question of whether cultural differences, in the definition and experience of unwanted intrusions, affect how others respond to these symptoms, as well as their effect on functioning.

As reported in Chapter 4, research on hoarding suggests that many people who hoard are unmarried and live alone. Likewise, similar research on OCD also indicates less effective social functioning (Chapter 2), and these conditions, as well as BDD, are associated with considerable social anxiety (Chapters 2–4). What is not yet clear is whether social discomfort and poor social functioning share similar causal factors with OC spectrum conditions, or whether both sets of symptoms are reciprocally influential (e.g., OC spectrum conditions lead to social dysfunction, or social discomfort exacerbates OC spectrum symptoms). Clearly, much work remains to be done in the family and social arena to better understand the possible effects on symptoms and on treatment outcomes.

Assessment

Much has been accomplished in developing and testing assessment instruments that capture well the symptoms and related functioning problems associated with OCD, and with the several spectrum conditions described in this volume. Nonetheless, a number of challenges remain. With regard to OCD, symptom patterns are well studied, and several useful instruments are available for identifying these from multiple perspectives (patient, independent assessor, clinician). Several remaining concerns are articulated by Dorfan and Woody (Chapter 13). It is not clear whether beliefs can be accurately measured at different levels of specificity; for example, can interpretations/appraisals be distinguished from beliefs, as a number of researchers have attempted to do? Assessments of information processing deficits have been used in research settings, but are these useful or feasible in clinical practice? Depression is closely entwined with serious OCD symptoms, and measures of OCD severity are often not independent of this negative mood; perhaps it is neither possible nor fruitful to attempt to separate these conditions.

Carmin, Calamari, and Ownby (Chapter 24) raise several concerns about the psychometrics of standard OCD symptom measures when used with older adults. They suggest a need to distinguish OCD and other OC spectrum disorders from other anxiety and mood disorders, in order to reliably diagnose confusing comorbid conditions in this population. For example, in the elderly, it seems essential to develop methods that reliably distinguish geriatric psychiatric disorders from the emotional sequelae of late-life cognitive and physical decline, in order to provide better targeted interventions. These authors point to a need to assess OCD in elders living in retirement and nursing facilities, especially given that higher-care facilities will have higher incidences of significant mental and physical impairment problems and comorbid psychiatric conditions. For example, accurate assessments that distinguish disorders will facilitate collection of more accurate epidemiological data about the prevalence of hoarding among older people.

With regard to the spectrum condition of hoarding, a significant problem with the first studies of this problem, and even now, with some research, is the frequent use of OCD samples and OCD assessment measures to study hoarding. These assessments were not developed to measure the severity of hoarding, and thus lack essential validity and may seriously overestimate hoarding symptoms (see Frost and Rasmussen's discussion in Chapter 4). However, recently developed, well-validated hoarding measures are now available in self-report forms (e.g., Frost et al., 2004), observational instruments (Frost et al., 2008), and interview measures (Tolin, Frost, & Steketee, 2010). Other OC spectrum conditions also have reliable and valid measures of symptoms and related functioning aspects, as indicated in the relevant chapters on these disorders. However, with regard to BDD, Kelly and Phillips (Chapter 3) raise concerns about why BDD is frequently missed in clinical settings; effective methods for screening for conditions that patients often hide on initial clinic presentation (e.g., BDD, hoarding) seems an important goal for research and clinical practice.

How culture affects patients' responses to measures of OCD and OC spectrum disorders, and how these conditions can be assessed more reliably across cultures, remains a concern in the assessment literature (see Nedeljkovic et al., Chapter 26). An additional need raised by McLaughlin and Greenberg in Chapter 10 is for better ways to assess the clinical effectiveness of neurosurgeries for OCD patients who are not responsive to other treatments. Such measures may need to go beyond mere symptom severity to detecting improvements in functioning, social spheres, and general quality of life.

Treatment
Mechanisms of Action and Predictors of the Therapeutic Change Process
An important goal of treatment research is to shed light on how and why the therapy produces (or does not produce) the desired benefits. Cassin and Rector (Chapter 11) express concern that to date, there is insufficient study of the mechanisms of change in behavioral treatments for OCD (exposure and response prevention, or ERP), including factors that interfere with successful habituation and extinction of obsessive fears. With regard to cognitive therapy (CT) for OCD, Whittal and Robichaud (Chapter 18) concur, noting that because this is a relatively new therapy method, more studies of predictors of treatment are needed to elucidate how it works. Apropos of both suggestions, Abramowitz and colleagues (Chapter 17) recommend that specialized symptoms of OCD, such as "not just right experiences," need more study with regard to their response to ERP; this can be extended to CT methods, as well. In a very similar vein, Grisham et al. (Chapter 22) call for investigation of possible subtypes of hoarding (e.g., those with or without comorbid OCD) that might respond differentially to CBT methods, and might benefit from combining specialized hoarding methods with standard CBT methods for OCD symptoms.

Improving Treatments to Enhance their Effects

Both CBT and serotonergic medications for OCD have produced very positive outcomes, as articulated in Chapters 15, 17, and 18. However, how to modify therapy methods for those who do not respond well to standard treatments remains an issue. Abramowitz et al. raise this issue with regard to ERP in Chapter 17. Among the suggested options is modification of the existing therapy methods—for example, by extending the treatment period, or expanding the purview and methods within the therapy, to address comorbid conditions (see Whittal and Robichaud, Chapter 18). A further suggested option is to add psychosocial methods, such as family treatment (see Purdon, Chapter 14). In this regard Renshaw, Caska, Rodrigues and Blais (Chapter 9) encourage research that will clarify best practices for incorporating family members into treatment—for example, identifying the characteristics of family members and clients who are likely to benefit from such treatment, and best methods for conducting the family treatment.

Additional strategies focus on additive therapies such as D-cycloserine (DCS), which might be used to augment ERP methods and possibly improve treatment outcomes for subgroups such as OCD patients with poor insight (see Chapter 17 by Abramowitz et al. on adults, and Chapter 25 by Storch et al. on children). Tolin (Chapter 19) raises questions about whether non-serotonergic medications (SRIs) such as benzodiazepines, atypical antipsychotics, or cognitive enhancers or other neuroplasticity compounds, might improve the effects of CBT. He also suggests that understanding how such additive medications have their impact is an important element for understanding treatment mechanisms better, and for improving outcomes.

Some authors provide specific suggestions for further research on improving treatments for OC spectrum conditions. For example, Grisham et al. (Chapter 22) recommend comparing intensive treatment vs. weekly outpatient therapy for hoarding, in order to better study how hoarding patients respond when therapy intensity is varied. They also suggest the need to test the specific benefits of motivational interviewing in improving outcomes for hoarding treatment (see Steketee & Frost's treatment manual, 2007). Since most medication treatments for hoarding have been studied only retrospectively, an important remaining need is to determine prospectively whether a range of medications will provide significant benefit. Storch and

colleagues (Chapter 25) indicate that researchers need to study child treatments to better understand which treatments, and which augmentation strategies, are most effective, in which combinations, for whom. This work has begun for children, and also for adults with OCD and OC spectrum conditions, but will require considerable additional development over time. Finally, in Chapter 26, Nedeljkovic et al. are concerned that elucidation of cultural factors are likely to require revision of CBT models of OCD that will need to be integrated (not merely added to) treatment protocols. For example, van Noppen and colleagues are currently developing and testing a family treatment intervention for Latino OCD patients and their families, by modifying both the content and therapy procedures to fit cultural expectations (personal communication, October, 2010).

Medication and CBT + Medication Regimens

With regard to medications for OCD, Dougherty, Rauch, and Jenike (Chapter 15) point to the need for research that tailors individual medication regimens to individual people. This entails not only determining the most effective monotherapies for specific individuals, but also when augmentation would be helpful. Tolin (Chapter 19) raises the question of whether serotonergic medications are effective for CBT nonresponders and partial responders. He expands on Dougherty et al.'s goals to tailor treatment to individual patient characteristics (such as severity of illness, previous treatment history, comorbidity) with regard not only to monotherapies (e.g., CBT or medications alone) but also to combined therapies (CBT plus medications). These treatments must also be examined for costs and benefits to better understand the overall impact on patients and their families. For example, both Tolin (Chapter 19) and Grisham (Chapter 22) raise questions about whether under-studied subtypes such as hoarding will benefit more from combined treatments, rather than monotherapies.

Complementary and Alternative Treatments

Muroff, Ross, and Rothfarb's Chapter 20 on complementary and alternative treatments notes the very serious methodological problems in much of the published research on these methods. These include small samples that provide very limited power, the lack of comparison groups, overreliance on self-report assessments without additional perspectives, inconsistency in using intent-to-treat versus completers-only analyses, and higher attrition rates for studies of OCD than for those of other anxiety disorders. Clearly, more rigorous studies of these interesting methods are needed to determine which complementary and alternative treatments are most effective and for whom, but in some cases, the personalized therapy methods may require research methodologies that do not fit the randomized clinical trial (RCT) model well. Among the substantive questions these authors raise about alternative methods is whether they may be effective for dealing with certain physical problems exacerbated by the mental health symptoms, and also whether there is a somatic subtype of OCD that would benefit especially from such interventions.

Dissemination

Concerns about dissemination of therapies for OCD and spectrum conditions are also raised in this volume. For example, might current research on healthcare utilization be helpful in informing the field about how best to disseminate effective treatment strategies, so they could become widely available in clinical practice settings and readily utilized by patient groups (see Ricketts et al., Chapter 5)? Greenberg, Chosak, Fang and Wilhelm (Chapter 21) raise concerns about how to disseminate treatments for BDD, because they are relatively new and not widely known. Similar needs are evident for making available newly developed CBT methods for hoarding. This problem of dissemination is not small, but in recent years the availability and interest of the media makes it possible to alert the public to opportunities that create demand with the mental health profession. As public demand increases, it become essential to study the most effective ways of moving treatments from sophisticated research settings into community settings. Franklin, Antinoro, Ricketts, and Woods (Chapter 23) suggest studying a "train the trainers" model to move treatments more rapidly to patient populations in need.

Special Issues

A variety of special issues for particular disorders are raised in the chapters in this book, mainly concerned with BDD and trichotillomania and tic disorders. These are discussed below.

Body Dysmorphic Disorder

Chapters 3 (Kelly & Phillips) and 21 (Greenberg et al.) on BDD point to several specialized concerns about this problem and those that suffer from it. For example, it is clear that researchers simply do not know enough about BDD from a longitudinal perspective, with only one prospective study identified to date. Nor are its neurobiological bases and risk factors, or cultural features, clear at this stage of the research. These authors also note concerns about possible differences between delusional and nondelusional forms of BDD, especially with regard to the need for treatments that adequately resolve convictions about body problems that are not evident to others. In particular, Greenberg and colleagues describe a clear need for research on prevention and early intervention for BDD during childhood, and especially adolescence, when concerns about appearance are common and can become ingrained in the form of mistaken and delusional beliefs that affect adult lives. The need for comprehensive intervention efforts is also evident given the complex combination of biological, psychological, and socioenvironmental factors that affect the onset, course, and treatment for this condition. As the OC spectrum condition most associated with suicidality and physical damage, BDD may require specialized attention from researchers in order to manage the substantial risks associated with this condition if left untreated.

Trichotillomania and Tic Disorders

Another condition that poses special challenges for basic research into its neurobiological and neuroanatomical pathways is trichotillomania (Franklin et al., Chapter 23). Needed are studies of etiological and maintaining variables, such as emotional states, cognitive events, and physical sensations, such as a sense of inner pressure and "not just right" feelings that have also been identified for OCD (e.g., Ghisi, Chiri, Marchetti, Sanavio, & Sica, 2010). These symptoms may be associated with escaping or avoiding unpleasant emotions or thoughts. Another concerns raised in the discussion of these disorders is whether nonclinical or subclinical forms of tics and trichotillomania predict future onset, or instead are distinct and stable conditions (see Ricketts et al., Chapter 5). Further, as for other OC spectrum conditions, it is not clear whether there are distinct subtypes of these problems with differing severity (e.g., automatic versus focused hair pulling) that will shed light on possible differences in etiology, maintenance, and treatment outcomes. Another problem (also raised by Carmin et al. for OCD in elderly patients) is the difficulty in distinguishing functional impairment due to tics and trichotillomania from functional impairment due to comorbid conditions. As for other conditions, Ricketts et al. question whether there are cultural differences in the expression of these conditions, which might increase understanding as well as suggest strategies for treatment. Finally, Franklin et al. (Chapter 23) point to the need for more research on medications for tics and trichotillomania; while these conditions tend to be treated like OCD because of the repetitive behavior, they do not appear to respond well to medication protocols designed for OCD. Thus, more work is clearly needed on differential treatment(s), because at present, clinicians do not have access to an integrated, well-studied treatment protocol such as is available for OCD, BDD, hoarding, and other conditions. As Franklin et al. note, this problem might benefit greatly from a public advocacy campaign among peers and providers to alert the public and research funders to this problem.

Concluding Comments

Clearly, much research remains to be done on OCD and the several conditions we have come to call OC spectrum disorders. Not least among these is actually establishing the relationship and differences between these disorders. It is our hope that this volume assists the reader in better understanding the conditions detailed here with regard to their phenomenology, biological and psychosocial features, their assessment, and interventions. Of course, our most important goal is to understand each of these problems with such clarity that effective treatments can be identified that alleviate the suffering of the hundreds of thousands of people who have these problems around the world.

References

Abramowitz, J. S., & Houts, A. C., Eds. (2005). *Concepts and controversies in obsessive-compulsive disorder.* NY: Springer.

Chambless, D. L., & Steketee, G. (1999). Expressed emotion and behavior therapy outcome: A prospective study with obsessive compulsive and agoraphobic outpatients. *Journal of Consulting and Clinical Psychology, 67,* 658–665.

de Silva, P. (2006). Culture and obsessive-compulsive disorder. *Psychiatry, 5,* 402–405.

Foa, E. B., Steketee, G., & Milby, J. (1980). Differential effects of exposure and response prevention in obsessive-compulsive washers. *Journal of Consulting and Clinical Psychology, 48,* 71–79.

Frost, R. O., Steketee, G., & Grisham, J. (2004). Measurement of compulsive hoarding: Saving Inventory-Revised. *Behaviour Research and Therapy, 42,* 1163–1182.

Frost, R. O., Steketee, G., Tolin, D. F., & Renaud, S. (2008). Development and validation of the Clutter Image Rating. *Journal of Personality and Behavioral Assessment. 30,* 193–203.

Ghisi, M., Chiri, L. R., Marchetti, I., Sanavio, E., & Sica, C. (2010). "Not just right experiences" and obsessive-compulsive symptoms in non-clinical and clinical Italian individuals. *Journal of Anxiety Disorders, 24,* 879–886.

Goodman, W. K., & Insel, T. R. (2009). Deep brain stimulation in psychiatry: concentrating on the road ahead. *Biological Psychiatry, 65*(4), 263–266.

Gottesman, I. I., & Gould, T. D. (2003). The endophenotype concept in psychiatry: etymology and strategic intentions. *American Journal of Psychiatry, 160,* 636–645.

McKay, D., & Moretz, M. W. (2009). The intersection of disgust and contamination fear. In B.O. Olatunji & D. McKay (Eds.), *Disgust and its disorders: Theory, assessment, and treatment implications* (pp. 211–227). Washington, DC: American Psychological Association.

Najmi, S., & Amir, N. (2010). The effect of attention training on a behavioral test of contamination fears in individuals with subclinical obsessive-compulsive symptoms. *Journal of Abnormal Psychology, 119,* 136–142.

Obsessive Compulsive Cognitions Working Group (1997). Cognitive assessment of obsessive-compulsive disorder. *Behavior Research and Therapy, 35,* 667–681.

Rachman, S., & de Silva, P. (1978). Abnormal and normal obsessions. *Behaviour Research and Therapy, 16,* 233–248.

Rachman, S., & Hodgson, R. (1980). *Obsessions and compulsions.* Englewood Cliffs, NJ: Prentice-Hall.

Salkovskis, P., & Harrison, J. (1984). Abnormal and normal obsessions: A replication. *Behaviour Research and Therapy, 22,* 549–552.

Steketee, G., Chambless, D. L., & Tran, G. (2001). Effects of Axis I and II comorbidity on behavior therapy outcome for obsessive compulsive disorder and agoraphobia. *Comprehensive Psychiatry, 42,* 76–86.

Steketee, G., & Frost, R. O. (2007). *Treatment of compulsive hoarding: Therapist guide.* New York: Oxford.

Steketee, G., Frost, R. O., Tolin, D. F., Rasmussen, J., & Brown, T. A. (2010). Waitlist controlled trial of cognitive behavior therapy for hoarding disorder. *Depression and Anxiety, 27,* 476–484.

Steketee, G., & Shapiro, L. (1995). Predicting behavioral treatment outcome for agoraphobia and obsessive compulsive disorder. *Clinical Psychology Review, 15,* 317–346.

Tolin, D. F., Frost, R. O., & Steketee, G. (2010). A brief interview for assessing compulsive hoarding: The Hoarding Rating Scale. *Psychiatry Research, 178,* 147–152.

INDEX